University Casebook Series

March, 1989

ACCOUNTING AND THE LAW, Fourth Edition (1978), with Problems Pamphlet (Successor to Dohr, Phillips, Thompson & Warren)

George C. Thompson, Professor, Columbia University Graduate School of Business.
Robert Whitman, Professor of Law, University of Connecticut.
Ellis L. Phillips, Jr., Member of the New York Bar.
William C. Warren, Professor of Law Emeritus, Columbia University.

ACCOUNTING FOR LAWYERS, MATERIALS ON (1980)

David R. Herwitz, Professor of Law, Harvard University.

ADMINISTRATIVE LAW, Eighth Edition (1987), with 1983 Problems Supplement (Supplement edited in association with Paul R. Verkuil, Dean and Professor of Law, Tulane University)

Walter Gellhorn, University Professor Emeritus, Columbia University.
Clark Byse, Professor of Law, Harvard University.
Peter L. Strauss, Professor of Law, Columbia University.
Todd D. Rakoff, Professor of Law, Harvard University.
Roy A. Schotland, Professor of Law, Georgetown University.

ADMIRALTY, Third Edition (1987), with Statute and Rule Supplement

Jo Desha Lucas, Professor of Law, University of Chicago.

ADVOCACY, see also Lawyering Process

AGENCY, see also Enterprise Organization

AGENCY—PARTNERSHIPS, Fourth Edition (1987)

Abridgement from Conard, Knauss & Siegel's Enterprise Organization, Fourth Edition.

AGENCY AND PARTNERSHIPS (1987)

Melvin A. Eisenberg, Professor of Law, University of California, Berkeley.

ANTITRUST: FREE ENTERPRISE AND ECONOMIC ORGANIZATION, Sixth Edition (1983), with 1983 Problems in Antitrust Supplement and 1988 Case Supplement

Louis B. Schwartz, Professor of Law, University of Pennsylvania.
John J. Flynn, Professor of Law, University of Utah.
Harry First, Professor of Law, New York University.

BANKRUPTCY (1985)

Robert L. Jordan, Professor of Law, University of California, Los Angeles.
William D. Warren, Professor of Law, University of California, Los Angeles.

BANKRUPTCY AND DEBTOR–CREDITOR LAW, Second Edition (1988)

Theodore Eisenberg, Professor of Law, Cornell University.

BUSINESS ORGANIZATION, see also Enterprise Organization

UNIVERSITY CASEBOOK SERIES—Continued

BUSINESS PLANNING, Temporary Second Edition (1984)
David R. Herwitz, Professor of Law, Harvard University.

BUSINESS TORTS (1972)
Milton Handler, Professor of Law Emeritus, Columbia University.

CHILDREN IN THE LEGAL SYSTEM (1983) with 1988 Supplement
Walter Wadlington, Professor of Law, University of Virginia.
Charles H. Whitebread, Professor of Law, University of Southern California.
Samuel Davis, Professor of Law, University of Georgia.

CIVIL PROCEDURE, see Procedure

CIVIL RIGHTS ACTIONS (1988), with 1988 Supplement
Peter W. Low, Professor of Law, University of Virginia.
John C. Jeffries, Jr., Professor of Law, University of Virginia.

CLINIC, see also Lawyering Process

COMMERCIAL AND DEBTOR–CREDITOR LAW: SELECTED STATUTES, 1988 EDITION

COMMERCIAL LAW, Second Edition (1987)
Robert L. Jordan, Professor of Law, University of California, Los Angeles.
William D. Warren, Professor of Law, University of California, Los Angeles.

COMMERCIAL LAW, Fourth Edition (1985)
E. Allan Farnsworth, Professor of Law, Columbia University.
John Honnold, Professor of Law, University of Pennsylvania.

COMMERCIAL PAPER, Third Edition (1984)
E. Allan Farnsworth, Professor of Law, Columbia University.

COMMERCIAL PAPER, Second Edition (1987) (Reprinted from COMMERCIAL LAW, Second Edition (1987))
Robert L. Jordan, Professor of Law, University of California, Los Angeles.
William D. Warren, Professor of Law, University of California, Los Angeles.

COMMERCIAL PAPER AND BANK DEPOSITS AND COLLECTIONS (1967), with Statutory Supplement
William D. Hawkland, Professor of Law, University of Illinois.

COMMERCIAL TRANSACTIONS—Principles and Policies (1982)
Alan Schwartz, Professor of Law, University of Southern California.
Robert E. Scott, Professor of Law, University of Virginia.

COMPARATIVE LAW, Fifth Edition (1988)
Rudolf B. Schlesinger, Professor of Law, Hastings College of Law.
Hans W. Baade, Professor of Law, University of Texas.
Mirjan P. Damaska, Professor of Law, Yale Law School.
Peter E. Herzog, Professor of Law, Syracuse University.

COMPETITIVE PROCESS, LEGAL REGULATION OF THE, Third Edition (1986), with 1987 Selected Statutes Supplement
Edmund W. Kitch, Professor of Law, University of Virginia.
Harvey S. Perlman, Dean of the Law School, University of Nebraska.

UNIVERSITY CASEBOOK SERIES—Continued

CONFLICT OF LAWS, Eighth Edition (1984), with 1987 Case Supplement

Willis L. M. Reese, Professor of Law, Columbia University.
Maurice Rosenberg, Professor of Law, Columbia University.

CONSTITUTIONAL LAW, Eighth Edition (1989)

Edward L. Barrett, Jr., Professor of Law, University of California, Davis.
William Cohen, Professor of Law, Stanford University.
Jonathan D. Varat, Professor of Law, University of California, Los Angeles.

CONSTITUTIONAL LAW, CIVIL LIBERTY AND INDIVIDUAL RIGHTS, Second Edition (1982), with 1987 Supplement

William Cohen, Professor of Law, Stanford University.
John Kaplan, Professor of Law, Stanford University.

CONSTITUTIONAL LAW, Eleventh Edition (1985), with 1988 Supplement (Supplement edited in association with Frederick F. Schauer, Professor of Law, University of Michigan)

Gerald Gunther, Professor of Law, Stanford University.

CONSTITUTIONAL LAW, INDIVIDUAL RIGHTS IN, Fourth Edition (1986), (Reprinted from CONSTITUTIONAL LAW, Eleventh Edition), with 1988 Supplement (Supplement edited in association with Frederick F. Schauer, Professor of Law, University of Michigan)

Gerald Gunther, Professor of Law, Stanford University.

CONSUMER TRANSACTIONS (1983), with Selected Statutes and Regulations Supplement and 1987 Case Supplement

Michael M. Greenfield, Professor of Law, Washington University.

CONTRACT LAW AND ITS APPLICATION, Fourth Edition (1988)

Arthur Rosett, Professor of Law, University of California, Los Angeles.

CONTRACT LAW, STUDIES IN, Third Edition (1984)

Edward J. Murphy, Professor of Law, University of Notre Dame.
Richard E. Speidel, Professor of Law, Northwestern University.

CONTRACTS, Fifth Edition (1987)

John P. Dawson, Professor of Law Emeritus, Harvard University.
William Burnett Harvey, Professor of Law and Political Science, Boston University.
Stanley D. Henderson, Professor of Law, University of Virginia.

CONTRACTS, Fourth Edition (1988)

E. Allan Farnsworth, Professor of Law, Columbia University.
William F. Young, Professor of Law, Columbia University.

CONTRACTS, Selections on (statutory materials) (1988)

CONTRACTS, Second Edition (1978), with Statutory and Administrative Law Supplement (1978)

Ian R. Macneil, Professor of Law, Cornell University.

COPYRIGHT, PATENTS AND TRADEMARKS, see also Competitive Process; see also Selected Statutes and International Agreements

COPYRIGHT, PATENT, TRADEMARK AND RELATED STATE DOCTRINES, Second Edition (1981), with 1988 Case Supplement, 1987 Selected Statutes Supplement and 1981 Problem Supplement

Paul Goldstein, Professor of Law, Stanford University.

UNIVERSITY CASEBOOK SERIES—Continued

COPYRIGHT, Unfair Competition, and Other Topics Bearing on the Protection of Literary, Musical, and Artistic Works, Fourth Edition (1985), with 1985 Statutory Supplement

Ralph S. Brown, Jr., Professor of Law, Yale University.
Robert C. Denicola, Professor of Law, University of Nebraska.

CORPORATE ACQUISITIONS, The Law and Finance of (1986), with 1988 Supplement

Ronald J. Gilson, Professor of Law, Stanford University.

CORPORATE FINANCE, Third Edition (1987)

Victor Brudney, Professor of Law, Harvard University.
Marvin A. Chirelstein, Professor of Law, Columbia University.

CORPORATE READJUSTMENTS AND REORGANIZATIONS (1976)

Walter J. Blum, Professor of Law, University of Chicago.
Stanley A. Kaplan, Professor of Law, University of Chicago.

CORPORATION LAW, BASIC, Third Edition (1989), with Documentary Supplement

Detlev F. Vagts, Professor of Law, Harvard University.

CORPORATIONS, see also Enterprise Organization

CORPORATIONS, Sixth Edition—Concise (1988), with Statutory Supplement (1988)

William L. Cary, late Professor of Law, Columbia University.
Melvin Aron Eisenberg, Professor of Law, University of California, Berkeley.

CORPORATIONS, Sixth Edition—Unabridged (1988), with Statutory Supplement (1988)

William L. Cary, late Professor of Law, Columbia University.
Melvin Aron Eisenberg, Professor of Law, University of California, Berkeley.

CORPORATIONS AND BUSINESS ASSOCIATIONS—STATUTES, RULES AND FORMS (1988)

CORPORATIONS COURSE GAME PLAN (1975)

David R. Herwitz, Professor of Law, Harvard University.

CORRECTIONS, SEE SENTENCING

CREDITORS' RIGHTS, see also Debtor-Creditor Law

CRIMINAL JUSTICE ADMINISTRATION, Third Edition (1986), with 1988 Case Supplement

Frank W. Miller, Professor of Law, Washington University.
Robert O. Dawson, Professor of Law, University of Texas.
George E. Dix, Professor of Law, University of Texas.
Raymond I. Parnas, Professor of Law, University of California, Davis.

CRIMINAL LAW, Fourth Edition (1987)

Fred E. Inbau, Professor of Law Emeritus, Northwestern University.
Andre A. Moenssens, Professor of Law, University of Richmond.
James R. Thompson, Professor of Law Emeritus, Northwestern University.

CRIMINAL LAW AND APPROACHES TO THE STUDY OF LAW (1986)

John M. Brumbaugh, Professor of Law, University of Maryland.

UNIVERSITY CASEBOOK SERIES—Continued

CRIMINAL LAW, Second Edition (1986)

Peter W. Low, Professor of Law, University of Virginia.
John C. Jeffries, Jr., Professor of Law, University of Virginia.
Richard C. Bonnie, Professor of Law, University of Virginia.

CRIMINAL LAW, Fourth Edition (1986)

Lloyd L. Weinreb, Professor of Law, Harvard University.

CRIMINAL LAW AND PROCEDURE, Seventh Edition (1989)

Ronald N. Boyce, Professor of Law, University of Utah.
Rollin M. Perkins, Professor of Law Emeritus, University of California, Hastings College of the Law.

CRIMINAL PROCEDURE, Third Edition (1987), with 1988 Supplement

James B. Haddad, Professor of Law, Northwestern University.
James B. Zagel, Chief, Criminal Justice Division, Office of Attorney General of Illinois.
Gary L. Starkman, Assistant U. S. Attorney, Northern District of Illinois.
William J. Bauer, Chief Judge of the U.S. Court of Appeals, Seventh Circuit.

CRIMINAL PROCESS, Fourth Edition (1987), with 1988 Supplement

Lloyd L. Weinreb, Professor of Law, Harvard University.

DAMAGES, Second Edition (1952)

Charles T. McCormick, late Professor of Law, University of Texas.
William F. Fritz, late Professor of Law, University of Texas.

DECEDENTS' ESTATES AND TRUSTS, Seventh Edition (1988)

John Ritchie, Late Professor of Law, University of Virginia.
Neill H. Alford, Jr., Professor of Law, University of Virginia.
Richard W. Effland, Professor of Law, Arizona State University.

DISPUTE RESOLUTION, Processes of (1989)

John S. Murray, President and Executive Director of The Conflict Clinic, Inc., George Mason University.
Alan Scott Rau, Professor of Law, University of Texas.
Edward F. Sherman, Professor of Law, University of Texas.

DOMESTIC RELATIONS, see also Family Law

DOMESTIC RELATIONS, Successor Edition (1984) with 1988 Supplement

Walter Wadlington, Professor of Law, University of Virginia.

EMPLOYMENT DISCRIMINATION, Second Edition (1987), with 1988 Supplement

Joel W. Friedman, Professor of Law, Tulane University.
George M. Strickler, Professor of Law, Tulane University.

EMPLOYMENT LAW (1987), with 1987 Statutory Supplement and 1988 Case Supplement

Mark A. Rothstein, Professor of Law, University of Houston.
Andria S. Knapp, Adjunct Professor of Law, University of California, Hastings College of Law.
Lance Liebman, Professor of Law, Harvard University.

ENERGY LAW (1983) with 1986 Case Supplement

Donald N. Zillman, Professor of Law, University of Utah.
Laurence Lattman, Dean of Mines and Engineering, University of Utah.

UNIVERSITY CASEBOOK SERIES—Continued

ENTERPRISE ORGANIZATION, Fourth Edition (1987), with 1987 Corporation and Partnership Statutes, Rules and Forms Supplement

Alfred F. Conard, Professor of Law, University of Michigan.
Robert L. Knauss, Dean of the Law School, University of Houston.
Stanley Siegel, Professor of Law, University of California, Los Angeles.

ENVIRONMENTAL POLICY LAW 1985 Edition, with 1985 Problems Supplement (Supplement in association with Ronald H. Rosenberg, Professor of Law, College of William and Mary)

Thomas J. Schoenbaum, Professor of Law, University of Georgia.

EQUITY, see also Remedies

EQUITY, RESTITUTION AND DAMAGES, Second Edition (1974)

Robert Childres, late Professor of Law, Northwestern University.
William F. Johnson, Jr., Professor of Law, New York University.

ESTATE PLANNING, Second Edition (1982), with 1985 Case, Text and Documentary Supplement

David Westfall, Professor of Law, Harvard University.

ETHICS, see Legal Profession, Professional Responsibility, and Social Responsibilities

ETHICS AND PROFESSIONAL RESPONSIBILITY (1981) (Reprinted from THE LAWYERING PROCESS)

Gary Bellow, Professor of Law, Harvard University.
Bea Moulton, Legal Services Corporation.

EVIDENCE, Sixth Edition (1988 Reprint)

John Kaplan, Professor of Law, Stanford University.
Jon R. Waltz, Professor of Law, Northwestern University.

EVIDENCE, Eighth Edition (1988), with Rules, Statute and Case Supplement (1988)

Jack B. Weinstein, Chief Judge, United States District Court.
John H. Mansfield, Professor of Law, Harvard University.
Norman Abrams, Professor of Law, University of California, Los Angeles.
Margaret Berger, Professor of Law, Brooklyn Law School.

FAMILY LAW, see also Domestic Relations

FAMILY LAW Second Edition (1985), with 1988 Supplement

Judith C. Areen, Professor of Law, Georgetown University.

FAMILY LAW AND CHILDREN IN THE LEGAL SYSTEM, STATUTORY MATERIALS (1981)

Walter Wadlington, Professor of Law, University of Virginia.

FEDERAL COURTS, Eighth Edition (1988)

Charles T. McCormick, late Professor of Law, University of Texas.
James H. Chadbourn, late Professor of Law, Harvard University.
Charles Alan Wright, Professor of Law, University of Texas, Austin.

UNIVERSITY CASEBOOK SERIES—Continued

FEDERAL COURTS AND THE FEDERAL SYSTEM, Hart and Wechsler's Third Edition (1988), with the Judicial Code and Rules of Procedure in the Federal Courts (1988)

    Paul M. Bator, Professor of Law, University of Chicago.
    Daniel J. Meltzer, Professor of Law, Harvard University.
    Paul J. Mishkin, Professor of Law, University of California, Berkeley.
    David L. Shapiro, Professor of Law, Harvard University.

FEDERAL COURTS AND THE LAW OF FEDERAL–STATE RELATIONS, Second Edition (1989)

    Peter W. Low, Professor of Law, University of Virginia.
    John C. Jeffries, Jr., Professor of Law, University of Virginia.

FEDERAL PUBLIC LAND AND RESOURCES LAW, Second Edition (1987), with 1984 Statutory Supplement

    George C. Coggins, Professor of Law, University of Kansas.
    Charles F. Wilkinson, Professor of Law, University of Oregon.

FEDERAL RULES OF CIVIL PROCEDURE and Selected Other Procedural Provisions, 1988 Edition

FEDERAL TAXATION, see Taxation

FOOD AND DRUG LAW (1980), with Statutory Supplement

    Richard A. Merrill, Dean of the School of Law, University of Virginia.
    Peter Barton Hutt, Esq.

FUTURE INTERESTS (1958)

    Philip Mechem, late Professor of Law Emeritus, University of Pennsylvania.

FUTURE INTERESTS (1970)

    Howard R. Williams, Professor of Law, Stanford University.

FUTURE INTERESTS AND ESTATE PLANNING (1961), with 1962 Supplement

    W. Barton Leach, late Professor of Law, Harvard University.
    James K. Logan, formerly Dean of the Law School, University of Kansas.

GOVERNMENT CONTRACTS, FEDERAL, Successor Edition (1985)

    John W. Whelan, Professor of Law, Hastings College of the Law.

GOVERNMENT REGULATION: FREE ENTERPRISE AND ECONOMIC ORGANIZATION, Sixth Edition (1985)

    Louis B. Schwartz, Professor of Law, Hastings College of the Law.
    John J. Flynn, Professor of Law, University of Utah.
    Harry First, Professor of Law, New York University.

HEALTH CARE LAW AND POLICY (1988)

    Clark C. Havighurst, Professor of Law, Duke University.

HINCKLEY, JOHN W., JR., TRIAL OF: A Case Study of the Insanity Defense (1986)

    Peter W. Low, Professor of Law, University of Virginia.
    John C. Jeffries, Jr., Professor of Law, University of Virginia.
    Richard C. Bonnie, Professor of Law, University of Virginia.

INJUNCTIONS, Second Edition (1984)

    Owen M. Fiss, Professor of Law, Yale University.
    Doug Rendleman, Professor of Law, College of William and Mary.

UNIVERSITY CASEBOOK SERIES—Continued

INSTITUTIONAL INVESTORS, (1978)
David L. Ratner, Professor of Law, Cornell University.

INSURANCE, Second Edition (1985)
William F. Young, Professor of Law, Columbia University.
Eric M. Holmes, Professor of Law, University of Georgia.

INTERNATIONAL LAW, see also Transnational Legal Problems, Transnational Business Problems, and United Nations Law

INTERNATIONAL LAW IN CONTEMPORARY PERSPECTIVE (1981), with Essay Supplement
Myres S. McDougal, Professor of Law, Yale University.
W. Michael Reisman, Professor of Law, Yale University.

INTERNATIONAL LEGAL SYSTEM, Third Edition (1988), with Documentary Supplement
Joseph Modeste Sweeney, Professor of Law, University of California, Hastings.
Covey T. Oliver, Professor of Law, University of Pennsylvania.
Noyes E. Leech, Professor of Law Emeritus, University of Pennsylvania.

INTRODUCTION TO LAW, see also Legal Method, On Law in Courts, and Dynamics of American Law

INTRODUCTION TO THE STUDY OF LAW (1970)
E. Wayne Thode, late Professor of Law, University of Utah.
Leon Lebowitz, Professor of Law, University of Texas.
Lester J. Mazor, Professor of Law, University of Utah.

JUDICIAL CODE and Rules of Procedure in the Federal Courts, Students' Edition, 1988 Revision
Daniel J. Meltzer, Professor of Law, Harvard University.
David L. Shapiro, Professor of Law, Harvard University.

JURISPRUDENCE (Temporary Edition Hardbound) (1949)
Lon L. Fuller, late Professor of Law, Harvard University.

JUVENILE, see also Children

JUVENILE JUSTICE PROCESS, Third Edition (1985)
Frank W. Miller, Professor of Law, Washington University.
Robert O. Dawson, Professor of Law, University of Texas.
George E. Dix, Professor of Law, University of Texas.
Raymond I. Parnas, Professor of Law, University of California, Davis.

LABOR LAW, Tenth Edition (1986), with 1986 Statutory Supplement
Archibald Cox, Professor of Law, Harvard University.
Derek C. Bok, President, Harvard University.
Robert A. Gorman, Professor of Law, University of Pennsylvania.

LABOR LAW, Second Edition (1982), with Statutory Supplement
Clyde W. Summers, Professor of Law, University of Pennsylvania.
Harry H. Wellington, Dean of the Law School, Yale University.
Alan Hyde, Professor of Law, Rutgers University.

LAND FINANCING, Third Edition (1985)
The late Norman Penney, Professor of Law, Cornell University.
Richard F. Broude, Member of the California Bar.
Roger Cunningham, Professor of Law, University of Michigan.

UNIVERSITY CASEBOOK SERIES—Continued

LAW AND MEDICINE (1980)

Walter Wadlington, Professor of Law and Professor of Legal Medicine, University of Virginia.
Jon R. Waltz, Professor of Law, Northwestern University.
Roger B. Dworkin, Professor of Law, Indiana University, and Professor of Biomedical History, University of Washington.

LAW, LANGUAGE AND ETHICS (1972)

William R. Bishin, Professor of Law, University of Southern California.
Christopher D. Stone, Professor of Law, University of Southern California.

LAW, SCIENCE AND MEDICINE (1984), with 1989 Supplement

Judith C. Areen, Professor of Law, Georgetown University.
Patricia A. King, Professor of Law, Georgetown University.
Steven P. Goldberg, Professor of Law, Georgetown University.
Alexander M. Capron, Professor of Law, University of Southern California.

LAWYERING PROCESS (1978), with Civil Problem Supplement and Criminal Problem Supplement

Gary Bellow, Professor of Law, Harvard University.
Bea Moulton, Professor of Law, Arizona State University.

LEGAL METHOD (1980)

Harry W. Jones, Professor of Law Emeritus, Columbia University.
John M. Kernochan, Professor of Law, Columbia University.
Arthur W. Murphy, Professor of Law, Columbia University.

LEGAL METHODS (1969)

Robert N. Covington, Professor of Law, Vanderbilt University.
E. Blythe Stason, late Professor of Law, Vanderbilt University.
John W. Wade, Professor of Law, Vanderbilt University.
Elliott E. Cheatham, late Professor of Law, Vanderbilt University.
Theodore A. Smedley, Professor of Law, Vanderbilt University.

LEGAL PROFESSION, THE, Responsibility and Regulation, Second Edition (1988)

Geoffrey C. Hazard, Jr., Professor of Law, Yale University.
Deborah L. Rhode, Professor of Law, Stanford University.

LEGISLATION, Fourth Edition (1982) (by Fordham)

Horace E. Read, late Vice President, Dalhousie University.
John W. MacDonald, Professor of Law Emeritus, Cornell Law School.
Jefferson B. Fordham, Professor of Law, University of Utah.
William J. Pierce, Professor of Law, University of Michigan.

LEGISLATIVE AND ADMINISTRATIVE PROCESSES, Second Edition (1981)

Hans A. Linde, Judge, Supreme Court of Oregon.
George Bunn, Professor of Law, University of Wisconsin.
Fredericka Paff, Professor of Law, University of Wisconsin.
W. Lawrence Church, Professor of Law, University of Wisconsin.

LOCAL GOVERNMENT LAW, Second Revised Edition (1986)

Jefferson B. Fordham, Professor of Law, University of Utah.

MASS MEDIA LAW, Third Edition (1987)

Marc A. Franklin, Professor of Law, Stanford University.

UNIVERSITY CASEBOOK SERIES—Continued

MENTAL HEALTH PROCESS, Second Edition (1976), with 1981 Supplement

Frank W. Miller, Professor of Law, Washington University.
Robert O. Dawson, Professor of Law, University of Texas.
George E. Dix, Professor of Law, University of Texas.
Raymond I. Parnas, Professor of Law, University of California, Davis.

MUNICIPAL CORPORATIONS, see Local Government Law

NEGOTIABLE INSTRUMENTS, see Commercial Paper

NEGOTIATION (1981) (Reprinted from THE LAWYERING PROCESS)

Gary Bellow, Professor of Law, Harvard Law School.
Bea Moulton, Legal Services Corporation.

NEW YORK PRACTICE, Fourth Edition (1978)

Herbert Peterfreund, Professor of Law, New York University.
Joseph M. McLaughlin, Dean of the Law School, Fordham University.

OIL AND GAS, Fifth Edition (1987)

Howard R. Williams, Professor of Law, Stanford University.
Richard C. Maxwell, Professor of Law, University of California, Los Angeles.
Charles J. Meyers, Dean of the Law School, Stanford University.
Stephen F. Williams, Judge of the United States Court of Appeals.

ON LAW IN COURTS (1965)

Paul J. Mishkin, Professor of Law, University of California, Berkeley.
Clarence Morris, Professor of Law Emeritus, University of Pennsylvania.

PATENTS AND ANTITRUST (Pamphlet) (1983)

Milton Handler, Professor of Law Emeritus, Columbia University.
Harlan M. Blake, Professor of Law, Columbia University.
Robert Pitofsky, Professor of Law, Georgetown University.
Harvey J. Goldschmid, Professor of Law, Columbia University.

PLEADING AND PROCEDURE, see Procedure, Civil

POLICE FUNCTION, Fourth Edition (1986), with 1988 Case Supplement

Reprint of Chapters 1–10 of Miller, Dawson, Dix and Parnas's CRIMINAL JUSTICE ADMINISTRATION, Third Edition.

PREPARING AND PRESENTING THE CASE (1981) (Reprinted from THE LAWYERING PROCESS)

Gary Bellow, Professor of Law, Harvard Law School.
Bea Moulton, Legal Services Corporation.

PROCEDURE (1988), with Procedure Supplement (1988)

Robert M. Cover, late Professor of Law, Yale Law School.
Owen M. Fiss, Professor of Law, Yale Law School.
Judith Resnik, Professor of Law, University of Southern California Law Center.

PROCEDURE—CIVIL PROCEDURE, Second Edition (1974), with 1979 Supplement

The late James H. Chadbourn, Professor of Law, Harvard University.
A. Leo Levin, Professor of Law, University of Pennsylvania.
Philip Shuchman, Professor of Law, Cornell University.

UNIVERSITY CASEBOOK SERIES—Continued

PROCEDURE—CIVIL PROCEDURE, Fifth Edition (1984), with 1988 Supplement

Richard H. Field, late Professor of Law, Harvard University.
Benjamin Kaplan, Professor of Law Emeritus, Harvard University.
Kevin M. Clermont, Professor of Law, Cornell University.

PROCEDURE—CIVIL PROCEDURE, Fourth Edition (1985), with 1988 Supplement

Maurice Rosenberg, Professor of Law, Columbia University.
Hans Smit, Professor of Law, Columbia University.
Harold L. Korn, Professor of Law, Columbia University.

PROCEDURE—PLEADING AND PROCEDURE: State and Federal, Fifth Edition (1983), with 1988 Supplement

David W. Louisell, late Professor of Law, University of California, Berkeley.
Geoffrey C. Hazard, Jr., Professor of Law, Yale University.
Colin C. Tait, Professor of Law, University of Connecticut.

PROCEDURE—FEDERAL RULES OF CIVIL PROCEDURE, 1988 Edition

PRODUCTS LIABILITY (1980)

Marshall S. Shapo, Professor of Law, Northwestern University.

PRODUCTS LIABILITY AND SAFETY (1980), with 1985 Case and Documentary Supplement

W. Page Keeton, Professor of Law, University of Texas.
David G. Owen, Professor of Law, University of South Carolina.
John E. Montgomery, Professor of Law, University of South Carolina.

PROFESSIONAL RESPONSIBILITY, Fourth Edition (1987), with 1989 Selected National Standards Supplement

Thomas D. Morgan, Dean of the Law School, Emory University.
Ronald D. Rotunda, Professor of Law, University of Illinois.

PROPERTY, Fifth Edition (1984)

John E. Cribbet, Professor of Law, University of Illinois.
Corwin W. Johnson, Professor of Law, University of Texas.

PROPERTY—PERSONAL (1953)

S. Kenneth Skolfield, late Professor of Law Emeritus, Boston University.

PROPERTY—PERSONAL, Third Edition (1954)

Everett Fraser, late Dean of the Law School Emeritus, University of Minnesota.
Third Edition by Charles W. Taintor, late Professor of Law, University of Pittsburgh.

PROPERTY—INTRODUCTION, TO REAL PROPERTY, Third Edition (1954)

Everett Fraser, late Dean of the Law School Emeritus, University of Minnesota.

PROPERTY—REAL AND PERSONAL, Combined Edition (1954)

Everett Fraser, late Dean of the Law School Emeritus, University of Minnesota.
Third Edition of Personal Property by Charles W. Taintor, late Professor of Law, University of Pittsburgh.

PROPERTY—FUNDAMENTALS OF MODERN REAL PROPERTY, Second Edition (1982), with 1985 Supplement

Edward H. Rabin, Professor of Law, University of California, Davis.

PROPERTY—PROBLEMS IN REAL PROPERTY (Pamphlet) (1969)

Edward H. Rabin, Professor of Law, University of California, Davis.

UNIVERSITY CASEBOOK SERIES—Continued

PROPERTY, REAL (1984), with 1988 Supplement
Paul Goldstein, Professor of Law, Stanford University.

PROSECUTION AND ADJUDICATION, Third Edition (1986), with 1988 Case Supplement
Reprint of Chapters 11–26 of Miller, Dawson, Dix and Parnas's CRIMINAL JUSTICE ADMINISTRATION, Third Edition.

PSYCHIATRY AND LAW, see Mental Health, see also Hinckley, Trial of

PUBLIC REGULATION OF DANGEROUS PRODUCTS (paperback) (1980)
Marshall S. Shapo, Professor of Law, Northwestern University.

PUBLIC UTILITY LAW, see Free Enterprise, also Regulated Industries

REAL ESTATE PLANNING, Second Edition (1980), with 1980 Problems, Statutes and New Materials Supplement
Norton L. Steuben, Professor of Law, University of Colorado.

REAL ESTATE TRANSACTIONS, Revised Second Edition (1988), with Statute, Form and Problem Supplement (1988)
Paul Goldstein, Professor of Law, Stanford University.

RECEIVERSHIP AND CORPORATE REORGANIZATION, see Creditors' Rights

REGULATED INDUSTRIES, Second Edition, (1976)
William K. Jones, Professor of Law, Columbia University.

REMEDIES, Second Edition (1987)
Edward D. Re, Chief Judge, U. S. Court of International Trade.

RESTITUTION, Second Edition (1966)
John W. Wade, Professor of Law, Vanderbilt University.

SALES, Second Edition (1986)
Marion W. Benfield, Jr., Professor of Law, University of Illinois.
William D. Hawkland, Chancellor, Louisiana State Law Center.

SALES AND SALES FINANCING, Fifth Edition (1984)
John Honnold, Professor of Law, University of Pennsylvania.

SALES LAW AND THE CONTRACTING PROCESS (1982)
Reprint of Chapters 1–10 of Schwartz and Scott's Commercial Transactions.

SECURED TRANSACTIONS IN PERSONAL PROPERTY, Second Edition (1987) (Reprinted from COMMERCIAL LAW, Second Edition (1987))
Robert L. Jordan, Professor of Law, University of California, Los Angeles.
William D. Warren, Professor of Law, University of California, Los Angeles.

SECURITIES REGULATION, Sixth Edition (1987), with 1988 Selected Statutes, Rules and Forms Supplement and 1988 Cases and Releases Supplement
Richard W. Jennings, Professor of Law, University of California, Berkeley.
Harold Marsh, Jr., Member of California Bar.

SECURITIES REGULATION, Second Edition (1988), with Statute, Rule and Form Supplement (1988)
Larry D. Soderquist, Professor of Law, Vanderbilt University.

UNIVERSITY CASEBOOK SERIES—Continued

SECURITY INTERESTS IN PERSONAL PROPERTY, Second Edition (1987)

Douglas G. Baird, Professor of Law, University of Chicago.
Thomas H. Jackson, Professor of Law, Stanford University.

SECURITY INTERESTS IN PERSONAL PROPERTY (1985) (Reprinted from Sales and Sales Financing, Fifth Edition)

John Honnold, Professor of Law, University of Pennsylvania.

SENTENCING AND THE CORRECTIONAL PROCESS, Second Edition (1976)

Frank W. Miller, Professor of Law, Washington University.
Robert O. Dawson, Professor of Law, University of Texas.
George E. Dix, Professor of Law, University of Texas.
Raymond I. Parnas, Professor of Law, University of California, Davis.

SOCIAL RESPONSIBILITIES OF LAWYERS, Case Studies (1988)

Philip B. Heymann, Professor of Law, Harvard University.
Lance Liebman, Professor of Law, Harvard University.

SOCIAL SCIENCE IN LAW, Cases and Materials (1985)

John Monahan, Professor of Law, University of Virginia.
Laurens Walker, Professor of Law, University of Virginia.

TAX, POLICY ANALYSIS OF THE FEDERAL INCOME (1976)

William A. Klein, Professor of Law, University of California, Los Angeles.

TAXATION, FEDERAL INCOME (1989)

Stephen B. Cohen, Professor of Law, Georgetown University

TAXATION, FEDERAL INCOME, Second Edition (1988)

Michael J. Graetz, Professor of Law, Yale University.

TAXATION, FEDERAL INCOME, Sixth Edition (1987)

James J. Freeland, Professor of Law, University of Florida.
Stephen A. Lind, Professor of Law, University of Florida and University of California, Hastings.
Richard B. Stephens, Professor of Law Emeritus, University of Florida.

TAXATION, FEDERAL INCOME, Successor Edition (1986), with 1988 Legislative Supplement

Stanley S. Surrey, late Professor of Law, Harvard University.
Paul R. McDaniel, Professor of Law, Boston College.
Hugh J. Ault, Professor of Law, Boston College.
Stanley A. Koppelman, Professor of Law, Boston University.

TAXATION, FEDERAL INCOME, VOLUME II, Taxation of Partnerships and Corporations, Second Edition (1980), with 1988 Legislative Supplement

Stanley S. Surrey, late Professor of Law, Harvard University.
William C. Warren, Professor of Law Emeritus, Columbia University.
Paul R. McDaniel, Professor of Law, Boston College.
Hugh J. Ault, Professor of Law, Boston College.

TAXATION, FEDERAL WEALTH TRANSFER, Successor Edition (1987)

Stanley S. Surrey, late Professor of Law, Harvard University.
Paul R. McDaniel, Professor of Law, Boston College.
Harry L. Gutman, Professor of Law, University of Pennsylvania.

UNIVERSITY CASEBOOK SERIES—Continued

TAXATION, FUNDAMENTALS OF CORPORATE, Second Edition (1987)
Stephen A. Lind, Professor of Law, University of Florida and University of California, Hastings.
Stephen Schwarz, Professor of Law, University of California, Hastings.
Daniel J. Lathrope, Professor of Law, University of California, Hastings.
Joshua Rosenberg, Professor of Law, University of San Francisco.

TAXATION, FUNDAMENTALS OF PARTNERSHIP, Second Edition (1988)
Stephen A. Lind, Professor of Law, University of Florida and University of California, Hastings.
Stephen Schwarz, Professor of Law, University of California, Hastings.
Daniel J. Lathrope, Professor of Law, University of California, Hastings.
Joshua Rosenberg, Professor of Law, University of San Francisco.

TAXATION, PROBLEMS IN THE FEDERAL INCOME TAXATION OF PARTNERSHIPS AND CORPORATIONS, Second Edition (1986)
Norton L. Steuben, Professor of Law, University of Colorado.
William J. Turnier, Professor of Law, University of North Carolina.

TAXATION, PROBLEMS IN THE FUNDAMENTALS OF FEDERAL INCOME, Second Edition (1985)
Norton L. Steuben, Professor of Law, University of Colorado.
William J. Turnier, Professor of Law, University of North Carolina.

TAXES AND FINANCE—STATE AND LOCAL (1974)
Oliver Oldman, Professor of Law, Harvard University.
Ferdinand P. Schoettle, Professor of Law, University of Minnesota.

TORT LAW AND ALTERNATIVES, Fourth Edition (1987)
Marc A. Franklin, Professor of Law, Stanford University.
Robert L. Rabin, Professor of Law, Stanford University.

TORTS, Eighth Edition (1988)
William L. Prosser, late Professor of Law, University of California, Hastings.
John W. Wade, Professor of Law, Vanderbilt University.
Victor E. Schwartz, Adjunct Professor of Law, Georgetown University.

TORTS, Third Edition (1976)
Harry Shulman, late Dean of the Law School, Yale University.
Fleming James, Jr., Professor of Law Emeritus, Yale University.
Oscar S. Gray, Professor of Law, University of Maryland.

TRADE REGULATION, Second Edition (1983), with 1987 Supplement
Milton Handler, Professor of Law Emeritus, Columbia University.
Harlan M. Blake, Professor of Law, Columbia University.
Robert Pitofsky, Professor of Law, Georgetown University.
Harvey J. Goldschmid, Professor of Law, Columbia University.

TRADE REGULATION, see Antitrust

TRANSNATIONAL BUSINESS PROBLEMS (1986)
Detlev F. Vagts, Professor of Law, Harvard University.

TRANSNATIONAL LEGAL PROBLEMS, Third Edition (1986) with Documentary Supplement
Henry J. Steiner, Professor of Law, Harvard University.
Detlev F. Vagts, Professor of Law, Harvard University.

TRIAL, see also Evidence, Making the Record, Lawyering Process and Preparing and Presenting the Case

UNIVERSITY CASEBOOK SERIES—Continued

TRUSTS, Fifth Edition (1978)
>George G. Bogert, late Professor of Law Emeritus, University of Chicago.
>Dallin H. Oaks, President, Brigham Young University.

TRUSTS AND SUCCESSION (Palmer's), Fourth Edition (1983)
>Richard V. Wellman, Professor of Law, University of Georgia.
>Lawrence W. Waggoner, Professor of Law, University of Michigan.
>Olin L. Browder, Jr., Professor of Law, University of Michigan.

UNFAIR COMPETITION, see Competitive Process and Business Torts

UNITED NATIONS LAW, Second Edition (1967), with Documentary Supplement (1968)
>Louis B. Sohn, Professor of Law, Harvard University.

WATER RESOURCE MANAGEMENT, Third Edition (1988)
>Charles J. Meyers, Esq., Denver, Colorado, formerly Dean, Stanford University Law School.
>A. Dan Tarlock, Professor of Law, II Chicago-Kent College of Law.
>James N. Corbridge, Jr., Chancellor, University of Colorado at Boulder, and Professor of Law, University of Colorado School of Law.
>David H. Getches, Professor of Law, University of Colorado School of Law.

WILLS AND ADMINISTRATION, Fifth Edition (1961)
>Philip Mechem, late Professor of Law, University of Pennsylvania.
>Thomas E. Atkinson, late Professor of Law, New York University.

WORLD LAW, see United Nations Law

WRITING AND ANALYSIS IN THE LAW (1989)
>Helene S. Shapo, Professor of Law, Northwestern University
>Marilyn R. Walter, Professor of Law, Brooklyn Law School
>Elizabeth Fajans, Writing Specialist, Brooklyn Law School

University Casebook Series

EDITORIAL BOARD

DAVID L. SHAPIRO
DIRECTING EDITOR
Professor of Law, Harvard University

EDWARD L. BARRETT, Jr.
Professor of Law, University of California, Davis

ROBERT C. CLARK
Professor of Law, Harvard University

OWEN M. FISS
Professor of Law, Yale Law School

JEFFERSON B. FORDHAM
Professor of Law, University of Utah

GERALD GUNTHER
Professor of Law, Stanford University

THOMAS H. JACKSON
Dean of the School of Law, University of Virginia

HARRY W. JONES
Professor of Law, Columbia University

HERMA HILL KAY
Professor of Law, University of California, Berkeley

PAGE KEETON
Professor of Law, University of Texas

ROBERT L. RABIN
Professor of Law, Stanford University

CAROL M. ROSE
Professor of Law, Northwestern University

SAMUEL D. THURMAN
Professor of Law, Hastings College of the Law

FEDERAL INCOME TAXATION:

A CONCEPTUAL APPROACH

By

STEPHEN B. COHEN

Associate Professor of Law
Georgetown University

Westbury, New York
THE FOUNDATION PRESS, INC.
1989

COPYRIGHT © 1989 By THE FOUNDATION PRESS, INC.
615 Merrick Ave.
Westbury, N.Y. 11590

All rights reserved
Printed in the United States of America

Library of Congress Cataloging-in-Publication Data

Cohen, Stephen B.
    Federal income taxation: a conceptual approach/by Stephen B. Cohen.
        p. cm. — (University casebook series)
    Includes index.
    ISBN 0-88277-707-6
    1. Income tax—Law and legislation—United States—Cases.
I. Title. II. Series.
KF6368.C64 1989
343.7305'2—dc19
[347.30352]

                                      88-27030
                                         CIP

for lord, sam, and max

Bastard Chateaux and smoky demoiselles,
No more. I can build towers of my own,
There to behold, there to proclaim, the grace

And free requiting of reponsive fact,
To project the naked man in a state of fact,
As acutest virtue and ascetic trove.

Item: The cocks crow and the birds cry and
The sun expands, like a repetition on
One string, an absolute, not varying

Toward an inaccessible pure sound.
Item: The wind is never rounding O
And, imageless, it is itself the most,

Mouthing its constant smatter throughout space.
Item: the green pensive fish pensive in green reeds
Is an absolute. Item: The cataracts

As facts fall like rejuvenating rain,
Fall down through nakedness to nakedness,
To the auroral creature musing in the mind.

Item: Breathe, breathe upon the centre of
The breath life's latest, thousand senses.
But let this one sense be the single main.

And yet what good were yesterday's devotions?
I affirm and then at midnight the great cat
Leaps quickly from the fireside and is gone.

                        Wallace Stevens, Montrachet-le-Jardin

Gertrude, what is the answer?

Alice, what is the question?

                        A reported conversation between
                        Alice B. Toklas and Gertrude Stein

*

PREFACE

This is not a conventional casebook. Its primary goal is to teach the deeper structure, or what might be called the conceptual or theoretical map, which underlies the federal income tax—not an easy task. A massive amount of dry and difficult detail is necessarily part of learning federal taxation. Students are often so mesmerized by the technical detail that they fail to grasp the basic concepts.

This casebook, therefore, emphasizes a conceptual approach. The emphasis does not mean that technical details of the law are neglected, and there should be enough in these materials to satisfy anyone.[1] But my guiding principle has been that technical detail should always be conceptually anchored and never presented in a theoretical vacuum. Detail, in other words, is used to illustrate and illuminate fundamental ideas but not for its own sake or for the sake of mere coverage.

This approach has significantly affected the casebook's organization. Readings are structured around basic concepts, rather than formal legal issues as is often the case. As a result, familiar material is often juxtaposed in unconventional ways. For example:

—Because excluding an item raises the same conceptual issues as deducting the item, exclusion and deduction issues are considered together, rather than separately as in most casebooks.[2] Thus, the *exclusion* for meals and lodging provided by an employer is presented along with the *deduction* for meals and lodging with a business connection.[3]

—The principal consequence of characterizing a loss as capital is to permit recognition only to the extent that the taxpayer also has capital gains. Therefore, the question of *how* to characterize a gain or loss is integrated with the question of *when* the gain or loss should be taken into account. Limits on the deduction of capital losses are juxtaposed with pro-

---

1. See, for example, the effect of mortgages on like-kind exchanges in Chapter 24.
2. The analytic equivalence of exclusion and deduction was reflected in the 1984 enactment of Section 132(a)(3) and (d). Working condition fringe benefits, paid for by an employer, may be excluded only if deductible when paid for by the employee.
3. In terms of cases, Benaglia v. Commissioner, 36 B.T.A. 838 (1937), acq., 1940–1 C.B. 1 (may a hotel manager exclude the value of meals and lodging provided by his employer on the hotel premises), is juxtaposed with Rosenspan v. United States, 438 F.2d 905 (2d Cir. 1971) (may a salesperson, with no permanent abode, deduct the cost of meals and lodging while traveling on business).

Preface

visions requiring nonrecognition of losses from related party sales and wash sales.[4]

—Bond discount, deferred and accelerated payments, sales and gifts of carved-out term and future interests, insurance contracts, below-market interest loans, and premature accruals are all considered together as involving a common underlying problem—the tax system's failure to account accurately for the time value of money.

There are a number of other ways in which I believe this casebook represents a significant departure:

—Present value theory is introduced at an early point and used repeatedly to analyze the tax consequences of a variety of transactions, creating an emphasis on the importance of integrating financial and legal analysis.[5]

—The issue of form and substance—when may the government disregard the taxpayer's choice of form and when is it bound to follow it—is a recurrent theme, raised in connection with three-party exchanges, sales and leasebacks, wash sales, related party sales, tax shelters, and time value of money transactions. The casebook attempts to give questions of form and substance the same prominence as in the course on federal income taxation of corporations and shareholders.

—Tax shelters are examined in depth. The different policy issues that arise in connection with "ordinary" tax shelters, on the one hand, and "abusive" tax shelters, on the other, are contrasted with the legal doctrines and statutory reforms used to attack both ordinary and abusive tax shelter transactions.

The first chapter provides the flavor of the conceptual approach. In most casebooks, the first chapter provides a smattering of information on a dozen or more different topics: the history and constitutionality of the income tax, the tax expenditure budget, the economic effects of taxation, the criteria for tax policy, the choice of income as a tax base, the taxable unit, tax accounting, the time value of money, research in federal tax law, the tax legislative process, the administration of the tax laws, procedure in federal tax cases, realization and recognition, the definition of capital gains, and so on.

In my experience, students understand little, and retain even less, of such introductory reading. Therefore, the first chapter of this casebook focuses on the importance of a conceptual approach in order to build a foundation for what follows. Most of the topics usually covered in a first chapter are instead raised as appropriate later on. For example, the choice

---

4. Most casebooks use Eisner v. Macomber, 252 U.S. 189 (1920), to introduce students to the concept of realization, a purpose for which it is poorly suited, given the complexity of the transaction and the unfamiliarity of most students with the basic mechanics of taxing corporations and shareholders. This casebook uses the Supreme Court decision in Higgins v. Smith, 308 U.S. 473 (1940), to present the realization concept. Higgins v. Smith involves a much simpler transaction (the sale of securities at a loss to a wholly-owned corporation), but at the same time raises fundamental issues of form and substance in determining whether a "true" realization has occurred. Eisner v. Macomber is used, not to introduce the concept of realization, but to illustrate one of the justifications for preferential capital gains treatment, namely alleviating the double taxation of corporate-shareholder taxation.

5. In placing considerable stress on the use of present value theory, I have been influenced by another casebook on a different legal subject, Corporate Finance by Victor Brudney and Marvin Chirelstein.

Preface

of forum is discussed in connection with Commissioner v. Duberstein[6] and Stanton v. U.S.,[7] where it helps to explain results that appear inconsistent.

In format, this casebook is only slightly unconventional. Legal opinions predominate, although the casebook includes a fair amount of other material: excerpts from law review articles, congressional reports, newspapers, and even correspondence between the Treasury and taxpayers.

In addition, I have written extensive notes for each chapter, usually titled "Notes and Questions." The notes serve a number of distinct purposes. They place the reading in a conceptual and analytic context. Where the reading involves sophisticated financial or economic analysis, the notes attempt to lead the reader through the analysis, *step by step*, so that even those without a background in finance or economics will be able to follow.[8] The notes can also serve as a structure for class discussion and constitute, in effect, suggested "lesson plans" for each chapter.

After the introductory first chapter, the casebook is divided into five parts: Part One—Compensation for Personal Services; Part Two—Gains and Losses on Property; Part Three—Costs of "For Profit" Activities; Part Four—Tax Shelters; and Part Five—Assignment of Income.

There are fifty-six chapters. Each chapter can be covered in one class hour (usually a fifty-five minute period, rather than a full sixty minutes). The typical course in basic income tax meets for fifty-six class hours. (It is a four credit course, meeting four hours a week for fourteen weeks.) If a different chapter occupies every class hour, it will be possible to cover all fifty-six chapters in this casebook during the typical four credit basic course. But if some chapters take more than one hour, or if some class hours are devoted to review, some of the material will have to be skipped.

I usually cover between fifty and fifty-four chapters in the basic course. Assuming that most others will do about the same, I recommend the following possible variations on which chapters to omit.

1) For those who want to skip most of capital gains, 26–29.
2) For those who want to skip tax shelters, 38–43.
3) For those who want to skip most of time value of money transactions, 52–56.
4) For those who want to skip the most difficult material, 6, 16, 49, 52, 54, and 55.
5) What I often skip, 27, 34, 46, 49, 52, and 53.

A number of law schools devote two semesters to basic income tax so that the material may be covered more slowly and in greater depth. If this option is chosen, the first semester might include Part One (Compensation for Personal Services), Part Two (Gains and Losses on Property), Part Three (Costs of "For Profit" Activities), and Subpart A of Part Five (Intrafamily Assignments of Income) - 42 chapters in all. The following 11 chapters could occupy two class hours: 9, 15, 16, 17, 18, 23, 24, 25, 34, 35, and 36. With the other 31 chapters each occupying one class hour, 53 of the 56 hours in a four credit first semester course would be taken up, leaving a

---

6. 363 U.S. 278 (1960).
7. Ibid.
8. For example, see the extensive note material on commodity straddles in Chapter 16.

Preface

few hours for review. The more difficult material of Part Four (Tax Shelters) and Subpart B of Part Five (Time Value of Money Transactions) could then be reserved for a second semester course.

Teaching the basic course in federal income tax has never been easy, perhaps because so many different things are being taught at once. The student is simultaneously asked to speak a new language, understand a prolix and opaque statute, decipher complex financial transactions, and apply economic analysis to the effects of the tax law. There is obviously no one right way to structure the course. Any casebook involves hundreds of judgments about what to teach and when and how to teach it. These judgments necessarily reflect the author's personal values and easily could have been made in other ways.

The multitude of possibilities means that the casebook author should always be open to different approaches. I hope that teachers and students who use these materials will offer suggestions for improving them.

I have already benefited from numerous criticisms made by colleagues while this casebook was in draft. Patricia Cain, Charles Gustafson, Calvin Johnson, David Shakow, Peter Weidenbruch, and Patricia White all provided helpful comments.

I have also been blessed with exceptionally talented research assistants. Mary Jo Weigman helped assemble the first version of the casebook. Maura Caffrey edited the entire text and made substantial improvements in clarity and logic. Linda Lenartowicz proofread the final draft and checked every citation and quotation.

Dana Wall, a certified public accountant, detected numerous technical errors. Janis Oppelt, a professional editor, made sure that the manuscript was consistent in matters of style and punctuation.

Special thanks are due Anne Collins, Director of Technical Support Services at Georgetown Law Center, and Mary Ann DeRosa, Word Processing Manager. Whenever I had difficulty relating to my computer or its software, they managed to find a solution. Without their help, this manuscript might still be lost somewhere between DOS and RAMBIOS.

I also wish to acknowledge Marvin Chirelstein and Boris Bittker who taught me federal income taxation when I was in law school.[9] No student could hope for more inspiring or challenging teachers.

Finally, I am particularly indebted to Daniel Halperin for his perceptive comments on the manuscript and for all that I have learned from teaching with him at Georgetown. No law professor could hope for a better colleague.

STEPHEN COHEN

Washington, D.C. and
Santa Fe, N.M.
February, 1989

---

9. The first three opinions in these materials are U.S. v. Drescher, 179 F.2d 863 (2d Cir. 1950), Commissioner v. Lobue, 351 U.S. 243 (1956), and Benaglia v. Commissioner, 36 B.T.A. 838 (1937). In deciding to start with these cases, I am following earlier editions of Professor Bittker's casebook.

SUMMARY OF CONTENTS

	Page
PREFACE	xxiii
ACKNOWLEDGMENTS	xliii
EDITORIAL NOTICE	xlvii
1. Introduction	1

PART ONE. COMPENSATION FOR PERSONAL SERVICES

2. Limited Choice and Restricted Property	16
3. Distinguishing Compensation in Kind From Investment Gain: Compensatory Stock Options	24
4. Working Conditions and Business Expenses	33
5. Distinguishing Business From Personal Consumption Expenses: Commuting	44
6. Education	55
7. Travel and Entertainment	77
8. Imputed Income and Employee Discounts	101
9. Personal Expenditures for Child Care, Medical Care, and Charity	128
10. Disguising Gifts as Compensation (and Vice Versa)	161
11. Stock Options Revisited: Do Tax Considerations Always Predominate?	180

PART TWO. GAINS AND LOSSES ON PROPERTY

SUBPART A. When Has Enough Happened to Account for Gain or Loss?	192
12. The Realization Principle	193
13. Sales for Deferred Payment	206
14. Losses From Related Party and Wash Sales	215
15. Capital Losses and Inventory Losses	227
16. Commodity Straddles	244
17. Like-Kind Exchanges: Potential Loss	274
18. Like-Kind Exchanges: Potential Gain	294
19. Involuntary Realizations	311
20. Forgiveness of Debt and the Annual Accounting Principle	322

Summary of Contents

Page

SUBPART B. When Enough Has Happened, How Much Is the Gain or Loss? 330
21. Piecemeal and Installment Sales 331
22. Part Gift/Part Sale 339
23. After a Nonrecognition Transaction 347
24. Effect of Mortgages on Basis and Amount Realized 358

SUBPART C. Should the Gain Be Preferentially Taxed? 369
25. Justifications for Preferential Treatment 371
26. Inventory Versus Investment Property 388
27. Dual Character Assets 400
28. Property Versus Compensation for Personal Services 418
29. Property Versus Contract 426

PART THREE. COSTS OF "FOR PROFIT" ACTIVITIES

30. Comparing "for Profit" and "for Pleasure" Property 445
31. Distinguishing "for Profit" from "for Pleasure" Activities 461
32. The Capitalization Requirement 471
33. When Should Salaries Be Capitalized? 490
34. Allocating Capital Expenditures Between Wasting and Non-wasting Assets 512
35. Depreciation 526
36. Recapture and the Tax Benefit Rule 553
37. Implications of Recapture 567

PART FOUR. TAX SHELTERS

38. Airplane (and Other Equipment-Leasing) Tax Shelters of the 1960s 576
39. Will the Airplane Tax Shelter Work? 590
40. Is the Airplane Tax Shelter an Abuse? 605
41. The Supreme Court Steps In 644
42. Abusive Tax Shelters: Real Estate 663
43. Abusive Tax Shelters: Copyrights 671
44. The Elusive and Puzzling Interest Deduction 700

PART FIVE. ASSIGNMENT OF INCOME

SUBPART A. Intrafamily Transactions 721
45. The Common Law 722
46. Circumventing the Common Law: Family Partnerships, Self-Created Property, and Professional Service Corporations 745
47. Statutory Modification of Common Law Principles 767
48. Gift and Leaseback 775
49. Private Annuities and Alimony 785

Summary of Contents

	Page
SUBPART B. Time Value of Money Transactions	797
50. Bond Discount	798
51. Unstated Interest on Sales for Deferred Payment	813
52. OID on Future Interests: Ignoring the Temporal Division	833
53. Insurance, Interest-Free Loans, and Prepayments	849
54. Premature Accruals, the All Events Test, and Economic Performance	867
55. Premature Accruals as Implicit Loans	890
56. Accounting Methods, Deferred Compensation, and Qualified Pension Plans	898
Table of Cases	919
Table of Internal Revenue Code Sections	923
Table of Treasury Regulations	931
Table of Revenue Rulings and Procedures	933
Index	935

DETAILED TABLE OF CONTENTS

	Page
Preface	xxiii
Acknowledgments	xliii
Editorial Notice	xlvii

Chapter 1. Introduction ... 1
A. To the Reader ... 1
B. Introductory Problems ... 4
C. The Income Tax: Basic Mechanics ... 6
D. Appearances Are Deceiving: The Hidden 33% Tax Rate ... 8
E. Before Tax and After Tax: The Critical Importance of the Marginal Rate ... 10
F. Why Tax Income? Alternative Methods of Financing Government ... 11
G. Alternative Rate Structures ... 12
H. Suggestions for Further Reading ... 14

PART ONE. COMPENSATION FOR PERSONAL SERVICES

Chapter 2. Limited Choice and Restricted Property ... 16
A. *U.S. v. Drescher* ... 16
B. Notes and Questions ... 20

Chapter 3. Distinguishing Compensation in Kind From Investment Gain: Compensatory Stock Options ... 24
A. *Commissioner v. LoBue* ... 24
B. Notes and Questions ... 27

Chapter 4. Working Conditions and Business Expenses ... 33
A. *Benaglia v. Commissioner* ... 33
B. Notes and Questions ... 36
C. *Rosenspan v. U.S.* (Part One) ... 40
D. Notes and Questions ... 41

Chapter 5. Distinguishing Business From Personal Consumption Expenses: Commuting ... 44
A. Introductory Note ... 44
B. *Commissioner v. Flowers* ... 44
C. *Rosenspan v. U.S.* (Part Two) ... 49
D. Notes and Questions ... 50

Detailed Table of Contents

	Page
Chapter 6. Education	55
A. Introductory Notes and Questions	55
B. *Greenberg v. Commissioner*	57
C. Notes and Questions	61
D. *Bingler v. Johnson*	62
E. Notes and Questions	68
F. *Armantrout v. Commissioner*	71
G. Notes and Questions	75
Chapter 7. Travel and Entertainment	77
A. *Rudolph v. U.S.*	77
B. Notes and Questions	83
C. *Schulz v. Commissioner*	85
D. Notes and Questions	90
E. Kinsley, The Mystery Of The Free Lunch	91
F. Wasserman, Drawing Board	95
G. The 1986 Tax Reform Act	96
H. *Moss v. Commissioner*	97
I. Notes and Questions	100
Chapter 8. Imputed Income and Employee Discounts	101
A. *Commissioner v. Minzer*	101
B. Notes and Questions	102
C. Fringe Benefit Provisions, House Committee on Ways and Means	104
D. Notes and Questions	115
E. Newman, Fly Me, Fly My Mother	119
F. Other Tax-Favored Fringe Benefits	126
Chapter 9. Personal Expenditures for Child Care, Medical Care, and Charity	128
A. *Smith v. Commissioner*	128
B. Notes and Questions	129
C. The Tax Expenditure Concept	135
D. General Accounting Office, Tax Expenditures: A Primer	137
E. The Medical Expense Deduction, from Andrews, Personal Deductions in an Ideal Income Tax	138
F. *Mattes v. Commissioner*	141
G. Notes and Questions	144
H. The Charitable Contribution Deduction, from Andrews, Personal Deductions in an Ideal Income Tax	147
I. *Oppewal v. Commissioner*	153
J. Deductible to the Extent Permitted By Law, Tax Notes Editorial	155
K. Notes and Questions	156

Detailed Table of Contents

	Page
Chapter 10. Disguising Gifts as Compensation (and Vice Versa)	161
A. *Eller v. Commissioner*	161
B. Notes and Questions	163
C. *Commissioner v. Duberstein*	164
D. A Critique of *Duberstein* and *Stanton*, from Griswold, Forward: Of Time and Attitudes—Professor Hart and Judge Arnold, The Supreme Court, 1959 Term	173
E. Notes and Questions	174
Chapter 11. Stock Options Revisited: Do Tax Considerations Always Predominate?	180
A. N.D. Plume, Incentive Stock Options	180
B. Testimony of Daniel Halperin	182
C. Letter of Ed Zschau	183
D. Letter of Daniel Halperin	185
E. Notes and Questions	186
F. Executives Get Bonus For Swap In Stock Options, The Wall Street Journal	189

PART TWO. GAINS AND LOSSES ON PROPERTY

SUBPART A. When Has Enough Happened to Account for Gain or Loss?	192
Chapter 12. The Realization Principle	193
A. Introductory Note	193
B. Practical Problems With Taxing Unrealized Gain, from Andrews, A Consumption-Type or Cash Flow Personal Income Tax	193
C. Slawson, Taxing as Ordinary Income the Appreciation of Publicly Held Stock	194
D. Notes and Questions	196
E. Time and Economic Value	197
F. Miller and Moody, Quantitative Techniques in Financial Decision Making	199
G. Present Value, from Alchian and Allen, University Economics	200
H. Notes and Questions	201
Chapter 13. Sales for Deferred Payment	206
A. Introductory Note	206
B. *Nye v. U.S.*	206
C. Notes and Questions	209
D. Pledging or Mortgaging as a Taxable Event	212

Detailed Table of Contents

	Page

Chapter 14. Losses From Related Party and Wash Sales — 215
A. *Higgins v. Smith* — 215
B. Notes and Questions — 220
C. *McWilliams v. Commissioner* — 224
D. Notes and Questions — 225

Chapter 15. Capital Losses and Inventory Losses — 227
A. Introductory Notes and Questions — 227
B. Warren, The Deductibility by Individuals of Capital Losses Under the Federal Income Tax — 228
C. Notes and Questions — 229
D. Comparing Inventory Losses With Capital Losses — 230
E. *Thor Power Tool Co. v. Commissioner* — 234
F. Notes and Questions — 242

Chapter 16. Commodity Straddles — 244
A. Introductory Note — 244
B. How the Commodity Tax Straddle Works, The New York Times — 245
C. The Commodity Tax Straddle, Staff of the Joint Committee on Taxation — 245
D. Letter of Donald C. Lubick — 254
E. *Smith v. Commissioner* — 255
F. Notes and Questions — 263
G. The Butterfly Straddle, Staff of Joint Committee on Taxation — 271

Chapter 17. Like-Kind Exchanges: Potential Loss — 274
A. Introductory Note — 274
B. *Cottage Savings Association v. Commissioner* — 274
C. Notes and Questions — 284
D. *Jordan Marsh Co. v. Commissioner* — 288
E. Notes and Questions — 291

Chapter 18. Like-Kind Exchanges: Potential Gain — 294
A. Introductory Questions — 294
B. *Alderson v. Commissioner* — 295
C. Notes and Questions — 299
D. *Starker v. U.S.* (District Court) — 300
E. *Starker v. U.S.* (Circuit Court) — 302
F. Notes and Questions — 308

Chapter 19. Involuntary Realizations — 311
A. *Helvering v. Bruun* — 311
B. Notes and Questions — 313
C. Bush Made a $198,000 Payment to I.R.S. in June for Back Taxes, The New York Times — 316
D. Is the Maine House the Main House? — 317
E. Forgiveness of Debt — 318
F. A Closing Question — 321

Detailed Table of Contents

	Page
Chapter 20. Forgiveness of Debt and the Annual Accounting Principle	322
A. *Bowers v. Kerbaugh-Empire Co.*	322
B. *U.S. v. Kirby Lumber Co.*	323
C. Notes and Questions	324
D. *Bradford v. Commissioner*	325
E. Questions	328
SUBPART B. When Enough Has Happened, How Much Is the Gain or Loss?	350
Chapter 21. Piecemeal and Installment Sales	331
A. *Inaja Land Co. v. Commissioner*	331
B. Notes and Questions	333
C. *Burnet v. Logan*	334
D. Notes and Questions	336
Chapter 22. Part Gift/Part Sale	339
A. Gifts With Unrealized Gain	339
B. *Diedrich v. Commissioner*	340
C. Notes and Questions	343
Chapter 23. After a Nonrecognition Transaction	347
A. The Parable of "Sam Who Never Forgets"	347
B. Introductory Note	347
C. Like-Kind Exchanges	348
D. Wash Sales	349
E. Related Party Sales	350
F. Inter Vivos and Testamentary Gifts	350
G. Kurtz and Surrey, Reform of Gift and Death Taxes: The 1969 Treasury Proposals, the Criticisms and a Rebuttal	351
Chapter 24. Effect of Mortgages on Basis and Amount Realized	358
A. *Commissioner v. Tufts*	358
B. Notes and Questions	365
C. Like-Kind Exchanges of Mortgaged Property	367
SUBPART C. Should the Gain Be Preferentially Taxed?	369
Chapter 25. Justifications for Preferential Treatment	371
A. Introductory Note	371
B. *Hellerman v. Commissioner*	371
C. Critique of Traditional Justifications, From Andrews, A Consumption-Type or Cash-Flow Personal Income Tax	372
D. Notes and Questions	375
E. *Eisner v. Macomber*	378
F. Notes and Questions	384
Chapter 26. Inventory Versus Investment Property	388
A. Introductory Note	388
B. *Corn Products Refining Co. v. Commissioner*	388

Detailed Table of Contents

		Page
C.	Notes and Questions	391
D.	*Arkansas Best Corp. v. Commissioner*	394
E.	Notes and Questions	398

Chapter 27. Dual Character Assets 400
- A. *Malat v. Riddell* 400
- B. Notes and Questions 401
- C. *Biedenharn Realty Co. v. U.S.* 402
- D. Notes and Questions 411
- E. *International Shoe Machine Corp. v. Commissioner* 413
- F. Notes and Questions 416

Chapter 28. Property Versus Compensation for Personal Services 418
- A. *McFall v. Commissioner* 418
- B. Notes and Questions 420
- C. *Miller v. Commissioner* 420
- D. Notes and Questions 423

Chapter 29. Property Versus Contract 426
- A. *Commissioner v. Pittston Co.* 426
- B. Notes and Questions 431
- C. *Commissioner v. Ferrer* 432
- D. Notes and Questions 438

PART THREE. COSTS OF "FOR PROFIT" ACTIVITIES

Chapter 30. Comparing "for Profit" and "for Pleasure" Property 445
- A. Imputed Rent of Owner-occupied Dwellings, from R. Goode, The Individual Income Tax 445
- B. Imputed Rental Income, from U.S. Treasury, Blueprints for Basic Tax Reform 446
- C. Notes and Questions 447
- D. Epstein, The Consumption and Loss of Personal Property Under the Internal Revenue Code 448
- E. Notes and Questions 451
- F. *Gevirtz v. Commissioner* 452
- G. Notes and Questions 454
- H. Bittker, Income Tax Deductions, Credits, and Subsidies for Personal Expenditures 455
- I. *Carpenter v. Commissioner* 456
- J. *Rev. Rul. 63–232* 458
- K. Notes and Questions 458
- L. Nonrecognition of Forgiveness of Debt: The Difference Between "for Profit" and "for Pleasure" Property 460

Detailed Table of Contents

	Page
Chapter 31. Distinguishing "for Profit" From "for Pleasure" Activities	461
A. *Nickerson v. Commissioner*	461
B. Notes and Questions	467
Chapter 32. The Capitalization Requirement	471
A. Introductory Note: What the Disputes Are About	471
B. *Welch v. Helvering*	471
C. Notes and Questions	473
D. *Midland Empire Packing Co. v. Commissioner*	475
E. Notes and Questions	479
F. *Commissioner v. Idaho Power Co.*	480
G. Notes and Questions	485
H. New Inventory Expense Rules Increase Costs at Many Firms, The Wall Street Journal	488
Chapter 33. When Should Salaries Be Capitalized?	490
A. Introductory Note	490
B. *Encyclopaedia Britannica, Inc. v. Commissioner*	491
C. Notes and Questions	495
D. Kitty Kelley, Only the Rich Will Write, Newsweek	496
E. *North Carolina National Bank Corp. v. U.S.*	498
F. *Central Texas Savings & Loan Ass'n. v. U.S.*	506
G. Notes and Questions	510
Chapter 34. Allocating Capital Expenditures Between Wasting and Non-wasting Assets	512
A. Introductory Note	512
B. Notes and Questions on Premium Leases	513
C. *Commissioner v. Moore* (Part One)	514
D. Notes and Questions	518
E. Notes and Questions on Premium Bonds	520
F. *Commissioner v. Moore* (Part Two)	522
G. Notes and Questions	524
Chapter 35. Depreciation	526
A. Introductory Notes and Questions	526
B. Sinking Fund Method Depreciation, from M. Chirelstein, Federal Income Taxation	530
C. Depreciation Methods and Rates, from B. Bittker, Federal Taxation of Income, Estates and Gifts	532
D. Notes and Questions	535
E. Steines, Income Tax Allowances for Cost Recovery	537
F. Capital Cost Provisions, Conference Committee Report on the 1986 Tax Reform Act	546
G. Depreciation and the Minimum Tax	548
H. Calculating Depreciation: An Explanation and Some Problems	551

Detailed Table of Contents

	Page
Chapter 36. Recapture and the Tax Benefit Rule	553
A. Introductory Notes and Questions	553
B. *Alice Phelan Sullivan Corp. v. U.S.*	556
C. *U.S. v. Bliss Dairy, Inc.*	558
D. Notes and Questions	563
E. *Haverly v. U.S.*	564
F. Notes and Questions	566
Chapter 37. Implications of Recapture	567
A. Introductory Notes and Questions	567
B. *Redwing Carriers, Inc. v. Tomlinson*	567
C. Notes and Questions	572

PART FOUR. TAX SHELTERS

	Page
Chapter 38. Airplane (and Other Equipment-Leasing) Tax Shelters of the 1960s	576
A. The Talk Of The Town, The New Yorker	576
B. Zeitlin, Tax Planning in Equipment-Leasing Shelters	577
C. Notes and Questions	581
D. Exit Gracefully, from Zeitlin, Tax Planning in Equipment-leasing Shelters	586
E. Notes and Questions	588
Chapter 39. Will the Airplane Tax Shelter Work?	590
A. Introductory Note	590
B. *Helvering v. Lazarus*	590
C. Notes and Questions	591
D. *Estate of Starr v. Commissioner*	592
E. Notes and Questions	594
F. Lease Versus Sale, from Zeitlin, Tax Planning in Equipment-leasing Shelters	596
G. Notes and Questions	599
H. Statutory Reform	602
Chapter 40. Is the Airplane Tax Shelter an Abuse?	605
A. Introductory Note	605
B. The Economics of Leasing, from Note, "Safe Harbor" as Tax Reform: Taxpayer Election of Lease Treatment	605
C. The Revenue Consequences of Shifting Tax Preferences	608
D. Safe Harbor Leasing, Staff of the Joint Committee on Taxation	610
E. New Tax Law Makes Once-Unusable Credits a Boon for Many Firms, The Wall Street Journal	614
F. Ford Sells IBM $200 Billion in 1981 Tax Breaks, The Washington Post	617
G. The Great Business Giveaway, The Washington Post	618

Detailed Table of Contents

	Page
H. Testimony of John Chapoton	619
I. Testimony of Paul McDaniel	623
J. Notes and Questions	625
K. Galper and Lubick, the Defects of Safe Harbor Leasing and What to Do About Them	630
L. Auerbach and Warren, Transferability of Tax Incentivies and the Fiction of Safe Harbor Leasing	634
M. Notes and Questions	638
N. Forman, Tax Considerations in Renting a Navy	640
O. Notes and Questions	643
Chapter 41. The Supreme Court Steps In	644
A. *Frank Lyon Co. v. U.S.*	644
B. Notes and Questions	656
C. *Swift Dodge v. Commissioner*	659
D. Notes and Questions	662
Chapter 42. Abusive Tax Shelters: Real Estate	663
A. *Estate of Franklin v. Commissioner*	663
B. Notes and Questions	667
Chapter 43. Abusive Tax Shelters: Copyrights	671
A. Abusive Tax Shelter Recipe	671
B. *Dean v. Commissioner*	672
C. *Barnard v. Commissioner*	688
D. Notes and Questions	690
E. Passive Activity Losses	696
F. Instead of a Condo, a Cabin Hotel Suite, The New York Times	698
Chapter 44. The Elusive and Puzzling Interest Deduction	700
A. Introductory Note	700
B. Investments in Real Estate and Stock	701
C. Personal Consumption	701
D. Municipal Bonds	704
E. Categorizing Interest	707
F. *The Wisconsin Cheeseman, Inc. v. U.S.*	708
G. *Rev. Proc. 72–18*	711
H. Notes and Questions	716

PART FIVE. ASSIGNMENT OF INCOME

SUBPART A. Intrafamily Transactions	721
Chapter 45. The Common Law	722
A. Introductory Note	722
B. *Lucas v. Earl*	722
C. *Corliss v. Bowers*	723

Detailed Table of Contents

		Page
D.	*Poe v. Seaborn*	724
E.	*Blair v. Commissioner*	728
F.	*Helvering v. Clifford*	731
G.	*Helvering v. Horst*	736
H.	*Harrison v. Schaffner*	740
I.	• Notes and Questions	742

Chapter 46. Circumventing the Common Law: Family Partnerships, Self-Created Property, and Professional Service Corporation — 745

A.	*Commissioner v. Culbertson*	745
B.	Notes and Questions	752
C.	*Heim v. Fitzpatrick*	755
D.	Notes and Questions	758
E.	*Fogelsong v. Commissioner*	758
F.	Notes and Questions	764

Chapter 47. Statutory Modification of Common Law Principles — 767

A.	Joint Returns	767
B.	The Taxable Unit	769
C.	Grantor Trusts	770
D.	Below-market Interest Gift Loans	773

Chapter 48. Gift and Leaseback — 775

A.	*Rosenfeld v. Commissioner*	775
B.	Notes and Questions	782

Chapter 49. Private Annuities and Alimony — 785

A.	*Lafargue v. Commissioner*	785
B.	Notes and Questions	789
C.	*Bernatschke v. U.S.*	790
D.	Notes and Questions	795

SUBPART B. Time Value of Money Transactions — 797

Chapter 50. Bond Discount — 798

A.	Introductory Notes and Questions	798
B.	*Commissioner v. Caulkins*	802
C.	*U.S. v. Midland-Ross Corp.*	804
D.	Notes and Questions	806
E.	Amortization of Original Issue Discount on Bonds, Staff of Joint Committee on Taxation	808
F.	Notes and Questions	811

Chapter 51. Unstated Interest on Sales for Deferred Payment — 813

A.	Introductory Notes and Questions	813
B.	Imputing Interest on Sales for Deferred Payment [Section 1274], Staff of the Joint Committee on Taxation	815

Detailed Table of Contents

	Page
C. Notes and Questions	817
D. *Commissioner v. [Clay] Brown*	818
E. Notes and Questions	829

Chapter 52. OID on Future Interests: Ignoring the Temporal Division — 833
- A. Introductory Notes and Questions — 833
- B. *Alstores Realty Corp. v. Commissioner* — 836
- C. Notes and Questions — 840
- D. *Commissioner v. P.G. Lake, Inc.* — 842
- E. Notes and Questions — 843
- F. *Irwin v. Gavit* — 845
- G. Notes and Questions — 847

Chapter 53. Insurance, Interest-Free Loans, and Prepayments — 849
- A. Annuities and Life Insurance — 849
- B. *Dean v. Commissioner* — 853
- C. Notes and Questions — 855
- D. Interest-free and Below-market Interest Loans, Staff of Joint Committee on Taxation — 856
- E. Notes and Questions — 857
- F. *RCA Corp. v. U.S.* — 858
- G. Notes and Questions — 863

Chapter 54. Premature Accruals, the All Events Test, and Economic Performance — 867
- A. *Mooney Aircraft, Inc. v. U.S.* — 867
- B. Notes and Questions — 871
- C. *U.S. v. Hughes Properties, Inc.* — 875
- D. *U.S. v. General Dynamics Corp.* — 883
- E. Notes and Questions — 888

Chapter 55. Premature Accruals as Implicit Loans — 890
- A. The Implicit Loan Analysis — 890
- B. Deferred Compensation — 893

Chapter 56. Accounting Methods, Deferred Compensation, and Qualified Pension Plans — 898
- A. *Amend v. Commissioner* — 898
- B. *Rev. Rul. 60–31* — 902
- C. Notes and Questions — 906
- D. Statement of Daniel Halperin — 909
- E. Deferred Compensation Plans [Section 457] — 910
- F. Notes and Questions — 912
- G. Nonqualified Deferred Compensation, from Halperin, Interest in Disguise: Taxing the "Time Value of Money" — 912
- H. Notes and Questions — 916
- I. A Last Word — 916

Detailed Table of Contents

	Page
Table of Cases	919
Table of Internal Revenue Code Sections	923
Table of Treasury Regulations	931
Table of Revenue Rulings and Procedures	933
Index	935

ACKNOWLEDGMENTS

I wish to express my deep appreciation to the authors and publishers who gave permission to reprint from the following publications, listed in the order in which they appear in this volume:

Montrachet-le-Jardin, The Collected Poems of Wallace Stevens, by permission of Alfred A. Knopf, Inc. Copyright 1942 by Wallace Stevens.

Kinsley, The Mystery Of The Free Lunch, The New Republic (May 23, 1981).

Wasserman, Drawing Board, Los Angeles Times Syndicate (Sept. 12, 1981).

Newman, *Fly Me, Fly My Mother,* 35 Tax Notes 291 (April 20, 1987). Reprinted with permission of Tax Analysts, Arlington, Virginia, All rights reserved.

Andrews, *Personal Deductions in an Ideal Income Tax*, 86 Harv. L. Rev. 309 (1972). Copyright 1972 by the Harvard Law Review Association.

Deductible to the Extent Permitted By Law, 31 Tax Notes 1557 (March 28, 1988). Reprinted with permission of Tax Analysts, Arlington, Virginia, All rights reserved.

Griswold, *Forward: Of Time and Attitudes—Professor Hart and Judge Arnold, The Supreme Court, 1959 Term,* 74 Harv. L. Rev. 81 (1960). Copyright 1960 by the Harvard Law Review Association.

N. D. Plume, *Incentive Stock Options,* 13 Tax Notes 402 (August 31, 1981). Reprinted with permission of Tax Analysts, Arlington, Virginia, All rights reserved.

Ed Zschau, former Member of Congress and currently General Partner of Brentwood Associates, Letter to Senator Packwood.

Daniel Halperin, Letter to Ed Zschau.

Executives Get Bonus For Swap In Stock Options, The Wall Street Journal (July 28, 1987).

Andrews, *A Consumption-Type or Cash Flow Personal Income Tax*, 87 Harv. L. Rev. 1113 (1974). Copyright 1974 by the Harvard Law Review Association.

Slawson, *Taxing as Ordinary Income the Appreciation of Publicly Held Stock*, 76 Yale L. J. 623 (1967).

Alchian and Allen, University Economics, Wadsworth Publishing Company.

Acknowledgments

Miller and Moody, *Quantitative Techniques in Financial Decision Making*, 59 Taxes 831 (1981), Commerce Clearing House, Inc. Reprinted with permission.

Warren, *The Deductibility by Individuals of Capital Losses under the Federal Income Tax*, 40 U. Chi. L Rev. 291 (1973).

How The Commodity Tax Straddle Works, The New York Times (July 10, 1981). Copyright 1981 by The New York Times Company. Reprinted by permission.

Bush Made a $198,000 Payment to I.R.S. in June for Back Taxes, The New York Times (October 4, 1984). Copyright 1984 by The New York Times. Reprinted by permission.

Eve Rice, Sam Who Never Forgets. Copyright 1977 by Eve Rice. Reprinted by permission of Greenwillow Books (A Division of William Morrow & Co., Inc.).

Kurtz and Surrey, *Reform of Gift and Death Taxes: The 1969 Treasury Proposals, The Criticisms and a Rebuttal*, 70 Col. L. Rev. 1365 (1970). Copyright 1970 by the Directors of the Columbia Law Review Association, Inc. All rights reserved. Reprinted by permission.

Goode, The Individual Income Tax (1976). Published by the Brookings Institution.

Epstein, *The Consumption and Loss of Personal Property Under the Internal Revenue Code*, 23 Stan. L. Rev. 454 (1971). Copyright 1971 by the Board of Trustees of Leland Stanford Junior University.

Bittker, *Income Tax Deductions, Credits, and Subsidies for Personal Expenditures*, 16 J. Law and Econ. 193 (1973). Published by the University of Chicago Press. Copyright 1988 by the University of Chicago. All rights reserved.

New Inventory Expense Rules Increase Costs At Many Firms, The Wall Street Journal (June 29, 1987).

Only The Rich Will Write, Newsweek (August 24, 1987). Published by Newsweek, Inc. All rights reserved. Reprinted by permission.

Chirelstein, Federal Income Taxation (1988). Copyright 1988 by The Foundation Press, Inc. All rights reserved.

Bittker, Federal Taxation Of Income, Estates and Gifts (1981). Copyright 1981 by Warren, Gorham, and Lamony, Inc. All rights reserved.

Paul McDaniel, Statement before the Senate Budget Committee.

Steines, *Income Tax Allowances For Cost Recovery*, 40 Tax L. Rev. 483 (1985).

The Talk Of The Town, The New Yorker (October 17, 1970). Reprinted by permission. Copyright 1970 by The New Yorker Magazine, Inc.

Zeitlin, *Tax Planning in Equipment-leasing Shelters*, 21 Major Tax Planning 621 (1969). Published for the University of Southern California Law Center's Institute on Federal Taxation by Matthew Bender.

Note, *'Safe Harbor' as Tax Reform: Taxpayer Election of Lease Treatment*, 95 Harv. L. Rev. 1648 (1982). Copyright 1982 by the Harvard Law Review Association.

New Tax Law Makes Once-Unusable Credits a Boon for Many Firms, The Wall Street Journal (August 27, 1981).

Acknowledgments

Ford Sells IBM $200 Billion In 1981 Tax Breaks, The Washington Post (November 6, 1981). Copyright by The Washington Post.

The Great Business Giveaway, The Washington Post, (December 3, 1981). Copyright by The Washington Post.

Galper and Lubick, *The Defects of Safe Harbor Leasing and What to Do About Them*, 14 Tax Notes 643 (March 15, 1982). Reprinted with permission of Tax Analysts, Arlington, Virginia, All rights reserved.

Auerbach and Warren, *Transferability of Tax Incentives and the Fiction of Safe Harbor Leasing*, 95 Harv. L. Rev. 1752 (1982). Copyright 1982 by the Harvard Law Review Association.

Instead Of A Condo, A Cabin Hotel Suite, The New York Times (July 19, 1987). Copyright 1987 by The New York Times Company. Reprinted by permission.

Halperin, *Interest in Disguise: Taxing the "Time Value of Money,"* 95 Yale L. J. 506 (1987).

EDITORIAL NOTICE

Ellipses indicate deletions from quoted material. Brackets indicate additions to quoted material. Most footnotes from quoted material are omitted. All footnotes, textual as well as the few retained from quoted material, are numbered consecutively from the beginning of each chapter.

*

FEDERAL INCOME TAXATION:

A CONCEPTUAL APPROACH

*

Chapter 1

INTRODUCTION

"We are about to consider the unpleasant subject of taxes."
L. Eisenstein, The Ideologies of Taxation

A. TO THE READER

Federal income tax is reputedly a dry, difficult, and highly technical subject, and it is easy to understand why. The income tax statute—the Internal Revenue Code—often seems incomprehensible and is unbelievably lengthy.

Just how prolix is the law of federal income taxation? The Sixteenth Amendment to the Constitution, which authorizes Congress to impose an income tax, contains a modest thirty words. The income tax provisions of the 1987 edition of the Internal Revenue Code occupy more than 1,000 pages.[1]

The statute is, moreover, frequently amended. Until recently, the number of amendments in any year tended to be relatively modest. In the 1980s, however, Congress grew more accustomed to enacting major "reforms" of the income tax statute every year or so. The first of these, the Economic Recovery Tax Act (ERTA) of 1981, ran 185 pages.[2] A year later, the Tax Equity and Fiscal Responsibility Act of 1982 (TEFRA) was, at 384 pages, over twice as long.[3] Two years later, the Deficit Reduction Act of 1984 (DEFRA) surpassed both combined with 717 pages of statutory

---

1. Internal Revenue Code, U.S. Code Cong. and Admin. News (1989).
2. Economic Recovery Tax Act of 1981, Pub. L. 97–34, 95 Stat. 172, 172–356 (1981). The number of pages in the present Code, as well as in various tax revision acts, are offered merely to suggest the volume of material involved. They should not be used for making exact comparisons. The text of the current Code is printed in smaller type than is the text of the various tax revision acts. Moreover, a portion of each tax revision act is devoted to non-income tax provisions.
3. Tax Equity and Fiscal Responsibility Act of 1982, Pub. L. 87–248, 96 Stat. 324, 324–707 (1982).

changes.[4] In 1986, Congress enacted a massive overhaul of the tax law, occupying nearly 900 pages.[5]

While these reform efforts, in particular the 1986 Tax Reform Act, promised simplification, each has in fact made the Code considerably longer and somewhat more complex. One commentary, contrasting the promise with the reality, described the 1986 Act as the "tunnel at the end of the light."[6] Nor is the end in sight.

> The effects of this [1986 Tax Reform] Act will take years to unfold, and cannot yet be predicted with any degree of certainty. Further . . . the reforms are unlikely to stop there. Since 1981 there have been three other major tax bills; if history . . . is any guide, more changes will occur. . . . Because the development and creation of tax policy is a never ending process, the reader is well advised to view the Tax Reform Act of 1986 as a very large step in tax reform, but by no means the last.[7]

The 1987 and 1988 tax acts began to fulfill this prediction. At 91 and 471 pages, respectively, they were appreciably shorter than the 1986 tax act but still effected important changes in the federal income tax statute.[8]

The statute, furthermore, is just the beginning. The Treasury has been charged by Congress with issuing regulations interpreting the Code. These interpretive regulations already occupy nearly 5,000 pages in three volumes.[9] And they would (and will) continue to grow, even if the process of changing the Code came to a complete halt, since there is a considerable backlog of Code sections amended or enacted in 1981, 1982, 1984, 1986, 1987 and 1988 for which regulations are still being written. It is hardly surprising that the Treasury has fallen so far behind, given the volume of statutory changes during this decade.

In addition to the regulations, the Internal Revenue Service (IRS) issues a constant stream of legal interpretations, usually denoted *Revenue Rulings* or *Revenue Procedures,* which are published in the IRS Cumulative Bulletin. Besides the published rulings and revenue procedures, the IRS also issues thousands of private rulings each year.[10]

---

4. Deficit Reduction Act of 1984, Pub. L. 98–369, 98 Stat. 494, 494–1210 (1984).
5. Tax Reform Act of 1986, Pub. L. 99–514, 100 Stat. 2085, 2085–2963 (1986).
6. J. Eustice, et. al., The Tax Reform Act of 1986, 1–5 (1987).
7. An Analysis of the Tax Reform Act of 1986, 3 (1986).
8. Omnibus Budget Reconciliation Act of 1987, Pub. L. 100–203, 101 Stat. 1330, 1330–382 to 1330–472 (1987) and The Technical and Miscellaneous Revenue Act of 1988, Pub. L. 100–647, 102 Stat. 3342, 3342–3812 (1988). The 1987 Act changed the treatment of home mortgages, partnerships, and installment sales. The 1988 Act was ostensibly a "technical corrections measure" to cure technical defects in the massive 1986 overhaul of the Code, but Congress could not resist also making nontechnical changes in the taxation of creative artists, life insurance, and savings for education.
9. Income Tax Regulations, Volumes I–III, U.S. Code Cong. and Admin. News (1989).
10. A private ruling applies the tax law to specific facts submitted to the IRS by an attorney or accountant on behalf of a client. Since 1974, the IRS has been required to make such rulings available to the public. Tax Analysts and Advocates v. Internal Revenue Service, 505 F.2d 350 (D.C. Cir. 1974) interpreted the Freedom of Information Act to require public disclosure of private rulings. The decision was codified, with some modification, in the 1976 Tax Reform Act. See Section 6110.

Finally, there are judicial opinions arising from litigation between taxpayers and the government. In a typical year, the Supreme Court decides just a handful of income tax cases, and the Circuit Courts of Appeal, perhaps several hundred. But the trial courts—the Tax Court, the Court of Claims, and federal district courts—decide tens of thousands of tax cases annually.[11]

How does a law student begin to make sense of, let alone master, this subject? Not even the most knowledgeable tax lawyer knows more than a tiny fraction of the federal income tax law. Fortunately, lurking beneath the mass of technical detail is a deeper structure, a conceptual or theoretical map, that enables the practitioner to spot problems and identify issues even before the actual legal research begins.

The principal objective of this casebook is to convey that conceptual or theoretical map. While a fair amount of technical detail is also presented, the technical detail is not an end in itself. In a basic course, it primarily serves as a reflection of the deeper structure.

In contemplating this deeper structure, it is useful to recall the statement of purpose for Professor Bittker's *five-volume* treatise on federal taxation:

> My objective in this work has been to provide guidance and orientation by emphasizing the purpose, structure, and principal effects of the Internal Revenue Code, without bogging down in details. . . . These are challenging objectives and some may think they are doomed to fail because the Internal Revenue Code is a quagmire of detail in which no structural principles or logic can be discerned. I do not minimize the difficulties. . . . Nevertheless, I am convinced that the Code is more than a laundry list of discrete items . . . and that routes through the bog can be picked out.[12]

A second objective of these materials is to place the tax law in a broader social and economic context. The tax law has an enormous impact, pervading every sphere of public and even private life. It may be a major cause of our society's primary reliance on private automobiles, rather than mass transit, for transportation and on single-family dwellings, rather than apartment buildings, for housing. It may also affect a couple's decision to marry or have children. To study the tax law, then, can be to hold up a mirror to ourselves and to examine the basic value choices that we, as a people, have made.

Being so all-pervasive, taxation is naturally an intensely political subject. A myriad of groups lobby Congress to amend the tax laws to serve their particular, and often conflicting, interests. The degree to which one group succeeds, rather than another, reflects the distribution of political power in our society.

> Our taxes reflect a continuing struggle among contending interests for the privilege of paying the least. . . . Tax legislation commonly derives from

---

11. These figures are estimates. In fiscal year 1983, taxpayers disputed over 34,000 cases in the Tax Court. U.S. General Accounting Office, Report to the Chief Judge United States Tax Court: Tax Court Can Reduce Growing Case Backlog and Expenses Through Administrative Improvement 1 (1984).

12. B. Bittker, Federal Taxation of Income, Estates and Gifts, p. vii (1981).

private pressures exerted for selfish ends. . . . Class politics is of the essence of taxation.[13]

Because of the massive amount of technical detail in the statute and regulations, most students approach the basic tax course with low expectations (and considerable foreboding). By the end, however, they are often pleasantly surprised by its conceptual character, as well as by the basic value questions and political issues that are raised.

B. INTRODUCTORY PROBLEMS

Each chapter includes at least one set of problems (usually denoted "Notes and Questions"). Trying to answer them is indispensable to learning these materials. Because taxation is concerned with the economics of everyday life, many of the problems will involve economic or financial analysis, and numerical examples will be used throughout. It is critical to work with numbers from the start. If numbers induce panic, try Lamaze breathing or say a mantra. But don't give up. The math isn't all that hard.

The introductory problems in this chapter raise some of the basic questions that occur under an income tax. For each, first try to think through for yourself what the answer should be *and why*. Don't worry about the actual result provided under the Internal Revenue Code.

1) The President of Georgetown University lives for free in a university-owned house on the main campus. Should the rental value of the house be reported as income? If it should be, how would you determine the amount?

2) Sara Eder, the drama critic for The New York Times, reviews three plays a week. All theater tickets are provided to her by producers at no cost. Should the value of the tickets be taxed to her as income?

3) Susan Thomas, an amateur art historian, is an expert on early twentieth century American paintings. One Saturday, during an auction at the Berry-Hill Gallery, Susan saw an original Raphael Soyer mislabeled as the work of another artist. (The mistake occurred, in part, because the painting was unsigned.) None of the other bidders noticed the error, and Ms. Thomas' offer of $1,000 was the winning bid. Three weeks later, her insurance company appraised the painting (which was hanging in Ms. Thomas' bedroom) at $6,000. Should the difference between what she paid and its appraised value be taxable income to her?

4) Harry Stassen holds Texaco stock for which he paid $5,000 at the end of last year. It has recently doubled in value. Should the increase in value be counted as income?

5) Sheila Alexander is a free lance writer. She earns $50,000 a year, $5,000 of which she puts in a money market fund for her retirement. Should her retirement savings be included in her taxable income?

6) Ambrose Bierce, an IBM executive, is paid a cash salary of $45,000 a year. In addition, IBM contributes $5,000 a year to a pension fund for

---

13. L. Eisenstein, The Ideologies of Taxation 3–5 (1961).

Bierce. He will be entitled to annual payments from the fund after he reaches 65 years of age. Should the pension fund contribution be counted as income to Bierce when it is made?

7) Frances Morgan owns a farm in Baraboo, Wisconsin. The farm produces and sells milk, beef, and fresh vegetables. She and her family consume about 10% of the farm's output for their own needs. Should the value of the food that she and her family produce and consume be taxed as income?

Read Section 61(a) of the Internal Revenue Code. Under Section 61(a), how does it appear that these problems will be decided? In fact, *none* of the transactions described above will produce taxable income, in most cases because of a specific Internal Revenue Code section or regulation. Citations are provided below to the authority for nontaxation in each case.

1) Section 119(a) (provided that specified conditions are met).
2) Section 132(a)(3) and (d).
3) Reg. § 1.61-6(a)—first sentence only.
4) Same as above.
5) Self-employed individuals are permitted to deduct savings placed in a designated retirement account, up to the limits specified in Section 415(c)(1).
6) Employees are not taxed on amounts contributed on their behalf by employers to so-called "qualified pension plans" until "actually distributed." Section 402(a)(1) (first sentence).
7) Although Section 61(a) might be read to cover such income, the IRS has never tried to assert that it does. According to one leading authority, such "income is not exempted from tax by a specific statutory provision, but congressional silence on the subject is clearly tantamount to an affirmative grant of immunity."[14] However, the IRS tells farmers not to deduct the cost of raising home-consumed produce.[15] Suppose that Frances Morgan raises $50,0000 worth of produce at a cost of $20,000, consuming 10% of it at home and selling the rest. What is her income?

If a decision is made not to treat any of the seven transactions above as producing income, might taxation nevertheless occur at a later date when further steps are taken? In such cases, the decision whether to tax the transaction is simply a matter of now or later. This means that the issue is when the income will be taxed, or timing. In other cases, however, the decision is a matter of now or never. This means that the issue is whether the income will be taxed now or excluded for all time. Which of the problems above involve timing issues and which involve exclusion issues?

If the issue is "merely" timing, what is the advantage to taxpayers of postponing the reporting of income? One possibility is that, if the income is reported later rather than sooner, it will be taxed at a lower rate. But even if the rate of tax is not expected to change, why would it still be advantageous to report income later rather than sooner? What could be done with the amount that would otherwise be paid in taxes during the period of postponement?

---

14. B. Bittker, Federal Taxation of Income, Estates and Gifts 5–22 n.1 (1980).
15. See IRS Pub. No. 225, Farmer's Tax Guide 22 (1986 ed.) and Nowland v. Commissioner, 244 F.2d 450 (4th Cir. 1957) (deduction representing costs of producing food for family properly disallowed).

C. THE INCOME TAX: BASIC MECHANICS

Although this casebook emphasizes a conceptual approach, readers should be familiar with the basic mechanics of calculating taxes due under the federal income tax statute. Vastly simplified, the steps are as follows.

1) Calculating Taxable Income

The first step is to list all items which must be reported. This produces a category known as *gross income* or GI (defined in Section 61(a)). The taxpayer is then instructed to take deductions for certain expenses that are primarily (although not exclusively) incurred in business activities. GI minus these deductions equals *adjusted gross income* or AGI (defined in Section 62). The final step is to take additional deductions that are primarily (although not exclusively) of a nonbusiness nature and are generally referred to by the Code as *itemized deductions*. AGI minus these amounts equals *taxable income* or TI (defined in Section 63).

One reason for taking deductions in two separate steps, to produce AGI first and TI second, is that the availability of some itemized deductions depends on the level of AGI. For example, unreimbursed medical expenses are deductible only to the extent that they exceed 7.5% of AGI and casualty losses only to the extent that they exceed 10% of AGI.[16]

Suppose that in 1988 Joanna Miller, a single person, living alone, earns a salary of $50,000, has dividend income of $10,000 from stock, spends $5,000 on business travel for which she is reimbursed by her employer, has unreimbursed medical expenses of $10,000, and contributes $5,000 to charities. Her GI equals her salary, plus dividend income, plus the amount that she is reimbursed for her business travel, or $65,000. She has business expenses of $5,000 which she can deduct from GI to produce AGI of $60,000. See Section 62(a)(2)(A).[17]

From AGI, she is entitled to deduct a personal exemption of $1,950. See Section 151(a), (b), and (d)(1)(B).[18] In addition, she may deduct all of her $5,000 in charitable contributions and $5,500 of her medical expenses, which is the excess over 7.5% of AGI. See Section 213(a). Thus, her personal exemption plus itemized deductions equal $12,450, and her TI is $47,550.

A taxpayer who does not elect to list separately the itemized deductions allowed by Section 63 is entitled to take the standard deduction provided by Section 63(c). The size of the standard deduction depends on one's family status. For a single taxpayer in 1988, the amount is $3,000. For a married couple filing a joint return, it is $5,000. In general, a taxpayer

---

16. However, corporations and other entities do not separately calculate AGI but simply take all deductions from GI in one step. See the reference in Section 62(a) to the "individual" taxpayer.

17. Some readers may ask why taxpayers should have to go to the trouble of reporting and then deducting reimbursed business expenses. Under Reg. § 1.274–5T(f)(2), the Treasury permits employees to *not* report reimbursed business expenses if an "adequate accounting" is made to the employer and if reimbursements equal expenses.

18. For 1989, the personal exemption rises to $2,000. Section 151(d)(1)(C). Thereafter, the amount is to be adjusted annually for inflation. Section 151(d)(3).

should claim the standard deduction only if it exceeds the taxpayer's separately listed and allowable itemized deductions.

2) Determining the Tax Due: Income Tax Rates

The tax due is determined by multiplying the individual's taxable income by the appropriate tax rates. The number and level of rates have varied considerably over the years. The Revenue Act of 1913, passed after enactment of the Sixteenth Amendment, contained low rates ranging from 1% to 7%. World War I produced a dramatic change, as the top individual rate rose to 77% to help finance the war effort. After the war, the top rate fell to 24% but rose in the aftermath of the Great Depression to 63% in 1932 and to 79% in 1936. To finance military expenditures during World War II, Congress imposed substantially higher taxes with individual rates as high as 94%. The rates fell slightly after World War II, rose again during the Korean War, and then in 1965 the top rate settled at 70%. In 1982, the range was reduced further, to thirteen rates ranging from 11% to 50%. The 1986 Tax Reform Act explicitly provides, beginning in 1988, for a structure with just two individual rates of 15% and 28%. See Section 1(a)-(e).

Tax rates for corporations have varied somewhat less than individual rates. For over three decades until 1986, a flat rate applied to all corporate income over a minimum amount. Although periodically modified, the flat rate hovered at just above, or just below, 50%. Beginning in 1987, the corporate rate is stated to be 34% on income over $75,000. See Section 11.

Each tax rate is applied by the Code to a range of income or *tax bracket*. Under Section 1(a)-(d), each bracket varies according to an individual's family status and according to whether the individual, if married, files jointly or separately. Beginning in 1989, the brackets are to be adjusted for inflation. See Section 1(f).

Income within each bracket is taxed at the designated rate, no matter what the taxpayer's total income. Only income in excess of the bracket's upper limit is taxed at a different rate. For example, the first bracket, to which the 15% rate applies, starts at zero and rises to $17,850 for single individuals. If a single individual's taxable income is less than or equal to $17,850, the tax rate will obviously be 15%. But even if taxable income exceeds the upper limit of the 15% bracket, or $17,850, the first $17,850 is still taxed at 15%. Only income in excess of $17,850 is taxed at a higher rate.[19]

Which tax brackets and rates apply to Joanna Miller, whose tax status is described above? How much will she owe? See Sections 1(a)-(d). In order to determine their tax liability, most individuals do not have to actually multiply each bracket of their taxable income by the designated rate. Instead, they consult tax tables provided by the Treasury, which incorporate such calculations.

---

19. However, the rate applied to income in excess of the 15% bracket can be designed to eliminate the benefit of the lower rate bracket as income rises. See Section D, below.

D. APPEARANCES ARE DECEIVING: THE HIDDEN 33% TAX RATE

The new "simplified" structure of only two brackets and rates for individuals, 15% and 28%, provided under Section 1(a)-(e), is deceptive. By virtue of Section 1(g), the tax rate on additional income may actually reach 33%! How can this happen?

Once a taxpayer's income reaches a certain level, extra dollars of income become subject to a 5% surcharge in addition to the 28% rate, for a total tax rate of 33%. However, at some point, the 5% surcharge is lifted, so that additional dollars revert back to being taxed at only 28%.

To illustrate, Code Section 1(c) represents single individuals as facing the following tax brackets and rates:

Not over $17,850 ....15%
Over $17,850..28%

But when account is taken of the 5% surcharge of Section 1(g), the actual tax brackets and rates are:

Not over $17,850 ....15%
Over $17,850 up to $43,150......................28%
Over $43,150 up to $100,480 ....33%
Over $100,480 ....28%[20]

Recalculate how much Joanna Miller owes (in the example under section C), above) taking account of the 5% surcharge.

Section 1(g)(3) specifies the level at which the surcharge kicks in, based on the taxpayer's family status. How do you determine the level of income at which the surcharge is *removed* and the tax rate falls back to 28%? The purpose of the surcharge is to phase out the benefit of the 15% bracket and of personal exemptions for higher-income taxpayers. Thus, the surcharge is removed when the extra tax that it imposes equals the amount of tax "saved" by:

a) lower levels of income being taxed at the rate of 15% as opposed to 28%; and

b) personal exemptions allowed under Section 151 for the taxpayer and his or her dependents. See Section 1(g)(2).

To illustrate, a single individual with taxable income in excess of $17,850 saves 13% of $17,850, or $2,320.50, because lower levels of the taxpayer's income are taxed at 15% instead of 28%. This individual also saves 28% of $1,950, or $546, by virtue of the Section 151 personal exemption (without it, the taxpayer would have that much additional income taxable at 28%).[21]

---

20. This table assumes that the taxpayer has no dependents. See the discussion below.

21. This assumes that the personal exemption is set at the 1988 level of $1,950. In 1989, with the personal exemption rising to $2,000, the income level at which the 5% surcharge is removed—in this example—will increase by 28% of $50, or $14.

Ch. 1   Introduction

The total savings from both sources is $2,866.50. The 5% surcharge kicks in at $43,150 and applies to the next $57,330 so that the Treasury can make back the $2,866.50 that it lost by virtue of the 15% bracket and personal exemptions.

Similar computations are incorporated in tax tables for taxpayers of different family status. For example, a married couple, with no dependents, filing jointly appears to face the following tax bracket and rates under Section 1(a):

Not over $29,750 ....15%
Over $29,750...28%

But when account is taken of the surcharge of Section 1(g), the actual tax brackets and rates are:

Not over $29,750 ....15%
Over $29,750 up to $71,900........................28%
Over $71,900 up to $171,090 ....33%
Over $171,090 ....28%[22]

A surcharge also applies to corporations. Section 11 appears to provide for taxing corporate income at three separate brackets and rates:

Not over $50,000 ....15%
Over $50,000 up to $75,000........................25%
Over $75,000...34%

However, corporate income above $100,000 is subject to a 5% surcharge. The purpose is to phase out the benefit of the two lower brackets of 15% and 25%. Thus, when account is taken of the surcharge, the actual corporate rates are:

Not over $50,000 ....15%
Over $50,000 up to $75,000........................25%
Over $75,000 up to $100,000 ....34%
Over $100,000 up to $335,000....................39%
Over $335,000 ....34%

Was it misleading of the President and Congress to trumpet, as they did, the 1986 Tax Reform Act as providing *only* two tax rates for individuals, 15% and 28%? Would it have been more straightforward to provide explicitly for a third higher rate and fairer to apply that rate to all income above a certain level, instead of only within a limited bracket?

---

22. This table also assumes that the personal exemption is set at the 1988 level of $1,950. See the preceding footnote.

E. BEFORE TAX AND AFTER TAX: THE CRITICAL IMPORTANCE OF THE MARGINAL RATE

Suppose that your employer pays you a $100 end-of-the-year bonus. The benefit of that $100 can be examined from two different perspectives: first, without taking the income tax into account, or *before tax;* and second, after taking such effects into account, or *after tax.*

From a before-tax perspective, a $100 bonus is obviously worth just that—$100. An after-tax perspective, however, is more complicated and depends on how much of the $100 must be paid for federal income taxes. The amount due in federal taxes is determined, in turn, by the rate at which the income is taxed. This rate is not constant but depends on your tax bracket, as explained above. And the tax bracket depends on how much other income you have. Thus, in determining the after-tax benefit of the $100 bonus, the critical variable is the *marginal* tax rate—the rate at which this additional income is taxed.

For example, assuming that you are a single individual with taxable income of $17,000, then an additional $100 of income will be taxed at 15%. After taxes, you will have $85 left out of the $100. But if your other income is between $17,850 and $43,050, then the additional $100 will be taxed at 28% and be worth $72 after taxes. If you believe that there are currently only two tax rates for individuals—the two explicitly provided of 15% and 28%—you might mistakenly conclude that the after-tax benefit of $100 must be at least $72. But if the 5% surcharge applies to you—because your other income is between $43,150 and $100,380—then the actual rate of tax on the additional $100 is 33%, and after taxes you have only $67 left.

The two different perspectives—before tax and after tax—are also important in evaluating the effect of deducting an expenditure. Suppose that you give $100 to charity. The cost of the expenditure can be examined from either the before-tax or after-tax perspective. Before tax, a $100 charitable contribution obviously costs $100. The after-tax cost is a more complicated matter. It depends on how much you save in taxes as a result of having made a contribution. Because of the deduction for charitable contributions (Section 170(a)), you will be able to reduce your taxable income by $100. The amount saved depends on the rate at which the $100 of income would have been taxed but for the charitable contribution deduction. And that, in turn, *also* depends on your marginal tax rate.

For example, if the income would have been taxed at only 15%, then the tax saving is $15 and the after-tax cost of the $100 charitable contribution is $85. But if the income would have been taxable at 28% (or even 33%), then the tax saving is $28 (or $33), and the after-tax cost is $72 (or $67).[23]

---

23. In addition to federal income taxes, the effect of state or local taxes on income should also be taken into account. This is more complicated than it seems, because state or local income taxes are deductible for federal income tax purposes under Section 164. To illustrate, suppose that your federal income tax bracket is 33% and that your state income tax bracket is 10%. Because state income taxes are deductible, the after-tax cost of $100 of such taxes is only $67. The after-tax state income tax rate is 10%, minus 33% times 10%, which equals 6.7%. Thus, the combined federal and state income tax rate is not 43% (the 33% federal rate plus the 10% state rate) but rather 39.7% (the 33% federal rate plus the state after-tax rate of 6.7%).

Learning to analyze problems from an after-tax perspective is neither easy nor automatic. But it is a critical skill whether you are making tax policy or advising a private client. Thus, one of the goals of these materials is to teach you the mental habit of analyzing transactions from both before-tax and after-tax points of view.

F. WHY TAX INCOME? ALTERNATIVE METHODS OF FINANCING GOVERNMENT

The primary purpose of the income tax is to pay for government expenditures. Yet there are alternative ways of financing government. Try to evaluate each of the methods and standards described below in terms of how fairly each allocates the burden of paying taxes.

1) Printing Money

In theory, the government could pay all its bills simply by printing money. Why isn't this method exclusively used? Wouldn't it be much simpler than having to collect taxes? If this method were adopted, how would the burden of paying for government be allocated? Would such an allocation be fair?

2) User Fees: The Benefit Principle

Another possibility is to charge each individual according to how much he or she uses government goods and services. Under this method, a heavy user would pay more than a moderate user, and a moderate user more than a light user, and so on. Apportioning taxes in this way is said to be justified by the Benefit Principle: the idea that taxes should be apportioned according to benefits received.

User fees, in whole or in part, finance a few government programs. For example, the interstate highway system was partly paid for by federal taxes on gasoline. What are the practical limits of the Benefit Principle? Can it help to determine how to apportion taxes to pay for the Federal court system, the Defense Department, or foreign policy? Why not?

3) The Per Capita or Head Tax

Why not simply take the total amount that needs to be raised by taxes, divide it by the number in the population, and require each person to pay his or her proportionate share? For example, if federal expenditures are one trillion dollars and the population is 250 million, then each person would pay $4,000 under a head tax.

In reality, a head tax would not be that simple. Disabled citizens and minor children might pay only a fractional share or be exempted altogether. But a head tax would be infinitely easier to administer than an income tax.

Under what conditions would a head tax be consistent with the Benefit Principle? How do you react to the idea of a head tax? Can you explain your reaction?

4) The Ability-to-Pay Principle: Does it Justify an Income Tax?

Apportioning taxes on the basis of income is explained most often by the Ability-to-Pay Principle. The higher one's income, the more one is considered able to pay for the cost of government. Therefore, it is argued, the measure of taxes due should be an individual's income.

Income can be defined as the amount by which a taxpayer's wealth *increases* during a given period of time. Is income, thus defined, necessarily the best measure of Ability-to-Pay? Doesn't wealth itself provide a better measure of ability to pay for the cost of government? What are the practical obstacles to taxing wealth?

5) The Standard-of-Living Principle: Consumption as a Tax Base

An individual's income can be spent for two basic purposes: consumption (such as food and clothing) and saving (such as stocks). Some people believe that consumption is a fairer measure of how taxes should be apportioned than total income and therefore that savings should not be included in the tax base. The exclusion of savings is justified by the Standard-of-Living Principle: it is only to the extent that an individual actually uses up economic resources that he or she should be taxed. Amounts saved are not consumed and remain part of society's productive resources. Therefore, savings should be taxed only when they are withdrawn and spent on personal consumption.

Does the Standard-of-Living Principle suggest that items 4–6 in the problems under section C), above, should not be taxed? How do you react to the idea that savings should be excluded from income? Is a savings exclusion consistent with levying taxes according to Ability-to-Pay?

G. ALTERNATIVE RATE STRUCTURES

For the entire history of the federal income tax, the rate structure has been *progressive,* meaning that as a taxable income rises, a *larger* proportion is due in taxes. Progression in rates is usually contrasted with *proportionality* under which, as a taxpayer's income rises, the *same* proportion remains due in taxes. A third possibility is a *regressive* rate structure, under which, as a taxpayer's income rises, a *smaller* proportion is due in taxes.

Table 1–1 illustrates the difference between progressive, proportional, and regressive rate structures. It assumes a society with only four taxpayers, whose incomes are $20,000, $40,000, $60,000, and $80,000. Revenues of $50,000 must be raised to pay for government, and the tax will be imposed on income.

The progressive rate structure is assumed to be:

Not over $20,000	15%
Over $20,000 up to $40,000	25%
Over $40,000 up to $60,000	35%
Over $60,000	45%

The proportional rate is assumed to be 25% for taxpayers at all income levels. The regressive rate structure is assumed to be:

Not over $20,000 ....35%
Over $20,000 up to $40,000 ....25%
Over $40,000 up to $60,000 ....15%
Over $60,000 ....5%

As explained above, the progressive and regressive schedules contain marginal rates, which apply only to a range of income or tax bracket. Another important figure, indicated in Table 1–1, is the average rate of tax at different income levels. The average rate is the weighted average of the marginal rates and can be derived by dividing taxes due by total income.

TABLE 1–1. COMPARISON OF PROGRESSIVE, PROPORTIONAL, AND REGRESSIVE RATE STRUCTURES

Income	Progressive Rates		Proportional Rates		Regressive Rates	
	Taxes Due	Ave. Rate	Taxes Due	Ave. Rate	Taxes Due	Ave. Rate
20,000	3,000	15%	5,000	25%	7,000	35%
40,000	8,000	20%	10,000	25%	12,000	30%
60,000	15,000	25%	15,000	25%	15,000	25%
80,000	24,000	30%	20,000	25%	16,000	20%
Total	50,000		50,000		50,000	

Under what assumptions are either progressive, proportional, or regressive rates consistent with the Benefit Principle (discussed in section F), above)? Consider the following comments:

> [John Stuart] Mill ... argued that the persons who would suffer most if the protection of government were to be withdrawn would be those "who were weakest in mind or body, either by nature or position," so that a tax system geared to the taxpayer's benefits would impose the heaviest burden on "those who are least capable of helping or defending themselves."
>
> In asserting that the poor benefit more from government than the rich, Mill may have been contrasting the England of his day with a feudal society, on the unstated assumption that the rich (primarily great landlords) would have been powerful and independent feudal barons if "the protection of government" were withdrawn; at any rate, if this were the only alternative model, there would be some validity in his argument. It is surprising, however, that the French revolution did not suggest another model to him, *viz.*, that "those to whom the protection of government is the most indispensable" are the lords and their ladies, not the wretched of the earth. If wealth is seen as dependent for its protection on the existence of a legal order, rather than as an attribute of man which antedates government and can be preserved by self-help, Mill's argument collapses. What good are stock certificates, or even deeds to real estate, in a society in which ownership depends on brute force?[24]

---

24. B. Bittker in B. Bittker and C. Galvin, The Income Tax: How Progressive Should It Be? 48–49 (1969).

How is the distribution of wealth affected by a decision to adopt more progressive rates? How are the relative after-tax incomes of the four individuals in Table 1–1 affected by progressive, as opposed to proportional, rates? By proportional, as opposed to regressive?

One argument for more progressive rates is to redistribute income from higher to lower income groups. How can redistribution be justified? By a moral obligation to aid those who are less well off? By a judgment that individuals may sometimes have very large incomes as a result of luck (including the advantage of having been born to affluent parents) rather than merit?

In 1988, about 50,000 Americans had incomes in excess of half a million dollars, and about 20,000 had incomes of $1 million or more.[25] Is it fair to tax such high incomes at a rate of only 28%, as our tax system has since 1988?

H. SUGGESTIONS FOR FURTHER READING

Many students find M. Chirelstein, Federal Income Taxation: A Law Student's Guide to Leading Cases and Concepts to be helpful, or even indispensable, to learning basic income tax. Both Commerce Clearing House and Prentice-Hall publish looseleaf services, organized by Code section, which cite and summarize most regulations, cases, and public rulings. Readers wishing to pursue any particular subject in more depth might begin with B. Bittker, Federal Taxation of Income, Estates and Gifts, which is also available in an abridged student edition. Professor Bittker's treatise lists leading law review articles in footnotes at the beginning of each section dealing with a particular topic. In addition, Federal Tax Articles, published by Commerce Clearing House provides a comprehensive listing of law review articles organized by Code section. Readers interested in exploring the social and economic dimension of federal income taxation might consult the multivolume series published by the Brookings Institution on tax policy issues. Finally, Tax Notes, published weekly by Tax Analysts, surveys current developments in tax law and policy.

---

25. These are estimates based on 1985 figures. See Internal Revenue Service, Individual Income Tax Returns—1985, p. 12 (1988).

PART ONE

Compensation for Personal Services

Part One deals with the taxation of compensation for personal services, also referred to as income from labor or as earned income. When compensation for services consists of cash, the federal income tax treatment is usually straightforward. Cash compensation is covered by Section 61(a)(1) and included in gross income.

Most of the issues discussed in Part One arise when compensation is paid in a form other than cash. The generic name applied to such noncash compensation is *income in kind* (as distinguished from income in cash). The broad language of Section 61(a)(1) appears to include income in kind just as clearly as income in cash. Nevertheless, the taxation of income in kind has raised special problems throughout the history of the Internal Revenue Code.

For example, suppose that an automobile salesperson receives, in addition to a regular salary, a free car. Should this in-kind benefit be reported as income? What if the employee does not especially like the car provided? For example, what if the car is a two-door convertible and the employee would prefer a four-door sedan? What if the employee is required to return the car in the event she takes another job within two years? What difference does it make if the employee does not receive the car free of charge but is given a substantial discount, for example, 20% below the automobile dealer's cost? Should the car be excluded from income altogether if the employee uses it to commute to work and as a demonstration vehicle for potential customers? Should it be excluded even if the employee's family uses the car on weekends and vacations?

Chapter 2

LIMITED CHOICE AND RESTRICTED PROPERTY

A. UNITED STATES v. DRESCHER
179 F.2d 863 (2d Cir. 1950), cert. denied, 340 U.S. 821 (1950)

SWAN, CIRCUIT JUDGE.

This appeal brings up for review an action against the United States to recover additional income taxes for the years 1939 and 1940 which the plaintiff asserts were illegally assessed and collected. He was an officer and director of Bausch & Lomb Optical Company, and in each of the taxable years the Company purchased from an insurance company at a cost of $5,000 a single premium annuity contract naming him as the annuitant. The taxes in dispute resulted from the Commissioner's including such cost as additional compensation received by the plaintiff in the year when the annuity contract was purchased. The district court awarded the plaintiff judgment for overpayments . . . ruling that he received no income in 1939 or 1940 attributable to the purchase of the annuity contracts. The correctness of this ruling is presented by the appeal.

The facts are not in dispute. In 1936 the Optical Company inaugurated a plan to provide for the voluntary retirement at the age of 65 of its principal officers then under that age. There were five such, of whom Mr. Drescher was one. He was born April 28, 1894. Pursuant to this plan and in "recognition of prior services rendered," the Company purchased on December 28, 1939, and on the same date in 1940, a single premium, non-forfeitable annuity contract which named Mr. Drescher as the annuitant. Each policy was issued by Connecticut General Life Insurance Company and was delivered to the Optical Company which retained possession of it. It was the Company's intention, and so understood by the annuitant, that possession of the policy should be retained until the annuitant should reach the age of 65. The premium paid for each policy was $5,000. . . .

By the terms of the policy the Insurance Company agrees to pay the annuitant, commencing on December 28, 1958, a life income of $54.70 monthly under the 1939 policy and $44.80 monthly under the 1940 policy, with a minimum of 120 monthly payments. If the annuitant dies before receiving 120 monthly payments, the rest of them are payable to the beneficiary named in the policy. Each policy gives the annuitant an option to accelerate the date when monthly payments shall commence, but this option must be exercised by the annuitant in writing and endorsed on the policy. Consequently so long as the Optical Company retains possession of the policy the annuitant cannot exercise the option. If the annuitant dies before December 28, 1958, or before the acceleration date if he has exercised the option to accelerate monthly income payments, a death benefit is payable to the beneficiary designated by him (his wife). The policy reserves to him the right to change the beneficiary. The policy declares that "Neither this contract nor any payment hereunder may be assigned, and the contract and all payments shall be free from the claims of all creditors to the fullest extent permitted by law." The policy has no cash surrender, salable, or loan value . . . .

This case is governed by the provisions of the Internal Revenue Code as they existed in 1939 and 1940. The appellant contends that the contracts are taxable to the annuitant in the year of purchase by the employer because § 22(a), 26 U.S.C.A., sweeps into gross income "compensation for personal service, of whatever kind and in whatever form paid, . . . and income derived from any source whatever." . . .

[I]n Ward v. Commissioner . . . a single premium annuity contract [was] delivered to the annuitant and assignable by him. We there held that "the petitioner became taxable in 1941 upon whatever value was, by the delivery of the policy to him in that year, then unconditionally placed at his disposal. . . . This was the then assignable value of the policy." . . . We then considered whether it was error to value the policy in the amount of the premium paid for it. We recognized that the assignable value of the policy in 1941 might be less than the single premium paid for it, but as the purchaser had offered no proof that it was we held that the Tax Court was right in treating "cost to the purchaser as the assignable value of the policy when received by the taxpayer." . . .

As we shall not overrule the Ward case, the question is narrowed to determining whether the present case is distinguishable because the plaintiff's policies are non-assignable and were retained in the possession of the employer. We do not think these facts are sufficient to distinguish the cases with respect to taxability of the contracts, although they may affect the value of the rights the respective annuitants acquired. It cannot be doubted that in 1939 the plaintiff received as compensation for prior services something of economic benefit which he had not previously had, namely, the obligation of the insurance company to pay money in the future to him or his designated beneficiaries on the terms stated in the policy. That obligation he acquired in 1939 notwithstanding the employer's retention of possession of the policy and notwithstanding its non-assignability. The perplexing problem is how to measure the value of the annuitant's rights at the date he acquired them. The taxpayer contends that they then had no present value, while the appellant argues that their value was equal to the premium paid by the employer. We are unable to accept either contention.

The prohibition against assignment does not prove complete absence of present value.... [The annuity] may not have been worth to him the amount his employer paid for it; but it cannot be doubted that there is a figure, greater than zero although less than the premium cost, which it would have cost him to acquire identical rights.... Another element of value inheres in the possibility that the annuitant could realize cash by contracting with a putative third person to hold in trust for him any payments to be received under the annuity contract. True, the promisee would run the risk that the annuitant might die before becoming entitled to any payments, in which event they would be payable to the beneficiary designated in the policy, but by exercising the reserved power to change the beneficiary the annuitant could designate his promisee. The power to make such a contract based on the policy may well have had some present value. No proof was offered as to this.... [T]he plaintiff had the burden of proving the amount by which he was overtaxed. On the other hand, it seems clear that the policy was worth less to the annuitant than the premium paid because the employer's retention of possession precluded him from exercising the privilege of accelerating the date of annuity payments since the insurance company's approval had to be endorsed upon the policy. The granting of this privilege must have been one of the factors taken into account in fixing the premium—at least, we may so assume in the absence of evidence. Hence deprivation of ability to exercise the privilege would decrease the value of the policy to the annuitant below its cost to the employer.... [I]t is unnecessary on the present appeal to determine the precise valuation of the policies.

As already mentioned the burden of proving by how much he was overtaxed was on the plaintiff.... He relied upon the terms of the contract to prove that it had no present value whatever. But for reasons already stated we are satisfied that the 1939 policy had some present value and since he did not prove that such value was less than $5,000, the judgment in his favor cannot stand....

CLARK, CIRCUIT JUDGE (DISSENTING IN PART).

I agree that the judgment must be reversed, but do not share in the view that some amount less than the $5,000 expended by the employer for this taxpayer in each of the years in question may be found to be the value of the annuity and hence the amount of additional compensation for which he is to be taxed....

In the light of modern conditions of life, the satisfying of the highly natural and indeed burning desire of most men of middle age to obtain security for their old age and for their widows at death seems so clearly an economic benefit that I wonder it has been questioned as much as it has. Nor do I see the need to support this conclusion by looking for some highly theoretical possibility of turning this benefit into immediate dollars and cents any more than in the case where an employee is furnished living quarters or meals. Just as the latter are valued as additional compensation, though not assigned or assignable, so I think this highly valuable security is a purchased benefit for these company executives. Consequently the making of nice distinctions in either taxability or the amount thereof between assignable or accelerable annuities or their delivery or retention by the company—after careful forethought and advice of its attorneys with naturally an eye on both pension and tax possibilities[1]—seems to me improper, when the general purpose to make adequate retirement provisions for these employees was made so clear.

Hence for any issues here involved I do not think it is important to discover what reasons impelled the employer to make the slightly differing provisions from those before this court in Ward v. Commissioner. . . . Perhaps the employer may have had the prescience to foresee these tax problems which are troubling my brothers and did trouble the court below and may result in at least postponement, if not non-collectibility, of most, if not all, of the tax on the additional return provided by the employer for these executives. Perhaps, rather, the employer was providing only for a surer provision "free from the claims of all creditors to the fullest extent permitted by law" for this taxpayer and his wife. So in retaining possession of the policies and cherishing the present intent not to permit acceleration of the annuities, the employer may have had in mind a way of both securing the purchased services to the retirement age in normal cases and guarding against unusual situations due to disability or other special cause. In any event the fact is that the employer purchased at the going insurance rate those contracts which for the parties fulfilled the conditions desired.[2] Actually they would return to the annuitant, or to his widow, total amounts at least well in excess of the premiums paid and increasing yet more the longer he lived. The parties got just what they paid for in the insurance market, and its cost price is the additional compensation the executive received. The two features stressed in the opinion, namely, the nonassignability and the present nonaccelerability of the annuities, may add to their usability for the particular purpose, but would seem not to change the basis of value. Perhaps, indeed, they render the contracts more desirable not only to the employer, but also to the annuitant's wife, as making the security provisions less easily impaired, and thus have a special appeal to a husband solicitous of his wife's future. At least, I do not see what basis we have for thinking they adversely affect values of provisions for a particular purpose, *viz.*, security. If, in fact, these conditions do affect the amount of the premium, as the opinion rather naturally assumes, then all the more is the bargain of the parties to be respected as made; even the annuitant would doubtless be interested in a maximum return though it be strictly limited to himself or his wife. It seems to me that there is being set up some premise,

---

1. The annuity contracts for the earlier years, 1936 and 1937, were actually delivered by the president to the taxpayer and the other annuitants, but were retrieved after counsel had advised this course.
2. This was a tightly controlled corporation, so much so that the executives receiving the annuities and their families owned approximately 35 per cent of the voting stock, while the older officers and directors owned approximately 57 per cent. Hence there was never a sharp divergency of interest between these executives and their employer.

not found in any of the precedents, of a fictitious partly-impaired transferability which is now somehow to be given a value in place of the wholly practical values set upon these contracts in the insurance market itself. . . .

[T]he fact that the annuities in [other] cases were assignable should not make their purchase price any more accurate a gauge of their value than is the purchase price here. . . .

Hence unless these benefits are now taxed, this small group of top executives will be given a tax advantage not accruing to less fortunate or less well-advised persons. Such taxation should not be confused or rendered abortive by directions for valuation impossible of execution in any realistic way.

B. NOTES AND QUESTIONS

1) Nontax Aspects

The compensation in kind paid to Drescher consisted of an annuity contract. Under the annuity, an insurance company promised to pay him a stated monthly amount for life, starting when he retired. How much would Drescher be paid if he died before or soon after he was due to retire? In the event that he lived to be 100?

If his employer had not provided the annuity, Drescher could have purchased it himself from an insurance company. Why might he have wanted an annuity? What is the principal advantage of an annuity over other forms of saving for retirement, such as a mutual fund or money market account?

The annuity in *Drescher* was a form of insurance.[3] Against what risk did the annuity insure? Insurance against fire is usually called "fire insurance," insurance against earthquakes is "earthquake insurance," and so on. Is what we ordinarily call "life insurance" misnamed? Is it the annuity that is true "life insurance"? In that case, how might so-called "life insurance" be more accurately described?

2) The Stakes in *Drescher*

Assume that Drescher lives for exactly ten years after he retires, so that he receives $6,564 ($54.70 × 120 months) under the first annuity contract during his retirement. If Drescher is *not* taxed on the annuity in 1939 when it is purchased for him, how much income should he report during his retirement years from payments under the annuity contract? If Drescher *is* taxed on $5,000 in 1939, representing the value of the annuity at that

---

[3]. In its most general sense, the term, annuity, refers to any series of payments made at regular intervals. In more specialized usage, it refers to a series of payments made at regular intervals for the annuitant's life, as in *Drescher*.

time, why should the amount reported during retirement be reduced? Exactly what was at stake in *Drescher?*[4]

3) The Factor of Limited Choice

Suppose that Bausch & Lomb had simply given Drescher $5,000 in 1939 as a cash bonus and that Drescher had then purchased the annuity on his own. In that case, Drescher clearly would have to report the $5,000. Why should the result be any different if the employer buys the annuity and delivers it to Drescher? (Notice that taxing income in kind is equivalent to treating the employee as if he or she received income in cash and then used the cash to buy the item in question.)

Is it unfair to tax Drescher on the annuity at its full market price since it may not be what Drescher would have chosen for himself? Suppose we decide to tax compensation in kind at less than its cost because of the factor of limited choice. Wouldn't employees arrange to be paid as much as possible in kind rather than in cash in order to reduce their taxable income? As a practical matter, can special treatment be limited to cases where the compensation in kind is chosen by the employer and "forced" on the employee? Was *Drescher,* in fact, such a case? See footnote 2 to Judge Clark's concurring opinion.

4) The Assignability Issue

Much of the *Drescher* opinion is devoted to discussing the fact that the annuity contract was nonassignable. How is this logically related to the factor of limited choice? If the contract had been assignable, would Drescher's choice still have been limited? If Drescher were able to sell the contract, what price would he be able to charge?

How does the majority deal with the nonassignability issue? How does Judge Clark? What is the difference between the two approaches?

5) Hanrahan v. Commissioner

In Hanrahan v. Commissioner, 50 T.C.M. 440 (1985), an inmate at the Joliet, Illinois Correctional Center worked as a prison plumber and was paid about $3,000 for his services. Under prison rules, the amounts were not paid to Hanrahan directly but were deposited in a General Inmate Trust Fund and credited to his account. Inmates were allowed to use their accounts either to purchase items from the prison commissary or to send

---

4. At this very early point in the course, I have found it advisable *not* to do a rigorous present value analysis of the benefits of deferral. Present value theory and the time value of money are formally presented only in Chapter 12. At that point, I begin to quantify the benefits of deferral in a variety of situations.

In addition, one of the complicating aspects of the annuity in *Drescher* is that not taxing it currently might provide *no* benefit at all *if* the investment income earned on the annuitant's behalf is taxed to the insurance company. This counter-intuitive result is discussed more fully in Chapters 55 and 56 at the casebook's end.

money to relatives and friends. Hanrahan had not used his funds for either purpose and argued that he was not taxable on them.

The Tax Court held that the amounts deposited and credited to Hanrahan's account were income under IRC Section 61(a), noting, "We have carefully reviewed the relevant law and have failed to find a provision that would specifically exempt the payments received by petitioner." (The Court offered no other explanation for its decision.)

Is the argument for not taxing Hanrahan stronger or weaker than the argument for not taxing Drescher on the annuity? Is the factor of limited choice more compelling in *Hanrahan* than in *Drescher*?

6) Valuation of Restricted Property

Because Bausch & Lomb retained physical possession of the annuity contract, Drescher was unable to use the acceleration option. The annuity sold for $5,000 with the acceleration option, so the policy was presumably worth something less without it.

Suppose Drescher had proved that the value of the annuity was reduced by $200 because his employer retained possession and consequently restricted use of the acceleration option. Would such proof have affected the outcome of the case? Under the majority opinion? Under Judge Clark's separate opinion?

Should the effect of restrictions be taken into account? What is the danger if they are? See footnote 1 to Judge Clark's opinion.

Section 83(a), enacted in 1969, states that if an employee is paid in kind, his or her income shall include "the fair market value of such property (determined without regard to any restriction other than a restriction which by its terms will never lapse)..." How would the annuity contract in *Drescher* be valued under this language? Is the restriction "never lapsing"? Suppose that it is viewed as never lapsing and that five years after buying the contract, Bausch & Lomb gives Drescher physical possession. What are the tax consequences, assuming that Section 83 applies? See Section 83(d)(2).

7) Section 83(a) and the Risk of Forfeiture

Although Section 83(a) generally requires that restrictions be ignored in valuing compensation in kind, it contains one other important exception: when the property is subject to a substantial risk of forfeiture *and* is nontransferable. In that case, the employee is not taxed until either the risk of forfeiture disappears *or* the restriction on transferability is lifted. Why make this exception?

Apply Section 83(a) to the following problem. Harold Ickes has just been hired by International Business Machines (IBM). His employment contract provides that he will receive, in addition to a cash salary, ten shares of IBM stock as a bonus for joining IBM. However, the IBM stock is subject to a special restriction printed on the stock certificates. It may not be sold or otherwise transferred to any other party for five years. It is generally agreed that such a restriction reduces the value of stock by 20%. Assume that IBM stock trades for $100 per share on the New York Stock Exchange on the date of the transfer to Ickes.

a) When will Ickes be taxed under Section 83(a)? On what amount?

b) What difference does it make in your answer to a), above, if the contract also provides that Ickes must return the stock to IBM if he does not remain with the company for at least two years after receiving it? Assume that two years later, the stock is trading for $150 per share.

c) What difference does it make in your answer to a), above, if the contract also provides that the IBM stock may be resold only to IBM at a price equal to its current market value less 10%?

Chapter 3

DISTINGUISHING COMPENSATION IN KIND FROM INVESTMENT GAIN: COMPENSATORY STOCK OPTIONS

A. COMMISSIONER v. LOBUE
351 U.S. 243 (1956)

MR. JUSTICE BLACK delivered the opinion of the Court.

This case involves the federal income tax liability of respondent LoBue for the years 1946 and 1947. From 1941 to 1947 LoBue was manager of the New York Sales Division of the Michigan Chemical Corporation, a producer and distributor of chemical supplies. In 1944 the company adopted a stock option plan making 10,000 shares of its common stock available for distribution to key employees at $5 per share over a 3-year period. LoBue and a number of other employees were notified that they had been tentatively chosen to be recipients of nontransferable stock options contingent upon their continued employment. LoBue's notice told him: "You may be assigned a greater or less amount of stock based entirely upon your individual results and that of the entire organization." About 6 months later he was notified that he had been definitely awarded an option to buy 150 shares of stock in recognition of his "contribution and efforts in making the operation of the Company successful." As to future allotments he was told "It is up to you to justify your participation in the plan during the next two years."

LoBue's work was so satisfactory that the company in the course of 3 years delivered to him 3 stock options covering 340 shares. He exercised all these $5 per share options in 1946 and in 1947,[1] paying the company only $1,700 for stock having a market value when delivered of $9,930. Thus, at the end of these transactions, LoBue's employer was worth $8,230

---

1. There may be some question as to whether the first option was exercised in 1945 or 1946. See the discussion, *infra*, as to when the transactions were completed.

less to its stockholders and LoBue was worth $8,230 more than before. The company deducted this sum as an expense in its 1946 and 1947 tax returns but LoBue did not report any part of it as income. Viewing the gain to LoBue as compensation for personal services the Commissioner levied a deficiency assessment against him, relying on § 22(a) of the Internal Revenue Code of 1939 . . . which defines gross income as including "gains, profits, and income derived from . . . compensation for personal service . . . of whatever kind and in whatever form paid . . . ."

LoBue petitioned the Tax Court to redetermine the deficiency, urging that "The said options were not intended by the Corporation or the petitioner to constitute additional compensation but were granted to permit the petitioner to acquire a proprietary interest in the Corporation and to provide him with the interest in the successful operation of the Corporation deriving from an ownership interest." The Tax Court held that LoBue had a taxable gain if the options were intended as compensation but not if the options were designed to provide him with "a proprietary interest in the business." Finding after hearings that the options were granted to give LoBue "a proprietary interest in the corporation, and not as compensation for services" the Tax Court held for LoBue. . . .

Relying on this finding the Court of Appeals affirmed, saying: "This was a factual issue which it was the peculiar responsibility of the Tax Court to resolve. From our examination of the evidence we cannot say that its finding was clearly erroneous." . . . Disputes over the taxability of stock option transactions such as this are longstanding. We granted certiorari to consider whether the Tax Court and the Court of Appeals had given § 22(a) too narrow an interpretation. . . .

We have repeatedly held that in defining "gross income" as broadly as it did in § 22(a) Congress intended to "tax all gains except those specifically exempted." . . . [T]he Tax Court found that the stock option plan was designed to achieve more profitable operations by providing the employees "with an incentive to promote the growth of the company by permitting them to participate in its success." . . .

The Tax Court held there was no taxable income . . . on the ground that one purpose of the employer was to confer a "proprietary interest." But there is not a word in § 22(a) which indicates that its broad coverage should be narrowed because of an employer's intention to enlist more efficient service from his employees by making them part proprietors of his business. In our view there is no statutory basis for the test established by the courts below. When assets are transferred by an employer to an employee to secure better services they are plainly compensation. It makes no difference that the compensation is paid in stock rather than in money. Section 22(a) taxes income derived from compensation "in whatever form paid." And in another stock option case we said that § 22(a) "is broad enough to include in taxable income any economic or financial benefit conferred on the employee as compensation, whatever the form or mode by which it is effected." . . . LoBue received a very substantial economic and financial benefit from his employer prompted by the employer's desire to get better work from him. This is "compensation for personal service" within the meaning of § 22(a).

LoBue nonetheless argues that we should treat this transaction as a mere purchase of a proprietary interest on which no taxable gain was "realized" in the year of purchase. It is true that our taxing system has ordinarily treated an arm's length purchase of property even at a bargain price as giving rise to no taxable gain in the year of purchase. . . .

But that is not to say that when a transfer which is in reality compensation is given the form of a purchase the Government cannot tax the gain. . . . The transaction here was unlike a mere purchase. It was not an arm's length transaction between strangers. Instead it was an arrangement by which an employer transferred valuable property to his employees in recognition of their services. We hold that LoBue realized taxable gain when he purchased the stock.

A question remains as to the time when the gain on the shares should be measured. LoBue gave his employer promissory notes for the option price of the first 300 shares but the shares were not delivered until the notes were paid in cash. The market value of the shares was lower when the notes were given than when the cash was paid. The Commissioner measured the taxable gain by the market value of the shares when the cash was paid. LoBue contends that this was wrong, and that the gain should be measured either when the options were granted or when the notes were given.

It is of course possible for the recipient of a stock option to realize an immediate taxable gain. . . . The option might have a readily ascertainable market value and the recipient might be free to sell his option. But this is not such a case. These three options were not transferable and LoBue's right to buy stock under them was contingent upon his remaining an employee of the company until they were exercised. Moreover, the uniform Treasury practice since 1923 has been to measure the compensation to employees given stock options subject to contingencies of this sort by the difference between the option price and the market value of the shares at the time the option is exercised. . . . Under these circumstances there is no reason for departing from the Treasury practice. The taxable gain to LoBue should be measured as of the time the options were exercised and not the time they were granted.

It is possible that a bona fide delivery of a binding promissory note could mark the completion of the stock purchase and that gain should be measured as of that date. Since neither the Tax Court nor the Court of Appeals passed on this question the judgment is reversed and the case is remanded to the Court of Appeals with instructions to remand the case to the Tax Court for further proceedings.

MR. JUSTICE HARLAN, whom MR. JUSTICE BURTON joins, concurring in part and dissenting in part.

In my view, the taxable event was the grant of each option, not its exercise. When the respondent received an unconditional option to buy stock at less than the market price, he received an asset of substantial and immediately realizable value, at least equal to the then-existing spread between the option price and the market price. It was at that time that the corporation conferred a benefit upon him. At the exercise of the option, the corporation "gave" the respondent nothing; it simply satisfied a previously-created legal obligation. That transaction, by which the respondent merely converted his asset from an option into stock, should be of no consequence for tax purposes. The option should be taxable as income when given, and any subsequent gain through appreciation of the stock, whether realized by sale of the option, if transferable, or by sale of the stock acquired by its exercise, is attributable to the sale of a capital asset and, if the other requirements are satisfied, should be taxed as a capital gain. Any other result makes the division of the total gains between ordinary income (compensation) and capital gain (sale of an asset) dependent solely upon the fortuitous circumstance of when the employee exercises his option.[2]

The last two options granted to respondent were unconditional and immediately exercisable, and thus present no further problems. The first option, however, was granted under somewhat different circumstances. Respondent was notified in January 1945 that 150 shares had been "allotted" to him, but he was given no right to purchase them until June 30, 1945, and his right to do so then was expressly made contingent upon his still being employed at that date. His right to purchase the first allotment of stock was thus not vested until he satisfied the stated condition, and it was not until then that he could be said to have received income, the measure of which should be the value of the option on that date.

Accordingly, while I concur in the reversal of the judgment below and in the remand to the Tax Court, I would hold the granting of the options to be the taxable events and would measure the income by the value of the options when granted.

B. NOTES AND QUESTIONS

1) The Nontax Purpose of Compensatory Stock Options

The holder of a stock option is entitled to buy a stated number of shares of stock at a fixed price (or *strike price*) during a stated period of time (or *term*). Why might a corporation decide to compensate its employees with stock options? Why not instead pay them additional compensation in cash? There are two basic nontax reasons for using stock options. First, cash is conserved for other purposes, such as capital investment, and that may be especially important if the corporation is just starting out. Second, the employee receives an ownership interest in the corporation and therefore may be motivated to work harder.

---

2. Suppose two employees are given unconditional options to buy stock at $5, the current market value. The first exercises the option immediately and sells the stock a year later at $15. The second holds the option for a year, exercises it, and sells the stock immediately at $15. Admittedly the $10 gain would be taxed to the first as capital gain; under the Court's view, it would be taxed to the second as ordinary income because it is "compensation" for services. I fail to see how the gain can be any more "compensation" to one than it is to the other.

But why won't the transfer of stock also conserve scarce cash and provide employees with an ownership interest? Suppose that the option's terms are written so that (a) the strike price equals the market value of the stock when the option is granted and (b) the option is nontransferable. Why might stock options with such terms motivate employees more effectively than stock? Why is the nontransferability restriction essential to achieving that advantage?

2) Preferential Tax Treatment for Investment (or Capital) Gains

If a taxpayer invests in property and later sells it at a profit, the income is generally known as a *capital gain*. For most of the period since the adoption of the Sixteenth Amendment, such gains in investment property, or capital gains, have been preferentially treated. A primary justification for the so-called capital gains preference has been the asserted need to encourage investment.[3]

The precise form of the preference has been subject to frequent legislative modification. During the tax years involved in *LoBue*, the top rate on ordinary income was 85.5%, while the top individual capital gains rate was only 25%. More recently, from 1978 until 1986, individuals were allowed to deduct 60% of all capital gains. Thus, if an individual bought AT&T stock for $200 and later resold it for $300, $60 of the $100 gain was deductible, and only $40 was taxable.

The capital gains preference had seemed one of the more enduring structural features of the Code. However, in 1986 Congress repealed the basic preference and provided that, beginning in 1988, capital gains would be taxed at the same rate as other income.

How does this change affect the issue in *LoBue*, which was how to apportion the gain arising from the stock option transaction between compensation for services and investment gain? Does repeal of the capital gains preference make the issue irrelevant, since the gain will be taxed at the same rate, whether characterized as compensation or as investment gain? Or might its character still affect the time when taxation occurs? The answers can be derived by working through the problems under 3) and 4), below.

3) Distinguishing Compensation for Services from Investment Gain: The Case of Compensatory Stock

Suppose that Michigan Chemical transfers 100 shares of its stock to LoBue and that the market value at the time of the transfer is $7 per share. Four years later, LoBue sells the stock for $10 per share. Taxes aside, what is the total gain that he derives from this transaction? How should it be allocated between compensation for personal services and investment gain? *When* is each component taxable? What difference would it make if Michigan Chemical requires LoBue to pay $5 for each share? See Section 83(a).

---

3. This and other justifications are explored in Chapter 25.

4) Distinguishing Compensation for Services from Investment Gain: The Case of Compensatory Stock Options

Suppose that X Corp. grants stock options to A and B, permitting each to purchase ten shares of its stock for $1 per share. The term of the option is three years. Six months later, when X Corp. is selling for $2 per share, A exercises her option. Two years later, when X Corp. is selling for $3 per share, B exercises his option. Both A and B eventually sell the stock for $6 per share. Assume that the option right—that is, the right to buy ten shares for $1 a share during the next three years—has a market value of $5 when it is granted.

a) Taxes aside, how much total gain does each have as a result of these transactions?

b) Applying the same method as used in the case of compensatory stock (under 3), above), how should the total gain be apportioned between compensation for services and investment gain? When should each component of the gain be taxed? (Assume that exercise of the option is not a taxable event.) Your answer should be the same as that provided by Justice Harlan's separate opinion in *LoBue*.

c) Under the majority opinion in *LoBue*, how in fact will A and B be taxed?

d) Rework a), b), and c), above, assuming that the options are never exercised (perhaps because the market value of the underlying stock plummets to less than the strike price).

e) Describe the differences between the majority and Justice Harlan in *LoBue*. Why does the majority opt for what appears to be a less accurate method of allocating income between compensation for personal services and investment gain? One possible virtue is that it avoids having to value the stock option, a problem described in more detail below.

5) Factors That Affect a Stock Option's Value

Justice Harlan wrote that the value of a stock option must be "at least equal to . . . the spread between the [strike] price and the market price." Suppose that there is no spread because the current market value of the stock is less than or equal to the strike price? Would the option have no value? What if it is not due to expire for three years? What if it is due to expire in ten minutes?

In 1946, LoBue received an option entitling him to buy 150 shares of the Michigan Chemical Corporation stock for $5 a share. Suppose that when LoBue received his option, the market value of the underlying stock was $7 a share. Wouldn't its value be exactly $300 (the spread of $2 per share times the number of shares that LoBue is entitled to buy at the strike price)? Or should it be worth more?

6) Ascertaining Fair Market Value

Reg. § 1.83–7(a) and (b)(1) provides that compensatory stock options are to be taxed when received (that is, according to the method prescribed by Justice Harlan) *if* they have an "ascertainable fair market value." (Otherwise, they are to be taxed on exercise under the method of the *LoBue* majority.)

"Fair market value" means the price for which the option would sell in an arms' length, or market, transaction. Without an *actual* sale, how can the price for which it *would* sell be ascertained? One possibility is to use the price for which identical items are selling in an established market. This provides a clear, objective measure. For example, the fair market value of one's AT&T stock is easily ascertained, without an actual sale, simply by looking up the price for which identical shares are selling on the New York Stock Exchange.

The Chicago Board Options Exchange operates a national market for options in the stocks of most companies listed on the New York and American Stock Exchanges. However, the options traded are usually of three, six, or nine months duration, whereas most compensatory stock options have a term of at least a year or more. The value of an option depends, among other things, on the chance that the underlying stock will appreciate. The longer the term of the option, the more chances there are that the stock will appreciate, and the more valuable the option will be—just as the more chances a lottery ticket gives you to win, the more expensive it will be. This makes it virtually impossible to use the market prices of options traded on the Options Exchange to value compensatory stock options.

In the absence of an objective market benchmark, an appraiser might estimate the value of a stock option, by taking the sales price of similar (but not identical) property and adjusting for the differences. For example, the fair market value of an office building can be estimated by using the price for which a similar office building in the same general location has recently sold. But, because no two office buildings are identical, adjustments have to be made for differences in location, square footage, age, architectural style, and so on.

The process of appraising fair market value, in the absence of an *objective* market benchmark, is a highly *subjective* process. Identifying property similar to the property being appraised, as well as making adjustments to account for differences between the properties, involves a myriad of judgments. Appraisals vary considerably, depending on what assumptions the appraiser makes, and disputes over appraisals generate a steady stream of litigation between taxpayers and the IRS.

The IRS, however, does not consider the need for appraisal as an obstacle to taxing most forms of compensation in kind under Section 83(a). For example, if compensation takes the form of closely held corporate stock, for which there is no market, the employee will be taxed on its appraised value. *Yet, over the years, the IRS has rarely been willing to appraise compensatory stock options in order to tax them when received.* Economists consider the valuation of stock options to be especially complex, which may explain the IRS reluctance to appraise this particular form of compensation in kind.[4]

---

4. See R. Brealey and S. Myers, Principles Of Corporate Finance 444–48 (1984).

7) Pinpointing the Time of Exercise

Under Reg. § 1.83–7(b)(1), a compensatory option with *no* "ascertainable fair market value" is taxed on exercise under the method prescribed by the *LoBue* majority. In *LoBue,* the taxpayer and IRS disagreed as to when exercise occurred. In 1945 and 1946, the taxpayer used some of his options to buy stock, but instead of paying the strike price in cash, he gave promissory notes. A few years later, the notes were paid. The taxpayer claimed that exercise occurred when he gave promissory notes in exchange for the stock. The IRS disagreed and argued that exercise really occurred only when the notes were paid. What was at stake if the market value of the stock rose between the date that the notes were given and the date that the notes were paid off?

The majority opinion stated that exercise occurs when a note is exchanged for stock, provided that the note is "binding," and remanded the case for a determination of this question. By binding, the Court appeared to mean that the promisor, or obligor, must be *personally* liable.

What difference does it make if the promisor is *not* personally liable? Suppose that the note is secured by the stock but is without recourse? This means that, in case of default, the creditor can only look to the security of the stock to satisfy the note; the promisor is not personally liable. If LoBue gives a nonrecourse note, is he likely to pay it off if the value of the stock falls below the amount owed on the note? Should the "purchase" of stock with a nonrecourse note therefore be regarded as just another form of stock option?

8) The Proprietary Interest Doctrine

a) How did the Tax Court in *LoBue* propose taxing compensatory stock options? Apply its method to the problem in question 3), above.

b) How did the Tax Court justify allocating all of the income to investment gain? What is the flaw in the Tax Court's logic? What covert social and economic policy judgments might the Tax Court's opinion reflect?

c) Congress has periodically provided for the *LoBue* Tax Court's method of taxing compensatory stock options when certain requirements are met. Options entitled to favorable tax treatment have been referred to at various times as *restricted, qualified,* or *incentive* stock options. Options which do not meet the statutory requirements for special treatment are referred to as *regular, nonqualified,* or *ordinary.* The most recent Code provision, allowing the entire gain resulting from compensatory stock options to be taxed as capital gain, is Section 422A, which will be examined in more detail in Chapter 11.

9) Sections 61(a) and 83(a): A Hard Line?

These two sections appear to establish a fairly hard line on compensation in kind. It is to be taxed at its fair market value, even though it may not be worth that much to the employee. Moreover, restrictions on using the compensation in kind are generally disregarded. (See Chapter 2.)

Despite Sections 61(a) and 83(a), a large variety and amount of in-kind compensation goes untaxed. In some cases, this is due to judicial decisions or administrative practice; in other cases, it is due to specific statutory provisions. These exceptions are examined in more detail in Chapters 4–9.

Chapter 4

WORKING CONDITIONS AND BUSINESS EXPENSES

A. BENAGLIA v. COMMISSIONER
36 B.T.A. 838 (1937), acq. 1940–1 C.B. 1

FINDINGS OF FACT.

The petitioners are husband and wife, residing in Honolulu, Hawaii, where they filed joint income tax returns for 1933 and 1934.[1]

The petitioner has, since 1926 and including the tax years in question, been employed as the manager in full charge of the several hotels in Honolulu owned and operated by Hawaiian Hotels, Ltd., a corporation of Hawaii, consisting of the Royal Hawaiian, the Moana and bungalows, and the Waialae Golf Club. These are large resort hotels, operating on the American plan. Petitioner was constantly on duty, and, for the proper performance of his duties and entirely for the convenience of his employer, he and his wife occupied a suite of rooms in the Royal Hawaiian Hotel and received their meals at and from the hotel.

Petitioner's salary has varied in different years, being in one year $25,000. In 1933 it was $9,625, and in 1934 it was $11,041.67. These amounts were fixed without reference to his meals and lodging, and neither petitioner nor his employer ever regarded the meals and lodging as part of his compensation or accounted for them.

OPINION.

STERNHAGEN: The Commissioner has added $7,845 each year to the petitioner's gross income as "compensation received from Hawaiian Hotels, Ltd.", holding that this is "the fair market value of rooms and meals furnished by the employer." . . . The . . . notice seems to hold that the rooms and meals were not in fact supplied "merely as a convenience to the hotels" of the employer.

---

1. Since the wife is party only because she was party to the joint returns, she is not further referred to in this report, and the term petitioner may be read to mean the husband alone.

From the evidence, there remains no room for doubt that the petitioner's residence at the hotel was not by way of compensation for his services, not for his personal convenience, comfort or pleasure, but solely because he could not otherwise perform the services required of him. The evidence of both the employer and employee shows in detail what petitioner's duties were and why his residence in the hotel was necessary. His duty was continuous and required his presence at a moment's call. He had a lifelong experience in hotel management and operation in the United States, Canada, and elsewhere, and testified that the functions of the manager could not have been performed by one living outside the hotel, especially a resort hotel such as this. The demands and requirements of guests are numerous, various, and unpredictable, and affect the meals, the rooms, the entertainment, and everything else about the hotel. The manager must be alert to all these things day and night. He would not consider undertaking the job and the owners of the hotel would not consider employing a manager unless he lived there. This was implicit throughout his employment, and when his compensation was changed from time to time no mention was ever made of it. Both took it for granted. The corporation's books carried no accounting for the petitioner's meals, rooms, or service.

Under such circumstances, the value of meals and lodging is not income to the employee, even though it may relieve him of an expense which he would otherwise bear. In *Jones v. United States*, ... the subject was fully considered in determining that neither the value of quarters nor the amount received as commutation of quarters by an Army officer is included within his taxable income. There is also a full discussion in the English case of *Tennant v. Smith*. ... A bank employee was required to live in quarters located in the bank building, and it was held that the value of such lodging was not taxable income. The advantage to him was merely an incident of the performance of his duty, but its character for tax purposes was controlled by the dominant fact that the occupation of the premises was imposed upon him for the convenience of the employer....

ARNOLD, dissenting: I disagree with the conclusions of fact that the suite of rooms and meals furnished petitioner and his wife at the Royal Hawaiian Hotel were entirely for the convenience of the employer and that the cash salary was fixed without reference thereto and was never regarded as part of his compensation.

Petitioner was employed by a hotel corporation operating two resort hotels in Honolulu—the Royal Hawaiian, containing 357 guest bed rooms, and the Moana, containing 261 guest bed rooms, and the bungalows and cottages in connection with the Moana containing 127 guest bed rooms, and the Waialae Golf Club. His employment was as general manager of both hotels and the golf club.

His original employment was in 1925, and in accepting the employment he wrote a letter to the party representing the employer, with whom he conducted the negotiations for employment, under date of September 10, 1925, in which he says:

Confirming our meeting here today, it is understood that I will assume the position of general manager of both the Royal Waikiki Beach Hotel (now under construction) and the Moana Hotel in Honolulu, at a yearly salary of $10,000.00, payable monthly, together with living quarters, meals, etc., for myself and wife. In addition I am to receive $20.00 per day while travelling, this however, not to include any railroad or steamship fares, and I [am] to submit vouchers monthly covering all such expenses.

While the cash salary was adjusted from time to time by agreement of the parties, depending on the amount of business done, it appears that the question of living quarters, meals, etc., was not given further consideration and was not thereafter changed. Petitioner and his wife have always occupied living quarters in the Royal Hawaiian Hotel and received their meals from the time he first accepted the employment down through the years before us. His wife performed no services for the hotel company.

This letter, in my opinion, constitutes the basic contract of employment and clearly shows that the living quarters, meals, etc., furnished petitioner and his wife were understood and intended to be compensation in addition to the cash salary paid him. Being compensation to petitioner in addition to the cash salary paid him, it follows that the reasonable value thereof to petitioner is taxable income. . . .

Conceding that petitioner was required to live at the hotel and that his living there was solely for the convenience of the employer, it does not follow that he was not benefited thereby to the extent of what such accommodations were reasonably worth to him. His employment was a matter of private contract. He was careful to specify in his letter accepting the employment that he was to be furnished with living quarters, meals, etc., for himself and wife, together with the cash salary, as compensation for his employment. Living quarters and meals are necessities which he would otherwise have had to procure at his own expense. His contract of employment relieved him to that extent. He has been enriched to the extent of what they are reasonably worth.

The majority opinion is based on the finding that petitioner's residence at the hotel was solely for the convenience of the employer and, therefore, not income. While it is no doubt convenient to have the manager reside in the hotel, I do not think the question here is one of convenience or of benefit to the employer. What the tax law is concerned with is whether or not petitioner was financially benefited by having living quarters furnished to himself and wife. He may have preferred to live elsewhere, but we are dealing with the financial aspect of petitioner's relation to his employer, not his preference. He says it would cost him $3,600 per year to live elsewhere.

It would seem that if his occupancy of quarters at the Royal Hawaiian was necessary and solely for the benefit of the employer, occupancy of premises at the Moana would be just as essential so far as the management of the Moana was concerned. He did not have living quarters or meals for himself and wife at the Moana and he was general manager of both and both were in operation during the years before us. Furthermore, it appears that petitioner was absent from Honolulu from March 24 to June 8 and from August 19 to November 2 in 1933, and from April 8 to May 24 and from September 3 to November 1 in 1934—about 5 months in 1933 and 3½ months in 1934. Whether he was away on official business or not we do not know. During his absence both hotels continued in operation. The $20 per day travel allowance in his letter of acceptance indicates his duties were not confined to managing the hotels in Honolulu, and the entire letter indicates he was to receive maintenance, whether in Honolulu or elsewhere, in addition to his cash salary.

At most the arrangement as to living quarters and meals was of mutual benefit, and to the extent it benefited petitioner it was compensation in addition to his cash salary, and taxable to him as income.

The Court of Claims in the case of *Jones* v. *United States,* relied on in the majority opinion, was dealing with a governmental organization regulated by military law where the compensation was fixed by law and not subject to private contract. The English case of *Tennant* v. *Smith,* involved the employment of a watchman or custodian for a bank whose presence at the bank was at all times a matter of necessity demanded by the employer as a condition of the employment.

The facts in both these cases are so at variance with the facts in this case that they are not controlling in my opinion.

B. NOTES AND QUESTIONS

1) The Board of Tax Appeals

The Board of Tax Appeals, which decided *Benaglia,* was created by Congress in 1924 to hear disputes between taxpayers and the IRS.[2] Originally designated as an administrative agency in the Treasury Department, the members of the Board were called "Commissioners," following the model of other administrative agencies, such as the Interstate Commerce Commission and the Federal Communications Commission. In 1942, Congress changed the name of the Board to the Tax Court of the United States and redesignated the former "Commissioners" as "Judges."[3] These name changes had no effect on the board's function or method of handling cases.[4]

Why did Congress bother to alter the names of this body and its members without making any other changes? One explanation is that the name changes were a reform to deter members of Congress from trying to influence the Board. The relabeling is supposed to have had the desired effect, as even unscrupulous members of Congress had qualms about med-

---

2. Revenue Act of 1924, Pub. L. No. 176, Sec. 900, 43 Stat. 253, 336. The board provided a forum in which a taxpayer could be heard prior to the payment of the assessed tax. See H.R. Rep. No. 179, 68th Cong., 1st Sess. 7 (1924).
3. Revenue Act of 1942, Pub. L. No. 753, § 504(a), 56 Stat. 798, 957 (1942).
4. See H.R. Rep. No. 2333, 77th Cong., 2d Sess. 172 (1942). In 1969, the court was granted full status as a legislative court under Article I of the Constitution and its name was changed to the United States Tax Court. See Section 7441.

dling in judicial, as opposed to administrative, proceedings.[5] If true, it is an example of how to achieve the maximum social effect with the minimum action. See "Spell My Name With An S" in I. Asimov, Nine Tomorrows (1959).

2) "Convenience of the Employer," Working Conditions and Kleinwachter's Conundrum

The "convenience of the employer" doctrine used to decide *Benaglia* is perhaps inaptly named. The idea behind the doctrine is that in-kind benefits should not be taxed if furnished by the employer to enable the employee to perform the job satisfactorily. Such benefits are known as *working conditions*.

Why generally don't we try to tax working conditions? Would it be administratively feasible? Would it be fair, given the fact that the benefits *must* be consumed to enable the employee to work? Kleinwachter's conundrum illustrates the difficulty with taxing working conditions as income to the employee:

> Let us consider here another of Kleinwachter's conundrums. We are asked to measure the relative incomes of the ordinary officer serving with his troops and a *Flugeladjutant* to the sovereign. Both receive the same nominal pay; but the latter receives quarters in the palace, food at the royal table, servants, and horses for sport. He accompanies the prince to the theater and opera, and, in general, lives royally at no expense to himself and is able to save generously from his salary. But suppose, as one possible complication, that the *Flugeladjutant* detests opera and hunting.
>
> The problem is clearly hopeless. To neglect all compensation in kind is obviously inappropriate. On the other hand, to include the perquisites as a major addition to the salary implies that all income should be measured with regard to the relative pleasurableness of different activities—which would be the negation of measurement. There is hardly more reason for imputing additional income to the *Flugeladjutant* on account of his luxurious wardrobe than for bringing into account the prestige and social distinction of a (German) university professor. Fortunately, however, such difficulties in satisfactory measurement of relative incomes do not bulk large in modern times; and, again, these elements of unmeasurable psychic income may be presumed to vary in a somewhat continuous manner along the income scale. . . .[6]

Towards the end of this excerpt, the author argues that the nontaxation of working conditions is not a serious problem. Why not, if the value of working conditions varies, in the author's words, "in a somewhat continuous manner along the income scale"? Later in the same work, the author appears less complacent about the fairness of not taxing working conditions.

> There is here an essential and insuperable difficulty, even in principle. The problem of Kleinwachter's *Flugeladjutant* is insoluble and certainly is

---

5. This explanation, possibly apocryphal, was related to the casebook's author by Professor Marvin Chirelstein.
6. H. Simons, Personal Income Taxation 53 (1938).

not amenable to reasonable solution on the basis of simple rules which could be administered by revenue agents. Obviously there are many instances where taxpayers are too favorably treated.... Yet one must surely hesitate to propose ... income taxes according to the pleasurableness of people's occupations.[7]

Working conditions (aside from meals and lodging) have been excluded from taxation by common understanding and administrative practice, rather than by any explicit statutory exception or court decision. Only in 1984 did Congress enact Section 132(a)(3), which specifically provides for the nontaxation of "fringe benefits" that qualify as a "working condition fringe." Section 132(d) defines "working condition fringe" as "any property or services provided to an employee ... to the extent that, if the employee paid for such property or services, such payment would be allowable as a deduction under Section 162...." Section 162, which allows deductions for business expenses, is examined later in this chapter.

3) *Drescher*, *Benaglia*, and *LoBue* Compared

If Benaglia had *not* been required to reside at the Royal Hawaiian Hotel to perform his duties, the meals and lodging would clearly have been taxable. Why should the employer's convenience make such a critical difference? Does the employer's convenience justify taking the factor of limited choice more seriously than in *Drescher* or in *LoBue*?

One reason why Bausch & Lomb provided the annuities was to enable Drescher to feel secure about his retirement and thereby make him a more loyal and efficient employee. Similarly, Michigan Chemical granted LoBue the stock options in order to make him a part owner and thereby motivate him to be more productive. True, neither item was strictly required for the performance of the employees' duties but, then, neither are other morale-boosting working conditions, such as a plush office with modern art. Why, then, weren't the items provided to Drescher and LoBue also "for the employer's convenience" and therefore tax exempt?

4) Are Meals and Lodging Like Other Working Conditions?

Consider some other examples of working conditions: the spacious office of the successful law firm partner, tastefully decorated with modern art; the trips to France, enjoyed by the airline pilot who works the New York to Paris route; the plays attended by the theater critic with tickets supplied by producers. Do the objections to taxing these working conditions (indicated in Kleinwachter's conundrum, above) apply with equal force to the special case of meals and lodging which are necessities?

The meals and lodging in *Benaglia* were valued at $7,845. The taxpayer admitted that, if not furnished by his employer, he would have spent about $3,600 on such items. Even if the Board of Tax Appeals decides not to tax the *full* value of meals and lodging, why not tax that $3,600? Why decide

---

7. Ibid. at 123.

to tax *nothing* at all? Is a rule administratively feasible that would tax what the employee would have spent if meals and lodging had not been provided? If not, can you suggest a practical alternative which would lead to at least some income being taxed when meals and lodging are provided for the employer's convenience?

Perhaps Benaglia would have preferred a modest bungalow and fast food. But would that make it necessarily unfair to tax him on the full value of a suite in the Royal Hawaiian Hotel and meals in the elegant hotel restaurant?

> Should the want of a free choice mean that whatever value meals and lodging do possess is not taxable income?
>
> Many taxpayers are forced by their work to live or eat as their fancy would not have dictated. . . . The miner must live near the dust of the mine, and the atomic scientist must live in the isolation of Oak Ridge; should it matter whether they engage their own quarters or get them from their employer? Hordes of employees are required by their work to eat hurriedly and in whatever ptomaine palaces are close by; how do they differ from restaurant workers? I have never been persuaded that the value of meals or lodging should be excluded because the employee must accept whatever is offered or available . . .[8]

5) Section 119

Section 119, enacted in 1954, codifies the result in *Benaglia* by excluding meals and lodging provided to an employee "for the convenience of his employer," if furnished "on the business premises." In the case of lodging, there is an additional requirement that the employee "accept such lodging . . . as a condition of his employment." Compare Section 119(a)(1) with Section 119(a)(2). Reg. § 1.119–1(b) states that the requirement is met if the employee must accept the lodging "in order to enable him properly to perform the duties of his employment." Does this add anything to the employer's convenience language that is already in the statute?

The regulations go on to state that lodging may be excluded if the employee is "required to be available for duty at all times" or if, because of the isolation of the job site, alternative housing is unavailable. See Reg. § 1.119–1(f), examples 5–7. Meals are covered if the employee must be available for "emergency call during his meal period" or if "there are insufficient eating facilities in the vicinity of the employer's premises." Reg. § 1.119–1(a)(2)(ii)(a) and (c). In addition, meals are also excluded if "the business is such that the employee must be restricted to a short meal period, such as 30 or 45 minutes, and because the employee could not be expected to eat elsewhere in such a short meal period." Reg. § 1.119–1(a)(2)(ii)(b). One commentator sees this last regulation as a cause for hope: "It is heartening to know that *some* places have not been invaded by fast-food outlets."[9]

---

8. Bittker, The Individual as Wage Earner, 11 Inst. on Fed. Tax'n. 1147, 1155–56 (1953).
9. B. Bittker, Federal Taxation of Income, Estates and Gifts 14–18, n. 10 (1980).

C. ROSENSPAN v. UNITED STATES [PART ONE]
438 F.2d 905 (2d Cir. 1971)

FRIENDLY, CIRCUIT JUDGE:

This appeal is from the dismissal on the merits of an action for refund of income taxes, brought in the District Court for the Eastern District of New York. . . . The taxes were paid as a result of the Commissioner's disallowance of deductions for unreimbursed expenses for meals and lodging, allegedly incurred "while away from home in the pursuit of a trade or business," I.R.C. § 162(a)(2), in 1962 and 1964.

Plaintiff, Robert Rosenspan, was a jewelry salesman who worked on a commission basis, paying his own traveling expenses without reimbursement. In 1962 he was employed by one and in 1964 by two New York City jewelry manufacturers. For some 300 days a year he traveled by automobile through an extensive sales territory in the Middle West, where he would stay at hotels and motels and eat at restaurants. Five or six times a year he would return to New York and spend several days at his employers' offices. There he would perform a variety of services essential to his work—cleaning up his sample case, checking orders, discussing customers' credit problems, recommending changes in stock, attending annual staff meetings, and the like.

Rosenspan has grown [up] in Brooklyn and during his marriage had maintained a family home there. After his wife's death in 1948, he abandoned this. From that time through the tax years in question he used his brother's Brooklyn home as a personal residential address, keeping some clothing and other belongings there, and registering, voting, and filing his income tax returns from that address. The stipulation of facts states that, on his trips to New York City, "out of a desire not to abuse his welcome at his brother's home, he stayed more often" at an inn near the John F. Kennedy Airport. It recites also that "he generally spent his annual vacations in Brooklyn, where his children resided, and made an effort to return to Brooklyn whenever possible," but affords no further indication where he stayed on such visits. In 1961 he changed the registration of his automobile from New York to Ohio, giving as his address the address of a cousin in Cincinnati, where he also received mail, in order to obtain cheaper automobile insurance. Rosenspan does not contend that he had a permanent abode or residence in Brooklyn or anywhere else.

The basis for the Commissioner's disallowance of a deduction for Rosenspan's meals and lodging while in his sales territory was that he had no "home" to be "away from" while traveling. . . .

What is now § 162(a)(2) was brought into the tax structure by . . . the Revenue Act of 1921. . . . Prior to that date, [the Code] had permitted the deduction of "ordinary and necessary expenses paid or incurred . . . in carrying on any trade or business," Revenue Act of 1918 . . . , without further specification. In a regulation, the Treasury interpreted the statute to allow deduction of "traveling expenses, including railroad fares, and meals and lodging *in an amount in excess of any expenditures ordinarily required for such purposes when at home,*" (emphasis supplied). A formula was provided for determining what expenditures were thus "ordinarily required"; the taxpayer was to compute such items as rent, grocery bills, light, etc. and servant hire for the periods when he was away from home, and divide this by the number of members of his family.... The puzzlement of the man without a home was dealt with in a cryptic pronouncement ... :

> Living expenses paid by a single taxpayer who has no home and is continuously employed on the road may not be deducted in computing net income.

The 1921 amendment, inserting what is now § 162(a)(2)'s allowance of a deduction for the entire amount of qualified meals and lodging, stemmed from a request of the Treasury based on the difficulty of administering the "excess" provision of its regulation.... There is ... nothing to indicate that the Treasury sought, or that Congress meant to require, any change in the ruling that disallowed deductions for living expenses [for a traveler without a home]. The objective was to eliminate the need for computing the expenses "ordinarily required" at home by a taxpayer who had one....

... [W]e find it impossible to read the words "away from home" out of the statute, as Rosenspan, in effect, would have us do and allow a deduction to a taxpayer who had no "home" in the ordinary sense. The limitation reflects congressional recognition of the rational distinction between the taxpayer with a permanent residence—whose travel costs represent a duplication of expense or at least an incidence of expense which the existence of his permanent residence demonstrates he would not incur absent business compulsion—and the taxpayer without such a residence.

... The judgment dismissing the complaint must therefore be affirmed.

D. NOTES AND QUESTIONS

1) Section 119

Could Rosenspan have argued that Section 119 authorizes excluding the amount spent on meals and lodging in order to perform his duties as a traveling salesman? There are several possible obstacles to applying Section 119.

First, Section 119 excludes only meals and lodging provided to an employee by his or her employer. This language does not appear to cover self-employed taxpayers. Rosenspan would probably be viewed as self-employed because he worked on a commission basis (without salary) for several different jewelry manufacturers. Could Rosenspan have overcome this problem by forming a wholly owned corporation to conduct his activities and directing the corporation to hire him?

Second, the employer apparently must furnish the meals and lodging in kind and may not simply reimburse the employee for such expenses. See Reg. § 1.119–1(e). Will this requirement be satisfied if Rosenspan forms a wholly owned corporation which hires him *and* which contracts directly with selected motels and restaurants to provide meals and lodging to its sole employee while he is on the road?

Third, the meals and lodging must be provided on the "business premises" of the employer. Could Rosenspan argue that his entire sales territory—the Middle West of the United States—constitutes his "business premises"? A number of cases have held that meals provided to state troopers in public restaurants occur on the business premises, which include every state road and highway. The current validity of that interpretation, however, may be open to question, and, in any event, it is doubtful that it would be extended beyond the special case of state police.[10]

2) Exclusion versus Deduction

The formal issue in *Benaglia* was whether the meals and lodging were excludable, despite the all-inclusive language of the Code that gross income includes "all income . . . from whatever source derived." The formal issue in *Rosenspan* was whether amounts, conceded to be includable in gross income under Section 61(a), were deductible. Although, formally, these appear to be different issues, functionally they have the same consequence. Excluding an item is equivalent to including it and permitting a deduction in full.

For example, although Section 119 treats meals and lodging provided for the employer's convenience as excludable, the same result could be reached by including such items and providing an offsetting deduction. Similarly, although Section 162(a)(2) treats amounts spent for meals and lodging while away from home on business as deductible, the same result could be reached by excluding such amounts from gross income.

3) The Duplication Requirement

Until 1948, when Rosenspan's wife died and he abandoned their home in Brooklyn, he apparently was allowed to deduct the cost of meals and lodging as a traveling salesman. Then, suddenly, when Rosenspan abandoned the home, the cost was no longer deductible because he was no longer duplicating expenses. Why require duplication before allowing a deduction for the cost of meals and lodging incurred as a business necessity?

Is the duplication requirement unfair to Rosenspan? Suppose that he spends $8,000 for meals and lodging while working as a traveling salesman but would spend only $3,000 if he had a fixed job location? What is the best measure of the amount that Rosenspan should be allowed to deduct? Which method, in principle, provides the better result, the excess rule of the Treasury regulation under the 1918 statute or the duplication requirement of Section 162(a)(2)?

How is the duplication requirement of Section 162(a)(2) inconsistent with *Benaglia* and Section 119? Was the exclusion of the meals and lodging

---

10. Compare, for example, United States v. Keeton, 383 F.2d 429 (10th Cir. 1967) (meal allowance to state troopers nontaxable) with Wilson v. United States, 412 F.2d 694 (1st Cir. 1969) (meal allowance taxable). The conflict was presented to the Supreme Court in Commissioner v. Kowalski, 434 U.S. 77 (1977). The Court decided the case on the basis of the requirement that the meals be "furnished in kind," holding that the cash allowances involved in *Kowalski* did not qualify for exclusion under Section 119. Id. at 84. The Court did not decide whether business premises included state roads and highways.

provided to Benaglia conditioned on his having some other residence? Does Section 119 have a duplication requirement? Isn't it shockingly unfair for Rosenspan to be taxed in full on the relatively modest amounts that he spends for meals and lodging while Benaglia is not taxed at all on the value of his lavish quarters and meals?

In view of the duplication requirement, what should Rosenspan's attorney advise him to do in the future?

4) The Effect of Section 67

The Code generally favors the employee who is reimbursed for the cost of business-related meals and lodging over the employee who must pay out of his or her own pocket without reimbursement. Section 67, enacted as part of the 1986 Tax Reform Act, provides that employee business expenses that are *not reimbursed* may be deducted only to the extent that they (and other designated expenses) exceed 2% of the taxpayer's Adjusted Gross Income. See Section 67(a) and (b). However, employee expenses that are reimbursed may be deducted from Gross Income in calculating Adjusted Gross Income, and, as a result, are not itemized deductions subject to the 2% floor. See Sections 62(a)(2)(A) and 63(d)(1).[11]

Might the difference in treatment reflect an assumption that the non-reimbursed expenses are more likely to represent an abuse problem? Is such an assumption justified by the facts of *Rosenspan* and *Benaglia*?

Readers interested in the performing arts may appreciate the special treatment afforded the nonreimbursed expenses of performing artists. See Section 62(a)(2)(B). If they meet the requirements of Section 62(b), such artists may deduct nonreimbursed expenses from Gross Income and, as a result, are not subject to the 2% floor.

---

11. In contrast, nonreimbursed employee expenses may only be deducted from Adjusted Gross Income in calculating Taxable Income, and, as a result, are itemized deductions subject to the 2% floor. See Section 62(a)(1).

Chapter 5

DISTINGUISHING BUSINESS FROM PERSONAL CONSUMPTION EXPENSES: COMMUTING

A. INTRODUCTORY NOTE

Distinguishing business expenses from nonbusiness, personal consumption expenses is critical to the design and implementation of an income tax. Suppose that A, employed as in-house counsel to a corporation, receives a $50,000 salary and that B, a sole practitioner, earns $80,000 in fees but also spends $30,000 for office rent, supplies, and secretarial help. Clearly, A and B end up with the same amount of purchasing power, and it would be a mistake to calculate B's income without allowing deductions for the cost of earning it, that is, the business expenses. If business expenses were not deductible, we would have a tax on *gross* receipts rather than on income, which equals receipts *net* of business expenses.

Suppose that C and D are both employed at an annual salary of $50,000 and that C spends $40,000 on meals, lodging, and other personal consumption expenses, while D spends only $20,000 on such items. Why is no deduction permitted for these expenses? How do they differ from B's expenses of running a law office? If personal consumption expenses were generally deductible, we would not have an income tax but a tax on income less amounts spent for personal consumption—in other words, a tax on savings.

While, in theory, the difference between business and personal consumption expenditures may seem reasonably clear, in practice, the distinction quickly becomes muddied as Chapters 5 through 9 illustrate.

B. COMMISSIONER v. FLOWERS
326 U.S. 465 (1946)

Mr. Justice Murphy delivered the opinion of the Court.

This case presents a problem as to the meaning and application of the provision of § [162(a)(2)] of the Internal Revenue Code allowing a deduction for income tax purposes of "traveling expenses (including the entire amount expended for meals and lodging) while away from home in the pursuit of a trade or business."

The taxpayer, a lawyer, has resided with his family in Jackson, Mississippi, since 1903. There he has paid taxes, voted, schooled his children and established social and religious connections. He built a house in Jackson nearly thirty years ago and at all times has maintained it for himself and his family. He has been connected with several law firms in Jackson, one of which he formed and which has borne his name since 1922.

In 1906 the taxpayer began to represent the predecessor of the Gulf, Mobile & Ohio Railroad, his present employer. He acted as trial counsel for the railroad throughout Mississippi. From 1918 until 1927 he acted as special counsel for the railroad in Mississippi. He was elected general solicitor in 1927 and continued to be elected to that position each year until 1930, when he was elected general counsel. Thereafter he was annually elected general counsel until September, 1940, when the properties of the predecessor company and another railroad were merged and he was elected vice president and general counsel of the newly formed Gulf, Mobile & Ohio Railroad.

The main office of the Gulf, Mobile & Ohio Railroad is in Mobile, Alabama, as was also the main office of its predecessor. When offered the position of general solicitor in 1927, the taxpayer was unwilling to accept it if it required him to move from Jackson to Mobile. He had established himself in Jackson both professionally and personally and was not desirous of moving away. As a result, an arrangement was made between him and the railroad whereby he could accept the position and continue to reside in Jackson on condition that he pay his traveling expenses between Mobile and Jackson and pay his living expenses in both places. This arrangement permitted the taxpayer to determine for himself the amount of time he would spend in each of the two cities and was in effect during 1939 and 1940, the taxable years in question.

The railroad company provided an office for the taxpayer in Mobile but not in Jackson. When he worked in Jackson his law firm provided him with office space, although he no longer participated in the firm's business or shared in its profits. He used his own office furniture and fixtures at this office. The railroad, however, furnished telephone service and a typewriter and desk for his secretary. It also paid the secretary's expenses while in Jackson. Most of the legal business of the railroad was centered in or conducted from Jackson, but this business was handled by local counsel for the railroad. The taxpayer's participation was advisory only and was no different from his participation in the railroad's legal business in other areas.

The taxpayer's principal post of business was at the main office in Mobile. However, during the taxable years of 1939 and 1940, he devoted nearly all of his time to matters relating to the merger of the railroads. Since it was left to him where he would do his work, he spent most of his time in Jackson during this period. In connection with the merger, one of the companies was involved in certain litigation in the federal court in Jackson and the taxpayer participated in that litigation.

During 1939 he spent 203 days in Jackson and 66 in Mobile, making 33 trips between the two cities. During 1940 he spent 168 days in Jackson and 102 in Mobile, making 40 trips between the two cities. The railroad paid all of his traveling expenses when he went on business trips to points other than Jackson or Mobile. But it paid none of his expenses in traveling between these two points or while he was at either of them.

The taxpayer deducted $900 in his 1939 income tax return and $1,620 in his 1940 return as traveling expenses incurred in making trips from Jackson to Mobile and as expenditures for meals and hotel accommodations while in Mobile.[1] The Commissioner disallowed the deductions, which action was sustained by the Tax Court. But the Fifth Circuit Court of Appeals reversed the Tax Court's judgment, . . . and we granted certiorari because of a conflict between the decision below and that reached by the Fourth Circuit Court of Appeals in *Barnhill* v. *Commissioner*. . . .

§ [162(a)(2)] is to be contrasted with the provision of § [262] of the Internal Revenue Code disallowing any deductions for "personal, living, or family expenses." . . .

Three conditions must thus be satisfied before a traveling expense deduction may be made under § [162(a)(2)]:

(1) The expense must be a reasonable and necessary traveling expense, as that term is generally understood. This includes such items as transportation fares and food and lodging expenses incurred while traveling.

(2) The expense must be incurred "while away from home."

(3) The expense must be incurred in pursuit of business. This means that there must be a direct connection between the expenditure and the carrying on of the trade or business of the taxpayer or of his employer. Moreover, such an expenditure must be necessary or appropriate to the development and pursuit of the business or trade.

Whether particular expenditures fulfill these three conditions so as to entitle a taxpayer to a deduction is purely a question of fact in most instances. . . . And the Tax Court's inferences and conclusions on such a factual matter, under established principles, should not be disturbed by an appellate court. . . .

In this instance, the Tax Court without detailed elaboration concluded that "The situation presented in this proceeding is, in principle, no different from that in which a taxpayer's place of employment is in one city and for reasons satisfactory to himself he resides in another." It accordingly disallowed the deductions on the ground that they represent living and personal expenses rather than traveling expenses incurred while away from home in the pursuit of business. The court below accepted the Tax Court's findings of fact but reversed its judgment on the basis that it had improperly construed the word "home" as used in the second condition precedent to a traveling expense deduction under §[162(a)(2)]. The Tax Court, it was said, erroneously construed the word to mean the post, station or place of

---

1. No claim for deduction was made by the taxpayer for the amounts spent in traveling from Mobile to Jackson.

business where the taxpayer was employed—in this instance, Mobile—and thus erred in concluding that the expenditures in issue were not incurred "while away from home." The court below felt that the word was to be given no such "unusual" or "extraordinary" meaning in this statute, that it simply meant "that place where one in fact resides" or "the principal place of abode of one who has the intention to live there permanently."... Since the taxpayer here admittedly had his home, as thus defined, in Jackson and since the expenses were incurred while he was away from Jackson, the court below held that the deduction was permissible.

The meaning of the word "home" in §[162(a)(2)] with reference to a taxpayer residing in one city and working in another has engendered much difficulty and litigation.... The Tax Court and the administrative rulings have consistently defined it as the equivalent of the taxpayer's place of business.... On the other hand, the decision below... ha[s] flatly rejected that view and ha[s] confined the term to the taxpayer's actual residence. See also *Coburn v. Commissioner*....

We deem it unnecessary here to enter into or to decide this conflict. The Tax Court's opinion, as we read it, was grounded neither solely nor primarily upon that agency's conception of the word "home." Its discussion was directed mainly toward the relation of the expenditures to the railroad's business, a relationship required by the third condition of the deduction. Thus even if the Tax Court's definition of the word "home" was implicit in its decision and even if that definition was erroneous, its judgment must be sustained here if it properly concluded that the necessary relationship between the expenditures and the railroad's business was lacking. Failure to satisfy any one of the three conditions destroys the traveling expense deduction.

Turning our attention to the third condition, this case is disposed of quickly. There is no claim that the Tax Court misconstrued this condition or used improper standards in applying it. And it is readily apparent from the facts that its inferences were supported by evidence and that its conclusion that the expenditures in issue were non-deductible living and personal expenses was fully justified.

The facts demonstrate clearly that the expenses were not incurred in the pursuit of the business of the taxpayer's employer, the railroad. Jackson was his regular home. Had his post of duty been in that city the cost of maintaining his home there and of commuting or driving to work concededly would be non-deductible living and personal expenses lacking the necessary direct relation to the prosecution of the business. The character of such expenses is unaltered by the circumstance that the taxpayer's post of duty was in Mobile, thereby increasing the costs of transportation, food and lodging. Whether he maintained one abode or two, whether he traveled three blocks or three hundred miles to work, the nature of these expenditures remained the same.

The added costs in issue, moreover, were as unnecessary and inappropriate to the development of the railroad's business as were his personal and living costs in Jackson. They were incurred solely as the result of the taxpayer's desire to maintain a home in Jackson while working in Mobile, a factor irrelevant to the maintenance and prosecution of the railroad's legal business. The railroad did not require him to travel on business from Jackson to Mobile or to maintain living quarters in both cities. Nor did it compel him, save in one instance, to perform tasks for it in Jackson. It simply asked him to be at his principal post in Mobile as business demanded and as his personal convenience was served, allowing him to divide his business time between Mobile and Jackson as he saw fit. Except for the federal court litigation, all of the taxpayer's work in Jackson would normally have been performed in the headquarters at Mobile. The fact that he traveled frequently between the two cities and incurred extra living expenses in Mobile, while doing much of his work in Jackson, was occasioned solely by his personal propensities. The railroad gained nothing from this arrangement except the personal satisfaction of the taxpayer.

Travel expenses in pursuit of business within the meaning of §[162(a)(2)] could arise only when the railroad's business forced the taxpayer to travel and to live temporarily at some place other than Mobile, thereby advancing the interests of the railroad. Business trips are to be identified in relation to business demands and the traveler's business headquarters. The exigencies of business rather than the personal conveniences and necessities of the traveler must be the motivating factors. Such was not the case here.

It follows that the court below erred in reversing the judgment of the Tax Court.

Reversed.

MR. JUSTICE RUTLEDGE, dissenting.

I think the judgment of the Court of Appeals should be affirmed. When Congress used the word "home" in §[162(a)(2)] of the Code, I do not believe it meant "business headquarters." And in my opinion this case presents no other question. . . .

[In Jackson, Mississippi] he kept hold upon his place as a lawyer, though not substantially active in practice otherwise than to perform his work as general counsel for the railroad. This required his presence in Mobile, Alabama, for roughly a third of his time. The remainder he spent in Jackson at the same work, except for the time he was required to travel to points other than Mobile.

The company's principal offices were there, including one set aside for respondent's use. But the bulk of its trackage was in Mississippi and much of its legal work, with which he was concerned, was done there. His choice to keep his home in Jackson must have been affected by this fact, although it was motivated chiefly by more purely personal considerations. It is doubtful indeed, though perhaps not material, whether by not moving to Mobile he did not save the Government from larger deductions on account of traveling expense than those he claimed. . . .

I agree with the Court of Appeals that if Congress had meant "business headquarters," and not "home," it would have said "business headquarters." When it used "home" instead, I think it meant home in everyday parlance, not in some twisted special meaning of "tax home" or "tax headquarters." I find no purpose stated or implied in the Act, the regulations or the legislative history to support such a distortion or to use §[162] as a lever to force people to move their homes to the locality where their employer's chief business headquarters may be, although their own work may be done as well in major part at home. The only stated purpose, and it is clearly stated, not in words of art, is to relieve the tax burden when one is away from home on business.

The Government relies on administrative construction, by the Commissioner and the Tax Court, and says that unless this is accepted the Act creates tax inequality. If so, it is inequality created by Congress, and it is not for the Commissioner or the Tax Court, by administrative reconstruction, to rewrite what Congress has written or to correct its views of equality. . . .

Administrative construction should have some bounds. It exceeds what are legitimate when it reconstructs the statute to nullify or contradict the plain meaning of nontechnical terms not artfully employed. . . .

C. ROSENSPAN v. UNITED STATES [PART TWO]
438 F.2d 905 (2d Cir. 1971)

. . . The basis for the Commissioner's disallowance of a deduction for Rosenspan's meals and lodging while in his sales territory was that he had no "home" to be "away from" while traveling. Not denying that this would be true if the language of § 162(a)(2) were given its ordinary meaning, Rosenspan claimed that for tax purposes his home was his "business headquarters," to wit, New York City where his employers maintained their offices, and relied upon the Commissioner's long advocacy of this concept of a "tax home." . . . The Commissioner responded that although in most circumstances "home" means "business headquarters," it should be given its natural meaning of a permanent abode or residence for purposes of the problem here presented. Rosenspan says the Commissioner is thus trying to have it both ways. . . .

Proper analysis of the problem has been beclouded, and the Government's position in this case has been made more difficult than it need be, by the Commissioner's insistence that "home" means "business headquarters," despite the Supreme Court's having thrice declined to endorse this, and its rejection by several courts of appeals, see Flowers v. C. I. R. . . .

When Congress uses such a non-technical word in a tax statute, presumably it wants administrators and courts to read it in the way that ordinary people would understand, and not "to draw on some unexpressed spirit outside the bounds of the normal meaning of words." . . . The construction which the Commissioner has long advocated not only violates this principle but is unnecessary for the protection of the revenue that he seeks. That purpose is served, without any such distortion of language, by the third condition laid down in *Flowers* . . . namely, "that there must be a direct connection between the expenditure and the carrying on of the trade or business of the taxpayer or of his employer" and that "such an expenditure must be necessary or appropriate to the development and pursuit of the business or trade." These requirements were enough to rule out a deduction for Flowers' lodging and meals while in Mobile even if he was "away from home" while there. . . .

Since the Commissioner's definition of "home" as "business headquarters" will produce the same result as the third *Flowers* condition in the overwhelming bulk of cases arising under § 162(a)(2), courts have often fallen into the habit of referring to it as a ground or an alternate ground of decision.... But examination of the string of cases cited by plaintiff as endorsing the "business headquarters" test has revealed almost none ... which cannot be explained on the basis that the taxpayer had no permanent residence, or was not away from it, or maintained it in a locale apart from where he regularly worked as a matter of personal choice rather than business necessity. This principle likewise affords a satisfactory rationale for the "temporary" employment cases.... When an assignment is truly temporary, it would be unreasonable to expect the taxpayer to move his home, and the expenses are thus compelled by the "exigencies of business"; when the assignment is "indefinite" or "indeterminate," the situation is different and, if the taxpayer decides to leave his home where it was, disallowance is appropriate, not because he has acquired a "tax home" in some lodging house or hotel at the worksite but because his failure to move his home was for his personal convenience and not compelled by business necessity....

Shifting the thrust of analysis from the search for a fictional "tax home" to a questioning of the business necessity for incurring the expense away from the taxpayer's permanent residence thus does not upset the basic structure of the decisions which have dealt with this problem.... It merely adopts an approach that better effectuates the congressional intent in establishing the deduction and thus provides a sounder conceptual framework for analysis while following the ordinary meaning of language.... We see no basis whatever for believing that ... Congress ... meant to disallow a deduction to someone who had the expense of maintaining a home from which business took him away but possessed no business headquarters....

D. NOTES AND QUESTIONS

1) The Definition of "Home" in Section 162

How did the IRS' reading of the word "home" almost backfire in *Rosenspan*? Is there any difference between interpreting the word "home" to mean "personal residence" and imposing the duplication requirement of *Rosenspan*?

How did the IRS's reading of the word "home" almost backfire in *Rosenspan*? Is there any difference between interpreting the word "home" to mean "personal residence" and imposing the duplication requirement of *Rosenspan*?

2) Commuting Expenses and Section 162(a)

In *Flowers,* the Court analogized the taxpayer's expenditure for meals and lodging in Mobile, Alabama to commuting expenses. Reg. § 1.162–2(e) states that "commuter's fares" are not considered business expenses and are not deductible. The regulation probably involves a judgment that commuting is a personal consumption expense—reflecting one's personal choice of where to reside—and so might also have cited Section 262 as justifying nondeductibility.

However, is it realistic to assume that the choice of where to reside—and therefore the distance one commutes to work—is necessarily a voluntary personal consumption decision that one is free to alter? What if restrictive zoning limits the availability of low-income housing? Faced with a choice between allowing low-income taxpayers to deduct their commuting costs or providing federal government subsidies for mass transit, which would you prefer?

3) Employer-provided Mass Transit and Parking

Suppose that Kodak Corp. runs a special bus service from residential areas to its offices and that employees may ride the bus free of charge. Should the free ride generate taxable income? Suppose Kodak charges a fare that covers only 50% of the value? Should the other 50% be taxable to the employees? Section 124, in effect *only* for taxable years from 1979 through 1985, states that gross income does not include the value of such transportation, provided that the employer's plan does not discriminate in favor of employees who are "officers, shareholders, or other highly compensated employees." Section 124(c).

If commuting expenses are not deductible under Section 162(a), why should the value of employer-provided commuting be excluded? Can the exclusion be defended on the ground that Kodak's subsidy for bus service is not appreciably different from federal or municipal subsidies for mass transit (which, like most government services, are not considered taxable income)?

Suppose Kodak also offers free parking to its employees. Should that generate taxable income? Under the Code, free parking provided by an employer is considered a working condition and, as such, its value is not included in gross income. Section 132(h)(4). Under Section 162(a)(2), however, the cost of parking is considered a commuting expense and, hence, may not be deducted. Is it fair to exclude the value of employer-provided parking as a working condition, while denying a Section 162(a)(2) deduction to employees who must pay for their parking?[2]

Perhaps Sections 124 and 132(h)(4) reflect our ambivalence about the general rule that commuting expenses reflect personal consumption choices and are therefore nondeductible. But *should* the treatment of commuting expenses depend on whether they result from voluntary personal consumption choices? Or should national transportation and energy policies determine the outcome so that, for example, the cost of commuting by

---

2. This is one instance where the status of an item as a working condition is *not* dependent on its being deductible, if paid for by the employee, under Section 162(a). See Chapter 8.

mass transit might be deductible, but not the cost of commuting by private automobile?[3]

4) Was Flowers Treated Unfairly?

If Flowers had actually resided in Mobile during 1939 and 1940, would he have been entitled to any Section 162(a)(2) deductions for meals and lodging in Jackson, Mississippi? Should the fact that his personal residence was in Jackson affect his right to those deductions? How might Flowers have been advised to conduct the negotiations regarding his employment as counsel in order to lay a better foundation for deducting his meals and lodging while in Mobile, Alabama?

5) Other Issues Implicit, But Not Raised, in *Flowers*

Flowers' former law firm provided him with office space in Jackson. Does this represent income to Flowers, which is includible under Section 61(a)? If it is, might Flowers be entitled to an offsetting deduction?

Flowers made no attempt to deduct the cost of train travel between Mobile and Jackson during the tax years in question. Why do you suppose not?

6) The "Sleep or Rest" Rule: U.S. v. Correll

Suppose that a taxpayer who lives in New York City flies to Washington, D.C. for the day on business. May the taxpayer deduct the cost of lunch in Washington, D.C. as a traveling expense "while away from home"? In U.S. v. Correll, 389 U.S. 299 (1967), the Supreme Court upheld the IRS position that the cost of meals is deductible only if the trip requires the taxpayer to stop for "sleep or rest."

> Any rule in this area must make some rather arbitrary distinctions, but at least the sleep or rest rule avoids the obvious inequity of permitting the New Yorker who makes a quick trip to Washington and back . . . to deduct the cost of his lunch merely because he covers more miles than the salesman who travels locally and must finance all his meals without the help of the Federal Treasury. . . .
>
> [T]he statute speaks of "meals and lodging" as a unit, suggesting—at least arguably—that Congress contemplated a deduction for the cost of meals only where the travel in question involves lodging as well. Ordinarily, at least, only the taxpayer who finds it necessary to stop for sleep or rest incurs significantly higher expenses as a direct result of his business travel. . . .[4]

7) Temporary Jobs

Rev. Rul. 83–82, 1983–1 C.B. 45, permits a taxpayer who is away from home in a temporary job to deduct the costs of meals and lodging.

---

3. This assumes, of course, that there is a policy to encourage mass transit and discourage private automobiles.

4. 389 U.S. at 303–304.

Employment is temporary . . . only if its termination can be foreseen within a reasonably short period of time. . . . Where a taxpayer anticipates employment to last for less than one year, whether such employment is temporary will be determined on the basis of the facts and circumstances.

If a taxpayer anticipates employment to last for 1 year or more and that employment does, in fact, last for 1 year or more, there is a presumption that the employment is not temporary but rather is indefinite. . . . However, . . . this 1-year presumption may be rebutted where the employment is expected to, and does, last for 1 year or more, but less than 2 years. An expected or actual stay of 2 years or more will be considered an indefinite stay . . . regardless of any other facts and circumstances.

To rebut the 1-year presumption of indefiniteness with respect to employment that lasts for 1 year or more but less than 2 years, the taxpayer must clearly demonstrate by objective factors that the taxpayer realistically expected that the employment in issue would last less than 2 years and that the taxpayer would return to the claimed tax home after the job terminates. In addition, the taxpayer must show that the claimed tax home is the taxpayer's regular place of abode in a real and substantial sense. There are three objective factors that may be used. . . . They are:

(1) Whether the taxpayer has used the claimed abode (for purposes of the taxpayer's lodging) while performing work in the vicinity thereof immediately prior to the current job and the taxpayer continue[s] to maintain bona fide work contacts (e.g., job seeking, leave of absence, on-going business, etc.) in that area during the alleged temporary employment;

(2) Whether the taxpayer's living expenses at the claimed abode are duplicated . . .; and

(3) Whether the taxpayer (a) has a family member or family members (marital or lineal only) currently residing at the claimed abode, or (b) continues to [use] the claimed abode frequently for purposes of the taxpayer's lodging. . . .

If a taxpayer clearly demonstrates the requisite realistic expectation as to job duration and return to the claimed abode, and the taxpayer satisfies all three of the claimed abode factors set forth above, the Internal Revenue Service will recognize [the deduction]. If a taxpayer demonstrates such . . . realistic expectation, but satisfies only two of the three claimed abode factors, then all the facts and circumstances of the case will be [scrutinized] to determine whether the taxpayer is [entitled to the deduction]. If a taxpayer demonstrates such . . . realistic expectation, but fails to satisfy at least two of the three claimed abode factors, the Service [will not recognize the deduction].[5]

8) The *Hantzis* Decision

In Hantzis v. Commissioner, 638 F.2d 248 (1st Cir. 1981), *cert. denied*, 453 U.S. 962 (1982), Mrs. Hantzis attended law school in the Boston area where she lived with her husband who was employed in Boston. After failing to obtain employment in Boston during the summer after her second year of law school, Mrs. Hantzis accepted a job with a New York City firm. On their joint return, Mr. and Mrs. Hantzis deducted her costs during the

---

5. 1983–1 C.B. 46.

summer for meals and lodging in New York City and for traveling between New York and Boston.

The Tax Court sustained the deductions, holding that Mrs. Hantzis' home was Boston, that her summer employment was temporary, and that her expenses were required by temporary employment away from home. The Circuit Court of Appeals reversed:

> Mrs. Hantzis' *trade or business* did not require that she maintain a home in Boston as well as one in New York. Though she returned to Boston at various times during the period of employment in New York, her visits were all for personal reasons. It is not contended that she had a business connection in Boston that necessitated her keeping a home there.... The home in Boston was kept up for reasons involving Mr. Hantzis, but those reasons cannot substitute for a showing by *Mrs.* Hantzis that the exigencies of *her* trade or business required *her* to maintain two homes. Mrs. Hantzis' decision to keep two homes must be seen as a choice dictated by personal, albeit wholly reasonable, considerations and not a business or occupational necessity....
>
> We are not dissuaded from this conclusion by the temporary nature of Mrs. Hantzis' employment in New York.... The Tax Court here held that Boston was the taxpayer's home because it would have been unreasonable for her to move her residence to New York for only ten weeks....
>
> The temporary employment doctrine does not, however, purport to eliminate any requirement that continued maintenance of a first home have a business justification. We think the rule has no application where the taxpayer has no business connection with the usual place of residence. If no business exigency dictates the location of the taxpayer's usual residence, then the mere fact of his taking temporary employment elsewhere cannot supply a compelling business reason for continuing to maintain that residence.[6]

If Mrs. Hantzis were single and living in Boston while attending law school, would she be allowed to deduct the costs of living and working in New York City at a "temporary" summer job? If not, why should she be treated differently simply because she is married?

Suppose that, after graduating from law school, Mrs. Hantzis is unable to find work in the Boston area and reluctantly accepts employment in New York City. In that event, is the case for allowing her to deduct the cost of living in New York and traveling to and from Boston more appealing? In terms of the underlying equities, how does Mrs. Hantzis' situation differ from that of a) Flowers, b) Rosenspan, and c) a married couple when both spouses are able to find jobs in the same location?

---

6. 638 F.2d at 254-255.

Chapter 6

EDUCATION

A. INTRODUCTORY NOTES AND QUESTIONS

1) Education as Personal Consumption

Consider the following three examples of education: a) a course in French cooking (for amateur chefs); b) an undergraduate liberal arts program; and c) law school. The tax law generally does not allow a deduction for the cost of any of these educational programs. Can the disallowance of deductions be explained by the presence, in each example, of *significant* personal consumption benefits? Even in the case of law school? One commentator seems to think so.

> [A] significant difficulty is determining what portion, if any, of education expenses such as tuition and fees does in fact amount to a cost of producing income, as distinguished from personal consumption. . . . For a professional student such as a law student, would income producing costs include all his tuition and educational or instructional fees? Or, are part of those fees paid [for] the purely personal delights of legal instruction, the elevated social status . . ., bettered marital opportunities, parental approval, daily classroom entertainment, generally sharpened intellectual powers, and other personal benefits of a legal education? Educational expenditures, in other words, can be seen as, at least in part, expenditures for present or future consumption. To separate . . . the consumption component of tuition charges, even for vocational, professional, or graduate school, proves very difficult, if not impossible.[1]

Do you agree with this statement? Is separating out the personal consumption component of law school education all that difficult? How much

---

1. McNulty, Tax Policy and Tuition Credit Legislation: Federal Income Tax Allowances for Personal Costs of Higher Education, 61 Cal. L. Rev. 1, 18 (1973).

would you personally be willing to pay for law school if it would neither qualify you for a new profession, nor otherwise enhance your career prospects? How much would you pay, in other words, if the only possible benefit of law school were personal consumption?

2) The Timing Problem

In principle, a business expenditure should be deductible over the period of time during which the expenditure produces income. For example, if a machine costs $5,000 and is expected to last five years, its cost should be spread out and deducted over the five-year period.[2]

Assume that one views law school as providing no significant personal consumption benefits. If the cost of law school *is* regarded as a business expenditure, *when* should it be deductible? Over what period of time does legal education produce income? Can that period be specified with reasonable accuracy? Even if it can be, how should the cost be spread over that period?

Suppose that, for practical reasons, we limit ourselves to two choices in the treatment of expenses for law school—an immediate deduction in full, or no deduction at all. Which choice more closely approximates spreading the cost over the period during which it produces income? Hint: Which is closer to the value of deducting the cost of law school over the period during which it produces income: (a) no deduction at all or (b) an immediate deduction in full?

Consider the case of a practicing lawyer who attends a two-day seminar on current developments in tax law. Does the cost of this educational program raise the same kinds of timing problems as the cost of law school? Can the period of time during which this program produces revenue be more easily specified? Why might an immediate deduction (rather than no deduction at all) be appropriate?

3) Deductible Education

Reg. § 1.162–5 allows a deduction for the cost of education which meets two separate requirements. First, it must be business related. This means education which "[m]aintains or improves skills required by the individual in his employment or other trade or business" or "[m]eets the express requirements of the individual's employer, or the requirements of applicable law ..." that are "imposed as a condition to the retention by the individual of an established employment relationship ..." Reg. § 1.162–5(a). Second, the education must not provide the "minimum education necessary to qualify for a position" or for a "new trade or business." Reg. § 1.162–5(b)(2) and (3).

4) Are Capital Expenditures for Education Sometimes Deductible?

Reg. § 1.162–5 states that its purpose is to prevent the deduction of "[e]ducational expenditures [which] are personal expenditures or constitute

---

2. This issue is addressed in considerably more detail in Chapter 35 on depreciation.

an inseparable aggregate of personal and capital expenditures ...." Reg. § 1.162–5(b)(1). Capital expenditures can be defined as expenditures that provide benefits over a period of more than one year.

Does the regulation appear to permit an immediate deduction in full for some capital expenditures? Suppose that, after completing law school, you decide to pursue an LL.M. in taxation. Are the tuition fees deductible? Does it depend on whether you have already begun to practice law (and take the LL.M. courses at night) or wait until after you obtain the advanced degree? Section 162(a) refers to expenses incurred while "carrying on a trade or business" which suggests that unless the student is already an established employee or worker, the deductions will not be allowed. But even if you have already begun to practice law, why should a capital expenditure—that will probably last over your entire professional life—be immediately deductible in full?

B. GREENBERG v. COMMISSIONER
367 F.2d 663 (1st Cir. 1966)

[Editor's Note: The second requirement of Reg. § 1.162–5—that education not qualify the taxpayer for a new trade or business—applies an *objective* test. Education which does qualify a taxpayer for a new trade or business is not deductible *even if* the taxpayer does not intend to so qualify. An earlier version of the regulation, in effect until 1965, applied a *subjective* test. Education which did qualify the taxpayer for a new trade or business satisfied the requirement, *provided* that the taxpayer did not intend to qualify. The *Greenberg* case, which follows, was decided under the earlier subjective test.]

COFFIN, CIRCUIT JUDGE.

The sole question in this case is whether the Tax Court erred in denying a deduction claimed by petitioner, a psychiatrist, as an "ordinary and necessary" business expense, for the cost of his own analysis as part of an extensive training program in psychoanalysis.

The availability of the deduction claimed under ... § 162(a) depends upon the pertinent 1954 Treasury Regulations, which are set forth in the margin. The critical question raised by these regulations is whether petitioner's psychoanalytic studies, including his own analysis, were undertaken to improve his skills as a psychiatrist or were for the purposes of obtaining a new position, obtaining a substantial advancement in position, or fulfilling his general educational aspirations.

The facts found by the Tax Court, apart from stipulated data concerning the profession of psychiatry and the purpose of the Boston Psychoanalytic Institute, covered the psychiatric education and experience of petitioner and his undertaking a six or seven year training program at the Boston Institute. ...

In this case, ... a psychiatrist, having completed medical school, internship, and at least one year of psychiatric residency, qualified for the practice of psychiatry, and, while engaging in such practice, pursued a lengthy institute-sponsored training program in psychoanalysis. Such a program consisted of several years of the taxpayer's own analysis, seminars and courses in psychoanalytical theory, and the supervised handling of several patients over a lengthy period. On the satisfactory completion of such a program, the psychiatrists would be eligible for membership in the particular psychoanalytical institute and recognized as full-fledged psychoanalysts. . . . [T]he taxpayer unsuccessfully claimed that the training in psychoanalysis was undertaken primarily to improve his skills as a psychiatrist, the Tax Court holding that the dominant purpose was to prepare for the practice of a separate specialty, psychoanalysis.

Omitted from the findings of fact in this case is the considerable testimony of petitioner, the only witness, relating to his purpose in taking extended training in psychoanalysis. Since the regulations . . . make purpose of the taxpayer central in the determination of such questions, since the judge who heard this testimony found it not only "uncontradicted" but "believable" . . . it is appropriate to summarize it briefly.

Petitioner, even while in medical school, became interested in the application of psychoanalytical thinking to neurophysiological data, writing a paper on the subject. Although he had resolved, during his time in medical school, to become a psychiatrist, he postponed his psychiatric residency one year to allow him to study neurology, which he felt to be important to his future work as a psychiatrist. He then took two succeeding years of psychiatric residency. These two years, together with his year in neurology, met the minimum psychiatric board requirement. He did not seek additional years of psychiatric residency because, he said, he then had in mind obtaining psychoanalytic training as "a continuation of my psychiatric training."

As he began his practice as a psychiatrist with the Boston Veterans Administration Hospital, he also applied for admission to the Boston Psychoanalytic Society and Institute, writing in his application, "At this point, my choice of psychiatry as a specialty seems a happy one. . . . I feel that with psychoanalytic training, I may be able to gain more understanding of the function of the mind and also will be able to help emotionally ill patients achieve a better living adjustment."

In defending this purpose as not being unusual, petitioner testified that over 90 per cent of those associated with the Boston Institute spend "more or less of their time" teaching psychiatric residents, teaching psychiatry to medical students, and doing psychiatric research. He referred to articles in professional journals on the place of psychoanalysis in psychiatric training; a foundation grant to train young psychiatrists in psychoanalysis to further their work in psychiatric research; and National Institute of Health career fellowships in psychiatry, which included psychoanalytic training.

Petitioner gave testimony at length on the connection of each part of the psychoanalytic training program to the work of a psychiatrist. Personal analysis helped, he said, to remove one's own "blind spots" and to work more easily with a patient. The study of basic psychoanalytical theory, covered only sparsely in medical school and psychiatric residencies, was "one of the basic sciences in psychiatric thinking" and, more particularly, was useful in his own work in teaching psychiatric residents and as a prerequisite to research. The supervised handling of several cases in depth and at length, petitioner testified, was "one of the main dividends", giving insights into the problems of other patients he would see in the course of his regular work.

As to petitioner's future plans, he testified that he would continue to work part-time at the Boston Veterans Administration Hospital, where he teaches and does research, and to continue to conduct a private practice. He would apply psychoanalytical methods, either "classical" or "modified" as the needs of the patient indicated. As to referrals, he testified, "I think in terms of my being a better psychiatrist, for having this training, that the referrals will come."

Finally, respondent's counsel, at the conclusion of his cross-examination, asked: "Is it your position in this case that you undertook the analytic training and the supervised clinical work and the theoretical instruction to improve your field [sic] as a psychiatrist?" To which petitioner answered, "That is right." . . . [The Tax Court] pointed out (1) that, while petitioner had stated his reason as that of improving his skills as a psychiatrist, he did not say that this was his "primary" reason; (2) that he did not say that he did not intend to practice psychoanalysis upon graduation; (3) that in fact petitioner's testimony indicated his intention to treat some patients with psychoanalysis; and (4) that it is a reasonable inference that when petitioner testified about hoped-for referrals, he meant referrals for psychoanalytic treatment. From these specific observations the Tax Court arrives at its final conclusion, phrased in the negative: "This record would hardly warrant a finding that petitioner did not intend to hold himself out as a practicing psychoanalyst when he completed his six-year course at the Institute."

We reverse. We have set forth the substance of petitioner's testimony and the Tax Court's opinion at some length to illuminate our difficulty. For we do not take issue either with any specific finding of fact or with any inference drawn therefrom except the final conclusion. Our action is based on our conviction that, reviewing the entire evidence, "a mistake has been committed". . . .

The error lies in the automatic assumption, which contravenes the overwhelming weight of the evidence in this case, that the acquisition of a "specialty" is inconsistent with the improvement of skills required for the practice of a preexisting profession. To put the difficulty in terms of the facts of this case, the Tax Court majority deemed it sufficient to ask only two questions: is psychoanalysis a specialty? and is it reasonable to infer that the petitioner intended to use the knowledge and methods which he was learning? Affirmative answers to both questions effectively disposed of the case. The question unasked was: did the petitioner have a primary (and reasonable) purpose of using the lore of this new specialty in improving his skills as a practicing and teaching psychiatrist? Since this is the question required by existing regulations, the failure to answer it in the light of the evidence constitutes reversible error.

What is involved in the improvement of skills of a taxpayer in his employment, trade, or business reflects the complexity and variety of our society itself. Perhaps the worker tightening bolts on an assembly line may be said to require only one skill. But most occupations require a bundle of skills. And, to the extent that one is engaged in a learned profession, he must employ a multiplicity of skills. The fact that what is newly acquired by a taxpayer may be recognized as a "skill" or a "specialty"—or, as is usually the case, another group of skills—is irrelevant if the taxpayer's primary purpose is to add to his equipment in carrying on his preexisting vocation. Some of the cases cited in the margin have gone quite far in allowing deductions for training of less proximate relevance than that indicated by the testimony in this case. Most of them involved a new "specialty".

The regulations attempt to delineate the area of deductible education not only by the positive language referring to improving skills but by proscriptive language. Education pursued primarily to obtain "a new position or substantial advancement in position" and to satisfy "general educational aspirations or other personal purposes" is beyond the pale. Most of the cases holding against the taxpayer do so, not on the ground that he was studying another field of learning, but on the ground that his intent was to change the direction or nature of his career or to qualify for a specific job opportunity. . . .

Primary purpose under the quoted regulations is to be determined by the facts of each case. The petitioner testified at length on the interrelationship of psychoanalytic knowledge and methods and the work of one engaged in practicing psychiatry, teaching psychiatric residents, and doing psychiatric research. There was no evidence to the contrary.

The unrebutted testimony even went so far as to indicate that it was not unusual for other members of petitioner's profession to undertake such education. Under the regulations, if customary conduct is proved, ". . . the taxpayer will ordinarily be considered to have undertaken this education for the purposes [of improving skills]. . . ." While the evidence on this point might not compel a finding of custom, it at least forecloses any inferences which might be drawn from unusual conduct.

There was no evidence that petitioner had any other "position" in mind than that of continuing his part-time work at the Boston VA Hospital and his part-time psychiatric practice. There was no hint of any purpose to secure a "substantial advancement in position", except the obvious aim to increase in stature in his profession. Nor could it be said that the six or seven year program was to fulfill his general educational aspirations or other personal purposes.

The Tax Court's difficulty seems to stem from its appropriate findings and inferences that petitioner intended to apply what he was learning when it was applicable. Without addressing itself to the question required by the regulations, i. e., whether or not the petitioner had succeeded in showing that he was motivated principally to improve his skills as a psychiatrist, it took a long leap in concluding that petitioner's primary purpose was to hold himself out as a practicing psychoanalyst. If this means that petitioner intended wholly or substantially to abandon his practice of psychiatry and his position at the Hospital, there is no support whatsoever in the evidence. If this means that petitioner would, in the course of his practice, administer psychoanalysis in varying degrees without having to refer patients to others, it does not support the court's decision under the regulations.

Without making any generalizations as to how far the Tax Court can, with propriety, disregard uncontradicted evidence, we believe in this case that if the court's decision did not reflect an erroneous application of the regulations, it reflected an unjustified rejection of unimpeached and credible testimony. In either case, the decision must be reversed.

C. NOTES AND QUESTIONS

1) The Current Version of § Reg. 1.162–5

Could Greenberg still win under the current regulation? The relevant language states that the cost is deductible *only if* the education does not prepare the taxpayer to enter a "new trade or business." The regulation further explains that this test is satisfied if the education involves "the same general type of work as . . . the individual's present employment." Reg. § 1.162–5(b)(3). Greenberg's prospects may therefore seem uncertain to readers familiar with the differences between psychiatry and psychoanalysis. One writer described them:

> [P]atients in analysis . . . come four or five times a week and lie on the couch . . . [while] patients . . . come for psychotherapy once or twice or three times a week and sit in a chair.[3]
>
> The analyst as far as possible confines himself to listening to the patient and (sparingly) offering him his conjectures—which are called "interpretations"—about the unconscious meaning of his communications. He does not give advice, . . . he does not let himself be provoked . . . into discussions of abstract subjects, . . . he does not show like or dislike of the patient, or approval or disapproval of his actions. His behavior toward the patient is as neutral, mild, colorless, self-effacing, uninterfering, and undemanding as he is able to make it . . . with the paradoxical (and now absolutely predictable) result that the patient reacts with stronger, more vivid and intense personal feelings to this bland, shadowy figure than he does to the more clearly delineated and provocative figures in his life outside the analysis. On this paradox—on the patient's quickness to overfill the emotional vacuum created by the analyst's reticence—the analysis is poised. . . .[4]
>
> Psychoanalysis, alone among today's psychotherapies, remains strictly a talking cure. Even the most far-out theorist will confine himself to telling his patients what he believes to be true about them, rather than attempting to manipulate or act on them.[5]
>
> [N]o analyst ever knows with certainty when the time has come to set a termination date. However, over the years, the consensus about what constitutes an appropriate length of time for analysis has had a steady upward trend. In the twenties, one to two years was deemed sufficient; in the thirties and forties, two to four years was the norm; in the fifties and sixties, four to six years; today, six to eight.[6]

3. J. Malcom, Psychoanalysis: The Impossible Profession 3 (1980).
4. Ibid. at 38.
5. Ibid. at 145.
6. Ibid. at 151.

Although psychoanalysis and psychiatry may seem no more similar than, say, law and accounting, the regulation explicitly states that, for a psychiatrist, psychoanalysis does *not* constitute "a new trade or business." Reg. § 1.162–5(b)(3), Example 4. An accountant studying for a law degree does not fare as well. Even if the accountant has no intention of practicing law, the latter is regarded as a new trade. Reg. § 1.162–5(b)(3), Example 1.

One answer for the accountant may be to attend an unaccredited law school. Since completion of the program would not qualify the student to sit for a state bar examination, the IRS has ruled that expenses incurred in attending such unaccredited institutions are deductible. See Rev. Rul. 76–62, 1976–1 C.B. 12.

2) Subjective versus Objective Standards

Which is preferable, a subjective test under the old regulation or an objective test under the current one? Which is easier to administer?

3) The Additional Limit Imposed by Section 67 on Otherwise Deductible Educational Expenses

Notice that Section 67, discussed in Chapter 4, above, also applies to business-related education expenses. If the expenses are not reimbursed by the taxpayer's employer, the allowable deduction is limited to the extent that education costs and other designated expenditures exceed 2% of Adjusted Gross Income.

D. BINGLER v. JOHNSON
394 U.S. 741 (1969)

[Editor's Note: The issue in this case was whether an amount could be excluded as a "scholarship" under Section 117 of the Code. In order to make sense of the opinion below, the student should note the following differences between the earlier version of Section 117 under which the case was decided and Section 117 as it is today.[7]

1) Previously, Section 117 excluded both tuition and living expenses. Today, Section 117 excludes only "tuition and related expenses." Section 117(b)(2).

2) Previously, Section 117 generally did not exclude "any amount which represents payment for teaching, research, or other services in the nature of part-time employment required as a condition to receiving the scholarship . . ." In 1986, the reference to "in the nature of part-time employment" was dropped. Section 117(c).

3) Previously, nondegree candidates could qualify under Section 117, although their exclusion was limited to $300 per month and was subject to a number of additional requirements. Since 1986, Section 117 has applied

---

7. Section 117 was substantially revised by the 1986 Tax Reform Act.

only to candidates for a degree. Nondegree candidates may no longer benefit.]

Mr. Justice Stewart delivered the opinion of the Court.

We are called upon in this case to examine for the first time § 117 of the Internal Revenue Code of 1954, which excludes from a taxpayer's gross income amounts received as "scholarships" and "fellowships." The question before us concerns the tax treatment of payments received by the respondents from their employer, the Westinghouse Electric Corporation, while they were on "educational leave" from their jobs with Westinghouse.

During the period here in question the respondents held engineering positions at the Bettis Atomic Power Laboratory in Pittsburgh, Pennsylvania, which Westinghouse operates under a "cost-plus" contract with the Atomic Energy Commission. Their employment status enabled them to participate in what is known as the Westinghouse Bettis Fellowship and Doctoral Program. That program, designed both to attract new employees seeking further education and to give advanced training to persons already employed at Bettis, offers a two-phase schedule of subsidized postgraduate study in engineering, physics, or mathematics.

Under the first, or "work-study," phase, a participating employee holds a regular job with Westinghouse and in addition pursues a course of study at either the University of Pittsburgh or Carnegie-Mellon University. The employee is paid for a 40-hour work week, but may receive up to eight hours of "release time" per week for the purpose of attending classes. "Tuition remuneration," as well as reimbursement for various incidental academic expenses, is provided by the company.

When an employee has completed all preliminary requirements for his doctorate, he may apply for an educational leave of absence, which constitutes the second phase of the Fellowship Program. He must submit a proposed dissertation topic for approval by Westinghouse and the AEC. Approval is based, *inter alia*, on a determination that the topic has at least some general relevance to the work done at Bettis. If the leave of absence is secured, the employee devotes his full attention, for a period of at least several months, to fulfilling his dissertation requirement. During this period he receives a "stipend" from Westinghouse, in an amount based on a specified percentage (ranging from 70% to 90%) of his prior salary plus "adders," depending upon the size of his family. He also retains his seniority status and receives all employee benefits, such as insurance and stock option privileges. In return he not only must submit periodic progress reports, but under the written agreement that all participants in the program must sign, also is obligated to return to the employ of Westinghouse for a period of at least two years following completion of his leave.[8] Upon return he is, according to the agreement, to "assume . . . duties commensurate with his

---

8. Respondent Wolfe began his leave at a time when Westinghouse did not require agreement in writing to the two-year "return" commitment. He was formally advised before he went on leave, however, that he was "expected" to return to Westinghouse for a period of time equal to the duration of his leave, and he in fact honored that obligation.

education and experience," at a salary "commensurate with the duties assigned."

The respondents all took leaves under the Fellowship Program at varying times during the period 1960–1962, and eventually received their doctoral degrees in engineering. Respondents Johnson and Pomerantz took leaves of nine months and were paid $5,670 each, representing 80% of their prior salaries at Westinghouse. Respondent Wolfe, whose leave lasted for a year, received $9,698.90, or 90% of his previous salary. Each returned to Westinghouse for the required period of time following his educational leave.

Westinghouse, which under its own accounting system listed the amounts paid to the respondents as "indirect labor" expenses, withheld federal income tax from those amounts.[9] The respondents filed claims for refund, contending that the payments they had received were "scholarships," and hence were excludable from income under § 117 of the Code. . . .

When those claims were rejected, the respondents instituted this suit in the District Court for the Western District of Pennsylvania, against the District Director of Internal Revenue. After the basically undisputed evidence regarding the Bettis Program had been presented, the trial judge instructed the jury in accordance with Treas. Reg. . . . § 1.117–4(c), . . . which provides that amounts representing "compensation for past, present, or future employment services," and amounts "paid . . . to . . . an individual to enable him to pursue studies or research primarily for the benefit of the grantor," are not excludable as scholarships. The jury found that the amounts received by the respondents were taxable income. Respondents then sought review in the Court of Appeals for the Third Circuit, and that court reversed, holding that the Regulation referred to was invalid, that the jury instructions were therefore improper, and that on the essentially undisputed facts it was clear as a matter of law that the amounts received by the respondents were "scholarships" excludable under § 117. . . .

The holding of the Court of Appeals with respect to Treas. Reg. § 1.117–4(c) was contrary to the decisions of several other circuits . . . which explicitly sustained the Regulation against attack and held amounts received under an arrangement quite similar to the Bettis Program to be taxable income. Accordingly, upon the District Director's petition, we granted certiorari to resolve the conflict and to determine the proper scope of § 117 and Treas. Reg. § 1.117–4(c) with respect to payments such as those involved here. . . .

In holding invalid the Regulation that limits the definitions of "scholarship" and "fellowship" so as to exclude amounts received as "compensation," the Court of Appeals emphasized that the statute itself expressly adverts to certain situations in which funds received by students may be thought of as remuneration. After the basic rule excluding scholarship funds from gross income is set out in § 117(a), for instance, [one] subsection . . . stipulates:

---

9. Tuition and incidental fees were also paid by Westinghouse, but no withholding was made from those payments, and their tax status is not at issue in this case. Although conceptually includable in income, such sums presumably would be offset by educational expense deductions. See Treas. Reg. on Income Tax (1954 Code) § 1.162–5, 26 CFR § 1.162–5.

In the case of an individual who is a candidate for a degree at an educational institution . . . , subsection (a) shall not apply to that portion of any amount received which represents payment for teaching, research, or other services in the nature of part-time employment required as a condition to receiving the scholarship or the fellowship grant.

In addition, [another] subsection . . . limits the exclusion from income with regard to nondegree candidates in two respects: first, the grantor must be a governmental agency, an international organization, or an organization exempt from tax under §§ 501(a), (c)(3) of the Code; and second, the maximum exclusion from income available to a nondegree candidate is $300 per month for not more than 36 months. Since these exceptions are expressly set out in the statute, the Court of Appeals, relying on the canon of construction that *expressio unius est exclusio alterius*, concluded that no additional restrictions may be put on the basic exclusion from income granted by subsection (a)—a conclusion forcefully pressed upon us by the respondents.

Congress' express reference to the limitations just referred to concededly lends some support to the respondents' position. The difficulty with that position, however, lies in its implicit assumption that those limitations are limitations on an exclusion of *all funds* received by students to support them during the course of their education. Section 117 provides, however, only that amounts received as "scholarships" or "fellowships" shall be excludable. And Congress never defined what it meant by the quoted terms. As the Tax Court has observed:

> [A] proper reading of the statute requires that before the exclusion comes into play there must be a determination that the payment sought to be excluded has the normal characteristics associated with the term 'scholarship.' . . .

The regulation here in question represents an effort by the Commissioner to supply the definitions that Congress omitted. And it is fundamental, of course, that as "contemporaneous constructions by those charged with administration of" the Code, the Regulations "must be sustained unless unreasonable and plainly inconsistent with the revenue statutes," and "should not be overruled except for weighty reasons." . . . In this respect our statement last Term in *United States v. Correll*, [Chapter 5] bears emphasis:

> [W]e do not sit as a committee of revision to perfect the administration of the tax laws. Congress has delegated to the Commissioner, not to the courts, the task of prescribing 'all needful rules and regulations for the enforcement' of the Internal Revenue Code. . . . In this area of limitless factual variations, 'it is the province of Congress and the Commissioner, not the courts, to make the appropriate adjustments.' . . . .

Here, the definitions supplied by the Regulation clearly are prima facie proper, comporting as they do with the ordinary understanding of "scholarships" and "fellowships" as relatively disinterested, "no-strings" educational grants, with no requirement of any substantial *quid pro quo* from the recipients.

The implication of the respondents' *expressio unius* reasoning is that any amount paid for the purpose of supporting one pursuing a program of study or scholarly research should be excludable from gross income as a "scholarship" so long as it does not fall within the specific limitations of § 117. . . . Pay received by a $30,000 per year engineer or executive on a leave of absence would, according to that reasoning, be excludable as long as the leave was granted so that the individual could perform work required for a doctoral degree. This result presumably would not be altered by the fact that the employee might be performing, in satisfaction of his degree requirements, precisely the same work which he was doing for his employer prior to his leave and which he would be doing after his return to "employment"—or by the fact that the fruits of that work were made directly available to and exploited by the employer. Such a result would be anomalous indeed, especially in view of the fact that under § 117 the comparatively modest sums received by part-time teaching assistants are clearly subject to taxation. Particularly in light of the principle that exemptions from taxation are to be construed narrowly, we decline to assume that Congress intended to sanction—indeed, as the respondents would have it, to compel—such an inequitable situation.

The legislative history underlying § 117 is, as the Court of Appeals recognized, "far from clear." We do not believe, however, that it precludes, as "plainly inconsistent" with the statute, a definition of "scholarship" that excludes from the reach of that term amounts received as compensation for services performed. The 1939 Internal Revenue Code, like predecessor Codes, contained no specific provision dealing with scholarship grants. Whether such grants were includable in gross income depended simply upon whether they fell within the broad provision excluding from income amounts received as "gifts." Thus case-by-case determinations regarding grantors' motives were necessary. The cases decided under this approach prior to 1954 generally involved two types of financial assistance: grants to research or teaching assistants—graduate students who perform research or teaching services in return for their stipends—and foundation grants to post-doctoral researchers. In cases decided shortly before the 1954 Code was enacted, the Tax Court, relying on the "gift" approach to scholarships and fellowships, held that amounts received by a research assistant were taxable income, but reached divergent results in situations involving grants to post-doctoral researchers.

In enacting § 117 of the 1954 Code, Congress indicated that it wished to eliminate the necessity for reliance on "case-by-case" determinations with respect to whether "scholarships" and "fellowships" were excludable as "gifts." Upon this premise the respondents hinge their argument that Congress laid down a standard under which all case-by-case determinations—such as those that may be made under Treas. Reg. § 1.117–4(c)—are unnecessary and improper. We have already indicated, however, our reluctance to believe that § 117 was designed to exclude from taxation all amounts, no matter how large or from what source, that are given for the support of one who happens to be a student. The sounder inference is that Congress was merely "recogni[zing] that scholarships and fellowships are sufficiently unique . . . to merit [tax] treatment separate from that accorded gifts," and attempting to provide that grants falling within those categories should be treated consistently—as in some instances, under the generic provisions of the 1939 Code, they arguably had not been. Delineation of the precise contours of those categories was left to the Commissioner.

Furthermore, a congressional intention that not all grants received by students were necessarily to be "scholarships" may reasonably be inferred from the legislative history. In explaining the basis for its version of § 117 . . . , the House Ways and Means Committee stated that its purpose was to "tax those grants which are in effect merely payments of a salary during a period while the recipient is on leave from his regular job." This comment related, it is true, to a specific exception to the exclusion from income set out in subsection (a). But, in view of the fact that the statute left open the definitions of "scholarship" and "fellowship," it is not unreasonable to conclude that in adding [specific exceptions] to the statute Congress was merely dealing explicitly with those problems that had come explicitly to its attention—*viz.*, those involving research and teaching assistantships and post-doctoral research grants—without intending to forbid application to similar situations of the general principle underlying its treatment of those problems. One may justifiably suppose that the Congress that taxed funds received by "part-time" teaching assistants, presumably on the ground that the amounts received by such persons really represented compensation for services performed, would also deem proper a definition of "scholarship" under which comparable sorts of compensation—which often, as in the present case, are significantly greater in amount—are likewise taxable. In providing such a definition, the Commissioner has permissibly implemented an underlying congressional concern. We cannot say that the provision of Treas. Reg. § 1.117–4(c) that taxes amounts received as "compensation" is "unreasonable or plainly inconsistent with the . . . statut[e]."

Under that provision, as set out in the trial court's instructions, the jury here properly found that the amounts received by the respondents were taxable "compensation" rather than excludable "scholarships." The employer-employee relationship involved is immediately suggestive, of course, as is the close relation between the respondents' prior salaries and the amount of their "stipends." In addition, employee benefits were continued. Topics were required to relate at least generally to the work of the Bettis Laboratory. Periodic work reports were to be submitted. And, most importantly, Westinghouse unquestionably extracted a *quid pro quo*. The respondents not only were required to hold positions with Westinghouse throughout the "work-study" phase of the program, but also were obligated to return to Westinghouse's employ for a substantial period of time after completion of their leave. The thrust of the provision dealing with compensation is that bargained-for payments, given only as a *"quo"* in return for the *quid* of services rendered—whether past, present, or future—should not be excludable from income as "scholarship" funds. That provision clearly covers this case.

Accordingly, the judgment of the Court of Appeals is reversed, and that of the District Court reinstated.

E. NOTES AND QUESTIONS

1) Exclusion Rules versus Deduction Rules for Education

The Section 117 exclusion for fellowships and scholarships is the functional equivalent of including such items and allowing an offsetting deduction. Are the Section 117 exclusion rules consistent with the Reg. § 1.162–5 deduction rules? What kinds of tuition fees are excluded by Section 117(a) that cannot be deducted under Reg. § 1.162–5?

2) Justifying Section 117

Shouldn't the rules governing exclusion of fellowships and scholarships and the deduction of educational expenses be the same? Can you defend the considerably broader scope of Section 117? Most universities charge tuition that covers only a portion of the actual costs. Do students report income resulting from the gap between actual costs and the tuition charged? Does it depend on whether the university is public or private? Can fellowships and scholarships be analogized to the gap between education costs and tuition that goes untaxed?

3) Justifying Bingler v. Johnson

The Latin maxim cited by the Court of Appeals in *Johnson* states a principle of statutory construction: "When certain things are specified in a law . . ., an intention to exclude all others . . . may be inferred."[10] Is the Supreme Court's stated reason for ignoring the maxim convincing? Is there a more plausible justification for reading the Section 117 restrictions as not being exclusive?

4) The Special Case of Government-provided Employee Benefits

In 1980, Congress amended the Code to provide that Section 117 shall apply to scholarships provided by the federal government *even if* the recipient is "required to perform future service as a federal employee . . ." (The language was repealed six years later in the 1986 Tax Reform Act.) Could the taxpayer in Bingler v. Johnson arguably have qualified under this language had it been in effect at the time?

What is the justification for this exception to the general rule that employer-provided scholarships are taxable income if the employee is required to render a quid pro quo? Compare the *Jones* case (cited in the *Benaglia* dissent in Chapter 4) which held that living quarters provided by the federal government to military personnel are exempt from taxation. What both cases have in common is that employee benefits were provided by the federal government rather than by a private employer.

Why might the federal government decide not to tax in-kind benefits that it provides even though it insists on taxing similar benefits provided

---

10. Black's Law Dictionary 1266 (5th ed. 1979).

by the private sector? How is a decision *not* to tax government benefits likely to affect the dollar amount of benefits provided? How is a decision to tax benefits likely to affect the dollar amount?

Assuming that the dollar amount is adjusted to take account of whether benefits are taxed, isn't it simpler to provide for nontaxation? But what about the impact of differences in marginal tax rates? Why does nontaxation treat lower bracket taxpayers unfairly compared to higher bracket taxpayers?

In the past, the IRS has ruled that Section 61(a) does not reach such government payments as welfare, unemployment compensation, and social security.[11] Congress has since provided, however, for taxing unemployment compensation in full and one-half of social security payments when AGI exceeds a certain level.[12] Welfare remains exempt from taxes. Might the decision to tax unemployment compensation reflect a judgment that the simplicity of nontaxation is not justified by the unfair impact of nontaxation due to differences in marginal tax rates? Why, in the case of welfare, is this trade-off arguably different and nontaxation therefore appropriate?

5) Bingler v. Johnson Today

As noted above, an earlier version of Section 117 applied to living expenses as well as tuition. The Tax Reform Act of 1986 limited the exclusion to amounts spent on tuition and course-related equipment. See Section 117(b)(2). Living expenses, such as room, board, and incidental expenses, are thus no longer excludible under Section 117. If Bingler v. Johnson were litigated today, how would this change affect the outcome? Was the actual dispute over tuition or living expenses? Given the 1986 changes, would there even be an issue to litigate?

6) Applying Reg. § 1.162–5 to Bingler v. Johnson

Even though the payments in Bingler v. Johnson did not qualify for exclusion under Section 117, were they nonetheless deductible? In a footnote, the Supreme Court suggests that they were, under the pre-1965 Reg. § 1.162–5. Would this still be the case today under the revised regulation's objective standard?[13] Even if the tuition payments are deductible, how could the stipend for living expenses possibly qualify given Section 262? What might you advise Johnson to do in order to make the living expenses deductible? See Reg. § 1.162–5(e).

7) Employer-provided Education

Suppose that you go to work as a management executive for IBM and spend your first six months in a special training program to familiarize

---

11. Rev. Rul. 76–144, 1976–1 C.B. 17; Rev. Rul. 76–63, 1976–1 C.B. 14; and Rev. Rul. 70–217, 1970–1 C.B. 13.
12. Sections 85 and 86.
13. Today, education which does qualify a taxpayer for a new trade or business is not deductible *even if* the taxpayer does not intend to so qualify. See the discussion of Reg. § 1.162–5, immediately preceding the opinion in *Greenberg*, above.

yourself with company operations. Is the education that you receive taxable income? If it is, are you entitled to an offsetting business expense deduction? Suppose that the training program, instead of specifically focusing on IBM operations consists of a short course in general principles of business management and is required only of new executives lacking an MBA degree. Should this make a difference?

Suppose that IBM starts a free adult education program for its employees, offering courses in literature, mathematics, and science. IBM tells employees that the program will make them more productive workers and strongly encourages them to enroll. Should the value of the courses be taxable to employees who do enroll?

Under Section 127, an employee could exclude up to $5,250 of "educational assistance" furnished by his or her employer. Educational assistance includes both tuition and course-related material but not living or travel expenses. Also, it does not cover courses in "sports, games, or hobbies." Section 127(c)(1)(B). This last provision, one commentator has noted, "rejects the wisdom of classical Greece and seems un-American to boot."[14]

Section 127 is due to expire after 1988. For taxable years through 1988, what is the effect of Section 127 on IBM's free adult education program described above? Beginning in 1989, does the IRS have to determine whether the employee may deduct the value of the employer-provided education under Reg. § 1.162–5?[15]

8) Athletic Scholarships

Does a college athletic scholarship qualify for exclusion under Section 117? Rev. Rul. 77–263, 1977–2 C.B. 47, considered the question:

> In the instant case, the university requires no particular activity of any of its scholarship recipients. Although students who receive athletic scholarships do so because of their special abilities in a particular sport and are expected to participate in the sport, the scholarship is not cancelled in the event the student cannot participate and the student is not required to engage in any other activities in lieu of participating in the sport.
>
> Accordingly, in the instant case, the athletic scholarships are awarded by the university primarily to aid the recipients in pursuing their studies, and therefore, the value is excludible from the recipients' gross income under Section 117 of the Code.

Do you agree that athletic scholarships, under the stated facts, "are awarded primarily to aid recipients in pursuit of their studies"? Even in the absence of an explicit requirement that the recipient participate in a particular sport, might the expectations of the parties indicate that the scholarship was intended to compensate the recipients for participating in sports? But if so, why doesn't a scholarship awarded to a promising high

---

14. B. Bittker, Federal Taxation of Income, Estates and Gifts 4–14 (1981). In addition, for 1988 only, Section 127 does not exclude expenditures for graduate or professional education.

15. Or might its value be excluded as a nontaxable fringe benefit under Section 132? See the discussion of Section 132 in Chapter 8.

school math student constitute compensation for specializing in mathematics? Is the athletic scholarship case different only where the college has a "big-time" athletic program that makes significant profits?

Would you feel confident advising Westinghouse that, based on Rev. Rul. 77–263, employee scholarships will not be taxable, even if recipients are told they are "expected" to return to Westinghouse for two years, provided that their returning is *not* explicitly required? Would you expect the IRS to grant a favorable ruling on this issue if you requested one?

F. ARMANTROUT v. COMMISSIONER
67 T.C. 996 (1977), aff'd per curiam, 570 F.2d 210 (7th Cir. 1978)

GOFFE, JUDGE: . . .

FINDINGS OF FACT

. . . Hamlin, Inc., a Delaware corporation (Hamlin), is engaged in the business of manufacturing, distributing, and selling electronic components. During the taxable years 1971 through 1973, petitioner Richard T. Armantrout was employed by Hamlin as vice president in charge of marketing. Petitioner Francis H. Pepper was employed as plant manager during the taxable year 1973. Petitioner Llewellyn G. Owens was employed as secretary-treasurer throughout the taxable year 1971.

Educo, Inc. (Educo), a Delaware corporation, is engaged in the business of designing, implementing, and administering college education benefit plans for corporate employers.

Sometime in 1969, petitioner Llewellyn G. Owens noticed an advertisement in the Wall Street Journal which outlined, in a general way, the potential benefits of the Educo plan. Upon subsequent investigation, Mr. Owens suggested that such a plan be implemented by Hamlin, Inc.

On September 2, 1969, Hamlin entered into an agreement with Funds for Education, Inc., a Delaware corporation. Subsequently, on November 17, 1969, Funds for Education changed its corporate name to Educo, Inc.

Pursuant to the agreement, Educo undertook to administer an Educo education plan to provide funds for college expenses for the children of certain key employees of Hamlin. Hamlin, upon becoming a participant of the Educo plan, agreed to make contributions to the Continental Illinois National Bank & Trust Co. of Chicago which acted as trustee under a trust agreement entered into with Educo on December 9, 1969.

Pursuant to the Educo plan, children of Hamlin's key employees named in the enrollment schedules which formed a part of the plan would be entitled to receive sums from the trustee to defray college education expenses. Upon receipt of the appropriate information from Hamlin, Educo would direct the trustee to pay, in accordance with the enrollment schedule, the expenses incurred by the employees' children in attending a college or university, trade or vocational school.

The education expenses which could be defrayed under the terms of the plan included:

(1) Tuition, registration, and other fees payable to any college;

(2) Rental of living quarters provided by a college or a reasonable allowance for same, if not so provided;

(3) Cost of meals if provided by a college or by a club, fraternity, sorority, or boarding house, or a reasonable allowance for such meals if not so furnished by any of the foregoing;

(4) Cost of books, supplies, equipment, and other extras required to be purchased in connection with attendance at any such college;

(5) Hospitalization insurance; and

(6) Such other expenses as, in the opinion of Educo, Inc., were necessary and reasonable and directly related to the education of the child.

The Educo plan as implemented by Hamlin provided for a maximum of $10,000 to be made available to the children of any one employee with an upper limit of $4,000 available to any one child. Payments to or on behalf of a child enrolled in the plan were limited during any one year to one-fourth of the total amount scheduled for that child; however, the unused funds of a prior year could be used to defray expenses in a subsequent academic year. Children otherwise qualified who did not utilize any of the available funds before reaching age 21 or within 2 years after completing the 12th grade would be ineligible to participate in the plan.

In adopting the Educo plan, it was Hamlin's intention to make available sufficient funds to enable at least two children of each key employee to attend college. Consonant therewith, the plan was in general administered so that $4,000 was scheduled to be received by each of the employee's two eldest children while $2,000 would be provided to a third younger child; funds not utilized by the older children were in turn made available to younger children, thus it was possible that more than three children of each key employee could ultimately participate in the plan. However, this administrative policy was not required by the terms of the plan and, moreover, prior to the adoption of the first enrollment schedule the employee-parents were given the opportunity to allocate the available funds within the maximum allowed by the plan to their children in amounts different from those described above.

Children would be designated to receive the trust benefits through the use of enrollment schedules which could be changed or amended. . . . If any child covered by the Educo plan did not utilize the funds scheduled for his benefit within the period prescribed by the plan, Hamlin could enroll a replacement child of the same or younger age to use any unused funds. Moreover, Hamlin could allocate the unused funds to children already enrolled in the plan or it could apply the funds toward the reduction of its future obligation to make payments to the Educo trust.

Typically, payments of the children's expenses were made directly to the school or creditor providing the service which qualified under the Educo plan. On a few occasions, parents of children attending college made advances for the educational expenses of their respective children which were reimbursed by the Educo trust. In addition, payments were on occasion made directly from the Educo trust to the students attending college to reimburse the purchase of supplies and other qualifying expenses incurred by the students.

The Hamlin Educo plan was adopted, in part, to relieve Hamlin's most important employees from concern and trepidation about the cost of providing a college education for their children and, thus, enable those employees to better perform their duties as employees of Hamlin. Moreover, it was felt by Hamlin that the Educo plan was a benefit which the key employees wanted it to provide. The cost of higher education would be defrayed by the Educo trust for all the children enrolled in the plan without regard to any objective scholastic criteria such as admissions test scores, rank in high school class, or financial need.

Children eligible to participate in the Educo plan were those whose parents were regarded as key employees in the Hamlin organization and although the selection of such employees bore a rough correlation to salary, the determinative factor was the employees' value to the company. Compensation of key employees who did not have children was not increased to counterpoise the effect of the Educo plan on those employees with children. Children of lesser employees could be included as the value of the parents to Hamlin increased.

The employees whose children participated in the Educo plan had no right or claim to the benefits which flowed from the trustees in discharge of their children's educational expenses as outlined in the plan. It was, moreover, impossible for the parent of any child enrolled in the plan to receive benefit from any unused portion of the available funds not expended by their children.

Under the terms of the plan, benefits were payable in accordance with the applicable enrollment schedule to defray the costs incurred by the employee's child in attending college. However, should an employee-parent cease to be employed by Hamlin, the plan would become inoperable for each of his children except that education expenses incurred prior to the termination of the parent's employment would continue to be eligible for payment in accordance with the terms of the Educo plan.

Considering the Educo plan to be a unique benefit made available to its most important employees, Hamlin would describe in a general way the nature and advantages offered by the plan to prospective employees. The existence of the plan has enabled Hamlin to be successful in recruiting and retaining key employees and to do so without the assistance of higher salaries competitive with those in larger urban areas.

By statutory notices of deficiency issued to the respective taxpayers in the cases consolidated herein, the Commissioner determined that the amounts distributed by the Educo trust were scholarships which formed a part of the employees' compensation and were directly related to each employee's pattern of employment and, therefore, compensation for services includable in gross income.

OPINION

Respondent contends that the amounts distributed by the Educo trust in discharge of certain of the educational expenses of petitioners' children constitute taxable income to petitioners because the payments were attributable to petitioners' employment relationship with Hamlin rather than on the basis of any competitive criteria such as need, motivation, or merit.

Petitioners in essence argue, however, that while the amounts distributed by the Educo trust were perhaps "generated" by their efforts as employees of Hamlin, they do not constitute gross income because they were neither beneficially received by them nor did they have the right to receive such distributions and, moreover, because they did not possess an ownership interest in such amounts. In addition, petitioners assert that the mere realization of some familial satisfaction is not sufficient to occasion the recognition of income. For reasons which will hereinafter be expressed, we hold that the distributions from Educo trust to petitioners' children were in the nature of deferred compensation to petitioners and, therefore, includable in their gross income according to the provisions of section 83.

Proper analysis of this issue must begin with the notion often called "the first principle of income taxation: that income must be taxed to him who earns it." . . . It is also important to recall that the income tax consequences of a particular transaction are not to be accorded by reference to "anticipatory arrangements" or "attenuated subtleties" but rather income must be attributed to the tree upon which it grew. . . . In addition, in apportioning the income tax consequence of a particular factual pattern, it is the substance of the transaction which must govern. . . .

While we might agree with petitioners that mere realization of some "familial" satisfaction is perhaps not sufficient to occasion a tax, we must nevertheless take cognizance of the context in which such a benefit accrues. When such a benefit is created in an employment situation and in connection with the performance of services, we are unable to conclude that such a benefit falls outside the broad scope of section 61. . . . This view is especially compelling herein because there is a specific, additional, and identifiable cost incurred by petitioners' employer. . . .

In any event, we do not understand respondent's position to be that the mere "generation" of income is sufficient to occasion a tax. Instead, respondent argues that the amounts paid by the Educo trust were "generated" by petitioners in connection with their performance of services for Hamlin and were, therefore, compensatory in nature. We find this view to be amply supported by the record. The Educo plan was adopted by Hamlin to relieve its most important employees from concern about the high costs of providing a college education for their children. It was hoped that the plan would thereby enable the key employees to render better service to Hamlin.

Employees eligible to participate were selected on the basis of their value to the company; selection was thus inexorably linked to the quality of the employee's performance of services. Moreover, the eventual payment of benefits by the Educo trust was directly related to petitioners' employment. This is illustrated quite graphically by the fact that only those expenses incurred by petitioners' children while the parent was employed by Hamlin were covered by the plan.

In recruiting new employees, Hamlin would describe the benefits accorded by the plan and how an employee could become entitled to participate upon attaining a level at which he was sufficiently valuable to the company. The plan was successful in aiding the recruitment and retention of key employees. Moreover, the utilization of the Educo plan at the corporate level was clearly a substitute for salary because it enabled Hamlin to compete with employers in more populated areas which paid higher salaries.

It is fundamental that anticipatory arrangements designed to deflect income away from the proper taxpayer will not be given effect to avoid tax liability. . . . In substance, by commencing or continuing to be employed by Hamlin, petitioners have allowed a portion of their earnings to be paid to their children. Petitioners have acquiesced in an arrangement designed, at least in part, to shift the incidence of tax liability to third parties unconnected in any meaningful way with their performance of services. . . .

Hamlin and petitioners were acting at arm's length in an employment situation. By accepting employment or continuing to be employed by Hamlin, cognizant of the trust payments, petitioners in effect consented to having a portion of their earnings paid to third parties. There is no evidence to indicate that petitioners were unable to bargain with Hamlin about the terms of their employment and the available avenues of compensation. Hamlin could have made available a direct salary benefit to those employees who so desired, and by supplemental enrollment schedule continued to make available the Educo plan to others. We also think significant petitioners' power, whether exercised or not, to designate which of their children would be enrolled in the Educo plan. Under the facts of this case, such power lends substantial compensatory flavor to the Educo arrangement. Petitioners were in a position to influence the manner in which their compensation would be paid. . . .

Although the legislative history is somewhat vague and the parties have chosen not to argue this case based upon interpretation of section 83, we must point out that our decision is supported by the specific language of section 83 which provides:

> (a) GENERAL RULE.—If, in connection with the performance of services, property is transferred to *any person* other than the person for whom such services are performed, [such property]
>
> shall be *included in the gross income of the person who* performed such services . . .
>
> [Emphasis added.]

Accordingly, we hold that the amounts paid by the Educo trust constituted additional compensation to petitioners and, therefore, are includable in gross income.

Decisions will be entered for the respondent.

G. NOTES AND QUESTIONS

1) Section 117

Why didn't the grants to Armantrout's children qualify for exclusion under Section 117? Did they fail to qualify under the language of Section

117(c)? If so, how can you justify concluding that Section 117 does not apply?

Suppose that each year a business provides college scholarships to five students selected on the basis of ability. Are the amounts covered by Section 117 if the scholarship program is open to the general public? Suppose that the program is open only to children of employees and the business employs 20,000 persons? If the program is open only to the children of employees and the business employs 20 persons?

2) Timing in *Armantrout*

In *Drescher*, the employee was taxable when Bausch & Lomb purchased the annuity contracts, guaranteeing future monthly payments upon his retirement. Why wasn't Armantrout taxable as soon as the special educational trust fund was created, guaranteeing future payments for his children when they attend college? Why wait to tax him until the amounts are actually paid out? Perhaps when the trust was created, there existed a "substantial risk of forfeiture" so that taxation was deferred under Section 83(a). What circumstances might have created such a risk? Why were the benefits also not "transferable" within the meaning of that statute?

Chapter 7

TRAVEL AND ENTERTAINMENT

A. RUDOLPH V. UNITED STATES
370 U.S. 269 (1962)

PER CURIAM.

The petition for certiorari in this case was granted because it was thought to present important questions involving the definition of "income" and "ordinary and necessary" business expenses under the Internal Revenue Code. . . . An insurance company provided a trip from its home office in Dallas, Texas, to New York City for a group of its agents and their wives. Rudolph and his wife were among the beneficiaries of this trip, and the Commissioner assessed its value to them as taxable income. It appears to be agreed between the parties that the tax consequences of the trip turn upon the Rudolphs' "dominant motive and purpose" in taking the trip and the company's in offering it. In this regard the District Court, on a suit for a refund, found that the trip was provided by the company for "the primary purpose of affording a pleasure trip . . . in the nature of a bonus, reward, and compensation for a job well done" and that from the point of view of the Rudolphs it "was primarily a pleasure trip in the nature of a vacation. . . ." The Court of Appeals approved these findings. . . . Such ultimate facts are subject to the "clearly erroneous" rule, cf. *Commissioner v. Duberstein*, [Chapter 10], and their review would be of no importance save to the litigants themselves. The appropriate disposition in such a situation is to dismiss the writ as improvidently granted. . . .

Separate opinion of MR. JUSTICE HARLAN.

Although the reasons given by the Court for dismissing the writ as improvidently granted should have been persuasive against granting certiorari, now that the case is here I think it better to decide it, two members of the Court having dissented on the merits.

The courts below concluded (1) that the value of this "all expense" trip to the company-sponsored insurance convention constituted "gross income" to the petitioners within the meaning of § 61 of the Internal Revenue

Code of 1954, and (2) that the amount reflected was not deductible as an "ordinary and necessary" business expense under § 162 of the Code. Both conclusions are, in my opinion, unassailable unless the findings of fact on which they rested are to be impeached by us as clearly erroneous. . . .

The basic facts, found by the District Court, are as follows. Petitioners, husband and wife, reside in Dallas, Texas, where the home office of the husband's employer, the Southland Life Insurance Company, is located. By having sold a predetermined amount of insurance, the husband qualified to attend the company's convention in New York City in 1956 and, in line with company policy, to bring his wife with him. The petitioners, together with 150 other employees and officers of the insurance company and 141 wives, traveled to and from New York City on special trains, and were housed in a single hotel during their two-and-one-half-day visit. One morning was devoted to a "business meeting" and group luncheon, the rest of the time in New York City to "travel, sight-seeing, entertainment, fellowship or free time." The entire trip lasted one week.

The company paid all the expenses of the convention-trip which amounted to $80,000; petitioners' allocable share being $560. When petitioners did not include the latter amount in their joint income tax return, the Commissioner assessed a deficiency which was sustained by the District Court, . . . and also by the Court of Appeals, one judge dissenting, in a *per curiam* opinion. . . . The District Court held that the value of the trip being "in the nature of a bonus, reward, and compensation for a job well done," was income to Rudolph, but being "primarily a pleasure trip in the nature of a vacation," the costs were personal and nondeductible.

I.

Under § 61 of the 1954 Code was the value of the trip to the taxpayer-husband properly includible in gross income? That section defines gross income as "all income from whatever source derived," including, among other items, "compensation for services." Certain sections of the 1954 Code enumerate particular receipts which are included in the concept of "gross income," including prizes and awards (with certain exceptions); while other sections, §§ 101–121, specifically exclude certain receipts from "gross income," including, for example, gifts and inheritances (see *Commissioner* v. *Duberstein* [Chapter 10]), and meals or lodgings furnished for the convenience of the employer. The Treasury Regulations emphasize the inclusiveness of the concept of "gross income."

In light of the sweeping scope of § 61 taxing "all gains except those specifically exempted," . . . and its purpose to include as taxable income "any economic or financial benefit conferred on the employee as compensation, whatever the form or mode by which it is effected," . . . it seems clear that the District Court's findings, if sustainable, bring the value of the trip within the reach of the statute.

Petitioners do not claim that the value of the trip is within one of the statutory exclusions from "gross income". . . . [R]ather they characterize the amount as a "fringe benefit" not specifically excluded from § 61 by other sections of the statute, yet not intended to be encompassed by its reach. Conceding that the statutory exclusions from "gross income" are not exhaustive, as the Government seems to recognize is so . . . , it is not now necessary to explore the extent of any such nonstatutory exclusions. For it was surely within the Commissioner's competence to consider as "gross income" a "reward, or a bonus given to . . . employees for excellence in service," which the District Court found was the employer's primary purpose in arranging this trip. I cannot say that this finding, confirmed as it has been by the Court of Appeals, is inadequately supported by this record.

There remains the question whether, though income, this outlay for transportation, meals, and lodging was deductible by petitioners as an "ordinary and necessary" business expense under § 162. . . .

Where, as here, it may be arguable that the trip was both for business and personal reasons, the crucial question is whether, under all the facts and circumstances of the case, the purpose of the trip was "related primarily to business" or was, rather, "primarily personal in nature." That other trips to other conventions or meetings by other taxpayers were held to be primarily related to business is of no relevance here; that certain doctors, lawyers, clergymen, insurance agents or others have or have not been permitted similar deductions only shows that in the circumstances of those cases, the courts thought that the expenses were or were not deductible as "related primarily to business."

The husband places great emphasis on the fact that he is an entrapped "organization man," required to attend such conventions, and that his future promotions depend on his presence. Suffice it to say that the District Court did not find any element of compulsion; to the contrary, it found that the petitioners regarded the convention in New York City as a pleasure trip in the nature of a vacation. Again, I cannot say that these findings are without adequate evidentiary support. . . .

The trip not having been primarily a business trip, the wife's expenses are not deductible. It is not necessary, therefore, to examine whether they would or would not be deductible if, to the contrary, the husband's trip was related primarily to business.

Where, as here, two courts below have resolved the determinative factual issues against the taxpayers, according to the rules of law set forth in the statute and regulations, it is not for this Court to re-examine the evidence, and disturb their findings, unless "clearly erroneous." That is not the situation here.

I would affirm.

MR. JUSTICE DOUGLAS, with whom MR. JUSTICE BLACK joins, dissenting.

I.

It could not, I think, be seriously contended that a professional man, say a Senator or a Congressman, who attends a convention to read a paper or conduct a seminar *with all expenses paid* has received "income" within the meaning of the Internal Revenue Code. Nor would it matter, I assume, that he took his wife and that her expenses were also paid. Income has the connotation of something other than the mere payment of expenses. . . .

The formula "all expenses paid" might be the disguise whereby compensation "for services" is paid. Yet it would be a rare case indeed where one could conclude that a person who gets only his expenses for attendance at one convention gets "income" in the statutory sense. If this arrangement were regular and frequent or if it had the earmarks of a sham device as a cloak for remuneration, there would be room for fact-finders to conclude that it was evasive. But isolated engagements of the kind here in question have no rational connection with compensation "for services" rendered.

It is true that petitioner was an employee and that the expenses for attending the convention were paid by his employer. He qualified to attend the convention by selling an amount of insurance that met a quota set by the company. Other salesmen also qualified, some attending and some not attending. They went from Dallas, Texas, to New York City, where they stayed two and a half days. One day was given to a business session and a luncheon; the rest of the time was left for social events.

On this record there is no room for a finding of fact that the "expenses paid" were "for services" rendered. They were apparently a proper income tax deduction for the employer. The record is replete with evidence that from management's point of view it was good business to spend money on a convention for its leading agents—a convention that not only kept the group together in New York City, but in transit as well, giving ample time for group discussions, exchanges of experience, and educational training. It was the exigencies of the employment that gave rise to the convention. There was nothing dishonest, illegitimate, or unethical about this transaction. No services were rendered. New York City may or may not have been attractive to the agents and their wives. Whether a person enjoys or dislikes the trip that he makes "with all expenses paid" has no more to do with whether the expenses paid were compensation "for services" rendered than does his attitude toward his job. . . .

II.

The expenses, if "income," are plainly deductible. . . .

The test of deductibility to be applied here is whether the expenses are "ordinary and necessary" in the carrying on of petitioner's business. . . .

The Regulations are even more explicit. Section 1.162–2(b)(1) provides:

> If a taxpayer travels to a destination and while at such destination *engages in both business and personal activities*, traveling expenses to and from such destination are deductible only if the trip is related *primarily* to the taxpayer's trade or business. If the trip is primarily personal in nature, the traveling expenses to and from the destination are not deductible even though the taxpayer engages in business activities while at such destination. (Italics added.)

Thus, by the very terms of the Regulations a taxpayer who combines business and pleasure may deduct all "traveling expenses," provided the business purpose is dominant.

Section 1.162–2(b)(2) of the Regulations states:

Whether a trip is related primarily to the taxpayer's trade or business or is primarily personal in nature depends on the facts and circumstances in each case. The amount of time during the period of the trip which is spent on personal activity compared to the amount of time spent on activities directly relating to the taxpayer's trade or business is an important factor in determining whether the trip is primarily personal. If, for example, a taxpayer spends one week while at a destination on activities which are directly related to his trade or business and subsequently spends an additional five weeks for vacation or other personal activities, the trip will be considered primarily personal in nature in the absence of a clear showing to the contrary.

Where, as here, at least one-half of the time is spent on mundane "business" activities,[1] the case is nowhere near the colorable transaction described in § 1.162–2(b)(2).

I see no reason to take this case out of the main stream of precedents and establish a special rule for insurance conventions. Judge Brown, dissenting in the Court of Appeals, shows how discriminatory this decision is:

Deductions have been allowed as 'ordinary and necessary' to clergymen attending a church convention; to expenses of an employee attending conventions of a related business group; to a lawyer attending a meeting of the American Bar Association; to a legal secretary attending the national convention of the National Association; to physicians attending medical conventions; to certified public accountants attending conventions; to university teachers in attending conventions or scientific meetings; to professional cartoonists attending political conventions; to persons attending the Red Cross Convention; to school teachers attending summer school; to attorneys attending an institute on Federal taxation; to employees sent to refresher courses to become more acquainted with new processes in the industry; to a furniture store sending its buyers to the annual furniture mart; to representatives to annual conventions of trade associations; and to an insurance agent away from home on business. . . .

Insurance conventions go back at least to 1924 (Report No. 15, Life Insurance Sales Research Bureau, Nov. 1924) and are premised on the idea that agents and companies benefit from the knowledge and increase in morale which result from them. Why they should be treated differently from other conventions is a mystery. It cannot be, as the district judge thought and as the Government seems to argue, because going to New York City is, as a matter of law, a "pleasure trip." If we are in the field of judicial notice, I would think that some might conclude that the weekend in New York City was a chore and that those who went sacrificed valuable time that might better have been spent on the farm, in the woods, or along the seashore.

Moreover, federal revenue agents attending their convention are given a deduction for the expenses they incur. We are advised that

---

1. The travel to and from the convention was in a group, so arranged as to develop solidarity among the agents, and to provide a continuing seminar.

> ... the Commissioner has recently withdrawn his objections in two Tax Court cases to the deduction of convention expenses incurred by two IRS employees in attending conventions of the National Association of Internal Revenue Employees.
>
> No explanation has been given publicly for the Tax Court action of the Commissioner, it being generally presumed that the IRS employees met the tests of Reg. § 1.162–2(d) by showing a sufficient relationship between the trade or business of being an IRS employee and attendance at conventions of the NAIRE. The National Association of Internal Revenue Employees has hailed the Commissioner's actions as setting a precedent which can be cited by IRS employees when taking deductions for expenses incurred in attending NAIRE conventions. . . .

It is odd, indeed, that revenue agents need make no accounting of the movies they saw or the nightclubs they attended, in order to get the deduction, while insurance agents must.

III.

The wife's expenses are, on this record, also deductible. The Treasury Regulations state in § 1.162–2(c):

> Where a taxpayer's wife accompanies him on a business trip, expenses attributable to her travel are not deductible unless it can be adequately shown that the wife's presence on the trip has a bona fide business purpose. The wife's performance of some incidental service does not cause her expenses to qualify as deductible business expenses. The same rules apply to any other members of the taxpayer's family who accompany him on such a trip.

The civil law philosophy, expressed in the community property concept, attributes half of the husband's earnings to the wife—an equitable idea that at long last was reflected in the idea of income splitting under the federal income tax law. The wife's contribution to the business productivity of the husband in at least some activities is well known. It was specially recognized in the insurance field long before the issue of deductibility of her expenses arose under the federal income tax. Business reasons motivated the inclusion of wives in this particular insurance convention. An insurance executive testified at this trial:

> Q. I hand you Plaintiff's Exhibit 15, and you will notice it is a letter addressed to 'John Doe'; also a bulletin entitled 'A New Partner Has Been Formed.' Will you tell us what that consists of?
>
> A. This is a letter addressed to the wife of an agent, a new agent, as we make the contract with him. This letter is sent to his wife within a few days after the contract, enclosing this booklet explaining to her how she can help her husband in the life insurance business. . . .
>
> Q. Please tell us, as briefly as you can and yet in detail, how you as agency director for Southland attempt to integrate the wives' performance with the performance of agents in the life insurance business.
>
> A. One of the important functions we have in mind is the attendance at these conventions. In addition to that communication, occasionally there

are letters that will be written to the wife concerning any special sales effort that might be desired or promoted. The company has a monthly publication for the agents and employees that is mailed to their homes so the wife will have a convenient opportunity to see the magazine and read it.

At most of our convention program[s], we have some specific reference to the wife's work, and in quite a few of the convention programs we have had wives appear on the program.

Q. Suppose you didn't have the wives and didn't seek to require their attendance at a convention, would there be some danger that your meetings and conventions would kind of degenerate into stag affairs, where the whole purpose of the meeting would be lost?

A. I think that would definitely be a tendency.

I would reverse the judgments below and leave insurance conventions in the same category as conventions of revenue agents, lawyers, doctors, business men, accountants, nurses, clergymen and all others, until and unless Congress decides otherwise.

B. NOTES AND QUESTIONS

1) The Theoretically Correct Treatment of a Combined Business and Pleasure Trip

If Rudolph's trip were purely for business or purely for personal consumption, his tax treatment would present no real difficulty, in theory or in practice. But when travel combines both business and pleasure—as it often does—difficulties may arise.

In theory, how should Rudolph be taxed on a business trip that also provides some personal consumption benefit? Even if the trip serves important business goals, should the entire cost be deductible if he also obtains some personal consumption pleasure? For example, suppose that the trip costs $1,000 and that Rudolph, had he been free to choose, would have willingly spent $600 to go. Should he be permitted to deduct only $400, the excess of the $1,000 cost over the $600 that he would have paid? As an administrative matter, would it be practical to tax employees on the personal consumption benefit derived from business travel? How can the trip be distinguished from working conditions, such as a pleasant office decorated with modern art, that also provide personal consumption pleasure to the employee and that presumably we are unwilling to tax?

2) The Primary Purpose Test

Reg. § 1.162–2(b)(2), cited in *Rudolph,* provides that the deductibility of a combined business-pleasure trip depends on a subjective standard: whether the taxpayer's primary purpose was business or personal. Absent the invention of a mental X-ray or the establishment of thought police, how can primary purpose be ascertained? And in Rudolph's case, *whose* purpose is relevant, the employee's or the employer's?

The regulation states that the primary purpose can be inferred from the "facts and circumstances" of the case, such as the "amount of time . . .

spent on personal activity compared to the amount of time spent on . . . business." How reliable are such facts and circumstances as an indicator of primary purpose? To what extent are they subject to manipulation by the taxpayer or the employer? What might Rudolph's employer have done to assure the trip's deductibility under the primary purpose rule?

3) Foreign Travel

Section 274(c), enacted in 1962, imposes an additional limitation on the deduction of travel outside the United States, even when the primary purpose is business. If (a) the trip exceeds one week *and* (b) the nonbusiness portion is 25% or more of the total travel time, then the deduction is disallowed for a portion of the travel expenses of reaching the foreign destination. The proportion disallowed is the same as the proportion of the trip spent on nonbusiness activities.

Consider, for example, the case of a taxpayer who travels to London for eight days, conducting business for five days and vacationing for the remaining period of time. The travel outside the United States exceeds one week, and time devoted to nonbusiness activities is 25% or more of the total travel time. Consequently, three-eighths of the expenses for transportation to and from London will be disallowed. See Reg. § 1.274–4(g), example 7.

What does Section 274(c) assume about the personal consumption value of traveling abroad for more than one week on business? Is there a good reason not to apply these rules to travel abroad that lasts no more than a week? To travel abroad lasting more than a week where the nonbusiness portion is less than 25%? Even if these distinctions make sense, why is domestic travel altogether excluded? If you travel to San Diego and spend five days on business and three days vacationing, why should the *entire* transportation cost be deductible when the same schedule in London results in deduction of only five-eighths?

4) Foreign Conventions

In 1976, the Senate Finance Committee noted a "proliferation of conventions, educational seminars, and cruises . . . ostensibly held for business or educational purposes, but which . . . are held at locations outside the United States primarily because of the recreational and sightseeing opportunities."[2] For example, a state bar association would schedule a continuing legal education course in estate planning on a mediterranean cruise ship, or pediatricians would meet in Paris to discuss the treatment of ear infections. Why do you suppose Section 274(c), discussed above, did not disallow at least a portion of the costs of such meetings?

In reaction to the perceived abuse, Congress enacted Section 274(h)(1) to limit deductions for attending "a convention, seminar, or similar meeting . . . outside the North American area." No deduction is allowed unless "it

---

2. S. Rep. No. 938, 94th Cong., 2d Sess. 156.

is as reasonable for the meeting to be held outside the North American area as within the North American area."

Conventions on cruise ships are subject to even stricter requirements of Section 274(h)(2). In general, no deduction is allowed. However, special dispensation is granted if the cruise ship is registered in the United States and all ports of call are located in the United States or U.S. possessions. In that event, an individual may deduct up to $2,000 for cruise ship conventions in any calendar year, provided that the meeting is "directly related" to business. Why do you suppose Congress allowed this limited exception for American flag ships, rather than simply denying all such deductions?

5) Luxury Travel

Suppose an employer pays for employees to fly first class on business trips. Should the excess cost of first class over economy air travel be taxable income to an employee, without any offsetting deduction, even when a legitimate business trip is involved? Some businesses own and operate their own aircraft, that are often more convenient and comfortable than commercial airliners. Suppose that the cost of a trip on a business-owned aircraft exceeds the cost of the same trip on a commercial airline. Should the excess cost produce taxable income to the employee traveling on business?

Section 274(m)(1), enacted in 1986, limits deductions for "luxury water transportation." The allowable deduction is set equal to twice the highest per diem travel allowance for federal government employees. But Congress has not limited deductions for luxurious air travel so that executives, and members of Congress, can still fly first class (or even the supersonic Concorde) on business trips without concern.

C. SCHULZ v. COMMISSIONER
16 T.C. 401 (1951), acq. 1951–2 C.B. 4

FINDINGS OF FACT.

... Petitioner is engaged in the business of manufacturing and importing fine watches and jewelry. ...

The petitioner sells only to stores and wholesale houses. He keeps merchandise on hand for sale to his customers and also fills special orders placed by them. The wholesale price of his watches ranges from $100 to $10,000 and averages about $200 each. The average order during 1945 was between $2,000 and $4,000. His firm is patronized by stores handling expensive jewelry. The buyers for these stores frequently come to New York and often bring their wives and families with them. It is customary in the petitioner's business to entertain such buyers in order to gain and hold their patronage.

During the year 1945, petitioner could not produce enough merchandise to fill his customers' orders, and such unfilled orders amounted to several hundred thousand dollars in 1945. Buyers came from all over the country and from as far away as the Philippines and Honolulu begging for merchandise and offered "bonuses" to the petitioner if he would sell to them. Because of this shortage of supply, the buyers came to New York City more frequently than usual. During 1945 petitioner entertained customers to maintain or promote good will, not to "drum up" business.

In earlier years the petitioner had employed salesmen, paying them a salary and commission, but during 1945 he could not make enough merchandise to fill the orders his customers had placed with him and employed no salesmen.

The petitioner claimed a deduction for entertainment expense in the amount of $9,304.40 on his 1945 income tax return. That amount was arrived at by the petitioner through the use of three types of records, hereinafter referred to as chits, petty cash vouchers and checks. The chits represented $6,150.08 of the total $9,304.40 and were made up as follows: The petitioner's wife, who worked in his office as bookkeeper and office manager, would draw checks payable to cash and place the proceeds thereof in a safe in the office. Such checks totaled $6,350.08 for the year 1945. When a check for this cash fund was drawn, a charge therefore was made at the end of the month to the entertainment account in the general ledger. The petitioner would advise his wife that he had expended a certain sum for entertainment, and she would then make out a chit, setting forth the amount given to her by the petitioner and a brief description of the purpose of the expenditure. The information given to her by the petitioner was also recorded by him in a book which he carried. Sometimes he would tell her what he had spent on the day he spent it, but sometimes as much as a week would elapse before he would inform her of the expenditure. When his wife had made out the chit, she would give the petitioner cash from the aforementioned fund in the amount reported as spent. When the fund began to get low, she would replenish it by cashing another check. The checks were drawn in varied amounts.

In all of the chits for the year 1945 there was included the cost of the petitioner's own entertainment and food, and in the chits relating to the evening entertainment there was also included the cost of his wife's entertainment and food. The petitioner had known many of the people referred to on the chits for a long time. Some of those people also entertained the petitioner.

Of the total expenditures recorded on the chits, approximately $3,400 was spent for suppers, theaters and nightclubs. The balance was spent mainly on luncheons. The following table shows the information contained on the chits for the months of January, June, September and October, 1945. Each date represents an individual chit and the numbers following the written notation show the number of people entertained. Chits set forth in this table are typical of those for the other months of 1945.

Date	January	Amount
1945		
1–5	For luncheon, Myron Everts—3	$ 12.45
1–6	For Brotherhood luncheon—Keller, Schaeffer, Kelly	24.25
1–6	For cocktails & supper, Brecht plus 4	37.00
1–8	Pay to luncheon, for Hausmann (New Orleans)	8.50
1–9	Pay to JS, for luncheon, Al Schulz—3	16.40
1–9	Pay to Woods, for luncheon, Elebash—4	22.50
1–9	For theater, Fri. Jan. 12, Red Mill	75.20

Ch. 7 Travel and Entertainment

Date	January	Amount
1945		
1–10	For luncheon, Hy Schliessman—2	8.75
1–12	Pay to tips—Wivels	28.00
1–12	For 16 at Wivel's after theater	135.00
1–12	Pay to tips N.Y.A.C., Julius	20.00
1–12	Pay to Waldorf, for luncheon—Leon Binard	12.50
1–12	For tips—Waters	15.00
1–12	For theater, Sat. matinee–4	11.00
1–12	For Garden tickets, Sonja Henie	14.40
1–13	Pay to Sat. luncheon, for Simard, McCayne, Vogt, ELS	18.85
1–13	Pay to Sat. supper, Simard, Lyons, ELS	32.25
1–13	Pay to tips, Waldorf, for banquet dept., hat check, etc., Hans & waiters	95.00
1–14	For M. J. Lyons, Barclay reservation	66.20
1–17	Pay to supper & theater, for Vogt—4	56.00
1–22	For luncheon, Grauat	22.50
1–22	For supper & theater Laykin—4	43.75
1–25	Pay to luncheon, for Helzberg	18.00
1–26	For supper & evening, Reingold & Maurice	93.50

June

6–1	For Memorial Day & weekend, Detroit	$316.00
6–4	For cocktails, Commodore	14.00
6–7	For theater & Wivels—7	155.00
6–7	For overnight, N.Y.	34.00
6–11	For luncheon	31.00
6–15	For theater & "21" club	180.50
6–20	For luncheon, Oberman	7.50
6–21	For luncheon, Lichtey	12.00

September

9–5	For cocktails & supper, Higginbotham	47.00
9–9	For Labor Day weekend	225.00
9–14	For luncheon, Hansen	13.00
9–17	For Helzberg, cocktails	15.00
9–18	For luncheon, Chris Brodersen	7.00
9–20	For lunch, Bud Tobias	17.00
9–21	For supper, Clawson	18.00
9–24	For supper—Habe, Chicago	42.00

October

10–1	For luncheon—M. Caplan	11.00
10–5	For luncheon—Pongrace	9.00
10–6	For supper & theater—4	63.00
10–8	For theater & supper, Lichtenstein	129.00
10–15	For luncheon—Kleska & Gutowitz	35.00
10–18	For supper—Stegmeier	84.00
10–31	For luncheon—M. Wethered	18.00

Two chits, one for $34 and the other for $25, represented the cost to the petitioner of a hotel room, meals, and tips when, after a night of entertaining customers, he missed his train home and remained overnight in New York.

The second type of records kept by the petitioner was petty cash vouchers, which represented $1,870.97 of the total $9,304.40 claimed as entertainment expenses. Such vouchers were small memoranda similar to the chits.

The expenditures by petitioner's wife and employees for the entertainment of customers were recorded on these vouchers. Thereafter, they were listed in a "Petty Cash" disbursements journal where they were consolidated by months and recorded in the entertainment expense account in the general ledger. The cash so expended was drawn from the petty cash fund, a fund separate from the previously mentioned revolving fund from which petitioner was reimbursed.

The third type of record of entertainment expense kept by the petitioner was cancelled checks. Such checks were made payable to the persons who provided the entertainment, and the amount thereof, which totaled $1,083.35 for 1945, was charged to the entertainment account. Included in these checks were checks payable to the New York Athletic Club, checks for bon voyage baskets that petitioner sent to customers leaving on a steamer, and checks representing the cost of tickets and entertainment at jewelers' conventions. Among these cancelled checks was one for $25.40 in payment of repairs on the petitioner's automobile.

Gross profits of the petitioner's business for the years 1943, 1944, and 1945 were $67,523.68, $120,007.56, and $204,483.37, respectively. Petitioner claimed entertainment and traveling expenses in 1943 in the amount of $4,490.24, and entertainment expenses in 1944 in the amount of $8,256.64.

The petitioner's advertising account was charged with the amount of $400 representing money expended by the petitioner for entering a horse named "Schulztime" which he owned in horse shows, for horse show programs, and for trophies for certain classes of shows. This expenditure was not an ordinary and necessary business advertising expense.

Petitioner's ordinary and necessary business expense for entertainment in the taxable year 1945 totaled $5,500.

OPINION.

ARUNDELL, JUDGE: The respondent has disallowed as a deduction from the petitioner's 1945 taxable income the sum of $9,304.40 claimed as entertainment expense, and a $400 item claimed as advertising expense. There is no serious dispute as to whether either of these sums was spent; the issue is whether they are deductible.

Entertainment expenses are allowed as a deduction from gross income only to the extent that they are "ordinary and necessary" in carrying on a trade or business. Section [162(a)(1)] of the Internal Revenue Code. The requirements that the expense must be both ordinary and necessary must be strictly complied with, . . . and whether contested expenditures are ordinary and necessary is primarily a question of fact. . . . Proof is required that the purpose of the expenditure was primarily business rather than social or personal, and that the business in which taxpayer is engaged benefited or was intended to be benefited thereby. . . .

During 1945 petitioner elaborately entertained buyers and others connected with the jewelry business, personally spending about $7,000. In addition thereto approximately $2,000 was expended by his wife and employees on luncheons, drinks, weekend visits, conventions, suppers, theaters, and nightclubs. Approximately $3,400 of the $7,000 expended by petitioner personally was spent on suppers, theaters and nightclubs and other forms of evening entertainment. On these occasions petitioner would bring his wife and the party or parties he was entertaining would also bring their wives. There is little to distinguish these occasions from the usual social gatherings among friends to renew acquaintanceship and enjoy a pleasant evening. They bear little semblance to the usual gatherings of business people at restaurants or other places of entertainment which serve primarily as congenial meeting places for the discussion or negotiation of business matters. Petitioner made no attempt to show that the evening entertainment he offered his guests served this purpose or that all of it was directly related to the operations of his business.

These gatherings may have been desirable and helpful to the present and future success of petitioner's business, but this is usually true of all entertaining done by business or professional people for the purpose of acquiring or retaining the favor of patrons and clients. Such expenditures are nonetheless nondeductible absent a showing that they were ordinary and necessary to the taxpayer's business within the meaning of section [162(a)(1)] of the Internal Revenue Code. In *Louis Boehm*, . . . we stated:

> We do not think the burden of proof is met by the petitioner's argument that in general, membership in social, political, and fraternal organizations is helpful in obtaining clients through contacts made thereby or the citing of one instance of gaining a client through acquaintance made at a political club. No evidence has been introduced to show that any part or all of the expenditures in question were so closely related to the conduct of the petitioner's business as to have been appropriate, helpful, usual, or necessary. It is noted that in cases where expenditures of a social nature have been held to be deductible business expenses proof was presented to show that such expenditures had a direct relation to the conduct of a business or the business benefits expected. Such proof has not been presented here to show that the expenditures are deductible. . . .

After taking into consideration the nature of the entertainment provided by the petitioner and the fact that it was undertaken at a time when he had more business than he could handle, we are not convinced that all of the expenditures in issue were made for purely business reasons or that the entire cost of such entertainment may be characterized as ordinary and necessary expense incident to the carrying on of the petitioner's business. An expense is deductible only if it complies with the strict requirements of section [162(a)(1)] and does not constitute a personal expense expressly disallowed by section [262].

Moreover, the petitioner's attempt to deduct such nondeductible items as the cost of repairing an automobile, the cost of hotel rooms, tips, and meals on two occasions when, after a night of entertaining customers, he remained in New York after missing the train home, and the inclusion of $200 which had been placed in the petty cash fund but was not expended on entertainment, all create doubt as to the accuracy of the total deduction.

On the other hand, we are convinced that some part of the expenditures was prompted by strictly business considerations and should be characterized as ordinary and necessary expenses. Applying the rule of *Cohan v. Commissioner*, . . . , we have reached an approximation after a careful consideration of the testimony of petitioner and his wife and a close examination of the memoranda and other exhibits received in evidence. From all this evidence, we have concluded that $5,500 fairly represents the amount spent by the petitioner for ordinary and necessary business entertainment in 1945 and that amount is properly deductible under section [162(a)(1)] of the Internal Revenue Code.

The petitioner has included in his advertising expense the sum of $400 spent in entering his horse named "Schulztime" in a horse show and for such items as horse show programs and trophies. Petitioner has not satisfactorily shown how these expenditures were calculated to advertise or publicize his business. There is no evidence that the petitioner called the attention of those persons attending the horse shows to the fact that he was a dealer in watches by advertising in the horse show program. . . . There is an inference in the record that the name "Schulztime" was relied on by petitioner to publicize his business but if this be true the name chosen was so subtle and the entry of a horse in a show so far removed from the petitioner's business that it could not reasonably have been expected to publicize the business. In our opinion, the $400 so expended was not an ordinary and necessary business expense. . . .

D. NOTES AND QUESTIONS

1) The Primary Purpose Test in *Schulz*

The Tax Court in *Schulz* stated that the claimed expenses were deductible if "the purpose of the expenditure was primarily business rather than social or personal." Again, absent a mental X-ray or thought police, how can the primary purpose be ascertained? How did the court in *Schulz* decide to allow about half of the deductions? Does it appear that the court tried to determine the taxpayer's subjective intent or state of mind when each expenditure was made?

2) The 1962 Reforms

Sections 274(a), (d), and (e) were enacted in 1962 to curb abuse of entertainment expense deductions. Section 274(d) imposes special record-keeping requirements. Taxpayers must keep records substantiating the amount, time, place, and business relationship to the persons entertained. What business, do you suppose, has been the principle beneficiary of Section 274(d)?

Under Section 274(a)(1)(A), a deduction is allowed only if entertainment is either (a) "directly related to" business *or* (b) preceded or followed by "a substantial and bona fide business discussion" and is "associated with . . . business." Reg. § 1.274–2(c)(4) provides, as an example of "directly related to business," the "entertainment of business representatives and civic leaders at the opening of a new hotel . . . where the clear purpose . . . is to obtain business publicity." Thus, if Schulz entertained a customer at the Superbowl or the World Series, the expense would not be "directly related to" business and presumably could be deducted only if actually preceded or followed by business discussions.

Until 1987, however, business *meals* (as contrasted with other forms of entertainment) were generally exempted from the Section 274(a)(1)(A) requirement that the activity be directly related to business or accompanied by a business discussion. Thus, if Schulz took a customer out to dinner and no business discussion occurred before, during, or after the meal, the cost would still be deductible provided that the meal was "of a type generally considered to be conducive to a business discussion."[3] An IRS publication used questions and answers to explain the difference in the requirements for entertainment on the one hand and meals on the other:

> Question: What must a taxpayer be able to show in order to deduct an entertainment expense under these new rules?
> Answer: He must show that the amount of the expense for which he is claiming a deduction was:
> (1) "directly related" to the active conduct of his business . . . or
> (2) "associated with" the active conduct of his business and that the entertainment occurred directly before or after a substantial and bona fide business discussion. . . .
> Question: If, for business reasons, I take a customer to breakfast, lunch, or dinner at a restaurant or hotel, or to a bar for a few drinks, but we do not discuss business, can I deduct the cost of the entertainment under the new rules?
> Answer: Yes, the statute provides that if the circumstances are of a type generally considered to be conducive to business discussion, an expense for meals or beverages will be deductible to the extent the expenses were ordinary and necessary business expenses as under prior law.[4]

E. KINSLEY, THE MYSTERY OF THE FREE LUNCH
The New Republic (May 23, 1981)

. . . [T]here are two kinds of money—Before Tax (BT) and After Tax (AT)—and that BT money buys a lot more goodies than AT money. Anyone who denies the reality of this distinction . . . hasn't experienced the joys of tax-free consumption. . . .

A few weeks ago I had lunch with the editor of a rival publication I sometimes write for. It was a nice restaurant, a treat for both of us. He suggested we split the check. Instead, I paid the whole thing and will deduct it as a business expense ("lunch with customer, $25"). This will reduce my taxes by about the cost of his lunch. If (unlikely, but let's suppose) he picks up the check next time ("lunch with supplier, $25"), we will have lunched twice for the same cost as if we'd lunched once and split the check. Who

---
3. This exception—formerly contained in Section 274(e)(1)—was repealed by the 1986 Tax Reform Act.
4. Rev. Rul. 63-144, 1963-2 C.B. 129, 130-132.

is paying for that second lunch? I wouldn't presume to say. It must have something to do with supply-side economics. . . .

Most industries in what might be called the luxury sector of the economy are deeply dependent on untaxed money. Of the consumer items associated with high living, only wearables—clothes, furs, and jewels—are really rarely paid for with BT money. (Though even here, the *Wall Street Journal* has reported an arrangement whereby corporations lease business suits for their executives.) Relatively little luxury housing gets written off as a business expense. . . .

At the opposite extreme are luxury restaurants, almost all of which would fold if they had to rely on AT customers. In a city like Washington, 80 to 90 percent of the lunch crowd and perhaps half the dinner crowd at top restaurants is eating on "business." This is an unscientific estimate, but experienced Washington trencherpersons don't challenge it.

The travel industry—airlines, hotels, resorts—is only somewhat less dependent than restaurants on tax-deductible customers. As with restaurants, the fancier the circumstances, the more likely the money is BT. According to the Air Transport Association, 55 percent of commercial air travel was for business purposes in 1979, up from 46 percent in 1973. Some of this represents traveling salesmen or computer engineers off to training sessions in Topeka, but much of it is doctors and lawyers heading for conventions in Hawaii and corporate executives attending conferences at the Greenbriar. The airlines won't say whether business is more heavily represented in first class or coach, but the question answers itself. The hotel industry has been developing its own equivalent of "first class" in recent years—a special section of rooms with extra services like little chocolate bars on the pillow at night. The newly opened Marriott in downtown Washington charges $30 extra a night (about $125 for a double room) for its "Concierge Level." According to the *Wall Street Journal,* "Hotels say the bulk of luxury customers are on expense accounts." Surprise, surprise. . . .

. . . There is a conceptual trap awaiting inequality buffs here. If such luxury is considered compensation for services rendered, to specific businesses and to general prosperity, then the money that pays for it should be subject to tax like all other compensation. We can argue about the proper tax *rate,* as of course we are doing these days, but even the Laffer Curve recognizes that a tax rate of zero is not fiscally sound. . . .

. . . [L]et us consider the problem from a strictly supply-side point of view. From this perspective, favored tax treatment for "business" luxury has three defects.

First, it encourages consumption over productive investment, at a time when the nation requires the opposite priority. Should Pickaname Corporation spend $100,000 on modernizing its rusty plant, or on a lavish weekend at the Superbowl for Mr. Pickaname and some "clients"? Ordinarily the government doesn't try to second-guess businesses about how they spend their money, figuring that they know best how to maximize their profits, and therefore the government's tax take. But Mr. Pickaname is not likely to make a cool and rational business decision here if one option will let him stage a grand exercise in hospitality at about half of what it would otherwise cost him. If Mr. Pickaname has passed from the scene, and his firm is now run by professional executives, their preference for the Superbowl weekend is likely to be even more pronounced, since it won't cost them anything at all. Furthermore, even when "investing" in lavish entertainment is a sound decision for an individual business, it rarely brings any return for the economy as a whole. At best, competitive orgies of consumption merely redirect demand; they do not create new supply.

Second, tax-free "business" consumption is inflationary. A customer who is paying only about half the cost (if he deducts it), or none of it at all (if she's on expense-account) is not going to be as sensitive to prices as people who have to pay with their own after-tax money. By any standard, the value-for-money ratio at establishments that cater primarily to business customers is lower than at places where most people pay their own way. The cost of a fancy meal or top hotel room has outpaced most consumer prices in recent years, whereas restaurant meals in general, for example, have lagged behind.

Third, business consumption deductions reduce tax revenues—about three billion dollars a year for meals alone. This money could be used to cut marginal tax rates or to reduce the federal deficit, the two key conservative economic nostrums. Of course the money could also be used in other ways. The Congressional Black Caucus has proposed making restaurant meals only half-deductible, and using the money to restore Reagan's cuts in spending for child nutrition. But I suppose that suggestion smacks of envy.

Periodic crackdown attempts over two decades have added verses of sonorously forbidding language to the statute and regulation books. In practice, though, almost any sort of self-indulgence remains deductible. For example, the regulations state quite sternly that for a social occasion to be deductible, the "active conduct of business" must be the "principal aspect" of the occasion. The atmosphere must be "conducive to a business discussion." But read on. "Principal aspect," it develops, does not mean more than half of the time. And social occasions of any sort are deductible if they are "preceding or following a substantial business discussion." So are meals while traveling on business, and almost anything to do with a convention, and on and on.

And how about this passage from the IRS regulations for taking away with one hand and giving back with the other?

> 41. Question: Are there limitations on deductions for entertainment expenditures which are lavish or extravagant?
>
> Answer: Yes. To the extent that the expenditure is lavish or extravagant it is not allowable as a deduction.
>
> 42. Question: Will entertainment expenses be subject to disallowance on grounds of being lavish or extravagant merely because they exceed a fixed dollar amount or are incurred at deluxe restaurants, hotels, night clubs and resort establishments?
>
> Answer: No. An expense for entertainment will not be considered lavish or extravagant merely because it includes first class accommodations or services. An expense which, considering the facts and circumstances, is reasonable will not be considered lavish or extravagant.

The most complex rules surround the recondite question of deducting club dues. Business use of the club must be computed two different ways, one to determine whether the dues are deductible at all, and the other to determine how much. This can be a nuisance, but it isn't much of a limitation. Unofficial tax guides contain pages of hints like this:

> Make a point of having a quiet business lunch on the same day as you play golf. That makes it a directly related day. ANOTHER POINT: a few drinks . . . at the bar can also transform a casual golf date into a full-fledged business day.

The rules for writing off yachts and hunting lodges used to be the same as for club dues. But the only crackdown that survived from President Carter's "three martini lunch" campaign (besides a restriction on foreign conventions that was mainly for the benefit of the US tourist industry) was a new rule disallowing all deductions for fun-and-games "facilities." Even here, however, there is an exception for "out-of-pocket costs" of entertaining at such facilities. In the case of hunting lodges, this includes the guides, the dogs, the guns, the bullets, the food, the booze, . . . the private planes to get there—in short, almost everything except the roof.

Even under present rules, with their loopholes and self-immolating limitations, the IRS estimates that 20 percent of all entertainment and travel deductions people take are illegitimate. The problem is not that the rules are too lax or that they're not enforced, but that such rules are conceptually unenforceable. How long must angels talk business before they can deduct the cost of going out dancing on the head of a pin? Faced with meaningless concepts like "principal aspect," impossible demands for precision in apportioning life's moments between business and pleasure, and restrictions on what counts as "business" that only a clairvoyant could supervise, taxpayers naturally treat themselves generously. The IRS, boxed in by the statute and by limited enforcement resources, is powerless to prevent billions of dollars a year of the most superfluous consumption from being subsidized by the taxpayers. (Sorry Mr. Kristol, that just popped out.)

Money spent on meals, parties, sports tickets, vacations, and lavish living in general should not escape taxation. Permitting so much of it to do so is both bad for the economy and, just by the way, terribly unfair. A few very simple and easily enforceable rules would solve the problem. Expenditures for food and entertainment should not be deductible unless they are also reported as taxable income to the recipients. Deductions for business travel should be limited to some modest but not spartan standard, such as coach air fare plus the daily allowance the government sets for its own employees. One or two conventions a year should be all that is considered necessary for fraternal comity within the professions.

There are three standard objections to proposals like these. One is that jobs in the luxury industries would be sacrificed. The answer is that subsidizing extravagant consumption by the already prosperous is a silly and costly way to create jobs for the deprived. A second objection is that some truly legitimate and necessary business spending would be caught unfairly in the tax maw. The answer is, not much, not nearly so much as the properly

Ch. 7 **Travel and Entertainment** 95

taxable consumption that now escapes, and not the kind that really contributes to national prosperity. A third objection is that defining consumption is an impossible task, and cracking down on only certain kinds is unfair. Should executives be taxed on offices beyond a certain size, or carpet above a certain thickness? Should doctors have to declare the value of their satisfaction at saving lives or their status in the community? The simplest answer to this is that the people who enjoy these inchoate forms of business income are the same ones who have been deducting the more material gratifications of their caste. Starting to tax just one category of income of this sort makes the tax code more fair, not less fair.

If people still wished to live high on the hog, they would be free to do so. Relieved of the need to pretend that they're not enjoying it, they could instead reflect that this was their just reward for their contribution to society, as accurately measured by a free market economic system. Whether this reflection would have any basis in fact is a question for another day.

F. WASSERMAN, DRAWING BOARD
Los Angeles Times Syndicate, (September 12, 1981)

THE PRESIDENT CUT MY SCHOOL LUNCH

BUT HE DID IT FOR MY OWN GOOD

HE WANTS ME TO KNOW THAT BEING POOR IS NO FUN

THAT YOU CAN'T GET SOMETHING FOR NOTHING

AND THAT YOU HAVE TO WORK VERY HARD...

BEFORE YOU CAN DEDUCT LUNCH FROM YOUR TAXES

G. THE 1986 TAX REFORM ACT

1) Must Business be Discussed for the Meal Cost to be Deducted?

Until recently, Section 274(e)(1) allowed a deduction for business meals (not otherwise "directly related to" business) even if no business was discussed before, during, or after the meal. The 1986 Tax Reform Act repealed this provision. Such meals are now subject to the Section 274(a)(1)(A) requirement that business be discussed. Do you believe this change is meaningful and will help curb abuse of the deduction?

2) The 20% Disallowance Rule

In response to complaints about abuse of the deduction for entertainment and meal expenses, Congress also voted in 1986 to limit deductions to 80% of the actual cost. Section 274(n). Thus, if an employer pays directly or reimburses an employee for a $100 business lunch, the employer may deduct only $80. Or if an employee pays for a $100 business lunch and is not reimbursed, the employee may deduct only $80.

The employee who pays for the lunch out of his or her own pocket, without reimbursement, is also subject to Section 67, discussed in Chapter 4, which permits certain designated expenses to be deducted only to the extent they exceed 2% of the taxpayer's Adjusted Gross Income. The Section 67 limit is applied separately from and only after Section 274(n)'s disallowance of 20% of the cost.

The Conference Committee Report states that Section 274(n) is to apply not only to meals where an employee entertains a client or customer but also to "meals away from home and meals furnished on an employer's premises to its employees (whether or not such meals are excludible from the employee's gross income under Section 119)."[5] Congress, however, made no explicit reference to Section 274(n) in either Section 162(a)(2) (allowing a deduction for "meals away from home") or Section 119 (excluding employee meals provided for the employer's convenience). In the absence of an explicit reference in the Code itself, is the Conference Committee's expansive reading of Section 274(n) justified?

3) Should the 20% Rule Apply to the Employer or to the Employee?

Section 274(n) presumably reflects the idea that business meals and entertainment necessarily provide some personal consumption benefits and therefore constitute disguised compensation. See the notes and questions following *Rudolph*. In that event, the 20% disallowance figure might be viewed as a rough guess as to how to measure the personal consumption benefits of business entertainment and meals to the employee.

However, if taxing the *employee* on the personal consumption benefits is the objective, wouldn't it make more sense to allow the employer the full

---

5. 2 Conf. R. No. 841 (to Accompany H.R. 3838), 99th Cong., 2d Sess. II-25 (1986).

deduction but then to require the employee to include 20% of the cost as income? After all, even if the cost of entertainment is intended as disguised compensation for the employee, it is still a business expense and therefore deductible in full. The remedy should be to tax the employee on what is really salary (rather than a working condition)—not to deny part of the employer's deduction.

If employer and employee are in the same tax bracket, it may not matter whether we disallow 20% of the deduction to the employer or allow 100% of the deduction but tax the employee on 20%. To illustrate, suppose that both employer and employee are taxed at a rate of 34%. On a $100 business lunch, the first approach denies the employer a $20 deduction, increasing the employer's taxes by $6.80 ($20 times 34%). The second approach results instead in the employee having to report an extra $20 of income and having to pay $6.80 additional in taxes. From the Treasury's perspective, the same amount of revenue is gained.[6]

The figures used in this example are probably an accurate reflection of the tax brackets of large numbers of employers and employees. Most employers are corporations which are taxed at 34% on income above $100,000. See section 11. The marginal rate applicable to many employees will be 33%.[7]

H. MOSS v. COMMISSIONER
758 F.2d 211 (7th Cir. 1985)

POSNER, CIRCUIT JUDGE.

The taxpayers, a lawyer named Moss and his wife, appeal from a decision of the Tax Court disallowing federal income tax deductions of a little more than $1,000 in each of two years, representing Moss's share of his law firm's lunch expense at the Cafe Angelo in Chicago.... The Tax Court's decision in this case has attracted some attention in tax circles because of its implications for the general problem of the deductibility of business meals....

Moss was a partner in a small trial firm specializing in defense work, mostly for one insurance company. Each of the firm's lawyers carried a tremendous litigation caseload, averaging more than 300 cases, and spent most of every working day in courts in Chicago and its suburbs. The members of the firm met for lunch daily at the Cafe Angelo near their office. At lunch the lawyers would discuss their cases with the head of the firm, whose approval was required for most settlements, and they would decide which lawyer would meet which court call that afternoon or the next morning. Lunchtime was chosen for the daily meeting because the courts were

---

6. This analysis applies to the client being entertained as well as to the employee doing the entertaining. Section 274(n) presumably reflects the judgment that the personal consumption benefit to the client is also 20% of the cost.

7. But suppose that the employee's tax bracket is only 28%. In that case, the second method increases employee taxes by only $5.60 ($20 times 28%), and it does appear to matter which approach is adopted. Denying 20% of the deduction at the employer rather than the employee level may appear to impose too heavy a tax in the 28% bracket employee case.

in recess then. The alternatives were to meet at 7:00 a.m. or 6:00 p.m., and these were less convenient times. There is no suggestion that the lawyers dawdled over lunch, or that the Cafe Angelo is luxurious.

The framework of statutes and regulations for deciding this case is simple, but not clear. Section 262 of the Internal Revenue Code (Title 26) disallows, "except as otherwise expressly provided in this chapter," the deduction of "personal, family, or living expenses." Section 119 excludes from income the value of meals provided by an employer to his employees for his convenience, but only if they are provided on the employer's premises; and section 162(a) allows the deduction of "all the ordinary and necessary expenses paid or incurred during the taxable year in carrying on any trade or business, including—. . . (2) traveling expenses (including amounts expended for meals . . .) while away from home. . . ." Since Moss was not an employee but a partner in a partnership not taxed as an entity, since the meals were not served on the employer's premises, and since he was not away from home (that is, on an overnight trip away from his place of work, see *United States v. Correll* [chapter 5], neither section 119 nor section 162(a)(2) applies to this case. The Internal Revenue Service concedes, however, that meals are deductible under section 162(a) when they are ordinary and necessary business expenses (provided the expense is substantiated with adequate records, see section 274(d)) even if they are not within the express permission of any other provision and even though the expense of commuting to and from work, a traveling expense but not one incurred away from home, is not deductible. Treasury Regulations on Income Tax § 1.262–1(b)(5). . . .

The problem is that many expenses are simultaneously business expenses in the sense that they conduce to the production of business income and personal expenses in the sense that they raise personal welfare. This is plain enough with regard to lunch; most people would eat lunch even if they didn't work. Commuting may seem a pure business expense, but is not; it reflects the choice of where to live, as well as where to work. Read literally, section 262 would make irrelevant whether a business expense is also a personal expense; so long as it is ordinary and necessary in the taxpayer's business, thus bringing section 162(a) into play, an expense is (the statute seems to say) deductible from his income tax. But the statute has not been read literally. There is a natural reluctance, most clearly manifested in the regulation disallowing deduction of the expense of commuting, to lighten the tax burden of people who have the good fortune to interweave work with consumption. To allow a deduction for commuting would confer a windfall on people who live in the suburbs and commute to work in the cities; to allow a deduction for all business-related meals would confer a windfall on people who can arrange their work schedules so they do some of their work at lunch.

Although an argument can thus be made for disallowing *any* deduction for business meals, on the theory that people have to eat whether they work or not, the result would be excessive taxation of people who spend more money on business meals because they are business meals than they would spend on their meals if they were not working. Suppose a theatrical agent takes his clients out to lunch at the expensive restaurants that the clients demand. Of course he can deduct the expense of their meals, from which he derives no pleasure or sustenance, but can he also deduct the expense of his own? He can, because he cannot eat more cheaply; he cannot munch surreptitiously on a peanut butter and jelly sandwich brought from home while his client is wolfing down tournedos Rossini followed by soufflé au grand marnier. No doubt our theatrical agent, unless concerned for his longevity, derives personal utility from his fancy meal, but probably less than the price of the meal. He would not pay for it if it were not for the business benefit; he would get more value from using the same money to buy something else; hence the meal confers on him less utility than the cash equivalent would. The law could require him to pay tax on the fair value of the meal to him; this would be (were it not for costs of administration) the economically correct solution. But the government does not attempt this difficult measurement; it once did, but gave up the attempt as not worth the cost. . . . The taxpayer is permitted to deduct the whole price, provided the expense is "different from or in excess of that which would have been made for the taxpayer's personal purposes.". . .

Because the law allows this generous deduction, which tempts people to have more (and costlier) business meals than are necessary, the Internal Revenue Service has every right to insist that the meal be shown to be a real business necessity. This condition is most easily satisfied when a client or customer or supplier or other outsider to the business is a guest. Even if Sydney Smith was wrong that "soup and fish explain half the emotions of life," it is undeniable that eating together fosters camaraderie and makes business dealings friendlier and easier. It thus reduces the costs of transacting business, for these costs include the frictions and the failures of communication that are produced by suspicion and mutual misunderstanding, by differences in tastes and manners, and by lack of rapport. A meeting with a client or customer in an office is therefore not a perfect substitute for a lunch with him in a restaurant. But it is different when all the participants in the meal are coworkers, as essentially was the case here (clients occasionally were invited to the firm's daily luncheon, but Moss has made no attempt to identify the occasions). They know each other well already; they don't need the social lubrication that a meal with an outsider provides—at least don't need it daily. If a large firm had a monthly lunch to allow partners to get to know associates, the expense of the meal might well be necessary, and would be allowed by the Internal Revenue Service. . . . But Moss's firm never had more than eight lawyers (partners and associates), and did not need a daily lunch to cement relationships among them.

It is all a matter of degree and circumstance (the expense of a testimonial dinner, for example, would be deductible on a morale-building rationale); and particularly of frequency. Daily—for a full year—is too often, perhaps even for entertainment of clients, as implied by *Hankenson v. Commissioner*, . . . where the Tax Court held nondeductible the cost of lunches consumed three or four days a week, 52 weeks a year, by a doctor who entertained other doctors who he hoped would refer patients to him, and other medical personnel.

We may assume it was necessary for Moss's firm to meet daily to coordinate the work of the firm, and also, as the Tax Court found, that lunch was the most convenient time. But it does not follow that the expense of the lunch was a necessary business expense. The members of the firm had to eat somewhere, and the Cafe Angelo was both convenient and not too expensive. They do not claim to have incurred a greater daily lunch expense than they would have incurred if there had been no lunch meetings. Although it saved time to combine lunch with work, the meal itself was not an organic part of the meeting, as in the examples we gave earlier where the business objective, to be fully achieved, required sharing a meal.

The case might be different if the location of the courts required the firm's members to eat each day either in a disagreeable restaurant, so that they derived less value from the meal than it cost them to buy it. . . . ; or in a restaurant too expensive for their personal tastes, so that, again, they would have gotten less value than the cash equivalent. But so far as appears, they picked the restaurant they liked most. Although it must be pretty monotonous to eat lunch the same place every working day of the year, not all the lawyers attended all the lunch meetings and there was nothing to stop the firm from meeting occasionally at another restaurant proximate to their office in downtown Chicago; there are hundreds.

An argument can be made that the price of lunch at the Cafe Angelo included rental of the space that the lawyers used for what was a meeting as well as a meal. There was evidence that the firm's conference room was otherwise occupied throughout the working day, so as a matter of logic Moss might be able to claim a part of the price of lunch as an ordinary and necessary expense for work space. But this is cutting things awfully fine; in any event Moss made no effort to apportion his lunch expense in this way.

Affirmed.

I. NOTES AND QUESTIONS

1) Equity

Was the taxpayer in *Moss* treated unfairly? As compared with the advertising executive who entertains clients at fancy lunches twice a week and deducts the cost? As compared with the attorney who generally pays for and does not deduct the cost of lunch?

2) The Meaning of *Moss*

Suppose that the Cafe Angelo were the only restaurant accessible to the courthouse and that the menu was limited to Southern Italian food. In those circumstances, if the taxpayer could demonstrate a profound dislike for this type of cuisine, *should* he be entitled to the deduction?

Chapter 8

IMPUTED INCOME AND EMPLOYEE DISCOUNTS

A. MINZER v. COMMISSIONER
279 F.2d 338 (5th Cir. 1960)

JONES, CIRCUIT JUDGE.

In 1954 the taxpayer was an insurance agent or broker. During that year he procured or kept in force policies of insurance upon his life. As a representative of the insurance companies which had issued the policies he became entitled to commissions on the policies to the same extent as though the insurance had been on the life of someone else. He received the commissions, or the benefit of them, upon these policies on his own life either by remitting the premiums, less commissions, to the companies, or by remitting the premiums in their entirety and receiving back from the companies their checks to him for the amounts of the commissions. The taxpayer did not include these commissions as taxable income in his return for 1954. The Commissioner of Internal Revenue recomputed the tax by the inclusion of the commissions as income and made a deficiency determination. The Tax Court held for the taxpayer.... Seven judges dissented. The Commissioner brings the case to us for review....

The Tax Court, or those of the Court who subscribed to the prevailing opinion, placed their decision upon the narrow ground that the taxpayer was a broker and not an employee and hence the transactions were outside the terms of Income Tax Regulations Section 61–2(d) (2).[1] In the prevailing opinion of the Tax Court an unwillingness is expressed to apply the prior administrative rulings holding that commissions received or retained by a life insurance agent on policies upon his own life are income to the agent.

---

1. "Except as otherwise provided..., if property is transferred by an employer to an employee for an amount less than its fair market value, regardless of whether the transfer is in the form of a sale or exchange, the difference between the amount paid for the property and the amount of its fair market value at the time of the transfer is compensation and shall be included in the gross income of the employee."

[Editor's Note: The current version of this regulation applies to independent contractors as well as to employees.]

This ruling would have been followed by the Tax Court if it had found an employer-employee relationship between the insurance companies and the taxpayer.

... It does not seem to us that the tax incidence is dependent upon the tag with which the parties label the connection between them. The agent or broker, or by whatever name he be called, is to receive or retain a percentage of the premiums on policies procured by him, called commissions, as compensation for his service to the company in obtaining the particular business for it. The service rendered to the company, for which it was required to compensate him, was no different in kind or degree where the taxpayer submitted his own application than where he submitted the application of another. In each situation there was the same obligation of the company, the obligation to pay a commission for the production of business measured by a percentage of the premiums. In each situation the result was the same to the taxpayer. The taxpayer obtained insurance which the companies were prohibited by law from selling to him at any discount.... It cannot be said that the insurance had a value less than the amount of the premiums. It must then be said that a benefit inured to the taxpayer to the extent of his commissions. The benefit is neither diminished nor eliminated by referring, as does the Tax Court, to the word "commission" as a verbal trap. The commissions were, we conclude, compensation for services and as such were income within the meaning of ... § 61(a)(1).

B. NOTES AND QUESTIONS

1) Imputed Income from Services versus Employee Discounts

Was *Minzer* correctly decided? If a lawyer prepares her own will or if a carpenter builds her own desk, should she be taxable on the benefit? The value of services provided to oneself is called *imputed income from services* and, under long-established practice, is excluded from tax.

> If A works nine hours a day and pays for care of his garden with the proceeds of one hour's work, he would be overtaxed relative to B, who works eight hours at the same hourly rate and maintains a similar garden by giving daily one hour of his own time....
>
> On the other hand, if the value of goods and services produced within the household are to be accounted for, one must face, first of all, the necessity of stopping somewhere; and no convenient stopping-place is discernible. Shall one include the value of shaves? of instruction to children?[2]

> The consumption of one's own services is a form of income. Housekeeping, dressmaking, painting, carpentry, and gardening are examples of services that may either be done by family members or purchased. The performance of these chores, moreover, often competes for time with work for wages and salaries. Because it takes account of the salaries and wages, but not the value of services performed for oneself, the income tax results in inequities and penalizes specialization. If a homeowner takes time off

---

2. H. Simons, Personal Income Taxation 110–111 (1938).

from his regular job and repaints his house, his taxable income is reduced by much more than his real income. . . .

Any attempt to value the services performed within the household, however, would immediately come up against insurmountable obstacles of both a theoretical and practical nature. It would be impossible to distinguish activities that produce valuable services from relaxation or to separate the commercial from the noncommercial, the significant from the trivial.[3]

Minzer held that the taxpayer must report income equal to the difference between the usual cost of life insurance and the cost to him. In effect, the court held that this amount—equal to his commission for selling life insurance—should be taxable like other discounts on goods and services provided by employers to employees. See Reg. § 1.61–2(d)(2) cited in the opinion. But did *Minzer* mistake a case of imputed income from services for an employee discount?

Suppose that an automobile salesperson is entitled to a 10% commission on every car that she sells. If the salesperson buys a new car from her employer at a 50% discount, should the *entire* benefit produce taxable income? Or should only four-fifths of the discount be taxable? Isn't one-fifth of the discount (10% divided by 50%) attributable to the salesperson performing the service of selling to herself? And doesn't that constitute imputed income which is ordinarily tax exempt?

Should it make any difference whether (a) Minzer paid the insurance company an amount equal to the usual premium minus his commission (as he sometimes did) or (b) he paid the usual premium and was refunded the commission (as he did at other times)?

2) Income in Kind Exempted by Administrative Practice

The definition of gross income in Section 61(a)—"all income from whatever source derived"—suggests that *all* compensation for services is taxable, whether provided in cash or in kind, unless excluded by some specific Code provision.[4] However, the IRS has, over the years, exhibited a fairly relaxed attitude toward many forms of income in kind; its aggressive posture in *Drescher, LoBue,* and *Minzer* is atypical. More often, the IRS has not pressed the issue, at least if the amount was not too large. Particularly favored were special discounts on (or even free use of) employer products and employer-provided recreational, parking, and eating facilities. For years, airline workers received free plane travel, auto company executives received free cars, and employees used company swimming pools and golf courses, without the IRS attempting to tax the benefits under Section 61(a) and Reg. § 1.61–2(d)(2) (cited in *Minzer*). Because Congress had never expressly authorized the exclusion of these items from taxable income, they came to be known as *nonstatutory fringe benefits.*

---

3. R. Goode, The Individual Income Tax 142 (1976).
4. The phrase "fringe benefits" in Section 61(a)(1) appears to cover compensation in kind. But it was added to the Code only in 1984 and thus should not have influenced pre-1984 administrative decisions and case law.

It was only in 1975 that the Treasury articulated a comprehensive approach in a discussion draft of proposed regulations on the taxation of nonstatutory fringe benefits. However, the discussion draft generated considerable opposition from taxpayers who were benefiting from tax-free fringe benefits, and the Treasury took no further steps to implement its proposal. In 1978, Congress, preferring to devise its own solution, prohibited the Treasury from issuing any regulations in this area. Congress' answer, finally enacted in 1984 as Section 132, is discussed below.

C. FRINGE BENEFIT PROVISIONS

House Committee on Ways and Means,
H. R. Rep. No. 432, 98th Cong.,
2d Sess. at 1590–1610 (1984)

Present Law

General rules

The Internal Revenue Code defines gross income for purposes of the Federal income tax as including "all income from whatever source derived," and specifies that it includes "compensation for services" (sec. 61). Treasury regulations provide that gross income includes compensation for services paid other than in money (Reg. sec. 1.61–1(a)). Further, the U.S. Supreme Court has stated that Code section 61 "is broad enough to include in taxable income any economic or financial benefit conferred on the employee as compensation, whatever the form or mode by which it is effected.". . .

Moratorium on issuance of regulations

In 1975, the Treasury Department issued a discussion draft of proposed regulations which contained a number of rules for determining whether various nonstatutory fringe benefits constitute taxable compensation. Public Law 95–427, enacted in 1978, prohibited the Treasury Department from issuing, prior to 1980, final regulations under section 61 of the Internal Revenue Code relating to the income tax treatment of fringe benefits. That statute further prohibited Treasury from proposing regulations relating to the treatment of fringe benefits under section 61 which would be effective prior to 1980.

Public Law 96–167, enacted in 1979, extended the moratorium on issuance of fringe benefit regulations through May 31, 1981. . . .

The Economic Recovery Tax Act of 1981 (Public Law 97–34) extended the moratorium on issuance of fringe benefit regulations through December 31, 1983. . . .

Reasons for Change

In providing statutory rules for exclusion of certain fringe benefits for income and payroll tax purposes, the committee has attempted to strike a balance between two competing objectives.

First, the committee is aware that in many industries, employees may receive, either free or at a discount, goods and services which the employer sells to the general public. In many cases, these practices are long established, and have been treated by employers, employees, and the IRS as not giving rise to taxable income. Although employees may receive an economic benefit from the availability of these free or discounted goods or services, employers often have valid business reasons, other than simply providing compensation, for encouraging employees to avail themselves of the products which they sell to the public. For example, a retail clothing business will want its salespersons to wear, when they deal with customers, the clothing which it seeks to sell to the public. In addition . . . the selection of goods and services . . . usually is restricted. . . . The committee believes, therefore, that many present practices under which employers may provide to a broad group of employees, either free or at a discount, the products and services which the employer sells or provides to the public do not serve merely to replace cash compensation. . . .

The second objective of the committee's bill is to set forth clear boundaries for the provision of tax-free benefits. Because of the moratorium on the issuance of fringe benefit regulations, the Treasury Department has been precluded from clarifying the tax treatment of many of the forms of noncash compensation commonly in use. As a result, the administrators of the tax law have not had clear guidelines in this area, and hence taxpayers in identical situations have been treated differently. The inequities, confusion, and administrative difficulties for businesses, employees, and the IRS resulting from this situation have increased substantially in recent years. The committee believes that it is unacceptable to allow these conditions—which have existed since 1978—to continue any longer.

In addition, the committee is concerned that without any well-defined limits on the ability of employers to compensate their employees tax-free by using a medium other than cash, new practices will emerge that could shrink the income tax base significantly, and further shift a disproportionate tax burden to those individuals whose compensation is in the form of cash. . . .

The nondiscrimination rule is an important common thread among the types of fringe benefits which are excluded under the bill from income and employment taxes. Under the bill, most fringe benefits may be made available tax-free to officers, owners, or highly compensated employees only if the benefits are also provided on substantially equal terms to other employees. The committee believes that it would be fundamentally unfair to provide tax-free treatment for economic benefits that are furnished only to highly paid executives. Further, where benefits are limited to the highly paid, it is more likely that the benefit is being provided so that those who control the business can receive compensation in a nontaxable form; in that situation, the reasons stated above for allowing tax-free treatment would not be applicable. Also, if highly paid executives could receive free from taxation economic benefits that are denied to lower-paid employees, while the latter are compensated only in fully taxable cash, the committee is concerned that this situation would exacerbate problems of noncompliance among taxpayers. . . .

In summary, the committee believes that by providing rules which essentially codify many present practices under which employers provide their own products and services tax-free to a broad group of employees, and by ending the uncertainties arising from a moratorium on the Treasury Department's ability to clarify the tax treatment of these benefits, the bill substantially improves the equity and administration of the tax system. . . .

Explanation of Provisions

1. Overview

Under the bill, certain fringe benefits provided by an employer are excluded from the recipient employee's gross income for Federal income tax purposes. . . .

The excluded fringe benefits are those benefits that qualify under one of the following five categories as defined in the bill: (1) a no-additional-cost service, (2) a qualified employee discount, (3) a working condition fringe, (4) a de minimis fringe, and (5) a qualified tuition reduction. Special rules apply with respect to certain parking or eating facilities provided to employees, on-premises athletic facilities, and demonstration use of an employer-provided car by auto salespersons. Some of the exclusions under the bill apply to benefits provided to the spouse and dependent children of a current employee, to former employees who separated from service because of retirement or disability (and their spouses and dependent children), and to the widow(er) of a deceased employee (and the dependent children of deceased employees).

In the case of no-additional-cost service, a qualified employee discount, employee parking or eating facilities, or a qualified tuition reduction, the exclusion applies with respect to benefits provided to officers, owners, or highly compensated employees only if the benefit is made available to employees on a basis which does not discriminate in favor of officers, owners, or highly compensated employees.

Any fringe benefit that does not qualify for exclusion under the bill (for example, free or discounted goods or services which are limited to corporate officers) and that is not excluded under another statutory fringe benefit provision of the Code is taxable to the recipient under Code sections 61 and 83, and is includible in wages for employment tax purposes, at the excess of its fair market value over any amount paid by the employee for the benefit. . . .

2. No-additional-cost Service (Sec. 502 of the bill and new Code sec. 132(b))

General rule

Under this category, the entire value of any no-additional-cost service provided by an employer to an employee for the use of the employee (or of the employee's spouse or dependent children) is excluded. . . . However, the exclusion applies only if the service is available to employees on a nondiscriminatory basis (see description below of the nondiscrimination rules of the bill). The exclusion applies whether the service is provided directly for no charge or at a reduced price or whether the benefit is provided through a cash rebate of all or part of the amount paid for the service.

To qualify under this exclusion, the employer must incur no substantial additional cost in providing the service to the employee, computed without regard to any amounts paid by the employee for the service. For this purpose, the term cost includes any revenue forgone because the service is furnished to the employee rather than to a nonemployee. In addition, the service provided to the employee must be of the type which the employer offers for sale to nonemployee customers in the ordinary course of the line of business of the employer in which the employee is performing services.

Generally, situations in which employers incur no additional cost in providing services to employees are those in which the employees receive, at no substantial additional cost to the employer, the benefit of excess capacity which otherwise would have remained unused because nonemployee customers would not have purchased it. Thus, employers that furnish airline, railroad, or subway seats or hotel rooms to employees working in those lines of business in such a way that nonemployee customers are not displaced, and telephone companies that provide telephone service to employees within existing capacity, incur no substantial additional cost in the provision of these services to employees, as this term is used in the bill.

Line of business limitation

To be excluded under this category, a service must be the same type of service which is sold to the public in the ordinary course of the line of business of the employer in which the employee works. (Thus, types of services most of the employer's production of which are provided or sold to the employer's employees do not qualify for this exclusion.) For purposes of this limitation, a single employer is treated as consisting of more than one line of business if, after aggregating businesses under common control (see "definition of employer," below), the products or services the employer sells to nonemployee customers fall into more than one industry group.... .

Under this limitation, for example, an employer which provides airline services and hotel services to the general public is considered to consist of two separate lines of business. As a consequence, the employees of the airline business of the employer may not exclude the value of free hotel rooms provided by the hotel business of the employer, and vice versa. The purpose of the line of business limitation is to avoid, to the extent possible, the competitive imbalances and inequities which would result from giving the employees of a conglomerate or other large employer with several lines of business a greater variety of tax-free benefits than could be given to the employees of a small employer with only one line of business. Thus, small businesses will not be disadvantaged in their ability to compete with large businesses providing the same goods or services, and employees of small business will not be disadvantaged, in comparison to employees of multi-faceted businesses, in terms of receiving tax-free economic benefits.

If an employee provides services that directly benefit more than one line of business of the employer, then the individual is treated as performing services in all such lines of business. Thus, for example, the chief executive officer, payroll department employees, and similar "headquarters" employees may exclude the value of no-additional-cost services provided by either the airline or hotel lines of business of the employer if they provide services which directly benefit both those lines of business.

Reciprocal arrangements

Under the bill, the employees of one employer are allowed the no-additional-cost service exclusion for services provided by an unrelated employer (i.e., another employer not under common control) only if the services provided to the employee are the same type of services as provided to nonemployee customers by both the line of business (of the first employer) in which the employee works and the line of business (of the other employer) in which the services are provided to the employee. In addition, both employers must be parties to a written reciprocal agreement under which the employees of each such line of business may receive the service from the other employer, and neither employer may incur any substantial additional cost (including forgone revenue or payments to the other employer) in providing such service or pursuant to such agreement.

The criteria for determining whether two unrelated employers are providing the same type of service are the same as described above (under "line of business limitation") for determining the composition of the distinct lines of business comprised by a single employer. Thus, for example, the exclusion is available if two unrelated airlines provide free standby flights to each other's airline employees, but is not available to a hotel's employees if they receive free standby flights from an airline line of business (whether the airline is operated by the employees' employer or another employer).

Definition of employee

The bill provides that, with respect to a line of business of an employer, the term employee means (1) an individual who is currently employed by the employer in that line of business; (2) an individual who separated from service with the employer in that line of business by reason of retirement or disability; and (3) a widow or widower of an individual who died while employed by the employer in that line of business or of an individual who had separated from service with the employer in that line of business by reason of retirement or disability. The bill also provides that any use (e.g., of a standby airline flight) by the spouse or a dependent child of the employee (as so defined) is to be treated as use by the employee. These definitions are relevant both for purposes of eligibility for the exclusion under the bill and for purposes of defining nonemployee customers.

Examples

As an illustration of the no-additional-cost service category of excludable benefits, assume that a corporation which operates an airline as its only line of business provides all of its employees (and their spouses and dependent children) with free travel, on the same terms to all employees, as stand-by passengers on the employer airline if the space taken on the flight has not been sold to the public shortly before departure time. In such a

Ch. 8   Imputed Income, Employee Discounts   109

case, the entire fair market value of the free travel is excluded under the no-additional-cost service rule in the bill. This conclusion follows because the service provided by the employer to its employees who work in the employer's airline line of business is the same as that sold to the general public (airline flights), the service is provided at no substantial additional cost to the employer (the seat would have been unsold to nonemployees if the employee had not taken the trip), and the eligibility terms satisfy the nondiscrimination rules of the bill since all employees are eligible for the benefit on the same terms.

This exclusion also applies where employees of the airline line of business of an employer receive free stand-by flights from the airline line of business of another employer through a written reciprocal agreement, if the benefit to the employee would have been excluded under this provision of the bill had it been provided in the same manner by the employee's employer. Thus, for example, the free flights furnished by the other employer must be available to the employees of the first employer on the same nondiscriminatory basis as required for the exclusion when furnished by the first employer, and neither employer may incur any substantial cost (including forgone revenue or any payment from one employer to the other) in providing the service or pursuant to the agreement.

Another example of a no-additional-cost service is the provision of utility services to the employees of the utility where there is excess capacity, such as the provision by a telephone company of free or reduced-cost telephone service to its employees. Because the phone lines, switching capacity, and other overhead already exist, the telephone calls which employees may make without charge or at a reduced price impose no substantial additional cost on the employer. Thus, assuming the telephone service is provided to employees on a nondiscriminatory basis, the requirements of this exclusion category are met, and the value of the service is excluded from gross income and wages.

Under the bill, the exclusion for no-additional-cost service is not available, for example, to employees in the hotel line of business of a corporation for receipt of free stand-by travel on an airline operated by the same corporation, or to employees of a consumer goods manufacturer who travel for personal purposes on a company plane (even if the plane is otherwise making a trip on company business). In each of these cases, even assuming that there were no substantial additional cost to the employer in providing the service on a space-available basis, the service is not the same type generally provided to the general public in the specific line of business of the employer in which the employee-recipient works. Accordingly, the requirements of the no-additional-cost exclusion are not satisfied.

3. Qualified Employee Discount (Sec. 502 of the bill and new Code sec. 132(c))

General rule

Under the bill, certain employee discounts allowed from the selling price of qualified goods or services of the employer are excluded for income and employment tax purposes, but only if the discounts are available to employees on a nondiscriminatory basis (see description below of the nondiscrimination rules of the bill). The exclusion applies whether the qualified employee discount is provided through a reduction in price or through a cash rebate from a third party.

The exclusion is not available for discounts on any personal property (tangible or intangible) of a kind commonly held for investment or for discounts on any real property. Thus, for example, the exclusion does not apply to discounts on any employee purchases of securities, gold coins, residential or commercial real estate, or interests in mineral-producing property (regardless of whether a particular purchase is made for investment purposes). This limitation is provided because the committee does not believe that favorable tax treatment should be provided when noncash compensation is provided in the form of property which the employee could typically sell at close to the same price at which the employer sells the property to its nonemployee customers. Under the discount exclusion of the bill, an employee of a brokerage house may purchase stock and receive an excludable discount on a commission (subject to the 20-percent limitation discussed below for discounts on services.) However, any discount allowed on the price of the stock itself is not eligible for the discount exclusion.

Line of business limitation

To qualify under this exclusion, the goods or services on which the discount is available must be those which are offered for sale by the employer to nonemployee customers in the ordinary course of the employer's line of business in which the employee works. (Thus, types of goods or services most of the employer's production of which are provided or sold to the employer's employees do not qualify for this exclusion.) The rules for treatment of a single employer as consisting of more than one line of business are the same as those described above in connection with the exclusion for a no-additional-cost service. However, the discount exclusion is not available for goods or services provided by another employer, whether or not a reciprocal agreement exists, except where commonly controlled businesses are treated as one employer (see "definition of employer," below).

For example, merchandise held for sale in the retail department store line of business of a firm is eligible for the discount exclusion if purchased at a discount by an employee of the firm who works in that line of business. Similarly, an employee who works for a manufacturer assembling appliances is eligible for the discount exclusion if the employee purchases the assembled appliances from the manufacturer-employer at a discount.

On the other hand, if an employee works for a company that consists of more than one line of business, such as a company consisting of a retail department store business, a hotel business, and an electrical component manufacturing business, an employee is eligible for the discount exclusion only for merchandise or services offered to customers in the ordinary course of business in the particular line of business in which the employee works. This is the case regardless of whether the employer makes discounts available to the employees in the other two lines of business. Thus, in this example, employees of the hotel business or of the electrical component manufacturing business are not eligible for the discount exclusion if these employees purchase merchandise at a discount from the employer's department store. However, employees of units of the employer that provide repair, or financing services with respect to, or that sell by catalog, retail merchandise are considered as providing services in the retail merchandise line of business and hence are eligible for excludable discounts on merchandise items. . . .

Definition of employee

The bill provides that, with respect to a line of business of an employer, the term employee means (1) an individual who is currently employed by the employer in that line of business; (2) an individual who separated from service with the employer in that line of business by reason of retirement or disability; and (3) a widow or widower of an individual who died while employed by the employer in that line of business or of an individual who had separated from service with the employer in that line of business by reason of retirement or disability. The bill also provides that any use (e.g., of discounted goods) by the spouse or a dependent child of the employee (as so defined) is to be treated as use by the employee. These definitions are relevant both for purposes of eligibility for the exclusion under the bill and for purposes of defining nonemployee customers.

Amount of exclusion

General rule.—Under the bill, an employee discount is excluded only up to a specified limit. In the case of merchandise, the excludable amount of the discount is limited to the selling price of the merchandise, multiplied by the employer's gross profit percentage. The discount exclusion for a service may not exceed 20 percent of the selling price, regardless of the actual gross profit percentage.

Merchandise.—In the case of merchandise, the excludable amount of the discount may not exceed the selling price of the merchandise, multiplied by the employer's gross profit percentage. For this purpose, the employer's gross profit percentage for a period means the excess of the aggregate sales price for the period of merchandise sold by the employer in the relevant line of business over the aggregate cost of such merchandise to the employer, then divided by the aggregate sales price.

For example, if total sales of such merchandise during a year were $1,000,000 and the employer's cost for the merchandise was $600,000, then the gross profit percentage for the year is 40 percent ($1,000,000 minus $600,000 equals 40 percent of $1,000,000). Thus, an employee discount with respect to such merchandise is excluded from income to the extent it does not exceed 40 percent of the selling price of the merchandise to nonemployee customers. If in this case the discount allowed to the employee exceeds 40 percent (for example, 50 percent), the excess discount on a purchase (10 percent in the example) is included in the employee's gross income. . . .

4. Working Condition Fringe (Sec. 502 of the bill and new Code sec. 132(d))

General rules

Under the bill, the fair market value of any property or services provided to an employee of the employer is excluded for income and employment tax purposes to the extent that the costs of the property or services would be deductible as ordinary and necessary business expenses (under Code secs. 162 or 167) if the employee had paid for such property or services. The nondiscrimination rules applicable to certain other provisions of Title V of the bill do not apply as a condition for exclusion as a working condition fringe, except for employee parking (as described below).

Examples

By way of illustration, the value of use by an employee of a company car or airplane for business purposes is excluded as a working condition fringe. (However, use of a company car or plane for personal purposes is not excludable. Merely incidental personal use of a company car, such as a small detour for a personal errand, might qualify for exclusion as a de minimis fringe.) As another example, assume the employer subscribes to business periodicals for an employee (e.g., a brokerage house buys a financial publication for its brokers). In that case, the fair market value of the subscriptions is an excluded working condition fringe, since the expense could have been deducted as a business expense if the employee had directly paid for the subscription.

Examples of other benefits excluded as working condition fringes are those provided by an employer primarily for the safety of its employees, if such safety precautions are considered ordinary and necessary business expenses. For example, if for security reasons the U.S. Government or a private business provides a bodyguard or car and driver to an employee, the value of the bodyguard or use of the car and driver is treated as a working condition fringe and hence is not includible in income of the employee. Other examples of excluded working condition fringes are employer expenditures for on-the-job training or travel by an employee if such expenditures meet the present-law requirements for deductibility under section 162. . . .

The fair market value of the use of consumer goods which are manufactured for sale to nonemployee customers and which are provided to employees for product testing and evaluation outside the employer's office is excluded as a working condition fringe only if (1) consumer testing and evaluation of the product is an ordinary and necessary business expense of the employer, (2) business reasons necessitate that the testing and evaluation be performed off-premises by employees (i.e., the testing and evaluation cannot be carried out adequately in the employer's office or in laboratory testing facilities), (3) the item is furnished to the employee for purposes of testing and evaluation, (4) the item is made available to the employee for no longer than necessary to test and evaluate its performance, and the item must be returned to the employer at completion of the testing and evaluation period, (5) the employer imposes limitations on the employee's use of the item which significantly reduce the value of any personal benefit to the employee, and (6) the employee must submit detailed reports to the employer on the testing and evaluation. The fifth requirement above is satisfied, for example, if (i) the employer places limitations on the employee's ability to select among different models or varieties of the consumer product which is furnished for testing and evaluation purposes, (ii) the employer's policy provides for the employee, in appropriate cases, to purchase or lease at his or her own expense the same type of item as that being tested (so that personal use by the employee's family will be limited), and (iii) the employer requires that members of the employee's family generally cannot use the item. If products are furnished under a testing and evaluation program only to officers, owners, or highly compensated employees, this fact may be considered in a determination of whether the goods are furnished for testing and evaluation purposes or for compensation purposes, unless the employer can show a business reason for the classification of employees to whom the products are furnished (e.g., that automobiles are furnished for testing and evaluation by an automobile manufacturing company to its design engineers and supervisory mechanics.)

Employee parking

Under a special rule in the bill, the fair market value of free or reduced-cost parking provided to an employee on or near the business premises of the employer is excludable as a working condition fringe. For officers, owners, or highly compensated employees, however, this exclusion applies only if such parking is available on a nondiscriminatory basis (see description below of the nondiscrimination rules of the bill).

Demonstration use by auto salespersons

Under a special rule, the fair market value of any use of an employer-provided automobile by an automobile salesperson in the geographic sales area in which the dealer's sales office is located is an excludable working condition fringe if (1) such use of the car is provided primarily for the purpose of facilitating the salesperson's performance of services for the employer, and (2) there are substantial restrictions on the personal use of the car by the salesperson. For example, if an auto salesperson is required to have a car available for showing to customers during working hours, is required to drive the make of car which the auto dealer sells, is limited in the amount of miles he or she may drive the auto, may not store personal possessions in the auto, and is prohibited from using the car for vacation trips, then use of the car in the sales area qualifies for the exclusion under the bill.

5. De Minimis Fringe (Sec. 502 of the bill and new Code sec. 132(e))

General rules

Under the bill, if the fair market value of any property or a service that otherwise would be a fringe benefit includible in gross income is so small that accounting for the property or service would be unreasonable or administratively impracticable, the value is excluded for income and employment tax purposes. The nondiscrimination rules applicable to certain other provisions of the bill do not apply as a condition for exclusion of property or a service as a de minimis fringe, except for subsidized eating facilities (as described below).

In determining whether the de minimis exclusion applies, the fair market values of all property or services provided to an individual during a calendar year are to be aggregated, *except* for (1) property or services that are excluded from taxation under another specific statutory exclusion provision of the Code, as amended by this bill (such as health benefits or qualified employee discounts) and (2) any nonexcluded property or service provided to the employee that (without regard to the aggregation rule) does not qualify as a de minimis fringe because the value of the individual item is too large.

To illustrate, benefits which generally are excluded from income and employment taxes as de minimis fringes (without regard to the aggregation rule) include the typing of personal letters by a company secretary, occasional personal use of the company copying machine, monthly transit passes provided at a discount not exceeding $15, occasional company cocktail parties or picnics for employees, occasional supper money or taxi fare because of overtime work, traditional holiday gifts of property with a low fair market value, occasional theatre or sporting event tickets, and coffee and doughnuts furnished to employees.

Subsidized eating facilities

If an employer provides and operates an eating facility for its employees on or near the employer's business premises and if revenue derived from the facility normally equals or exceeds the direct operating costs of the facility, the excess of the value of the meals over the fees charged to employees is excluded under the bill if the nondiscrimination rules (see description below) are satisfied. . . . While the benefits provided to a particular employee who eats regularly at such a facility may not qualify as a de minimis fringe absent this rule, the recordkeeping difficulties involved in identifying which employees ate which meals on particular days, as well as the values and costs for each such meal, led the committee to conclude that a general exclusion should be provided for subsidized eating facilities as defined in the bill.

6. Qualified Tuition Reductions (Sec. 503 of the bill and Code sec. 117)

The bill adds a new provision to Code section 117 . . . to exclude, for income and employment tax purposes, the amount of qualified tuition reductions, including cash grants for tuition, provided to an employee of an educational institution. . . . To qualify for the exclusion, the tuition reductions must be made available to employees on a nondiscriminatory basis. . . .

7. Athletic Facilities (Sec. 502 of the bill and new Code sec. 132(h)(5))

In general, the fair market value of any on-premises athletic facility provided and operated by an employer for its employees, where substantially all the use of the facility is by employees of the employer (or their spouses or dependent children) is excluded under the bill for income and employment tax purposes. The athletic facility need not be in the same location as the business premises of the employer, but must be located on premises of the employer and may not be a facility for residential use. Examples of athletic facilities are swimming pools, gyms, tennis courts, and golf courses.

The exclusion for certain employer-provided athletic facilities does not apply to the providing of memberships in a country club or similar facility unless the facility itself is owned and operated by the employer and satisfies the employee-use and other requirements for the exclusion. . . .

D. NOTES AND QUESTIONS

1) Arguments for Excluding Nonstatutory Fringe Benefits

The House Report on Section 132 deserves careful and critical reading. Are you convinced by the Report's arguments for excluding the enumerated fringe benefits from taxation? First, it notes that the practice of not taxing these items is "long-established." Does this mean that a practice (or provision) in the tax law should be changed only if it has existed for a short or medium period of time?

One could argue that, because the practice is long-established, taxpayers have justifiably relied on it. Therefore, it would be unfair to such taxpayers to repeal the exclusion. For example, Jones may have chosen to work as a flight attendant believing that free plane trips would constitute a substantial part of his income not subject to tax. If Jones had thought that such benefits might be taxed, he might have pursued a different career. Or an airline company may have planned on a certain level of cash salary expenditures. With free plane trips subject to taxation, the airline may be forced to raise salaries to continue to compete with other sectors of the economy for workers.

Do you find such reliance arguments convincing? Do they suggest that, when the tax law is amended, Congress should provide for a transition period so that taxpayers can have time to adjust? Or does the risk that the tax law may change differ little from other economic risks that accompany career or business decisions?

The second argument made for excluding so-called nonstatutory fringe benefits is that "employers often have valid business reasons for providing them." But if the fringe benefit is truly provided for business reasons, then it should be either excludable as a working condition (see the Sara Eder example in the problems in Chapter 1, Section 132(a)(3), and Chapter 4) or deductible as a business expense (see Section 162(a)). Is there any need for additional statutory exclusions for "no additional cost service," "qualified employee discounts," and the like?

The third argument is that "the selection of goods and services... usually is restricted." But taking into account the employee's restricted choice is contrary to the result in *Drescher*, not to mention the explicit language of Section 83(a). The factor of restricted choice is generally irrelevant for goods or services produced by someone other than the employer (as in *Drescher*). Why should it suddenly become relevant simply because goods or services are produced by the employer or consist of free parking or subsidized meals?

2) Sections 132(a)(2) and (c): Qualified Employee Discounts

Sections 132(a)(2) and (c) permit the exclusion of "qualified employee discounts." There may be other justifications, not mentioned in the House Report, for this particular exclusion.

At one time or another, most goods and services are sold to consumers at a discount from the usual market price. (These discounts will be referred to as *consumer discounts* to distinguish them from the special case of discounts offered to employees or *employee discounts*.) Consumer discounts are typically aimed at special groups who are unwilling to buy a product at the usual market price but who may be willing to buy at a specially reduced price. In general, a seller will offer such a discount only if it believes that sales at the usual market price will not be appreciably affected.

For example, a department store may announce a special $200 reduction in the price of washing machines for buyers over the age of 65 (in effect, a senior citizen discount). The store may have calculated that buyers age 65 and over are generally unwilling to pay the usual market price and that younger customers are unlikely to engage in subterfuge to obtain the special discount.

Consumers who buy the washing machines at the $200 discount are not treated by the tax law as having $200 of income. Why not? Perhaps because they are viewed as constituting a separate market for washing machines; therefore, the discounted price that they pay *is* the market price in that separate market.

Employee discounts on a company's products might be analogized to consumer discounts *if* a company's employees constitute a separate market for goods or services in which there are too few customers at the usual market price. Do you find the comparison with consumer discounts convincing? For example, suppose that Maytag employees may purchase Maytag washing machines at a $200 discount from the usual price. How likely is it that Maytag employees truly constitute a separate market for the company's products?

There may be another justification for excluding employee discounts. The discount from market value may reflect the value added to the company's product by the services of its employees. If a company has just one employee, to tax the discount would be to tax the employee on the value created by his or her services. Excluding the discount in the case of the business with one employee might therefore be justified by the nontaxation of imputed income from services. (See the Notes and Questions following *Minzer,* above.) When a company has several, or even many, employees, why should they be treated any differently? Doesn't the discount reflect the value created by their collective services? Wouldn't taxing that discount be to tax the imputed income from their collective services?

3) Sections 132(a)(1) and (b): No Additional Cost Service

Section 132(a)(1) permits the exclusion of services provided at no substantial additional cost. "Cost" is defined by Section 132(b)(2) to include not just actual expenditures but also "foregone revenue."

This provision was intended, among other things, to exclude the value of airline seats provided to airline employees on a standby basis. But what if the airline also offers (as many airlines have) discount standby fares to the general public? Should airline employees benefit from the exclusion only if they are seated *after* all nonemployee standby passengers have been accommodated? If an airline employee is seated *before* all nonemployee standbys are seated, wouldn't the airline have "foregone revenue," so that the fringe benefit involves "substantial additional cost"?

One commentator finds another example of "no additional cost service" in the House Report on Section 132—free telephone service for telephone company employees—even "more troublesome."

> The telephone company's estimate of required capacity surely takes into account the potential needs of its employees (even if we could assume that an airline does not). For one thing, employees are not required to make phone calls on a standby basis. Therefore, it does not seem sensible to view the sale to the employee as a sale of a good that would otherwise be wasted.[5]

4) The Administrative Feasibility of Allocating Benefits

One possible justification for excluding the value of subsidized meals (Section 132(e)(2)) and athletic facilities (Section 132(h)(5)) is the difficulty of determining the value of benefits received by any individual employee. One employee may eat every day in the subsidized cafeteria and spend every evening working out in the company gym. Another may prefer to bring bag lunches and may shun all forms of exercise. The House Report emphasizes "the recordkeeping difficulties involved in identifying which employees ate which meals on particular days, as well as the values and costs for each such meal."

---

5. Halperin, Broadening the Base—The Case of Fringe Benefits, 37 Nat'l. Tax J. 271, 277 (1984).

However, even if it is difficult to determine how much each individual employee actually benefits, what about other possible solutions? Why not simply allocate the value of such fringe benefits to employees on a pro rata basis? Or how might denying the employer a deduction compensate for failing to tax the employees?

5) Qualified Tuition Reduction

Section 117(d) was enacted at the same time as Section 132. It excludes from income the amount of any reduction in tuition provided to an employee of an educational organization. Why was this provision necessary? Why isn't free tuition already excluded as "additional no-cost service" under Sections 132(a)(1) and (b)?

6) Section 132 as a Political Compromise

Is it a worthwhile exercise to try to rationalize Section 132? Perhaps the legislation is better understood as codifying "long-established" IRS practices which have been retained—not for *bona fide* reasons of tax policy—but because special interest groups, such as airline employees, car salespersons, and university faculty, wield significant political influence. Or might Section 132 (and Section 117(d)) be defended as clarifying what those "long-established" practices are and as setting precise limits to prevent even more erosion of the tax base? For example, while the practice of excluding discounts on employer products is recognized, the allowable discount is limited to 20% in the case of services and to the "gross profit percentage" in the case of goods.

In thinking about these questions, consider the possibility that even attempting to imagine a principled justification of a provision like Section 132 may disguise social reality.

> Social inequalities . . . present certain specific problems for inquiry, as regards their specific nature and their relationship to the total social system of which they form a part. We are faced . . . with the problem of mystification. . . .
> This problem (with which both Marxist and Freudian social science have been systematically concerned . . .) refers to the fact that things do not often seem what they are; more specifically, to the fact that the specific form of a social reality, its specific outward appearance and manifestation, is often not a clear picture of, a clear window on to, its specific nature—its reality—as it is actually, as opposed to apparently, constituted and determined. Inquiry is consequently faced with the task of penetrating behind the mask of specific form and appearance to specific nature, of un-masking and de-mystifying and thus elucidating specific nature.[6]

In light of this statement, consider Section 132(f)(3) and the following account of its enactment.

---

6. F. Johnstone, Race, Class, and Gold, pp. 5–6 (1971).

E. NEWMAN, FLY ME, FLY MY MOTHER
35 Tax Notes 291, 291–300 (April 20, 1987)

Introduction

The life of a flight attendant has changed markedly since commercial airlines began. In the fifties and sixties, flight attendants were mostly young, single females. The average tenure on the job was relatively short. In fact, many airlines had specific provisions stating a maximum age for female flight attendants, and some had provisions stating that marriage was prohibited.

Subsequently, the maximum age restrictions were abolished, as were the restrictions on marriage. Average job tenure increased dramatically. Ironically, during the same period, the job became less pleasant, due to a combination of factors. In the 1970s, a series of advertising campaigns reinforced the image of flight attendants as sex objects. Not surprisingly, this image led to increased harassment of flight attendants in the air.

Later, increasing cost competition resulting from deregulation and changes in technology led to larger, longer range, more crowded planes. The ratio of passengers to flight attendants increased from 25 to one in the fifties to the current 50 to one. In addition, the flight attendant's working day grew longer, and the layover time decreased. Finally, flight attendants became more aware of the health hazards associated with the job.

As a result, flight attendants had something to improve, and could foresee enough time on the job to make a long range improvement effort worthwhile. Therefore, flight attendants in the last 10 years have banded together for the first time as a political and economic force to be reckoned with. A remarkable example of this new political activity occurred when Congress and the IRS changed the taxation of airline employee fringe benefits.

Perhaps the most well known fringe benefit of airline employees is the opportunity to take a free flight, if a commercial airliner has an unsold seat. This fringe benefit has existed for a long time, but the airlines have not always loved it. These pass privileges were complex, therefore costly to administer. Moreover, they were sometimes abused, and they created image problems for the airlines.

The first problem was the complexity. Interline agreements—the right of an employee on one airline to obtain a free or reduced price flight on another airline—proliferated. Pass privileges were extended to the immediate families of the employee, and, to a limited extent, to the parents of the employee. More recently, some airlines allowed the "buddy pass"—the right of an airline employee to obtain a free flight for his or her live-in companion. Many of these interline passes and passes for relatives or friends of airline employees were not free. In fact, some airlines had varying discounts for various relatives of the employee. Moreover, many airlines had "positive space" passes even for their employees, which gave the user some priority in standby boarding, for a higher price. These varying fares made the pass privileges increasingly costly for the airlines to administer.

In addition, with complexity came abuse. While it was the airlines that unilaterally determined who received the passes, the system was really administered by the airline employees at the airport departure gates. Some have alleged that these employees at the gates were abusing their discretion, sometimes even bumping revenue passengers in favor of an employee friend. Finally, a series of articles in major newspapers commenting on the magnitude of these privileges were thought by some to have given the airlines a bad image. For all of these reasons, by 1983, at least some of the airlines would have been just as happy to see the privileges disappear.

The Congress Acts

It was at this juncture that Congress finally decided to let the last moratorium on the taxation of fringe benefits run out, and do something about them. The series of moratoria on fringe benefits taxation were a cumulative embarrassment to Congress, as they were a continuing admission of the inability of Congress to legislate. Moreover, the proliferation of nonstatutory, tax-free fringe benefits went against the growing mood of Congress to broaden the base for taxation.

Although Congressman Dan Rostenkowski, Chairman of the House Ways and Means Committee, decided to take up fringe benefits, they were still a very controversial subject. There were many who thought that their fringe benefits were simply gifts from God, and therefore not to be taxed. As a result, even though a subject of this magnitude ordinarily would have been considered by the whole Committee, Rostenkowski sent this one to the Subcommittee on Select Revenue Measures. In that way, the issue would not be quite so much in the public eye, and, if it blew up, it could be quietly buried.

Rostenkowski's instructions to Congressman Fortney H. (Pete) Stark, D-Calif., Chairman of the Subcommittee, were simple. Either the Subcommittee was to come up with a bill, or the moratorium would be allowed to expire so that IRS could draft regulations. No further moratoria were to be allowed.

Stark decided to draft a bill. His strategy was to placate those interested in fringe benefits largely by codifying the existing tax-free treatment. In return, the proliferation of tax-free benefits would be frozen; no further tax-free benefits would be allowed. He hoped that, in this way, the bill would not generate too much controversy, and would pass relatively easily. Stark also wanted to prohibit discrimination in favor of one employee group over another, and to rationalize the treatment of fringe benefits in some respects. It was in this latter attempt that Stark generated a heavy lobbying effort from the airlines and their employees.

As to airline passes, Stark's first proposal was that they would be tax free only to airline employees, and only when the trip was on the employee's own airline. This proposal generated a lobbying response from the Air Transport Association, the International Association of Machinists, and the various flight attendant unions.

The Air Transport Association, the industry trade group, decided that . . . employee morale was paramount. Therefore, in spite of the ambivalence of some of its members, the ATA lobbied to retain the existing, more generous tax-free treatment of airline fringe benefits. It lobbied especially for tax-free treatment for interline passes, since these passes had been sold to employees, usually at 25 percent of the standard coach fare, almost since the inception of the airlines. By the time Stark's bill became part of the Deficit Reduction Act of 1984, interline passes were tax free.

The International Association of Machinists (IAM) also mounted a lobbying effort. Its position was that there should be no change in the taxation of fringe benefits. IAM officials had numerous meetings with Congressman Stark. In addition, IAM members mounted a letter-writing campaign, with Stark as a particular target. Some 8,000 IAM members live in Stark's district, and many of them work at nearby San Francisco Airport. The IAM's all-or-nothing approach, however, did not work.

The flight attendant unions also mounted a heavy lobbying effort. The Independent Union of Flight Attendants (IUFA), which represents Pan American flight attendants, was especially effective. IUFA members were informed of the proposed legislation in their newsletter, and sample forms of letters to their congressmen were provided. Members were urged to send letters to their own representatives, those from the districts in which they grew up, and especially to members of Stark's subcommittee.

The IUFA newsletter asked that any member who sent in such a letter send a copy of the letter and any response to the union. At the time, the IUFA had 6,500 members. Twelve hundred of them sent copies of their letters to the union. The union built files from the responses, telling who was for and who was against. Finally, the IUFA urged its members to lobby the members of Congress when they found them as passengers on their airplanes. Stark and Rostenkowski were targeted especially for this treatment.

Congressman Rostenkowski was lobbied hard, on and off airplanes. However, Rostenkowski had two daughters who were flight attendants, one for United, and one for Delta. As a parent of airline employees himself, Rostenkowski was thought by many to be reluctant to support parent passes, in that it would be viewed as a self-serving position. However, others feel that Rostenkowski used the fact of his flight attendant daughters as a convenient shield to allow him to refuse to take a position which he did not want to make.

Congressman Pete Stark also was courted assiduously. Stark has represented his district in Oakland, California since 1973. For all of that time, he has flown back to his district twice a month. As a frequent, first class passenger, Stark already was well known to the flight attendants. Therefore, when their unions told them of the proposed legislation, they knew what to do. Twice a month, on those long flights from Washington to California and back, Stark was lobbied vigorously by the flight attendants in the first class cabin.

In addition to the inflight lobbying and the mail campaign, there was a "hill visit." In the spring of 1984, the IUFA organized a two-day legislative conference in Washington. Both IUFA members and members of other flight attendant unions were invited, and about 70 people attended. Conference members were briefed on who to see and what to say. Once again, they were urged to see not only their own representatives, but representatives from the districts in which they had grown up. It was known that members of the Subcommittee on Aviation of the House Committee on Public Works and Transportation were especially friendly to the cause of the flight attendants.

After the briefing, the conference members spent an afternoon seeing members of Congress and reporting their results back to the union. Not surprisingly, it always has been easy for a flight attendant to get an appointment with a member of Congress.

As a result of all of these lobbying efforts, by the time the fringe benefit legislation was enacted in November 1984 as part of DEFRA, the tax-free treatment had been extended to airline employees, their spouses, and their dependents. That, however, left the parents. Congressman Barber Conable, another key player, did not see why the airline industry should be treated differently from other industries. Fringe benefit packages in most industries, such as employee discounts, were available to employees and their immediate families, but not the parents. Even though fringe benefits had been extended to the parents in the airline industry, Conable did not see why a special case should be made.

Congressman Stark also was opposed initially to tax-free treatment for parent passes. According to some, Stark felt that a deal had been cut. In his view, Congress already had conceded enough erosion of the tax base in allowing tax-free treatment for interline passes and passes for immediate families. In asking for tax-free treatment for parent passes as well, the airline employees were asking too much. The airline employees should have been content with the concessions granted, and terminated their lobbying effort.

The parent passes, however, were particularly important to the flight attendants. Being still predominantly young and single, many of them had no immediate families. Therefore, eliminating the tax-free treatment of parent passes was tantamount to limiting the tax-free treatment to the flight attendants themselves. This especially was true given the reaction of the airlines.

Making parent passes an item of taxable income meant further administrative burdens for the airlines. Now, every time a parent flew at free or reduced rates, the airline would have to report the bargain element of the flight as taxable income to the employee. The paperwork burden was exacerbated by the difficulties in valuing what was a unique standby pass, with no comparable passes sold in the open market. These difficulties, plus the ambivalence of some of the airlines to the passes, led them to act.

As to parent passes, the airlines reacted to DEFRA in one of three ways. Some airlines merely cancelled all parent passes. Most airlines continued parent passes, but those who had given them to employees for nothing or at a nominal price now began to charge a fee for them, usually 25 percent of the standard coach fare. Alleging that this fee was equal to the fair market value of the passes, these airlines took the position that there was no longer any bargain element, hence no reportable free parent passes, and notified its employees as to how it proposed to [treat parent discounts for tax purposes].

Interline passes had a different fate. Since they had been taxable in a prior version of the legislation, some confusion remained. As a result, most airlines cancelled all interline passes as soon as DEFRA was enacted. However, these interline passes were reinstated by some airlines once the confusion dissipated.

The Battle Shifts to IRS

During this period, the IRS was not idle. In 1983, when it became apparent that Congress would pass something, IRS knew that it would have to promulgate regulations. In the L & R Division of IRS, a supervisor approached a gathering of his underlings and asked if anyone was interested in fringe benefits. One employee, thinking that he meant the fringe benefit package of IRS employees, of course answered that she was. As a result of that misunderstanding, she was given the project.

When DEFRA was enacted, both IRS and the lobbyists set to work trying to determine how taxable passes should be valued. James Landry, General Counsel of the ATA, discovered an average system yield formulation, which had been developed by the General Accounting Office for valuation of free passes given to Amtrak employees. Delta picked up this idea, and began reporting the taxable income of parent passes at a value of 25 percent of average system yield. The same suggestion was made to IRS by ATA's counsel, Morgan, Lewis & Bockius. However, IRS and Treasury officials decided to promulgate regulations valuing free flights at 50 percent of the standard coach fare, and see what happened.

By January 1985, the first draft of the proposed regulations, valuing parent passes at 50 percent, was out. The first impact was on the telephone. In the beginning, IRS was getting 35 phone calls per hour, on this and other issues. The IRS official responsible for drafting the regulations answered every one, even though she was sometimes as much as two weeks behind in her answers. However, right behind the phone calls came the letters, postcards, and petitions.

Ultimately, more than 10,000 pages of written commentary were mailed to the IRS. Although these comments covered all of the issues raised by the proposed regulations, airline employee fringe benefits accounted for a substantial portion of the volume. Through 1985 and early 1986, over 4,100 letters and postcards were received on the topic of airline employee fringe benefits. In addition, petitions containing almost 10,000 signatures were received from airline employees.

About half of the cards and letters were generalized complaints, often in the form of standardized postcards merely stating disapproval of the proposed regulations and noting that the writer's union representatives would be following up with details. The generalized complaints that were not form postcards often exhibited considerable confusion and emotion. There was often confusion as to what was being taxed, and who was being taxed. Moreover, relatively few writers were aware of the differences between IRS' responsibility for the regulations and Congress' responsibility for the statute.

The following excerpt expresses typical sentiments, although more strongly worded than was common:

> You are a bunch of bloodsuckers!
>
> ... As a major airline employee, we are *furious* beyond words. ... My parents dedicated 20 years of their life with lots of love and care to me and my brothers and sisters and you had to go and swipe the one thing (besides my love) that I would give them in return!!! Why can't you just leave us ALONE?!

The argument of an assistant high school principal was more unique: "Because airlines strive to employ only people with impeccable character traits, I feel these parental benefits are just a small reward for parents who have done a good job of raising their children."

There were, however, quite a few letters that did comment on what IRS, not Congress, had done. These letters universally took the position that the IRS valuation of 50 percent of standard coach fares was unrealistically high. Numerous letters enclosed ads from local papers showing the latest discount fares, in order to prove that one could pay considerably less than 50 percent.

Many also pointed out that the passes were standby seats, and should be discounted accordingly. Examples of the hazards of standby were numerous. In one instance, an airline employee had arranged for her mother to fly from Pennsylvania to Australia, to visit her relatives. Her mother made it to the West Coast with no problem, but then found herself bumped off flight after flight, with the attendant costs of a hotel in Los Angeles, and long distance calls to Australia to assuage her frantic relatives. Finally, she purchased a discount flight to Honolulu, and managed to make it from there to Australia.

On the way back, she was stuck in Japan for a number of days, paying exorbitant Tokyo hotel prices while waiting for an open flight. By the time she made it back to Pennsylvania, she was 10 days beyond her vacation leave from her job. As a result, she was fired.

An American Airlines flight attendant reported that she spent three days in Honolulu International Airport trying to get on a flight to Sydney. Then she gave up. Her luggage, however, made it to Sydney, and spent a month there. This same attendant spent three days in San Francisco Airport trying to get on a flight to London. She gave up, and went to the Bahamas, instead. She enjoyed what was left of her vacation, but the sweaters and woolen pants which she had packed for London were not of much use.

Many cited a host of other restrictions on employee travel. For example, employees have no recourse if their baggage is lost, and no guarantee of a meal on a flight. In earlier days, airline employees had to comply with a dress code if they desired a free flight. All of these things arguably further reduced the value of the employee passes.

Recommendations as to valuation varied wildly. Of those making specific suggestions, the great majority keyed their suggestions to the average system yield proposals initiated by ATA and put into effect by Delta. Although some 161 letters specifically supported Delta's valuation of 25 percent of average system yield, others suggested other valuations based upon average system yield, ranging from 10 percent to 50 percent of average system yield.

Others keyed their suggestions to the standard, stated coach fare. Of the 50 letters that took this position, the bulk of them suggested either 10 percent or 25 percent of the coach fare. Other suggestions ranged as low as five percent of coach fare. Still others suggested that airline passes be valued at a flat amount, ranging from $5 per flight to $100 per flight.

One may well ask how all of these people knew to write. Presumably, very few were reading the *Federal Register* on a daily basis. The regulations did receive some coverage in the media, and this did lead to some letters.

... [I]t was not until Senator William Armstrong, R-Colo., weighed in that Congress showed movement. Being on a tax-writing committee can make all the difference. Senator Armstrong was interested in the airlines because Denver is an important hub for both United and Continental Airlines, not to mention the now defunct Frontier Airlines. Of course, he also was lobbied heavily when he travelled on airplanes.

Senator Armstrong introduced his bill on May 8, 1965. Given the reluctance of Rostenkowski and Stark to take action with respect to parent passes, it was not deemed possible to start the legislation in the House, even though tax legislation is supposed to begin there. It was clear that the bill would not pass if voted on all by itself. Moreover, as a tax bill originating in the Senate, it would have to be attached to a larger bill. The only bill going through Congress in the summer of 1985 that had an appropriate subject matter for the insertion of a tax amendment was COBRA—the Consolidated Omnibus Budget Reconciliation Act.

Once Armstrong's bill was introduced, the lobbyists went into action. The Airline Labor Coordinating Committee of the AFL-CIO was a preexisting organization which coordinated the efforts of the International Association of Machinists, the Transport Workers Union, the Brotherhood of Railway and Airline Clerks, the Air Line Pilots Association, the Flight Engineers International, and the Association of Flight Attendants. Sensing a real possibility of success, the ATA pitched in as well.

The language of Senator Armstrong's bill was inserted in the Senate version of COBRA in the Senate Finance Committee on September 9, 1985. The amendment passed, by a vote of 11 to 7. COBRA, as thus amended, passed the full Senate on November 14. Disagreement on other matters prevented final passage of the Conference Report until the next session of Congress.

At this point, it was quite clear to IRS that Congress was likely to act. The IRS was concerned that a reversion of the tax-free status of the parent passes would result in a loss of tax revenue. Thus, in part due to the mail campaign, but more due to their desire to pre-empt Congress and maintain a source of tax revenue, IRS decided in December to reduce the valuation of parent and other taxable airline passes from 50 percent of the standard coach fare to 25 percent. It was hoped that this reduction in the taxable value would reduce the pressure on Congress sufficiently so that the legislative drive would stall, and the tax base would be preserved.

Congressional supporters of the parent pass legislation, however, were aware of the IRS strategy. IRS had attempted this ploy many times before.

Had the IRS concessions been greater, it might have worked. However, the reduction from 50 percent to 25 percent was not enough.

At this point, the International Association of Machinists played a major role, on the House side. The goal was not positive support; it was simply to ensure that key figures in the House would not oppose the bill. Congressman Stark, with some 8,000 machinists in his district, again was a significant target. He had gone against the wishes of the IAM in 1983. Presumably, he could not afford to go against them again.

Therefore, on March 18 and 20, 1986, both houses agreed to the Conference Report, which essentially substituted the entire language of the Senate bill for that of the House. President Reagan signed COBRA on April, 7, 1986, and parent passes were again tax free, retroactive to January 1, 1985. . . .

Conclusion

Reams of paper, dollars and dollars of stamps, miles of walking through the corridors of the congressional office buildings. What was accomplished? The taxation of airline employee fringe benefits was tightened, and then it was returned to what it had been before.

F. OTHER TAX–FAVORED FRINGE BENEFITS

1) Employer-provided Insurance, Legal Services, Transportation, and Educational and Dependent Care Assistance

In addition to fringe benefits excluded by Section 132, Congress has from time to time mandated the statutory exclusion from income of certain other fringe benefits: term life insurance under Section 79; medical insurance under Section 106; legal services under Section 120; transportation to and from work under Section 124; educational assistance programs under Section 127; and dependent care assistance under Section 129.

In order to qualify for exclusion, the fringe benefit must generally be provided under a plan which does not discriminate in favor of highly compensated employees. Section 89. The exclusion for transportation expired after 1985. The exclusions for transportation expired after 1985. The exclusions for legal services and educational assistance are due to expire after 1988.

2) Justifications

Can the exclusion from income of the programs described above be defended on principle? One possibility is that the programs benefit, not only the direct participants, but society as well. For example, society as a whole may benefit from reduced pollution and congestion when a private employer provides mass transit for employees who ordinarily would commute to work in private cars. Do prospective social benefits justify excluding *all* these programs from taxation?

Even if incentives should be provided, why through the tax system rather than with direct grants? The precise benefit of an exclusion depends on the recipient's tax bracket and therefore varies according to income. An upper-middle-class taxpayer saves 33% on the dollar, while a lower income taxpayer saves only 15%. Does it make sense for the benefit per dollar to vary in this fashion? Doesn't this reduce the tax burden more for upper income taxpayers than for lower income taxpayers? Or can the greater reduction in tax burdens for higher income taxpayers be corrected by generally increasing tax rates that apply to them?

3) Section 125: Cafeteria Plans

Section 125, enacted in 1978, permits individual employees to choose how to allocate salary among a variety of nontaxable fringe benefits and taxable cash compensation, rather than requiring all employees to accept fringe benefits of a certain kind and amount. These arrangements are known as *cafeteria* plans because each employee is free to decide how much and what kind of each available fringe benefit portion to place on his or her salary tray. Among the excluded fringe benefits that are or have been eligible to be part of cafeteria plans are: group term life insurance; medical insurance; legal services; and dependent care assistance.

Section 125 has been criticized for loosening the usual restraints on employers providing untaxed fringe benefits in place of taxable cash salary:

> Prior to the establishment of cafeteria plans, there was a practical limitation on the extent to which employers could provide compensation to employees in the form of non-taxable fringe benefits.... The need for additional fringe benefits would differ from employee to employee. As a consequence, the provision of additional fringe benefits would be sought by some employees and opposed by others....
>
> The establishment of cafeteria plans eliminates "employee jealousy" as a constraint upon the use of fringe benefits.... Under a properly designed cafeteria plan, an employee will never bear any portion of the economic cost of fringe benefits enjoyed by other employees.... [L]ooking to the example of medical insurance, an employee will not care if another employee receives tax-free comprehensive health insurance coverage for an entire family so long as he or she can receive either cash or an equivalent amount of compensation in the form of a desired tax-free fringe benefit.[7]

---

7. Overview of Administration Proposal to Cap Exclusion for Employer-Provided Medical Care (§ 640) and of Tax Treatment of Other Fringe Benefits before the Senate Committee on Finance, 98th Cong., 1st Sess. 31 (1983) (statement of John Chapoton, Ass't. Sec. of the Treasury for Tax Policy).

Chapter 9

PERSONAL EXPENDITURES FOR CHILD CARE, MEDICAL CARE, AND CHARITY

A. SMITH v. COMMISSIONER
40 B.T.A. 1038 (1939), aff'd. without opinion,
113 F.2d 114 (2d Cir. 1940)

OPPER: Respondent determined a deficiency of $23.62 in petitioner's 1937 income tax. This was due to the disallowance of a deduction claimed by petitioners, who are husband and wife, for sums spent by the wife in employing nursemaids to care for petitioners' young child, the wife, as well as the husband, being employed. The facts have all been stipulated and are hereby found accordingly.

Petitioners would have us apply the "but for" test. They propose that but for the nurses the wife could not leave her child; but for the freedom so secured she could not pursue her gainful labors; and but for them there would be no income and no tax. This thought evokes an array of interesting possibilities. The fee to the doctor, but for whose healing service the earner of the family income could not leave his sickbed; the cost of the laborer's raiment, for how can the world proceed about its business unclothed; the very home which gives us shelter and rest and the food which provides energy, might all by an extension of the same proposition be construed as necessary to the operation of business and to the creation of income. Yet these are the very essence of those "personal" expenses the deductibility of which is expressly denied. [Section 262].

We are told that the working wife is a new phenomenon. This is relied on to account for the apparent inconsistency that the expenses in issue are now a commonplace, yet have not been the subject of legislation, ruling, or adjudicated controversy. But if that is true it becomes all the more necessary to apply accepted principles to the novel facts. We are not prepared to say that the care of children, like similar aspects of family and household life, is other than a personal concern. The wife's services as custodian of the home and protector of its children are ordinarily rendered without monetary compensation. There results no taxable income from the performance of this service and the correlative expenditure is personal and not susceptible of deduction. . . . Here the wife has chosen to employ others to discharge her domestic function and the services she performs are rendered outside the home. They are a source of actual income and taxable as such. But that does not deprive the same work performed by others of its personal character nor furnish a reason why its cost should be treated as an offset in the guise of a deductible item.

We are not unmindful that, as petitioners suggest, certain disbursements normally personal may become deductible by reason of their intimate connection with an occupation carried on for profit. In this category fall entertainment . . . and traveling expenses . . . and the cost of an actor's wardrobe. . . . The line is not always an easy one to draw nor the test simple to apply. But we think its principle is clear. It may for practical purposes be said to constitute a distinction between those activities which, as a matter of common acceptance and universal experience, are "ordinary" or usual as the direct accompaniment of business pursuits, on the one hand; and those which, though they may in some indirect and tenuous degree relate to the circumstances of a profitable occupation, are nevertheless personal in their nature, of a character applicable to human beings generally, and which exist on that plane regardless of the occupation, though not necessarily of the station in life, of the individuals concerned. . . .

In the latter category, we think, fall payments made to servants or others occupied in looking to the personal wants of their employers. . . . And we include in this group nursemaids retained to care for infant children.

B. NOTES AND QUESTIONS

1) The "But For" Argument

The taxpayer in *Smith* argued that child-care costs should be deductible as Section 162(a) business expenses, since "but for" the child care, the taxpayer could not have worked. The court rejected the "but for" argument by comparing child care to other personal consumption expenditures for clothing, food, and housing which everyone must incur in order to survive. The court's analogy is inexact, since clothing, food, and housing expenses must be incurred whether or not the taxpayer is employed, whereas child care is necessary only for employed taxpayers. Nevertheless, at the simplest causation level, "but for" food, clothing, and shelter, an individual indeed could not work. And, as the court observes, such costs have always been treated as personal consumption and have never been considered deductible business expenses.[1]

Although the court correctly states the law, doesn't it also beg the question? In theory, why shouldn't minimum survival expenses be deductible?

---

1. Wouldn't it be more exact to analogize child care to commuting? Like child care, commuting is nondeductible *and* necessary only for employed taxpayers.

One possible answer is that the minimum amount needed is accounted for by the combination of the standard deduction plus the personal exemptions of Section 151.

For 1988, this combined amount was $4,950 for a single individual, living alone, and $8,900 for a married couple with no children, filing a joint return. Do these amounts seem adequate if the purpose of the standard deduction and personal exemption is to provide, in effect, an allowance for the necessities of life? In 1988, the Bureau of the Census estimated the poverty line—the minimum annual amount needed for the bare necessities of life—at $6,036 for a single individual and at $7,985 for a married couple with no children. Should the standard deduction and exemption levels in the Internal Revenue Code be periodically adjusted to conform to the Census Bureau's poverty line estimates? Note that under Sections 63(c)(4) and 151(d)(3), the standard deduction and personal exemption are adjusted for inflation.

In addition to the standard deduction and personal exemption, taxpayers are entitled to an additional exemption for each dependent. A dependent is defined to include the taxpayer's children if the taxpayer provides more than half of their support. See Sections 151(c)(1)(B) and 152(a). For 1988, the dependency exemption equaled $1,950 and supposedly reflected the minimum annual amount needed to support a child.

2) Equity Considerations: The Imputed Income Factor

The *Smith* court noted that if a spouse stays home and provides child care, "[t]here results no taxable income from the performance of this service." Why not? The court then concluded that nontaxation when the services are provided by and for oneself does not "furnish a reason why its cost [when purchased] should be treated as ... deductible."

In stating this conclusion, the *Smith* court appears to have misunderstood the economic significance of not taxing imputed income from services. To illustrate, suppose that A and B are married, that A works for a salary of $40,000 and that B provides child care for their children, generating imputed income from services worth $20,000. Suppose further that C and D, who are also married, each earn a salary of $30,000 and also pay $20,000 for child care during the working day. Before child-care expenses, each couple has $60,000 of income. Why? After child-care expenses, each couple has $40,000 of income. Why?

The two couples appear to be in the same economic position. Yet C and D will report more taxable income than A and B, unless we either (a) tax the imputed service income generated by B (resulting in both couples reporting $60,000 of income), *or* (b) allow a deduction for the child care costs of C and D (resulting in both couples reporting $40,000 of income). Assuming that taxing imputed income from services is impractical, doesn't equity between one-earner and two-earner couples "furnish a reason why" (to use the words of *Smith*) the cost of child care in two-earner couples "should be treated as deductible"?

But if this equity argument for a child-care deduction is valid, shouldn't it also apply to *childless* two-earner couples who hire someone to do housework? To illustrate, consider the example of the following two couples without children. E and F are married; E earns a salary of $40,000, and F does housework, generating imputed income from services worth $20,000. G and H are married, each earns $30,000, and they pay someone else $20,000 to do housework. Before housework expenses, each couple has $60,000 of income; after housework expenses, each couple has $40,000. Thus, the two couples appear to be in the same economic position. Doesn't equity between one-earner and two-earner couples justify a deduction for housekeeping as well as child-care expenses of two-earner couples?

What about the fact that, ordinarily, no deduction is allowed for personal consumption expenditures even if the taxpayer might have furnished equivalent services in imputed and, therefore, nontaxable form. For example, suppose that J and K each earn a $50,000 salary and that J pays a gardener $3,000 a year for yard work, while K generates equivalent services in imputed form by taking care of his or her own backyard. K's income consists of $50,000 in salary plus $3,000 in imputed gardening services and, therefore, may appear higher than J's income which consists of $50,000 in salary. Yet, we neither tax K on the imputed service income nor allow J a deduction for expenditures on equivalent services. What is different about the comparison between one-earner and two-earner couples? Why might that difference justify a deduction for the two-earner couple in order to take account of the nontaxation of imputed income of the one-earner couple?

In 1981, Congress enacted Section 221 to permit two-earner couples—with or without children—to deduct 10% of the earnings of the spouse earning less, up to a maximum of $3,000. In 1986, Congress repealed this provision at the same time that it reduced individual tax rates (Chapter 1). Why is there less need for a two-earner deduction when marginal tax rates are lower?

3) Efficiency Considerations: Does the Income Tax Deter Parents From Entering the Work Force?

Another argument often made for the child-care deduction is based on considerations of economic efficiency. The argument assumes that the income tax distorts the decision to take care of one's children rather than to enter the work force.

> [P]arents ... are given the choice between work in the labor force, the income from which is taxable, and child care, the imputed income from which is not taxed. This is hardly a neutral system of taxation. It may induce a [parent] whose productivity in the labor force is higher than [his or her] productivity as a [parent] (measured by the fair market value of ... services as a [parent]) to stay out of the labor force even if [the parent] prefers paying work to caring for ... children. This would be an irrational allocation of labor. Normally, the price system would attract such a [parent] into the labor force but may be frustrated when the income from one kind of work is taxed, and that from another is not. ...
>
> A way to make the tax system more neutral as to a [parent's] choice of work would be to tax the imputed income which [he or she] generates. ...

> The only other solution is a child care deduction. . . . Those who see the deduction as one for a personal expense would say that it reduces the rate of income tax imposed on a [parent's] earned income below that imposed on other taxpayers. The justification is that the usual rates of income tax would have an unusually deterring effect on the entrance into the labor force of one who could work (as a parent) without being taxed at all.
>
> We do not know if the theoretical disincentive which arises from taxing labor force income, but not the imputed child care services income of a [parent], really results in a large misallocation of labor. We can calculate the income tax penalty for entering the labor force in the case of any given [parent], if we value . . . child care services and know [the] income tax bracket, but we do not know whether the income tax penalty influences a [parent's] choice of work often, sometimes, rarely, or never.[2]

It is difficult to predict the impact of a child-care deduction on the willingness of potential second-earners to enter the work force, because of what economists call the competing "substitution" and "income" effects. On the one hand, a child-care deduction increases the after-tax income from earning a given amount of salary. As a result, some individuals will decide to enter the work force rather than to stay home and care for their children. This is called a substitution effect because work in the marketplace is substituted for work in one's household.

On the other hand, a child-care deduction makes it possible to earn the same amount after-taxes by working less. As a result, other individuals will decide to spend fewer hours working than they would in the absence of a child-care deduction. This is called an income effect because work in the marketplace is reduced in order to achieve no more than a given level of after-tax income.

> [The child care deduction] obviously makes work more attractive and should tend to increase the amount of work undertaken, especially by secondary workers [the substitution effect]. . . . At the same time, however, the increase in the net income that will be earned from working a given number of hours may make additional hours of work less attractive than increased leisure. This [income] effect would tend to decrease the amount of work undertaken, at least in situations in which the number of hours of work can fairly readily be varied. Accordingly, it is not possible, a priori, to predict the net effect of the deduction on the amount of work undertaken. It does seem safe to predict that some unemployed people will be induced by the newly increased level of after-tax economic reward to join the work force, but this [substitution] effect may be offset by a reduction of working hours by other people.[3]

4) Child-care Deductions in the Code: Section 214

In 1954, Congress enacted Section 214 to authorize a deduction for child care. The deduction was available not only to two-earner couples but

---

2. Schaffer and Berman, Two Cheers for the Child Care Deduction, 28 Tax L. Rev. 535, 538–539 (1973).

3. Klein, Tax Deductions for Family Care Expenses, 14 B.C. Indus. & Com. L. Rev. 917, 935 (1973).

also to single women and divorced men. It also covered care for disabled adults, as well as for children, and therefore was designated a "*dependent care deduction.*" Initially, the maximum permissible deduction was a modest $600. For married couples, the $600 was reduced by one dollar for each dollar that adjusted gross income (AGI) rose above $4,500 and so was entirely eliminated for couples whose AGI was $5,100 or more.

Over the years, Section 214 was revised periodically, the most important changes being increases in the dollar limits. In 1964, the maximum allowable deduction rose to $900, and the AGI level at which the deduction began to be phased out went to $6,000, thereby enabling couples to obtain some benefit until their AGI exceeded $6,900. In 1971, even more dramatic changes were enacted. The maximum allowable deduction was increased to $4,800, the AGI phase-out level rose to $18,000, and the phase-out rate was cut in half. For every two dollars that AGI exceeded $18,000, the allowable deduction was reduced by only one dollar. Thus, some benefit was available until a married couple's AGI exceeded $27,600.

5) The Child-care Credit: Section 21

In 1976, Congress repealed the Section 214 deduction and in its place substituted a *credit* for dependent care expenses. What is the basic difference between a deduction and a credit? A deduction reduces taxable income. Therefore, the benefit depends on the taxpayer's marginal rate. A $1,000 deduction saves a 50% bracket taxpayer $500 but saves a 15% bracket taxpayer only $150. A credit, on the other hand, directly reduces tax liability. For example, a $500 credit enables the taxpayer to reduce the amount he or she owes in tax payments by $500. Therefore, the amount saved is the same for both the 50% and the 15% bracket taxpayer, provided only that both owe at least the amount of the credit in taxes.

The dependent care credit—now contained in Section 21—equals 30% of dependent care expenses, which include "household services" as well as dependent care. Section 21(b)(2). The percentage allowed as a credit is reduced by one percentage point for each $2,000 (or fraction thereof) by which the taxpayer's AGI exceeds $10,000. However, the allowable percentage may not fall below 20%, regardless of the size of AGI. Section 21(a)(2). To illustrate, the allowable percentage is 30% for taxpayers with an AGI of $10,000 or less, declines to 21% as AGI rises to $28,000, and remains at the 20% level for all taxpayers with AGI over $28,000. Thus, some benefit is available, no matter how high a taxpayer's AGI.

Whatever the applicable percentage, however, Section 21 permits a maximum of $4,800 in expenses to be taken into account in computing the credit. Section 21(c). Thus, the maximum allowable credit is 30% of $4,800 or $1,440.

6) Comparing the Effects of a Deduction versus a Credit

Consider three taxpayers, A, B and C, each of whom spends $1,000 on child care. Assume that child-care expenses are fully deductible for all three. If A is in the 33% bracket, what is the benefit to A of the $1,000 deduction?

If B is in the 28% bracket, what is the benefit to B? If C is in the 15% bracket, what is the benefit to C? Is the deduction arguably a perverse method of furnishing federal aid for child care?

On the other hand, suppose instead that there is a credit for 25% of child care expenses. What is the benefit to A? to B? to C? Does the credit appear to provide a better way of providing child care benefits? But what about D, who also spends $1,000 on child care, but whose taxable income is below the sum of the standard deduction plus D's personal and dependency exemptions? In that case—in which D's income is taxed at a zero rate—does D derive any benefit from a credit at all?

What economic class was the primary beneficiary of the original version of Section 214, enacted in 1954? Of the increase in the dollar limits in 1964 and then in 1971? What economic class is the primary beneficiary of Section 21? Have low-income groups—at or below the poverty line—benefited from these provisions? Why not? Don't both a deduction and a credit fail to provide any assistance whatsoever to those who owe very little or nothing in taxes and, presumably, have the greatest need? Is the tax system the proper medium for providing federal child-care assistance?

7) Other Tax Policy Considerations and Sections 214 and 21

Might the dollar limits imposed on Section 214 and the replacement of the Section 214 deduction with the Section 21 credit indicate a judgment that a greater share of federal tax assistance for child care should be targeted toward lower- and middle-income groups? But if one accepts the equity or efficiency arguments for a child care deduction, do the dollar limits and the adoption of a credit make any sense? Or might they reflect a conviction that as AGI rises, both the equity and efficiency arguments for a child-care allowance become less compelling?

8) Dependent Care as a Nontaxable Fringe Benefit

Section 129 permits an employee to exclude up to $5,000 of dependent care assistance paid for by one's employer.[4] In order to qualify for the exclusion, the dependent care plan must "not discriminate in favor of employees who are highly compensated" and also must satisfy other non-discrimination requirements specified in Section 129(d).

What economic class do you suppose to be the chief beneficiary of Section 129? What is the maximum benefit available to a 33% bracket taxpayer? A 28% bracket taxpayer? A 15% bracket taxpayer?

---

4. As originally enacted in 1981, the amount of the Section 129 exclusion was limited (a) in the case of unmarried taxpayers, to the earned income of the taxpayer and (b) in the case of married taxpayers, to the lesser of the earned income of the taxpayer or the taxpayer's spouse. Section 129(b). The additional $5,000 cap was added a year later. Section 129(a)(2). Query: If the value of employer-provided dependent care exceeds $5,000, can the employee claim a percentage of the excess as a credit under Section 21? See Section 21(c).

9) The Section 32 Earned Income Credit

Section 32 provides a credit for low-income taxpayers equal to a percentage of their earned income. Section 32 has a number of interesting features. Although taxpayers must have at least one dependent child to qualify, the credit is not contingent on child care expenditures. Even taxpayers who pay nothing for child care are eligible. In addition, the credit is *refundable*. If it exceeds the tax owed, the Treasury issues the "taxpayer" a check for the excess amount.

The credit equals 14% of earned income up to $5,714 (or a maximum of $800). Once either earned income or AGI exceeds $9,000, a reduction of the credit begins so that it is fully phased out when taxable income reaches $17,000. The Code provides for inflation adjustments in these dollar amounts.

Why is a refundable credit a better method of providing benefits to low-income individuals than either a deduction or an ordinary nonrefundable credit? How does a refundable credit appear to compare with a direct expenditure program, such as Aid to Families with Dependent Children (AFDC)?

C. THE TAX EXPENDITURE CONCEPT

The tax expenditure concept—the idea that tax preferences are the functional equivalent of direct expenditures—was popularized by Professor Stanley Surrey, who served as Assistant Secretary of the Treasury for Tax Policy in the Kennedy and Johnson administrations. As he explained it:

> The federal income tax system consists really of two parts: one part comprises the structural provisions necessary to implement the income tax . . .; the second part comprises a system of tax expenditures under which Governmental financial assistance programs are carried out through special tax provisions rather than through direct Government expenditures. This second system is grafted on to the structure of the income tax proper; it has no basic relation to that structure and is not necessary to its operation. Instead, the system of tax expenditures provides a vast subsidy apparatus that uses the mechanics of the income tax as the method of paying the subsidies. The special provisions under which the subsidy apparatus functions take a variety of forms, covering exclusions from income, exemptions, deductions, credits against tax, preferential rates of tax, and deferrals of tax.
>
> These special tax provisions serve ends which are similar in nature to those served in the same or other areas by direct government expenditures in the form of grants, loans, interest subsidies, and federal insurance or guarantees of private loans. The interplay is such that for any given program involving federal monetary assistance, the program may be structured to use the tax system to provide that assistance—where it will usually be called a "tax incentive"—or structured to use a direct Government expenditure. As a consequence of history, design, lack of analysis, and similar factors our present tax system is replete with these special provisions, or tax expendi-

tures, under which many existing Government assistance programs operate through the tax system rather than the direct expenditure route.

The tax expenditure concept in essence considers these special provisions as composed of two elements: the imputed tax payment that would have been made in the absence of the special provision ... and the simultaneous expenditure of that payment as a direct grant to the person benefited by the special provision.[5]

As Professor Surrey indicates, the tax expenditure concept depends on a critical distinction between:

a) income-defining provisions of the Code, which help to refine the proper amount subject to tax, and

b) other provisions which represent departures from the proper definition of income and therefore are tax expenditures.

There is considerable controversy over whether this distinction can be made with enough objectivity to justify labeling designated Code provisions as "tax expenditures."

> There are many problem areas in which the search for "preferences" is doomed to fail because we cannot confidently say which provisions are "rules" and which are "exceptions." In these areas, we cannot comply with [the] advice to "lean over backward" to avoid "[tax] preferences" because, in the absence of a generally acceptable or scientifically determinable vertical, we cannot know whether we are leaning forward or backward. The central source of difficulty is the fact that the income tax structure cannot be discovered, but must be constructed; it is the final result of a multitude of debatable judgments.
>
> If we were dealing not with an income tax but with a tax whose label described its reach with greater precision, an "exception" would be easier to identify. For example, in constructing a poll tax, we would have at the outset a consensus on what constitutes a natural person whose "head" is to be taxed. To be sure, even here there would be marginal cases—conceived but unborn children, persons who have been legally declared dead but who reappear, Siamese twins and so on. These peripheral cases aside, a consensus on the base to which the tax is to be applied would be feasible, and it would warrant the use of terms like "exception" [or "tax expenditure"] to describe proposals to exempt from the tax such persons as children, foreign tourists and diplomats, or incompetents. ... When we turn to the field of income taxation, however, we do not begin with a consensus on the meaning of income, but with a myriad of arguments about what should be taxed, when, and to whom.[6]

Do you believe that a child-care deduction should be classified as an income-defining provision or as a tax expenditure? If the child-care deduction is considered an income-defining provision, would there be any justification for the dollar limits imposed in Section 214 or for the replacement of the deduction with the Section 21 credit? Might the dollar limits

---

5. S. Surrey, Pathways To Tax Reform, 6–7 (1973).
6. Bittker, A "Comprehensive Tax Base" as a Goal of Income Tax Reform, 80 Harv. L. Rev. 925, 985 (1967).

and the eventual adoption of a credit reflect uncertainty about how to classify an allowance for child care?

Whatever the difficulty of distinguishing income-defining provisions from tax expenditures, it seems indisputable that the income tax system is a major vehicle for providing federal financial assistance. This observation is based on both economic theory and political reality.

A basic axiom of public finance is that equivalent financial benefits can be furnished by government either through a tax provision or through direct aid. Consider three examples of support for higher education: tuition subsidies, assistance for teachers' salaries, and aid that supplements private donations. Tuition could be subsidized either by reimbursing parents with cash or by allowing them a tax deduction or credit for higher education tuition. Grants could be provided for teachers' salaries, or teachers could be allowed special tax benefits. Gifts to schools from private donors could be matched by government grants, or instead a tax deduction or credit could be permitted for private donations. It is therefore evident that the benefits of a direct expenditure program could alternatively be provided through the tax system.

Political reality confirms this principle of public finance. When particular groups request direct federal assistance, Congress will typically consider the tax system as an alternative vehicle for furnishing the requested aid.

D. GENERAL ACCOUNTING OFFICE, TAX EXPENDITURES: A PRIMER 1–2 (1979)

The Federal Government sponsors many programs to promote the health of its citizens. They include such familiar examples as Medicare and Medicaid, the medical research programs of the National Institutes of Health, and the medical care provided in Veterans Administration hospitals. A less familiar program is one in which the Government forgoes $3 billion of revenue to assist one-fifth of the population to pay its medical and dental bills. This program's benefits are somewhat oddly structured; the program gives no benefits to persons unless their medical bills exceed 3 percent of their income, then pays 14 to 18 percent of the excess to low income persons, 20 to 30 percent of the excess to middle income persons, and nearly 70 percent of the excess to persons with the highest incomes. The program's best feature is administrative simplicity: the beneficiary does not have to apply to a Government office and wait for approval and payment; instead he simply reduces his income tax. Since the percentage of medical expenses above the floor that is borne by the Government is by law equal to the highest income tax rates paid by the beneficiary, and since the program applies only to persons who itemize deductions on their income tax returns, the reduction in taxes is accomplished by including medical expenses in the taxpayers' itemized deductions.

The Government's dedication of money to an activity by allowing a special reduction in taxes rather than a direct payment is called a "tax expenditure." Looking at provisions of the tax law this way emphasizes their similarity to direct expenditures and suggests that the Federal revenue losses they create could be "budgeted" the way direct expenditures are. By implication, they *must* be accounted for in the budget process if the total Government effort in a program area is to be known. This is the concept of the "tax expenditures budget," which was added to the budget-making process by the Congressional Budget and Impoundment Control Act of 1974.

The tax expenditures concept is merely one way of looking at tax provisions. The Congressmen who enacted the deduction for medical expenses probably did not think of themselves as appropriating money to pay some taxpayers' medical bills. The deduction is identified as a tax expenditure because its effect is to subsidize medical care (regardless of its original purpose).

Identifying such effects as subsidies is exactly the reason for constructing tax expenditures budgets. By lumping together the total Government support for an activity, including direct payments, loans, loan guarantees, and tax expenditures, it is possible to evaluate that support in ways that might not otherwise be apparent. One type of support may be far more (or less) effective than others, leading to a restructuring of the support. The effects of the tax expenditure may conflict with the goals of the direct payment programs, and hence one or the other should be changed. It might be that the existence of one type of program makes another redundant. Both tax expenditure and direct expenditure policies can benefit from this type of analysis. . . .

E. THE MEDICAL EXPENSE DEDUCTION

Andrews, Personal Deductions in an Ideal Income Tax, 86 Harv. L. Rev. 309, 309–313, 331, 333, 335–337 (1972)

A variety of provisions in the income tax law are now described as tax expenditures and evaluated as if they involved direct government expenditures equivalent in amount and distribution to the revenue reduction they produce. The medical expense deduction, for example, is described as the equivalent of a direct expenditure program by which the federal government provides partial reimbursement for extraordinary medical expenses. So viewed, of course, the provision seems to reflect an upside-down idea of policy because the rate of reimbursement is the taxpayer's marginal tax rate; this results in relatively generous rates of reimbursement for the well-to-do, while it provides nothing at all for the very poor who presumably have the greatest need.

Similarly, the charitable contribution deduction has been described as a kind of government matching gift program for the support of taxpayers' charities. Again the distribution of matching grants is effectively skewed to favor the charities of the wealthy because of their higher marginal tax rates: in the 70% bracket, for example, the Government contributes $70 to match the taxpayer's $30 contribution, while in the 20% bracket the Government's matching grant is only $20 for each $80 contributed by the taxpayer. Furthermore, there are other difficulties. Presumably, we would not permit direct government expenditures to provide matching gifts for churches. And if we were to have programs of direct support for other charities, it seems likely that we would insist upon a much more rigorous evaluation of priorities than the tax expenditure mechanism provides.

These are devastating criticisms. If they are correct, it seems to me the provisions in question are indefensible. But my feeling is that the criticisms are somehow overstated and that more sense can be made out of these two provisions than tax expenditure analysis immediately indicates. . . .

The principal lesson to be derived from the tax expenditure analysis, I think, is that deductions (or exclusions) in the individual income tax are inferior devices for implementing objectives extraneous to those of the tax itself. This is mostly because of graduated rates. It will not generally make sense to distribute government funds according to the graduated rates in the personal income tax unless the purpose of the distribution is intrinsically related to the distribution of tax burdens that those rates are designed to effect.

But this lesson makes it imperative to focus very carefully upon the question whether the purposes underlying a particular provision are indeed extraneous to the purposes of the tax. Put the other way, it makes it imperative to consider carefully whether a provision can be defended by reference to intrinsic matters of tax policy before evaluating it as if it were something else. The tax expenditure analysis itself does not lead us to focus on that question because characterization as a tax expenditure and analogy to a direct expenditure generally imply that the provision serves purposes outside those of the tax system. The crucial judgment about underlying purpose tends, therefore, to get made by implication when a provision is classified as a tax expenditure, before the analysis itself begins. . . .

Since 1942 our income tax law has allowed a deduction for medical expenses. . . .

The medical expense deduction has been called a tax preference, and the reduction in tax liabilities it produces is commonly listed as a tax expenditure. The notion is that the tax law is merely being used as a device to provide partial reimbursement of medical expenses. Viewed in this way, of course, the deduction appears to represent a perverse means of distributing government funds since it has the effect of reimbursing a higher percentage of medical expenses for wealthy taxpayers than for poor taxpayers, who presumably have the greater need.

But this analysis is inadequate. Essentially, it assumes away the best reasons for the deduction by taking a tax on income without a medical expense deduction as its norm and asserting that any departure from that norm must rest on purposes extraneous to those of the tax. I believe we can come to a better understanding of this deduction, and of what an ideal personal income tax would be like, by asking whether there are good, intrinsic reasons for elaborating the notion of taxable consumption—the consumption component of taxable personal income—in a way that excludes medical services, so that the medical expense deduction is a device for approaching the ideal, not a departure from it. . . .

*The Case for Excluding Medical Services
from Personal Consumption as a Component of Taxable Income*

The medical expense deduction should be evaluated primarily by considering whether there are good reasons to exclude medical services generally from the category of taxable personal consumption. Or perhaps the issue is more clearly expressed the other way around: are there sound reasons to define or elaborate the category of personal consumption, as a component of an ideal personal tax base, so as to exclude medical services? . . .

. . . [D]ifferences in health affect relative material well-being. It would be impractical to try to include robust good health directly as an element of personal consumption for those who have it, but the difference between good and poor health can be partially reflected—or the failure to include the difference directly can be partially offset—by also excluding or allowing a deduction for the medical services that those in poorer health will generally need more of.

Put a slightly different way, medical services are in the end only a means, an intermediate good whose ultimate object is good health. The right basis for making interpersonal welfare comparisons on which to base the distribution of tax burdens is that ultimate object, good health, rather than the intermediate good. Furthermore, it is not expedient to take medical services as a proxy for the ultimate object, good health, because it is not the case, at least between people in otherwise similar financial circumstances, that good health will vary in direct proportion to medical services utilized. If anything, the relation is apt to go the other way. . . .

What distinguishes medical expenses from other personal expenses at bottom is a sense that large differences in their magnitude between people in otherwise similar circumstances are apt to reflect differences in need rather than choices among gratifications. The distinction holds, to be sure, only as a general matter. First, people may need different amounts of food, for example, because of differences in physical make-up. Yet we do not allow any deduction for food, presumably because we think substantial differences in expenditures for food mostly reflect differences in taste and means. As a further complication, some of the people with a greater need for food may get greater pleasure out of life by reason of their greater appetite or greater size or higher energy levels. It is impossible to make any generalization about whether a large appetite is a boon or a burden, let alone to assign it any monetary value.

Second, particular medical expenses may reflect a considerable component of voluntary personal gratification. It is difficult to find any difference in principle, for example, between expenditures for elective plastic surgery and for cosmetics. But such borderline difficulties are inevitable whatever general policies we choose to pursue. Taxation in particular, like politics in general, is the art of the possible. It seems reasonable to act upon the proposition that disease or injury is a burden, not a boon, and that large differences in utilization of medical services go less than all the way toward offsetting differences in health and need. This is, in any event, the judgment on which defense of the deduction ultimately depends. . . .

F. MATTES v. COMMISSIONER
77 T.C. 650 (1981)

[Editor's Note: Consider whether the opinion in this case affects the argument that the medical expense deduction is an income-defining provision.]

WILBUR, JUDGE: ... The sole issue for our decision is whether the expense of a surgical hair transplant performed by a physician qualifies as a deductible medical expense under section 213. ...

In January 1976, petitioner, a 24-year-old male who suffered from premature baldness, began the process of surgical hair transplants which was completed in October 1976 at a total cost to him of $1,980. Petitioner underwent the surgery for purely cosmetic reasons, and his general emotional well-being was improved as a result of the hair transplants.

Hair transplantation is a surgical procedure whereby small plugs of tissue are transferred surgically from one part of the scalp to another part of the scalp. This procedure requires specialized training and is performed, for the most part, by dermatologists and, to a lesser extent, by plastic surgeons.

The surgical hair transplants were performed on the petitioner by a physician, Herbert L. Kronthal, M.D., at his office and involved the use of a local anesthetic. Under Maryland law, surgical hair transplants are required to be performed by a licensed physician.

Male pattern baldness, medically termed androgenic alopecia, is a physiological condition caused by normal levels of androgenic steroids acting on follicles that are genetically predisposed to shed hair. There are no commercially available drugs which will effectively treat pattern baldness. The surgical hair transplant technique is widely accepted in the medical community as an effective treatment for male pattern baldness, baldness from scars due to accidents, operations, or radiation, and baldness due to inflammatory or infectious diseases of the scalp. Various complications can arise subsequent to the surgery such as scalp infection, scarring, osteomyelitis of the skull, and local trauma.

On his return for 1976, petitioner claimed the $1,980 expended by him for the surgical hair transplants as a medical expense in computing his allowable medical expense deduction. ...

Petitioner contends simply that since the respondent has ruled that facelifts are a deductible medical expense, this Court should accord similar treatment for hair transplantations. We find on the basis of the statute, regulations, and case law that the surgical hair transplantation undergone by petitioner is a deductible medical expense.

Section 213(a) provides a deduction for expenses paid for "medical care," a term defined in section 213(e)(1) as follows:

> (1) The term "medical care" means amounts paid—
> (A) for the diagnosis, cure, mitigation, treatment, or prevention of disease, or for the purpose of affecting any structure or function of the body.

Medical care is further defined in section 1.213–1(e)(1), Income Tax Regs.:

> (e) *Definitions*—(1) *General.* (i) The term "medical care" includes the diagnosis, cure, mitigation, treatment, or prevention of disease. Expenses paid for "medical care" shall include those paid for the purpose of affecting any structure or function of the body or for transportation primarily for and essential to medical care. . . .
>
> (ii) Amounts paid for operations or treatments affecting any portion of the body, including obstetrical expenses and expenses of therapy or X-ray treatments, are deemed to be for the purpose of affecting any structure or function of the body and are therefore paid for medical care. Amounts expended for illegal operations or treatments are not deductible. Deductions for expenditures for medical care allowable under section 213 will be confined strictly to expenses incurred primarily for the prevention or alleviation of a physical or mental defect or illness. Thus, payments for the following are payments for medical care: Hospital services, nursing services (including nurses' board where paid by the taxpayer), medical, laboratory, surgical, dental and other diagnostic and healing services, X-rays, medicine and drugs . . . artificial teeth or limbs, and ambulance hire. However, an expenditure which is merely beneficial to the general health of an individual, such as an expenditure for a vacation, is not an expenditure for medical care.

The statutory definition of medical care is a broad one, encompassing amounts paid either for the treatment of a disease or for the purpose of affecting any structure of the body. Since it cannot be doubted that the scalp is a part of the human body, the transplantation of hair from one portion of the scalp to another through a surgical procedure certainly affects a structure of the body. Furthermore, we think it is clear that the hair transplant operation undergone by petitioner was a treatment for a specific physical defect, that of baldness, medically termed alopecia. The most common type of baldness is male pattern baldness, medically termed androgenic alopecia. Such baldness is caused by normal levels of androgenic steroids acting on follicles that are generally predisposed to shed hair. Therefore, hair transplantation is a treatment for a physical defect within the meaning of "medical care."

Respondent however emphasizes the fact that since petitioner underwent the hair transplant for purely cosmetic reasons the cost of the procedure was essentially a nondeductible personal expense. We cannot agree. Of course, there is the need to distinguish between those expenses which are primarily medical in nature and those which are personal. Indeed, courts have long been forced to draw such a line in situations where the character of the expense is a personal one, that is, one that is normally expended in the ordinary course of one's life without health care motives. Commissioner v. Bilder . . . (Florida living expenses incurred by taxpayer who suffered from a severe heart condition and who was ordered by his doctor to abandon his home and legal practice in order to spend the winter months in Florida not deductible under sec. 213); *Randolph v. Commissioner,* . . . (difference in cost between a normal diet and a special, medically prescribed diet deductible).

The regulations preclude a deduction of expenses for personal enjoyment disguised as a medical expense. Thus, "an expenditure which is *merely* beneficial to the general health of an individual, such as an expenditure for a vacation, is not an expenditure for medical care." Sec. 1.213–1(e)(1)(ii), Income Tax Regs. (Emphasis added.) In short, the tension between section 213 and section 262 exists where an expense is personal in nature and "merely" beneficial to the taxpayer's general emotional or spiritual well-being without having a direct or proximate therapeutic relation to the bodily condition in question. See, e.g., *Adler v. Commissioner,* . . . (cost of dancing lessons which taxpayer considered therapy for his varicose veins not deductible as medical expenses); *Brown v. Commissioner,* . . . (expenses incurred in Scientology processing were not deductible since they were for taxpayers' "spiritual well-being" and not for the purpose of alleviating a specific illness); *Ring v. Commissioner,* . . . (expenses incurred for a trip to the Shrine of Our Lady of Lourdes (France) to seek spiritual help to alleviate physical defect were not deductible).

In the instant case, however, the character of the expense was wholly medical in nature. The hair transplant operation was a specific medical treatment to alleviate a specific condition of the body. In fact, the regulations in stating that "Deductions for expenditures for medical care allowable under section 213 will be confined strictly to expenses incurred primarily for the . . . alleviation of a physical . . . defect (sec. 1.213–1(e)(1)(ii), Income Tax Regs.), cite surgical service as an example of such deductible medical care payment. Hair transplantation is a surgical procedure whereby small cylinders of hair-bearing scalp are transferred surgically from the occipital area of the scalp to the bald area. This procedure involves local anesthesia and is performed in the doctor's office. The procedure requires specialized training, and, under Maryland law, surgical hair transplants are required to be performed by a licensed physician. In fact, medical expertise is especially necessary in view of the myriad complications that could arise subsequent to such surgery such as scalp infection, scarring, osteomyelitis of the skull, and local trauma. In addition, since there are no commercially available drugs which will effectively restore hair growth, surgical procedures remain the only acceptable means of alleviating alopecia.

Admittedly, the decision to undergo hair transplantation stems from a personal choice. Living with baldness does not constitute a risk to one's health. Baldness may in fact be appealing to some. Nonetheless, the fact that the surgical procedure of hair transplantation was undertaken by petitioner for cosmetic reasons and that the efficacy of the procedure undoubtedly improved petitioner's general well-being does not render the expense personal and thus nondeductible. Rather, since the expense is for a medical surgical procedure to correct a specific physiological condition, performed in accordance with usual physician practice, it is deductible under section 213 without the necessity of examining a taxpayer's motive for undergoing such treatment. In such context, we need not draw the fine line between medical and personal expenses. Accordingly, we hold that petitioner is allowed to deduct the cost of the hair transplant as a medical expense under section 213.

G. NOTES AND QUESTIONS

1) Is the Medical Expense Deduction an Income-defining Provision or a Tax Expenditure?

Consider five individuals—A, B, C, D, and E. A earns a salary of $40,000 a year and is in perfect health. B earns $20,000 and is also in perfect health. A, with more income, will be taxed more heavily than B. C earns $40,000 and spends $20,000 on coronary bypass surgery. Should C be taxed like A or B? D earns $40,000 and spends $20,000 on elective cosmetic surgery. Should D be taxed like A or B? What about E, who earns only $20,000 and needs coronary bypass surgery, but cannot afford it and therefore goes without?

How do you react to the argument that the medical expense deduction should be regarded as an income-defining provision rather than as a "tax expenditure"? Is allowing a deduction for the cost of coronary bypass surgery consistent with this argument? Is allowing a deduction for the cost of cosmetic surgery, as in *Mattes*?

2) The Significance of Private Health Insurance

The majority of Americans have private insurance to cover medical bills. The proportion of taxpayers with private medical insurance coverage rises with income. Higher income taxpayers are more likely to have medical insurance than lower income taxpayers. Moreover, the quality of the coverage also increases with income. The medical insurance of higher income taxpayers is likely to provide significantly better coverage than the insurance of lower income taxpayers.

When insurance pays for medical bills, the amounts are generally excluded from the beneficiary's gross income by Section 104 or Section 105. What justifies excluding these amounts from income? Is it the same as the argument for viewing the medical expense deduction as an income-defining provision?

An insured individual may claim a Section 213 deduction only for expenditures *not* covered by health insurance. Section 213(a). How does this observation affect the argument for viewing the medical expense deduction as an income-defining provision? Does it suggest that when an *insured* taxpayer claims a Section 213 deduction, it is likely to be for elective, rather than necessary, medical care, particularly if the taxpayer is in an upper income group? According to a Congressional Budget Office Study:

> Where outlays for necessary uninsured services are concerned, the ability of the deduction to subsidize uninsured medical expenses promotes taxation on the basis of taxpayers' ability to pay. However, the deduction can also subsidize the cost of elective medical items not generally covered by insurance, such as cosmetic surgery and elaborate physical examinations. In these cases, the deduction serves more to promote consumption of medical care than to fill important gaps left by private health insurance.[7]

---

7. Congressional Budget Office, Tax Subsidies for Medical Care: Current Policies and Possible Alternatives 35 (1980).

As a result, the study concludes:

> With the rapid growth of health insurance ... the medical deduction has become for many families a source of tax subsidies for medical costs not covered by their health-insurance policies. For affluent households, who are the primary beneficiaries of the deduction, it can provide generous subsidies for plastic surgery ... and other types of elective care. Thus, it may be more reasonable to view the deduction as a tax subsidy than as an [income-defining] provision.[8]

Should Section 213 be amended to take account of differences between insured and uninsured taxpayers? For example, should the deduction be unavailable to taxpayers who are already insured and are more likely to be deducting the cost of elective medical care? What about the fact that some medical insurance may only pay a stated percentage (for example, 80%) of medical costs and require the insured to pay the balance? Or that some medical insurance plans may not cover even necessary medical expenses that exceed a fixed dollar amount?

3) Statutory Limits on Medical Expense Deductions

The reader should note that Section 213(a), as revised in 1986, permits the taxpayer to deduct uninsured medical costs only in excess of 7.5% of AGI. (The floor has been gradually raised over the years from 3% of AGI, to 5%, and now to 7.5%.) Is the floor consistent with the view of the deduction as an income-defining provision? Will the floor effectively deter the deduction of the costs of elective medical care—such as cosmetic surgery and psychoanalysis—which are generally not covered by medical insurance?

In addition, the medical expense deduction may be claimed only by taxpayers who itemize their Section 63 deductions instead of claiming the standard deduction. Is that result consistent with either the income-defining or the tax expenditure view of the deduction?

4) The Exclusion for Employer-provided Health Insurance: Section 106

Although the cost of insurance is considered a Section 213 medical expense, it will rarely exceed the 7.5% of AGI floor. Thus, if a taxpayer purchases medical insurance on his or her own, the cost in general may not be deducted. However, if medical insurance is provided by the taxpayer's employer, the employee will not be taxed on the value of the insurance provided that certain coverage and nondiscrimination requirements are met. Section 106(a). In this regard, employer-provided medical insurance resembles other tax-favored employee fringe benefits, such as for dependent care under Section 129 (discussed earlier in this chapter). But unlike dependent care and most other tax-favored fringe benefits, there is no limit on the amount of coverage that can be excluded.

---

8. Ibid. at xv.

Assuming that Section 106 is a tax expenditure, can it be justified? Which economic class benefits most and which benefits least from Section 106? Is that an equitable way to subsidize medical insurance? Even if the benefits were distributed differently, why should middle- and upper-income workers receive any subsidy for medical insurance at all? What is the aggregate effect of Section 106 on the after-tax cost of medical insurance? Why might a lower after-tax cost tend to encourage the overconsumption of medical services? Consider the following comments from a Congressional Budget Office study:

> The ... exclusion exempts from taxable income all employer contributions to health and accident insurance plans. ... Employees, therefore, receive a discount equal to their marginal tax rate for each dollar of health insurance purchased through employer contributions. This saving provides a powerful incentive for employees to bargain for employer-provided health and accident insurance. It also encourages employers to provide ... health coverage, since a dollar of direct cash compensation [which is taxable] may be less attractive to employees than a smaller amount of employer-provided health benefits [which is not]. ...
>
> [T]he employer exclusion ... has adverse consequences for the level of medical spending. The exclusion encourages employees to buy more health insurance coverage than they otherwise would, and this in turn encourages more frequent use and more elaborate forms of medical care. As a result, total medical expenditures tend to increase. The incentive to obtain more health insurance is particularly strong because employer contributions are excluded from taxable income without limit. This feature of the exclusion [tends to eliminate] most of the incentive to choose health insurance with cost-containment features.[9]
>
> The exclusion of employers' health contributions from taxable income generates higher medical spending, to the extent it brings about greater health insurance coverage. Coverage, in turn, tends to stimulate medical spending in at least three ways. First, because it lowers the out-of-pocket cost of health care, it encourages consumers to seek care. Second, it reduces patients' awareness of and sensitivity to the difference in price among providers. Third, by lowering the risk of nonpayment, insurance promotes unconstrained use of costly forms of care. When insurance covers the full cost of care, as is true for inpatient hospital care under many current plans, doctors in particular have little incentive to restrain costs. On the contrary, they are encouraged to order more tests and use more services, because the gains from saving money are small while the risks in potential malpractice liability for deferring services are great. The cumulative effect of these patterns, many analysts believe, contributes significantly to inflation in the medical sector.[10]
>
> Besides its adverse effect on medical spending, the exclusion has other defects. For example, the tax savings generated by the exclusion are concentrated disproportionately among persons with higher incomes, since the rate of tax subsidy equals the employee's marginal tax rate and tax rates rise with taxable income.[11]

9. Ibid. at xi.
10. Ibid. at 13.
11. Ibid. at xii.

The employer exclusion has two effects on tax liabilities that could be said to create inequities in the tax system. First, the exclusion favors persons who receive part of their incomes in the form of health benefits over those whose earnings come entirely in taxable forms.... Although the differences in tax liabilities are not great for low- and moderate-income families, they can be significant for workers in relatively high marginal tax brackets. A worker in the 40% bracket, for example, whose employer offers a health insurance plan worth $500, saves $200 in income taxes as a result of the exclusion....

Second, the exclusion also tends to reduce the progressivity of the income tax. Because tax benefits from the exclusion of income depend on a taxpayer's marginal tax rate, upper-income taxpayers with employer-provided health plans benefit more from the exclusion than do other workers. For example, the hypothetical employee in the 40 percent marginal tax bracket, whose employer contributes $500 a year to a health plan, receives $200 in tax savings from the exclusion. Another worker with the same health benefits but with a marginal tax rate of only 20 percent saves only $100. The exclusion also benefits upper-income taxpayers more than others to the extent that upper-income employees work for organizations that provide more generous health insurance packages.[12]

Do these criticisms assume that the Section 106 exclusion for employer-provided health insurance is a tax expenditure? Would the criticisms remain valid if Section 106 were regarded as an income-defining provision? Can the arguments for viewing the medical expense deduction as an income-defining provision be applied to justify the exclusion of employer-provided health insurance? Is there any plausible argument for regarding the exclusion as income-defining? Or can a persuasive case be made that Section 106 is almost without question a "true" tax expenditure?

H. THE CHARITABLE CONTRIBUTION DEDUCTION

Andrews, Personal Deductions in an Ideal Income Tax, 86 Harv. L. Rev. 309, 344–349, 352, 354–358, 370 (1972)

Since 1917 a deduction has been allowed for contributions to religious, educational, and charitable organizations. The deduction is subject to some rather complicated but relatively generous percentage limitations; it also contains some quite complicated provisions and restrictions dealing with contributions of appreciated property and of limited interests in property. . . .

The charitable contribution deduction is generally described as a subsidy to charitable giving and thus to the activities of qualified charitable organizations. The effect of the deduction has been likened to a matching gift program under which an employer makes matching gifts to charities supported by its employees. There is something peculiar, of course, about the Government spending funds with so little control over their allocation or use. Furthermore, this is an unusual matching gift program because the rate at which gifts are matched varies directly with the taxpayer's marginal tax rate bracket; wealthy taxpayers find their gifts much more generously

---

12. Ibid. at 9–10.

matched than do lower bracket taxpayers. A 70% bracket taxpayer can make a $100 contribution at an after-tax cost of only $30; by way of tax reduction, therefore, the Government can be seen as contributing $70 to match the taxpayer's $30, for a matching rate of 233%. By similar computation, a 40% bracket taxpayer will find that the Government provides a matching grant of only $40 for his charitable contributions of $60, or a 66 ⅔% matching rate; a 20% bracket taxpayer will find the Government's rate for matching his contributions to be only $1 for every $4 he contributes, or 25%; and one too poor to pay any income tax in any event will find the Government unwilling to make any matching grant at all. . . .

But I do not believe, nor do I think most serious practical students of the subject believe, that the charitable contribution deduction is as irrational as this explanation makes it sound. To be sure, there are anomalies arising out of the allowance of a deduction for the fair market value of appreciated property without any offsetting recognition of gain. But as to simple cash contributions, the charitable deduction makes more sense than tax expenditure analysis would indicate. If we want our theories to express our judgments, therefore, we should seek to give the deduction a better explanation.

As in the case of the medical expense deduction, there are substantial grounds for excluding from our definition of taxable personal consumption whatever satisfactions a taxpayer may get from making a charitable contribution. The charitable contribution deduction is quite different from the medical expense deduction since there is no reason to view the charitable contribution as offsetting some particular personal hardship like disease or injury. But there are other good reasons why a charitable contribution may rationally be excluded from the concept of taxable personal consumption. In the case of alms for the poor, for instance, the charitable contribution results in the distribution of real goods and services to persons presumably poorer and in lower marginal tax brackets than the donor. These goods and services, therefore, should not be taxed at the higher rates intended to apply to personal consumption by the donor. In the case of philanthropy more broadly defined—the support of religion, education, and the arts—benefits often do not flow exclusively or even principally to very low bracket taxpayers. But the goods and services produced do have something of the character of common goods whose enjoyment is not confined to contributors nor apportioned among contributors according to the amounts of their contributions. There are a number of reasons for defining taxable personal consumption not to include the benefit of such common goods and services. The personal consumption at which progressive personal taxation with high graduated rates should aim may well be thought to encompass only the private consumption of divisible goods and services whose consumption by one household precludes their direct enjoyment by others. . . .

A. Alms for the Poor

Consider a taxpayer who simply contributes some of his earnings to an organization which redistributes them to or for the needy. In such a case the consumption or accumulation of real goods and services represented by the funds in question has been shifted to the recipients rather than the donor and should not be subjected to taxation at rates designed to apply to the donor's standard of living and saving. If the redistributed funds are used for ordinary consumption by the recipients, then in principle the funds should be taxed to the recipients at their rates—although in practice the recipients' total income may often fall below a taxable level. The matter is essentially one of rates. Under a graduated rate schedule the personal consumption and accumulation of well-to-do taxpayers is intended to be curtailed much more than that of the poor. Yet if a wealthy taxpayer were to be taxed at his high rate even on the income that he donated to the poor, the probable effect would be a reduction in the amount received by the donees. For all practical purposes, such a scheme would tax the consumption of the poor at the rate intended for the wealthy taxpayer. The effect of the charitable contribution is to avoid this result. . . .

More to the point, perhaps, a doctor might choose to spend one day a week in a clinic without charging for his services. More generally he might simply treat inpecunious patients for less than the going rate. In either case he has foregone in favor of the patients whom he treats some of the personal consumption and accumulation he could have had. We do not tax the doctor on the value of his services or the excess of the value of his services over the fee he charges. We tax the doctor only on the personal consumption and accumulation he achieves by the exercise of his profession, not on what he could have achieved if he chose to maximize his personal financial gain.

Another professional man, a tax lawyer for example, may have skills that are not so directly useful to the poor as those of the doctor. If he wishes to devote part of his professional energies to the welfare of the poor, the efficient way to do it may well be to continue practicing his profession for paying clients but to turn over part of his fees for distribution among the poor or for the purchase of other services to meet their needs. The charitable contribution deduction operates to treat the tax lawyer like the doctor, by taxing him only on the amount of personal consumption and accumulation he realizes from the practice of his profession, not on what he could have realized if he had not given part of his fees away. . . .

1. *The Problem of Ordinary Gifts.*—In the case of an ordinary gift between friends or relations, the donor is allowed no deduction even though he has in one sense given up the personal consumption or accumulation that the donated funds might have purchased. On the other hand, we do not tax the recipient of the gift, even though clearly his personal consumption or accumulation will be enhanced. The result is that income earned by one taxpayer and then given to another who devotes it to personal consumption or accumulation is taxed once and only once, albeit to the donor rather than the donee whose consumption and accumulation it ultimately supports. Ideally, perhaps, the tax should be on the donee rather than the donor. But it is much simpler for everyone concerned to leave ordinary interpersonal gifts out of the computation of income on both sides. And if the income tax rates of the donor are appropriate for consumption or accumulation by the donee, the result is perfectly acceptable.

What warrant is there, however, for thinking that the donor's rates are fit for the donee's consumption or accumulation? Perhaps it is assumed that interpersonal gifts occur mostly between members of the same family or between people of similar social and economic status whose income tax rates are likely to be similar. But that is not a very realistic assumption, particularly in the case of intrafamily gifts which often go from a high bracket adult to a child in a lower bracket.

A sounder explanation for our treatment of at least intrafamily gifts may rest upon the fact that consumption is largely a household rather than an individual function. In the most usual case one member of a household earns the income which supports the whole household, and the convenient way to collect a tax is to impose it on the earner individually. But the rate and exemption schedules applicable to the breadwinner are designed to cover consumption and accumulation by the whole household without regard to the precise way in which consumption is distributed among household or family members and without distinctions between intrafamily transfers by way of support and transfers by way of gift. In other words, income is ultimately to be taxed at rates appropriate to the household whose consumption it supports although those rates are expressed in terms of an individual rate schedule applied to the breadwinner.

I do not suppose the tax has been consciously designed on this premise. . . . [But] while people participate in the production sector on an individual basis, consumption and accumulation are largely household functions. Therefore, it is sensible to view the individual income tax on the breadwinner as an indirectly measured tax on the consumption and accumulation of the household. . . .

3. Consumption as Power.—A more general argument against a deduction for almsgiving is that the tax should be apportioned on taxpayers' power to consume, however that power may be exercised. The income tax is supposed to be a tax based on ability to pay, not on what one does with that ability. To say that the ultimate object of the tax is consumption plus accumulation does not foreclose that argument, because consumption can be construed to embrace any exercise of power over the disposition of consumer goods and services even if that exercise does operate to benefit others.

The difficulty with defining taxable consumption as the exercise of power over the disposition of goods and services is that we cannot, and probably would not want to, carry such an approach very far. Only a part of the power that people exercise over the allocation and distribution of economic resources is represented by the expenditure of money. The direct influence of people participating in political and economic affairs cannot practically be subjected to income taxation. Moreover, we probably would not want to tax the exercise of power as such because the effect would be to channel some of the energies of the people involved away from these activities toward earning the funds with which to pay the taxes.

We do not tax people who exercise power through direct participation on what they could have earned if they had devoted their full energies to earning money. By analogy, it is reasonable not to tax others on what they have earned and could have kept for their own use if they choose not to keep it. If we take a broad view of how the tax falls on people who lead different kinds of lives, of how we intend it to fall, and of how it is practical to make it fall, it is not according to their powers that we should tax people but according to their standards of living and personal saving. And that is very much a matter of what they have chosen to do with their powers. . . .

4. *The Pleasure of Giving.*—Finally, there is a kind of argument against the allowance of a deduction for alms to the poor which is based not on power but on pleasure. The argument is that one who makes a charitable contribution must get some pleasure or satisfaction from his act which he considers equal to what he could have gotten from some other use of his funds. Some wealthy people dress for dinner; some ride to hounds; others make substantial charitable contributions. *Chacun à son goût.* Whatever a man chooses to do with his money should be classed as personal consumption for him.

But there is a difference between dinner clothes and charitable contributions. Wearing dinner dress represents some diversion of economic resources, real goods and services, *away from* the satisfaction of other people's needs. The effect of almsgiving, on the other hand, is to cause real economic resources to be directed *toward* the satisfaction of the needs of the poor. Thus, the imposition of a tax on this latter kind of expenditure will ultimately fall on the poor in a sense that it will not in the case of dinner dress. The satisfaction one gets from making a charitable contribution is in this respect like a great many of the rest of life's best satisfactions which people can enjoy without diverting economic resources away from other people and which we do not try to take into account in assessing income taxes. . . .

B. *Philanthropy More Broadly Defined*

For many kinds of charitable contributions the foregoing analysis will not quite do because the benefits of the contributions do not go entirely to the poor. More than half of all charitable deductions are for contributions to churches, whose activities are conducted for rich and poor alike and often on a more comfortable and expensive scale in wealthy neighborhoods than in poor ones. Many contributions are to private schools, whose student bodies are probably still disproportionately representative of the affluent part of the population. Some contributions go to support artistic enterprises, ordinary and esoteric, in which most of the poor are likely to have little interest. Moreover, the activities of such organizations are frequently ones in which contributors participate more or less directly for their own edification or pleasure.

Such contributions also differ from alms for the poor because they represent an affirmative allocation of resources by the contributor to a particular activity whose benefits are not taxed to the recipients. In theory, though not in practice (and it is typically not important in practice), alms should be counted as income to the recipient, so that deduction by the donor is only a matter of reassigning taxability to the person whose consumption is supported, as in the case of alimony. But when a group of wealthy people support a church, a school, a research institute, or a symphony orchestra, the effect of the charitable contribution deduction is to eliminate the enjoyment of the output of that activity from the tax base altogether. A community of people that supports a church will pay less in taxes than a community of people with the same total income, similarly distributed, that spends less on its church and more on its private homes.

Nevertheless, the benefits produced by charitable contributions have certain shared characteristics which provide the basis for principled arguments in favor of deduction. Almost all charitable organizations other than those that distribute alms to the poor produce something in the nature of common or social goods or services. The benefit produced by a contribution to a private school, for example, may not inure primarily to the poor, but neither does it inure solely to the contributor. Even when contributors are almost all members who share in the product of the organization, as in the case of a church, the product is essentially a common good to be enjoyed by the members without regard to relative contributions and usually is at least open to enjoyment by others.

Common goods have several characteristics relevant for our purposes. Principally, their enjoyment is not limited exclusively or even primarily to those who pay for them. That might be stated merely as a matter of external benefits: a wealthy man cannot purchase and enjoy the sound of a new church organ without conferring a benefit on his fellow parishioners. Unlike the typical external effect of private consumption, however, the benefit conferred on others is of the same kind as that enjoyed by the contributor himself.

Moreover, it is typically the case that the benefits produced by a charitable organization are free goods in the sense that one person's enjoyment of them will not directly impair another's enjoyment. Attendance at church on a particular Sunday, use of the town library, or listening to a symphony orchestra broadcast will not immediately prevent someone else from doing the same thing. Of course, pure public goods are relatively rare. Use of the library does not immediately prevent others from using it; but if too many use it too much, then its utility will be impaired. The conditions under which a town common can serve effectively for common use are very limited. And students' places in schools are sometimes quite scarce. But as among the students, once admitted to a school or to a particular class, many of the educational opportunities offered have this quality of common goods.

The underlying problem with respect to contributions to churches, schools, museums, and similar charities is whether the common goods they produce should be reflected in the consumption component of personal income of any of the individuals associated with them. . . .

It is sometimes said that the charitable contribution deduction is justified because charitable organizations provide services that otherwise the Government might have to provide directly. One abstract sense in which that statement seems true is that charitable organizations produce common goods. To some extent the basic reason underlying taxation and governmental provision of common or public goods is that people acting individually will not tend to pay voluntarily for the provision of public goods or services up to an optimum level. Insofar as that is the reason for taxation, it may well seem counterproductive to lay the tax on that very kind of activity—production of common goods for shared enjoyment—even if the common goods produced by private philanthropic institutions differ substantially from the ones the Government would purchase or produce in the absence of such institutions. . . .

I. OPPEWAL v. COMMISSIONER
468 F.2d 1000 (1st Cir. 1972)

[Editor's Note: Consider how the following opinion affects the argument that the charitable contribution deduction is an income-defining provision.]

HAMLEY, CIRCUIT JUDGE.

In their federal income tax return for 1968, Jacob and Leona G. Oppewal, of Whitinsville, Massachusetts, deducted as a charitable contribution, the sum of nine hundred dollars they had paid that year to the Whitinsville Society for Christian Instruction (Society). The Commissioner of Internal Revenue disallowed this to the extent of six hundred and forty dollars on the ground that this sum, representing the cost to the Society of educating taxpayers' two children that year, constituted a non-deductible personal expense under section 262 of the Internal Revenue Code. . . .

On this ground the Commissioner declared a 1968 tax deficiency in the amount of $153.22. Taxpayers petitioned the Tax Court to redetermine the asserted deficiency. The Tax Court adhered to the Commissioner's determination. . . . Taxpayers appeal to this Court.

The controlling facts are not in dispute. The Society was organized in 1924 ". . . for the purpose of advancing the cause of education. . . ." It was, during the taxable year 1968, an organization exempt from tax under section 501 of the Code. . . . The membership of the Society consisted of three hundred and twenty contributing individuals and families, some ninety of which had children attending the school. The Society solicited and received gifts from members, non-members, churches and other organizations.

Members who were parents with children in the Society's school were solicited in the same manner as were non-parents. Money received was not put into donor or students accounts but was put into a general operating fund. No child obtained the opportunity to attend the Society's school by reason of any contribution made, nor was any child barred for lack of a contribution. Approximately forty percent of the total Society receipts was collected from the contributions of parents who had children in the school, though a record or tally was not kept. Funds were solicited on the basis of what a person could afford to give rather than on a per capita basis.

Funds normally came to the Society on a regular established basis rather than as a result of a drive or newly-initiated program. Solicitations were made from time to time on a personal basis. The academic training received at the Society's school was no better or worse than that available at the public schools in taxpayers' community, consisting of about ten thousand people.

During the 1967 to 1968 school year, one hundred and ninety-three children attended the school operated by the Society. The cost of operating the school amounted to about three hundred and thirty-eight dollars per student. During the taxable year 1968, two of the taxpayers' children attended this school for a period of thirty-nine weeks.

Section 170 of the Code ... allows as a deduction any charitable contribution payment of which is made during the taxable year. Section 170(c) defines a "charitable contribution" as including a "contribution or gift to or for the use of ... [a] corporation ... or ... fund ... organized and operated exclusively for religious ... or educational purposes."

The Tax Court ... held that to the extent of six hundred and forty dollars, the taxpayers' payment to the Society was not a "contribution or gift" to the Society, because it proceeded primarily from the incentive of anticipated benefit to the taxpayers "beyond the satisfaction which flows from the performance of a generous act. . ." Said the Tax Court:

> ... we are persuaded that the contributions made by petitioner to the Society in 1968 were substantially induced by the benefits anticipated by him from the enrollment of his two children in the Society's school and were, to a substantial extent, in the nature of tuition.

In their brief in this court, taxpayers apparently accepted the subjective test applied by the Tax Court involving taxpayers' motive and intent in making the payment to the Society. However, they argued that, under the facts, it was not reasonable to conclude that the payment was induced by the educational benefits taxpayers expected to derive for their children. In oral argument taxpayers urged that objective rather than subjective standards should be applied. The objective test taxpayers would apply is whether there was certainty as to the beneficiaries of their payment. . . . They assert that this test was not met because no part of the payment was earmarked for the education of taxpayers' children.

We have heretofore expressed our dissatisfaction with such subjective tests as the taxpayer's motives in making a purported charitable contribution. In Crosby Valve & Gage Company v. C.I.R. . . . , we said:

> While agreeing with the holding of the Tax Court, we think it necessary to register our disagreement with the [Tax Court] majority's emphasis upon a purely charitable motive as a prerequisite for a deductible charitable contribution. Were the deductibility of a contribution under section 170(c) of the Internal Revenue Code of 1954 to depend on 'detached and disinterested generosity', an important area of tax law would become a mare's nest of uncertainty woven of judicial value judgments irrelevant to eleemosynary reality. . . .

But while we believe it important to solve this tax problem through the application of an objective test, we do not regard taxpayers' proposed objective inquiry—was the payment earmarked for the education of taxpayers' children—appropriate. Classification of a payment as a gift, or as payment of family expenses, should depend upon something more fundamental than the particular bookkeeping methods used by the educational institution.

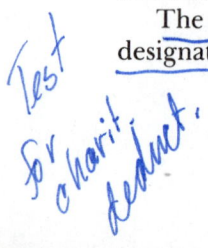

The more fundamental objective test is—however the payment was designated, and whatever motives the taxpayers had in making it, was it, to any substantial extent, offset by the cost of services rendered to taxpayers in the nature of tuition? If so, the payment, to the extent of the offset, should be regarded as tuition for, in substance, it served the same function as tuition.

Applying that test here, the conclusion is inescapable that six hundred and forty dollars of taxpayers' payment to the Society was non-deductible tuition. The taxpayers' two children obtained a year of education in the Society's religiously-oriented school, as desired by taxpayers. The cost to the Society of providing that service was at least six hundred and forty dollars. In effect, if not in form or by design, taxpayers paid this cost.

Affirmed.

J. DEDUCTIBLE TO THE EXTENT PERMITTED BY LAW
31 Tax Notes 1557–1558 (March 28, 1988)

... In this era of reform and close scrutiny of "shelters," the fund-raising activities of many charities should be examined closely. Many appear quite questionable under existing law, to state the proposition "charitably." It appears the IRS should act promptly and aggressively (including imposition of penalties on fund-raisers where appropriate) to prevent the transformation of nondeductible items of personal consumption into purported charitable contributions. Let us look at a few of the fund-raising techniques currently in vogue:

1. The Benefit Dinner. A charity holds a benefit dinner with tickets costing $50, of which $35 is paid to the hotel and other suppliers for the costs of the affair. The notice typically states the cost of the ticket is "deductible to the extent provided by law." Come now—the cost is only deductible to the extent it exceeds "the value" of the dinner, which under the postulated facts is probably $35. In many cases, the cost and value may well be $50 as suggested by ... the lavish Roman circus atmosphere and costs of many benefit dinners. ...

[C]harities ought to be required to state to donors the costs of putting on the affair (whether donated or out-of-pocket) unless it is less than some *de minimis* amount. It should not be open to defend deductions for benefit dinners on the ground that the food provided is uniformly bad and the affair is boring.

2. The Benefit Auction. A variation on the benefit dinner is the benefit auction, attended by people who bid on everything from garage sale bric-a-brac to fully paid, all-inclusive tours to China or luxury cars. At many, the array of available goods is as broad as a Neiman Marcus catalog or a Christie's auction. By and large, nobody pays more than "list price." The typical disclosures on tax consequences say nothing. Most organizers of these events take the position that the attendees should not ask about tax consequences because they would not want to know, but gratefully accept the checks made payable to charity. I suspect that some checks bear a prominent notation "contribution." The charities should be required to stamp on the check "Payment for goods or services."

3. Free Lectures. An educational institution promotes lectures by various learned professors. Rather than charging admission, it requires attendees to make a donation of a specified amount.

4. Tuition Alchemy. A private school has a fund-raising drive by students to raise contributions with all money raised being credited to that student's tuition. Your child, a student at the institution, approaches you for a contribution, and [you] contribute $X thousand knowing that your tuition cost has just been eliminated and (by a process of alchemy) converted into a deductible charitable contribution. About all that can be said of this variant is that at least the deduction is limited in amount, unlike some of the rumored practices of bygone days when parishioners could secure currency for weekly expenses by merely dropping a check made out to the church in exchange for cash from the collection plate.

5. Group Travel. More sophisticated perhaps is the practice of various institutions of selling group travel with part of the tour cost designated as a contribution. An exempt organization has a travel packager use its membership mailing list and may also advertise the tour in magazines to non-members. The "contribution" undoubtedly represents the fee paid by the tour packager to the institution for use of its mailing list. . . .

6. TV Premiums. A public television station solicits donations of $60 and as a premium to subscribers awards them a free book and magazine subscription worth $40.

The very persistence and pervasiveness of these fund-raising techniques is explicable on several alternative grounds: (1) a possibility that IRS employees are never exposed to these practices; (2) a belief that uprooting many of these practices could require substantial audit time; (3) a disinclination to pursue those perceived to be "doing good"; or (4) the deterrent effect of opprobrium for anyone speaking out on charitable matters. . . .

Another irony here is that some of the guardians of the "public fisc" who inveigh against "tax expenditures" for the benefit of the commercial sector may be indirect beneficiaries of these activities (as employees of tax-exempt institutions) and have remained mute while the conduct takes place literally under their noses. Where are their shrill voices?

Whatever the reasons for IRS lethargy, it is high time to take action through a concerted series of public announcements, required actions by donees, and aggressive audits. . . .

K. NOTES AND QUESTIONS

1) Is the Charitable Contribution Deduction an Income-defining Provision?

What are the arguments for regarding the charitable contribution deduction as an income-defining provision, rather than as a tax expenditure? Do you find them convincing? Why does Professor Andrews distinguish between "Alms for the Poor" and other charitable contributions?

2) The Significance of *Oppewal*

Donors often receive tangible benefits in return for their charity. Contributors to public television are offered Sesame Street sleeping bags, attendees at a fundraiser often receive food and drink, patrons of the ballet and opera get free tickets to rehearsals and the chance to buy the best seats for scheduled performances before tickets are offered to the general public. Under the principle of *Oppewal*, the charitable deduction in each case should be reduced by the value of the real goods and services that the contributor receives in return for the contribution. In practice, why do you suppose that this happens only rarely? Is it the difficulty of valuing what is received in return? Or the difficulty of changing the behavior of taxpayers accustomed to deducting the *full* amount of contributions? Is enforcing the *Oppewal* rule beyond the capabilities of the IRS?

3) Church and Synagogue Dues

May a church or synagogue member deduct a weekly offering or membership dues? Historically, such payments have always been treated as charitable contributions. But why doesn't the member, as much as the taxpayer in *Oppewal*, receive a quid pro quo? According to Murphy v. Commissioner, 54 T.C. 249 (1970), such dues are deductible because:

> [T]he benefits are merely incidental to making the organization function according to its charitable purposes and the only return benefit is the satisfaction of participating in the furtherance of its ... religious cause. Such privileges, we think, are not significant return benefits that have a monetary value within the meaning of [S]ection 170.[13]

Do you find this reasoning convincing? Is there a better explanation (cultural or historical) for why the cost of church or synagogue membership may be deducted as a charitable contribution? Should this allowance be viewed as a tax expenditure? If it is, does it violate the First Amendment prohibition on government aid to religion?[14]

4) Contributions to Segregated Private Schools

A gift is deductible as a Section 170(a) charitable contribution if the recipient qualifies for tax-exempt status under Section 501(c)(3). Section 170(c)(2)(D).[15] Section 501(c)(3) includes organizations operated exclusively for:

---

13. 54 T.C. at 253.
14. In Walz v. Tax Commission, 397 U.S. 664, the plaintiff challenged a state property tax exemption for religious institutions as violating the Establishment Clause. While conceding that direct financial aid might be unconstitutional, the Court upheld the tax exemption. Citing Justice Holmes dictum that "a page of history is worth a volume of logic," the Court noted that exemptions for churches had been considered constitutional for the nation's entire history. In other areas (notably state aid to parochial schools), the Court has retreated from its position in *Walz* that "tax [provisions] occupy a different constitutional status than do direct grants." Committee for Public Education v. Nyquist, 413 U.S. 756, 806 (J. Rhenquist dissenting) (1973).
15. Besides contributions to Section 501(c)(3) organizations, contributions to other organizations may be deducted as specified in Section 170(c)(1), (3), (4), and (5).

> ... religious, charitable, scientific, testing for public safety, literary, or educational purposes, or to foster international sports competition ..., or for the prevention of cruelty to children or animals, no part of the net earnings of which inures to the benefit of any private shareholder or individual, no substantial part of the activities of which is ... attempting to influence legislation ..., and which does not participate in ... any political campaign ...

Before 1970, segregated private schools were considered eligible for tax-exempt status under Section 501(c)(3) as "educational" organizations, and contributions to such schools were therefore tax deductible. As a result, civil rights groups sued to prevent segregated private schools from receiving federal tax benefits, including tax-exempt status. In Green v. Connally, 330 F. Supp. 1150 (D.D.C. 1971), a federal court construed the Code to prohibit tax-exempt status for such schools. Noting that the Constitution prohibited government aid to segregated education, the court added:

> [Any other construction of the Code] would raise serious constitutional questions.... [I]t would be difficult indeed to establish that such [tax] support can be provided consistently with the Constitution.[16]

Does the *Green* court's reading of the Constitution assume that the deduction of contributions to private schools is a tax expenditure rather than an income-defining provision? (Note that the principal consequence of Section 501(c)(3) status for these schools was to permit donors to deduct contributions to them.) Professor Andrews argued that the deduction should, in general, be viewed as income-defining because "[t]he benefit produced by a contribution to a private school" is a "common good." But does this general argument apply to the specific case of racially segregated institutions?[17]

On appeal, *Green* was affirmed by the Supreme Court, 404 U.S. 997 (1971). Therefore, its construction of the Code appeared to be the law of the land, and the IRS issued a series of rulings to implement the decision. Nevertheless, on January 8, 1982, the Reagan administration announced that tax-exempt status would be granted to segregated schools because the IRS lacked authority to deny it. *Green* was dismissed as the work of "judicial activists."[18]

After critical public reaction, however, the administration backed off and said it would wait until the Supreme Court ruled in litigation challenging the previous denial of tax-exempt status to segregated private in-

---

16. 330 F. Supp. at 1164–1165.

17. Readers interested in pursuing this subject might compare Bittker and Kauffman, Taxes and Civil Rights: "Constitutionalizing" the Internal Revenue Code, 82 Yale L.J. 51 (1972) with Cohen, Exempt Status for Segregated Private Schools: Does the Constitution Permit Lower Standards for Tax Benefits than for Direct Grants?, 17 Tax Notes 259 (October 25, 1982).

18. Testimony of Deputy Attorney General Schmults, Administration's Change in Federal Policy Regarding the Tax Status of Racially Discriminatory Private Schools: Hearing Before the House Comm. on Ways and Means, 97th Cong., 2d Sess. 155 (1982).

stitutions. In Bob Jones University v. United States, 461 U.S. 574 (1983), the Court held that the IRS was authorized to deny tax-exempt status to segregated schools.

5) The Percentage Limits of Section 170

Section 170, which allows the charitable contribution deduction, has some unusual and complicated percentage limits, which will be briefly noted. In general, the deduction for individuals is subject to an overall limit of 50% of AGI. Thus, if X has AGI of $300,000 and gives $180,000 to Georgetown University, only $150,000 is deductible. The overall limit is subject to further qualifications and restrictions which are beyond the scope of this introductory casebook.

Are such limits consistent with the view that the charitable contribution deduction is an income-defining provision? Or are they defensible only if one regards the deduction as a subsidy for charitable organizations and if one wants to limit the amount of subsidy that can be directed by any individual?

6) The Deduction for State and Local Taxes

Section 164 allows taxpayers to deduct state and local income and property taxes (but not sales or excise taxes). Is the deduction for state and local taxes an income-defining provision or a tax expenditure? A 1984 Treasury Department study regarded the deduction as a tax expenditure:

> The current deduction for State and local taxes in effect provides a Federal subsidy for the public services provided by State and local governments, such as public education, road construction and repair, and sanitary services. When taxpayers acquire similar services by private purchase (for example, when taxpayers pay for water or sewer services), no deduction is allowed for the expenditure. Allowing a deduction for State and local taxes simply permits taxpayers to finance personal consumption expenditures with pre-tax dollars. . . .
>
> The subsidy provided by the current deduction for State and local taxes is distributed in an uneven and unfair manner. . . . [S]tate and local taxes are deductible only by taxpayers who itemize, and among itemizers, those with high incomes and high marginal tax rates receive a disproportionate benefit.[19]

The Treasury's characterization of the deduction as a tax expenditure has been challenged:

> [In] any state and local tax transaction, two basic events take place: (1) A taxpayer makes tax payments to the government, and (2) the same taxpayer receives certain goods and services for those payments. Since step (1), the payment of taxes, is neither consumption nor savings, the payment of

---

19. 2 Department of the Treasury, Tax Reform for Fairness, Simplicity, and Growth, 62–63 (1984).

taxes [should] not be included in the tax base.... [H]owever, the value of the benefits received by the taxpayer in step (2) does constitute income and should be included in the base....

If [a] person ... paid $50 of state and local taxes and received $50 in goods and services in return, although the tax payments [should be] deductible in computing taxable income (because they represent neither consumption nor savings), the $50 in goods and services received would represent consumption (and thus income) creating a wash.... In other words, in cases in which the amount of taxes paid equals goods and services received, the ... income tax [should] allow no ... deduction for state and local taxes....

[D]enying a deduction for state and local taxes only produces the proper result if the state and local taxes are imposed on a benefits received basis. If, for example, the above taxpayer paid $50 in state and local taxes, but received only $25 in goods and services in return ... [c]ompletely denying a deduction ... would result in the person being overtaxed....[20]

Under current law, payments to charities and state and local governments are generally treated consistently. In each case, not every payment to such an entity is deductible. In both cases, if a taxpayer receives ... a direct benefit, no deduction is allowed....

On the other hand, if a payment to a charity or a state and local government can only be said to be indirectly in exchange for any specific service or benefit, the payment is usually deductible.... As long as payments (whether charitable contributions or taxes) are not directly linked to benefits received, they should be deductible.

There is yet another similarity between the function of charities and state and local governments that makes any differentiation in the tax treatment of [the two] difficult to defend. In many cases, governments and charities provide similar services to the public at large....[21]

Which of these two views do you find more persuasive? Is the analogy between state and local taxes and charitable contributions convincing?

---

20. Billman and Cunningham, Nonbusiness State and Local Taxes: The Case for Deductibility, 28 Tax Notes 1107, 1111–1112 (September 2, 1985).
21. Ibid. at 1119.

Chapter 10

DISGUISING GIFTS AS COMPENSATION (AND VICE VERSA)

A. ELLER v. COMMISSIONER
77 T.C. 934 (1981)

DAWSON, JUDGE:

... During 1972, 1973, and 1974, the Ellers' children performed a variety of services for various of their parents' businesses. They performed these services on a continuing basis after school, on weekends, and during their summer vacations, devoting considerable time and expending considerable effort. The services performed were necessary for the operation of the businesses and could not have been performed by the existing "staff." Thus, had these services not been performed by the children, a third party (or parties) would have had to have been hired.

At Alimur Trailer Park, the children were assigned a variety of responsibilities, including maintenance of the swimming pool, landscaping, and park grounds. They also read the gas and electric meters, cleaned and set up the recreation hall for various events, and mopped and cleaned the laundry room. Moreover, they delivered leaflets and messages to the tenants, answered the phones in the absence of the secretary, and swept and cleaned the trailer pads and new mobile homes which were offered for sale. Finally, they performed minor repair work and assisted their father or tradesmen on larger projects and in emergency situations.

At Voyage West, the children were responsible for maintaining the grounds and cleaning and mopping the office and laundry room. They also performed minor repair work.

At Golden Wheels, the children were responsible for maintaining the swimming pool, the landscaping, and the park grounds. They registered the transient tenants, assisted in making the necessary electrical connections, and collected the nightly rental. They also cleaned the mobile homes which were offered for sale. Finally, they performed a variety of secretarial and office services.

At El Rancho, the children were responsible for cleaning the parking lot and sidewalks with an industrial sweeper and blower. They also had janitorial duties related to the public restrooms, hallways, and stairways. Moreover, they cleaned the premises after the tenants vacated. Finally, they maintained the landscaping, answered complaints, performed minor repairs, and assisted their father at all hours in emergency situations.

The children were compensated for their services by the various Eller-owned businesses which deducted the amounts paid as "outside services." These amounts were as follows:

1972	Michael	Patti	John	Total
Voyage West	$ 550	$ 550	$ 550	$1,650
Golden Wheels	550	550	550	1,650
Alimur Trailer Park	557	770	550	1,877
	1,657	1,870	1,650	5,177
1973				
Golden Wheels	1,334	1,334	1,434	4,102
Alimur Trailer Park	25	25	0	50
	1,359	1,359	1,434	4,152
1974				
Modesto	$3,028	$3,000	$2,000	$8,028
El Rancho	156	116	68	340
	3,184	3,116	2,068	8,368

In the notices of deficiency issued to the Ellers . . . , respondent determined that approximately 90 percent of the compensation paid to the children was unreasonable and disallowed that amount. The 10 percent allowed was allocated as follows:

1972	Michael	Patti	John	Total
Alimur Trailer Park	$300	$300	0	$600
1973				
Golden Wheels	275	275	0	550
Alimur Trailer Park	25	25	0	50
1974				
Modesto				
El Rancho	300	300	0	600

. . . Compensation is deductible under section 162(a)(1) only if it is (1) reasonable in amount, (2) based on services actually rendered, and (3) paid or incurred. See also sec. 1.162–7(a), Income Tax Regs. In the notices of deficiency issued to the Ellers . . . , respondent disallowed part of the compensation paid to the children on the ground that it was unreasonable and excessive. On brief, however, respondent argues that at least part of the amount paid to the children was not based on services actually rendered.

Whether amounts paid as compensation are reasonable and represent payments purely for services are questions of fact to be resolved on the

Ch. 10 Disguising Gifts as Compensation

basis of all of the surrounding facts and circumstances. . . . The burden of proof is, of course, on the petitioners. . . . The fact that payments are made to minor children by a related party does not preclude their deductibility. . . .

As found above, we think that the Ellers' children performed substantial services the reasonable value of which was as follows:

1972	Michael	Patti	John	Total
Voyage West	$ 550	$ 550	$ 400	$1,500
Golden Wheels	550	550	400	1,500
Alimur Trailer Park	557	770	400	1,727
	1,657	1,870	1,200	4,727
1973				
Golden Wheels	1,334	1,334	934	3,602
Alimur Trailer Park	25	25	0	50
	1,359	1,359	934	3,652
1974				
Modesto	2,528	2,500	1,800	6,828
El Rancho	156	116	68	340
	2,684	2,616	1,868	7,168

Our findings differ somewhat from the amounts deducted by petitioners for two reasons. First, we think that the reasonable value of John's services must reflect the age differential between him and his brother and sister.[1] In 1972, John was 7; Michael and Patti were 12 and 11, respectively.[2] Experience teaches that 11- and 12-year old children can generally handle greater responsibility and perform greater services than 7-year old children. Moreover, [the father] testified that it was his practice to promote youngsters as they demonstrated their aptitude, acquired experience, and developed greater responsibility. And as Michael testified, with greater responsibility came greater remuneration.

Second, we think that there should be some relationship between the reasonable value of the children's services over the 3-year period. After all, the record does not indicate that the children rendered significantly greater services (whether measured quantitatively or qualitatively) during 1974 than they did during either 1972 or 1973. . . .

B. NOTES AND QUESTIONS

1) The Stakes in *Eller*

The formal legal issue was whether compensation paid to Eller's children was "reasonable" under Section 162(a)(1) and therefore deductible as a business expense. Compensation that was reasonable and deductible by Eller was presumably taxable income to the children. To the extent that

---

[1]. There is nothing in the record to suggest that John performed a greater quantum of services than his siblings so as to neutralize the age differential.
[2]. In our opinion, the age differential between Michael and Patti was inconsequential.

the compensation was "unreasonable" and nondeductible by Eller, would it still have been taxable income to the children? How should the unreasonable compensation have been recharacterized? See Section 102(a). What was at stake in *Eller?* Was the dispute over *how much* income should be reported? Or *to whom* income should be taxed?

2) The Gift Exclusion of Section 102(a)

Suppose that Eller makes a gift of $1,000 to each of his children. Under the Code, Eller—the donor—is not entitled to a deduction for the gift, and the children—the donees—do not report the receipt of the gift as income. Is this result necessarily correct?

Why shouldn't Eller be allowed to deduct the amount of the gift? Has he personally either consumed or saved it? Isn't his buying power diminished by having made it? What is the only sense in which he has benefited from the gift? Does he benefit any differently from the director of a charity who designates the beneficiaries of the charity's largesse? From a dance instructor who enjoys his work? From someone who derives satisfaction from a beautiful sunset? Would these benefits produce taxable income? Why not?

Why don't the children have income as a result of the gift? Is the cash any less useful to them because it was given rather than earned? Isn't their buying power increased at least as much by a gift as by earnings?

These questions may suggest that, instead of allowing no deduction to the donor and exclusion for the donee, perhaps we should give the donor a deduction and tax the donee. But if we changed to this system, what would happen to the structure of tax brackets and rates under which higher levels of income are taxed at higher rates? How might taxpayers cause income to be taxed at the lowest possible rate by making gifts to family members?

C. COMMISSIONER v. DUBERSTEIN
363 U.S. 278 (1960)

MR. JUSTICE BRENNAN delivered the opinion of the Court.

These two cases concern the provision of the Internal Revenue Code which excludes from the gross income of an income taxpayer "the value of property acquired by gift." They pose the frequently recurrent question whether a specific transfer to a taxpayer in fact amounted to a "gift" to him within the meaning of the statute. The importance to decision of the facts of the cases requires that we state them in some detail.

No. 376, *Commissioner v. Duberstein.* The taxpayer, Duberstein, was president of the Duberstein Iron & Metal Company, a corporation with headquarters in Dayton, Ohio. For some years the taxpayer's company had done business with Mohawk Metal Corporation, whose headquarters were in New York City. The president of Mohawk was one Berman. The taxpayer and Berman had generally used the telephone to transact their companies' business with each other, which consisted of buying and selling metals. The taxpayer testified, without elaboration, that he knew Berman "personally" and had known him for about seven years. From time to time in their telephone conversations, Berman would ask Duberstein whether the latter knew of potential customers for some of Mohawk's products in which Duberstein's company itself was not interested. Duberstein provided the names of potential customers for these items.

One day in 1951 Berman telephoned Duberstein and said that the information Duberstein had given him had proved so helpful that he wanted to give the latter a present. Duberstein stated that Berman owed him nothing. Berman said that he had a Cadillac as a gift for Duberstein, and that the latter should send to New York for it; Berman insisted that Duberstein accept the car, and the latter finally did so, protesting however that he had not intended to be compensated for the information. At the time Duberstein already had a Cadillac and an Oldsmobile, and felt that he did not need another car. Duberstein testified that he did not think Berman would have sent him the Cadillac if he had not furnished him with information about the customers. It appeared that Mohawk later deducted the value of the Cadillac as a business expense on its corporate income tax return.

Duberstein did not include the value of the Cadillac in gross income for 1951, deeming it a gift. The Commissioner asserted a deficiency for the car's value against him, and in proceedings to review the deficiency the Tax Court affirmed the Commissioner's determination. It said that "The record is significantly barren of evidence revealing any intention on the part of the payor to make a gift. . . . The only justifiable inference is that the automobile was intended by the payor to be remuneration for services rendered to it by Duberstein." The Court of Appeals for the Sixth Circuit reversed. . . .

No. 546, *Stanton v. United States*. The taxpayer, Stanton, had been for approximately 10 years in the employ of Trinity Church in New York City. He was comptroller of the Church corporation, and president of a corporation, Trinity Operating Company, the church set up as a fully owned subsidiary to manage its real estate holdings, which were more extensive than simply the church property. His salary by the end of his employment there in 1942 amounted to $22,500 a year. Effective November 30, 1942, he resigned from both positions to go into business for himself. The Operating Company's directors, who seem to have included the rector and vestrymen of the church, passed the following resolution upon his resignation: "BE IT RESOLVED that in appreciation of the services rendered by Mr. Stanton . . . a gratuity is hereby awarded to him of Twenty Thousand Dollars, payable to him in equal instalments of Two Thousand Dollars at the end of each and every month commencing with the month of December, 1942; provided that, with the discontinuance of his services, the Corporation of Trinity Church is released from all rights and claims to pension and retirement benefits not already accrued up to November 30, 1942."

The Operating Company's action was later explained by one of its directors as based on the fact that, "Mr. Stanton was liked by all of the Vestry personally. He had a pleasing personality. He had come in when Trinity's affairs were in a difficult situation. He did a splendid piece of work, we felt. Besides that . . . he was liked by all of the members of the Vestry personally." And by another: "[W]e were all unanimous in wishing to make Mr. Stanton a gift. Mr. Stanton had loyally and faithfully served Trinity in a very difficult time. We thought of him in the highest regard. We understood that he was going in business for himself. We felt that he was entitled to that evidence of good will."

On the other hand, there was a suggestion of some ill-feeling between Stanton and the directors, arising out of the recent termination of the services of one Watkins, the Operating Company's treasurer, whose departure was evidently attended by some acrimony. At a special board meeting on October 28, 1942, Stanton had intervened on Watkins' side and asked reconsideration of the matter. The minutes reflect that "resentment was expressed as to the 'presumptuous' suggestion that the action of the Board, taken after long deliberation, should be changed." The Board adhered to its determination that Watkins be separated from employment, giving him an opportunity to resign rather than be discharged. At another special meeting two days later it was revealed that Watkins had not resigned; the previous resolution terminating his services was then viewed as effective; and the Board voted the payment of six months' salary to Watkins in a resolution similar to that quoted in regard to Stanton, but which did not use the term "gratuity." At the meeting, Stanton announced that in order to avoid any such embarrassment or question at any time as to his willingness to resign if the Board desired, he was tendering his resignation. It was tabled, though not without dissent. The next week, on November 5, at another special meeting, Stanton again tendered his resignation which this time was accepted.

The "gratuity" was duly paid. So was a smaller one to Stanton's (and the Operating Company's) secretary, under a similar resolution, upon her resignation at the same time. The two corporations shared the expense of the payments. There was undisputed testimony that there were in fact no enforceable rights or claims to pension and retirement benefits which had not accrued at the time of the taxpayer's resignation, and that the last proviso of the resolution was inserted simply out of an abundance of caution. The taxpayer received in cash a refund of his contributions to the retirement plans, and there is no suggestion that he was entitled to more. He was required to perform no further services for Trinity after his resignation.

The Commissioner asserted a deficiency against the taxpayer after the latter had failed to include the payments in question in gross income. After payment of the deficiency and administrative rejection of a refund claim, the taxpayer sued the United States for a refund in the District Court for the Eastern District of New York. The trial judge, sitting without a jury, made the simple finding that the payments were a "gift," and judgment was entered for the taxpayer. The Court of Appeals for the Second Circuit reversed. . . .

The Government, urging that clarification of the problem typified by these two cases was necessary, and that the approaches taken by the Courts of Appeals for the Second and the Sixth Circuits were in conflict, petitioned for certiorari in No. 376, and acquiesced in the taxpayer's petition in No.

546. On this basis, and because of the importance of the question in the administration of the income tax laws, we granted certiorari in both cases. . . .

The exclusion of property acquired by gift from gross income under the federal income tax laws was made in the first income tax statute passed under the authority of the Sixteenth Amendment, and has been a feature of the income tax statutes ever since. The meaning of the term "gift" as applied to particular transfers has always been a matter of contention. Specific and illuminating legislative history on the point does not appear to exist. . . . The meaning of the statutory term has been shaped largely by the decisional law. With this, we turn to the contentions made by the Government in these cases.

First. The Government suggests that we promulgate a new "test" in this area to serve as a standard to be applied by the lower courts and by the Tax Court in dealing with the numerous cases that arise. We reject this invitation. We are of opinion that the governing principles are necessarily general and have already been spelled out in the opinions of this Court, and that the problem is one which, under the present statutory framework, does not lend itself to any more definitive statement that would produce a talisman for the solution of concrete cases. The cases at bar are fair examples of the settings in which the problem usually arises. They present situations in which payments have been made in a context with business overtones—an employer making a payment to a retiring employee; a businessman giving something of value to another businessman who has been of advantage to him in his business. In this context, we review the law as established by the prior cases here.

The course of decision here makes it plain that the statute does not use the term "gift" in the common-law sense, but in a more colloquial sense. This Court has indicated that a voluntary executed transfer of his property by one to another, without any consideration or compensation therefor, though a common-law gift, is not necessarily a "gift" within the meaning of the statute. For the Court has shown that the mere absence of a legal or moral obligation to make such a payment does not establish that it is a gift. . . . And, importantly, if the payment proceeds primarily from "the constraining force of any moral or legal duty," or from "the incentive of anticipated benefit" of an economic nature, . . . it is not a gift. And, conversely, "[w]here the payment is in return for services rendered, it is irrelevant that the donor derives no economic benefit from it." . . . A gift in the statutory sense, on the other hand, proceeds from a "detached and disinterested generosity," *Commissioner v. LoBue;* "out of affection, respect, admiration, charity or like impulses." . . . And in this regard, the most critical consideration, as the Court was agreed in the leading case here, is the transferor's "intention." . . .

The Government says that this "intention" of the transferor cannot mean what the cases on the common-law concept of gift call "donative intent." With that we are in agreement, for our decisions fully support this. Moreover, . . . the donor's characterization of his action is not determinative—that there must be an objective inquiry as to whether what is called a gift amounts to it in reality. . . . It scarcely needs adding that the parties' expectations or hopes as to the tax treatment of their conduct in themselves have nothing to do with the matter.

It is suggested that the . . . criterion would be more apt if rephrased in terms of "motive" rather than "intention." We must confess to some skepticism as to whether such a verbal mutation would be of any practical consequence. We take it that the proper criterion, established by decision here, is one that inquires what the basic reason for his conduct was in fact—the dominant reason that explains his action in making the transfer. Further than that we do not think it profitable to go.

Second. The Government's proposed "test," while apparently simple and precise in its formulation, depends frankly on a set of "principles" or "presumptions" derived from the decided cases, and concededly subject to various exceptions; and it involves various corollaries, which add to its detail. Were we to promulgate this test as a matter of law, and accept with it its various presuppositions and stated consequences, we would be passing far beyond the requirements of the cases before us, and would be painting on a large canvas with indeed a broad brush. The Government derives its test from such propositions as the following: That payments by an employer to an employee, even though voluntary, ought, by and large, to be taxable; that the concept of a gift is inconsistent with a payment's being a deductible business expense; that a gift involves "personal" elements; that a business corporation cannot properly make a gift of its assets. The Government admits that there are exceptions and qualifications to these propositions. We think, to the extent they are correct, that these propositions are not principles of law but rather maxims of experience that the tribunals which have tried the facts of cases in this area have enunciated in explaining their factual determinations. Some of them simply represent truisms: it doubtless is, statistically speaking, the exceptional payment by an employer to an employee that amounts to a gift. Others are overstatements of possible evidentiary inferences relevant to a factual determination on the totality of circumstances in the case: it is doubtless relevant to the over-all inference that the transferor treats a payment as a business deduction, or that the transferor is a corporate entity. But these inferences cannot be stated in absolute terms. Neither factor is a shibboleth. The taxing statute does not make nondeductibility by the transferor a condition on the "gift" exclusion; nor does it draw any distinction, in terms, between transfers by corporations and individuals, as to the availability of the "gift" exclusion to the transferee. The conclusion whether a transfer amounts to a "gift" is one that must be reached on consideration of all the factors.

Specifically, the trier of fact must be careful not to allow trial of the issue whether the receipt of a specific payment is a gift to turn into a trial of the tax liability, or of the propriety, as a matter of fiduciary or corporate law, attaching to the conduct of someone else. The major corollary to the Government's suggested "test" is that, as an ordinary matter, a payment by a corporation cannot be a gift, and, more specifically, there can be no such thing as a "gift" made by a corporation which would allow it to take a deduction for an ordinary and necessary business expense. As we have said, we find no basis for such a conclusion in the statute; and if it were applied as a determinative rule of "law," it would force the tribunals trying tax cases involving the donee's liability into elaborate inquiries into the local law of corporations or into the peripheral deductibility of payments as business expenses. The former issue might make the tax tribunals the most frequent investigators of an important and difficult issue of the laws of the several States, and the latter inquiry would summon one difficult and delicate problem of federal tax law as an aid to the solution of another. Or perhaps there would be required a trial of the vexed issue whether there was a "constructive" distribution of corporate property, for income tax purposes, to the corporate agents who had sponsored the transfer. These considerations, also, reinforce us in our conclusion that while the principles urged by the Government may, in nonabsolute form as crystallizations of experience, prove persuasive to the trier of facts in a particular case, neither they, nor any more detailed statement than has been made, can be laid down as a matter of law.

Third. Decision of the issue presented in these cases must be based ultimately on the application of the fact-finding tribunal's experience with the mainsprings of human conduct to the totality of the facts of each case. The nontechnical nature of the statutory standard, the close relationship of it to the data of practical human experience, and the multiplicity of relevant factual elements, with their various combinations, creating the necessity of ascribing the proper force to each, confirm us in our conclusion that primary weight in this area must be given to the conclusions of the trier of fact. . . .

This conclusion may not satisfy an academic desire for tidiness, symmetry and precision in this area, any more than a system based on the determinations of various fact-finders ordinarily does. But we see it as implicit in the present statutory treatment of the exclusion for gifts, and in the variety of forums in which federal income tax cases can be tried. If there is fear of undue uncertainty or overmuch litigation, Congress may make more precise its treatment of the matter by singling out certain factors and making them determinative of the matter, as it has done in one field of the "gift" exclusion's former application, that of prizes and awards. Doubtless diversity of result will tend to be lessened somewhat since federal income tax decisions, even those in tribunals of first instance turning on issues of fact, tend to be reported, and since there may be a natural tendency of professional triers of fact to follow one another's determinations, even as to factual matters. But the question here remains basically one of fact, for determination on a case-by-case basis.

One consequence of this is that appellate review of determinations in this field must be quite restricted. Where a jury has tried the matter upon correct instructions, the only inquiry is whether it cannot be said that reasonable men could reach differing conclusions on the issue. . . . Where the trial has been by a judge without a jury, the judge's findings must stand unless "clearly erroneous." Fed. Rules Civ. Proc., 52(a). "A finding is 'clearly erroneous' when although there is evidence to support it, the reviewing court on the entire evidence is left with the definite and firm conviction that a mistake has been committed.". . . .

Fourth. A majority of the Court is in accord with the principles just outlined. And, applying them to the *Duberstein* case, we are in agreement, on the evidence we have set forth, that it cannot be said that the conclusion of the Tax Court was "clearly erroneous." It seems to us plain that as trier of the facts it was warranted in concluding that despite the characterization of the transfer of the Cadillac by the parties and the absence of any obligation, even of a moral nature, to make it, it was at bottom a recompense for Duberstein's past services, or an inducement for him to be of further service in the future. We cannot say with the Court of Appeals that such a conclusion was "mere suspicion" on the Tax Court's part. To us it appears based in the sort of informed experience with human affairs that fact-finding tribunals should bring to this task.

As to *Stanton,* we are in disagreement. To four of us, it is critical here that the District Court as trier of fact made only the simple and unelaborated finding that the transfer in question was a "gift." To be sure, conciseness is to be strived for, and prolixity avoided, in findings; but, to the four of us, there comes a point where findings become so sparse and conclusory as to give no revelation of what the District Court's concept of the determining facts and legal standard may be. . . . Such conclusory, general findings do not constitute compliance with Rule 52's direction to "find the facts specially and state separately . . . conclusions of law thereon." While the standard of law in this area is not a complex one, we four think the unelaborated finding of ultimate fact here cannot stand as a fulfillment of these requirements. It affords the reviewing court not the semblance of an indication of the legal standard with which the trier of fact has approached his task. For all that appears, the District Court may have viewed the form of the resolution or the simple absence of legal consideration as conclusive. While the judgment of the Court of Appeals cannot stand, the four of us think there must be further proceedings in the District Court looking toward new and adequate findings of fact. In this, we are joined by MR. JUSTICE WHITTAKER, who agrees that the findings were inadequate, although he does not concur generally in this opinion.

Accordingly, in No. 376, the judgment of this Court is that the judgment of the Court of Appeals is reversed, and in No. 546, that the judgment of the Court of Appeals is vacated, and the case is remanded to the District Court for further proceedings not inconsistent with this opinion.

MR. JUSTICE BLACK, concurring and dissenting.

I agree with the Court that it was not clearly erroneous for the Tax Court to find as it did in No. 376 that the automobile transfer to Duberstein was not a gift, and so I agree with the Court's opinion and judgment reversing the judgment of the Court of Appeals in that case.

I dissent in No. 546, *Stanton v. United States.* The District Court found that the $20,000 transferred to Mr. Stanton by his former employer at the end of ten years' service was a gift and therefore exempt from taxation under I.R.C. of 1939, § 22(b)(3) (now I.R.C. of 1954, § 102(a)). I think the finding was not clearly erroneous and that the Court of Appeals was therefore wrong in reversing the District Court's judgment. While conflicting inferences might have been drawn, there was evidence to show that Mr. Stanton's long services had been satisfactory, that he was well liked personally and had given splendid service, that the employer was under no obligation at all to pay any added compensation, but made the $20,000 payment because prompted by a genuine desire to make him a "gift," to award him a "gratuity." . . . The District Court's finding was that the added payment "constituted a gift to the taxpayer, and therefore need not have been reported by him as income. . . ." The trial court might have used more words, or discussed the facts set out above in more detail, but I doubt if this would have made its crucial, adequately supported finding any clearer. For this reason I would reinstate the District Court's judgment for petitioner.

MR. JUSTICE FRANKFURTER, concurring in the judgment in No. 376 and dissenting in No. 546.

As the Court's opinion indicates, we brought these two cases here partly because of a claimed difference in the approaches between two Courts of Appeals but primarily on the Government's urging that, in the interest of the better administration of the income tax laws, clarification was desirable for determining when a transfer of property constitutes a "gift" and is not to be included in income for purposes of ascertaining the "gross income" under the Internal Revenue Code. As soon as this problem emerged after the imposition of the first income tax authorized by the Sixteenth Amendment, it became evident that its inherent difficulties and subtleties would not easily yield to the formulation of a general rule or test sufficiently definite to confine within narrow limits the area of judgment in applying it. While at its core the tax conception of a gift no doubt reflected the non-legal, non-technical notion of a benefaction unentangled with any aspect of worldly requital, the divers blends of personal and pecuniary relationships in our industrial society inevitably presented niceties for adjudication which could not be put to rest by any kind of general formulation.

. . . The Court has rejected the invitation of the Government to fashion anything like a litmus paper test for determining what is excludable as a "gift" from gross income. Nor has the Court attempted a clarification of the particular aspects of the problem presented by these two cases, namely, payment by an employer to an employee upon the termination of the employment relation and non-obligatory payment for services rendered in the course of a business relationship. While I agree that experience has shown the futility of attempting to define, by language so circumscribing as to make it easily applicable, what constitutes a gift for every situation where the problem may arise, I do think that greater explicitness is possible in isolating and emphasizing factors which militate against a gift in particular situations.

Thus, regarding the two frequently recurring situations involved in these cases—things of value given to employees by their employers upon the termination of employment and payments entangled in a business relation and occasioned by the performance of some service—the strong implication is that the payment is of a business nature. The problem in these two cases is entirely different from the problem in a case where a payment is made from one member of a family to another, where the implications are directly otherwise. No single general formulation appropriately deals with both types of cases, although both involve the question whether the payment was a "gift." While we should normally suppose that a payment from father to son was a gift, unless the contrary is shown, in the two situations now before us the business implications are so forceful that I would apply a presumptive rule placing the burden upon the beneficiary to prove the payment wholly unrelated to his services to the enterprise. The Court, however, has declined so to analyze the problem and has concluded "that the governing principles are necessarily general and have already been spelled out in the opinions of this Court, and that the problem is one which, under the present statutory framework, does not lend itself to any more definitive statement that would produce a talisman for the solution of concrete cases."

. . . What the Court now does sets fact-finding bodies to sail on an illimitable ocean of individual beliefs and experiences. This can hardly fail to invite, if indeed not encourage, too individualized diversities in the administration of the income tax law. I am afraid that by these new phrasings the practicalities of tax administration, which should be as uniform as is possible in so vast a country as ours, will be embarrassed. By applying what has already been spelled out in the opinions of this Court, I agree with the Court in reversing the judgment in *Commissioner v. Duberstein.*

But I would affirm the decision of the Court of Appeals for the Second Circuit in *Stanton v. United States*. I would do so on the basis of the opinion of Judge Hand and more particularly because the very terms of the resolution by which the $20,000 was awarded to Stanton indicated that it was not a "gratuity" in the sense of sheer benevolence but in the nature of a generous lagniappe, something extra thrown in for services received though not legally nor morally required to be given. This careful resolution, doubtless drawn by a lawyer and adopted by some hardheaded businessmen, contained a proviso that Stanton should abandon all rights to "pension and retirement benefits." The fact that Stanton had no such claims does not lessen the significance of the clause as something "to make assurance doubly sure." . . . The business nature of the payment is confirmed by the words of the resolution, explaining the "gratuity" as "in appreciation of the services rendered by Mr. Stanton as Manager of the Estate and Comptroller of the Corporation of Trinity Church throughout nearly ten years, and as President of Trinity Operating Company, Inc." The force of this document, in light of all the factors to which Judge Hand adverted in his opinion, was not in the least diminished by testimony at the trial. Thus the taxpayer has totally failed to sustain the burden I would place upon him to establish that the payment to him was wholly attributable to generosity unrelated to his performance of his secular business functions as an officer of the corporation of the Trinity Church of New York and the Trinity Operating Co. Since the record totally fails to establish taxpayer's claim, I see no need of specific findings by the trial judge.

D. A CRITIQUE OF *DUBERSTEIN* AND *STANTON*

Griswold, Forward: Of Time and Attitudes—Professor Hart and Judge Arnold, The Supreme Court, 1959 Term, 74 Harv. L. Rev. 81, 89–91 (1960)

Now what is the result of all this? In these "gift" cases we are told that it is a matter for the fact finder in each case. We are advised that this will not "satisfy an academic desire for tidiness," and I concur. I venture the thought that it will not please practical lawyers either, within or without the Government. Surely some guides and standards could be developed and laid down in cases like these. . . . Where the transaction clearly has commercial or economic elements, where there is a quid pro quo, and no aspect of family love and affection, it would be more satisfactory, it seems to me, to rule as a matter of law that property transferred is not a "gift," rather than to leave each such case to the apparently unguided surmise of the trier of the facts. It is no doubt true that a standard established by the Court as a construction of the statutory provision would not decide every conceivable case that might arise. It is the nature of legal questions that many of them fall between earlier decisions, or very close to the line, and thus require further refinement, or even qualification, of earlier decisions in the field. But that is no reason for not providing guidance which will resolve a larger proportion of the cases, and, even more important as a practical matter, will enable administrative officers and counsel advising clients to resolve many of the problems long before they develop into disputes or litigation.

It is true that Congress can step into this situation, and make the statute more explicit. It could be that such action by Congress is one of the reasons for some of the great length and complexity of the taxing statute, and it is somewhat painful to contemplate the statutory verbiage that will have to be written to deal with this problem. Such a statutory solution would surely be more difficult to apply than would have been a fairly simple, straightforward opinion dealing with the questions in these cases (in which no direct fact was disputed) as questions of law. . . .

[*Duberstein* states]: "Decision of the issue presented in these cases must be based ultimately on the application of the fact-finding tribunal's experience with the mainsprings of human conduct to the totality of the facts of each case." That should cover the situation and make everything clear and easy. Still, one may find himself asking: How are the triers of the facts to proceed with this? Is every case to be another guess? Is that a sound way to lead the administration of the tax system? Is there any standard of fact-finding or of trial by jury that requires such a result?—or, indeed, should tolerate such a result? Is this not an example of an undue and unfortunate yielding of responsibility to juries and other triers of the facts, when what was called for was some clarification of the law applicable in cases of this sort? . . .

In considering these cases, I find myself reminded of a story told of Dr. Henry Churchill King, the great president of Oberlin College in the early years of this century. Two of the students had taken a cow up to the top floor of a tall building, and locked her in a belfry, where she made herself known quite audibly on a Sunday morning. It is one thing to take a cow upstairs, and another thing to bring her down. Considerable damage was done in the process; feelings and sensibilities were much ruffled. A meeting of the faculty was called to consider what should be done with the culprits when they were discovered. The matter was taken very seriously, and two leading members of the faculty made speeches to the effect that the students should be turned over to the police, charged with malicious destruction of property, and given their just deserts. This obviously impressed the faculty, who were about to vote to follow this procedure. At this point, President King spoke up. "Come, gentlemen," he said, "you can't do that." And it was so obvious that they couldn't and shouldn't that a suitable academic punishment was quickly devised. From my point of view, *Duberstein* . . . would be [a] "Come, gentlemen, you can't do that" [case].

E. NOTES AND QUESTIONS

1) *Duberstein* versus *Drescher*

What value should have been assigned to the Cadillac when Duberstein reported it? The cost to Mohawk? Its resale value? Is it clear which would be the measure of value under Section 83(a) today? Should the factor of limited choice have been given more weight in *Duberstein* than in *Drescher*? Why?

2) The Meaning of "Gift" in Section 102(a)

The Supreme Court held that the word "gift" in Section 102(a) cannot be given its common-law definition. Why not? If it were so defined, would employees be taxable on end-of-the-year bonuses payable at the employer's option?

3) Will the Real Donor Please Stand Up?

In *Duberstein*, the government argued that business corporations were incapable of making gifts. What do you suppose was the government's reasoning? Does it suggest that if there was really a gift—so that Duberstein was not taxable under Section 102(a)—the real donor may have been someone other than the corporation? If so, who? If that other person were treated as the real donor, would he have to report income as a result of the gift being made by the corporation on his behalf? See Section 61(a)(7).

4) Choice of Forum in Tax Cases

Why was *Duberstein* tried in the Tax Court but *Stanton* in the Federal District Court? In litigation with the IRS the taxpayer has a choice of forums. If the disputed taxes are paid in advance, the taxpayer can sue for a refund either in the Federal District Court where the taxpayer resides or in the Court of Claims (but is precluded from the Tax Court). Alternatively, the taxpayer can choose not to pay in which case the dispute will be heard by the Tax Court.

For many years, there was a powerful financial incentive for choosing not to pay—and thereby choosing the Tax Court. Unpaid taxes accumulate interest at a rate determined under the Code. Until 1976, the Code rate was far below commercial rates. Thus, if a taxpayer who refused to pay eventually lost, he or she would benefit from a government "loan" below the market rate of interest.[3]

This benefit began to erode in 1976, when the rate charged by the government was raised to 90% of the prime rate, and in 1981, when it was raised to 100% of prime. Two changes made in the 1986 Tax Reform Act virtually eliminated the benefit. First, the interest rate charged on unpaid taxes was raised to the "short-term Federal rate,"[4] plus three percentage points. Sections 6601(a) and 6621(a)(2). Second, prior to 1987, interest paid on tax deficiencies was fully deductible. The 1986 Act phases out this deduction—at least for individual taxpayers—and thus increases the after-tax cost of refusing to pay a tax deficiency and losing.[5]

Will these changes discourage taxpayers from using the Tax Court? Perhaps not. Once a petition is filed for Tax Court review, the tax can be paid to avoid the accumulation of interest without losing Tax Court jurisdiction.

A number of other considerations affect the choice of forum. Judges of the Court of Claims and the Tax Court sit without a jury, while there is a right to a jury trial in the District Court. Appellate review of a Tax Court or District Court decision lies with the Federal Court of Appeals for the circuit in which the taxpayer resides; Court of Claims decisions may be reviewed only by the U.S. Court of Appeals for the District of Columbia. Therefore, careful study of both trial and appellate court precedents ought to precede choosing a forum.

5) The Effect of the Choice of Forum in *Duberstein* and *Stanton*

Duberstein chose to litigate his case in the Tax Court and lost; Stanton chose the District Court and won. On the facts, however, Duberstein's case, if anything, may appear to have more merit. Whereas Stanton was a regular employee of the church, Duberstein never expected to be paid for the service he performed for Mohawk. Might the results be explained by a difference in the natural sympathies of the two forums? Why might local District courts be more sympathetic to taxpayers and the Tax Court more sensitive to the national interest in effective administration of the tax law?

---

3. See Chapter 12 for a discussion of why deferral of tax can be viewed as the equivalent of an interest-free government loan.

4. The "short-term Federal rate" is defined as the average interest rate paid by the U.S. government on obligations with a maturity of three years or less. Section 1274(d)(1)(C)(i).

5. The disallowance of the interest deduction is examined in greater detail in Chapter 44.

Or was the vague legal standard adopted by *Duberstein* responsible for the arguably inconsistent outcomes?[6] Would the results have been more consistent if a more precise legal standard had been adopted? Professor Griswold criticized *Duberstein* for leaving too much discretion to the trial court, thereby inviting taxpayers to litigate doubtful cases. In fact, the decision failed to produce an outpouring of litigation for reasons indicated below.

6) Section 274(b) and the Stakes in *Duberstein*

Read the first two sentences of Section 274(b)(1). What is the consequence today of characterizing a payment from an employer to an employee as a "gift" rather than as compensation? How is the employee affected? The employer? Hint: Assume that compensation for services is ordinarily deductible by employers. Overall, what is at stake?

The key to answering these questions is understanding that the true cost of an expenditure to an employer is its cost after taking taxes into account, or *after-tax cost*. For example, assume that an employer in the 40% tax bracket pays an employee $200. The before-tax expenditure of $200 overstates the true cost if the employer can deduct it as a business expense and save $80 in taxes. In that event, the true cost is the $200 before-tax expenditure, minus the $80 tax savings, or $120 net. If the payment is to be characterized as a gift, rather than as taxable salary, the deduction and the tax savings will be lost. The employer therefore probably would reduce the payment to the employee to $120 in order to maintain the same after-tax cost.

Does the employee gain anything when the payment is characterized as a gift and reduced to $120? What if the employee's tax bracket is also 40% (that is, the same as the employer's)? What if the employee's tax bracket is 30% (that is, less than the employer's)? Why is there *no* advantage to disguising *compensation as a gift* if the employee's tax rate is equal to or less than the employer's (and how does this differ from *Eller* where there was an advantage to disguising *a gift as compensation*)?

Today, individual employees are taxable at rates of 15%, 28%, and 33%. Most employers are corporations taxed at a flat rate of 34% on income over $75,000. See Section 11. However, for much of the history of the modern income tax, the top rate for individuals has been *greater* than the rate for most corporations. There was an advantage to disguising compensation as a gift, thereby avoiding taxation under the employee's higher tax rate, even if that meant losing the employer's deduction.

Assume that Duberstein's tax bracket was equal to or less than Mohawk Corporation's. Why was it still advantageous to characterize the transaction as a gift rather than as compensation? Hint: Section 274(b) was not enacted until 1962.

---

6. Stanton won his case not only the first time around but also on remand after the Supreme Court's decision in *Duberstein*. See 186 F. Supp. 393 (E.D.N.Y. 1960), aff'd. per curiam 287 F.2d 876 (2d Cir. 1961).

Ch. 10 Disguising Gifts as Compensation 177

7) After Section 274(b): Disguising Compensation as a Gift

Given current tax rates and Section 274(b), when might it still be advantageous to disguise compensation as a gift? Is the incentive in *Stanton* diminished by the enactment of Section 274(b)? The IRS has ruled that payments to retiring clergy may be excluded if not made pursuant to past practice or agreement. Rev. Rul. 55–422, 1955–1 C.B. 14. Should this ruling have been issued?

Suppose you employ a full time babysitter for $15,000 a year. At the end of the year, you make him a "gift" of $200. Does it matter whether the amount is recharacterized as compensation? Should it be? Hint: Assume that babysitting expenses are ordinarily *non*deductible.[7]

8) Gift versus Entertainment

Suppose that on Duberstein's next trip to New York City, Mohawk Corporation provides him with a "gift" ticket to a Broadway show which costs $100. What is the after-tax cost to Mohawk (assume that the exception for the first $25 under Section 274(b)(1) has already been used up)?

Suppose that instead Berman decides to accompany Duberstein to the theater (at Mohawk Corporation's expense) after they meet to discuss business. Does Section 274(b) still apply? What is the after-tax cost of two $100 tickets? Does either Berman or Duberstein report income as a result of attending the show?

To answer these questions, first assume that Mohawk Corporation faces a 50% tax rate and second, a 34% tax rate. Don't forget to take into account the effect of new Section 274(n), which allows the deduction of only 80% of entertainment expenses.

9) Exceptions to Section 274(b): Employee Achievement Awards

The general principle of Section 274(b)—that an employer may deduct an amount as compensation only if the employee also reports it as income—is subject to a number of detailed exceptions for "Employee Achievement Awards." If an award is made for "length of service" or "safety" and if its cost does not exceed $400 per employee in a given year, then the employee may exclude it from income under Section 74(c) *and* the employer may deduct it under Section 274(j)(1) and (2)(A). The permitted cost increases to $1,600 if the award is made under a "qualified plan." Section 274(j)(2)(B). A plan is "qualified" if it is in writing and "does not discriminate in favor of highly compensated employees." Section 274(j)(3)(B)(i).

These exceptions are hedged with additional limitations. For example, the award must be given "as part of a meaningful presentation." Section 274(j)(3)(A)(ii). And, although under a qualified plan an employee may be awarded up to $1,600 in any given year, the average cost of all awards may not exceed $400. Section 274(j)(3)(B)(ii).

---

7. The tax treatment of expenditures for child care is explored more fully in Chapter 9.

Thus, if Mohawk Corporation awards Berman a $400 watch for promoting employee safety, it may deduct the cost, and he may exclude the amount from income. If Mohawk has a written plan under which janitors as well as officers are awarded watches for promoting safety, then the company may be able to spend up to $1,600 on Berman's watch. But the award of a $1,600 watch will not qualify if the average cost of watches exceeds $400 or if the plan is discriminatory because officers consistently receive Rolexes while the janitors get Timexes.

Is the employee award exception defensible? Does it add unnecessary clutter to the Code and give some employees an unfair tax advantage? Or does it facilitate administration of the tax law by excluding items with a relatively low value, while providing desirable incentives for increased employee productivity?

10) Employee Achievement Awards as Excludable Fringe Benefits

Even if an employee achievement award fails to meet the requirements of Sections 74 and 274, it may be excludable by the employee, yet deductible by the employer, as a Section 132(e) de minimis fringe benefit. According to the Senate Finance Committee:

> [N]o serious potential for avoiding [taxes] arises from transfers by employers to employees of items of minimal value. Therefore, the committee wishes to clarify that the [S]ection 132(e) exclusion . . . for de minimis fringe benefits can apply to employee awards of low value, including traditional awards (such as a gold watch) upon retirement after lengthy service for an employer.[8]

Should a gold watch qualify as a de minimis fringe benefit? Might its value exceed the maximum of $1,600 permitted under Section 274(j)(2)(B) for qualified achievement awards? Does the Committee's statement "clarify" or confuse the tax law?

11) New Section 102(c)

In 1986, when it enacted Section 74(c) and 274(j), Congress also added Section 102(c), which provides that the gift exclusion of Section 102(a) shall not apply to "any amount transferred by or for an employer to, or for the benefit of, an employee." This provision appears to state an *irrebuttable* presumption: *No* employer-employee transfer may be regarded as a gift. So understood, it reverses the ruling in *Duberstein* (that an employer-employee transfer that proceeds from "detached and disinterested generosity" is a gift) and goes considerably further than the mere *rebuttable* presumption urged by the government in that case.

This reading of Section 102(c) could produce questionable results where an employer-employee gift is clearly not intended to provide compensation. For example, suppose an employee invites his employer and a number of

---

8. S. Rep. No. 313, 99th Cong., 2d Sess. 49 (1986).

his co-workers to his wedding. Any wedding gift from the employer—even if no more expensive than the average gift from other guests—would be treated as taxable compensation to the employee. Gifts received from co-workers would, on the other hand, continue to be excludable under Section 102(a).

Such a literal reading of new Section 102(c), however, is not inevitable. The Senate Finance Committee Report can be understood to suggest a much more restricted purpose.

> The committee believes that, in general, an award to an employee from his or her employer does not constitute a "gift" comparable to such excludible items as intra-family holiday gifts. . . .[9]

According to this explanation, the objective was to make Sections 74(c) and 132(e) the sole basis for excluding employee awards. If an award does not qualify under these sections, Section 102(c) prevents the employee from arguing that the award may nevertheless be excluded as a Section 102(a) gift. Outside of the award context, however, an employee might still receive an excludable gift from an employer if it proceeded from "detached and disinterested generosity," as in the case of a *bona fide* wedding gift.

If this is what Congress in fact meant, why didn't it say so clearly? Consider the pressure of enacting a complex and lengthy tax bill, over 900 pages in length, in a fairly short period of time.

---

9. Ibid.

Chapter 11

STOCK OPTIONS REVISITED: DO TAX CONSIDERATIONS ALWAYS PREDOMINATE?

A. N. D. PLUME, INCENTIVE STOCK OPTIONS
13 Tax Notes 493, 493–494 (August 31, 1981)

The 1981 Tax Cut Act brings back in slightly modified form what used to be known as a "qualified stock option." The new option is christened "incentive stock option," but I will refer to it generically as a statutory option. Both statutory and nonstatutory options are typically granted to highly compensated top executives. The reason is that these persons have the capacity by their good performance to cause an increase in the value of the company's shares. The stock option gives them a personal financial incentive to do so.

Statutory and Nonstatutory Options

The statutory option is a right granted to a corporate employee to purchase a given number of shares at a price equal to the value of the shares at the time the option is granted. If the price of the shares declines, the employee loses nothing, but if the price rises, the employee may purchase the shares at the price originally stated. There are no tax consequences at the time the option is exercised. When the purchased shares are sold, however, the employee must pay a capital gain tax on the difference between the selling price and his cost.

A nonstatutory option is in large part equivalent to a statutory option, except that it need not qualify under the technical rules for incentive stock options. When a nonstatutory option is exercised, the "spread" between the market price and the option price is taxed as ordinary income to the employee. The corporate employer, however, receives a corresponding deduction, because the spread is treated as compensation paid by the corporation to the employee.

Which Type of Option is More Attractive?

Because the statutory options are free upon exercise, they seem much more attractive to executives. But when the corporate tax implications are considered, the opposite appears to be the case. The marginal corporate tax rate on income over $100,000 is 46 percent. Even though effective tax rates will be substantially slashed by the 1981 Act, most major corporations will still experience the 46 percent marginal rate. On the other hand, the marginal rate for corporate executives will not exceed 50 percent starting in 1982, and may even be lower if income is successfully sheltered or taxation is deferred. Thus, if $1 million in gain is realized by exercising a nonstatutory option, the corporation receives a $460,000 tax benefit, while the executive must pay no more than $500,000 in tax.

The corporation could instead grant a statutory option for half the number of shares, leading to a $500,000 gain to the employee, which will be tax free, and costing the corporation $460,000 in tax. In this case, the corporation would come out slightly ahead (by $40,000). If the employee sold his stock, however, the $500,000 spread which went untaxed at the time of exercise would be subject to a 20 percent capital gain tax, totaling $100,000. Thus, the statutory option is less favorable when the taxes paid by the executive and the corporation are considered together. In the typical case, the present value of the tax burden on the capital gain is likely to be less than 20 percent, because of the possibility of deferral and basis step-up at death, but it is likely to be greater than four percent, which is the difference between the corporate and individual rates. Of course, smaller corporations or corporations in a loss position do not experience a 46 percent marginal rate, so they may find statutory options relatively more attractive.

But Will Rationality Prevail?

Despite this analysis, many corporations intend to make use of the incentive stock option provision. Indeed, many will modify their outstanding nonqualified options so that they will be treated as statutory options, as the 1981 Act permits. Thus, highly compensated executives will get a windfall (limited to $200,000 in stock options as to options granted before 1981 and $100,000 per year thereafter) on options they already held and which were granted with the expectation that they would be taxable, while the electing corporations will suffer a corresponding loss of tax savings.

The reason for this apparent irrationality appears to be that the loss of the tax deduction need not appear on the corporate proxy statements as additional compensation. Thus, corporations can actually reduce the amount of options granted to top executives, pleasing their shareholders, even though in practical terms the reduced level represents an increase in compensation because the options will be tax free.

Shareholder Involvement

Furthermore, outstanding options can in most cases be converted into statutory options without shareholder approval. The statute requires that incentive stock options be granted pursuant to a plan which has received shareholder approval but if the existing plan happens to qualify under the new rules it will not have to be amended and hence will not be subject to shareholder scrutiny. Even if plan amendments are required to retroactively qualify outstanding options, in most cases shareholder approval appears not to be required. This is because the regulations under identical language in the old qualified stock option provision somewhat inexplicably state that only limited terms of the option plan require shareholder approval. Other plan terms can simply be amended by the Board of Directors.

It will be interesting to see to what extent major corporations make use of incentive stock options, and how these corporations report this use to their shareholders. Of particular interest will be corporate willingness to essentially grant their executives windfalls with respect to currently outstanding options. This sort of corporation action would not be reprehensible if the detriment to the corporation were reported as additional compensation, or made up for by a reduction in other compensation. It remains to be seen whether this will be done, however, or whether corporate executives will assume that shareholders will raise no objections.

B. TESTIMONY OF DANIEL HALPERIN
Deputy Assistant Secretary of the Treasury for Tax Policy, before the House Committee on Ways and Means, September 18, 1980

H.R. 7618 would create an "incentive stock option" subject to tax in a manner similar to the previously available "qualified" stock option.

Present law permits employers to grant only "nonqualified" options, under which the employee recognizes taxable income, and the employer receives a corresponding deduction, equal to the bargain "spread" between the market value of stock purchased and the employee's purchase price under the option. A "qualified" option, on the other hand, permits the employee to defer paying tax until he or she sells the stock (assuming it is held for three years) and then to recognize capital gain rather than compensation income. The employer is denied any deduction under the qualified option approach.

The qualified stock option was removed from the Code in 1976, primarily because Congress believed it did not provide key employees any more incentive than other forms of compensation and, in any case, because it should not be taxed more favorably than other compensation.

This rationale is correct, since employers can provide benefits essentially identical to a qualified option under present law. This can be done by giving an employee a nonqualified stock option together with a cash stock appreciation right ("SAR"). Under an SAR, the employee receives cash equal to the difference between the value of the stock when the option is exercised and the value when the SAR was granted.

. . . Why should employers and employees adopt a method of compensation which will increase the overall tax cost. Apparently, some employers may favor the qualified option if it permits them to pay compensation without clear disclosure to shareholders and without adding an expense item to the profit and loss statement. We question whether facilitating such reporting motivations can be good tax policy.

Accordingly, we strongly oppose reinstituting qualified options.

C. LETTER OF ED ZSCHAU
Chairman of the Board, System Industries, Inc., to Senator Packwood, Chairman of the Senate Finance Committee

Dear Senator Packwood:

... In his testimony, Secretary Halperin raised four issues or concerns which, he said, gave him "serious reservations" as to the wisdom of reinstituting restricted stock [options].

The first argument raised by Secretary Halperin is that a restricted (or qualified) stock option is not needed because Congress concluded in 1976 that "it did not provide key employees any more incentives than other forms of compensation, and in any case, it should not be taxed any more favorably than than [sic] other compensation." Secretary Halperin also contends that restricted stock options are unnecessary because the combination of nonqualified options with cash stock appreciation rights (SAR's) would be just as effective and would avoid the "complexity" of restricted stock options.

Although I may not be an expert on what motivates Treasury employees, I do feel that I and my colleagues are experts in what motivates employees in small, rapidly growing companies. Therefore, we feel more qualified than Treasury to give an opinion on the effectiveness of restricted stock options and alternatives.

When I started System Industries in 1968, after getting some seed money I immediately sought some talented people. I assembled my initial team by getting one person from IBM in New York, one from Univac in Minneapolis, one from Texas Instruments in Dallas, one from McKinsey & Company in San Francisco, and one from Hewlett Packard in Palo Alto. All of these people were on very fast career paths and had reached levels of significant responsibility with their companies. Without the qualified stock options, which were permissible at that time, they wouldn't have left those positions, moved their families, and joined a company just starting up at a time when it had no products and no sales. The reason why they joined System Industries was that they wanted to invest in a start-up, high technology company. However, unlike venture capital investors, they did not have funds to invest. All they had to invest was their talents and their energies. In a sense, these employees were "partners" with the financial investors. Just as it's appropriate and necessary to offer capital gains treatment to investors risking their money in new ventures, it is also appropriate and necessary to offer capital gains treatment to those people risking their careers in the same ventures. Stock options are not compensation: They are the method by which employees can invest their talents and energies side by side with others investing money. Both groups should receive the same types of benefits from taking the same kinds of risks that enable companies like mine to get started and grow. . . .

I feel that the opinion of those who have started and grown companies should receive proper weight in the debate on Secretary Halperin's first point. We believe that restricted stock options are extremely effective when compared with other compensation schemes and that they should receive capital gains tax treatment because they are a form of investment by employees rather than ordinary compensation.

Secretary Halperin's argument that nonqualified options coupled with cash stock appreciation rights would be just as good as restricted stock options overlooks two admittedly subtle problems.

1. The nonqualified option plus an SAR is *more complex,* not less complex, than the restricted stock option. Complications may be tolerable, even desirable, by lawyers, but our experience is that a complicated incentive plan is much less effective than a simple one. It's difficult to explain to the employee whom you are trying to motivate a scheme under which he gets an option on which he owes ordinary income at the time of exercise but the company will take care of that by paying him some additional money that will cover the taxes. That explanation lacks the simplicity of telling the same employee that he is being granted an opportunity to purchase a number of shares of the company's stock and he will get all the benefits of ownership even though he does not have to make the cash investment until some time in the future. The Treasury's proposal is viewed by employees as a convoluted scheme whereas the restricted stock option program is simple, straightforward, and, therefore, more effective as an alternative.

2. The second problem with the SAR proposal is that it can produce a significant drag on a company's reported earnings which can have a distorting effect on its financial statements. In particular, the more that a company's good profit performance causes its stock price to rise, the greater will be the gain to the employee upon the exercise of the nonqualified options and the greater will be the SAR payment to the employee. Such SAR payments are expenses for financial reporting purposes. Therefore, in the case of good profit performance, the greater will be the reduction of the company's reported profit. For a small company growing rapidly, the payment of cash stock appreciation rights can cause significant fluctuations in reported profit which will affect its stock price adversely. Therefore, only large companies with a significant base of profitability can afford to use this scheme and even those must restrict its use to a limited number of employees.

For the two reasons described above, stock appreciation rights are not equivalent to restricted stock options. We need restricted stock options in order to provide attractive incentives to employees that can actually be used without detrimental effects by smaller, rapidly growing companies. . . .

Secretary Halperin's final point was a little bit on the insulting side. He suggested that companies like mine could only be supporting a bill that might result in their paying higher taxes if there was some evil, ulterior motive. The one he suggests is that such companies desire to compensate people excessively and in a manner to prevent their shareholders from finding out. If that were our desire, restricted stock options wouldn't fill the bill. Shareholders must approve the establishment of a restricted stock option plan and, in addition, as options are granted (even before they are exercised), they are taken into account when computing a company's earnings per share which is the primary measure of performance that the shareholders use in determining the value of their investment.

Again, the Treasury fails to understand the motivations of today's businessmen. Although the companies using restricted stock options will pay higher taxes than if they had used cash bonuses or nonqualified options, they are willing to pay these higher taxes because they believe in the efficacy of restricted stock options in motivating employees to be more productive, more loyal, more concerned with the overall success of the enterprise. The value of the increased incentives can far outweigh their extra costs in increased tax payments. That's why shareholders approve such stock option plans. Of course, those companies who do not believe that the benefits of using restricted stock options would outweigh their added cost to the corporation will simply not use them. . . .

Sincerely,

Ed V. W. Zschau
Chairman of the Board

D. LETTER OF DANIEL HALPERIN

Deputy Assistant Secretary of the Treasury for Tax Policy, to Ed Zschau, Chairman of the Board, System Industries, Inc.

Dear Dr. Zschau:

I have read the transcript of your testimony at the April 25th Senate Finance Subcommittee hearing, and have been sent a copy of your April 29th letter to Senator Packwood, regarding S. 2239, a bill to reintroduce restricted stock options. Apparently, you have concluded that direct communication with the Treasury is not possible. However, I would like to take this opportunity to address a number of issues you have raised. . . .

You . . . indicate that my testimony regarding stock appreciation rights overlooks "two admittedly subtle problems." You first state that the nonqualified option together with a stock appreciation right (SAR) is "more complex" than a restricted stock option. However, you do an adequate job of explaining the SAR in your letter to Senator Packwood. Thus, it is perhaps not as complex as you claim. Further, when we refer to simplicity, we refer not only to perceptions by employees, but to the standards to be applied under the Internal Revenue Code. We are firmly convinced that the current provisions allowing nonqualified options with an SAR are substantially less complex from the point of view of administering the tax law than the proposal you recommend.

You indicate that the "second problem with the SAR proposal is that it can produce a significant drag on a company's reported earnings." You later state that the restricted option proposal would not have this result.

We believe that the earnings statement in the case of the SAR approach does give a fair indication of the cost to shareholders of the compensation provided.

However, the basic questions which must be addressed are why two essentially equivalent forms of compensation are treated so differently for income statement purposes and whether it is appropriate to juggle, and otherwise tamper with, the tax law to take advantage of this inconsistency.

Although it is true that the shareholders must approve the establishment of a restricted stock option plan, the options are still not totally reflected in the company's earnings per share. We are convinced by your letter that indeed one of the underlying considerations for the restricted options proposal is the ability to avoid full disclosure of the option on the company's reported earnings. We do not mean this to be insulting, as you suggest, but rather an accurate reflection of the reasons for this bill. . . .

> Sincerely yours,
>
> Daniel I. Halperin
> Deputy Assistant Secretary
> (Tax Legislation)

E. NOTES AND QUESTIONS

1) The Tax Treatment of Ordinary and Incentive Stock Options Compared

There is not much reading in this chapter, although the topic is the most complex so far. These notes and questions are designed to help make sense of the material.

The tax law currently employs two different methods for taxing compensatory stock options. First, an ordinary stock option—which will be referred to as an OSO—is generally taxed under the method endorsed by the Supreme Court majority in *LoBue*:

a) assuming the option has no "ascertainable fair market value" (Chapter 3), the grant, or transfer, of the option to the employee is ignored;

b) the spread (market value of the stock less strike price) at the time of exercise is treated as compensation for services; and

c) all other gain that results from the transaction is treated as investment or capital gain, taxable only when the stock is sold.

However, if certain requirements are met (see Sections 422A(a) and (b)), then the option qualifies as an incentive stock option—which will be referred to as an ISO—and is taxed under the method endorsed by the Tax Court in *LoBue*:

a) the grant of the option to the employee is ignored;

b) the exercise of the option is ignored; and

c) all gain resulting from the transaction is treated as capital gain when the stock is sold.

The purpose of these questions is to help you focus more closely on the differences between an OSO and an ISO. In answering, assume that, whether the option is an OSO or ISO, the holder, an executive:

    a) is entitled to buy one share of stock at a strike price of $50;

    b) exercises the option when the market value of the stock is $150; and

    c) eventually sells the stock for $180.

2) OSO versus ISO From the Executive's Perspective

a) Taxes aside (or *before taxes*), what is the overall gain to the executive from the entire stock option transaction?

b) If the option is an OSO, when and how is it taxed? If the option is an ISO, when and how is it taxed?

c) A certain amount is taxed the same whether the option is an OSO or ISO. What is that amount, and what does it represent?

d) A certain amount is taxed differently depending on whether the option is an OSO or ISO. What is that amount, and what does it represent?

e) Looking at your answers to questions 2)c) and 2)d), above, what advantage is the ISO to the executive? Is that advantage significant?

f) Would you expect executives always to prefer ISOs to OSOs, all other things being equal? Even after repeal of the capital gains preference?

3) OSO versus ISO From the Corporation's Perspective

a) Suppose we now broaden the perspective to include the tax differences between an OSO and an ISO for the corporation. It is ordinarily entitled to a deduction for business expenses, including employee compensation. If the option is an OSO, how would you measure the cost to the corporate employer? Hint: Pretend that the employer compensated the employee with cash instead of with a bargain purchase. Having determined the amount of the employer's deduction for an OSO, *when* should it be deductible? See Section 83(h).

b) Suppose instead that the option is an ISO. What happens to the corporation's deduction? See Section 421(a)(2).

c) Looking at your answers to questions 3)a) and 3)b), above, what is the precise disadvantage to the corporation of an ISO? Is that disadvantage significant?

4) Putting Both Perspectives Together

a) When Section 422A was enacted in 1981, corporate income above $100,000 was taxed at a flat rate of 46%; individual income was taxed at rates ranging from 11% to 50%; and 60% of capital gains were deductible. Suppose that, at that time, a corporation with income in excess of $100,000 granted the option described in 1), above, to an executive in the top individual tax bracket. What is the net tax burden on both parties combined of an OSO? Of an ISO? Hint: To simplify, you need focus only on the tax imposed with respect to the spread on exercise (the market value of the stock on exercise minus the strike price).

b) Which involves the least overall tax burden on both parties combined—an OSO or ISO? How is your answer affected as the period of time increases between when the option is exercised and when the stock is sold? How is your answer affected if the corporation is experiencing losses?

c) Your answers to 4)a), above, should indicate that the net tax burden of an OSO for both parties combined will generally be lower than the net tax burden of an ISO. From the perspective of the executive receiving the option, the OSO involves a disadvantage or *tax detriment*. But the detriment to the executive is more than offset by the tax benefit of an OSO to the corporation. If a corporation decides to use an OSO rather than an ISO, it can be expected to increase the compensation provided to the executive (in the form of additional stock options or stock appreciation rights) so that he or she is at least no worse off than with an OSO.

d) In 1950, when special treatment for stock options first entered the code, individual rates were appreciably higher than they were in 1981. At that earlier time, the top individual rate was 80%, the top individual capital gains rate was 25%, and the flat rate on corporate income over $100,000 was 42%. Under that rate regime, was the overall tax cost of an OSO greater or less than that of an ISO?

5) A Comparison of Two OSOs With One ISO

a) Suppose that the corporation is planning to transfer to an executive either *two* OSOs or *one* ISO. To simplify the arithmetic, assume that both the corporation and the executive face a 50% tax rate. Using the numbers specified under 1), above, is there any difference in the after-tax cost of these two plans to the corporation? Hint: Again, in this and the remaining questions, you need focus only on the tax imposed with respect to the spread on exercise.

b) Is there any difference in the after-tax benefits to the executive?

c) Looking at the tax consequences to both corporation and executive, is the ISO overall a net advantage or disadvantage?

6) OSO With Stock Appreciation Rights (SAR)

a) Suppose that the option is an OSO and that the corporation promises, when the option is exercised, to pay the executive cash equal to the spread on exercise. Such payments of cash are known as stock appreciation rights or SAR. When the option is exercised, what does the executive have left after taxes (assuming that the executive faces a tax rate of 50% and that 60% of capital gains are deductible)? What is the precise advantage for the executive of an OSO with SAR over an ISO?

b) What is the after-tax cost to the corporation of using an OSO with SAR (assuming that the corporate tax rate is 50%)? How does it compare to the after-tax cost of an ISO alone?

7) Nontax Considerations

a) Corporate executives generally supported Section 422A and its so-called "preferential" tax treatment of ISOs. Many lobbied hard for its enactment in 1981. Was their behavior tax-motivated?

b) Under federal law, publicly traded corporations must tell their shareholders how much top executives are paid. This includes reporting both the grant and exercise of stock options and the amount of SAR. Suppose that the president of IBM is granted an OSO to purchase 10,000 shares with SAR. What is IBM required to tell the shareholders when the option is granted? When it is exercised?

c) Suppose, instead, that the president of IBM is granted an ISO to purchase 10,000 shares. What must be reported when the option is granted? When it is exercised?

d) Compare your answers to questions 6)b) and 6)c), above. If you are the President of IBM, what nontax considerations might lead you to recommend to the board of directors that you be paid with an ISO instead of an OSO with SAR (even though the OSO with SAR appears to leave you in a better position financially at no extra cost to the corporation)?

e) What is the precise problem suggested by your answer to question 6)d), above? What additional information might corporations be required to disclose in order to resolve that problem?

F. EXECUTIVES GET BONUS FOR SWAP IN STOCK OPTIONS
The Wall Street Journal (July 28, 1987)

Should a company ask its executives to give up a valuable personal tax break to save the company taxes?

Hundreds of the nation's largest companies are wrestling with that question because of changes approved in last year's tax-law overhaul. The employers stand to reap millions of dollars in tax savings if they can persuade executives to give up the special tax status of their incentive stock options. . . .

Before the tax changes, incentive options were a popular form of compensation for executives because the arrangement deferred taxes and, moreover, because capital gains were taxed at a much lower rate than personal income.

After this year, however, capital gains and personal income will be taxed at the same rate, making the incentive options less attractive to many executives. In response, many companies are asking executives to convert their incentive options to so-called nonqualified options—which trigger taxes earlier for the executive but provide a tax break for the employer.
. . .

Although such conversions may benefit the employer, many executives may be better off keeping the incentive options because of the tax deferral they provide. "Clearly, if you're planning to hold the stock for 20 years, you're better off with incentive options," says Webb Bassick, a partner in Hewitt Associates, a Lincolnshire, Ill.-based consulting firm.

Unlike incentive options, nonqualified options trigger taxes as soon as they are exercised. The executives have to pay taxes on the "bargain element"—the difference between the exercise price and the stock's current trading price. That same amount is the deduction that the employer gets when the options are exercised.

For executives who are asked to convert incentive options, "the key issue is what inducement the company will give" to get the executive to go along, says Jude Rich, president of Sibson & Co., a Princeton, N.J.-based consulting firm.

Even before the tax law went into effect, companies began devising cash bonus plans that would entice executives into converting their incentive options. Such bonuses are meant to compensate executives for having to pay taxes sooner on nonqualified options than they would if they held on to the incentive options. . . .

For many executives, the bonuses won't make up for the loss of the tax deferral. "Generally, these bonuses aren't being calculated using a holding period" for the stock, says Steve Pennachio, a Peat Marwick tax partner. "If an executive sells the stock sooner than the company estimates he will, he wins. But if he holds the stock longer than that, he loses."

If the stock's price has soared since an executive received the incentive options, the executive would have to pay a sizable tax when the options are exercised. "It's possible the bonus wouldn't make up for having to pay the tax early," says Mr. Pennachio. . . .

PART TWO

Gains and Losses on Property

Part Two deals with the taxation of gains and losses in the value of property. Suppose that a taxpayer purchases farmland for $50,000 at the end of 1985. During 1986, the farmland decreases in value to $25,000. In 1987, the taxpayer exchanges the farmland for an office building worth $30,000. In 1988, the building is sold for $60,000 in cash.

This series of transactions raises three distinct questions. First, *when* should the taxpayer report gain or loss? In 1986 when the farmland first decreases in value? In 1987 when the farmland is exchanged for the office building? In 1988 when the office building is sold for cash? Or perhaps on all three occasions?

Second, *how much* income should be reported? The taxpayer ends up with $60,000 in cash at the end but started with $50,000. Is the taxpayer's overall gain measured by the entire $60,000 received from selling the office building? Or must an allowance first be made for the $50,000 originally invested so that the actual income arising from the transactions is only $10,000? And how much gain or loss arises from each separate step?

Finally, *how* should the gain (if any) be taxed? Should it be treated as ordinary income or accorded preferential capital gains treatment?

Each of these three questions is addressed in turn in Subparts A, B, and C, below.

SUBPART A

When Has Enough Happened to Account for Gain or Loss?

Suppose you purchase land for $1,000 and the land increases in value to $1,500. When should the $500 gain be taxed? Is it ever appropriate to tax the gain *before* you sell the land? Or should the gain be taxable only *after* you sell, in order to measure the amount of gain accurately and to insure that you have funds to pay the tax due?

Assume that the gain may be taxed when you sell the property but not before. If the sales contract allows the buyer to defer paying the purchase price (for example, until one year after the sale), should taxation also be deferred until you are actually paid?

Suppose the land purchased for $1,000 decreases in value to $700. When should you be allowed to deduct the $300 loss? Is it ever appropriate to allow the deduction *before* you sell the land? Or should the loss be deductible only *after* you sell?

Assume that the loss may generally be deducted when the property is sold but not before. Suppose you sell the land for $700 to your child. Should the $300 loss be ignored because the land continues to be owned by a family member? Suppose you sell the land to an unrelated party for $700 but retain an option to buy back the land for the same price. Should the loss be ignored on the theory that no "real" sale has occurred?

Suppose you purchase ten shares of GM stock in 1970 for $100 per share and ten shares in 1980 for $200 per share. Assume that in 1990—when the price of GM stock is $150 per share—you sell the stock for which you paid $200 per share in 1980. Should you get to deduct the loss? Or should the deduction be postponed until you also sell the shares acquired in 1970 that have increased in value?

Suppose you exchange an office building in one city for an office building in another. Is the exchange an appropriate time to account for any increase or decrease in the value of the first building? Or should an accounting be postponed until you sell the second building for cash?

Subpart A focuses on these and other questions.

Chapter 12

THE REALIZATION PRINCIPLE

A. INTRODUCTORY NOTE

Under Section 61(a)(3), gross income includes "[g]ains derived from dealings in property." This phrase is explained by Reg. § 1.61–6(a) as meaning "[g]ain *realized* on the *sale* or *exchange* of property" (emphasis added). An increase in the value of property that has been neither sold nor exchanged is commonly referred to as *unrealized gain* or *unrealized appreciation*. The idea that gains on property are taxable only when the property is sold or exchanged is known as the *realization principle*. The readings that follow discuss the policy underpinnings of the realization principle.

B. PRACTICAL PROBLEMS WITH TAXING UNREALIZED GAIN

Andrews, A Consumption-Type or Cash Flow Personal Income Tax, 87 Harv. L. Rev. 1113, 1141–1143 (1974)

Comprehensive inclusion of unrealized appreciation in taxable income would entail enormous practical problems. These involve the necessity of valuing investment property in order to measure unrealized appreciation, and of raising funds with which to pay the tax.

1. *Valuation.*—Unrealized appreciation can only be measured by valuing property on hand at the end of each taxable period in order to see how much that value exceeds cost or prior value. Experience shows, however, that valuation of property is not a matter that can be handled adequately by taxpayers on unaudited returns. Except in the case of fungible property traded on a regular exchange, and even in that case when unusually large blocks are involved, valuation is a matter of reasonable ranges rather than discrete figures, and many taxpayers will naturally tend to pick figures in the favorable end of the range so far as their tax liability is concerned. Taxpayers will vary in the degree to which they will push their own interest

in appraising property. Evenhanded application of the tax laws therefore cannot be obtained unless taxpayers' judgments on questions of valuation are subjected to rather regular examination by auditing authorities. Even then, however, there are not easily applicable criteria for arriving at uniformly fair figures. One has the sense that valuation questions take up a relatively large amount of time on audit, and that even so results are not very uniform as between different taxpayers.

The present income tax depends on property valuation in a relatively few isolated situations, principally when a taxpayer receives compensation in kind for services or for property given up in a barter exchange.... These situations represent sore points in the administration of the income tax as it is. The practical efficacy of the existing tax is heavily dependent upon the fact that it is mostly computed from cash transactions that do not raise questions of valuation. Any change that would make computation of tax liabilities depend generally on the valuation of ... assets would represent an enormous transformation in the tax from a practical operating viewpoint....

2. *Forced Liquidation.*—Taxes are payable in cash. Inclusion of unrealized appreciation in taxable income would create a tax liability without any corresponding immediate source of funds with which to pay the tax. In some cases this would not be a serious problem: part of the property could be sold, or the taxpayer could pay the tax with other funds. But in other cases—small farm owners, other owners of family businesses, elderly homeowners with small fixed incomes, and speculative investors heavily committed to a single project—the necessity of paying tax on unrealized appreciation might work a substantial hardship. It might compel the liquidation of all or part of an investment at a price below what it would otherwise be worth, because the sale is forced. Or, in any event, it might force a sale at a price below what the taxpayer himself thinks the property is worth. Moreover, a taxpayer may be discouraged from making vigorous selling efforts with respect to a small part of his investment, because of the adverse tax effect on the valuation of the remaining holdings if he secures a favorable price. Borrowing to avoid such a sale may be difficult or expensive, especially where the property is stock in a very speculative enterprise, and in any event would make the taxpayer's net investment even riskier than before. A tax on unrealized appreciation might therefore tend to discourage investment in illiquid and risky ventures.

C. SLAWSON, TAXING AS ORDINARY INCOME THE APPRECIATION OF PUBLICLY HELD STOCK
76 Yale L. J. 623, 624–626 and 644–645 (1967)

[I]ncome tax laws barely touch what has become one of the most important and highly concentrated kinds of individual income: the annual increment in value of publicly traded corporate stock....

Shareholders with other sufficient sources of income can allow this stock appreciation to continue indefinitely; if they should need to sell, their assets are as liquid as a bank deposit....

If appreciation of publicly traded stock were taxed annually as ordinary income, whether or not the stock was sold, the tax system would become [fairer]. . . .

A conceptual difficulty with this proposal is its frank treatment of what has not been sold—what is "unrealized"—as "income."

Liquidity and measurability characterize the kind of appreciation that can also be regarded as "income." Liquidity is here used in its broadest sense, taking into account any reasonable obstacle to converting property to cash—factual, legal or subjective. When all the barriers to conversion are low, the increased value of appreciated property is indistinguishable from cash in its effect on the owner's ability to pay, and ability to pay is the touchstone of liability for an income tax.

Measurability is necessary simply because if appreciation is taxed before property is sold, there must be some convenient measure of its amount other than the price realized on an actual sale. Measurability thus operates as a practical limit on how close the individual income tax can approach its own ideal of matching tax liability to ability to pay.

A few illustrations may clarify the use of the terms. Unimproved real estate held as an investment and located in or near a populated area is usually highly liquid, because buyers are not hard to find and because a sale of the property, by hypothesis, will deprive the seller of nothing except its investment value. But since every parcel of real estate is to an extent different from every other, smoothly functioning markets or "exchanges" in which they can be bought and sold at predictable prices do not exist. On the other hand, real estate which the owner occupies as a residence or operates for a profit, for example, a farm or a restaurant, is normally neither readily measurable in value nor readily liquidable, because a sale would materially inconvenience the seller.

But publicly traded stocks amply meet both the test of liquidity and of measurability. . . . [T]heir sale . . . imposes no extraordinary hardship on the selling shareholder. Appreciation of publicly held stock therefore must be regarded as income if the income tax is to remain true to its own basic rationale, ability to pay, within the limits of measurability. . . .

Public stock appreciation could be taxed annually. The stockholder would be taxed on the amount, if any, by which his stock increased in value during the year, each year, for as long as he had it. If he sold it, he would be taxed on the amount by which the sale price exceeded its value for the previous year. A large amount of untaxed appreciation thus would never be permitted to accrue, and there would be no tax-imposed obstacle to selling the shares whenever a more attractive use for the invested funds appeared.

The common argument against imposing a tax on the increased value of an asset before it has been sold is the difficulty of assessing the extent of the increase. The exchanges, however, eliminate this difficulty for public stocks. A shareholder could not justly complain if in his opinion the market was too low a measure of the value of his shares for tax purposes, because the tax difference would be in his favor. He could not justly complain that it was too high either, because . . . he could sell the shares and, with no tax penalty for liquidating his investment, make an extra profit on the market's apparent miscalculation.

D. NOTES AND QUESTIONS

1) Taxing Unrealized Appreciation

In the case of assets that are not publicly traded, taxing unrealized appreciation would require annual appraisals. This would substantially increase the administrative costs of the income tax law, and so taxing unrealized appreciation is often regarded as impractical. However, the realization principle itself is a major source of complexity in the income tax law. Over half of this casebook—Chapters 12–37 and 51–56—would be largely unnecessary if we systematically took unrealized appreciation into account.

> If taxpayers were required to value their assets annually, and to take the current increase or decrease into account currently, a number of complexities in existing law would evaporate. . . . I do not mean to imply that there would be no offsetting social costs in complying with an income tax taking account of annual changes in the taxpayer's net worth. The appraisal industry would flourish, and its fees would no doubt be very considerable. I doubt, however, that they would approach the cost of administering the concept of realization as it operates in existing law.[1]

2) The Realization Principle in Operation: Taxable Income versus Economic Gain

Suppose that you buy land for $100 in January, 1980. As of December 31, 1980 the land is worth $150. Do you have economic gain as a result? Do you have taxable income under Section 61(a)(3)? What are the practical obstacles to taxing the gain in 1980?

Suppose that during 1981 the land does not change in value. In November, 1981, you sell the land for $150. Do you have economic gain in 1981? Do you have taxable income in that year? Are there any practical obstacles to taxing the gain after the land has been sold for cash?

Suppose that in 1981 you exchange the land for a $150 yacht. Do you have taxable income under Section 61(a)(3)? Are there any practical obstacles to imposing a tax on the exchange? If so, why not wait to tax the gain until the yacht is sold for cash?

Suppose that you buy AT&T Stock for $100 on January 20, 1980. As of December 31, 1980, the stock is worth $150. Are there any practical obstacles (such as difficulty of valuation or lack of liquidity) to taxing the gain in 1980? If no such obstacles exist, why not tax the gain?

To what extent is the realization principle, as articulated in Reg. § 1.61–6(a), consistent with the policy of taxing gain only when it can be accurately measured and only when the taxpayer has liquid assets with which to pay the tax?

3) The Realization Principle and Gifts

Should transferring appreciated property by gift produce realization? What benefit does the donor receive in return for making a gift? Could a

---

1. Bittker, Tax Reform and Tax Simplification, 29 Univ. of Miami Law Rev. 1, 3 (1974).

gift be analogized to a barter transaction, that is, a noncash exchange of one property for another property?

Since its inception, the Internal Revenue Code has provided that making a gift of appreciated property generally does not produce realization. Instead, under rules discussed in Chapter 22, the gain is considered to be realized only when the donee sells or exchanges the property. Thus, if the donee's tax bracket is lower than the donor's, the appreciation may be taxed at a lower rate (in addition to being taxed at a later point in time).

4) Marital Property Settlements: The Realization Principle and Transfers of Property in Separation or Divorce

Suppose that property is transferred from one spouse to the other as part of a separation or divorce. *Should* the transfer produce realization? Could the transferring spouse be viewed as selling the property for something, namely the satisfaction of marital obligations owed to the transferee spouse?

Prior to 1984, the answer depended on whether marital property rights under state law were determined by community property or common law principles. In general, community property law makes each spouse a co-owner of property acquired by the other spouse during the marriage. Since the division of property between *unrelated* co-owners was not considered a taxable event, neither was a division of community property as part of a divorce.

In common law jurisdictions, a spouse is given, not an ownership interest in the other spouse's property, but rather the right to sue for a portion of the property in the event of separation or divorce. Thus, the transfer of property in a common law jurisdiction was held to be in exchange for the satisfaction of spousal rights and therefore to cause realization. See United States v. Davis, 370 U.S. 65 (1962).

In 1984, Congress enacted Section 1041(a)(2) to eliminate the disparity between community property and common law states by providing that such transfers between spouses would not produce a taxable event. Transfers of property that are "incident to divorce" are treated as if they were "gifts." No gain is reported when the transfer occurs; rather, the gain is taxed only when the transferee spouse sells or exchanges the property.

5) How Sides are Chosen

In a dispute over whether gain has been realized, which side is the taxpayer likely to take? Which side is the IRS likely to take? In this connection, consider the following materials on the time value of money.

E. TIME AND ECONOMIC VALUE

1) The Critical Importance of Timing

The relationship between time and economic value may be the most important idea in the basic income tax course. *Most tax disputes do not involve* the question of WHETHER something will be taxed but WHEN it will be taxed—in other words, the issue of timing. This note and the readings that follow attempt to explain the relationship between time and economic value using both language and numbers. Even if you are apprehensive about working with numbers, it is crucial to take the time to master this material.

2) The Basic Relationship

You know intuitively that a dollar available *today* is worth more (or has a higher value) than a dollar available only *one year from today*. The dollar today can be deposited in a savings account (or otherwise invested) and in one year will earn interest, growing to something more than a dollar. If, for example, the interest rate equals 10% a year, one dollar deposited today will grow to $1.10 in one year. And a dollar today is worth even more than a dollar in two years. If the interest rate is 10%, a dollar deposited today which has grown to $1.10 after one year will grow to $1.21 at the end of two years.[2]

These observations about time and money can be stated as a simple theorem: *The earlier in time one receives a dollar, the more it is worth.* To restate the obvious, it is better to be paid earlier than later.

Suppose that instead of receiving a dollar, you must pay it out. In that case, you will prefer to pay later, rather than earlier. The cost of paying one dollar is less, the later in time it must be paid. Referring again to the savings account example, you will prefer paying out a dollar in one year to paying out a dollar today because, in the interim, the dollar can be invested to earn interest. For example, if a dollar of taxes can be deferred for one year and invested at 10%, it will grow to $1.10. At the end of the year, the dollar of taxes is due, but the taxpayer is 10 cents richer as a result of earning interest on the deferred amount for one year.

3) Quantifying the Relationship

How does one quantify the difference between the value of a dollar today and a dollar at some future date? We need some method for comparing dollars at different points in time. The problem is like that of comparing a sum of dollars with a sum of francs or other foreign currency. To compare dollars with francs, we need to transform dollars into francs or vice versa. Once we know the prevailing currency exchange rate, the comparison is easy.

It is also possible to transform a *future* dollar into an equivalent amount of dollars *today*. The process of calculating the value today of some future amount is known as *discounting*. (In everyday language, a discount is a reduction, as in a discount price.) The result of discounting a future amount (that is, reducing it to obtain its value today) is called the *present value of a future amount*, or *present value* for short.

---

2. The $1.10 on hand after one year will increase by 10%, or 11 cents, during the second year.

How exactly does discounting work? Suppose that the interest rate is 10%. What is the present value of a dollar in one year? It is the amount which, if invested today, will grow by 10% to equal a dollar in one year. Mathematically, the present value (PV) times 1.10 equals 1. Rearranging terms, PV equals 1/1.10, which is about 90.9 cents. In other words, 90.9 cents is the value today, or present value, of one dollar in one year.

What is the present value of one dollar in two years? It is the amount which, if invested today, will equal one dollar after two years. At the end of the first year, the amount will have grown by 10% and equal the present value times 1.10. During the second year, the amount will grow by an additional 10%. Mathematically, PV times 1.10 times 1.10 equals 1. Rearranging terms, PV equals 1/(1.10)(1.10), which is about 83 cents.

Students of basic income taxation do not actually need to be able to compute present values, since tables are available which indicate the present value of one dollar available at different future dates and discounted at different interest rates. Such tables are included in the reading that follows.

F. MILLER AND MOODY, QUANTITATIVE TECHNIQUES IN FINANCIAL DECISION MAKING
59 Taxes 831, 831–832 (1981)

The tax consultant is, by virtue of the role he serves, frequently called upon to quantitatively analyze the financial consequences of contemplated financial transactions and economic alternatives. Unfortunately, once most tax people get beyond such questions as "What will my client save if he makes a charitable contribution this year or next?" into the arena of broader-based financial issues, they become increasingly uncomfortable. The purpose of this article is to increase the tax consultant's comfort with the quantitative aspects of financial decision-making for taxes by reviewing the basic concepts in the area, and building from there.

Discounting/Present Value.—Regardless of the nature of the financial alternatives under consideration, they must be evaluated and compared in terms of quantity, timing, and quality. Quantity refers to the amount of the cash flows. Timing refers to when the cash flows occur. Quality refers to the relative certainty of the cash flows occurring in the amounts and at the times expected—risk.

Some traditional quantitative methods for evaluating financial alternatives fail to properly account for timing as well as quantity. . . . As it is universally held (or at least should be) that the timing of anticipated cash flows is as important as their amount, techniques that ignore either one are inadequate as a measure of the financial consequences of the alternatives. The ideal measure of the financial consequences of alternatives, then, looks not only to the sum of the cash flows but also reflects the differences in the expected time of their receipt.

A common element of all time-adjusted techniques is that they "discount" expected future cash flows to make them comparable to those receivable in the present. The conceptual basis for discounting is formed by two fundamental propositions, neither of which is startling: "more is better than less" (quantity) and "sooner is better than later" (timing). In connection with this latter proposition, there is an inherent presumption that the cash flows associated with an alternative will be put to good use as soon as they are received (or were being put to use before they were disbursed).

The basic concept of discounting is demonstrated by the following example. If A were to give B the choice of receiving $200 today or $500 10 years from now, B would need a common basis for comparing his alternatives in order to make a decision. From the standpoint of timing, he would take the $200. But, as already established, timing is every bit as important as quantity, and vice versa. The question, then, is how much the $500 is worth compared to the $200. One approach to the solution is to compute how much B would need to invest today to yield $500 10 years from now. That would be the present value of the $500, discounted using the after-tax annual yield on his investments—assume 10%. The present value of $500 received 10 years hence, discounted at 10% (compounded annually), is $193. This is less favorable than the $200 alternative; and so, assuming equal quality (certainty or risk), B would take the $200 now. Without discounting (adjusting the quantity for the timing), B might have been unable to make the correct economic decision.

G. PRESENT VALUE

Alchian and Allen, University Economics 205–209 (1967)

The *more distant* the deferred service (or income, or goods), the *lower* its present price. At an interest rate of 6 percent, the current price of $1 deferred a year is 94 cents—the amount that will grow at 6 percent in one year to $1. This is given by the formula

$$p_1 = \frac{A}{(1 + r)} = \frac{\$1.00}{(1 + .06)} = \$.943.$$

To get the present price for $1 deferred *two* years, simply repeat the above operation. If $1 deferred one year is now worth 94 cents, then deferring the dollar an additional year again reduces its present value by the same proportion. For two years, this is .943 × .943 = .890. A dollar due in two years is worth 89 cents today.

This can be expressed by noting that at 6 percent per year 89 cents will grow in one year to 94 cents, and then in the second year the 94 cents will grow to exactly $1. This can be written in algebraic form

$$p_2(1 + r)(1 + r) = A.$$

where *p* represents the price now that will in two years grow at the 6 percent annual rate of interest to the amount A. Solving for *p*, we get

$$p_2 = \frac{A}{(1 + r)(1 + r)} = \frac{A}{(1 + r)^2} = \frac{\$1.00}{(1.06)^2} = \$.890.$$

Two years' discounting is measured by the factor $1/(1 + .06)^2 = .890$; three years of discounting is obtained by multiplying the future amount due in three years by $1/(1.06)^3 = .839$. The present value of $1 deferred t years from today is obtained by use of the "present value factor" $1/(1.06)^t$. Multiplying an amount due at the end of t years by this present-value factor gives the present value (or present price, or discounted value) of the deferred amount, A, due in t years. A set of these present-value factors is given in Table [12–1] for various rates of interest and years of deferment. The present-value factor decreases as t is larger: the farther into the future an amount is deferred, the lower is its *present* value. This is in no way dependent upon an assumption of inflation of prices.

Instead of working from future amounts to present values, we can derive for any annual rate of interest the future amount that will be purchasable for any present value. How much will $1 paid now purchase if the future amount is due in one year, or in two years, or in three years? At 15 percent per year, $1 will be worth $1.15 in one year. And at 15 percent for the next year, that $1.15 will in turn grow to $1.32. Hence, $1 today is the present price or value of $1.32 in two years. In terms of our formula, this can be expressed

$$p_2(1 + r)(1 + r) = A.$$

$$\$1(1.15)(1.15) = \$1(1.32) = \$1.32.$$

If the future amount is deferred three years, the term (1.15) enters three times, and if deferred t years, it enters t times. For three years, the quantity (1.15) is multiplied together three times, denoted $(1.15)^3$, and equals 1.52. Therefore, in three years $1 will grow to $1.52. In general, the formula is

$$p_t(1 + r)^t = A$$

for any present payment, p_t, that is paid for an amount A available t years later. The multiplicative factor $(1 + r)^t$ is called the *future-value* (or *amount*) *factor*. Values of this future-amount factor for different combinations of t and r are given in Table [12–2]. For example, at 6 percent in five years, the future-amount factor is 1.34, which means that a present payment of $1 will buy, or grow to, the future amount $1.34 at the end of five years. Notice that the entries in Table [12–2] are simply the reciprocals of the entries in Table [12–1].

H. NOTES AND QUESTIONS

1) The Relationship Between the Period of Deferral and the Present Value of a Future Amount

Given an interest rate of 8%, what is the present value of $5,000 payable in six years? In four years? In eight years? What is the relationship between the period of deferral and the present value of a future amount? As the period of deferral increases, what happens to the present value? As it decreases?

TABLE 12–1. PRESENT VALUE OF A FUTURE $1: WHAT A DOLLAR AT END OF SPECIFIED FUTURE YEAR IS WORTH TODAY

Year	3%	4%	5%	6%	7%	8%	10%	12%	15%	20%	Year
1	.971	.962	.952	.943	.935	.926	.909	.893	.870	.833	1
2	.943	.925	.907	.890	.873	.857	.826	.797	.756	.694	2
3	.915	.890	.864	.839	.816	.794	.751	.711	.658	.578	3
4	.889	.855	.823	.792	.763	.735	.683	.636	.572	.482	4
5	.863	.823	.784	.747	.713	.681	.621	.567	.497	.402	5
6	.838	.790	.746	.705	.666	.630	.564	.507	.432	.335	6
7	.813	.760	.711	.665	.623	.583	.513	.452	.376	.279	7
8	.789	.731	.677	.627	.582	.540	.466	.404	.326	.233	8
9	.766	.703	.645	.591	.544	.500	.424	.360	.284	.194	9
10	.744	.676	.614	.558	.508	.463	.385	.322	.247	.162	10
11	.722	.650	.585	.526	.475	.429	.350	.287	.215	.134	11
12	.701	.625	.557	.497	.444	.397	.318	.257	.187	.112	12
13	.681	.601	.530	.468	.415	.368	.289	.229	.162	.0935	13
14	.661	.577	.505	.442	.388	.340	.263	.204	.141	.0779	14
15	.642	.555	.481	.417	.362	.315	.239	.183	.122	.0649	15
16	.623	.534	.458	.393	.339	.292	.217	.163	.107	.0541	16
17	.605	.513	.436	.371	.317	.270	.197	.146	.093	.0451	17
18	.587	.494	.416	.350	.296	.250	.179	.130	.0808	.0376	18
19	.570	.475	.396	.330	.277	.232	.163	.116	.0703	.0313	19
20	.554	.456	.377	.311	.258	.215	.148	.104	.0611	.0261	20
25	.478	.375	.295	.232	.184	.146	.0923	.0588	.0304	.0105	25
30	.412	.308	.231	.174	.131	.0994	.0573	.0334	.0151	.00421	30
40	.307	.208	.142	.0972	.067	.0460	.0221	.0107	.00373	.000680	40
50	.228	.141	.087	.0543	.034	.0213	.00852	.00346	.000922	.000109	50

TABLE 12–2. COMPOUND AMOUNT OF $1: AMOUNT TO WHICH $1 NOW WILL GROW BY END OF SPECIFIED YEAR AT COMPOUNDED INTEREST

Year	3%	4%	5%	6%	7%	8%	10%	12%	15%	20%	Year
1	1.03	1.04	1.05	1.06	1.07	1.08	1.10	1.12	1.15	1.20	1
2	1.06	1.08	1.10	1.12	1.14	1.17	1.21	1.25	1.32	1.44	2
3	1.09	1.12	1.16	1.19	1.23	1.26	1.33	1.40	1.52	1.73	3
4	1.13	1.17	1.22	1.26	1.31	1.36	1.46	1.57	1.74	2.07	4
5	1.16	1.22	1.28	1.34	1.40	1.47	1.61	1.76	2.01	2.49	5
6	1.19	1.27	1.34	1.41	1.50	1.59	1.77	1.97	2.31	2.99	6
7	1.23	1.32	1.41	1.50	1.61	1.71	1.94	2.21	2.66	3.58	7
8	1.27	1.37	1.48	1.59	1.72	1.85	2.14	2.48	3.05	4.30	8
9	1.30	1.42	1.55	1.68	1.84	2.00	2.35	2.77	3.52	5.16	9
10	1.34	1.48	1.63	1.79	1.97	2.16	2.59	3.11	4.05	6.19	10
11	1.38	1.54	1.71	1.89	2.10	2.33	2.85	3.48	4.66	7.43	11
12	1.43	1.60	1.80	2.01	2.25	2.52	3.13	3.90	5.30	8.92	12
13	1.47	1.67	1.89	2.13	2.41	2.72	3.45	4.36	6.10	10.7	13
14	1.51	1.73	1.98	2.26	2.58	2.94	3.79	4.89	7.00	12.8	14
15	1.56	1.80	2.08	2.39	2.76	3.17	4.17	5.47	8.13	15.4	15
16	1.60	1.87	2.18	2.54	2.95	3.43	4.59	6.13	9.40	18.5	16
17	1.65	1.95	2.29	2.69	3.16	3.70	5.05	6.87	10.6	22.2	17
18	1.70	2.03	2.41	2.85	3.38	4.00	5.55	7.70	12.5	26.6	18
19	1.75	2.11	2.53	3.02	3.62	4.32	6.11	8.61	14.0	31.9	19
20	1.81	2.19	2.65	3.20	3.87	4.66	6.72	9.65	16.1	38.3	20
25	2.09	2.67	3.39	4.29	5.43	6.85	10.8	17.0	32.9	95.4	25
30	2.43	3.24	4.32	5.74	7.61	10.0	17.4	30.0	66.2	237	30
40	3.26	4.80	7.04	10.3	15.0	21.7	45.3	93.1	267.0	1470	40
50	4.38	7.11	11.5	18.4	29.5	46.9	117	289	1080	9100	50

2) Comparing Deferral With Exclusion

Suppose you are able to defer paying one dollar in taxes for one year. Using an interest rate of 8%, what is the present value of the tax due in one year? Suppose deferral is instead for two years? Three years? Five years? Ten years? Twenty years? Thirty years? As the length of time increases, what happens to the present value of the future tax liability? What is the difference between deferral and exclusion?

3) The Relationship Between the Interest Rate and the Present Value of a Future Amount

What is the present value of $5,000 payable in five years, given an interest rate of 7%? 5%? 10%? What is the relationship between the interest rate at which a future amount is discounted and its present value? As the rate increases, what happens to the present value? As it decreases?

4) Choosing an Interest Rate to Calculate the Value of Deferral

Your answers above should indicate that the *higher* the interest rate, the *lower* the present value of a future amount and, therefore, the *greater* the benefit from deferring payment of taxes to some future date. Conversely, the *lower* the interest rate, the *higher* the present value, and the *less* the benefit of deferral. The choice of a proper interest rate is thus critical to calculating the precise benefits of deferral. How does one go about choosing the proper rate?

The ability to defer paying taxes is generally equivalent to obtaining an interest-free loan from the government for the period of deferral. For example, suppose that a 28% bracket taxpayer delays reporting $1,000 of income for five years. If the income were reported today, $280 in taxes would be due. By delaying reporting, payment of $280 is deferred. During the period of deferral, the taxpayer can use the $280. But at the end of the period, the $1,000 of income is reported and—assuming that the taxpayer's bracket remains at 28%—$280 in taxes must be paid. The result is the same as if there were *no* deferral and the taxpayer obtained a $280 loan for five years with no interest charge.

This equivalence suggests that the benefit of deferral consists of the interest that would have to be paid to a commercial lender if an interest-free loan were not available. Therefore, the value of deferral should be calculated using the rate of interest, *after taxes*, that would have to be paid on a commercial loan. For example, suppose a bank would charge 10%, the interest would be deductible (a subject explored in greater detail in Chapter 44), and the marginal tax rate is 28%. Then the appropriate interest rate for calculating the benefit of deferral is 10%, minus 10% times 28%, or 7.2%. Rounding off the 7.2% to 7%, what is the benefit from deferring payment of $280 for five years?

But does the after-tax commercial rate of interest fully reflect the value of an interest-free government loan—which is made on terms that no commercial lender would ever agree to?

> The postponement of tax liabilities ... is often analogized to an interest free loan by the Government to the taxpayer....
>
> [T]he "loan" that is obtained by postponing a tax liability has features that are overlooked by the academician but critical to the businessman. Loans from banks and other nongovernmental lenders can be procured only if the lender is satisfied with the debtor's financial ability, and are often accompanied by restrictions on the borrower's freedom.... The loan that results from a postponement of tax liabilities, by contrast, is obtainable at the borrower's will, regardless of his financial condition, and entails no restrictions on his freedom. Moreover, it does not appear on the balance sheet as a liability and hence does not reduce his power to get other loans. Finally, an ordinary loan carries a fixed maturity date, imposed by the lender, and is subject to extension only at his sufferance. Postponed tax liabilities, on the other hand, become "due" only if the taxpayer takes whatever step ... is required to realize the income in question. Thus, even if interest [were charged for the privilege of deferring taxes], he would be well advised to "borrow" from the Government by postponing his tax liability whenever possible rather than to borrow from a private lender.[3]

Could the commercial rate of interest be adjusted to reflect these advantages? How?

Using the after-tax cost of borrowing from a commercial lender assumes that, if the "loan" from the U.S. government is unavailable, the taxpayer will borrow from a commercial lender. But suppose that the taxpayer would *not* borrow commercially. We might view the benefit of deferral as consisting of the amount earned by investing the deferred taxes. Under this view, we would choose the rate of interest, *after taxes*, that is earned on the deferred payment. For example, if it is invested in tax-exempt bonds[4] earning 6%, then the interest rate for calculating the benefit of deferral is 6%. Using this rate, what is the benefit of deferring payment of $280 for five years?

---

3. Bittker, A "Comprehensive Tax Base" as a Goal of Income Tax Reform, 80 Harv. L. Rev. 925, 959–961 (1967).

4. The interest paid on bonds issued by state and local governments is generally tax exempt. Section 103(a). Tax-exempt bonds are discussed further in Chapter 44.

Chapter 13

SALES FOR DEFERRED PAYMENT

A. INTRODUCTORY NOTE

Even if property has been sold or exchanged so that *realization* has occurred, the Internal Revenue Code may provide for not recognizing the gain or loss, or *nonrecognition*. In that event, the gain or loss is usually taken into account at some later date, although in some instances it may be forgotten altogether.[1]

To the student, the terms *realization* and *recognition* are often confusing. We might be better off if they were banished from the tax law. Certainly, all the issues could be discussed without these terms simply by asking, "*When is it appropriate to account for an increase or decrease in the value of property?*"

The first of the so-called nonrecognition sections to be discussed is Section 453, which provides for a delay in reporting when property is sold but the seller is not paid, in whole or in part, until some time after the sale. Although the gain (if any) is *realized* when the property is sold, Section 453 permits the seller to *recognize*—that is, pay tax on the gain—only as he or she is actually paid. Such sales for deferred payment are commonly referred to as *installment sales*.

B. NYE v. UNITED STATES
407 F. Supp. 1345 (M.D.N.C. 1975)

GORDON, CHIEF JUDGE.

This action is before the Court on cross motions for summary judgment. The parties have stipulated to all material facts, which stipulations constitute the Court's Findings of Fact. . . .

11. Charles B. Nye is a practicing attorney and a partner in a law firm in Durham, North Carolina.

---

1. This issue is explored further in Chapter 23.

12. Mary Jane Nye is a licensed medical physician engaged in private practice in Durham, North Carolina.

13. At all times material to this action plaintiffs were engaged in the practicing of their respective professions.

14. As such, plaintiffs Charles B. and Mary Jane Nye maintained separate checking accounts for the proceeds derived from the practice of their respective professions as well as for the proceeds of their investments.

15. Plaintiffs, however, maintained a joint checking account for living expenses.

16. In 1964, upon the advice of her husband, plaintiff Mary Jane Nye invested $30,134.00 in the stock of Colorcraft Corporation.

17. The monies used for the aforesaid purchase of Colorcraft stock by plaintiff Mary Jane Nye were drawn from her separate checking account.

18. Plaintiff Mary Jane Nye has always listed the Colorcraft stock as her separate property on her North Carolina Intangible Tax Return.

19. Subsequent to plaintiff Mary Jane Nye's purchasing the Colorcraft stock, Colorcraft Corporation merged with Fuqua Industries, which resulted in plaintiff Mary Jane Nye receiving eight hundred thirty-four shares of Preferred "B" stock in Fuqua Industries in exchange for her Colorcraft stock.

20. In the fall of 1968, plaintiff Charles B. Nye became a principal financier for a construction project to be undertaken by the Nello Teer Company for the construction of a building for the Wright Machinery Company, Inc.

21. As a direct result of plaintiff Charles B. Nye's venture in the aforesaid construction project, he was contractually obligated, *inter alia*, to make a $100,000.00 payment to a third party in June of 1969.

22. Although plaintiff Charles B. Nye had ample resources of his own at his disposal to meet the said $100,000.00 contractual obligation, he and his wife (i.e., plaintiff Mary Jane Nye) decided upon a course of action at his instigation wherein he would purchase the aforesaid Fuqua stock from his wife and then subsequently sell the same in order to realize proceeds with which to meet the said $100,000.00 contractual obligation.

23. To this end, plaintiff Charles B. Nye acquired, on February 3, 1969, 334 shares of Fuqua Industries stock from his wife (i.e., plaintiff Mary Jane Nye) on the following basis: $10,125.00 in cash and a promissory note from Charles B. Nye made payable to Mary Jane Nye in the amount of $111,375.00 payable in eleven equal annual installments plus interest at the annual rate of four per cent.

24. There is neither any dispute that the price paid by plaintiff Charles B. Nye to plaintiff Mary Jane Nye for the 334 shares of Fuqua Industries stock did in fact constitute the fair market value of the Fuqua stock, nor is there any dispute that plaintiff Charles B. Nye has in fact paid the annual installments plus the specified interest called for by said promissory note.

25. As a result of this transfer between plaintiffs, plaintiff Mary Jane Nye recognized a long-term capital gain in the amount of $109,432.58,

which she reported on the installment basis on Schedule D of plaintiffs' 1969 Joint Individual Income Tax Return (Form 1040).

26. Shortly after the aforesaid transaction between plaintiffs, plaintiff Charles B. Nye converted the 334 preferred Fuqua shares acquired from his wife into common stock, whereby he received 2,672 shares of Fuqua common stock.

27. On or about June 25, 1969, plaintiff Charles B. Nye sold 2,500 shares of the aforesaid Fuqua common stock through a registered broker for $100,381.72 recognizing a short-term capital loss of $13,297.44, which he reported on Schedule D of plaintiffs' 1969 Joint Individual Income Tax Return (Form 1040). Plaintiff Charles B. Nye still holds the balance of his Fuqua common stock and plaintiff Mary Jane Nye still owns 4,596 shares of Fuqua common stock, having converted her preferred to common.

28. At the time (February 3, 1969) plaintiff Mary Jane Nye transferred the Fuqua stock to plaintiff Charles B. Nye, both parties were aware that the latter intended to sell the same stock in order to meet his contractual liabilities some four months hence.

29. The underlying purpose of structuring the purported installment sale of the Fuqua stock by plaintiff Mary Jane Nye to plaintiff Charles B. Nye and the subsequent resale by the latter on the open market was to enable plaintiff Mary Jane Nye to pay less taxes on the resulting capital gain as well as affording plaintiff Charles B. Nye access to monies at a four per cent rate of interest rather than eight per cent. . . .

31. Plaintiff Charles B. Nye had ample resources of his own that would have enabled him to pay plaintiff Mary Jane Nye the entire purchase price on the date of purchase if he so desired.

32. Plaintiff Mary Jane Nye would have sold some or all of her Fuqua stock on the open market had she not consummated the installment transaction with plaintiff Charles B. Nye. . . .

Discussion and Conclusions of Law

Upon the foregoing facts, the Internal Revenue Service (I.R.S.) concluded that Charles B. Nye acted as the agent of Mary Jane Nye in the sale of the Fuqua Industries securities. Accordingly, the I.R.S. disallowed Mary Jane Nye's use of Section 453(b) of the Internal Revenue Code of 1954 . . . to report her gain on the sale by the installment method.

This is not an easy case. Although both parties have submitted excellent and comprehensive briefs, no case has been found which cannot be readily distinguished. Therefore, the Court has searched for what appears to be the most appropriate standard or test to apply to the transaction at issue here. It is believed that standard is found in *Rushing v. Commissioner of Internal Revenue Service.* . . . Although *Rushing* is not factually similar to the case at bar, its discussion of the principles applicable to a contested installment sale is deemed to be an accurate and comprehensive exposition of the controlling law.

We think it clear from a reading of these cases that a taxpayer may, if he chooses, reap the tax advantages of the installment sales provision if he actually carries through an installment sale, even though this method was used at his insistence and was designed for the purpose of minimizing his tax. . . . On the other hand, a taxpayer certainly may not receive the benefits of the installment sales provisions if, through his machinations, he achieves in reality the same result as if he had immediately collected the full sales price, or, in our case, the full liquidation proceeds. As we understand the test, in order to receive the installment sale benefits the seller may not directly or indirectly have control over the proceeds or possess the economic benefit therefrom. In *Griffiths v. Helvering*, . . . the Supreme Court denied installment sale benefits to a seller who arranged for an intermediate corporation which he wholly controlled to collect the full sales price from the buyer and pay it over to him in installments. . . .

It is evident that the sole reason the I.R.S. has denied Mary Jane Nye the benefit of the installment method of reporting her gain is because of the marriage relationship existing between her and the purported installment purchaser. Obviously, such a relationship renders the transaction suspect, but here the I.R.S. has automatically and perfunctorily concluded that any person is the agent of his or her spouse for the purposes of section 453(b) installment method reporting. This rule would probably be valid in the vast majority of installment sale transactions between spouses. But the facts of the present dispute make plain that under no objective analysis could Charles B. Nye be said to be the agent of Mary Jane Nye.

The plaintiffs are two, separate, and, evidently, very healthy economic entities. Both maintain substantial personal estates separate and apart from each other. Given the facts of this case, it is impossible to conclude that Mary Jane Nye "directly or indirectly [had] control over the proceeds or possess[ed] the economic benefit" from the sale of the Fuqua stock by Charles B. Nye. Mary Jane Nye retained no effective benefit or control over the proceeds of the sale by her husband; she received only what section 453(b) entitles her to—a tax benefit. The absence of retained control or benefit by Mary Jane Nye significantly distinguishes this transaction from those involved in the cases cited by defendant. . . .

By way of summary, it should be reemphasized that the facts of this case are rather uncommon. Good reason exists for the I.R.S. to be suspicious of tax saving transactions between spouses, but here nothing was done between Dr. and Mr. Nye which could not have been legitimately done between Mary Jane Nye and any stranger. The simple fact of their marriage relationship, standing alone without anything more to support an adverse inference, is insufficient to deprive Mary Jane Nye of the benefits of section 453(b).

Accordingly, a judgment will be entered.

C. NOTES AND QUESTIONS

1) Policy Considerations

Why might it be appropriate to tax installment sale gain only as payment is actually received rather than when the sale occurs and gain is realized.

In 1980, when Congress made major revisions in Section 453, the Senate Finance Committee explained:

> The function of the installment method of reporting income is to permit the spreading of the income tax over the period during which payments of the sales price are received. Thus, the installment method alleviates possible liquidity problems which might arise from the bunching of gain in the year of sale when a portion of the selling price has not been actually received.[2]

Might the installment method also be justified on accurate measurement of income grounds? The seller's gain should equal the selling price minus the seller's cost for the property. While it is true that the selling price is usually stated in the installment contract, the seller does not know for certain that the buyer will pay in full until all deferred payments have been made. If the buyer does not pay in full, then immediate taxation of the seller on the basis of the selling price in the contract will overstate the amount of the seller's gain.

2) Do Installment Sellers Enjoy an Unfair Advantage?

Are the liquidity and measurement obstacles sufficient to justify special treatment of installment sellers relative to sellers for immediate cash payment in full? Consider this criticism of the installment method:

> The apparently benign object of Section 453 is to make it easier for installment sellers to pay their taxes by associating gain recognition with the receipt of cash. . . . However, the section . . . imposes different burdens on taxpayers who appear to be similarly situated. Thus, property sellers who desire or are willing to invest in their vendee's installment obligations [benefit from deferral], while those who sell for cash because they prefer to invest the funds received in securities issued by other borrowers [obtain no such benefit.][3]

In 1987, Congress revised Section 453 to deny the installment method to businesses that sell to customers for deferred payment. See Sections 453(b)(2)(A) and 453(*l*)(1). Might these provisions reflect a belief that businesses that sell to customers for deferred payment should not obtain an advantage over competitors that do not?

Could the advantage afforded by Section 453 be eliminated by charging installment sellers interest on their deferred tax payments? See Sections 453A(a)(1) and (c)(1), enacted in 1987. This new provision, however, applies only to taxpayers who hold installment obligations with a total sales price exceeding $5 million.

3) Installment Sales of Liquid Assets

Should the installment method be denied when the property sold is publicly traded stock? See finding #32 in the *Nye* opinion. Would Professor

---

2. S. Rep. No. 1000, 96th Cong., 2d Sess. 7 (1980).
3. M. Chirelstein, Federal Income Taxation, 253–254 (1985).

Slawson (whose article on taxing unrealized appreciation in publicly traded stock was excerpted in Chapter 12) favor exempting such property from Section 453?

In 1986, Congress enacted new Section 453(j)(2) to deny the installment method for "a sale of . . . stock or securities which are traded on an established securities market. . . ." Thus, were the *Nye* transaction to occur today, Ms. Nye would not be entitled to defer taxation under Section 453 and presumably would be taxed on the entire gain when she sold the stock.

The careful Code reader may notice a technical error made by Congress in denoting this provision as Section 453(j). There was already in existence another Section 453(j) that deals with an entirely different problem and remains in effect! Thus, in some editions of the Code, the 1986 provision is referred to as Section 453(j)[(k)].[4]

4) The Stakes in *Nye*

Why didn't Ms. Nye simply sell her stock on the open market and then lend the proceeds to her husband? Suppose that Ms. Nye originally paid $30,000 for her stock and sold it to her husband for $120,000, to be paid at the rate of $12,000 a year for ten years, plus interest. How much gain does Ms. Nye report in the year of the sale if her installment method is respected? See Section 453(c). How much gain does her husband report if he immediately resells the stock for $120,000? What were the Nyes trying to achieve by structuring the transaction as they did?

5) The Legal Issues

In *Nye*, the issue was whether an intermediate event (the resale of the property by Mr. Nye for cash) should result in suspending Section 453 and effecting immediate taxation of gain to the installment seller, Ms. Nye. In *Griffiths* (cited in *Nye*), the Supreme Court held that when a shareholder makes an installment sale of stock to a wholly owned corporation, the resale of the stock by the corporation for cash triggers immediate taxation of the installment sale gain to the shareholder. What was the rationale of *Griffiths*? How did the *Nye* court distinguish *Griffiths*? See findings #14 and #17.

Did the *Nye* opinion confuse "equality" with "independence"? Was the confusion possibly aggravated by the IRS' argument that Mr. Nye should be viewed as Ms. Nye's agent? How might the IRS have used finding #29 to support its position?

6) The Statutory Response

What would happen to the Nyes today under Section 453(e)(1), enacted in 1980? See Section 453(f)(1) which defines the term "related person" with reference to Section 318(a). Can you explain the "more than two year" exception of Section 453(e)(2)(A)?

---

4. See, for example, 1 Internal Revenue Code of 1986, Commerce Clearing House 5161 (1986).

Also, consider Section 1041(a)(1), enacted in 1984. Under this provision, *any transfer* of property from one spouse to another, including any transfers for consideration, is treated as if it were a gift. The transferring spouse reports no gain. The gain is taxed only to the transferee spouse when he or she sells or exchanges the property. How does Section 1041(a)(1) affect the *Nye* transaction?

7) Some Other Nonrecognition Events

The *Nye* case implicitly treats a number of *realization* events as being entitled to *nonrecognition*. Ms. Nye originally purchased Colorcraft common stock. When Colorcraft was merged into Fuqua Industries, she received Fuqua preferred stock in exchange for her Colorcraft common. After Mr. Nye purchased the Fuqua preferred, he converted the stock (that is, exchanged it with the corporation) for Fuqua common (which he was entitled to do under the terms of the preferred stock investment contract). Why did neither of these two exchanges (of Colorcraft common for Fuqua preferred and of Fuqua preferred for Fuqua common) produce taxation? Under Section 368, stock exchanges in corporate mergers and in the conversion of one class of stock into another class are treated as nonrecognition events provided that certain requirements are met. Section 368 is usually the subject of an advanced course in corporate-shareholder taxation and is therefore beyond the scope of this casebook.

D. PLEDGING OR MORTGAGING AS A TAXABLE EVENT

1) Pledging an Installment Sales Contract

Are there any other events (besides a related party resale) that should trigger recognition of installment sale gain, even though all payments have not yet been received?

Suppose Ms. Nye sells her installment contract to a third party for cash. Is there any longer a reason to defer taxing her on the installment sale gain?

If Ms. Nye goes to a bank and obtains a $100,000 loan, pledging the installment contract as security, is there any longer a reason to defer taxation? What about the risk that the installment buyer may default? Suppose the installment contract is secured by a third party guarantee or bank letter of credit?

If Ms. Nye pledges the installment contract as security for a loan, will she have "disposed of" it and have to report gain under Section 453B(a)? Courts have been more willing to treat a pledge as a taxable disposition when there is a similarity between the timing of payment on the installment contract and the loan and when the installment payments are made directly to the lender. See Town and Country Food Co., Inc. v. Commissioner, 51 T.C. 1049 (1969). Is it logical to treat similarity in timing as the relevant factor? Shouldn't the critical factor be whether there is a serious risk of default on the installment contract, so that the taxpayer will have to make up any deficiency? See United States Surgical Steel v. Commissioner, 54

T.C. 1215 (1970). If the contract is itself secured, it may be difficult for a taxpayer to argue that pledging is not a taxable disposition. Why?

In 1984, the Treasury proposed that the pledge of *any* installment contract be treated as triggering recognition.[5] Did the proposal go too far by treating the pledge of an unsecured installment contract like the secured one? The proposal was partially enacted into law in 1987 and 1988. See Section 453A(d)(1). This new provision only applies to installment obligations arising from the sale of property held "for profit" where the sale price exceeds $150,000. See Section 453A(b)(1). Thus, it does not affect installment sales of (i) property used for personal consumption (such as a taxpayer's principal residence or vacation home) or (ii) any property sold for $150,000 or less.

2) Mortgaging Property: Loans With and Without Recourse

Suppose that Ms. Nye takes her Colorcraft stock and (without selling it) pledges it as security for a $100,000 loan. Should the pledging of the stock produce realization, that is, has enough happened to justify taxing the gain? If Ms. Nye originally bought the stock for $30,000, why hasn't she cashed out at least a $70,000 gain? Is lack of liquidity an obstacle to taxing her? Inaccurate measurement? If Colorcraft goes bankrupt and its stock becomes worthless, must Ms. Nye still repay the loan?

Suppose that, in the example above, Ms. Nye is able to pledge the stock and borrow the money without recourse. This means that in case of default, the bank can only look to the security of the stock to satisfy the loan obligation; Ms. Nye is not personally liable. Is this transaction distinguishable from a sale of the stock for cash? Should this transaction be treated as a taxable event, producing realization?

3) The *Woodsam* Case

In Woodsam Associates v. Commissioner, 198 F.2d 357, 359 (2d Cir. 1952), the court declined to treat the mortgaging of property to secure a nonrecourse loan as a realization event.

> The contention of the petitioner may now be stated quite simply. It is that, when the borrowing of Mrs. Wood . . . became charges solely upon the property itself, the cash she received for the repayment of which she was not personally liable was a gain then taxable to her as income to the extent that the mortgage indebtedness exceeded her [cost of the mortgaged property]. . . .
>
> While this conclusion would be sound if the premise on which it is based were correct, we cannot accept the premise. It is that [Mrs. Wood] made a taxable disposition of property . . . when the . . . mortgage was executed, because she had, by then, dealt with it in such a way that she had received cash . . . which, at that time, she was freed from any personal obligation to repay. Nevertheless, whether or not personally liable on the mortgage, [the

---

5. U.S. Department of Treasury, Tax Reform for Fairness, Simplicity and Economic Growth-General Explanation of the Treasury Department Proposals 212–214 (1984).

mortgagor remained the owner of the property].... Mrs. Wood, ... far from closing the venture, remained in a position to borrow more if and when circumstances permitted and she so desired. And so, she never "disposed" of the property to create a taxable event which [is] a condition precedent to the taxation of gain. "Disposition" ... is the "getting rid, or making over, of anything; relinquishment." ... Nothing of that nature was done here by the mere execution of the ... mortgage; Mrs. Wood was the owner of this property in the same sense after the execution of this mortgage that she was before. "[The mortgagor] has all the income from the property; he manages it; he may sell it; any increase in its value goes to him; any decrease falls on him, until the value goes below the amount of the lien." Realization of gain was, therefore, postponed ... until there was a final disposition of the property....

4) A Quick Review

As a review, again consider the following four transactions. Has enough happened to make it appropriate to require reporting of the gain? Under the current law, will gain have to be reported? Are the results of current law logically consistent?

a) Ms. Nye pledges her stock as security for an ordinary loan.

b) Ms. Nye makes an installment sale of her stock and pledges the installment contract as security for a bank loan. The installment contract itself is unsecured. Payments under the installment contract and payments under the loan are due at the same time, and the bank is authorized to receive the installment payments directly and apply them to pay off the loan.

c) Ms. Nye pledges her stock as security for a nonrecourse loan.

d) Ms. Nye makes an installment sale of her stock and pledges the installment contract as security for a loan. The installment contract is secured by a third party guarantee or bank letter of credit.

5) Making a Gift of an Installment Sales Contracts

A gift of Ms. Nye's Colorcraft stock to her favorite nephew will not produce realization. Instead the gain will be taxed to the nephew (under rules to be discussed) if and when he sells the stock. However, if Ms. Nye makes an installment sale of the stock and gives the installment contract to her nephew, the gift will be treated by the IRS as a taxable disposition under Section 453B(a).[6] Are these results consistent? If Ms. Nye is well-advised, will the difference in treatment matter? What must be true in order for the difference to matter?

---

6. Rev. Rul. 67–167, 1967–1 C.B. 107.

Chapter 14

LOSSES FROM RELATED PARTY AND WASH SALES

A. HIGGINS v. SMITH
308 U.S. 473 (1940)

Mr. Justice Reed delivered the opinion of the Court.

Certiorari was allowed from the judgment of the Circuit Court of Appeals for the Second Circuit on account of an asserted conflict between the decision below and that of the Circuit Court of Appeals for the Seventh Circuit in *Commissioner v. Griffiths*.

The issue considered here is whether a taxpayer under the circumstances of this case is entitled to deduct a loss arising from the sale of securities to a corporation wholly owned by the taxpayer. The statute involved is § [165(a)].

The Innisfail Corporation was wholly owned by the taxpayer, Mr. Smith. It was organized in 1926 under the laws of New Jersey. The officers and directors of the corporation were subordinates of the taxpayer. Its transactions were carried on under his direction and were restricted largely to operations in buying securities from or selling them to the taxpayer. While its accounts were kept completely separate from those of the taxpayer, there is no doubt that Innisfail was his corporate self....

[A] number of shares of stock were sold to the corporation by the taxpayer at market. The securities sold had cost the taxpayer more than the price charged to the corporation, and in carrying out the transaction the taxpayer had in mind the tax consequences to himself.

In computing his net taxable income for 1932, the taxpayer deducted as a loss the difference between the cost of these securities and their sale price to his wholly owned corporation. The Commissioner of Internal Revenue ruled against the claim, whereupon respondent paid the tax and brought this suit for refund in the United States District Court for the Southern District of New York. The case was tried before a jury and the verdict was adverse to the taxpayer's claim that the purported sales of these securities to Innisfail marked the realization of loss on their purchase. On appeal the judgment was reversed and the case remanded to the District Court for a new trial. It was the opinion of the Court of Appeals that the facts as detailed above, as a matter of law, established the transfer of the securities to Innisfail as an event determining loss.

Under §[165(a)] deductions are permitted for losses "sustained during the taxable year." The loss is sustained when realized by a completed transaction determining its amount. In this case the jury was instructed to find whether these sales by the taxpayer to Innisfail were actual transfers of property "out of Mr. Smith and into something that existed separate and apart from him" or whether they were to be regarded as simply "a transfer by Mr. Smith's left hand, being his individual hand, into his right hand, being his corporate hand, so that in truth and fact there was no transfer at all." The jury agreed the latter situation existed. There was sufficient evidence of the taxpayer's continued domination and control of the securities, through stock ownership in the Innisfail Corporation, to support this verdict, even though ownership in the securities had passed to the corporation in which the taxpayer was the sole stockholder. Indeed this domination and control is so obvious in a wholly owned corporation as to require a peremptory instruction that no loss in the statutory sense could occur upon a sale by a taxpayer to such an entity.

It is clear an actual corporation existed. Numerous transactions were carried on by it over a period of years. It paid taxes, state and national, franchise and income. But the existence of an actual corporation is only one incident necessary to complete an actual sale to it under the revenue act. Title, we shall assume, passed to Innisfail but the taxpayer retained the control. Through the corporate forms he might manipulate as he chose the exercise of shareholder's rights in the various corporations, issuers of the securities, and command the disposition of the securities themselves. There is not enough of substance in such a sale finally to determine a loss. . . .

. . . The purpose here is to tax earnings and profits less expenses and losses. If one or the other factor in any calculation is unreal, it distorts the liability of the particular taxpayer to the detriment or advantage of the entire tax-paying group.

The taxpayer cites *Burnet v. Commonwealth Improvement Company* as a precedent for treating the taxpayer and his solely owned corporation as separate entities. In that case the corporation sold stock to the sole stockholder, the Estate of P. A. B. Widener. The transaction showed a book profit and the corporation sought a ruling that a sale to its sole stockholder could not result in a taxable profit. This Court concluded otherwise and held the identity of corporation and taxpayer distinct for purposes of taxation. In the *Commonwealth Improvement Company* case, the taxpayer, for reasons satisfactory to itself voluntarily had chosen to employ the corporation in its operations. A taxpayer is free to adopt such organization for his affairs as he may choose and having elected to do some business as a corporation, he must accept the tax disadvantages.

On the other hand, the Government may not be required to acquiesce in the taxpayer's election of that form for doing business which is most advantageous to him. The Government may look at actualities and upon determination that the form employed for doing business or carrying out the challenged tax event is unreal or a sham may sustain or disregard the effect of the fiction as best serves the purposes of the tax statute. To hold otherwise would permit the schemes of taxpayers to supersede legislation in the determination of the time and manner of taxation. It is command of income and its benefits which marks the real owner of property.

Such a conclusion, urges the respondent, is inconsistent with the prior interpretations of the income tax laws and consequently unfair to him. He points to the decisions of four courts of appeals which have held losses determined by sales to controlled corporations allowable and further calls attention to the fact that the Board of Tax Appeals has consistently reached the same conclusion. But this judicial and administrative construction has no significance for the respondent. The Bureau of Internal Revenue has insistently urged since February 18, 1930, the date of the Board of Tax Appeals' decision in Jones v. Helvering, that a transfer from a taxpayer to a controlled corporation was ineffective to close a transaction for the determination of loss. Every case cited by respondent in the courts of appeals and before the Board of Tax Appeals found the Government supporting that contention. The Board's ruling in the *Jones* case was standing unreversed at the time of the transaction here involved, December 29, 1932. It was only after the transactions here involved and after the reversal of the Board in the *Jones* case on April 23, 1934, or this Court's refusal of certiorari on October 8, 1934, that the Board of Tax Appeals and the courts of appeals, over Government protests, ruled in line with the opinion of the Court of Appeals of the District of Columbia in the *Jones* case. If the Bureau's stand in the *Jones* case represented a change in administrative practice, there can be no doubt that the change operated validly at least from 1930 on. After the *Jones* defeat the Government sought relief in Congress and after the judgment in *Commissioner v. Griffiths* . . . certiorari here on a conflict in principle between circuits. Certainly there was no acquiescence by the Government which would justify the taxpayer in relying upon prior interpretations of the law.

Respondent makes the further point that the passage of [§ 267] of the Revenue Act of 1934 which explicitly forbids any deduction for losses determined by sales to corporations controlled by the taxpayer is convincing proof that the law was formerly otherwise. This does not follow. At most it is evidence that a later Congress construed the 1932 Act to recognize separable taxable identities between the taxpayer and his wholly owned corporation. As the new provision goes much farther than the former decisions in disregarding transfers between members of the family it may well have been passed to extend as well as clarify the existing rule. The suggestion is not sufficiently persuasive to give vitality to a futile transfer. . . .

The judgment of the Circuit Court of Appeals is reversed and that of the District Court affirmed.

Reversed.

Mr. Justice Roberts, dissenting.

I think the judgment should be affirmed. To reverse it is to disregard a rule respecting the separate entity of corporations having basis in logic and practicality and which has long been observed in the administration of the revenue acts.

Since the inception of the system of federal income taxation, capital gains have been taxed and certain capital losses have been allowed as credits against such gains. In order that this system might be practical it has been necessary to select some event as the criterion of realization of gain or loss. The revenue laws have selected the time of the closing of a capital transaction as the occasion for reckoning gain or loss on a capital asset. A typical method of closure is a sale of the asset.

As the sale is voluntarily made by the taxpayer, his determination when he shall sell affects his capital gain or loss. He, therefore, in a sense, controls the question whether, in a given taxable year, he must pay tax on a realized gain or may claim credit for a realized loss. Of course such a sale must be bona fide and title must pass absolutely. In the present instance the sale and transfer were such, and, as the Circuit Court of Appeals held, there was not a scintilla of evidence to the contrary for the jury's consideration. A taxpayer who pretends he has made a sale when in fact he has a secret agreement which leaves him still, for all practical purposes, the owner of the thing sold, is but committing a fraud upon the revenue. . . .

. . . The sole question, then, is whether, as matter of law, a bona fide and absolute sale to a wholly owned corporation can constitute a completed transaction, determining a loss.

The problem as to how a sale to a corporation wholly owned or wholly controlled by an individual taxpayer is to be treated is not a new one. The existence of such corporations and the dealings between them and their stockholder or stockholders have long been understood. Congress was not ignorant of the problem. At the outset Congress might well have adopted the policy that a sale by the stockholder to the corporation, or vice versa, should be disregarded, and the stockholder treated as in effect the owner of the capital asset until its sale to a stranger. On the other hand, it would be a practical policy to recognize the separate entity of the corporation, to treat a transfer at current value for adequate consideration occurring between it and its sole stockholder as closing a transaction for the purpose of reckoning either gain or loss, and then to tax the vendee upon his or its gain or loss upon a subsequent transfer by comparison of the [cost] on which the asset was acquired and the amount realized on final disposition by the vendee. In fact, the latter course was adopted and was consistently followed until 1934 when Congress dealt with the subject. . . .

This court has found that a taxable gain was realized in a case where a wholly owned corporation sold securities to its sole stockholder. Every element appearing in that case is paralleled here, as a comparison of the facts stated in the opinions in the two cases will demonstrate. This court said, in the earlier case, referring to the corporation: "The fact that it had only one stockholder seems of no legal significance," and held the corporation a separate taxable entity. It is now said, however, that there is no inequity in not applying the same rule to losses as to gains because the taxpayer who exercises the option to conduct a portion of his business through the instrumentality of a wholly owned corporation does so in the full knowledge that, if he does, gains shown on sales by him to the corporation will be taxed whereas losses on such sales will not be allowed as deductions. As hereafter will be shown, this is now true in virtue of the amendment embodied in the Revenue Act of 1934 but it was not true as the law stood before the adoption of that amendment.

In 1921 the Treasury was first called upon to deal with a loss deduction arising out of a sale to a wholly owned corporation. In that year it published Law Opinion 1062. It was held that if the sale was bona fide and passed title absolutely to the controlled corporation, even though the sale was made with the intent of reducing the tax liability of the vendor it fell within the provisions of the revenue act concerning the reckoning of gain or loss upon a closed transaction. So far as I am informed, the Treasury followed this rule in administering the various revenue acts for years after it was issued. The first evidence of a change in its position was the refusal of the Commissioner of Internal Revenue to recognize losses resulting to taxpayers from a bona fide sale of bonds owned by them to a wholly owned corporation at the current market price. The Board of Tax Appeals sustained the Commissioner, but the Court of Appeals of the District of Columbia reversed the Board in *Jones* v. *Helvering*. . . . The decision was rendered April 23, 1934. The Commissioner sought certiorari which was denied October 8, 1934. The same result has been reached by three other Circuit Courts of Appeals. The Board of Tax Appeals followed these decisions. In the meantime the Circuit Courts of Appeal had decided numerous cases which are, in principle, indistinguishable. . . .

So well settled had the judicial interpretation become that the Treasury determined to recommend that Congress amend the statute. The result was the adoption of § [267] of the Revenue Act of 1934. The committee reports disclose that Congress thought it necessary to change the statute in order to render nondeductible a loss claimed on a sale to a wholly owned or a controlled corporation. Subsequent hearings before the Joint Commission on Tax Evasion and Avoidance . . . indicate the same understanding on the part of the Bureau of Internal Revenue and of Congress that the rule of law in effect prior to the adoption of the amendment in 1934 was changed by that legislation. . . .

Plainly, prior to 1934, taxpayers were justified in relying, first, upon the Treasury ruling on the subject and, secondly, upon the uniform decisions of the courts in claiming deductions for losses on sales to controlled corporations. After the passage of the amendment they were on notice that this was no longer permissible.

I turn then to the situation here presented. The claims of this taxpayer, as I have said, had been sustained for prior years by the Board of Tax Appeals. The Congress had enacted that subsequent to 1934 the taxpayer could not claim such losses. Notwithstanding the earlier decisions of the respondent's case and those of other taxpayers against the Government's present contention, the Commissioner of Internal Revenue, *after* the adoption of the Act of 1934, namely on March 11, 1935, served a notice of deficiency upon the respondent respecting losses claimed in his return for the year 1932 on sales to Innisfail. Thus the Treasury repudiated the position it had taken in asking that the law be amended to cover cases of this kind; reversed its position in acquiescing in the adjudication of the respondent's tax liability for earlier years and sought, now that it had obtained an amendment of the law operating prospectively, to reach back into sundry unclosed ones,—this one amongst others,—and to attempt to obtain decisions reversing the settled course of decision. I think this court should not lend its aid to the effort.

I am of opinion that where taxpayers have relied upon a long unvarying series of decisions construing and applying a statute, the only appropriate method to change the rights of the taxpayers is to go to Congress for legislation. In my view, the resort to Congress, on the one hand, for amendment, and the appeal to the courts, on the other, for a reversal of construction, which, if successful, will operate unjustly and retroactively upon those who have acted in reliance upon oft-reiterated judicial decisions, are wholly inconsistent.

I am of opinion that the courts should not disappoint the well-founded expectation of citizens that, until Congress speaks to the contrary, they may, with confidence, rely upon the uniform judicial interpretation of a statute. The action taken in this case seems to me to make it impossible for a citizen safely to conduct his affairs in reliance upon any settled body of court decisions.

B. NOTES AND QUESTIONS

1) The Stakes in *Nye* and *Higgins v. Smith* Compared

In *Nye*, the IRS argued that a taxable event had already occurred and sought to accelerate reporting; in Higgins v. Smith, it argued that realization had not yet occurred and sought to delay reporting. Why would tax revenue be increased by accelerating reporting in one case and by delaying reporting in the other?

2) The Realization Principle and Losses

In Higgins v. Smith, the Supreme Court held that the claimed losses could not be deducted because they had not yet been realized. The Court found a statutory basis for applying the realization principle to losses in the predecessor of Section 165(a), which allows a deduction only if a loss is "sustained."

What are the policy reasons for not taking account of a loss in the value of property until there has been a sale or exchange? Do the same policy reasons which justify the realization principle for gains also apply to losses? Is liquidity an obstacle to allowing deduction of unrealized losses? In the case of publicly traded stock, is accurate measurement of the loss an obstacle? In the case of farmland?

Suppose that you earn an annual salary of $60,000. At the beginning of the year you invest $200,000 in the stock market. During the year, half of your stocks increase in value by $40,000, and the other half decrease in value by $25,000. How would permitting deduction of unrealized losses (while continuing to require realization before taxing gains) distort the measurement of income? Also, how would tax revenues be affected?

3) Measuring the Loss in Related Party Sales

In Higgins v. Smith, the taxpayer measured the amount of his loss by the difference between what he paid for the property and what he was paid when he sold it to Innisfail Corp. For example, if the stock cost the taxpayer $200 and was sold by him for $50, then the claimed loss would have been $150.

But was the amount paid by Innisfail, a related party, necessarily an accurate reflection of the property's fair market value and therefore of the amount of the loss? Isn't there an incentive for a related party to pay less than the fair market value in order to overstate the amount of the loss? Why is this incentive absent in sales between *unrelated* parties, conducted at arm's length? Why is it also absent in sales between related parties when the property is publicly traded stock (as in Higgins v. Smith)?

4) Form and Substance

In Higgins v. Smith, how did the Supreme Court justify holding that realization had not occurred even though the property had been sold? What did the Court mean when it said there was no sale in "substance" even though "[t]itle passed"?

How did Higgins v. Smith distinguish *Commonwealth Improvement* in which, on nearly identical facts, it held that realization had occurred? According to the Court, when is a taxpayer allowed to argue that substance should prevail over form? When is the IRS permitted to make that argument?

How is Higgins v. Smith at odds with both *Nye* and *Woodsam*? In both *Nye* and *Woodsam*, how was form arguably elevated over substance? Can these differences between Higgins v. Smith, on the one hand, and *Nye* and *Woodsam*, on the other, be reconciled? Consider the following views on form and substance in the federal tax law:

> The courts themselves follow no single and consistent set of rules in deciding when to accept and when to disregard the taxpayer's choice of form, although there is a conclusory commonplace for either type of determination. Thus, when declining to accept the taxpayer's choice of form the courts commonly assert as a matter of principle that the incidence of taxation depends upon the substance of the transaction and that mere form is not controlling. When, on the other hand, the choice of form is accepted, the appropriate maxim is that "there is nothing sinister in so arranging one's affairs as to keep taxes as low as possible."[1]

> [I]n deciding federal tax cases the courts are ordinarily willing if not eager to take account of the substance behind the veil of form.... The appeal from form to substance is frequently deplored as more confusing than helpful,... but it is hard to imagine how a mature jurisprudence could consistently adhere to formalities in all circumstances. To reach no further back than the Europe of the Middle Ages and Renaissance, for example, the Catholic Church's prohibition of usury set into motion a never-ceasing

---

1. Chirelstein, Learned Hand's Contribution to the Law of Tax Avoidance, 77 Yale L. J. 440, 440–441 (1968).

inquiry into the form of transactions designed to evade the restriction, including sales of property with an option in the seller to repurchase for a higher price at a later date—a device that is still sometimes used in the hope of avoiding the tax results of a mortgage....

The substance-over-form doctrine is invoked by the government with greatest success when the transaction under examination entails self-dealing, since in these circumstances the form used often has minimal, if any, nontax consequences and is often chosen solely because it is expected to reduce taxes.... Recognizing that "sales" within the family may not be what they purport to be and that evidence of their true nature is peculiarly within the control of the taxpayer, Congress has laid down a number of statutory rules that treat intra-family sales differently from sales to third parties. An example is IRC § 267(a)(1), forbidding taxpayers to deduct losses on such sales, even if effected at the property's fair market value.

But even if a transaction is not explicitly condemned by the statute, its form may be disregarded by the courts in appropriate circumstances....

Transactions at arm's length between the taxpayer and outsiders are far less vulnerable to substance-over-form attacks by the government than self-dealing transactions. For nontax reasons, the parties usually fully express their understanding in documents, so that the chosen form ordinarily embodies the substance of their transaction. This fusion of form and substance is fostered if, as often occurs, they have divergent tax interests. Thus, when a business pays an employee for services, the desire to deduct the payment as business expense usually leads the employer to resist suggestions by the recipient that the payment be disguised as a tax-free gift rather than reported as taxable wages.

This frequent opposition of interests does not mean that the characterization adopted by the parties to an arm's length bargain is invariably conclusive. The employer, to continue with the example just used, may be a tax exempt organization or a persistently unsuccessful enterprise with more deductions than it can use; if so, it may be willing to cooperate with the employee as a costless gesture of benevolence or in return for a concession by him. A similar bargain may be struck when two parties expect to be taxed at very different rates; if they can devise a legal form that will assign the tax advantages to the party who can best "use" them, the tax savings thus achieved can be divided between them.[2]

5) The Relevance of Tax Avoidance Purpose

What was the primary function of Innisfail Corp., which was created by the taxpayer in Higgins v. Smith? What does that tell you about the purpose of the sale of stock to Innisfail? Suppose that the taxpayer had created Innisfail to conduct a taxicab business and that Innisfail was managed for the taxpayer by unrelated parties who did not consult him about day-to-day management decisions. Suppose further that Innisfail's management placed an order with a broker to invest excess cash in stock and that on the same day Smith—unaware of Innisfail's order—told the same broker to sell identical stock. If the broker matched these orders—selling

---

2. B. Bittker, Federal Income Taxation of Income, Estates and Gifts, pp. 4–36 to 4–40 (1980).

Smith's stock to Innisfail—*should* Smith be prohibited from deducting the loss? How does Smith's purpose in this hypothetical situation differ from his purpose in the actual case?

Today, would the language of Section 267 apply to both the actual case and the hypothetical above? See Sections 267(a)(1) and 267(b)(2). Should Congress have required a finding of tax avoidance purpose before disallowing losses under Section 267? Or, as an objective matter, is a sale of stock to a related party not a sale in substance, even when it is inadvertent?

Higgins v. Smith involved the interpretation of the word "sustained" in Section 165(a), rather than the application of Section 267, which was enacted only *after* the tax year in question. If the case had involved the *inadvertent* related party sale described above, would the IRS have been more likely to lose? Why?

6) When is a Taxpayer Entitled to Rely on Prior Administrative Practice and Judicial Decisions?

The dissent argued that the taxpayer should have won because the IRS had allowed the deduction of losses on sales to a wholly owned corporation from 1921 until 1930. Once the IRS decides that it was mistaken in an earlier interpretation of the Code, shouldn't it be allowed to modify its position? Or should the IRS instead ask Congress to amend the statute to overrule its mistaken interpretation?

The dissent also noted that four other courts of appeal had interpreted the Code, prior to the 1934 enactment of the predecessor of Section 267, as allowing such losses. Shouldn't a taxpayer be entitled to rely on favorable decisions of the Circuit Court of Appeal? Or should it depend on whether the IRS has indicated that it regards the decisions as erroneous and intends to continue litigating the issue in other circuits?

When the IRS loses in the Tax Court, it usually announces its "acquiescence" or "nonacquiescence" in the result. This provides some guidance for taxpayers as to whether the IRS will accept the unfavorable decision or continue to litigate the issues in hope of eventually reversing the outcome.

7) Analogous Transactions

What other kinds of sales might be covered by the principle of Higgins v. Smith? See Sections 267(a)(1) and (b)(1)-(10) and 1091(a). Suppose that a taxpayer sells shares at a loss and then repurchases identical shares on the open market after 31 days. Will the loss be disallowed by Section 1091(a)? If not, is there a serious abuse problem?

If a transaction is not covered by Section 267 or Section 1091, can the loss still be disallowed if it is "without substance"? In Horne v. Commissioner, 5 T.C. 250 (1945), a taxpayer owned a seat on a commodities exchange that had been acquired for $24,000 in July of 1929, just before the stock market crash and the "Great Depression." In November of 1941, he purchased a second seat on the exchange and then ten days later sold his old seat for $1,000, realizing a $23,000 loss. The Tax Court held that the transaction was not covered by Section 1091, since the seat was not "stock or securities." See Section 1091(a). It nevertheless disallowed a deduction, stating that the taxpayer's only *purpose* was to establish a loss while continuing to hold his seat on the exchange without interruption.

C. McWILLIAMS v. COMMISSIONER
331 U.S. 694 (1947)

MR. CHIEF JUSTICE VINSON delivered the opinion of the Court.

John P. McWilliams . . . had for a number of years managed the large independent estate of his wife . . . as well as his own. On several occasions in 1940 and 1941 he ordered his broker to sell certain stock for the account of one of the two and to buy the same number of shares of the same stock for the other, at as nearly the same price as possible. He told the broker that his purpose was to establish tax losses. On each occasion the sale and purchase were promptly negotiated through the Stock Exchange, and the identity of the persons buying from the selling spouse and of the persons selling to the buying spouse was never known. Invariably, however, the buying spouse received stock certificates different from those which the other had sold. Petitioners filed separate income tax returns for these years, and claimed the losses which he or she sustained on the sales as deductions from gross income.

The Commissioner disallowed these deductions on the authority of § [267] of the Internal Revenue Code, which prohibits deductions for losses from "sales or exchanges of property, directly or indirectly . . . Between members of a family," and between certain other closely related individuals and corporations. . . .

[The] purpose of § [267] was to put an end to the right of taxpayers to choose, by intra-family transfers and other designated devices, their own time for realizing tax losses on investments which, for most practical purposes, are continued uninterrupted.

We are clear as to this purpose, too, that its effectuation obviously had to be made independent of the manner in which an intra-group transfer was accomplished. Congress, with such purpose in mind, could not have intended to include within the scope of § [267] only simple transfers made directly or through a dummy, or to exclude transfers of securities effected through the medium of the Stock Exchange, unless it wanted to leave a loophole almost as large as the one it had set out to close.

Petitioners suggest that Congress, if it truly intended to disallow losses on intra-family transactions through the market, would probably have done so by an amendment to the wash sales provisions, making them applicable where the seller and buyer were members of the same family, as well as where they were one and the same individual. This extension of the wash sales provisions, however, would bar only one particular means of accomplishing the evil at which § [267] was aimed, and the necessity for a comprehensive remedy would have remained.

Nor can we agree that Congress' omission from § [267] of any prescribed time interval, comparable in function to that in the wash sales provisions, indicates that § [267] was not intended to apply to intra-family transfers through the Exchange. Petitioners' argument is predicated on the difficulty which courts may have in determining whether the elapse of certain periods of time between one spouse's sale and the other's purchase of like securities on the Exchange is of great enough importance in itself to break the continuity of the investment and make § [267] inapplicable.

Precisely the same difficulty may arise, however, in the case of an intra-family transfer through an individual intermediary, who, by pre-arrangement, buys from one spouse at the market price and a short time later sells the identical certificates to the other at the price prevailing at the time of sale. The omission of a prescribed time interval negates the applicability of § [267] to the former type of transfer no more than it does to the latter. But if we should hold that it negated both, we would have converted the section into a mere trap for the unwary.

Petitioners also urge that, whatever may have been Congress' intent, its designation in § [267] of sales "between" members of a family is not adequate to comprehend the transactions in this case, which consisted only of a sale of stock by one of the petitioners to an unknown stranger, and the purchase of different certificates of stock by the other petitioner, presumably from another stranger.

We can understand how this phraseology, if construed literally and out of context, might be thought to mean only direct intra-family transfers. But petitioners concede that the express statutory reference to sales made "directly or indirectly" precludes that construction. Moreover, we can discover in this language no implication whatsoever that an indirect intra-family sale of fungibles is outside the statute unless the units sold by one spouse and those bought by the other are identical. Indeed, if we accepted petitioners' construction of the statute, we think we would be reading into it a crippling exception which is not there. . . .

D. NOTES AND QUESTIONS

1) A Statutory Gap?

Would the loss in *McWilliams* be disallowed under the literal language of either Sections 267 or 1091? Why not? How did *McWilliams* fill the statutory gap? Did the Court adequately justify its expansive reading of Section 267? Could it just as easily have tried to fill the gap by an expansive reading of Section 1091?

2) The Relevance of the Time Interval

Suppose that McWilliams ordered his broker to wait one day between selling stock for his account and buying it for his wife's. Or, suppose that he instructed the broker to wait one week, thirty days, or thirty-one days. As the interval between the two transactions lengthens, should we be more willing to allow the loss? How can a court determine where the line should be drawn?

3) The Relevance of Tax Avoidance Purpose

Suppose that a taxpayer sells 100 Chrysler shares at a loss on the New York Stock Exchange and that, on the same day, a related party (as defined in Section 267(b))—for example, the taxpayer's brother, sister, grandparent, or grandchild—buys 100 Chrysler shares on the New York Stock Exchange. The orders are not part of a coordinated transaction. Neither party has advance knowledge of the other's plans. Can this example be distinguished from *McWilliams*? Would you advise the taxpayer that he or she can safely deduct the loss without fear of being challenged by the IRS? Might it depend on whether the related party is a member of the taxpayer's household or maintains a separate household?

Chapter 15

CAPITAL LOSSES AND INVENTORY LOSSES

A. INTRODUCTORY NOTES AND QUESTIONS

1) Recognition and Nonrecognition of Capital Losses

The basic capital gains preference was repealed by the 1986 Tax Reform Act. But *capital losses*—defined roughly as losses from the sale or exchange of investment property[1]—were essentially unaffected. Capital losses may be deducted *only to the extent that the taxpayer has recognized capital gains*. There is an exception for the first $3,000 for noncorporate taxpayers. Apart from this exception, capital losses may *not* be deducted against ordinary income. See Section 1211(b).

Capital losses that may not be deducted under Section 1211(b) may be applied to other tax years. Corporations may carry the losses backward up to three years and forward up to five years. Individuals may carry the losses forward only but are allowed to do so *indefinitely*.

When an unused capital loss is applied to another year, it remains subject to the limits in Section 1211(b). Thus, the loss is deductible only to the extent of reported capital gains in that other year, except for the first $3,000 of losses for noncorporate taxpayers which are fully deductible.

Why is Section 1211, in effect, a nonrecognition provision? When may even *realized* capital losses be subject to nonrecognition? What has to happen in order for realized capital losses to be *recognized*?

2) Why Limit the Deductibility of Capital Losses?

Suppose that you earn an annual salary of $60,000. At the beginning of the year, you invest $200,000 in the stock market. During the year, half of your stocks increase in value by $40,000 and the other half decrease in value by $25,000. If there were no limits on the deductibility of realized

---

1. The Code defines capital losses as losses from the sale or exchange of *capital assets*. See Section 1222. Capital assets are defined as *property*, subject to stated exceptions. See Section 1221.

capital losses, what tax minimization strategy might you be advised to pursue? Why might the Treasury regard such a strategy as excessively damaging to revenues? As providing some taxpayers with an unfair advantage over others?

If gains and losses were accounted for annually, whether realized or not, would there be any need to limit the deduction of capital losses? Are the arguments for limiting the deduction of capital losses analytically distinct from the arguments, discussed in Chapter 14, for applying the realization principle to losses?

The following article argues for repeal of limits on deducting realized capital losses.

B. WARREN, THE DEDUCTIBILITY BY INDIVIDUALS OF CAPITAL LOSSES UNDER THE FEDERAL INCOME TAX
40 U. Chi. L. Rev. 291, 291–295, 297–298, 300 (1973)

The federal income tax consequences for individuals who realize capital losses have undergone a bewildering number of changes since the adoption of the sixteenth amendment. Originally denied deductibility from ordinary income, capital losses were for a short period fully deductible; since 1924 they have been only partially deductible. The limitations imposed since 1924 include an offset against capital gains only. . . .

The Case for Full Deductibility

The Net Income Concept . . .

Suppose now that two taxpayers each have ordinary business income of $10,000; B has a capital loss of $5,000, while A has no losses of any kind. B has acquired the power to command $5,000 in additional goods and services while A can command $10,000 more than formerly. Unless there is reason to believe that B's $5,000 loss is unworthy of recognition solely because it is a capital rather than a business loss, he should be permitted the deduction to reflect the fact that he has not achieved as great a net economic gain as the taxpayer who sustained no losses. . . .

The argument for full deductibility of capital losses as a matter of equity—treating like cases alike—was made before the Senate Finance Committee as early as 1916, along with the assertion that this had been the intent of Congress when the income tax was first enacted in 1913. Two years later, when Congress expressly embraced full deductibility, the chairman of the House Ways and Means Committee defended the measure as a matter of equity:

> Under the present act a loss to the taxpayer can only be deducted if it is connected with the transactions of the business, while a casual loss on the outside cannot be deducted. To illustrate, suppose that I am a player of the stock market, and that is my business. Suppose I lose $50,000. I can deduct that from my total year's earnings. . . . [B]ut if I am a merchant, a farmer, or a lawyer, and happen to see something in the paper which makes me think I can make a big sum of money, and then I go out and buy a future contract, and make a loss of $10,000, I cannot deduct that from my income under the existing law or under the act of 1913. . . . Now, this bill permits

all taxpayers to deduct their losses that are made in their business or outside of their business during the year. If I make $10,000 in the practice of law and lose $10,000 on the stock market I can deduct it, because in the case I have supposed I would have no income left.

Because Congress has, since 1924, refused to allow full deduction of capital losses, references in subsequent legislative history to the theoretical validity of unlimited deductions have necessarily been minimal. Among commentators, however, there is a fair amount of agreement that full deductibility is theoretically justified, but the expected revenue and avoidance effects of such a policy have led many of them to refrain from advocating it in practice. . . .

Economic Incentives for Risk Taking

In addition to the theoretical argument based on the net income concept, the primary rationale for making capital losses fully deductible is in the economic incentive for risk taking it would provide. The securities industry has long complained that new capital ventures are made less attractive because the government insists upon having so large a share of capital gains and so small a share of the losses. Equity investment, particularly in new enterprises of greater than usual risk, is discouraged by the failure of the tax system to permit full deduction of losses. Yet the legislative history of loss limitations only occasionally manifests congressional recognition of the argument that taxpayers would be more willing to take substantial risks, subjecting any profit to the possibility of taxation, if losses could be deducted from other income. . . .

In summary, the case for full deductibility rests primarily on two grounds: (1) in its impact on a taxpayer's ability to command goods and services, a capital loss is indistinguishable from any other loss incurred in a gain seeking transaction; and (2) full deductibility would have beneficial economic effects.

C. NOTES AND QUESTIONS

1) Equity Considerations: Is Limiting the Deduction of Capital Losses Unfair?

The preceding article argues that fairness, or *equity*, requires unlimited deduction of capital losses. An example is cited of two individuals who both have earnings and losses. The first individual's losses arise in business and so are immediately deductible in full, while the second individual's losses arise from an investment and so cannot be deducted, absent capital gains.

But is there another way to look at the issue of fairness? Consider a different example involving two individuals, X and Y, who both earn $50,000 during the year. X has no investment property. Y owns a stock portfolio, which, during the year, experiences $20,000 in unrealized gains and $20,000 in unrealized losses. If Y decides to sell the stock with unrealized losses (but continues to hold the stock with unrealized gains), *should* the losses be deductible without limit? If they are, then Y's reported income will be only $30,000 while X's income will be $50,000. But is Y's economic income for the year really less than X's?

Whether limiting the deduction of capital losses is fair seems to depend on the example chosen. Which example seems more appropriate?

2) Efficiency Considerations: Does Limiting the Deduction of Capital Losses Deter Risk Taking?

The preceding article also argues that limiting the deduction of capital losses discourages risk taking and, therefore, causes a decline in the amount of risky investment. What about all the other kinds of government regulation that affect investment decisions? Does it make sense to oppose the limitation on capital loss deductions without first trying to estimate the net impact of all other government measures that affect risk taking, both positively and negatively?

D. COMPARING INVENTORY LOSSES WITH CAPITAL LOSSES

1) The Special Treatment of Inventory Losses

Inventory can be defined as the goods sold by a business to its customers as, for example, when General Motors sells cars, IBM sells computers, or Texaco sells gasoline. Losses on inventory are treated differently from losses on investment property (or capital losses). First, although capital losses may generally be deducted only to the extent of capital gains, inventory losses are not so limited and may be deducted even if there are no gains on inventory or on other property.[2] Second, although capital losses are deductible only if *realized*, even *unrealized* losses on inventory are deductible under certain circumstances!

This Note explores the reasons why inventory losses are not subject to the same limits as capital losses. In order to understand these reasons, the reader must first know something of the rudiments of inventory accounting, which are explained below.

2) Accounting for the Cost of Inventory: Constant Wholesale Prices

Suppose that a jelly bean store:
a) at the end of 1984, has in stock 1,200 pounds of jelly beans;
b) during 1985, acquires 800 additional pounds;
c) during 1985, sells 1,000 pounds to customers for $2 per pound; and
d) during 1986, goes out of business, selling the remaining 1,000 pounds to customers for $2 per pound (having acquired no additional jelly beans during 1986).

Assume that the wholesale price of jelly beans has remained constant at $1 per pound. How much income should the store report during 1985 (ignoring all expenses other than the wholesale cost of jelly beans)? During 1986? The critical problem is to assign a cost to the goods sold in each year. Do you need to know which particular beans were sold during 1985 and

---

2. Section 1221 defines the scope of the Section 1211 limit on deducting losses. The definition is written in terms of what is not covered rather than what is. Capital assets—which produce capital losses—are defined to include all "property," with certain stated exceptions (denoted "exclusions"). The most important exclusion is that for "inventory, stock-in-trade, and property held primarily for sale to customers . . ." See Section 1221(1).

which were sold during 1986? Since all beans cost the same, income for each year can be determined without making assumptions about which beans were actually sold in each year.

3) Rising Wholesale Prices

Assume that the wholesale price is $1 per pound for jelly beans acquired prior to 1985, but rises to $2 per pound for jelly beans acquired during 1985. How much income should the store report for 1985 and for 1986, respectively? Why might you want to know which beans were sold in each year? Why might such knowledge be unattainable?

The Internal Revenue Code solves this problem by adopting certain conventions about which inventory was sold first. The first-in, first-out method, or FIFO, is the basic convention adopted by the Code. Under FIFO, when inventory is sold, it is presumed to have been that which was first or earliest acquired. Under FIFO, how much income is reported by the jelly bean store each year?

Businesses may instead elect the last-in, first-out method, or LIFO. Under LIFO, when inventory is sold, it is presumed to have been the last acquired. Under LIFO, how much income is reported by the jelly bean store each year?

A third possibility would be to compute income on the basis of the *average* wholesale cost of inventory. Using this method, how much would the jelly bean store report each year?

Compare the results of calculating the jelly bean store's income for 1985 and 1986 using each of the three methods. Your answers should correspond to Table 15-1, below. [3]

TABLE 15-1.

	FIFO	LIFO	AVG. COST
1985	1,000	200	600
1986	200	1,000	600

---

3. Each year, gross receipts from selling 1,000 pounds of jelly beans at $2 a pound equal $2,000.

Using FIFO—The 1,000 pounds sold during 1985 are presumed to come from the first acquired jelly beans, which cost $1 a pound or $1,000 altogether. Thus, 1985 income equals gross receipts of $2,000, minus jelly bean costs of $1,000, or $1,000 net. The 1,000 pounds sold during 1986 are presumed to consist of 200 pounds acquired before 1985 for $1 a pound, or $200, and 800 pounds acquired during 1985 for $2 a pound, or $1,600. Thus, the cost of all jelly beans sold in 1986 is $1,800. 1986 income equals gross receipts of $2,000, minus costs of $1,800, or $200 net.

Using LIFO—The 1,000 pounds sold during 1985 are presumed to come from the 800 pounds last acquired during 1985 for $2 a pound, or $1,600, and 200 pounds acquired before 1985 for $1 a pound, or $200. Thus, the cost of all jelly beans sold in 1985 is $1,800. 1985 income equals gross receipts of $2,000, minus costs of $1,800, or $200 net. The 1,000 pounds sold during 1986 are presumed to consist of the jelly beans acquired before 1985, which cost $1 a pound or $1,000 altogether. Thus, 1986 income equals gross receipts of $2,000, minus costs of $1,000, or $1,000 net.

Using Average Cost—With 1,200 pounds costing $1 a pound and 800 pounds costing $2 a pound, the average cost per pound is $1.40. Thus, the average cost of 1,000 pounds sold each year is $1,400. Each year's income equals gross receipts of $2,000, minus costs of $1,400, or $600 net.

Which inventory method most accurately reflects income? Which understates income? Which overstates income? Which results in the least variation in the amount of income reported over the two years?

LIFO is elected by only about one-third of all businesses. Can this result be explained, at least in part, by the requirement that if LIFO is used for tax reporting, it must also be used for financial reporting? See Section 472(c). When wholesale prices are rising, what is the effect of LIFO on income for financial reporting purposes? Why might corporate managers be reluctant to use LIFO?

4) Falling Wholesale Prices

Assume that the wholesale price is $2 per pound for jelly beans acquired prior to 1985 but falls to $1 per pound for jelly beans acquired during 1986. How much income is reported each year under the FIFO, LIFO, and average cost methods? Note that FIFO taxpayers are permitted to deduct any unrealized losses (which would occur when wholesale prices are falling), while LIFO taxpayers are not. Reg. §§ 1.471–4 and 1.471–2(b).

Compare the results of calculating the jelly bean store's income for 1985 and 1986 using each of the three methods. Your answers should correspond to Table 15-2, below.[4]

TABLE 15-2.

	FIFO	LIFO	AVG. COST
1985	−200	800	400
1986	1000	0	400

---

4. Each year, gross receipts from selling 1,000 pounds of jelly beans at $2 a pound equal $2,000.

Using FIFO—The 1,000 pounds sold during 1985 are presumed to come from the first acquired jelly beans which cost $2 a pound or $2,000 altogether. Thus, 1985 income *appears* to equal gross receipts of $2,000, minus jelly bean costs of $2,000, or zero net. However, unrealized losses on unsold inventory may also be deducted. Although the current wholesale price of jelly beans is $1 a pound, there are still on hand 200 pounds acquired before 1985 for $2 a pound, with unrealized losses of $1 a pound, or $200 altogether. Thus, the zero income from selling jelly beans, with the $200 of unrealized inventory losses, produces a 1985 income figure of −$200. In addition, the cost of the 200 pounds acquired before 1985— which are still on hand—has to be adjusted down to $1 a pound to reflect the deduction of the unrealized loss.

The 1,000 pounds sold during 1986 are presumed to consist of 200 pounds acquired before 1985 for an adjusted cost of $1 a pound, or $200, and 800 pounds acquired during 1985 for $1 a pound, or $800. Thus, the cost of all jelly beans sold in 1986 is $1,000. 1986 income equals gross receipts of $2,000, minus costs of $1,000, or $1,000 net.

Using LIFO—The 1,000 pounds sold during 1985 are presumed to come from the 800 pounds last acquired during 1985 for $1 a pound or $800, and 200 pounds acquired before 1985 for $2 a pound or $400. Thus, the cost of all jelly beans sold in 1985 is $1,200. 1985 income equals gross receipts of $2,000, minus costs of $1,200 or $800 net. The 1,000 pounds sold during 1986 are presumed to consist of the jelly beans acquired before 1985, which cost $2 a pound or $2,000 altogether. Thus, 1986 income equals gross receipts of $2,000, minus costs of $2,000, or zero net.

Using Average Cost—With 1,200 pounds costing $2 a pound and 800 pounds costing $1 a pound, the average cost per pound is $1.60. Thus, the average cost of 1,000 pounds sold each year is $1,600. Each year's income equals gross receipts of $2,000, minus costs of $1,600, or $400 net.

Which inventory method most accurately reflects income? Which method understates income? Which overstates income? Which results in the least variation in the amount of income reported over the two years?

5) Accounting for Inventory Costs in the Real World

The reader should note two important characteristics of inventory accounting, which may not be apparent from the highly stylized example presented above. First, inventory methods are not assumed to reflect the order in which goods are actually sold.

> [T]he "flow of goods" for inventory purposes does not refer to their *physical movement*, but to the order in which *costs* are assigned in computing ... costs of goods sold, and this order is unaffected by whether the taxpayer draws from the bottom of the pile or the top when shipping goods to customers ... [It] describes an accounting practice, not the physical movement of goods.[5]

Second, in practice, inventory costs are not calculated directly by adding up the costs of goods sold but indirectly by subtracting (a) inventory on hand at the end of the year from (b) inventory on hand at the beginning plus inventory acquired during the year.

> [T]he cost of goods sold is not computed ... by assigning inventory costs to the goods as sold, but by a process of elimination; costs are assigned to the closing inventory, which is then deducted from the cost of goods available for sale (opening inventory plus additions during the taxable year) to ascertain the cost of goods sold. The size of the hole in the doughnut, in short, is determined by measuring the ring.[6]

6) Explaining the Special Treatment of Inventory Losses

Why are inventory losses deductible without limit? Doesn't the same potential for manipulation exist with inventory as with investment property? Why can't a business choose to sell its inventory with unrealized losses as early as possible and to delay selling its inventory with unrealized gains? Is it because the discipline imposed by inventory accounting under either FIFO or LIFO restricts the potential for manipulation by picking which items to sell?

If inventory accounting effectively eliminates manipulation, why not repeal Section 1211 (which limits the deduction of capital losses) and require inventory accounting of investment property? Can it be done easily where an investor holds a diversified portfolio of thirty different stocks? Or a diversified portfolio consisting of stocks, bonds, and real estate? Why is inventory accounting practical only with fungible assets?

---

5. B. Bittker, 4 Federal Taxation of Income, Estates and Gifts 105–89 (1980).
6. Ibid. at 105–89 to 105–90.

How can the deduction for *unrealized* inventory losses be explained? By the absence of a measurement obstacle because the current market value of inventory can be easily determined from the cost of inventory most recently acquired? And because the discipline imposed by inventory accounting prevents the seller from manipulating this allowance to distort income? But then why are unrealized losses deductible only if FIFO is used and not when LIFO is used? Because LIFO causes income to be undertaxed when prices are rising, while FIFO causes it to be overtaxed?

E. THOR POWER TOOL CO. v. COMMISSIONER
439 U.S. 522 (1979)

MR. JUSTICE BLACKMUN delivered the opinion of the Court.

A

Taxpayer is a Delaware corporation with principal place of business in Illinois. It manufactures hand-held power tools, parts and accessories, and rubber products. At its various plants and service branches, Thor maintains inventories of raw materials, work-in-process, finished parts and accessories, and completed tools. At all times relevant, Thor has used, both for financial accounting and for income tax purposes, the "lower of cost or market" method of valuing inventories. . . .

Thor's tools typically contain from 50 to 200 parts, each of which taxpayer stocks to meet demand for replacements. Because of the difficulty, at the time of manufacture, of predicting the future demand for various parts, taxpayer produced liberal quantities of each part to avoid subsequent production runs. Additional runs entail costly retooling and result in delays in filling orders. . . .

In 1960, Thor instituted a procedure for writing down the inventory value of replacement parts and accessories for tool models it no longer produced. It created an inventory contra-account and credited that account with 10% of each part's cost for each year since production of the parent model had ceased. . . . The effect of the procedure was to amortize the cost of these parts over a 10-year period. For the first nine months of 1964, this produced a write-down of $22,090. . . .

In late 1964, new management took control and promptly concluded that Thor's inventory in general was overvalued. After "a physical inventory taken at all locations" of the tool and rubber divisions, . . . management wrote off approximately $2.75 million of obsolete parts, damaged or defective tools, demonstration or sales samples, and similar items. . . . The Commissioner allowed this writeoff because Thor scrapped most of the articles shortly after their removal from the 1964 closing inventory. Management also wrote down $245,000 of parts stocked for three unsuccessful products. . . . The Commissioner allowed this write-down, too, since Thor sold these items at reduced prices shortly after the close of 1964. . . .

This left some 44,000 assorted items, the status of which is the inventory issue here. Management concluded that many of these articles, mostly spare parts, were "excess" inventory, that is, that they were held in excess of any reasonably foreseeable future demand. It was decided that this inventory should be written down to its "net realizable value," which, in most cases, was scrap value. . . .

Two methods were used to ascertain the quantity of excess inventory. Where accurate data were available, Thor forecast future demand for each item on the basis of actual 1964 usage, that is, actual sales for tools and service parts, and actual usage for raw materials, work-in-process, and production parts. Management assumed that future demand for each item would be the same as it was in 1964. Thor then applied the following aging schedule: the quantity of each item corresponding to less than one year's estimated demand was kept at cost; the quantity of each item in excess of two years' estimated demand was written off entirely; and the quantity of each item corresponding to from one to two years' estimated demand was written down by 50% or 75%. . . .

Thor presented no statistical evidence to rationalize these percentages or this time frame. In the Tax Court, Thor's president justified the formula by citing general business experience, and opined that it was "somewhat in between" possible alternative solutions. This first method yielded a total write-down of $744,030. . . .

At two plants where 1964 data were inadequate to permit forecasts of future demand, Thor used its second method for valuing inventories. At these plants, the company employed flat percentage write-downs of 5%, 10%, and 50% for various types of inventory. Thor presented no sales or other data to support these percentages. Its president observed that "this is not a precise way of doing it," but said that the company "felt some adjustment of this nature was in order, and these figures represented our best estimate of what was required to reduce the inventory to net realizable value." . . . This second method yielded a total write-down of $160,832. . . .

Although Thor wrote down all its "excess" inventory at once, it did not immediately scrap the articles or sell them at reduced prices, as it had done with the $3 million of obsolete and damaged inventory, the write-down of which the Commissioner permitted. Rather, Thor retained the "excess" items physically in inventory and continued to sell them at original prices. . . . The company found that, owing to the peculiar nature of the articles involved, price reductions were of no avail in moving this "excess" inventory. As time went on, however, Thor gradually disposed of some of these items as scrap; the record is unclear as to when these dispositions took place.

Thor's total write-down of "excess" inventory in 1964 therefore was:

Ten-year amortization of parts for discontinued tools	$22,090
First method (aging formula based on 1964 usage)	744,030
Second method (flat percentage write-downs)	160,832
Total	$926,952

Thor credited this sum to its inventory contra-account, thereby decreasing closing inventory, increasing cost of goods sold, and decreasing taxable income for the year by that amount. The company contended that, by writing down excess inventory to scrap value, and by thus carrying all inventory at "net realizable value," it had reduced its inventory to "market" in accord with its "lower of cost or market" method of accounting. On audit, the Commissioner disallowed the write-down in its entirety, asserting that it did not serve clearly to reflect Thor's 1964 income for tax purposes.

The Tax Court, in upholding the Commissioner's determination, found as a fact that Thor's write-down of excess inventory did conform to "generally accepted accounting principles"; indeed, the court was "thoroughly convinced . . . that such was the case.". . . The court found that if Thor had failed to write down its inventory on some reasonable basis, its accountants would have been unable to give its financial statements the desired certification. . . . The court held, however, that conformance with "generally accepted accounting principles" is not enough; § 446 (b), and § 471 as well, . . . prescribe, as an independent requirement, that inventory accounting methods must "clearly reflect income." The Tax Court rejected Thor's argument that its write-down of "excess" inventory was authorized by Treasury Regulations . . . and held that the Commissioner had not abused his discretion in determining that the write-down failed to reflect 1964 income clearly.

B

Inventory accounting is governed by §§ 446 and 471 of the Code, 26 U.S.C. §§ 446 and 471. Section 446(a) states the general rule for methods of accounting: "Taxable income shall be computed under the method of accounting on the basis of which the taxpayer regularly computes his income in keeping his books." Section 446(b) provides, however, that if the method used by the taxpayer "does not clearly reflect income, the computation of taxable income shall be made under such method as, in the opinion of the [Commissioner], does clearly reflect income." Regulations promulgated under § 446, and in effect for the taxable year 1964, state that "no method of accounting is acceptable unless, in the opinion of the Commissioner, it clearly reflects income." Treas. Reg. § 1.446–1(a)(2). . . .

Section 471 prescribes the general rule for inventories. It states:

> Whenever in the opinion of the [Commissioner] the use of inventories is necessary in order clearly to determine the income of any taxpayer, inventory shall be taken by such taxpayer on such basis as the [Commissioner] may prescribe as conforming as nearly as may be to the best accounting practice in the trade or business and as most clearly reflecting the income.

As the Regulations point out, § 471 obviously establishes two distinct tests to which an inventory must conform. First, it must conform "as nearly as may be" to the "best accounting practice," a phrase that is synonymous with "generally accepted accounting principles." Second, it "must clearly reflect the income." Treas. Reg. § 1.471–2(a)(2). . . .

It is obvious that on their face, §§ 446 and 471, with their accompanying Regulations, vest the Commissioner with wide discretion in determining whether a particular method of inventory accounting should be disallowed as not clearly reflective of income. This Court's cases confirm the breadth of this discretion. In construing § 446 and its predecessors, the Court has held that "[t]he Commissioner has broad powers in determining whether accounting methods used by a taxpayer clearly reflect income.". . . Since the Commissioner has "[m]uch latitude for discretion," his interpretation of the statute's clear-reflection standard "should not be interfered with unless clearly unlawful. . . ." In construing § 471, the Court held that the taxpayer bears a "heavy burden of [proof]," and that the Commissioner's disallowance of an inventory accounting method is not to be set aside unless shown to be "plainly arbitrary. . . ."

As has been noted, the Tax Court found as a fact in this case that Thor's write-down of "excess" inventory conformed to "generally accepted accounting principles" and was "within the term, 'best accounting practice,' as that term is used in section 471 of the Code and the regulations promulgated under that section.". . . Since the Commissioner has not challenged this finding, there is no dispute that Thor satisfied the first part of § 471's two-pronged test. The only question, then, is whether the Commissioner abused his discretion in determining that the write-down did not satisfy the test's second prong in that it failed to reflect Thor's 1964 income clearly. Although the Commissioner's discretion is not unbridled and may not be arbitrary, we sustain his exercise of discretion here, for in this case the write-down was plainly inconsistent with the governing Regulations which the taxpayer, on its part, has not challenged.

It has been noted above that Thor at all pertinent times used the "lower of cost or market" method of inventory accounting. The rules governing this method are set out in Treas. Reg. § 1.471–4. . . . That Regulation defines "market" to mean, ordinarily, "the current bid price prevailing at the date of the inventory for the particular merchandise in the volume in which usually purchased by the taxpayer." § 1.471–4(a). The courts have uniformly interpreted "bid price" to mean replacement cost, that is, the price the taxpayer would have to pay on the open market to purchase or reproduce the inventory items. Where no open market exists, the Regulations require the taxpayer to ascertain "bid price" by using "such evidence of a fair market price at the date or dates nearest the inventory as may be available, such as specific purchases or sales by the taxpayer or others in reasonable volume and made in good faith, or compensation paid for cancellation of contracts for purchase commitments." § 1.471–4(b).

The Regulations specify two situations in which a taxpayer is permitted to value inventory below "market" as so defined. The first is where the taxpayer in the normal course of business has actually offered merchandise for sale at prices lower than replacement cost. Inventories of such merchandise may be valued at those prices less direct cost of disposition, "and the correctness of such prices will be determined by reference to the actual sales of the taxpayer for a reasonable period before and after the date of the inventory." . . . The Regulations warn that prices "which vary materially from the actual prices so ascertained will not be accepted as reflecting the market." . . .

The second situation in which a taxpayer may value inventory below replacement cost is where the merchandise itself is defective. If goods are "unsalable at normal prices or unusable in the normal way because of damage, imperfections, shop wear, changes of style, odd or broken lots, or other similar causes," the taxpayer is permitted to value the goods "at bona fide selling prices less direct cost of disposition." § 1.471–2(c). The Regulations define "bona fide selling price" to mean an "actual offering of goods during a period ending not later than 30 days after inventory date." . . . The taxpayer bears the burden of proving that "such exceptional goods as are valued upon such selling basis come within the classifications indicated," and is required to "maintain such records of the disposition of the goods as will enable a verification of the inventory to be made.". . .

From this language, the regulatory scheme is clear. The taxpayer must value inventory for tax purposes at cost unless the "market" is lower. "Market" is defined as "replacement cost," and the taxpayer is permitted to depart from replacement cost only in specified situations. When it makes any such departure, the taxpayer must substantiate its lower inventory valuation by providing evidence of actual offerings, actual sales, or actual contract cancellations. In the absence of objective evidence of this kind, a taxpayer's assertions as to the "market value" of its inventory are not cognizable in computing its income tax.

It is clear to us that Thor's procedures for writing down the value of its "excess" inventory were inconsistent with this regulatory scheme. Although Thor conceded that "an active market prevailed" on the inventory date . . . it "made no effort to determine the purchase or reproduction cost" of its "excess" inventory. . . . Thor thus failed to ascertain "market" in accord with the general rule of the Regulations. In seeking to depart from replacement cost, Thor failed to bring itself within either of the authorized exceptions. Thor is not able to take advantage of § 1.471–4(b) since, as the Tax Court found, the company failed to sell its excess inventory or offer it for sale at prices below replacement cost. . . . Indeed, Thor concedes that it continued to sell its "excess" inventory at original prices. Thor also is not able to take advantage of § 1.471–2(c) since, as the Tax Court and the Court of Appeals both held, it failed to bear the burden of proving that its excess inventory came within the specified classifications. . . . Actually, Thor's "excess" inventory was normal and unexceptional, and was indistinguishable from and intermingled with the inventory that was not written down.

More importantly, Thor failed to provide any objective evidence whatever that the "excess" inventory had the "market value" management ascribed to it. The Regulations demand hard evidence of actual sales and further demand that records of actual dispositions be kept. The Tax Court found, however, that Thor made no sales and kept no records. . . . Thor's management simply wrote down its closing inventory on the basis of a well-educated guess that some of it would never be sold. The formulae governing this write-down were derived from management's collective "business experience"; the percentages contained in those formulae seemingly were chosen for no reason other than that they were multiples of five and embodied some kind of anagogical symmetry. The Regulations do not permit this kind of evidence. If a taxpayer could write down its inventories on the basis of management's subjective estimates of the goods' ultimate salability, the taxpayer would be able, as the Tax Court observed... "to determine how much tax it wanted to pay for a given year."

For these reasons, we agree with the Tax Court and with the Seventh Circuit that the Commissioner acted within his discretion in deciding that Thor's write-down of "excess" inventory failed to reflect income clearly. In the light of the well-known potential for tax avoidance that is inherent in inventory accounting, the Commissioner in his discretion may insist on a high evidentiary standard before allowing write-downs of inventory to "market." Because Thor provided no objective evidence of the reduced market value of its "excess" inventory, its write-down was plainly inconsistent with the Regulations, and the Commissioner properly disallowed it.

C

The taxpayer's major argument against this conclusion is based on the Tax Court's clear finding that the write-down conformed to "generally accepted accounting principles." Thor points to language in Treas. Reg. §1.446–1 (a)(2) ... to the effect that "[a] method of accounting which reflects the consistent application of generally accepted accounting principles ... *will ordinarily be regarded* as clearly reflecting income" (emphasis added).... [The] Regulations likewise stated that an inventory taken in conformity with best accounting practice "can, *as a general rule*, be regarded as clearly reflecting ... income" (emphasis added). These provisions, Thor contends, created a *presumption* that an inventory practice conformable to "generally accepted accounting principles" is valid for income tax purposes. Once a taxpayer has established this conformity, the argument runs, the burden shifts to the Commissioner affirmatively to demonstrate that the taxpayer's method does *not* reflect income clearly. Unless the Commissioner can show that a generally accepted method "demonstrably distorts income," ... or that the taxpayer's adoption of such method was "motivated by tax avoidance," ... the presumption in the taxpayer's favor will carry the day. The Commissioner, Thor concludes, failed to rebut that presumption here.

If the Code and Regulations did embody the presumption petitioner postulates, it would be of little use to the taxpayer in this case. As we have noted, Thor's write-down of "excess" inventory was inconsistent with the Regulations; any general presumption obviously must yield in the face of such particular inconsistency. We believe, however, that no such presumption is present. Its existence is insupportable in light of the statute, the

Court's past decisions, and the differing objectives of tax and financial accounting.

First, as has been stated above, the Code and Regulations establish two distinct tests to which an inventory must conform. The Code and Regulations, moreover, leave little doubt as to which test is paramount. While § 471 of the Code requires only that an accounting practice conform "as nearly as may be" to best accounting practice, § 1.446–1(a)(2) of the Regulations states categorically that "*no* method of accounting is acceptable unless, in the opinion of the Commissioner, it clearly reflects income" (emphasis added). Most importantly, the Code and Regulations give the Commissioner broad discretion to set aside the taxpayer's method if, "in [his] opinion," it does not reflect income clearly. This language is completely at odds with the notion of a "presumption" in the taxpayer's favor. The Regulations embody no presumption; they say merely that, in most cases, generally accepted accounting practices will pass muster for tax purposes. And in most cases they will. But if the Commissioner, in the exercise of his discretion, determines that they do not, he may prescribe a different practice without having to rebut any presumption running against the Treasury.

Second, the presumption petitioner postulates finds no support in this Court's prior decisions. It was early noted that the general rule specifying use of the taxpayer's method of accounting "is expressly limited to cases where the Commissioner believes that the accounts clearly reflect the net income." . . . More recently, it was held in *American Automobile Assn.* v. *United States* that a taxpayer must recognize prepaid income when received, even though this would mismatch expenses and revenues in contravention of "generally accepted commercial accounting principles." . . . "[T]o say that in performing the function of business accounting the method employed by the Association 'is in accord with generally accepted commercial accounting principles and practices,'" the Court concluded, "is not to hold that for income tax purposes it so clearly reflects income as to be binding on the Treasury." . . . "[W]e are mindful that the characterization of a transaction for financial accounting purposes, on the one hand, and for tax purposes, on the other, need not necessarily be the same." . . . Indeed, the Court's cases demonstrate that divergence between tax and financial accounting is especially common when a taxpayer seeks a current deduction for estimated future expenses or losses. . . . The rationale of these cases amply encompasses Thor's aim. By its president's concession, the company's write-down of "excess" inventory was founded on the belief that many of the articles inevitably would become useless due to breakage, technological change, fluctuations in market demand, and the like. Thor, in other words, sought a current "deduction" for an estimated future loss. Under the decided cases, a taxpayer so circumstanced finds no shelter beneath an accountancy presumption.

Third, the presumption petitioner postulates is insupportable in light of the vastly different objectives that financial and tax accounting have. The primary goal of financial accounting is to provide useful information to management, shareholders, creditors, and others properly interested; the major responsibility of the accountant is to protect these parties from being misled. The primary goal of the income tax system, in contrast, is the equitable collection of revenue; the major responsibility of the Internal Revenue Service is to protect the public fisc. Consistently with its goals and responsibilities, financial accounting has as its foundation the principle of conservatism, with its corollary that "possible errors in measurement [should] be in the direction of understatement rather than overstatement of net income and net assets." In view of the Treasury's markedly different goals and responsibilities, understatement of income is not destined to be its guiding light. Given this diversity, even contrariety, of objectives, any presumptive equivalency between tax and financial accounting would be unacceptable.

This difference in objectives is mirrored in numerous differences of treatment. Where the tax law requires that a deduction be deferred until "all the events" have occurred that will make it fixed and certain . . . accounting principles typically require that a liability be accrued as soon as it can reasonably be estimated. Conversely, where the tax law requires that income be recognized currently under "claim of right," "ability to pay," and "control" rationales, accounting principles may defer accrual until a later year so that revenues and expenses may be better matched. Financial accounting, in short, is hospitable to estimates, probabilities, and reasonable certainties; the tax law, with its mandate to preserve the revenue, can give no quarter to uncertainty. This is as it should be. Reasonable estimates may be useful, even essential, in giving shareholders and creditors an accurate picture of a firm's overall financial health; but the accountant's conservatism cannot bind the Commissioner in his efforts to collect taxes. . . .

Finally, a presumptive equivalency between tax and financial accounting would create insurmountable difficulties of tax administration. Accountants long have recognized that "generally accepted accounting principles" are far from being a canonical set of rules that will ensure identical accounting treatment of identical transactions. "Generally accepted accounting principles," rather, tolerate a range of "reasonable" treatments, leaving the choice among alternatives to management. Such, indeed, is precisely the case here. Variances of this sort may be tolerable in financial reporting, but they are questionable in a tax system designed to ensure as far as possible that similarly situated taxpayers pay the same tax. If management's election among "acceptable" options were dispositive for tax purposes, a firm, indeed, could decide unilaterally—within limits dictated only by its accountants—the tax it wished to pay. Such unilateral decisions would not just make the Code inequitable; they would make it unenforceable.

D

Thor complains that a decision adverse to it poses a dilemma. According to the taxpayer, it would be virtually impossible for it to offer objective evidence of its "excess" inventory's lower value, since the goods cannot be sold at reduced prices; even if they could be sold, says Thor, their reduced-price sale would just "pull the rug out" from under the identical "non-excess" inventory Thor is trying to sell simultaneously. The only way Thor could establish the inventory's value by a "closed transaction" would be to scrap the articles at once. Yet immediate scrapping would be undesirable, for demand for the parts ultimately might prove greater than anticipated. The taxpayer thus sees itself presented with "an unattractive Hobson's choice: either the unsalable inventory must be carried for years at its cost instead of net realizable value, thereby overstating taxable income by such overvaluation until it is scrapped, or the excess inventory must be scrapped prematurely to the detriment of the manufacturer and its customers.". . .

If this is indeed the dilemma that confronts Thor, it is in reality the same choice that every taxpayer who has a paper loss must face. It can realize its loss now and garner its tax benefit, or it can defer realization, and its deduction, hoping for better luck later. Thor, quite simply, has suffered no present loss. It deliberately manufactured its "excess" spare parts because it judged that the marginal cost of unsalable inventory would be lower than the cost of retooling machinery should demand surpass expectations. This was a rational business judgment and, not unpredictably, Thor now has inventory it believes it cannot sell. Thor, of course, is not so confident of its prediction as to be willing to scrap the "excess" parts now; it wants to keep them on hand, just in case. This, too, is a rational judgment, but there is no reason why the Treasury should subsidize Thor's hedging of its bets. There is also no reason why Thor should be entitled, for tax purposes, to have its cake and eat it too.

F. NOTES AND QUESTIONS

1) The Stakes in *Thor Power Tool*

When would the taxpayer be able to deduct the claimed loss? Never? When the unsold inventory is scrapped? What was at stake?

2) The Rationale of *Thor Power Tool*

Why did the Supreme Court reject the taxpayer's method of valuing FIFO inventory? Did this method use an objective benchmark? Or was it based on subjective estimates? Were those subjective estimates supported by any data?

What was the purpose of financial accounting, as contrasted with tax accounting, in *Thor Power Tool*? Why might those subjective estimates of the inventory's value be acceptable for purposes of financial accounting but not income tax accounting?

If the taxpayer had substantiated the estimates with data, should it have been permitted to deduct the unrealized loss? That is to say, does this case basically involve a measurement problem? Or should substantiation have made no difference, since the taxpayer was currently selling identical items at a price considerably in excess of scrap value?

3) Consistency Between Tax and Nontax Accounting

Under Section 472(c), taxpayers may elect LIFO accounting for tax purposes only if they also use LIFO for nontax financial reporting. The Code requires consistency between tax and nontax accounting. In *Thor Power Tool*, however, the IRS was permitted to require inconsistent accounting methods. Unrealized losses on inventory could not be deducted for tax purposes even though the identical losses were deducted for nontax purposes. Try to explain why the tax law requires consistency in the one area and permits inconsistency in the other. Readers should note that the tension between the different objectives of tax and nontax accounting is a recurring theme in federal tax law.

Chapter 16

COMMODITY STRADDLES

A. INTRODUCTORY NOTE

The commodity straddle is a complex financial arrangement that in the past enabled investors to avoid paying billions of dollars in taxes. This chapter attempts to provide a step-by-step explanation of what a commodity straddle is and how it has been used for tax avoidance.

The commodity straddle works by manipulating the realization principle as it applies to losses. As you read the materials, consider the following questions. What is the precise connection between the realization principle and the use of commodity straddles for tax avoidance? Why is Section 1211, which limits the deduction of capital losses, not effective at preventing tax avoidance with commodity straddles? Why were special rules needed? Why is the kind of tax avoidance created by commodity straddles generally not a problem with other kinds of investments?

B. HOW THE COMMODITY TAX STRADDLE WORKS

The New York Times (July 10, 1981)

How a Commodity Tax Straddle Works

In which a taxpayer has real capital gain that he wants to offset with a capital loss in order to defer his current-year tax liability.

1. STARTING THE STRADDLE	2. TAKING THE LOSS	3. CLOSING THE STRADDLE
The taxpayer establishes what is known in the futures markets as a spread or straddle. The straddle involves two steps: first, establishing a "long," or buy position in [one] month and, simultaneously, a "short," or sell position in a [different] month.	Suppose the straddle is in silver and, further, that the price of silver falls. When the price has dropped enough to give the taxpayer a loss that will offset the tax liability, the taxpayer takes a loss on the long contracts.	At the end of the tax year the taxpayer closes out his position, realizing the gain in the short contracts, which should offset the loss on the original long contracts.
The straddle is usually undertaken in a nonagricultural commodity, such as silver or interest rate futures, because the prices of contracts for different delivery months tend to move in tandem.	The taxpayer closes out the long contract by selling the long contract but re-establishes the straddle by buying another silver futures contract for delivery in a different month. (This way the taxpayer locks in the unrealized gain on the short contracts, which will be realized after the close of the tax year.)	The taxpayer has at least deferred his income tax liability by taking the capital loss on the short contracts in the current tax year. But that loss is offset by a gain in the next tax year, a gain that might conceivably be deferred again by another straddle.
Now, if prices rise the taxpayer will have a loss on the short contracts and a gain on the long contracts; if prices decline he will have a loss on long contracts, but a gain on the short contracts.		

C. THE COMMODITY TAX STRADDLE

Staff of the Joint Committee on Taxation, 97th Cong., 1st Sess., Background on Commodity Tax Straddles and Explanation of H.R. 1293, 1–8 and 11–13 (Joint Comm. Print 1981)

[Editor's Note: The next three excerpts refer to capital gains as being either *short term* or *long term*. When a capital asset is held for one year or less, it produces short term gain (or loss). When held for more than one year, it produces long term gain (or loss). Before the 1986 Tax Reform

Act, preferential rates applied only to long term gains, with short-term gains taxed at the same rate as ordinary income.[1] The short term versus long term distinction, while maintained in the Code, no longer has much practical relevance now that the basic capital gain preference has been repealed.[2]]

A. Development of the Commodities Industry

Present day commodity futures exchanges can trace their origins to medieval European markets usually held at the principal regional center of production for a particular commodity. Initially, only physical ("cash") commodities were traded. However, as commerce grew in size and complexity, markets expanded to year-round operations and trade in contracts for future delivery developed. Trading practices became standardized and over the centuries, some trade practices were adopted as law.

In the United States, regional cash markets for agricultural commodities developed in the Eighteenth Century. Trade in cash commodities was marked by wide seasonal variations in supply and demand resulting in large fluctuations in prices. At harvest time, farmers glutted the markets with their produce, which far exceeded merchants' immediate needs. Inadequate transportation and storage facilities compounded farmers' economic difficulties. Prices were low; some commodities were kept off the markets; others spoiled and remained unsold. Within months, however, demand would increase and prices would soar as the supply of produce sought by merchants, processors and individuals dwindled and fell short of demand.

In order to increase their control over supply and demand, producers and users of agricultural commodities began to enter forward contracts with each other. Forward contracts are individualized agreements directly negotiated between a particular buyer and a particular seller, and always requiring actual delivery. These contracts called for delivery of a fixed quantity of a commodity at a specific place at a particular time for a fixed price. Forward contracts provided that actual delivery of the commodity would occur in the future, but title to the commodity was transferred when the parties executed the contract.

Although some individual speculation in forward contracts occurred, such speculation was too irregular and insufficient to reduce the risk of price fluctuations. Forward contracts permitted a shifting of the risk of future price fluctuations from the seller to the buyer, but because they required actual delivery of the commodity, they were not very attractive to speculators who might otherwise have been willing to assume the risks of price changes. Futures contracts and futures exchange developed as a means of encouraging speculators to enter the commodities markets and assume

---

1. Short term and long term gains and losses are netted out to produce a net capital gain or loss figure. Individual taxpayers were entitled to deduct 60% of any net long term capital gain.

2. Note, however, that a taxpayer who makes a gift of appreciated property to charity may not deduct the property's full value if the appreciation represents either ordinary income *or* short term capital gain. See Section 170(e)(1)(A), discussed in the introduction to Subpart C of Part Two.

the risk of price fluctuations. Knowledgeable, well-capitalized price speculators typically make markets more efficient because their trading responds quickly to information about changes in supply and demand. Also, the active trading of speculators usually makes markets more liquid; that is, it reduces the gap between the prices at which the public is able to buy and sell the commodity.

In this century, futures trading has become increasingly regulated, both by the industry itself and by the Federal Government. Initially futures trading in agricultural commodities was regulated by the Agriculture Department under the Commodity Exchange Act. Later additional commodities were made subject to regulation. The Commodity Futures Trading Commission Act of 1974 created an independent federal agency, the Commodity Futures Trading Commission, and granted its exclusive jurisdiction over futures trading.

B. Commodity Futures Contracts

A commodity futures contract is a standardized agreement either to buy or to sell a fixed quantity of a commodity to be delivered at a particular location in a specified month in the future. Currently, exchanges list contracts for agricultural commodities, heating oil, precious metals, financial paper and currencies. Called "futures," these contracts require payment at the time of delivery. . . .

All futures contracts are subject to the rules and regulations of the exchange where they are traded. For each contract, an exchange establishes a standard contract size. For example, a soybean futures contract consists of 5,000 bushels. Each contract specifies delivery of a particular grade of the contract commodity. Exchange rules may allow a seller to substitute delivery of the standard grade with other specified grades of the commodity, at stated premiums or discounts from the delivery price.

Exchanges list contracts for delivery only in certain designated months, some over three years into the future. In June 1981, the Chicago Board of Trade, for example, listed wheat contracts for July, September and December 1981 and March, May and July 1982. The New York Commodity Exchange (COMEX) listed gold contracts for delivery in June, July, August, October and December of 1981; February, April, June, August, October and December of 1982; and February and April of 1983. Closing futures prices are listed daily in the financial pages of many newspapers.

C. Futures Trading

1. Types of traders

Hedging
Commodities futures trading involves two types of trading: hedging and speculation. A hedger is a business person who produces, sells, or processes the actual "cash" commodity and engages in futures trading for price protection of inventories. For example, a wheat farmer who expects

to harvest a crop several months in the future may enter a futures contract to sell wheat to protect against a price decline between the current date and the date when the actual wheat will be available. Also, a flour manufacturer may enter a futures contract to buy wheat to protect against a price increase between the current date and the time when the manufacturer will need the actual wheat. Similarly, financial institutions, which realize ordinary income or loss on the disposition of their securities, may use financial futures to hedge such securities.

Speculation

A speculator does not trade futures for price protection, as the hedger does. Instead, the speculator risks his capital in the hope of profiting from price movements.

Speculators buy if they think prices are too low; they sell, if they consider prices too high. Speculators generally do not take delivery of the physical commodity but instead "liquidate" (i.e., close out or cancel) their futures.... Speculators generally hold their contracts for short periods; some are day-traders, often called scalpers, who get out of the market the same day they get in....

Obviously, any one person may trade futures contracts, sometimes as a hedger and other times as a speculator, depending on the purpose and the type of transactions which are executed.

2. Trading strategy

Futures v. cash prices

Speculators employ a variety of trading strategies. Traders expecting prices to increase may take a "long" position, that is, enter into contracts to buy a commodity. If a trader expects prices to fall, he may go "short," that is, enter into contracts to sell. Speculators who are "long" or "short" in the futures markets expect to profit from the difference between the subsequent price of the physical (or cash) commodity and the price at which they purchased the futures contract.

Spreads

Many professional traders employ a trading strategy, frequently referred to interchangeably as spread or straddle trading, which is usually considered more conservative than outright long or short positions. Spreads involve the simultaneous holding of a long position (contract to buy) in one futures contract and a short position (contract to sell) in a related futures contract. The two positions are called the "legs" of the spread. Spread traders hope to profit from changes in the difference between the prices of the two positions. They try to trade spreads when they think prices for the different months are "out of line." This trading strategy is similar to and sometimes referred to as arbitrage.

For example, there is normally a relatively stable relationship between the price of June gold and the price of September gold. This relationship is based on the costs of storing gold (including financing costs) from June to September. Should there be an influx of buy orders for June gold, there would be upward pressure on the price of June gold contracts. Spread traders could then sell June contracts and buy September contracts, which would tend to restore the normal relationship between the two contracts. Because of the large number of spread traders, many markets trade spreads as a single unit; that is, they allow traders to buy and sell the two legs of the spread simultaneously.

3. Mechanics of trading

An individual can trade futures contracts by opening a commodity account with a brokerage firm which holds a membership in one or more commodity exchanges through its officers or partners or with a firm which is registered with the Commodity Futures Trading Commission as futures commission merchant (FCM) placing orders through an exchange member. The firm arranges execution of the individual's order to buy or sell and charges a commission for these transactions. In addition, the firm requires that the individual sign a margin agreement and maintain at least a minimum amount of cash in a margin account.

4. Comparison: futures v. corporate stock

In general

Although aspects of futures trading appear similar to practices and terminology used in securities trading, there are substantial differences between futures and securities trading. Some of these differences are very significant. Unlike corporate stock which a purchaser may hold indefinitely, futures contracts have a limited life span. Holders of futures either must liquidate them prior to their final delivery date, or must make or accept delivery of the commodity pursuant to the contracts.

Payment

When corporate stock is purchased, the buyer must pay the seller the full amount of the purchase price. However, commodity traders do not make any payment for their futures contracts until the contracts' delivery dates. When they enter the contracts, traders merely make a deposit, similar to earnest money, to guarantee performance in the future.

Margin

Margin requirements in futures trading differ greatly from margin requirements in securities trading. The margin established for securities purchases constitutes partial payment for the securities. The remainder of the securities' purchase price is loaned by the broker to the customer, who pays the broker interest for the borrowed portion of the purchase price. Minimum margin requirements may range well over 50 percent of the price of securities.... [P]ublicly traded stock margin requirements are subject to Federal regulation.

In futures trading, however, a margin deposit is not a partial payment on the contracts. The margin deposit required for futures trading technically is "earnest money," a cash deposit made as a financial guarantee to the broker that the individual will fulfill his or her future obligations. Margin required for commodity futures accounts generally amounts to 5 to 10 percent of the face amount of a contract. Margin on individual accounts is set by the broker, who as an exchange member, must meet in turn margin requirements established by the exchange. Margin requirements for futures are not regulated by the Government. Thus, broker-set margins reflect exchange requirements.

Margins for futures are higher for positions involving greater risk and lower for positions with less risk. Hedgers have significantly lower margin requirements than speculators because hedgers hold the underlying physical commodity. Speculators' margin requirements depend on the risk of their net position. Spread or straddle positions, usually less risky than outright long or short positions, often have margin requirements of only one percent of the face amount of the two positions.

Exchanges require two types of margin deposits: initial and maintenance. Initial margin is the deposit amount required when the futures positions are established. Maintenance margin is the minimum amount of margin which must be maintained in the margin account at all times to support a position. Maintenance margin is usually set at 75 percent of initial margin. Margin requirements are computed daily based on the contract's settlement price, the official price set daily by the exchange. If a trader's overall position declines in value, the amount of the decline will be withdrawn from the margin deposit and paid over to the exchange clearing association. If the trader's margin drops below the maintenance level, the trader will have to deposit additional margin, called variation margin, before the next business day to bring the trader's margin back up to the initial level, or his undermargined positions will be liquidated.

Marking-to-market

If a trader's position has increased in value during the day, the net increase in the position is computed and transferred to the trader's account before the beginning of trading the next day. The trader has the right to withdraw the full amount of such gains immediately every trading day. However, if a trader's position decreases in value, the trader will have to meet a margin call, that is, deposit additional funds before the next business day. Money paid on position losses is paid into the exchange clearing association which transfers such amounts to those accounts which gained during the trading day. This daily determination of contract settlement prices and margin adjustments to reflect gains and losses is called "marking-to-market."

Marking-to-market requires daily cash adjustments through the exchange clearing association to reconcile exchange members' net gains and losses on their positions. At the close of trading each day, every member must mark all customer accounts to the settlement prices (current market value) for the day. Gains and losses are immediately deposited into or withdrawn from the customer accounts. And, customers in turn are entitled to withdraw their gains, or are required to deposit any margin required because of losses in their accounts at the close of every day under this marking-to-market system.

Leverage

Because the margin deposits required for commodity accounts are so small, leverage—the relation between the amount of money required to control property and the value of the property—is significant. Moreover, unlike an investor who purchases stock on margin, a commodity futures trader does not buy or sell the commodity when he enters the contract. In acquiring a futures contract, a commodity trader only promises to buy or sell the commodity at a future time. If the trader is a speculator, the trader probably does not plan to hold the contract to maturity, but instead intends to liquidate it by executing an offsetting contract. Thus, the speculator would never be required to pay the full face amount of the contract (or to accept or deliver the commodity itself). When a trader liquidates his position, he receives back the amount in his margin account, as of the date of liquidation, less any commission. If the value of his contracts has increased since they were executed, the trader's margin account will have increased by the amount of the gain (unless the trader previously withdrew the gain). Losses on the contracts will be reflected by the total decrease in the original deposit in the margin account as well as any additional amounts paid in by the trader to meet margin calls. With a very small deposit, as low as five or even one percent of the value of the commodity covered by the contracts, a futures trader can speculate for the profits to be earned (or loss to be incurred) on the full 100 percent of the value of the commodity in the contracts.

Commissions

In securities transactions, brokers immediately charge customers a commission for any security purchases. Brokers also impose an additional commission for any subsequent sales. In futures transactions, however, commissions are charged only after the entire transaction is completed. Ordinarily, no commission is charged when a contract is purchased; the commission is assessed subsequently on a "round-trip" basis when the contract is liquidated. . . .

D. Tax Shelters

The tax potential of certain transactions in commodity futures to defer income and to convert ordinary income and short-term capital gains into long-term capital gains has been recognized by the investment industry for decades. However, only in the last ten to fifteen years has the use of such tax shelters in commodity futures extended beyond commodity and investment professionals to significant numbers of taxpayers, individual and corporate, throughout the economy. The tax advantages of spread transactions in futures are touted in commodity manuals, tax services and financial journals. Brokerage firms have promoted tax spreads or straddles to their clients. Domestic and offshore syndicates advertise tax straddle shelters for which purchasers pay an amount equal to a percentage of their desired tax loss.

1. *Tax straddles*

Use of tax straddles

Simple commodity tax straddles generally are used to defer tax on short-term capital gains from one tax year to the next tax year and, in many cases, to convert short-term capital gain realized in the first year into preferentially taxed long-term capital gain in a later year. However, in some cases (described below) straddles are used to defer tax on ordinary income and convert that income into short- or long-term capital gain. A simple straddle is constructed by taking equal long and short positions in the same property in the same market. The two positions, called "legs," are expected to move in opposite directions but with approximately equal absolute changes. Thus, for example, if one leg of a straddle in futures contracts increases $500 in value, the other leg can be expected to decrease in value by about the same amount. By maintaining balanced positions, the risks of the transaction are minimized.

A taxpayer using a simple futures straddle as a tax shelter will establish a position in contracts with contract prices of about, say, $10,000 each. The two contracts, one to buy, the other to sell, are identical in every respect, except for their delivery months. Because the taxpayer's position is a straddle, his margin deposit will be very low—as little as one percent of the value of the position ($200). The taxpayer will wait for the market to move, so that one leg of the straddle shows a loss, e.g., $500, and the other leg shows an almost identical gain. The taxpayer will liquidate the loss by entering into the opposite futures contract for the same month. (A contract to sell December wheat, for example, is liquidated by executing a contract to buy December wheat.) In order to maintain a balanced, minimal-risk position, the taxpayer will replace the liquidated leg with a contract which is identical, except for its delivery month. (The replacement contract will have a contract price of about $9,500, if the original long leg was liquidated at a loss, or a contract price of about $10,500, if the original short leg was liquidated at a loss.)

The taxpayer will claim the decrease in value in the liquidated leg as a $500 short-term capital loss and deduct it from his income, thereby eliminating a $500 short-term gain for the tax year. At the same time, the taxpayer will continue to hold the other leg, which will have an unrealized gain approximately equal to his "realized loss," that is, about $500. However, the taxpayer will not have paid out any money because no money is due on a futures contract until its delivery date. In addition, because the taxpayer maintained a balanced position, he ordinarily will not be required to put up any additional margin.

The taxpayer will hold the two legs into the following year. In the second year, the taxpayer will close out the two positions. Assuming the holdover contract has increased another $500 in value, the taxpayer will recognize a total gain of about $1,000 on the original leg and about a $500 loss on the replacement leg. If the gain is on the long (buy) position and that position was held for over six months, the taxpayer will report a $1,000 long-term capital gain on the long position and a $500 short-term capital loss on the short position. If he has no other capital transactions for the year, he will report the $500 difference between these legs as long-term capital gain. (His margin, less commissions, will be returned.) Thus, he will have succeeded in deferring his short-term capital gain for one year and converting it to a long-term capital gain. If the gain is in the short (sell) position, the gain will be short-term capital gain. In this case, the taxpayer gets a one-year deferral, but no conversion.

Certain commodity futures trading practices have facilitated tax straddle transactions. Exchange rules at the New York Commodity Exchange (COMEX), for example, provided for "after-hours" trading in spreads under extraordinary circumstances. During such trading sessions, only spreads were traded. In the late 1970s, however, COMEX after-hour sessions in silver futures occurred almost daily. Special sessions at the end of the calendar year lasted hours and drew press attention and comment. In 1980, after investigations suggested that abuses and violations of the Commodity Exchange Act rules, as well as significant tax-oriented trading, occurred during after-hours trading, the Commodity Futures Trading Commission suspended the sessions. In April 1981, the Commission announced its intention to disapprove the COMEX rule providing for these sessions.

Revenue Ruling 77–185

In 1977, the Internal Revenue Service issued Revenue Ruling 77–185, which disallowed deductions for losses and expenses in a simple two-contract silver straddle transaction. The ruling stated that the loss claimed by the taxpayer in connection with the disposition of one leg of the straddle was not *bona fide* because the disposition represented no real economic change and was not a closed and completed transaction. Moreover, the deductions for the loss and expenses were denied because, the ruling held, the transaction was not entered into for profit, but for tax-avoidance purposes.

Although the ruling discusses a two-contract (two-leg) silver straddle, many commodity experts have interpreted the ruling as applying to more complex "butterfly" straddles which involve four (or more) legs. Butterfly straddles, like simple straddles, are structured to create tax benefits regardless of the direction in which the market moves. [See sections E and G, below.] Thus, Butterfly straddles avoid risks entailed in single-spread straddles. The ruling has aroused controversy. Two lead cases involving IRS deficiency determinations under the theory in Revenue Ruling 77–185, are currently being litigated in the United States Tax Court.

Despite resistance to the IRS position, the ruling has caused some investment advisers to counsel greater caution with respect to tax straddle activity. Some have encouraged clients to vary their trading pattern from the facts outlined in the ruling; others arrange multiple, difficult-to-audit futures trades for their clients in order to give greater evidence of a profit-making motive. Because the IRS ruling dealt with a silver straddle, some tax straddlers switched to other commodities, particularly gold and Treasury bills. Some investment counselors now discourage tax straddles altogether.

Silver was a popular tax-shelter commodity because there generally has been a stable relationship between the price of silver contracts in different months. As noted above, this relationship is based on the costs of holding silver from one month to the other. Thus, the risks of spread trading were considered smaller than in other commodities. However, daily trading in silver was highly volatile, resulting in significant upward and downward price movement. This pattern was conducive to planning significant losses for tax purposes because the typical spread position provided a sizable gain on one leg and an almost precisely equal loss on the other leg. . . . [B]ecause the supply of silver was considered relatively stable, the price increases over time were largely a function of interest and storage for the silver until the commodity's delivery date, and not generally a function of sudden changes in supply.

The 1977 IRS ruling caused some tax straddlers to abandon silver. The extraordinary silver market crisis in March 1980, which some observers attributed to an attempt to corner the market, while others attributed to interference with market operations by short traders, led most remaining tax straddlers to abandon silver. Subsequently, tax straddle traders turned to other, more predictable commodities with premium market features similar to those which had previously characterized silver. Other precious metals and financial paper became the primary shelter commodities. However, tax straddles also can be executed in agricultural commodities, particularly those commodities which can be stored for long periods. . . .

D. LETTER OF DONALD C. LUBICK
Assistant Secretary of the Treasury for Tax Policy, reprinted in 12 Tax Notes 83, 83–84 (January 19, 1981)

December 23, 1980

Dear Senator Moynihan:

I have your letter of December 18, 1980 with respect to the use of commodity tax straddles and related devices to defer and, in some cases, permanently reduce tax liabilities.

. . . Both the Office of Tax Policy and the Internal Revenue Service have been concerned about this issue for some time. The Internal Revenue Service first published its position disapproving the use of tax-motivated commodity straddles in 1977, and since that time it has been attacking this device through increased audits and court actions. . . .

The reasons for our concern can be understood when you consider some of the tax returns that the IRS has uncovered in its investigation of these transactions. By virtue of straddles one taxpayer who sold stock in a closely held business at a $10 million gain in 1976 still had not paid tax on any of this income three years later. . . .

Tax-oriented commodity transactions are so attractive to some promoters that tax shelter limited partnerships have been formed that claim to act as dealers in commodities and money market instruments. In its first full year of operations, one of these partnerships, with almost a hundred partners, recognized an ordinary loss of about $46 million. At the same time, in commodity futures transactions which it claimed were of an investment nature, the partnership registered $20 million of short-term loss. Remarkably, its long-term investment transactions resulted in gains totalling almost $37 million. Such dismal results so impressed investors, that the partnership doubled in size the following year, and investor interest proved fully justified. The enlarged partnership proceeded to lose close to $70 million—an average of about $400,000 of ordinary losses for each partner. Meanwhile, "investment" activities again showed a remarkable dichotomy—short-term capital transactions produced a net loss of almost $240 million, while long term transactions resulted in gains of almost $280 million.

It is clear that investment interest in this partnership (most investors contributed at least $100,000 to the partnership) was not sparked by a desire to lose money in a real economic sense. The losses recorded on this partnership's tax return reflect only paper losses, leavened, to be sure, by some aggressive positions as to the tax consequences of certain transactions. (All the returns described above are now under audit by the IRS.) It is estimated, very conservatively, that about $1 billion is lost to the Treasury every year from these transactions. If it is not made clear soon, to all taxpayers, that these transactions do not have the consequences that are claimed for them, the figure for revenue loss will surely increase dramatically in the years to come. While the IRS should prevail in court on many of the issues raised by these returns, it is likely to take a number of years before definitive judicial decisions are handed down. In the interim, many more of these transactions will be carried out, and it cannot be expected that they can all be discovered by the IRS and questioned. . . .

> Sincerely yours,
> Donald C. Lubick
> Assistant Secretary
> (Tax Policy)

E. SMITH v. COMMISSIONER
78 T.C. 350 (1982), affirmed, 1820 F.2d 1220 (4th Cir 1988)

NIMS, JUDGE:

FINDINGS OF FACT

. . . During the early 1970's, Smith and Jacobson were both successful real estate developers. In 1971, the two men formed a partnership to develop apartments at La Costa, Calif., with a view to resale. On October 17, 1972, Smith and Jacobson sold their partnership interests to third parties at a substantial gain. The proceeds of these sales were to be received in the years 1972 through 1974, inclusive, with profits from the sale to be recognized for tax purposes on the installment sales method. Pursuant to the sales, the Smiths reported a $69,745 short-term capital gain in 1973; the Jacobsons reported a $68,802 short-term capital gain in such year.

Myron Shelley (Shelley) was a stockbroker working at the San Diego offices of Merrill Lynch, Pierce, Fenner & Smith, Inc. (Merrill Lynch), in 1973. Sometime after 1966, he had attended a seminar given by Thomas O'Hare (O'Hare), who headed Merrill Lynch's "Tax Straddle Department." O'Hare's presentation at Shelley's seminar was, in summary, as follows.

First, O'Hare explained that commodity tax straddles were useful for high-bracket taxpayers with large short-term capital gains. (O'Hare recommended a minimum of $20,000 in short-term capital gain and a 50-percent tax bracket before putting a client into a straddle.)

Second, O'Hare explained the mechanics of a typical tax straddle.

Third, O'Hare noted the beneficial tax results that a straddle was supposed to produce: (1) Deferring short-term capital gain from the current taxable year to the succeeding taxable year; and (2) depending on whether the price of the underlying commodity moved generally up or down over the course of the straddle, possibly converting the short-term capital gain in the second taxable year into long-term capital gain.

Commission costs were likely to amount to 10 percent of the short-term capital gain offset by the straddle, O'Hare explained. Customers should also be prepared for "difference" or "spread" losses of an equal amount.

Finally, O'Hare urged his audience to solicit business for the tax straddle department, located in New York. Stockbrokers would be paid in commissions for finding appropriate business.

Shelley first met Jacobson through mutual friends. At a luncheon meeting between the two men in 1973, Shelley learned that Jacobson had a large short-term capital gain that year. Shelley explained to Jacobson that there was a possibility the latter could enter into a series of commodity transactions that might result in deferral of his gain and possibly convert it to a long-term capital gain. Jacobson showed interest in Shelley's ideas and Shelley then set up a meeting with Clifford Schmidt (Schmidt), a commodities trader in the San Diego Merrill Lynch office.

The meeting with Schmidt was held on or about June 7, 1973, in the offices of Henry Sussman (Sussman), Jacobson's accountant. Attending the meeting were Schmidt, Shelley, Jacobson, Sussman, and Mrs. Jacobson. At this meeting, Schmidt explained basically how a tax straddle worked and detailed the potential market risks of straddling. Jacobson was primarily concerned with how much he would be at economic risk of losing in a tax straddle. Not counting commissions, Schmidt quoted Jacobson a figure of approximately 25 percent of margin. Jacobson then inquired whether that meant he could also make a gain of 25 percent of margin. Schmidt said, "yes." Schmidt also briefly discussed commission costs, giving the impression that they would be in the range of $4,000. Schmidt told Jacobson that O'Hare's tax straddle department in New York was expert in this area. Jacobson agreed to go ahead with the straddle, but asked that O'Hare's department, not Schmidt, handle the transactions.

Jacobson later told Smith about the commodity straddle he was planning, and Smith became interested in straddling to reduce his large short-term capital gain, also. Smith contacted Schmidt by phone. After a brief conversation wherein Schmidt gave a quick summary of what he had told Jacobson at the June 7 meeting, Smith requested that he, too, be put into a commodity tax straddle.

Notes made by George Peterson, Smith's accountant, of a telephone conversation he had with Smith on June 26, 1973, indicate that as of that date, Smith anticipated his 1973 short-term capital gain to amount to $84,752. Smith also told the accountant that he intended to "straddle" to convert that amount of short-term capital gain to long-term capital gain and to move the gain into 1974.

Schmidt next contacted O'Hare's tax straddle department in New York. O'Hare's department wanted to know what the size of the tax problem was. Schmidt replied that it was $85,000 of short-term capital gain, each, for both Smith and Jacobson.

Schmidt filled out forms entitled "New Account Information for Commodity Speculative Accounts" for Mr. and Mrs. Jacobson and for Smith.

On a long blank line near the bottom of the Jacobsons' form, Schmidt wrote, "This will be an 85K tax straddle thru N.Y." Smith's form contained a similar notation. . . .

After having received a request from Schmidt to place Smith and the Jacobsons into commodity straddles, O'Hare (or some other member of the tax straddle department in New York) filled out "holding pages" for the two new accounts. Near the top of each of these pages was the printed word "Objective" followed by a blank line. The blank line was then filled in with the notation "85M" for each account. This meant that the objective was to take a loss of $85,000 in each account before December 31, 1973. . . .

On February 13, 1974, O'Hare liquidated all of petitioners' butterfly straddle positions. . . .

On March 5, 1974, O'Hare wrote two letters to Schmidt. The letters related to Smith's account and the Jacobson's account and were identical in all respects, except as to the account numbers in the text. The letter regarding the Smith account read as follows:

> Dear Cliff:
> In reviewing our completed tax straddles, I find that your account 291–59604 realized a loss last year of $95,424 and his net gain in 1974 is $90,342. This latter figure is made up of $974,526 in long-term gain on the closeout of his May and September silver position and a $884,184 short-term loss in his July position.
> The overall cost of doing this business was $5,082 which is made up of $4,032 in commissions and exchange fees and a $1,050 difference loss. Since his overall cost ran approximately 5½% of the amount of money moved and the gains this year show net long-term, I would consider the entire transaction very satisfactory.

On their 1973 joint tax return, petitioners Harry Lee Smith and Patricia Ann Smith reported a short-term capital loss from "commodity transactions (silver)" of $95,424. On their 1973 joint tax return, petitioners Herbert J. Jacobson and Ruth D. Jacobson reported short-term capital losses of $50,022 attributable to "March Silver" and $45,402 attributable to "December Silver."

OPINION

This case presents, to our knowledge, one of the first occasions for a court to rule on the deductibility of losses sustained in what is commonly referred to as a "commodity tax straddle." As a preliminary matter, we note that Congress has dealt with this subject extensively in the Economic Recovery Tax Act of 1981, Pub. L. 97–34, secs. 501–509, 95 Stat. 323–335. Since the act is not intended to have retroactive application, the instant case, involving as it does trades in the years 1973 and 1974, is not governed by the act. Economic Recovery Tax Act of 1981, *supra* at sec. 508.

The device of the commodity tax straddle has been known for many years to the tax bar. See, e.g., Goldfein and Hochberg, "Use of Commodity Straddles Can Effect Impressive Tax Savings," 29 J. Tax. 342 (1968). The appeal of a commodity tax straddle is that it appears to offer a way to postpone the taxability of short-term capital gains by moving them into future years and possibly converting them to long-term capital gains, all at a minimum economic risk.

Since we have made extensive findings of what we deem to be the salient facts underlying this controversy, they will not, for the most part, be repeated here. The record contains very extensive testimony by Thomas O'Hare, the head of Merrill Lynch's tax straddle department during the years in question, and others, as to the nature and objectives of trading in commodity (specifically silver) tax straddles. The following, we believe, is an acceptable general explanation of the Federal income tax objectives of commodity tax straddles in silver based upon the entire record.

The typical tax straddle in silver futures is intended to work as follows: First, the taxpayer simultaneously acquires long and short futures positions in the identical quantity of silver. The long and short futures positions are in futures contracts having different delivery months so that under the rules of the commodity exchanges and the tax laws, the long and short positions do not cancel each other out. See sec. 1233(e)(2)(B).

Next, the taxpayer awaits a rise or fall in the market price of the underlying commodity. Such a rise or fall will usually cause futures contracts prices to rise or fall in a parallel fashion. The particular direction of the market movement is immaterial to the taxpayer: If the market rises by, say, $10 (and if each delivery month's futures price also rises by $10, in sympathy), the taxpayer will have an unrealized gain of $10 in the long position, or "leg," and an offsetting unrealized loss of $10 in the short position, or "leg." If the market falls by $10, on the other hand, the taxpayer will have a $10 unrealized loss in the long leg and a $10 unrealized gain in the short leg. In either case, the taxpayer has one loss leg and one gain leg with economically offsetting unrealized gains and losses of $10 each.

As stated above, the goal of a silver tax straddle is to "move" a certain quantity of short-term capital gain into a future year and possibly convert it into a long-term capital gain. Assume, for example, that the amount of short-term capital gain the taxpayer desires to move is $25. To move that $25, the taxpayer must hope for the market price of silver (and the parallel-traveling delivery months' futures prices) to rise or fall by $25. At this point, one leg of the straddle will possess an unrealized gain of $25 and the other an unrealized loss in that amount. The taxpayer then proceeds to the next step: the liquidation of the loss leg position and the realization of the $25 loss.

If the loss leg was held for less than 6 months before it was liquidated (and assuming the taxpayer was not in the commodities market as an integral part of his other businesses), the closing of the loss leg will produce a claimed $25 short-term capital loss. This $25 short-term capital loss will offset the $25 short-term capital gain which originally prompted the straddle.

At this point, only one leg of the initial straddle remains. This leg possesses an unrealized gain of $25. If the taxpayer can postpone realization of the gain until the next taxable year, he will have succeeded in shifting the $25 short-term capital gain from one taxable year to the next. If, in addition, he has held the remaining leg over the requisite holding period to convert it to long-term at the time of final liquidation, and this gain leg was the long leg of the initial straddle . . . he will have realized a long-term, rather than short-term, capital gain of $25 in the second taxable year. In this latter instance, the goals of both deferral and conversion of the short-term capital gain will be claimed to have been realized. In the event that the short leg of the initial straddle produced the gain, on the other hand, only the goal of deferral would be claimed. . . .

The taxpayer locks in the $25 unrealized gain by acquiring a new offsetting futures position (either long or short, as required) in an as yet unused delivery month. This new delivery month's prices will also be expected to move in tandem with the gain leg's delivery month's prices. The taxpayer then holds this new straddle position for the period necessary to achieve deferral and possible conversion (i.e., into the next year and over the requisite long-term holding period), and then liquidates both legs of this new straddle. This effectively locks in the $25 of unrealized gain no matter how volatile the underlying price of the commodity is during this holding period (assuming parallel futures price movements): any loss from price movement in the gain leg's delivery month will be compensated for by an offsetting gain from price movement in the new leg's delivery month, and vice versa. Upon liquidating this new straddle position, the taxpayer will claim to have realized a net capital gain of $25.

In the event that only the goal of deferral has been realized, and not that of converting the gain to long-term, the taxpayer may go back to step one in the second taxable year and straddle again to move the short-term capital gain from the second year to the third year. In fact, if petitioners' analysis of the tax law is correct, nothing but commission costs and death would prevent a taxpayer from perpetually straddling, achieving perhaps the ultimate tax goal of permanent deferral of taxation of an initial short-term capital gain.

A commodity tax straddle employing "butterfly" straddles works generally on the same principle as the typical commodity tax straddle described above, but with less economic risk. A butterfly straddle is, in essence, two separate straddles—one, for example, which is long March 1974/short July 1974 and another which is short July 1974/long December 1974. Thus, a butterfly straddle is one in which the positions are a combination of two separate straddles having one common intermediate delivery month.

If the market price of silver futures rises after the butterfly position in the example above is acquired, the two short July 1974 legs are loss legs which will be disposed of; if the market price of silver futures falls, the long March 1974 and long December 1974 legs are the loss legs to be disposed of. In the latter example, there will be gain in the short July 1974 legs which can be locked in by acquiring, for example, new long May 1974 and long September 1974 positions, achieving a new butterfly straddle position. As indicated earlier, butterfly straddles are often employed in preference to using an equal number of straddles sharing common delivery months in *both* legs of the straddles, the reason being that a butterfly position reduces even further the risk of "difference" loss or gain—i.e., the net difference (exclusive of commission costs) between loss and gain when all of the positions have been closed out.

With this background in mind, we turn now to the specifics of this case. On August 7, 1973, after the close of the COMEX regular trading session and during the after-hours trading session of that date, O'Hare sold 21 March 1974/July 1974 straddles and purchased 21 July 1974/December 1974 straddles, each, for both Smith's account and the Jacobsons' account. As we have set out in our findings of fact, August 7 was a day on which the prices of silver futures fluctuated widely during the regular trading session. Contracts of March 1974 silver and December 1974 silver traded as high as 302.30 cents per ounce and 314.20 cents per ounce, respectively, and as low as 290.00 cents and 306.00 cents, respectively. Settlement prices at the end of the regular trading session were near the lows of the day: 291.20 cents per ounce and 306.10 cents per ounce for March 1974 and December 1974 silver, respectively. . . . [Traders] in the after-hours session were given fairly wide latitude to agree on the respective prices to be assigned to the legs of the straddles they bought and sold. Under the rules, buyers and sellers of straddles could agree to price the long and short legs of the straddles using any prices at which the respective legs had traded during the regular trading session. The only limitation on the choice of these leg prices was that the spread differential between the prices had to exactly reflect the spread at which the straddle was actually bought and sold.

O'Hare took maximum advantage of this pricing latitude. He assigned prices to the . . . straddles at the highest possible prices of the day, given the spread limitation. This he did despite the fact that settlement prices had been near the lows of the day's prices. By choosing prices deviating substantially upward from the actual closing, or "settlement," prices on the trading day, O'Hare, in effect, locked in substantial unrealized losses in the . . . long legs of the straddles and locked in equally offsetting unrealized gains in the short . . . legs of the straddles.

Must the Losses Be Integrated?

In Rev. Rul. 77–185, 1977–1 C.B. 48, respondent first took the position that first-year losses in a commodity tax straddle should be integrated with second-year gains and recognized, if at all, only in the second year. He pursues this argument here. Respondent asserts that petitioners' scheme of maintaining a balanced position in long and short silver futures merely to stagger economically offsetting gains and losses in different years should [result in] gain or loss recognizable, if at all, at the close of the scheme.

Amicus points out that if we were to accept respondent's argument, we would be essentially writing a wash sale provision into the Code for straddle trading. Amicus notes that a number of courts, including this one, have held that commodity futures do not constitute stock or securities within the meaning of the wash sale provisions of the Code—currently Section 1091. . . .

The question we are faced with, then, is whether switches in the course of an attempt to maintain a continuous *straddle* position are, or should be, subject to any . . . common law wash sale doctrine. . . .

While respondent is deeply troubled by the use of unrealized gain to offset realized losses, we do not think this a sufficiently grave reason to integrate and postpone the recognition of such losses. It is well-settled tax law that a taxpayer may borrow out the unrealized gain inherent in an asset and use the proceeds for any purpose he likes without triggering a sale of the underlying asset. *Woodsam Associates, Inc. v. Commissioner* [Chapter 13].

Respondent's real, if obliquely articulated, objection, it seems to us, is that it is unfair to let petitioners recognize their losses because they knew ahead of time that there would likely be sufficient unrealized gain in their short July 1974 legs to borrow against so that they would not have to suffer any economic discomfiture on the switch. We might be more sympathetic with respondent's argument if in fact petitioners were guaranteed to have an exact offsetting unrealized gain available on August 9. However, here, they were not so assured. Contracts in different delivery months could, and in fact, did, show varying relative prices during the course of petitioners' straddles trades. While the actual pricing differences may have been small considering the size of petitioners' investments, we are not prepared to say such differences were de minimis. For us to draw a line, here, by saying that investments in these different assets must be integrated for tax purposes because their prices travel too much in tandem, simply begs the question: How nearly parallel is too nearly parallel? If platinum and gold futures prices travel roughly in tandem, are we to integrate a straddle in opposing platinum and gold futures? If the prices of certain utility stocks travel in a parallel fashion, are we to integrate a long position in utility A stock with a short position in utility B stock? A little reflection shows that straddles may be maintained in almost anything. . . .

We conclude that in the instant case . . . a nonstatutory wash sale doctrine [is] inappropriate to achieve respondent's result. In the past, nonstatutory wash sale consequences have resulted in cases where a party has failed to completely relinquish an economic investment in the same or a substantially identical asset. *McWilliams v. Commissioner* [Chapter 14]. In the instant case, after the switch, petitioners were not holding the same assets, March 1974 and December 1974 futures, but were instead holding May 1974 and September 1974 futures. These new positions were not substantially identical assets for purposes of the statutory wash sale provision, . . . nor were they substantially identical for any other wash sale approach. . . .

Section 165(c)(2)

Respondent next argues that even if petitioners incurred real, measurable losses in 1973, such losses are not allowable because they were not "incurred in any transaction entered into for profit" within the meaning of section 165(c)(2).

. . . Petitioners' expert demonstrated that historically an investment in a silver butterfly straddle potentially could have resulted in a profit exceeding commission costs if the right straddle and right date to get out of the straddle were chosen. Respondent's expert, on the other hand, demonstrated that an investor acquiring a silver butterfly straddle position during the latter half of the taxable year, holding it until a particular tax loss was achieved, and then switching position into a new butterfly straddle to be held for 6 months and then liquidated, was much less likely to achieve a profit. We agree with respondent that what petitioners invested in with Merrill Lynch were commodity tax straddles—i.e., a prearranged, planned sequence of trading along the lines studied by respondent's expert—not simple investments in butterfly straddles held solely for nontax profit objectives....

The mere fact that petitioners may have had a strong tax-avoidance purpose in entering into their commodity tax straddles does not in itself result in the disallowance of petitioners' losses under section 165(c)(2), provided petitioners also had a nontax profit motive for their investments at the time.... Such hope of deriving an economic profit aside from the tax benefits need not be reasonable so long as it is bona fide.... However, the existence of a nontax profit objective is a question of fact on which the petitioners bear the burden of proof.... In ascertaining petitioners' subjective intent, this Court is not bound by the taxpayer's uncontradicted assertions of proper motive made 8 years after the events in issue....

Contemporaneous evidence, we think, belies any nontax motive on petitioners' part. First, it is clear that petitioners were solicited for these investments solely because they possessed large short-term capital gains which these investments could defer. Merrill Lynch did not solicit clients for these investments who could not take advantage of the tax consequences. To us, this indicates that Merrill Lynch did not view the potential nontax benefits of such an investment large enough on their own to justify the cost. In light of Merrill Lynch's own doubts about the nontax benefits, we think it unlikely that Merrill Lynch stressed these benefits (or, more accurately, lack of benefits) to petitioners.

Indeed, information (discussed subsequently) which was made available to petitioners at the time of their investments indicated that there was no probability of earning an economic profit on their investments. Such information is a strong factor to consider in evaluating a taxpayer's subjective profit intent....

Jacobson achieved his albeit limited understanding of the nature of a commodity tax straddle from the meeting with Schmidt held at the offices of Sussman, Jacobson's accountant. Jacobson, according to Schmidt, was concerned primarily with how much he was at economic risk of losing, not gaining, in a commodity tax straddle; not counting commissions....

... Jacobson's subsequent investment in the tax straddle in light of the information he possessed (not to mention his primary preoccupation with economic losses at the meeting) is, we think, strong evidence of a lack of any economic profit objective on his part....

Smith acquired his knowledge of the risks of a tax straddle from both Jacobson and Schmidt. In a brief telephone conversation, Schmidt repeated to Smith the substance of what he had told Jacobson. These facts, we believe, also point to a lack of a nontax profit objective on the part of Smith.

Secondly, petitioners have failed to introduce any contemporaneous documents showing anything but tax objectives in their straddle investments. Notes of a telephone conversation between Smith and his accountant only refer to the tax benefits of the investment he planned. Both Smith's and the Jacobsons' "New Account Information for Commodity Speculative Accounts" forms indicate their investments to be $85,000 tax straddles through New York. So-called holding pages kept by O'Hare's tax straddle department contain the words "Objective *85M*," which, as interpreted by O'Hare, meant an $85,000 short-term capital loss in the first year was desired. Finally, O'Hare's letters to Schmidt at the conclusion of the straddles note the $5,082 of economic losses (difference losses and commission costs) and yet still term the transactions "very satisfactory," as losses ran only approximately 5½ percent of the amount of money moved. (Jacobson admitted at trial that he never later complained to O'Hare or Schmidt about these economic losses.)

The only evidence introduced by petitioners to support their contention that they possessed nontax profit objectives in 1973 is their own, uncorroborated testimony which we are inclined to find of no probative value.

In light of the above facts, we find that petitioners lacked the requisite economic profit objective necessary to enable them to deduct their commodity tax straddle losses in 1973. Sec. 165(c)(2).

Economic Recovery Tax Act of 1981

Petitioners and amicus' final argument is that Congress' closing of the tax straddle "loophole" in 1981 indicates that Congress felt that that loophole was open and available to be used by petitioners in 1973. . . .

. . . [W]e think it clear that Congress in passing the new act did not intend to influence the resolution of the issues in this case. Throughout the consideration of the new act, constant reference was made to the fact that the Internal Revenue Service disputed the tax benefits claimed by pre-1981 tax straddlers. . . . Tax benefits from pre-1981 tax straddles were referred to only as "allegedly available" in the Senate Finance Committee report. . . . In committee prints prepared by the Joint Committee on Taxation to explain the proposed Senate and House of Representatives versions of the new tax straddle legislation, specific references were made to the instant cases, both by name and Tax Court docket number. . . . Rarely can a court be as certain as we are here that the provisions of a new law were not to affect the case before it.

In addition, there is no evidence whatsoever that Congress sought to retroactively modify the longstanding principles of how gain and loss are computed or how losses under section 165(c)(2) are deducted.

Consequently, we reject petitioners' attempt to justify their loss deductions on the basis of congressional actions occurring 8 years later. . . .

F. NOTES AND QUESTIONS

1) A Simple Two-Leg Silver Straddle

Suppose that it is October, 1980 and that you have just completed a very successful real estate deal. Farmland that you purchased in June for $2 million has been sold for $3 million, producing a $1 million profit.

However, because you held the property for only four months, the gain is short term and therefore taxable at ordinary income rates. This would not be a problem if you had other capital losses to offset against the gain—but you do not. In 1980, the top individual rate on unearned income was 70%. Assuming that you are already in the top bracket, you will owe $700,000 in federal income taxes on the short-term gain.

To delay paying the $700,000 tax liability, you enter into a two-leg commodities straddle in silver. Each leg involves a contract known as a commodities future, which is an agreement between two parties for the sale of a commodity at a fixed price at a specified future date.[3] Suppose that on the first leg, you commit yourself to *buy* 1 million ounces of silver at a fixed price in April, 1981; and on the second leg, you commit yourself to *sell* 1 million ounces of silver at a fixed price in July, 1981.

2) How the Fixed Price in a Futures Contract is Determined

With a commodity like silver—of which there is a stable supply, not subject to weather and other growing conditions—a straightforward relationship exists between the current market value of silver and the price that is fixed in the futures contract. The difference—known as the price spread—normally equals the *current* market value plus the costs of carrying the silver until the futures contract is executed.

Thus, if the current market value of silver is $10 an ounce in October, 1980, the contract price for an April, 1981 sale will be fixed at $10 an ounce plus carrying costs. Similarly, the contract price for a July, 1981 sale will be $10 an ounce plus carrying costs. (The July, 1981 contract made in October, 1980 would be at a slightly higher fixed price than the April, 1981 contract made in October, 1980, because of the costs of carrying silver for an additional three months.)

3) Volatility in the Price of the Underlying Commodity

While the price spread between delivery months for silver shows little variation, the price of the underlying commodity itself is fairly volatile. Suppose that in November, 1980, one month after the straddle is established, the current market value of silver has risen to $11 an ounce.

In that event, the first leg of the straddle will show a gain of about $1 million. Where does the gain come from? You have the right to buy 1 million ounces of silver in April, 1981 for only $10 an ounce plus carrying charges. But the current market value of silver is $11 an ounce. Assuming the price spread between delivery dates remains stable, a futures contract written in November, 1980 for the sale of silver in April, 1981 would fix the price at $11 an ounce, plus carrying charges. Therefore, the value of the first leg should equal (a) what someone contracting today would have to agree to pay ($11 million plus carrying costs) less (b) what you will have

---

3. A single contract involves a standardized amount of the commodity, which in the case of silver is usually 10,000 ounces. Thus, a leg committing to buy or sell 1 million ounces would actually require 100 contracts, rather than a single contract.

to pay under your existing contract right (only $10 million plus carrying costs).

The second leg of the straddle will show a corresponding loss of about $1 million for precisely analogous reasons. You are obligated to sell 1 million ounces of silver in July, 1981 for $10 an ounce plus carrying charges. But the current market value of silver is $11 an ounce. The second leg involves a loss equal to (a) what someone contracting today would be able to charge ($11 million plus carrying costs) minus (b) what you will have to charge ($10 million plus carrying costs). In other words, someone would be willing to take on your obligation only if paid the difference between the November, 1980 price for July delivery of 1 million ounces of silver ($11 million plus carrying costs) and what you are obligated to charge in July ($10 million plus carrying costs).

Suppose that in November the price of silver had fallen to $9 an ounce. How much of a gain or loss would you show on each leg of the straddle at that time? Why?

4) Understanding the Straddle: The Analogy of Betting for and Against the Same Thing

Investing in the two-leg silver straddle can be analogized to betting both for and against the same thing. When you make the commitment to buy silver in the future at a fixed price, you are betting that the price will rise. When you make the commitment to sell silver in the future, you are betting that the price will fall. If the price goes up, you have a gain as a future buyer but a loss as a future seller. If the price falls, the reverse is true. Provided only that the price spread between future delivery dates remains stable, the amount of gain on one leg will about equal the amount of loss on the other.

It appears that there is nothing to be either gained or lost from entering the commodity straddle as long as you maintain balanced positions as both buyer and seller. *Aside from the tax consequences,* it makes little difference if the price of the underlying commodity rises or falls.

5) Disposing of One Leg and Realizing a Loss in 1980

Return to the example of the two-leg silver straddle where the November price of silver has risen, causing a loss to occur on the second leg, the commitment to sell. You will dispose of the second leg of the straddle in order to realize the loss. Disposition means finding someone else to take your place as obligated to sell 1 million ounces of silver for $10 an ounce in July, 1981. But in order to induce someone to take your position, you will have to put up about $1 million. This represents the difference between what you are obligated to charge for selling silver—$10 million plus carrying charges—and the November, 1980 price for July delivery—$11 million plus carrying charges.

This $1 million is also the measure of your realized loss. The initial cost for this leg of the straddle is zero. Although you were required to make a cash deposit when you entered the second leg, the deposit is refunded when it is disposed of. In effect, the cost of your investment in the second leg can be viewed as $1 million, while your return is zero, so that the net is a $1 million loss.

Where will this $1 million come from? It is about equal to the appreciation on the first leg. The commodities exchanges allow you to use the appreciation on the first leg to fund the loss on the second leg (see the Joint Committee on Taxation Report, above).

Notice that if the price of silver had fallen by $1 an ounce (instead of rising), the $1 million loss would have occurred with respect to the first leg of the straddle and basically the same steps would be taken to dispose of that leg and realize the loss.

6) Re-establishing and Then Disposing of the Straddle

Continue with the case of rising silver prices. By disposing of the second leg of the straddle, you have realized a $1 million loss in 1980. This can be used to offset the $1 million short-term gain from investing in farmland. But there is still $1 million of unrealized gain on the first leg of the straddle. And if you dispose of that first leg in 1980 and realize the gain in that year, you will have achieved no tax saving. You will save taxes only if you can delay realizing the gain on the first leg until at least 1981. In that event, you will be able to defer a $1 million short-term gain for one year.

There is substantial risk involved, however, in simply doing nothing until 1981. With the sale of the second leg, your position is now unbalanced. You are subject to all the economic risks associated with the up and down movements in the price of silver. With only a buy position, you are now betting that the price of silver will rise. If it falls while you are waiting for 1981, however, you will suffer an immediate economic loss and have to deposit cash to cover it.

Commodities exchange rules require an investor to deposit cash whenever his or her position in a futures contract falls in value. Moreover, even though your position in the first leg shows a $1 million gain, you are missing that cushion, having used it to fund the cost of disposing of the second leg. Should the current value of silver drop at all, you will have to put up cash.

In order to avoid these risks, you must re-establish the straddle by entering another contract to sell silver at a fixed price at a specified future date. Suppose that you commit yourself to sell 1 million ounces of silver for $11 an ounce (the current market value) plus carrying charges in October, 1981. You are now protected. If the price of silver falls, your first leg will decrease in value, but your re-established second leg should increase in value by about the same amount. Any cash deposit required on the first, losing leg will be funded by the gain on the second, winning leg.

If the price rises, your first leg will increase further in value, but the second leg should decrease in value by about the same amount. Any cash deposit required on the second, losing leg will be funded by the gain on the first, winning leg. No matter what happens to the price of silver until you dispose of your positions, you have eliminated the risks and also "locked in" the $1 million gain.

As soon as 1981 arrives, you dispose of the straddle. No matter what has happened to the price of silver, the net gain—from disposing of the entire straddle in 1981—should equal about $1 million (the 1980 loss). You have successfully deferred reporting that amount for one year.

Notice that if the price of silver had fallen (rather than risen) and the first leg had been disposed of in 1980 in order to realize a loss, you could have re-established the straddle by entering a futures contract to buy silver for a fixed price in October, 1981.

7) Manipulating Prices in Order to Minimize Risks

Assuming that the spread between prices for different delivery dates remains stable, virtually the only economic risk is that the price of the underlying commodity will stabilize and not vary enough to produce the desired loss. How did commodity exchange rules enable straddle investors to lessen this risk? Should the IRS have stopped this practice? For example, should it have required that the price assigned to an after-hours transaction be the closing price for the day?

8) A Financial Analysis: Are the Benefits Worth the Costs?

Assuming that you are in the 70% bracket, deferring $1 million of short-term capital gain for one year means deferring payment of $700,000 in taxes for one year. If the $700,000 is invested in tax-exempt securities earning 6%, it will earn $42,000 during the year of deferral.

Two sorts of costs must be considered. First, as long as positions in straddles are maintained, the commodities exchange requires a cash deposit (referred to as a margin deposit), usually equal to 1% of the price in the futures contract. In the example, each contract is for the sale of 1 million ounces for about $10 an ounce, or $10 million.[4] Thus, each contract would require a $100,000 deposit (1% of $10 million). For a period of about three months, from the time the straddle is established until the time it is disposed of, you must maintain a deposit on two contracts or a total of $200,000. Assume that if no deposit were required, this amount would be invested in tax-exempt bonds earning 6%. The cost of making the deposit is equal to the lost interest that would have been earned on tax exempt bonds or about $3,000.

You must also consider the brokerage fees. You have entered into and disposed of three separate futures contracts with a total face amount (or contract price for silver) of about $30 million.[5] If the brokerage fee is

---

4. Actually, the third contract—entered to reestablish the straddle after the sell leg is disposed of—has a slightly higher contract price of about $11 an ounce for 1 million ounces, or $11 million. The $10 an ounce figure is used here to simplify the calculations.

5. See the preceding footnote.

small—say one-tenth of 1% or $30,000—then you have made $42,000 (the benefit of tax deferral) at a total cost of $33,000.[6]

This produces a $9,000 profit or 27% ($9,000/$33,000) return on the amount invested in just three months. If the three-month return is annualized by multiplying 27% times four, it is the equivalent of earning annual interest at a rate of over 100%! The straddle investment looks particularly attractive next to tax-exempt bonds, earning over seventeen times as much. The only real economic risk incurred by the investor is the insignificant risk that silver prices may stabilize and vary hardly at all during the remainder of the year.

You should note how the overall profitability of the straddle depends on a number of factors. Suppose the tax rate applicable to the amount deferred were much lower, say 28% instead of 70%. Then the straddle would enable you to save only $280,000 for one year, and the interest earned from investing in tax-exempt securities paying 6% (which is the benefit of deferral) would be about $17,000. The tax benefits are then only about one-half the $33,000 in costs, and so the straddle investment would be a losing proposition.

Or suppose the margin requirement were higher, say 5% of the face amount of the contracts. The required deposit would then be $1 million and the cost of the deposit would be the lost interest on that amount for three months or about $15,000. In that event, too, total costs of $45,000 ("lost" interest of $15,000 plus brokerage fees of $30,000) would exceed the $42,000 in tax benefits. Or if the brokerage fees were higher, say one-half of 1% or $150,000, the costs would also exceed the benefits.

---

6. To simplify the example, this calculation of benefits and costs ignores the different points in time at which the benefits and costs are incurred and therefore disregards the time value of money. Ideally, the calculation of costs and benefits would take account of these differences in the timing of when the margin amount must be deposited, when brokerage fees must be paid and when tax benefits begin. Such a precise calculation would discount both benefits and costs to a common point in time before comparing them.

The margin deposit is due in October, 1980 when the straddle position is first established and is not refunded until the straddle is disposed of in January, 1981. The brokerage fees, on the other hand, are due only when a future is disposed of. In the example, above, some fees are due in November, 1980 when one leg is disposed of to establish a loss. The rest of the fees are due when the re-established straddle is disposed of several months later, in early 1981.

Tax returns are ordinarily due on April 15 for the preceding year so that the straddle may *appear* to defer the payment of $700,000 from April 15, 1981 until April 15, 1982. Estimated taxes must be paid, however, in quarterly installments, with the final April 15 payment simply making up for any difference between estimated and actual taxes due. Suppose it is anticipated in the first quarter of 1980 that there will be a straddle loss in the fourth quarter and that payments of 1980 estimated taxes are adjusted accordingly. In that event, the benefit of deferring $700,000 in taxes for one year begins to be realized as early as April of 1980, six months before the taxpayer even establishes the first straddle position.

Peculiarities of calculating estimated taxes may also have the effect of increasing the period of deferral considerably beyond one year. Estimated taxes are assessed on the assumption that current year taxes will *not* increase over the prior year's taxes. If taxes due are actually higher, reconciliation will occur on April 15, but there is no penalty for underpaying the estimated tax. Thus, a straddle loss realized in 1980 may reduce the estimated tax bill for both 1980 and 1981 when estimated taxes for 1981 are based on 1980 taxes. The final reconciliation for 1981 will not occur until April 15, 1982. Estimated taxes are due more or less quarterly, so that tax payments will effectively be deferred, on average, for about another six months.

Suppose you invest in a commodity straddle that produces tax savings of $42,000 but costs the same amount in lost interest on the deposit and brokerage commissions. In that event, who really gains from the straddle? The investor or the broker? Even if the total costs are only $21,000, how is the revenue lost to the Treasury (the $42,000 in tax savings) allocated between investor and broker?

Even if the straddle appeared to provide an attractive return, there was the legal risk that the loss would not be allowed and the costs would have been incurred without any benefit. This legal risk is examined below.

9) The Straddle as a Wash Sale

Returning to the two-leg silver straddle example, in November, 1980 you disposed of the second leg, which consisted of a commitment to sell silver in July, 1981. You then re-established the straddle by committing to sell silver in October, 1981. Why don't these transactions constitute a wash sale under Section 1091? Section 1091 has been consistently interpreted by both the IRS and the courts as *not* applying to commodity futures. It was only in 1981 that Congress enacted Section 1092(b) to apply to wash sales involving commodity futures.

But apart from the specific wash sale provisions in the Code, why doesn't the doctrine of Higgins v. Smith apply to disallow the loss? At virtually the same time, the taxpayer disposes of the commitment to sell July, 1981 silver and enters into a commitment to sell October, 1981 silver. Doesn't this involve a sale "without substance" not very different from the sale of securities to a wholly owned corporation in Higgins v. Smith? The two commitments appear identical, except for the three-month difference in due dates. Is that difference significant in the case of a commodity like silver which is in stable supply?

In Rev. Rul. 77–185, 1977–1 C.B. 49, the IRS disallowed deductions for losses in a two-leg silver straddle like the one described above. Among the reasons given was that the "loss" lacked substance. While the ruling did not mention Higgins v. Smith, it did cite *Horne* (Chapter 14).

Why did Smith v. Commissioner refuse to adopt the "no sale in substance" analysis? Do you find the reasoning convincing, given the fact that the case involved a butterfly straddle that was designed to eliminate virtually all the risk of variation in price spreads between different delivery dates? Would you have been more convinced if it were a case of a simple two-leg silver straddle?

10) The Anti-*Woodsam* Solution

In *Woodsam* (Chapter 13), the Supreme Court refused to treat the mortgaging of property without recourse as a realization event. When the straddle investor re-establishes the position and locks in the unrealized gain, isn't that equivalent to taking out a nonrecourse mortgage? If *Woodsam* had gone the other way, would the straddle scheme have ever been viable? Would re-establishing the straddle then be viewed as producing realization of locked-in gain?

11) The Tax Avoidance Purpose Rationale

The Tax Court in Smith v. Commissioner disallowed the loss because the taxpayer's only purpose was tax avoidance, and there was no bona fide expectation of economic profit.

Is this rationale convincing? How relevant is tax avoidance motive to whether the loss should be disallowed? How can the motive be ascertained without a mental X-ray or thought police? Or can it be inferred from the fact that no reasonable person would expect to profit from this particular straddle except by creating artificial tax losses?

But are there no circumstances in which straddles might be acquired for a bona fide nontax purpose? Suppose an investor believes that spreads between delivery dates for silver, although stable in the past, may become volatile in the future and invests in two-leg silver straddles in order to profit from those changed circumstances. If the changed circumstances do not materialize and the investor shows a loss, should it still be disallowed?

> [A]lthough the taxpayers lost the *Smith* case, the Service did not win it. . . . [It] represents the first judicial determination that straddles are a permissible means for deferring . . . income, *so long as the taxpayer enters into the straddles with a legitimate profit motive and the pricing of the straddle positions is not manipulated to create an immediate loss* (emphasis added). This result leaves the Service in the uncomfortable position of having to litigate profit motive in every case.[7]

12) The Statutory Solution

Initially, the Treasury proposed legislation that would allow straddle losses to be deducted only against gains *recognized* from the *same* transaction. Later, the Treasury proposed, in addition, the annual taxation of gains and losses on commodity straddles, *whether realized or not*. Congress enacted both Section 1256 to require accrual taxation of straddle gains and losses, with Section 1092 (discussed above) to provide back-up.

Although Section 1256 does not, in so many words, purport to limit the deductibility of straddle losses, why does it amount to that? Can it be viewed as a nonrecognition provision, analogous to Section 1211? Analogous to Sections 267 and 1091?

13) Straddles in Other Commodities

Why were futures in a perishable commodity like wheat, with an unstable supply, not attractive as a basis for two-leg straddles? Why is the price

---

7. Rothenberg and Balbus, Securities Partnerships—Straddle Opportunities and Limitations, 36 Major Tax Planning 1–1, 1–10 (1984). The quoted comments may be too pessimistic. Butterfly straddles, which use four legs, are designed to eliminate volatility in price spreads. (See the discussion below.) When taxpayers invest in a four-legged butterfly straddle, as they did in *Smith*, the absence of a profit motive might not be that difficult to demonstrate. Moreover, in 1984 and 1986, Congress enacted special legislation affecting straddle losses resulting from positions entered into on or before June 23, 1981. Such losses are not deductible unless the taxpayer's *primary* motive was to make a profit. See Boswell v. Commissioner, 91 T.C. (1988). Losses on positions entered into after June 23, 1981 are disallowed under Sections 1092 and 1256, discussed below.

spread between future delivery dates for wheat relatively unstable? What affects the supply of wheat that does not affect the supply of silver? What is the unattractive economic risk this creates for the person who buys straddles solely to reduce taxes?

The four-leg butterfly straddle permits the use of commodities such as wheat for tax reduction, without incurring such risks. (It reduced even further the risks on straddling *via* a commodity like silver with very stable price spreads.) The butterfly straddle also offered the opportunity not simply for deferring a short-term capital gain but also for converting it into long term gain, with the effect of permanently excluding 60% of it. A fuller description of the butterfly straddle follows these notes and questions, for those heroic readers who wish to explore the subject further.

G. THE BUTTERFLY STRADDLE

Staff of Joint Committee on Taxation, 97th Cong., 1st Sess., Background on Commodity Tax Straddles and Explanation of H.R. 1293 16, 17–19 (Joint Comm. Print 1981)

A butterfly straddle is a commodity futures spread entailing at least four positions. A butterfly straddle generally is composed of two simple, mirror-image spreads with the same intermediate delivery date.

The butterfly straddle can consist of a long position in a futures contract with a near delivery date, a long position in a futures contract with a distant delivery date, and two short positions in a futures contract with an interim delivery date. A butterfly straddle also may be structured with one near and one distant short position and two interim long positions.

Because the two spreads in the butterfly are established as mirror images of each other, the butterfly provides protection against a change in the price of the commodity whether the market moves up or down and also against any change in the price of the spread. It also makes it more likely that at least one long position will produce a gain and will be held for more than six months, so that short-term gain will be converted into long-term gain.

EXAMPLE: Gold Butterfly Straddle

The following example outlines the steps in executing a butterfly straddle in gold futures contracts (100 troy oz.). The following prices are rounded from closing prices listed for contracts traded on the New York Commodity Exchange (COMEX) in the middle of April, 1981.

Gold Futures—100 Troy oz.

Contract:	Cost per oz.
February 1982	$550.00
April 1982	560.00
June 1982	570.00

August 1982	585.00
October 1982	600.00
December 1982	610.00
February 1983	625.00

Step I: April 1981

Establish straddle:
Buy Feb. 1982—Sell June 1982, Sell June 1982—Buy Oct. 1982
Taxpayer deposits one percent of contracts' face value ($229,000) as margin: $2,290.

Step II: September 1981

Assume price of gold increased 10 percent: **September 1981**

February 1982	$605
June 1982	627
October 1982	660

The straddle has potential losses in its two June short positions and approximately equal gains in its two long, February and October, positions:

February 1982	+5,500
October 1982	+6,000
June 1982	−5,700
June 1982	−5,700
Economic gain	+100

Because the taxpayer wants tax losses, he closes out the loss legs (June) with two new straddles:

Sell April—Buy June,   Buy June—Sell August

As a result of executing these two straddles, the taxpayer's position now is:

Buy February—Sell April,   Sell August—Buy October

The taxpayer thus has the two long, February and October contracts still in place with profits of $11,500, all the while maintaining the spread positions. The profit of $11,500 belongs to the taxpayer as a matter of right. The taxpayer may have already withdrawn the profits as they were credited daily to his account. The taxpayer has a tax loss of $11,400 for 1981. Generally this will be a capital loss deductible against capital gains and up to $3,000 of ordinary income.

Step III: March 1982

Assume additional 10-percent increase: **March 1982**

February 1982	$665.50
April 1982	677.60
August 1982	707.85
October 1982	726.00

The taxpayer liquidates all positions by executing offsetting spreads which cancel his positions:

Sell February—Buy April,   Buy August—Sell October

The two long positions have gain $24,150:

February	+11,550
October	+12,600

The April position lost $6,160 since it was entered at $161 per oz. in September 1981:
April .... −6,160

The August position lost $6,435 since it was entered in September 1981 at $643.5 per oz.:
August .... −6,435

Taxpayer recognizes net gain of $11,555 for 1982. (Of course, gain credited to the taxpayer's account in 1981 may have been withdrawn by him in that year.)

Summary

If gain is recognized on a long position held over 6 months, as in this example, it is taxed as long-term capital gain even though the losses in the prior year were deducted against short-term capital gains.

Taxpayer's actual economic change on the butterfly is determined by reducing total gains by total losses:

All gains	+11,550
	+12,600
All losses	−6,160
	−6,435
	−11,400
Net economic change	+155

Alleged tax savings for 1981: $7,980 (assuming 70-percent bracket).

The taxpayer can enter into a new straddle to generate losses to deduct against the $11,555 of gain for 1982. Alternatively, he can pay tax of $3,235.40 on the long-term gain (assuming a 70-percent tax bracket). In this case, the tax benefit is $4,744.60 ($7,980−$3,235.40) plus the advantage of a one-year deferral.

Chapter 17

LIKE–KIND EXCHANGES: POTENTIAL LOSS

A. INTRODUCTORY NOTE

Before proceeding further, it may help to summarize the basic ideas developed so far regarding the deduction of losses on property. First, the realization principle dictates that, in general, the losses are deductible only when the property has been sold or exchanged. (There are, however, exceptions for FIFO inventory and commodity straddles, for which even unrealized losses are deductible.)

Second, a formal realization alone may not permit deduction of a loss. Under Higgins v. Smith, *Horne*, and *McWilliams* (Chapter 14), the loss must be realized in substance as well as in form.

Third, even if a loss is truly realized, Congress may provide for not taking it into account, or nonrecognition. For example, losses from related party and wash sales are subject to nonrecognition under Sections 267 and 1091.

B. COTTAGE SAVINGS ASSOCIATION v. COMMISSIONER
90 T.C. 372 (1988)

Background

Since 1883, petitioner has been in the business of receiving savings deposits from the public and in turn making loans secured by residential and commercial real estate.... Petitioner, a State-chartered mutual savings association, was a federally insured savings and loan institution subject to the regulations of the Federal Home Loan Bank Board (hereinafter sometimes referred to as the FHLBB)....Petitioner was required to file semiannual financial reports to the FHLBB reporting petitioner's financial condition in conformity with accounting principles adopted by the FHLBB and commonly referred to as regulatory accounting principles (hereinafter sometimes referred to as RAP). . . .

[B]ecause of the increases in market interest notes, the market values of existing fixed-interest loan portfolios held by savings and loan institutions were substantially less than the book values of these loan portfolios. . . .

FHLBB regulations required petitioner (and other federally insured savings and loan institutions) to meet certain net worth requirements. . . .

If petitioner had sold the loan participations described *infra,* and had been required by the FHLBB's RAP to reduce its net worth by the amounts of the losses that it would have sustained . . . then petitioner's net worth would have been reduced to such a level that it would have barely exceeded the FHLBB's minimum requirements.

Memorandum R-49

On June 27, 1980, the Director of the Office of Examination and Supervision (OES) of the FHLBB issued Memorandum R-49 relating to "reciprocal sales" of mortgage loans, with the following stated synopsis: "A LOSS NEED NOT BE RECORDED FROM 'RECIPROCAL SALES' OF SUBSTANTIALLY IDENTICAL MORTGAGE LOANS". The body of Memorandum R-49 states as follows:

> The purpose of this memorandum is to advise OES staff on the proper accounting for reciprocal sales of mortgage loans.
>
> A loss resulting from a difference between market value and book value in connection with reciprocal sales of substantially identical mortgage loans need not be recorded [under RAP]. Mortgage loans are considered substantially identical only when each of the following criteria is met. The loans involved must:
> 1. involve single-family residential mortgages,
> 2. be of similar type (e.g., conventionals for conventionals),
> 3. have the same stated terms to maturity (e.g., 30 years),
> 4. have identical stated interest rates,
> 5. have similar seasoning (i.e., remaining terms to maturity),
> 6. have aggregate principal amounts within the lesser of 2½% or $100,000 (plus or minus) on both sides of the transaction, with any additional consideration being paid in cash,
> 7. be sold without recourse,
> 8. have similar fair market values,
> 9. have similar loan-to-value ratios at the time of the reciprocal sale, and
> 10. have all security properties for both sides of the transaction in the same state. . . .

Memorandum R-49 was the FHLBB's response to a desire of the savings and loan industry to structure exchanges of mortgage loans to create losses for income tax reporting purposes which would not be reported under RAP or under general accepted accounting principles (hereinafter sometimes referred to as GAAP).

The criteria selected in Memorandum R-49 represented an attempt by the FHLBB, OES, to maintain the regulated institution's position with respect to three types of risk in a loan portfolio. These risks related to credit or collectibility, rate or future earnings potential, and repayment or extent of principal repayments and prepayments. In the opinion of the OES, a change in any of these risks would change the economic factors underlying a savings and loan institution's loan portfolio and, as a result, require recording the resulting gain or loss under RAP.

A memorandum dated August 10, 1981, from the Director of the OES to the Executive Staff Director of the FHLBB, sets forth the following explanation with respect to the criteria listed in Memorandum R-49.

> When developing the criteria contained in Memorandum R-49, we worked closely with the AICPA Committee on Savings & Loan Associations. In addition to communication with this committee, we also obtained agreement with our stance from prominent CPAs serving the industry. . . . Our objective at that time was to structure a transaction which was as close as possible to the IRS "materially different" definition which would still not change the economic position of the association after it engaged in the swap. It was and remains our opinion that Memorandum R-49 represents a transaction which is on a fine line between "substantially identical" and "materially different."
>
> These criteria represented our attempt to maintain the association's position with respect to the three types of risks in a loan portfolio. These risks relate to credit (collectibility), rate (future earnings potential), and repayment (extent of principal repayments and prepayments). In our opinion, a change in any of these risks would change the economic factors underlying an association's loan portfolio and, as a result, require recording the resulting gain or loss. . . .

Transactions in Issue

Before and during 1980, the independent accounting firm engaged by petitioner was Frank Milostan & Associates (hereinafter sometimes referred to as Associates). In October 1980, Frank Milostan (hereinafter sometimes referred to as Milostan) of Associates attended a week-long seminar given by an accounting firm in Houston, Texas. This seminar concerned the banking and savings and loan industries. At this seminar, Milostan was introduced to the concept of reciprocal loan sales. On his return to Cincinnati, Milostan asked the staff of Associates to consider the benefits of such a concept to Associates' clients.

On November 6, 1980, Associates gave a seminar in which the speakers highlighted the use of reciprocal sales to obtain refunds of Federal income taxes. The registration form mailed to Associates' clients and to the other savings and loan institutions which were invited to the seminar captioned the seminar "1980 TAX STRATEGIES FOR FINANCIAL INSTITUTIONS (Your Contribution to the National Debt!!)". Petitioner's president, William C. Kordis (hereinafter sometimes referred to as Kordis), was invited to attend on behalf of petitioner, and he and at least one other officer of petitioner attended the seminar.

Before attending the seminar, Kordis had discussed with Milostan the possibility of reciprocal sales of mortgage loans as a method of obtaining cash-flow resulting from tax refunds. After the seminar, Kordis discussed with petitioner's board of directors the possibility of entering into such transactions, and invited Milostan to come and explain the possibility in more depth to the board of directors. On November 10, 1980, Milostan and Stanley Quay (an associate of Milostan) discussed reciprocal sale transactions with petitioner's board of directors, and on that date the board of directors passed the following resolution to enter into such transactions:

> RESOLVED: To enter into reciprocal sales of mortgage loans to other nonrelated financial institutions in exchange for mortgage loans of identical interest rates, stated maturities and seasoning. The reciprocal sale of mortgage loans will not result in a gain or loss for finfncial [sic] reporting purposes. (R-49) However, the reciprocal sale of mortgage loans will result in an ordinary loss for Federal Income Tax purposes equal to the difference between the book value of the portfolio sold and the fair market value of the portfolio purchased on the date of sale. (Rev. Rul. 71–558)

On December 31, 1980, petitioner as "Seller" entered into a series of loan participation sale and trust agreements as shown in table 1.

TABLE 1

Buyer	Number of loans	Total consideration
Rosemont Savings Association	8	$99,388.66
Civic Savings Association	44	655,575.72
First Financial Savings Association	188	3,432,714.35
Kenwood Savings & Loan Association	12	271,176.09

Also on December 31, 1980, petitioner as "Buyer" entered into a series of loan participation sale and trust agreements as shown in table 2.

TABLE 2

Seller	Number of loans	Total consideration
Rosemont Savings Association	8	$98,257.50
Civic Savings Association	45	655,488.29
First Financial Savings Association	240	3,431,868.28
Kenwood Savings & Loan Association	12	271,298.43

... Each of petitioner's trading partners was unrelated to petitioner, was run by other people, and had a board of directors that was separate from that of any of the other of petitioner's trading partners.

In each of the transactions described in table 1 or table 2, *supra* (hereinafter sometimes referred to as the December 31, 1980, transactions), the "Buyer" delivered to the "Seller" a check for the total consideration stated in the applicable agreement. ...

Each of the loan participation sale and trust agreements entered into by petitioner on December 31, 1980, states "Seller hereby sells and issues to buyer . . . a 90-percent participation ownership (subject to the terms and conditions of said Participation Agreement) in loans described in the list . . . attached hereto." The subject loans were described in packages by interest rate, total term, and term to maturity. The packages which were subject to the agreements were matched under the criteria of FHLBB Memorandum R-49.

As a result of the December 31, 1980, transactions, petitioner was required to undertake additional administrative activity. Petitioner continued to service the loans in which it had sold the participations. Monthly reports of the transferred loan participations were prepared by each of the transferor institutions for each of the transferee institutions. In addition, payments on the participations were made monthly. Petitioner also had to record and maintain records relative to the payments on the participation packages received from petitioner's trading partners.

Petitioner and Associates considered it advantageous to sell 90-percent participation interests in the loans rather than selling the loans outright. Petitioner thus was able to maintain its relationship with the obligors on the loans, since these obligors were not aware that participation interests in their loans had been transferred. In addition, petitioner was not required to transfer the records associated with the mortgages to the buyers of the participation interests.

In entering into the December 31, 1980, transactions, petitioner relied on its officers' knowledge of the trustworthiness of the individuals from petitioner's trading partners and the assumed increase in value of the collateral from the date of the loans. In selecting the loans for inclusion, petitioner and petitioner's trading partners did not investigate individual loan files, employment histories of the individual borrowers, or the underlying value of the real estate securing the individual loans. Only current, i.e., nondelinquent, loans were considered.

The participations sold and bought by petitioner all were in loans that had different obligors, that were "conventional" loans secured by mortgages on single-family residential properties, and that were current as of December 31, 1980. The underlying security for each loan was different, in that each property had a different location. Most of the properties are inside the Cincinnati "beltway" (U.S. Highway I-275). Most of the in-beltway properties where petitioner was the seller are east of downtown Cincinnati, while the in-beltway properties where petitioner was the buyer are more evenly distributed throughout the area. Some of the properties where petitioner was the buyer are as far north as Dayton, Ohio (about 55 miles from Cincinnati), and some are as far east as Jackson, Ohio (about 120 miles from Cincinnati). Of the properties where petitioner was the seller, some are as far north as Middletown, Ohio (about 35 miles from Cincinnati), and some are as far east as Batavia, Ohio (about 25 miles from Cincinnati).

Sales or purchases of participations, such as the 90-percent participations involved in this case, are customary; and loans that are sold or purchased are usually sold or purchased in a group by savings and loan institutions. Reciprocal sales of loans by savings institutions occurred before the December 31, 1980, transactions. Although diversification by geography and other factors may be reasons for reciprocal sales transactions generally, such factors were not considered in the December 31, 1980, transactions.

In the savings and loan industry, it is recognized that, generally, mortgage loans do not run to the completion of the terms of the loans. Petitioner made no attempt to determine, on a loan-by-loan basis or an aggregate basis, whether there was a difference between the prepayment potential or anticipated income stream of the loan participations received by petitioner and those transferred by petitioner on December 31, 1980. Actual collections did not achieve the equality anticipated at the time of the transfers. . . .

Participation interests are less liquid than whole loans in the secondary market. That is, there is an active secondary market for mortgage loans but very little market for participation interests. As a result, after the December 31, 1980, transactions, petitioner and its trading partners all were in a less liquid position (except for their income tax refunds) than they had been before the December 31, 1980, transactions.

The December 31, 1980, transactions met the criteria of Memorandum R-49 of the FHLBB and qualified for nonrecognition of loss under RAP. Petitioner did not report under RAP any losses on the December 31, 1980, transactions.

The December 31, 1980, transactions were between independent parties; the transactions were closed and completed; the transactions were bona fide. At the time of the transactions, petitioner and its trading partners anticipated that the income stream earned from the loan participations that were acquired would be substantially equal to the income stream earned from the loan participations that were sold. If this anticipated equality did not occur, absent misrepresentations, the party receiving less in actual collections had no recourse against the party receiving more.

Before the December 31, 1980, transactions, petitioner's loan portfolio had decreased in market value because of economic conditions general to the savings and loan industry. The losses claimed by petitioner accurately reflect the decrease in petitioner's assets from book value to market value.

The December 31, 1980, transactions were motivated solely by the desire of petitioner and its trading partners to recognize for tax purposes (but not for regulatory purposes) the losses in market values of the loan portfolios each institution owned before the December 31, 1980, transactions.

OPINION. . . .

Sales v. Exchanges

As a preliminary matter, we reject petitioner's contentions that the four pairs of transactions occurring on December 31, 1980, were not reciprocal and cannot be regarded as "exchanges" as distinguishable from "sales". Petitioner argues that the loan sales transactions occurred between petitioner, on the one hand, and four other savings and loan institutions, on the other, solely as a matter of expediency. Petitioner denies that the transactions were reciprocal, interdependent, or conditioned on one another, and points out that the agreements do not expressly make them interdependent.

The obvious and expressed intention of the contracting parties was to come within the terms of Memorandum R-49. That memorandum specifically referred to "reciprocal sales of substantially identical mortgage loans". The testimony at trial, including that of Kordis, referred to the transactions as reciprocal.... Petitioner's counsel conceded, in his opening statement at trial, that petitioner bought about as much as it sold, "in order to comply with the regulatory accounting principle known as R-49, which required that loans be purchased in order not to recognize the loss [for] financial accounting purposes which, in most instances, if it had to be recognized, would have brought these savings and loans beneath the net worth requirements of the Federal Home Loan Bank." The only practical interpretation of the simultaneous purchases and sales were that they were interdependent in order to avoid the necessity of reporting losses under GAAP or RAP. Under these circumstances, the separate agreements will be regarded together as an overall transaction rather than as separate sales between the contracting parties.... Thus, we have adopted, for purposes of our opinion, respondent's characterization of the transactions as exchanges.

However, this conclusion does not resolve the case before us; it merely sets the framework for the remainder of our analysis....

Basic Analysis

Under section 1001, if there has been a sale or other disposition of property ... then the resulting loss is to be recognized unless subtitle A provides otherwise. Respondent does not contend that any nonrecognition provision in subtitle A applies to the transfers of the mortgage loan participations in dispute in the instant case (except to the extent that section 1001 may be viewed as a nonrecognition provision). Under section 165(a) the losses are deductible for 1980 ... if they were sustained during 1980.

On December 31, 1980, petitioner simultaneously bought and sold 90-percent participations in residential mortgage loans. The transfers were at then-current fair market values which, in the case of the participations that petitioner sold, were substantially below petitioner's cost.... The loans that were affected were carefully selected by petitioner and by petitioner's trading partners to satisfy the equivalence criteria set forth in FHLBB Memorandum R-49, and also to match as nearly as practicable the aggregate fair market values of the loan participations transferred in the opposite direction.... The transfers were bona fide, completed transactions. That is, petitioner assumed all the benefits and burdens of the loan participations it acquired and petitioner's trading partners assumed all the benefits and burdens of the loan participations they acquired from petitioner.

The transfers were solely tax-motivated. That is, although participations often are sold for a variety of business reasons, in the instant case, the loan participation sales and offsetting purchases were effectuated solely to reduce petitioner's tax liabilities (and, presumably, the tax liabilities of petitioner's trading partners).[1] This, by itself, is not fatal to petitioner's claimed deduction in the context of the instant case . . . but it does require us . . . to scrutinize the record with particular care. . . .

The loan participations are not fungible, unlike cash . . . or shares of stock of the same class in a given corporation (see *McWilliams v. Commissioner* [Chapter 14]. The underlying securities and the obligors on the loans differed one from another. The claimed losses were the market economic losses that petitioner had in fact suffered as a result of changes in interest rates. Actual collections on these loan participations after December 31, 1980, the date of the transfers, did not achieve the equality anticipated at the time of the transfers. . . . The transfers clearly did change the flow of economic benefits from the loan participations.

In addition, before the December 31, 1980, transactions, petitioner owned real estate mortgage loans. After these transactions, petitioner owned (1) real estate mortgage loans diminished by 90-percent participations and (2) 90-percent participations in other real estate mortgage loans. Ownership of participations in loans has a number of characteristics that differ from ownership of entire loans. . . .

We conclude that petitioner realized and sustained the claimed losses in 1980, that petitioner is required to recognize these losses for 1980, and that petitioner is entitled to deduct these losses for 1980.

Realization and Recognition

Respondent contends that "The resolution of this case rests largely upon the application of Treasury Reg. sec. 1.1001–1(a) which limits the realization of gain or loss under section 1001 to transactions in which property is exchanged for 'other property differing materially either in kind or in extent' ".

The first sentence of this section of the regulation may be read as providing that income or loss is sustained if the income or loss is realized, and if this realization occurs from an "exchange of property for other property differing materially either in kind or in extent". The regulation could have, but does not state that this is the only way in which income or loss is sustained. However, respondent reads that sentence as restricting

---

1. Petitioner contends that there were other reasons, specifically geographic diversification, improving relations with other institutions, increasing its servicing portfolio, and the possibility of faster payoffs. The record would not support a finding that any of these possible concerns played any part in the transactions of Dec. 31, 1980. In fact, the record supports a finding that they did not, and we have so found. Petitioner also states that "Milostan stated in his testimony that another reason to sell and repurchase loans was to reinvest the proceeds of the sale at prevailing market rates." However . . . almost 99.96 percent of petitioner's proceeds from the sales of participations were immediately used to buy participations from petitioner's trading partners. . . . The only significant benefit petitioner received from the transactions was the tax loss deduction, which generated the net operating loss carrybacks, which in turn generated the tax refunds that led to the instant case. . . . We conclude, and we have so found, that the generation of the tax loss deduction was the sole motive for the transactions in dispute.

"the occurrence of realization to situations where exchanged property differs materially in kind or extent." This appears to be equivalent to the converse of the language that is actually in the regulation.[2]

Our disagreement with respondent's conclusion does not rest on whether his regulation should be given the interpretation for which he contends. Rather, assuming that respondent is correct in his interpretation of his regulation, we conclude that the property petitioner acquired differs "materially . . . in kind" from the property petitioner transferred. We conclude, further, that the cases and concepts to which respondent directs our attention either are distinguishable or support petitioner's conclusion. . . .

Respondent devotes a substantial portion of his brief to the history of predecessor statutes to section 1001 . . . . Respondent summarizes his position as follows:

> In limiting the realization of gains and losses to exchanges involving materially different property, Treas. Reg. sec. 1.1001–1(a) is a vestige of the prior regulations and early Revenue Acts and reflects a position that gain or loss arises upon a change in the substance, not merely in the form, of the taxpayer's property. In general, sections 165 and 1001 require that gain or loss be realized by a specific event involving either a conversion or exchange of property. The requirement embodied in Treas. Reg. sec. 1.1001–1(a) that a conversion or exchange take place before gain or loss is sustained implies that a material change in the taxpayer's property is necessary before a realization of gain or loss occurs under section 1001.

Respondent claims that his position is supported by Horne v. Commissioner [Chapter 14]. . . .

In *Horne*, for the conceded purpose of establishing a tax loss . . . , the taxpayer sold a certificate representing his membership (or "seat") in the New York Coffee & Sugar Exchange, Inc. Eight days before the sale, in

---

2. For an illustration of the danger of assuming that converses are equivalents, see the following colloquy from "A Mad Tea-Party":

> The Hatter opened his eyes very wide on hearing this; but all he *said* was "Why is a raven like a writing-desk?"
>
> "Come, we shall have some fun now!" thought Alice. "I'm glad they've begun asking riddles—I believe I can guess that," she added aloud.
>
> "Do you mean that you think you can find out the answer to it?" said the March Hare.
>
> "Exactly so," said Alice.
>
> "Then you should say what you mean," the March Hare went on.
>
> "I do," Alice hastily replied; "at least—at least I mean what I say—that's the same thing, you know."
>
> "Not the same thing a bit!" said the Hatter. "Why, you might just as well say that 'I see what I eat' is the same thing as 'I eat what I see'!"
>
> "You might just as well say," added the March Hare, "that 'I like what I get' is the same thing as 'I get what I like'!"
>
> "You might just as well say," added the Dormouse, which seemed to be talking in its sleep, "that 'I breathe when I sleep' is the same thing as 'I sleep when I breathe'!"
>
> "It *is* the same thing with you," said the Hatter, and here the conversation dropped, and the party sat silent for a minute, while Alice thought over all she could remember about ravens and writing-desks, which wasn't much.

C.L. Dodgson, The Complete Works of Lewis Carroll (Alice's Adventures in Wonderland) 75–76 (Modern Library ed.).

order to assure uninterrupted membership in the exchange and in the use of the exchange's facilities, he bought another certificate that differed from the first only by [the] identifying number on the certificate. Respondent contended in *Horne* that the wash sales provision . . . applied. We rejected that argument. . . Nevertheless, we concluded that the claimed deduction must be disallowed. . . .

In our penultimate paragraph in *Horne,* we stated as follows . . . :

> Putting aside other considerations, the persuasive fact is that after consummation of the plan which petitioner had put into operation eight days previously he stood in exactly the same position as before . . . . One "seat" was exactly like another. . . . Petitioner never divested himself of the rights which he enjoyed by reason of his membership in the exchange, and never intended to do so. . . .

In the instant case, in contrast, petitioner exchanged participations in some loans for participations in other loans. Although the loans were similar, there were important differences. Specifically, the loans had different obligors and were secured by different pieces of realty. The subsequent history of payments on the loans . . . shows that the transactions were real, not feigned, and that the assets received were not the same as the assets given up. In the instant case (unlike . . . *Horne*), when the smoke cleared away petitioner was left with assets that were different (and performed differently) from what petitioner had at the start. Thus, application of the principle of *Horne* . . . leads us to conclude that the property is materially different, and petitioner is entitled to the claimed deductions.

As in *Smith v. Commissioner* [Chapter 16] respondent is asking us to create a nonstatutory wash sale doctrine.

Our problem in accepting respondent's position is analogous to that we faced in *Smith* dealing with the proper tax treatment of silver futures "straddle" trading on the Commodity Exchange.

In *Smith,* we stated. . . :

> [A] nonstatutory wash sale doctrine [is] inappropriate to achieve respondent's result. In the past, nonstatutory wash sale consequences have resulted in cases where a party has failed to completely relinquish an economic investment in the same or a substantially identical asset. *McWilliams v. Commissioner* [Chapter 14]; *Horne v. Commissioner* [Chapter 14]. In the instant case, after the switch, petitioners were not holding the same assets, March 1974 and December 1974 futures, but were instead holding May 1974 and September 1974 futures. These new positions were not substantially identical assets for purposes of the statutory wash sale provision . . . nor were they substantially identical for any other wash sale approach. . . .

Section 165

Respondent's final contention is that petitioner is not entitled to a loss deduction under section 165(a). Respondent states as follows:

A transaction involving legally enforceable arrangements between legitimate entities may lack substance and fail to achieve the desired tax effect because it is purposeless apart from tax motivations. . . .

[But] in the instant case—

(1) By December 31, 1980, petitioner had already suffered the real economic losses in transactions originally entered into for profit.

(2) On December 31, 1980, petitioner really did dispose of and acquire the loan participations; there were no limitations on the transfers that would cause petitioner to retain benefits or burdens on the loan participations it disposed of, or require shifting of benefits and burdens on the loan participations it acquired.

(3) The December 31, 1980, transactions were real transfers of real assets to and from unrelated parties.

We conclude that petitioner's realized, recognizable losses are deductible under section 165.

Respondent has drawn our attention to a recent opinion in *Centennial Savings Bank FSB v. United States*, 682 F. Supp. 1389 (N.D. Tex. 1988), in which the taxpayer lost on a record apparently essentially similar to that in the instant case. In *Centennial*, the court concluded that the transactions there in dispute were exchanges and not merely sales (we have come to the same conclusion as to the December 31, 1980, transactions in the instant case), that the parties to the transactions there in dispute paid little or no attention to individual characteristics of the loan there involved (we have come to the same conclusion as to the December 31, 1980, transactions in the instant case), and that no loss was realized as a result of the transactions there in dispute. . . .

The *Centennial* opinion stresses the taxpayer's compliance with Memorandum R-49 and concludes that "If Centennial claims the benefits of alleged business purposes for entering into the R-49 transaction, it must also bear the burdens. It cannot have its cake and eat it too." As we have pointed out, the requirements of RAP do not control the tax laws. We do not believe it is appropriate to judicially modify the tax laws in order to offset (or to enhance) the effects of benefits and burdens that may be dispensed by regulatory agencies. . . . We take the tax law as we find it.

We disagree with part of the analysis in *Centennial* and with the conclusion in *Centennial*.

B. NOTES AND QUESTIONS

1) Background to *Cottage Savings:* The S & L Crisis

For the past decade, the savings and loan industry has faced financial crisis. The crisis stemmed initially from the dramatic rise in interest rates in the late 1970s. Historically, the primary function of savings and loan institutions (S&Ls) has been to make long-term (twenty-five or thirty-year) home mortgage loans using the money provided by depositors. During the 1960s and early 1970s, S&Ls extended a large volume of home mortgage loans at the relatively low interest rates prevailing during that period. When interest rates rose dramatically during the late 1970s, many S&Ls found themselves earning much less on these mortgage loans than they had to pay depositors.

The crisis was aggravated by federal deregulation of the banking industry in the early 1980s. As a result of deregulation, S&Ls were allowed to lend money to a broad range of business ventures. Many S&Ls, hoping to recoup losses on home mortgage loans, extended loans at relatively high interest rates to risky ventures. When many of these ventures failed, an astonishing proportion of S&Ls—perhaps 20%–40%—found themselves close to insolvency. Memorandum R-49 was developed in this context.

2) A Nontax Accounting Perspective: *Thor Power Tool* versus *Cottage Savings*

In *Thor Power Tool* (Chapter 15), the company's accountants insisted on reporting the unrealized inventory loss in order to present an accurate picture of the company's finances for nontax purposes. In *Cottage Savings*, the conservative accounting practice also would have been to report the unrealized losses on loans in order to accurately portray the institution's financial condition. Yet the federal banking authorities did not even require the reporting of *realized* losses for nontax financial reporting purposes if the Memorandum R-49 conditions were met. Didn't the banking authorities thereby encourage an inaccurate representation of the bank's true financial position? Did their apparent objective—to maintain public confidence in the ailing savings and loan industry—justify this perhaps unorthodox accounting practice?

3) When is a Reciprocal Sale Really an Exchange?

In *Cottage Savings*, the reciprocal sales of mortgages were recast as an exchange; the intermediate cash step was ignored. Why?

4) The Nonrecognition Issue: Why Section 1031 Did Not Apply

Section 1031 provides for nonrecognition of gain or loss on exchanges of certain like-kind properties. For example, if one commercial office building is exchanged for another, the realized gain or loss will go unrecognized under Section 1031. The rationale appears to be that, despite the formal realization event, the taxpayer's underlying economic position is essentially unchanged when the taxpayer continues to own the same kind of asset. The taxpayer, therefore, should be treated as if no disposition had occurred.

The exchanges of mortgages in *Cottage Savings* might appear to qualify as Section 1031 like-kind exchanges, resulting in the nonrecognition of realized losses. There is a specific exception, however, for loans (including mortgages). See Section 1031(a)(2)(B) and (C). Therefore, the IRS could not—and did not—try to argue that Section 1031 should apply to disallow the claimed loss in *Cottage Savings*.

5) The Realization Issue in *Cottage Savings*: Form and Substance

As a formal matter, the exchange in *Cottage Savings* produced realization. The IRS attempted to argue, however, that there was no realization in substance, as in *Horne* (Chapter 14). In rejecting this argument, how did the Tax Court distinguish *Horne*? Are you persuaded by the distinction? How did the Tax Court use *Smith* (Chapter 16) to buttress its reasoning?

6) The Materially Different Requirement of Reg. § 1.1001(a)

The IRS also argued that the loss in *Cottage Savings* could not be deducted because the original mortgages did not differ materially from the mortgages for which they were exchanged. Why did the Tax Court conclude that the two groups of mortgages were materially different? The Tax Court's reasoning was criticized in First Federal Savings & Loan Association of Temple v. U.S., (USDC WTex July 26, 1988):

> It is, indeed, tempting when considering any two loans . . . which meet the requirements of Memorandum R-49 to pick out the fact that they have two entirely different individual obligors, thus, allowing for the possibility that subsequent performance may be radically different . . . and thereby conclude that such a potential difference in performance is, in and of itself, a significant economic or "material" difference. However, this is post hoc reasoning. The market value of an outstanding and unmatured loan can never take into account the *actual* future performance of a loan (this is merely to say one cannot know the future). . . .
>
> Therefore, the question arises, "What does one look at in determining whether R-49 loans are materially different. . . ?" The answer to this question in the context of an outstanding, unmatured loan is the notion of "risk.'" When someone . . . attempts to evaluate the economic distinctions between two loans, they do not look at the eventual actual performance because it is unknown and unknowable. However, they attempt to make their best *guess* as to the eventual performance of the loan which is the crux of the value of a loan. The guess can be described as a calculation of the overall "risk" involved in a loan. In making this calculation of the "risk" underlying a loan, one would look at a variety of factors including interest rate, geographic area, etc. (factors all of which are included in the requirements of Memorandum R-49). These factors all combine to form the notion of "risk"—not *actual* future performance, but *potential* future performance. . . .
>
> Memorandum's R-49's very purpose . . . was to describe a certain class of loans which were identical with respect to their underlying "risk." Memorandum R-49 represents the opinion of experts in the field of lending that where the ten criteria are met the underlying risk between any two loans is equivalent and *at that point in time* the loans are economically equivalent. The government's expert . . . pointed out that on the secondary mortgage market loans meeting the criteria of Memorandum R-49 are considered economically indistinguishable. Thus, the fact that there are different obligors on loans or different collateral on loans only becomes economically significant if it alters the "risk" involved.
>
> Memorandum R-49 carefully limits the type of collateral (single-family homes) and the general type of obligor (similarly seasoned notes for relatively equivalent principal amounts) available for an R-49 exchange. The

obvious economic effect is to render the differences in collateral and obligors "mere" differences rather than economically significant or "material" differences. Certainly [the banks] were unconcerned with these differences. No examination of individual obligors or collateral was ever done. The two savings and loan institutions simply matched up loans on the basis of the Memorandum R-49 criteria and traded them, fully convinced that they were trading what at that time were economic substitutes for one another.

It is true that these loans later showed slightly different performance histories, as one would expect. Nonetheless, this does not alter the fact that *at the time of the transaction* it was impossible to predict which set of loans this slight variation would favor.... To anyone looking at any two loans meeting the criteria of Memorandum R-49, or two loan pools which meet the same criteria ... the loans will be economically indistinguishable. When asked, "Which one of these Memorandum R-49 loans would you prefer," such an observer would respond, "It makes no difference, the underlying risks of the loans are so similar that they are economically identical at this time. I'll take either one."

When it is established that Memorandum R-49's very purpose for existing was to fashion a transaction that involves the exchange of what are in essence economic substitutes for one other ... it becomes almost ludicrous to suggest that R-49 loans are at the same time "substantially identical" for financial accounting purposes and "materially different" for tax accounting purposes.... Therefore, the court finds that the loans transferred ... are not "materially different" from those it received....[3]

7) The Significance of Section 1031

Even though the *First Federal Savings* court found the loans not to be materially different, it nevertheless held that Reg. 1.1001–1(a) (as interpreted by the IRS) was invalid and therefore allowed the losses:

Having concluded that the loans exchanged ... were not materially different, the Court must now address the validity of the Government's proposed interpretation of Reg. § 1.1001–1(a)....

In adopting nonrecognition sections such as the Like-kind Exchange Rule, Congress easily could have included the exchange of like-kind "loans (i.e., "notes or other evidences of indebtedness"), but explicitly chose to exclude them from the coverage of the rule. [Section] 1031(a)(2)(B) & (C). No where in the Code can a nonrecognition section be found that applies to loans, notes, or evidence of indebtedness....

To read Treasury Regulation § 1.1001–1(a) in the manner proposed by the Government would make ... all of the nonrecognition sections meaningless surplusage in the Code. The interpretation of the Regulation proposed by the Government would effectively make Treasury Regulation § 1.1001–1(a) a universal and all-encompassing like-kind exchange rule....
If Treasury Regulation § 1.1001–1(a) is intended to disallow losses on any and all exchanges of property that is not materially different, then the exceptions of Section 1031 are an absurd effort in futility. Such an inter-

---

3. First Federal Savings & Loan Association of Temple v. U.S., (USDC WTex July 26, 1988)

pretation of Treasury Regulation 1.1001–1(a) is simply not consistent with the remainder of the Code. To read the regulation as requiring property exchanged to be materially different before a loss may be recognized would make it a "super-nonrecognition" statute rendering all other nonrecognition sections superfluous.[4]

Is this reasoning consistent with the Supreme Court decision in *McWilliams* (Chapter 14) and the Tax Court decision in *Horne* (Chapter 14)? In those cases, wasn't a realized loss subject to nonrecognition even though not really covered by any nonrecognition provision of the Code?

8) The Issue of Backdoor Funding Through the Tax System

The Federal Home Loan Bank Board (FHLBB) is a federal agency established by Congress. The FHLBB designed the Memorandum R-49 plan to provide federal tax benefits for ailing Savings and Loans. Would it have been more politically responsible of the FHLBB to ask Congress for a direct subsidy for troubled S&Ls? Was Memorandum R-49 an attempt to provide backdoor funding by manipulating the tax system?

D. JORDAN MARSH COMPANY v. COMMISSIONER
269 F.2d 453 (2d Cir. 1959)

HINCKS, CIRCUIT JUDGE.

... The transactions giving rise to the dispute were conveyances by the petitioner in 1944 of the fee of two parcels of property in the city of Boston where the petitioner, then as now, operated a department store. In return for its conveyances the petitioner received $2,300,000 in cash which, concededly, represented the fair market value of the properties. The conveyances were unconditional, without provision of any option to repurchase. At the same time, the petitioner received back from the vendees leases of the same properties for terms of 30 years and 3 days, with options to renew for another 30 years if the petitioner-lessee should erect new buildings thereon. The vendees were in no way connected with the petitioner. The rentals to be paid under the leases concededly were full and normal rentals so that the leasehold interests which devolved upon the petitioner were of no capital value.

In its return for 1944, the petitioner, claiming the transaction was a sale, ... sought to deduct from income the difference between the [cost] of the property and the cash received. The Commissioner disallowed the deduction, taking the position that the transaction represented an exchange of property for other property of like kind. Under Section [1031] such exchanges are not occasions for the recognition of gain or loss; and even the receipt of cash or other property in the exchange of the properties of like kind is not enough to permit the taxpayer to recognize loss. Section

---

4. Ibid.

[1031(c)]. Thus the Commissioner viewed the transaction, in substance, as an exchange of a fee interest for a long term lease, justifying his position by . . . Regulation § [1.1031] which provides that a leasehold of more than 30 years is the equivalent of a fee interest. . . .

Upon this appeal, we must decide whether the transaction in question here was a sale or an exchange of property for other property of like kind within the meaning of [Section 1031(a)(1) and (c)] of the Internal Revenue Code cited above. If we should find that it is an exchange, we would then have to decide whether the Commissioner's regulation, declaring that a leasehold of property of 30 years or more is property "of like kind" to the fee in the same property, is a reasonable gloss to put upon the words of the statute. The judge in the Tax Court felt that Century Electric Co. v. Commissioner . . . was dispositive of both questions. In the view which we take of the first question, we do not have to pass upon the second question. For we hold that the transaction here was a sale and not an exchange.

The controversy centers around the purposes of Congress in enacting [Section 1031], dealing with non-taxable exchanges. The section represents an exception to the general rule . . . that upon the sale or exchange of property the entire amount of gain or loss is to be recognized by the taxpayer. The first Congressional attempt to make certain exchanges of this kind non-taxable occurred in . . . 1921. . . . [N]o gain or loss was recognized from an exchange of property unless the property received in exchange had a "readily realizable market value." In 1924, this . . . was amended to the form in which it is applicable here. Discussing the old section the House Committee observed:

> The provision is so indefinite that it cannot be applied with accuracy or with consistency. It appears best to provide generally that gain or loss is recognized from all exchanges, and then except specifically and in definite terms those cases of exchanges in which it is not desired to tax the gain or allow the loss. This results in definiteness and accuracy and enables a taxpayer to determine prior to the consummation of a given transaction the tax liability that will result. . . .

Thus the "readily realizable market value" test disappeared from the statute. A later report, reviewing the section, expressed its purpose as follows:

> The law has provided for 12 years that gain or loss is recognized on exchanges of property having a fair market value, such as stocks, bonds, and negotiable instruments; on exchanges of property held primarily for sale; or on exchanges of one kind of property for another kind of property; but not on other exchanges of property solely for property of like kind. In other words, profit or loss is recognized in the case of exchanges of notes or securities, which are essentially like money; or in the case of stock in trade; or in case the taxpayer exchanges the property comprising his original investment for a different kind of property; but *if the taxpayer's money is still tied up in the same kind of property* as that in which it was originally invested, he is not allowed to compute and deduct his theoretical loss on the exchange, nor is he charged with a tax upon his theoretical profit. The calculation of the profit or loss is deferred until it is realized in cash, marketable securities, or other property not of the same kind having a fair market value. . . .

These passages lead us to accept as correct the petitioner's position with respect to the purposes of the section. Congress was primarily concerned with the inequity, in the case of an exchange, of forcing a taxpayer to recognize a paper gain which was still tied up in a continuing investment of the same sort. If such gains were not to be recognized, however, upon the ground that they were theoretical, neither should equally theoretical losses. And as to both gains and losses the taxpayer should not have it within his power to avoid the operation of the section by stipulating for the addition of cash, or boot, to the property received in exchange. These considerations, rather than concern for the difficulty of the administrative task of making the valuations necessary to compute gains and losses, were at the root of the Congressional purpose in enacting [Section 1031]. Indeed, if these sections had been intended to obviate the necessity of making difficult valuations, one would have expected them to provide for nonrecognition of gains and losses in all exchanges, whether the property received in exchanges were "of a like kind" or *not* of a like kind. And if such had been the legislative objective, [Section 1031(b)], providing for the recognition of gain from exchanges not wholly in kind, would never have been enacted.

That such indeed was the legislative objective is supported by Portland Oil Co. v. Commissioner of Internal Revenue. . . . There Judge Magruder, in speaking of a cognate provision [said]

> It is the purpose . . . to save the taxpayer from an immediate recognition of a gain, or to intermit the claim of a loss, in certain transactions where gain or loss may have accrued in a constitutional sense, but where in a popular and economic sense there has been a mere change in the form of ownership and the taxpayer has not really "cashed in" on the theoretical gain, or closed out a losing venture.

In conformity with this reading of the statute, we think the petitioner here, by its unconditional conveyances to a stranger, had done more than make a change in the *form of ownership:* it was a change as to the *quantum* of ownership whereby, in the words just quoted, it had "closed out a losing venture." By the transaction its capital invested in the real estate involved had been completely liquidated for cash to an amount fully equal to the value of the fee. This, we hold, was a sale—not an exchange within the purview of [Section 1031].

The Tax Court apparently thought it of controlling importance that the transaction in question involved no change in the petitioner's possession of the premises: it felt that the decision in Century Electric Co. v. Commissioner of Internal Rev., supra, controlled the situation here. We think, however, that that case was distinguishable on the facts. For notwithstanding the lengthy findings made with meticulous care by the Tax Court in that case . . . , there was no finding that the cash received by the taxpayer was the full equivalent of the value of the fee which the taxpayer had conveyed to the vendee-lessor, and no finding that the lease back called for a rent which was fully equal to the rental value of the premises. Indeed, in its opinion the Court of Appeals pointed to evidence that the fee which the taxpayer had "exchanged" may have had a value substantially in excess of the cash received. And in the Century Electric case, the findings showed . . . that the taxpayer-lessee, unlike the taxpayer here, was not required to pay "general state, city and school taxes" because its lessor was an educational institution which under its charter was exempt from such taxes. Thus the leasehold interest in Century Electric on this account may well have had a premium value. In the absence of findings as to the values of the properties allegedly "exchanged," necessarily there could be no finding of a loss. And without proof of a loss, of course, the taxpayer could not prevail. Indeed, in the Tax Court six of the judges expressly based their concurrences on that limited ground. . . .

. . . Here plainly the petitioner by the transfer finally closed out a losing venture. And it cannot justly be said that the economic situation of the petitioner was unchanged by a transaction which substituted $2,300,000 in cash for its investment in real estate and left it under a liability to make annual payments of rent for upwards of thirty years. . . .

In ordinary usage, an "exchange" means the giving of one piece of property in return for another—not, as the Commissioner urges here, the return of a lesser interest in a property received from another. It seems unlikely that Congress intended that an "exchange" should have the strained meaning for which the Commissioner contends. For the legislative history states expressly an intent to correct the indefiniteness of prior versions of the Act by excepting from the general rule "specifically and in definite terms those cases of exchanges in which it is not desired to tax the gain or allow the loss."

But even if under certain circumstances the return of a part of the property conveyed may constitute an exchange for purposes of [Section 1031] we think that in this case, in which cash was received for the full value of the property conveyed, the transaction must be classified as a sale. . . .

E. NOTES AND QUESTIONS

1) Preliminary Issues

The *Jordan Marsh* opinion stated that the buyer and seller were not connected. But suppose they had been connected, for example, the buyer being a corporation wholly owned by the seller. How would that relationship have made a difference under Higgins v. Smith and Section 267?

The opinion also noted that the seller had no option to repurchase the building. What would be the relevance of such an option? Would its relevance depend on whether the option price was likely to be less than the building's fair market value so that the option would probably be exercised? What if the option price were set equal to the $2.3 million for which the building was sold? What if the option were to repurchase the building for its fair market value at the time of exercise as estimated by an independent appraiser?

2) The Hidden Issue: Realization

The taxpayer sold the building for less than it cost and tried to deduct the loss. The IRS did not try to argue that the loss was *unrealized*. Did it miss an opportunity? How might it have tried to use the ruling of Higgins v. Smith that a sale does not produce realization unless it is a sale in substance as well as in form? Hint: Does the *Jordan Marsh* transaction really involve two *different* properties?

When the taxpayer sold the building to the city of Boston for cash, the city simultaneously agreed to lease the building back to the taxpayer for thirty years and a few days. Do you see a way to recharacterize, or recast, these two transactions? Instead of "selling" the building for cash and paying back "rent" over thirty years, what might you view the taxpayer as doing? What might you call the present value of the taxpayer's future obligations to pay "rent" under the lease? How would this recharacterization help the IRS to argue that the loss was unrealized?

Under the kind of arguments suggested above, would all of the claimed loss be disallowed when the "sale" occurs or just most of it? How would you go about calculating the exact fraction that should be deductible when the sale and leaseback transaction occurs? When should the disallowed loss be deductible?

3) The Explicit Issue: Nonrecognition

Assuming that two different properties were involved and that they were "like-kind,"[5] the critical question is whether or not the sale and leaseback transactions constituted a Section 1031 "exchange." Would the transfer of an ownership interest in one building in return for a thirty-year leasehold in another building constitute a Section 1031 exchange? What about the transfer of an ownership interest in one building in return for a thirty-year leasehold in another building plus cash? See Section 1031(c). Why was the *Century Electric* case covered by Section 1031(c)?

The *Jordan Marsh* opinion concluded that the transactions could not be viewed as involving partly an exchange and partly a sale for cash, as in *Century Electric*. Why not?

4) The Significance of an Intermediate Cash Step

Even if the taxpayer received from the City of Boston cash equal to the full fair market value of the building, should that have entitled the taxpayer to avoid Section 1031? Should the creation of an intermediate cash step be given significance? If you sell property to W for cash and then immediately use the cash to buy like-kind property from W, instead of *directly* trading one piece of property for another, shouldn't Section 1031 still apply?

---

5. Reg. 1.1031(a)–1(b) states that like-kind refers to "the nature or character of the property and not to its grade or quality. One kind or class of property may not be exchanged tax-free for property of a different kind or class." The definition of "like-kind" is discussed in Chapter 18.

What if you sell property to W for cash and then buy like-kind property from W, not for cash, but for a deferred payment? Why should the deferred payment make any difference? How can *Jordan Marsh* be viewed as the sale of property for cash, followed by the acquisition of like-kind property for a deferred payment?

In *Jordan Marsh,* the court refused to treat the reciprocal sale of the building and thirty-year lease back as an exchange; the intermediate cash step was accorded independent significance. From this perspective, isn't *Jordan Marsh* inconsistent with *Cottage Savings?*

Suppose Section 1031 is interpreted *not* to apply when there is an intermediate cash step. What will taxpayers do when they wish to recognize a loss arising from the exchange of like-kind properties? Is that result consistent with the approach to form and substance taken in Higgins v. Smith—that the taxpayer's form may be recast by the IRS to prevent the deduction of artificial losses?

5) The *Redwing Carriers* Decision

In Redwing Carriers, Inc. v. Tomlinson, 399 F.2d 652 (5th Cir. 1968), the taxpayer sold used trucks for cash to a truck manufacturer and several weeks later bought new trucks for cash from the same manufacturer. The court held that the taxpayer could not avoid Section 1031 by using an intermediate cash step and recast the transaction as the taxpayer exchanging used trucks plus cash for new trucks. Is *Jordan Marsh* consistent with *Redwing Carriers?*[6]

6) Juxtaposing the Realization and Recognition Issues

Would it have been possible for the IRS to argue both that the loss was unrealized because there was no real sale *and* that the loss was unrecognized because there was a like-kind exchange? Or are these positions logically contradictory? If only one or the other positions can be argued, did the IRS choose the weaker argument? Or did the IRS miss a chance to argue in the alternative?

---

6. Suppose that you sell property to W for cash and then use the cash to buy like-kind property from Z. Should Section 1031 apply? How does this transaction differ from *Redwing Carriers?* The opinion in *Redwing Carriers* appears in Chapter 37. The case is also cited (and its facts are inaccurately described) in T.J. Starker v. United States, 602 F.2d 1341 (9th Cir. 1979), which appears in Chapter 18.

Chapter 18

LIKE-KIND EXCHANGES: POTENTIAL GAIN

A. INTRODUCTORY QUESTIONS

Consider the following hypothetical. A taxpayer named Alderson owns *appreciated* real estate known as Buena Park. Alderson wishes to exchange Buena Park for another real estate parcel known as Salinas. If the owner of Salinas is willing to trade, then the transaction will constitute a direct exchange and (assuming the other requirements are met) the realized gain should qualify for nonrecognition under Section 1031.

Suppose, however, that the owner of Salinas is not interested in Buena Park and will take only cash for the property. Since a direct exchange is no longer possible, Alderson might sell Buena Park to a third party for cash and immediately use the cash to purchase Salinas. The IRS, however, is likely to oppose Section 1031 treatment because of the intermediate cash step, even though the cash would be held by Alderson for only an instant. Can the IRS position be reconciled with its argument that a Section 1031 exchange occurred in *Jordan Marsh*, notwithstanding the existence of an intermediate cash step? See the Supreme Court's attempt to reconcile Higgins v. Smith and *Burnet Commonwealth* in Chapter 14.

In response to the likelihood that even the momentary receipt of cash is fatal to Section 1031 nonrecognition[1], lawyers have devised the so-called *three-party exchange transaction*. Under such an arrangement, the third party would purchase Salinas for cash and then trade Salinas to Alderson in exchange for Buena Park. Although from Alderson's perspective this appears to be a direct exchange, the IRS initially argued that nonrecognition was unavailable on two grounds: first, that Section 1031 was intended to apply only to direct two-party trades and not to transactions involving three parties; and second, that the third party had really purchased Buena Park for cash, not in exchange for Salinas. Do you find the IRS' arguments persuasive, given the underlying policies of the section, as described in *Jordan Marsh*

---

1. But see Biggs v. Commissioner, 69 T.C. 905 (1978), aff'd 632 F.2d 1171 (5th Cir. 1980).

(Chapter 17)? After losing in the courts, the IRS acquiesced in the grant of nonrecognition to properly structured three-party transactions.

What is the difference between holding that Section 1031 applies (a) when Alderson sells Buena Park for cash and immediately uses the cash to buy Salinas and (b) in a three-party transaction in which Alderson never actually receives cash? Is there any principled reason to validate method (b) for achieving nonrecognition but not method (a)?

In the opinion that follows, a real taxpayer named Alderson tried to exchange a parcel of real estate, known as Buena Park, for another parcel, known as Salinas. However, Alderson failed to adhere closely to the usual three-part exchange transaction described above. As a result, the IRS challenged his claim that the transaction qualified for nonrecognition under Section 1031.

B. ALDERSON v. COMMISSIONER
317 F.2d 790 (9th Cir. 1963)

CRARY, DISTRICT JUDGE.

... The question presented is whether the transactions whereby taxpayers transferred one parcel of realty and acquired another constituted a sale, the gain from which is recognizable under Section 1002 of the Internal Revenue Code of 1954, or a non-taxable exchange within the meaning of Section 1031 of said Code.

On May 21, 1957, following negotiations between petitioners and Alloy Die Casting Company, hereinafter referred to as Alloy, representatives of petitioners and Alloy executed escrow instructions to the Orange County Title Company, hereinafter referred to as Orange, constituting a purchase and sale agreement whereby petitioners agreed to sell their Buena Park property, consisting of 31.148 acres of agricultural property, to Alloy for $5,550.00 per acre, a total price of $172,871.40. Pursuant to the terms of said agreement, Alloy deposited $17,205.00 in the Orange escrow toward purchase of the Buena Park property.

Some time after the execution of the May 21st escrow petitioners located 115.32 acres of farming land in Monterey County, California, hereinafter referred to as the Salinas property, which they desired to obtain in exchange for their Buena Park property.

On August 19, 1957, petitioners and Alloy executed an amendment to their May 21, 1957, escrow providing that "the Salinas property be acquired by Alloy and exchanged for the Buena Park property in lieu of the original contemplated cash transaction." ... The amendment further provides that if the exchange was not effected by September 11, 1957, the original escrow re the purchase for cash would be carried out. On the same day (August 19th) petitioners' daughter, Jean Marie Howard, acting for petitioners, executed escrow instructions to the Salinas Title Guarantee Company, hereinafter referred to as Salinas Title, in the form of "Buyer's Instructions."

The parties have agreed that the acts of petitioners' daughter, Jean Marie Howard, with respect to the transactions here involved, are to be considered as acts of the petitioners, and any acts of said daughter are hereinafter referred to as acts of petitioners. The escrow instructions last mentioned provided for payment of $190,000.00 for the Salinas property, that title was to be taken in the name of Salinas Title, that $19,000.00 had been deposited with Orange and that the remaining $171,000.00 would also be deposited with Orange. The instructions also stated that Salinas Title was authorized to deed the Salinas property to Alloy, provided Salinas Title could "immediately record a deed from Alloy . . . to James Alderson and Clarissa E. Alderson, his wife, issuing final title evidence in the last mentioned grantees. . . ."

On August 20, 1957, petitioners authorized Orange to pay $19,000.00 into the Salinas escrow, which was done, and directed Orange to pay $171,000.00 into the Salinas escrow when these funds became available. . . .

On August 22, 1957, Alloy, by letter to petitioners, summarized the agreements of the parties *re the manner of accomplishing the transfer of the properties between them.* . . . The letter further stated that Alloy's representative would deposit $172,871.40 (the cash amount for the Buena Park property as per May 21st escrow) with Salinas Title on assurance that the agreements would be effected. The letter was countersigned by petitioners.

By deed dated August 20, 1957, title to the Salinas property was transferred to Salinas Title. By deed dated August 21, 1957, Salinas Title conveyed the Salinas property to Alloy. By deed dated August 26, 1957, petitioners conveyed the Buena Park property to Alloy and deed dated August 29, 1957, conveyed the Salinas property from Alloy to petitioners. All four of these deeds were recorded September 4, 1957. . . .

On September 3, 1957, Alloy, acting through its attorney, Elliott H. Pentz, deposited $172,871.40, *belonging to Alloy,* into the Salinas escrow, *on Alloy's behalf,* with instruction that said sum should be used to complete the purchase of the Salinas property. . . . The said $172,871.40, plus the $19,000.00 previously deposited with Salinas Title by Orange, made up something more than the $190,000.00 purchase price for the Salinas property, and the excess was returned to the petitioners. Alloy's original deposit of $17,205.00 in the Orange escrow was returned to it sometime after August 28, 1957. . . .

The Commissioner determined that the transfer of the Buena Park property to Alloy constituted a sale upon which petitioners realized a long term capital gain . . . and the Tax Court sustained the decision of the Commissioner . . . holding ". . . that the transactions in which petitioners disposed of the Buena Park property and acquired the Salinas property did not constitute an exchange within the meaning of Section 1031(a)."

In considering the question involved, there are certain findings of the Tax Court which this court believes to be particularly pertinent. Said findings are as follows:

> *From the outset, petitioners desired to exchange their Buena Park property for other property of a like kind. They intended to sell the property* for cash *only* if they were unable to locate a suitable piece of property to take in exchange. . . . (Emphasis ours.)

The deposit by Alloy of $172,871.40 in the Salinas escrow was made by Elliott Pentz, an attorney, pursuant to the commitment of his client, Alloy. The funds were received from Alloy by Pentz; *were the property of Alloy;* and *were deposited by him in Alloy's behalf.*

Alloy acquired title to the Salinas property solely to enable it to perform its agreement to exchange that property for the Buena Park property." . . . (Emphasis ours.)

The Buena Park property and the Salinas property were of like kind. . . .

By the findings of the Tax Court, supra, it was determined that there was from the outset no intention on the part of the petitioners to sell the Buena Park property for cash if it could be exchanged for other property of like kind. There is no question that the desired property of like kind was located (Salinas property) and that, as determined by the findings, petitioners had no intention other than to exchange the Buena Park property for the Salinas property. It also follows from the findings that petitioners had no intention to purchase the Salinas property and that title to the Salinas property was to come to the petitioners by exchange thereof for the Buena Park property. The intention of the parties and what actually occurred re the obtaining of the Salinas property for the exchange is further established by the finding that the $172,871.40 deposited by Alloy's attorney, Pentz, in the Salinas escrow was the *"property of Alloy"* and deposited by Pentz *"in Alloy's behalf."* Further, "Alloy acquired title to the Salinas property solely to enable it to perform its agreement to exchange the property for the Buena Park property.". . .

It is the position of respondent that from the facts and circumstances outlined above it must be concluded the Buena Park property was sold by petitioners to Alloy and the Salinas property was purchased by petitioners, not Alloy. However, it does not appear from the terms of the amended Orange escrow (August 19, 1957) that there was ever any obligation on the part of Alloy to pay cash for the Buena Park property or for the petitioners to receive cash for said property as provided in the May 21, 1957, escrow, by reason of the fact that *prior* to September 11, 1957, Alloy did deposit with Orange a deed to the Salinas property conveying same to petitioners. Neither liability of Alloy to petitioners for payment of cash for the Buena Park property nor liability of petitioners to sell the said property to Alloy for money ever matured because under no conditions was there to be a sale of the Buena Park property for cash until September 11, 1957, and *then only* if the Salinas property *was not* acquired by Alloy and exchanged for the Buena Park property as of that date. . . . Deed of Alloy to petitioners conveying the Salinas property and deed of petitioners to Alloy conveying the Buena Park property were exchanged and recorded September 4, 1957. Consequently, an agreement on the part of petitioners to sell to Alloy the Buena Park property for money did not come into being.

Petitioners, on finding the Salinas property, took steps to make it available to Alloy for the exchange by signing buyer's instructions in the escrow of August 19, 1957, opened at Salinas Title, but the fact is, as found by the Tax Court, that petitioners at that time intended to accomplish an exchange of properties and that the Salinas property was "acquired by Alloy" for the sole purpose of such exchange.

True, the intermediate acts of the parties could have hewn closer to and have more precisely depicted the ultimate desired result, but what actually occurred on September 3 or 4, 1957, was an exchange of deeds between petitioners and Alloy which effected an exchange of the Buena Park property for the Salinas property. It is also noted by the court that the buyer's instructions in the Salinas escrow did not conform to the seller's instructions although the transfer from the original owner of the Salinas property to Salinas Title was, as to the provision at variance, pursuant to the terms of the buyer's instructions. If Alloy had signed the said "Buyer's Instructions" this litigation would have been avoided, but even in the circumstances here involved the court concludes that the intended exchange was accomplished.

Respondent argues the Tax Court found only that petitioners from the outset "desired" to exchange their Buena Park property and not that from the outset they "intended" to do so. This would appear in the circumstances to be a distinction without a difference since it does not seem logical that one would intentionally take steps to accomplish a result not desired, and that, therefore, all acts of the petitioners may be considered as having been performed with the intent to accomplish their desired result, to wit, "exchange their Buena Park property for other property of a like kind. . . ."

In the case at bar, the ultimate objective appears without question to have been the exchange of property of like kind. . . . In the instant case we find a plan to exchange the properties within the intent of the statute . . . and the acquiring of the Salinas property by Alloy with the sole purpose of trading same for the Buena Park property which does not make the transaction one within Section 1002. . . .

Petitioners place strong reliance on the case of Mercantile Trust Company of Baltimore v. Commissioner of Internal Revenue. . . . Respondent observes . . . it is in accord with the petitioners that "the multi-party situation should be governed by the principle enunciated in the Mercantile Trust Co. case, supra." In that case, the taxpayers, owners of Baltimore Street property, agreed with a Title Company to exchange said property for a certain property on Lexington Street, owned by an estate, plus the sum of $33,000.00 in cash. The agreement also provided that if the Title Company was unable to purchase the Lexington Street property the taxpayer could require the Title Company to pay cash for the Baltimore Street property. . . . The Board of Tax Appeals held there had been an exchange of property within the statute. Pertinent to the case at bar, the court . . . states:

> The above-mentioned agreement of March 7 evidenced an intention to exchange the Baltimore Street property, if certain conditions were met, and to sell it, if those conditions were not met. Those conditions were met. The property was, in fact, exchanged. That fact is controlling here.

The title to the Lexington Street property was acquired by the Title Company for the purpose of the exchange, and it follows by analogy that there was no need for Alloy to acquire a "real" interest in the Salinas property by assuming the benefits and burdens of ownership to make the exchange qualify under the statute although respondent asserts that failure of Alloy to hold a "real" interest in the Salinas property precluded the transactions involved from being construed as constituting an exchange.

The Mercantile case appears to hold that one need not assume the benefits and burdens of ownership in property before exchanging it but may properly acquire title *solely for the purpose of exchange* and accept title and transfer it in exchange for other like property, all as a part of the same transaction with no resulting gain which is recognizable under Section 1002. . . .

Referring again to the Salinas escrow and the instructions to Orange, it is to be noted that the terms of the buyer's instructions in the Salinas escrow and the instructions to Orange were not carried out in important details not heretofore mentioned. Although the petitioners authorized Orange to pay $19,000.00 into the Salinas escrow and to pay $171,000.00, when available, into the Salinas escrow, and although the Salinas escrow provided for the depositing of $171,000.00 into the Orange escrow . . . , *this was not done.* The $171,000.00 nor any part thereof was ever paid into the Orange escrow, but on the contrary $172,871.40, *property of Alloy*, was by its attorney, Pentz, deposited in the Salinas escrow *in Alloy's behalf.*

The court concludes the holding of the Tax Court, "that in essence petitioners acquired the Salinas property in a separate transaction; that payment of the $172,871.40, made by Alloy, was a payment made for petitioners" . . . is not supported by the Tax Court's Findings of Fact, Stipulation of Facts or by the evidence in the case when considered in all of its aspects.

The court further concludes that there was no sale by petitioners of the Buena Park property to Alloy, but that the pertinent transactions resulted in an exchange of the Buena Park property for property of like kind to be held either for productive use in trade or for investment, and that by reason thereof there was no gain or loss from said exchange which should be recognized for income tax purposes. For the reasons set forth above, the Decision of the Tax Court of the United States . . . is reversed.

C. NOTES AND QUESTIONS

1) *Alderson* versus *Jordan Marsh*

In *Jordan Marsh* (Chapter 17), where a loss was involved, the taxpayer sought to avoid Section 1031, while the IRS argued for its application. In *Alderson*, where a gain was at stake, the reverse occurred. The IRS sought to avoid Section 1031, while the taxpayer was arguing for its application. In other words, depending on whether a gain or loss is at stake, the IRS may argue for either a broad or narrow construction of Section 1031.

2) The Obstacles to *Alderson* Being Treated as a Three-party Exchange

Why didn't the *Alderson* transaction *as originally structured* qualify for nonrecognition as a three-party exchange transaction? Even after the original contract was amended, how did the escrow instructions to Orange Title appear to treat the transaction as involving the cash purchase of Salinas by Alderson (rather than by Alloy)? Leaving aside the problem created by these escrow instructions, how did the amended contract fail to conform to the usual three-party exchange, using the criteria described in the introductory questions?

3) Fairness to Alderson

Would it have been fair to penalize Alderson for not initially adopting the correct contractual form? Or for failing to conform the Orange Title escrow instructions to the three-party exchange transaction form? Or for not having identified like-kind property when the real estate contract was signed?

D. STARKER v. UNITED STATES
432 F. Supp. 864 (D. Ore. 1977)

SOLOMON, JUDGE.

Plaintiff T. J. Starker (plaintiff) filed this action for a tax refund, claiming that he is entitled to non-recognition treatment under [Section] 1031(a), for property transferred to Crown Zellerbach Corporation (Crown).

On April 1, 1967, plaintiff and plaintiff's son and daughter-in-law, Bruce and Elizabeth Starker (Starkers), entered into a Land Exchange Agreement (Agreement) with Crown. In accordance with this Agreement, plaintiff and the Starkers conveyed 1,843 acres of timberland to Crown and Crown entered an "Exchange Value" balance (exchange balance) on its books of $1,502,500 for plaintiff and $73,500 for the Starkers.

Under the Agreement, plaintiff and the Starkers were to locate acceptable parcels of real property which Crown would then buy and convey to them. As each parcel was purchased, the exchange balance was reduced by the purchase price and the acquisition costs.

Plaintiff and the Starkers received an additional credit for a six per cent annual "growth factor" based on the exchange balance remaining on Crown's books at the end of each month. This growth factor was added to the exchange balance.

The Agreement also provided that if there was an exchange balance in favor of the plaintiff or the Starkers after five years, Crown could pay the balance in cash rather than property.

Between July 1967 and May 1969, twelve parcels of property were located by plaintiff. They were acquired by Crown and conveyed to plaintiff. The total value of the twelve parcels was $1,577,387.91.

During the time the twelve parcels were being located and acquired, a six per cent growth factor of $74,887.91 was added to plaintiff's exchange balance. Plaintiff did not receive any cash because the exchange balance, including the growth factor, equalled the cost of the twelve parcels.

In 1967, Crown conveyed three parcels of property to the Starkers. The value of these parcels equalled their exchange balance of $73,500, and the Starkers did not receive any cash.

In their income tax returns for 1967, plaintiff and the Starkers treated the transfers to Crown as non-recognition transactions under § 1031 of the Internal Revenue Code. The Internal Revenue Service (IRS) ruled that the transactions were not tax exempt and assessed a tax deficiency of $300,930.31 plus interest against the plaintiff and $35,248.41 against the Starkers. They paid the deficiencies and filed claims for refunds, which the IRS disallowed.

The Starkers filed an action for a tax refund [Starker I]. Although no case was directly in point, on May 1, 1975, I held that under *Alderson v. Commissioner of Internal Revenue* ..., the transfer was entitled to non-recognition treatment. The government appealed, but the appeal was voluntarily dismissed and the Starkers received their refund.

On January 26, 1976, plaintiff filed this action for a tax refund. . . .

The government denies that it was an exchange of like-kind property held for investment or productive use in trade or business. It asserts that it was a sale and therefore not entitled to non-recognition treatment. . . .

Section 1031 was enacted to defer recognition of gain or loss when a taxpayer makes a direct exchange of property with another party. . . . Its object is to provide for non-recognition in transactions which do not change the nature of the investment. . . . Section 1031 is strictly construed because it is an exception to the general rule that the entire gain or loss realized on disposition of property is recognized. *See* Treas.Reg. § 1.1002–1(b) (1962). Plaintiff must bring himself squarely within the explicit provisions of the exception to qualify for non-recognition treatment. . . .

In *Starker* I, I held that the taxpayers were entitled to non-recognition treatment under § 1031 because I believed that *Alderson v. Commissioner of Internal Revenue* ... required this result. I realized that *Alderson* was not directly in point, but at the time, I thought that the reasoning of *Alderson* required that result. . . .

Plaintiff contends that the government is estopped from litigating whether his transfer to Crown qualifies for non-recognition treatment under § 1031 because of *Starker* I.

I have reconsidered my opinion in *Starker* I. I now conclude that I was mistaken in my holding as well as in my earlier reading of *Alderson*. Even if *Alderson* can be interpreted as contended by plaintiff, I think that to do so would be improper. It would merely sanction a tax avoidance scheme and not carry out the purposes of § 1031.

In *Alderson*, the taxpayer agreed to sell his property (Buena Park) through an escrow agreement to Alloy Die (Alloy). Before the sale was consummated, Alderson located a second parcel (Salinas) which he wanted to exchange for the Buena Park property. The escrow agreement was therefore amended to reflect this change. Alloy bought the Salinas parcel, and then, through the escrow, the parties exchanged deeds. The Court held that this transfer was entitled to non-recognition treatment under § 1031.

The taxpayer in *Alderson* did not give up his rights to the Buena Park property until Alloy had purchased and tendered a deed to the Salinas property. As a result of the amendment in the escrow, there was a reciprocal, simultaneous exchange of like-kind property.[2]

Here, plaintiff did not make either a reciprocal or a simultaneous exchange. He transferred all of his rights in the timberland to Crown in return for a promise, here called an exchange balance. At the time of the transfer, Crown did not own any of the twelve parcels which Crown either transferred or caused to be transferred to plaintiff or to plaintiff's nominees. When plaintiff made the Agreement, he did not know whether he would find acceptable property to exchange for his property or whether he would eventually be paid in cash. . . .

Plaintiff seeks to expand the definition of "exchange" to include not only reciprocal transfers, but also transactions in which the taxpayer transfers his property in return for a promise that he will receive like-kind property in the future. . . .

I find that plaintiff exchanged his property for a promise to convey like-kind property in the future, and I hold that plaintiff's transfer to Crown does not qualify for non-recognition treatment under § 1031. . . .

The Agreement provided that plaintiff would be paid a growth factor of six per cent on the exchange balance and that this growth factor was to be added to the exchange balance "at the time of the last offsetting charge to [the plaintiff]."

In my view, the term "growth factor" was used in the Agreement to conceal the true nature of the transaction. It was really interest and should be taxed as ordinary income. . . .

E. STARKER v. UNITED STATES
602 F.2d 1341 (9th Cir. 1979)

GOODWIN, CIRCUIT JUDGE:

T. J. Starker appeals from the dismissal, on stipulated facts, of his tax refund action. We affirm in part and reverse in part. . . .

The trial court's opinion in *Starker I* dealt with Bruce and Elizabeth Starker's reciprocal, but not simultaneous, transfers of title to Crown and another corporation. The *Starker I* court noted that at the time the Starkers transferred their land to Crown, Crown did not own the land ultimately transferred to them. If "a taxpayer disposes of all his rights in property for a promise from the transferee to convey like-kind property in the future", the court said, that transaction is still an exchange "solely for properties of a like kind". . . . The opinion said nothing to indicate that the court considered significant the amount of time elapsed between the taxpayers' transfer of title and their receipt of title. Under a fair reading of *Starker I*, the length of the time lapse is inconsequential. Thus, *Starker II* cannot be distinguished on that ground. Indeed, in its opinion in *Starker II*,

---

2. I do not decide that there must always be a simultaneous exchange to qualify for non-recognition treatment under § 1031. There may be such cases, but this is not one of them.

the court did not distinguish the facts of *Starker I*; it straightforwardly overruled it, recognizing "that many of the transfers here are identical to those in *Starker I*.". . . . Hence, as to the nine properties to which T. J. Starker himself actually received title directly from Crown, collateral estoppel is warranted. . . .

On the other hand, as to the three other properties received by T. J. Starker under the contract, collateral estoppel should not apply. . . . These are the Bi-Mart, Timian, and Booth properties. Title to the Bi-Mart and Timian properties was transferred by Crown, not to T. J. Starker, but to his daughter, Jean Roth. Crown never acquired title to the Booth property; instead, it acquired a right to purchase, which it transferred to T. J. Starker. Not having such transfers before it in *Starker I*, the district court could not have considered the effects of such circuitous transfers on the nonrecognition issue. . . .

In sum, collateral estoppel is inapplicable to T. J. Starker's receipt of the Timian, Bi-Mart, and Booth properties. . . . But . . . collateral estoppel is applicable to the other nine parcels he received. . . .

The government, having lost its case against this taxpayer's son based on the same contract to transfer the same family lands, decided not to pursue an appeal in that case, but instead to pursue this taxpayer. Although T. J. Starker's transactions involving three of the parcels differed in a relevant way from those of his son, the legal issues and facts surrounding the other nine are so similar that collateral estoppel applies. Except as to the Timian, Bi-Mart, and Booth properties, the government should have been held collaterally estopped by *Starker I* from relitigation of the applicability of I.R.C. § 1031 in *Starker II*.

As to Timian, Bi-Mart, and Booth properties, the facts of *Starker I* are so different from those of this case that the entire issue of the applicability of section 1031 to them was properly before the district court in *Starker II*. The court therefore correctly went to the merits of the litigants' arguments as they pertained to these parcels. We now turn to those arguments.

As with the other nine parcels T. J. Starker received, none of these three properties was deeded to him at or near the time he deeded his timberland to Crown. T. J. Starker admits that he received no interest in these properties until a substantial time after he conveyed away title to his property. Thus, the question whether section 1031 requires simultaneity of deed transfers is presented as to all three. In addition, each of these parcels presents its own peculiar issues because of the differing circumstances surrounding their transfers.

A. Timian and Bi-Mart Properties

The Timian property is a residence. Legal title to it was conveyed by Crown at T. J. Starker's request to his daughter, Jean Roth, in 1967. T. J. Starker lives in this residence, and pays rent on it to his daughter. The United States argues that since T. J. Starker never held legal title to this property, he cannot be said to have exchanged his timberland for it. Furthermore, the government contends, because the property became the taxpayer's personal residence, it is neither property "held for investment" nor of a like kind with such property under the meaning of the Code. On the other hand, the taxpayer argues that there was, in economic reality, a transfer of title to him, followed by a gift by him to his daughter.

The Bi-Mart property, a commercial building, was conveyed by Crown to Roth in 1968. The government raises the same issue with regard to the Bi-Mart property: since T. J. Starker never had title, he did not effect an exchange. T. J. Starker points out, however, that he expended substantial time and money in improving and maintaining the structure in the three months prior to the conveyance of the property to his daughter, and he emphasizes that he controlled and commanded its transfer to her.

We begin our analysis of the proper treatment of the receipt of these two properties with a consideration of the Timian residence. T. J. Starker asserts that the question whether such property can be held "for investment" is unsettled. We disagree. It has long been the rule that use of property solely as a personal residence is antithetical to its being held for investment.... Thus, nonrecognition treatment cannot be given to the receipt of the Timian parcel.

Moreover, T. J. Starker cannot be said to have received the Timian or Bi-Mart properties in exchange for his interest in the Columbia County timberland because title to the Timian and Bi-Mart properties was transferred by Crown directly to someone else, his daughter.... Although in some cases a father and his daughter may be seen as having an identity of economic interests (*cf. McWilliams v. Commissioner,* [Chapter 14]), that unity is not sufficient to make transfer of title to one the same as transfer of title to the other. T. J. Starker has not shown that he has any legally cognizable interest in the Timian or Bi-Mart properties that would entitle him to prevent Jean Roth from exercising full ownership rights. In case of a disagreement about the use or enjoyment of these properties, her wishes, not his, would prevail. In these circumstances, T. J. Starker cannot be said to have "exchanged" properties under section 1031, because he never received any property ownership himself.

B. Booth Property

The Booth property is a commercial parcel, title to which has never been conveyed to T. J. Starker. The transfer of this property to him was achieved in 1968 by Crown's acquiring third parties' contract right to purchase the property, and then reassigning the right to T. J. Starker. In addition to emphasizing the lack of simultaneity in the transfers, the government points here to the total lack of deed transfer.

An examination of the record reveals that legal title had not passed by deed to T. J. Starker by the time of the trial. He continued to hold the third-party purchasers' rights under a 1965 sales agreement on the Booth land. That agreement notes that one of the original transferors holds a life interest in the property, and that legal title shall not pass until that life interest expires. In the meantime, the purchasers are entitled to possession, but they are subject to certain restrictions. For example, they are prohibited from removing improvements and are required to keep buildings and fences in good repair. Under the agreement, a substantial portion of the purchase price must be invested, with a fixed return to be paid to the purchaser of the life interest. Should any of these conditions fail, the agreement provides, the sellers may elect, *inter alia*, to void the contract.

Despite these contingencies, we believe that what T. J. Starker received in 1968 was the equivalent of a fee interest for purposes of section 1031. Under Treas. Regs. § 1.1031(a)–1(c), a leasehold interest of 30 years or more is the equivalent of a fee interest for purposes of determining whether the properties exchanged are of a like kind. Under the assigned purchase rights, Starker had at least the rights of a long-term lessee, plus an equitable fee subject to conditions precedent. If the seller's life interest lasted longer than 30 years, the leasehold interest would be the equivalent of a fee; the fact that the leasehold might ripen into a fee at some earlier point should not alter this result. Thus, we hold that what T. J. Starker received in 1968 was the equivalent of a fee.

This does not solve the riddle of the proper treatment of the Booth parcel, however. Since the taxpayer did not receive the fee equivalent at the same time that he gave up his interest in the timberland, the same issue is presented as with the nine parcels on which the government was estopped, namely, whether simultaneity of transfer is required for nonrecognition treatment under section 1031.

The government's argument that simultaneity is required begins with Treas.Reg. § 1.1002–1(b). That regulation provides that all exceptions to the general rule that gains and losses are recognized must be construed narrowly:

> ... Nonrecognition is accorded by the Code only if the exchange is one which satisfies both (1) the specific description in the Code of an excepted exchange, and (2) the underlying purpose for which such exchange is excepted from the general rule.

There are two problems, however, with applying this regulation to section 1031.

First, the "underlying purpose" of section 1031 is not entirely clear. The legislative history reveals that the provision was designed to avoid the imposition of a tax on those who do not "cash in" on their investments in trade or business property. Congress appeared to be concerned that taxpayers would not have the cash to pay a tax on the capital gain if the exchange triggered recognition. This does not explain the precise limits of section 1031, however; if those taxpayers sell their property for cash and reinvest that cash in like-kind property, they cannot enjoy the section's benefits, even if the reinvestment takes place just a few days after the sale. Thus, some taxpayers with liquidity problems resulting from a replacement of their business property are not covered by the section. The liquidity rationale must therefore be limited.

Another apparent consideration of the drafters of the section was the difficulty of valuing property exchanged for the purpose of measuring gain or loss....

But this valuation rationale also has its limits.... [T]he nonrecognition provision applies only to like-kind exchanges, and not to other exchanges in which valuation is just as difficult. Therefore, valuation problems cannot be seen as the controlling consideration in the enactment of section 1031.

In addition to the elusive purpose of the section, there is a second sound reason to question the applicability of Treas.Regs. § 1.1002–1: the long line of cases liberally construing section 1031. If the regulation purports to read into section 1031 a complex web of formal and substantive requirements, precedent indicates decisively that the regulation has been rejected. . . . We therefore analyze the Booth transaction with the courts' permissive attitude toward section 1031 in mind.

Two features of the Booth deal make it most likely to trigger recognition of gain: the likelihood that the taxpayer would receive cash instead of real estate, and the time gap in the transfers of the equivalents of fee title.

In assessing whether the possibility that T. J. Starker might receive cash makes section 1031 inapplicable, an important case is *Alderson v. Commissioner*. . . . There, this court held that a "three corner" exchange qualified for nonrecognition treatment. The taxpayer and Alloy entered into an agreement for the simple cash sale of the taxpayer's property, but later amended the agreement to provide that Alloy would purchase another parcel to effect a swap with the taxpayer. This amendment did not totally eradicate the possibility that the cash transaction would take place; it provided, in the words of the court, that "if the exchange was not effected by September 11, 1957, the original escrow re the purchase for cash would be carried out. . . ." The exchange was effected when reciprocal deeds were recorded. Said the court:

> True, the intermediate acts of the parties could have hewn closer to and have more precisely depicted the ultimate desired result, but what actually occurred on September 3 or 4, 1957, was an exchange of deeds between the petitioners and Alloy which effected an exchange of the Buena Park property for the Salinas property. . . .

The court stressed that, although at the time the contract was amended there was a possibility that a cash sale would take place, there was from the outset no intention on the part of the taxpayer to sell his property for cash if it could be exchanged for other property of a like kind. . . .

Thus, the mere possibility at the time of agreement that a cash sale might occur does not prevent the application of section 1031. . . .

In this case, the taxpayer claims he intended from the very outset of the transaction to get nothing but like-kind property, and no evidence to the contrary appears on the record. Moreover, the taxpayer never handled any cash in the course of the transactions. Hence, the *Alderson* line of cases would seem to control.

The government contends, however, that *Alderson* and other precedents of its type are distinguishable. It points out that in those cases, there may have been a possibility of a receipt of cash at the time of the exchange *agreement*, but there was no possibility of receiving cash at the time the taxpayer *transferred* the property pursuant to the agreement. This difference in timing, says the commissioner, renders the *Alderson* line of cases inapplicable.

At least one appellate decision indicates, however, that title may not have to be exchanged simultaneously in order for section 1031 to apply. In *Redwing Carriers, Inc. v. Tomlinson* [Chapter 37], the government argued successfully that mutual transfers of trucks that occurred "at or about" the same time were in fact an "exchange" under section 1031. In *Redwing Carriers,* the taxpayer was attempting to deduct a loss in the purchase of new trucks to replace old trucks; the government disallowed recognition of the loss on the ground that section 1031(c) applied. To keep its replacement transactions outside the scope of the section, a parent corporation transferred its old trucks to a subsidiary, bought new trucks for cash, and had the subsidiary sell the old trucks to the manufacturer for cash. The court viewed the transactions as a whole, and disallowed the loss under section 1031. Some lack of simultaneity was apparently "tolerated" by the commissioner and the court. As the court explained, the transfers to the subsidiary by the parent and to the parent by the manufacturer took place "at or about" the same time. . . . Nonetheless, the government urges this court to distinguish *Redwing Carriers,* and *Alderson* and its kin, on the ground that the transfers of title in T. J. Starker's case were separated by a "substantial" period of time. We decline to draw this line.

The government also argues that the contract right to receive property or cash was not "like" title to property, because it was like cash. . . .

Against this background, the government offers the explanation that a contract right to land is a "chose in action", and thus personal property instead of real property. This is true, but the short answer to this statement is that title to real property, like a contract right to purchase real property, is nothing more than a bundle of potential causes of action: for trespass, to quiet title, for interference with quiet enjoyment, and so on. The bundle of rights associated with ownership is obviously not excluded from section 1031; a contractual right to assume the rights of ownership should not, we believe, be treated as any different than the ownership rights themselves. Even if the contract right includes the possibility of the taxpayer receiving something other than ownership of like-kind property, we hold that it is still of a like kind with ownership for tax purposes when the taxpayer prefers property to cash before and throughout the executory period, and only like-kind property is ultimately received. . . .

. . . Here, the statute's purposes are somewhat cloudy, and the precedents are not easy to reconcile. But the weight of authority leans in T. J. Starker's favor, and we conclude that the district court was right in *Starker I,* and wrong in *Starker II.* Thus, on the merits, the transfer of the timberland to Crown triggered a like-kind exchange with respect to the Booth property.

[C.] *Six Per Cent "Growth Factor"*

The next issue presented is whether the 6 per cent "growth factor" received by T. J. Starker was properly treated as capital gain or as ordinary income. The government successfully argued below that this amount should be treated as ordinary income because it was disguised interest. The taxpayer, on the other hand, contends that the 6 per cent "growth" provision merely compensated him for timber growth on the Columbia County property he conveyed to Crown.

The taxpayer's argument is not without some biological merit, but he was entitled to the 6 per cent regardless of the actual fate of the timber on the property. He retained no ownership rights in the timber, and bore no risk of loss, after he conveyed title to Crown. We agree with the government that the taxpayer is essentially arguing "that he conveyed $1,502,500 to a stranger for an indefinite period of time [up to five years] without any interest." The 6 per cent "growth factor" was "compensation for the use or forbearance of money", that is, for the use of the unpaid amounts owed to Starker by Crown. Therefore, it was disguised interest. . . .

[D.] *Timing of Inclusion*

Our final task, having characterized the proper nature of T. J. Starker's receipts, is to decide in which years they are includable in income. The Timian and Bi-Mart properties do not qualify for nonrecognition treatment, while the other 10 properties received do qualify. In this situation, we believe the proper result is to treat T. J. Starker's rights in his contract with Crown, insofar as they resulted in the receipt of the Timian and Bi-Mart properties, as "boot," received in 1967 when the contract was made. We hold that section 1031(b) requires T. J. Starker to recognize his gain on the transaction with Crown in 1967, to the extent of the fair market values of the Timian and Bi-Mart properties as of the dates on which title to those properties passed to his appointee.

We realize that this decision leaves the treatment of an alleged exchange open until the eventual receipt of consideration by the taxpayer. Some administrative difficulties may surface as a result. Our role, however, is not necessarily to facilitate administration. It is to divine the meaning of the statute in a manner as consistent as possible with the intent of Congress and the prior holdings of the courts. If our holding today adds a degree of uncertainty to this area, Congress can clarify its meaning. . . .

F. NOTES AND QUESTIONS

1) Redwing Carriers, Inc. v. Commissioner

In *Redwing Carriers*, the IRS successfully argued that a Section 1031 exchange did not require *simultaneous* transfers. How was this argument used against the IRS in *Starker*? How did the government try to distinguish *Redwing Carriers*? If you were arguing *Starker* for the government, how would you try to distinguish *Redwing Carriers*?

2) The Policy Behind Section 1031 and the Result in *Starker*

Starker permitted identification of like-kind property up to several years after the transfer of the property being exchanged. Is this result consistent with (a) the policy behind Section 1031, as explained in *Jordan Marsh*, and (b) the identification of the 6% growth factor as interest income?

3) Congress Restricts *Starker:* Section 1031(a)(3)

In 1984, Congress restricted *Starker* by enacting Section 1031(a)(3). Like-kind property must now be identified within forty-five days of settlement and received within either 180 days of settlement or the due date for the taxpayer's return, whichever occurs earlier.

4) Can Section 1031(a)(3) Be Circumvented?

Is there a way to revise the *Starker* transaction to avoid Section 1031(a)(3)? Suppose that Starker leases the property to Crown for five years and simultaneously agrees to sell the property to Crown at some time during the lease term. The sales price is to be paid not with cash but with other real estate to be designated by Starker. If no such property is designated before the lease is over, then Crown is to pay cash. How might this revised plan still be vulnerable to IRS attack? Does the "real" transfer to Crown occur when the property is leased rather than when title is transferred? Consider what J. H. Baird Publishing Co. v. Commissioner, 39 T.C. 608 (1962), summarized below, suggests about the chances of avoiding Section 1031(a)(3)?

In *Baird,* title to property was transferred in 1956, but the owner retained use of the property rent-free until a new lot was acquired and a new building constructed on the lot. In 1957, when construction was completed, the owner relinquished use of the old property and obtained title to the new lot and building. The Tax Court held that the transaction qualified for nonrecognition under Section 1031:

> [The Commissioner] states that there could have been no exchange in 1957 when [the other party] transferred title to the new property to the petitioner since at that time the petitioner itself did not have any property to exchange, having transferred its property away in the prior year. . . .
>
> [U]nder the contract . . . the petitioner was to retain the use of [the] property rent free until the [other party] should provide a suitable new building. . . . [T]he deed executed . . . [in] 1956 . . . had the effect of transferring only legal title to the property. The petitioner in effect retained beneficial ownership of the property until the new . . . property was available for its use. Thus the petitioner's transfer of ownership of the [old] property and the transfer of ownership of the [new] property to the petitioner were reciprocal and mutually dependent. When [in] 1957, the [new] property was deeded to the petitioner . . . , beneficial ownership of the [old] property passed. . . . At that time there was effected, within the meaning of section 1031 of the Code, an exchange by the petitioner of its [old] property for the [new] property. . . .[3]

5) The Definition of Like-Kind

In order for Section 1031 to apply, each property must be either used in a "trade or business" or "held for investment" by the taxpayer and,

---

3. 39 T.C. 608, 615, 618 (1962).

therefore, neither may be used for personal consumption. In addition, the properties must be "like-kind." Reg. §1.1031(a)–1(b) states that like-kind refers to "the nature or character of the property and not to its grade or quality. One kind or class of property may not be exchanged tax-free for property of a different kind or class."

In general, all real estate qualifies as like-kind with respect to other real estate. Thus, the exchange of a farm for a commercial office building can qualify under Section 1031. However, the regulations indicate that there will be less latitude afforded to nonreal property. See Reg. § 1.1031–1(a)–(c). Moreover, trading a cow for a bull can never qualify for nonrecognition, since, under Section 1031(e), "livestock of different sexes are not property of a like-kind."

Note also that Section 1031(a)(2)(A)–(C) prevents Section 1031 from applying to exchanges of corporate securities. Instead, such transactions must run the gamut of complex rules in Section 368(a), which are beyond the scope of this book and are usually the subject of an advanced tax course.

Is it possible to construct a clear and principled definition of like-kind? Why should the exchange of an apartment house for a farm qualify for nonrecognition under Section 1031 but not the exchange of an office building for General Motors stock? Would it be better simply to afford nonrecognition whenever the exchanged properties are used in a "trade or business" or "held for investment," without regard to any other differences between them?

Chapter 19

INVOLUNTARY REALIZATIONS

A. HELVERING v. BRUUN
309 U.S. 461 (1940)

MR. JUSTICE ROBERTS delivered the opinion of the Court.

The controversy had its origin in the petitioner's assertion that the respondent realized taxable gain from the forfeiture of a leasehold, the tenant having erected a new building upon the premises. The court below held that no income had been realized. . . .

[On] July 1, 1915, the respondent, as owner, leased a lot of land and the building thereon for a term of ninety-nine years.

The lease provided that the lessee might, at any time, upon giving bond to secure rentals accruing in the two ensuing years, remove or tear down any building on the land. . . . The lessee was to surrender the land, upon termination of the lease, with all buildings and improvements thereon.

In 1929 the tenant demolished and removed the existing building and constructed a new one which had a useful life of not more than fifty years. July 1, 1933, the lease was cancelled for default in payment of rent and taxes and the respondent regained possession of the land and building.

The parties stipulated "that as at said date, July 1, 1933, the building which had been erected upon said premises by the lessee had a fair market value of $64,245.68 and that the unamortized cost of the old building, which was removed from the premises in 1929 to make way for the new building, was $12,811.43, thus leaving a net fair market value as at July 1, 1933, of $51,434.25, for the aforesaid new building erected upon the premises by the lessee."

On the basis of these facts, the petitioner determined that in 1933 the respondent realized a net gain of $51,434.25. . . .

The course of administrative practice and judicial decision in respect of the question presented has not been uniform. In 1917 the Treasury ruled that the adjusted value of improvements installed upon leased premises is income to the lessor upon the termination of the lease. The ruling

311

was incorporated in two succeeding editions of the Treasury Regulations. In 1919 the Circuit Court of Appeals for the Ninth Circuit held in *Miller v. Gearin* . . . that the regulation was invalid as the gain, if taxable at all, must be taxed as of the year when the improvements were completed.

The regulations were accordingly amended to impose a tax upon the gain in the year of completion of the improvements, measured by their anticipated value at the termination of the lease and discounted for the duration of the lease. Subsequently the regulations permitted the lessor to spread the depreciated value of the improvements over the remaining life of the lease, reporting an aliquot part each year, with provision that, upon premature termination, a tax should be imposed upon the excess of the then value of the improvements over the amount theretofore returned.

In 1935 the Circuit Court of Appeals for the Second Circuit decided in *Hewitt Realty Co. v. Commissioner* . . . that a landlord received no taxable income in a year, during the term of the lease, in which his tenant erected a building on the leased land. The court, while recognizing that the lessor need not receive money to be taxable, based its decision that no taxable gain was realized in that case on the fact that the improvement was not portable or detachable from the land, and if removed would be worthless except as bricks, iron, and mortar. It said . . . : "The question as we view it is whether the value received is embodied in something separately disposable, or whether it is so merged in the land as to become financially a part of it, something which, though it increases its value, has no value of its own when torn away."

This decision invalidated the regulations then in force.

In 1938 this court decided *M. E. Blatt Co. v. United States*. . . . There, in connection with the execution of a lease, landlord and tenant mutually agreed that each should make certain improvements to the demised premises and that those made by the tenant should become and remain the property of the landlord. The Commissioner valued the improvements as of the date they were made, allowed depreciation thereon to the termination of the leasehold, divided the depreciated value by the number of years the lease had to run, and found the landlord taxable for each year's aliquot portion thereof. His action was sustained by the Court of Claims. The judgment was reversed on the ground that the added value could not be considered rental accruing over the period of the lease; that the facts found by the Court of Claims did not support the conclusion of the Commissioner as to the value to be attributed to the improvements after a use throughout the term of the lease; and that, in the circumstances disclosed, any enhancement in the value of the realty in the tax year was not income realized by the lessor within the Revenue Act.

The circumstances of the instant case differentiate it from the *Blatt* and *Hewitt* cases; but the petitioner's contention that gain was realized when the respondent, through forfeiture of the lease, obtained untrammeled title, possession and control of the premises, with the added increment of value added by the new building, runs counter to the decision in the *Miller* case and to the reasoning in the *Hewitt* case.

The respondent insists ... that ... improvements cannot be separately valued or treated as received in exchange for the improvements which were on the land at the date of the execution of the lease: that they are, therefore, in the same category as improvements added by the respondent to his land, or accruals of value due to extraneous and adventitious circumstances. Such added value, it is argued, can be considered ... gain only upon the owner's disposition of the asset. The position is that the economic gain consequent upon the enhanced value of the recaptured asset is not gain ... realized. ...

We hold that the petitioner was right in assessing the gain as realized in 1933. ...

While it is true that economic gain is not always taxable as income, it is settled that the realization of gain need not be in cash derived from the sale of an asset. Gain may occur as a result of exchange of property. ... The fact that the gain is a portion of the value of property received by the taxpayer in the transaction does not negative its realization.

Here, as a result of a business transaction, the respondent received back his land with a new building on it, which added an ascertainable amount to its value. It is not necessary to recognition of taxable gain that he should be able to sever the improvement begetting the gain from his original capital. If that were necessary, no income could arise from the exchange of property; whereas such gain has always been recognized as realized taxable gain. ...

B. NOTES AND QUESTIONS

1) Taxing the Building to Bruun in the Year of Construction

Should the landlord in *Bruun* have reported income in 1929 when the tenant erected the building? In that year, didn't the landlord receive income in kind consisting of the right to the building when the lease ended? *Drescher* (Chapter 2) held that an employee had income in kind when he received the right, under an annuity, to monthly payments on retirement. Why is the right to the building upon expiration of the lease in *Bruun* any different?

Assume that when the building in *Bruun* was constructed, it was expected to have a useful life of fifty years. Why would no income, in fact, have to be reported under either version of the Treasury regulations described in the opinion?

Even if no tax would be due under Treasury regulations in effect at the time, why not tax Bruun in 1929 on the present value of his right to possess the building? Although the lease was originally expected to run until the year 2014, didn't the right to the building have some positive value if there was some chance of the tenant defaulting? But why would it have been difficult to value Bruun's right when the remaining term of the lease exceeded the useful life of the building? How does this resemble the difficulty of valuing compensatory stock options? And even if the right to the building could have been valued, was it arguably subject to a substantial risk of forfeiture?

2) The Realization Issue

The principal issue in *Bruun* was whether the gain had been *realized*. What analogy did the taxpayer use to argue that the gain was *unrealized*? In deciding that the gain was realized, what competing analogy did the Supreme Court adopt? Why did the Court also state that to treat the gain as realized was "counter to the decision in the *Miller* case and to the reasoning in the *Hewitt* case"?

Suppose that the real estate rented out by Bruun had consisted simply of unimproved land. In that event, would the Supreme Court's analogy justify taxing Bruun on gain attributable to a building erected by the tenant? Alternatively, would it be possible to view the building as liquidated damages paid in kind?

Even if the gain were considered unrealized, why couldn't it be taxed? At the time that *Bruun* was decided, the taxation of unrealized gain was thought to be unconstitutional. A prior Supreme Court decision had held that the Sixteenth Amendment authorized taxing only realized gains. That decision, Eisner v. Macomber, appears in Chapter 25.[1]

3) *Bruun* as a Like-kind Exchange

Even if the gain in *Bruun* was realized, why didn't the exchange of the old building for the new building qualify for nonrecognition as a Section 1031 like-kind exchange?

4) The Hidden Issue: The Unrealized Loss

Suppose that the land underneath the building originally cost Bruun $70,000 but, as of 1929, had declined in value to only $10,000. Could Bruun use the loss on the land to offset the gain on the building? Hadn't there been a sale or exchange of the land with Bruun's tenant? Why might the principle of Higgins v. Smith prevent deduction of the loss? If, taking into account both the gain on the building and the loss on the land, the transaction *as a whole* was a loss, was Bruun treated unfairly?

5) Nonrecognition of Involuntary Conversions

Section 1033(a)(1) and (a)(2)(A) provides for nonrecognition of gain when property is "compulsorily or involuntarily converted," provided that it is converted into or replaced by other property which is "similar or related in service or use." Suppose that you own a commercial office building which is destroyed by a fire and that you use the insurance proceeds to acquire another office building. Has realization occurred? If so, what are the policy reasons for granting nonrecognition? Could Section 1033(a) be interpreted to apply to Bruun's case? See also Section 109, enacted after *Bruun* was decided.

---

1. 252 U.S. 189 (1920). Today, most experts believe that the Sixteenth Amendment would be interpreted to permit taxation of unrealized gain.

6) The "Similar or Related in Use" Requirement of Section 1033

Why does Section 1033 deny nonrecognition if the new property is "dissimilar" to the old, for example, if insurance proceeds from the destruction of a valuable work of art are reinvested in a yacht? Suppose that a Pablo Picasso painting hanging in your living room is stolen. The painting is done in a cubist style. You receive insurance proceeds and are considering the following possible acquisitions: (a) a Picasso painting from his Harlequin period; (b) a cubist painting by Braque; (c) a Picasso lithograph; (d) a sofa with upholstery taken from a Picasso design; (e) a Jacques Lipschutz sculpture; and (f) a working color television designed by Andy Warhol. Which acquisition should qualify under Section 1033(a)?

"Similar or related in ... use" has been interpreted to mean a similar relationship to the property:

> [W]hen the taxpayer-owner ... uses the converted property, the Tax Court is correct in comparing the actual physical ... use which the end user makes of the ... properties. However, if the taxpayer-owner is an investor rather than a user, it is not the lessee's actual physical use but the nature of the lessor's relation ... which must be examined.[2]

This interpretation appears to cover the replacement of rental residential realty with rental commercial realty, since in both cases the role of the owner as landlord is unchanged, even though the actual physical use of the property by the tenant is different. But it does not appear to provide relief to the owner-user of an office building who replaces it with rental commercial realty, since the role of the owner is changed from a user-occupier to a landlord. However, the "similar or related in ... use" test now applies only to nonreal property. See Section 1033(g).

7) The Exclusion of Damages for Personal Injury or Sickness

Section 104(a)(2) excludes from income "damages received ... on account of personal injuries or sickness." For example, if X loses a limb in a car accident and recovers $1 million as compensation for the loss, the recovery is untaxed. Can the exclusion be explained as a special instance of involuntary conversion in which it would be silly to require, or to try to judge whether there was, reinvestment in similar or related property? Or is the exclusion better understood as assuming, in effect, that the taxpayer's cost equals the amount received? Or is nontaxation appropriate because the taxpayer who receives such damages is really no better off than the taxpayer who was never damaged in the first place and is, if anything, probably worse off? (See the discussion of the medical expense deduction in Chapter 9.)

The IRS has ruled that Section 104 excludes damages, not only for physical injuries but also for injury to one's *personal* reputation. In addition, the courts have interpreted Section 104, over the IRS' objection, as applying as well to damages for injury to one's *professional* reputation. Under these

---

2. Liant Record, Inc. v. Commissioner, 303 F.2d 326, 328–29 (2d Cir. 1962).

decisions, recoveries for libel, slander, malicious prosecution, and the like generally will not be taxed.[3]

8) Nonrecognition on Sale of Personal Residence

Section 1034(a) grants nonrecognition to the sale of the taxpayer's principal residence, provided that the taxpayer buys a new principal residence within a two-year period before or after the sale of the old residence. Why does Section 1034 grant nonrecognition? Can the move into a new home be analogized to a Section 1033 involuntary conversion?

Section 121 permits taxpayers fifty-five years of age and older to elect not to recognize up to $125,000 on sale of a "principal residence." The election is available only once in a lifetime. How can Section 121 be justified? Perhaps on the ground that an older taxpayer, whose children are grown and who desires to move to smaller and possibly less expensive quarters, should be treated the same as the older taxpayer who elects not to move? Does Section 121 promote or retard the efficient allocation of housing resources?

9) Sections 1031, 1033, and 1034 Compared

There are a number of other important differences among the nonrecognition provisions of Sections 1031, 1033, and 1034. Section 1031 applies to both gains and losses; Sections 1033 and 1034 apply only to gains.[4] Section 1031 refers to an "exchange" of properties, whereas both Sections 1033 and 1034 expressly permit an intermediate cash step. In addition, the latter two provisions contain explicit time limits on the permissible interval between sale of the old property and acquisition of the new—two years after the end of the taxable year if there is an involuntary conversion (Section 1033(a)(1)(B)), and either two years before or two years after the sale of the old principal residence (under Section 1034). Could the IRS have used the specified time intervals in Sections 1033 and 1034 to argue in *Starker* (Chapter 18) that Section 1031, lacking such a provision, must have been intended to apply only to simultaneous exchanges?

C. BUSH MADE A $198,000 PAYMENT TO I.R.S. IN JUNE FOR BACK TAXES

The New York Times, October 4, 1984

Vice President Bush paid the Internal Revenue Service $198,000 in back taxes and interest last June after the service ruled that he had failed to report about $500,000 in income from the sale of his house on his 1981 tax return....

---

3. Compare Roemer v. Commissioner, 716 F.2d 693 (9th Cir. 1983), in which the court refused to distinguish between injuries to personal and professional reputation, with Rev. Rul. 85–143, 1985–2 C.B. 55.

4. Although Section 1034 applies only to gains on the sale of a taxpayer's principal residence, losses are generally disallowed by Section 165(c). See Chapter 30.

Mr. Bush had believed that he did not have to report the income and . . . intend[s] to sue the revenue service in an effort to recover the additional taxes. . . .

The issue in the house sale is the definition, under tax law, of Mr. Bush's principal residence. If, as he says, it is his home in Kennebunkport, [Maine], which he bought in 1981, then he could apply the $600,000 in profits he made when he sold his home in Houston in 1981 to the purchase of the Maine home, and not pay taxes on the capital gain from the Houston sale. If, however, his principal residence is deemed to be the Vice-Presidential residence in Washington, as the I.R.S. contends, he must report the gain and pay taxes at a rate of 20 percent.

Mr. Yorty, Mr. Bush's tax attorney, said the decision to call the Maine home Mr. Bush's principal residence was a "borderline" call because there were a number of previous rulings and decisions not favorable to their position.

One decision that Mr. Yorty said he was aware of was a 1974 ruling by the Congressional Joint Taxation Committee in which the committee found that President Nixon had improperly claimed a house in San Clemente, Calif., as his principal residence rather than the White House. After the committee finding and a similar ruling by the I.R.S., Mr. Nixon paid back taxes on the gain he realized in 1969 from the sale of a cooperative apartment in New York. . . .

Mr. Bush had been "enraged" at the tax decision. A prepared statement issued by the Vice President's press secretary today said that the decision "raises not only legal questions, but questions of fairness" since "the Kennebunkport house is the only house Vice President Bush owns."

The statement says Mr. Bush's occupancy of the Vice President's house in Washington, which is owned by the Federal Government, is "temporary and is incidental to the Vice President's duties." . . .

BUSH FEELS SINGLED OUT

Mr. Bush said that he felt he had been "singled out" by the I.R.S. because he was not entitled by a ruling by the agency to do "what any other taxpayer" can do and roll over the capital gains. . . .

Mr. Bush said that he had "been taken to the cleaners" by the I.R.S. . . . .

The Vice President said he did not see why he should be treated any differently than a Navy officer who was provided a home by the Government but might also buy private property.

"If a guy is provided a house in the Navy, that doesn't mean he can't sell a home in Virginia and buy another home in Maine or Texas or any place else, even though he has quarters provided," Mr. Bush said.

D. IS THE MAINE HOUSE THE MAIN HOUSE?

1) The "Principal Residence" Test of Section 1034

Section 1034 permits gain on the sale of a homeowner's "principal residence" to be tax free if another house is purchased *and used* as "principal residence" within two years. If a taxpayer occupies two different houses, the "principal residence" is defined as where he or she spends more time. Thus, Mr. Bush owed no tax, provided he used the Maine house more than any other residence within two years of the Texas sale. During this period, however, Mr. Bush and his family appear to have resided principally at the Vice President's Official residence on the grounds of the naval observatory in Washington, D.C. and to have occupied the Maine house only on weekends and holidays.

2) Was Mr. Bush Unfairly Singled Out?

Shortly after his election, former President Richard Nixon sold his New York City apartment and used the cash to buy a San Clemente estate. Mr. Nixon claimed that no tax was due on the New York sale because he intended to live full time in San Clemente after leaving the White House. In 1974, the Joint Committee on Taxation, investigating Mr. Nixon's tax returns, determined that taxes were owed on the New York sale because Mr. Nixon's "principal residence" at the time was not San Clemente but the White House. Mr. Nixon paid the taxes without further protest.

Other taxpayers have argued that a newly acquired home, although used only for vacations, could qualify as their "principal residence" if they were required to work temporarily in a different location but intended to live in the home full time at some future date. However, the courts have uniformly ruled against them, and the IRS has consistently followed these rulings in applying the tax law.

3) Military Personnel

Congress has decided to allow military personnel four years after the sale of an old residence, instead of the usual two, to purchase and occupy a new house as "principal residence" and still qualify for nonrecognition under Section 1034. Section 1034(h)(1).[5] (This exception explains the reference to "a Navy officer" in Vice President Bush's remarks.)

Should Congress extend this exception to politicians who hold public office? Or should the "principal residence" test be relaxed whenever a taxpayer is away from home for an extended period and resides in lodgings that are either rented or provided by an employer?

E. FORGIVENESS OF DEBT

1) Are Loans Income?

Under the Code, a loan is treated as not producing income to the borrower because the cash received is offset by a corresponding liability, producing no net gain. For identical reasons, the repayment *in full* of a

---

5. Military personnel stationed outside the United States are allowed up to eight years. Section 1034(h)(2)(A).

loan is treated as not producing a loss because the cash paid out is offset by a decrease in liabilities, resulting in no net loss. To illustrate, if you borrow $10,000 to pay law school tuition, you do not have income because the receipt of an asset (the cash) is balanced by the obligation to repay $10,000. When you repay the $10,000 loan, you do not have a loss because the decrease in assets is balanced by a decrease in your loan obligations.

2) The Logic of Treating Forgiveness of Debt as Producing Income

The income tax treatment of the borrower on receipt and repayment of a loan is, if not intuitively obvious, at least reasonably understandable. More difficult is understanding why forgiveness of debt (lender agreement to accept less than the full principal amount due) causes income to the borrower. For example, suppose that the lender agrees to accept $9,000 in full satisfaction of a $10,000 loan. The $1,000 difference between what was owed and what was repaid (that is, the amount "forgiven") is treated as income to the borrower. Section 61(a)(12).

There are at least two possible ways to understand why forgiveness of debt produces income. One is to compare the overall effects of the decrease in assets to the decrease in loan obligations. In the case of forgiveness of debt, the decrease in assets is *more* than offset by a decrease in loan obligations. Your assets are diminished by the $9,000 you repaid, but your liabilities have fallen by $10,000, and the overall effect is a $1,000 gain.

Because this first explanation may be less comprehensible to students unfamiliar with the concept of balance sheet accounting, there is an alternative approach. Whenever money is borrowed, the borrower is, in effect, selling property, where the property consists of the IOU or contractual promise to repay. The amount loaned represents the price for which the IOU is sold. Thus, if you borrow $10,000, you might be viewed as selling an IOU for $10,000. The gain, if any, from selling this property depends on its cost. The cost of the IOU is equivalent to the amount that you repay. If you repay the entire $10,000, the cost equals the selling price, and there is no gain. If you repay only $9,000, the cost is $1,000 less than the selling price, producing an equivalent amount of gain. It is as if you purchased property for $9,000 and later resold it for $10,000.

Despite this logic, the idea that forgiveness of debt produces income has encountered some resistance. This might explain the surprisingly peremptory tone of another federal income tax casebook:

> The notion that a person can have income from the discharge of indebtedness may not be intuitively obvious to a person who is not versed in tax law, but it is a matter of pure tax logic and is not reasonably debatable. The task of the student is to master the logic.[6]

Courts have at times shared the reluctance of students to view forgiveness of debt as a taxable event. One possible explanation is a sensitivity to

---

6. W. Klein, B. Bittker, and L. Stone, Federal Income Taxation 249 (1987).

the circumstances that usually accompany forgiveness of debt. A lender typically agrees to be repaid less than what is fully owed only when the debtor is experiencing serious financial distress and, for that reason, is unable to repay in full. Furthermore, the lender is often concerned that insisting on full repayment may drive the debtor out of business. The lender hopes that partial forgiveness will enable the debtor to regain at least a modicum of financial health and thereby maximize the amount eventually repaid. In these circumstances, IRS insistence on payment of taxes could upset the bargain. Liquid assets that the debtor requires in order to regain a sound financial state would instead be siphoned off to pay the tax bill arising from forgiveness of debt.

> [F]requently when creditors agree to accept less than the amount due, it is because the debtor is in financial distress; taxing such debtors may have seemed anomalous, even heartless, especially since the closer the debtor approaches the abyss of bankruptcy, the greater the discount creditors are willing to grant and therefore the heavier the potential tax burden if the discount were taxed.[7]

Congress has recognized this problem by providing in Section 108(a) for nonrecognition of income arising from "discharge . . . of indebtedness." The current version of Section 108 applies *only* when the forgiveness occurs (a) in connection with bankruptcy proceedings or (b) when the taxpayer is insolvent. Thus, if a taxpayer is experiencing serious financial distress, but is neither insolvent nor in bankruptcy court, Section 108(a) nonrecognition is not available.

Whether a taxpayer is involved in bankruptcy proceedings should be easy to determine. But how does one determine whether a taxpayer is insolvent?[8] Will some taxpayers be encouraged to file for bankruptcy solely in order to avoid ambiguity as to whether they are entitled under Section 108(a) to delay taxation of income arising from forgiveness of debt? Is it sensible to encourage such tax-motivated use of the bankruptcy process?

Farmers are entitled to avail themselves of Section 108(a) even if they are neither bankrupt nor insolvent. Under Section 108(g), forgiveness of debt incurred "in connection . . . with the trade or business of farming" shall be treated "in the same manner as if . . . the taxpayer was insolvent." How do you explain the more liberal treatment of farmers?

3) Forgiveness of Debt versus Reduction of Purchase Price

Suppose that property costing $10,000 is purchased for $2,000 cash down plus an $8,000 note. One month after the sale, the seller agrees to

---

7. Bittker and Thompson, Income From the Discharge of Indebtedness: The Progeny of United States v. Kirby Lumber, 66 Cal. L. Rev. 1159, 1160 (1978).

8. When originally enacted in 1939, Section 108(a) was limited to taxpayers in "unsound financial condition"—a requirement which proved too difficult to administer and was later dropped. Until 1987, Section 108 applied, without restriction, to debt arising in connection with a trade or business. However, when the debt was not connected with the taxpayer's trade or business, Section 108 nonrecognition was available only if the debtor was bankrupt or insolvent. The distinction between debts that are business-related and debts that are not has now been dropped.

reduce the amount owed on the note by $1,000. Section 108(e)(5) treats the adjustment as a reduction in the purchase price of the property. Ordinarily, a reduction in the price of property does not result in recognition of gain.[9]

What is the rationale for Section 108(e)(5)? Does it assume that the reduction in debt reflects a reduction in the original purchase price, perhaps because the buyer was overcharged or because the property has not performed as advertised? What about the possibility that the seller does not attempt to collect the full amount owed because the buyer, although neither insolvent nor bankrupt, is in unsound financial condition? Is it practical to try to determine in each case what motivated the seller to collect less than the full amount owed?

4) Forgiveness of Student Loans for Public Service

Section 108(f)(1), enacted in 1984, excludes income arising from forgiveness of a student loan in return for the student performing public service. Only loans made by a governmental entity qualify.[10]

Can Section 108(f) be rationalized on the ground that such a forgiveness of debt closely resembles a scholarship under Section 117? And, conversely, can't a scholarship be viewed as the immediate forgiveness of tuition debt? Is this rationalization consistent with the rule of Bingler v. Johnson (Chapter 6) that an amount does not qualify as a scholarship if the recipient is required to render future services?

Suppose the student loan covered, not tuition, but living expenses. Will Section 108(f) apply if the loan is forgiven in return for public service? If Section 108(f) does apply, is it consistent with Section 117, which currently does not exclude a scholarship to the extent that it pays for living expenses? Is consistency less important than providing a tax incentive for students with large education loans to take low-paying jobs in the public interest sector?

F. A CLOSING QUESTION

This chapter has covered a grab bag of different provisions that grant nonrecognition when: (1) improvements are conveyed to a landlord on termination of a lease (Section 109); (2) property is destroyed, stolen, seized, or condemned (Section 1033); (3) damages are paid on account of personal injury or sickness (Section 104); (4) a principal residence is sold and the proceeds are reinvested in a new principal residence (Section 1034); and (5) a debt of a bankrupt or insolvent taxpayer is forgiven (Section 108).

Why was this chapter entitled Involuntary Realizations? In what sense is the realization in each of these circumstances involuntary?

---

9. Section 108(e)(5) applies only to debtors who are neither in bankruptcy court nor insolvent. However, the debtor who fails to meet this requirement is already covered by the general rule of Section 108(a). Another way of putting this is that, under Section 108(a) and 108(e)(5), forgiveness of debt is treated as producing income only if (a) the taxpayer is neither insolvent nor in bankruptcy, *and* (b) the debt did not arise from the purchase of property from the creditor.

10. See Section 108(f)(2) which covers loans made by the U.S. government, state and local governments, and by corporations which have assumed control over a "State, county, or municipal hospital" and which meet other specified requirements.

Chapter 20

FORGIVENESS OF DEBT AND THE ANNUAL ACCOUNTING PRINCIPLE

A. BOWERS v. KERBAUGH–EMPIRE CO.
271 U.S. 170 (1926)

Mr. Justice Butler delivered the opinion of the Court.

Defendant . . . owned all the capital stock of H. S. Kerbaugh, Incorporated, engaged in the performance of large construction contracts, and applied to the Deutsche Bank of Germany, through its New York representative, for loans to finance the work being done by its subsidiary. The bank agreed that it would make the loans by cabling to the credit of its New York representative German marks equivalent in dollars to the requirements of defendant in error, upon condition that the loans would be evidenced by notes payable as to principal and interest in marks or their equivalent in United States gold coin. . . .

The several amounts from time to time borrowed by defendant . . . were contemporaneously advanced to its subsidiary and were expended and lost in and about the performance of the construction contracts. These losses were sustained in 1913, 1914, 1916, 1917, and 1918, and were allowed as deductions in the subsidiary's income tax returns for those years. The excess of its losses over income was more than the amount here claimed by plaintiff in error to be income of defendant . . . in 1921.

After the United States entered the War the Deutsche Bank was an alien enemy. In 1921, on the demand of the Alien Property Custodian, defendant in error paid him $113,688.23 in full settlement of principal and interest owing on the note belonging to the bank. . . . The settlement was on the basis of two and one-half cents per mark. Measured by United States gold coin the difference between the value of the marks borrowed at the time the loans were made and the amount paid to the Custodian was $684,456.18. The Commissioner of Internal Revenue, notwithstanding the claim of defendant in error that the amount borrowed had been lost in construction operations carried on by it and its subsidiary and that no income resulted from the transaction, held the amount to be income and chargeable to defendant . . . for 1921. . . .

The question for decision is whether the difference between the value of marks measured by dollars at the time of payment to the Custodian and the value when the loans were made was income. . . .

. . . The essential facts set forth in the complaint are the loans . . . the loss in 1913 to 1918 of the moneys borrowed, the excess of such losses over income by more than the item here in controversy, and payment in the equivalent of marks greatly depreciated in value. The result of the whole transaction was a loss. . . .

The contention that the item in question is cash gain disregards the fact that the borrowed money was lost, and that the excess of such loss over income was more than the amount borrowed. When the loans were made and notes given, the assets and liabilities of defendant in error were increased alike. The loss of the money borrowed wiped out the increase of assets, but the liability remained. The assets were further diminished by payment of the debt. The loss was less than it would have been if marks had not declined in value; but the mere diminution of loss is not gain, profit or income. . . .

B. UNITED STATES v. KIRBY LUMBER CO.
284 U.S. 1 (1931)

MR. JUSTICE HOLMES delivered the opinion of the Court.

In July, 1923, the plaintiff, the Kirby Lumber Company, issued its own bonds for $12,126,800 for which it received their par value. Later in the same year it purchased in the open market some of the same bonds at less than par, the difference of price being $137,521.30. The question is whether this difference is a taxable gain or income of the plaintiff for the year 1923. . . .

In *Bowers* v. *Kerbaugh-Empire Co.*, . . . the defendant in error owned the stock of another company that had borrowed money repayable in marks or their equivalent for an enterprise that failed. At the time of payment the marks had fallen in value, which so far as it went was a gain for the defendant in error, and it was contended by the plaintiff in error that the gain was taxable income. But the transaction as a whole was a loss, and the contention was denied. Here there was no shrinkage of assets and the taxpayer made a clear gain. As a result of its dealings it made available $137,521.30 assets previously offset by the obligation of bonds now extinct. . . . The defendant in error has realized within the year an accession to income, if we take words in their plain popular meaning, as they should be taken here. . . .

C. NOTES AND QUESTIONS

1) The Principle of Annual Accounting

A general principle of the tax law is that each year's taxable income and the tax due are calculated without reference to any other year. Suppose, for example, that X Corp. starts in business in 1920 and loses $10,000, but in 1921 turns a $10,000 profit. X Corp. will obviously pay no income taxes in 1920, since it had no income in that year. However, because of the principle that each tax year stands on its own, X Corp. will not be permitted (absent special statutory dispensation) to use its 1920 losses in calculating its 1921 taxable income. Thus, it will owe taxes on its 1921 profits, even though over its history the corporation has merely broken even. Any unfairness created in particular cases is thought to be less significant than the overall importance of adhering to the annual accounting principle.

In the same year that it decided *Kirby Lumber*, the Supreme Court affirmed the annual accounting principle in Burnet v. Sanford & Brooks Co., 282 U.S. 359, 364 (1931):

> A taxpayer may be in receipt of net income in one year and not in another. The net result of the two years, if combined in a single taxable period, might still be a loss; but it has never been supposed that that fact would relieve him from a tax on the first, or that it affords any reason for postponing assessment of the tax until the end of a lifetime....
>
> It is the essence of any system of taxation that it should produce revenue ascertainable, and payable to the government, at regular intervals. Only by such a system is it practicable to produce a regular flow of income and apply the methods of accounting, assessment, and collection capable of practical operation. It is not suggested that there has ever been any general scheme for taxing income on any other basis....

Did *Kerbaugh-Empire*, decided five years before Burnet v. Sanford & Brooks, respect the principle that each tax year stands on its own? How did *Kerbaugh–Empire* adopt a transactional accounting, rather than an annual accounting, approach? See also Sections 172(a), (b)(1)(A), and (b)(1)(B). Are these sections an appropriate relaxation of the rigors of the annual accounting principle?

2) The Meaning of *Kirby Lumber*

Did *Kirby Lumber*, in which forgiveness of debt did produce income, overrule or distinguish *Kerbaugh-Empire*? The *Kirby Lumber* opinion states that, despite the taxpayer's repurchase of its bonds for less than their issue price, there was "no shrinkage of [the company's] assets." As a matter of economics, why is the court's statement nonsense?

> In point of fact, a taxpayer's ability to repurchase its bonds for less than their issue price is almost always evidence either (a) that its creditors have come to doubt its ability to pay the interest and principal on the due dates or (b) that the market rate of interest on bonds of comparable risk have

risen, making the taxpayer's bonds less attractive than similar new issues. If the bonds in *Kirby Lumber* dropped in value because of creditor doubts about the taxpayer's financial stability, there presumably was a decline of at least an equal amount in the value of the taxpayer's business as a going concern. A similar loss of going concern value would result from an increase in the market rate of interest; one of the few reliable stock market phenomena is that an increase in interest rates almost invariably causes stock prices to drop, reflecting a lower present value for the stream of income expected from corporate assets. Whichever of these events accounted for the taxpayer's ability in *Kirby Lumber* to repurchase its bonds at a discount, "the transaction as a whole" was not necessarily anymore profitable in *Kirby Lumber* than in *Kerbaugh-Empire*.[1]

By definition, the value of a corporation's assets equals the value of its stock and bonds, that is, the value of the business is the value of the ownership interests. If the value of a company's bonds falls, there is likely to be a corresponding decrease in the value of the corporation's assets. If there is a decrease in asset values, why isn't the loss available to offset the gain due to forgiveness of debt? Does your answer suggest that *Kirby Lumber* should be read as overruling, rather than distinguishing, *Kerbaugh-Empire*? And as rejecting transactional accounting rather than accepting it? Also, in this respect, how is *Kirby Lumber* like *Bruun*?

D. BRADFORD v. COMMISSIONER
233 F.2d 935 (6th Cir. 1956)

STEWART, CIRCUIT JUDGE.

The question here is whether the petitioner realized $50,000 income in 1946 when her liability upon a note for $100,000 was discharged for $50,000.

In 1938 the petitioner's husband owed a Nashville bank approximately $305,000. The debt had grown out of investment banking ventures he had engaged in prior to the depression. He had pledged most of his assets to the bank as collateral, but the greater part of the indebtedness was unsecured. The brokerage firm of which he was a member held a seat on the New York Stock Exchange. In October of 1938 the Exchange adopted a rule requiring each general partner of a member firm to submit a detailed report of his indebtedness. Fearing that disclosure of so much indebtedness might impair the position of his firm with the Exchange, he persuaded the bank to substitute the note of his wife, the petitioner, for a portion of his indebtedness. Accordingly, the petitioner executed her note to the bank for $205,000 without receiving any consideration in return. Her husband remained the obligor on two notes to the bank for $100,000 and so reported to the New York Stock Exchange.

---

1. Bittker and Thompson, Income from the Discharge of Indebtedness: The Progeny of United States v. Kirby Lumber Co., 66 Cal. L. Rev. 1159, 1163–1164 (1978).

About two years later the petitioner at the bank's request executed two notes to replace her $205,000 note, one for $105,000, on which all the collateral was pledged, and another for $100,000 which was unsecured. In 1943 a bank examiner required the bank to write off $50,000 of the petitioner's $100,000 unsecured note. In 1946 the bank advised petitioner that it was willing to sell the $100,000 note for $50,000, its then value on the bank's books. The petitioner's husband accordingly persuaded his half-brother, a Mr. Duval, to purchase the note from the bank for $50,000 with funds furnished by the petitioner and her husband. The Tax Court found that this transaction "was, in essence, a discharge of Mrs. Bradford's indebtedness for $50,000." The petitioner accepts the correctness of that finding, conceding that Duval "purchased the note as agent for the Bradfords and with no intention of enforcing same." The petitioner was solvent both before and after the note was discharged.

Upon these facts the Tax Court concluded that the petitioner had realized unreported ordinary income of $50,000 in 1946. . . . The petitioner asks us to reverse the Tax Court's decision upon two separate grounds: (1) that the cancellation of her $100,000 note for $50,000 was a "gratuitous forgiveness" upon the part of the bank and therefore a gift within the meaning of § [102(a)], and (2) that because she received nothing when the original note was executed by her in 1938, she did not realize income in 1946 when the note was cancelled for less than its face amount, even if the cancellation was not a gift.

The contention that what the petitioner received from the bank was a gift is grounded upon the testimony of the bank's president. He stated that the petitioner's husband had done a great deal of business with the bank, had met all his obligations during the depression, and that the bank looked forward to substantial future business with him. He further testified that although it might have been possible for the bank to collect the entire face amount of the note, "if I foreclosed on the proposition, put Mrs. Bradford out of her home, taken the furniture and liquidated everything he had, . . ." he considered it to the bank's best interest under the circumstances to forego a lawsuit so long as the bank could get the book value of the note paid. Upon cross-examination he stated explicitly that he considered the transaction a donation or gift by the bank of the $50,000 charged off.

The Tax Court found that the discharge of the note for $50,000 "was not a gift. . . . The bank's motive in selling the note for $50,000 was to liquidate its investment for book value. [The bank] was of the opinion that this was the best price available. Also by selling at this price the bank avoided the realization of taxable income on the recovery of a charged-off debt as well as the difficulties and uncertainties of enforced collection. . . . Also the bank did not wish to alienate petitioner and lose his future business by bringing suit against his wife.

"The instant transaction did not represent the discharge of a $50,000 indebtedness 'for nothing.' . . . We can only interpret the bank president's testimony as meaning that the bank was willing to sell the note at book value, and, if the transaction benefited petitioner, so much the better.". . .

. . . We cannot say that the Tax Court's ultimate finding that there was no gift in the present case was clearly erroneous, and we therefore accept it as we must. . . .

It was the view of the Tax Court that if there was no gift, the discharge of the $100,000 note for $50,000 clearly resulted in ordinary income in the amount of $50,000. . . . The Commissioner in effect adopts that view in his argument here. "It has become well settled," we are told, "that a profit is realized by a debtor whose obligation is extinguished by payment of an amount less than that which is owing, and that such profit constitutes gain which is taxable income within the broad sweep of Section [61(a)] of the Internal Revenue Code of 1939."

The statement quoted can be accepted without question as a correct general proposition of tax law, where the debtor is solvent [and] where there is no finding of a gift. . . . The proposition was first clearly announced by the Supreme Court in United States v. Kirby Lumber Co. . . . .

It is also a well settled general rule that each year's transactions are to be considered separately, without regard to what the net effect of a particular transaction might be if viewed over a period of several years. . . .

A mechanical application of these principles would of course support the Tax Court's decision. Looking alone to the year 1946 . . . it is obvious that when $100,000 of the petitioner's indebtedness was discharged for $50,000 in that year, she realized a balance sheet improvement of $50,000 which would be taxable as ordinary income under the rule of the Kirby Lumber Co. case. We cannot agree with the Commissioner, however, that these principles are to be applied so mechanically.

The fact is that by any realistic standard the petitioner never realized any income at all from the transaction in issue. In 1938 "without receiving any consideration in return," she promised to pay a prior debt of her husband's. In a later year she paid part of that debt for less than its face value. Had she paid $50,000 in 1938 to discharge $100,000 of her husband's indebtedness, the Commissioner could hardly contend that she thereby realized income. Yet the net effect of what she did do was precisely the same. We cannot agree that the transaction resulted in taxable income to her.

The conclusion we have reached is not without authority to support it. In Bowers v. Kerbaugh-Empire Co. . . . , the corporate taxpayer had borrowed money from a bank in Germany repayable in marks. The marks were immediately converted into dollars, and the money was lost in the performance of construction contracts by a subsidiary company over a period of years. In a subsequent year, the taxpayer repaid the loan with greatly devalued marks. The question for decision was "Whether the difference between the value of marks measured by dollars at the time of payment . . . and the value when the loans were made was income." The Court decided that it was not, saying that "The loss was less than it would have been if marks had not declined in value; but the diminution of loss is not gain, profit, or income." . . .

The Kerbaugh-Empire Co. case was decided before the Kirby Lumber Co. . . . . The case has been called "a frequently criticized and not easily understood decision.". . . . It is nonetheless a decision which has not been overruled.[2] Whatever validity the Kerbaugh-Empire Co. decision may now

---

2. The Supreme Court distinguished the Kerbaugh-Empire Co. case in . . . the Kirby Lumber Co. opinion.

have on its own facts, it remains an authority for the proposition that in deciding the income tax effect of cancellation of indebtedness for less than its face amount, a court need not in every case be oblivious to the net effect of the entire transaction. . . .

Courts have not hesitated in appropriate circumstances to look behind the cancellation of indebtedness in a given calendar year, and in doing so to evaluate in its entirety the transaction out of which the cancellation arose. Thus, it has been consistently held that the partial forgiveness of indebtedness in a given year does not constitute taxable income to the debtor if the actual effect of the entire transaction was simply to reduce the purchase price of property acquired in a prior year. . . .

Before concluding it should be emphasized that there is not before us on this review the question of the tax liability of petitioner's husband either in 1938 when his indebtedness was assumed by his wife, or in 1946 when it was discharged, nor do we have for decision any question as to the petitioner's gift tax liability. We have decided only that the petitioner herself under the circumstances of this case did not realize $50,000 of unreported income in 1946.

E. QUESTIONS

1) Why did Mr. Bradford arrange for his wife to assume his debt? Was this act a fraud on the New York Stock Exchange? Or was the Exchange at fault for writing loose disclosure rules?

2) Mr. Bradford and Mrs. Bradford filed separate returns for the tax years in question. Originally, the IRS brought cases against both of them, arguing that each had to report income arising from the forgiveness of debt. The IRS argued in the Tax Court that the assumption of Mr. Bradford's note by Mrs. Bradford produced taxable income to Mr. Bradford. The Tax Court disagreed and found that Mr. Bradford had no taxable income. Was that finding correct? Didn't Mr. Bradford's net worth increase when his wife assumed the liability? Wasn't that income? What statutory provision might justify excluding the gain?

3) The IRS also argued, before the Tax Court, that Mrs. Bradford realized $50,000 of income when the bank agreed to cancel her $100,000 note for $50,000. Mrs. Bradford responded that the gain was not taxable because the loan forgiveness was a "gift" under Section 102(a). The Tax Court held that Section 102(a) did not apply and found Mrs. Bradford taxable. Was its decision consistent with *Duberstein* (Chapter 10)?

4) The Tax Court treated Mrs. Bradford as if her note had been canceled by the bank for $50,000. But the actual facts were different. The bank actually sold the note to a Mr. Duval (Mr. Bradford's half-brother) for $50,000, a sum supplied to Duval by the Bradfords. Why was the Tax Court justified in ignoring Duval? Why did Mr. Bradford use Duval? What did he hope to achieve? Hint: If the transaction had not been recast, the note would have been sold at a discount, but no actual forgiveness of debt would have occurred.

5) Mrs. Bradford appealed her adverse decision from the Tax Court. The IRS did not appeal the decision against it in Mr. Bradford's case. Was the IRS decision not to appeal a mistake? After the Circuit Court found for Mrs. Bradford, should the IRS have been allowed to appeal Mr. Bradford's case, even though the time for filing had long passed?

6) How did the Circuit Court justify concluding that Mrs. Bradford realized no income in 1946? Didn't she have a gain in that year? What else did the Circuit Court take into account? Didn't the Circuit Court violate the basic rule that, absent specific statutory exception, each year's income must be calculated independently? How did the court use *Kerbaugh-Empire*?

7) Would you characterize Mrs. Bradford's assumption of her husband's liability in 1936 as a business transaction or as a gift? If characterized as a gift, then how can the "loss" be allowed to offset gain? Doesn't that violate Section 262?

8) If you view the Bradfords as one unit, then isn't it clear that the unit should have taxable income of $50,000 from forgiveness of debt?

9) Did the court in *Bradford* ignore all the considerations raised in the questions above and thereby permit a manifestly unjust result? Or was there some underlying equitable reason to give the Bradfords relief, unstated but hovering in the opinion? What did Mr. Bradford do with the $100,000 that he originally borrowed? What do you suppose happened to the assets he purchased? Is it possible that he was unable to deduct his losses? In the end, the result in *Bradford* may recall the claim of Alan Greenspan (chairperson of the President's Council of Economic Advisors under President Ford and head of the Federal Reserve Board under Presidents Reagan and Bush) that stockbrokers were hurt worse by the economic downturn of 1972–75 than anyone else.

10) Suppose Mrs. Bradford purchases stock for $50,000 and makes a gift of the stock to Mr. Bradford, who then sells it for $100,000. Under rules to be discussed in Chapter 22, the entire increase in the value of the stock is taxable to Mr. Bradford, the donee, when he sells the property. Instead of making a gift by giving property, Mrs. Bradford actually made a gift by assuming a liability. What is the difference between these two methods of making a gift? When a gift is made by the donor assuming a donee liability, what is the donor's cost? What is the benefit received by the donee? Why will a gain occur when the donor pays off the assumed donee liability for less than the full amount owed? Should the gain occurring in this context, like the gain on stock, be taxed to the donee? When?

SUBPART B

When Enough Has Happened, How Much Is the Gain or Loss?

Suppose that you buy Blackacre for $100,000 and later sell the property. How much gain should you report on the sale? The entire amount that you are paid—the "amount realized"—is obviously not the correct measure of gain. Gain arises only to the extent that the amount realized exceeds the cost or the *capital* invested. In other words, before determining gain from the sale of property, an allowance must be made for the *return of capital*. Similarly, if the amount realized is less than the cost, then the owner's capital has not been fully returned and the transaction has produced a loss.

These principles are implemented through a concept known as *basis*, which is one of the major themes of a basic course in federal income tax. Roughly speaking, basis equals the allowance that must be made for return of capital in order to determine gain or loss on property. In the simplest case, like that of Blackacre above, the basis equals the taxpayer's cost.

Readers may wish to refer to:

1) Section 1001(a), defining "gain from the sale or other disposition of property" as "the excess of the amount realized therefrom over the adjusted basis" and defining "loss" as the "excess of the adjusted basis over the amount realized."

2) Section 1001(b), defining "amount realized" as "any money received plus the fair market value of the property (other than money) received. . . ."

3) Section 1011(a), defining "adjusted basis for determining the gain or loss from the sale or other disposition of property" as "the basis [d]etermined under Section 1012 or other appropriate sections. . . ."

4) Section 1012, providing that "[t]he basis of property shall be the cost except as otherwise provided. . . ."

Chapter 21

PIECEMEAL AND INSTALLMENT SALES

A. INAJA LAND CO. v. COMMISSIONER
9 T.C. 727 (1947)

... The issue is whether petitioner received taxable income of $48,945 under a certain indenture of August 11, 1939, whereby it granted the city of Los Angeles, California, certain easements over its land and settling all claims arising out of the release of foreign waters from the city's Mono Craters Tunnel project. . . .

On or about January 26, 1928, petitioner acquired approximately 1,236 acres of land in Mono County, California, together with all water and water rights appurtenant or belonging thereto, at a cost of approximately $61,000. This property was located along the banks of the Owens River, which flows through and over petitioner's land, involved in this controversy. . . .

Petitioner's purpose in acquiring its properties was to operate a private fishing club thereon, with incidental rental of its properties for grazing livestock. It has conducted these activities since the time of its incorporation to date. . . .

The principal value of petitioner's lands to petitioner arose from the fishing facilities offered by the Owens River as it flowed through and over petitioner's land; but it also had some value for grazing purposes. The property was not used for agricultural purposes, other than livestock grazing. . . .

The Department of Water and Power of the City of Los Angeles, a municipal corporation, is responsible for the construction, operation, and maintenance of the water supply of that city. On or about September 25, 1934, the Department of Water and Power commenced the construction of Mono Craters Tunnel. . . .

During the entire period of the construction of the Mono Craters Tunnel, seepage waters from the tunnel in a substantial amount of between 10 and 15 cubic second feet flowed out of the east portal of the tunnel into the Owens River and through and over petitioner's lands. These seepage waters were polluted to a substantial extent by concrete dust, sediment, and foreign matter, which injured and killed fish and interfered with the fishing on petitioner's lands. . . .

Between September 25, 1934, the date the Mono Craters Tunnel project was commenced, and August 11, 1939, petitioner and its attorneys complained to the city and its officials. . . . Petitioner threatened to institute injunctive and other legal proceedings. After extended negotiations, petitioner and the city entered into an arm's length agreement settling their differences on August 11, 1939. . . .

Under the indenture of August 11, 1939, the petitioner reserved substantial beneficial interests in its properties and has continued to function and operate as a fishing club, with incidental leasing out of its lands for grazing livestock from the date of the indenture to the present time. The indenture permits the city to release foreign waters into the Owens River. . . .

The amounts of water released from the Mono Craters Tunnel into Owens River in the years 1939 to date have resulted in substantial injury and damage to petitioner and its properties in that (a) the quality and quantity of the fish have been reduced; (b) grazing lands have been damaged and grazing fodder reduced from 25 per cent to 35 per cent below its former quality and quantity; (c) irrigation ditches and intake gates have been damaged, necessitating repairs. . . .

The adjusted basis of petitioner's properties was more than $50,000 on January 1, 1939. Disregarding the sum in controversy, no event occurred in 1939 which would cause or require the adjusted basis of these properties to be reduced below $50,000 for the taxable year involved.

The petitioner's income . . . tax return for the taxable year 1939 did not report receipt of any income from the city of Los Angeles. . . .

Opinion

Leech, Judge: The question presented is whether the . . . amount . . . received by petitioner in the taxable year 1939 under a certain indenture constitutes taxable income . . . or is chargeable to capital account. . . . Petitioner maintains that the language of the indenture and the circumstances leading up to its execution demonstrate that the consideration was paid for the easement granted to the city of Los Angeles and the consequent damage to its property rights; that the loss of past or future profits was not considered or involved; that the character of the easement rendered it impracticable to attempt to apportion a basis to the property affected; and, since the sum received is less than the basis of the entire property, taxation should be postponed until the final disposition of the property.

The recitals in the indenture of August 11, 1939, indicate its principal purpose was to convey to the city of Los Angeles a right of way and perpetual easements to discharge water upon and flood the lands of petitioner, in connection with the water supply of the city. . . .

. . . Capital recoveries in excess of cost do constitute taxable income. Petitioner has made no attempt to allocate a basis to that part of the property covered by the easements. It is conceded that all of petitioner's lands were not affected by the easements conveyed. Petitioner does not contest the

Ch. 21   Piecemeal and Installment Sales

rule that, where property is acquired for a lump sum and subsequently disposed of a portion at a time, there must be an allocation of the cost or other basis over the several units and gain or loss computed on the disposition of each part, except where apportionment would be wholly impracticable or impossible. . . . Petitioner argues that it would be impracticable and impossible to apportion a definite basis to the easements here involved, since they could not be described by metes and bounds; that the flow of the water has changed and will change the course of the river; that the extent of the flood was and is not predictable. . . .

. . . Apportionment with reasonable accuracy of the amount received not being possible, and this amount being less than petitioner's cost basis for the property, it can not be determined that petitioner has, in fact, realized gain in any amount. Applying the rule as above set out, no portion of the payment in question should be considered as income, but the full amount must be treated as a return of capital and applied in reduction of petitioner's cost basis. . . .

B. NOTES AND QUESTIONS

1) How to Apportion Basis to the Part Sold

Suppose that in 1980 you buy four acres of farmland for $10,000. In 1982, you sell one acre to a real estate developer for $5,000. In 1986, you sell the remaining three acres for $30,000. How much gain should you report and when? One possibility would be to permit you to wait until the amount realized from selling the land piecemeal exceeds the cost (or basis) of the entire parcel. Under this method, since the $5,000 amount realized from selling the first acre does not exceed the $10,000 basis of the whole, no gain would be reported in 1982. Since $5,000 of basis is used up in 1982—to offset the amount realized in that year—the basis (or adjusted basis) for the remaining three acres would be $5,000. When these acres are sold in 1986 for $30,000, you would report $25,000 of gain, which is the excess of the amount realized over the adjusted basis.

In fact, Reg. § 1.61–6 prescribes a different method:

> When a part of a larger property is sold, the cost or other basis of the entire property shall be equitably apportioned among the several parts. . . .

Thus, assuming that the four acres are of equal value, $2,500 of the basis for the entire property would be allocated to the 1982 sale of one acre, producing $2,500 of gain at that time, and $7,500 would be allocated to the 1986 sale of three acres, producing $22,500 of gain. The total amount realized from disposing of all four acres would equal $25,000.

Notice that the choice of one basis allocation method or the other does not affect the total gain arising from selling all four acres. The choice only affects *when* the gain is reported.

2) Basis Allocation in *Inaja*

Does *Inaja* follow the instruction of Reg. § 1.61–6 that basis be "apportioned among the several parts"? What difficulty would arise if one attempted to allocate the basis for the whole between the part sold and the part retained? But see Example (2) of Reg. § 1.61–6.

3) The Stakes in *Inaja*

Suppose that (a) the land in *Inaja* originally cost $60,000; (b) the easement is sold for $50,000 in 1938; and (c) the land without the easement is sold for $130,000 in 1944.

How much total gain arises from both transactions? Under the *Inaja* decision, when is the gain taxed? If Reg. § 1.61–6 applied, when would the gain be taxed, assuming that the easement's value equals one-third of the value of the whole property? What was at stake in *Inaja*?

C. BURNET v. LOGAN
283 U.S. 404 (1931)

MR. JUSTICE MCREYNOLDS delivered the opinion of the Court.

... Prior to March, 1913, and until March 11, 1916, respondent, Mrs. Logan, owned 250 of the 4,000 capital shares issued by the Andrews & Hitchcock Iron Company. It held 12% of the stock of the Mahoning Ore & Steel Company, an operating concern. In 1895 the latter corporation procured a lease for 97 years upon the "Mahoning" mine and since then has regularly taken therefrom large, but varying, quantities of iron ore—in 1913, 1,515,428 tons; in 1914, 1,212,287 tons; in 1915, 2,311,940 tons; in 1919, 1,217,167 tons; in 1921, 303,020 tons; in 1923, 3,029,865 tons. The lease contract did not require production of either maximum or minimum tonnage or any definite payments. Through an agreement of stockholders (steel manufacturers) the Mahoning Company is obligated to apportion extracted ore among them according to their holdings.

On March 11, 1916, the owners of all the shares in Andrews & Hitchcock Company sold them to Youngstown Sheet & Tube Company, which thus acquired, among other things, 12% of the Mahoning Company's stock and the right to receive the same percentage of ore thereafter taken from the leased mine.

For the shares so acquired the Youngstown Company paid the holders $2,200,000 in money and agreed to pay annually thereafter for distribution among them 60 cents for each ton of ore apportioned to it. Of this cash Mrs. Logan received 250/4000ths—$137,500; and she became entitled to the same fraction of any annual payment thereafter made by the purchaser under the terms of sale. . . .

During 1917, 1918, 1919 and 1920 the Youngstown Company paid large sums under the agreement. Out of these respondent received on account of her 250 shares $9,900.00 in 1917, $11,250.00 in 1918, $8,995.50 in 1919, $5,444.30 in 1920—$35,589.80. . . .

Reports of income for 1918, 1919 and 1920 were made by Mrs. Logan. ... They included no part of what she had obtained from annual payments by the Youngstown Company. She maintains that until the total amount actually received by her from the sale of her shares equals their value on March 1, 1913, no taxable income will arise from the transaction. ...

On March 1, 1913, the value of the 250 shares then held by Mrs. Logan *exceeded* $173,089.80—the total of all sums actually received by her prior to 1921 from their sale ($137,500.00 cash in 1916 plus four annual payments amounting to $35,589.80). ...

The Commissioner ruled that the obligation of the Youngstown Company to pay 60 cents per ton had a fair market value of $1,942,111.46 on March 11, 1916; that this value should be treated as so much cash and the sale of the stock regarded as a closed transaction with no profit in 1916. He also used this valuation as the basis for apportioning subsequent annual receipts between income and return of capital. His calculations, based upon estimates and assumptions, are too intricate for brief statement.[1] He made deficiency assessments according to the view just stated and the Board of Tax Appeals approved the result.

The Circuit Court of Appeals held that, in the circumstances, it was impossible to determine with fair certainty the market value of the agreement by the Youngstown Company to pay 60 cents per ton. Also, that respondent was entitled to the return of her capital—the value of 250 shares on March 1, 1913. ... As this had not in fact been returned, there was no taxable income.

We agree with the result reached by the Circuit Court of Appeals. ...

... As annual payments on account of extracted ore come in they can be readily apportioned first as return of capital and later as profit. The liability for income tax ultimately can be fairly determined without resort to mere estimates, assumptions and speculation. When the profit, if any, is actually realized, the taxpayer will be required to respond. The consideration for the sale was $2,200,000.00 in cash and the promise of future money payments wholly contingent upon facts and circumstances not possible to foretell with anything like fair certainty. The promise was in no proper sense equivalent to cash. It had no ascertainable fair market value.

---

1. In the brief for petitioner the following appears:

"The fair market value of the Youngstown contract on March 11, 1916, was found by the Commissioner to be $1,942,111.46. This was based upon an estimate that the ore reserves at the Mahoning mine amounted to 82,858,535 tons; that all such ore would be mined; that 12 per cent (or 9,942,564.2 tons) would be delivered to the Youngstown Company. The total amount to be received by all the vendors of stock would then be $5,965,814.52 at the rate of 60 cents per ton. The Commissioner's figure for the fair market value on March 11, 1916, was the then worth of $5,965,814.52, upon the assumption that the amount was to be received in equal annual installments during 45 years, discounted at 6 per cent, with a provision for a sinking fund at 4 per cent. For lack of evidence to the contrary this value was approved by the Board. ...

"During the years here involved the Youngstown Company made payments in accordance with the terms of the contract, and respondents respectively received sums proportionate to the interests in the contract which they acquired by exchange of property. ...

"The Board held that respondents' receipts from the contract, during the years in question, represented 'gross income'; that respondents should be allowed to deduct from said gross income a reasonable allowance for exhaustion of their contract interests; and that the balance of the receipts should be regarded as taxable income."

The transaction was not a closed one. Respondent might never recoup her capital investment from payments only conditionally promised. Prior to 1921 all receipts from the sale of her shares amounted to less than their value on March 1, 1913. She properly demanded the return of her capital investment before assessment of any taxable profit based on conjecture.

> In order to determine whether there has been gain or loss, and the amount of the gain, if any, we must withdraw from the gross proceeds an amount sufficient to restore the capital value that existed at the commencement of the period under consideration. . . .

D. NOTES AND QUESTIONS

1) Burnet v. Logan and *Inaja* Compared

In both cases, the taxpayer was allowed to offset the entire basis against what amounted to only partial payment for the property. And in both the result was justified by uncertainty as to whether the taxpayer had any gain at all. What was the reason for the uncertainty in Burnet v. Logan? How does it compare with the reason for the uncertainty in *Inaja*?

2) The Stakes in Burnet v. Logan

Assume that (a) the basis of Ms. Logan's stock was $200,000, (b) she sold the stock for $150,000 in cash plus the right to future payments based on the amount of ore extracted from the Mahoning mine, and (c) the present value of the right to future payments was $150,000. Under the IRS approach, what was her gain when the stock was sold? Under the Supreme Court's approach?

Today, if her gain were taxed under the installment method, how much would she report when the stock was sold? Hint: Refer to Chapter 13 to determine how much of the stock's basis would offset the immediate cash payment?

3) Applying the Installment Method to Ms. Logan

Because the amount and timing of future payments was uncertain, Ms. Logan was not required to report any gain until total payments exceeded her basis. Today, although Section 453 may permit installment sellers to defer reporting gain until payment is received, it does not allow deferral until total payments exceed basis. Instead, Section 453(c) (like Reg. § 1.61–6) requires the basis to be apportioned so that gain is taxed ratably as each payment is received.

Section 453 provides for this apportionment of basis even when the timing and amount of future payments is uncertain. Under Section 453(j), the Treasury is authorized to issue regulations "providing for ratable basis recovery in transactions where the gross profit or the total contract price (or both) cannot be readily ascertained." The regulations provide three different methods. Where it is possible to ascertain a maximum amount that will be paid, that amount is treated as the selling price. Where a maximum price cannot be determined, but a maximum payment period can be, the basis is spread ratably over that time period. Where neither a maximum sales price nor time period can be determined, the basis is allocated evenly over fifteen years. Reg. § 15A.453–1(c).

4) Is Burnet v. Logan Dead?

If Section 453(j) and the regulations issued thereunder applied to Burnet v. Logan, how would the taxpayer's gain be accounted for? Would they, in fact, apply to her case today? Or, even with the enactment of Section 453(j), might the holding in Burnet v. Logan—permitting the taxpayer to defer reporting any gain until the amount realized exceeds her basis—have some continuing relevance? According to the Senate Finance Committee Report:

> [T]he effect of [Section 453(j)] is to reduce substantially the justification for treating transactions as "open" and permitting the use of the cost recovery method sanctioned by *Burnet v. Logan* . . . Accordingly, it is the Committee's intent . . . that its use be limited to those rare and extraordinary cases involving sales for a contingent price where the fair market value of the purchaser's obligation cannot reasonably be ascertained.[2]

Is this statement consistent with the reference in Section 435(j)(2) to "transactions where the gross profit or the total contract price (or both) cannot be readily ascertained." Given this language, why should Burnet v. Logan have any effect today at all?

5) Did Ms. Logan Really Make a Sale?

In Burnet v. Logan, was there a sale in substance—as well as in form—of the Andrews and Hitchcock Iron Company stock? A principal asset of Andrews and Hitchcock appears to have been stock of Mahoning Ore and Steel Co., and Mahoning's business was to operate the Mahoning iron ore mine. Although Ms. Logan transferred legal title of the Andrews and Hitchcock Iron Company stock, her future payments were contingent on the amount of ore produced by the Mahoning mine. Does this suggest that she did not really dispose of her entire investment?

6) Statutory Depletion

Congress has provided various methods, known as *depletion allowances*, for allocating basis to mineral deposits of uncertain extent. Under *cost depletion*, the basis is allocated over the estimated number of recoverable units. For example, if a coal deposit has a basis of $100,000 and is estimated to contain 10,000 tons of coal, then the basis of each ton mined and sold is treated as $10. If the mine turns out to contain less than 10,000 tons,

---

2. S. Rep. No. 1000, 96th Cong., 2d Sess. 24 (1980).

then the remaining basis may be deducted when the mine is sold. If the mine turns out to have more than 10,000 tons, then once 10,000 tons have been mined the entire basis has been deducted and the basis for any additional coal that is recovered is zero.

Under *percentage depletion,* a fixed percentage of income may be deducted each year. For coal mines, the statutory percentage is 10%. Section 613(b)(4). Percentage depletion may be deducted each year as long as the mine operates. As a result, *total depletion deductions often exceed the original basis.* This allowance for deductions in excess of basis can provide substantial tax incentives for mineral extraction, depending on the level of percentage depletion and the nature of the specific mining operation.

For years, the availability of high levels of percentage depletion (as much as 27½%) for producers of oil and gas was a major factor in stimulating petroleum production and consequently our society's reliance on the private automobile for transportation. The percentage has now been reduced to 22%, and percentage depletion is no longer available to large oil and gas producers.

Chapter 22

PART GIFT/PART SALE

A. GIFTS WITH UNREALIZED GAIN

Suppose that (a) in 1975, a donor buys AT&T stock for $1,000; (b) in 1980, the donor makes a gift of the stock when its value is $2,000; and (c) in 1982, the donee sells the stock for $2,500. Total appreciation, or gain, is $1,500 (the excess of the amount realized over the amount invested), $1,000 occurring while the donor owns the stock and $500 while the donee owns the stock. When should the gain be taxed and to whom?

One possibility would be to treat the making of the gift as producing realization. The donor could be taxed as if he or she had sold the property to the donee for cash in an amount equal to the fair market value of the property when the gift occurred. The donor would then report $1,000 in 1980 and the donee $500 in 1982.

Under the Code, however, a gift generally is not treated as a taxable event that produces realization of gain either to the donor or to the donee. Instead, appreciation in the gift is realized only when the donee sells or exchanges the property. In the above example, the donee would report the entire $1,500 appreciation in the value of the stock in 1982. The statutory provisions implementing this system are Section 102(a), which excludes, from the donee's income, property acquired by gift and Section 1015(a), which provides that "the basis [of property acquired by gift] shall be the same as it would be in the hands of the donor . . . ."

Which of these two methods of taxing gifts of appreciated property more accurately reflects the underlying economic realities—treating the gift as a sale for cash or treating the gift as not producing realization? What are the advantages for taxpayers of the second system over the first? What else is at stake besides when gain is taxed?

B. DIEDRICH v. COMMISSIONER
457 U.S. 191 (1982)

[Editor's Note: In *Diedrich*, parents made a gift of property to their children on condition that the children agree to assume a liability of the parents. The issue is whether the quid pro quo means that the so-called gift should be recharacterized, at least in part, as a sale.

The particular liability involved in *Diedrich* was of a type that may be unfamiliar to some readers and so a brief explanation may be helpful. The liability assumed by the children was the parents' obligation to pay a federal gift tax on the property transferred. The federal gift tax constitutes a separate and distinct tax from the income tax. It is imposed on the making of gifts and is payable by donors. Most people do not pay gift taxes because the tax comes into play only for gifts involving relatively large amounts. Each donor may exclude, from gift tax, the first $10,000 given to any single donee in a given year. In addition, each donor has a lifetime exemption of $600,000. Donors must pay a tax on gifts that do not qualify for either the annual per donee exclusion or the lifetime exemption.]

CHIEF JUSTICE BURGER delivered the opinion of the Court.

We granted certiorari to resolve a Circuit conflict as to whether a donor who makes a gift of property on condition that the donee pay the resulting gift tax receives taxable income to the extent that the gift tax paid by the donee exceeds the donor's adjusted basis in the property transferred.... The United States Court of Appeals for the Eighth Circuit held that the donor realized income.... We affirm.

I

In 1972 Petitioners Victor and Frances Diedrich made gifts of approximately 85,000 shares of stock to their three children.... The gifts were subject to a condition that the donees pay the resulting federal and state gift taxes. There is no dispute concerning the amount of the gift tax paid by the donees. The donors' basis in the transferred stock was $51,073; the gift tax paid in 1972 by the donees was $62,992. Petitioners did not include as income on their 1972 federal income tax returns any portion of the gift tax paid by the donees. After an audit the Commissioner of Internal Revenue determined that petitioners had realized income to the extent that the gift tax owed by petitioners but paid by the donees exceeded the donors' basis in the property....

II

A

Pursuant to its constitutional authority, Congress has defined "gross income" as income "from whatever source derived," including "[i]ncome from discharge of indebtedness." 26 U. S. C. § 61 (a)(12). This Court has recognized that "income" may be realized by a variety of indirect means. In *Old Colony Trust Co.* v. *Commissioner* . . . the Court held that payment of an employee's income taxes by an employer constituted income to the employee. Speaking for the Court, Chief Justice Taft concluded that "[t]he payment of the tax by the employe[r] was in consideration of the services rendered by the employee and was a gain derived by the employee from his labor." . . . The Court made clear that the substance, not the form, of the agreed transaction controls. "The discharge by a third person of an obligation to him is equivalent to receipt by the person taxed." . . . The employee, in other words, was placed in a better position as a result of the employer's discharge of the employee's legal obligation to pay the income taxes; the employee thus received a gain subject to income tax.

The holding in *Old Colony* was reaffirmed in *Crane* v. *Commissioner* [cited in Chapter 24]. In *Crane* the Court concluded that relief from the obligation of a nonrecourse mortgage in which the value of the property exceeded the value of the mortgage constituted income to the taxpayer. The taxpayer in *Crane* acquired depreciable property, an apartment building, subject to an unassumed mortgage. The taxpayer later sold the apartment building, which was still subject to the nonrecourse mortgage, for cash plus the buyer's assumption of the mortgage. This Court held that the amount of the mortgage was properly included in the amount realized on the sale, noting that if the taxpayer transfers subject to the mortgage,

> the benefit to him is as real and substantial as if the mortgage were discharged, or as if a personal debt in an equal amount had been assumed by another. . . .

Again, it was the "reality," not the form, of the transaction that governed. . . . The Court found it immaterial whether the seller received money prior to the sale in order to discharge the mortgage, or whether the seller merely transferred the property subject to the mortgage. In either case the taxpayer realized an economic benefit.

B

The principles of *Old Colony* and *Crane* control. A common method of structuring gift transactions is for the donor to make the gift subject to the condition that the donee pay the resulting gift tax, as was done in each of the cases now before us. When a gift is made, the gift tax liability falls on the donor under 26 U. S. C. §2502(d). When a donor makes a gift to a donee, a "debt" to the United States for the amount of the gift tax is incurred by the donor. Those taxes are as much the legal obligation of the donor as the donor's income taxes; for these purposes they are the same kind of debt obligation as the income taxes of the employee in *Old Colony, supra*. Similarly, when a donee agrees to discharge an indebtedness in consideration of the gift, the person relieved of the tax liability realizes an economic benefit. In short, the donor realizes an immediate economic benefit by the donee's assumption of the donor's legal obligation to pay the gift tax....

It cannot be doubted that the donors were aware that the gift tax obligation would arise immediately upon the transfer of the property; the economic benefit to the donors in the discharge of the gift tax liability is indistinguishable from the benefit arising from discharge of a preexisting obligation. Nor is there any doubt that had the donors sold a portion of the stock immediately before the gift transfer in order to raise funds to pay the expected gift tax, a taxable gain would have been realized.... The fact that the gift tax obligation was discharged by way of a conditional gift rather than from funds derived from a pregift sale does not alter the underlying benefit to the donors.

C

Consistent with the economic reality, the Commissioner has treated these conditional gifts as a discharge of indebtedness through a part gift and part sale of the gift property transferred. The transfer is treated as if the donor sells the property to the donee for less than the fair market value. The "sale" price is the amount necessary to discharge the gift tax indebtedness; the balance of the value of the transferred property is treated as a gift. The gain thus derived by the donor is the amount of the gift tax liability less the donor's adjusted basis in the entire property. Accordingly, income is realized to the extent that the gift tax exceeds the donor's adjusted basis in the property. This treatment is consistent with § 1001 of the Internal Revenue Code, which provides that the gain from the disposition of property is the excess of the amount realized over the transferor's adjusted basis in the property....

JUSTICE REHNQUIST, dissenting.

It is a well-settled principle today that a taxpayer realizes income when another person relieves the taxpayer of a legal obligation in connection with an otherwise taxable transaction.... In neither *Old Colony* nor *Crane* was there any question as to the existence of a taxable transaction; the only question concerned the amount of income realized by the taxpayer as a result of the taxable transaction. The Court in this case, however, begs the question of whether a taxable transaction has taken place at all when it concludes that "[t]he principles of *Old Colony* and *Crane* control" this case....

In *Old Colony*, the employer agreed to pay the employee's federal tax liability as part of his compensation. The employee provided his services to the employer in exchange for compensation. The exchange of compensation for services was undeniably a taxable transaction. The only question was whether the employee's taxable income included the employer's assumption of the employee's income tax liability.

In *Crane*, the taxpayer sold real property for cash plus the buyer's assumption of a mortgage. Clearly a sale had occurred, and the only question was whether the amount of the mortgage assumed by the buyer should be included in the amount realized by the taxpayer....

Unlike *Old Colony* or *Crane*, the question in this case is not the amount of income the taxpayer has realized as a result of a concededly taxable transaction, but whether a taxable transaction has taken place at all. Only *after* one concludes that a partial sale occurs when the donee agrees to pay the gift tax do *Old Colony* and *Crane* become relevant in ascertaining the amount of income realized by the donor as a result of the transaction. Nowhere does the Court explain why a gift becomes a partial sale merely because the donor and donee structure the gift so that the gift tax imposed by Congress on the transaction is paid by the donee rather than the donor.

In my view, the resolution of this case turns upon congressional intent: whether Congress intended to characterize a gift as a partial sale whenever the donee agrees to pay the gift tax. Congress has determined that a gift should not be considered income to the donee. [Section] 102. Instead, gift transactions are to be subject to a tax system wholly separate and distinct from the income tax.... Both the donor and the donee may be held liable for the gift tax.... Although the primary liability for the gift tax is on the donor, the donee is liable to the extent of the value of the gift should the donor fail to pay the tax. I see no evidence in the tax statutes that Congress forbade the parties to agree among themselves as to who would pay the gift tax upon pain of such an agreement being considered a taxable event for the purposes of the income tax. Although Congress could certainly determine that the payment of the gift tax by the donee constitutes income to the donor, the relevant statutes do not affirmatively indicate that Congress has made such a determination.

I dissent.

C. NOTES AND QUESTIONS

1) Characterization and Context

In *Diedrich*, the parents were relieved of a debt in return for transferring property to their children. In that context, the debt relief is treated as an amount paid for the property. Does *Diedrich* involve a forgiveness of debt as in *Bradford*? If the gift tax had been paid by Diedrich's employer (and if the employer had deducted the amount as a business expense), what would have been the income tax consequences for Diedrich? What if the gift tax had been paid by Diedrich's mother?

2) Bargain Sales at Arms' Length Between Two Unrelated Parties

Suppose that A transfers property worth $200 to B in exchange for property worth only $150. If A and B are relatives, then it may be proper to characterize as a gift the excess of the value of the property transferred by A over the value of the property received by A. In other words, it is as if A made a gift of $50 to B. Or if A is B's employer, then the excess may represent compensation for personal services.

But suppose the two parties have no relationship whatsoever, either familial or business, outside of the particular exchange. Would it then be proper to characterize the $50 excess as a gift from A to B? Or is it more likely that A simply made a bad deal?

3) Basis Allocation in *Diedrich*

Suppose that a parent has stock worth $200 with a basis of $40. The parent transfers the stock to a child in 1979 in return for the child assuming a $50 debt of the parent.

a) If the parent-child transfer is considered a gift (as argued by the taxpayer in *Diedrich*), how much is taxed to the parent when the gift is made?

b) Under *Diedrich*, how much income will the parent report when the stock is transferred? In order to answer this question, you need to consider separately the part treated as the subject of a parent-child gift and the part treated as the subject of a parent-child sale. How much gain will the parent report on the part that is a gift? How much gain will the parent report on the part that is sold? What is the amount realized on the part sold? How much of the $40 basis is allocated under *Diedrich* to the part sold? How does *Diedrich* resemble *Inaja*? Why is the method of allocating basis to the part sold in *Diedrich* inconsistent with Reg. § 1.61–6?

c) Suppose that the parent sells one-fourth of the stock to a third party for $50 in cash and gives the remaining three-fourths to the child. Under Reg. § 1.61–6, how much gain will be taxed to the parent when one-fourth of the stock is sold to an outsider (rather than to the child)?

d) Compare your answers to a), b), and c), above. In each instance, how much gain is taxable to the parent when the stock is transferred? In this example, how much is at stake in deciding whether to characterize the *Diedrich* transaction as entirely a gift or as a part gift/part sale? Once the transaction is characterized as partly a sale, how much is at stake in deciding whether to use the basis allocation method of *Inaja* or Reg. § 1.61–6? Which issue appears to be more important?

4) Is *Diedrich* Like *Inaja*?

Why did the IRS permit an *Inaja*-like basis allocation in *Diedrich*? Is there an appraisal problem as in *Inaja*? In order to allocate only a portion of the basis to the part sold, there must be some estimate of the stock's value. If this is closely held stock, why might such an estimate be difficult to obtain? In this particular case, hadn't an estimate already been made in order to levy the gift tax?

5) Sales to a Related Party at Cost: Has Enough Occurred to Justify Taxing the Gain?

If the difficulty of appraisal does not justify the basis allocation method adopted in *Diedrich*, is another rationale available? Suppose that the donor sells the stock to the donee but asks to be paid only what it cost. Under *Diedrich*'s method of allocating basis, how much gain does the donor realize from this part gift/part sale transaction? Under the method prescribed by

Ch. 22   **Part Gift/Part Sale**   345

Reg. § 1.61–6? (Use the numerical example from 3), above.) Which result do you prefer? Should the sale of appreciated property to a related party at cost produce realization? Has enough happened to make it an appropriate occasion for taxing the gain? In such a case, won't allocation of the entire basis to the part sold insure that no realization occurs?

Suppose that a parent buys a $100,000 house with $20,000 cash down and an $80,000 mortgage. Several years later, when the mortgage principal amount has been reduced to $50,000 and the house's value has risen to $125,000, the parent makes a gift of the house to his or her child in return for the child's agreement to assume the mortgage obligations. Should this gift produce realization of gain to the parent? Would it produce realization of gain under the basis allocation method of Reg. § 1.61–6?

Initially, the question of whether enough has happened to make it appropriate to tax a gain or a loss may seem separate and distinct from the question of how to measure the gain or loss. But *Diedrich* should indicate that these questions are often intertwined. How to measure the gain in *Diedrich*—that is, which basis allocation method to use—may depend on whether we think the sale of property at cost should be an occasion for taxing gain.

6) The Overall Stakes in *Diedrich*

Return to the numerical example in 3), above, in which a parent transfers stock worth $200 and with a $40 basis to a child in return for the child assuming a $50 debt of the parent. Suppose the child eventually sells the stock for $200 in cash.

a) Taxes aside, what is the total gain arising from the stock in this transaction?

b) How much of the gain is taxed to the child when she sells the stock?

In answering these questions, you need to consider three possibilities: (i) the parent-child transfer is considered to be entirely a gift (that is, the taxpayer's position in *Diedrich*); (ii) the parent-child transfer is considered to be part gift/part sale and an *Inaja*-like basis allocation method applies to the part sold by the parent (the IRS position in *Diedrich*); and (iii) Reg. § 1.61–6 applies to apportion basis for the parent between the sale part and the gift part (as it would if the parent made the gift and sale to different persons, rather than to the same person).

In addition, you need to determine the child's basis for the stock. What is the child's basis for the stock acquired by purchase? For the stock acquired by gift?

7) Bargain Sales to Charity

Section 1011(b) adopts the basis method of Reg. § 1.61–6 when the part gift/part sale is to a charity. Can you explain why Congress might have concluded that the sale of property at cost should not produce realization, except in the case of sale to a charity?

Suppose that stock costing $40 and now worth $200 is transferred to a charity for $50. Under *Diedrich*, the donor is considered to have sold $50 worth of stock and to have made a gift of $150. How much gain does the donor report as a result of the sale under the basis allocation method prescribed by Section 1011(b)? If the *Inaja-Diedrich* method is applied? How much gain will the charity report if and when it sells the stock, whichever basis allocation method applies to the donor?

Can Section 1011(b) be explained by the fact that if and when the charity sells the stock it will not have to recognize any gain at all since it is tax exempt? Or by the circumstance that the owner gets a charitable contribution deduction under Section 170(a) for the full value of the $150 gift, without ever being taxed on the unrealized stock gain?

Chapter 23

AFTER A NONRECOGNITION TRANSACTION

A. THE PARABLE OF "SAM WHO NEVER FORGETS"

(from a children's story)[1]

[E]very day at three o'clock Sam the zookeeper feeds the animals. Sam never forgets.

"Good afternoon, Giraffe," says Sam. "I have lovely green leaves for your dinner." "Hello Monkeys!" Sam says and hands them yellow bananas. Next is Seal. Sam throws him fish. And then comes Bear, who loves red berries. Sam feeds the hungry Crocodiles and long-legged Ostrich. He gives fresh meat to Lion and oats to quiet Zebra. Then Sam's wagon is empty. And off he goes.

But Elephant has not been fed! And poor Elephant, who is very hungry, bellows: "Did you forget? Oh, Sam! Did you forget?" But just as a tear starts to fall from Elephant's eye, just as Elephant starts to cry, Sam calls out, "Forget? I NEVER forget!"

And there is Sam with a wagon full of golden hay. Elephant trumpets: "Hooray for Sam! Sam who never, ever, never, Sam who never, never, forgets!"

B. INTRODUCTORY NOTE

How is the Internal Revenue Code sometimes like "Sam Who Never Forgets" but sometimes not? Suppose property previously acquired in a *nonrecognition* transaction is disposed of in a *taxable* sale or exchange. Will the *earlier* gain or loss, which was not recognized, be remembered and taken into account when the *later* taxable transaction occurs? In some cases, the

---

1. Eve Rice, Puffin Books, 1977. Although the text is abridged, ellipses are omitted to avoid distracting the reader. The complete text, with illustrations, is highly recommended to readers with, and without, children.

Code, like Sam, never forgets the earlier gain or loss; in other cases, the Code, unlike Sam, does forget. It depends on the character of the previous nonrecognition transaction.

Gains and losses arising from like-kind exchanges (Section 1031), losses arising from wash sales of stock (Section 1091), and gains on property transferred by inter vivos gift (Section 1015(a)) are all remembered. (These sections are like Sam.) But losses from related party sales (Section 267), losses on property transferred by inter vivos gift (Section 1015(a)), and gains and losses on testamentary gifts (Section 1014(a)) are not remembered. (These sections, in other words, are unlike Sam.)

The principal mechanism for determining whether the earlier gain or loss will be taken into account is the basis assigned to the property acquired in a nonrecognition transaction. When the earlier gain or loss is to be forgotten, the basis assigned to such property is its cost (or, if the property was acquired by gift, the fair market value when the gift occurred). When the earlier gain or loss is to be remembered, it usually becomes necessary to assign to the property a "basis" *other than its cost*. In that event, special rules determine the basis of property acquired in a nonrecognition transaction.

The following problems require you to apply the different rules for determining the basis of property acquired in a nonrecognition transaction in order to calculate the gain or loss arising from a subsequent taxable event.

C. LIKE–KIND EXCHANGES

1) You buy land A for $10,000. Later you exchange land A for land B, worth $80,000. Finally, you sell land B for $100,000. These events involve investments in two separate properties, land A and land B.

How much economic gain arises from each investment? How much is *realized* when land A is traded for land B? How much is *recognized* when land A is traded for land B? When land B is sold for cash, the amount that went unrecognized in the earlier like-kind exchange of A for B is to be taken into account. Thus, the realized gain when B is sold should equal (a) the gain that was not recognized on land A plus (b) the gain arising on land B. For this to happen, what must the basis for land B equal? (Recall that gain is the amount realized less the adjusted basis.)

What is the cost of land B (Hint: If you had paid cash for land B, what amount would you have had to pay?) What is its basis under Section 1031(d)? (The Section 1031(d) basis is referred to as a *carryover* basis, because the basis of the property traded in the like-kind exchange is *carried over* to the property received.) Why doesn't the basis of land B equal its cost? If the basis of land B equaled its cost, why would Section 1031 lead to exclusion, rather than deferral?

Does this problem assume that at the time of the exchange land A must be worth $80,000? Does it make any difference whether land A is actually worth $80,000, or less (say $70,000), or more (say $90,000)?

2) Assume that at the time of the exchange land A is worth only $70,000, but that land B is worth $80,000 and that, as a result, you have to exchange not only land A but also $10,000 in cash in order to receive land B. How does that affect your answers to the questions under 1), above? Why? See Section 1031(b).

It may help to recast the transaction, viewing it partly as a like-kind exchange of land A for land B and partly as a purchase of land B for cash. Then, the basis for the portion of land B acquired in a like-kind exchange must preserve for later taxation the earlier unrecognized amount. The basis for the portion of land B acquired for cash will be its cost.

3) Assume that at the time of the exchange land A is worth $100,000. Suppose that you exchange land A and receive not only land B (still worth $80,000) but also $20,000 in cash. How does that change your answers to the questions under 1), above? Will Section 1031(a) apply to grant nonrecognition to this transaction? What about Section 1031(b)?

Can this transaction be viewed as a part sale/part exchange? How does Section 1031(d) allocate basis between the part sold and the part exchanged? Suppose that you sold a 20% interest in land A to a third party and then exchanged the remaining 80% interest in land A for land B. How would the basis be allocated under Reg. § 1.61–6? Are the results consistent? Compare with the discussion of *Inaja* in Chapter 21 and *Diedrich* in Chapter 22.

4) Suppose that you exchange land A for land B, which is worth $80,000, plus a diamond necklace worth $20,000. After the exchange, what is the basis of land B? What is the basis of the necklace? Why not divide the total between land B and the necklace, for example, in proportion to their relative market values? Why does Section 1031 assign to land B a carryover basis and to the necklace a basis equal to its cost? Given the method of assigning basis between like-kind and non-like-kind property following a Section 1031 exchange, how much gain would be reported if land B were sold immediately for cash? If the necklace were sold immediately for cash? Why does Section 1031(d) allocate all of the unrecognized gain to land B and none of it to the necklace?

D. WASH SALES

Suppose that you buy five shares of Chrysler common stock for $100, sell them for $80 and, twenty days later, purchase another five shares of Chrysler common for $60. A year later, you sell the stock for $130. How much economic gain or loss arises from the first purchase and sale transaction? From the second? How much is recognized on the first transaction? See Section 1091(a).

In the second transaction, any unrecognized loss from the first transaction is taken into account. Thus, the realized gain or loss in the second transaction should equal (1) the loss arising on the first transaction, which was not recognized, plus (2) the gain or loss arising on the second transaction. In order for the second transaction to produce this result, what must be the basis of the stock acquired in the wash sale?

What is the cost of the stock acquired in the wash sale? What is its basis under Section 1091(d)? And why is it easier to figure out the basis (1) by thinking through what it must be if the earlier loss is to be taken into account at some later time than (2) by trying to understand and apply the mechanical rule of Section 1091(d)? Why is the basis not equal to its cost? If basis equaled cost, why would Section 1091 lead to exclusion, rather than deferral?

Without the special substituted basis provided under Section 1091(d), wouldn't Section 1091 be a more effective deterrent to tax avoidance through wash sales of stock? Or would it unfairly penalize taxpayers who sell stock and repurchase identical shares, not to avoid taxes, but because they have re-evaluated the stock's prospects?

E. RELATED PARTY SALES

Suppose that Parent buys Chrysler stock for $500 and later sells it to Child for $100. Child resells the stock for $20. How much economic gain or loss arises while Parent owns the stock? While Child owns the stock? How much is recognized when Parent sells the stock? See Section 267(a). When Child sells the stock? Note that Section 267 does not provide for any special adjustment in the child's stock basis.

How does Section 267 provide for exclusion, rather than deferral, of losses realized from related party sales? Is there any justification for not allowing the earlier loss to be "remembered" and taken into account in a later taxable transaction?[2]

What difference does it make if the stock is resold by Child for $100? For $200? See Section 267(d). In what limited circumstances does Section 267 "remember" the earlier loss and provide for it to be taken into account in a later taxable transaction?

F. INTER VIVOS AND TESTAMENTARY GIFTS

Suppose that the stock referred to in E, above, is transferred by inter vivos gift instead of by sale. How does that change your answers to the questions posed in E? See Section 1015(a), lines 4–7.[3]

When the stock is resold by the child for $200, the basis for determining gain produces a loss and the basis for determining loss produces a gain. In that event, what should the donee report? In what limited circumstances does Section 1015(a) remember the earlier loss and provide that it be taken into account in a later taxable transaction? How is the result parallel to that provided by Section 267(d) in the case of related party sales at a loss?

---

2. If the seller and buyer are spouses, however, the buyer's basis will apparently be the seller's basis. See Section 1041 (Chapter 12). Thus, the earlier loss will be remembered and taken into account on the buyer's disposition.

3. If the donor and donee are spouses, however, the donee's basis will apparently be the donor's basis for determining loss as well as gain. See Section 1041 (Chapter 12). Thus, the donor's loss will be remembered and taken into account on donee disposition.

Suppose that the stock referred to in E, above, is transferred by testamentary gift. How does that change your answers to the questions in E, above? See Section 1014(a)(1).

G. KURTZ AND SURREY, REFORM OF DEATH AND GIFT TAXES: THE 1969 TREASURY PROPOSALS, THE CRITICISMS, AND A REBUTTAL
70 Col. L. Rev. 1365, 1381–1389, 1397–1399 (1970)

INCOME TAXATION ON APPRECIATION OF ASSETS AT DEATH

A. The Existing System

The most serious defect in our federal tax structure today is an income tax defect associated with death. This defect is the failure of the income tax to reach the appreciation in value of assets transferred at death. Our income tax system does not tax the annual appreciation in value of an asset. Yet it is clear that such appreciation is "income" and that the person benefiting from such appreciation has the same ability to pay tax on it as does the recipient of income in the form of salary or dividends. In most cases—particularly where marketable securities are involved—the taxpayer could reach out his hand and obtain the income, i.e., sell the asset and thereby acquire the actual funds. But if he stays his hand, our income tax stays its demand and the income—the increase in value—goes currently untaxed. In more technical terms, the income tax for a variety of reasons will await the time when the income is "realized." In some cases the person may not be readily able to sell the asset; in some cases valuation may be troublesome; other problems might arise in the taxation of accrued but unrealized gains. The aspect here relevant is not the decision to leave such unrealized gains currently untaxed, but rather the consequences of that decision under the present system.

One might suppose that the decision not to tax the unrealized gain would result only in a postponement of the tax and not its complete forgiveness. And indeed, if an[d] when the asset is sold and the gain is realized, that gain will then be taxed even though it in fact may be attributable to prior years. The tax will be based on capital gains rates rather than on the higher ordinary income rate, but that aspect of the income tax system turns on other issues. But suppose a sale is steadily postponed and the owner dies, so that he cannot himself sell the asset. Is the postponement then to mean complete forgiveness? Our income tax structure today has just that effect—it turns postponement into forgiveness by not including the appreciation in the decedent's final income tax return while at the same time allowing the heirs to take as *their* income tax basis, i.e. *their* tax cost on a later sale by them, the asset's fair market value at the time of the decedent's death. The appreciation ipso facto becomes capital and beyond the reach of the income tax. This change from postponement to forgiveness has two far-reaching consequences. From a revenue standpoint, it results in a large escape from the income tax and a consequent serious revenue loss under that tax. As far as equitable considerations are concerned, it has the effect of seriously discriminating between those families who can build their estates through such untaxed appreciation and those who have to build them out of after-tax dollars. . . .

The complete illogic of the present system can be illustrated in many ways. The following example, furnished by Gerard Brannon, should suffice: Assume that each of two individuals, A and B, obtains throughout his adult life a salary of $40,000, all of which is used for current consumption and for the payment of income tax thereon. Assume that each also has an investment account used for saving. In the case of A, all of the yield is in the form of dividends and interest, averaging $50,000 a year and subject to the income tax at, say a 50% rate. A's 40 years of after-tax accumulation in this account comes to $1,000,000. B has his investment account in growth securities with no current yield and with no lifetime realization of the appreciation. Assume that B's average annual appreciation is $50,000, the same amount as A's before-tax yield. B's accumulation over 40 years aggregates $2,000,000. By hypothesis, the two individuals have comparable consumption patterns, i.e., they live in the same kind of house, eat the same kind of food, take similar vacations. The difference is that B's savings, and hence his estate, are built from unrealized and untaxed appreciation, while A's savings and his estate are built out of after-tax income. B has been able to build up the larger estate because the income tax system stayed its hand. But once B has died, there is no reason for that system to continue the postponement and leave the appreciation forever untaxed. The factors which stayed the tax initially when the appreciation accrued are clearly no longer pertinent. B's assets must now be valued for estate tax purposes and some presumably will have to be sold to pay that tax.

It is certainly no answer—though some continue to assert it as if it were—that the appreciation is not wholly untaxed inasmuch as B must pay an *estate tax* on the appreciation. The pertinent tax under consideration is the *income tax* which B escapes. As the Treasury proposals state:

> The estate tax will fall on both A and B so it is not relevant to say that B ought not to pay any income tax on his accumulation of wealth "because he pays an estate tax." A has paid income tax on the money that he earned to build an estate *and* an estate tax. B avoided income tax on his wealth increase and *only* an estate tax is paid on it.

Suppose B had decided to sell all his securities in order either to embark on a new investment plan or to increase his consumption, but unfortunately died soon after the sale. B would then have paid his income tax on the appreciation so that his savings are now "after-tax" as are A's savings, but B's estate will also pay an estate tax on the savings. No one has seriously attempted to justify on any logical ground why B should go untaxed under the *income tax* if he had decided not to sell and had then died holding the appreciated assets. There are other arguments advanced to perpetuate the present illogic and inequity, but these can be considered after the Treasury proposal has been described.

B. The Treasury Proposal

Under the Treasury proposal the appreciation in value of assets held at death would be subject to income taxation at that time and would be included in the decedent's final income tax return. The appreciation in capital assets would be treated as long-term capital gain, taxable at the preferential rates applicable to that gain. The assets would, as under present law, take as their new basis the value at death or at the ultimate valuation date. (The appreciation on other assets, and accrued income items, would be taxed as ordinary income.) Declines in value of capital assets would be treated as capital losses, which could be carried back for three years against capital gains and, after appropriate reductions to reflect the excluded portion of gains, against ordinary income. . . .

OBJECTIONS TO THE PROPOSALS

Over a year has passed since the Treasury proposals were made public. While the testimony at the Ways and Means Committee Hearing in 1969 was not extensive, a majority of the witnesses testifying on this subject opposed the proposals. In view of the extent to which these witnesses were self-selected, however, their testimony is not a good measure of the general reaction to the proposals on their merit. This seems also to be true of those who have written on the proposals since that time. Different critics of the proposals state the arguments differently, but most of the adverse criticism can be classified into a few broad categories for purposes of analysis.

None of the critics of the proposals, however, has dealt directly with the inequities in the existing system. Their comments instead have generally been directed to some of the anticipated effects of the proposed changes, usually without suggesting any alternatives to cure the problems discussed at the beginning of this article and usually without any satisfactorily articulated reasoning as to why the changes are perceived as undesirable.

A. Income Taxation of Asset Appreciation at Death

Most of the objections to the proposal for income taxation of the appreciation in assets transferred at death are either specious or are directed at debating points that are minor indeed when considered in the perspective of the stakes involved. Thus, some critics persist in contending that the unrealized capital gain at death does not escape taxation since the estate tax rates apply to the full asset at death—and in so contending never bother to point out that those estates built up from "after-income tax" dollars also pay the estate tax. Others state that it is unfair to tax the appreciation at death since the asset may later decline in value—but conveniently overlook the fact that the estate tax itself is applied, often at much higher rates than the capital gain rate, to those same values at death, despite the possibility that they may decline. Of course, the assets may, on the other hand, appreciate still more in value, but any subsequent value changes are properly treated as gain or loss to the heirs. Some critics make much of the contention that the executor may not have adequate records to show the income tax basis of the appreciated assets. But most of the assets involved will be marketable securities and their basis can usually be reconstructed in the cases where it is not recorded. Moreover, improved record-keeping, if improvement is necessary, will come about. The situation must be kept in perspective: we are considering . . . billion[s] in appreciation each year, and the taxation of such a significant amount of gain, if otherwise appropriate, can hardly be faulted because some records are found wanting. Finally, in this category is the argument that such income taxation on appreciation at death has not been imposed before in this country. This observation of course is correct—and is the reason why change is now needed....

Others raise the argument that the appreciation in the value of the transferred assets mirrors inflationary change so that taxation is unfair. But this contention would apply as well to lifetime sales, and indeed it is one of the principal contentions pushed by opponents of any capital gains tax. Our tax system has rejected the contention and does include capital gains in income, though at a preferred rate. There is no reason after rejecting the contention when lifetime sales are involved to turn around and accept the contention when the asset is transferred at death. Nor does the contention itself have merit. As the Treasury proposals state, "over the long run the principal assets involved in appreciation [in asset value at death], land and stocks, have increased in price over twice as fast as consumer prices." This actually understates the case; between World War II and 1970 consumer prices have risen about 2½ times, but stock prices have increased eightfold. Even the part of the asset appreciation that corresponds to general price inflation does in fact represent a "gain" to the asset holders compared with those not so fortunately situated—those, for example, who hold cash, bonds, pension rights, and other fixed claims. Persons holding property such as stocks and land are able to avoid the losses that are imposed by inflation on those who hold such fixed claims. As the Treasury proposals further state:

> The entire tax system is based on money income. Inflation gains are not excluded, nor are deductions allowed for inflation losses. An obvious reason for taxing inflation gains is that to the extent of inflation gains an individual benefits by escaping from the reduction of purchasing power that inflation imposes on holders of fixed dollar claims. The burden can be shared more equally if some tax is imposed on the benefit from escaping inflation.

There are more pragmatic critics who see that the sheer unfairness and illogic of the present system are beginning to be understood by both Congress and the public at large. They also recognize that, as a consequence, the time for change appears to be at hand; and hence an orderly retreat is more appropriate than a diehard defense of the present system. They therefore agree that the present system is wrong. However, they urge that the corrective course is not to tax the appreciation at death but rather to adopt a carry-over of basis system under which the decedent's basis would become the tax basis for the heirs. But this suggestion does indeed represent no more than ground yielded in retreat, rather than a solution possessing any real advantages over the Treasury proposal. Moreover, the carry-over basis suggestion involves serious disadvantages. To turn back to our example of individuals A and B, the former with an after-tax estate and the latter with untaxed appreciation, why should B's advantages persist even after his death and result in his family having a larger inheritance simply because he has thus far escaped an income tax? And why should his heirs be able to keep that larger inheritance until they sell the property? Whatever the validity of the reasons that underlie the policy decision not to tax B's accrued but unrealized appreciation during his lifetime—e.g., that he may not be able to sell the asset, that it may be hard to value the asset, that he may not have the cash to pay the tax without a sale of the asset—those reasons no longer obtain at B's death when the imposition of an estate tax requires valuation and most likely a sale of at least some of the assets in order to pay the tax. Moreover, further postponement of the tax can only harden the lock-in effect, for under a carry-over system B's heirs would face the prospect that sale by them would result in tax liability while continued holding would not.

It is important in this connection not to lose sight of the overall situation. The problem is one of determining the amount of tax that should be levied on a decedent's wealth when he dies. The Treasury proposals would require a final income tax tally on a decedent's hitherto untaxed appreciation in asset values. This would result in a settling of accounts as between estates with much untaxed appreciation and those with little such appreciation. Death is the appropriate occasion for these final accountings. There is no reason to hold some of the books open and, at some future occasion when the heirs sell the assets, to close the books on the appreciation. The untaxed appreciation was experienced by the decedent, and his death is the appropriate occasion for closing that account.

A last point urged by some critics—and really the only relevant one—is the possible effect of this proposal on estates consisting of closely held businesses or farms with significantly appreciated values. The real issue here is that of the liquidity, or rather the possible illiquidity, of such estates in that income taxation at death could aggravate any difficulties that may be present in finding the funds to pay the taxes occasioned by death. But this point also must be kept in perspective. By far the major share of those estates of which asset appreciation is a significant part consist largely of diversified stocks and securities; such estates do not present this illiquidity problem. Criticism based on illiquidity in estates where closely held businesses are involved should not, therefore, be permitted to cloak opposition to the change over the broad area where that aspect is not present. We will return to the aspect of liquidity after considering the objections to the remainder of the Treasury proposals. . . .

[Critics] treated the liquidity problem as the basis for an argument against the imposition of a capital gains tax at death on the ground that this tax would be particularly burdensome to "moderate" estates with illiquid business interests. It is true that a moderate size estate with illiquid business interests and with substantially appreciated assets may in some situations have difficulty meeting the death tax burdens. It is also true that such an estate may have a higher deathtime tax burden under the Treasury proposals than it now has. It is equally true, however, that decedents leaving estates with substantially appreciated assets have been preferentially taxed during life compared with others whose estates of equal size are composed of unappreciated, after-tax, wealth accumulations. The burden is relatively heavier at death only because it has been relatively lighter during life, and there seems no good reason to perpetuate this inequity by foregoing at death all or a part of the tax that has been paid by others during life.

Moreover, any general argument against the capital gains tax at death on the grounds of illiquidity overemphasizes the magnitude of the liquidity problem. By far the greatest element of appreciation in assets held in taxable estates is in marketable securities. If closely held businesses or farms present a special problem, then the special problem should be dealt with as such. The existing inequity of permanently omitting appreciation in assets held at death from the income tax base should not be continued on the ground that problems may exist in regard to a small percentage of such assets. The liquidity problems that may be faced by a small minority of estates should not be permitted to shield all other estates from proper tax rules.

The suggestion for providing special lower values for closely held business interests and farms, while having the virtue of being limited to illiquid assets, seems inequitable and perhaps self-defeating in the long run. Our transfer tax system is based on ability to pay as measured by wealth in economic terms. A grant of preferential tax treatment to certain types of assets over others must be based on non-tax considerations, and these considerations are articulated at least by the proponents of special valuation rules for farms. The principal reason advanced is the desirability of encouraging the family farm. But if the family farm is in fact worth much more than is indicated by its earning capacity as a farm, it is because there is some use for the land on which the marketplace puts a higher value than farming. It may be that there is a reason to encourage family farming as a matter of national policy, but, if there is, the reduction in estate tax seems an inefficient way of providing it. Moreover, one explanation given for high farm land values is that nonfarmers bid the land up for personal reasons—for use as hunting preserves, country homes, gentlemen farms, or for the acquisition of income tax "farm losses." Granting estate tax preference to these assets as compared to other "investments" could well lead to greater demands for these properties, with a further increase in their values, thereby adding to the problems of farmers in finding economical farm land.

Some witnesses argued against the Treasury proposals granting time extensions for the payment of tax in illiquid estates on the ground that the farms involved would never produce enough income to pay the tax. If this argument is true, it is because the farm produces a low rate of return on the value of the investment. If the return from farming is lower than that which optimal economic use of the land could command, it follows that the owner continues to farm, not for business reasons, but rather for consumption purposes—he perhaps enjoys the life or likes the land for sentimental reasons. Other individuals may have equally strong emotional reasons for wanting to hold other non-businesss assets such as art works, a family estate, collections of all kinds. But these latter preferences are not recognized for tax purposes, and the preference for a farm should not be recognized either. It seems unwise, as a matter of tax policy, to encourage or reward one type of consumption more than another.

The same general reasoning applies to closely held businesses. If the business has a certain fair market value, the estate should pay the tax on that value, since it represents wealth accumulated but untaxed during the decedent's lifetime. It should not be treated preferentially in relation to other assets accumulated out of after-tax income or in relation to investments in other assets. If the business yields are unusually low, the business assets are not being put to their best use, and it is reasonable to infer that there are non-business consumption reasons for wanting to continue such an uneconomic employment of assets. . . .

[Editor's Note: The 1969 Treasury Proposals were never adopted. In 1976, Congress did enact Section 1023 to provide that gains or losses on property transferred by testamentary gift be preserved for later recognition by the donee.[4] However, after the new provision generated controversy, Congress postponed its effective date and then repealed it altogether, restoring the primacy of Section 1014(a).]

---

4. Section 1023 was written to apply only to gains or losses arising after its effective date. If property was acquired *after* the effective date, the testamentary donee's basis was to be the donor's basis. If property was acquired *before* the effective date of Section 1023, its basis in the hands of a testamentary donee was to be the property's fair market value on the effective date.

Chapter 24

EFFECT OF MORTGAGES ON BASIS AND AMOUNT REALIZED

A. COMMISSIONER v. TUFTS
461 U.S. 300 (1983)

JUSTICE BLACKMUN delivered the opinion of the Court.

Over 35 years ago, in *Crane v. Commissioner* . . . this Court ruled that a taxpayer, who sold property encumbered by a nonrecourse mortgage (the amount of the mortgage being less than the property's value), must include the unpaid balance of the mortgage in the computation of the amount the taxpayer realized on the sale. The case now before us presents the question whether the same rule applies when the unpaid amount of the nonrecourse mortgage exceeds the fair market value of the property sold.

I

On August 1, 1970, respondent Clark Pelt, a builder, and his wholly owned corporation, respondent Clark, Inc., formed a general partnership. The purpose of the partnership was to construct a 120-unit apartment complex in Duncanville, Tex., a Dallas suburb. . . . Six days later, the partnership entered into a mortgage loan agreement with the Farm & Home Savings Association (F&H). Under the agreement, F&H was committed for a $1,851,500 loan for the complex. In return, the partnership executed a note and a deed of trust in favor of F&H. The partnership obtained the loan on a nonrecourse basis: neither the partnership nor its partners assumed any personal liability for repayment of the loan. . . .

. . . [The] partnership's adjusted basis in the property in August 1972 was $1,455,740.

In 1971 and 1972, major employers in the Duncanville area laid off significant numbers of workers. As a result, the partnership's rental income was less than expected, and it was unable to make the payments due on the mortgage. Each partner, on August 28, 1972, sold his partnership interest to an unrelated third party, Fred Bayles. As consideration, Bayles agreed to reimburse each partner's sale expenses up to $250; he also assumed the nonrecourse mortgage.

On the date of transfer, the fair market value of the property did not exceed $1,400,000. Each partner reported the sale on his federal income tax return and indicated that a partnership loss of $55,740 had been sustained.[1] The Commissioner of Internal Revenue, on audit, determined that the sale resulted in a partnership capital gain of approximately $400,000. His theory was that the partnership had realized the full amount of the nonrecourse obligation. . . .[2]

II

Section 752(d) of the Internal Revenue Code of 1954, 26 U.S.C. § 752(d), specifically provides that liabilities involved in the sale or exchange of a partnership interest are to "be treated in the same manner as liabilities in connection with the sale or exchange of property not associated with partnerships." Section 1001 governs the determination of gains and losses on the disposition of property. Under § 1001(a), the gain or loss from a sale or other disposition of property is defined as the difference between "the amount realized" on the disposition and the property's adjusted basis. Subsection (b) of § 1001 defines "amount realized": "The amount realized from the sale or other disposition of property shall be the sum of any money received plus the fair market value of the property (other than money) received." At issue is the application of the latter provision to the disposition of property encumbered by a nonrecourse mortgage of an amount in excess of the property's fair market value.

A

In *Crane v. Commissioner,* supra, this Court took the first and controlling step toward the resolution of this issue. Beulah B. Crane was the sole beneficiary under the will of her deceased husband. At his death in January 1932, he owned an apartment building that was then mortgaged for an amount which proved to be equal to its fair market value. . . . The widow, of course, was not personally liable on the mortgage. She operated the

---

1. The loss was the difference between the adjusted basis of $1,455,740, and the fair market value of the property, $1,400,000. On their individual tax returns, the partners did not claim deductions for their respective shares of this loss. In their petitions to the Tax Court, however, the partners did claim the loss.

2. The Commissioner determined the partnership's gain on the sale by subtracting the adjusted basis of $1,455,740, from the liability assumed by Bayles, $1,851,500. . . .

building for nearly seven years ... but did not make payments upon the mortgage principal....

In November 1938, with her hopes unfulfilled and the mortgage threatening foreclosure, Mrs. Crane sold the building. The purchaser took the property subject to the mortgage and paid Crane $3,000; of that amount, $500 went for the expenses of the sale.

Crane reported a gain of $2,500 on the transaction. She reasoned that her basis in the property was zero ... and that the amount she realized from the sale was simply the cash she received. The Commissioner disputed this claim. He asserted that ... the amount realized was the net cash received plus the amount of the outstanding mortgage assumed by the purchaser.

In upholding the Commissioner's interpretation ... the Court observed that to regard merely the taxpayer's equity in the property as her basis would ... require the basis to be recomputed with each payment on the mortgage.... The effect of the Court's ruling was that the taxpayer's basis was the value of the property undiminished by the mortgage....

The Court next proceeded to determine the amount realized.... In order to avoid the "absurdity" ... of Crane's realizing only $2,500 on the sale of property worth over a quarter of a million dollars, the Court treated the amount realized as it had treated basis, that is, by including the outstanding value of the mortgage. To do otherwise would have permitted Crane to recognize a tax loss unconnected with any actual economic loss....

Crane, however, insisted that the nonrecourse nature of the mortgage required different treatment. The Court, for two reasons, disagreed. First, excluding the nonrecourse debt from the amount realized would result in the same absurdity and frustration of the Code.... Second, the Court concluded that Crane obtained an economic benefit from the purchaser's assumption of the mortgage identical to the benefit conferred by the cancellation of personal debt. Because the value of the property in that case exceeded the amount of the mortgage, it was in Crane's economic interest to treat the mortgage as a personal obligation; only by so doing could she realize upon sale the appreciation in her equity represented by the $2,500 boot. The purchaser's assumption of the liability thus resulted in a taxable economic benefit to her, just as if she had been given, in addition to the boot, a sum of cash sufficient to satisfy the mortgage.

In a footnote, pertinent to the present case, the Court observed:

> Obviously, if the value of the property is less than the amount of the mortgage, a mortgagor who is not personally liable cannot realize a benefit equal to the mortgage. Consequently, a different problem might be encountered where a mortgagor abandoned the property or transferred it subject to the mortgage without receiving boot. That is not the case....

B

This case presents that unresolved issue. We are disinclined to overrule *Crane*, and we conclude that the same rule applies when the unpaid amount of the nonrecourse mortgage exceeds the value of the property transferred.

Crane ultimately does not rest on its limited theory of economic benefit; instead, we read *Crane* to have approved the Commissioner's decision to treat a nonrecourse mortgage in this context as a true loan. This approval underlies *Crane's* holdings that the amount of the nonrecourse liability is to be included in calculating both the basis and the amount realized on disposition. That the amount of the loan exceeds the fair market value of the property thus becomes irrelevant.

When a taxpayer receives a loan, he incurs an obligation to repay that loan at some future date. Because of this obligation, the loan proceeds do not qualify as income to the taxpayer. When he fulfills the obligation, the repayment of the loan likewise has no effect on his tax liability.

Another consequence to the taxpayer from this obligation occurs when the taxpayer applies the loan proceeds to the purchase price of property used to secure the loan. Because of the obligation to repay, the taxpayer is entitled to include the amount of the loan in computing his basis in the property; the loan, under § 1012, is part of the taxpayer's cost of the property. Although a different approach might have been taken with respect to a nonrecourse mortgage loan,[3] the Commissioner has chosen to accord it the same treatment he gives to a recourse mortgage loan. The Court approved that choice in *Crane*, and the respondents do not challenge it here. The choice and its resultant benefits to the taxpayer are predicated on the assumption that the mortgage will be repaid in full.

When encumbered property is sold or otherwise disposed of and the purchaser assumes the mortgage, the associated extinguishment of the mortgagor's obligation to repay is accounted for in the computation of the amount realized. . . . Because no difference between recourse and nonrecourse obligations is recognized in calculating basis, *Crane* teaches that the Commissioner may ignore the nonrecourse nature of the obligation in determining the amount realized upon disposition of the encumbered property. He thus may include in the amount realized the amount of the nonrecourse mortgage assumed by the purchaser. The rationale for this treatment is that the original inclusion of the amount of the mortgage in basis rested on the assumption that the mortgagor incurred an obligation to repay. Moreover, this treatment balances the fact that the mortgagor originally received the proceeds of the nonrecourse loan tax-free on the same assumption. Unless the outstanding amount of the mortgage is deemed to be realized, the mortgagor effectively will have received untaxed income

---

3. The Commissioner might have adopted the theory, implicit in Crane's contentions, that a nonrecourse mortgage is not true debt, but, instead, is a form of joint investment by the mortgagor and the mortgagee. On this approach, nonrecourse debt would be considered a contingent liability, under which the mortgagor's payments on the debt gradually increase his interest in the property while decreasing that of the mortgagee. . . . Because the taxpayer's investment in the property would not include the nonrecourse debt, the taxpayer would not be permitted to include that debt in basis. . . .

We express no view as to whether such an approach would be consistent with the statutory structure and, if so, and *Crane* were not on the books, whether the approach would be preferred over *Crane's* analysis. We note only that the *Crane* Court's resolution of the basis issue presumed that when property is purchased with proceeds from a nonrecourse mortgage, the purchaser becomes the sole owner of the property. . . . Under the *Crane* approach, the mortgagee is entitled to no portion of the basis. . . . The nonrecourse mortgage is part of the mortgagor's investment in the property, and does not constitute a coinvestment by the mortgagee. . . .

at the time the loan was extended and will have received an unwarranted increase in the basis of his property. The Commissioner's interpretation of § 1001(b) in this fashion cannot be said to be unreasonable.

C

The Commissioner in fact has applied this rule even when the fair market value of the property falls below the amount of the nonrecourse obligation. . . . Because the theory on which the rule is based applies equally in this situation . . . we have no reason, after *Crane,* to question this treatment.[4]

Respondents received a mortgage loan with the concomitant obligation to repay by the year 2012. The only difference between that mortgage and one on which the borrower is personally liable is that the mortgagee's remedy is limited to foreclosing on the securing property. This difference does not alter the nature of the obligation; its only effect is to shift from the borrower to the lender any potential loss caused by devaluation of the property. If the fair market value of the property falls below the amount of the outstanding obligation, the mortgagee's ability to protect its interests is impaired, for the mortgagor is free to abandon the property to the mortgagee and be relieved of his obligation.

This, however, does not erase the fact that the mortgagor received the loan proceeds tax-free and included them in his basis on the understanding that he had an obligation to repay the full amount. See *Woodsam Associates, Inc. v. Commissioner* [Chapter 13]. When the obligation is canceled, the mortgagor is relieved of his responsibility to repay the sum he originally received and thus realizes value to that extent within the meaning of § 1001(b). From the mortgagor's point of view, when his obligation is assumed by a third party who purchases the encumbered property, it is as if the mortgagor first had been paid with cash borrowed by the third party from the mortgagee on a nonrecourse basis, and then had used the cash to satisfy his obligation to the mortgagee. . . .

. . . To permit the taxpayer to limit his realization to the fair market value of the property would be to recognize a tax loss for which he has suffered no corresponding economic loss. Such a result would be to construe "one section of the Act . . . so as . . . to defeat the intention of another or to frustrate the Act as a whole." . . .

In the specific circumstances of *Crane,* the economic benefit theory did support the Commissioner's treatment of the nonrecourse mortgage as a

---

4. Professor Wayne G. Barnett, as *amicus* in the present case, argues that the liability and property portions of the transaction should be accounted for separately. Under his view, there was a transfer of the property for $1.4 million, and there was a cancellation of the $1.85 million obligation for a payment of $1.4 million. The former resulted in a capital loss of $50,000, and the latter in the realization of $450,000 of ordinary income. Taxation of the ordinary income might be deferred under § 108 by a reduction of respondents' bases in their partnership interests.

Although this indeed could be a justifiable mode of analysis, it has not been adopted by the Commissioner. Nor is there anything to indicate that the Code requires the Commissioner to adopt it. We note that Professor Barnett's approach does assume that recourse and nonrecourse debt may be treated identically. . . .

personal obligation. The footnote in *Crane* acknowledged the limitations of that theory when applied to a different set of facts. *Crane* also stands for the broader proposition, however, that a nonrecourse loan should be treated as a true loan. We therefore hold that a taxpayer must account for the proceeds of obligations he has received tax-free and included in basis. Nothing in either § 1001(b) or in the Court's prior decisions requires the Commissioner to permit a taxpayer to treat a sale of encumbered property asymmetrically, by including the proceeds of the nonrecourse obligation in basis but not accounting for the proceeds upon transfer of the encumbered property. . . .

IV

When a taxpayer sells or disposes of property encumbered by a nonrecourse obligation, the Commissioner properly requires him to include among the assets realized the outstanding amount of the obligation. The fair market value of the property is irrelevant to this calculation. We find this interpretation to be consistent with *Crane v. Commissioner* . . . and to implement the statutory mandate in a reasonable manner. . . .

The judgment of the Court of Appeals is therefore reversed.

JUSTICE O'CONNOR, concurring.

I concur in the opinion of the Court, accepting the view of the Commissioner. I do not, however, endorse the Commissioner's view. Indeed, were we writing on a slate clean except for the decision in *Crane v. Commissioner*, . . . I would take quite a different approach—that urged upon us by Professor Barnett as *amicus*. [See footnote 4.]

Crane established that a taxpayer could treat property as entirely his own, in spite of the "coinvestment" provided by his mortgagee in the form of a nonrecourse loan. That is, the full basis of the property, with all its tax consequences, belongs to the mortgagor. That rule alone, though, does not in any way tie nonrecourse debt to the cost of property or to the proceeds upon disposition. I see no reason to treat the purchase, ownership, and eventual disposition of property differently because the taxpayer also takes out a mortgage, an independent transaction. In this case, the taxpayer purchased property, using nonrecourse financing, and sold it after it declined in value to a buyer who assumed the mortgage. There is no economic difference between the events in this case and a case in which the taxpayer buys property with cash; later obtains a nonrecourse loan by pledging the property as security; still later, using cash on hand, buys off the mortgage for the market value of the devalued property; and finally sells the property to a third party for its market value.

The logical way to treat both this case and the hypothesized case is to separate the two aspects of these events and to consider, first, the ownership and sale of the property, and, second, the arrangement and retirement of the loan. Under *Crane*, the fair market value of the property on the date of acquisition—the purchase price—represents the taxpayer's basis in the property, and the fair market value on the date of disposition represents the proceeds on sale. The benefit received by the taxpayer in return for the property is the cancellation of a mortgage that is worth no more than the fair market value of the property, for that is all the mortgagee can expect to collect on the mortgage. His gain or loss on the disposition of the property equals the difference between the proceeds and the cost of acquisition. Thus, the taxation of the transaction *in property* reflects the economic fate of the *property.* If the property has declined in value, as was the case here, the taxpayer recognizes a loss on the disposition of the property. The new purchaser then takes as his basis the fair market value as of the date of the sale....

In the separate borrowing transaction, the taxpayer acquires cash from the mortgage. He need not recognize income at that time, of course, because he also incurs an obligation to repay the money. Later, though, when he is able to satisfy the debt by surrendering property that is worth less than the face amount of the debt, we have a classic situation of cancellation of indebtedness, requiring the taxpayer to recognize income in the amount of the difference between the proceeds of the loan and the amount for which he is able to satisfy his creditor. 26 U.S.C. § 61(a)(12). The taxation of the financing transaction then reflects the economic fate of the loan.

The reason that separation of the two aspects of the events in this case is important is, of course, that the Code treats different sorts of income differently. A gain on the sale of the property may qualify for capital gains treatment ... while the cancellation of indebtedness is ordinary income, but income that the taxpayer may be able to defer. §§ 108, 1017.... Not only does Professor Barnett's theory permit us to accord appropriate treatment to each of the two types of income or loss present in these sorts of transactions, it also restores continuity to the system by making the taxpayer-seller's proceeds on the disposition of property equal to the purchaser's basis in the property. Further, and most important, it allows us to tax the events in this case in the same way that we tax the economically identical hypothesized transaction.

Persuaded though I am by the logical coherence and internal consistency of this approach, I agree with the Court's decision not to adopt it judicially. We do not write on a slate marked only by *Crane.* The Commissioner's longstanding position ... is now reflected in the regulations. Treas. Reg. § 1.1001–2.... In the light of the numerous cases in the lower courts including the amount of the unrepaid proceeds of the mortgage in the proceeds on sale or disposition, ... it is difficult to conclude that the Commissioner's interpretation of the statute exceeds the bounds of his discretion. As the Court's opinion demonstrates, his interpretation is defensible. One can reasonably read § 1001(b)'s reference to "the amount realized *from* the sale or other disposition of property" (emphasis added) to permit the Commissioner to collapse the two aspects of the transaction. As long as his view is a reasonable reading of § 1001(b), we should defer to the regulations promulgated by the agency charged with interpretation of the statute....

B. NOTES AND QUESTIONS

1) Amount Realized on the Sale of Mortgaged Property

When mortgaged property is sold, the buyer will sometimes assume the seller's obligations under the mortgage. If this occurs, the amount realized from the sale includes not only cash and other assets received by the seller but also the principal amount of the mortgage assumed by the buyer. This is simply a particular instance of the general rule that the amount realized from the sale of property includes any liabilities assumed by the buyer as part of the transaction. See Diedrich v. Commissioner, Chapter 22.

For example, suppose that Blackacre, with a market value of $100 and a $70 mortgage, is sold for $30 in cash plus the buyer's agreement to assume the mortgage obligation. The amount realized by the seller is $100—the sum of the cash received plus the principal amount of the mortgage assumed by the buyer. Why will the buyer pay no more than $30 in cash for property worth $100 if the buyer takes the property subject to the mortgage?

2) Does Assumption of a Nonrecourse Mortgage Produce an Economic Benefit?

In Crane v. Commissioner (discussed extensively in *Tufts*), the taxpayer sold land subject to a nonrecourse mortgage. She argued that her amount realized did not include the mortgage because she was not personally liable and therefore received no "economic benefit."

Why did the Supreme Court reject the argument that no economic benefit resulted? If the mortgage had been foreclosed before the sale, how much could the lender have collected from Ms. Crane? Why was it critical to the economic benefit analysis that the value of her property exceeded the principal amount owed on the mortgage?

Why didn't the *Crane* reasoning apply to the full amount of the nonrecourse mortgage in *Tufts*? If the nonrecourse mortgage had been foreclosed before the sale in *Tufts*, how much could the lender have collected? Why was the economic benefit—derived from transferring the property subject to a nonrecourse mortgage—limited to the property's value? Did the lender have the right to collect the excess of the mortgage amount over the property's value?

3) The Accurate Measurement of Gain or Loss Rationale

In *Tufts*, the Supreme Court conceded that the economic benefit rationale of *Crane* did not apply to the excess of the mortgage loan over the property's value. Nevertheless, the Supreme Court justified counting that excess in the amount realized by invoking the need to avoid "absurdity and frustration of the Code." By this, the Court appears to have meant the need to measure the taxpayer's income accurately.

To illustrate, assume that the property in *Tufts* was purchased for $200, with a $20 down payment and a $180 mortgage loan. Some time later, when the value of the property falls to $140 and $10 of the mortgage principal has been repaid, the owner transfers it subject to the $170 mortgage. According to the Commissioner, the amount realized is the full amount of the unpaid mortgage or $170, the basis is $200 (assuming there have been no basis adjustments since the property was purchased), and the taxpayer reports a $30 loss. According to the taxpayer, the amount realized consists of the mortgage principal only up to the property's value, or $140, and the loss is therefore $60.

Which figure, $30 or $60, is the accurate measure of the taxpayer's loss? To answer this question, consider the following two methods of measuring gain or loss on the sale of mortgaged property.

a) *The Cash Flow Method*—How much cash of his own has the taxpayer paid out to acquire the property? How much cash did the taxpayer receive when the property was sold? What is the difference between cash received and cash paid out? This method of calculating gain or loss is called the "cash flow" approach, because it focuses on the flow of cash: cash received, or cash inflow, minus cash paid out, or cash outflow. Notice that, under the cash flow method, the loan is ignored. It is not treated as part of the taxpayer's cost nor is it taken into account in figuring the amount realized.

b) *The Code Method*—This method counts the mortgage liability as part of both the basis and the amount realized. Using this method, what is the amount realized? What is the property's basis? What is the gain or loss, as measured by the difference between the two? Is the answer any different than under the cash flow method?

4) Alternative Ground for *Crane* and *Tufts*

Both *Crane* and *Tufts* hold that the amount realized when property is sold includes the amount of any unpaid mortgage to which the property remains subject. Is there an alternative ground for decision in both cases? Could both opinions have conceded that the nonrecourse mortgage should be excluded from the amount realized but then also required the taxpayer to exclude the nonrecourse mortgage from the property's basis? See Judge Magruder's concurring opinion in Parker v. Delaney, 186 F. 2d 455 (1st Cir. 1950).

5) Disaggregating the Transaction: Justice O'Connor's Concurrence

Justice O'Connor suggested a third method of calculating the gain arising from the transaction in *Tufts*. Did she agree with the taxpayer that the amount realized should exclude the excess of the nonrecourse mortgage over the property's value? If so, how did she measure accurately the gain or loss arising from the transaction? If the final net figure is the same, how does Justice O'Connor's approach make a difference?

6) Administrative Feasibility and the Treatment of Nonrecourse Debt

Under the code, the taxpayer's basis in property generally equals its cost, even if partly financed by nonrecourse debt. What are the reasons for this approach? Suppose cost were defined to include only the purchaser's actual cash investment plus debt for which the purchaser is personally liable. In other words, suppose cost were defined to exclude nonrecourse debt financing. In that event, what kinds of frequent adjustments to basis might be required? Despite the administrative difficulties, the Code effectively treats the cost of property as excluding nonrecourse debt in the case of certain tax shelters (see Section 465, examined in Chapter 39).

7) *Tufts* versus *Woodsam*

In both *Tufts* and *Woodsam*, the general issue concerned whether a transaction involving a nonrecourse mortgage produced realization of gain. But the specifics were very different. In *Woodsam*, the issue was whether gain was realized when a taxpayer mortgaged property, without recourse, for more than its basis. In *Tufts*, the issue was whether, on the transfer of property, the amount realized included a nonrecourse mortgage that exceeded the property's value.

To illustrate, suppose that property with a basis of $20 is mortgaged, without recourse, for $80. The *Woodsam* issue is whether the receipt of the $80 in mortgage proceeds should be treated as a realization event so that the taxpayer reports a gain of $60. Suppose that, several years later, the property falls in value to $40 and is transferred subject to a nonrecourse mortgage of $60. The *Tufts* issue is whether the amount realized on the transfer is $40, the property's value, or $60, the full amount owed on the nonrecourse mortgage.

8) Codification of *Tufts*

The result in *Tufts* is now codified in Section 7701(g) of the Code.

C. LIKE–KIND EXCHANGES OF MORTGAGED PROPERTY

1) Assume land A cost $100,000 and is encumbered by an $80,000 mortgage. Suppose that you trade land A, subject to the mortgage (for which the other party is to assume responsibility), in exchange for land B, worth $120,000 and unencumbered by any mortgage. How much gain have you *realized*? Don't forget that the amount realized includes not only cash received but also relief from mortgage liability. How much of the realized gain would you *recognize*? Note that Reg. § 1.1031(b)–1(c) defines non-like-kind property to include the relief of mortgage liabilities. See also Example 1 under Reg. § 1.1031(d)–2. ★ *Study this reg.*

Using the cash flow approach, how much cash profit have you actually received? Does your answer suggest that, in this example, the regulation produces a result inconsistent with the purpose of Section 1031 and might therefore be challenged as invalid?

2) Other than by challenging the regulation's validity, how might you try to avoid recognition in question 1), above? Suppose that instead of trading for land B, you trade for land C, worth $200,000 and encumbered by an $80,000 mortgage? How much gain is realized? How much is recognized? Note that Reg. § 1.1031(b)–1(c) provides that the amount of non-like-kind property received is reduced for any mortgages assumed by the taxpayer. See also Example 2 under Reg. § 1.1031(d)–2.

3) Suppose that you buy land A for $100,000 in a cash deal with no mortgage financing. Later you mortgage land A for $80,000, use the cash to buy a yacht, and then trade land A, encumbered by the mortgage, for land B, worth $120,000 and unencumbered. How much gain is realized? Will any gain be recognized? In this example, does the regulation produce a result consistent with the theory of Section 1031?

4) Suppose that in question 3), above, instead of mortgaging land A, you trade it for land C worth $200,000. You then mortgage land C for $80,000 and use the cash to buy a yacht. How much gain is realized? How much is recognized? What is the effect of Reg. § 1.1031(b)–1(c)?

5) What problem is illustrated by questions 1)–4), above? Suppose that you buy property for $100,000 cash, that it increases in value to $200,000, and that you then mortgage the property for $80,000. Is any gain realized? Why not? Is Reg. § 1.1031(b)–1(c) consistent with *Woodsam* (Chapter 13)? Is it an advisable departure from the general principle that taking out a mortgage is not a taxable event? Even if it is, should the regulation be rewritten to provide that the assumption of debt constitutes non-like-kind property only to the extent that the debt exceeds the basis of the property exchanged?

SUBPART C

Should the Gain be Preferentially Taxed?

Capital gains, which are generally defined as gains from the sale or exchange of investment property, have received preferential treatment during most of the history of the modern income tax. The capital gains preference was first enacted in 1921, eight years after the tax came into being. For the next sixty-five years, Congress periodically modified the precise nature of the preference but never seriously questioned whether it should exist at all. It was only in 1986 that Congress voted to eliminate the basic preference and to tax capital gains at the same rate as ordinary income.

In view of the abolition of the preference, readers might justifiably demand to know why a significant portion of this casebook is devoted to the subject of capital gains. First, its historical importance alone might be enough to require some attention in an introductory course.

Second, Congress, while abolishing the basic preference in 1986, served notice that it might be resurrected at any time. The Conference Report on the 1986 Tax Reform Act stated, "The current statutory structure for [defining] capital gains is retained in the Code to facilitate reinstatement of a capital gains rate differential. . . ."[1]

Third, while abolishing the lower tax rate for capital gains, Congress continued the distinct (and disadvantageous) treatment of capital losses. Such losses are deductible only to the extent of capital gains (except for the first $3,000 for noncorporate taxpayers). Therefore, the cases deciding whether property produces capital gain or ordinary income are still relevant to determining whether the same property, if sold for less than its adjusted basis, produces a capital or ordinary loss. Moreover, it remains important to know whether a gain is capital, in which case it may be offset by capital losses, or whether the gain is ordinary, in which case it may not be.

Fourth, capital gains still retain some other advantages, principally when a taxpayer makes a charitable contribution of real or intangible property that has appreciated in value. If the appreciation represents potential or-

---

1. 2 Conf. R. No. 841 (to Accompany H.R. 3838), 99th Cong., 2d Sess. at II-106 (1986).

dinary income *or* short-term capital gain, then the deduction is limited to the property's basis. See Section 170(e)(1)(A). In addition, if appreciated property is sold for a deferred payment, then the installment method may not be available to the extent that the appreciation reflects potential ordinary income. See Section 453(i), discussed in Chapter 37.

Chapter 25

JUSTIFICATIONS FOR PREFERENTIAL TREATMENT

A. INTRODUCTORY NOTE

The 1986 Tax Reform Act ended the basic capital gain preference for tax years beginning in 1988. For decades, many tax reformers considered the capital gains preference to have been the single worst "loophole" from the perspective of overall fairness or equity. Why, they asked, should the wage earner be taxed in full on the product of labor, while the wealthy investor is taxed on only 50% or less of capital gains? In addition, determining whether income is capital or ordinary complicated the administration of the Code and was one of the most frequently litigated tax issues.

Given these costs in equity and administrative feasibility, it might appear that proponents of special treatment have a heavy burden of justification. The readings that follow provide a critical look at four of the principal arguments made in support of special treatment—the lock-in argument, the inflation argument, the bunching argument, and the savings incentive argument.

B. HELLERMANN v. COMMISSIONER
77 T.C. 1361 (1981)

EKMAN, JUDGE: ... The sole issue for our decision is whether that portion of gain from the sale of property, which is attributable solely to inflation, is income within the meaning of the 16th Amendment. ...

Petitioners purchased four buildings in 1964 for $93,312. They sold the buildings in 1976 for $264,000, and reported a capital gain of $170,688 on their 1976 return. ...

Petitioners [argue] ... that they are entitled to a refund of capital gains tax paid in 1976. [They] claim that much of their reported gain on the sale of the four buildings was due to inflation. They point out that the Consumer Price Index (CPI) had approximately doubled between 1964 and 1976. Thus, even though they received more dollars on the sale than they had paid to purchase the buildings, each 1976 dollar they received was worth less than each 1964 dollar they paid. From this they concluded that their economic gain on the sale was $88,167. However, they concede that they had a nominal gain of $170,688.

Petitioners assert that they should not be taxed on their nominal gain, but only on their economic gain. They argue that the portion of their nominal gain which is attributable solely to inflation does not constitute taxable income within the meaning of the 16th Amendment. Instead, they contend that, economically speaking, such gain is a return of capital. . . . They conclude that the Code must be interpreted in a manner which does not permit such gain to be taxed as income. As an appropriate means to that end, petitioners suggest that we adjust nominal gain to reflect the effects of inflation.

Respondent rejects as irrelevant petitioners' use of the CPI, or other measures of inflation, to calculate taxable income. He contends that nominal capital gain is taxable income whether or not such gain represents an increase in economic value. We agree with respondent. . . .

We reject petitioners' contention that nominal gain is not taxable income within the meaning of the 16th Amendment on two grounds. First, we rely on the well-established doctrine that Congress has the power and authority to establish the dollar as a unit of legal value with respect to the determination of taxable income, independent of any value the dollar might also have as a commodity. . . .

As our second ground for rejecting petitioners' arguments, we rely upon the doctrine of common interpretation. As was stated by Judge Learned Hand, "[the] meaning [of income] is . . . to be gathered from the implicit assumptions of its use in common speech." . . . Thus, the meaning of income is not to be construed as an economist might, but as a layperson might. Petitioners received many more dollars for the buildings than they paid for them. The extra dollars they received are well within the common perception of income, even though each 1976 dollar received represents less purchasing power than each 1964 dollar paid. Petitioners' nominal gain may or may not equal their real gain in an economic sense. Nonetheless, neither the Constitution, nor the tax laws "embody perfect economic theory."

Based on the foregoing, we find that petitioners' nominal gain represented a change in legal value. Thus, petitioners' nominal gain is taxable income within the meaning of the 16th Amendment.

C. CRITIQUE OF TRADITIONAL JUSTIFICATIONS

Andrews, A Consumption-Type or Cash-Flow Personal Income Tax, 87 Harv. L. Rev. 1113, 1131–1135, 1140–1141, 1146, 1148–1149, 1151–1153 (1974)

. . . Even if realized and recognized, gain from the sale or exchange of a capital asset held for more than six months is taxed at not more than half the rate applicable to other income. "Capital asset" is defined broadly to include corporate securities and investment real estate and most other kinds of property most individuals are likely to hold for accumulation, except property held primarily for sale in the ordinary course of business.

As compared with the nonrecognition provisions, the capital gain provisions may only eliminate about half the current tax on a realized gain, but the elimination is permanent and outright, not a mere matter of deferral....

... One common assumption about the purpose of the capital gain provisions is that they are to give relief from the hardship, under a graduated rate schedule, of having several years' appreciation (accumulation) taxed in a single year upon realization. But this explanation is painfully inadequate. Most obviously, it is inconsistent with the statutory provision requiring only a six-month holding period for long-term capital gain treatment. Moreover, while a single capital gain may represent realization of a gain that accrued over an extended period, there is no reason to think that capital gain income is generally a widely fluctuating item for many taxpayers. In many cases the timing of realization of capital gains is subject to more control than the timing of other income items. And capital gain treatment is not generally denied even when the gain from a single sale is spread out through several years, through use of installment sale reporting or other deferral provisions. Finally, the explanation in terms of bunching fails utterly to provide any justification for relief in the case of taxpayers whose ordinary income puts them in high brackets year after year in any event. A very substantial amount of capital gains are reported by very high-bracket taxpayers for whom capital gain rates probably represent something far below the regular marginal rates that could be produced by any kind of spreading of their income among taxable periods.

If the problem of capital gains were truly one of bunching, the sensible remedy would be one of spreading or averaging total income over a period of years. Such a remedy would have no value or effect for regular capital gain repeaters or for regular high-bracket taxpayers, who probably are the biggest beneficiaries of the present provisions.

Another popular justification for capital gain rates has to do with inflation. If a person has invested a dollar of after-tax income in an asset that has grown in value, and later sells the asset, the proceeds should be regarded as taxpaid to the full extent of the real value of his original taxpaid investment, undiluted by inflation. In a very rough way, if capital gains were in fact about half due to inflation, the capital gain provisions would serve on average to accomplish this objective. At least, one might say, the capital gain provisions should not be repealed until something else is done about inflation.

This explanation is still, of course, much too rough, even though inflation is a very real problem. The capital gain provisions exempt half the realized gain from tax; the more one gains the more relief he will be granted. There is no very high correlation, however, between the amount of gain one enjoys and the burden of inflation he bears, except insofar as both are functions of wealth and time. For any two taxpayers with similar amounts of wealth held over the same period of time, the burden of inflation will be just as heavy for the one with no gains as for the one with large gains, and if relief is to be provided for the latter it should be provided for the former, too. Justification of the existing capital gain provisions because *on average* they may compensate for inflation is essentially no justification at all, since the essence of justice in taxation is to treat individuals fairly in relation to one another, according to their relevant individual circumstances, without having one taxpayer bear another's share of the burden to make the average come out right.

The most nearly satisfactory explanation for the capital gain provisions is simply that capital gain rates serve to mitigate disparity of treatment between unrealized gains and gains that are realized and recognized but reinvested. This explanation has both an efficiency and an equity aspect. It is economically inefficient to have a tax that gives people an incentive not to make otherwise desirable changes in investments. Indeed it has been argued that the existing tax on capital gains is too high and that even the tax yield itself might be greater if the rate were reduced. But whatever the incentive or inducement effects, it would be inequitable to impose a tax at ordinary rates on taxpayers with realized but reinvested gains while unrealized gains are allowed to accumulate taxfree. . . .

This explanation, while it does not tie justification of capital gain treatment to a long prior period of accumulation, does presuppose reinvestment. It is true that the most typical kind of capital gain is gain from the sale of corporate securities. And it is also true that by tradition a prudent owner of wealth is supposed to try to live off dividends without dipping into capital, and that under this rule of behavior the whole proceeds from sales of securities, including any capital gain, would ordinarily be reinvested. Discussion of capital gains is sometimes seemingly conducted under the assumption that capital gains are in fact mostly reinvested. But there is nothing in the law confining capital gain treatment to reinvested gains. . . .

Nontaxation of unrealized gains and special rates on realized capital gains are often defended by general reference to the need to encourage saving and capital formation. Full taxation of capital gains at ordinary rates, it is said, would represent an undesirable increase in the total tax burden on investment and savings. This defense also depends on the assumption that capital gains are saved, and it provides no justification for distinguishing between capital gains and other forms of saving or investment return. . . .

According to prevailing doctrine, the way to deal with the problems [of capital gains taxation] is to move closer to a true accretion-type tax. Accordingly, we should impose a tax on unrealized gains, at least on transfer at death or by gift, if not currently as they accrue. In addition, we should eliminate special rates of tax on capital gains, allowing averaging to deal with any problem of bunching that may exist. . . .

If all accumulation were taxed currently as it occurred, even when it takes the form of unrealized appreciation in the value of property or contract rights, then indeed most of the difficulties . . . would be eliminated. Problems in the definition of realization and nonrecognition would disappear since gains and losses would be recognized in every case, whether realized or not. Insofar as special treatment of capital gains is to reduce the dichotomy in treatment between realized and unrealized gains, it would no longer be necessary. . . .

[But] [c]omprehensive inclusion of unrealized appreciation in taxable income would entail enormous practical problems. These involve the necessity of valuing investment property in order to measure unrealized appreciation, and of raising funds with which to pay the tax. . . .

In practice, few people advocate a true accretion-type personal income tax in which all the changes in value would be currently and comprehensively reflected in taxable income....

[An alternative solution is to adopt a] consumption-type personal income tax. [Such a tax] would ... be computed on personal income ... minus ... savings....

The most obvious difference about a consumption-type income tax would be that ordinary investments would be accounted for on a pure cash flow basis. The cost of investment assets would be deductible in the year paid, while the proceeds of sale would be fully included in taxable income in the year received. This does not necessarily mean that there would be a large tax in a year when substantial sales are made, since it is likely that taxable proceeds would be largely offset by deductions for reinvestment in that year....

[This] treatment of ordinary investments would eliminate a whole host of complications in the existing income tax.... Furthermore, there would be no problems concerning realization and recognition of gain or loss when an individual changes investments. If a taxpayer receives new investment property in exchange for old ... it would make no difference whether the transaction is one on which the gain is realized and recognized under present law, since any gain recognized would in effect be offset by a deduction for the fresh investment....

... [T]his treatment for ordinary investments would eliminate any need for special rates of tax for capital gains. The best justification for capital gains treatment is to mitigate the disparity in treatment between unrealized gains and realized but reinvested gains. A cash flow treatment of ordinary investments would eliminate that disparity entirely. Proceeds from the sale of investment property would be taxed only if devoted to personal consumption, in which event there would be no reason to distinguish them from ordinary earned income also directed to consumption....

D. NOTES AND QUESTIONS

1) The Lock-in Argument

Suppose that you own property with a basis of $100, that the property has a current value of $200, that the property pays 10% of its value each year, and that you are in a 50% tax bracket. Suppose further that there is *no* capital gains preference.

a) What is the annual cash return from the property?

b) Suppose that you find an alternative investment that pays 12% a year of its value. If you sell the investment that you now hold for cash, how much is left after taxes to invest in the alternative?

c) Assume that you invest the entire after-tax amount in the alternative investment that pays 12%. What is the annual cash return from the alternative?

d) Would you be willing to switch to this alternative investment, assuming that the only thing you care about is the annual cash return from the property?

e) How high does the percentage return on the alternative investment have to rise in order for you to switch? The difference between this figure and the percentage return on your original investment property is called a *tax wedge*.

f) Because of the tax wedge, you tend to be "locked-in" to your current investments (that is, unwilling to consider switching to alternative investment properties), unless you can identify alternatives offering not just somewhat higher but *appreciably* higher percentage returns. Economists consider the lock-in effect undesirable because it produces an "inefficient allocation of resources." What do you think this means?

g) Now suppose that 60% of all capital gains are deductible. (For a 50% bracket taxpayer, a 60% deduction is equivalent to a 20% tax on the full amount of the capital gain.) How does that change your answers to questions b) through e), above?

h) With the repeal of the capital gains preference, what has happened to the size of the tax wedge? Under the 1986 Tax Reform Act, the maximum tax rate for individuals on capital gains rises explicitly to 28% and, where the 5% surcharge applies, goes to 33%. How does this change affect the lock-in problem compared with the pre-1986 maximum capital gains tax rate of 20%?

i) Suppose that nonrecognition were afforded to all sales of investment property, provided only that the receipts are used to buy other investment property. In effect, this would be like modifying Section 1031 to (i) eliminate the like-kind requirement and (ii) permit the receipt of cash as an intermediate step on the way to acquiring other investment property. The gain would be taxable only if the receipts were spent for personal consumption but would then be taxable in full. Would this scheme, permitting tax-free rollover of investments, eliminate the lock-in problem?

j) Suppose, alternatively, that we taxed unrealized appreciation in property. Would this scheme, sometimes referred to as accrual taxation, eliminate the lock-in problem?

k) Both proposals discussed in i) and j), above, represent rejection, albeit at different extremes, of the realization principle. The tax-free rollover scheme ignores realization and focuses instead on the spending of resources for personal consumption. Accrual taxation accounts for property appreciation in the year it occurs, whether the property in question is sold or not. What do your answers to i) and j), above, indicate about the relationship of the lock-in effect to the realization principle?

l) If property has a useful life of five years or less, how serious a problem is the lock-in effect?

2) The Inflation Argument

a) Suppose that you buy land A for $100 in 1975 and sell it for $200 in 1980. How much is your nominal or money gain? Suppose that the consumer price index, a common measure of inflation, has risen by 60% between the time you bought the property and the time you sold it. How much of your nominal gain is real gain (in 1980 dollars)? Ideally, how might inflationary gains be excluded on the sale of property? How accurately does an across-the-board 60% deduction achieve that objective in this specific example? If inflation has been only 10% while you held the property? If it has been 25%? 150%?

b) How closely related is the objective of not taxing inflationary gains to the capital gains preference as it existed in 1986, that is, a 60% deduction for individuals and a flat 28% tax rate for corporations?

c) Is there a more exact solution to the inflation problem? The Department of Treasury's 1984 tax reform proposals recommended that the capital gains preference be eliminated and that the basis of property be adjusted to reflect inflation (as measured by the consumer price index) in the period since the property was purchased.[1]

d) Under either tax-free rollover of investments or accrual taxation of appreciation in property, would inflation remain a problem? Again, what does this indicate about the relationship between the realization principle and the inflation argument for the capital gains preference?

3) The Bunching Argument

a) Suppose that you buy land in 1960 for $10,000 and then sell it in 1980 for $100,000. How much is your gain, and when is it reported? How is reporting the entire gain in 1980 likely to affect the rate at which the gain is taxed? Compare this with the rate that would apply if the gain were taxed as it arose (an average of $4,500 a year). How might allowing a deduction for 60% of the gain provide relief from the rigors of reporting (or "bunching") the entire amount in one year instead of over a period of years?

b) How closely is the objective of providing relief from "bunching" related to the capital gains preference as it existed in 1986?

c) Does the bunching of gain necessarily produce a disadvantage? If the taxpayer is already in the top bracket? (Note that studies indicate that the great majority of individual capital gains are realized by such investors.) If the investor realizes more or less the same amount of capital gains each year so that the effect of bunching is evened out?

d) Even if bunching produces a significant disadvantage, doesn't the taxpayer benefit from an offsetting advantage, namely the delay in taxing the gain that has arisen over a period of years?

e) Suppose that the taxpayer is a corporation. Is the bunching argument valid, except in very limited circumstances?

f) What kind of help-yourself device is available to taxpayers who sell property and realize in one year a large gain that has accumulated over many years?

g) If accrual taxation were to be adopted, would bunching present a problem? Again, what is the relation between the realization principle and the bunching argument for the capital gains preference?

---

1. Dept. of the Treasury, Tax Reform for Fairness, Simplicity, and Economic Growth (Report to the President) 100–105 (1984).

4) The Savings Incentive Argument

If a savings incentive is the objective, would it be preferable to replace the capital gains preference with a partial or full deduction for savings?

E. EISNER v. MACOMBER
252 U.S. 189 (1920)

MR. JUSTICE PITNEY delivered the opinion of the court.

This case presents the question whether, by virtue of the Sixteenth Amendment, Congress has the power to tax, as income of the stockholder and without apportionment, a stock dividend. . . .

. . . "A stock dividend really takes nothing from the property of the corporation, and adds nothing to the interests of the shareholders. Its property is not diminished, and their interests are not increased. . . . The proportional interest of each shareholder remains the same. The only change is in the evidence which represents that interest, the new shares and the original shares together representing the same proportional interest that the original shares represented before the issue of the new ones. *Gibbons v. Mahon*. . . . In short, the corporation is no poorer and the stockholder is no richer than they were before." . . .

The Sixteenth Amendment must be construed in connection with the taxing clauses of the original Constitution and the effect attributed to them before the Amendment was adopted. In *Pollock v. Farmers' Loan & Trust Co.* . . . it was held that taxes upon rents and profits of real estate and upon returns from investments of personal property were in effect direct taxes upon the property from which such income arose, imposed by reason of ownership; and that Congress could not impose such taxes without apportioning them among the States according to population, as required by Art. I, § 2, cl. 3, and § 9, cl. 4, of the original Constitution.

Afterwards, and evidently in recognition of the limitation upon the taxing power of Congress thus determined, the Sixteenth Amendment was adopted, in words lucidly expressing the object to be accomplished: "The Congress shall have power to lay and collect taxes on incomes, from whatever source derived, without apportionment among the several States, and without regard to any census or enumeration." As repeatedly held, this did not extend the taxing power to new subjects, but merely removed the necessity which otherwise might exist for an apportionment among the States of taxes laid on income. . . .

In order, therefore, that the clauses cited from Article I of the Constitution may have proper force and effect, save only as modified by the Amendment, and that the latter also may have proper effect, it becomes essential to distinguish between what is and what is not "income," as the term is there used; and to apply the distinction, as cases arise, according to truth and substance, without regard to form. . . .

The . . . fundamental conception is clearly set forth in the Sixteenth Amendment—"incomes, *from* whatever *source derived*"—the essential thought being expressed with a conciseness and lucidity entirely in harmony with the form and style of the Constitution.

Can a stock dividend, considering its essential character, be brought within the definition? To answer this, regard must be had to the nature of a corporation and the stockholder's relation to it. . . .

. . . [T]he interest of the stockholder is a capital interest, and his certificates of stock are but the evidence of it. They state the number of shares to which he is entitled. . . . They show that he or his assignors, immediate or remote, have contributed capital to the enterprise, that he is entitled to a corresponding interest proportionate to the whole, entitled to have the property and business of the company devoted during the corporate existence to attainment of the common objects, entitled to vote at stockholders' meetings, to receive dividends out of the corporation's profits if and when declared, and, in the event of liquidation, to receive a proportionate share of the net assets, if any, remaining after paying creditors. Short of liquidation, or until dividend declared, he has no right to withdraw any part of either capital or profits from the common enterprise; on the contrary, his interest pertains not to any part, divisible or indivisible, but to the entire assets, business, and affairs of the company. Nor is it the interest of an owner in the assets themselves, since the corporation has full title, legal and equitable, to the whole. The stockholder has the right to have the assets employed in the enterprise, with the incidental rights mentioned; but, as stockholder, he has no right to withdraw, only the right to persist, subject to the risks of the enterprise, and looking only to dividends for his return. If he desires to dissociate himself from the company he can do so only by disposing of his stock. . . .

. . . If profits have been made and not divided they create . . . bookkeeping liabilities under the head of "profit and loss," "undivided profits," "surplus account," or the like. None of these, however, gives to the stockholders as a body, much less to any one of them, either a claim against the going concern for any particular sum of money, or a right to any particular portion of the assets or any share in them unless or until the directors conclude that dividends shall be made and a part of the company's assets segregated from the common fund for the purpose. The dividend normally is payable in money . . . and when so paid, then only (excluding, of course, a possible advantageous sale of his stock or winding-up of the company) does the stockholder realize a profit or gain which becomes his separate property, and thus derive income from the capital that he or his predecessor has invested.

In the present case, the corporation had surplus and undivided profits invested in plant, property, and business, and required for the purposes of the corporation, amounting to about $45,000,000, in addition to outstanding capital stock of $50,000,000. In this the case is not extraordinary. The profits of a corporation, as they appear upon the balance sheet at the end of the year, need not be in the form of money on hand in excess of what is required to meet current liabilities and finance current operations of the company. Often, especially in a growing business, only a part, sometimes a small part, of the year's profits is in property capable of division;

the remainder having been absorbed in the acquisition of increased plant, equipment, stock in trade, or accounts receivable, or in decrease of outstanding liabilities. When only a part is available for dividends, the balance of the year's profits is carried to the credit of undivided profits, or surplus, or some other account having like significance. If thereafter the company finds itself in funds beyond current needs it may declare dividends out of such surplus or undivided profits; otherwise it may go on for years conducting a successful business, but requiring more and more working capital because of the extension of its operations, and therefore unable to declare dividends approximating the amount of its profits. Thus the surplus may increase until it equals or even exceeds the par value of the outstanding capital stock. This may be adjusted upon the books in the mode adopted in the case at bar—by declaring a "stock dividend." This, however, is no more than a book adjustment, in essence not a dividend but rather the opposite; no part of the assets of the company is separated from the common fund, nothing distributed except paper certificates that evidence an antecedent increase in the value of the stockholder's capital interest resulting from an accumulation of profits by the company, but profits so far absorbed in the business as to render it impracticable to separate them for withdrawal and distribution. In order to make the adjustment, . . . the new stock is issued . . . and the certificates delivered to the existing stockholders in proportion to their previous holdings. This, however, is merely bookkeeping that does not affect the aggregate assets of the corporation or its outstanding liabilities; it affects only the form, not the essence. . . .

[I]t does not alter the pre-ëxisting proportionate interest of any stockholder or increase the intrinsic value of his holding or of the aggregate holdings of the other stockholders as they stood before. The new certificates simply increase the number of the shares, with consequent dilution of the value of each share.

A "stock dividend" shows that the company's accumulated profits have been capitalized, instead of distributed to the stockholders or retained as surplus available for distribution in money or in kind should opportunity offer. Far from being a realization of profits of the stockholder, it tends rather to postpone such realization, in that the fund represented by the new stock has been transferred from surplus to capital, and no longer is available for actual distribution.

The essential and controlling fact is that the stockholder has received nothing out of the company's assets for his separate use and benefit; on the contrary, every dollar of his original investment, together with whatever accretions and accumulations have resulted from employment of his money and that of the other stockholders in the business of the company, still remains the property of the company, and subject to business risks which may result in wiping out the entire investment. Having regard to the very truth of the matter, to substance and not to form, he has received nothing that answers the definition of income within the meaning of the Sixteenth Amendment. . . .

It is said that a stockholder may sell the new shares acquired in the stock dividend; and so he may, if he can find a buyer. It is equally true that if he does sell, and in doing so realizes a profit, such profit, like any other, is income, and so far as it may have arisen since the Sixteenth Amendment is taxable by Congress without apportionment. The same would be true were he to sell some of his original shares at a profit. But if a shareholder sells dividend stock he necessarily disposes of a part of his capital interest, just as if he should sell a part of his old stock, either before or after the dividend. What he retains no longer entitles him to the same proportion of future dividends as before the sale. His part in the control of the company likewise is diminished. Thus, if one holding $60,000 out of a total $100,000 of the capital stock of a corporation should receive in common with other stockholders a 50 per cent stock dividend, and should sell his part, he thereby would be reduced from a majority to a minority stockholder, having six-fifteenths instead of six-tenths of the total stock outstanding. A corresponding and proportionate decrease in capital interest and in voting power would befall a minority holder should he sell dividend stock; it being in the nature of things impossible for one to dispose of any part of such an issue without a proportionate disturbance of the distribution of the entire capital stock, and a like diminution of the seller's comparative voting power—that "right preservative of rights" in the control of a corporation. Yet, without selling, the shareholder, unless possessed of other resources, has not the wherewithal to pay an income tax upon the dividend stock. Nothing could more clearly show that to tax a stock dividend is to tax a capital increase, and not income, than this demonstration that in the nature of things it requires conversion of capital in order to pay the tax.

Throughout the argument of the Government, in a variety of forms, runs the fundamental error already mentioned—a failure to appraise correctly the force of the term "income" as used in the Sixteenth Amendment, or at least to give practical effect to it. Thus, the government contends that the tax "is levied on income derived from corporate earnings," when in truth the stockholder has "derived" nothing except paper certificates which, so far as they have any effect, deny him present participation in such earnings. It contends that the tax may be laid when earnings "are received by the stockholder," whereas he has received none; that the profits are "distributed by means of a stock dividend," although a stock dividend distributes no profits; that under the Act of 1916 "the tax is on the stockholder's share in corporate earnings," when in truth a stockholder has no such share, and receives none in a stock dividend; that "the profits are segregated from his former capital, and he has a separate certificate representing his invested profits or gains," whereas there has been no segregation of profits, nor has he any separate certificate representing a personal gain, since the certificates, new and old, are alike in what they represent—a capital interest in the entire concerns of the corporation.

We have no doubt of the power or duty of a court to look through the form of the corporation and determine the question of the stockholder's right, in order to ascertain whether he has received income taxable by Congress without apportionment. But, looking through the form, we cannot disregard the essential truth disclosed; ignore the substantial difference between corporation and stockholder; treat the entire organization as unreal; look upon stockholders as partners, when they are not such. . . . We must treat the corporation as a substantial entity separate from the stockholder, not only because such is the practical fact but because it is only by recognizing such separateness that any dividend—even one paid in money or property—can be regarded as income of the stockholder. Did we regard corporation and stockholders as altogether identical, there would be no income except as the corporation acquired it; and while this would be taxable against the corporation as income under appropriate provisions of law, the individual stockholders could not be separately and additionally taxed with respect to their several shares even when divided, since if there were entire identity between them and the company they could not be regarded as receiving anything from it, any more than if one's money were to be removed from one pocket to another.

Conceding that the mere issue of a stock dividend makes the recipient no richer than before, the Government nevertheless contends that the new certificates measure the extent to which the gains accumulated by the corporation have made him the richer. There are two insuperable difficulties with this: In the first place, it would depend upon how long he had held the stock whether the stock dividend indicated the extent to which he had been enriched by the operations of the company; unless he had held it throughout such operations the measure would not hold true. Secondly, and more important for present purposes, enrichment through increase in value of capital investment is not income in any proper meaning of the term.

The complaint contains averments respecting the market prices of stock such as plaintiff held, based upon sales before and after the stock dividend, tending to show that the receipt of the additional shares did not substantially change the market value of her entire holdings. This tends to show that in this instance market quotations reflected intrinsic values—a thing they do not always do. But we regard the market prices of the securities as an unsafe criterion in an inquiry such as the present, when the question must be, not what will the thing sell for, but what is it in truth and in essence.

It is said there is no difference in principle between a simple stock dividend and a case where stockholders use money received as cash dividends to purchase additional stock contemporaneously issued by the corporation. But an actual cash dividend, with a real option to the stockholder either to keep the money for his own or to reinvest it in new shares, would be as far removed as possible from a true stock dividend, such as the one we have under consideration, where nothing of value is taken from the company's assets and transferred to the individual ownership of the several stockholders and thereby subjected to their disposal. . . .

. . . [T]he Government, . . . virtually abandoning the contention that a stock dividend increases the interest of the stockholder or otherwise enriches him, insisted as an alternative that . . . the tax is imposed not upon the stock dividend but rather upon the stockholder's share of the undivided profits previously accumulated by the corporation; the tax being levied as a matter of convenience at the time such profits become manifest through the stock dividend. If so construed, would the act be constitutional?

That Congress has power to tax shareholders upon their property interests in the stock of corporations is beyond question; and that such interests might be valued in view of the condition of the company, including its accumulated and undivided profits, is equally clear. But that this would be taxation of property because of ownership, and hence would require apportionment under the provisions of the Constitution. . . .

Thus, from every point of view, we are brought irresistibly to the conclusion that neither under the Sixteenth Amendment nor otherwise has Congress power to tax without apportionment a true stock dividend made lawfully and in good faith, or the accumulated profits behind it, as income of the stockholder. The Revenue Act of 1916, in so far as it imposes a tax upon the stockholder because of such dividend, contravenes the provisions of Article I, § 2, cl. 3, and Article I, § 9, cl. 4, of the Constitution, and to this extent is invalid notwithstanding the Sixteenth Amendment.

Judgment affirmed.

Mr. Justice Brandeis, dissenting, delivered the following opinion, in which Mr. Justice Clarke concurred.

. . . The argument which appears to be most strongly urged for the stockholders is, that when a stock dividend is made, no portion of the assets of the company is thereby segregated for the stockholder. . . . Clearly segregation of assets in a physical sense is not an essential of income. The year's gains of a partner are taxable as income, although there, likewise, no segregation of his share in the gains from that of his partners is had.

The objection that there has been no segregation is presented also in another form. It is argued that until there is a segregation, the stockholder cannot know whether he has really received gains; since the gains may be invested in plant or merchandise or other property and perhaps be later lost. But is not this equally true of the share of a partner in the year's profits of the firm or, indeed, of the profits of the individual who is engaged in business alone? And is it not true, also, when dividends are paid in cash? . . .

The Government urges that it would have been within the power of Congress to have taxed as income of the stockholder his *pro rata* share of undistributed profits earned, even if no stock dividend representing it had been paid. Strong reasons may be assigned for such a view. . . . The undivided share of a partner in the year's undistributed profits of his firm is taxable as income of the partner, although the share in the gain is not evidenced by any action taken by the firm. Why may not the stockholder's interest in the gains of the company? . . . The stockholder's interest in the property of the corporation differs, not fundamentally but in form only, from the interest of a partner in the property of the firm. There is much authority for the proposition that, under our law, a partnership or joint stock company is just as distinct and palpable an entity in the idea of the law, as distinguished from the individuals composing it, as is a corporation. No reason appears, why Congress, in legislating under a grant of power so comprehensive as that authorizing the levy of an income tax, should be limited by the particular view of the relation of the stockholder to the corporation and its property which may, in the absence of legislation, have been taken by this court. . . .

. . . If stock dividends representing profits are held exempt from taxation under the Sixteenth Amendment, the owners of the most successful businesses in America will, as the facts in this case illustrate, be able to escape taxation on a large part of what is actually their income. . . . That stock dividends representing profits are so regarded, not only by the plain people but by investors and financiers, and by most of the courts of the country, is shown, beyond peradventure, by their acts and by their utterances. It seems to me clear, therefore, that Congress possesses the power which it exercised to make dividends representing profits, taxable as income, whether the medium in which the dividend is paid be cash or stock, and that it may define, as it has done, what dividends representing profits shall be deemed income. It surely is not clear that the enactment exceeds the power granted by the Sixteenth Amendment. And, as this court has so often said, the high prerogative of declaring an act of Congress invalid, should never be exercised except in a clear case. "It is but a decent respect due to the wisdom, the integrity and the patriotism of the legislative body, by which any law is passed, to presume in favor of its validity, until its violation of the Constitution is proved beyond all reasonable doubt." . . .

F. NOTES AND QUESTIONS

1) The Effect of a Stock Dividend

Suppose that X Corp. is worth $10 million and has 1 million outstanding common shares. X Corp. distributes a stock dividend consisting of one new share of common stock for each existing share of common. What is the effect of the stock dividend on the number of shares? On value per share? On the value of any shareholder's interest? In what sense is the issuance of the stock dividend in this example a "paper transaction," which changes nothing of substance?

2) Reasons for Issuing Stock Dividends

If issuance of a stock dividend is just a "paper transaction," why are stock dividends ever issued? There are three reasons commonly offered. First, as a result of the stock dividend, the price per share is halved and the lower price may make the stock more attractive to investors. Second, if the corporation decides not to pay its usual cash dividend because earnings are needed for reinvestment, the stock dividend may make shareholders feel that they are receiving something. Third, the stock dividend may be used to send the message that management feels especially optimistic about the corporation's future prospects.

Do these arguments suggest that shareholders are influenced by illusory changes? Why should halving the price of the stock make the corporation's stock more attractive if the number of outstanding shares are doubled? Does a stock dividend really represent something that shareholders would not have received without it? Why can't management announce that it is feeling optimistic, rather than relying on stock dividends to convey the message obliquely?

3) The Basic Structure for Taxing Corporate-Shareholder Income

Since 1921, the Internal Revenue Code has maintained a sharp distinction between corporate earnings distributed to shareholders (dividends) and corporate earnings retained for reinvestment. In general, distributed earnings are taxed as ordinary income to the individual shareholder at the time of distribution. Retained earnings are not directly attributed or imputed to shareholders but are taxed as gain on the sale of stock to the extent that the stock's value reflects earnings retained. Like all gain on the sale of stock, retained earnings receive (a) capital gain treatment, (b) tax deferral until the disposition of stock (which may not occur until many years after the earnings are generated), and (c) complete tax forgiveness if the shareholder holds the stock until death so that any gain attributable to retention escapes taxation under the basis rule of Section 1014(a) (Chapter 23). Consequently, individual investors obtain a significant tax advantage when corporate earnings are retained for reinvestment.

Eisner v. Macomber was decided in 1920, one year before the enactment of the capital gains preference. Therefore, when the case was decided, the special treatment afforded retained earnings consisted only of (b) and (c), above.

4) The Effect of Taxing Stock Dividends

Taxation of any *stock* dividend constitutes a departure from the basic tax distinction between distributed and retained earnings. A dividend in cash reduces earnings available for reinvestment, but a dividend in stock does not. The stock dividend in Eisner v. Macomber was issued to reflect the amount by which retained earnings had increased the value of shareholder equity. The taxation of the stock dividend, therefore, was identified as a shareholder ordinary income tax on undistributed and retained corporate earnings.

5) The Realization Principle in Eisner v. Macomber

The narrow legal question before the Court was whether Congress could impose an income tax on the *pro rata* distribution of a common stock dividend on common stock. The Court decided that realization must occur in order for the tax to be constitutional under the Sixteenth Amendment. By this, the Court meant that the mere accrual of gain (that is, a mere increase in net worth) is not by itself sufficient to permit taxation. Some "separation or transformation" of the gain must occur. Although the Court left unclear what kind of separation or transformation is necessary for realization, it held that the stock dividend before it was a paper transaction and did not rise to the level of a realization.

Once a tax on stock dividends is identified as a shareholder tax on undistributed corporate profits, how persuasive is the reasoning in Eisner v. Macomber? Why is such a tax more violative of the realization principle than the rule that all partnership profits are taxed annually to partners, whether distributed or reinvested in the business? Eisner v. Macomber distinguished the partnership case on the ground that each partner has the legal right to compel distribution of his or her share of the earnings, while the stockholder ordinarily does not. Is the Court's distinction persuasive in the case of a closely held corporation? In the case of publicly held stock, which is easily valued and highly liquid? Does Eisner v. Macomber imply that it would be unconstitutional to tax a partner on undistributed profits if the partnership agreement permits a distribution only by vote of a majority of the partners?[2]

6) Legal Realism and Eisner v. Macomber

How might a legal realist explain Eisner v. Macomber? Was the Court motivated by the same philosophy as in Lochner v. New York, 198 U.S. 45 (1905), which held that a law regulating the working hours of bakery employees violated the Fourteenth Amendment's due process clause. Should the stock dividend opinion be understood as another example of early twentieth century substantive due process, with the aim of preserving the interests of property against undue state interference?

7) Justifying the Nontaxation of Stock Dividends

If the legal rationale for Eisner v. Macomber is weak, can the nontaxation of stock dividends be justified on broader tax policy grounds? The usual rationale for affording preferential treatment to retained earnings is that it affords some relief from the double taxation of corporate-shareholder income. Compensation for personal services is ordinarily taxed only once—to the wage earner. Similarly, income from property held in noncorporate form is generally taxed just once—to the property's owner. But the profits on corporate capital are effectively subject to a double burden, taxed once at the corporate level and again a second time at the shareholder level.

Assume that mitigating the double burden of corporate-shareholder taxation is an adequate justification for taxing retained earnings to shareholders only on the sale of stock. Is there any valid reason for departing from the principle when a stock dividend is paid?

Note also that relief from the double burden of corporate-shareholder taxes provides a fifth justification for the capital gains preference, in addition to the lock-in, bunching, inflation, and savings incentive arguments.

8) Is Corporate-Shareholder Income Taxed More or Less Heavily Than Noncorporate Income?

At first glance, the answer may appear to be *more* heavily. Income earned by a corporation is, after all, taxed twice, whereas noncorporate income is

---

2. Domestic shareholders of foreign personal holding companies and certain other foreign corporations are taxed on their shares of undistributed corporate income. Sections 551 and 951. How likely is it today that these sections would be held to violate the constitutional realization requirement?

Although the Supreme Court has never overruled Eisner v. Macomber, concepts of what constitutes realization have broadened considerably. Since 1920, the Supreme Court has found an absence of realization in only one other case, Weiss v. Stearn, 265 U.S. 242 (1924).

taxed only once. In fact, however, the answer depends on the relative levels of corporate and individual rates.

Until 1981, corporate income above $100,000 was taxed at a flat rate of 46%, while the top individual tax rate was 70% on ordinary income and 20% on capital gains. Given this rate structure, corporate-shareholder income was always taxed more heavily than noncorporate income when the shareholder's tax rate was 46% or less. Why? In addition, corporate-shareholder income was also taxed more heavily to the extent that corporate earnings were distributed, no matter what the shareholder's tax rate. Why? However, corporate-shareholder income might be taxed less heavily when earnings were retained *and* the shareholder's tax rate exceeded 46%. Why?

Another factor is the size of incentives provided by the tax law for corporate investment in plant and machinery, through accelerated depreciation and the investment tax credit, both of which are examined in more detail in Chapter 35. Between 1981 and 1986, the benefit provided by these incentives was roughly equivalent to taxing corporate income at a zero rate. Under this regime, was corporate-shareholder income (regardless of the relative levels of individual and corporate rates) taxed more or less heavily than an individual's wage earnings? Than income from property held in noncorporate form?

9) Rationale for the Separate Corporate Tax

Partnership income is subject only to a one-level tax. The partnership itself is not treated as a separate taxable entity, and all income is allocated and taxed to the partners, whether distributed or retained.

Why is a separate corporate level tax imposed on corporate-shareholder income? Why not simply tax corporations in the same way as partnerships, allocating to each shareholder the appropriate portion of annual corporate income, whether distributed or retained?

Would taxing corporations like partnerships be difficult to administer if a corporation simply has an all common stock capital structure? What complications are introduced if the corporation has preferred stock as well as common? Or preferred stock that may be converted into common?

Chapter 26

INVENTORY VERSUS INVESTMENT PROPERTY

A. INTRODUCTORY NOTE

Capital gain arises from the sale or exchange of *capital assets*. Section 1222. Capital assets are defined by Section 1221 as *property*, subject to certain exclusions. The basic (but not only) statutory exclusion is for "inventory, stock-in-trade, and property held primarily for sale to customers in the ordinary course of business." Section 1221(1).

Why is preferential treatment withheld for such items? When such items are sold, is there likely to be a lock-in, inflation, or bunching problem? To what is most of the gain on such items attributable? To the extent that inflationary gains are a problem with inventory, the Code already provides a solution by allowing taxpayers to elect the LIFO method of accounting.[1]

In most instances, whether property should be regarded as inventory is easily determined, as, for example, when General Motors sells cars, IBM sells computers, or Texaco sells gasoline. The cases in this chapter and the following chapter involve borderline instances in which the possible inventory character of property is not self-evident.

B. CORN PRODUCTS REFINING CO. v. COMMISSIONER
350 U.S. 46 (1955)

Mr. Justice Clark delivered the opinion of the Court.

This case concerns the tax treatment to be accorded certain transactions in commodity futures.[2] In the Tax Court, petitioner Corn Products Refining Company contended that its purchases and sales of corn futures in 1940

---

1. When prices are rising, LIFO tends to eliminate the taxation of inflationary gains (Chapter 15).

2. A commodity future is a contract to purchase some fixed amount of a commodity at a future date for a fixed price. Corn futures, involved in the present case, are in terms of some multiple of five thousand bushels to be delivered eleven months or less after the contract. . . .

and 1942 were capital-asset transactions under § [1221]. . . .[W]e hold that these futures do not constitute capital assets in petitioner's hands. . . .

Petitioner is a nationally known manufacturer of products made from grain corn. It manufactures starch, syrup, sugar, and their byproducts, feeds and oil. Its average yearly grind of raw corn during the period 1937 through 1942 varied from thirty-five to sixty million bushels. Most of its products were sold under contracts requiring shipment in thirty days at a set price or at market price on the date of delivery, whichever was lower. It permitted cancellation of such contracts, but from experience it could calculate with some accuracy future orders that would remain firm. While it also sold to a few customers on long-term contracts involving substantial orders, these had little effect on the transactions here involved.

In 1934 and again in 1936 droughts in the corn belt caused a sharp increase in the price of spot corn. With a storage capacity of only 2,300,000 bushels of corn, a bare three weeks' supply, Corn Products found itself unable to buy at a price which would permit its refined corn sugar, cerelose, to compete successfully with cane and beet sugar. To avoid a recurrence of this situation, petitioner, in 1937, began to establish a long position in corn futures "as a part of its corn buying program" and "as the most economical method of obtaining an adequate supply of raw corn" without entailing the expenditure of large sums for additional storage facilities. At harvest time each year it would buy futures when the price appeared favorable. It would take delivery on such contracts as it found necessary to its manufacturing operations and sell the remainder in early summer if no shortage was imminent. If shortages appeared, however, it sold futures only as it bought spot corn for grinding. In this manner it reached a balanced position with reference to any increase in spot corn prices. It made no effort to protect itself against a decline in prices.

In 1940 it netted a profit of $680,587.39 in corn futures, but in 1942 it suffered a loss of $109,969.38. In computing its tax liability Corn Products reported these figures as ordinary profit and loss from its manufacturing operations for the respective years. It now contends that its futures were "capital assets" under § [1221] and that gains and losses therefrom should have been treated as arising from the sale of a capital asset. In support of this position it claims that its futures trading was separate and apart from its manufacturing operations and that in its futures transactions it was acting as a "legitimate capitalist." . . .

Both the Tax Court and the Court of Appeals found petitioner's futures transactions to be an integral part of its business designed to protect its manufacturing operations against a price increase in its principal raw material and to assure a ready supply for future manufacturing requirements. Corn Products does not level a direct attack on these two-court findings but insists that its futures were "property" entitled to capital-asset treatment . . . and as such were distinct from its manufacturing business. We cannot agree.

We find nothing in this record to support the contention that Corn Products' futures activity was separate and apart from its manufacturing operation. On the contrary, it appears that the transactions were vitally important to the company's business as a form of insurance against increases in the price of raw corn. Not only were the purchases initiated for just this reason, but the petitioner's sales policy, selling in the future at a fixed price or less, continued to leave it exceedingly vulnerable to rises in the price of corn. Further, the purchase of corn futures assured the company a source of supply which was admittedly cheaper than constructing additional storage facilities for raw corn. Under these facts it is difficult to imagine a program more closely geared to a company's manufacturing enterprise or more important to its successful operation.

Likewise the claim of Corn Products that it was dealing in the market as a "legitimate capitalist" lacks support in the record. There can be no quarrel with a manufacturer's desire to protect itself against increasing costs of raw materials. Transactions which provide such protection are considered a legitimate form of insurance.... However, in labeling its activity as that of a "legitimate capitalist" exercising "good judgment" in the futures market, petitioner ignores the testimony of its own officers that in entering that market the company was "trying to protect a part of [its] manufacturing costs"; that its entry was not for the purpose of "speculating and buying and selling corn futures" but to fill an actual "need for the quantity of corn [bought] . . . in order to cover . . . what [products] we expected to market over a period of fifteen or eighteen months. It matters not whether the label be that of "legitimate capitalist" or "speculator"; this is not the talk of the capital investor but of the far-sighted manufacturer. For tax purposes petitioner's purchases have been found to "constitute an integral part of its manufacturing business" by both the Tax Court and the Court of Appeals, and on essentially factual questions the findings of two courts should not ordinarily be disturbed. . . .

Petitioner also makes much of the conclusion by both the Tax Court and the Court of Appeals that its transactions did not constitute "true hedging." It is true that Corn Products did not secure complete protection from its market operations. Under its sales policy petitioner could not guard against a fall in prices. It is clear, however, that petitioner feared the possibility of a price rise more than that of a price decline. It therefore purchased partial insurance against its principal risk, and hoped to retain sufficient flexibility to avoid serious losses on a declining market.

Nor can we find support for petitioner's contention that hedging is not within the exclusions of § [1221]. Admittedly, petitioner's corn futures do not come within the literal language of the exclusions set out in that section. They were not stock in trade, actual inventory, property held for sale to customers or depreciable property used in a trade or business. But the capital-asset provision . . . must not be so broadly applied as to defeat rather than further the purpose of Congress. . . . Congress intended that profits and losses arising from the everyday operation of a business be considered as ordinary income or loss rather than capital gain or loss. The preferential treatment provided by § [1221] applies to transactions in property which are not the normal source of business income. It was intended "to relieve the taxpayer from . . . excessive tax burdens on gains resulting from a conversion of capital investments, and to remove the deterrent effect of those burdens on such conversions." . . . Since this section is an exception from the normal tax requirements of the Internal Revenue Code, the definition of a capital asset must be narrowly applied and its exclusions interpreted broadly. This is necessary to effectuate the basic congressional purpose. This Court has always construed narrowly the term "capital assets" in § [1221]. . . .

The problem of the appropriate tax treatment of hedging transactions first arose under the 1934 Tax Code revision. Thereafter the Treasury issued G.C.M. 17322, supra, distinguishing speculative transactions in commodity futures from hedging transactions. It held that hedging transactions were essentially to be regarded as insurance rather than a dealing in capital assets and that gains and losses therefrom were ordinary business gains and losses. The interpretation outlined in this memorandum has been consistently followed by the courts as well as by the Commissioner. While it is true that this Court has not passed on its validity, it has been well recognized for 20 years; and Congress has made no change in it though the Code has been re-enacted on three subsequent occasions. This bespeaks congressional approval. . . . Furthermore, Congress has since specifically recognized the hedging exception here under consideration in the short-sale rule of § 1233(a) of the 1954 Code.[3]

We believe that the statute clearly refutes the contention of Corn Products. Moreover, it is significant to note that practical considerations lead to the same conclusion. To hold otherwise would permit those engaged in hedging transactions to transmute ordinary income into capital gain at will. The hedger may either sell the future and purchase in the spot market or take delivery under the future contract itself. But if a sale of the future created a capital transaction while delivery of the commodity under the same future did not, a loophole in the statute would be created and the purpose of Congress frustrated.

C. NOTES AND QUESTIONS

1) Illustrating the *Corn Products* Problem

Suppose that Corn Products, Inc. (CPI) contracts with a customer to deliver manufactured corn products (corn syrup, popcorn, etc.) in six months. CPI plans to start manufacturing the products in about five months (about one month before the specified delivery date). It does not yet have on hand the raw corn that it will use because it lacks storage facilities. The raw corn will be acquired only a few days before manufacturing begins.

---

3. Section 1233(a) provides that gain or loss from "the short sale of property, other than a hedging transaction in commodity futures," shall be treated as gain or loss from the sale of a capital asset to the extent "that the property, including a commodity future, used to close the short sale constitutes a capital asset in the hands of a taxpayer." The legislative history recognizes explicitly the hedging exception. . . . "Under existing law bona fide hedging transactions do not result in capital gains or losses. This result is based upon case law and regulations. To continue this result hedging transactions in commodity futures have been specifically excepted from the operation of this subsection."

CPI's customer wants the price of the manufactured goods specified in the contract in advance. However, it is difficult for CPI to know in advance what price to charge since CPI does not know today how much it will have to pay in five months for the raw corn that it will use in manufacturing its products. The price of raw corn is highly sensitive to variations in supply and may rise or fall significantly, depending on such factors as the weather, insects, and foreign imports that affect the overall supply.

To resolve this problem, CPI takes a position in corn futures as a buyer. The future is a contractual commitment to buy a certain amount of raw corn at a specified date at a fixed cost. See Chapter 16. For this example, assume that the date is five months in the future and that the fixed cost is $1,000.

The corn future enables CPI to know exactly how much it will have to pay for the raw corn at the time CPI needs it. With this, no matter what happens to the price of raw corn in the interim, CPI knows that it can buy the raw corn for no more than $1,000. Thus, CPI is able to set a fixed contract price in advance for the manufactured corn products of, say, $3,000.

2) Rising Prices

Suppose that, in the above example, five months down the road, a plague of beetles attacks the nation's corn crop, curtailing supplies and causing the price of raw corn to rise to $1,500.

a) If CPI uses the future to acquire raw corn and then sells the manufactured products, how much and what kind of gain does it report (ignoring all other costs)?

b) Suppose that, instead of exercising its rights under the future, CPI sells the future. For how much can CPI sell it just prior to the delivery date? If CPI is allowed to treat the corn future as a capital asset, how much and what kind of gain does it report? If CPI then uses the proceeds to buy the raw corn, how much and what kind of gain does it report from selling the manufactured products (again, ignoring all other costs)?

c) Compare your answers to a) and b), above. Why is there a difference? What does this difference represent? *Assuming that corn futures are a capital asset*, which is the more accurate result? How is this reminiscent of the basic issue that arises with compensatory stock options (Chapter 3)?

d) If CPI may choose between a) or b), above, which will it choose?

3) Falling Prices

Suppose that five months down the road, warm weather and plentiful rains lead to a record corn crop, dropping the price of raw corn to $500. Now answer questions a), b), c), and d), under 2), above, for these changed circumstances.

4) The Specific Abuse Problem

What will CPI do with the future if corn prices rise (the answer to 2)d), above)? What will it do with the future if corn prices fall (the answer to

3)d), above)? What is the underlying abuse problem? Why were corn futures treated as noncapital assets by the *Corn Products* decision?

Writing for the Court in *Corn Products,* Justice Clark stated that "[t]o hold otherwise would permit those engaged in hedging transactions to transmute ordinary income into capital gain at will." Is that an accurate statement of the abuse problem? Would it be more accurate to say that it would permit the transmutation of "capital loss into ordinary loss"? Is Justice Clark more on the mark when he writes, in closing, "But if a sale of the future created a capital transaction while delivery of the commodity under the same future did not, a loophole would be created"?

5) Alternative Solutions

Are there any alternative solutions to the *Corn Products* problem that would allow the futures to be treated as Section 1221 property? For example, could taking delivery of the commodity be treated as a taxable event? Or, could the IRS prohibit the manufacturer from ever taking delivery on futures and instead require that they be sold in order to separate clearly the investment and manufacturing activities?

6) Literalism versus Nonliteralism in Interpreting the Code

Which side in *Corn Products* argued for a more literal interpretation of the language of Section 1221? Which side argued for a less literal interpretation? What does the Supreme Court cite as evidence of what Congress intended?

7) Legislative Intent and the Reenactment Doctrine

Prior to the decision in *Corn Products,* the Treasury had ruled that commodity futures were not Section 1221 "property" when the taxpayer's purpose was to hedge against a future increase in the price of raw materials. On three subsequent occasions, Congress reenacted the Internal Revenue Code without rejecting the Treasury ruling. Therefore, the Supreme Court reasoned, Congress intended to accept the Treasury interpretation.

What is the doctrine of statutory construction implicit in the Court's reasoning? As a common-sense matter, do you believe that reenactment of Section 1221 proved that Congress intended to accept the Treasury ruling? Why didn't reenactment simply mean that Congress wanted the courts to decide the meaning of Section 1221?

8) The Significance of Hedging

Why should the hedging purpose make a difference? Suppose that when sales of sweeteners made from corn go up, sales of sugar tend to fall, and vice versa. If Corn Products uses excess cash to purchase stock in a sugar refinery in order to hedge against a decline in its corn products business, should the stock be regarded as a noncapital asset? Or suppose that a Honda dealer buys Chrysler stock because when sales of Hondas fall, Chrysler sales tend to rise. Should the Chrysler stock be regarded as a noncapital asset because of the hedging purpose? If the stock in these two examples *should* constitute a capital asset, notwithstanding the hedging purpose, how can *Corn Products* be distinguished?

9) Corn Futures as Equivalent to Raw Corn

Had the taxpayer sold off excess stores of raw corn at a profit, the gain would have been ordinary. Raw material used to manufacture a business' output is considered inventory. See Reg. § 1.471–1. Could the IRS have argued that the corn futures, representing a contractual commitment to buy raw corn, should have exactly the same character in the taxpayer's hands as the raw corn would?

But would all raw corn owned by Corn Products necessarily be inventory? Could Corn Products sometimes acquire raw corn for its manufacturing activities and at other times buy raw corn as an investment because it anticipates a rise in prices and plans to resell the corn at a profit? If both purposes are conceivable, would it be easy for the IRS to determine which corn was, in fact, acquired as inventory and which was acquired for investment?

D. ARKANSAS BEST CORP. v. COMMISSIONER
_____ U.S. _____ (1988)[4]

JUSTICE MARSHALL delivered the opinion of the Court.

The issue presented in this case is whether capital stock held by petitioner Arkansas Best Corporation (Arkansas Best) is a "capital asset" as defined in § 1221 of the Internal Revenue Code regardless of whether the stock was purchased and held for a business purpose or for an investment purpose.

I

Arkansas Best is a diversified holding company. In 1968 it acquired approximately 65% of the stock of the National Bank of Commerce (Bank) in Dallas, Texas. Between 1969 and 1974, Arkansas Best more than tripled the number of shares it owned in the Bank, although its percentage interest in the Bank remained relatively stable. These acquisitions were prompted principally by the Bank's need for added capital. Until 1972, the Bank appeared to be prosperous and growing, and the added capital was necessary to accommodate this growth. As the Dallas real estate market declined, however, so too did the financial health of the Bank, which had a heavy concentration of loans in the local real estate industry. In 1972, federal examiners classified the Bank as a problem bank. The infusion of

---

4. 108 S. Ct. 971, 99 L. Ed. 2d 183 (1988).

capital after 1972 was prompted by the loan portfolio problems of the bank.

Petitioner sold the bulk of its Bank stock on June 30, 1975, leaving it with only a 14.7% stake in the Bank. On its federal income tax return for 1975, petitioner claimed a deduction for an ordinary loss of $9,995,688 resulting from the sale of the stock. The Commissioner of Internal Revenue disallowed the deduction, finding that the loss from the sale of stock was a capital loss, rather than an ordinary loss, and that it therefore was subject to the capital loss limitations in the Internal Revenue Code.

Arkansas Best challenged the Commissioner's determination in the United States Tax Court. The Tax Court, relying on cases interpreting *Corn Products Refining Co. v. Commmissioner* . . . held that stock purchased with a substantial investment purpose is a capital asset which, when sold, gives rise to a capital gain or loss, whereas stock purchased and held for a business purpose, without any substantial investment motive, is an ordinary asset whose sale gives rise to ordinary gains or losses. . . . The court characterized Arkansas Best's acquisitions through 1972 as occurring during the Bank's " 'growth' phase," and found that these acquisitions "were motivated primarily by investment purpose and only incidentally by some business purpose." . . . The stock acquired during this period therefore constituted a capital asset, which gave rise to a capital loss when sold in 1975. The court determined, however, that the acquisitions after 1972 occurred during the Banks' " 'problem' phase" . . . and . . . "were made exclusively for business purposes and subsequently held for the same reasons." . . . These acquisitions, the court found, were designed to preserve petitioner's business reputation, because without the added capital the Bank probably would have failed. . . . The loss realized on the sale of this stock was thus held to be an ordinary loss.

The Court of Appeals for the Eighth Circuit reversed the Tax Court's determination that the loss realized on stock purchased after 1972 was subject to ordinary-loss treatment, holding that all of the Bank stock sold in 1975 was subject to capital-loss treatment. . . . The court reasoned that the Bank stock clearly fell within the general definition of "capital asset" in Internal Revenue Code § 1221, and that the stock did not fall within any of the specific statutory exceptions to this definition. The court concluded that Arkansas Best's purpose in acquiring and holding the stock was irrelevant to the determination whether the stock was a capital asset. We granted certiorari . . . and now affirm.

II

Section 1221 of the Internal Revenue Code defines "capital asset" broadly, as "property held by the taxpayer (whether or not connected with his trade or business)," and then excludes five specific classes of property from capital-asset status. In the statute's present form, the classes of property exempted from the broad definition are (1) "property of a kind which would properly be included in the inventory of the taxpayer"; (2) real property or other depreciable property used in the taxpayer's trade or business; (3) "a copyright, a literary, musical, or artistic composition," or similar property; (4) "accounts or notes receivable acquired in the ordinary course of trade or business for services rendered" or from the sale of inventory; and (5) publications of the Federal Government. Arkansas Best acknowledges that the Bank stock falls within the literal definition of capital asset in § 1221, and is outside of the statutory exclusions. It asserts, however, that this determination does not end the inquiry. Petitioner argues that in *Corn Products Refining Co. v. Commissioner* . . . this Court rejected a literal reading of § 1221, and concluded that assets acquired and sold for ordinary business purposes rather than for investment purposes should be given ordinary-asset treatment. Petitioner's reading of *Corn Products* finds much support in the academic literature and in the courts. Unfortunately for petitioner, this broad reading finds no support in the language of § 1221.

In essence, petitioner argues that "property held by the taxpayer (whether or not connected with his trade or business)" does not include property that is acquired and held for a business purpose. In petitioner's view an asset's status as "property" thus turns on the motivation behind its acquisition. This motive test, however, is not only nowhere mentioned in § 1221, but it is also in direct conflict with the parenthetical phrase "whether or not connected with his trade or business." The broad definition of the term "capital asset" explicitly makes irrelevant any consideration of the property's connection with the taxpayer's business, whereas petitioner's rule would make this factor dispositive.

In a related argument, petitioner contends that the five exceptions listed in § 1221 for certain kinds of property are illustrative, rather than exhaustive, and that courts are therefore free to fashion additional exceptions in order to further the general purposes of the capital-asset provisions. The language of the statute refutes petitioner's construction. Section 1221 provides that "capital asset" means "property held by the taxpayer[,] . . . but does not include" the five classes of property listed as exceptions. We believe this locution signifies that the listed exceptions are exclusive. The body of § 1221 establishes a general definition of the term "capital asset," and the phrase "does not include" takes out of that broad definition only the classes of property that are specifically mentioned. The legislative history of the capital asset definition supports this interpretation . . . ("[T]he definition includes all property, except as specifically excluded"); . . . ("[A] capital asset is property held by the taxpayer with certain exceptions"), as does the applicable Treasury regulation, see 26 CFR § 1.1221–1(a) (1987) ("The term 'capital assets' includes all classes of property not specifically excluded by section 1221").

Petitioner's reading of the statute is also in tension with the exceptions listed in § 1221. These exclusions would be largely superfluous if assets acquired primarily or exclusively for business purposes were not capital assets. Inventory, real or depreciable property used in the taxpayer's trade or business, and accounts or notes receivable acquired in the ordinary course of business, would undoubtedly satisfy such a business-motive test. Yet these exceptions were created by Congress in separate enactments spanning 30 years. Without any express direction from Congress, we are unwilling to read § 1221 in a manner that makes surplusage of these statutory exclusions.

In the end, petitioner places all reliance on its reading of *Corn Products Refining Co. v. Commissioner* . . . a reading we believe is too expansive. . . .

The Court in *Corn Products* proffered the oft-quoted rule of construction that the definition of capital asset must be narrowly applied and its exclusions interpreted broadly, but it did not state explicitly whether the holding was based on a narrow reading of the phrase "property held by the taxpayer," or on a broad reading of the inventory exclusion of § 1221. In light of the stark language of § 1221, however, we believe that *Corn Products* is properly interpreted as involving an application of § 1221's inventory exception. Such a reading is consistent both with the Court's reasoning in that case and with § 1221. The Court stated in *Corn Products* that the company's futures transactions were "an integral part of its business designed to protect its manufacturing operations against a price increase in its principal raw material and to assure a ready supply for future manufacturing requirements." . . . The company bought, sold, and took delivery under the futures contracts as required by the company's manufacturing needs. As Professor Bittker notes, under these circumstances, the futures can "easily be viewed as surrogates for the raw material itself" . . . The Court of Appeals for the Second Circuit in *Corn Products* clearly took this approach. That court stated that when commodity futures are "utilized solely for the purpose of stabilizing inventory cost[,] . . . [they] cannot reasonably be separated from the inventory items," and concluded that "property used in hedging transactions, properly comes within the exclusions of [§ 1221]." . . . [A]lthough the corn futures were not "actual inventory," their use as an integral part of the taxpayer's inventory-purchase system led the Court to treat them as substitutes for the corn inventory such that they came within a broad reading of "property of a kind which would properly be included in the inventory of the taxpayer" in § 1221.

Petitioner argues that by focusing attention on whether the asset was acquired and sold as an integral part of the taxpayer's everyday business operations, the Court in *Corn Products* intended to create a general exemption from capital-asset status for assets acquired for business purposes. We believe petitioner misunderstands the relevance of the Court's inquiry. A business connection, although irrelevant to the initial determination of whether an item is a capital asset, is relevant in determining the applicability of certain of the statutory exceptions, including the inventory exception. The close connection between the futures transactions and the taxpayer's business in *Corn Products* was crucial to whether the corn futures could be considered surrogates for the stored inventory of raw corn. For if the futures dealings were not part of the company's inventory-purchase system, and instead amounted simply to speculation in corn futures, they could not be considered substitutes for the company's corn inventory, and would fall outside even a broad reading of the inventory exclusion. We conclude that *Corn Products* is properly interpreted as standing for the narrow proposition that hedging transactions that are an integral part of a business' inventory-purchase system fall within the inventory exclusion of § 1221. Arkansas Best, which is not a dealer in securities, has never suggested that the Bank stock falls within the inventory exclusion. *Corn Products* thus has no application to this case.

It is also important to note that the business-motive test advocated by petitioner is subject to the same kind of abuse that the Court condemned in *Corn Products*. The Court explained in *Corn Products* that unless hedging transactions were subject to ordinary gain and loss treatment, taxpayers engaged in such transactions could "transmute ordinary income into capital gain at will." . . . The hedger could garner capital-asset treatment by selling the future and purchasing the commodity on the spot market, or ordinary-asset treatment by taking delivery under the future contract. In a similar vein, if capital stock purchased and held for a business purpose is an ordinary asset, whereas the same stock purchased and held with an investment motive is a capital asset, a taxpayer such as Arkansas Best could have significant influence over whether the asset would receive capital or ordinary treatment. Because stock is most naturally viewed as a capital asset, the Internal Revenue Service would be hard pressed to challenge a taxpayer's claim that stock was acquired as an investment, and that a gain arising from the sale of such stock was therefore a capital gain. Indeed, we are unaware of a single decision that has applied the business-motive test so as to require a taxpayer to report a gain from the sale of stock as an ordinary gain. If the same stock is sold at a loss, however, the taxpayer may be able to garner ordinary-loss treatment by emphasizing the business purpose behind the stock's acquisition. The potential for such abuse was evidenced in this case by the fact that as late as 1974, when Arkansas Best still hoped to sell the Bank stock at a profit, Arkansas Best apparently expected to report the gain as a capital gain. . . .

III

We conclude that a taxpayer's motivation in purchasing an asset is irrelevant to the question whether the asset is "property held by a taxpayer (whether or not connected with his business)" and is thus within § 1221's general definition of "capital asset." Because the capital stock held by petitioner falls within the broad definition of the term "capital asset" in § 1221 and is outside the classes of property excluded from capital-asset status, the loss arising from the sale of the stock is a capital loss. *Corn Products Refining Co. v. Commissioner*, . . . which we interpret as involving a broad reading of the inventory exclusion of § 1221, has no application in the present context. Accordingly, the judgment of the Court of Appeals is affirmed.

E. NOTES AND QUESTIONS

1) The Reinterpretation of *Corn Products*

Do you find the reinterpretation of *Corn Products* by *Arkansas Best* persuasive? Even if justified on purely analytic grounds, can the *Arkansas Best* court justify omitting all discussion whatsoever of the re-enactment doctrine, which played such a significant role in the *Corn Products* decision?

2) The Whipsaw Danger

Suppose that the taxpayer had won in *Arkansas Best Corp.* If the stock fell in value, the Court notes that the owner could be expected to claim that it was acquired for a noninvestment purpose and therefore produced an ordinary loss. But if the stock rose in value, the owner might claim an investment purpose and report a capital gain. Could this danger of the Treasury being whipsawed have been avoided if the taxpayer in *Arkansas Best* had been required to declare either an investment or noninvestment purpose when the stock was acquired?

3) Designating Property Clearly on Acquisition

Section 1236 permits a dealer in securities to hold some securities as "investments," provided that they are clearly labeled as such, thus preventing the taxpayer from claiming preferential treatment if sold at a gain but taking an ordinary deduction if sold at a loss. Should Section 1236 be extended to the kind of property involved in *Corn Products* and *Arkansas Best Corp.*? Would labeling solve the *Corn Products* problem only if (a) taking delivery were also viewed as a taxable event or (b) taxpayers were forbidden to take delivery of a future labeled a capital asset?

4) Bad Debts

Under Section 166, a taxpayer is entitled to a bad debt deduction for the year in which a loan becomes worthless. If the loan is considered a *business* bad debt, the deduction is an ordinary loss. Section 166(a). However, if considered a *non*business bad debt, the deduction is treated as a short-term capital loss. Section 166(d). The Supreme Court has held that whether a debt is business or nonbusiness depends on the taxpayer's "dominant motivation." United States v. Generes, 405 U.S. 93 (1972).

Suppose that Arkansas Best Corp. had made a loan to the National Bank of Commerce and that at some point the loan became uncollectible. Under the *Generes* rule would Arkansas Best Corp. be entitled to an ordinary loss or capital loss deduction for the bad debt? Is the *Generes* rule, that applies when the taxpayer holds a debt interest, consistent with the rule of *Arkansas Best*, that applies when the taxpayer holds an equity interest?

Chapter 27

DUAL CHARACTER ASSETS

A. MALAT v. RIDDELL
383 U.S. 569 (1966)

PER CURIAM.

Petitioner was a participant in a joint venture which acquired a 45-acre parcel of land, the intended use for which is somewhat in dispute. Petitioner contends that the venturers' intention was to develop and operate an apartment project on the land; the respondent's position is that there was a "dual purpose" of developing the property for rental purposes or selling, whichever proved to be the more profitable. In any event, difficulties in obtaining the necessary financing were encountered, and the interior lots of the tract were subdivided and sold. The profit from those sales was reported and taxed as ordinary income.

The joint venturers continued to explore the possibility of commercially developing the remaining exterior parcels. Additional frustrations in the form of zoning restrictions were encountered. These difficulties persuaded petitioner and another of the joint venturers of the desirability of terminating the venture; accordingly, they sold out their interests in the remaining property. Petitioner contends that he is entitled to treat the profits from this last sale as capital gains; the respondent takes the position that this was "property held by the taxpayer primarily for sale to customers in the ordinary course of his trade or business," and thus subject to taxation as ordinary income.

The District Court made the following finding:

> The members of [the joint venture], as of the date the 44.901 acres were acquired, intended either to sell the property or develop it for rental, depending upon which course appeared to be most profitable. The venturers realized that they had made a good purchase price-wise and, if they were

unable to obtain acceptable construction financing or rezoning ... which would be prerequisite to commercial development, they would sell the property in bulk so they wouldn't get hurt. The purpose of either selling or developing the property continued during the period in which [the joint venture] held the property.

The District Court ruled that petitioner had failed to establish that the property was not held *primarily* for sale to customers in the ordinary course of business, and thus rejected petitioner's claim to capital gain treatment for the profits derived from the property's resale. The Court of Appeals affirmed.... We granted certiorari ... to resolve a conflict among the courts of appeals with regard to the meaning of the term "primarily" as it is used in § 1221 (1) of the Internal Revenue Code of 1954.

The statute denies capital gain treatment to profits reaped from the sale of "property held by the taxpayer *primarily* for sale to customers in the ordinary course of his trade or business." (Emphasis added.) The respondent urges upon us a construction of "primarily" as meaning that a purpose may be "primary" if it is a "substantial" one.

As we have often said, "the words of statutes—including revenue acts—should be interpreted where possible in their ordinary, everyday senses." ... Departure from a literal reading of statutory language may, on occasion, be indicated by relevant internal evidence of the statute itself and necessary in order to effect the legislative purpose.... But this is not such an occasion. The purpose of the statutory provision with which we deal is to differentiate between the "profits and losses arising from the everyday operation of a business" on the one hand ... and "the realization of appreciation in value accrued over a substantial period of time" on the other.... A literal reading of the statute is consistent with this legislative purpose. We hold that, as used in § 1221 (1), "primarily" means "of first importance" or "principally."

Since the courts below applied an incorrect legal standard, we do not consider whether the result would be supportable on the facts of this case had the correct one been applied. We believe, moreover, that the appropriate disposition is to remand the case to the District Court for fresh fact-findings, addressed to the statute as we have now construed it.

B. NOTES AND QUESTIONS

1) The Specific Abuse Problem

What specific tax avoidance problem concerned the IRS in Malat v. Riddell? Was it that the property in question would be labeled inventory or investment, after the fact, depending on whether commercial development or subdividing the land turned out to be the more attractive course to follow? How is this like the problem in *Corn Products* and *Arkansas Best Corp.*?

C. BIEDENHARN REALTY CO. v. UNITED STATES
526 F.2d 409 (5th Cir. 1976), cert. denied 429 U.S. 819 (1976)

GOLDBERG, CIRCUIT JUDGE:

. . . Biedenharn listed profits of $254,409.47 from the sale of 38 residential lots. Taxpayer divided this gain, attributing 60% to ordinary income and 40% to capital gains. Later, having determined that the profits from these sales were entirely ordinary income, the Internal Revenue Service assessed and collected additional taxes and interest. In its present action, plaintiff asserts that the whole real estate profit represents gain from the sale of capital assets. . . . [W]e reject plaintiff's claim. . . .

I.

Because of the confusing state of the record in this controversy and the resulting inconsistencies among the facts as stipulated by the parties, as found by the District Court, and as stated in the panel opinion, we believe it useful to set out in plentiful detail the case's background and circumstances as best they can be ascertained.

A. *The Realty Company.* Joseph Biedenharn organized the Biedenharn Realty Company in 1923 as a vehicle for holding and managing the Biedenharn family's numerous investments. . . . The investment company controls, among other interests, valuable commercial properties, a substantial stock portfolio, a motel, warehouses, a shopping center, residential real property, and farm property.

B. *Taxpayer's Real Property Sales—The Hardtimes Plantation.* Taxpayer's suit most directly involves its ownership and sale of lots from the 973 acre tract located near Monroe, Louisiana, known as the Hardtimes Plantation. The plaintiff purchased the estate in 1935 for $50,000.00. B. W. Biedenharn, the Realty Company's president, testified that taxpayer acquired Hardtimes as a "good buy" for the purpose of farming and as a future investment. The plaintiff farmed the land for several years. Thereafter, Biedenharn rented part of the acreage to a farmer. . . .

1. *The Three Basic Subdivisions.* Between 1939 and 1966, taxpayer carved three basic subdivisions from Hardtimes—Biedenharn Estates, Bayou DeSiard Country Club Addition, and Oak Park Addition—covering approximately 185 acres. During these years, Biedenharn sold 208 subdivided Hardtimes lots in 158 sales, making a profit in excess of $800,000.00. These three basic subdivisions are the source of the contested 37 sales of 38 lots. . . .

2. *Additional Hardtimes Sales.* Plaintiff lists at least 12 additional Hardtimes sales other than lots vended from the three basic subdivisions. The earliest of these dispositions occurred in November, 1935, thirteen days after the Plantation's purchase. Ultimately totaling approximately 275 acres, most, but not all, of these sales involved large parcels of non-subdivided land.

C. *Taxpayer's Real Property Activity: Non-Hardtimes Sales.* The 208 lots marketed from the three Hardtimes subdivisions represent only part of Biedenharn's total real property sales activities. Although the record does not in every instance permit exactitude, plaintiff's own submissions make clear that the Biedenharn Realty Company effectuated numerous non-Hardtimes retail real estate transactions. From the Company's formation in 1923 through 1966, the last year for which taxes are contested, taxpayer sold 934 lots. Of this total, plaintiff disposed of 249 lots before 1935 when it acquired Hardtimes. Thus, in the years 1935 to 1966, taxpayer sold 477 lots apart from its efforts with respect to the basic Hardtimes subdivisions. . . . [There were] sales in all but two years, 1932 and 1970, since the Realty Company's 1923 inception.

Unfortunately, the record does not unambiguously reveal the number of *sales* as opposed to the number of *lots* involved in these dispositions. Although some doubt exists as to the actual *sales* totals, even the most conservative reading of the figures convinces us of the frequency and abundance of the non-Hardtimes sales. . . .

Each of these parcels has its own history. Joseph Biedenharn transferred much of the land to the Realty Company in 1923. The company acquired other property through purchases and various forms of foreclosure. Before sale, Biedenharn held some tracts for commercial or residential rental. . . . Also, the length of time between acquisition and disposition differed significantly among pieces of realty. However, these variations in the background of each plot and the length of time and original purpose for which each was obtained do not alter the fact that the Biedenharn Realty Company regularly sold substantial amounts of subdivided and improved real property, and further, that these sales were not confined to the basic Hardtimes subdivisions.

D. *Real Property Improvements.* Before selling the Hardtimes lots, Biedenharn improved the land, adding in most instances streets, drainage, water, sewerage, and electricity. The total cost of bettering the Plantation acreage exceeded $200,000. . . .

E. *Sale of the Hardtimes Subdivisions.* Bernard Biedenharn testified that at the time of the Hardtimes purchase, no one foresaw that the land would be sold as residential property in the future. Accordingly, the District Court found, and we do not disagree, that Biedenharn bought Hardtimes for investment. Later, as the City of Monroe expanded northward, the Plantation became valuable residential property. The Realty Company staked off the . . . subdivision so that prospective purchasers could see what the lots "looked like." As demand increased, taxpayer opened the Oak Park and Biedenharn Estates Unit 2 subdivisions and resubdivided the Bayou DeSiard section. Taxpayer handled all Biedenharn Estates and Bayou DeSiard sales. Independent realtors disposed of many of the Oak Park lots. . . . Of the 37 sales consummated between 1964 and 1966, Henry Biedenharn handled at least nine transactions . . . while "independent realtors" effected some, if not all, of the other 28 transactions. . . .

Taxpayer delegated significant responsibilities to these brokers. In its dealings with [brokers], Biedenharn set the prices, general credit terms, and signed the deeds. Details, including specific credit decisions and advertising, devolved to [brokers], who utilized on-site signs and newspapers to publicize the lots.

In contrast to these broker induced dispositions, plaintiff's non-brokered sales resulted after unsolicited individuals approached Realty Company employees with inquiries about prospective purchases. At no time did the plaintiff hire its own real state salesmen or engage in formal advertising. Apparently, the lands' prime location and plaintiff's subdivision activities constituted sufficient notice to interested persons of the availability of Hardtimes lots. Henry Biedenharn testified:

> [O]nce we started improving and putting roads and streets in people would call us up and ask you about buying a lot and we would sell a lot if they wanted it.

The Realty Company does not maintain a separate place of business but instead offices at the Biedenharn family's Ouachita Coca-Cola bottling plant. A telephone, listed in plaintiff's name, rings at the Coca-Cola building. Biedenharn has four employees: a camp caretaker, a tenant farmer, a bookkeeper and a manager. The manager, Henry Biedenharn, Jr., devotes approximately 10% of his time to the Realty Company, mostly collecting rents and overseeing the maintenance of various properties. The bookkeeper also works only part-time for plaintiff. Having set out these facts, we now discuss the relevant legal standard for resolving this controversy.

II.

The determination of gain as capital or ordinary is controlled by the language of the Internal Revenue Code. The Code defines capital asset, the profitable sale or exchange of which generally results in capital gains, as "property held by the taxpayer." 26 U.S.C. § 1221. Many exceptions limit the enormous breadth of this congressional description and consequently remove large numbers of transactions from the privileged realm of capital gains. In this case, we confront the question whether or not Biedenharn's real estate sales should be taxed at ordinary rates because they fall within the exception covering "property held by the taxpayer primarily for sale to customers in the ordinary course of his trade or business." 26 U.S.C. § 1221(1).

The problem we struggle with here is not novel. We have become accustomed to the frequency with which taxpayers litigate this troublesome question. Chief Judge Brown appropriately described the real estate capital gains-ordinary income issue as "old, familiar, recurring, vexing and ofttimes elusive." . . . The difficulty in large part stems from ad-hoc application of the numerous permissible criteria set forth in our multitudinous prior opinions. Over the past 40 years, this case by case approach with its concentration on the facts of each suit has resulted in a collection of decisions not always reconcilable. Recognizing the situation, we have warned that efforts to distinguish and thereby make consistent the Court's previous holdings must necessarily be "foreboding and unrewarding." . . . Litigants are cautioned that "each case must be decided on its own peculiar facts. . . . Specific factors, or combinations of them are not necessarily controlling." . . . Nor are these factors the equivalent of the philosopher's stone, separating "sellers garlanded with capital gains from those beflowered in the garden of ordinary income." . . .

Assuredly, we would much prefer one or two clearly defined, easily employed tests which lead to predictable, perhaps automatic, conclusions. However, the nature of the congressional "capital asset" definition and the myriad situations to which we must apply that standard make impossible any easy escape from the task before us. No one set of criteria is applicable to all economic structures. Moreover, within a collection of tests, individual factors have varying weights and magnitudes, depending on the facts of the case. The relationship among the factors and their mutual interaction is altered as each criteria increases or diminishes in strength, sometimes changing the controversy's outcome. As such, there can be no mathematical formula capable of finding the X of capital gains or ordinary income in this complicated field.

Yet our inability to proffer a panaceatic guide to the perplexed with respect to this subject does not preclude our setting forth some general, albeit inexact, guidelines for the resolution of many of the § 1221(1) cases we confront. This opinion does not purport to reconcile all past precedents or assure conflict-free future decisions. Nor do we hereby obviate the need for ad-hoc adjustments when confronted with close cases and changing factual circumstances. Instead, with the hope of clarifying a few of the area's mysteries, we more precisely define and suggest points of emphasis for the major . . . factors as they appear in the instant controversy. . . .

III.

We begin our task by evaluating in the light of *Biedenharn's* facts the main . . . factors—substantiality and frequency of sales, improvements, solicitation and advertising efforts, and brokers' activities—as well as a few miscellaneous contentions. A separate section follows discussing the keenly contested role of prior investment intent. Finally, we consider the significance of the Supreme Court's decision in *Malat v. Riddell.*

A. Frequency and Substantiality of Sales

Scrutinizing closely the record and briefs, we find that plaintiff's real property sales activities compel an ordinary income conclusion. In arriving at this result, we examine first the most important of . . . factors—the frequency and substantiality of taxpayer's sales. Although frequency and substantiality of sales are not usually conclusive, they occupy the preeminent ground in our analysis. The recent trend of Fifth Circuit decisions indicates that when dispositions of subdivided property extend over a long period of time and are especially numerous, the likelihood of capital gains is very slight indeed. . . . Conversely, when sales are few and isolated, the taxpayer's claim to capital gain is accorded greater deference. . . .

On the present facts, taxpayer could not claim "isolated" sales or a passive and gradual liquidation. . . . Although only three years and 37 sales (38 lots) are in controversy here, taxpayer's pre-1964 sales from the Hardtimes acreage as well as similar dispositions from other properties are probative of the existence of sales "in the ordinary course of his trade or business." ... Biedenharn sold property, usually a substantial number of lots, in every year, save one, from 1923 to 1966. ...

... [T]he District Court sought to overcome this evidence of dealer-like real estate activities and property "primarily held for sale" by clinging to the notion that the taxpayer was merely liquidating a prior investment. We discuss later the role of former investment status and the possibility of taxpayer relief under that concept. Otherwise, the question of liquidation of an investment is simply the opposite side of the inquiry as to whether or not one is holding property primarily for sale in the ordinary course of his business. In other words, a taxpayer's claim that he is liquidating a prior investment does not really present a separate theory but rather restates the main question currently under scrutiny. ...

B. Improvements

Although we place greatest emphasis on the frequency and substantiality of sales over an extended time period, our decision in this instance is aided by the presence of [other] taxpayer activity—particularly improvements. ... Biedenharn vigorously improved its subdivisions, generally adding streets, drainage, sewerage, and utilities.... In *Barrios Estate v. Commissioner of Internal Revenue* ... heavily relied on by plaintiff, the Court reasoned that improvements constituted an integral part of the sale of subdivided realty and were therefore permissible in the context of a liquidating sale. As discussed above, Biedenharn's activities have removed it from any harbor of investment liquidation. Moreover, the additional sales flexibility permitted the *Barrios Estate* taxpayer might be predicated on the forced change of purpose examined in section IV. ...

C. Solicitation and Advertising Efforts

Substantial, frequent sales and improvements such as we have encountered in this case will usually conclude the capital gains issue against taxpayer. ... Minimizing the importance of its own sales activities, taxpayer points repeatedly to its steady avoidance of advertising or other solicitation of customers. Plaintiff directs our attention to stipulations detailing the population growth of Monroe and testimony outlining the economic forces which made Hardtimes Plantation attractive residential property and presumably eliminated the need for sales exertions. We have no quarrel with plaintiff's description of this familiar process of suburban expansion, but we cannot accept the legal inferences which taxpayer would have us draw.

The Circuit's recent decisions ... implicitly recognize that even one inarguably in the real estate business need not engage in promotional exertions in the face of a favorable market. As such, we do not always require a showing of active solicitation where "business ... [is] good, indeed brisk," ... and where other ... factors make obvious taxpayer's ordinary trade or business status. ... Plainly, this represents a sensible approach. In cases such as *Biedenharn*, the sale of a few lots and the construction of the first homes, albeit not ... by the taxpayer, as well as the building of roads, addition of utilities, and staking off of the other subdivided parcels constitute a highly visible form of advertising. Prospective home buyers drive by the advantageously located property, see the development activities, and are as surely put on notice of the availability of lots as if the owner had erected large signs announcing "residential property for sale." We do not by this evaluation automatically neutralize advertising or solicitation as a factor in our analysis. This form of inherent notice is not present in all land sales, especially where the property is not so valuably located, is not subdivided into small lots, and is not improved. . . . Media utilization and personal initiatives remain material components of this criterion. When present, they call for greater Government oriented emphasis on [the] solicitation factor.

D. Brokerage Activities

. . . [T]he Realty Company hired brokers who, using media and on site advertising, worked vigorously on taxpayer's behalf. We do not believe that the employment of brokers should shield plaintiff from ordinary income treatment. . . . Their activities should at least in discounted form be attributed to Biedenharn. To the contrary, taxpayer argues that "one who is not already in the trade or business of selling real estate does not enter such business when he employs a broker who acts as an independent contractor. . . ." Without presently entangling ourselves in a dispute as to the differences between an agent and an independent contractor . . . we find the cases cited [by the taxpayer] distinguishable from the instant circumstances. In [those cases], the taxpayer turned the entire property over to brokers, who, having been granted total responsibility, made all decisions including the setting of sales prices. In comparison, Biedenharn determined original prices and general credit policy. Moreover, the Realty Company did not make all the sales in question through brokers. . . . Biedenharn sold the Bayou DeSiard and Biedenharn Estates lots and may well have sold some of the Oak Park land. In other words . . . Biedenharn's brokers did not so completely take charge of the whole of the Hardtimes sales as to permit the Realty Company to wall itself off legally from their activities.

E. Additional Taxpayer Contentions

Plaintiff presents a number of other contentions and supporting facts for our consideration. Although we set out these arguments and briefly discuss them, their impact, in the face of those factors examined above, must be minimal. Taxpayer emphasizes that its profits from real estate sales averaged only 11.1% in each of the years in controversy. . . . Whatever the percentage, plaintiff would be hard pressed to deny the substantiality of its Hardtimes sales in absolute terms (the subdivided lots alone brought in over one million dollars) or, most importantly, to assert that its real estate business was too insignificant to constitute a separate trade or business.

The relatively modest income share represented by Biedenharn's real property dispositions stems not from a failure to engage in real estate sales activities but rather from the comparatively large profit attributable to the Company's 1965 ($649,231.34) and 1966 ($688,840.82) stock sales. The fact of Biedenharn's holding, managing, and selling stock is not inconsistent with the existence of a separate realty business. If in the face of taxpayer's numerous real estate dealings this Court held otherwise, we would be sanctioning special treatment for those individuals and companies arranging their business activities so that the income accruing to real estate sales represents only a small fraction of the taxpaying entity's total gains.

Similarly, taxpayer observes that Biedenharn's manager devoted only 10% of his time to real estate dealings and then mostly to the company's rental properties. This fact does not negate the existence of sales activities. Taxpayer had a telephone listing, a shared business office, and a few part-time employees. Because, as discussed before, a strong seller's market existed, Biedenharn's sales required less than the usual solicitation efforts and therefore less than the usual time. Moreover, plaintiff . . . hired brokers to handle many aspects of the Hardtimes transactions—this further reducing the activity and time required of Biedenharn's employees.

Finally, taxpayer argues that it is entitled to capital gains since its enormous profits (74% to 97%) demonstrate a return based principally on capital appreciation and not on taxpayer's "merchandising" efforts. We decline the opportunity to allocate plaintiff's gain between long-term market appreciation and improvement related activities. . . .

IV.

The District Court found that "[t]axpayer is merely liquidating over a long period of time a substantial investment in the most advantageous method possible." . . . In this view, the original investment intent is crucial, for it preserves the capital gains character of the transaction even in the face of normal real estate sales activities.

The Government asserts that Biedenharn Realty Company did not merely "liquidate" an investment but instead entered the real estate business in an effort to dispose of what was formerly investment property. Claiming that Biedenharn's activities would result in ordinary income if the Hardtimes Plantation had been purchased with the intent to divide and resell the property, and finding no reason why a different prior intent should influence this outcome, the Government concludes that original investment purpose is irrelevant. Instead, the Government would have us focus exclusively on taxpayer's intent and the level of sales activity during the period commencing with subdivision and improvement and lasting through final sales. Under this theory, every individual who improves and frequently sells substantial numbers of land parcels would receive ordinary income.

While the facts of this case dictate our agreement with the Internal Revenue Service's ultimate conclusion of taxpayer liability, they do not require our acquiescence in the Government's entreated total elimination of . . . "the nature and purpose of the acquisition." Undoubtedly, in most subdivided-improvement situations, an investment purpose of antecedent origin will not survive into a present era of intense retail selling. The antiquated purpose, when overborne by later, but substantial and frequent selling activity, will not prevent ordinary income from being visited upon the taxpayer. . . . Generally, investment purpose has no built-in perpetuity nor a guarantee of capital gains forever more. Precedents, however, in certain circumstances have permitted landowners with earlier investment intent to sell subdivided property and remain subject to capital gains treatment. . . .

We reject the Government's sweeping contention that prior investment intent is always irrelevant. There will be instances where an initial investment purpose endures in controlling fashion notwithstanding continuing sales activity. We doubt that this aperture, where an active subdivider and improver receives capital gains, is very wide; yet we believe it exists. We would most generally find such an opening where the change from investment holding to sales activity results from unanticipated, externally induced factors which make impossible the continued pre-existing use of the realty. *Barrios Estate* . . . is such a case. There the taxpayer farmed the land until drainage problems created by the newly completed intercoastal canal rendered the property agriculturally unfit. The Court found that taxpayer was "dispossessed of the farming operation through no act of her own." . . . Similarly, Acts of God, condemnation of part of one's property, new and unfavorable zoning regulations, or other events forcing alteration of taxpayer's plans create situations making possible subdivision and improvement as a part of a capital gains disposition. . . .

The distinction drawn above reflects our belief that Congress did not intend to automatically disqualify from capital gains bona fide investors forced to abandon prior purposes for reasons beyond their control. At times, the Code may be severe, and this Court may construe it strictly, but neither Code nor Court is so tyrannical as to mandate the absolute rule urged by the Government. However, we caution that although permitting a land owner substantial sales flexibility where there is a forced change from original investment purpose, we do not absolutely shield the constrained taxpayer from ordinary income. That taxpayer is not granted *carte blanche* to undertake intensely all aspects of a full blown real estate business. . . .

Clearly, under the facts in this case, the distinction just elaborated undermines Biedenharn's reliance on original investment purpose. Taxpayer's change of purpose was entirely voluntary and therefore does not fall within the protected area. Moreover, taxpayer's original investment intent, *even if* considered a factor sharply supporting capital gains treatment, is so overwhelmed by the other . . . factors discussed supra, that that element can have no decisive effect. However wide the capital gains passageway through which a subdivider with former investment intent could squeeze, the Biedenharn Realty Company will never fit.

V.

The District Court, citing *Malat v. Riddell* . . . stated that "the lots were not held . . . primarily for sale as that phrase was interpreted . . . in *Malat*. . . ." . . . Finding that Biedenharn's primary purpose became holding for sale and consequently that *Malat* in no way alters our analysis here, we disagree with the District Court's conclusion. *Malat* was a brief per curiam in which the Supreme Court decided only that as used in Internal Revenue Code § 1221(1) the word "primarily" means "principally," "of first importance." The Supreme Court, remanding the case, did not analyze the facts or resolve the controversy which involved a real estate dealer who had purchased land and held it at the time of sale with the dual intention of developing it as rental property or selling it, depending on whichever proved to be the more profitable. . . . In contrast, having substantially abandoned its investment and farming intent, Biedenharn was cloaked primarily in the garb of sales purpose when it disposed of the 38 lots here in controversy. With this change, the Realty Company, lost the opportunity of coming within any dual purpose analysis. . . .

VI.

Having surveyed the Hardtimes terrain, we find no escape from ordinary income. The frequency and substantiality of sales over an extended time, the significant improvement of the basic subdivisions, the acquisition of additional properties, the use of brokers, and other less important factors persuasively combine to doom taxpayer's cause. Applying [the] criteria, this case clearly falls within the ordinary income category delineated in that decision. . . .

We cannot write black letter law for all realty subdividers and for all times, but we do caution in words of red that once an investment does not mean always an investment. A simon-pure investor forty years ago could by his subsequent activities become a seller in the ordinary course four decades later. The period of Biedenharn's passivity is in the distant past; and the taxpayer has since undertaken the role of real estate protagonist. The Hardtimes Plantation in its day may have been one thing, but as the plantation was developed and sold, Hardtimes became by the very fact of change and activity a different holding than it had been at its inception. No longer could resort to initial purpose preserve taxpayer's once upon a time opportunity for favored treatment. The opinion of the District Court is reversed. . . .

GEE, CIRCUIT JUDGE, with whom BELL, COLEMAN, AINSWORTH and DYER, CIRCUIT JUDGES, join, dissenting.

. . . [T]o permit a finding of continuing investment purpose in the face of major sales activity only . . . when that activity "results from unanticipated, externally induced factors which make impossible the continued pre-existing use of the realty," . . . makes impossible any voluntary disposition of investment property at capital gains rates, exalts one factor—sales activity—over all others. . . . This circuit's long-standing inclusion of factors other than sales activity in the capital gains/ordinary income calculus implicitly recognized that an investor could engage in a voluntary liquidation and begin selling property without a change of purpose. Holding that property is not part of a business only so long as it is sold in large blocs, but not if it is sold in small parcels, discriminates irrationally against an investor who decides on liquidation but cannot locate purchasers interested in large acquisitions. . . .

D. NOTES AND QUESTIONS

1) Apportioning the Gain Between Investment and Development Activities

Suppose that you buy the Hardtimes Plantation for $100,000 and rent it out for cultivation. Twenty years later, you sell it to a real estate developer for $400,000. The real estate developer spends $100,000 improving and subdividing the property and then sells off all the lots for a total of $800,000. How much and what kind of gain do you and the real estate developer each report?

Suppose that you decide to develop the plantation yourself. Should the apportionment of gain between capital and ordinary income be denied simply because one person is both investor and developer? The taxpayer in *Biedenharn* originally attempted to apportion the gain realized from the sale of lots. Neither the IRS nor the Court of Appeals was willing to accept apportionment as the solution. What are the practical obstacles to apportioning the gain on dual character property between investment and development activities?

If apportionment were permitted, how might taxpayers attempt to convert ordinary income into capital gain? Suppose a taxpayer sells undeveloped farmland to her spouse at an artificially high price (perhaps as an installment sale, with payments due only as lots are developed and sold by the spouse)? See Section 1041(a). What about a sale to one's child?

2) *Biedenharn, Corn Products*, and the Realization Principle

Why not treat the conversion of property from an investment to a development as a realization event? How is such a conversion analogous to taking delivery on a corn future in *Corn Products*?

3) Inventory versus Property Held for Sale to Customers in Business

The issue in *Biedenharn* was whether the lots sold were excluded from capital asset treatment under Section 1221(1) as "property held primarily for sale to customers in the ordinary course of a trade or business." Why didn't the IRS try to argue that the lots sold constituted inventory, which is also excluded by Section 1221(1)? Does inventory include only those items whose cost is accounted for by an inventory method? Was the cost of the lots accounted for under either the LIFO or FIFO method?

If the lots constituted inventory at some point, does it matter whether they were held primarily as inventory or not? In the statute, the word "primarily" appears not to modify the holding of property as inventory. But might it be interpreted to apply generally to the 1221(1) exclusion?

4) The Conversion of Investment Property

Another issue in *Biedenharn* was the nature and extent of activity sufficient to convert what was once investment property into "property held primarily for sale to customers in the ordinary course of a trade or business." What two factors were cited by the Court of Appeals as conclusive?

Suppose that you buy a 1,000 acre farm and rent it out for cultivation. Under which of the following circumstances *should* the farmland be excluded by Section 1221(1) when it is resold? Consider separately the relevance of improvements and frequency of sales as indicating whether capital gain treatment is appropriate. When is the making of improvements enough by itself to justify 1221(1) treatment? When is it not enough? When is the existence of frequent sales enough by itself to justify 1221(1) treatment? When is it not enough?

a) No improvements have been made, and the land is sold as a single parcel.

b) Considerable improvements have been made to upgrade the farmland for cultivation. The barn has been rebuilt, new fences have been erected, and additional land has been cleared. No other improvements have been made, and the land is sold as a single parcel.

c) No improvements have been made, and the farmland is sold off in twenty separate fifty-acre parcels to different real estate developers. Is this case any different from that of the investor who buys 1,000 shares of IBM and then sells fifty shares at a time?

d) No improvements have been made, and the farmland is sold off in 100 separate ten acre lots as future homesites. (Purchasers are told they will be charged dues by a homeowners' association to pay for the cost of roads, sewers, and utilities.) Why is this case arguably different from the preceding one? Because 100 sales are significantly more than fifty? Or because of the nature of the market in which lots are sold?

e) The farm buildings have been removed, the land has been platted into ten-acre lots, roads have been constructed providing access to each lot, and sewers and electric utilities have been installed. But the entire parcel is sold to *one* real estate dealer. If the lots had been sold separately, they would almost certainly fall within the Section 1221(1) exclusion. Should the fact that they are all sold to one customer make a difference? What makes this case arguably different from b), above? Is it the nature of the improvements?

5) *Biedenharn's* Treatment of Malat v. Riddell

Is the *Biedenharn* holding—that the business purpose is "of first importance" if the later business activity is substantial—consistent with the Malat v. Riddell holding that the business character controls only if it is "of first importance"? How is Malat v. Riddell like the comedian Rodney Dangerfield?

6) Forced Liquidations

Why does *Biedenharn* make an exception for "forced liquidations"? How does this situation differ from the usual case where an investor decides to assume the role of developer and the entire gain is taxed as ordinary income? From the case where an investor decides to sell the land without attempting development and the gain receives preferential treatment?

7) Section 1237

Section 1237 provides that if certain conditions are met, then real property is not "held primarily for sale to customers in the ordinary course of ... business" solely because of subdividing and sales activities. To qualify, a taxpayer must not be a dealer in real estate, must not have made a substantial improvement in the property, and must have held the property for five years. In that event, the taxpayer will realize capital gain on the sale of the lots with one important qualification. In the year in which the sixth lot is sold, and in any subsequent sales, 5% of the *gross proceeds* are treated as producing ordinary income gain.

According to the Senate Finance Committee Report, Section 1237 is intended to provide relief when "an individual holding real property for investment ... find[s] that the only way to dispose of it at a reasonable price is to subdivide it into lots."[1] Section 1237 thus permits gain on the sale of real estate to be apportioned between investment and development gain, creating an exception to the general antiapportionment rule approved in *Biedenharn*.

What is the relationship of Section 1237 to the "forced liquidation" exception described in *Biedenharn*? Does Section 1237 mean that if a forced liquidation occurs, the seller has to apportion 5% of the gross proceeds to ordinary income once the sixth lot is sold? Or will the apportionment formula be inapplicable if investor status is granted, not because of the Section 1237 "safe harbor," but under the forced liquidation doctrine of *Biedenharn*?

E. INTERNATIONAL SHOE MACHINE CORP. v. COMMISSIONER
491 F.2d 157 (1st Cir. 1974), cert. denied 419 U.S. 834 (1974)

COFFIN, CHIEF JUDGE.

Appellant taxpayer contends that the Commissioner of Internal Revenue erroneously treated income realized from the appellant's sales of certain shoe machines as "property held by the taxpayer primarily for sale to customers in the ordinary course of his trade or business", 26 U.S.C. § 1231(b)(1)(B), thereby taxing it as ordinary income instead of treating it under the capital gains provisions of the Code, and assessing deficiencies against the taxpayer. After having paid the deficiencies, the appellant filed claims for refunds, which were denied, and then instituted the present case. The district court upheld the Commissioner's disposition.

---

1. S. Rep. No. 1622, 83d Cong., 2d Sess. 415 (1954).

It is undisputed that during the years in question, 1964 through 1966, appellant's main source of income derived from the leases of its shoe machinery equipment, rather than from their sales. The revenue from sales of the leased machinery comprised, respectively, only 7 per cent, 2 per cent, and 2 per cent of appellant's gross revenues. In fact, because the appellant preferred the more profitable route of leasing its machines, it never developed a sales force, never solicited purchases, set prices high to make purchasing unattractive, and even attempted to dissuade customers from purchasing them.

Yet the district court found that, beginning in 1964, when the investment tax credit made it more attractive for shoe manufacturers to buy shoe machinery rather than to lease it, the selling of machinery became an accepted and predictable, albeit small, part of appellant's business. Since appellant's chief competitor was selling leased shoe machines, it was necessary for appellant to offer its customers the same option. During the years in issue, appellant never declined to quote a price, nor did it ever decline to make a sale if the customer was persistent. Unlike previous years, purchase inquiries were referred to the appellant's vice president for sales, normally charged with selling new, nonleased machines, whereupon a price was negotiated. A schedule was prepared, indicating the sales price of leased machines, based upon the number of years that the machines had been leased. In total, 271 machines were sold to customers who, at the time of the sales, had been leasing the machines for at least six months.

The case raises what has become a repeating source of difficulty in applying § 1231(b)(1)(B), which denies highly favored capital gains tax treatment to "property held ... primarily for sale to customers in the ordinary course of his trade or business". In particular, does the word "primarily" invoke a contrast between sales and leases, as the appellant contends, or between sales made in the ordinary course of business and non-routine sales made as a liquidation of inventory? And, if the latter, how can sales made in the ordinary course of business be distinguished from a liquidation of inventory?

In support of its contention that "primarily" refers to a contrast between sales and leases, appellant relies upon Malat v. Riddell.... There, the taxpayer purchased a parcel of land, with the alleged intention of developing an apartment project. When the taxpayer confronted zoning restrictions, he decided to terminate the venture, and sold his interest in the property, claiming a capital gain. The lower courts found, however, that the taxpayer had had a "dual purpose" in acquiring the land, a "substantial" one of which was to sell if that were to prove more profitable than development. Therefore, since the taxpayer had failed to establish that the property was not held primarily for sale to customers in the ordinary course of his business, his gain was treated as ordinary income. The Supreme Court vacated and remanded the case, stating that the lower courts had applied an incorrect legal standard when they defined "primarily" as merely "substantially" rather than using it in its ordinary, everyday sense of "first importance" or "principally". Although the Court in *Malat* was dealing with § 1221, rather than § 1231, the same clause appears in both sections. Appellant argues that the present case is analogous, since the "first" and "principal" reason for holding the shoe machinery was clearly for lease rather than for sale.

We cannot agree that *Malat* is dispositive. Even if "primarily" is defined as "of first importance" or "principally", the word may still invoke a contrast between sales made in the "ordinary course of . . . business" and those made as liquidations of inventory, rather than between leases and sales. *Malat* itself concerned the dual purposes of developing an apartment complex on the land and selling the land. Although these two possible sources of income might be characterized as income from "lease" or "sale", a more meaningful distinction could be made between on-going income generated in the ordinary course of business and income from the termination and sale of the venture. . . .

The real question, therefore, concerns whether or not the income from the sales of appellant's shoe machinery should have been characterized as having been generated in the "ordinary course of . . . business". Appellant contests the conclusion of the district court that selling was "an accepted and predictable part of the business" by pointing out that sales were made only as a last resort, after attempts to dissuade the customer from purchasing had failed. We think that the district court was correct in its finding. While sales were made only as a last resort, it seems clear that after 1964 such sales were expected to occur, on an occasional basis, and policies and procedures were developed for handling them. Purchase inquiries were referred to the vice president for sales, a price schedule was drawn up, and discounts were offered to good customers. Appellant may not have desired such sales. It is likely that appellant would never have developed a sales policy for its leased machines had it not been forced to do so by the pressure of competition. But it was justifiable to find that such occasional sales were indeed "accepted and predictable".

Even "accepted and predictable" sales might not, however, occur in the "ordinary course of . . . business". For example, a final liquidation of inventory, although accepted and predictable, would normally be eligible for capital gains treatment. Appellant's final contention, therefore, is that the sales in question represented the liquidation of an investment. Appellant points out that the machines were leased for an average of eight and one half years before they were sold, during which time depreciation was taken on them and repairs were made. Thus, appellant seeks to bring itself within the scope of the "rental-obsolescence" decisions, which hold that the sale of rental equipment, no longer useful for renting, is taxable at capital gains rates. . . .

In the "rental obsolescence" decisions, however, equipment was sold only after its rental income-producing potential had ended and "such sales were . . . the natural conclusion of a vehicle rental business cycle". . . . Moreover, the equipment was specifically manufactured to fit the requirements of lessees; it was sold only when lessees no longer found the equipment useful. . . . In the present case, however, the shoe manufacturing equipment was sold, not as a final disposition of property that had ceased to produce rental income for the appellant, but, rather, as property that still retained a rental income producing potential for the appellant. Had appellant chosen not to sell the shoe machinery, the machinery would have continued to generate ordinary income in the form of lease revenue. Thus, the sale of such machinery, for a price which included the present value of that future ordinary income, cannot be considered the liquidation of an investment outside the scope of the "ordinary course of . . . business".

Affirmed.

F. NOTES AND QUESTIONS

1) The Section 1221(2) Exclusion and Quasi-capital Assets

Section 1221(2) excludes from the capital asset definition real and depreciable property used in a trade or business. However, such property may still qualify for favored treatment as a Section 1231 quasi-capital asset. Section 1231(b) defines "quasi-capital assets" as real and depreciable property used in a trade or business. The same exceptions apply, however, under Section 1231(b), as under Section 1221(1), for "inventory" and "property held primarily for sale to customers in the ordinary course of a trade or business."

If the gains from quasi-capital assets exceed the losses, the net figure is treated as a long-term capital gain. Section 1231(a)(1). The effect is about the same as if the Section 1221(2) exclusion was eliminated. However, if losses from quasi-capital assets exceed gains, the net figure is treated as an ordinary loss. Section 1231(a)(2).

2) Justifications for Preferential Treatment and Quasi-capital Assets

As a matter of tax policy, why should gains on quasi-capital assets receive preferential treatment? Are the gains on such property subject to a lock-in effect? Do they represent inflation? Is there a bunching problem? (Despite Section 1231(b), the sale of such assets often produces ordinary income, for reasons explained in Chapter 36.)

3) Liquidating versus Retailing Used Assets

Does *International Shoe* suggest that the machinery became Section 1221(1) property because the taxpayer began to act as a dealer in used machinery? Might the outcome have been different if the machinery had been sold, perhaps in bulk, to a used machinery dealer? Is that what the opinion meant by "a more meaningful distinction . . . between on-going income generated in the ordinary course of business and income from the termination and sale of the venture"?

4) The Distinction Between Investment and Trade or Business Activities

Biedenharn supplies a list of factors that distinguish investment from trade or business activities, but provides no real explanation or justification for its list. *International Shoe Machinery* merely asserts, somewhat cryptically, that the critical factor is whether the taxpayer is selling in bulk or acting as a dealer. It should be possible to articulate more analytically what *should* distinguish an investment from a trade or business.

One possibility is to consider the activities performed vis-a-vis the property. The investor is usually thought of as buying property and simply holding it in the hope that it will appreciate in value. In that event, property appreciation, if any, is the result of increased demand, decreased supply, inflation, or some combination of the above. In a trade or business, however, there is some processing of the property. The processing may take one of two forms. It may involve (a) manufacturing which physically transforms the property (development in the case of land) or (b) making the property available for sale in a different market (as in buying wholesale and selling retail). In either case, profit arises (for the most part) from the value added by processing the property.

If a trade or business involves either manufacturing or marketing, as defined above, what is the relevance of the *Biedenharn* factors? For example, do frequent sales necessarily indicate that the landowner has become a "retailer"? Does advertising the sale of land prove that an investment is not involved? How about the hiring of a sales force? Conversely, does the lack of frequent sales, advertising, or a sales force necessarily indicate that the owner is not acting as a dealer or retailer of land? Or is it merely suggestive?

5) Adam v. Commissioner

In Adam v. Commissioner, 60 T.C. 996 (1973), a full-time accountant (Adam) bought and sold nine separate parcels of waterfront property in Maine over a two and one-half year period. Adam purchased eight of the nine properties on the advice of a professional real estate broker, with whom he agreed to share one-half of his profits.

No improvements were made on any of the parcels. None was ever advertised for sale. In each case, it was the potential buyer who contacted Adam and initiated negotiations for Adam to sell the property.

The real estate broker, who advised Adam, was in the business of buying and selling real estate. Since Adam bought on the basis of the broker's advice and split the profits with the broker, the IRS argued that he, too, should be viewed as engaging in the real estate business. Therefore, the IRS concluded, Adam's real estate gains should be taxable as ordinary income. The Tax Court rejected the IRS position, holding that the broker's status should not automatically be imputed to Adam. Was this case correctly decided? By acting on the advice of the broker, was the taxpayer effectively engaged in the same kind of business activity as the broker?

Chapter 28

PROPERTY VERSUS COMPENSATION FOR PERSONAL SERVICES

A. MCFALL v. COMMISSIONER
34 B.T.A. 108 (1936)

FINDINGS OF FACT

After preliminary negotiations, the petitioners, under date of December 31, 1926, made written contracts with the Sparta Foundry Co. whereby petitioners agreed to give their services as superintendent and metallurgist, respectively, and the corporation employed them as such for five years and agreed to pay them each $100 a week, plus one sixth of its annual profits computed as prescribed. The contract, as far as appears, was continuously performed in 1927 and 1928 by both employer and employee....

On April 2, 1929, A. W. Clutter & Co. made a written agreement with each petitioner whereby petitioner agreed to sell and Clutter & Co. to buy "all right, title and interest of the vendor in and to said employment contract for the sum of $175,000 payable at ... Grand Rapids ... on or before June 5, 1929, against delivery of the original employment contract ... accompanied by a valid assignment of said contract which in the opinion of counsel for the purchaser validly transfers to the purchaser all right, title and interest of the vendor in said employment contract." ... Clutter & Co., among other terms, agreed with the corporation ... to secure petitioners' release of the corporation from the employment contracts in consideration for 8,088 shares. Petitioners caused their contracts to be delivered to Clutter & Co. in May 1929, and received the latter's promissory notes for $175,000 each. On June 5, 1929, they received checks for $175,000 and releases from the Sparta corporation from their obligations under the employment contracts....The corporation, on its 1929 income tax return, deducted $404,400, the value of the 8,088 shares, as "Expense of Obtaining Release of Liability and Cancellation of Profit-sharing Contracts", and the Commissioner allowed the deduction. The petitioners each treated the

$175,000 as capital net gain. . . . The Commissioner has determined the amount to be ordinary income.

OPINION

STERNHAGEN:

. . . The petitioners' contention is that they sold their contracts in 1929, that the contracts were property, that they had owned the contracts since 1926, more than two years, and that the resulting gain, admitted to be $175,000 each, was a capital net gain . . . and not ordinary income. . . .

The determination of deficiencies must, we think, be sustained. Petitioners did not sell their contracts, for inherently this they could not do. The contracts bound them to perform services of skill. *Arkansas Valley Smelting Co. v. Belden Mining Co.* . . . Before they had any contractual rights which they could sell, they were obligated to perform services for the company. . . . On April 2, 1929, there was a right of petitioners to continue to perform service and then to be paid—to persist in their contractual relation for its agreed term. While this right is property in the constitutional sense in that it could not be arbitrarily legislated away, it is not capital. . . . It is a continuing right which goes hand in hand with performance. Before performance it is in embryo, and after payment it is exhausted. Obviously it is not the sort of property which is susceptible of ownership for a length of time as is a share of stock, a bond, or a thing. . . .

There is, we think, no need to attempt a discussion of the various meanings in law of the word "property", or to define the term as used in section [1221]. The purpose of the statute, whether it be liberal or strict, is not served by including within it the contractual expectation of receiving pay for services not yet performed. . . .

Holding, for this reason, that the amount received was not a statutory capital gain, it is not necessary to agree with respondent's argument that petitioners were receiving in advance the pay which they would have received and for that reason the amount was ordinary income. . . . Our decision is sufficiently founded, we think, upon the transactions as they were stated by the parties themselves. It may be, however, that the anomalous sale by petitioners of their rights in a personal contract which they had yet to perform, to another, not in position to perform it, for cash, straightens out in the subsequent treatment of the contract. For notwithstanding the legal forms which were employed or the artificial conception that the contract was sold for cash, ultimately the parties to it abrogated it in the full light of the earlier transactions. It is not, therefore, a stretch of reason to say that this is what, in a layman's way, the petitioners had intended throughout their negotiations and agreement with Clutter & Co. to be understood as promising to do—to hold themselves bound, for a price, to terminate their employment contracts. Clearly, if the agreement with Clutter & Co. had been thus stated, the cash consideration received would have had no semblance of sale of property. . . .

B. NOTES AND QUESTIONS

1) Requirement of a Sale or Exchange

Section 1222 defines capital gains and losses as arising from the "sale or exchange" of a capital asset. Why did *McFall* hold that this sale or exchange requirement was not met? Wasn't there a sale of the contract rights, at least in form? In order to find that there was no sale in substance, how did *McFall* recast the transaction?

2) Justifying the *McFall* Result

In addition to the absence of a sale or exchange, what additional ground did *McFall* offer for denying capital gains treatment? Other than asserting that the transaction *should* not produce capital gain, did *McFall* provide any reasoning to support that result?

Suppose that the contract rights had been sold to a third party after the services were performed but before the taxpayer was paid for performance. In that event, would either of the technical grounds mentioned in *McFall* apply? But, in that event, should capital gain treatment result? If it did, what would happen to the taxation of compensation for services? Is there a better way to justify the result in *McFall* than the highly artificial reasons offered in the opinion?

3) Compensation for Personal Services as a Component of Investment Gain

Suppose that you hold an investment portfolio of stocks that you manage for yourself. You make the decisions about what to buy and sell. In theory, should some of the gains on the sale of stock be attributed to your management activities and therefore be taxable as ordinary income? While precise apportionment might be impractical, why not adopt a rule of thumb (see Section 1237, discussed in Chapter 27) and apportion some arbitrary percentage of such gains to ordinary income, as representing compensation for personal services?

C. MILLER v. COMMISSIONER
299 F.2d 706 (2d Cir. 1962), cert. denied 370 U.S. 923 (1962)

KAUFMAN, CIRCUIT JUDGE.

Petitioner is the widow of Glenn Miller, a band leader who achieved world fame about twenty-five years ago. Although Glenn Miller died in 1944, petitioner has been able to engage in a number of enterprises actively exploiting his continuing popularity. Apparently "the good that men do," if sufficiently publicized, does live after them, for petitioner's commercial efforts have met with appreciable financial success.

Thus, in 1952, she entered into a contract with Universal Pictures Company, Inc. (Universal) in connection with the production of a motion picture film entitled "The Glenn Miller Story"; and in the calendar year 1954, she received $409,336.34 as her share of the income derived from that theatrical venture. According to the terms of the 1952 contract, petitioner had purportedly granted to Universal "the exclusive right to produce, release, distribute and exhibit . . . one or more photoplays based upon the life and activities of Glenn Miller throughout the world"; and had warranted that she was "the sole and exclusive owner of all the rights" conveyed by her.

Petitioner now contends that the payment received in 1954 from Universal pursuant to that contract should be considered, for income tax purposes, as a "gain from the sale or exchange of a capital asset held for more than 6 months . . ." 26 U.S.C. § 1222; while the Commissioner, whose position was sustained by the Tax Court, contends that the 1954 payment must be treated as ordinary income. . . .[1]

. . . [T]he specific question dividing the parties relates to the meaning of the term "capital asset." Furthermore, since Section 1221 of the Internal Revenue Code of 1954, 26 U.S.C. § 1221, defines the term "capital asset" as "*property* held by the taxpayer . . ." (emphasis supplied), and since, if anything was held by anyone it was held by the petitioner,[2] the conflict is narrowed to the meaning of the word "property" for purposes of this section of the Code.

One would assume that since the question is so easily narrowed, the answer would be correspondingly free of difficulty. The assumption is unwarranted. The narrowing of a question does, ordinarily, reduce the *complexity* of the answer; but it also tends to increase the difficulty of reaching it. Moreover, in order to avoid creating more problems than we resolve, we wish to emphasize that throughout the ensuing discussion, our analysis of the term "property" is made within the context of capital gains taxation; universality in definition is not only unlikely, but undesirable.

The Internal Revenue Code does not define "property" as used in Section 1221. "It is here that the Code itself discloses the enormity of the problem." . . . This is one of those instances in which the drafters of that statute have (for obvious reasons) declined the challenge of preserving a chameleon in a pithy phrase. . . . Therefore, we must look outside the eight corners of the code for some elucidation. The ordinary technique is to refer to principles of state property law for, if not an answer, at least a hint. Since ultimately it is the Congressional purpose which controls, such non-tax definitions are certainly not binding on us. . . . On the other hand,

---

1. The Tax Court concluded that, (a) petitioner was compensated by Universal for services which she had agreed to render in connection with the photoplay; (b) petitioner accepted a share in the proceeds of the motion picture as an advance settlement of any liability which Universal might incur because of an invasion of privacy; and (c) petitioner had no "property right" in the name, image, reputation etc. of Glenn Miller which could qualify as a capital asset. Although the Tax Court's discussion of issues (a) and (b) suggests that there are alternative theories upon which this Court might affirm its decision, we prefer to dispose of the matter by accepting, *arguendo*, petitioner's theory that the contract dealt with a conveyance of "property" only. For this purpose we ignore the fact that taxpayer's original petition characterized the contract proceeds as constituting both a payment for taxpayer's services and a settlement of tort liability.

2. It is clear that whatever was sold to Universal was either created by petitioner, or owned by her deceased husband during his life. In addition, there is no dispute that under his will petitioner was the decedent's sole beneficiary.

Congress may be presumed to have had ordinary property concepts in mind so they are relevant to our inquiry.

Most people trained in the law would agree that for many purposes one may define "property" as a bundle of rights, protected from interference by legal sanctions.... This concept is behind one prong of petitioner's attack. She cites several cases, claiming they indicate that if Universal had made its motion picture without contracting with her, it would have been the victim of a substantial lawsuit.

Even if this were so, those cases would not compel this court to recognize, for income tax purposes, a "property right" in Glenn Miller himself if he were still alive. However, it is not necessary for us to reach a determination upon such an assertion. Those cases do not even remotely bear on the question whether such a property right, if it existed, could pass to the sole beneficiary under his will; and certainly they lend no support to petitioner's theory that the reputation or fame of a dead person could give rise to such "property rights."... Indeed, petitioner is well aware of this, for she concedes that at the time of the "sale" there were "no *clear-cut* decisions ... protecting publicity rights of a deceased celebrity"....

Undeterred by her failure to find case authority which would substantiate the existence of "property rights" petitioner invokes the authority of logic. With considerable ingenuity, she argues:

(1) Universal paid petitioner $409,336.34 in 1954, which is a great deal of money.[3]

(2) Universal was a sophisticated corporate being to which donative intent would be difficult to ascribe.

(3) If there was no danger in free use of Glenn Miller material, why did Universal pay?

Petitioner appears to find this question unanswerable unless it is conceded that there was a sale of a "property right." Petitioner is wrong.

It is clear to this Court, at least, that many things can be sold which are not "property" in any sense of the word. One can sell his time and experience, for instance, or, if one is dishonest, one can sell his vote; but we would suppose that no one would seriously contend that the subject matter of such sales is "property" as that word is ordinarily understood. Certainly no one would contend that such subject matter was inheritable. We conclude, therefore, that not everything people pay for is "property."

In the instant case, "something" was indeed sold. And the expedient business practice may often be to sell such "things." But the "thing" bought, or more appropriately "bought off," seems to have been the chance that a new theory of "property" might be advanced, and that a lawsuit predicated on it might be successful. It was a purchase, so to speak, of freedom from fear. In effect, it was a hedge against the chance that the Miller "property" *might* exist. Because Universal feared that it might sometime in the future be held to have infringed a property right does not mean, however, that a

---

3. It should be noted that petitioner received a fixed percentage of the income produced by the motion picture. Only the ultimate success of the venture, the extent of which was unknown at the time of the signing of the contract, made the sum actually paid so high.

court presently considering whether that property right *did* exist in 1952 must realize Universal's worst fears. That does not mean that Universal's payment was foolish or illusory. It got what it contracted for in 1952 and what it later paid Mrs. Miller for: freedom from the danger that at a future date a defensible right constituting "property" *would* be found to exist. But it didn't pay for "property." . . .

In any event we are unwilling to accept the fact of substantial payment as proof that "property" within the meaning of Section 1221 of the Code exists; and for the reasons stated, we must reject this argument as being in reality a makeweight. Petitioner concedes that at the time of the "sale" there had been no authoritative decision holding that a decedent's successors had any "property right" to the public image of a deceased entertainer; and therefore it follows that their bargain was not, at that time, a bargain that both parties knew involved a "property right." Furthermore, we do not find it necessary to decide whether the parties were then bargaining for a property right. The case before us only involves the meaning of language in a highly technical statute and the legal effects flowing from that language. . . .

. . . We do not believe that for income tax computation purposes the beneficiaries of the estate of a deceased entertainer receive by descent a capitalizable "property" in the name, reputation, right of publicity, right of privacy or "public image" of the deceased; or that in this case the petitioner, for tax purposes, owned any "property" which came into existence after Glenn Miller's death.[4] Therefore, income received by Mrs. Miller from contractual arrangements made by her with Universal dealing with deceased's intangible rights of the nature above specified is "ordinary" income as opposed to capital gain or loss under § 1221 of the Internal Revenue Code of 1954.

Affirmed.

D. NOTES AND QUESTIONS

1) The Relevance of State Law

Suppose that the "right" sold by Mrs. Miller were to be recognized as "property" under New York law. For example, the legislature might pass a statute providing that a surviving spouse has a property right consisting of the right to make a motion picture about his or her deceased spouse. *Should* that change the result of *Miller?*

---

4. Petitioner insists that in Thomas D. Armour . . . we have a "reasonably definite indication". . . that the Tax Court would, under some circumstances, hold that a right of publicity is property which qualifies as a capital asset. In that case a living celebrity granted the use of his name to a golf ball manufacturer. The court did not discuss the issue of whether there was "property," but held that on the facts of that case there was no "sale." Petitioner regards this as an implied recognition of the "property right"; but we think, to the contrary, that the absence of a "sale" was used to avoid that very issue.

2) The Nature of the Asset Sold by Miller's Widow

What kind of asset was sold by Mrs. Miller? Who created it? What Shakespeare play did Judge Kaufman quote in the *Miller* opinion?

3) The Tax Treatment of Self-created Intangible Assets

Suppose that Glenn Miller composes and sells a tune. If Glenn Miller is a professional songwriter, how is the gain taxed? See Section 1221(1). If Miller is a full-time accountant but only an occasional, amateur songwriter, will that make a difference? See Section 1221(3)(A). Also, note the special treatment afforded patents by Section 1235.

4) Donees of Self-created Intangible Assets

Suppose Glenn Miller composes a tune and gives it to Mrs. Miller. If she sells it, how will her gain be taxed? See Section 1221(3)(C). Why is her basis determined with reference to the basis of the tune's creator? What is the relationship between Section 1221(3)(C) and Section 1015(a)?

Suppose that Miller sells the tune to his child for its fair market value and that the child later resells it at a profit. Will Section 1221(3)(C) apply to the sale by the child? Why isn't the child's basis determined with reference to Miller's basis? What is the relationship between Section 1221(3)(C) and Section 1012?

Suppose that Miller sells the tune to his child for less than its fair market value. Will Section 1221(3)(C) apply? Is the child's basis determined "in whole or in part" by his basis? See *Diedrich* in Chapter 22.

Suppose that Miller sells the tune to his wife. Will Section 1221(3)(C) apply? Is her basis determined with reference to his basis? What is the effect of Section 1041 (Chapter 12)?

If Mrs. Miller inherits the tune under her husband's will and then sells it, will Section 1221(3)(C) apply to her? Is her basis determined with reference to the basis of the tune's creator? What is the relationship between Section 1221(3)(C) and Section 1014(a)?

5) *Miller* Reconsidered

If the asset sold by Mrs. Miller had been a tune, created by her husband and passed on to her by inheritance, how would she have been taxed? Why should the fact that the asset is his life story make any difference? Is she treated unfairly in comparison with the heirs of other kinds of self-created property? Should the asset that she sold have been regarded as "similar property" under Section 1221(3)?

But suppose Mrs. Miller has been selling not only the right to make a movie about her husband's life but also rights to make Glenn Miller T-shirts, running shoes, pens, etc. so that she is in the business of franchising her husband's name? Would the Section 1221(1) exclusion apply, even if Section 1221(3) would not? Would her situation then be comparable to the taxpayer who inherits 100 different musical compositions and sells them off? Would the compositions then become "property held primarily for sale to customers in the ordinary course of a trade or business"? (Or does that depend, as in *International Shoe Machinery*, on whether the songs are sold in one lot or sold piecemeal, with Mrs. Miller acting as a dealer in songs?)

6) The Ordinary Income Component of Deferred Payment for a Capital Asset

Suppose that what is sold by Mrs. Miller is regarded as Section 1221 "property," not excluded either by Section 1221(1) as "held primarily for sale to customers in the ordinary course of a trade or business" or by Section 1221(3)(C) as "similar property" with a basis determined by the creator's basis. Then, presumably, it is a capital asset, and she is entitled to capital gains treatment if she sells for immediate payment in cash or other property.

But if she sells for a deferred payment (as she did in this case) doesn't some of each payment represent interest? Shouldn't the amount she is paid be taxable as ordinary income to that extent, even if not explicitly labeled as interest? Special rules for imputing interest in deferred payment transactions, not in effect when Mrs. Miller sold her rights, are discussed in Chapter 51.

7) Was There Really a Sale?

Mrs. Miller sold her rights for a fixed percentage of the profits of the motion picture to be made of her husband's life. Had she effectively transferred the economic risks associated with those rights to another party? Or was she still "at risk" with respect to what she sold? Should she, therefore, be regarded as still owning the rights, despite the formal transfer? Perhaps as having entered a joint venture with Universal Pictures to make a movie based on her husband's life? See the discussion following Burnet v. Logan in Chapter 21. If Mrs. Miller is regarded as having sold her rights only in form and not in substance, should her share of the movie profits be taxed as ordinary income or as capital gain?

Chapter 29

PROPERTY VERSUS CONTRACT

A. COMMISSIONER v. PITTSTON CO.
252 F.2d 344 (2d Cir. 1958), cert. denied 357 U.S. 919 (1958)

SMITH, DISTRICT JUDGE.

This is a petition by the Commissioner of Internal Revenue for review of a decision of the Tax Court . . . , holding the taxpayer The Pittston Company entitled to treat the sum of $500,000 received in 1949 as consideration for the termination of an exclusive contract to purchase the output of Russell Fork Coal Company's leased Pike County coal mines, as long term capital gain. . . .

On January 25, 1944, taxpayer (as buyer) and Russell (as seller) entered into a written contract, which provided, in part, as follows:

> That in consideration of the mutual covenants and conditions herein set forth and of an agreement executed and delivered simultaneously with the execution and delivery of this agreement, it is agreed as follows:
>
> (1) . . . [T]he Seller (Russell Fork) agrees to sell to the Buyer (Pattison & Bowns) . . . all of the coal which shall be mined and sold for resale from the mining plant or plants which the Seller expects to install or does install upon its leased property in Pike County, Kentucky, as set forth in the agreement executed simultaneously herewith. . . .
>
> (3) The title to all coal sold to the Buyer hereunder shall pass to the Buyer at the time said coal is loaded into cars or trucks at the mines for transportation and before transportation begins.
>
> (4) The Buyer shall be entitled to and is hereby authorized to deduct a discount of 8% of the gross selling price on all coal purchased by it. . . .
>
> (6) The Buyer agrees . . . that it . . . will at all times have and maintain proper facilities and employees so as to be able efficiently to resell the said coal and agrees to endeavor with diligence and in every proper manner to resell the largest available amount of said coal at prices specified from time to time by the Seller. . . .
>
> [I]f the Buyer . . . complies with the obligations binding upon it and them, then this agreement shall be irrevocable for a period of ten (10) years from this date. . . .

On the same date, January 25, 1944, taxpayer and Russell entered into another contract, under the terms of which taxpayer agreed to loan Russell $250,000, which loan was to be repaid in periodic installments over a period of 10 years and was to bear interest at 4 per cent per annum. During the period January 25, 1944 to October 14, 1949, taxpayer purchased from Russell 1,959,563.15 tons of coal for $9,855,089.64 which it resold at a gross profit of $273,411.14. Taxpayer carried out its agreement to loan Russell $250,000 and it also made various additional advances on open account; these loans were finally liquidated by Russell during 1948. On October 14, 1949, Russell paid $500,000 to taxpayer in consideration of taxpayer's surrender of all of its rights under the coal agreement of January 25, 1944. The transaction was reflected in a letter agreement dated October 14, 1949; the letter was sent to Russell by taxpayer, and read as follows:

> In consideration of the payment by you to us of the sum of Five Hundred Thousand Dollars ($500,000), receipt of which is hereby acknowledged, it is understood that you have as of this day acquired all of our right and interest in and to the agreement dated January 25, 1944 between us, which agreement provides for the exclusive right by Pattison & Bowns, Inc. to purchase all of the coal produced by you at your Russell Fork Mine, said contract expiring by its terms on January 25, 1954.

In its income tax return for the year 1949, taxpayer reported the $500,000 as long-term capital gain. In his notice of deficiency, the Commissioner determined that this amount "was not received as the result of a sale or exchange and therefore is reportable as ordinary income." The Tax Court held that the $500,000 was taxable as long-term capital gain, not as ordinary income, and accordingly overruled the Commissioner.

The courts have not been entirely consistent in their treatment of lump sum payments received by a taxpayer for the termination of jural relations between the taxpayer and another as falling within or without the area entitled to more favored treatment as long-term capital gains rather than ordinary income. This circuit has steered a middle course. . . . The court . . . held in C. I. R. v. Starr Bros. . . . that payment received by a taxpayer, a New London retail druggist, for relinquishing its rights under a provision in a contract with a manufacturer, binding the manufacturer not to sell drugs to taxpayer's competitors in New London, was ordinary income and not a capital gain. In the same year, consistently with Starr, the court in General Artists Corp. v. C. I. R. . . . held that payments received by a taxpayer for transfer of its contracts with a singer as his exclusive booking agent to another such agent by an agreement providing for cancellation of the contracts and execution of new contracts with the singer by the transferee were ordinary income and not capital gains received as gain from sale of a capital asset. However, in C. I. R. v. McCue Bros. & Drummond, Inc., . . . the court held a payment received by a taxpayer lessee from a landlord for vacating premises where the taxpayer had a right to continued possession under rent control laws was a capital gain from the sale or exchange of a capital asset held more than six months. In so doing the court followed the third circuit in C. I. R. v. Golonsky . . . holding payment received by a lessee from the landlord for cancelling the lease and surrendering the premises to be a capital gain. The court distinguished Starr and General Artists because there the contractual right was not transferred, but was released and merely vanished. The right to possession of the realty was considered a more substantial property right which does not lose its existence when it is transferred.

The Tax Court in the instant case concluded that the contractual right held by the taxpayer constituted capital assets, which petitioner does not dispute, and concluded that the right was not extinguished by its cancellation, but continued to exist as property of the transferee-payor. It distinguished Starr and General Artists on the ground that the court had held in those cases the contractual right was not transferred, but was released and merely vanished. The Tax Court says in effect that the extinguishment of a contract duty to deal only with one person transfers to the one formerly bound a right to deal with all the world. It would be more in accord with common understanding to say that the payment is solely for the termination of the right-duty relationship between the two parties to the agreement. To be sure, the same might be said of the termination of lessee's or life tenant's rights, but they have been distinguished as relating to matters of greater "substance" than mere contract rights. . . .

While the contract right here surrendered was "property" of value it carried with it no direct interest in the mine itself, or in the coal produced until delivery f. o. b. car or truck. It was a naked contract right, not in the nature of a lease or profit *à prendre*. If Russell Fork was able to do better elsewhere it might have sold its coal through anyone, responding in damages to the taxpayer, for so far as appears similar coal would have been obtainable elsewhere by taxpayer at a price. The large amount received by the taxpayer for the 4½ years the contract had to run compared with its gross returns for the 5½ years already expired, while not explained on the record, may reflect an expectation of lower expense to the taxpayer since taxpayer no longer is financing Russell. . . .

The Congress has since the tax year here in question more fully provided for the application of the sale or exchange concept when a lease or distribution agreement is cancelled, by Section 1241 of the Internal Revenue Code of 1954, 26 U.S.C.A § 1241, allowing the more favorable capital gains treatment of the amount received on cancellation, but in case of distributorships only where the distributor has a "substantial investment" in the distributorship, as in facilities for storing, processing, etc. the physical product or as in maintaining a substantial inventory. This amendment is not applicable in this case, and of course no showing was made as to whether such a substantial investment in facilities or inventory was or was not maintained. The amendment is of little assistance in interpreting the original provision for we cannot tell whether the intent of Congress was to broaden or narrow the capital gains on sale or exchange exception to the income tax, and its apparent result falls somewhere between the contentions of the opposing parties here. . . . The heavy burden of income taxation inevitably leads to the broadening of exceptions such as the capital gains provision.

This court has endeavored to define what it conceived to be the limits to this exception in Starr and United Artists by a somewhat literal definition of "sale or exchange." Even though the logic of setting the limit by drawing the line where it now is may be open to debate, any line set must be to some degree arbitrary. This case falls outside the limit thus far set for the exception by this court. We should leave further expansion of the exception, to include the release of naked contract rights as a "sale," to legislative action.

The judgment of the Tax Court is reversed and the case is remanded for entry of judgment in favor of the Commissioner in accordance herewith.

MOORE, CIRCUIT JUDGE.

I dissent. The assumption of the majority that mere "naked contract rights" form the basis of this transaction is, in my opinion, contrary to the undisputed facts and the law applicable thereto.

The only question involved upon this appeal is whether the sum of $500,000 paid by Russell to Pittston on October 14, 1949 for which Russell "acquired all of our [Pittston's] right and interest in and to the agreement dated January 25, 1944 between us," should be taxed as a long-term capital gain or as ordinary income. The answer to this question depends upon a precise analysis of the rights and interests then existing between the parties.

In 1944 Russell held a lease on certain real estate in Pike County, Kentucky. In order to enable it to install a coal mining plant thereon Pittston, pursuant to a contract with Russell dated January 25, 1944, agreed to loan Russell $250,000 to be advanced in such amounts as required for "the installation by it of a coal mining plant, and for the operation thereof".... Pittston was given the right to designate a director or directors to the extent of one-third of the board and Russell's expenditures of the proceeds of the loan had to be approved by him or them. Restrictions were placed upon the payment of salaries to Russell's officers and the use of net earnings. Notes evidencing the loan were to be secured by a mortgage upon the lease and structures to be placed upon the property. At the same time Russell and Pittston made a second contract whereby Russell agreed to sell to Pittston "all of the coal which shall be mined and sold for resale from the mining plant or plants which the Seller expects to install or does install upon its leased property in Pike County, Kentucky, as set forth in the agreement executed simultaneously herewith," i.e., the loan agreement, for a period of ten years. Ten cents per ton was to be deducted by Pittston from all coal sold "pursuant to the coal sales agreement entered into simultaneously herewith" to be applied on the loan. By reason of these provisions the $250,000 loan was repaid by the end of 1948.

Thus, the business arrangement between these companies was not confined to a "naked contract right" (as the majority holds) to buy coal but was an integrated transaction whereby Pittston financed the construction of a coal mining plant on Russell's leasehold and agreed to take the entire output, f. o. b. the mine, for ten years with conditional extension possibilities. The two simultaneous agreements, each referring to the other, evidenced the transaction. These contract rights can only be rendered "naked" by stripping from them and discarding the raiments which the parties found to be essential. To say that Russell despite its commitment could sell to anyone responding only in damages on the assumption that similar coal could have been obtained elsewhere (as to which there is no proof in the record) is, first, to suggest that these companies would not honor their mutual obligations and, second, that the courts in view of the investment of Pittston in the Russell operation and the nature of the agreement (entire output for a period of years) would restrict relief to damages. "Contracts for the delivery of goods will be specifically enforced, when by their terms the deliveries are to be made and the purchase price paid in installments running through a considerable number of years".... Specific performance is particularly applicable to a contract "to continue over a period of years without rigidity of price"....

The mutual rights and obligations created by these two agreements were most substantial. Russell as effectively deprived itself of any other use of its property for ten years as the owner of a building granting a leasehold for ten years to a tenant who had loaned the money to construct it. Russell could only regain for itself the unrestricted use of its property by a surrender by Pittston tantamount to the voluntary termination of a leasehold prior to the expiration date. Pittston, in turn, not only had an investment in Russell's lease, plant and equipment but had a property right to acquire the entire output of the Russell mine which proved to be a right of substantial value....

... The $500,000 paid was the value to Russell to get its property back and also represented Pittston's opinion of the contract's worth. If the contract were assigned to a third party there would be no question that the consideration received would reflect the value of the asset sold. Yet for all practical purposes Pittston by such assignment would thereby have terminated or cancelled its right to purchase coal from Russell.

In endeavoring to find a guide as to the type of transaction which will be construed as resulting in a capital gain as distinguished from ordinary income, the decisions reveal uniform consistency in holding that the surrender, termination or cancellation for monetary consideration of a capital asset results in a capital gain. Neither the petitioner nor the majority assail the correctness of the Tax Court's conclusion that the contract right here was in itself a capital asset. For this reason I must disagree with the majority that "the termination of the right-duty relationship between the two parties" results in ordinary income to the taxpayer; particularly since they concede that "the same might be said of the termination of the lessee's or life tenant's rights" which clearly produces a capital gain....

Legal rights should not be adjudicated by mere choice of words. "There surely cannot be that efficacy in lawyers' jargon that termination or cancellation or surrender carries some peculiar significance vastly penalizing laymen whose counsel have chanced to use them"... Moreover, here the parties did not even use the word "surrender" but said that Russell had "acquired all of our right and interest." That "there was a 'surrender' to the remainderman, rather than a 'transfer' to third persons ... does not change the essentially dispositive nature of the transaction so far as the former property owner is concerned". . . . So here Pittston had effectively disposed of its property interest. Whether by surrender or transfer or acquisition the legal consequences should be the same. . . .

I cannot agree that the property rights created by the two agreements between Pittston and Russell were mere "naked contract right" but find them clothed not only with a mortgage interest in the Russell leasehold until the repayment of the loan but also with sufficient substance to justify specific performance. . . .

In no branch of the law is it more important that there be as much certainty as possible than in the field of taxes. Businessmen and their corporations must often make decisions involving future plans and the expenditure of large sums of money upon the advice of counsel as to the tax consequences of the contemplated transactions. The decision of the majority in the present case injects an unwarranted inconsistency into this field. In my opinion the Tax Court correctly construed the decisions in this as well as the other circuits referred to and its judgment below should be affirmed.

B. NOTES AND QUESTIONS

1) Earlier Cases Cited in *Pittston*

Pittston cites four earlier opinions involving the question of whether an amount received for termination of contractual rights is ordinary income or capital gain. How does *Pittston* explain the difference between the outcomes in *Starr Brothers* and *General Artists* on the one hand, and *McCue* and *Golonsky* on the other? Do you find the distinction made by *Pittston* persuasive? Or is it a highly artificial "legalism"? Can you think of a more satisfying way to distinguish the results in these four cases, using the *underlying* principle of *McFall*? Does Section 1241, discussed in *Pittston*, suggest a better way to explain these four cases?

2) The Rationale of *Pittston*

Why do the majority and dissent disagree? Despite their differences, do they nevertheless agree that the issue is whether the contract rights are enforceable by specific performance or only by money damages? *Should* capital gain treatment hinge on that issue? How is the approach of both the majority and dissent in *Pittston* similar to that of the opinions in both *McFall* and *Miller* (Chapter 28)?

3) Is *Pittston* Like *Corn Products*?

Can you think of better grounds for justifying the denial of capital gain treatment? Suppose that Pittston is a steel producer and has been using the coal in its manufacturing operations. Does the contract right fall under any of the explicit statutory exclusions in Section 1221? If not, how might *Corn Products* be used to justify the *Pittston* result?

4) The Significance of the Simultaneous Loan

At the same time that Russell agreed to sell coal to Pittston for ten years at an 8% discount from the market price, Pittston loaned Russell $250,000 at 4% interest. When an employer sells property to an employee at less than fair market value "[i]n connection with the performance of services," the discount is generally treated as compensation under Section 83(a). When a borrower sells property to a lender at less than fair market value in connection with a loan, what might the discount represent? What other evidence might you want to examine in order to answer this question? Whether the 4% interest charged on the loan from Pittston to Russell was equal to or less than the market rate of interest? Whether the 8% discount on the price of the coal was equal to or greater than the discount generally available to purchasers who made a long-term commitment to buy the entire output of a coal mine?

C. COMMISSIONER v. FERRER
304 F.2d 125 (2d Cir. 1962)

FRIENDLY, CIRCUIT JUDGE.

This controversy concerns the tax status of certain payments received by José Ferrer with respect to the motion picture "Moulin Rouge" portraying the career of Henri de Toulouse-Lautrec. The difficulties Mr. Ferrer must have had in fitting himself into the shape of the artist can hardly have been greater than ours in determining whether the transaction here at issue fits the rubric "gain from the sale or exchange of a capital asset . . ." or constitutes ordinary income, as the Commissioner contends. We have concluded that neither party is entirely right, that some aspects of the transaction fall on one side of the line and some on the other, and that the Tax Court must separate the two.

In 1950 Pierre LaMure published a novel, "Moulin Rouge," based on the life of Toulouse-Lautrec. He then wrote a play, "Monsieur Toulouse," based on the novel. On November 1, 1951, LaMure as "Author" and Ferrer, a famous actor but not a professional producer, as "Manager" entered into a contract, called a Dramatic Production Contract, for the stage production of the play by Ferrer. . . .

Shortly after signature of the Dramatic Production Contract, John Huston called Ferrer to ask whether he would be interested in playing Toulouse-Lautrec in a picture based upon "Moulin Rouge." On getting an affirmative indication, Huston said he would go ahead and acquire the motion picture rights. Ferrer replied, in somewhat of an exaggeration, "When you get ready to acquire them talk to me because I own them."

Both Huston and Ferrer then had discussions with LaMure. Ferrer expressed a willingness "to abandon the theatrical production in favor of the film production, provided that, if the film production were successful, I would be recompensed for my abandoning the stage production." On the strength of this, LaMure signed a preliminary agreement with Huston's corporation. In further negotiations, Huston's attorney insisted on "either an annulment or conveyance" of the Dramatic Production Contract. LaMure's lawyer prepared a letter of agreement, dated February 7, 1952, whereby Ferrer would cancel and terminate the Contract. Ferrer signed the letter but instructed his attorney not to deliver it until the closing of a contract between himself and the company that was to produce the picture; the letter was not delivered until May 14, 1952.

Meanwhile, on May 7, 1952, Ferrer entered into a contract with Huston's company, Moulin Productions, Inc. ("Moulin"), hereafter the Motion Picture Contract. . . .

The Motion Picture Contract said that Romulus Films Limited, of London, proposed to produce the picture "Moulin Rouge," that Moulin would be vested with the Western Hemisphere distribution rights, and that Moulin on behalf of Romulus was interested in engaging Ferrer's service to play the role of Toulouse-Lautrec. Under clause 4(a), Ferrer was to receive $50,000 to cover 12 weeks of acting, payments to be made weekly as Ferrer rendered his services. Ferrer's performance was to begin between June 1 and July 1, 1952. . . . Finally, clauses 4(d) and (e) provided "percentage compensation" equal to stipulated percentages of the net profits from distribution of the picture in the Western and Eastern Hemispheres respectively—17% of the Western Hemisphere net profits until Ferrer had received $25,000 and thereafter 12¾% (such payments to "be made out of sixty-five (65%) percent of the net profits," whatever that may mean), and 3¾% of the Eastern Hemisphere net profits. If Ferrer's services were interrupted by disability or if production of the picture had to be suspended for causes beyond Moulin's control, but the picture was thereafter completed and Ferrer's "acts, poses and appearances therein" were recognizable to the public, he was to receive a proportion of the compensation provided in clauses. . .[4] (d) and (e) corresponding to the ratio of his period of acting to 12 weeks. . . . Over objections by the Commissioner, Ferrer offered testimony by Huston's attorney, who was also president of Moulin, that in the negotiation "it was said that the ultimate percentage payment to be made to Ferrer would be his compensation for giving up his interest in the dramatization guild," and a letter from the same attorney, dated March 3, 1953, confirming that in the negotiations with Ferrer's attorney "for the sale of the dramatic rights held by you to the property entitled 'Monsieur Toulouse' and the novel 'Moulin Rouge,' it was understood that the consideration for such sale price was the payments due, or to become due, to you under Clause 4(d) and Clause 4(e)," and also that LeMure "refused to sell the motion picture rights for the production of the motion picture known as 'Moulin Rouge' unless you sold the aforesaid dramatic rights." Ferrer's agent testified, again over objection, that the largest salary Ferrer had previously received for a moving picture appearance was $75,000. . . .

[Section 1221], tells us, not very illuminatingly, that " 'capital asset' means property held by the taxpayer (whether or not connected with his trade or business), but does not include" four (now five) types of property therein defined. However, it has long been settled that a taxpayer does not bring himself within the capital gains provision merely by fulfilling the simple syllogism that a contract normally constitutes "property," that he held a contract, and that his contract does not fall within a specified exclusion. . . . This is easy enough; what is difficult, perhaps impossible, is to frame a positive definition of universal validity. Attempts to do this in terms of the degree of clothing adorning the contract cannot explain all the cases, however helpful they may be in deciding some, perhaps even this one; it would be hard to think of a contract more "naked" than a debenture, yet no one doubts that is a "capital asset" if held by an investor. Efforts to frame a universal negative, e.g., that a transaction can never qualify if the taxpayer has merely collapsed anticipation of future income, are equally fruitless; a lessor's sale of his interest in a 999 year net lease and an investor's sale of a perpetual bond sufficiently illustrate why. . . .

Perhaps we can get more help from analyzing the fact situations in cases in adjacent areas, including those decided since Judge Smith's careful review in C. I. R. v. Pittston Company. . . . [T]he principal relevant authorities on the two sides of the line in the Supreme Court and in the courts of appeals are as follows: There is no sale or exchange of a capital asset when a lessor receives payment for releasing a lessee from an obligation to pay future rent, Hort v. C. I. R. . . . The same was true of the cancellation of an exclusive distributorship, C. I. R. v. Starr Bros., Inc. . . . although § 1241 of the 1954 Code, 26 U.S.C.A. § 1241 now rules otherwise if the distributor has a substantial capital investment therein. The transfer of exclusive agency rights to a third person likewise did not qualify, General Artists Corp. v. C. I. R. . . . Whether it now does if the capital investment requirement of § 1241 is met is another question. . . .

One common characteristic of the group held to come within the capital gain provision is that the taxpayer had either what might be called an "estate" in . . . , or an "encumbrance" on, or an option to acquire an interest in . . . property which, if itself held, would be a capital asset. In all these cases the taxpayer had something more than an opportunity, afforded by contract, to obtain periodic receipts of income, by dealing with another . . . or by rendering services . . . or by virtue of ownership of a larger "estate."
. . . We are painfully aware of the deficiencies of any such attempt to define the wavering line even in this limited area, but it is the best we can do. We add, with greater confidence, that more recent cases . . . have moved away from the distinction . . . between a sale to a third person that keeps the "estate" or "encumbrance" alive, and a release that results in its extinguishment. Indeed, although reasoning from another section of a statute so full of anomalies is rather treacherous business, we take § 1241 of the 1954 Code as indicating Congressional disenchantment with this formalistic distinction. In the instant case we can see no sensible business basis for drawing a line between a release of Ferrer's rights to LaMure for a consideration paid by Moulin, and a sale of them, with LaMure's consent, to Moulin or to a stranger who would then release them. Moulin's attorney, as we have seen, did not care a fig whether there was "an annulment or conveyance" of the Dramatic Production Contract. Tax law is concerned with the substance, here the voluntary passing of "property" rights allegedly constituting "capital assets," not with whether they are passed to a stranger or to a person already having a larger "estate." So we turn to an analysis of what rights Ferrer conveyed.

Two issues can be eliminated before we do this. We need no longer concern ourselves, as at one time we might have been obliged to do, over the alleged indivisibility of a copyright; the Commissioner is now satisfied that sales and exchanges of less than the whole copyright may result in capital gain. . . . Neither do we have in this case any issue of excludability under . . . § [1221(1)]; Ferrer was not in the "trade or business" of acquiring either dramatic production rights or motion picture rights.

When Huston displayed an interest in the motion picture rights in November, 1951, Ferrer was possessed of a bundle of rights, three of which are relevant here. First was his "lease" of the play. Second was his power, incident to that lease, to prevent any disposition of the motion picture rights until June 1, 1952, or, on making an additional $1500 advance, to December 1, 1952, and for a period thereafter if he produced the play, and to prevent disposition of the radio and television rights even longer. Third was his 40% share of the proceeds of the motion picture and other rights if he produced the play. All these, in our view, Ferrer "sold or exchanged," although the parties set no separate price upon them. To be sure, Moulin had no interest in producing the play. But Ferrer did, unless a satisfactory substitute was provided. Hence Moulin had to buy him out of that right, as well as to eliminate his power temporarily to prevent a sale of the motion picture, radio and television rights and to liquidate his option to obtain a share of their proceeds.

Surrender of the "lease" of the play sounds like the transactions held to qualify for capital gain treatment in Golonsky and McCue Bros. & Drummond, see § 1241 of the 1954 Code. . . . [C]ourts would have enjoined LaMure, or anyone else, from interfering with this, unless the Dramatic Production Contract dictated otherwise. None of its many negations covered this basic grant. Ferrer thus had an "equitable interest" in the copyright of the play.

The Commissioner did not suggest in the Tax Court, and does not here, that this interest or, indeed, any with which we are concerned in this case, fell within . . . § [1221(3)], excluding from the term "capital asset" "a copyright; a literary, musical, or artistic composition; or similar property; held by—"(i) a taxpayer, whose personal efforts created such property. . . ." He was right in not doing this. In one sense the lease of the play was "created" simply by the agreed advance of $1500. If it be said that this is too narrow an approach and that we must consider what Ferrer would have had to do in order to make the lease productive, the result remains the same. Although the Dramatic Production Contract demanded Ferrer's personal efforts in the play's production, much else in the way of capital and risk-taking was also required. Yet the legislative history . . . shows that § [1221(3)] . . . was intended to deal with personal efforts and creation in a rather narrow sense. . . . Ferrer's role as producer, paying large sums to the theatre, the actors, other personnel, and the author, is not analogous to that of the writer or even the "creator" of a radio program mentioned by the Committee. Moreover, the dramatic producer does not normally "sell" the production to a single purchaser, as an author or radio program "creator" usually does—he offers it directly to public custom.

We see no basis for holding that amounts paid Ferrer for surrender of his lease of the play are excluded from capital gain treatment because receipts from the play would have been ordinary income. The latter is equally true if a lessee of real property sells or surrenders a lease from which he is receiving business income or subrentals; yet Golonsky and McCue Bros. & Drummond held such to be the sale or exchange of a capital asset, as § 1241 now provides. Likewise, we find nothing in the statute that forbids capital gain treatment because the payment to Ferrer might be spread over a number of years rather than coming in a lump sum; although prevention of the unfairness arising from applying ordinary income rates to a "bunching" of income may be one of the motivations of the "capital gain" provisions, the statute says nothing about this. . .

Ferrer's negative power, as an incident to the lease, to prevent any disposition of the motion picture, radio and television rights until after production of the play, was also one which, under the cases previously cited . . . would be protected in equity unless he had contracted to the contrary, and would thus constitute an "equitable interest" in this portion of the copyright. . . . As a practical matter, this feature of the Dramatic Production Contract "clouded" LaMure's title, despite the Contract's contrary assertion. Huston would not conclude with LaMure and LaMure would not conclude with Huston unless Ferrer released his rights; Huston's attorney testified that a contract like Ferrer's "imposes an encumbrance on the motion picture rights." Ferrer's dissipation of the cloud arising from the negative covenant seems analogous to the tenant's relinquishment of a right to prevent his landlord from leasing to another tenant in the same business, held to be the sale or exchange of a capital asset. . . .

We take a different view with respect to the capital assets status of Ferrer's right to receive 40% of the proceeds of the motion picture and other rights if he produced "Monsieur Toulouse."

We assume, without deciding, that there is no reason in principle why if the holder of a copyright grants an interest in the portion of a copyright relating to motion picture and other rights contingent on the production of a play, or, to put the matter in another way, gives the producer an option to acquire such an interest by producing the play, the option would not constitute a "capital asset". . . . However, it is equally possible for the copyright owner to reserve the entire "property" both legal and equitable in himself and agree with the producer that a percentage of certain avails shall be paid as further income from the lease of the play—just as the lessor of real estate might agree to pay a lessee a percentage of what the lessor obtained from other tenants attracted to the building by the lessee's operations. In both instances such payments would be ordinary income. If the parties choose to cast their transaction in the latter mold, the Commissioner may take them at their word.

Here the parties were at some pains to do exactly that. LaMure was to "retain for his sole benefit, complete title, both legal and equitable, in and to all rights whatsoever" other than the right to produce the play. Ferrer was to "have no right, title or interest, legal or equitable, in the motion picture rights, other than the right to receive the Manager's share of the proceeds"; even as to that, he was to have "no recourse, in law or in equity" against a purchaser, a lessee, or the Negotiator, but only a right to arbitration against the Author. We cannot regard all this as mere formalism. The Contract is full of provisions designed to emphasize the Negotiator's freedom to act—provisions apparently stemming from a fear that, without them, the value of the motion picture rights might disintegrate in controversy.... [D]espite the contrary language of the Contract, Ferrer [never] had, or ... would have, an affirmative equitable interest in the motion picture or other rights, as distinguished from his temporary negative "encumbrance" on them....

It follows that if Ferrer had produced the play and LaMure had sold the motion picture, radio and television rights for a percentage of the profits, Ferrer's 40% of that percentage would have been ordinary income and not the sale or exchange of a capital asset....

The situation is thus one in which two of the rights that Ferrer sold or exchanged were "capital assets" and one was not. Although it would be easy to say that the contingent contract right to a percentage of the avails of the motion picture, radio and television rights was dominant and all else incidental, that would be viewing the situation with the inestimable advantage of hindsight. In 1952 no one could tell whether the play might be a huge success and the picture a dismal failure, whether the exact opposite would be true, whether both would succeed or both would fail. We cannot simply dismiss out of hand the notion that a dramatic production, presenting an actor famous on the speaking stage and appealing to a sophisticated audience, might have had substantial profit possibilities, perhaps quite as good as a film with respect to a figure, not altogether attractive and not nearly so broadly known then as the success of the picture has made him now, which presumably would require wide public acceptance before returning production costs. At the very least, when Ferrer gave up his lease of the play, he was abandoning his bet on two horses in favor of a bet on only one.

In such instances, where part of a transaction calls for one tax treatment and another for a different kind, allocation is demanded.... If it be said that to remand for this purpose is asking the Tax Court to separate the inseparable, we answer that no one expects scientific exactness; that however roughly hewn the decision may be, the result is certain to be fairer than either extreme....

Still we have not reached the end of the road. The Commissioner contends that, apart from all else, no part of the payments here can qualify for capital gain treatment, since Ferrer could receive "percentage compensation" only if he fulfilled his acting commitments, and all the payments were thus for personal services.... [T]he Commissioner says it was error for the Tax Court to rely on extrinsic evidence to vary the written contract....

... [N]o such issue is here presented. No one argued the contract provided anything other than what was plainly said. Huston's attorney did not assert that Ferrer would become entitled to the percentage compensation without fulfilling his acting commitment; what the attorney said in his testimony, as he had earlier in his letter, was that Ferrer was selling two things to Moulin—his services as an actor and his rights under the Dramatic Production Contract—and that the parties regarded the payments under clause 4(a)... as the consideration for the former and those under clauses 4(d) and (e) as the consideration for the latter.

On the basis of this evidence the Tax Court found that the percentage compensation was not "to any extent the consequence of, or consideration for, petitioner's personal services." In one sense, this is hardly so. Under the Motion Picture Contract, Ferrer would receive no percentage compensation if he wrongfully refused to furnish acting services, and none or only a portion if, for reasons beyond his control, he furnished less than all. Since that must have been as plain to the Tax Court as to us, we read the finding to mean rather that Ferrer and Moulin adopted the percentage of profits formula embodied in clauses 4(d) and (e) as an equivalent and in lieu of a fixed sum payable in all events for the release of the Dramatic Production Contract. If they had first agreed on such a sum and had then substituted the arrangement here made, it would be hard to say that although payments under their initial arrangement would not be disqualified for capital gain treatment, payments under the substituted one would be. Ferrer was already bound to play the role of Toulouse-Lautrec, at a salary implicitly found to constitute fair compensation for his services; adoption of a formula whereby his receipt of percentage compensation for releasing his rights was made contingent on his fulfilling that undertaking does not mean that the percentage compensation could not be solely for his release of the Contract. The Tax Court was not bound to accept the testimony that this was the intent—it could lawfully have found that the percentage compensation was in part added salary for Ferrer's acting services and in part payment for the release. However, it found the contrary, and we cannot say that in doing so it went beyond the bounds to which our review of its fact findings is confined. . . . Since, on the taxpayer's own evidence, the percentage compensation was for the totality of the release of his rights under the Dramatic Production Contract, allocation is required as between rights which did and rights which did not constitute a "capital asset."

We therefore reverse and remand to the Tax Court to determine what portion of the percentage compensation under clauses 4(d) and (e) of the Motion Picture Contract constituted compensation for Ferrer's surrendering his lease of the play and his incidental power to prevent disposition of the motion picture and other rights pending its production, as to which the determination of deficiency should be annulled, and what part for the surrender of his opportunity to receive 40% of the proceeds of the motion picture and other rights as to which it should be sustained. . . .

D. NOTES AND QUESTIONS

1) The Nature of the Asset

What was the precise nature of the asset in *Ferrer*? How was LaMure, the original seller, taxed on its sale? What was the status of the asset in Ferrer's hands? Did it fall within the exclusions of Section 1221(1), Section 1221(3)(C), or Section 1221(3)(A)?

How did Judge Friendly define Section 1221 "property"? How is his approach like that of the court in *Pittston*? Judge Friendly accepted the distinction between "property" and "contract" but rejected the distinction between "sale" and "extinguishment" of property rights as empty and formalistic? Were these positions logically consistent?

2) Allocating the Total Paid to Ferrer Between Services and Property

Ferrer simultaneously agreed to sell his rights in the literary property and to act in the movie. Why did Ferrer have an incentive to allocate as much of the total paid as possible to the sale of property, rather than to the sale of his services? How did the allocation problem in *Ferrer* resemble the *Biedenharn* problem (Chapter 27) of allocating the gain from the sale of real estate between investment and development activities?

The Tax Court accepted Ferrer's representation as to how much was paid for his acting services and how much was paid for the literary property rights. How did this finding conflict with the express terms of the contract between Ferrer and John Huston? Do you think that Judge Friendly agreed with the Tax Court finding? If not, why not reverse it? Was the artificial distinction between rights subject to specific performance and rights enforceable only through money damages a *sub rosa* method of reversing the Tax Court's finding? How did the "clearly erroneous" rule of the Federal Rules of Civil Procedure appear to have led Friendly to rely on this artificial distinction?

3) The Position of the Purchaser on Allocating the Total Paid Between Property and Services

Was Huston, the purchaser of both Ferrer's property and services, affected by the allocation? Ordinarily, expenditures for salary are immediately deductible in full, while expenditures for property may be deducted only over the property's useful life. However, in this particular circumstance, the expenditures for property and services receive the same treatment. The expenditures for both the literary property and for Ferrer's acting services are considered to have the same useful life as the movie that is being made, and the cost of both can be deducted only over that period.

This does not mean, however, that Huston will be indifferent to the allocation of the purchase price between property and services. He has an incentive to agree to overallocate that price to property and to ask Ferrer to share the benefits with him by reducing the total that Huston must pay.

To illustrate, suppose that the fair market value of the property is $300, the services $200, and that the total price initially agreed on for both is therefore $500. Assume that Ferrer is in the 50% tax bracket and that only 40% of capital gains are taxable. If $100 of the amount being paid for services is designated as being for property, Ferrer saves $30 (50% of $100, minus 50% of 40% of $100). But, as the price for agreeing to overallocate the total paid to property, Huston may ask that the $30 in tax savings be shared. For example, the overall amount paid to Ferrer could be reduced by $15 to $485.

4) Netting Out the Effects of Tax Benefits and Detriments

In other circumstances, expenditures for property and services may be treated differently. Usually the expenditure for property can be deducted only over a period of years, but the expenditure for salary can be deducted in full at once. In that event, the purchaser and the seller appear to have divergent interests. The purchaser appears to benefit from allocating as much of the total price as possible to services, immediately deductible in full, whereas the seller appears to benefit from allocating as much as possible to property, taxable as capital gain.

But the appearances may be deceiving. Both purchaser and seller have the same interest in misallocating the price, provided only that the tax benefit to one is greater than the tax detriment to the other. Suppose that the tax benefit to the seller outweighs the tax detriment to the purchaser (or vice versa). Then, overallocating the price to property (or overallocating the price to services) produces a *net* tax benefit overall. The purchaser can be compensated for the detriment and allowed to share in the net benefit in the form of a reduced total price (or the seller can be compensated for the detriment and allowed to share in the net benefit in the form of an increased total price). *Both* purchaser and seller will have an incentive to overallocate. They will not have divergent interests.

To illustrate, return to the example, above, in which $100 of the total price is allocated from services to property, saving the seller $30 in taxes. The tax detriment to the purchaser equals the difference between immediately deducting $100 and deducting $100 over the life of the property. If the purchaser's tax bracket is 50%, deducting $100 saves $50 in taxes. The detriment equals the difference between saving $50 at once and saving $50 over a number of years. If the present value of deducting $100 in the future (rather than all at once) is $30, the tax detriment to the purchaser is $20.

The net tax benefit equals the difference between the seller's tax savings of $30 and the purchaser's tax detriment of $20, or $10. If the purchase price is reduced to, say, $475, the purchaser will have an incentive to agree to misallocation, notwithstanding the tax detriment. In that event, the purchaser gets to pay $25 less, which equals the tax detriment plus one-half of the net tax benefits. The seller receives $25 less (a nontax detriment) but saves $30 in taxes and so also comes out $5 ahead.

5) The Effect of Taxing Capital Gains and Ordinary Income at the Same Rate

Today, with capital gains taxed basically the same as ordinary income, would there be much of an incentive for Ferrer and Huston to overallocate the price to property? If Huston could take a current deduction in full for services, why would the incentive today be to overallocate the price to services?

6) Must Seller and Purchaser Take Consistent Positions?

Can seller and purchaser take inconsistent positions on the allocation of the purchase price between property and services, at least where the contract is ambiguous, as in *Ferrer*? For example, could Ferrer try to claim that the greater part of the total price was for property and Huston that it was for services?

Suppose that, in a sale in which consistent positions are taken, the IRS argues that too much of the total price has been allocated to property and collects extra taxes from the seller based on a reallocation to services. Can the buyer file an amended return, claiming that the reallocated amount is currently deductible as salary, rather than as a capital expenditure for property? Or, will the buyer be stuck with the allocation that the buyer chose? In other words, is reallocation a one-way street, available only to the IRS, and not to the taxpayer? Recall the materials on form and substance in Chapter 14.

7) The Ordinary Income Component of Deferred Payment for a Capital Asset

Even if all of what Ferrer sold was Section 1221 property and the allocation between payment for property and for services was accurate, shouldn't some of the sales proceeds be treated as interest income, since payment is deferred? Aren't these amounts, to some extent, analogous to the "growth factor" in *Starker* (Chapter 18)? In this way, isn't *Ferrer* like Burnet v. Logan (Chapter 21) and *Miller* (Chapter 28).

8) Was There Really a Sale?

Since Ferrer was still "at risk" with respect to what was allegedly sold, had there been a real sale? Again, see the notes and questions following Burnet v. Logan and *Miller.*

PART THREE

Costs of "For Profit" Activities

Part Three deals with the costs of business and investment activities, sometimes referred to as activities engaged in "for profit." If these costs were not deductible, the tax would be imposed on gross receipts instead of on income. Therefore, the costs of "for profit" activities are generally deductible in order to arrive at a "true" income figure.

Exceptions to this rule are occasionally made, the most notable examples being the disallowance of deductions for bribes, kickbacks, and other illegal payments under Section 162(c), fines under Section 162(f), and two-thirds of antitrust treble damage payments under Section 162(g). What is the effect of disallowance on the after-tax cost of these payments? Can disallowance be defended as preventing the tax law from subsidizing antisocial behavior? Or does it impose an unwarranted additional penalty on certain kinds of antisocial behavior, above and beyond whatever criminal or civil penalties have been otherwise provided by law? Also, note Section 162(e)(2) which in effect denies business deductions for contributions to political campaigns.[1]

Outside of these special cases, *whether* to allow a deduction for the costs of a "for profit" activity is rarely an issue. A deduction must be allowed at some point so that a tax will be imposed on income, rather than on gross receipts. *When* to permit the deduction, however, is the source of many contentious disputes between taxpayers and the IRS. Therefore, Part Three is almost exclusively concerned with issues of timing.

In order to understand Part Three, the reader needs to be familiar with three basic categories used to classify the costs of a "for profit" activity. The

---

1. Although federal law prohibits corporations from contributing to presidential and congressional candidates, corporations may be permitted to contribute to candidates for state and local office. Does Section 162(e), therefore, unjustifiably deny deductions for business expenses of a corporation that may be regarded as legitimate under state and local law? Or is the question of the legality of a contribution different from whether it should be tax deductible? Even if such contributions are legal, wouldn't a tax deduction permit businesses an unfair political advantage over individual taxpayers whose contributions are nondeductible personal consumption expenses?

classification system is based on the length of time that an item is expected to produce revenues before it wears out and is no longer productive.

1) *Items expected to last no longer than the end of the current taxable year*—The cost can be fully deducted at once. Such items are said to be *expensed* or subject to *expensing*.

2) *Items expected to last beyond the end of the current taxable year but expected to wear out within some ascertainable period of time*—In this case, the cost generally cannot be fully deducted at once. Instead, it must be spread out over the item's productive life. Such items are labeled *depreciable* or subject to *depreciation*.

3) *Items expected to last more or less indefinitely or not expected to wear out within any ascertainable period of time*—Here, the cost cannot be deducted except to offset the amount realized when the item is sold. Such items are referred to as *nonwasting* or *nondepreciable*.

There are several other important terms of art. *Wasting assets* refers to items not expected to last indefinitely, that is, the expensed and depreciable assets of categories 1) and 2), above. *Capital expenditures* refers to items expected to last beyond the end of the current taxable year, that is, the depreciable and nonwasting assets of categories 2) and 3), above.

In allowing deductions, the Code mentions two kinds of "for profit" activities: *trade or business* and *production of income*. Section 162(a) authorizes a trade or business to deduct items subject to expensing, while Section 212(1) provides similar authorization in connection with the production of income. Section 167(a) authorizes depreciation deductions for both a trade or business and for the production of income.

The terms *trade or business* and *production of income* are not defined by the Code or regulations. Nor has there ever been a clear judicial definition, although nontrade or business activities are generally thought to include investments in stock, bonds, real estate, and the like.

"For profit" activities that do not constitute a trade or business but are merely for the production of income may suffer from several disadvantages. An individual may deduct the costs only if he or she itemizes deductions under Section 62. If the taxpayer claims the standard deduction rather than itemizing, the costs of conducting the activity are generally not deductible. See Sections 62(a), 63(b), and 63(d)(1).[2] In addition, even the itemizer's costs may be deducted only to the extent that they and certain other miscellaneous deductions exceed 2% of AGI. See Section 67(a).

---

2. Note, however, the exception for the costs of producing rent or royalty income under Section 62(a)(4).

Chapter 30

COMPARING "FOR PROFIT" AND "FOR PLEASURE" PROPERTY

A. IMPUTED RENT OF OWNER–OCCUPIED DWELLINGS
R. Goode, The Individual Income Tax, 117–118 (1976)

A person who resides in his own house or apartment obtains an income in the form of consumer services. This imputed return is classified as personal income in national income and product accounts, and individuals often recognize that homeownership is an alternative to other income-yielding investments.

Homeowners are often puzzled by economists' assertions that they derive an income from their houses; these owners look on their houses as a source of expense rather than income. They are right in insisting that homeownership entails expense, but they overlook the fact that part of their shelter cost is covered by the imputed return on their equity. A homeowner is an investor who takes his return in the form of services. If he wishes, he can convert his imputed return to cash by moving and renting his house.

Imputed rent of owner-occupied dwellings is taxable in a number of countries, but is not included in AGI in the United States. The United Kingdom taxed imputed rent from the beginning of the income tax early in the nineteenth century but allowed the provision to become ineffective after World War II, owing to obsolete assessments, and dropped it in 1963.

Under a net income tax, the item to be included in income would be imputed net rent, defined as gross rental value minus necessary expenses of ownership. The expenses consist of interest on mortgage debt, property taxes, depreciation, repairs and maintenance, and casualty insurance. Homeowners may now deduct interest and taxes, even though imputed rent is not included in AGI. The taxation of imputed net rent, therefore, would involve an addition to taxable income equal to gross rent minus expenses other than interest and taxes. This increase in the tax base would equal the sum of imputed net rent and the personal deductions now allowed for mortgage interest and property taxes on owner-occupied dwellings.

Merely to increase the tax base by the amount of net rent would imply double deductions for interest and property taxes, one set in the form of the personal deductions now granted and a second set in the computation of net rent. . . .

B. IMPUTED RENTAL INCOME
U.S. Treasury, Blueprints for Basic Tax Reform, 85–86 (1977)

Any dwelling, whether owner-occupied or rented, is an asset that yields a flow of services over its economic lifetime. The value of this service flow for any time period represents a portion of the market rental value of the dwelling. For rental housing, there is a monthly contractual payment (rent) from tenant to landlord for the services of the dwelling. In a market equilibrium, these rental payments must be greater than the maintenance expenses, related taxes, and depreciation, if any. The difference between these continuing costs and the market rental may be referred to as the "net income" generated by the housing unit.

An owner-occupier may be thought of as a landlord who rents to himself. On his books of account will also appear maintenance expenses and taxes, and he will equally experience depreciation in the value of his housing asset. What do not appear are, on the sources side, receipts of rental payment and, on the uses side, net income from the dwelling. Viewed from the sources side, this amount may be regarded as the reward that the owner of the dwelling accepts in-kind, instead of the financial reward he could obtain by renting to someone other than himself. Since a potential owner-occupier faces an array of opportunities for the investment of his funds, including in housing for rental to himself or others, the value of the reward in-kind must be at least the equal of these financial alternatives. Indeed, this fact provides a possible method for approximating the flow of consumption he receives, constituting a portion of the value of his consumption services. Knowing the cost of the asset and its depreciation schedule, one could estimate the reward necessary to induce the owner-occupier to rent to himself.

In practice, to tax this form of imputed income, however desirable it might be from the standpoint of equity or of obtaining neutrality between owning and renting, would severely complicate tax compliance and administration. Because the owner-occupier does not explicitly make a rental payment to himself, the value of the current use of his house is not revealed. Even if market rental were estimated, perhaps as a fixed share of assessed value of the dwelling, the taxpayer would face the difficulties of accounting for annual maintenance and depreciation to determine his net income.

The present tax system does not attempt to tax the imputed income from housing. This is, perhaps, because there would be extreme administrative difficulties in determining it and because there is a general lack of understanding of its nature. The incentive for home ownership that results from including net income from rental housing in the tax base while excluding it for owner-occupied housing also has strong political support, although the result is clearly a distortion from the pattern of consumer housing choices that would otherwise prevail.

C. NOTES AND QUESTIONS

The Internal Revenue Code establishes two basic methods for taxing property, depending on whether the property is held "for profit" or "for pleasure." The following material illustrates and compares the basic structural differences between these two methods.

1) A Sailboat Example: Taxing the First Year's Receipts

Suppose you purchase a sailboat at the beginning of the year for $2,000. Assume that the sailboat can be rented for $1,400 during the year and that, at the end of the year, the sailboat will be worth $1,200. The decline in value during the year, or *economic depreciation*, reflects wear and tear due to ordinary use.

a) If the sailboat is held "for profit" and rented out, how much is included in Gross Income for the year under Section 61(a)? In addition, Section 167(a) allows a depreciation deduction for the cost of the sailboat. If the deduction equals the decline in value due to ordinary wear and tear (in other words, if tax depreciation deductions equal economic depreciation), what is the net income arising from the sailboat?

b) If the sailboat is instead held "for pleasure" and devoted to personal consumption, how much imputed rent is realized during the year? How much must be reported under Section 61(a)? May a deduction be taken for the decline in the sailboat's value due to ordinary wear and tear? See Sections 167(a) and 262.

c) Compare the two methods for taxing income from property, depending on whether it is held "for profit" or "for pleasure." What are the differences?

2) Sale of the Sailboat at the End of the Year

a) If the sailboat held "for profit" is sold at the end of the year, how much gain or loss is realized under the Code? Assuming that the sailboat is sold for its fair market value, what is the amount realized from the sale? (Recall that, at the end of the year, the sailboat is assumed to be worth $1,200.) What is the adjusted basis of the sailboat at the time of the sale? See Sections 1011, 1012, and 1016(a)(2)(A). Is the result provided by the Code correct? Even though the sailboat is sold for *less* than its cost, why should no loss be realized?

b) If the sailboat held "for pleasure" is sold, how much gain or loss is realized under the Code? How much of the realized loss may be deducted? See Code Section 165(c)(1) and (2). Even though there is a realized loss, why should no deduction be allowed? If Section 165(c) did not exist, would Section 262 deny deduction of the realized loss?

c) Compare the two methods for taxing the sale of property. What are the differences?

3) Increase in Sailboat Prices at the End of the Year

Suppose that, at the end of the year, used sailboat prices increase by $500 due to a surge in demand. The used sailboat in this example can then be sold for $1,700.

a) If the sailboat held "for profit" is sold, how much gain or loss is realized under the Code? Is the result provided by the Code correct? Even though the sailboat is sold for *less* than the original cost, why should a gain be realized?

b) If the sailboat held "for pleasure" is sold, how much gain or loss is realized under the Code? Is the result provided by the Code correct? Why *should* a gain be realized, even though the sailboat is sold for less than the original cost? But what prevents a gain from being reported? Is this result consistent with the policy of Section 262?

4) Decrease in Sailboat Prices at the End of the Year

Suppose that at the end of the year, used sailboat prices plummet by $600 due to falling demand (perhaps induced by mass panic after the making of the movies "Jaws" and "Jaws II"). The used sailboat in this example can then be sold for only $600.

a) If the sailboat is held "for profit," how much gain or loss is realized under the Code? Why is the result provided by the Code correct?

b) If the sailboat is held "for pleasure," how much gain or loss is realized under the Code? How much may be deducted under Section 165(c)(1) and (2)? Is the result provided by the Code correct? Would a deduction for the loss attributable to falling prices violate the policy of Section 262?

5) Providing a More Correct Result on the Sale of Property Held "For Pleasure"

When the sailboat held "for pleasure" is sold and market prices have risen or fallen, the Code arguably produces an incorrect result. How might the Code be amended to provide for a better result? By requiring an adjustment in the basis of property held "for pleasure" to reflect wear and tear even though depreciation may not be deducted? And by repealing Section 165(c)(1) and (2)? Consider the following proposal.

D. EPSTEIN, THE CONSUMPTION AND LOSS OF PERSONAL PROPERTY UNDER THE INTERNAL REVENUE CODE
23 Stan. L. Rev. 454, 454–455, 457–462 (1971)

This Article examines the effects that the consumption and loss of personal property should have upon the determination of taxable income. The provisions of the Internal Revenue Code material to this inquiry are few in number and simple in form. The Code's general rule states that personal, living, and family expenses are not deductible from gross income, whereas deductions may be taken for the ordinary and necessary expenses paid or incurred in the production or collection of income or in the maintenance of income-producing property.... These provisions mark, for our purposes, the extent of the relevant statutory material. They have, over the years, received detailed examination in the literature. Almost without exception these inquiries have taken as their outer limit the Code's current structure and have attempted only to interpret the difficult points of statutory language in light of the cases decided in accordance with the Code's terms. But the structure itself needs reexamination, because the results it yields are incorrect when measured against the economic benefits that personal property provides its owner....

... As an economic matter taxation of imputed income has received vigorous and sound defense, but as an administrative matter the prospect has been greeted with horror because of difficulties in identifying and evaluating each item of imputed wealth. Hence today, as a universal rule, the rigor of the economic definition of income gives way to the administrative difficulties of its application.

The exemption of imputed income from taxation is unimportant in evaluating most business transactions, for profit and not consumption is the goal in business. In transactions with personal property, however, consumption must play a large, if not leading, role in the determination of income....

THE NEED FOR BASIS ADJUSTMENT IN PERSONAL PROPERTY

The administrative problems mentioned above seem to preclude the taxation of imputed wealth where it represents, in an economic sense, current income, but those problems are not decisive on basis questions.... When a taxpayer devotes property to personal use, he recovers his initial cost not in terms of cash, as does the businessman, but in terms of the pleasures afforded through consumption. The general rule of taxation requires appropriate adjustments in basis to reflect cost recovery. Basis adjustments can be made for personal property without administrative difficulty since they need be a function only of the expected life and the initial cost of the asset in question. Once basis adjustments for personal property are made, they will be reflected in the gain or loss recognized subsequently upon disposition or conversion of the property. Here, as a practical matter, some of the benefits of imputed wealth can be taken into account as income, but the Code entirely ignores this possibility.

Examining the results produced by the Code in specific cases illustrates its shortcomings. Consider first the treatment of depreciable property devoted to the personal use of the taxpayer. For the moment, assume that changes in value over the property's life reflect only its depreciation and not fluctuations in market demand. Under the current law, a taxpayer is not entitled to a writeoff against gross income for the depreciation of his personal property during the tax year. Since no writeoff is permitted against gross income, the Code then allows a taxpayer to retain, without downward adjustment, his cost basis in the property for use in the computation of gain or loss. The Code treatment is based on the assumption that a reduction in basis is required if and only if a writeoff against gross income is permitted.

... Personal and business property decline in value on account of wear and tear, and in both cases the taxpayer should be required to reduce basis to account for the recovery of capital through use. In the business case, however, a deduction must be allowed against income ... because the exhaustion of capital represents a loss and not consumption, even though that loss is ultimately offset by the income derived from the taxpayer's activities. Personal property, on the contrary, produces an increment to income in the form of consumption that itself offsets the loss from depreciation. Consequently ... the taxpayer should not be entitled to a writeoff against gross income for depreciation because his loss in property value has been offset by an equal benefit in consumption. Notwithstanding the Code's current provisions, a reduction in basis should be required regardless of the kind of property in question, whereas a writeoff is proper only for depreciation of business property.

An example illustrates the proper method of taxation for depreciable personal property. Consider a case of depreciable property, dedicated to personal use, with a cost of $100, with an expected life of 20 years, and with a value that does not fluctuate at any point in its life because of changes in market conditions. If the taxpayer makes uniform use of his property over its expected life, then he consumes in each taxable year $5 worth of that property. After 20 years, he will recover, in the form of consumption, an amount precisely equal to his initial investment in the property, or the full $100. Under current law his basis remains at $100 throughout, but no tax results turn on that fact, assuming no sale or disposition occurs after the property becomes worthless.

The proper computation of basis, however, is crucial whenever the property is disposed of before it has been exhausted. In the previous example, assume that the owner decides to sell the asset after he has used it for five years. Under the current law he need not reduce his basis because the asset was not used in his trade or business. Selling the property for its fair market value of $75 will produce a loss of $25 since the basis is still $100, but the loss is not recognized under present law because it is not a business loss. The net effect of the Code's rules is that the taxpayer recognizes no gain or loss at any time from the acquisition to the disposition of the property. In this particular case the Code's result conforms to the treatment required by Simons' definition. The reduction in the taxpayer's store of wealth is $100, representing the initial cost of the property in question. The benefits realized by the taxpayer are two: $25 in consumption over the previous 5 years and $75 in proceeds received upon its disposition. Since the benefits received exactly offset the costs incurred, gain or loss need not be recognized at the time of sale.

The Code achieves the proper result only because it makes two errors in principle that cancel themselves out in effect. First, the Code refuses to take consumption into account, even as an adjustment to basis. Second, it refuses, except in some limited cases, to take the losses into account in the computation of income because they are personal. The Code's result will be correct only when the property's value is unaffected by changes in market demand over the period it is held. Once that assumption is relaxed, the tax results are certain to be wrong in a way that does not systematically benefit either the government or the taxpayer.

To make this point clear, consider several variants of the example discussed above. First, assume that the property's market value doubles at the end of the fifth year, from $75 to $150. . . .

Assume that at the end of the [fifth] year of ownership the taxpayer sells the property in an arm's length transaction. . . . [T]he taxpayer will receive [$150] from the sale. Current law demands recognition of only [$50] in gain from the sale, because the undepreciated cost of the property, $100, is set off against the proceeds. . . . [$25] of the initial investment has been recovered in the form of rights enjoyed in consumption. . . . In addition, the taxpayer received at the end of the [fifth] year [$150] in cash, so the total amount of his benefit from the property equals $175. Since only $100 was invested initially, $75 ought to be taxed at some point, but under current law the gain upon sale, calculated by reference to cost ($100) basis, is only [$50]. . . . The taxpayer's basis should be not $100 but only [$75] allowing $5 of cost recovery for each of [5] years of use. Accordingly, the gain should be [$75] equal to the amount realized [$150] less the adjusted basis [$75].

These errors in principle do not always work to the taxpayer's advantage. Assume that the value of this same property has, on account of market forces, fallen from $100 to $80 shortly after purchase. Assume further that the property had been held and used for a period of five years and then sold for $60. In this situation, the taxpayer sustains, in terms of Simons' definition, a loss of $20 that under present law will go unrecognized for all time. . . . Because of the realization requirement that loss is unrecognized when sustained; it should, however, be recognized after sale. . . .

The current law provides, of course, that all losses on the sale of personal property shall not be recognized. . . . If the taxpayer were required to write down his basis to reflect consumption of personal property, loss upon sale would occur less frequently because the taxpayer would be required to use his depreciated, not his original, basis in all computations of gain or loss. Where losses, properly calculated, do occur on sale, they should be recognized, since realization has taken place. A consistent theory of cost recovery is applicable to both personal and business property, but the Code makes provision for it only in the latter case. . . .

E. NOTES AND QUESTIONS

1) Equity and the Proposal

If Professor Epstein's proposal were adopted, how would the annual decline in value of a *particular* item be determined? Even if some *average* amount could be ascertained, would it be fair to require all taxpayers to reduce the basis of property by the average amount? Suppose that, on average, the value of a new automobile falls by 15% during the first year it is owned. Should all owners be required to reduce the basis during the first year by the same 15%, even though some drive the car 30,000 miles and others only 5,000 miles? Or even though some ignore normal upkeep and maintenance requirements, while others change the oil every thousand miles?

2) Administrative Feasibility and the Proposal

Can individual taxpayers be expected to keep accurate records of the date and cost of a multitude of personal consumption items such as clothes, stereos, kitchenware, furniture, and so on? Or is the burden of record-keeping a spurious objection, since the proposal could be restricted to relatively expensive items, costing over a certain minimum amount—say, $10,000? For most taxpayers, this would mean keeping records on two items: one's car and one's home.

Recall that the objective is to tax market gains and allow a deduction for market losses that now go unaccounted for when property is held "for pleasure." But if restricted to the two items mentioned above—one's car and one's home—what real difference would the proposal make? How often are cars sold for a market gain—that is, for more than the original cost, less wear and tear? Obsolescence diminishes the market value of most automobiles. (Recall the commonplace that as soon as a new car is driven off the dealer's lot, it falls in value.) Given the obsolescence factor, aren't market gains limited to the special case of antique cars, such as an old Mercedes or Rolls-Royce?

Personal residences, on the other hand, usually do sell for more than the original cost, less wear and tear, given the increasing scarcity of housing, particularly in urban areas, and the rising population. Thus, requiring that the basis of an owner-occupied house be reduced to reflect wear and tear would undoubtedly produce more *realized* gain. But how much of a difference would that make, given the *nonrecognition* of gain on the sale of a taxpayer's personal residence under Section 1034 or Section 121?

F. GEVIRTZ v. COMMISSIONER
123 F.2d 707 (2d Cir. 1941)

FRANK, CIRCUIT JUDGE.

Taxpayer, a woman of considerable wealth, was, for some years prior to 1926, a resident of Mt. Vernon, where, at one time, she had built and later sold a garden apartment house. Conceiving the idea of constructing another garden apartment, she purchased a tract of several acres with this in view, but she became dissatisfied with the location and sold it in 1925. Shortly thereafter she advised a real estate agent at Mt. Vernon that she was interested in acquiring another tract of land upon which to build an apartment house. Early in 1926 she purchased a one-acre parcel for $32,000, paying $7,000 in cash and giving back a mortgage for $25,000. The deed

Ch. 30　Comparing "For Profit" and "For Pleasure"　453

contained restrictions, providing that no building could be erected on the premises for any trade, calling, or business whatever, the premises being restricted to dwelling purposes by means of homes for use or value of not less than $15,000, and built not more than one to each 75 feet of frontage, and that no building erected on the land could be used as a tenement house or apartment house. At the time of the hearing of the present proceeding by the Board, these restrictions had not been removed, although it was believed, we may assume with good reason, that they could be. Immediately following the acquisition of this property, the taxpayer learned, for the first time, that several large apartment house projects were being contemplated in Mt. Vernon, some of them not far distant from the property in question. She then decided that it would be a mistake to proceed with any plans to build an apartment house on that site, since the other projected apartment houses were more than sufficient to satisfy the demand and there would be difficulty in securing tenants at profitable rental rates.

She then erected on the property a 12-room residence costing in excess of $90,000. On the advice of her real estate agent, this residence was constructed with three separate wings, each of which could be made into a separate apartment with its own private entrance and driveway, so that the building could be converted into a 3-family dwelling. She knew at that time that it could not be rented at a profit as a private residence. She lived in it from the time of its completion in 1926 until December 31, 1931. She then vacated it and endeavored to sell or rent it, but without success. In November or December, 1934, she discharged the caretaker whom she had left in charge of the property and turned the keys to the house over to the attorneys for the original mortgagees with the request that she be released from personal liability on the bond and mortgage. In the last week of 1934, those attorneys informed her that she would not be thus released, as the mortgagees wished to foreclose, although they expressed the opinion that there would be no deficiency judgment against the taxpayer as the mortgagees thought that the market value of the property was in excess of the amount of the bond and mortgage. In the taxpayer's income tax return for the calendar year 1934 she claimed, on the basis of the foregoing, a deductible loss from gross income of $89,588.80 and also deductions for depreciation, cost of insurance and legal expenses. The Commissioner disallowed these deductions and the Board, after hearing, sustained the deficiency as determined by the Commissioner. The taxpayer petitioned this court for review.

Taxpayer is entitled to a deduction only for a loss incurred in a "transaction entered into for profit," § [165(c)(2)]. The evidence amply supports the finding of the Board that there was a "definite abandonment" by the taxpayer of her original profit motive in purchasing the land and a "definite devotion of the property to a personal residence use." The fact that the residence cost $90,000, coupled with the other facts found by the Board, answers the suggestion that the construction of the residence with three separate wings, so that it could, at some indefinite future date, be converted into three separate apartments, showed a retention of the original business purpose. That the taxpayer had in mind the possibility of later devoting the property to such a purpose is not sufficient to demonstrate that the profit motive remained dominant. Cases can be imagined where a taxpayer's motive might be mixed, with the profit motive so markedly preponderant that it should be regarded as if it were controlling. But that is not this case. Here the prospect of a future business use of the property was clearly subsidiary, only on the edge of the taxpayer's mind. Her attitude was not unlike that of the White Knight who carried a mouse-trap on his horse because, he said, "it's well to be provided for everything." At best, it was as if she had bought a residence for her personal use, intending to live in it for several years and then put it on the market.

Once the conclusion is reached that when the residence was built she did not have a business purpose, the case falls into a familiar category. There was no subsequent conversion of the property to a business use; the mere effort to rent it did not have that effect. . . . The claimed deductions, therefore, constituted items of personal loss and expense which are not deductible.

G. NOTES AND QUESTIONS

1) The Nature of the Loss in *Gevirtz*

Assume that the residence cost $120,000 and that, in 1934, when the bank foreclosed, the unpaid mortgage liability was $30,000. If the taxpayer had no equity in the property and the mortgage debt was discharged following foreclosure, how much gain or loss was realized? Under Section 165(c)(1) and (2), could the loss be deducted? Given the dates of the transactions, how much of the loss was probably attributable to the wear and tear of personal consumption and how much to a collapse in the price of housing? If taxpayers were forced to reduce the basis of owner-occupied housing to reflect wear and tear *and* if Section 165(c)(1) and (2) were repealed, would most of the loss in a case like *Gevirtz* be deductible?

2) Conversion of Property From Personal to Business or Investment Use

Suppose that the court had concluded that Mrs. Gevirtz converted her personal residence to business or investment property when she moved out in 1931 and tried to rent it. Even then, should all her loss have been deductible? Or only that amount not attributable to wear and tear while she occupied the house as her residence? Or only that loss occurring *after* she moved out?

For example, suppose that the property, which originally cost $120,000, fell $10,000 in value due to wear and tear during her occupancy and $60,000 in value due to the collapse of price levels between 1926 and 1931. See Reg. § 1.165–7(a)(5), which provides that when property is converted from personal use, the basis shall be its adjusted basis or market value on the date of conversion, *whichever is lower.* How does the regulation compare with Professor Epstein's proposal that basis be reduced to reflect wear and tear due to personal consumption?

H. BITTKER, INCOME TAX DEDUCTIONS, CREDITS, AND SUBSIDIES FOR PERSONAL EXPENDITURES
16 J.L. & Econ. 193, 196–198 (1973)

[Editor's Note: While losses on property held "for pleasure" generally are *not* deductible, Section 165(c)(3) contains an exception for losses that arise from "fire, storm, shipwreck, or other casualty, or from theft." In the following article, Professor Bittker argues that the so-called casualty loss deduction could be regarded as an income-defining provision (Chapter 11).]

... If the only relevant transactions during the taxable year were the receipt of a salary of $50,000, the expenditure of $20,000 of this amount for food and clothing, loss by fire of a residence worth $20,000, and the expenditure of $30,000 to replace it, one might think that the ... computation would be: Consumption of $20,000 (food and clothing) plus accumulation of $10,000 (that is, increase in net worth between the beginning of the period, $20,000, and the end $30,000) equals $30,000 of personal income for the period. That is the result achieved by current law: $50,000 of salary income, less a casualty deduction of $20,000, equals net income of $30,000.

To reach a contrary result ... it is necessary to argue that what is consumed by fire should be treated as consumed by the taxpayer, and brought back into income ... This theory is, of course, a satisfactory answer to a taxpayer who claims that he suffered a reduction in his net worth, and hence in "income," on smoking a pack of cigarettes or using up a bag of charcoal briquettes. It is also the reason why the gradual decline and ultimate loss of value which a taxpayer's residence suffers as a result of exposure to the elements or boisterous conduct by his children do not reduce his income ... The reduction in his net worth is counterbalanced by the value to him of occupying the building during its useful life—the "rights exercised [by him] in consumption," to use the language of the definition.

But to count the taxpayer's purposeful uses of his property as part of his consumption in calculating his income does not inevitably lead to the same treatment for unexpected and catastrophic losses. In a statistical sense, of course, destruction by fire is one of the hazards of home ownership, "voluntarily" assumed when the taxpayer chooses to buy a personal residence. But if a dog can distinguish between being kicked and being stumbled over, as Holmes asserted, we can properly distinguish between the minor frustrations of life—a cigarette burn in a rug, a dented fender, a quarter lost when fumbling for change to put in a parking meter—and major casualties ("sudden, unexpected, and unusual" events that do not "commonly occur in the ordinary course of day-to-day living," to quote a recent Revenue Ruling).

As interpreted, the Code's definition of the term "casualty" may be too lenient, and the $100 non-deductible floor may be too low; perhaps account should be taken of the taxpayer's income (as in the case of medical expenses) in distinguishing between the normal hazards of life and deductible casualties. But these are details. Casualties undeniably reduce the taxpayer's net worth—and should therefore presumptively reduce his income . . . and it is debatable whether they are offset by the satisfactions implied by the term "consumption." It does, I suggest, stretch the meaning of the words a bit to say that a casualty *loss* constitutes a *"gain"* to the taxpayer. . . .

I do not say that income is "wrongly" defined if casualty losses are not deducted; terms like "income" and "consumption" are irretrievably ambiguous. By the same token, however, to assert flatly that the casualty deduction departs from the . . . definition is sheer dogmatism; and the related allegation that it is a "subsidy" means only that the writer prefers one interpretation . . . over an alternative that is at least equally plausible.

A more cogent criticism of the casualty deduction is that taxpayers should be encouraged to insure against such losses and that the deduction mitigates the cost of neglecting this sensible precaution. Whatever its strength, this line of argument does not prove that a taxpayer whose uninsured home is destroyed by fire has the same "income" as an otherwise identical taxpayer whose house escapes. The first taxpayer's loss is real, no matter how stupid, pigheaded, or foolhardy his failure to insure. One might wish to deny him a deduction as a penalty for improvidence, as a warning to others, or as a mode of raising revenue; but these objectives should be openly acknowledged, not disguised as an effort to "define income" or to achieve . . . equity.

I. CARPENTER v. COMMISSIONER
25 T.C.M. 1186 (1966)

MEMORANDUM FINDINGS OF FACT AND OPINION

WITHEY, JUDGE: A deficiency in the income tax [of] petitioners for the taxable year 1962 has been determined by the Commissioner in the amount of $221.92. The sole issue to be decided is whether respondent has erred in disallowing a claimed casualty loss deduction.

FINDINGS OF FACT

During 1962 petitioner Nancy Carpenter owned a diamond engagement ring. At an undisclosed time in 1962 she placed the ring in a waterglass of ammonia for the purpose of cleaning it. The glass containing the ring was left "next" to the kitchen sink. While petitioner William Carpenter was washing dishes, he inadvertently "picked up the glass and emptied its contents down the" sink drain, not realizing the ring was part of such contents. He then activated the garbage disposal unit in the sink damaging the ring. The damaged ring was recovered and taken to a jeweler for appraisal. His appraisal was that the ring was a total loss.

The ring consisted of a platinum mounting, one diamond of .76 carat and four small diamonds of undisclosed weight. Immediately before going into the disposal unit the fair market value of the mounting was $235, that of the large diamond $725, and the aggregate of four small diamonds $50, or an aggregate fair market value of $1,010. This amount was deducted on petitioner's income tax return as a casualty loss.

The fair market value of the mounting immediately after being placed in the disposal unit was $5, that of the large diamond zero, and the aggregate of the small diamonds $25, or a total aggregate fair market value of $30. . . .

Nancy had a loss as a result of the above facts in the amount of the difference between the fair market value of her original ring immediately before it was damaged and its fair market value immediately after in the resulting amount of $980.

OPINION

Respondent's position here is that Nancy did not suffer a casualty loss within the meaning of section 165(a) and (c)(3) of the Internal Revenue Code of 1954 in that, by applying the principle of ejusdem generis, it cannot be said that the events which gave rise to the ring damage were like or similar to a "fire, storm, [or] shipwreck" and therefore do not amount to "other casualty" under that section. . . .

Because William's testimony and his demeanor on the witness stand satisfies us that he is not the type of person who would deliberately and knowingly do so, we have concluded that his placing of the original ring in the disposal unit was inadvertent and accidental. We in turn conclude from this that the damage to the ring resulted from the destructive force of the disposal coupled with the accident or mischance of placing it therein; that, because this is so, the damage must be said to have arisen from fortuitous events over which petitioners had no control.

While the application of the principle of ejusdem generis has been consistent in reported cases under this section of the Code and its predecessors, . . . the application has been clearly and consistently broadened. Automobile accidental damage has been likened to shipwreck . . . earthslide damage to a building, to fire, storm, and shipwreck . . . and drought damage to buildings, to storm damage. . . . Respondent has gone so far as to allow deduction for damage caused by the sonic boom of a speeding airplane as "other casualty. . . ." This Court has held that "other casualty" includes damage caused by an infestation by termites . . . in no way departing from the principle in doing so.

We think the principle of ejusdem generis as now applied fulfills congressional intent in the use of the phrase "other casualty" in that it is being generally held that wherever force is applied to property which the owner-taxpayer is either unaware of because of the hidden nature of such application or is powerless to act to prevent the same because of the suddenness thereof or some other disability and damage results, he has suffered a loss which is, in that sense, like or similar to losses arising from the enumerated causes. Of course, we do not mean to say that one may willfully and knowingly sit by and allow himself to be damaged in his property and still come within the statutory ambit of "other casualty."

Nancy sustained a loss here under circumstances which it is true may be due to her or her husband's negligence, but this has no bearing upon the question whether an "other casualty" has occurred absent any willfulness attributable thereto. . . .

J. REV. RUL. 63–232
1963–2 C.B. 97

The Internal Revenue Service has re-examined its position with regard to the deductibility of losses resulting from termite damage, as set forth in Revenue Ruling 59–277, C.B. 1959–2, 73. . . .

An extensive examination of scientific data regarding the habits, destructive power and other factors peculiar to termites discloses that the biological background of all termites found in the United States is generally the same, with one notable exception. The subterranean or ground dwelling termite attacks only wood which is in contact with the ground, while the other types of termites attack wood directly from the air.

Leading authorities on the subject have concluded that little or no structural damage can be caused by termites during the first two years after the initial infestation. It has been estimated that under normal conditions, if left unchecked, depending upon climate and other factors, an infestation of three to eight years would be required to necessitate extensive repairs. Even under extreme conditions, the period would be from one to six years. See "Our Enemy the Termite" by Thomas Elliott Snyder; "Termite and Termite Control" by Charles A. Kofoid; "Insects Their Ways and Means of Living" by Robert Evans Snodgrass; and other authorities.

Such authorities agree that termite infestation and the resulting damage cannot be inflicted with the suddenness comparable to that caused by fire, storm or shipwreck.

Accordingly, it is the position of the Service, based on the scientific data available in this area, that damage caused by termites to property not connected with the trade or business does not constitute an allowable deduction as a casualty loss within the meaning of section 165(c)(3) of the Code. Such damage is the result of gradual deterioration through a steadily operating cause and is not the result of an identifiable event of a sudden, unusual or unexpected nature. Further, time elapsed between the incurrence of damage and its ultimate discovery is not a proper measure to determine whether the damage resulted from a casualty. Time of discovery of the damage, in some situations, may affect the extent of the damage, but this does not change the form or the nature of the event, the mode of its operation, or the character of the result. These characteristics are determinative when applying section 165(c)(3) of the Code. . . .

K. NOTES AND QUESTIONS

1) The Special Deduction for Casualty Losses

Return to the example, in C, above, of the sailboat acquired "for pleasure," which costs $2,000 and falls in value by $800 due to ordinary wear and tear of the first year. Suppose, however, that one year after its purchase, the market value is only $500. Should the additional fall in value, for reasons other than ordinary wear and tear, be deductible? Should it depend on whether the additional loss is due to: (a) uninsured storm damage; (b) uninsured termite damage; (c) uninsured collision damage; (d) an unwar-

Ch. 30 Comparing "For Profit" and "For Pleasure"

ranted defect in construction causing the mast to crack; or (e) the collapse of sailboat prices generally? See Section 165(c)(3).

Do the lines drawn by Section 165(c)(3) make any sense? Why is the loss caused by a storm or collision (or throwing out the ring in *Carpenter* above) any more of a "casualty" and deserving of a deduction than the loss caused by The Great Depression in *Gevirtz*? Is Section 165(c)(3) consistent with the policy of Section 262? What is the difference between a fall in value due to "ordinary" wear and tear and a fall in value due to the "less ordinary" events described in (a), (b), and (c), above?

Are you persuaded by Professor Bittker's argument that the casualty loss might be viewed as an income-defining provision? As a matter of social policy, is Section 165(c)(3) desirable? Does it encourage reckless behavior? Does it subsidize people who neglect to insure the property they use? Is there a stronger case for allowing deduction of the *non*casualty losses described above (arising from an unwarranted defect or a general collapse of prices) than for so-called casualty losses?

2) Limits on the Casualty Loss Deduction

Section 165(h) imposes several different limits on the deduction of casualty losses. First, Section 165(h)(1) reduces the allowable loss from each separate casualty by $100. Second—and considerably more far-reaching—is Section 165(h)(2), enacted in 1982. It allows the deduction of "net casualty loss" only to the extent it exceeds 10% of the taxpayer's AGI. Net casualty loss is defined as the excess of casualty losses over recognized gains from any involuntary conversion arising from a casualty.

What is the practical effect of Section 165(h)(2)? Is it likely to permit most casualty loss deductions? Does it reflect the idea that most casualty losses arise from personal consumption and should therefore be nondeductible under the principle of Section 262? But if so, why still allow a deduction for casualty losses that exceed 10% of AGI?

In addition, Section 165(h)(4)(E), enacted in 1986, denies a casualty loss deduction for *insured* property unless the taxpayer has filed an insurance claim for the loss. Suppose that a collision causes $1,000 worth of damage to an automobile. If the owner's collision insurance carries a $500 deductible, why may the owner prefer not to file a claim? Because it is cheaper to absorb the loss than to report it and face higher insurance premiums in the future? What effect does Section 165(h)(4) have on this decision? The cost of insurance for a personal car is nondeductible under Section 262. Is Section 165(h)(4) designed to prevent the deduction of a casualty loss that is in essence a cost of obtaining such insurance?

3) Casualty Losses and the Realization Principle

In order for a casualty loss on property held "for pleasure" to be deductible, the damaged property need not be sold or exchanged. The loss is considered realized simply by virtue of it having occurred. In addition, if property held "for profit" is damaged by an event that would qualify as a casualty under Section 165(c)(3), realization is also deemed to have occurred. See Reg. § 1.165–7(b)(1).

4) The Amount Deductible

Section 165(b) states that the basis for determining the amount of a casualty loss is the adjusted basis of the property. Suppose that an automobile that cost $10,000 declines in value to $5,000 after four years of use and then is destroyed by fire. Does the casualty loss equal the entire adjusted basis? Would mechanical application of Section 165(b) be consistent with the policy of Section 262? In Helvering v. Owens, 305 U. S. 468 (1939), the Supreme Court held that the deduction is limited to the lesser of the property's adjusted basis or value immediately before the casualty.

Suppose that a 1924 Mercedes, purchased for $50,000, is worth $90,000 when it is destroyed by fire. How much is the deductible loss under Section 165(b)? Doesn't that understate the amount of the actual economic loss by $40,000? Or can the result be viewed as equivalent to requiring that the $40,000 of unrealized gain offset the $90,000 loss?

L. NONRECOGNITION OF FORGIVENESS OF DEBT: THE DIFFERENCE BETWEEN "FOR PROFIT" AND "FOR PLEASURE" PROPERTY

Return to the example of the sailboat purchased for $2,000. Suppose that the purchase is financed with a cash down payment of $400 and a $1,600 maritime mortgage. Shortly thereafter, the movies "Jaws" and "Jaws II" are released, the demand for sailboats plummets, and the sailboat is suddenly worth only $1,000. Suppose further that the owner becomes insolvent and that the mortgagee then agrees to forgive $600 of the mortgage debt (the amount in excess of the sailboat's value). Assume that the sailboat can now be rented out for only $750 a year and that its useful life is two years, after which it will be scrapped. For the purpose of answering the following questions, also assume that the basis of the sailboat is depreciable in equal amounts over the two years.

1) If the sailboat is held "for profit," calculate the taxable income for each year resulting from the forgiveness of debt plus rental of the sailboat, assuming that the taxpayer does not elect nonrecognition under Section 108. Next, calculate taxable income on the assumption that the taxpayer does elect nonrecognition of income due to the forgiveness of debt under Section 108. What is the effect of Section 1017 on the adjusted basis and on annual depreciation deductions? Compare the results. What difference does the election make?

2) Suppose instead the sailboat is held "for pleasure." What difference does the Section 108 election make? Why does nonrecognition lead to deferral with the sailboat held "for profit" but exclusion with the sailboat held "for pleasure"?

Chapter 31

DISTINGUISHING "FOR PROFIT" FROM "FOR PLEASURE" ACTIVITIES

A. NICKERSON v. COMMISSIONER
700 F.2d 402 (7th Cir. 1983)

PELL, CIRCUIT JUDGE.

Petitioners appeal the judgment of the United States Tax Court finding that profit was not their primary goal in owning a dairy farm. Based on this finding the tax court disallowed deductions for losses incurred in renovating the farm. The sole issue presented for our review is whether the tax court's finding regarding petitioners' motivation was clearly erroneous.

I. Facts

Melvin Nickerson (hereinafter referred to as petitioner) was born in 1932 in a farming community in Florida. He worked evenings and weekends on his father's farm until he was 17. Petitioner entered the field of advertising after attending college and serving in the United States Army. During the years relevant to this case he was self-employed in Chicago, serving industrial and agricultural clients. His wife, Naomi W. Nickerson, was a full-time employee of the Chicago Board of Education. While petitioners were not wealthy, they did earn a comfortable living.

At the age of forty, petitioner decided that his career in the "youth oriented" field of advertising would not last much longer, and he began to look for an alternative source of income for the future. Petitioners decided that dairy farming was the most desirable means of generating income and examined a number of farms in Michigan and Wisconsin. After several years of searching, petitioners bought an 80-acre farm in Door County, Wisconsin for $40,000. One year later they purchased an additional 40 acres adjoining the farm for $10,000.

The farm, which had not been run as a dairy for eight years, was in a run-down condition. What little equipment was left was either in need of repair or obsolete. The tillable land, about 60 acres, was planted with alfalfa, which was at the end of its productive cycle. In an effort to improve this state of affairs petitioners leased the land to a tenant-farmer for $20 an acre and an agreement that the farmer would convert an additional ten acres a year to the cultivation of a more profitable crop. At the time of trial approximately 80 acres were tillable. The rent received from the farmer was the only income derived from the farm.

Petitioner visited the farm on most weekends during the growing season and twice a month the rest of the year. Mrs. Nickerson and the children visited less frequently. The trip to the farm requires five hours of driving from petitioners' home in Chicago. During these visits petitioner and his family either worked on their land or assisted neighboring farmers. When working on his own farm petitioner concentrated his efforts on renovating an abandoned orchard and remodeling the farm house. In addition to learning about farming through this experience petitioner read a number of trade journals and spoke with the area agricultural extension agent.

Petitioners did not expect to make a profit from the farm for approximately 10 years. True to their expectations, petitioners lost $8,668 in 1976 and $9,872.95 in 1977. Although they did not keep formal books of account petitioners did retain receipts and cancelled checks relating to farm expenditures. At the time of trial, petitioners had not yet acquired any livestock or farm machinery. The farm was similarly devoid of recreational equipment and had never been used to entertain guests.

The tax court decided that these facts did not support petitioners' claim that the primary goal in operating the farm was to make a profit. We will examine the tax court's reasoning in more detail after setting out the relevant legal considerations.

II. The Statutory Scheme

Section 162(a) of the Internal Revenue Code of 1954 allows deduction of "all the ordinary and necessary expenses paid or incurred during the taxable year in carrying on any trade or business." Section 183, however, limits the availability of these deductions if the activity "is not engaged in for profit" to deductions that are allowed regardless of the existence of a profit motive and deductions for ordinary and necessary expenses "only to the extent that the gross income derived from such activity for the taxable year exceeds [otherwise allowable deductions]." I.R.C. § 183(b)(2). The deductions claimed by petitioners are only allowable if their motivation in investing in the farm was to make a profit.

Petitioners bear the burden of proving that their primary purpose in renovating the farm was to make a profit.... In meeting this burden, however, "it is sufficient if the taxpayer has a bona fide expectation of realizing a profit, regardless of the reasonableness of such expectation."... Although petitioners need only prove their sincerity rather than their realism the factors considered in judging their motivation are primarily objective. In addition to the taxpayer's statements of intent, which are given little weight for obvious reasons, the tax court must consider "all facts and circumstances with respect to the activity...." Treas.Reg. § 1.183–2(b)(1)–(9) [lists 9 factors that are to be considered]. None of these factors is determinative, nor is the decision to be made by comparing the number of factors that weigh in the taxpayer's favor with the number that support the Commissioner. . . . There is no set formula for divining a taxpayer's true motive, rather "[o]ne struggles in vain for any verbal formula that will supply a ready touchstone. The standard set by the statute is not a rule of law; it is rather a way of life. Life in all its fullness must supply the answer to the riddle." *Welch v. Helvering* [Chapter 32]. Nonetheless, we are given some guidance by the enumerated factors and by the Congressional purpose in enacting section 183.

> The legislative history surrounding section 183 indicates that one of the prime motivating factors behind its passage was Congress' desire to create an objective standard to determine whether a taxpayer was carrying on a business for the purpose of realizing a profit or was instead merely attempting to create and utilize losses to offset other income. . . .

Congressional concern stemmed from a recognition that "[w]ealthy individuals have invested in certain aspects of farm operations solely to obtain 'tax losses'—largely bookkeeping losses—for use to reduce their tax on other income. . . . One of the remarkable aspects of the problem is pointed up by the fact that persons with large nonfarm income have a remarkable propensity to lose money in the farm business." . . . With this concern in mind we will now examine the decision of the tax court.

III. Decision of the Tax Court

The tax court analyzed the relevant factors and determined that making a profit was not petitioners' primary goal in engaging in farming. The court based its decision on a number of factors that weighed against petitioners. The court found that they did not operate the farm in a businesslike manner and did not appear to have a concrete plan for improving the profitability of the farm. The court believed that these difficulties were attributable to petitioners' lack of experience, but did not discuss the steps actually taken by Melvin Nickerson to gain experience in farming.

The court found it difficult to believe that petitioners actually believed that the limited amount of time they were spending at the farm would produce a profit given the dilapidated condition of the farm. Furthermore, the court found that petitioners' emphasis on making the farm house habitable rather than on acquiring or repairing farm equipment was inconsistent with a profit motive. These factors, combined with the consistent history of losses borne by petitioners, convinced the court that "petitioner at best entertains the hope that when he retires from the advertising business and can devote his complete attention to the farming operation, he may at that time expect to produce a profit." The court did not think that this hope rose to the level of a bona fide expectation of profit.

IV. Review of the Tax Court's Findings

Whether petitioners intended to run the dairy farm for a profit is a question of fact, and as such our review is limited to a determination of whether the tax court was "clearly erroneous" in determining that petitioners lacked the requisite profit motive. Fed.R.Civ.P. 52(a). . . . This standard of review applies although the only dispute is over the proper interpretation of uncontested facts. *Commissioner v. Duberstein* [Chapter 5].

It is not enough, then, that we would have reached a different conclusion had the decision been ours to make. Rather, "[a] finding is 'clearly erroneous' when although there is evidence to support it, the reviewing court on the entire evidence is left with the definite and firm conviction that a mistake has been committed." . . . This is one of those cases in which we are convinced that a mistake has been made.

Our basic disagreement with the tax court stems from our belief that the court improperly evaluated petitioners' actions from the perspective of whether they sincerely believed that they could make a profit from their current level of activity at the farm. On the contrary, petitioners need only prove that their current actions were motivated by the expectation that they would later reap a profit, in this case when they finished renovating the farm and began full-time operations. It is well established that a taxpayer need not expect an immediate profit; the existence of "start up" losses does not preclude a bona fide profit motive.

> The presence of losses in the formative years of a business . . . is not inconsistent with an intention to achieve a later profitable level of operation, bearing in mind, however, that the goal must be to realize a profit on the entire operation, which presupposes not only future net earnings but also sufficient net earnings to recoup the losses which have meanwhile been sustained in the intervening years.

. . . The tax court was apparently of the view that petitioners' decision to spread these start-up losses over a period of years before starting full-time operation of the farm was inconsistent with a bona fide intention to make a profit. It is uncontested, however, that substantial time, effort, and money were needed to return the farm to a profitable operation, petitioners' only choice being when they would make this investment. We see no basis for distinguishing petitioners' actions from a situation in which one absorbs larger losses over a shorter period of time by beginning full-time operations immediately. In either situation the taxpayer stands an equal chance of recouping start-up losses. In fact, it seems to us a reasonable decision by petitioners to prepare the farm before becoming dependent upon it for sustenance. Keeping in mind that petitioners were not seeking to supplement their existing incomes with their current work on the farm, but rather were laying the ground work for a contemplated career switch, we will examine the factors relied upon by the tax court.

The tax court found that the amount of time petitioners devoted to the farm was inadequate. In reaching this conclusion the court ignored petitioners' agreement with the tenant-farmer under which he would convert 10 acres a year to profitable crops in exchange for the right to farm the land. In this situation the limited amount of time spent by petitioners, who were fully employed in Chicago, is not inconsistent with an expectation of profit. "The fact that the taxpayer devotes a limited amount of time to an activity does not necessarily indicate a lack of profit motive where the taxpayer employs competent and qualified persons to carry on such activity." Treas.Reg. § 1.183–2(b)(3). There is no indication in the record that the tenant-farmer was not qualified to convert the land, or that 10 acres a year was an unreasonable amount. In these circumstances the tax court erred in inferring a lack of profit motive from the amount of time personally spent by petitioners on renovating the farm.

The court also rested its decision on the lack of a concrete plan to put the farm in operable condition. Once again, this ignores petitioners' agreement with the tenant-farmer concerning reclamation of the land. Under this agreement the majority of the land would be tillable by the time petitioners were prepared to begin full-time farming. The tax court also believed that petitioners' decision to renovate the farm house and orchard prior to obtaining farm equipment evidenced a lack of profit motive. As petitioners planned to live on the farm when they switched careers refurbishing the house would seem to be a necessary first step. The court also failed to consider the uncontradicted testimony regarding repairs made to the hay barn and equipment shed, which supported petitioners' contention that they were interested in operating a farm rather than just living on the land. Additionally, we fail to understand how renovating the orchard, a potential source of food and income, is inconsistent with an expectation of profit.

The tax court took into account the history of losses in considering petitioners' intentions. While a history of losses is relevant, in this case little weight should be accorded this factor. Petitioners did not expect to make a profit for a number of years, and it was clear from the condition of the farm that a financial investment would be required before the farm could be profitable. Accordingly, that petitioners lost money, as they expected, does not cast doubt upon the sincerity of their motivation. In this regard, the tax court should have also considered the fact that petitioners were reaping what profit they could through leasing the land to a local farmer.

The court believed that most of petitioners' problems were attributable to their lack of expertise. While lack of expertise is relevant, efforts at gaining experience and a willingness to follow expert advice should also be considered. Treas.Reg. 1.183–2(b)(2). The court here failed to consider the uncontradicted evidence that Melvin Nickerson read trade journals and Government-sponsored agricultural newsletters, sought advice from a state horticultural agent regarding renovation of the orchard and gained experience by working on neighboring farms. In addition, petitioners' agreement with the tenant-farmer was entered into on the advice of the area agricultural extension agent. To weigh petitioners' lack of expertise against them without giving consideration to these efforts effectively precludes a bona fide attempt to change careers. We are unwilling to restrict petitioners in this manner and believe that a proper interpretation of these facts supports petitioners' claims.

The tax court recognized that the farm was not used for entertainment and lacked any recreational facilities, and that petitioners' efforts at the farm were "prodigious," but felt that this was of little importance. While the Commissioner need not prove that petitioners were motivated by goals other than making a profit, we think that more weight should be given to the absence of any alternative explanation for petitioners' actions. As we previously noted the standard set out by the statute is to be applied with the insight gained from a lifetime of experience as well as an understanding of the statutory scheme. Common sense indicates to us that rational people do not perform hard manual labor for no reason, and if the possibility that petitioners performed these labors for pleasure is eliminated the only remaining motivation is profit. The Commissioner has argued that petitioner was motivated by a love of farming that stems from his childhood. We find it difficult to believe that he drove five hours in order to spend his weekends working on a dilapidated farm soley for fun, or that his family derived much pleasure from the experience. Furthermore, there is no support for this contention in the record. At any rate, that petitioner may have chosen farming over some other career because of fond memories of his youth does not preclude a bona fide profit motive. Treas.Reg. § 1.183–2(b)(9). We believe that the absence of any recreational purpose strongly counsels in favor of finding that petitioners' prodigious efforts were directed at making a profit. . . .

Based upon these facts we conclude that the tax court erred in finding that petitioners had failed to prove a bona fide expectation of profit. We recognize that the scope of our review in this case is limited. In a similar situation the Supreme Court observed that:

> Decision of the issue presented in these cases must be based ultimately on the application of the factfinding tribunal's experience with the mainsprings of human conduct to the totality of the facts of each case. The nontechnical nature of the statutory standard, the close relationship of it to the data of practical human experience, and the multiplicity of relevant factual elements, with their various combinations, creating the necessity of ascribing the proper force to each, confirms us in our conclusion that primary weight in this area must be given to the conclusions of the trier of fact.

Commissioner v. Duberstein [Chapter 5]. Nonetheless, when the basic facts are not disputed and the inference drawn from them by the trier of fact is the result of an overly restrictive view of what a party must prove in order to prevail we will not hesitate to exercise our power to reverse. In this case the court erroneously concluded that petitioners were required to prove a bona fide expectation of profit from their current efforts at the farm. We think that it is sufficient that petitioners had a bona fide expectation that their current work would allow them to commence profitable farming in the future, and that the uncontested facts establish that they had this expectation.

If this were a case in which wealthy taxpayers were seeking to obtain tax benefits through the creation of paper losses we would hesitate to reverse. Before us today, however, is a family of modest means attempting to prepare for a stable financial future. The amount of time and hard work invested by petitioners belies any claim that allowing these deductions would thwart Congress's primary purpose, that of excluding "hobby" losses from permissible deductions. Accordingly, we hold that the tax court's finding was clearly erroneous and

Reverse.

B. NOTES AND QUESTIONS

1) The "Primary Purpose" Test

According to *Nickerson*, whether an activity is "for profit" or "for pleasure" depends on the taxpayer's "primary purpose." This resembles the test of whether travel and entertainment expenses are deductible, as articulated in *Rudolph* and *Schulz* (Chapter 8). As in those cases, "primary purpose" is said to be a factual issue, and the trial court's finding of fact controls unless "clearly erroneous" under the Federal Rules of Civil Procedure.[1]

What specific evidence did the Tax Court rely on to justify its finding? How did Nickerson's attorney appear to have convincingly argued that the nexus between that evidence and the Tax Court's finding was either weak or illogical? Reg. § 1.183–2(b) lists nine factors that are to be considered in determining whether an activity is "for profit." Which of these factors worked in Nickerson's favor? Which worked against him? Reg. § 1.183–2(c) lists six examples illustrating the method of determining whether an activity is "for profit." Which example did Nickerson's case most closely resemble?

2) Subjective versus Objective Standards

Did the Circuit Court apply an objective or subjective standard in finding that Nickerson had a "bona fide expectation of profit"? Which standard do you think should apply? Are there more compelling reasons for using an objective standard in *Greenberg* (which involved ordinarily nondeductible educational expenses) than in *Nickerson* (where such a test might penalize innovative entrepreneurs)?

3) The Hidden Issue: Timing

Even if Nickerson's farm is "for profit," making his costs deductible at some time, why permit an immediate deduction in full? When are the expenditures expected to begin to produce income?

Reg. § 1.162–12 permits farmers to expense many items that others must treat as capital expenditures. If the regulation had not been issued, would *Nickerson* have been litigated when it was? Could the issue have been resolved at a later date with a clearer record and less need to rely on a taxpayer's arguably self-serving assertions?

Section 446(b) permits the Treasury to direct that "the computation of taxable income be made under such method as ... does clearly reflect income." See *Thor Power Tool, Inc.* (Chapter 15). Might the government have argued in *Nickerson* that expensing preproduction expenditures under Reg. § 1.162–12 does not clearly reflect income, given the ten-year preproduction period, and that Nickerson should therefore have to capitalize the expenditures or at least not take a full deduction until full-time farming activities start? What political obstacle was there to making such an argu-

---

1. See *Ferrer* (Chapter 29).

ment? Whose wrath might have been incurred? Couldn't Nickerson's case be distinguished from that of most farmers?

Section 263A, enacted in 1986, now requires farmers to treat preproduction period expenses as capital expenditures if production is not to begin for more than two years. See Section 263A(d)(1)(A). How would this new provision have affected the outcome in *Nickerson*?

4) The Conversion of Farmland to Cultivation

Nickerson leased part of the farm for $20 an acre plus the promise to convert ten untillable acres to cultivation. Ignoring the cash rent (which is nominal in amount), what is the nature of this transaction? Does it result in the receipt of rental income in kind? Is the income in kind fully offset by a current deduction? If the rent had been paid solely in cash and Nickerson had then expended the cash for cultivation conversion, how would he have been treated?

Section 182, in effect from 1963 to 1986, allowed farmers to expense the costs of "the clearing of land for the purpose of making such land suitable for use in farming." However, the amount deductible was limited to the smaller of $5,000 or 25% of the taxable income derived from farming during the year. Having failed to characterize Nickerson's farm as "for pleasure," how might the IRS have used Section 182 to limit his deductions?

5) The Presumption of Section 183(d)

Section 183(d) creates a presumption that an activity is "for profit" if it is profitable in three out of five years. For activities involving horses—that is, the breeding, training, showing, or racing of horses—the activity must be profitable in two out of seven years. Why are these activities treated more leniently than others?

6) Deductible Hobby Expenses

Suppose that you are an amateur magician and spend $500 on your hobby. If you earn $200 a year for occasional performances at birthday parties, what is the effect of Sections 183(a), (b), and (c) on your allowable deductions? Note that the deductions permitted under Section 183 are also subject to Section 67 and therefore actually are deductible only to the extent that they and other designated deductions exceed 2% of AGI. (See Chapters 4 and 6.)

Why allow any deductions at all simply because you were paid for a few performances? Wouldn't you still have spent $500 on your hobby and, therefore, derived that amount of personal satisfaction? Suppose that, with no prospect of being paid, you would have spent only $400. In principle, how much of the $500 actually spent should you be allowed to deduct? Why isn't Section 183 written to permit deduction only of the excess amount spent on a hobby over what would have been spent if no sales were anticipated? Would an excess rule resemble the early Treasury ruling, cited in *Rosenspan* (Chapter 4), that limited meal deductions while away from home on business to the excess of what was spent over what would have been spent at home?

If an excess rule would be impractical, why not attempt to allocate costs between performing for pay and performing for pleasure with a formula that reduces the allowable deduction by some fixed percentage? Would this approach be similar to the rule of Section 274(n) disallowing 20% of deductions for meal and entertainment expenditures?

Suppose that you are an amateur painter and spend $500 a year on your hobby. If you earn $200 a year from selling paintings, what are your allowable deductions under Section 183? If you paint twenty pictures but sell only two, should deductions be allocated between sold and unsold paintings so that you deduct only 10% of your total costs?

Do Sections 183(a), (b), and (c) err on the side of permitting too large a deduction in order to limit the number of disputes? If an activity never produces an annual loss (that is, if it always either breaks even or makes a profit), does it matter (except for the possible application of Section 67) whether it is categorized as "for profit" or "for pleasure"? Why is the categorization question known as the "hobby *loss*" problem?

7) Home Offices and Vacation Homes

In the special cases of home offices and vacation homes, Section 183 is superceded by Section 280A which imposes much stricter limits on deductions. The cost of a home office may not be deducted at all unless it qualifies under one of the exceptions listed in Section 280A(c): (a) used exclusively and regularly as the taxpayer's principal place of business; (b) used to meet patients, clients, or customers in the normal course of business; or (c) a separate structure, not attached to the dwelling unit.[2]

In addition, the use of the space must be for the *employer's* convenience. Taxpayers will probably find it difficult to demonstrate why the work cannot be performed at the regular place of business, except for the *employee's* convenience.

When a vacation home is rented out to others, Section 280A(e) requires the costs to be allocated between rental and nonrental uses. For example, if the residence is rented for ninety days and used for a total of 100 days, then deductions are limited to 90% of the costs. In addition, if the taxpayer uses the property for personal purposes for more than fourteen days or 10% of the days that it is rented—whichever is greater—deductions are limited to rental income. Section 280A(c)(5).

If Section 280A did not exist, how would maintaining a home office or a vacation home be treated under Section 183? If found to constitute a "for profit" activity? If found to constitute a hobby? How does Section 280A modify the usual rule under Section 183 that hobby costs are deductible to the extent of hobby income? How does this reduce the Section 183 problem of permitting too large a deduction when property held "for

---

2. Does the second exception unduly favor taxpayers whose jobs involve contact with outsiders? Does the third exception discriminate against apartment dwellers?

pleasure" also generates income? If the farm in *Nickerson* were considered a vacation home, what deductions would be allowed under Section 280A?

8) Hobby Loss Litigation and Cultural Biases

Most of the litigation over whether an activity is a hobby or "for profit" involves farming and horse racing or breeding. Professional sports teams routinely appear to be treated as "for profit," even if their owners are independently wealthy individuals and the activity has had years of losses with little prospect of future profits. How do you explain the IRS's failure to litigate such cases? What kinds of cultural biases might it reflect?

9) Gambling Losses

Section 165(d) allows losses from gambling to be deducted only to the extent of winnings from gambling. In effect, this is equivalent to an irrebuttable presumption that the activity of gambling is always "for pleasure" and never "for profit." Is such a presumption unfair to professional gamblers? Can professionals still claim to be engaged in the trade or business of gambling and thus entitled to carry losses backward or forward to other tax years under Section 172?

Can gambling logically be distinguished from investment in very risky activities, such as commodities futures? How different in result is Section 165(d) from Section 1211, which generally allows the deduction of capital losses only against capital gains? (Note that Section 1211, unlike Section 165(d), allows excess losses to be carried forward to later years.)

10) Nickerson's Farm as a Tax Shelter

A tax shelter can be defined as an activity that produces losses which are used to offset, or *shelter*, other taxable income. The taxpayer in *Nickerson* presumably used the losses from farming to offset his salary as an advertising executive. Thus, *Nickerson* might be viewed as involving a kind of tax shelter.

If the Code provided that losses from one activity could only be used to offset gains from that particular activity and not from other activities, would "hobby losses" present a problem? A provision with this kind of effect was adopted in 1986 to curb the use of tax shelters generally (see Chapter 43).

Chapter 32

THE CAPITALIZATION REQUIREMENT

A. INTRODUCTORY NOTE: WHAT THE DISPUTES ARE ABOUT

Because of the time value of money, taxpayers want to take deductions as quickly as possible. Taxpayers generally prefer to classify a given expenditure as an item to be expensed (deductible immediately in full), rather than as depreciable (deductible over a period of time), and as depreciable, rather than as nonwasting (deductible only upon sale or exchange). Conversely, the Treasury wants deductions to be deferred as long as possible. It will generally prefer to classify an expenditure as nonwasting, rather than as depreciable, and as depreciable, rather than as an item to be expensed.

All the cases in this chapter and the two chapters following involve disputes over the proper categorization of "for profit" expenditures. The taxpayer seeks to accelerate the taking of deductions; the IRS seeks a delay.

B. WELCH v. HELVERING
290 U.S. 111 (1933)

Mr. Justice Cardozo delivered the opinion of the Court.

The question to be determined is whether payments by a taxpayer, who is in business as a commission agent, are allowable deductions in the computation of his income if made to the creditors of a bankrupt corporation in an endeavor to strengthen his own standing and credit.

In 1922 petitioner was the secretary of the E. L. Welch Company, a Minnesota corporation, engaged in the grain business. The company was adjudged an involuntary bankrupt, and had a discharge from its debts. Thereafter the petitioner made a contract with the Kellogg Company to purchase grain for it on a commission. In order to reëstablish his relations with customers whom he had known when acting for the Welch Company and to solidify his credit and standing, he decided to pay the debts of the Welch business so far as he was able. In fulfilment of that resolve, he made payments of substantial amounts during five successive years.... The Commissioner ruled that these payments were not deductible from income as ordinary and necessary expenses, but were rather in the nature of capital expenditures, an outlay for the development of reputation and good will. The Board of Tax Appeals sustained the action of the Commissioner ... and the Court of Appeals for the Eighth Circuit affirmed.... The case is here on certiorari.

"In computing net income there shall be allowed as deductions ... all the ordinary and necessary expenses paid or incurred during the taxable year in carrying on any trade or business." Revenue Act of 1924....

We may assume that the payments to creditors of the Welch Company were necessary for the development of the petitioner's business, at least in the sense that they were appropriate and helpful. *McCulloch v. Maryland*.... He certainly thought they were, and we should be slow to override his judgment. But the problem is not solved when the payments are characterized as necessary. Many necessary payments are charges upon capital. There is need to determine whether they are both necessary and ordinary. Now, what is ordinary, though there must always be a strain of constancy within it, is none the less a variable affected by time and place and circumstance. Ordinary in this context does not mean that the payments must be habitual or normal in the sense that the same taxpayer will have to make them often. A lawsuit affecting the safety of a business may happen once in a lifetime. The counsel fees may be so heavy that repetition is unlikely. None the less, the expense is an ordinary one because we know from experience that payments for such a purpose, whether the amount is large or small, are the common and accepted means of defense against attack.... The situation is unique in the life of the individual affected, but not in the life of the group, the community, of which he is a part. At such times there are norms of conduct that help to stabilize our judgment, and make it certain and objective. The instance is not erratic, but is brought within a known type.

The line of demarcation is now visible between the case that is here and the one supposed for illustration. We try to classify this act as ordinary or the opposite, and the norms of conduct fail us. No longer can we have recourse to any fund of business experience, to any known business practice. Men do at times pay the debts of others without legal obligation or the lighter obligation imposed by the usages of trade or by neighborly amenities, but they do not do so ordinarily, not even though the result might be to heighten their reputation for generosity and opulence. Indeed, if language is to be read in its natural and common meaning ... we should have to say that payment in such circumstances, instead of being ordinary is in a high degree extraordinary. There is nothing ordinary in the stimulus evoking it, and none in the response. Here, indeed, as so often in other branches of the law, the decisive distinctions are those of degree and not of kind. One struggles in vain for any verbal formula that will supply a ready touchstone. The standard set up by the statute is not a rule of law; it is rather a way of life. Life in all its fullness must supply the answer to the riddle.

The Commissioner of Internal Revenue resorted to that standard in assessing the petitioner's income, and found that the payments in controversy came closer to capital outlays than to ordinary and necessary expenses in the operation of a business. His ruling has the support of a presumption of correctness, and the petitioner has the burden of proving it to be wrong.... Unless we can say from facts within our knowledge that these are ordinary and necessary expenses according to the ways of conduct and the forms of speech prevailing in the business world, the tax must be confirmed. But nothing told us by this record or within the sphere of our judicial notice permits us to give that extension to what is ordinary and necessary. Indeed, to do so would open the door to many bizarre analogies. One man has a family name that is clouded by thefts committed by an ancestor. To add to his own standing he repays the stolen money, wiping off, it may be, his income for the year. The payments figure in his tax return as ordinary expenses. Another man conceives the notion that he will be able to practice his vocation with greater ease and profit if he has an opportunity to enrich his culture. Forthwith the price of his education becomes an expense of the business, reducing the income subject to taxation. There is little difference between these expenses and those in controversy here. Reputation and learning are akin to capital assets, like the good will of an old partnership.... For many, they are the only tools with which to hew a pathway to success. The money spent in acquiring them is well and wisely spent. It is not an ordinary expense of the operation of a business....

C. NOTES AND QUESTIONS

1) Justice Cardozo's Opinion

Are Justice Cardozo's analogies valid? Should Welch's payments to creditors of the Welch Co. be compared with payments for general education or to compensate the victim of a relative's crime? Doesn't Justice Cardozo's reading of the word "ordinary" in Section 162(a) penalize businesses that pursue extraordinary or innovative methods? Has Justice Cardozo given the phrase "ordinary and necessary" in Section 162(a) too literal a meaning? Professor Griswold has written of *Welch:*

> I yield to none in my admiration of Justice Cardozo. I knew him, and I count it one of the blessings of my life. His contributions to the law and to the literature of the law are very great and in many ways unique in our century. But occasionally even the masters slip. In Welch v. Helvering ... Justice Cardozo said: "Life in all its fullness must supply the answer to the riddle." Surely, though, this must have been one of the most empty sentences that Justice Cardozo ever wrote—nice words, no doubt, but essentially meaningless.[1]

---

1. Griswold, Foreword: Of Time and Attitudes, Professor Hart and Judge Arnold, 74 Harv. L. Rev. 81, 90 (1960).

2) The Capitalization Requirement

Is there a better statutory basis for denying the deduction in *Welch* than failure to comply with the "ordinary and necessary" language of Section 162(a)? Section 263 provides that no deduction shall be allowed for "any amount paid out for new buildings or for permanent improvements or betterments made to increase the value of any property or estate." Is payment of the Welch Co. debts an expenditure for a "permanent improvement or betterment"?

Reg. § 1.446-1(a)(4)(ii) provides that "expenditures made during the year shall be properly classified between capital and expense.... [E]xpenditures ... which have a useful life extending substantially beyond the taxable year, shall be charged to capital account and not to expense account." Does the useful life of the expenditure in *Welch* extend "beyond the taxable year"?

3) The Consequences of Capitalization

What are the consequences of capitalizing the expenditure in *Welch*? Recall that all capital expenditures are classified as wasting or nonwasting assets. The cost of a wasting asset may be depreciated over the asset's useful life, but the cost of a nonwasting asset may be deducted only when the asset is sold or exchanged. Assuming that capitalization is appropriate, should the expenditure in *Welch* be classified as wasting or nonwasting? Reg. § 1.167(a)−3 states:

> If an intangible asset is known from experience or other factors to be of use in the business or in the production of income for only a limited period, the length of which can be estimated with reasonable accuracy, such an intangible asset may be the subject of a depreciation allowance. Examples are patents and copyrights. An intangible asset, the useful life of which is not limited, is not subject to the allowance for depreciation. No allowance will be permitted merely because, in the unsupported opinion of the taxpayer, the intangible asset has a limited useful life. No deduction for depreciation is allowable with respect to good will.

Under the regulation, when can an expenditure for good will be deducted? Is the amount spent by Welch to pay off bad debts of the predecessor company an expenditure for good will? Even if not, is it an expenditure for an intangible asset? Assuming that it is of use "for only a limited period," can the length of that period "be estimated with reasonable accuracy"?

4) Advertising Expenditures

The IRS has ruled that advertising costs can be expensed provided they are reasonable in amount and have a reasonable relation to the taxpayer's business. See Rev. Rul. 56–181, 1956–1 C.B. 96 (expenses incurred from demonstrating installation of windows and awnings in private homes by manufacturer as part of an advertising campaign deductible as business expenses). Isn't this ruling inconsistent with the position taken by the IRS in *Welch* and in Reg. § 1.167(a)-3? Why isn't an expenditure for advertising like any other expenditure for good will? Or is expensing justified by the ephemeral nature of most advertising?

5) Research and Development Expenditures

In principle, should the cost of research and development be expensed or capitalized? If capitalized, will Reg. § 1.167(a)-3, quoted above, permit the cost to be depreciated? Section 174(a)(1), enacted in 1954, allows taxpayers to expense research and development costs. The Senate Finance Committee explained:

> No specific treatment is authorized by present law for research and experimental expenditures. To the extent that they are ordinary and necessary they are deductible; to the extent that they are capital in nature they are to be capitalized and amortized over useful life. . . . [R]ecovery through amortization is provided where the useful life of these capital items is determinable, as in the case of a patent. However, . . . where a useful life cannot be definitely determined, taxpayers have had no means of amortizing research expenditures.
>
> To eliminate uncertainty and to encourage taxpayers to carry on research and experimentation the House and your committee's bill provide that these expenditures . . . may, at the option of the taxpayer, be treated as deductible expenses.[2]

6) Intangible Drilling Costs

There is another important exception to the capitalization requirement, for the intangible costs of drilling and developing oil, gas, and geothermal deposits. Under Section 263(c), such costs—defined to include the costs of labor and of material without a salvage value—may be expensed. This favorable treatment provides a significant incentive for oil and gas exploration.

D. MIDLAND EMPIRE PACKING CO. v. COMMISSIONER
14 T.C. 635 (1950), acq. 1950–2 C.B. 3

. . . The issue presented for decision is whether or not the sum of $4,868.81 expended by the petitioner in oilproofing the basement of its meat-packing plant during the taxable year 1943 is deductible as an ordinary and necessary business expense under section [162(a)] of the Internal Revenue Code, or, in the alternative, as a loss sustained during the year and not compensated for by insurance or otherwise under section [165(c)] of the Internal Revenue Code. . . .

FINDINGS OF FACT

The petitioner, herein sometimes referred to as Midland, is . . . the owner of a meat-packing plant. . . .

---

2. S. Rep. No. 1622, 83d Cong., 2d Sess. 33 (1954).

The basement rooms of petitioner's plant were used by it in its business for the curing of hams and bacon and for the storage of meat and hides. These rooms have been used for such purposes since the plant was constructed in about 1917. The original walls and floors, which were of concrete, were not sealed against water. There had been seepage for many years and this condition became worse around 1943. At certain seasons of the year, when the water in the Yellowstone River was high, the underground water caused increased seepage in the plant. Such water did not interfere with petitioner's use of the basement rooms. They were satisfactory for their purpose until 1943.

The Yale Oil Corporation, sometimes referred to herein as Yale, was the owner of an oil-refining plant and storage area located some 300 yards upgrade from petitioner's meat-packing plant. The oil plant was constructed some years after petitioner had been in business in its present location. Yale expanded its plant and storage from year to year and oil escaping from the plant and storage facilities was carried to the ground surrounding the plant of petitioner. In 1943 petitioner found that oil was seeping into its water wells and into water which came through the concrete walls of the basement of its packing plant. The water would soon drain out through the sump, leaving a thick scum of oil on the basement floor. Such oil gave off a strong odor, which permeated the air of the entire plant. The oil in the basement and fumes therefrom created a fire hazard. The Federal meat inspectors advised petitioner to oilproof the basement and discontinue the use of the water wells or shut down the plant. . . .

The original walls and floor of petitioner's plant were of concrete construction. For the purpose of preventing oil from entering its basement, petitioner added concrete lining to the walls from the floor to a height of about four feet, and also added concrete to the floor of the basement. Since the walls and floor had been thickened, petitioner now had less space in which to operate. . . .

The oilproofing work was effective in sealing out the oil. While it has served the purposes for which it was intended down to the present time, it did not increase the useful life of the building or make the building more valuable for any purpose than it had been before the oil had come into the basement. The primary object of the oilproofing operation was to prevent the seepage of oil into the basement so that the petitioner could use the basement as before in preparing and packing meat for commercial consumption. . . .

OPINION

ARUNDELL, JUDGE: The issue in this case is whether an expenditure for a concrete lining in petitioner's basement to oilproof it against an oil nuisance created by a neighboring refinery is deductible as an ordinary and necessary expense under section [162(a)] of the Internal Revenue Code, on the theory it was an expenditure for a repair, or, in the alternative, whether the expenditure may be treated as the measure of the loss sustained during the taxable year and not compensated for by insurance or otherwise within the meaning of section [165(c)] of the Internal Revenue Code.

Ch. 32 The Capitalization Requirement 477

The respondent has contended, in part, that the expenditure is for a capital improvement and should be recovered through depreciation charges and is, therefore, not deductible as an ordinary and necessary business expense or as a loss.

...In *Illinois Merchants Trust Co., Executor* ... we discussed this subject in some detail and in our opinion said:

> ... In determining whether an expenditure is a capital one or is chargeable against operating income, it is necessary to bear in mind the purpose for which the expenditure was made. To repair is to restore to a sound state or to mend, while a replacement connotes a substitution. A repair is an expenditure for the purpose of keeping the property in an ordinarily efficient operating condition. It does not add to the value of the property, nor does it appreciably prolong its life. It merely keeps the property in an operating condition over its probable useful life for the uses for which it was acquired. Expenditures for that purpose are distinguishable from those for replacements, alterations, improvements, or additions which prolong the life of the property, increase its value, or make it adaptable to a different use. The one is a maintenance charge, while the others are additions to capital investment which should not be applied against current earnings.

It will be seen from our findings of fact that for some 25 years prior to the taxable year petitioner had used the basement rooms of its plant as a place for the curing of hams and bacon and for the storage of meat and hides. The basement had been entirely satisfactory for this purpose over the entire period in spite of the fact that there was some seepage of water into the rooms from time to time. In the taxable year it was found that not only water, but oil, was seeping through the concrete walls of the basement of the packing plant and, while the water would soon drain out, the oil would not, and there was left on the basement floor a thick scum of oil which gave off a strong odor that permeated the air of the entire plant, and the fumes from the oil created a fire hazard. It appears that the oil which came from a nearby refinery had also gotten into the water wells which served to furnish water for petitioner's plant, and as a result of this whole condition the Federal meat inspectors advised petitioner that it must discontinue the use of the water from the wells and oilproof the basement, or else shut down its plant.

To meet this situation, petitioner during the taxable year undertook steps to oilproof the basement by adding a concrete lining to the walls from the floor to a height of about four feet and also added concrete to the floor of the basement. It is the cost of this work which it seeks to deduct as a repair. The basement was not enlarged by this work, nor did the oilproofing serve to make it more desirable for the purpose for which it had been used through the years prior to the time that the oil nuisance had occurred. The evidence is that the expenditure did not add to the value or prolong the expected life of the property over what they were before the event occurred which made the repairs necessary. It is true that after the work was done the seepage of water, as well as oil, was stopped, but, as already stated, the presence of the water had never been found objectionable. The repairs merely served to keep the property in an operating condition over its probable useful life for the purpose for which it was used.

While it is conceded on brief that the expenditure was "necessary," respondent contends that the encroachment of the oil nuisance on petitioner's property was not an "ordinary" expense in petitioner's particular business. But the fact that petitioner had not theretofore been called upon to make a similar expenditure to prevent damage and disaster to its property does not remove that expense from the classification of "ordinary" for, as stated in *Welch v. Helvering* . . . "ordinary in this context does not mean that the payments must be habitual or normal in the sense that the same taxpayer will have to make them often. . . . the expense is an ordinary one because we know from experience that payments for such a purpose, whether the amount is large or small, are the common and accepted means of defense against attack. . . . The situation is unique in the life of the individual affected, but not in the life of the group, the community, of which he is a part." Steps to protect a business building from the seepage of oil from a nearby refinery, which had been erected long subsequent to the time petitioner started to operate its plant, would seem to us to be a normal thing to do, and in certain sections of the country it must be a common experience to protect one's property from the seepage of oil. Expenditures to accomplish this result are likewise normal.

In *American Bemberg Corporation* . . . we allowed as deductions, on the ground that they were ordinary and necessary expenses, extensive expenditures made to prevent disaster, although the repairs were of a type which had never been needed before and were unlikely to recur. In that case the taxpayer, to stop cave-ins of soil which were threatening destruction of its manufacturing plant, hired an engineering firm which drilled to the bedrock and injected grout to fill the cavities where practicable, and made incidental replacements and repairs, including tightening of the fluid carriers. In two successive years the taxpayer expended $734,316.76 and $199,154.33, respectively, for such drilling and grouting and $153,474.20 and $79,687.29, respectively, for capital replacements. We found that the cost (other than replacement) of this program did not make good the depreciation previously allowed, and stated in our opinion:

> In connection with the purpose of the work, the Proctor program was intended to avert a plant-wide disaster and avoid forced abandonment of the plant. The purpose was not to improve, better, extend, or increase the original plant, nor to prolong its original useful life. Its continued operation was endangered; the purpose of the expenditures was to enable petitioner to continue the plant in operation not on any new or better scale, but on the same scale and, so far as possible, as efficiently as it had operated before. The purpose was not to rebuild or replace the plant in whole or in part, but to keep the same plant as it was and where it was.

The petitioner here made the repairs in question in order that it might continue to operate its plant. Not only was there danger of fire from the oil and fumes, but the presence of the oil led the Federal meat inspectors to declare the basement an unsuitable place for the purpose for which it had been used for a quarter of a century. After the expenditures were made, the plant did not operate on a changed or larger scale, nor was it thereafter suitable for new or additional uses. The expenditure served only to permit petitioner to continue the use of the plant, and particularly the basement for its normal operations.

In our opinion, the expenditure of $4,868.81 for lining the basement walls and floor was essentially a repair and, as such, it is deductible as an ordinary and necessary business expense. . . .

E. NOTES AND QUESTIONS

1) *Midland Empire* versus *Welch*

If the cost of oilproofing in *Midland Empire* must be capitalized, when will it be deductible? Why is it much easier to demonstrate a limited life for the oilproofing in *Midland Empire* than for the good will in *Welch*? Why are the consequences of losing more severe for the taxpayer in *Welch* than in *Midland Empire*?

2) The Repair Exception to the Capitalization Requirement

What is the scope of the repair exception? If the storage facility were built near an existing refinery known to leak oil, could the expenditure for concrete lining be expensed? Or would it have to be capitalized? What is the distinction between an expenditure for oilproofing in this example and in *Midland Empire* where the storage facility existed for many years before the oil refinery was constructed? Do you find the distinction between foreseeable and unforeseeable repairs persuasive?

Suppose that General Motors opens a new plant to produce pickup trucks. Two years after the plant opens, GM discovers that it has installed an insufficient number of welding machines. Is GM permitted to expense the cost of additional machines simply because the need was unexpected?

3) Comparing the Repair Exception to the Casualty Loss Deduction

Suppose that you are an amateur hot dog maker and construct a small building in your backyard in which to conduct your hobby. Several years later, you spend $1,000 on oilproofing the building to protect your homemade hot dogs from oil leaking on a nearby property. Is the cost of oilproofing deductible? Does it depend on whether the oil leak was foreseeable or an unexpected and sudden occurrence? How do the contours of the repair exception resemble the contours of the casualty loss deduction of Section 165(c)(3)?

4) Rationalizing the Repair Exception

How can one rationalize the repair exception to the capitalization requirement? Why should there be immediate deduction in full for an expenditure that constitutes a "permanent improvement or betterment" under Section 263(a)(1), simply because it is a repair?

Assume that in *Midland Empire,* the storage facility originally cost $10,000 to construct; that the adjusted basis was $8,000 when the oil leak started; that the leak caused the facility to fall in value by $5,000; and that the taxpayer spent $5,000 to repair the damage. If property held "for profit" is damaged by a Section 165(c)(3) casualty, the amount of the loss may be deducted. See Reg. § 1.165–7(b)(1), discussed in Chapter 30. After deducting the loss, the basis of the property must be adjusted downwards to $3,000. Why? See Section 1016(a)(2)(A). If the taxpayer claims a casualty loss deduction, the repair may not also be expensed. See Reg. § 1.161–1. In that event, the $5,000 repair must be capitalized so that the basis is adjusted upwards to $8,000. Why is the taxpayer who deducts such a casualty loss not allowed, in addition, to expense the repair?

Why is (a) allowing an immediate deduction for the damage *and,* in that event, requiring capitalization of the repair equivalent to (b) simply permitting the repair to be expensed? Can the repair exception be justified by the equivalence? But if damage caused by a casualty to property held "for profit" is immediately deductible, why is the repair exception needed?

Suppose that the repair costs more than the fall in value caused by the damage. Suppose that, in the example above, $6,000 is spent on repairing $5,000 worth of damage. Should the entire $6,000 be deductible? A taxpayer is likely to spend more on the repair than the fall in value only if the repair increases the value of the property above its predamage level. Assume that the increase in value is $2,000. In that event, should the repair deduction be limited to $5,000 and should the excess be capitalized? Isn't that the equivalent of allowing an immediate deduction for the damage but requiring capitalization of the entire repair expenditure? Does *Midland Empire* recognize this possibility by noting that, after the repair, the storage facility did not increase in value?

Alternatively, suppose that, in the example above, the adjusted basis of the property before the damage is only $3,000. What is the maximum allowable deduction for damage caused by a casualty, even though the property has fallen in value by $5,000? See Reg. § 1.165–7(b)(1)(ii). Does your answer suggest that the repair deduction should be limited to the adjusted basis of the property, with capitalization required of any excess of the repair's cost over the adjusted basis?

F. COMMISSIONER v. IDAHO POWER CO.
418 U.S. 1 (1974)

MR. JUSTICE BLACKMUN delivered the opinion of the Court.

This case presents the sole issue whether, for federal income tax purposes, a taxpayer is entitled to a deduction from gross income, under § 167(a) of the Internal Revenue Code of 1954, 26 U.S.C. § 167(a), for depreciation on equipment the taxpayer owns and uses in the construction of its own capital facilities, or whether the capitalization provision of § 263(a)(1) of the Code, 26 U.S.C. § 263(a)(1), bars the deduction. . . .

I

Nearly all the relevant facts are stipulated. The taxpayer-respondent, Idaho Power Company, is a Maine corporation organized in 1915, with its principal place of business at Boise, Idaho. It is a public utility engaged in the production, transmission, distribution, and sale of electric energy. . . .

For many years, the taxpayer has used its own equipment and employees in the construction of improvements and additions to its capital facilities. The major work has consisted of transmission lines, transmission switching stations, distribution lines, distribution stations, and connecting facilities. . . .

During 1962 and 1963, the tax years in question, taxpayer owned and used in its business a wide variety of automotive transportation equipment, including passenger cars, trucks of all descriptions, power-operated equipment, and trailers. Radio communication devices were affixed to the equipment and were used in its daily operations. The transportation equipment was used in part for operation and maintenance and in part for the construction of capital facilities having a useful life of more than one year.

On its books, the taxpayer used various methods of charging costs incurred in connection with its transportation equipment either to current expense or to capital accounts. To the extent the equipment was used in construction, the taxpayer charged depreciation of the equipment, as well as all operating and maintenance costs (other than pension contributions and social security and motor vehicle taxes) to the capital assets so constructed. This was done . . . in accordance with procedures prescribed by the Federal Power Commission and adopted by the Idaho Public Utilities Commission.

For federal income tax purposes, however, the taxpayer treated the depreciation on transportation equipment differently. It claimed as a deduction from gross income *all* the year's depreciation on such equipment, including that portion attributable to its use in constructing capital facilities. The depreciation was computed on a composite life of 10 years and under straight-line and declining-balance methods. The other operating and maintenance costs the taxpayer had charged on its books to capital were not claimed as current expenses and were not deducted.

To summarize: On its books, in accordance with Federal Power Commission-Idaho Public Utilities Commission prescribed methods, the taxpayer capitalized the construction-related depreciation, but for income tax purposes that depreciation increment was claimed as a deduction under § 167(a).

Upon audit, the Commissioner of Internal Revenue disallowed the deduction for the construction-related depreciation. He ruled that that depreciation was a nondeductible capital expenditure to which § 263(a)(1) had application. He added the amount of the depreciation so disallowed to the taxpayer's adjusted basis in its capital facilities, and then allowed a deduction for an appropriate amount of depreciation on the addition, computed over the useful life (30 years or more) of the property constructed. A deduction for depreciation of the transportation equipment to the extent of its use in day-to-day operation and maintenance was also allowed. . . .

The taxpayer asserts that its transportation equipment is used in its "trade or business" and that depreciation thereon is therefore deductible under § 167(a)(1) of the Code. The Commissioner concedes that § 167 may be said to have a literal application to depreciation on equipment used in capital construction, . . . but contends that the provision must be read in light of § 263(a)(1) which specifically disallows any deduction for an amount "paid out for new buildings or for permanent improvements or betterments." He argues that § 263 takes precedence over § 167 by virtue of what he calls the "priority-ordering" terms (and what the taxpayer describes as "housekeeping" provisions) of § 161 of the Code, 26 U.S.C. § 161, and that sound principles of accounting and taxation mandate the capitalization of this depreciation.

It is worth noting the various items that are not at issue here. The mathematics, as such, is not in dispute. The taxpayer has capitalized, as part of its cost of acquisition of capital assets, the operating and maintenance costs (other than depreciation, pension contributions, and social security and motor vehicle taxes) of the transportation equipment attributable to construction. This is not contested. The Commissioner does not dispute that the portion of the transportation equipment's depreciation allocable to operation and maintenance of facilities, in contrast with construction thereof, qualifies as a deduction from gross income. There is no disagreement as to the allocation of depreciation between construction and maintenance. The issue, thus comes down primarily to a question of timing . . . that is, whether the construction-related depreciation is to be amortized and deducted over the *shorter* life of the equipment or, instead, is to be amortized and deducted over the *longer* life of the capital facilities constructed.

II

Our primary concern is with the necessity to treat construction-related depreciation in a manner that comports with accounting and taxation realities. Over a period of time a capital asset is consumed and, correspondingly over that period, its theoretical value and utility are thereby reduced. Depreciation is an accounting device which recognizes that the physical consumption of a capital asset is a true cost, since the asset is being depleted. As the process of consumption continues, and depreciation is claimed and allowed, the asset's adjusted income tax basis is reduced to reflect the distribution of its cost over the accounting periods affected. The Court stated in *Hertz Corp. v. United States* . . . : "[T]he purpose of depreciation accounting is to allocate the expense of using an asset to the various periods which are benefited by that asset." . . . When the asset is used to further the taxpayer's day-to-day business operations, the periods of benefit usually correlate with the production of income. Thus, to the extent that equipment is used in such operations, a current depreciation deduction is an appropriate offset to gross income currently produced. It is clear, however, that different principles are implicated when the consumption of the asset takes place in the construction of other assets that, in the future, will produce income themselves. In this latter situation, the cost represented by depreciation does not correlate with production of current income. Rather, the cost, although certainly presently incurred, is related to the future and is appropriately allocated as part of the cost of acquiring an income-producing capital asset. . . .

There can be little question that other construction-related expense items, such as tools, materials, and wages paid construction workers, are to be treated as part of the cost of acquisition of a capital asset. The taxpayer does not dispute this. Of course, reasonable wages paid in the carrying on of a trade or business qualify as a deduction from gross income. § 162(a)(1) of the 1954 Code, 26 U.S.C. § 162(a)(1). But when wages are paid in connection with the construction or acquisition of a capital asset, they must be capitalized and are then entitled to be amortized over the life of the capital asset so acquired. . . . See Treas. Reg. § 1.266–1(e).

Construction-related depreciation is not unlike expenditures for wages for construction workers. The significant fact is that the exhaustion of construction equipment does not represent the final disposition of the taxpayer's investment in that equipment; rather, the investment in the equipment is assimilated into the cost of the capital asset constructed. Construction-related depreciation on the equipment is not an expense to the taxpayer of its day-to-day business. It is, however, appropriately recognized as a part of the taxpayer's cost or investment in the capital asset. The taxpayer's own accounting procedure reflects this treatment, for on its books the construction-related depreciation was capitalized by a credit to the equipment account and a debit to the capital facility account. By the same token, this capitalization prevents the distortion of income that would otherwise occur if depreciation properly allocable to asset acquisition were deducted from gross income currently realized. . . .

An additional pertinent factor is that capitalization of construction-related depreciation by the taxpayer who does its own construction work maintains tax parity with the taxpayer who has its construction work done by an independent contractor. The depreciation on the contractor's equipment incurred during the performance of the job will be an element of cost charged by the contractor for his construction services, and the entire cost, of course, must be capitalized by the taxpayer having the construction work performed. The Court of Appeals' holding would lead to disparate treatment among taxpayers because it would allow the firm with sufficient resources to construct its own facilities and to obtain a current deduction, whereas another firm without such resources would be required to capitalize its entire cost including depreciation charged to it by the contractor.

Some, although not controlling, weight must be given to the fact that the Federal Power Commission and the Idaho Public Utilities Commission required the taxpayer to use accounting procedures that capitalized construction-related depreciation. Although agency-imposed compulsory accounting practices do not necessarily dictate tax consequences . . . they are not irrelevant and may be accorded some significance. . . . [Where] a taxpayer's generally accepted method of accounting is made compulsory by the regulatory agency *and* that method clearly reflects income, it is almost presumptively controlling of federal income tax consequences.

The presence of § 263(a)(1) in the Code is of significance. Its literal language denies a deduction for "[a]ny amount paid out" for construction or permanent improvement of facilities. The taxpayer contends, and the Court of Appeals held, that depreciation of construction equipment represents merely a decrease in value and is not an amount "paid out," within the meaning of § 263(a)(1). We disagree.

The purpose of § 263 is to reflect the basic principle that a capital expenditure may not be deducted from current income. It serves to prevent a taxpayer from utilizing currently a deduction properly attributable, through amortization, to later tax years when the capital asset becomes income producing. The regulations state that the capital expenditures to which § 263(a) extends include the "cost of acquisition, construction, or erection of buildings." Treas. Reg. § 1.263(a)–2(a). This manifests an administrative understanding that for purposes of § 263(a)(1), "amount paid out" equates with "cost incurred." The Internal Revenue Service for some time has taken the position that construction-related depreciation is to be capitalized. . . .

There is no question that the cost of the transportation equipment was "paid out" in the same manner as the cost of supplies, materials, and other equipment, and the wages of construction workers. The taxpayer does not question the capitalization of these other items as elements of the cost of acquiring a capital asset. We see no reason to treat construction-related depreciation differently. In acquiring the transportation equipment, taxpayer "paid out" the equipment's purchase price; depreciation is simply the means of allocating the payment over the various accounting periods affected. As the Tax Court stated in *Brooks v. Commissioner* . . . "depreciation—inasmuch as it represents a using up of capital—is as much an 'expenditure' as the using up of labor or other items of direct cost."

Finally, the priority-ordering directive of § 161—or, for that matter, § 261 of the Code, 26 U.S.C. § 261—requires that the capitalization provision of § 263 (a) take precedence, on the facts here, over § 167(a). Section 161 provides that deductions specified in Part VI of Subchapter B of the Income Tax Subtitle of the Code are "subject to the exceptions provided in Part IX." Part VI includes § 167 and Part IX includes § 263. The clear import of § 161 is that. . . an expenditure incurred in acquiring capital assets must be capitalized even when the expenditure otherwise might be deemed deductible under Part VI.

The Court of Appeals concluded, without reference to § 161, that § 263 did not apply to a deduction, such as that for depreciation of property used in a trade or business, allowed by the Code even though incurred in the construction of capital assets. We think that the court erred in espousing so absolute a rule, and it obviously overlooked the contrary direction of § 161. To the extent that reliance was placed on the congressional intent, in the evolvement of the 1954 Code, to provide for "liberalization of depreciation," . . . that reliance is misplaced. The House Report also states that the depreciation provisions would "give the economy added stimulus and resilience without departing from realistic standards of depreciation accounting." . . . To be sure, the 1954 Code provided for new and accelerated methods for depreciation, resulting in the greater depreciation deductions currently available. These changes, however, relate primarily to computation of depreciation. Congress certainly did not intend that provisions for accelerated depreciation should be construed as enlarging the class of depreciable assets to which § 167(a) has application or as lessening the reach of § 263(a)....

We hold that the equipment depreciation allocable to taxpayer's construction of capital facilities is to be capitalized.

The judgment of the Court of Appeals is reversed....

Mr. Justice Douglas, dissenting.

This Court has, to many, seemed particularly ill-equipped to resolve income tax disputes between the Commissioner and the taxpayers. The reasons are (1) that the field has become increasingly technical and complicated due to the expansions of the Code and the proliferation of decisions, and (2) that we seldom see enough of them to develop any expertise in the area. Indeed, we are called upon mostly to resolve conflicts between the circuits which more providently should go to the standing committee of the Congress for resolution.

That was the sentiment behind *Dobson v. Commissioner* ... written by Mr. Justice Jackson and enthusiastically promoted by Mr. Justice Black, Mr. Justice Frankfurter, and myself. *Dobson*, save for egregious error and constitutional questions, would have left picayune cases such as the present one largely to the Tax Court, whose expertise is well recognized. But *Dobson* was short-lived, as Congress made clear its purpose that we were to continue on our leaden-footed pursuit of law and justice in this field....

Now that we are on our own I disagree with the Court in disallowing the present claim for depreciation. A company truck has, let us say, a life of 10 years. If it cost $10,000, one would expect that "a reasonable allowance for the exhaustion, wear and tear" of the truck would be $1,000 a year within the meaning of 26 U.S.C. § 167(a). That was the provision in the House Report of the 1954 Code when it said that it provided for "a liberalization of depreciation with respect to both the estimate of useful life of property and the method of allocating the depreciable cost over the years of service...."

Not so, says the Government. Since the truck was used to build a plant for the taxpayer and the plant has a useful life of 40 years, a lower rate of depreciation must be used—a rate that would spread out the life of the truck for 40 years even though it would not last more than 10....

I suspect that if the life of the vehicle were 40 years and the life of the building were 10 years the Internal Revenue Service would be here arguing persuasively that depreciation of the vehicle should be taken over a 40-year period....

G. NOTES AND QUESTIONS

1) Applying the Capitalization Requirement to the Allowance for Depreciation

Section 167(a) allows "as a depreciation deduction a reasonable allowance for exhaustion, wear and tear...." The vehicles in *Idaho Power* were treated as having a ten-year useful life, with depreciation deductible in even amounts over the ten-year period. Assuming that the cost of a vehicle was $8,000 and that the salvage value at the end of its useful life was zero, deductions for depreciation would ordinarily have been allowed at the rate of $800 per year for ten years.

In *Idaho Power*, however, the IRS argued that: (a) the ordinary depreciation allowance had to be allocated between the vehicles' use in current operations and in power plant construction and (b) the depreciation allocated to construction had to be capitalized and deducted over the power plant's service life rather than currently. Assume that, during the year in question, the vehicle was used half of the time for regular operations and half of the time for power plant construction. Then, according to the IRS, only one-half of the $800 depreciation allowance for the year, or $400, could be deducted currently. The other half would be added to the plant's basis and deducted over the plant's service life. At the time of *Idaho Power*, power plants were treated as having a forty-year life and depreciation deductions were allowed in even amounts over that period. Thus, the taxpayer would get to deduct the capitalized depreciation allowance of $400 at the rate of $10 a year for forty years.

2) The Stakes in *Idaho Power*

Suppose that the company's tax bracket is 50%. How much does it save in taxes if it can deduct $400 at once? How much if it must capitalize the construction-related depreciation? Hint: The present value of $10 a year for forty years, assuming a discount rate of 8% is about $120. How much money is at stake if the vehicles cost, not $8,000, but $8 million?

3) Does Section 263(a)(1) Apply to Depreciation Allowances?

Idaho Power voluntarily capitalized the salaries paid to employees working on construction of the power plant. Instead of expensing them, Idaho Power added these salary expenditures to the facility's basis and, in effect, assigned them a forty-year life. The Circuit Court of Appeals agreed that such salary expenses had to be capitalized but balked at treating vehicle depreciation in the same fashion. How did the court justify applying Section 263(a)(1) to salaries but not to depreciation allowances?

In principle, which is the more accurate allowance for recovering the vehicle's cost when it is used to construct a power plant? Why does this use call for departure from the ordinary depreciation practices that apply when the vehicle is used to supply electricity currently (no pun intended) being generated for Idaho Power's customers?

4) The Relevance of Nontax Accounting

Justice Blackmun wrote the majority opinions in both *Thor Power Tool* (Chapter 15) and *Idaho Power*. In *Thor*, he held that the nontax method of accounting was not controlling and that a different method would apply for taxes. But, in *Idaho Power*, he described the nontax method of accounting as "almost presumptively controlling" and refused to allow a different method for taxes. Did Justice Blackmun take inconsistent positions? Or can the facts of the cases be distinguished and the apparent conflict reconciled?

What is the significance of the fact that in *Idaho Power* it was federal and state regulatory authorities who required capitalization of construction-related depreciation? Even if significant, does this fact adequately distinguish *Idaho Power*? Note that, in *Thor Power Tool,* the company's nontax accounting methods were subject to Securities and Exchange Commission regulations prohibiting deception in the financial statements of publicly traded corporations.

5) Does the Regulatory Agency's Method Clearly Reflect Income?

In upholding the IRS in *Idaho Power,* the Supreme Court stressed the fact that there was no difficulty in determining how much depreciation to allocate to construction, since the federal regulatory authorities already required Idaho Power to capitalize construction-related depreciation, and this method clearly reflected income. Why did the Court assume that the allocation imposed by regulatory authorities clearly reflected Idaho Power's income? Should the Court have considered the possibility that the allocation was not accurate? In this regard, consider the following questions about the impact of the allocation on the rates that Idaho Power was permitted to charge for electricity and about the role played by regulatory authorities in setting those rates.

The Federal Power Commission regulated the rates which Idaho Power charged for electricity transmitted across state lines. The Idaho Public Utilities Commission regulated the rates charged for electricity transmitted intrastate. The level of rates was supposed to be high enough to allow the company to earn a "fair return," but no higher. In order to set rates at a level that was fair to both the company and to consumers, the regulatory agency would presumably try to use the most accurate method for calculating Idaho Power's income. How is the company's income affected by capitalization of construction-related depreciation? How does this, in turn, affect the amount that the company is permitted to charge consumers for electricity? In rate-making proceedings, why might the company have an incentive to understate the extent to which vehicles were used in construction? Why might consumer groups have an incentive to overstate the extent to which vehicles were used in construction? Suppose that, in Idaho, public utilities have considerably more political influence than do consumer groups (or vice versa). In that event, might the regulatory agency's allocation of depreciation to construction reflect political pressures for higher (or lower) rates, rather than income?

6) *Duberstein* and Section 274(b) Revisited

Ordinarily, there is little or no incentive for disguising taxable compensation as a nontaxable gift, because the loss of an employer deduction under Section 274(b) offsets the advantage of nontaxation to the employee (Chapter 10). But if construction-related salary expense must be capitalized, is there a renewed incentive to disguise the salary payment as a gift? In these circumstances, does the loss of the employer's deduction offset the advantage of nontaxation to the employee?

H. NEW INVENTORY EXPENSE RULES INCREASE COSTS AT MANY FIRMS
The Wall Street Journal (June 29, 1987)

[Editor's Note: Section 263A, enacted in 1986, requires capitalization of many costs that were previously expensed. The following news article discusses business reaction to the new provision.]

Maintaining a hefty inventory is a matter of pride at Shamrock Chemicals Corp. It's also good business sense. The Newark, N.J., maker of wax compounds used in printing inks has sales of more than $15 million a year because it can ship any compound the same day a customer orders it.

But the Tax Reform Act of 1986 is undermining Shamrock's inventory strategy. The new law requires companies with sales of more than $10 million to record inventory-related expenses—such as purchasing, handling and warehousing—and add them to the cost of inventory. These capitalized expenses can't be deducted until the inventory is sold. And the less a company has in deductions, of course, the more it pays in taxes.

The new inventory rules create a dilemma for Shamrock. "We can't be lean and mean in our inventory policy because we can't afford to not have the stuff to ship," says William B. Neuberg, president and owner. And Shamrock can't pass on the added tax cost to customers because it has a number of overseas competitors, which aren't affected by the new rules. So, the inventory requirement, he says, "is a straight-up penalty for us."

Businesses throughout the country have been dismayed and confused by the new inventory rules. Bigger tax bills are only half of the problem. The other half is the complexity of the record-keeping the new rules require and the cost of installing an accounting system to keep track of the capitalized costs. . . .

The rules have come as a particularly rude surprise to companies that have owners or highly paid employees who spend a lot of time on purchasing, handling or warehousing inventory. In the past, the salary, travel and other expenses related to these functions were entirely deductible.

But now, the expenses associated with inventory-related activities must be segregated in the company's books and added to year-end inventory. If the owner, say, is paid $500,000 a year and spends half of his time buying merchandise, half of that compensation must be capitalized as an inventory cost and deducted as the inventory is sold. A portion of general and administrative costs also must be allocated to inventory.

One complication is that compliance will result in capitalizing costs for tax purposes that aren't capitalized for financial accounting purposes, such as warehousing finished goods. Owners say they will have to rely more heavily on outside accountants to reconcile the two, and that will mean greater expense. . . .

In many small businesses, of course, one employee may do several jobs, only some of which are related to inventory. The IRS has issued guidelines on how to allocate such an employee's time to inventory. But many small businesses operate informally, giving the owner plenty of discretion in deciding how to allocate an employee's time to inventory. That raises the question of how conscientious owners will be in complying with the new rules.

"I talked with one of our clients, who said, 'We're going to make a reasonable effort to estimate the amount of time our employees spend on inventory-related activities,'" says David A. Rooney of Newport, R.I., accountants Rooney, Plotkin & Willey. "But we're not going to do time-and-motion studies of how our drivers divide their time between the warehouse and our retail operation."

Barry Tovig, a tax manager in the Washington office of accountants Laventhol & Horwath, advises clients to estimate the time employees spend on inventory-related activities and document how they reached those estimates.

"Quite frankly," Mr. Tovig says, "it's going to be difficult for the IRS to rebut an employer's studies. They certainly don't have the resources to let an agent sit in your business for six weeks to see how your business works."

Despite the outcry from business owners, there is little prospect Congress will alter the measure. The new inventory rules will reap the Treasury $32.24 billion over the next five years, making it one of the richest provisions of the 1986 tax act. . . .

Chapter 33

WHEN SHOULD SALARIES BE CAPITALIZED?

A. INTRODUCTORY NOTE

Most employees contribute to both current *and* future revenues of a business. For example, a salesperson is engaged not only in making immediate sales of a company's product but also in building customer good will that will generate sales in the future. An assembly-line worker not only helps produce a company's current output but also acquires valuable experience which will make the worker more productive in the future. An executive not only manages this year's activities but may also engage in long-range planning. Although *Idaho Power* may imply that *all* salaries should be allocated between current and future production and that the portion allocable to the future should be capitalized, the salaries of all three employees ordinarily would be allocated entirely to current production.[1]

Two factors may explain why allocation of salaries between current and future production has generally not been required. First, in most instances, any allocation would depend on highly fallible subjective estimates. Recall that in *Idaho Power*, this difficulty was avoided. Only the salaries of employees working full time on power plant construction (where no allocation was necessary) appear to have been capitalized as a cost of the power plant.

Second, when salary is treated as a cost of future production, it is often difficult to demonstrate a limited life for the expenditure. When no such demonstration is possible—and it is the taxpayer who carries the burden of proof on this issue—the expenditure is treated as a nonwasting asset.[2] If treated as nonwasting, the expenditure is deductible only at some future date when the business is finally sold. Given the harsh consequences, courts

---

1. In the case of the salesperson and the executive, this means that the entire salary would be expensed, that is, deductible in full at once. In the case of the assembly-line worker, this means that the entire salary would be allocated to the current production of inventory. Section 263A(a)(1)(A) and (a)(2)(A).
2. In the case of good will, the taxpayer is not even permitted to try to prove a limited life; good will is conclusively presumed to be a nonwasting asset. Reg. § 1.167(a)–3 (Chapter 32).

have been sometimes reluctant to require taxpayers to allocate salary to future production.

As you read the cases in this chapter, ask yourself to what extent these two factors may have influenced the outcomes.

B. ENCYCLOPAEDIA BRITANNICA, INC. v. COMMISSIONER
685 F.2d 212 (7th Cir. 1982)

POSNER, CIRCUIT JUDGE.

Section 162(a) of the Internal Revenue Code of 1954, 26 U.S.C. § 162(a), allows the deduction of "all the ordinary and necessary expenses paid or incurred during the taxable year in carrying on any trade or business . . .," but this is qualified (see 26 U.S.C. § 161) by section 263(a) of the Code, which forbids the immediate deduction of "capital expenditures" even if they are ordinary and necessary business expenses. We must decide in this case whether certain expenditures made by Encyclopaedia Britannica, Inc. to acquire a manuscript were capital expenditures.

Encyclopaedia Britannica decided to publish a book to be called *The Dictionary of Natural Sciences*. Ordinarily it would have prepared the book in-house, but being temporarily short-handed it hired David-Stewart Publishing Company "to do all necessary research work and to prepare, edit and arrange the manuscript and all illustrative and other material for" the book. Under the contract David-Stewart agreed "to work closely with" Encyclopaedia Britannica's editorial board "so that the content and arrangement of the Work (and any revisions thereof) will conform to the idea and desires of [Encyclopaedia Britannica] and be acceptable to it"; but it was contemplated that David-Stewart would turn over a complete manuscript that Encyclopaedia Britannica would copyright, publish, and sell, and in exchange would receive advances against the royalties that Encyclopaedia Britannica expected to earn from the book.

Encyclopaedia Britannica treated these advances as ordinary and necessary business expenses deductible in the years when they were paid, though it had not yet obtained any royalties. The Internal Revenue Service disallowed the deductions and assessed deficiencies. Encyclopaedia Britannica petitioned the Tax Court for a redetermination of its tax liability, and prevailed. The Tax Court held that the expenditures were for "services" rather than for the acquisition of an asset and concluded that therefore they were deductible immediately rather than being, as the Service had ruled, capital expenditures. "The agreement provided for substantial editorial supervision by [Encyclopaedia Britannica]. Indeed, David-Stewart's work product was to be the embodiment of [Encyclopaedia Britannica's] ideas and desires. David-Stewart was just the vehicle selected by [Encyclopaedia Britannica] to assist . . . with the editorial phase of the Work." Encyclopaedia Britannica was "the owner of the Work at all stages of completion" and "the dominating force associated with the Work." . . .

As an original matter we would have no doubt that the payments to David-Stewart were capital expenditures regardless of who was the "dominating force" in the creation of *The Dictionary of Natural Sciences.* The work was intended to yield Encyclopaedia Britannica income over a period of years. The object of sections 162 and 263 of the Code, read together, is to match up expenditures with the income they generate. Where the income is generated over a period of years the expenditures should be classified as capital, contrary to what the Tax Court did here. From the publisher's standpoint a book is just another rental property; and just as the expenditures in putting a building into shape to be rented must be capitalized, so, logically at least, must the expenditures used to create a book. It would make no difference under this view whether Encyclopaedia Britannica hired David-Stewart as a mere consultant to its editorial board, which is the Tax Court's conception of what happened, or bought outright from David-Stewart the right to a book that David-Stewart had already published. If you hire a carpenter to build a tree house that you plan to rent out, his wage is a capital expenditure to you. See *Commissioner of Internal Revenue v. Idaho Power Co.* . . .

What does give us pause, however, is a series of decisions in which authors of books have been allowed to treat their expenses as ordinary and necessary business expenses that are deductible immediately even though they were incurred in the creation of long-lived assets—the books the authors were writing. The leading case is *Faura v. Commissioner* . . .; it was discussed with approval just recently by a panel of the Tenth Circuit . . ., and was relied on heavily by the Tax Court in the present case.

We can think of a practical reason for allowing authors to deduct their expenses immediately, one applicable as well to publishers though not in the circumstances of the present case. If you are in the business of producing a series of assets that will yield income over a period of years—which is the situation of most authors and all publishers—identifying particular expenditures with particular books, a necessary step for proper capitalization because the useful lives of the books will not be the same, may be very difficult, since the expenditures of an author or publisher (more clearly the latter) tend to be joint among several books. Moreover, allocating these expenditures among the different books is not always necessary to produce the temporal matching of income and expenditures that the Code desiderates, because the taxable income of the author or publisher who is in a steady state (that is, whose output is neither increasing nor decreasing) will be at least approximately the same whether his costs are expensed or capitalized. Not the same on any given book—on each book expenses and receipts will be systematically mismatched—but the same on average. Under these conditions the benefits of capitalization are unlikely to exceed the accounting and other administrative costs entailed in capitalization.

Yet we hesitate to endorse the *Faura* line of cases: not only because of the evident tension between them and *Idaho Power,* supra, where the Supreme Court said that expenses, whatever their character, must be capitalized if they are incurred in creating a capital asset, but also because *Faura,* and cases following it . . . fail in our view to articulate a persuasive rationale for their result. *Faura* relied on cases holding that the normal expenses of authors and other artists are deductible business expenses rather than nondeductible personal expenses, and on congressional evidence of dissatisfaction with the Internal Revenue Service's insistence that such expenses be capitalized. . . . But most of the cases in question . . ., are inapposite, because they consider only whether the author's expenditures are deductible at all—not whether, if they are deductible, they must first be capitalized. . . .

Yet despite all this we need not decide whether *Faura* is good law, and we are naturally reluctant to precipitate a conflict with the Tenth Circuit. The Tax Court interpreted *Faura* too broadly in this case. As we interpret *Faura* its principle comes into play only when the taxpayer is in the business of producing a series of assets that yield the taxpayer income over a period of years, so that a complex allocation would be necessary if the taxpayer had to capitalize all his expenses of producing them. This is not such a case. The expenditures at issue are unambiguously identified with *The Dictionary of Natural Sciences*. We need not consider the proper tax treatment of any other expenses that Encyclopaedia Britannica may have incurred on the project—editorial expenses, for example—as they are not involved in this case. Those expenses would be analogous to author Faura's office and travel expenses; they are the normal, recurrent expenses of operating a business that happens to produce capital assets. This case is like *Idaho Power*, supra. The expenditure there was on transportation equipment used in constructing capital facilities that Idaho Power employed in its business of producing and distributing electricity, and was thus unambiguously identified with specific capital assets, just as Encyclopaedia Britannica's payment to David-Stewart for the manuscript of *The Dictionary of Natural Sciences* was unambiguously identified with a specific capital asset.

It is also relevant that the commissioning of the manuscript from David-Stewart was somewhat out of the ordinary for Encyclopaedia Britannica. Now the word "ordinary" in section 162 of the Internal Revenue Code has two different uses: to prevent the deduction of certain expenses that are not normally incurred in the type of business in which the taxpayer is engaged ("ordinary" in this sense blends imperceptibly into "necessary") . . . and to clarify the distinction between expenses that are immediately deductible and expenses that must first be capitalized. . . . (A merging of these two distinct senses of the word is a possible explanation for the result in *Faura*.) Most of the "ordinary," in the sense of recurring, expenses of a business are noncapital in nature and most of its capital expenditures are extraordinary in the sense of nonrecurring. Here, as arguably in *Idaho Power* as well—for Idaho Power's business was the production and distribution of electricity, rather than the construction of buildings—the taxpayer stepped out of its normal method of doing business. In this particular project Encyclopaedia Britannica was operating like a conventional publisher, which obtains a complete manuscript from an author or in this case a compiler. The conventional publisher may make a considerable contribution to the work both at the idea stage and at the editorial stage but the deal is for a manuscript, not for services in assisting the publisher to prepare the manuscript itself. Yet we need not consider whether a conventional publisher should be permitted to deduct royalty advances made to its authors as current operating expenses, merely because those advances are for it[s] recurring business expenses because its business is producing capital assets. *Idaho Power,* though factually distinguishable, implies one answer to this question (no), *Faura* another (yes). . . But the principle of *Faura,* whatever its soundness, comes into play only when the expenditure sought to be immediately deducted is a normal and recurrent expense of the business, as it was not here. . . .

There is another point to be noted about the distinction between recurring and nonrecurring expenses and its bearing on the issue in this case. If one really takes seriously the concept of a capital expenditure as anything that yields income, actual or imputed, beyond the period . . . in which the expenditure is made, the result will be to force the capitalization of virtually every business expense. It is a result courts naturally shy away from. . . . It would require capitalizing every salesman's salary, since his selling activities create goodwill for the company and goodwill is an asset yielding income beyond the year in which the salary expense is incurred. The administrative costs of conceptual rigor are too great. The distinction between recurring and nonrecurring business expenses provides a very crude but perhaps serviceable demarcation between those capital expenditures that can feasibly be capitalized and those that cannot be. Whether the distinction breaks down where, as in the case of the conventional publisher, the firm's entire business is the production of capital assets, so that it is literally true that all of its business expenses are capital in nature, is happily not a question we have to decide here, for it is clear that Encyclopaedia Britannica's payments to David-Stewart were of a nonnormal, nonrecurrent nature.

In light of all that we have said, the contention that really what David-Stewart did here was to render consulting services to Encyclopaedia Britannica no different from the services of a consultant whom Encyclopaedia Britannica might have hired on one of its in-house projects, which if true would make the payments more "ordinary" in the *Faura* sense, is of doubtful relevance. But in any event, if that is what the Tax Court meant when it said that David-Stewart was not the "dominating force," its finding was, we think, clearly erroneous. We deprecate decision by metaphor. If the concept of a dominating force has any relevance to tax law, which we doubt, an attempt should have been made to operationalize it, as by computing the ratio of Encyclopaedia Britannica's in-house expenditures on *The Dictionary of Natural Sciences* to its payments to David-Stewart. If the ratio was greater than one, then Encyclopaedia Britannica could fairly be regarded as the dominant force in the enterprise. Although this computation was never made, we have no doubt that Encyclopaedia Britannica was dominant in the sense that, as the buyer, it was calling the tune; and it was buying a custom-made product, built to its specifications. But what it was buying was indeed a product, a completed manuscript. This was a turnkey project, remote from what is ordinarily understood by editorial consultation. While maybe some creators or buyers of capital goods—some authors and publishers—may deduct as current expenses what realistically are capital expenditures, they may not do so . . . when the expense is tied to producing or acquiring a specific capital asset. . . .

C. NOTES AND QUESTIONS

1) Economic Efficiency and the Capitalization Requirement

Suppose that an expenditure which in principle should be capitalized may instead be expensed (that is, currently deducted in full). What is the effect of expensing, as compared with capitalization, on the after-tax cost of the expenditure? Why will the after-tax cost be lower when the expenditure can be expensed? If the after-tax cost is lower, why will the expenditure be more likely to be made? Why will the lower after-tax cost cause investment to shift to expenditures that are capital in nature, but may be expensed? Why might such a shift cause a misallocation of resources?

The author of *Encyclopaedia Britannica,* Judge Richard Posner, is a leader of the so-called Law and Economics School, which argues that the primary objective of legal rules should be to promote the efficient allocation of resources. Might this explain why he decides that the expenditures for the manuscript should be capitalized and why he feels that *Faura* (permitting certain manuscript expenditures to be expensed) was wrongly decided?

2) The Capitalization Requirement in a Steady State

When a taxpayer's capital expenditures are "steady," Judge Posner writes, the benefits of capitalization are "unlikely to exceed the accounting and other administrative [costs]" because at some point it becomes irrelevant whether costs are expensed or depreciated. To illustrate, assume that a publisher goes into business in 1981 and spends $1 million each year on manuscripts and that the life of a book averages two years. It can be shown that, once the publisher has been in business for two years, deductions will be $1 million a year, whether costs are expensed or depreciated. With expensing, annual deductions for manuscripts are $1 million. If capitalized and depreciated evenly over two years, 1981 deductions would be only $500,000; 1982 deductions, however, would amount to $1 million. Half of this figure, or $500,000, would be the second year of depreciation for manuscripts acquired during 1981; the other half would be the first year of depreciation for manuscripts acquired during 1982.

As long as the publisher's capital expenditures remain in a "steady state," the level of deductions will remain at $1 million. For example, although no more depreciation may be taken in 1983 for manuscripts acquired in 1981, there would be the second year of depreciation for manuscripts acquired in 1982 and the first year of depreciation for manuscripts acquired in 1983, and so on. In general, the number of years that must pass before it becomes irrelevant whether costs are expensed or depreciated is the same as the number of years in the life of the capital expenditure. Thus, if the average life of a book were four years, it would become irrelevant in the fourth year whether costs were expensed or depreciated.

However, when capital expenditures are not steady, but expanding, it will always matter whether costs are expensed or depreciated. To illustrate, assume that each year the publisher expands the amount spent on manuscripts by 10%. Thus, $1 million is spent in 1981, $1,100,000 in 1982, $1,210,000 in 1983, and so on. With expensing, each year's deductions correspond to the amount spent. If expenditures are capitalized and depreciated evenly over two years, 1981 deductions again amount to $500,000. 1982 deductions rise to $1,050,000. $500,000 of this figure is the second year of depreciation for manuscripts acquired in 1981; the other $550,000 is the first year of depreciation for manuscripts acquired in 1982. By 1983, depreciation has risen to $1,155,000. $550,000 is depreciation for manuscripts acquired in 1982; $605,000 is the first year of depreciation for manuscripts acquired in 1983. Comparing 1982 and 1983, the gap between deductions under expensing and deductions under depreciation has widened. It was $50,000 in 1982 and $55,000 in 1983. This gap will continue to grow as long as capital expenditures continue to expand by at least a constant rate.

3) Distinguishing *Encyclopaedia Britannica* from Other Expenditures for Salary

In *Encyclopaedia Britannica*, the expenditure on the manuscript was basically compensation for the services of preparing a manuscript. What distinguishes this expenditure from the usual case where compensation for services is expensed, even though the expenditure is expected to produce some revenues beyond the current year? Is there an allocation problem here? If capitalization is required, will it be difficult to determine a limited useful life of the expenditure?

4) Does the Difficulty of Allocation Justify the *Faura* Rule?

Why did the Tax Court hold that the manuscript cost could be expensed? Suppose that Encyclopaedia Britannica had paid its own employees to produce the manuscript in-house. What justifies the *Faura* ruling that the cost may, in that event, be expensed? The Court of Appeals refers to an allocation problem. How does the court know that, in fact, an allocation problem would exist if the manuscript were produced in-house? Even if it did exist, how can it be distinguished from the usual difficulty with allocating salary expenditures between current and future production? Is the allocation problem referred to in *Encyclopaedia Britannica* arguably more manageable? Need an allocation even be made in order to require capitalization? Why not simply assign the expenditure a useful life equal to the average life of books published by the taxpayer?

In 1986, Congress reversed *Faura* by enacting Section 263A(a) and (b)(1). This provision required capitalization of the costs of producing "tangible personal property," which was defined to include "a film sound recording, video tape, book, or similar property." One writer reacted to the new law in the following commentary.

D. KITTY KELLEY, ONLY THE RICH WILL WRITE
Newsweek (August 24, 1987)

The self-employed writers of America, all 14,000 of us full timers and 47,000 part timers, face a financial guillotine. It could kill off many of our books, articles, plays and movies. We are the victims of a footnote in the 1986 Tax Reform Act, which states that we must capitalize our expenses.

This footnote, Section 263A(b), requires us to spread our expenses over the entire income-producing life of a book or other work. This means we can claim only a portion of our expenses in any one year—and none at all during the period we spend researching and writing, the time when we actually lay the money out. The new law further says that expenses may be applied only against income produced by the work in question and not against earnings from any other writing projects. This means that I must spend long, costly hours with my accountant trying to figure out how to apportion expenses among the books I write.

- Will "His Way: The Unauthorized Biography of Frank Sinatra" support my office rent? And for how long?
- Will the $4.12 I now receive in annual royalties from "Jackie Oh!," my 1978 book about Jacqueline Kennedy Onassis, cover paper clips for six weeks?
- Will the dwindling dollars from "Elizabeth Taylor: The Last Star" buy typing paper for another month?
- Does Liz, Jackie or Frank pay for photocopying? Which one picks up my phone bill? Health insurance? Postage?

Had this law been in effect when I was working on my first book, "The Glamour Spas," I would have gone broke in midstream because my research expenses in visiting America's fat farms far exceeded the publisher's advance. The book took two years to write and produced no income. And while I might have thought it worthy enough to be placed alongside "The American Way of Death," consumers in 1975 thought otherwise. Nevertheless, the new law requires writers to estimate the income-producing life of a book ... and that is like asking us to calculate the number of stars that shine over Spokane.

It is virtually impossible for anyone (except perhaps for Shirley MacLaine, who seems to have an extraterrestrial sense about such things) to compute with accuracy how long a book will produce income. Can a farmer say how long his cow will give milk? Can a plumber gauge the life of his wrench? Probably with better accuracy than a writer trying to estimate the life of a book.

With 50,000 books published in the United States every year, most writers would kill for one good income-producing year in hard-cover and another in paperback. However, the odds are against us because the shelf life of a book is about six weeks. If it doesn't sell in that time, it's returned to the publisher, dead on arrival. Resigned to the inevitability of the remainder tables, most writers only dream about publishers' backlists where books like "Goldilocks" and the Holy Bible are restocked and sold regularly.

Some among us get lucky and sell movie rights or see our books become mini-series on TV. About as many win lotteries, too. With the exception of superstars like Irving Wallace and James Michener and Judith Krantz, most writers must be content with a modest advance against royalties ($8,000 to $10,000), a small first printing (4,000 copies) and meager sales. And now because of the 1986 Tax Reform Act, writers—with an estimated median annual income of $7,900—will have to further penalize themselves for their creativity. People like David Halberstam ("The Reckoning: The Challenge to America's Greatness") and Edmund Morris ("The Rise of Theodore Roosevelt") and Robert A. Caro ("The Years of Lyndon Johnson: The Path to Power") will find it harder to enrich our understanding of American life. Their books require years of expensive research.

Under the current law, William Faulkner, whose works never earned much money while he was alive, might not have been able to produce "The Sound and the Fury." Eugene O'Neill might have been discouraged from writing "Desire Under the Elms." Could Joseph Heller have spent nearly eight years writing "Catch-22"?

. . . My friend Larry L. King, the funny man who wrote "The Best Little Whorehouse in Texas," has spent the last four years working on his second play, "The Night Hank Williams Died." He has invested thousands of dollars in this project, traveling around the country to meet with agents, producers and directors, trying to stage productions, hire talent, arrange music. The play has yet to produce any income and so, according to the new law, the playwright will have to swallow all of his expenses.

Even Ivan Boesky was allowed to deduct his losses in the stock market.

Surely Congress in its wisdom did not intend to punish the people who produce one of our nation's greatest resources. Did those senators and representatives who allocate hundreds of millions of dollars for Star Wars mean to plunder the libraries and bookstores of the United States? I can't believe that our lawmakers, many of them authors themselves, intended such artistic destruction. Aren't Sens. Daniel Patrick Moynihan, William S. Cohen, Paul Simon and Bill Bradley listed in "Books in Print"?

Without prompt congressional action, few American authors will be able to continue earning a living writing books. And the Faulkners of today, the budding O'Neills in the early stages of their careers won't be able to nurture their talents. Our lawmakers may not have recognized the import of that small footnote buried in 878 pages of tax legislation, but unless they do something now, those few phrases can render meaningless much of what the U.S. Constitution does to shield writers with copyright protection and First Amendment guarantees.

If you can't afford to write, all the protections in the world won't make a difference.

[Editor's Note: In 1988, Congress repealed the language in Section 263A that required writers to capitalize their expenses.]

E. NORTH CAROLINA NATIONAL BANK CORP. v. UNITED STATES
684 F.2d 285 (4th Cir. 1982)

WIDENER, CIRCUIT JUDGE:

I

At issue in this case is the proper treatment, for purposes of income tax computation, of certain expenditures incurred by NCNB in activities connected with its statewide branch banking system.... In the period between 1970 and 1973, for instance, the bank opened 57 new branches, including 21 offices in cities where the bank had not previously had operations.

As part of the expansion process and as a part of branch banking which is its business, NCNB incurred a variety of expenses. Besides the obvious cost of constructing and equipping new facilities, the bank conducted various market and feasibility studies, devoted staff time to planning and implementing expansion projects, and completed the process by applying for permission from the Comptroller of the Currency to open and relocate various facilities. During the years 1965–70 the bank capitalized the costs connected with building and equipping new facilities, pursuant to Internal Revenue Code § 263. The taxpayer, however, deducted as current expenses other costs incurred in the expansion process, pursuant to IRC § 162. The Commissioner of Internal Revenue asserted a deficiency with respect to the bank's tax returns, arguing that the costs taken as current expenses actually should have been capitalized. The Commissioner maintained that none of the expenditures were current expenditures because they related to the production of future income.... The taxpayer paid the assessed deficiencies and then timely sued for refunds in the district court. The trial court held for NCNB, concluding that the opening of a new branch bank "produces nothing corporeal or salable. It does not create a capital asset within the meaning of the Internal Revenue Code of 1954." The expenditures at issue were thus ordinary and necessary expenses and deductible under IRC § 162(a), it held.

This court's panel concluded, however, that the district court had applied an incorrect legal standard and reversed.... The panel concluded that benefits from the expenditures in question extended beyond the individual accounting years and thus the taxpayer could not deduct them as current expenses in the years incurred....

II

The question of whether particular expenditures are more properly charged to current expense or capitalized has long been a point of contention between those taxed and the Internal Revenue Service.... It should be noted, though, that neither courts nor the accounting profession have devised a universal, foolproof method of distinguishing current expenses from capital costs....

Section 162(a) of the Internal Revenue Code sets forth five criteria for evaluating whether an expenditure is a current expense.

> [A]n item must (1) be "paid or incurred during the taxable year," (2) be for "carrying on any trade or business," (3) be an "expense," (4) be a "necessary" expense, and (5) be an "ordinary" expense.

... The principal issue in this case as in most such cases is whether the expenditure is "ordinary and necessary."...

The [Supreme] Court has considered differences between capital and current expenditures ... most decisively in *Commissioner v. Lincoln Savings & Loan Association*. ... *Lincoln Savings & Loan* concerned the deductibility of a payment by a savings institution to a reserve fund held by a federal agency. ... In deciding whether the payment was a contribution to an asset or an expense, the Court said:

> What is important and controlling, we feel, is that the ... payment serves to create or enhance for Lincoln what is essentially a separate and distinct additional asset and that, as an inevitable consequence, the payment is capital in nature and not an expense, let alone an ordinary expense, deductible under § 162(a). ...

While concluding that the contribution to the reserve fund was capital, the Court in *Lincoln Savings & Loan* specifically rejected the argument that the expenditure was not deductible simply because it had an effect beyond one year:

> [T]he presence of an ensuing benefit that may have some future aspect is not controlling; many expenses concededly deductible have prospective benefit beyond the taxable year.

The latter language is particularly important in light of the decisions in this circuit, including the panel decision at hand, which hold that expenditures providing benefits for a taxpayer beyond one year must be capitalized. This court adopted the one-year rule in *Richmond Television Corp. v. United States*, ... where we said:

> Our system of income taxation attempts to match income and expenses of the taxable year so as to tax only net income. A taxpayer may, therefore, not deduct as a current business expense the full cost of acquiring an asset, tangible or intangible, which benefits the taxpayer for more than one year. ...

The one-year rule is certainly appealing in its conceptual simplicity, but as the *Lincoln Savings & Loan* opinion notes, numerous expenses with effects beyond one year are readily deductible. One need not consider further than the case of the corporate executive who spends a significant, though indeterminable, amount of his time on future planning to realize that universal application of the one year rule is impossible and that it has not been so applied in such cases. ...

... This does not mean that courts are to ignore the long term characteristics of expenditures in deciding whether particular costs are capital or current; rather, the length of the ensuing benefit is but one factor under consideration.

III

We turn now to application of the *Lincoln Savings & Loan* standard to the facts before us. The expenditures in question are of three types: metro studies, feasibility studies, and applications to the Comptroller of the Currency. Metro studies were long range planning reports making recommendations and plotting strategies for NCNB in various regions of North Carolina. These studies concerned both existing facilities and expansion opportunities and were prepared both internally and by outside consultants. Feasibility studies focused on particular proposed branch locations, evaluating the economics of various options. Preparation of these reports came after metro studies. . . . Applications to the Comptroller were for the statutorily required permission for a nationally chartered bank to open branch offices. Costs incurred included the application fee, internal staff time in preparation of the application, and attorneys' fees and related expenses connected with prosecution of the application.

It is important to recognize that all of these expenses were connected with NCNB's developing and operating a statewide network of branch banking facilities. In order to maintain its position in the industry, NCNB found it necessary to continually explore the market for its varied services and facilities. It is a long recognized principle of tax law that expenditures for the protection of an existing investment, the continuation of an existing business, or the preservation of existing income from loss or diminution are ordinary and necessary business expenses within the meaning of IRC § 162. . . .

The Second Circuit's *Briarcliff* opinion is of particular interest in the case before us. *Briarcliff* involved a candy company which had sold its products primarily through a chain of company owned stores in urban centers. Demographic changes forced the company to seek markets for its products in suburban areas. When company owned suburban stores failed to attract satisfactory business, the company decided to develop a network of franchised dealers. . . . The company, in preparing its income tax returns, treated the costs of developing the network, such as sales calls and advertisements in trade magazines, as deductible expenses. The Commissioner disallowed the deductions, however, reasoning that these promotional expenses were distinct from the operating expenses of the franchise division. The Commissioner said the expenses were actually capital in nature because they were incurred in obtaining 159 dealer contracts. The contracts were said to constitute the capital assets of the franchise division. . . . The Second Circuit, citing *Lincoln Savings & Loan,* rejected the Commissioner's argument that the expenditures were capital in nature because benefits from them extended into future years. . . . The court said the expenditures would be capital only if they served to create or enhance a separate and distinct additional asset. Turning to the issue of whether the contracts were such assets, the court stated that an expenditure is a "capital asset" only if "at the time it is furnished to the company, it has an ascertainable and measurable value—that is, a value in money or a fair market value.". . . Noting that there is no special statutory definition of "capital asset" for IRC §§ 162 and 263, the court said the term must be taken in its "usual and customary business sense as items of ownership of a permanent or fixed nature which are convertible into cash.". . . The Second Circuit concluded that the contracts were not capital assets and thus expenses incurred in obtaining them were not capital costs. . . . The *Briarcliff* reasoning is applicable in the instant case because NCNB, like the *Briarcliff* taxpayer, was expanding its business into new territories. We do not, however, hold as determinative the fact that the branch banks could not be turned into cash. But that is a factor to consider in determining whether they were "separate and distinct additional asset[s]" within the meaning of *Lincoln Savings & Loan*. The costs NCNB incurred in exploring such expansion are analogous to the costs in *Briarcliff* for developing the franchise network. Particularly relevant is the Second Circuit's rejection of the Commissioner's argument that the possible long term benefits of such expenditures mandated their capitalization.

Also applicable to the case before us is a series of cases, including one from this circuit, which have dealt with the costs incurred by banks in developing credit card systems. . . . The facts are generally the same in each case. The banks began issuing Master Charge or Bank-Americard credit cards either directly or through cooperative organizations, and, in the process, incurred various start-up expenses such as computer costs, computer services, advertising, credit bureau reports, travel, educational and entertainment expenses, and temporary clerical services, all of which were claimed as ordinary business expenses. In *First National Bank of South Carolina*, the taxpayer incurred its costs as part of an assessment by a cooperative association of which it was a member. We held that the assessment was not a membership fee and quoted approvingly from the *Colorado Springs* decision where the Tenth Circuit said:

> The start-up expenditures here challenged did not create a property interest. They produced nothing corporeal or salable. They are recurring. At the most they introduced a more efficient method of conducting an old business. . . .

Once again, the persuasive factual similarity between the credit card cases and the instant case is that costs incurred in expanding a business are not considered capital costs unless they meet the *Lincoln Savings & Loan* "separate and distinct additional asset" test. And this test holds whether or not the expenditures have benefits beyond the current taxation period. . . .

Still another indication that the expenditures in question are current expenses rather than capital costs is recent legislation dealing with amortization of certain expenses incurred by new businesses. A new statute, IRC § 195, provides that new businesses may apply a special amortization treatment to such expenditures if the costs would have been deductible,

> if paid or incurred in connection with the expansion of an existing trade or business (in the same field as the [new] trade or business . . .), would be allowable as a deduction for the taxable year in which paid or incurred.

IRC § 195(b)(2). As an example of expenditures which would be allowable deductions for an existing business, the Senate Report that accompanied § 195 explained:

> Under the provision, eligible expenses consist of investigatory costs incurred in reviewing a prospective business prior to reaching a final decision to

acquire or to enter that business. These costs include expenses incurred for the analysis or survey of potential markets, products, labor supply, transportation facilities, etc.

. . . Congress is thus under the impression that expenditures for market studies and feasibility studies, as at issue here, are fully deductible if incurred by an existing business undergoing expansion. An interpretation by us to the contrary would render § 195 meaningless for it would obliterate the reference point in the statute—"the expansion of an existing trade or business."

The government calls our attention to several cases which it says have held that license fees and other costs incurred in securing operating permits must be treated as capital expenditures which, at best, can be amortized over the life of the license. . . .

[It] is important to note that the Comptroller's permission to open a branch bank is factually different from certain other government licenses. The approval, if given, is only to "establish and operate [a] new branch." . . . It is not an exclusive territorial franchise; it is not transferable; and the branch bank is not readily salable as such. A branch bank has no value except its tangible and real assets apart from its parent as contrasted to the immense value of a TV station with construction permit or license, for example, which is the type of license usually encountered, and upon which precedents the government relies.

Still another reason for allowing NCNB to treat these expansion costs as current expenses is that such accounting is required by the Comptroller of the Currency. In an August 21, 1972 letter to the Assistant Secretary for Tax Policy, U. S. Treasury Department, the Comptroller wrote:

> It is the long-established policy of this office to require National Banks to charge to current operations all expenditures relating to the development and expansion of banking services, including those incurred in credit card programs. This policy has as its basis our responsibility of assuring the solvency and liquidity of National Banks and the concurrent protection of depositories and shareholders. . . .

When the taxpayer's accounting method is one specified by a governmental agency regulating the taxpayer, the Supreme court has said:

> [W]here a taxpayer's generally accepted method of accounting is made compulsory by the regulatory agency *and* that method clearly reflects income, it is almost presumptively controlling of federal income tax consequences.

Commissioner v. Idaho Power Co. [Chapter 32]. Thus, in the instant case, the Comptroller's accounting method is presumptively controlling as long as it accurately reflects income.

There is little doubt that the charging of expansion costs to current expenses represents a conservative accounting policy and, in fact, differs from that required of certain other federally regulated industries. Nevertheless, it is readily apparent to us that banking is a unique industry and that the Comptroller of the Currency has much more control over the daily operations of banks than regulators have over most other industries. The basis for this control, of course, is the overriding public interest in the stability and solvency of the nation's financial institutions. . . . [Banks] are unique in that a substantial portion of their assets must be readily available, as cash, for claims by their depositors on demand. To insure that a bank can meet these obligations, it must have an accounting system which gives an extraordinarily accurate picture of its financial position. Assets which cannot be quickly redeemed, or even redeemed at all, such as the items at issue here, are of little benefit to the liquidity of the bank when carried on its books as a capital asset. We think the Comptroller is in a unique position of expertise to determine what accurately reflects a bank's income. Thus, we conclude that NCNB should be entitled to the presumption explained in the *Idaho Power* decision.

. . . The money spent or obligated for metro studies, feasibility studies, and applications to the Comptroller of the Currency, it seems to us, adds nothing to the value of a bank's assets which can be so definitely ascertained that it must be capitalized. Certainly no "separate and distinct additional asset" is created. While the benefit of all of these classes of expenses may or may not endure for more than one year, that is but one factor to be considered. The branch has no existence separate and apart from the parent bank; as a branch bank, it is not readily salable and has no market value other than the real estate which it occupies and the tangible equipment therein.

IV

In conclusion, we emphasize that NCNB's business is operating a statewide network of branch banks. In order to maintain this network, NCNB must continually evaluate its market position through various means that utilize both internal and external resources. It has every right to keep abreast of demographic trends and the like in its necessary allocation of resources as well as in ascertaining where the public demand for its services exists. The bank must regularly take actions such as the opening and closing of branches so as to maintain profitability and a sound financial position. Where these actions result in the creation or retirement of separate and identifiable assets such as buildings and equipment, then the taxpayer must make adjustments to its capital accounts. But where these expenditures do not create or enhance separate and identifiable assets, they are properly considered "ordinary and necessary." IRC § 162(a).

The judgment of the district court is accordingly
Affirmed.

MURNAGHAN, CIRCUIT JUDGE, dissenting:

. . . I view somewhat wryly the controlling weight accorded by the *en banc* majority to justification language set forth in the legislative history of the new Internal Revenue Code Section 195. . . . The section was designed to benefit taxpayers by permitting them to elect to amortize, over a period no shorter than five years, expenditures which otherwise, insofar as the characteristics with which we are here concerned matter, would be recognized as deductible. The nature of the expenditures—planning costs—were like those with which we are here confronted, except that they involved start-up expenditures for new, rather than for existing businesses.

The nondeductibility perceived as requiring amelioration when IRC § 195 was passed arose not from the length of life of an expenditure, but from the non-business nature of expenditures paid or incurred before a new business began operation. Those expenditures were nondeductible whether their life spans were ten days or ten years....

Insofar as IRC § 195 is concerned, it is relevant to observe, at the outset, that amortization is a way, for tax purposes, to deal with capital items, not customarily a way to deal with items of ordinary and necessary expense. The statute thus focuses on broadening of the category of capital expenditure, not on an expansion of the deductible category. My panel opinion called for determinations to be made as to whether expenditures not qualifying for immediate 100% deduction should be amortizable, and, if so, over what duration of time. Such items not qualifying for 100% deductibility status under law extant when IRC § 195 was adopted were explicitly not the subject of, or affected by, IRC § 195. Expenditures amortizable at the taxpayer's election had to be such as "if paid or incurred in connection with the expansion of an existing trade or business . . . *would be allowable as a deduction* for the taxable year in which paid or incurred." 26 U.S.C. § 195(b)(2) (emphasis supplied).

It requires a giant, and unjustified leap, to derive from the justification set out in the legislative history any support for the proposition that *all* investigatory costs are automatically deductible, irrespective of length of life. Eligible expenses under IRC § 195 include "investigatory costs incurred in reviewing a prospective business prior to reaching a final decision to acquire or to enter that business.". . . But that is only one of the qualifications. In addition, to qualify as an eligible expense, an expenditure "must be one which would be allowable as a deduction for the taxable year in which it is paid or incurred if it were paid or incurred in connection with the expansion of an existing trade or business."...

Thus, the legislative history does not purport to say that all investigatory costs are deductible. To the contrary, it explicitly limits its application solely to those investigatory costs which are deductible in nature. The implication is inescapable that there are other investigatory costs which are not deductible, i.e. are to be capitalized. Consequently, we are brought straight back to the question we started with: In the case of each expenditure, was it deductible, or capitalizable? Hence, I submit that the authority relied on is illusory and not supportive of the conclusion reached by the *en banc* majority.

To sum it all up, we have here a case where an opportunity to resort to the golden mean is ignored. Start-up expenditures and other expenditures like start-up expenditures except that they concern existing businesses often have multi-year lives or applications. In such cases they should not be immediately fully deductible in the year paid or incurred as ordinary and necessary expenses. Rather they should be capitalized and prorated. That is to say that they should, over time, be deductible for income tax purposes, but not all at once, in one fell swoop.

Apparently Congress, in recently enacting IRC § 195 first decided that complete denial of any deductibility was unfair and unwise and that existing law to that effect should be changed. Second, Congress evidently appreciated that, as a matter of economic fact, a new enterprise often must operate, at the outset, at a loss, perhaps over a period of several years. Congress presumably appreciated that a new business could well see the losses altogether evaporate as deductions, because there had been no profit against which to apply them. Such a state of affairs would be inconsistent with a congressional desire to encourage formation of new businesses and the probable resulting increase in employment. So an election to amortize was extended to taxpayers to permit them to take some portions of early year expenditures as deductions in later, more probably profitable, years.

Congress by enacting IRC § 195 thus only emphasized the nature as capital, rather than as ordinary and necessary expenses, of the exploratory expenditures category. The congressional legislation, therefore, is fully consistent with, and strongly supports the result reached in my panel majority opinion. There is simply no justification for reading the legislative history as making *more* deductible than theretofore exploratory expenditures for existing businesses. To the extent such expenditures had been recognized as having the character of ordinary and necessary expenses (primarily short life span) they should remain deductible, and their counterparts among expenditures for new businesses, by IRC § 195, are made, at the taxpayer's election, amortizable. To the extent expenditures for existing businesses have characteristics of longer life, they will remain capitalizable. That is all that IRC § 195 and its justification language say. That is all that they should be deemed to mean. . . .

F. CENTRAL TEXAS SAVINGS & LOAN ASS'N v. UNITED STATES
731 F.2d 1181 (5th Cir. 1984)

REAVLEY, CIRCUIT JUDGE:

The government appeals the decision of the district court holding that expenditures made in investigating and establishing new branches of a savings and loan association were deductible expenses under 26 U.S.C. § 162(a) (1976). We agree with the government's contention that such expenditures should have been capitalized.

I. Statement of the Case

Central Texas Savings & Loan Association (Central Texas), with its principal place of business and home office in Marlin, Texas, opened Texas branch offices in Waco (1973), Temple (1974), Rosebud (1976), and Mart (1976). The taxpayer made several expenditures in investigating and in starting up the new branches, including professional fees for economic research and analysis to determine the potential market at each location and attorneys' fees and permit fees attendant upon licensing the new locations. . . .

In 1978 and 1979 Central Texas filed amended returns for the years 1972 through 1977, claiming current expense deductions under 26 U.S.C. § 162(a) . . . for the professional fees and the expenditures made in obtaining permits to open the branches. . . .

The district judge ruled in favor of Central Texas, stating that addition of the same services by a newly established branch did not create a separate and distinct asset; it merely enabled the institution to accommodate changing business conditions. The judge also ruled that the expenditures for the permits and studies had no measurable value beyond the date of approval for the branch offices. He relied chiefly on *NCNB Corp. v. United States* . . . in reaching these conclusions. For the reasons set out below, this court reaches a different result from that in *NCNB.*

II. Section 162(a) Deductions

. . . "Carrying on any trade or business" has been interpreted to mean that only an existing business, i.e., one that is fully operational, may take advantage of the provision. . . . Hence, if a taxpayer were to start a new business, the pre-operational or start-up expenses would not be deductible under section 162(a). Similarly, if the taxpayer were to investigate the feasibility of acquiring an existing business or stock in such a business, such costs would not be deductible under section 162(a) but would be capitalized. . . . It would seem anomalous to say that if a taxpayer purchases or merges with a savings and loan in another city, it must capitalize the investigative and start-up costs; but if it establishes a new office, these same costs may be deducted under § 162(a).

Section 162(a) further requires that an item be paid or incurred and the benefit exhausted during the taxable year to be deductible. While the period of the benefits may not be controlling in all cases, it nonetheless remains a prominent, if not predominant, characteristic of a capital item. *NCNB Corp. v. United States.* . . . We still consider, therefore, that the continuation of the permit's value to the taxpayer for a period exceeding one year is evidence that the permit or its costs of acquisition are capital items. . . . In this case, the permit was a one-time payment that gave the taxpayer the right to operate for an indefinite period of time. The benefit secured by the permit clearly extended beyond the year in which the fee payment was made. Furthermore, the fact that the fee payment was made only once supports the proposition that the outlay was a capital asset, rather than an annual expense. . . .

The third requirement of section 162(a) is that the expenditure be an ordinary and necessary expense. The courts have long had difficulty determining whether an expenditure is ordinary and necessary. The parties do not contest the necessity of the expenditures to establish the branches. Our inquiry is whether they were ordinary. In *Lincoln Savings,* the Supreme Court addressed the question whether a payment required by . . . the National Housing Act was deductible as an ordinary expense.... The savings and loan association was required to pay a two percent premium of the increase in the total of its insured accounts.... This premium was used to provide insurance for deposits in the participating institutions.... The institution retained a pro rata share in the reserve fund, but the interest was not transferable, except in case of merger or consolidation or similar transactions.... The taxpayer argued that the premium was an ordinary expense of doing business since it was an obligatory expenditure, made by all similarly situated savings and loan institutions, with little possibility of future benefit.... The Supreme Court disagreed and stated the test for distinguishing an ordinary expense from a capital expenditure:

> The presence of an ensuing benefit that may have some future aspect is not controlling. Many expenses concededly deductible have prospective effect beyond the taxable year.
>
> What is important and controlling, we feel, is that the ... payment serves to create or enhance for Lincoln what is essentially a separate and distinct additional asset and that, as an inevitable consequence, the payment is capital in nature and not an expense, let alone an ordinary expense, deductible under § 162(a)....

Our question, therefore, is whether the establishment of a new branch office creates a separate and distinct additional asset.

The district judge concluded that the expenditures in question related only to the acquisition of a permit and were of no use after the permit was received. We disagree. Section 162(a) must be read in tandem with section 263(a), which provides:

> No deduction shall be allowed for—(1) any amount paid out for new buildings or for permanent improvements on betterments made to increase the value of any property or estate....

This provision has been construed to mean that expenditures incurred in the acquisition of a capital asset must generally be capitalized.... Expenditures "made with the contemplation that they will result in the creation of a capital asset cannot be deducted as ordinary and necessary business expenses even though that expectation is subsequently frustrated or defeated."

... The district judge therefore erred by concluding that the expenditures had no measurable value to the savings and loan after it acquired approval to open the branch offices. The character of the item acquired determines the tax treatment of the expenditures made to acquire it....

The court must look to the character of the item for which the expenditure was made to determine if it was a separate and identifiable asset. The Fourth Circuit, in *NCNB Corp. v. United States*, held that a branch office for a bank was not an asset but merely an expansion of an existing business into new markets.... In reaching its conclusion it relied upon *Briarcliff Candy Corp. v. Commissioner* ... where a candy manufacturer, which owned its own retail stores, set up a "franchise" division within the company to promote sales of its product through other retail outlets such as pharmacies.

The manufacturer had no property interest in the space allocated to its product in these stores, and had no control over the store owners.... Based on these facts the court determined that the franchises had no ascertainable and measurable value at the time they were established and were, therefore, not [separate and distinct] assets....

The *NCNB* court also cited the "credit card cases" in which several circuits determined that the costs incurred by banks in providing credit card services to its customers were deductible as ordinary expenses. In *Colorado Springs National Bank v. United States*, ... for example, the court determined that credit cards were merely a new method for a bank to provide letters of credit to its customers. The court, adhering to the rule of *Briarcliff*, held that the bank had no property right in the new credit card procedures and that there was no way to determine the useful life of the asset....

We distinguish these cases from the situation where an association opens a new branch. *Briarcliff* itself distinguishes creation of a branch office from mere expansion of existing services to new markets: "[T]he changes which Loft made in its own internal organization to spread its sales into a new territory were not comparable to the acquisition of a new additional branch or division to make and sell a new and different product...." Following *Briarcliff*, we find that Central Texas had a property interest in its branch offices. It had a separate right to do business in a new territory which it acquired by virtue of the permit. It had the right to receive new accounts for new customers in a new market. It gained the right to challenge the entry of competitors into the local market. Even an intangible property right, such as the right to do business, may be a capital item.... Moreover, this right was easily valued at the time the permit was acquired. It was measurable by the value of its deposits and the income from its loans. That the branch was not transferable is not significant. This fact did not prevent the Supreme Court from holding that a non-transferable interest, except in limited circumstances, was nonetheless an asset. *Lincoln Savings*.... The taxpayer obtained a separate and identifiable business right that was exercised in a separate office by a separate staff in an exclusive territory. We therefore find the branch offices to be separate and distinct assets within the *Lincoln Savings* definition.

In finding branch banks not to be separate assets, the *NCNB* court also relied upon the Comptroller of Currency's requirement that banks treat expenditures for their establishment as expenses in their accounting procedures. Compulsory accounting rules of a regulatory agency, however, do not necessarily determine the tax consequences of the item.... An accounting practice must accurately reflect income in order to be presumptively controlling. *Idaho Power Co.* [Chapter 32]. For the reasons discussed above, we view the deduction of the investigatory and start-up expenses as an inaccurate reflection of the benefits or income of the taxpayer. Although the expenses are incurred in a single year, they procure benefits that endure for the life of the branch. The tax treatment should, therefore, reflect this longevity and the expenditures should be treated as a capital expense.... Furthermore, while the internal accounting procedures may treat the branches and the home office as a single entity, it is clear that each branch is also viewed separately, since the profitability of each branch must be assessed. This further supports our conclusion that each branch must be valued as a separate asset.

III. Amortization

The district court did not address whether the expenditures could be amortized, having determined that they would be deducted as expenses under section 162(a). Congress has now provided for amortization of certain expenditures:

> Election to amortize.—start-up expenditures may, at the election of the taxpayer, be treated as deferred expenses. Such deferred expenses shall be allowed as a deduction ratably over such period of not less than 60 months as may be selected by the taxpayer (beginning with the month in which the business begins).

26 U.S.C. § 195(a) (1981). Section (b) defines a start-up expenditure as "any amount—(1) paid or incurred in connection with—(a) investigating the creation or acquisition of an active trade or business. . . ." The expenditures involved, however, must also be those that would be deductible if they were paid in connection with the expansion of an existing business. 26 U.S.C. § 195(b)(2) (1981). We do not decide whether the expenditures in question in this case would meet this second requirement. This statute applies to amounts paid or incurred after July 29, 1980, and Central Texas cannot qualify for amortization of their expenditures. In the future, however, section 195(a) should encourage formation of new businesses without the attendant controversy and litigation to determine the proper tax classification of the start-up expenditures.

G. NOTES AND QUESTIONS

1) The Allocation Problem

The facts of *North Carolina National Bank (NCNB)* and *Central Texas Savings & Loan (CTS&L)* are almost identical. Both taxpayers paid for feasibility studies and legal work in order to establish new branch banks. Were these particular expenditures allocable to anything but the new branches? Were they capital in nature?

The taxpayer in *NCNB* also paid for so-called "metro studies." Were these costs allocable to anything besides the new branches? Even if they were allocable in part to existing branches, does that affect whether they were capital in nature? What was the exact subject of the "metro studies"?

2) If Capitalized, Are the Expenditures for Wasting or Nonwasting Assets?

If the expenditures to establish new branches were capitalized, would they be treated as wasting assets? Were they expenditures for intangibles subject to Reg. § 1.167(a)–3? Would the taxpayer be able to prove a limited useful life?

If Section 195 applied to the expenditures, what useful life would be assigned to them, notwithstanding Reg. § 1.167(a)–3? What views were expressed in *NCNB* and *CTS&L* as to whether Section 195 would apply?

3) The *Briarcliff* Rule

Briarcliff (cited in *NCNB*) held that planning expenses for an existing business could be expensed. If such expenditures were capitalized, would they be treated as wasting assets? Would the taxpayer be able to prove a limited useful life under Reg. § 1.167(a)–3?

4) Economic Efficiency and the Capitalization Requirement

NCNB compared the expenditures for new branches with planning expenditures for an *existing* business, which could be expensed under *Briarcliff*. Can this outcome, although arguably at odds with *Encyclopaedia Britannica*, also be justified on economic efficiency grounds? Given that some planning expenditures are expensed, might economic efficiency require treating all planning expenditures the same?

Should Section 195 be amended to provide five-year amortization of *all* planning expenses? Or would that favor companies whose planning is done by in-house employees on a part-time basis and thus discriminate against companies who pay outside consultants or assign employees to plan on a full-time basis?

5) The Relevance of Nontax Accounting

NCNB held that the nontax method of accounting was virtually controlling because it was compelled by regulatory authorities and clearly reflected income. *CTS&L* held that the nontax method was not controlling, even though compelled by regulatory authorities, because it did not clearly reflect income. Which opinion is more consistent with *Thor Power Tool* (Chapter 15) and *Idaho Power* (Chapter 32)?

Chapter 34

ALLOCATING CAPITAL EXPENDITURES BETWEEN WASTING AND NONWASTING ASSETS

A. INTRODUCTORY NOTE

1) The Incentive to Overallocate to Shorter-lived Assets

When a number of properties are acquired for a lump sum, the cost must be allocated among them. If those properties have different useful lives, the buyer usually has an incentive to overallocate the cost to the shorter-lived assets in order to deduct the cost as quickly as possible. This is particularly true when some of the properties acquired are nonwasting assets, a situation that arises whenever land is purchased with an existing structure. In that case, the buyer may try to allocate as much of the price as possible to the structure, so that it can be deducted as depreciation over the structure's life, and as little as possible to the land, the cost of which cannot be deducted until the land is sold.

Although overallocation of the purchase price to shorter-lived assets benefits the buyer, it may also produce a tax detriment to the seller. To illustrate, suppose the purchase price is overallocated to a noncapital asset and underallocated to a capital asset, increasing the amount of ordinary income and decreasing the amount of capital gain. If capital gains are taxed less heavily than ordinary income, the seller will suffer a tax detriment. But with repeal of the basic capital gains preference, the seller may not suffer at all. In other words, whether the seller has a tax detriment depends on how overallocation affects the character of the seller's gain (or loss) and also on whether capital gain receives preferential treatment (or whether a capital loss receives disadvantageous treatment).

Even if overallocation would cause the seller a tax detriment, it may be more than offset by the buyer's tax benefit so that there is a net savings to both parties. In that event, the buyer may try to induce the seller to agree to overallocation by increasing the total purchase price to compensate the seller for the tax detriment and possibly to share some of the net tax benefit with the seller. See the example following *Ferrer* (Chapter 29).

2) Allocation Issues and the Purchase of Professional Sports Teams

Allocation issues have been particularly contentious when a professional sports franchise is purchased. For example, in Laird v. United States, 556 F.2d 1224 (5th Cir. 1977), cert. denied, 434 U.S. 1014 (1978), the Atlantic Falcons professional football team was acquired for about $7,750,000. The purchaser allocated $50,000 of the cost to the National Football League franchise and $7,700,000 to the players' contracts. Under IRS rulings, the franchise was treated as a nonwasting asset, but the players' contracts were wasting assets with an estimated useful life of 5.25 years. The court held that $3,500,000 should be allocated to the players' contracts and $4,250,000 to the franchise. See also Section 1056(d), which now establishes a presumption that no more than 50% of the price of a sports franchise is allocable to players' contracts.

3) The Tax Lawyer's Ethical Obligations

What are the ethical obligations of a lawyer whose client purchases a number of properties for a lump sum? Should the lawyer advise the client to allocate the price among the various properties as accurately as possible? Suppose that the lawyer knows that, in negotiating a price and without taking tax consequences into account, buyer and seller agreed that shorter-lived assets were worth a certain figure. Even if a higher figure would appear reasonable, should a lawyer advise the client not to use it?

B. NOTES AND QUESTIONS ON PREMIUM LEASES

Ordinarily, land is considered a nonwasting asset. When land is purchased, the entire cost is capitalized and deducted only against the amount realized when the land is sold. Suppose, however, that land is purchased subject to an outstanding lease and that rent under the lease is higher than the current market rent for similar land. For example, suppose that the tenant is obligated to pay rent of $1,000 per month but that the current market rent for similar land is only $800 per month. Why will land with such a lease be worth more than the same land either without a lease or subject to a lease where lease rent equals current market rent?

A lease commanding rent higher than current market rent is called a *premium* lease. Land subject to such a lease should sell at a premium, or at a higher price than similar land without a lease or with a lease commanding only market rent. The amount of the premium is the difference between the price of the land with the premium lease and the price of the land without it. For example, if land with a premium lease sells for $1,100,000 and similar land without such a lease for $1 million, then the premium equals the difference, or $100,000.

What happens to the value of the premium lease over time? When the lease term is over, will the premium value be exhausted? If you purchase land subject to a premium lease, should the entire expenditure be allocated to the land and be considered a nonwasting asset? Or should part of the price be allocated to the premium lease and be considered a wasting asset? These questions are addressed in the opinion that follows.

C. COMMISSIONER v. MOORE
207 F.2d 265 (9th Cir. 1953) [Part One]

POPE CIRCUIT JUDGE. . . .

Taxpayer and her mother, Mrs. Mary C. Young, were the owners of the lot of land mentioned, when, on October 1, 1924, they executed a 99 year lease to Sun Realty Company as lessee. . . .

The mother died November 3, 1938, and by will left her half interest in the property to her daughter. The latter, as executrix, filed a Federal Estate Tax return, and by compromise with the Commissioner of Internal Revenue, the value of the estate's half interest in the property was fixed at $1,533,100. The estate tax proceedings made no segregation or itemization of the elements considered in making up that valuation.

There was no testimony (manifestly there could have been none), as to how the agreed figure of $1,533,100 was arrived at. However, expert witnesses for the taxpayer gave their opinions as to the values of the land. . . . They . . . attributed . . . $661,200 to "the favorable lease".

Two expert witnesses were likewise called by the Commissioner. One of them, who testified that a half interest in the land was worth $660,000 and a like interest in the building was worth $873,100 on November 3, 1938, (the two figures totaling the agreed sum of $1,533,100), expressed the opinion that the lease, when made, was at "the going rate"; that it at no time had a "bonus value", and he found no value attributable to a "favorable lease". The other witness, whose values for the half interest were $750,000 for the land and $783,000 for the building, was of the opinion that the lease produced substantially higher rentals than other rentals in the general area, and that the existence of the favorable lease was responsible for half of his $750,000 figure for the land. . . .

We now reach the point urged by taxpayer as petitioner, namely, that she should be permitted to amortize certain values claimed to attach to the lease, (or to take depreciation calculated with respect to those values). Three of the expert witnesses testified that the lease was a very favorable one. As one witness for the Commissioner put it, "the lease was on a basis very substantially above all of the other rentals in the general area". One witness for taxpayer described the lease as "favorable", and the increased values he attached to the property on account of the rentals paid as an "increment in lease, which is a vanishing investment". All of these witnesses were of the opinion that the rents reserved in the lease exceeded those obtainable for the same or similar property in 1938, and that this circumstance added materially to their estimate of the value of the property. . . . [The] witness called by the Commissioner who found added value in the favorable lease, gave it as his opinion that this increased value was properly reflected in the value of the land itself. . . .

In Young v. Commissioner, . . . this court had before it a question arising out of this same lease. As there appears, when this taxpayer and her mother entered into the 99 year lease, there were buildings on the lot which were demolished in order to make way for the new building. The owners also, in securing the lease, incurred expenses for real estate commissions, attorneys' fees, and title certificates. The question was whether taxpayer and her mother could deduct, in that year, the payments made for these expenses plus the full depreciated cost of the buildings demolished. This court affirmed the decision of the Board of Tax Appeals, . . . that these items constituted expenditures "in the acquisition of a capital asset and that any deduction allowable is by way of amortization over the life of the lease." This court stated that solution of the case depended upon "whether, by the acquisition of the long-term lease, the lessors added to their assets, or substituted property for another form of capital assets." In giving an affirmative answer this court said . . .: "On the other hand, where he finds it advantageous to remove substantial buildings in order to secure a lease which will result in his having erected on his property a new building, without money outlay on his part for its construction, and to have assured a large rental income for a long term of years, it would seem just and reasonable that the value of the buildings removed be charged as a contribution to the cost of securing his lease, and as a part of the investment then made for that purpose."

Thus this court there treated this 1924 transaction as the acquisition of a separate asset, apart from the land. The plan of amortization deductions there approved has been followed from that day down to and including the years here in controversy. (The record discloses that the Commissioner has allowed deductions for amortization of the items detailed in that former case from 1924 to 1945.) We perceive no reason why that lease should not be so regarded as a separate asset at this time.

Now, if we were dealing with a taxpayer who, on November 3, 1938, purchased a half interest in the whole property for $1,533,100, and if it appeared that at that time the rents being paid were in excess of the fair market rentals of the property, and if the price paid took this latter fact into consideration, it must have included a bonus or premium for the acquisition of the "favorable" features of the lease. Just as the benefits from the amounts representing demolition of the building and real estate commissions will have come to an end at the termination of the lease, so it may be possible to prove that the higher rents secured through the premium paid by such a purchaser would be exhausted and terminated when the lease ends, or when the 1938 rate of rental comes to an end. The lease, or rather the portion thereof providing the above-normal rents, is an intangible asset with a definitely limited life. . . . In our hypothetical case of a 1938 purchaser of this half interest, if the premium paid on account of the higher rents to be received under the lease may not be amortized by deductions over the period of the lease, his original investment will not be replaced as the Code contemplates. . . .

Here, of course, taxpayer is not a purchaser, but an heir. But the effect of Sec. [1014(a)(1)] is to put the heir in the same position as if he were a purchaser....

In the supposititious case of the purchaser of a half interest for $1,533,100, if taxpayer could prove the extent to which the lease was "favorable", or what part of the rents are "above normal", it should be feasible to ascertain the amount of the purchase price which represented a premium for the favorable aspects of the lease. Such would be no more difficult than the ascertainment of the proper basis for depreciation in the ordinary case where a purchaser buys a lot with a building thereon, all for a lump sum. A similar determination of an appropriate portion of the stipulated estate tax appraisal sum, is within the special competence of the Tax Court....

Thus we hold that if the lease was one whose favorable rentals are subject to ultimate exhaustion, that portion of the $1,533,100 attributable to what we here call, for want of a better term, its "premium" value, should be amortized through annual deductions allowable to the lessor.

Respecting the period of such amortization, our attention is called to the fact that Sunland Investment Company had succeeded Sun Realty Company as lessee prior to 1938. It may assign the lease without the consent of the lessor, and be relieved of further liability, and its assignee may do likewise. It is argued that at the end of 1960, when the sublease to Barker Bros. will terminate, the latter will have no reason to renew its lease, and Sunland will then withdraw and escape further obligation under the lease. Thus it is asserted that the useful life of the lease will end in 1960. We think we are not warranted in indulging in speculation that this will occur, and that the amortization here contemplated must be based on the term of the lease itself.

In theory, the lease was, in 1938, a favorable one if it then provided greater rentals than could have been obtained under a lease negotiated at that time. Whether this particular lease measured up to this test is a question of fact for the Tax Court to determine.

If we are considering what our hypothetical purchaser would offer, by way of bonus or premium, for the favorable lease, upon a purchase of the property in 1938, it would be fair to assume that, if he could arrive at the 1938 fair market rental value of the land he could calculate his premium by comparing the capitalized value of the rentals obtainable on a 1938 lease and payable over the remaining 85 years to 2023, with the capitalized value or the rentals of the existing lease, for the same period. Plainly reliable testimony as to what rents a similar lease would command if negotiated in 1938 may be hard to come by in the absence of a showing that other similar leases were made at or about that time.[1] On the other hand, the Tax Court

---

1. Thus the witness who found no evidence of the lease being "favorable", or that the rentals were above current market, testified: "There is no other piece of property in the metropolitan area that is comparable to that piece of property. It was the one large holding, you might say, that was available in the early 20s for development. It was in one ownership and at that time it had 300 and some feet of frontage upon Seventh Street, which was deemed the best street available for commercial development.... You can get on any streetcar traveling on Seventh Street and get to any portion of Los Angeles by transfer. That was true of Broadway. They are the only two streets in the town that could be done. Seventh Street comes as near traversing the center of the City of Los Angeles as any street did in town.... So Seventh

may arrive at the conclusion that the 1938 market value of the land would itself sufficiently reflect the present worth of the rentals normally to be expected to be obtainable from the land itself, by way of ground rents. Or, to put it another way, the possible prospective purchasers, whose opinions would have much to do with establishing market value, would no doubt arrive at those opinions by capitalizing the possible rentals. Should this be found to be a conclusion justified by the facts, the "premium", or sum representing the favorable features of the lease might be found to be the difference between the value of the land and the capitalized value of the rents reasonably to be expected under the lease.

Again the intangible property which we here consider must be found to be subject to ultimate exhaustion, if depreciation or amortization is to be allowed. When physical property is involved, such as a building, we know of a certainty that time and the elements will ultimately wear it away. In the case of the expenses, and the demolition costs which taxpayer and her mother incurred in order to procure this lease, we know that such amounts are gone and will not be recovered. What we are here considering, as a possible item of property for depreciation, is not the lease, as such, but rather the favorable aspects or part of the lease. If the terms of the lease are such that it could be renewed at any time on the same terms, there will be no exhaustion, or wasting, or wear and tear, and no occasion for depreciation or amortization. . . .

If we were the Tax Court we could proceed to put these difficulties of proof to the test by permitting the taxpayer, and the Commissioner, to submit such proof as they were able to adduce. If the taxpayer were unable to sustain her burden of proof as to what deductions she should be allowed, the judgment required would be plain. But since we are not the triers of the facts, we must drop these questions into the lap of the Tax Court. Possibly the Tax Court may be warranted in determining that there has been a failure of proof. On the other hand, it may find that although some speculation is involved, nevertheless some amount may be properly allocated as the value of that portion of the lease which represents its favorable features, or which is attributable to the excess of the actual rentals over those obtainable on a 1938 letting. That such allocations are somewhat speculative does not prevent their being made. . . . As stated in Bryant v. Commissioner, . . . : "In such cases though it be impossible to reach a certain conclusion, it has been several times held that the Board should exercise a sound judgment, though taking all chances against the taxpayer. . . . We

---

Street was the natural street to supplement Broadway in the commercial area, and this property, with this lease on it, and at the time the lease was made, it was made at the going rentals for the properties of that type. . . .

"Q. You heard the statements of estimates of land and building values given by Mr. Saint and Mr. Puffer, in which they testified to a certain value of the land and the building and an additional value due to the favorable lease. Do you remember that? A. Yes, sir.

"Q. Do you have an opinion as to whether or not there is any additional value attributable to that property due to the lease? A. I have an opinion, yes, sir.

"Q. What is your opinion? A. That there is no separate value. In my opinion, the value of that property is entirely in the ground, the owner of the fee, and that value is based upon the land and the improvement. That lease, at the time it was made, was the going rate. In other words, at no time, in my opinion, has that lease ever had a bonus value."

are quite aware that the result will be speculative, but the Treasury will be protected and some relief is juster than the denial of all." . . .

D. NOTES AND QUESTIONS

1) Nontax Aspects

Why did the lease in this case have a premium value? When the lease was signed, the lease rent presumably equaled current market rent. What later events probably caused the lease rent to become a premium rent? If the tenant under the lease was insolvent or bankrupt, would the lease still command a premium value? Compare *Moore* with *Bruun* (Chapter 19).

2) Can the Original Landlord Amortize the Value of a Premium Lease?

The word *amortize* has nothing to do with love or neckwear. It is roughly synonymous with depreciate and usually (but not always) connotes deductions for the cost of an *intangible* asset, taken in even amounts over the asset's useful life.

The taxpayer in *Moore* sought to amortize the value of the premium lease with respect to the half interest in the land that she inherited. But she made no attempt to amortize the premium value with respect to the half interest that she owned when the lease was signed. Why not? See Section 167(g). How does an original landlord differ from the taxpayer who purchases the land subject to a premium lease?

3) Can the Heir of the Original Landlord Amortize the Value of a Premium Lease?

How could the taxpayer justify an amortization deduction for the premium lease on the inherited interest when she paid nothing for it? What was the effect of the basis rule of Section 1014(a)? Would she have been able to claim an amortization deduction if she had acquired the same interest by inter vivos gift? See Section 1015(a).

4) Determining the Value of a Premium Lease

Why did the IRS resist an amortization deduction for the inherited interest in the premium lease? Because the premium lease was an intangible asset? Was there a *Welch* problem, that is, would the taxpayer have found it difficult to establish that the intangible asset had a limited life under Reg. § 1.167(a)-3?

How is a value assigned to a premium lease under Section 1014(a)? One possibility is to estimate the current market rent. The difference between this amount and the lease rent is the extra amount the landlord is entitled to receive. That amount should then be discounted to present value for the remaining term of the lease. For example, suppose that current market rent would be $80,000 per year and that the lease provides for $105,000 a year. If the remaining lease term is five years, the premium equals $25,000 a year for five years, discounted to present value. At an interest rate of 8%, how much is the premium? Consult the present value table in Chapter 12.

Note that two different subjective estimates are required in order to appraise the value of the inherited interest in a premium lease: (a) the current market rent for the land and (b) the appropriate interest rate. The IRS may have resisted amortization of the premium lease in *Moore* because of this need to rely on subjective estimates and because of the absence of any objective standard as a check against taxpayer abuse.

If property is acquired by purchase rather than inheritance, can the value of a premium lease (if any) be objectively determined or are subjective estimates still required? Is the danger of taxpayer abuse as great?

5) The Stakes in *Moore*

Suppose that land is purchased subject to a ten-year lease for $1,100,000 and that the purchaser allocates $100,000 of the price to the premium value of the lease. What is the effect of amortizing the lease premium on (a) the taxpayer's ordinary income over the next ten years and (b) the taxpayer's gain when the land is sold? Don't forget to include the effects of Section 1016(a)(2)(A). Why is there an incentive for the seller to overallocate the purchase price to the premium lease and underallocate it to the land?

How is this analogous to the effect of an incentive stock option from the employee's perspective? Recall that an incentive stock option affects only the taxation of the spread—that is, the difference between the market value of the stock on the option's exercise and the strike price (Chapter 11).

Why won't the seller of land with a premium lease be affected by the allocation of the purchase price between the land and the lease? (See *Hort*, discussed in Chapter 52.) How does the effect on the seller *differ* from the effect of an incentive stock option on the issuing corporation?

Overall, what are the net tax consequences to both parties combined if seller and buyer agree to overallocate the purchase price to a premium lease? How does this net effect on both differ from the net effect of using incentive stock options (Chapter 11)?

6) Applying the Capitalization Requirement to a Demolished Building

Suppose you buy land with a fifty-year-old office building in 1975. Ten years later, you demolish the existing building and construct a modern facility. How should the demolition of the old building be treated? As a sale? As a like-kind exchange for the new building? As part of the cost of the land? What are the different tax consequences of each of these approaches if the adjusted basis of the old building when it is demolished is $600,000? Suppose an appraiser testifies that the land is worth more vacant than with the old building? Does that help decide how demolition should be treated? See Section 280B.

In Young v. Commissioner, cited in *Moore,* the taxpayer demolished an existing building in order to secure the agreement of tenants to lease the land for ninety-nine years. The issue was whether the taxpayer was entitled to amortize the building's adjusted basis over the lease term. What does *Moore* say about this question? Does Section 280B reach the wrong result when an existing building is torn down in order to induce a tenant to lease a vacant lot, as in *Young*? In that event, should the demolition costs be viewed as a cost of the lease to be amortized over its life?

E. NOTES AND QUESTIONS ON PREMIUM BONDS

1) What Is a Bond?

A bond is a legal document that records the borrowing of funds by a debtor from a creditor. How does a bond differ from other loan transactions? The bond permits the debtor, usually a corporation or a government, to borrow funds *in one transaction* from a large number of separate lenders, rather than from a single lender. For example, suppose that AT&T wishes to borrow $100 million. It might obtain a loan from a single lender, such as a bank, insurance company, or pension fund. Alternatively, it might borrow a relatively small amount from each of tens of thousands of investors, typically individuals rather than institutions, by selling $100 million worth of AT&T bonds.

Bonds are usually issued in denominations (referred to as *principal amounts*) of $1,000. The bond itself consists of promises by the debtor to make payments to the creditor. There are two kinds of promises: first, a promise to pay *interest,* which is *stated* as a percentage of the principal amount (and thus referred to as *stated interest*); and, second, a promise to pay back the principal amount, due at a specified future time or *maturity date.* For example, suppose that in 1989, AT&T issues a bond promising to pay 10% annual interest and principal amount of $1,000 at maturity, five years from the issue date. Each year until maturity, AT&T must pay the stated annual interest of 10% of the principal amount, or $100 a year. In addition, AT&T is obligated to pay the bondholder the $1,000 principal amount in 1994.

2) The Relationship Between the Principal Amount and the Market Value

What determines the market value of bonds? A bond consists of the right to receive stated interest plus principal amount in the future. The market value of a bond is simply the sum of each of these future amounts discounted to present value. For example, the market value of the AT&T bond in the example above is the present value of the right to $100 a year for five years plus the right to $1,000 in five years. The discount rate used to calculate present value should equal the current market rate of interest for that particular kind of bond. What is the present value of the AT&T bond when the market rate of interest is 10%? When it is 8%? Consult the present value table in Chapter 12. Your answers should correspond to Table 34–1.

TABLE 34-1. CALCULATING THE MARKET VALUE OF A 5 YEAR $1,000 BOND, WITH 10% STATED INTEREST, GIVEN VARYING MARKET INTEREST RATES OF 10% AND OF 8%

Year	Payments of Interest and Principal	PV @ 10%	PV @ 8%
1	100	91	93
2	100	83	86
3	100	75	79
4	100	68	73
5	100	62	68
5	1000	621	681
Total	1500	1000	1080

Table 34–1 illustrates two propositions. First, if the stated interest on the bond *equals* the market rate of interest, then the market value of the bond *equals* the principal amount. Second, if the stated interest is *greater* than the market rate of interest, then the market value of the bond is *greater* than the principal amount.

In the second case, when the stated interest exceeds the market rate, the difference between the market value and principal amount is called a *premium*. What does the premium represent? What happens to the value of the premium over the term of the bond? When the bond is redeemed at maturity, has the premium value been exhausted?

3) The Economic Analogy Between Leases and Bonds

A lease arises when real estate is rented for a period of years at a stated rent. A bond arises when cash is loaned for a period of years at stated interest. In each instance, the owner conveys the use of an asset during a stated period for a stated fee. Just as a lease will have a premium value whenever the lease rent is greater than the market rent, a bond will have a premium value whenever the stated interest is greater than the market rate of interest. However, while the amount of a lease premium can be determined only by subjective appraisals, the amount of a bond premium can be objectively measured. How?

4) Amortizing the Value of a Bond Premium

Bonds are ordinarily considered nonwasting assets, because when you buy a bond, you expect to be repaid the full principal amount of your investment at maturity, without any diminution or waste. Thus, when a bond is purchased, the cost is capitalized and deducted only when the bond is sold or redeemed at maturity.

The Code, however, authorizes treatment of a bond premium as a wasting asset. Under Section 171(a)(1), the premium may be amortized over the term of the bond. Also, note that Section 1016(a)(2)(A) requires that the bond's basis be reduced to reflect the amortizable bond premium. Why?

5) Premiums on Tax-exempt Bonds

Suppose that a tax-exempt bond with a $1,000 principal amount sells for $1,100. Can you amortize the $100 premium over the life of the bond? See Section 171(a)(2). Why is a basis adjustment nonetheless required under Section 1016(a)(5)? Does this constitute adopting Professor Epstein's scheme for adjusting the basis of personal consumption property (see Chapter 30)?

F. COMMISSIONER v. MOORE
207 F.2d 265 (9th Cir. 1953) [Part Two]

POPE, CIRCUIT JUDGE.

... The lease required the lessee ... to construct at its own expense a new building thereon to cost not less than $2,000,000. ... The building called for in the original lease was completed January 1, 1926. ...

[The Tax Court upheld] taxpayer's claim to an allowance by way of depreciation on account of the building. ... After referring to the proposition that during the life of taxpayer's mother, neither of the lessors could deduct depreciation "for the reason that (they had) no investment or cost therein which is subject to exhaustion", the court expressed its ruling as to the half interest which taxpayer inherited from her mother by quoting from its decision in the Currier case as follows: "The basis of inherited property is accordingly not cost ... and to say that a property cost the taxpayer nothing makes no contribution to the solution of the present question. As opposed to cost, the basis of property acquired by devise is categorically fixed by statute as fair market value on the date of acquisition. Internal Revenue Code, sec. [1014(a)(1)]. Hence, if we can discover the fair market value of the property in question at the date of decedent's death ... (or the figure at which it was returned for estate tax purposes, which is recognized as the equivalent . . .), the upshot would ordinarily be its basis for depreciation in petitioner's hands, without any reference to its 'cost'. Having acquired a basis by the incident of the estate tax, the gradually disappearing value of a wasting asset can not be replaced except by periodic depreciation adjustments." Holding that the taxpayer "will suffer some loss due to depreciation", the court found that the fair market value of taxpayer's one-half of the building at the date of the mother's death, November 3, 1938, was $800,000, and that it had a 50 year life.

In attacking these conclusions the Commissioner says that they overlook important facts bearing on the real interest of the taxpayer. He points to the fact that because of the long term lease, taxpayer's interest in the building gives her no more than the prospect of possessing it in the year 2023, long after the building's useful life will have terminated and its value have been exhausted. This, says the Commissioner, is an interest "completely devoid of value". He argues that the essential error in the Tax Court's decision is that it arrived at a conclusion as to depreciable values in complete disregard of the lease, with its 99 year term extending beyond the useful life of the building.

We think the Commissioner's point is well taken. True it is that Internal Revenue Code, sec. [1014(a)(1)] provides: "If the property was acquired by bequest, devise, or inheritance . . . the basis shall be the fair market value of such property at the time of such acquisition." But "such property" is not the steel frame, brick and terra cotta loft and store building on the corner of Figueroa, Seventh and Flower Streets in the City of Los Angeles,—it is the taxpayer's *interest* in that property. And her interest is a limited one, not only because it is a fractional part, but also because it is subject to the lease. As the Tax Court said, dealing with another point in this case: "What petitioner inherited from her mother was an undivided half interest in the land under the Barker Bros. building *and a reversionary interest in the building.*" (Emphasis added.)

When it became necessary to appraise, for purposes of the Federal Estate Tax, the bundle of rights which passed to taxpayer from her mother's estate, it is plain that first to receive attention would be the interest in the fee, and the right to the rents reserved in the lease, which right to rents grew out of the ownership of the land. If there was any other right in this bundle, it was the right to possess the building in the year 2023. What would have been the fair market value of that right on November 3, 1938? No testimony before the Tax Court touched this question.

It is not the physical property itself, nor the title thereto, which alone entitles the owner to claim depreciation. The statutory allowance is available to him whose interest in the wasting asset is such that he would suffer an economic loss resulting from the deterioration and physical exhaustion as it takes place. Thus the lessee, obligated to make improvements, may recover his capital outlay by deductions for depreciation notwithstanding title to the improvements may be in the lessor. . . . And also, where the lessor erects the improvements, (and has title to them), but where the lessee undertakes to make good the physical exhaustion as it takes place, the lessor may not make such a deduction. . . . Here, so far as economic loss is concerned, taxpayer's interest in the building at the end of the 50 year life on November 3, 1988, will be fully as valuable as her interest therein on November 3, 1938. We think the Commissioner is right in his statement that "so far as the rights reserved by the lessors were concerned, the existence of the building and its depreciation, were matters of economic indifference. Their right to receive the ground rentals and to have possession of the property at a future time when the building would no longer possess value, was not diminished by the physical exhaustion of the building."

The Tax Court properly noted that section [1014(a)(1)] would operate to supply, for an inherited half interest, a "basis" which had theretofore not existed, and which continued to be nonexistent with respect to taxpayer's original half interest. But a "basis" is only one of the factors which must exist before depreciation may be claimed. More important is the necessity of a "depreciable interest" in exhausting and deteriorating property. If the taxpayer's interest is of such character that it is not affected by the deterioration, then it is not of a depreciable nature....

Here, the Tax Court, after referring to the provisions of Sec. [1014(a)(1)], and noting the acquisition of a "basis", assumed that this was an end of the matter. It said, in closing the foregoing quotation from the *Currier* case: "Having acquired a basis by the incident of the estate tax, the gradually disappearing value of a wasting asset can not be replaced except by periodic depreciation adjustment." But Sec. [1014(a)(1)], while providing a "basis". does not create a depreciable interest where none would otherwise exist.

The proof of values offered on behalf of the taxpayer ignored the difference between a building unaffected by a lease, and a building subject to a lease. Thus one of taxpayer's experts arrived at his testimony of value of the building by computing its reproduction cost as of November 3, 1938, then subtracting depreciation from the date of construction, and concluded with a figure of $802,000 as his value for the half interest....

It is thus apparent that the testimony of the witnesses, and the findings of the Tax Court, based upon the value of the building alone, viewed as a physical structure, do not reflect the taxpayer's true interest in that building, as that interest is, in fact, affected by a lease whose term exceeds the useful life of the building.

This brings us to the question as to whether that interest has a value, and if so, how it should be ascertained. The Commissioner says that necessarily the value is zero; hence, that there is no occasion for remanding the case for further findings. He says this must be true, first, because the ground rent which arises out of the taxpayer's ownership of the land, will come in forever; hence taxpayer must be a stranger to any economic loss as the building wears out. Also, he argues, since taxpayer could not conceivably sell her interest in the building apart from the land or the rentals, the value of her interest is nothing. We see no answer to this argument. And we suggest this further consideration that leads to the same result: Since, as above stated, taxpayer's interest in the building at the end of the 50 year life will be fully as valuable as her interest therein on November 3, 1938, we have no such wasting asset as is required for any depreciation.

An interesting sidelight upon the probable intent of the Code provisions in this situation is furnished by the rule relating to the right of the tenant to claim depreciation upon this building.... The right of the lessee to make such a deduction was upheld in Duffy v. Central R. Co.... A construction of the law to permit not only the lessee (who has a real economic interest) but also the taxpayer here to take depreciation on the same building would be somewhat anomalous....

G) NOTES AND QUESTIONS

1) Legal Title versus Depreciable Interest

Ordinarily, it is the owner of property who is entitled to depreciation deductions. The taxpayer in *Moore* appears to have had legal title to the building—that is, to have been the owner—yet is not allowed the depreciation. Why not? Why is the tenant, who does not hold legal title, allowed to deduct the depreciation? The court notes that allowing the landlord to depreciate the building at the same time as the tenant would be "anomalous." Why should only one taxpayer be allowed to depreciate the building at any time?

2) Tenant Improvements as Rent

Suppose that a tenant constructs a building, which the lease designates as "rent in kind." Should the landlord be *required* to report the entire value as income but *allowed* to depreciate the building's value? May the tenant deduct the value of the building as rent? If yes, should the tenant be required to capitalize the rent and deduct it ratably over some period? See *Idaho Power* (Chapter 32). If the tenant is required to capitalize the rent, should the landlord be allowed to report the rent as income over the same period, rather than all at once in the year when the building is constructed?

3) Sale and Leaseback of Tenant Improvements

Suppose that the tenant constructs a building, sells it to the landlord, and leases it back for thirty years. Assume that the landlord borrows 100% of the purchase price from the tenant, to be repaid over the lease term, and that each repayment on the loan exactly equals rent due under the lease for the same period. Since each period's rent equals each period's loan repayment, no money need ever change hands. Assuming the purchase price equals construction cost, the tenant reports no gain on the sale of the building.

Is the landlord entitled to deduct depreciation for the building plus interest on the loan? Will the tenant be entitled to deduct rent but also be required to report interest income? See Chapters 38–41.

Chapter 35

DEPRECIATION

A. INTRODUCTORY NOTES AND QUESTIONS

1) What Is a Depreciable Asset?

An asset is *depreciable* if it is expected (a) to produce income over a period of more than one year *and* (b) to wear out within some ascertainable period of time.

2) What Is a Depreciation Schedule?

A depreciation schedule shows how the cost of a depreciable asset is to be allocated over time. Any depreciation schedule has two critical variables. First, the Period Of Cost Recovery (POCR) designates the number of years over which the cost must be allocated. Second, the Method Of Cost Recovery (MOCR) determines how the cost is to be allocated among the years. The Code provides for two kinds of MOCRs. The straight-line method (SLM) allows even (or uniform) deductions each year of the POCR. Accelerated methods (AM) schedule larger deductions in early years and smaller deduction in later years of the POCR.

3) What Is at Stake?

In general, the particular depreciation schedule assigned to an asset does not affect either total deductions or total income over the asset's life. To illustrate, assume that a machine is purchased on January 1, 1980 for $3,000 and is expected to generate $1,300 in revenues each year for three years. Assume further that after three years the machine will be exhausted and have zero salvage or scrap value. Over its three-year life, the machine produces $3,900 in revenues, at a cost of $3,000, so that net income is $900.

Table 35–1 shows depreciation schedules for the machine using different POCRs and MOCRs. The center column assumes that the POCR is three years and that the MOCR is the straight-line method. With depreciation evenly spread over three years, the cost may be deducted at a rate of $1,000 per year. The left-hand column shows the schedule when the POCR is shortened to two years, but the MOCR is held constant. With depreciation evenly spread over two years, the cost may be deducted at a rate of $1,500 a year. In the right-hand column, the POCR remains at three years, but the MOCR is an accelerated method. With this particular accelerated method, about 67% of the cost is deducted in the first year, 23% in the second year, and 10% in the third year. Notice that either a shorter POCR or more accelerated MOCR produces faster deductions but does not affect the total deductions allowed over time.

TABLE 35-1. SCHEDULE OF DEPRECIATION DEDUCTIONS

	2 Years-SLM	3 Years-SLM	3 Years-AM
1	−1500	−1000	−2000
2	−1500	−1000	−700
3	—	−1000	−300
Total	−3000	−3000	−3000

Table 35–2 illustrates the effect of different depreciation schedules on taxable income. The income figure for each year is equal to annual revenues of $1,300 less allowable depreciation deductions. In the center column, when the POCR is three years and the MOCR is the straight-line method, income from the asset is $300 each year. In the left-hand column, with a shorter POCR, income is understated initially during the three-year period but overstated later during the period. In the right-hand column, with a more accelerated MOCR, the same pattern of initial understatement of income and later overstatement occurs.

Income not reported in the early years (as compared to three-year depreciation using the SLM) is reported in later years. The effect of speeding up depreciation, therefore, is not exclusion but, rather, deferral. Total income is *not* affected but the time for reporting income is.

Also, notice that with either of the faster depreciation schedules, early deductions more than offset revenues, and the machine initially *appears* to operate at a loss. This loss can be used to offset other income, illustrating that rapid depreciation is a basic ingredient in many tax shelters.

TABLE 35-2. TAXABLE INCOME = $1,300 MINUS DEPRECIATION

	2 Years-SLM	3 Years-SLM	3 Years-AM
1	−200	+300	−700
2	−200	+300	+600
3	+1300	+300	+1000
Total	+900	+900	+900

Table 35–3 illustrates the *change* in annual reported income when either of the faster depreciation schedules is used instead of the SLM over three years. In the left-hand column, when the POCR is shortened to two years, taxable income is $500 less during years 1 and 2 but $1,000 more in year 3. In the right-hand column, when the MOCR is accelerated, taxable income is $1,000 less in year 1 but $300 more in year 2 and $700 more in year 3.

TABLE 35-3. CHANGE IN TAXABLE INCOME FROM USING FASTER DEPRECIATION

	2 Years-SLM	3 Years-SLM	3 Years-AM
1	−500		−1000
2	−500		+300
3	+1000		+700
Total	zero		zero

Table 35–4 shows how faster depreciation affects the taxes owed by a 50% bracket taxpayer. In the left-hand column, when the POCR is shortened to two years, taxes are reduced by $250 in years 1 and 2 but increased by $500 in year 3. In the right-hand column, when the MOCR is accelerated, taxes are $500 less in year 1 but $150 more in year 2 and $350 more in year 3.

TABLE 35-4. CHANGE IN TAXES OWED FROM USING FASTER DEPRECIATION

	2 Years-SLM	3 Years-SLM	3 Years-AM
1	−250		−500
2	−250		+150
3	+500		+350
Total	zero		zero

To compare the advantage of paying less early on with the disadvantage of paying more later, the future amounts must be discounted to present value. The net tax benefit equals the present value of the tax saving minus the present value of the tax detriment.

Assuming an interest rate of 8%, shortening the POCR to two years saves $250 in the first year (with a present value of $231), plus $250 in the second year ($214 present value), but costs $500 in the third year ($397 present value). The net tax benefit is $231, plus $214, minus $397, which equals $48. Using a more accelerated method saves $500 in the first year ($463 present value) but costs $150 in the second year ($129 present value) and $350 in the third year ($278 present value). The net tax benefit is $463, minus $129, minus $278, which equals $56.

What is the effect of faster depreciation methods on aggregate tax revenues, taking account of all capital expenditures in the national economy? Recall the "steady state" model discussed in *Encyclopaedia Brittanica* (Chapter 33). If the level of capital expenditures is constant, faster and slower cost recovery methods produce the same result after a certain number of years. However, the economy as a whole is generally growing, and the amount of capital expenditures by business is increasing. Therefore, it is the "expanding state" model (also discussed in Chapter 33), in which the gap between faster and slower cost recovery continually widens, that mirrors the effect of permitting faster depreciation schedules. When Congress mandated radically shorter POCRs for depreciable assets as part of the 1981 Tax Act, the revenue cost was estimated at hundreds of billions of dollars.

4) Economic Depreciation

If the *only* objective is the accurate determination of income, how should depreciation deductions be scheduled? The answer is that depreciation schedules should correspond as closely as possible to *economic depreciation*—the decline in the market value of an asset during the year.

Suppose that an asset produces the same level of revenues each year (for example, the machine in the example above that produces $1,300 a year for three years). Intuitively, one might suppose that, if revenues are level, then level deductions under the SLM accurately reflect real economic wear and tear. As a matter of economics, however, this intuition turns out to be wrong. If revenues are level, then economic depreciation requires smaller deductions in early years and larger deductions in later years. Compared to economic depreciation, in other words, even the SLM turns out to be accelerated.

To understand why economic depreciation may correspond to a schedule of uneven deductions, smaller in early years and larger in later years, the reader needs to do a present value analysis of the revenues generated by an asset. Take the example of the machine costing $3,000 and generating revenues of $1,300 a year. When acquired, the machine's value equals the right to revenues at the end of each period or $1,300 in one year, plus $1,300 in two years, plus $1,300 in three years. At the beginning of the second year, the value equals the right to $1,300 in one year and $1,300 in two years. At the beginning of the third year, the value equals the right to only the remaining $1,300 in one year. At the end of the third year, the asset is exhausted and its value is zero. These figures are indicated in Table 35–5.

TABLE 35-5. VALUE AT BEGINNING OF EACH PERIOD

PV = Present Value

Start of Year 1—PV of $1,300 in one year, plus
PV of $1,300 in two years, plus
PV of $1,300 in three years.

Start of Year 2—PV of $1,300 in one year, plus
PV of $1,300 in two years.

Start of Year 3—PV of $1,300 in one year.

Start of Year 4—ZERO

Economic depreciation (the decline in value each year) is determined by subtracting from the value at the beginning of each period, the value at the start of the *next* period. The results are listed in Table 35–6. Because of the time value of money, economic depreciation is smallest in year 1, larger in year 2, and largest in year 3. This follows from the fact that the more distant in time a future amount, the lower its present value. The reading that follows provides additional examples to illustrate the principle that economic depreciation is slower than SLM depreciation.

TABLE 35-6. ECONOMIC DEPRECIATION

Year 1—PV of $1,300 in three years

Year 2—PV of $1,300 in two years

Year 3—PV of $1,300 in one year

B. SINKING FUND METHOD DEPRECIATION

M. Chirelstein, Federal Income Taxation 133–135 (1985)

Presumably the purpose of tax or accounting depreciation (putting fiscal policy aims aside) is to reflect the *annual loss in value* of the taxpayer's depreciable assets that results from their use in the taxpayer's business. The question which the depreciation allowance *ought* to answer is: how much less are such assets worth at the end of the year than they were at the beginning? The taxpayer's "true" annual income, then, is his gross income less the sum of (a) his current expenses plus (b) the decline for the year in the economic value of his capital equipment.

In our illustration..., [a] $4,000 machine is expected to generate income (after current maintenance expenses) of $1,200 a year for 5 years.

Ch. 35 Depreciation

The implied before-tax rate of return on the taxpayer's investment is a little more than 15%; that is, $1,200 a year for 5 years discounted at a rate of 15-plus% equals $4,000. If we apply this discount rate to each expected payment in turn, the schedule of present values looks roughly like this:

Year:	1	2	3	4	5	Totals
Expected receipt	$1,200	$1,200	$1,200	$1,200	$1,200	$6,000
Present value	$1,045	$ 905	$ 790	$ 687	$ 573	$4,000

The present value of all five payments must of course add up to $4,000, the original cost of the equipment.

How does this schedule look after the first year of use has passed? The second, the third, etc.? As each year of useful life expires the expected income stream becomes shorter and the present value of the sum of all remaining payments necessarily declines. There is just that much less to anticipate in the way of future returns. The taxpayer's economic loss from the year's operations—his annual cost—is measured by the decline in the present value of anticipated receipts which takes place between the beginning and the end of the taxable year. In effect, the difference between the value of the future income stream on January 1 and its value on December 31 represents the cost of using the machine for the year in question. If the object of the depreciation allowance is to reduce gross income by the true cost of operations, then the annual allowance should be no more or less than that amount.

Here is a schedule of the yearly decline in the present value of the taxpayer's investment:

	Present Value of Investment	\multicolumn{5}{c}{Present Value of Remaining Payments}	Annual Loss in Present Value
		1	2	3	4	5	
Start of Year 1	$4,000	$1,045	905	790	687	573	
End of Year 1	3,427		1,045	905	790	687	$ 573
End of Year 2	2,740			1,045	905	790	687
End of Year 3	1,950				1,045	905	790
End of Year 4	1,045					1,045	905
End of Year 5	–0–						1,045
						Total:	$4,000

The last column shows the true measure of economic cost from year to year and indicates that the correct apportionment method is one which *starts low and rises:* $573 in Year 1, then $687, $790, $905, and finally $1,045 in Year 5. The resulting schedule of taxable income, of course, is the inverse: $627 of taxable income in Year 1, $513 in Year 2, $410 in Year 3, $295 in Year 4 and finally $155 in Year 5. Income is thus *higher* in the earlier years than in the later.

This corrected depreciation method—sometimes called "sinking-fund" depreciation—looks peculiar and unfamiliar at first glance. Really, however, it is nothing more than the ordinary and conventional method by which a bank amortizes the principal amount of a mortgage loan. . . . [A]nyone who has ever paid off a home mortgage knows that principal payments are small in the early years and large in the later ones, with interest (income) being correspondingly greater in the beginning and smaller at the end. The machine-owner above occupies essentially the same status as a mortgage-lender: both invest their capital in the expectation of a future periodic return. Hence if the depreciation allowance were designed to produce an accurate measure of taxable income, the same cost-recovery procedure would seem to be appropriate for each.

It must be admitted, on the other hand, that the sinking-fund depreciation method is a great deal easier to apply in the case of mortgages, leases and other property whose future yield is fixed by contract than it is for tangible assets like machines. The income from a mortgage or a lease can be determined without engaging in predictions and projections which depend entirely on future events. By contrast, the cash-flow to be derived from the operation of a tangible asset is not a fixed quantity and would have to be estimated. Since such estimates are very hard to make, it is understandable why the sinking-fund method has never been used for machinery, equipment and other tangibles. In principle, nevertheless, sinking-fund is the *only* proper method of apportioning the taxpayer's capital investment in accordance with the economic cost of use. By comparison, even the straight-line method of depreciation turns out to be accelerated.

C. DEPRECIATION METHODS AND RATES

B. Bittker, Federal Taxation Of Income, Estates and Gifts, pp. 23–51 to 23–52 and 23–54 to 23–57 (1981)

From 1913 to 1954 the federal revenue acts permitted taxpayers to deduct "a reasonable allowance" for exhaustion, wear and tear, and obsolescence of depreciable assets without describing or listing any specific depreciation methods, and the regulations have long provided that the proper allowance is

> that amount which should be set aside for the taxable year in accordance with a reasonably consistent plan (not necessarily at a uniform rate), so that the aggregate of the amounts set aside, plus the salvage value, will, at the end of the estimated useful life of the depreciable property, equal the cost or other basis of the property. . . .

During these formative years, the straight-line method of computing the "reasonable allowance" allowed by Congress was almost universally used, except by public utilities, railroads, investors in rental real estate, and taxpayers in a few other industries.

The straight-line method's popularity was due in large part to its simplicity: The asset's cost (or other basis), less the estimated salvage value (if any), is divided by its estimated useful life in years, and the resulting amount is the annual deduction. For example, if an asset costs $10,000, has an estimated salvage value of $2,000, and is expected to last for ten years, the annual deduction is $800 (i.e., $8,000/10). Expressed as a rate of depreciation, the annual deduction is 10 percent of the amount to be depreciated. Because of its simplicity, the straight-line method is easily understood by the layman; and the fact that the same amount is deducted every year gives it an aura of fairness. For these reasons, it came to be regarded as the normal depreciation method, the reasonableness of which was self-evident. . . .

. . . [L]egislative deference to the straight-line method, coupled with its widespread use in practice, have given it an aura of normality and accuracy that, when subjected to financial analysis, proves to be insubstantial. Briefly stated, the straight-line method's deficiency lies in its failure to take account of the time value of money. By allocating an equal fraction of the aggregate amount to be depreciated to each year of the asset's useful life, it disregards the fact that each year's deduction represents a tax-free recovery of a portion of the taxpayer's original investment, so that the unrecovered investment continually declines.

For example, if a depreciable asset costing $2,487 will produce $1,000 of income (before deducting depreciation) at the end of each year during a three-year useful life and will have no salvage value, the straight-line method treats $829 of each year's receipts as depreciation ($2,487/3) and $171 as net income. For the first year this implies a return of 6.9 percent on the taxpayer's investment of $2,487 (i.e., $171/$2,487). For the second year the implied rate of return rises to 10.3 percent (i.e., $171/1,658), since the taxpayer recovered $829 of his original investment at the end of the first year and hence had a remaining investment of only $1,658 ($2,487 − $829) during the second year. This phenomenon of a rising rate of return is accentuated in the third year, when the remaining investment is only $829 ($1,658 − $829), with the result that the implied rate of return is 20.6 percent ($171/$829). The example used to illustrate this point presupposes that the pre-depreciation income from the depreciable asset is constant for the hypothesized three-year period; but the same principle applies if a declining flow is assumed to reflect deterioration of the asset or out-of-service periods for repairs.

As a corollary of its disregard of the time value of money, the straight-line method produces a series of year-end balances in the asset account that are out of line with reality. Thus, at the end of the first year, the adjusted basis of the asset just described is $1,658 (i.e., $2,487 less one year's depreciation), although its value at that time is the discounted value of the right to receive $1,000 at the end of each of the next two years. At a 10 percent discount, these amounts are $909 and $826, or a total of $1,735. At the end of the second year the asset's adjusted basis is $829, but its value—the discounted value of $1,000 to be received at the end of one year—is $909.

These results are set out [below]:

STRAIGHT-LINE METHOD OF COMPUTING DEPRECIATION

Year	1 Balance Jan. 1	2 Depre- ciation	3 Net Income ($1,000 Minus Col. 2)	4 Yield on Investment (Col. 3/ Col. 1)	5 Value as of Jan. 1 of Future Pre-depreciation Income
1	$2,487	$ 829	$171	6.9%	$2,487
2	1,658	829	171	10.3%	1,735
3	829	829	171	20.6%	909
		$2,487	$513		

Both these deficiencies in the straight-line method can be eliminated by using a compound-interest method of computing depreciation, under which the asset's yield is a constant percentage of the taxpayer's declining investment. In dividing the $1,000 of annual pre-depreciation income hypothesized in the example above between return *on* the taxpayer's investment (i.e., net income) and return *of* his investment (i.e., depreciation), the ratio must be changed every year. The part constituting return *on* the investment, being a constant fraction (10 percent) of the amount invested, declines each year because the amount invested declines, while the portion of the $1,000 constituting a return *of* the investment correspondingly increases from year to year. This phenomenon is analogous to the division between interest and amortization when a mortgage is serviced by equal annual payments over its life: The year-to-year decrease in the interest portion of the level payment is identical to the year-to-year decrease in the net income portion of the hypothesized $1,000 annual receipt, while the year-to-year increase in amortization of the mortgage is comparable to the year-to-year increase in the depreciation portion of the same $1,000 receipt.

Applying these principles, [the table below] divides the $1,000 received at the end of the first year into (a) $248 of net income (i.e., 10 percent of $2,487, the amount invested) and (b) a tax-free return of capital, or depreciation, of $752. The $1,000 received at the end of the second year consists of $174 of net income (10 percent of the taxpayer's remaining investment of $1,735) and a balance, representing depreciation, of $826. At the beginning of the third year, therefore, the remaining investment is $909 ($1,735 minus $826); and the $1,000 received at the end of that year consists of $91 of net income (10 percent of $909) and $909 of depreciation, which reduces the basis of the asset to zero.

When depreciation is computed in this manner (the so-called sinking fund method), the taxpayer's investments at the end of the first and second years are $1,735 and $909, respectively; and these amounts correspond exactly to the value at these dates of the income to be produced by the asset during its remaining useful life, discounted by the hypothesized 10 percent time value of money.

SINKING-FUND METHOD OF COMPUTING DEPRECIATION

Year	1 Balance Jan. 1	2 Depre- ciation	3 Net Income ($1,000 Minus Col. 2)	4 Yield on Investment (Col. 3/ Col. 1)	5 Value as of Jan. 1 of Future Pre-depreciation Income
1	$2,487	$ 752	$248	10%	$2,487
2	1,735	826	174	10%	1,735
3	909	909	91	10%	909
		$2,487	$513		

The propriety of computing depreciation on a sinking-fund or compound-interest basis can also be illustrated by starting with the fact that the value of a depreciable asset is the discounted value of the stream of income it will produce during its useful life, plus its salvage value (if any) when it is retired. Applying this analysis to the asset hypothesized above, its value ($2,487) is the sum of (a) $909, the present value of 10 percent discount of $1,000 to be received at the end of one year; (b) $826, the present value of $1,000 to be received at the end of two years; and (c) $752, the present value of $1,000 to be received at the end of three years.

At the end of the first year the owner will have received the anticipated income of $1,000, and the asset will be capable of producing $1,000 for each of the next two years—an income stream that is worth $1,735 at that time (i.e., $909 plus $826). Since the machine was worth $2,487 at the beginning of the first year and is worth $1,735 at the end of that year, the depreciation sustained in the first year is $752. At the end of the second year the owner will have received a second $1,000, and the asset will be capable of producing $1,000 in the third (and final) year of operation— an amount that is worth, at the end of the second year, $909. Hence, the depreciation sustained in the second year is $826 (i.e., $1,735 minus $909). Finally, the machine, which is worth $909 at the beginning of the third year, will be worthless at the end of that year, so that the depreciation sustained in the third year is $909.

D. NOTES AND QUESTIONS

1) Unstated Assumptions

Professors Chirelstein and Bittker calculate economic depreciation using present value analysis. On the basis of their calculations, both argue that sinking fund method (SFM) depreciation—which provides for lower deductions in the early years and higher deductions in later years—accurately reflects economic depreciation.

On what assumptions does their argument depend? Suppose that an asset is expected to produce declining rather than constant revenues over its productive life and that annual inflation is expected to be 10%. How will the calculation of economic depreciation using present values be affected? Why might the resulting schedule resemble straight-line or even accelerated depreciation?

Might straight-line and accelerated depreciation therefore be viewed as rough attempts to compensate for the effects of both declining productivity and inflation? Or is any correlation with both factors likely to be purely coincidental?

In principle, what would be the most accurate way to compensate for inflation? Suppose an asset, purchased in 1975, produces revenues for ten years. Does the cost in 1975 dollars adequately offset revenues paid in inflated dollars between 1976 and 1984? Should the depreciation allowance be adjusted upwards each year to reflect inflation since the asset was purchased?

2) Determining Economic Depreciation From Market Prices

Economic depreciation equals the market price of an asset at the year's beginning less the market price at the year's end. Why not determine economic depreciation directly by looking at market prices? But if the asset in question is not actually sold, how can its market price be known? By looking at the price for an identical or similar asset about the same age and in about the same condition? By appraising the value of the asset at annual intervals? (Recall the difficulties of implementation when the tax law depends on appraisals, discussed in Chapters 3 and 12.)

Although systematic studies of real world economic depreciation are rare, a few tentative observations might be offered. First, the sinking fund method probably understates real economic wear and tear on nonreal property such as machinery and vehicles. When the factors of inflation and declining productivity are taken into account, it may very well be that an accelerated method, faster than the straight-line method, most accurately reflects true economic wear and tear.

On the other hand, the straight-line method almost certainly overstates the amount of economic wear and tear on depreciable real estate, such as buildings. This observation is verified by the typical repayment schedule on a fixed interest mortgage that finances the purchase of real estate. Even if the mortgage is long term, say for thirty years, and even if it is for a high proportion of the price, say 80% or 90%, it is typically repaid in *even* monthly amounts over the entire period. Initially, most of each monthly payment pays off interest on the loan, and only a small fraction represents repayment of principal. As the years go by, however, the proportion representing principal slowly increases. This increase in the amount of payment allocated to principal corresponds to sinking fund depreciation. If the lender were concerned that the underlying security for the loan (the building) was depreciating more quickly, the lender would presumably demand that principal be repaid according to a faster schedule.

3) Sinking Fund Depreciation in Other Contexts: Annuities and Premium Bonds

An annuity typically guarantees the annuitant the right to an annual amount for as long as the annuitant lives. See *Drescher* (Chapter 2). The annuity can therefore be compared to a machine which is expected to produce constant revenues for a period equal to the annuitant's life expectancy. In that event, shouldn't the cost of the annuity be deducted by the annuitant according to a sinking fund schedule? Section 72(b)(1), however, permits annuitants to deduct the cost of an annuity on a straight-line schedule.[1]

A bond premium represents the amount paid for the right to receive stated interest above the market rate of interest for a fixed period (see Chapter 34). Can the premium therefore be compared to a machine that produces level revenues over a limited period? Shouldn't the bond premium therefore be deducted according to a sinking fund schedule? Prior to 1987, the Code authorized the straight-line deduction of bond premiums. In the 1986 Tax Reform Act, Congress amended Section 171(b)(3)(A) to require sinking fund deductions for bond premiums, but added no parallel provision to cover deductions for premium leases. Should the IRS issue regulations requiring that the sinking fund schedule also apply to premium leases? What Code Section would authorize such regulations? Perhaps Section 446(b)?

E. STEINES, INCOME TAX ALLOWANCES FOR COST RECOVERY
40 Tax L. Rev. 483, 483, 506, 521–540, 544–550 (1985)

[Editor's Note: The following article traces the history of depreciation methods under the Code, with an emphasis on changes made in the 1980s by the 1981 Economic Recovery Tax Act (ERTA), the 1982 Tax Equity and Fiscal Responsibility Act (TEFRA), and the 1984 Deficit Reduction Act (DRA). This article was written before and therefore does not address the most recent changes made by the 1986 Tax Reform Act.]

Introduction

The federal income tax purports to be a tax on income. Tax liability is determined by applying the tax rate schedule to taxable income. Roughly speaking, taxable income for a particular year is gross income for the year minus the costs of producing that income. Some of these costs—principally, costs of items exhausted during the year—are currently deductible for tax

---

1. Some annuities promise to pay an amount that varies depending on the performance of the annuity-funded investment. Since the annual payment may either *increase* or *decrease*, sinking fund depreciation may still be viewed as the theoretically correct allowance for the annuity's cost.

purposes. The cost of electricity to light an office is an example. Other costs are capital expenditures—items that remain productive for a longer period. Capital expenditures are not currently deductible in full. Cost recovery refers generally to the timing of reductions in the tax base on account of capital expenditures. These reductions usually take the form of depreciation deductions or other offsets against income. . . .

Expensing Cost of Property Is Equivalent to Exempting Its Yield From Tax

The most accelerated method of cost recovery is a deduction of the entire cost of an asset during its first year of use. This is known as expensing. It is said that . . . the deferral of tax caused by expensing is tantamount to exempting income from the expensed asset from tax. . . .

For example, at a tax rate of 60%, a $100 before-tax investment costs only $40 after taxes if the taxpayer can expense the investment and has enough other income so that the $100 deduction reduces tax liability by $60. . . . Because the asset has been expensed, the return is fully taxable. . . . The nominal 60% tax would normally reduce a 10% before-tax return to a 4% after tax return. [Thus,] expensing leaves the taxpayer with the equivalent of a tax-free 10% return on his net investment of $40. . . .

Before ERTA

The historical high points of the depreciation deduction and the investment credit are recounted here to show the trend preceding ERTA and the arguments influencing it. . . .

In 1920, the Bureau of Internal Revenue issued Bulletin F which, in recognition of the inherent inexactitude of depreciation, delegated to taxpayers the determination of accurate rates of depreciation in light of their judgment and experience. The rate chosen by a taxpayer was subject to the Bureau's approval, but only clearly unreasonable rates were challenged. In 1927, the Supreme Court said depreciation for a particular year should, in theory, be the portion of the cost of an asset disposed of during the year through use; aggregate depreciation throughout the asset's useful life was intended to restore original cost, less any salvage value.

Depreciation allowances grew substantially, causing revenue concerns, and in 1931 the Bureau revised Bulletin F and published a list of suggested useful lives for certain assets, broken down by industry groups. The revised Bulletin F also approved straight line depreciation and withheld judgment on other methods, including the declining balance method. In 1934, to ward off legislation that would have arbitrarily reduced depreciation allowances, the Treasury Department shifted to taxpayers the burden of proving the reasonableness of claimed depreciation allowances and insisted on cost recovery over useful life, either on the straight line method or in accordance with a recognized trade practice, such as the unit of production method. Bulletin F was again revised in 1942, providing an expanded list of useful lives. Given the taxpayer's burden of proof, Bulletin F lives were presumptively correct.

In 1946, the Bureau issued its first preaudit approval of declining balance depreciation, on the conditions that the same method be used for financial accounting and that it properly reflect net income. Disputes between taxpayers and the government continued, however, both as to useful lives and appropriate depreciation methods. To relieve the controversy, in 1953, the Service announced that it would not disturb claimed depreciation deductions unless there was a clear and convincing basis for change.

In 1954, for the first time, the Code allowed certain accelerated methods of depreciation, including the sum of the years digits method and declining balance depreciation at up to 200% of the straight line rate. These methods were only available, however, for new tangible property with a useful life of at least three years. The stated justifications for accelerated depreciation were that (1) it would reduce disputes with taxpayers over permissible methods, (2) it more closely approximated economic depreciation (decline in value) than the straight line method and, consequently, would more accurately reflect income, and (3) it would stimulate capital investment and result in increased growth, production, and standards of living. . . .

Several developments in 1962 continued the trend of more rapid cost recovery. Despite the allowance of accelerated methods, taxpayer dissatisfaction with the Bulletin F lives continued to cause numerous administrative disputes. In particular, it was thought that Bulletin F did not adequately account for obsolescence due to new technology. Revenue Procedure 62–21 withdrew Bulletin F and provided a list of "guideline lives" for rather broad classes of assets within four industry groups, as opposed to Bulletin F's asset-by-asset approach. Although the guideline lives were not intended as a departure from the useful life concept, on average, they were 30% to 40% shorter than the Bulletin F lives.

A taxpayer could use the new guideline lives, however, only if he showed that they were consistent with his asset retirement and replacement practices. The objective was to assure, within tolerances, that depreciation would be taken over the actual useful life of the asset to the taxpayer. Taxpayers could demonstrate this consistency by a factual showing or by the "reserve ratio test." The reserve ratio test was inordinately complicated and proved unworkable in practice. . . .

The most significant development concerning cost recovery in 1962 was the enactment of the investment credit. The credit was 7% of the cost of tangible personal property placed in service during the year with a useful life of eight years or more. The rate was $4\frac{2}{3}\%$ and $2\frac{1}{3}\%$ for property with useful lives of six to eight years and four to six years, respectively. No credit was allowed for property with a useful life of less than four years. The credit applied to new and used property, but no more than $50,000 of used property qualified. Also, the credit was limited to $25,000 plus 25% of tax liability in excess of that amount; unused credits could be carried to other years. A disposition of property before expiration of the useful life on which the amount of the credit was computed resulted in an addition to tax liability (recapture) of part or all of the credit. A provision that was repealed two years later reduced the basis of property by the amount of the credit, thus effecting a tradeoff of the credit for an equal amount of depreciation. The tradeoff was not equal in value, however, both because the tax savings from a deduction is only a fraction (the marginal tax rate) of the savings from an equal credit, and because the savings from a credit are immediate, whereas those from depreciation deductions are deferred. The purpose of the investment credit was to stimulate capital spending. . . .

To reduce inflation and the level of borrowing, Congress suspended the investment credit from late 1967 through all of 1968. The same measure increased the credit limitation to 50% of tax liability in excess of $25,000 for 1969 and afterward. In 1969, however, the credit was repealed. Again, the purpose was to fight inflation.

The same legislation, the Tax Reform Act of 1969, imposed limitations on accelerated depreciation of buildings. . . . Under the new rules, the most accelerated rates permissible were 200% declining balance for new residential property, 150% declining balance for new commercial property, 125% declining balance for used residential property, and straight line for used commercial property. . . . The purposes of these changes were to make depreciation on buildings a more accurate measure of decline in value and to diminish the advantages of real estate tax shelters. Also, the 1969 changes introduced the subsidiary judgments that residential property should be treated better than commercial property and new property better than used property. . . .

In 1971, attention turned once again to useful lives. Dissatisfied with the recent repeal of the investment credit and tightening of accelerated depreciation methods, taxpayers pressed for relief. The Treasury responded with the Asset Depreciation Range System (ADR), which Congress quickly embraced through legislation. ADR allowed taxpayers to choose useful lives for personal property anywhere within a range from 20% shorter to 20% longer than the guideline lives under Revenue Procedure 62–21. ADR, furthermore, dropped the reserve ratio rest. The stated justifications for ADR were that (1) it would minimize disputes over useful lives, (2) it would more accurately measure income by employing useful lives more reflective of changing technology, and (3) it was a necessary stimulant to a lagging economy.

Also, for the purpose of stimulating capital investment, Congress reinstated the investment credit in 1971, and shortened by one year the respective useful lives of property qualifying for the three available percentages. . . .

In 1975, Congress increased the investment credit percentages to 3⅓%, 6⅔%, and 10%, and increased the amount of used property qualifying for the credit from $50,000 to $100,000. These changes were to be effective for only two years, but, in 1976 they were extended, and in 1978 they were made permanent. The 1978 legislation also increased the limitation on the credit to 90% of tax liability in excess of $25,000. The argument in favor of these increases, again, was to stimulate capital investment. . . .

Debate Leading to ERTA

During the 1970's, a growing body of opinion, especially in the business community, held that inadequate cost recovery allowances were directly contributing to insufficient capital investment and, more generally, to a deteriorating economy. Those holding this view argued that cost recovery allowances had to be liberalized in order to encourage capital spending. The high inflation of the late 1970's fueled the argument. It was against this backdrop in 1980 that Congress began in earnest to deliberate on revising the cost recovery rules. During 1980 and 1981, Congress received a staggering volume of testimony on changes in tax law, particularly in the area of cost recovery, that were thought necessary to help revitalize the economy. Although there was general agreement that the existing rules should be simplified, there was wide diversity of opinion on the cost recovery formula best suited to economic recovery.

Several proposals combined a more generous investment credit, substantially shortened recovery periods, and various rates of accelerated recovery. The most reknowned of the proposals was the 10–5–3 proposal, which generally provided cost recovery for buildings over a ten-year period, and for personal property over three- and five-year periods. . . .

Proponents of 10–5–3 argued that the existing cost recovery allowances discouraged investment, and that 10–5–3, or something similar, was a necessary stimulus. No one seemed to doubt that 10–5–3 would result in increased capital spending, but several opponents maintained that its uneven effect across assets with different life spans would distort investment decisions and result in a capital composition less productive than the composition that would result from neutral cost recovery allowances. In other words, because 10–5–3 was perceived as relatively biased in favor of certain types of property, taxpayers would forego more productive investments in other property because the tax bias would more than compensate for the sacrificed pretax income; society, not the taxpayer, would suffer the loss. . . .

Others believed that 10–5–3 was relatively free of all these biases. One line of argument was: . . . Expensing the cost of property is tantamount to exempting income from the property from tax. . . . Within a range of discount rates thought to be realistic, the present value of cost recovery allowances for personal property under 10–5–3 (including the investment credit) approximated expensing. Thus, the argument ran, 10–5–3, by approximately eliminating income tax on capital, would substantially remove the income tax as a determinant of capital composition. . . .

Though couched in the language of cost recovery, this essentially was a dispute over whether the economy could afford to tax income from capital. Beyond that question, however, opponents of 10–5–3 argued that unlike expensing, it would not be the equivalent of a tax exemption for all income from capital; rather, it would be an uneven formula that would seriously distort investment decisions by subsidizing some investments at the expense of others. Without trying to decide who was right about precisely where the biases fell under 10–5–3, it is clear that biases did exist; 10–5–3 supporters did not entirely disagree. . . .

Apart from tinkering with details, ERTA embraced 10–5–3 with only one significant structural change: The cost of buildings is generally recovered under the ERTA rules over a 15-year period. That change alters the magnitude of objection voiced during the legislative process, but not the underlying complaints. The committee reports accompanying ERTA gave the following justification of the new cost recovery system. The real value of existing cost recovery allowances had been diminished by persistent inflation and did not provide the investment stimulus essential for economic expansion. A new system employing more rapid recovery and a greater investment credit was necessary to stimulate capital formation, increase productivity, and improve the nation's competitiveness in international trade. Also, the existing rules were too complex, involving unproductive disputes over such issues as useful life and salvage value, and entailing numerous exceptions and elections that were difficult to master and expensive to apply. A new system was necessary to minimize these complexities.

ERTA

Following is a very general summary of ERTA's cost recovery system. The system contains numerous qualifications and refinements that are omitted here. ERTA largely replaced the prior depreciation rules with the Accelerated Cost Recovery System (ACRS), which applies to tangible property placed in service after 1980 and is embodied in section 168. ACRS divides most property into three classes: personal property is either "3-year property" or "5-year property," and buildings (if placed in service before the effective date of a 1984 amendment described below) are "15-year real property."

A comparison of these periods with the corresponding guideline lives under prior law indicates the degree to which ERTA shortened recovery periods. Three-year property is property having a guideline life of four years or less; five-year property is property having a guideline life in excess of four years. Guideline lives for most buildings ranged from 40 to 60 years.

Under ACRS, the cost of property within each class is recovered over the period indicated in its title under tables that employ accelerated recovery methods. For personal property, the recovery rates given in the tables were computed using the 150% declining balance method with a half-year convention for the first year and a switch to straight line in later years. The recovery rates were scheduled to be further accelerated in two stages, the first for 1985 and the second for 1986 and subsequent years. The 1986 schedule was based on the 200% declining balance method. These further accelerations were later scuttled, however, and the original rates remain in effect. . . . For 15-year real property, the rate is 175% declining balance with a subsequent switch to straight line, but the deduction is based on actual months of use for the years of acquisition and disposition. Salvage value is ignored in all cases. ACRS does not distinguish between new and used property. . . .

ERTA also increased the investment credit, granting a 6% credit to three-year property and a 10% credit to five-year property, and raising the cap on qualifying used property to $150,000. . . .

During the deliberations on ERTA, the statement was often made that the new system approximated the tax benefits of expensing for personal property. The tables below compare (1) the immediate $50 tax savings a 50% taxpayer would reap from expensing a $100 investment with (2) the present value of tax reductions from ERTA's cost recovery allowances to such a taxpayer at alternative discount rates of 5%, 10%, and 15%. . . .

Three-Year Property

	Year 1	Year 2	Year 3	Total
Deduction	$25.00	$38.00	$37.00	$100.00
Credit	6.00			6.00
Tax savings	18.50	19.00	18.50	56.00
Present value at 5%	18.50	18.06	16.78	53.34
Present value at 10%	18.50	17.27	15.30	51.07
Present value at 15%	18.50	16.52	13.99	49.01

Five-Year Property

	Year 1	Year 2	Year 3	Year 4	Year 5	Total
Deduction	$15.00	$22.00	$21.00	$21.00	$21.00	$100.00
Credit	10.00					10.00
Tax savings	17.50	11.00	10.50	10.50	10.50	60.00
Present value at 5%	17.50	10.48	9.52	9.07	8.64	55.21
Present value at 10%	17.50	10.00	8.68	7.89	7.17	51.24
Present value at 15%	17.50	9.57	7.94	6.90	6.00	47.91

. . . The relativity of benefits under expensing and ERTA would not change significantly if the assumed tax rate were the maximum corporate rate of 46%. Interpolation of the figures based on discount rates of 10% and 15% demonstrates that ERTA approximates expensing to a 50% taxpayer at a discount rate of 13% for three-year property and 12% for five-year property. If the appropriate discount rate is less, ERTA exceeds the value of expensing; if the appropriate rate is greater, ERTA falls short of expensing.

TEFRA

If a cost recovery system is designed to provide the equivalent present value of expensing at a particular tax rate, the desired cost recovery schedule is a function of the discount rate used to compute present value. . . .

Several critics of ERTA believed that its cost recovery tables were premised on an unrealistically high discount rate. The rate of inflation had dropped considerably. Congress came to realize that if ERTA was an attempt to approximate expensing personal property, it had overshot the mark, and in the process had encouraged investment in unprofitable assets by effectively allowing more than 100% cost recovery.

The correction came in TEFRA. Congress decided that cost recovery allowances should be adjusted to approximate expensing at a 10% after-tax discount. This was effectuated through two measures. First, the faster recovery schedules that were to take effect in 1985 and 1986 were repealed. Second, section 48(q) was added. It reduces the basis recoverable through depreciation deductions by one half of the investment credit. TEFRA also reduced the limitation on the investment credit to 85% of tax liability in excess of $25,000. . . .

[Deficit Reduction] Act of 1984

... The recovery period for real estate was extended from 15 to 18 years.... The reason for the switch to 18 years was that ACRS had stimulated a rapid growth of real estate tax shelters, construction of unnecessary rental housing, and churning of ownership of existing property, all to the detriment of the revenue and of economic growth through more productive investments....

In short, Congress belatedly recognized, as it did when it enacted TEFRA, that ACRS was too seductive....

Summary and Conclusion

Until 1954, virtually all regulation of depreciation allowances was at the administrative level. Policy was dictated by the view that depreciation had the singular purpose to measure income. From time to time during this period, revenue concerns and a desire to minimize disputes precipitated changes in administrative oversight of this policy, but the policy itself remained constant and exclusive. In 1954, Congress assumed a more active role and sanctioned accelerated depreciation methods. Although the policy of accurate income measurement remained paramount, for the first time, depreciation allowances were justified on the alternative ground that they would stimulate investment.

From 1954 to 1981, virtually every liberalization of depreciation allowances was justified on the dual grounds that, relative to its predecessor, it would more accurately measure income, and would stimulate investment and consequently benefit the economy. And, virtually every direct or indirect tightening of depreciation allowances during this period was justified on converse grounds: Its predecessor exaggerated depreciation and consequently understated income, and harmed the economy by deflecting investment from the most productive assets to those with the greatest tax shelter. These tightenings often were also couched as revenue concerns. The turnings on and off of the investment credit were entirely justified by their anticipated effect on investment, inflation, and borrowing. Thus, for nearly three decades before ERTA, accurate measurement of income and economic goals shared the spotlight as objectives of cost recovery policy.

ERTA completed this evolution by eliminating accurate reflection of income as an objective of cost recovery allowances, and shifting entirely to a policy of influencing capital investment with a subsidiary emphasis on simplification of the rules. TEFRA and the Tax Reform Act of 1984 were simply applications of this policy, reflecting the judgments that ERTA stimulated an economically unhealthy mix of investment and threatened the revenue in the process, and that simplification must yield to refinements necessary to reach the desired quantity and quality of stimulus.

Economists, lawyers, and others have long questioned the wisdom and efficacy of using cost recovery allowances to influence private investment for the purpose of achieving greater economic good. Does government know which investments are best for the economy and, therefore, which investments to encourage? If it does not know, would not less targeted incentives, such as rate reductions, be superior? If it does know, is there a reasonable basis for predicting the extent to which liberalized cost recovery will actually induce the desired investments? Even if there is, do targeted tax incentives justify the resulting damage to traditional elements of tax policy, such as equity, simplicity, and neutrality? If targeted relief is necessary, would not a direct subsidy, outside the tax system, be more efficient and avoid collision with traditional elements of tax policy? No one can answer these questions definitively. The very existence of uncertainty makes a strong case for modest objectives—for not asking something of the tax system for which even hindsight cannot establish cause and effect.

Over the last 20 years or so, however, Congress has resolved these doubts in favor of cost recovery provisions that reward various investments relative to other investments in various degrees and ways.... New property is treated better than used property, real property better than personal property in some ways and vice versa in others, residential real property better than commercial real property, owner employed property better than leased property, and corporate owned property better than individually owned property in some ways and vice versa in others.

Most of these choices, standing alone, can be justified on one ground or another: social policy, economic effect, revenue concern, accurate measurement of income, or policing of tax shelters. But, some seem entirely without justification. And, the combined hodgepodge hardly instills confidence that Congress can identify and reward through the tax system the particular kinds of investment that will most benefit the economy.

Apart from the wisdom of Congress's choices of which investments to favor, a spot check shows mixed results on the extent to which the preference provisions have succeeded in stimulating the favored investments. There is opinion that investment in machinery and equipment has demonstrably responded to the turnings on and off of the investment credit. There is also opinion that the shortening of depreciable lives in 1971 spurred investment considerably. However, cause and effect are difficult, if not impossible, to establish, and some maintain that other factors, principally the emergence from recession, explain the increased investment activity. The most damning evidence is that for nearly two years after ERTA— arguably the greatest liberalization of cost recovery allowances this country has witnessed—capital investment did not significantly pick up, even in the midst of a healthy economic recovery. And, although some attribute to ERTA the impressive increase in capital spending that has occurred since, the new investment has primarily been in durable equipment, not in structures, and much of it has come from abroad. In short, ERTA added little weight to the argument that cost recovery allowances necessarily induce the desired investment, and did little to refute the claim that economic factors other than cost recovery allowances are equally plausible causes of the investment that does ensue.

This certainly is not proof that the economy would be in better shape if Congress had not departed from a cost recovery policy beholden exclusively to accurate measurement of income. But, no one can say for sure that the economy is better off because it did. And, the process has created a highly complicated set of rules which, by design or effect, has abandoned many of the traditional elements of income tax policy. Widespread awareness of this abandonment is manifested in a variety of complaints, some exaggerated, but all at least partially true, that the income tax has given way in an unduly complex manner to a system that discriminates among classes of capital and overall taxes capital less than services. Given the uncertainties in the consequences of this tradeoff, future reform of cost recovery allowances should deemphasize departures from the income standard that are grounded on the expectation of superior economic effects unless the case for relief is compelling and the efficacy and merit of the departure are solidly proved. This deemphasis would not dictate what the level of taxation should be, but would rather be only a stricter adherence to income as the tax base. . . .

But for the record budget deficits of recent years and projections of more of the same, significant change of the cost recovery provisions this soon after ERTA, TEFRA, and the [Deficit Reduction] Act would not have been likely. However, pressure to reduce the deficit and to reform the tax base has already begun to popularize reform proposals. . . .

The ensuing debate would give Congress the opportunity to scrutinize, more critically than it has before, the panacean claims of rapid cost recovery, and to reverse the primacy of stimulating investment as the most important determinant of cost recovery allowances. It would also give advocates of economic depreciation a chance to present their case more simply, with greater emphasis on the conceptual link between economic depreciation and an income tax, and with less optimism that economic depreciation will guarantee the optimal capital stock. The debate leading to ERTA suffered from lack of intellectual candor on both sides.

Obviously, tax measures cannot be adopted without regard to their effect on the economy. The point is simply that Congress should be reluctant to use a component of the tax system with selective impact—cost recovery allowances—in order to achieve a goal that is inconsistent with measuring income, unless there is demonstrable merit in doing so and no realistic way of achieving a similar end outside the tax system. This reluctance has not been shown. The consequence is a complicated and desultory set of rules, of dubious economic merit.

F. CAPITAL COST PROVISIONS

Conference Committee Report on the 1986 Tax Reform Act, 2 Conf. R. No. 841 (to Accompany H.R. 3838), 99th Cong., 2d Sess. II–38 to II–40 (1986)

[Editor's Note: The following congressional report summarizes the changes made in depreciation schedules by the 1986 Tax Reform Act.]

Present Law

. . . The cost of eligible personal property is recovered over a three-year, five-year, 10-year, or 15-year recovery period, using statutory percentages based on the 150-percent declining balance method. The cost of real property generally is recovered over a 19-year recovery period (15 years for low-income housing), using statutory percentages based on the 175-percent declining balance method (200-percent declining balance method for low-income housing).

Conference Agreement

In general.—The conference agreement modifies the Accelerated Cost Recovery System (ACRS) for property placed in service after December 31, 1986 [and repeals the investment tax credit for such property].

The conference agreement provides more accelerated depreciation for the revised three-year, five-year and 10-year classes, reclassifies certain assets according to their present class life . . . and creates a seven-year class, a 20-year class, a 27.5-year class, and a 31.5-year class. The conference agreement prescribes depreciation methods for each ACRS class. . . . Eligible personal property and certain real property are assigned among a three-year class, a five-year class, a seven-year class, a 10-year class, a 15-year class, or a 20-year class.

The depreciation method applicable to property included in the three-year, five-year, seven-year, and 10-year classes is the double declining balance method, switching to the straight-line method at a time to maximize the depreciation allowance. For property in the 15-year and 20-year class, the conference agreement applies the 150-percent declining balance method, switching to the straight-line method at a time to maximize the depreciation allowance. The cost of [most] real property . . . is recovered over 27.5 years for residential rental property and 31.5 years for nonresidential property, using the straight-line method.

Classes of property.—Property is classified as follows:

Three-year class.—ADR midpoints of 4 years or less, except automobiles and light trucks, and adding horses which are assigned to the three-year class under present law.

Five-year class.—ADR midpoints of more than 4 years and less than 10 years, and adding automobiles, light trucks, qualified technological equipment, computer-based telephone central office switching equipment, research and experimentation property, and geothermal, ocean thermal, solar, and wind energy properties, and biomass properties that constitute qualifying small power production facilities. . . .

Seven-year class.—ADR midpoints of 10 years and less than 16 years, and adding single-purpose agricultural or horticultural structures and property with no ADR midpoint that is not classified elsewhere.

10-year-class.—ADR midpoints of 16 years and less than 20 years.

15-year class.—ADR midpoints of 20 years and less than 25 years, and adding municipal wastewater treatment plants, and telephone distribution plant and comparable equipment used for the two-way exchange of voice and data communications.

20-year class.—ADR midpoints of 25 years and more, other than . . . real property. . . .

27.5-year class.—Residential rental property (including manufactured homes that are residential rental property and elevators and escalators).
31.5-year class.—Nonresidential real property. . . .

G. DEPRECIATION AND THE MINIMUM TAX

1) Depreciation Allowances After 1986

As the reading indicates, depreciation allowances have undergone substantial changes in the 1980s. Beginning in 1987, Section 168(c) establishes eight different POCR categories to which assets are assigned: 3, 5, 7, 10, 15, 20, 27.5, and 31.5 years.

Section 168(b) specifies MOCRs according to an assets's POCR. Three, five, seven, and ten-year property is depreciated under an accelerated method known as the 200% or double-declining balance method. Fifteen and twenty-year property is subject to a less accelerated method known as the 150% declining balance method. Twenty-seven-and-a-half-year and thirty-one-and-a-half-year property is depreciated under the straight-line method. The mechanics of calculating depreciation under these methods are explained in Section H, below.

2) Alternative Minimum Tax (AMT)

If all this weren't complex enough, Congress has complicated matters even further with the Alternative Minimum Tax (AMT). Briefly stated, AMT comprises a second income tax system in the Code under which the definition of taxable income is somewhat broader but the rate of tax is somewhat lower than under the "regular" income tax.

Sections 56–58 define Alternative Minimum Taxable Income (AMTI) by requiring the taxpayer to recompute taxable income without the benefit of specified tax preferences. Section 55(b) then imposes the alternative minimum tax on AMTI at a rate of 20% for corporations and 21% for noncorporate taxpayers. There is a basic exemption amount of $40,000 for corporations and for married couples filing jointly and $30,000 for single individuals. Taxpayers are required to pay either the regular tax or the alternative minimum tax, *whichever is higher.* See Section 55(a).

3) Alternative Minimum Taxable Income (AMTI)

In computing AMTI, *all* taxpayers must use somewhat slower depreciation schedules. For most real property placed in service after 1986, the POCR is lengthened to forty years. Section 168(g). For most nonreal property placed in service after 1986, there is no change in the POCR, but a less accelerated MOCR (the 150% declining balance method in place of the 200% declining balance method) is required. Section 56(a)(1)(ii). For assets placed in service before 1987 (whether real or nonreal), there are different adjustments in depreciation schedules.

Corporate taxpayers must make an additional calculation. The preliminary AMTI figure, computed using slower depreciation, is compared to "adjusted net book income," which is income calculated for nontax financial reporting purposes, after specified adjustments. If adjusted net book income exceeds the preliminary AMTI figure, 50% of the difference is added to produce a final AMTI figure. Section 56(f)(1).[2]

Why is the preliminary calculation of AMTI, using the alternative depreciation schedules, likely to exceed TI? When is adjusted net book income likely to exceed even the preliminary AMTI figure? See the discussions of the different objectives of tax and financial accounting in *Thor Power Tool* (Chapter 15) and *Idaho Power* (Chapter 32). Why is increasing AMTI to reflect adjusted net book income similar to calculating AMTI using even slower depreciation?

Although slower depreciation is probably the most significant difference between TI and AMTI, it is by no means the only one. Sections 56–58, which define AMTI, require numerous other adjustments. For example, AMTI, unlike TI, allows no deduction for: unrealized appreciation on property contributed to charity; unreimbursed employee business expenses; individual investment expenses; and state property and income taxes. Medical expenses are deductible only in excess of 10% of AGI (versus 7.5% for calculating TI). In addition, AMTI, unlike TI, includes certain installment sale gains, interest on municipal bonds that finance private activities, and the spread on the exercise of incentive stock options. This list is by no means complete. It is intended only to provide examples of some of the most important differences between TI and AMTI.

4) Policy Considerations

When the minimum tax was first enacted in 1969, Congress appeared most concerned with taxpayer morale. Three years earlier in 1966, the Treasury had issued a well-publicized study indicating that 154 very high income individuals paid no taxes at all due to the extensive use of tax preferences. The Senate Finance Committee Report on the minimum tax referred to the Treasury study:

> The fact that present law permits a small minority of high-income individuals to escape tax on a large proportion of their income has seriously undermined the belief of taxpayers that others are paying their fair share of the tax burden. It is essential that tax reform be obtained not only as a matter of justice but also as a matter of taxpayer morale. . . . [We] depend upon self-assessment and the cooperation of taxpayers. The loss of confidence on their part in the fairness of the tax system could result in a breakdown of taxpayer morale and make it far more difficult to collect the necessary revenues.[3]

---

2. Beginning in 1990, the preliminary calculation of AMTI is compared, not with adjusted net book income, but with a different income figure—denoted adjusted current earnings (ACE). In addition, if ACE exceeds the preliminary calculation of AMTI, 75% of the difference, rather than 50%, is added to produce a final AMTI figure. Section 56(g)(1). The complexities of ACE are mercifully beyond the scope of this introductory casebook. Basically, the taxpayer is required to compute ACE using depreciation methods which are generally slower than the methods used for the preliminary calculation of AMTI. For example, property placed in service after 1989 is depreciated according to either the method described in 168(g) *or* the method for nontax financial accounting—whichever "yields deductions with a smaller present value." Section 56(g)(4)(A)(i).

3. S. Rep. No. 552, 91st Cong., 1st Sess. 13 (1969).

Do these objectives, however laudable, justify the additional complexity of defining ordinary depreciation as a tax preference subject to the minimum tax? Is the AMT a rational method of limiting the financial advantage of rapid depreciation? Wouldn't it be more sensible to reduce depreciation allowances across the board and, simultaneously, to exempt depreciation from the AMT? Consider the following:

> Any minimum tax blunts the incentive effects of tax preferences. If a business engages only a little in activities or investments specifically encouraged by tax subsidies, no minimum tax will be imposed. But if the business is good at these activities and specializes in them, it will have to pay the minimum tax, putting it at a competitive disadvantage. If only efficiency considerations were relevant, the minimum tax would not receive very high marks. On efficiency grounds alone, no one should care if ten companies each invest a little in a tax-preferred activity or one company invests a lot.
>
> There clearly are economic efficiency costs in a tax world in which competing companies are subject to different depreciation systems and tax rates. . . . With the advent of the book-income preference, the corporate income tax can be viewed as involving three tax systems with three different depreciation rules and three different tax rates. Specifically there is a regular tax with incentive . . . depreciation and a 34 percent tax rate. There is an alternative minimum tax computation using specified nonincentive depreciation and a 20 percent tax rate. And there is a third tax on excess book income using even slower book-income depreciation and a 10 [later rising to 15] percent tax rate.[4]

Given the adverse effects on economic efficiency, not to mention the additional complexity in the tax law, how can the AMT be defended? The authors quoted above make a heroic effort:

> Purists would view . . . minimum taxes as a sign that . . . tax reform has failed or is unattainable. . . .
>
> We do not view the . . . minimum tax as a sign of failure. Instead, it is an admission that the U.S. income tax involves trade-offs among competing objectives. Congress wants to use income tax provisions to encourage particular economic investments or activities and to promote certain societal goals. At the same time, it wants to ensure that the income tax burden is distributed generally in accordance with taxpayers' ability to pay. A minimum tax is necessary because the ability of a few large, profitable companies or high-income families to pay little or no U.S. income tax is inherently unfair and undermines public confidence in the tax system by inducing widespread perceptions of tax inequity. A well-designed minimum tax should be able to ensure that no taxpayers with substantial economic income can reduce their tax liabilities to zero by combining tax-preferred exclusions, deductions, and credits. But this objective can be achieved only by incurring considerable complexity and by blunting the effectiveness of tax incentives. On balance, we favor minimum taxes for both individuals and corporations under the current income tax; the improvements in both the fairness of the distribution of the tax burden and the perception of tax fairness by the populace outweigh the costs.[5]

---

4. Graetz and Sunley, "Minimum Taxes and Comprehensive Tax Reform," in Uneasy Compromise 406 (H. Aaron, H. Galper, and J. Pechman eds 1988).
5. Ibid. at 387–388.

H. CALCULATING DEPRECIATION: AN EXPLANATION AND SOME PROBLEMS

1) The Basic Mechanics

To calculate straight-line method depreciation, take the asset's basis, subtract the salvage value, and divide the remaining basis by the estimated service life. If an asset costs $250, is expected to be worth $50 as scrap at the end of its life, and will last for ten years, then the annual depreciation deduction is ($250−$50)/10 or $20.

The declining balance method of depreciation is an accelerated method. The Code provides for two different declining balance methods, 200% and 150%. The designated percentage is divided by the asset's service life to produce a multiplier. This figure is multiplied by the adjusted basis to determine each year's depreciation. For example, the multiplier under the 200% declining balance method, for an asset with a ten year life, is 200%/10 or 20%. The 20% figure multiplied by the original basis of $250 equals the first year's depreciation of $50. After the first year's depreciation, the adjusted basis is reduced to $200. The second year's depreciation is 20% times $200 or $40.

The term *declining balance* refers to the declining amount of the adjusted basis against which the multiplier is applied each year to calculate depreciation. Notice that the percentage refers to the degree that first-year declining balance depreciation exceeds what would have been allowable under the straight-line method if salvage value were zero. Under the 200% method, it is twice as much and under the 150% method, one and one-half times as much.

No explicit allowance is made for a salvage value in the declining balance formula, but an arbitrary salvage value is implicit in the math. If the salvage value is higher than the arbitrary value, the Code limits depreciation deductions to the original basis minus actual salvage value. If the actual salvage value is lower, then the taxpayer will find it advantageous to change, at some point during the asset's life, from the declining balance method to the straight-line method. The Code explicitly permits such a change.

The Code directs taxpayers to make a number of simplifying assumptions in calculating tax depreciation allowances. First, salvage value is assumed to be zero for most assets placed in service since 1981. Section 168(b)(4). Second, rather than using the date during the year when an asset is actually placed in service, the Code adopts a convention or rule of thumb. When nonreal property is placed in service at any time during the year, it is treated as placed in service halfway through the year. When real property is placed in service at any time during a month, it is treated as placed in service halfway through the month. Section 168(d)(1), (2), and (4).

2) Some Problems

a) Herman Harried purchased a furniture factory near Mt. St. Helens in Washington state. The cost of the factory was $1.2 million, of which $900,000 was financed by a twenty-year mortgage. From 1971−1979 (inclusive), Harried depreciated the building on the straight-line method, using a service life of twenty years and a salvage value of $200,000. (The zero salvage value assumption of Section 168(b)(4) was not yet enacted.) On December 18, 1979, Mt. St. Helens erupted, damaging the factory and considerably reducing its output. Recognizing Harried's hard-pressed situation, the mortgagee agreed to forgive $300,000 of the outstanding principal still owed. At the time of forgiveness, Harried elected to have the forgiveness treated as a nonrecognition event. All other assets used in the business, including the land on which the factory was situated, were rented, except for raw material inputs which were purchased as needed. What was Harried's adjusted basis for the factory at the beginning of 1980?

b) Duane Hays is a wheat farmer in Salinas, Kansas. He owned a tractor which he purchased for $150,000 on January 1, 1978. Estimating the tractor's service life at ten years, he took depreciation at a double-declining balance rate during 1978. On January 1, 1979, Hays decided to trade in the 1978 model for a new air-conditioned 1979 tractor, which had a cash price of $200,000, a built-in stereo and TV, and a reclining seat. The International Harvester dealer transferred the new tractor to Hays in exchange for the old one plus $60,000 in cash. How much taxable income does Hays report as a result of the exchange, and what is Hays' basis for the new tractor?

c) Georgia Norman is a wheat farmer in Nebraska. On January 1, 1971, she purchased a tractor for $20,000, financed with a nonrecourse loan secured by the tractor. On December 31, 1971, she purchased a second tractor, costing $30,000. To finance this acquisition, she paid $9,000 in cash, obtained a $20,000 loan secured by the second tractor, and traded in the first tractor on which the outstanding mortgage balance was $9,000. How much depreciation may Norman deduct for the first tractor in 1971, using the double-declining balance method and a five-year service life? How much gain or loss does Norman recognize on disposition of the first tractor? What is Norman's initial basis for the second tractor? What difference does it make to your answers, if Norman must pay only $1,000 in cash to acquire the second tractor?

Chapter 36

RECAPTURE AND THE TAX BENEFIT RULE

A. INTRODUCTORY NOTES AND QUESTIONS

1) The Effect of Rapid Depreciation

Tax depreciation often occurs at a faster rate than economic depreciation. Faster-than-economic depreciation overstates deductions and understates income during the early years of an asset's life. But during the later years, depreciation deductions are understated and income is commensurately overstated. The understatement of income during the early years is exactly offset by the overstatement of income in the later years. *Provided that a taxpayer holds an asset for the asset's entire useful life,* the "only" effect of faster-than-economic depreciation is deferral. See Tables 35–1 and 35–2 in Chapter 35.

What happens, however, when the asset is *not* held by a taxpayer for its entire useful life *but is sold before its useful life is over?* Consider the following examples.

2) Nonreal Property

a) *When tax depreciation equals economic depreciation*—Suppose that a pickup truck is purchased for $10,000 on January 1, 1988, that economic depreciation during the first two years of use is $4,000, and that tax depreciation equals economic depreciation. After two years, why is the fair market value of the truck $6,000? And after two years, why is the adjusted basis also $6,000? Recall that basis must be reduced to reflect depreciation deductions. Section 1016(a)(2). When tax depreciation *equals* economic depreciation, what is the relationship between the market value and the adjusted basis? If the truck is sold for its fair market value at the very beginning of the third year, what is the realized gain or loss?

b) *When tax depreciation exceeds economic depreciation*—Suppose that tax depreciation for the pickup truck is determined under Section 168. Section 168(c) assigns a five-year POCR; Section 168(b) allows depreciation using the double declining balance method. During the first two years, then, tax depreciation equals $5,200.[1]

After two years, what is the adjusted basis of the truck? When tax depreciation *exceeds* economic depreciation, what is the relationship between the market value and the adjusted basis? If the truck is sold for its fair market value at the very beginning of the third year, what is the realized gain or loss? What does the realized gain represent? Why does the gain arise when tax depreciation exceeds economic depreciation but not when they are equal?

Ordinarily, if the pickup truck is used in business, how will the gain realized from the sale be taxed? What kind of asset is the truck? See Sections 1221(2) and 1231(b). If we want to limit the advantage of faster-than-economic depreciation to deferral (and thereby prevent conversion of ordinary income into capital gain), how *must* the gain be taxed?

In 1961, Congress enacted Section 1245 and, in 1964, Section 1250. These sections transform what might otherwise be capital gain into ordinary income on the sale or other disposition of depreciable assets. The Senate Report on Section 1245 stated:

> The depreciation deduction is a deduction against ordinary income. If either the useful life of the asset is too short, or the particular method of depreciation allows too much depreciation in the early years, the decline in value [sic] of the asset resulting from these depreciation deductions may exceed the actual decline. Wherever the depreciation deductions reduce the basis of the property faster than the actual decline in its value, then when it is sold there will be a gain. Under present law this gain is taxed as a capital gain, even though the depreciation deductions reduced ordinary income. The taxpayer who has taken excessive depreciation deductions and then sells an asset, therefore, has in effect converted ordinary income into a capital gain.[2]

How does Section 1245 affect the pickup truck example when tax depreciation is determined under Section 168? Section 1245 applies to depreciable nonreal property. Section 1245(a)(3)(A). When such property is sold, the gain is treated as ordinary income to the extent of all prior depreciation deductions. Section 1245(a)(1) and (2).

c) *The Case of Market Gains*—Suppose that after the pickup truck above is used for two years, there is a surge in demand for used pickup trucks. As a result, the fair market value of the two-year-old pickup truck increases from $6,000 to $8,000. When the truck is sold, how much gain is realized, assuming tax depreciation was determined under Section 168? To what two different factors is the realized gain attributable? In principle, how

---

1. First-year depreciation equals 200% divided by the 5-year POCR or 40%, times the $10,000 basis, which equals $4,000. Because of the half-year convention, this figure is divided by two, which equals $2,000. Second-year depreciation equals 40% times the end of first-year adjusted basis of $8,000, which equals $3,200. See Chapter 35.
2. S. Rep. No. 1881, 87th Cong., 2d Sess., 95 (1962).

should the gain be apportioned between ordinary income and capital gain? In fact, what is the effect of Section 1245?

Why might Section 1245 be described as recapturing too much or as over-recapturing? To produce the theoretically correct result, how would Section 1245 have to be rewritten? What are the practical obstacles to rewriting Section 1245? How often do true market gains arise on depreciable *nonreal* assets, given the factor of technological obsolescence? What about oil drilling rigs during the Middle East oil embargo? Or supertankers when the Suez Canal was closed?

3) Real Property

Suppose that a commercial office building costing $31.5 million is put into service on January 1, 1988; economic wear and tear during the first ten years of the building's life reduces its value by $1.5 million; and during the first ten years the building appreciates in value by $5 million due to the combination of inflation plus increased demand for commercial office space. Section 168(c) assigns the building a POCR of 31.5 years; Section 168(b) authorizes straight-line method depreciation. Thus, allowable depreciation for the first ten years is $10 million.

What is the adjusted basis of the building after ten years? What is its value? If it is sold after ten years, how much gain is realized? To what factors is that gain attributable? In principle, how should the gain be apportioned between ordinary income and capital gain?

What, in fact, is the effect of the recapture provisions? Section 1250 applies to *all* residential real property and to most nonresidential real property. Section 1250(c).[3] Section 1250 taxes the gain as ordinary income to the extent that depreciation deductions exceed what would be deductible under the straight-line method. Section 1250(a)(1)(A) and (b)(1).

Note that Section 1250 will have no impact on real property placed in service after 1986. All such property must be depreciated under the straight-line method. So-called accelerated methods are not permitted.

Why might Section 1250 be described as recapturing too little or as under-recapturing? What assumption about the rate of economic depreciation on buildings is implicit in the recapture formula of Section 1250? Why is that assumption often mistaken?

---

3. Residential real property includes apartment houses and other buildings that are rented out to individuals for use as "residences." Nonresidential real property includes all other real property.

All depreciable real estate was covered by Section 1250 when it was first enacted in 1964. In 1981, Congress amended the Code to allow nonresidential real estate to fall under Section 1250 only if it was subject to straight-line method depreciation. How did this change affect the willingness of nonresidential real estate owners to use more accelerated depreciation methods? Why do you suppose that residential real estate was exempted?

After 1981, if nonresidential real estate was depreciated using an accelerated method, Section 1245 applied. The 1986 Tax Reform Act disallows accelerated methods for *all* real estate (residential and otherwise). Thus, Section 1245, rather than Section 1250, applies to nonresidential real estate both acquired between January 1, 1982 and December 31, 1986, *and* depreciated using an accelerated method.

B. ALICE PHELAN SULLIVAN CORP. v. UNITED STATES
381 F.2d 399 (Ct. Cl. 1967)

COLLINS, JUDGE.

Plaintiff, a California corporation, brings this action to recover an alleged overpayment in its 1957 income tax. During that year, there was returned to taxpayer two parcels of realty, each of which it had previously donated and claimed as a charitable contribution deduction. The first donation had been made in 1939; the second, in 1940. Under the then applicable corporate tax rates, the deductions claimed ($4,243.49 for 1939 and $4,463.44 for 1940) yielded plaintiff an aggregate tax benefit of $1,877.49.[4]

Each conveyance had been made subject to the condition that the property be used either for a religious or for an educational purpose. In 1957, the donee decided not to use the gifts; they were therefore reconveyed to plaintiff. Upon audit of taxpayer's income tax return, it was found that the recovered property was not reflected in its 1957 gross income. The Commissioner of Internal Revenue disagreed with plaintiff's characterization of the recovery as a nontaxable return of capital. He viewed the transaction as giving rise to taxable income and therefore adjusted plaintiff's income by adding to it $8,706.93—the total of the charitable contribution deductions previously claimed and allowed. This addition to income, taxed at the 1957 corporate tax rate of 52 percent, resulted in a deficiency assessment of $4,527.60. After payment of the deficiency, plaintiff filed a claim for the refund of $2,650.11, asserting this amount as overpayment on the theory that a correct assessment could demand no more than the return of the tax benefit originally enjoyed, i.e., $1,877.49. The claim was disallowed.

This court has had prior occasion to consider the question which the present suit presents. In Perry v. United States, . . . it was recognized that a return to the donor of a prior charitable contribution gave rise to income to the extent of the deduction previously allowed. The court's point of division—which is likewise the division between the instant parties—was whether the "gain" attributable to the recovery was to be taxed at the rate applicable at the time the deduction was first claimed or whether the proper rate was that in effect at the time of recovery. The majority, concluding that the Government should be entitled to recoup no more than that which it lost, held that the tax liability arising upon the return of a charitable gift should equal the tax benefit experienced at time of donation. Taxpayer urges that the *Perry* rationale dictates that a like result be reached in this case.

A transaction which returns to a taxpayer his own property cannot be considered as giving rise to "income". . . . Yet the principle is well engrained in our tax law that the return or recovery of property that was once the subject of an income tax deduction must be treated as income in the year of its recovery. . . . The only limitation upon that principle is the so-called "tax-

---

4. The tax rate in 1939 was 18 percent; in 1940, 24 percent.

benefit rule." This rule permits exclusion of the recovered item from income so long as its initial use as a deduction did not provide a tax saving. . . . But where full tax use of a deduction was made and a tax saving thereby obtained, then the extent of saving is considered immaterial. The recovery is viewed as income to the full extent of the deduction previously allowed.

Formerly the exclusive province of judge-made law, the tax-benefit concept now finds expression both in statute and administrative regulations. Section 111 of the Internal Revenue Code of 1954 accords tax-benefit treatment to the recovery of bad debts, prior taxes, and delinquency amounts. Treasury regulations have "broadened" the rule of exclusion by extending similar treatment to "all other losses, expenditures, and accruals made the basis of deductions from gross income for prior taxable years. . . ."

Drawing our attention to the broad language of this regulation, the Government insists that the present recovery must find its place within the scope of the regulation and, as such, should be taxed in a manner consistent with the treatment provided for like items of recovery, i.e., that it be taxed at the rate prevailing in the year of recovery. We are compelled to agree.

Set in historical perspective, it is clear that the cited regulation may not be regarded as an unauthorized extension of the otherwise limited congressional approval given to the tax-benefit concept. While the statute (i.e., section 111) addresses itself only to bad debts, prior taxes, and delinquency amounts, it was, as noted in Dobson v. Commissioner, ... designed not to limit the application of the judicially designed tax-benefit rule, but rather to insure against its demise. "A specific statutory exception was necessary in bad debt cases only because the courts reversed the Tax Court and established as matter of law a 'theoretically proper' rule which distorted the taxpayer's income [i.e., taxation of a recovery though no benefit may have been obtained through its earlier deduction]." . . .

The *Dobson* decision insured the continued validity of the tax-benefit concept, and the regulation—being but the embodiment of that principle—is clearly adequate to embrace a recovered charitable contribution. . . . But the regulation does not specify which tax rate is to be applied to the recouped deduction, and this consideration brings us to the matter here in issue.

Ever since Burnet v. Sanford & Brooks Co., [Chapter 20] the concept of accounting for items of income and expense on an annual basis has been accepted as the basic principle upon which our tax laws are structured. "It is the essence of any system of taxation that it should produce revenue ascertainable, and payable to the government, at regular intervals. Only by such a system is it practicable to produce a regular flow of income and apply methods of accounting, assessment, and collection capable of practical operation." . . . To insure the vitality of the single-year concept, it is essential not only that annual income be ascertained without reference to losses experienced in an earlier accounting period, but also that income be taxed without reference to earlier tax rates. And absent specific statutory authority sanctioning a departure from this principle, it may only be said of *Perry* that it achieved a result which was more equitably just than legally correct.

Since taxpayer in this case did obtain full tax benefit from its earlier deductions, those deductions were properly classified as income upon recoupment and must be taxed as such. This can mean nothing less than the application of that tax rate which is in effect during the year in which the recovered item is recognized as a factor of income. We therefore sustain the Government's position and grant its motion for summary judgment. Perry v. United States, supra, is hereby overruled, and plaintiff's petition is dismissed.

C. UNITED STATES v. BLISS DAIRY, INC.
460 U.S. 370 (1983)

JUSTICE O'CONNOR delivered the opinion of the Court.

... We conclude that, unless a nonrecognition provision of the Internal Revenue Code prevents it, the tax benefit rule ordinarily applies to require the inclusion of income when events occur that are fundamentally inconsistent with an earlier deduction. . . .

[T]he respondent, Bliss Dairy, Inc., was a closely held corporation engaged in the business of operating a dairy. [I]t deducted upon purchase the full cost of the cattle feed purchased for use in its operations, as permitted by §162 of the Internal Revenue Code, 26 U.S.C. § 162. A substantial portion of the feed was still on hand at the end of the taxable year. On July 2, 1973, two days into the next taxable year, Bliss adopted a plan of liquidation, and, during the month of July, it distributed its assets, including the remaining cattle feed, to the shareholders. . . .

Bliss reported no income on the transaction. . . . On audit, the Commissioner challenged the corporation's treatment of the transaction, asserting that Bliss should have taken into income the value of the grain distributed to the shareholders. He therefore increased Bliss' income by $60,000. . . .

The Government . . . relies solely on the tax benefit rule—a judicially developed principle that allays some of the inflexibilities of the annual accounting system. An annual accounting system is a practical necessity if the federal income tax is to produce revenue ascertainable and payable at regular intervals. *Burnet v. Sanford & Brooks Co.* [Chapter 20]. Nevertheless, strict adherence to an annual accounting system would create transactional inequities. Often an apparently completed transaction will reopen unexpectedly in a subsequent tax year, rendering the initial reporting improper. For instance, if a taxpayer held a note that became apparently uncollectible early in the taxable year, but the debtor made an unexpected financial recovery before the close of the year and paid the debt, the transaction would have no tax consequences for the taxpayer, for the repayment of the principle would be recovery of capital. If, however, the debtor's financial recovery and the resulting repayment took place after the close of the taxable year, the taxpayer would have a deduction for the apparently bad debt in the first year under § 166(a) of the Code, 26 U.S.C. § 166(a). Without the tax benefit rule, the repayment in the second year, representing a return of capital, would not be taxable. The second transaction, then, although economically identical to the first, could, because of the differences in accounting, yield drastically different tax consequences. The Government, by allowing a deduction that it could not have known to be improper at the time, would be foreclosed from recouping any of the tax saved because of the improper deduction. Recognizing and seeking to avoid the possible distortions of income, the courts have long required the taxpayer to recognize the repayment in the second year as income....

The taxpayer ... and the Government ... propose different formulations of the tax benefit rule. The taxpayers contend that the rule requires the inclusion of amounts *recovered* in later years, and they do not view the events in these cases as "recoveries." The Government, on the other hand, urges that the tax benefit rule requires the inclusion of amounts previously deducted if later events are inconsistent with the deductions; it insists that no "recovery" is necessary to the application of the rule. Further, it asserts that the events in these cases are inconsistent with the deductions taken by the taxpayers. We are not in complete agreement with either view.

An examination of the purpose and accepted applications of the tax benefit rule reveals that a "recovery" will not always be necessary to invoke the tax benefit rule. The purpose of the rule is not simply to tax "recoveries." On the contrary, it is to approximate the results produced by a tax system based on transactional rather than annual accounting.... [T]he taxpayer['s] proposal would introduce an undesirable formalism into the application of the tax benefit rule. Lower courts have been able to stretch the definition of "recovery" to include a great variety of events.... Imposition of a requirement that there be a recovery would, in many cases, simply require the Government to cast its argument in different and unnatural terminology, without adding anything to the analysis.

The basic purpose of the tax benefit rule is to achieve rough transactional parity in tax ... and to protect the Government and the taxpayer from the adverse effects of reporting a transaction on the basis of assumptions that an event in a subsequent year proves to have been erroneous. Such an event, unforeseen at the time of an earlier deduction, may in many cases require the application of the tax benefit rule. We do not, however, agree that this consequence invariably follows. Not every unforeseen event will require the taxpayer to report income in the amount of his earlier deduction. On the contrary, the tax benefit rule will "cancel out" an earlier deduction only when a careful examination shows that the later event is indeed fundamentally inconsistent with the premise on which the deduction was initially based. That is, if that event had occurred within the same taxable year, it would have foreclosed the deduction. In some cases, a subsequent recovery by the taxpayer will be the only event that would be fundamentally inconsistent with the provision granting the deduction. In such a case, only actual recovery by the taxpayer would justify application of the tax benefit rule. For example, if a calendar-year taxpayer made a rental payment on December 15 for a 30-day lease deductible in the current year under § 162(a)(3) ... the tax benefit rule would not require the recognition of income if the leased premises were destroyed by fire on January 10. The resulting inability of the taxpayer to occupy the building would be an event not fundamentally inconsistent with his prior deduction as an ordinary and necessary business expense under § 162(a). The loss is attributable to the business and therefore is consistent with the deduction of the rental payment as an ordinary and necessary business expense. On the other hand, had the premises not burned and, in January, the taxpayer decided to use them to house his family rather than to continue the operation of his business, he would have converted the leasehold to personal use. This would be an event fundamentally inconsistent with the business use on which the deduction was based. In the case of the fire, only if the lessor—by virtue of some provision in the lease—had refunded the rental payment would the taxpayer be required under the tax benefit rule to recognize income on the subsequent destruction of the building. In other words, the subsequent recovery of the previously deducted rental payment would be the only event inconsistent with the provision allowing the deduction. It therefore is evident that the tax benefit rule must be applied on a case-by-case basis. A court must consider the facts and circumstances of each case in the light of the purpose and function of the provisions granting the deductions. . . .

Justice Stevens . . . suggests that we err in recognizing transactional equity as the reason for the tax benefit rule. It is difficult to understand why even the clearest recovery should be taxed if not for the concern with transactional equity. . . . Nor does the concern with transactional equity entail a change in our approach to the annual accounting system. Although the tax system relies basically on annual accounting, see *Burnet v. Sanford & Brook Co.*, . . . the tax benefit rule eliminates some of the distortions that would otherwise arise from such a system. . . . The limited nature of the rule and its effect on the annual accounting principle bears repetition: *only* if the occurrence of the event in the earlier year would have resulted in the disallowance of the deduction can the Commissioner require a compensating recognition of income when the event occurs in the later year. . . .

. . . Bliss took a deduction under § 162(a), so we must begin by examining that provision. Section 162(a) permits a deduction for the "ordinary and necessary expenses" of carrying on a trade or business. The deduction is predicated on the consumption of the asset in the trade or business. . . . If the taxpayer later sells the asset rather than consuming it in furtherance of his trade or business, it is quite clear that he would lose his deduction, for the basis of the asset would be zero, . . . so he would recognize the full amount of the proceeds on sale as gain. See §§ 1001(a), (c). In general, if the taxpayer converts the expensed asset to some other, nonbusiness use, that action is inconsistent with his earlier deduction, and the tax benefit rule would require inclusion in income of the amount of the unwarranted deduction. That nonbusiness use is inconsistent with a deduction for an ordinary and necessary business expense is clear from an examination of the Code. While § 162(a) permits a deduction for ordinary and necessary business expenses, § 262 explicitly denies a deduction for personal expenses. . . . The provision has been uniformly interpreted as providing a deduction only for those expenses attributable to the business of the taxpayer. . . . Thus, if a corporation turns expensed assets to the analog of personal consumption, as Bliss did here—distribution to shareholders—it would seem that it should take into income the amount of the earlier deduction. . . .

JUSTICE STEVENS, with whom JUSTICE MARSHALL joins . . . dissenting. . . .

This case requires us to apply the tax benefit rule. This rule has always had a limited, but important office: it determines whether certain events that enrich the taxpayer—recoveries of past expenditures—should be characterized as income. It does not create income out of events that do not enhance the taxpayer's wealth.

Today the Court declares that the purpose of the tax benefit rule is "to approximate the results produced by a tax system based on transactional rather than annual accounting." . . . . Whereas the rule has previously been used to determine the character of a current wealth-enhancing event, when viewed in the light of past deductions, the Court now suggests that the rule requires a study of the propriety of earlier deductions, when viewed in the light of later events. The Court states that the rule operates to "cancel out" an earlier deduction if the premise on which it is based is "fundamentally inconsistent" with an event in a later year. . . .

The Court's reformulation of the tax benefit rule constitutes an extremely significant enlargement of the tax collector's powers. In order to identify the groundbreaking character of the decision, I shall review the history of the tax benefit rule. . . . *Bliss Dairy* . . . fits comfortably within the class of cases to which the tax benefit rule has not been applied in the past. . . .

I

What is today called the "tax benefit rule" evolved in two stages, reflecting the rule's two components. The "inclusionary" component requires that the recovery within a taxable year of an item previously deducted be included in gross income. The "exclusionary component," which gives the rule its name, allows the inclusionary component to operate only to the extent that the prior deduction benefited the taxpayer.

The inclusionary component of the rule originated in the Bureau of Internal Revenue in the context of recoveries of debts that had previously been deducted as uncollectible. The Bureau sensed that it was inequitable to permit a taxpayer to characterize the recovery of such a debt as "return of capital" when in a prior year he had been allowed to reduce his taxable income to compensate for the loss of that capital. As one commentator described it, "the allowance of a deduction results in a portion of gross income not being taxed; when the deducted item is recouped, the recovery stands in the place of the gross income which had not been taxed before and is therefore taxable." This principle was quickly endorsed by the Board of Tax Appeals and the courts. . . .

The exclusionary component was not so readily accepted. The Bureau first incorporated it during the Great Depression as the natural equitable counterweight to the inclusionary component. . . . It soon retreated, however, insisting that a recovery could be treated as income even if the prior deduction had not benefited the taxpayer. . . . The Board of Tax Appeals protested . . . but the Circuit Courts of Appeals sided with the Bureau. . . .

At that point, Congress intervened for the first and only time. It enacted the forerunner of § 111 of the present Code . . . using language that by implication acknowledges the propriety of the inclusionary component by explicitly mandating the exclusionary component.

The most striking feature of the rule's history is that from its early formative years, through codification, until the 1960's, Congress, the Internal Revenue Service, courts, and commentators, understood it in essentially the same way. They all saw it as a theory that appropriately characterized certain recoveries of capital as income. Although the rule undeniably helped to accommodate the annual accounting system to multiyear transactions, I have found no suggestion that it was regarded as a generalized method of approximating a transactional accounting system through the fabrication of income at the drop of a fundamentally inconsistent event. An inconsistent event was always a necessary condition, but . . . inconsistency was never by itself a sufficient reason for applying the rule. Significantly, the first case from this Court dealing with the tax benefit rule emphasized the role of a recovery. And when litigants in this Court suggested that a transactional accounting system would be more equitable, we expressly declined to impose one, stressing the importance of finality and practicability in a tax system. . . .

II

In the *Bliss Dairy* case, the Court today reaches a result contrary to that dictated by a recovery theory. . . .

III

Because tax considerations play such an important role in decisions relating to the investment of capital, the transfer of operating businesses, and the management of going concerns, there is a special interest in the orderly, certain, and consistent interpretation of the Internal Revenue Code. Today's decision seriously compromises that interest. It will engender uncertainty, it will enlarge the tax gatherer's discretionary power to reexamine past transactions, and it will produce controversy and litigation.

Any inconsistent-event theory of the tax benefit rule would make the tax system more complicated than it has been under the recovery theory. Inconsistent-event analysis forces a deviation from the traditional pattern of calculating income during a given year: identify the transactions in which the taxpayer was made wealthier, determine from the history of those transactions which apparent sources of enrichment should be characterized as income, and then determine how much of that income must be recognized. Of course, in several specific contexts, Congress has already mandated deviations from that traditional pattern,[5] and the additional

---

5. E.g., §§ 1245, 1250 (mere dispositions of certain depreciable property and certain depreciable realty may give rise to income).

complications are often deemed an appropriate price for enhanced tax equity. But to my knowledge Congress has never even considered so sweeping a deviation as a general inconsistent-event theory. . . .

IV

Neither history nor sound tax policy supports the Court's abandonment of its interpretation of the tax benefit rule as a tool for characterizing certain recoveries as income. If Congress were dissatisfied with the tax treatment that I believe *Bliss Dairy* should be accorded under current law, it could respond by changing many of the . . . provisions that bear on this case. . . . It could modify the manner in which deductions are authorized under § 162. It could legislate another statutory exception to the annual accounting system, much as it did when it made the depreciation recapture provisions, §§ 1245, 1250. . . . But in the absence of legislative action, I cannot join the Court's attempt to achieve similar results by distorting the tax benefit rule. . . .

D. NOTES AND QUESTIONS

1) The Tax Benefit Rule as a Recapture Principle

The tax benefit rule can be understood as reflecting the same recapture principle as Sections 1245 and 1250, namely that faster-than-economic depreciation should lead only to deferral and not to conversion of ordinary income into capital gain. This is not to say that the tax benefit rule was consciously formulated with recapture in mind. The rule was first approved by the Board of Tax Appeals in 1929,[6] over three decades before Congress enacted Sections 1245 and 1250, the principal statutory recapture provisions. Moreover, none of the reasons offered by Congress for enacting statutory recapture provisions appear in judicial opinions endorsing the tax benefit doctrine.

The tax benefit rule appears most clearly as a recapture principle in cases of bad loans and expensed items. To illustrate, suppose that a bank lends out $1,000. In the ordinary course of events, the loan is considered nonwasting, and the bank is entitled to deduct its $1,000 cost only when the loan is repaid. If there is no prospect of repayment, however, the loan is considered "wasted," and the bank is entitled to a bad debt deduction of $1,000 under Section 166(a). If the loan is later paid off in full, the $1,000 represents the extent to which prior "depreciation" overstated economic "wear and tear." Under a recapture principle, the $1,000 would be taxed as ordinary income—the same result, in fact, provided by the tax benefit rule.

At the other end of the spectrum, suppose a company purchases feed for $1,000 and expenses the entire cost. Expensing, in effect, assumes that

---

6. Excelsior Printing Co. v. Commissioner, 16 B.T.A. 886 (1929).

the feed will be entirely used up by the taxpayer in the current year. If, however, the expensed items are sold for $300, that amount represents the extent to which expensing overstated economic wear and tear. Again, under a recapture principle, the amount should be taxed as ordinary income—the same result provided by the tax benefit rule.[7]

The preceding analysis may explain why there are explicit recapture provisions in the Code for depreciable assets but not for expensed or nonwasting items. The judge-made tax benefit rule already provides, in those cases, for recapture of prior deductions in excess of economic wear and tear.

2) The Principle of Annual Accounting

Section 111, which is described in *Alice Phelan Sullivan Corp.*, modifies the principle that each year's taxable income is computed without regard to events in other years. It is therefore similar to Sections 172 and 1212, which also mitigate the rigors of the annual accounting principle. Is Section 111 a sensible provision? Or does it haphazardly favor some taxpayers over others?

E. HAVERLY v. UNITED STATES
513 F.2d 224 (7th Cir.), cert. denied, 423 U.S. 912 (1975)

HASTINGS, SENIOR CIRCUIT JUDGE.

This case presents for resolution a single question of law which is of first impression: whether the value of unsolicited sample textbooks sent by publishers to a principal of a public elementary school, which he subsequently donated to the school's library and for which he claimed a charitable deduction, constitutes gross income to the principle within the meaning of Section 61 of the Internal Revenue Code of 1954, 26 U.S.C. § 61.

This action was brought by the plaintiffs in the district court for recovery of income taxes paid to the United States. Jurisdiction was based on 28 U.S.C. § 1346(a)(1). The parties stipulated to the relevant facts.

During the years 1967 and 1968 Charles N. Haverly was the principal of the Alice L. Barnard Elementary School in Chicago, Illinois. In each of these years publishers sent to the taxpayer unsolicited sample copies of textbooks which had a total fair market value at the time of receipt of $400. The samples were given to taxpayer for his personal retention or for whatever disposition he wished to make. The samples were provided, in the hope of receiving favorable consideration, to give taxpayer an opportunity to examine the books and determine whether they were suitable for the instructional unit for which he was responsible. The publishers did not intend that the books serve as compensation.

---

7. In *Bliss*, the only issue was whether the distribution of feed should be treated as a sale. In holding that it should be, the court equated the distribution with a sale of the feed for cash and a distribution of the cash.

In 1968 taxpayer donated the books to the Alice L. Barnard Elementary School Library. The parties agreed that the donation entitled the taxpayer to a charitable deduction under 26 U.S.C. § 170, in the amount of $400, the value of the books at the time of the contribution.

The parties further stipulated that the textbooks received from the publishers did not constitute gifts within the meaning of 26 U.S.C. § 102 since their transfer to the taxpayer did not proceed from a detached and disinterested generosity nor out of affection, respect, admiration, charity or like impulses.

Taxpayer's report of his 1968 income did not include the value of the textbooks received, but it did include a charitable deduction for the value of the books donated to the school library. The Internal Revenue Service assessed a deficiency against the taxpayer representing income taxes on the value of the textbooks received. Taxpayer paid the amount of the deficiency, filed a claim for refund and subsequently instituted this action to recover that amount.

The amount of income, if any, and the time of its receipt are not issues here since the parties stipulated that if the contested issue of law was decided in the taxpayer's favor, his taxable income for 1968 as determined by the Internal Revenue Service would be reduced by $400.00.

Upon agreement of the parties, the case was submitted to the district court on the uncontested facts and briefs for decision without trial. The district court issued a memorandum opinion which held that receipt of the samples did not constitute income. . . . The court subsequently ordered, in accordance with its decision, that plaintiffs recover from the United States the sum of $120.40 plus interest. The United States appeals from that judgment. We reverse. . . .

. . . We conclude that when the intent to exercise complete dominion over unsolicited samples is demonstrated by donating those samples to a charitable institution and taking a deduction therefore, the value of the samples received constitutes gross income.

The receipt of textbooks is unquestionably an "accession to wealth." Taxpayer recognized the value of the books when he donated them and took a $400 deduction therefor. Possession of the books increased the taxpayer's wealth. Taxpayer's receipt and possesion of the books indicate that the income was "clearly realized." Taxpayer admitted that the books were given to him for his personal retention or whatever disposition he saw fit to make of them. Although the receipt of unsolicited samples may sometimes raise the question of whether the taxpayer manifested an intent to accept the property or exercised "complete dominion" over it, there is no question that this element is satisfied by the unequivocal act of taking a charitable deduction for donation of the property.

The district court recognized that the act of claiming a charitable deduction does manifest an intent to accept the property as one's own. It nevertheless declined to label receipt of the property as income because it considered such an act indistinguishable from other acts unrelated to the tax laws which also evidence an intent to accept property as one's own, such as a school principal donating his sample texts to the library *without* claiming a deduction. We need not resolve the question of the tax consequences of this and other hypothetical cases discussed by the district court and suggested by the taxpayer. To decide the case before us we need only hold, as we do, that when a tax deduction is taken for the donation of unsolicited samples the value of the samples received must be included in the taxpayer's gross income. . . .

The Internal Revenue Service has apparently made an administrative decision to be concerned with the taxation of unsolicited samples only when failure to tax those samples would provide taxpayers with double tax benefits. It is not for the courts to quarrel with an agency's rational allocation of its administrative resources.

In light of the foregoing, the judgment appealed from is reversed and the case is remanded to the district court with directions to enter judgment for the United States.

Reversed.

F. NOTES AND QUESTIONS

1) An Alternative Rationale for the *Haverly* Decision

Is there a better way to reach the same result as the *Haverly* court? Suppose that the books are includable but that the taxpayer is entitled to an offsetting business expense deduction under either Section 162(a) or Section 179 so that income and deduction items are offsetting.[8] After this deduction, what is the books' adjusted basis? If the books were sold for cash, how much gain would be realized? How would the gain be characterized under the tax benefit rule of *Bliss Dairy*? How does the amount and character of the unrealized gain on the books affect the availability of a charitable contribution deduction under Section 170(e)(1)?

2) The Weakness of the *Haverly* Court's Rationale

Do you find convincing the court's distinction between gifts to charity and noncharitable gifts? If Haverly writes his name in the books, doesn't that show an intention to reduce them to possession? Consider the following two cases:

(a) Haverly gives the books to a personal friend.

(b) Haverly writes his name in the books, places them in his office bookcase, and consults them occasionally in his work.

Given the *Haverly* court's rationale, how would Haverly be taxed? Under the proposed alternative rationale, how would Haverly be taxed? Which rationale produces the better answer?

---

8. Even if the books are regarded as capital expenditures, Haverly should be able to deduct the cost under Section 179 which permits expensing of the first $10,000 in capital expenditures. Section 179 is intended to provide a modest tax incentive for small businesses. Notice the phase-out of Section 179(b)(2) which begins to reduce the amount that can be expensed dollar for dollar once capital expenditures for the year exceed $200,000.

Chapter 37

IMPLICATIONS OF RECAPTURE

A. INTRODUCTORY NOTES AND QUESTIONS

Review the facts of *International Shoe Machine* (Chapter 27). The controversy in this case arose before the enactment of Section 1245 in 1961. How was the issue largely mooted for future cases by Section 1245?

Suppose that you own a rental apartment building with fifty units. If you convert the property into a condominium and sell the units, does the character of the gain or loss depend on whether the units are investment or inventory property? Why would Section 1250 *not* moot the dual character asset question in this case, as Section 1245 has for shoe manufacturing machinery? Are your chances for preferential capital gain treatment increased if you first try to sell the apartment house as rental property to a single buyer and fail? What if condominium conversion occurs not from your own initiative but as a result of tenant action under a local ordinance permitting a stated majority of tenants to force you to sell the individual units? Might the forced liquidation exception of *Biedenharn Realty* (Chapter 27) apply?

B. REDWING CARRIERS, INC. v. TOMLINSON
399 F.2d 652 (5th Cir. 1968)

GOLDBERG, CIRCUIT JUDGE:

This case involves another attempt by a taxpayer to insulate himself from the incidence of taxation by means of paper armor. The question presented is whether a taxpayer may shape what is essentially an integrated purchase and trade-in transaction of new and used trucks into two separate transactions in order to recognize an immediate gain at capital gains rates and concomitantly to take a larger depreciation deduction from ordinary income. We agree with the district court that this transaction is an exchange rather than two sales, and thus comes within the coverage of Section 1031 of the Internal Revenue Code.

This appeal involves income tax liabilities for the calendar years 1958 through 1961 in the total amount of $66,630.33. The plaintiff below and appellant here, Redwing Carriers, Inc., paid the assessments in question and sued in the district court for a refund with interest.

The following facts were substantially stipulated, and the district court's findings on the few disputed fact questions were not clearly erroneous. Redwing is a Florida corporation engaged in the business of hauling bulk commodities as a common carrier, subject to regulation by the Interstate Commerce Commission. Trucksales, Inc., a Florida corporation engaged in the business of selling trucks, parts and equipment, is a wholly-owned subsidiary of Redwing. During the years in question Trucksales was a franchised dealer for G.M.C. trucks. Charles E. Mendez, as president and chairman of the board of both Redwing and Trucksales, was the moving force behind the transactions in question.

During 1958 Trucksales purchased twenty-eight new G.M.C. diesel tractor trucks from G.M.C. for cash. At or about the same time Redwing transferred title to twenty-seven used trucks to G.M.C. for cash. In 1959 and 1961 essentially identical transactions involving thirty-six and fourteen trucks, respectively, were executed. Also during 1959 transactions in like form were executed with White Motor Company.

Because it is an extremely profitable trucking concern, Redwing is considered a prestige account by both G.M.C. and White Motor Company. Thus Mendez, who handled all negotiations in these transactions, was in a strong bargaining position and was able to insist upon casting these purchases of new equipment and trade-ins in the form of separate purchases of the new and sales of the old.

Mendez did not specify which corporation he was representing at any time to either White or G.M.C., and it made no difference to the manufacturers whether they were dealing with Redwing or with Trucksales. Both Redwing and Trucksales used the same Tampa address on the checks used in these transactions, even though Trucksales is located in Fort Lauderdale and even though it used a Fort Lauderdale bank account for all of its other business activities. Most of the trucks involved were delivered by White and G.M.C. directly to Redwing in Tampa, despite the fact that they were ostensibly being sold to Trucksales in Fort Lauderdale for resale to Redwing.

In addition to the above indicia of transactional unity, the district court found a definite contractual interdependency between the sale of new trucks and the trade-in of old trucks. In its findings of fact the court noted: "There would have been no purchase by plaintiffs of new trucks or tractors without concurrent and binding agreements to purchase plaintiff's used equipment."[1]

---

1. This finding of fact was in fact substantiated by the testimony of Charles E. Mendez:
"Q. Mr. Mendez, when you negotiated these ideals with White and General Motors Corporation for the purchase of new equipment, did you insist that they agree to take your old equipment as a part of each of these deals?
A. Well, I was buying a certain number of trucks, and I was selling a certain number of trucks.
A. But as a part of the agreement to buy the new trucks, did you insist that they take these used trucks?
A. Well, it was part of the deal. Sure.
Q. It was part of the deal?
A. Yes, sir."

The district court further found that G.M.C. viewed these transactions as trade-ins which were occasioned by the purchase of new equipment and that the form of selling the old and purchasing the new was arranged *solely* on Mendez' insistence. A G.M.C. executive testified that the price which G.M.C. paid for the used trucks was in excess of their fair market value and that G.M.C would be able to calculate a profit only by viewing the purchases of used trucks and sales of new trucks as one transaction.

It is apparent that Mendez sculptured these transactions so as to achieve the best possible tax results for Redwing. Instead of obtaining customary discounts from the retail price of the new trucks, Mendez would insist that the manufacturers add the discount amount to the price of the used trucks being repurchased. The gain of the trade-in price over the depreciated basis of the used trucks would be recognized at capital gains rates, and the basis of the new trucks for depreciation purposes would be inflated. As a result, Redwing's depreciation deductions from ordinary income would also be inflated, resulting in considerable tax savings.

As is obvious from the above facts, these Mendez-dominated transactions were severable in form only. In substance, the sale was in bondage to the purchase and the purchase indissolubly dependent upon the sale. If Redwing had not carried out the agreement to buy the new trucks, the auto makers would have had no juristic obligation to purchase the used trucks. The buying and selling were synchronous parts meshed into the same transaction and not independent transactions.

Section 1031 requires the nonrecognition of gain or loss in transactions when in theory the taxpayer may have realized gain or loss, but in substance his economic interest in the property has remained virtually unchanged by the transaction. Century Electric Co. v. Commissioner [Chapter 17]. With its paper armor crumpled, Redwing's transactions are brought directly within the ambit of Section 1031, and, more specifically, within that of Treas. Reg. § 1.1031(a)–1(c):

> (c) No gain or loss is recognized if (1) a taxpayer exchanges property held for productive use in his trade or business, together with cash for other property of like kind for the same use *such as a truck for a new truck* or a passenger automobile for a new passenger automobile to be used for a like purpose; . . .

Because of the expertise of Internal Revenue Service in interpreting the Internal Revenue Code which it is charged with administering, Treasury regulations come to us with great persuasive force. . . . When, as here, the regulation has long continued without substantial change, applying to unamended or substantially reenacted statutes, the regulation is deemed to have the effect of law. . . . Judge Brown, speaking for our Court, articulated this rule of construction as follows:

> When a Treasury Regulation interprets a section of the Code and the Regulation remains in effect and unchanged for a long period of time, re-enactment of the statute without change is presumed to show congressional approval of the Regulation which thereby acquires the force and effect of law. . . .

The relevant part of Treas.Reg. § 1.1031(a)–1(c), as well as Section 1031(a) of the Internal Revenue Code, is identical to its predecessor under the 1939 Code. Despite extensive changes in the Internal Revenue Code in 1954, no change was made in what is now § 1031(a). Further amendments were made to other parts of § 1031 in 1958 and 1959, but § 1031(a) was left untouched. It is reasonable to assume, therefore, that Congress knew and approved of the application of § 1031(a) to trade-ins of trucks.

The Treasury's interpretation of § 1031(a) was also manifested in Revenue Ruling 61–119, 1961–1 Cum.Bull. 395. This Ruling bears directly on the exact question at bar:

> Where a taxpayer sells old equipment used in his trade or business to a dealer and purchases new equipment of like kind from the dealer under circumstances which indicate that the sale and the purchase are reciprocal and mutually dependent transactions, the sale and purchase is an exchange of property within the meaning of section 1031 of the Internal Revenue Code of 1954, even though the sale and purchase are accomplished by separately executed contracts and are treated as unrelated transactions by the taxpayer and the dealer for record keeping purposes.

The district court in its conclusions of law relied heavily on that Ruling, and we agree. Although the Ruling does not have the force and effect of law, we find it to be a persuasive interpretation of the Code and Regulations. . . .

Despite Redwing's arguments to the contrary, Revenue Ruling 61–119 is founded upon well established principles of tax law. Both the Supreme Court and our Court have on numerous occasions stated that when the realities of a transaction differ from its paper shell, the Internal Revenue Service and the courts may open the shell and look inside to determine the substance of the transaction. . . .

Equally well established is the corollary that an integrated transaction may not be separated into its components for the purposes of taxation by either the Internal Revenue Service or the taxpayer. . . .

> In determining the incidence of taxation, we must look through form and search out the substance of a transaction. . . . [cases cited] This basic concept of tax law is particularly pertinent to cases involving a series of transactions designed and executed as parts of a unitary plan to achieve an intended result. Such plans will be viewed as a whole regardless of whether the effect of so doing is imposition of or relief from taxation. The series of closely related steps in such a plan are merely the means by which to carry out the plan and will not be separated. . . .

The above cases show quite clearly that a tax-free exchange cannot be transformed into two sales by the arbitrary separation of time and exchange of cash. See Commissioner of Internal Revenue v. North Shore Bus Co., . . . which held that a trade-in of used busses in connection with a purchase of new ones was an exchange governed by the predecessor of Section 1031 despite the taxpayer's receipt of cash from the seller in order to pay off the mortgage on the used busses. . . .

The appellant attempts to bolster its defenses, however, with a decision from our Court, Carlton v. United States.... In that case the taxpayer had sold ranch property to a purchasing corporation for cash. As part of this sale, the purchaser had assigned to the taxpayer contracts to purchase two similar tracts of land, which purchases the taxpayer had immediately consummated. Although it was stipulated that both the taxpayer and the purchaser had intended to effect an exchange—indeed that they had performed the three-way transaction merely to avoid unnecessary duplication in title transfer—we refused to accept the taxpayer's classification of the overall transaction as a tax-free exchange under Section 1031.

The appellant would have us follow *Carlton* here as if that case had ignored transactional substance and instead had viewed the whole only as an aggregate of separate, unrelated transfers. On the contrary, in that case we gave weight to the various individual transfers *only* because they *were* separate and unrelated. In *Carlton* we were reviewing a three-way transaction in which the taxpayer had received, in return for property, cash which was not restricted in use to the purchase of like property. The most that could be said for the transactional relationship in *Carlton* was that the sale for cash between the taxpayer and a purchaser had been *complementary* with the later purchase of like property between the taxpayer and a seller. In the case at bar, however, there were only two parties to each exchange of trucks (ignoring intracorporate fictional distinctions), and the alleged "sale" and "trade-in sales," instead of being separate, were related by contractual interdependency.

In *Carlton* both the transfers of land and the interparty obligations were severable and, in fact, severed. Here we find, as did the district court, the same transactional twining from beginning to end. *Carlton,* then, is clearly distinguishable and certainly does not stand as an obstacle to the pertinent tax considerations which we have discussed supra.[2]

Taxation is transactional and not cuneiform. Our tax laws are not so supple that scraps of paper, regardless of their calligraphy, can transmute trade-ins into sales. Although Redwing's transfers may have been paper sales, they were actual exchanges. A taxpayer may engineer his transactions to minimize taxes, but he cannot make a transaction appear to be what it

---

2. *Carlton* is distinguishable on one ground other than those which have been previously discussed. *Carlton* involved the taxpayer's, not the Commissioner's, contention that documentary form was irrelevant in light of the "substance" of the transaction. In such circumstances the Commissioner's evidentiary problems became paramount because of the lack of insider information to prove or disprove true "substance." Moreover, since "substance" considerations can often be viewed effectively only from hindsight, the neglect of "form" could engender post-transactional tax planning on the part of many taxpayers. On the other hand, when as here the taxpayer insists that we abide by his forms and the Commissioner attempts to convince us otherwise, there is little danger, should we reject form, of our having been misled by insider reconstruction of a transaction after its effects have been determined. We, therefore, read *Carlton* as teaching that although a taxpayer's own documents are not conclusive, they normally override any conflicting subjective considerations advanced by that taxpayer.

Especially, in light of the above distinction, we see no need in comparing *Carlton* with preceding cases through obiter dicta for a determination of whether the vital missing ingredient there was (1) the lack per se of a two-party exchange of ownership rights in like property or merely (2) the failure of the cash transfer to be contractually intertwined to the immediate purchase of like property.

is not. Documents record transactions, but they do not always become the sole criteria for transaction analysis.

Affirmed.

C. NOTES AND QUESTIONS

1) Form and Substance

In *Redwing Carriers,* used trucks were sold for cash and new trucks purchased for cash in two different transactions, separated by several weeks. The IRS argued that both the intermediate cash step and the time interval should be ignored, and that the two separate transactions should be recast as a single like-kind exchange. Was this consistent with the IRS position, in two-party exchanges involving real estate, that the intermediate cash step should be given significance (Chapter 18)? And with the IRS position in *Starker* (Chapter 18) that Section 1031 requires simultaneous transfers? Or can the positions be reconciled on the basis of the general approach to questions of form and substance articulated in Higgins v. Smith (Chapter 14)? See footnote 2 to *Redwing Carriers.*

Suppose that the taxpayer had sold the used trucks to one dealer and bought new trucks from a different dealer. Do you think that the court would have been as willing to recast the two cash sales as a like-kind exchange? *Should* Redwing Carriers be treated differently if the deal involves three parties instead of two? Or if the deal involves only two parties but the trucks are not sold for a price in excess of fair market value?

2) The Stakes in *Redwing Carriers*

From the taxpayer's perspective, what was the point of designing the transaction as two separate sales for cash, rather than as a like-kind exchange? Note that the transaction occurred in 1958, four years before the enactment of Section 1245. Assume that each used truck had an adjusted basis of $90 and was sold for $150 in cash and that each new truck was purchased for $200 in cash. If the taxpayer's form is respected, how much and what kind of gain is reported from the sale of the used trucks? What is the adjusted basis for the new trucks? If recast as a like-kind exchange, how do the answers change (assume that the taxpayer is viewed as trading the used trucks plus $50 in cash for the new trucks)?

Suppose that the taxpayer has a capital gains tax rate of 25% and an ordinary income tax rate of 50%. What is the disadvantage of sale treatment? What is the more than offsetting advantage? Why is the higher basis for the new trucks desirable? What can it be used to reduce and when? How does the time value of money affect the taxpayer's calculation of potential tax savings?

3) The Effect of Section 1245

What does the enactment of Section 1245 do to the *Redwing Carriers* transaction? How does it affect the character of the gain reported when the used trucks are sold for cash? Why does the tax cost of obtaining a higher basis for the new trucks become unacceptable?

Suppose that after the enactment of Section 1245, Redwing Carriers designs the following transaction to avoid the statute's effect. Used trucks are sold on the installment method, with most of the payment not due for five years and new trucks are separately purchased. Why is this transaction preferable to trading used trucks plus cash for new trucks? How is Redwing Carriers able to obtain a higher basis for the new trucks at an acceptable tax cost?

Will this transaction be respected? Or will the IRS be able to recast the two separate sales as a like-kind exchange? See *Jordan Marsh* (Chapter 17). See also Section 453(i), which now denies the installment method of reporting to the extent of recapture gains. On the sale of property for deferred payment, the recapture gain is taxed immediately, even though reporting of other gain may be deferred.

4) The Overvaluation Problem

Redwing Carriers sold the used trucks for more than their fair market value. Why was the purchaser willing to pay an excess amount? How did Redwing Carriers return the excess when it purchased new trucks? What was the tax advantage for Redwing Carriers of being paid an excess amount for the used trucks and then paying the same excess amount for the new trucks? How did the excess affect the amount of gain reported on the sale of the used trucks and the basis allocable to the new trucks? What limits the amount of excess purchase price designated in the transaction?

*

PART FOUR

Tax Shelters

A tax shelter can be defined as an investment that produces artificial tax losses which are used to offset, or *shelter,* other taxable income. Two kinds of tax shelters have been examined previously in this casebook: the commodity straddle in connection with the realization principle (Chapter 16) and hobby losses in connection with the treatment of property not held "for profit" (Chapter 30).

Part Four attempts a more systematic examination of tax shelters. A historical perspective has been adopted in order to emphasize the evolution of judicial and Congressional responses to the problem. Part Four starts with a passenger airplane tax shelter that was primarily a 1960s phenomenon. Although this particular shelter has not been viable for fifteen years, it is worth studying because the basic structural principles are unchanged, and it provides a good vehicle for beginning to examine the evolution of the law.

Chapter 38

AIRPLANE (AND OTHER EQUIPMENT-LEASING) TAX SHELTERS OF THE 1960S

A. THE TALK OF THE TOWN
The New Yorker (October 17, 1970)

Now that the passengers hijacked by Arab guerrillas have been released unharmed, our attention has returned to a tantalizing sentence in one *Times* account of the guerrillas' destruction of the Pan American 747 jet in Cairo. "The jet, which is owned by the First National City Bank and another bank, not identified, is leased to Pan Am with the Bankers Trust Company as trustee," the *Times* said. Naïve enough to have believed that a Pan American jet would be owned by Pan American, we were amazed to have the *Times* inform us—in one sentence, as if reporting a routine business arrangement familiar to all—that the plane was owned by a jumble of banks, one of them anonymous. (Could it be, we wondered, that in the world of high finance there are not only numbered bank accounts but numbered banks?) We were curious enough to approach a financially astute friend of ours, a man we'll call Martin G. Cashflow, and ask him to explain who owns what.

"No big corporation owns what it appears to own," Cashflow said. "It wouldn't make sense taxwise."

"But why would a group of banks own a 747?" we asked.

"The banks don't actually own the 747," Cashflow said. "No bank owns what it appears to own."

We were more puzzled than ever, "You mean even the banks that aren't anonymous are not really the banks that own the 747?" we asked.

"That's not the point," Cashflow replied. "The banks probably represent a bunch of trust-account customers who have grouped together to buy a 747."

"But why would a bunch of trust-account customers want a 747?" we asked. "Would they all be going to the same place at the same time? Three hundred and sixty-two of them?"

"They don't want a 747," Cashflow said, in the manner of someone explaining the milk-producing property of cows to a well-behaved but slow-witted child. "They want the depreciation."

"Depreciation?"

"Depreciation," Cashflow said. "For tax purposes, depreciation cancels out income, and airplanes happen to have a very good depreciation picture. In five or six years, they can be totally depreciated, and then they can be sold."

"But who would want to buy a totally depreciated airplane?" we protested. "If it's totally depreciated, it doesn't exist."

"Of course it exists," Cashflow said, trying to keep a condescending smile from surfacing. "It's only for tax purposes that it's totally depreciated. It would still fly, and show movies, and all that. Also, it would be very valuable for the next owner, because he could totally depreciate it all over again."

We considered the hijacking for a while in the light of the new information provided by Cashflow. "Aha!" we said, at last. "Then the Arab guerrillas made a mistake. They're supposed to be against the American government. But by blowing up the 747 they destroyed twenty-four million dollars' worth of depreciation, and that means that the trust-account customers will now have to pay the American government taxes on the income from twenty-four million dollars that was going to be cancelled out by the depreciation, and the government can use the money to put armed guards on 747s and send Phantom jets to Israel and replace burned-out U.S.I.A. libraries."

"Don't be silly," Cashflow said. "The plane was fully insured, and nine and a half million dollars of the insurance was carried by the government, which will now have nine and a half million dollars less to spend on guards and jets and libraries. For people without professional tax advice, those guerrillas aren't so stupid."

"Except that they have one big problem left," we said. "They're Marxist revolutionaries, and what's the use of being Marxist revolutionaries if no one owns what he appears to own? If they took everything away from the big corporations and the banks, they still wouldn't have anything."

"Are you kidding?" Cashflow said. "They'd have some fantastically valuable depreciation."

B. ZEITLIN, TAX PLANNING IN EQUIPMENT-LEASING SHELTERS

21 Major Tax Planning 621, 621–629 and 675–676 (1969)

Last year the *Wall Street Journal* ran a front page article which began "Here's how to save money on income taxes," and continued:

> Get a bunch of friends, form a partnership, pool some money, borrow a lot more and use it all to buy railroad equipment or jetliners. Then lease the

equipment to railroads or airlines, taking the 7% tax credit on capital goods purchases to reduce your personal income tax.

The *Journal* described this as a "simple," "sophisticated," and "perfectly legal" "maneuver" which would save high-bracket taxpayers "tens of thousands of dollars in taxes in the first few years." While it noted that the tax benefit declines each year and that, after some years, the investor's tax liability actually increases, it stated that there was a "simple way" out of that problem—investing in a new equipment-leasing partnership. The *Journal* article went on to quote an unnamed "Official of the Internal Revenue Service in Washington" to the effect that the maneuver is just "intelligent tax planning" and therefore inferentially unassailable under present law.

This paper will examine the structure of the typical equipment-leasing syndicate described in the *Journal* article and will show that it is not nearly as simple a maneuver as it appears, that the anticipated tax benefits are not always assured under present tax law, and that it may not be quite so easy for the investor to extricate himself without adverse tax effect.

Parties Involved

The typical equipment-leasing syndicate is tailored to serve the needs and desires of two groups—the investors and the lessees. Typically, the investors are individuals with large amounts of ordinary income and consequently, high federal income tax brackets who are looking for ways of reducing their taxes, i.e., "sheltering" some of their ordinary taxable income by offsetting it with tax deductions, etc. They respond eagerly to a plan which requires a minimal investment but produces a return by way of tax reduction which is both quick and apparently riskless.

The lessees are businesses which need new equipment but would rather lease than purchase it. The last twenty years have witnessed a tremendous growth in leasing of all kinds. There are, of course, many reasons for leasing rather than purchasing; some real, some fancied. Among the more important are the following:

The lessee may have insufficient available cash to purchase the asset and its borrowing may be effectively limited by existing bond indentures or the exhaustion of its ordinary credit sources. Or the lessee may prefer to lease rather than buy because of a desire to improve the appearance of its balance sheet or to maintain a balance between debts and lease obligations. Finally, the lessee may lease because it fears rapid obsolescence or wants to test a new type of equipment without heavy initial investment.

Perhaps the most important reason for leasing is that the lessee is able to reduce his net cost, that is, the lessor offers him a better deal than the lender. Thus, the *Wall Street Journal* story states that United Airlines was able to lease planes for a cost equivalent to a 3.76 percent per year interest charge whereas it would have had to borrow at 5½ to 6 percent. In large measure the lower price offered by the lessor is attributable to the tax benefits the lessor believes it will obtain—tax benefits the lessee is willing to forego.

Thus the lessee may have no use for the investment tax credit even with the carryover. He can then reduce the real cost of the use of the equipment by bartering the investment credit to the lessor in exchange for lower rents. Similarly, the lessor may be able to make better use of the accelerated depreciation deductions than the lessee and may be willing to share that tax advantage with the lessee through lower rental charges. The lessee would, of course, obtain full deductions for reasonable rental payments.

Format

Typically, a limited partnership is formed with about fifty or so limited partners, each making a substantial investment (say $50,000 or more), and the promoters or their nominees as general partners, usually making only a nominal investment. The partnership leverages its capital by obtaining a nonrecourse loan of at least four times capital, so that its initial equity is usually not more than 20 percent of the cost of the equipment.

The partnership "purchases" the desired equipment and enters into a "lease" with the lessee. The lease terms vary widely but it is usually a full payout lease (i.e., rental payments over the initial term will repay the entire loan plus interest, the promoters' fees and management expense, and possibly some of the partnership capital investment). Because of the current competition for desirable equipment-leasing opportunities, it is no longer customary for the lessors to obtain any cash flow or return on their capital investment during the lease term. In any event the cash flow will not be sufficient for the investors to recoup their capital.

The lessee may have the right to release for a further term, or to purchase, or both, but usually at fair market value. The residual (that is, the value of the equipment for sale or re-lease at the end of the initial lease term) is to be shared between the limited and general partners, with the latter usually getting a share disproportionately large relative to their minimal capital contributions. The investment credit is retained by the partnership (and allocated among the partners) rather than being passed on to the lessee.

For federal income tax purposes, the partnership elects accelerated depreciation and a useful life about as long as the lease term. Determination of salvage value is either initially avoided by use of the double-declining-balance method of depreciation or set at a very low figure if the sum-of-the-years'-digits method is used.

In the early years of the lease, the large depreciation deductions plus the interest deductions exceed the rental income and the partnership sustains tax losses which are passed through to the partners. Each partner also claims his share of the investment credit earned by the partnership in the first year.

Assuming level rental payments, the early losses diminish as accelerated depreciation begins to run down and interest charges decline. About halfway through the lease term, the partnership (and hence the partners) begins to realize taxable income which increases for the remainder of the lease term. At the end of the lease term, the loan will have been repaid and the partnership will obtain the asset. It may then be sold or leased again, assuming it then has any value beyond scrap.

Superficially, the transaction looks very favorable from the investor's point of view. The only business risks he takes are that lessee will not meet the rental payments and that the tax deductions will not be of value to him because his other taxable income declines drastically. If these risks do not materialize, his after-tax return will be very large even if the residual is valueless. If the asset turns out to have a substantial residual value and the investor retains his interest to the end, he will have an additional bonanza. As illustrated in the Examples appended hereto, the investor anticipates that he will recover his entire investment in about two years by making effective use of his share of the investment credit and the partnership losses to reduce his taxes. He further envisions a continuing substantial return on his investment, through additional losses to be converted into tax savings, over roughly the first half of the lease term. Finally, he probably expects to dispose of his limited partnership interest (or to neutralize it) at or before the "crossover" point, that is, the time he would begin to realize taxable income from the partnership. . . .

Example

Two jet airplanes on a 15-year net lease to a major airline

```
Cost of planes .................................................. $13,000,000
Partnership capital ............................................... 3,000,000
Partnership debt ................................................. 10,000,000
```

. . .

A. *Economic return to all limited partners*

1. No cash flow during term of lease
2. 80 percent of value of planes (or further rentals) at end of 15 years

Value of residuals in 15 years necessary to give limited partners:

a. Return of capital = $3,750,000 or 29 percent of original cost.

b. Return of capital plus 5 percent per annum = $7,500,000 or 58 percent original cost.

B. *Anticipated after-tax return to limited partner investing $100,000 (3.3 percent), assuming 70 percent federal income tax bracket*

Year	Taxable Income	Tax Impact	Cash Payout	Net Investment ($100,000) or profit
1	(5,000)	(33,000)	0	(67,000)
2	(54,000)	(38,000)	"	(29,000)
3	(51,000)	(36,000)	"	7,000

Year	Taxable Income	Tax Impact	Cash Payout	Net Investment ($100,000) or profit
4	(47,000)	(33,000)	"	40,000
5	(44,000)	(30,000)	"	70,000
6	(40,000)	(28,000)	"	98,000
7	(12,000)	(8,000)	"	106,000
8	(6,000)	(4,000)	"	110,000
9	(1,000)	(1,000)	"	111,000
10	5,000	3,000	"	108,000
11	11,000	7,000	"	101,000
12	16,000	11,000	"	90,000
13	22,000	16,000	"	74,000
14	29,000	20,000	"	54,000
15	35,000	24,000	"	30,000
16	41,000	29,000	"	1,000
Totals	(101,000)	(100,000)	0	

C. NOTES AND QUESTIONS

1) The Basic Structure

The equipment-leasing tax shelter described in the preceding article by Professor Zeitlin is not the only way for an airline, say Pan Am, to acquire the use of a passenger airplane. Pan Am itself might purchase and own the airplane. Pan Am probably would pay cash for only a fraction of the cost and would borrow the balance. In Professor Zeitlin's example, where the airplane cost $13 million, Pan Am would pay $3 million down, borrow $10 million from a bank (pledging the airplane as security), and repay the loan in monthly installments over sixteen years.

Alternatively, Pan Am might opt to lease the airplane from a tax shelter syndicate. In Professor Zeitlin's example, a partnership of thirty individuals purchases the airplane with the same financing terms that would have been available to Pan Am. The partnership's role is that of owner and borrower, while Pan Am's status is that of lessee.

The leasing arrangement has three critical features. First, the lease is a *net* lease under which Pan Am is responsible for all maintenance, taxes, and insurance of the airplane. Rent is paid to the lessor after all the usual expenses of maintaining the airplane have been met. Therefore, the rent is an amount net of all such expenses.

Second, the lease is a full payout lease, which means that the rent will pay off the mortgage in full. Usually, there is an exact correspondence between the lease term and the mortgage term—both are for sixteen years—and that monthly rent due under the lease exactly equals monthly payments due on the mortgage.

Third, the mortgage obligation is without recourse to the tax shelter partnership but is secured by the lease as well as by the airplane. What is the effect of making the lease security for the mortgage? In the event of default on the mortgage, against whom does the lender have recourse?

2) Direct Ownership and Leasing Compared

Compare direct ownership with leasing from the perspective of each of the parties involved. Should the lender care which arrangement—direct ownership or leasing—Pan Am chooses? Does the particular choice affect the mortgage repayment schedule? Does the bank's security appear to be any greater with one arrangement or the other?

From Pan Am's perspective, how does owning differ from leasing? What does Pan Am gain by deciding to lease? What does it lose? If Pan Am believes that it is unlikely to have taxable income in the near future and that sixteen-year-old airplanes will be regarded as obsolete, which arrangement is Pan Am likely to prefer? How does Section 172 affect the attractiveness of leasing?

What do the partners get by investing $3 million in cash (with thirty partners, $100,000 each) in the airplane tax shelter? Will they receive any net cash flow from the lease, that is, will rent exceed expenses? At the end of the lease, the mortgage will have been paid off and the partnership will own, free and clear, a sixteen-year-old jet airplane. What are the chances that this residual interest in the airplane will provide an adequate return on the initial cash investment by the partners? (Conservative investment counselors would advise disregarding the residual altogether and so it will be for the remainder of this discussion.)

If neither the lease nor the residual provides any significant benefits, what are the partners getting in return for a cash investment of $100,000 apiece?

3) The Tax Benefits

From a before-tax perspective (that is, without taking tax benefits into account), the tax shelter is a losing proposition. Each partner has contributed $100,000 in cash but has received nothing in return. Over the sixteen-year term of the lease, cash received (in the form of rent for the use of the airplane) just equals cash paid out (for payments of principal and interest on the mortgage). The residual when the lease ends is too speculative to be counted. In effect, the transaction results in a $100,000 loss for each investor—*but only before the tax effects are taken into account.*

From an after-tax perspective, a radically different picture emerges. There are two distinct tax benefits associated with ownership of the airplane. First, each partner is entitled to a $30,000 investment tax credit. (There are thirty partners in the airplane costing $13 million, so that each partner's share of the cost is $433,333. The investment tax credit equals 7% of the cost.) Second, each partner is entitled to deduct any losses (and must report any gains) from leasing the airplane. The next step, therefore, is to determine how to calculate each partner's share of deductible loss (or taxable gain) under the lease.

4) Calculating Each Year's Loss (or Gain)

How is the amount of loss (or gain) determined? Each partner must report rental receipts under Section 61(a) but is permitted to deduct interest under Section 163 and depreciation under Section 167. The relative amounts of these three variables—rent, interest, and depreciation—affect the net loss or gain each year. How each of these amounts varies over the sixteen-year lease term is discussed below.

a) *Rent*—Under the lease, rent is a fixed monthly amount, equal to the monthly payment due on the mortgage. Thus, rental receipts are constant over the sixteen-year term of the lease.

b) *Interest*—Each monthly mortgage payment is allocated first to interest accumulating on the loan and second to repayment of principal. During the early years of the mortgage, almost all of each payment is composed of interest and only a small fraction is left to repay principal. But as time goes by and the principal is repaid, the amount of interest that accumulates each month falls (since interest is a constant percentage of unpaid principal). In the last few years of the mortgage, only a small fraction of each payment is composed of interest and most represents repayment of principal. Thus, interest deductions are high during the early years and gradually decline over the term of the mortgage.

c) *Depreciation*—Sinking fund method depreciation follows a pattern opposite that for interest deductions. As discussed in Chapter 35, depreciation would begin at a relatively low level and gradually increase over the life of the asset. One would expect the airplane to depreciate no faster than the sinking fund schedule according to which the bank requires repayment of principal on the mortgage. Otherwise, the value of the bank's security would fall more rapidly than the unpaid loan balance.

If the airplane were depreciated under the sinking fund method, total annual deductions for interest plus depreciation would be more or less constant. Interest deductions would start out high and gradually decline. Sinking fund depreciation would start low and gradually rise. As a result, with rent constant, the investor's $100,000 loss would be almost evenly spread over the sixteen-year period, about $6,250 a year.

However, with the accelerated method actually permitted, depreciation deductions are front-loaded. Three-quarters of the available depreciation is recovered in the first nine years. Because deductions for depreciation, as well as for interest, are very high in early years and gradually decline, the actual loss is overstated during the first part of the lease as being $261,000. During years 10–16, with little depreciation remaining, the investor reports artificially high gains of $161,000. The loss and gain for each year are set out in the left-hand column of Table 38-1, which is derived from the figures presented at the end of Professor Zeitlin's article.

Notice that the net loss over the sixteen-year period is still $100,000. This figure corresponds to the real economic loss of $100,000, incurred because the investor pays in $100,000 in cash and (ignoring the residual) receives zero return. But depreciation under the accelerated method greatly distorts the timing of the loss, to the taxpayer's advantage.

During the first nine years of the lease, what is the amount of excess losses created by using accelerated instead of sinking fund method depreciation? During years 10 through 16, what is the amount of excess gains? If you are a 70% bracket taxpayer, what is the extra amount saved in taxes during the first nine years? Paid back in taxes during years 10 through 16?

5) Financial Analysis: Valuation of the Losses

To measure the tax advantage of accelerated depreciation in the airplane tax shelter, the losses and gains over the sixteen-year lease term must be discounted to present value. In order to do these present value calculations, an interest rate must be chosen. One possibility is to choose a rate based on how the tax benefits from the shelter will be invested (Chapter 12). If the partners plan to invest their tax savings in tax-exempt bonds earning 5%, that rate could be used.

Table 38-1 uses a 5% discount rate to analyze the airplane tax shelter. This table assumes that both the first-year depreciation and the investment tax credit provide an immediate benefit and therefore neither has to be discounted to present value. Second-year depreciation is assumed to provide tax savings in one year, third-year depreciation is assumed to provide tax savings in two years, and so on.

Study the table carefully. What is the total present value of losses generated in years 1–9? Of gains generated in years 10–16? What is the net of the present value of the losses minus the present value of the gains? The answer to the last question is the present value of the accelerated depreciation deductions. What is it worth to a 70% bracket investor? To a 50% bracket investor? Considering the benefits of both accelerated depreciation and the investment tax credit, is $100,000 a fair price to pay for the tax shelter investment? Is this shelter a sensible investment for anyone whose marginal tax rate is no more than 50%?

TABLE 38-1. FINANCIAL ANALYSIS OF THE AIRPLANE TAX SHELTER

Year	Gain or Loss	PV Multiplier (5%)	Present Value
1	− 5,000	1.000	− 5,000
2	− 54,000	.952	− 51,408
3	− 51,000	.907	− 46,257
4	− 47,000	.864	− 40,608
5	− 44,000	.823	− 36,212
6	− 40,000	.784	− 31,360
7	− 12,000	.746	− 8,952
8	− 6,000	.711	− 4,266
9	− 1,000	.677	− 677
Sub-Total	− 260,000		− 224,740
10	+ 5,000	.645	+ 3,225
11	+ 11,000	.614	+ 6,754

Year	Gain or Loss	PV Multiplier (5%)	Present Value
12	+ 16,000	.585	+ 9,360
13	+ 22,000	.557	+ 12,254
14	+ 29,000	.530	+ 15,370
15	+ 35,000	.505	+ 17,675
16	+ 42,000[1]	.481	+ 20,202
Sub-Total	+ 160,000		+ 84,840
Total (Losses + Gains)	− 100,000		− 139,900
Net Tax Saving From Depreciation		50% bracket	+ 69,950
		70% bracket	+ 97,930
Investment Tax Credit			+ 30,000
Total Tax Saving		50% bracket	+ 99,950
		70% bracket	+127,930

6) Assessing the Risks

What risks does the taxpayer incur by investing in the airplane tax shelter? The purely economic risks appear minimal. The desired deductions will fail to materialize only if Pan Am defaults on its obligation to pay rent under the lease *and* the lender forecloses on the airplane. The deductions will not provide anticipated benefits only if the investor's tax bracket falls, probably as the result of a decline in earnings or in other investment income, or, if as now, tax rates are cut across the board.

Barring these eventualities, the primary contingency is legal—the risk that the IRS will successfully challenge the tax shelter arrangement and deny the tax benefits to the partners. Chapter 39 discusses how to assess this legal risk.

---

1. The table at the end of Professor Zeitlin's article actually shows a gain of $41,000 in year 16, subtotal gains of $159,000 for years 10–16, and total net loss for the entire 16 years of $101,000. The actual net loss figure should be only $100,000, corresponding to the $100,000 cash invested by each partner, with zero before-tax return when the residual is ignored. The extra $1,000 in net losses is probably the result of rounding off numbers in the table. To reach the correct net loss figure, income for the sixteenth year has been adjusted upward by $1,000.

D. EXIT GRACEFULLY

Zeitlin, Tax Planning in Equipment-Leasing Shelters, 21 Major Tax Planning 621, 663–671 (1969)

If the investor in an equipment-leasing syndicate is to realize fully the after-tax profit he anticipates, . . .the investor must arrange either for his safe exit from the partnership scene long before any realization on the residuals or must soon find a new and larger tax shelter.

About halfway through the term of the lease, the equipment-leasing syndicate, and hence its partners, will begin earning taxable income. Accelerated depreciation and interest deductions will by then have declined but rental income will ordinarily remain constant. At this point, if the situation of the investor-partner has not otherwise changed, he will be faced with a serious problem. In addition to the large ordinary income he originally sought to shield, he will have the income from the partnership piled on top and taxed at the highest rates. Moreover, the partnership will still be receiving no cash flow from the lease and will make no distributions to the partners. Thus the burden of additional tax liability will have to be met from the investor's other resources. The investor must then consider disposing of his partnership interest or shielding the taxable income it will throw off.

Sale of the Partnership Interest

The sale of the partnership interest in midstream would have three undesirable tax consequences—a large gain will probably be realized, much or all of the gain will be treated as ordinary income, and part or all of the investment credit will be recaptured.

Realization of gain

Gain on the sale of a partnership interest (like other assets) is measured by the excess of the amount realized over the adjusted basis. In addition to the cash and the fair market value of any property received by a partner on the sale of his interest, he will be treated as also realizing an amount equal to his share of the unpaid liability to which the leased asset is subject (i.e., the nonrecourse loan). Since the nonrecourse loan, like the typical real estate mortgage, is customarily repaid on a sinking fund basis, the outstanding indebtedness midway in the lease term will be large.

On the other hand the investor-partner's basis in his partnership interest will have been reduced [by the very large amount of accelerated depreciation] in earlier years which furnished the basis for his tax deductions in earlier years which furnished the basis for his tax deductions. Thus, the taxable spread between amount realized and adjusted basis should be substantial, at least if the residual then seems valuable and if a buyer in a low tax bracket (perhaps an exempt organization or a taxpayer with net operating losses) can be found. While such a buyer might not object to the prospect of years of taxable income with no cash flow, the partnership interest will probably sell for less than the apparent net value of the underlying assets because of the adverse tax effects it would have for the ordinary buyer.

Recognition of ordinary income—Section 1245

Gain on the sale of the partnership interest will probably be taxed as ordinary income. While gain on the sale of a partnership interest is generally treated as a capital gain, it is ordinary income to the extent attributable to unrealized receivables and appreciated inventory. "Unrealized receivables" includes potential Section 1245 income, that is, the amount which would have been treated as ordinary gain under Section 1245 if the partnership had then sold its Section 1245 property for fair market value. Since the principal partnership asset, the leased equipment, is Section 1245 property, the adjusted basis of which will have been reduced by the accelerated depreciation deductions, probably the entire gain on sale of the partnership interest will be taxed as ordinary income.

Investment credit recapture

In addition to the recognition of ordinary gain, the sale of a partnership interest is an event which will probably trigger investment credit recapture. Thus, if an eight-year or longer useful life was claimed by the partnership for the leased asset and a partner sells out within the first eight years, all or a portion of his investment credit must be repaid by way of a direct addition to his tax in the year of sale. For example, a sale of a partnership interest in the sixth or seventh year would result in a recapture of one-third of the seller's investment credit. . . .

Alternatives to a sale

Since the prospect of a large ordinary gain and investment credit recapture makes a sale of the partnership interest in the crossover year unpalatable, a number of alternative solutions have been proposed.

Pyramiding

Perhaps most frequently proposed is that the investor-partner pyramid or double-up, that is, invest in another equipment-leasing syndicate which will in its early years shelter the income originally shielded by the first venture and, provided the investor increases his capital investment, also shelter the income now being thrown off by that first syndicate.

Like all pyramiding schemes, this one depends on the continued availability of an ever-increasing source—here new equipment-leasing transactions that would be sound business investments as well as tax shelters. Thus, the potential investor in an equipment-leasing syndicate is betting that, some years from now (usually six to ten years), something like the present tax law and the present combination of business circumstances (money market, continuing expansion of our economy, etc.), which make equipment-leasing transactions financially feasible, will continue to exist. These are, I suspect, long-term predictions few economists or tax advisors would make with any degree of confidence, and the potential investor should be aware of the gamble. Of course, when the time arrives, the investor may be able to find another type of tax shelter.

Death or retirement

Among the other solutions for the problem of what to do when the partnership turns the taxable income corner, few are even as promising as pyramiding, although some may be quite satisfactory for persons in special circumstances. For example, if the investor-partner dies, his heirs may be able to sell out without tax consequence since they will arguably have a fair market value basis in the partnership interest and will not be subject to investment credit recapture.

Retaining the partnership interest to the end is a solution which is appropriate if the investor anticipates a reduction in his other taxable income. In such case he may not object to retaining his partnership interest and paying tax on the ordinary income at low rates as it rolls in (but without cash flow) over the last half of the lease term. He will have enjoyed his deductions against income otherwise taxable at higher rates in earlier years and both the rates and the timing are thus in his favor. The equipment-leasing syndicate will have served the investor as a kind of income averaging and tax-deferral device and the investment tax credit will have been a handsome bonus. In addition, by remaining in the partnership till the end of the lease, the investor may then share in the possible residual bonanza.

This type of planning may appeal to potential investors in equipment-leasing syndicates who anticipate retirement in a few years. But in this day and age of tax planning for retirement, the potential investor (particularly one sophisticated enough to contemplate an equipment-leasing investment) may find his post-retirement income larger than he realizes, after taking into account deferred compensation, pension and profit-sharing benefits, the fruits of stock options and other plans to defer income and tax to his post-retirement years.

Gifts

Another solution to the problem of unwanted taxable income in the later years of the lease that is often advanced is for the partner-investor to give away his partnership interest. Whether the donee of a gift is a tax-exempt charity, a relative in a low tax bracket, a controlled corporation, or another partnership, this "solution" raises many problems and seems questionable and even dangerous.

... To begin with, the gift would trigger investment credit recapture. Next, while there is considerable question as to whether the gift of property subject to a liability in excess of the donor's basis is a taxable event, at least two commentators have agreed that it is and their reasoning seems persuasive in the light of the existing authorities. It should also be noted that the charitable contribution deduction would in any event be reduced, probably to zero, by the amount that would have been treated as Section 1245 income if the partnership interest had been sold for its fair market value. . . .

E. NOTES AND QUESTIONS

1) The Significance of the Crossover Point: How Scrupulously Are Taxable Gains From Later Years Reported?

The crossover point is defined as the point at which the tax shelter no longer generates deductible losses and begins to show taxable income. In marketing shelter investments, promoters emphasized the tax benefits that arose from losses during the early years and glossed over the gains that had to be reported in later years when deductions for interest and depreciation declined. This may have overstated the value of the shelter for unsophisticated investors and induced below 50% bracket taxpayers to become involved.

The emphasis placed by promoters on deductible losses arising from shelters and the neglect of taxable gains may have had another consequence. While tax shelter losses from the early years were religiously reported, the taxable gains that arose in later years may not have been. Of course, the scrupulous taxpayer not only anticipated having to report taxable gains but also put aside some of the tax savings from early years to fund the taxes due after the crossover point was reached. But naive taxpayers, innocently equating cash flow with taxable income, may have believed that if they received no cash from the shelter investment, there could have been no income to report, no matter what the annual statement from the tax shelter partnership told them.

2) Can Reporting Shelter Gains Lawfully Be Avoided?

At the crossover point in the airplane tax shelter example, about three-quarters of available depreciation already has been deducted, so the original basis is reduced from $433,333 to $108,333. However, since mortgage principal is reduced according to a sinking fund schedule, considerably less than half of the $333,333 mortgage liability has been paid off. Suppose that, at the crossover point, the unpaid mortgage principal is $250,000. At this point, can the taxpayer lawfully avoid reporting future income by selling the tax shelter interest? In that event, what is the measure of the amount realized from a sale? Only the cash paid by the buyer? See *Tufts* (Chapter 24). What is the effect of Section 1245 on the character of the gain?

Suppose that, at the crossover point, an inter vivos gift is made of the tax shelter interest? What are the consequences of *Diedrich* (Chapter 22) when the donee is a lower bracket relative? What is the added effect of Sections 1011(b) and 170(e)(1) when the donee is a charity? How does a testamentary gift avoid the negative tax consequences of an inter vivos gift? See Section 1014(a).

Chapter 39

WILL THE AIRPLANE TAX SHELTER WORK?

A. INTRODUCTORY NOTE

Suppose that a client consults you on whether to invest in the airplane tax shelter described in Chapter 38. First, you should do a financial analysis to make sure that the tax shelter makes economic sense for your client. Table 38–1 indicates that your client should invest in the shelter only if his or her tax bracket is 50% or higher. Only in that event will the present value of the tax benefits equal or exceed the cost. Assuming that your client qualifies, you would next prepare a legal analysis to determine whether the IRS could successfully challenge the tax shelter arrangement. Consider what the following two cases indicate about the tax shelter's prospects.

B. HELVERING v. LAZARUS
308 U.S. 252 (1939)

MR. JUSTICE BLACK delivered the opinion of the Court.

In computing its net taxable income for 1930 and 1931, respondent claimed depreciation on three buildings occupied and used in its business as a department store. During those years, the legal title to two of these properties and an assignment of a ninety-nine year lease to the third were in a bank as trustee of certain land-trust certificate holders. These properties had been transferred to the trustee by the respondent in 1928 and the trustee had at the same time leased all three back to respondent for ninety-nine years, with option to renew and purchase. In claiming the deduction, respondent insisted that the capital loss from wear, tear, and exhaustion of the buildings was falling upon it, thus entitling it to the statutory allowance for depreciation of buildings. The Commissioner disallowed this deduction on the ground that the statutory right to depreciation follows legal title. . . .

[The] Board of Tax Appeals concluded that the transaction between respondent and the trustee bank was in reality a mortgage loan and ordered the deduction allowed, and the Circuit Court of Appeals affirmed. . . .

The federal income tax is aimed at net income determined from gross income less items such as necessary expenses incurred or capital consumed in earning it. Thus, the controlling statute permits a taxpayer in computing net income to deduct a "reasonable allowance for . . . exhaustion, wear and tear." While it may more often be that he who is both owner and user bears the burden of wear and exhaustion of business property in the nature of capital, one who is not the owner may nevertheless bear the burden of exhaustion of capital investment. Where it has been shown that a lessee using property in a trade or business must incur the loss resulting from depreciation of capital he has invested, the lessee has been held entitled to the statutory deduction.

Here, the taxpayer used business property in which it had a depreciable capital investment, provided it had not recovered its investment through a sale. The Board in substantial effect found that the instrument under which the taxpayer purported to convey legal ownership to the trustee bank was in reality given and accepted as no more than security for a loan on the property; the "rent" stipulated in the concurrently executed ninety-nine year "lease" back was intended as a promise to pay an agreed five per cent interest on the loan; and the "depreciation fund" required by the "lease" was intended as an amortization fund, designed to pay off the loan in forty-eight and one-half years. These findings are supported by evidence which permits, at most, conflicting inferences and are, therefore, conclusive here. And, unless the Board committed error of law we must affirm.

We think the Board justifiably concluded from its findings that the transaction between the taxpayer and the trustee bank, in written form a transfer of ownership with a lease back, was actually a loan secured by the property involved. General recognition has been given the "established doctrine that a court of equity will treat a deed, absolute in form, as a mortgage, when it is executed as security for a loan of money." In the field of taxation, administrators of the laws, and the courts, are concerned with substance and realities, and formal written documents are not rigidly binding. . . .

C. NOTES AND QUESTIONS

1) The Rationale of *Lazarus*

Why was Lazarus, the lessee, treated as the real owner of the building? The Supreme Court opinion is cursory and the reason for the holding is not clearly stated. Can it be deduced from the facts? Suppose that the property had been leased back for only fifteen years instead of ninety-nine years. Would Lazarus still have been treated as the owner? What was the relationship in *Lazarus* between the term of the lease and the expected useful life of the property?

2) Recharacterizing the Sale and Leaseback Transaction

Once Lazarus is treated as the owner, how should the sale and leaseback be recharacterized? If Lazarus is the owner, what does the receipt of cash on the "sale" really represent? What do rental payments under the "lease" really represent?

3) The Business Context

Why might the purchaser-lessor in *Lazarus* have wanted a sale and leaseback instead of a more conventional mortgage form? Might the purchaser-lessor have been concerned about foreclosing on its security in the event of default? Could one explain the choice of a sale and leaseback form by contrasting the property rights of a tenant defaulting on rent with an owner defaulting on a mortgage? If Lazarus were a tenant, rather than an owner, why might it be easier to force him off the property? Wouldn't it be just as effective to use a mortgage form and place the deed in escrow with instructions to record the lender as owner in case of default?

4) *Lazarus* versus *Jordan Marsh*

Jordan Marsh (Chapter 17) also involved a sale and leaseback transaction. The taxpayer sought to deduct the loss realized on the sale of a building that was simultaneously leased back for thirty years. Should the IRS have argued that, despite the formal "sale," the taxpayer remained the owner of the building and therefore had not yet realized a loss? What might distinguish the sale and leaseback in *Jordan Marsh* from the transaction in *Lazarus*? Was there arguably a different relationship between the term of the lease and the expected useful life of the building? Or was the relationship the same *if* the lease term in *Jordan Marsh* included renewal periods as well as the primary term?

5) Form and Substance

In *Lazarus*, which party is permitted to disregard form in favor of substance? Is *Lazarus* consistent with the approach to form and substance taken in Burnet v. Commonwealth Improvement, cited in Higgins v. Smith (Chapter 14)? How is *Lazarus* like *Alderson* (Chapter 18)?

D. ESTATE OF STARR v. COMMISSIONER
274 F.2d 294 (9th Cir. 1959)

CHAMBERS, CIRCUIT JUDGE.

Yesterday's equities in personal property seem to have become today's leases. This has been generated not a little by the circumstance that one who leases as a lessee usually has less trouble with the federal tax collector. At least taxpayers think so.

But the lease still can go too far and get one into tax trouble. While according to state law the instrument will probably be taken (with the consequent legal incidents) by the name the parties give it, the internal revenue service is not always bound and can often recast it according to what the service may consider the practical realities. . . . The principal case concerns a fire sprinkler system installed at the taxpayer's plant at Monrovia, California, where Delano T. Starr, now deceased, did business as the Gross Manufacturing Company. The "lessor" was "Automatic" Sprinklers of the Pacific, Inc., a California corporation. The instrument entitled "Lease Form of Contract" (hereafter "contract") is just about perfectly couched in terms of a lease for five years with annual rentals of $1,240. But it is the last paragraph thereof, providing for nominal rental for five years, that has caused the trouble. It reads as follows:

> 28. At the termination of the period of this lease, if Lessee has faithfully performed all of the terms and conditions required of it under this lease, it shall have the privilege of renewing this lease for an additional period of five years at a rental of $32.00 per year. If Lessee does not elect to renew this lease, then the Lessor is hereby granted the period of six months in which to remove the system from the premises of the Lessee.

Obviously, one renewal for a period of five years is provided at $32.00 per year, if Starr so desired. Note, though, that the paragraph is silent as to status of the system beginning with the eleventh year. Likewise the whole contract is similarly silent.

The tax court sustained the commissioner of internal revenue, holding that the five payments of $1,240, or the total of $6,200, were capital expenditures and not pure deductible rental. Depreciation of $269.60 was allowed for each year. Generally, we agree.

Taxpayers took the deduction as a rental expense under trade or business pursuant to Section [162(a)]. . . .

The law in this field for this circuit is established in Oesterreich v. Commissioner. . . . There we held that for tax purposes form can be disregarded for substance and, where the foreordained practical effect of the rent is to produce title eventually, the rental agreement can be treated as a sale.

In this, Starr's case, we do have the troublesome circumstance that the contract does not by its terms ever pass title to the system to the "lessee." Most sprinkler systems have to be tailor-made for a specific piece of property and, if removal is required, the salvageable value is negligible. Also, it stretches credulity to believe that the "lessor" ever intended to or would "come after" the system. And the "lessee" would be an exceedingly careless businessman who would enter into such contract with the practical possibility that the "lessor" would reclaim the installation. He could have believed only that he was getting the system for the rental money. And we think the commissioner was entitled to take into consideration the practical effect rather than the legal, especially when there was a record that on other such installations the "lessor", after the term of the lease was over, had not reclaimed from those who had met their agreed payments. It is obvious that the nominal rental payments after five years of $32.00 per year were just a service charge for inspection.

Recently the Court of Appeals for the Eighth Circuit has decided Western Contracting Corporation v. Commissioner, . . . reversing the tax court in its determination that the commissioner could convert leases of contractor's equipment into installment purchases of heavy equipment. The taxpayer believes that case strongly supports him here. We think not.

There are a number of facts there which make a difference. For example, in the contracts of Western there is no evidence that the payments on the substituted basis of rent would produce for the "lessor" the equivalent of his normal sales price plus interest. There was no right to acquire for a nominal amount at the end of the term as in *Oesterreich* and the value to the "lessor" in the personalty had not been exhausted as in Starr's case. And there was no basis for inferring that Western would just keep the equipment for what it had paid. It appears that Western paid substantial amounts to acquire the equipment at the end of the term. There was just one compelling circumstance against Western in its case: What it had paid as "rent" was apparently always taken into full account in computing the end purchase price. But on the other hand, there was almost a certainty that the "lessor" would come after his property if the purchase was not eventually made for a substantial amount. This was not even much of a possibility in *Oesterreich* and not a probability in Starr's case.

In Wilshire Holding Corporation v. Commissioner, . . . we referred the case back to the tax court to consider interest as a deductible item for the lessee. We think it is clearly called for here. Two yardsticks are present. The first is found in that the normal selling price of the system was $4,960 while the total rental payments for five years were $6,200. The difference could be regarded as interest for the five years on an amortized basis. The second measure is in clause 16 (loss by fire), where the figure of six per cent per annum discount is used. An allowance might be made on either basis, division of the difference (for the five years) between "rental payments" and "normal purchase price" of $1,240, or six per cent per annum on the normal purchase price of $4,960, converting the annual payments into amortization. We do not believe that the "lessee" should suffer the pains of a loss for what really was paid for the use of another's money, even though for tax purposes his lease collapses.

We do not criticize the commissioner. It is his duty to collect the revenue and it is a tough one. If he resolves all questions in favor of the taxpayers, we soon would have little revenue. However, we do suggest that after he has made allowance for depreciation, which he concedes, and an allowance for interest, the attack on many of the "leases" may not be worth while in terms of revenue. . . .

E. NOTES AND QUESTIONS

1) *Estate of Starr* versus *Lazarus*

How does *Estate of Starr* differ from *Lazarus* with respect to the relationship between the lease term and the property's expected useful life?

Why, despite these factual differences, is the lessee in *Estate of Starr* nevertheless treated as the real owner (just as the lessee in *Lazarus* was)? How do you distinguish *Western Contracting*, cited in *Estate of Starr*, in which the lessee is not treated as the owner?

2) Recharacterizing the Lease Transaction

Once the lessee in *Estate of Starr* is treated as the real owner, how should the lease transaction be recharacterized? If the lessee has really purchased the sprinkler system, what does the so-called "rent" represent? What does the difference between total rent payments and the immediate cash price of $4,960 reflect?

3) The Stakes in *Estate of Starr*

How does recharacterization affect the deductions claimed by the taxpayer? Of the $6,200 over five years ($1,240 a year) deducted as rent, how much is still deductible over the five years as interest? When is the balance deductible if the sprinkler system has an estimated useful life of eighteen years, a salvage value of $100, and is depreciated under the straight-line method? Exactly what was at stake in the case?

4) Applying the Capitalization Requirement of *Idaho Power*

Did the IRS have available an alternative argument in *Estate of Starr*—one that would not have recharacterized the lease as an installment sale? How might the IRS have recharacterized the term of the lease as being for eighteen years, rather than for five years? In that event, might it have challenged the expensing of the annual rental payment and required it to be capitalized, with rental deductions spread over eighteen years?

5) Comparing the Different Approaches

Table 39–1 compares the different results of (a) allowing the deductions as claimed by the taxpayer; (b) recasting the lease as a sale; and (c) respecting the lease arrangement but requiring the rental expenditures to be capitalized. The figures for (b) assume that $1,240 in interest is deductible over five years at the rate of $248 per year, that annual depreciation is $270 ($4,960, minus $100 salvage value, divided by eighteen), and that in the nineteenth year the sprinkler system is ripped out and the rusty pipes sold as scrap for $100. The figures for (c) assume that the $6,200 paid in rent is spread evenly over eighteen years and have been rounded off so that annual deductions are $1 higher for the first eight years than for the last ten years.

TABLE 39-1. DEDUCTING THE COST OF THE SPRINKLER SYSTEM

Year	(a) Taxpayer's Claim	(b) Recast As Sale	(c) Capitalizing Rent
1	1,240	518	345
2	1,240	518	345
3	1,240	518	345
4	1,240	518	345
5	1,240	518	345
6		270	345
7		270	345
8		270	345
9		270	344
10		270	344
11		270	344
12		270	344
13		270	344
14		270	344
15		270	344
16		270	344
17		270	344
18		270	344
19		100	

F. LEASE VERSUS SALE

Zeitlin, Tax Planning in Equipment-Leasing Shelters, 21 Major Tax Planning 621, 629–630, 638–643, 650–651, 656–659 (1969)

It is understood that the Internal Revenue Service has not issued any private rulings to individuals or syndicates covering the tax problems of equipment-leasing partnerships.[1] The transactions have all gone forward on advice of counsel, and thus the taxpayers have no assurance of protection against audit attack by the Service. . . .

The transaction between the equipment-leasing syndicate and the user of the equipment must be characterized as a lease rather than a sale or the

---

1. The Service has issued private rulings to corporate lessors. It is understood that these rulings apparently were conditioned on the following:
    (1) At least a 20 percent equity investment by the lessor;
    (2) At least some cash flow to the lessor;
    (3) Taxpayer representations that the residual will be worth at least 15 percent of the original cost at the end of the lease term;
    (4) Taxpayer representations that the useful life of the leased asset is at least two years longer than the lease term (or, if less, at least 20 percent longer);
    (5) Consistency between the useful life claimed for depreciation and investment credit purposes. (It is understood that the Service no longer requires a waiver of reliance on Depreciation Guidelines and Rules, Rev. Proc. 62–21, 1962–2 C.B. 418);
    (6) Level rental payments;
    (7) No option to purchase or release, except an option at fair market value when exercised;
    (8) No option to release for the full useful life.

leasing syndicate would not be entitled to depreciation deductions, the investment credit or interest deductions on nonrecourse loans secured by the equipment. In addition, if the transaction is a "sale," the syndicate would be faced with the problems of whether it realized any gain (or loss) on the "sale," how such gain would be characterized, and when such gain would be reportable.

The problem of distinguishing a lease from a sale is an old one in the tax law and has arisen in areas outside the tax law as well. Over the years the Internal Revenue Service and the courts have established numerous criteria for determining whether what is in form a lease should be treated as a sale. The inquiry begins, of course, with Section 162(a)(3) which allows a deduction for rent with respect to property in which the lessee "has no equity." Obvious cases of a sale rather than a lease (because the "lessee" will have "acquired practically all the equity interest in the property") may arise where the user is granted an option to purchase or to re-lease for a nominal price or a price lower than the then fair market value, where rental payments are to be offset against the purchase price, or where . . . more than a fair rental is charged, especially during the early portion of a lease term. These pitfalls are well known and are generally avoided in the typical equipment-leasing-syndicate transactions.

The most important criterion for distinguishing a lease from a sale as applicable to the situation of the equipment-leasing syndicate is whether the syndicate retains—in fact as well as in form—meaningful residual rights in the property after the term of the lease. It is clear that if property is "leased" for a period equal to or longer than its useful life, the Service would treat the "lease" as a sale since the "lessor" then has no real residual rights in the property. The user of the property has assumed the risk that the value of the use of the property for its entire life (and hence the value of the property itself) will unexpectedly decline and has also obtained the exclusive right to any unanticipated rise in its value. Indeed, it is difficult to conceive of why a "lease" for a period substantially equal to or in excess of the useful life of the property should not be treated as a sale.

Assuming, however, that the equipment-leasing syndicate avoids these obvious traps—the rent is fair, any option to purchase or re-lease is based on fair market value at the time of exercise, and the term of the lease is significantly shorter than the useful life—it would seem that the transaction would be characterized as a lease for tax purposes.

It is clear that under the tax law a transaction is either a lease or a sale; there is no real place for hybrids. In theory, however, this result may be questionable. It would seem that leases shade into sales and perhaps the tax consequences of being on one side or the other of the line should *not* be so disparate. For example, assume that property has an admitted useful life of exactly twenty years and that a "lease" for twenty years or more would be treated as a sale. In such case the "buyer" would be entitled to the investment credit, depreciation, and probably interest on a nonrecourse loan secured by the property, but would not be entitled to rental deductions. The "seller" would have income on the sale of property but would not be entitled to the investment credit, depreciation or to the deduction for interest on a nonrecourse loan secured by the property. On the other hand, if the property were leased for only eighteen years (and assuming that the last two years constituted a sufficient reversion to sustain lease treatment[2]) the situation would be reversed. The "lessee" would be entitled to rental deductions and no more, and the "lessor" would be entitled to the investment credit, depreciation, and interest deductions. The value of the reversion for the last two years might be a negligible factor in negotiating the transaction. At the outset, the parties might be almost entirely indifferent as to whether an eighteen or a twenty-year lease were involved since the present discounted value of the use of the property in the nineteenth and twentieth years would be relatively small.[3] The question then arises whether so much of a difference in tax treatment should hinge on what may be a relatively minor economic distinction.

The accounting profession, which is faced with somewhat similar problems, has made an attempt to cope with these matters of shading. While it requires leases which are really sales under criteria similar to those discussed above to be treated as such, it also requires disclosure by way of footnote of all meaningful long-term lease obligations. This solution may not be ideal and does not seem adaptable to the tax law, but perhaps some other tax treatment of the hybrid lease-sale should be devised.

Under present law, however, an equipment-leasing syndicate should, with some care, be able to arrange its transaction so as to qualify for treatment as a lease. . . .

Even if the equipment-leasing syndicate survives the tests of reality discussed above, it is not yet out of the woods. Indeed, the most difficult test is yet ahead of it. This is the test made famous by the *Gregory* case and recently epitomized by the Ninth Circuit as follows:

> *Gregory* v. *Helvering* . . . teaches that mere compliance with the Code provisions resulting in a tax advantage will be sanctioned by the courts only when there is, independent of the tax consequences, engagement in a business or corporate purpose intended by the statute utilized.

What will not be countenanced is "purposeful tax avoidance executed in compliance with the Code provisions."

Here we must inquire into the investor-partners' motives. The inquiry is not whether there is a tax-avoidance motive present, for a finding of a tax-avoidance intent will not alone defeat the equipment-leasing syndicate. (If it would, we could stop right here since such intent could almost be stipulated.) We all know that "a man's motive to avoid taxation will not establish his liability if the transaction does not do so without it." But the dubious efficacy of any transaction, step or zig-zag, taken *solely* to reduce taxes has often been made clear. . . .

---

2. Compare the Service's private ruling criteria (N. [1] supra) requiring a two-year residual worth (at the time of repossession) 15 percent of original cost.

3. Using a 5 percent discount factor (compounded semiannually), the value of $1 due 19 years hence is only 39 cents. . . . Under present money market conditions a considerably higher discount should be applied. Even at a 5 percent discount, however, the present value of the entire residual estimated to be worth 15 percent of original cost in nineteen years is less than 6 percent of the original cost (39 percent of 15 percent). The value of the *use* of the asset for the nineteenth and twentieth years would be far less than 6 percent, and, at a higher rate of discount, would be relatively trivial.

... Stanley S. Surrey, formerly Assistant Secretary of the Treasury for Tax Policy and long a leading tax scholar, saw it this way:

> Recently a number of investment syndicates have been formed by high-bracket taxpayers to buy an airplane and then lease the plane to an airline. The investors provide about 20 percent or so of the total cost and borrow the balance on a non-recourse basis....
>
> Now what is the point of a transaction that involves an investment of 20 percent of an asset for no cash flow in return; and also involves borrowing amounts at over 6 percent to, in effect, lend out at about 4 percent? There clearly is no economic point at all. But there *is* a 'tax method' in this 'economic madness.' The 20 percent investment by the syndicate members enables them to claim the depreciation deduction and investment credit for the entire cost of the plane. By offsetting that deduction against income taxable in the 60 or 70 percent brackets, and utilizing the investment credit, they obtain back both their investment and a handsome profit....
>
> The result is that the airline has sold its investment credit and depreciation deduction to higher bracket taxpayers who can better use them. The syndicate thus is formed to purchase tax benefits rather than to purchase and lease capital goods for the production of income....
>
> Without the tax system the transaction would not occur, for the only return offered the syndicate is the tax profit that the investors realize by offsetting tax benefits against high bracket income....
>
> But a real question emerges whether our income tax system does function this way—whether the transaction would be sustained by the courts under existing tax provisions. Certainly, depreciation deductions are not granted to be bartered away to bidders who have higher tax rates and who will divide with the seller the tax profits thus obtainable through the artificial acquisition of the deductions.

This view, while chilling, is clearly correct, at least as applied to the extreme cases in which the residuals have no significant value or their value will not restore the investor's capital plus some amount of profit....

In the Examples attached hereto the residuals must have a value of 20- to-30 percent of original cost for the investors to recover their capital and twice that for them to realize a 5 percent return on their investment. Is it realistic to predict such residual values? Of course, the answer will differ from case to case. In some instances the taxpayer may be able to demonstrate his realistic expectation of a high residual value and hence, an economic profit. In others any hope of recovering the initial investment—let alone a profit—may be quixotic....

G. NOTES AND QUESTIONS

1) The Financial Consequences of a Successful IRS Attack

The IRS might have challenged the airplane tax shelter (Chapter 38) by arguing that Pan Am, rather than the leasing partnership, was the "real" owner. If the partnership was not the owner, then the partners were not entitled to the tax benefits of ownership (the investment tax credit and accelerated depreciation).

In that event, how would the partners be treated? Perhaps each would be viewed as spending $100,000 to purchase tax benefits. Since those benefits did not materialize, each partner would have a $100,000 loss. *At best,* the loss would be an ordinary loss and immediately deductible in full. How would that outcome alter the financial analysis of the shelter? Would the investment make financial sense even for a 70% bracket taxpayer?

However, the partners might not be allowed to expense the cost of the failed shelter. Since the tax benefits—if available—would have been spread over the sixteen-year term of the airplane lease, the cost might be viewed as a capital expenditure which also has to be amortized over sixteen years. An even less desirable possibility is that the partnership would be viewed as having purchased a residual interest in the airplane. In that case, the cost could be recovered only when the residual is sold—which might not occur for many years—and then would produce only a capital loss.

2) Advising a Client

Assume that you are to prepare an opinion letter for a client on whether an investment in the airplane tax shelter will provide the desired tax benefits. Suppose that the estimated useful life of the airplane is eighteen years. Given the results in *Lazarus* and *Estate of Starr,* try to predict whether the IRS would succeed in arguing that Pan Am was the real owner of the airplane. How could you distinguish these two precedents? How could the IRS respond by arguing that the distinction is without a difference? Isn't the present value of the two-year residual only a tiny fraction of the value of the airplane as a whole? And if the investors ignore the residual for the purpose of valuing the investment, why should it be given significance for the purpose of determining who is the real owner?

3) Professor Zeitlin's View

Despite concerns that the airplane tax shelter might be vulnerable because the lessors have retained only a trivial residual, Professor Zeitlin predicted that it would probably not be attacked on that ground. What is the basis for his prediction? See footnote 2, which refers to condition (4) in footnote 1. How is condition (4)—that the lease term be two years less than the useful life—supplemented by conditions (7) and (8)?

The private rulings cited by Professor Zeitlin involved only *corporate* lessors. How could he feel confident about applying them to the airplane tax shelter, where the lessors are individuals, especially given the IRS refusal—which he notes—to issue rulings on leasing transactions involving individual lessors?

Why might the IRS have been willing to countenance leasing transactions between corporations but not between a corporate lessee and an individual lessor? Note the difference in the 1960s between the corporate tax rate (hovering between 48% and 52% on income above $100,000) and the top individual rate (which was 70%). Why is the magnitude of the tax benefit of accelerated depreciation a function of the owner's tax bracket? The IRS may have been concerned that leasing was being used to magnify the usual tax benefits of accelerated depreciation.

Why wasn't Professor Zeitlin deterred by such concerns? Because at the time Congress had not indicated that the tax benefits of accelerated depreciation were restricted to corporate taxpayers? Because the IRS' refusal to rule, even unfavorably, on leasing transactions with *individual* lessors indicated that it was uncertain about distinguishing corporate from individual lessors?

4) The Tax Shelter as an Activity not Engaged in "For Profit"

Recall *Smith* (Chapter 16), decided in 1982, in which losses from commodity straddles were not deductible because the transaction was not engaged in "for profit." Two years earlier, in Hilton v. Commissioner,[4] the Tax Court had held that losses from a real estate tax shelter were not deductible on similar grounds.

> We are . . . persuaded that an objective economic analysis of this transaction from the point of view of the buyer-lessor . . . should focus on the value of the cash flow derived from the rental payments and that little or no weight should be placed on the speculative possibility that the property will have a substantial residual value . . . . The low rents and almost nominal cash flow leave little room for doubt that, apart from tax benefits, the value of the interest acquired . . . is substantially less than they paid for it. . . . There is thus no justification for . . . participation in this transaction apart from its tax consequences.[5]

How is the requirement of before-tax profit reflected in the private rulings cited in footnote 1 of Professor Zeitlin's article? See conditions (2) and (3).

Writing over a decade before *Hilton* and *Smith* were decided, Professor Zeitlin predicted that the before-tax profit requirement *might* be used to deny the deduction of losses from the airplane tax shelter. The IRS, however, never really tried to use it to mount an aggressive attack on equipment-leasing shelters. Moreover, neither investors, nor their attorneys, seem to have been overly concerned about the possibility of such an argument being made. They relied, at least in part, on the circumstance that the IRS was relatively understaffed and lacked the personnel to audit more than a tiny fraction of all taxpayers filing returns.

There was another circumstance favoring aggressive investment in shelters. Most taxpayers would come out ahead even if they lost due to the low rate of interest charged by the government for underpaying taxes. This interest rate was considerably less than a commercial lender would charge. It was only in 1976 that the interest rate charged by the government was raised to 90% of the prime rate; and in 1981 to 100% of prime. As one court noted,

> [T]he rate of interest charged by the Government was less than that charged by commercial banks. . . . A particular tax strategy was not necessarily rejected merely because it might result in litigation or even ultimately

---

4. 74 T.C. 305 (1980), aff'd per curiam, 671 F.2d 316 (9th Cir. 1982).
5. 74 T.C. 305, 360–361.

fail. The more important criterion was the extent to which that strategy would promote the immediate availability of cash. . . .[6]

Thus, throughout the 1960s, investments by individuals in equipment-leasing tax shelters proliferated. Such tax shelters *began* to be affected only when Congress acted to amend the Code in the late sixties and in the seventies. These amendments are the subject of the following note.

H. STATUTORY REFORM

From 1969 to 1978, a number of different statutory measures were adopted to limit investment in tax shelters. Consider the effect of each of the following provisions on the airplane tax shelter.

1) The Minimum Tax

In 1969, Congress enacted the minimum tax (Chapter 35). In its original version, the minimum tax rate was 10%, there was a $30,000 exemption, and the excess of accelerated over straight-line method depreciation deductions on leased nonreal property was included in the list of tax preferences. Old Section 57(a)(3).[7] In addition, the minimum tax was an add-on (rather than an alternative) tax, so that minimum taxes were due *in addition to* (rather than instead of) regular taxes. How would the add-on minimum tax, as originally enacted, have affected the financial analysis of the airplane tax shelter? Don't forget that in 1969 the top individual rate was 70%.

2) Section 1348

In 1971, Congress imposed a maximum tax of 50% on "earned income," although investment income was still taxable at marginal rates up to 70%. Old Section 1348. How does the maximum tax affect the financial analysis of the airplane tax shelter?

3) Section 46(e)(3)(B)

Section 46(e)(3)(B), enacted in 1971, denies the investment tax credit to a *non*corporate lessor unless the lease is for less than half the property's useful life. How would the airplane tax shelter have to be restructured to avoid the effect of this section? What would such restructuring do to the

---

6. Foster v. Commissioner, 80 T.C. 34, 177 (1983), aff'd & rev'd, 756 F.2d 1430 (9th Cir. 1985), cert. denied, 474 U.S. 1055 (1986).

7. Since first enacted in 1969, the minimum tax has undergone considerable changes, which are beyond the scope of this introductory casebook. Note that the excess of accelerated over straight-line method depreciation is no longer used to calculate the minimum tax for most assets acquired after January 1, 1987. For real assets, a longer cost recovery period is assigned. For nonreal assets, the 150% declining balance method is used instead of the 200% declining balance method. See Chapter 35.

riskiness of the tax shelter investment? How would the change in riskiness affect the financial analysis of the airplane tax shelter?

4) Section 465

Section 465, enacted in 1976, limits the deduction of losses from certain designated activities to the amount "at risk." Section 465(a)(1). (Note that Section 465, like Section 46(e)(3)(B), generally applies only to *non*corporate lessors.) Is the airplane tax shelter one of the designated activities? See Section 465(c)(1)(C) and also Section 465(c)(3), added in 1978, to expand the list of covered activities.

What is the impact of Section 465 on the airplane tax shelter? What is the investor's initial amount "at risk"? See Section 465(b)(1) and (2). How soon will shelter losses equal that amount initially "at risk" (see Table 38–1 in Chapter 38)? How is the amount "at risk" affected as the mortgage principal is paid off? At what rate is the mortgage principal paid off? At what rate does the amount "at risk" increase? Why might the "at risk" rules be viewed as, in effect, requiring the investor to use sinking fund method depreciation?

How would the tax shelter have to be restructured to avoid the impact of Section 465? What would such restructuring do to the riskiness of the tax shelter investment? How would that change in riskiness affect the financial analysis of the airplane tax shelter?

How does Section 465, in effect, modify *Crane* (cited in *Tufts* in Chapter 24), where the Supreme Court held that the basis of property includes nonrecourse financing? Why might *Crane* be described as the "basis" of the tax shelter phenomenon?

5) The Relationship Between Sections 46(e)(3)(B) and 465

In order for the airplane tax shelter to avoid Section 46(e)(3)(B), the lease term can be for no more than nine years. What does this do to the full pay-out character of the lease? In order for the shelter to avoid Section 465, the investors must be personally liable on the mortgage. Why might a shorter lease term *or* an ordinary mortgage *alone* pose acceptable risks? Why is the *combined* effect of both requirements much more likely to make the risks unacceptable to potential investors (and to the lender as well)?

6) The Scope of Sections 46(e)(3)(B) and 465

Why are corporations generally exempted from Sections 46(e)(3)(B) and 465? Why is a corporation not an effective vehicle for individuals wishing to invest in the airplane tax shelter? The reason is that, corporations, unlike partnerships, are generally treated as separate taxable entities. Corporate losses and gains, therefore, do not pass through to the shareholders but are only reflected indirectly as loss or gain on the sale of stock.[8]

---

8. Under Section 7704, enacted in 1987, a publicly traded partnership will be treated for tax purposes as if it were a corporation. If Section 7704 applies, partnership losses and gains will be subject to separate taxation at corporate rates and not pass through to the partners.

The Code does permit certain corporations with a relatively small number of shareholders to elect to be taxed (more or less) as partnerships (see Sections 1361(b)(1), 1363(a), and 1366(a)(1)). Such "pass-through" corporations are treated as noncorporate taxpayers for the purposes of Sections 46(e)(3)(B) and 465.

7) The 1969–78 Reforms and Tax Shelters in Real Estate

Why were real estate tax shelters largely unaffected by the statutory reforms enacted between 1968 and 1978? Was there any investment tax credit to lose? (There was not.) Did the "at risk" rules of Section 465 apply to real estate? (Not until 1987.) Old Section 57(a)(2) defined the excess of accelerated over straight-line method depreciation on real property as a "tax preference." Why might real estate be depreciated on the straight-line method—to avoid the minimum tax—and still function as an efficient tax shelter? What kinds of taxpayers were unaffected by the maximum tax on earned income and therefore still likely to find tax shelters financially attractive? (Until 1981, the top rate applicable to *un*earned income, such as interest and dividends, remained 70%.)

Chapter 40

IS THE AIRPLANE TAX SHELTER AN ABUSE?

A. INTRODUCTORY NOTE

Tax shelters are commonly thought of as an abuse of our tax system. The very term "tax shelter" has highly pejorative connotations. But exactly what is objectionable about arrangements like the airplane tax shelter described in Chapter 38? The basic criticism of such transactions is that tax incentives, designed to encourage risky investment, go to the wrong party. Instead of benefiting the long-term lessee, who assumes the business risks, they benefit the shelter investors who avoid paying their fair share of taxes.

This chapter takes a close look at this criticism. After reviewing the economics of leasing transactions, it examines a transaction known as *safe harbor leasing* or SHL, which Congress provided for in the 1981 Economic Recovery Tax Act. Under SHL, leasing transactions which met certain requirements were immune from attack by the legal doctrines discussed in Chapter 39. A safe harbor lease was recognized for tax purposes even if the lessor retained no residual and had no prospect of a before-tax profit. The debate about SHL is used as a lens, or frame of reference, through which to evaluate equipment-leasing tax shelters in general and the airplane tax shelter in particular.

B. THE ECONOMICS OF LEASING

Note, "Safe Harbor" as Tax Reform: Taxpayer Election of Lease Treatment, 95 Harv. L. Rev. 1648, 1650–7 (1982)

The Effect of Tax Benefits on Equipment Lease Rentals

Three factors are central to the negotiation of long-term equipment leases: (1) rate of return, (2) depreciation deductions and the investment credit, and (3) residuals. It is from these three sources that the lessor can recover its original investment and make a profit.

1. Rate of Return.—The starting point for computing rent is the rate of return or "implied interest rate" sought by the lessor on the equipment's cost. For example, under a ten-year lease of $100,000 worth of equipment at an implied interest rate of twelve percent per year, the rental, before any adjustment, would be $1434.71 per month—the amount that would fully amortize a $100,000 loan at twelve percent over ten years. The lessor will then reduce the rent if it is to receive tax benefits or residuals.

2. Depreciation Deductions and Investment Credits.—The net value of the depreciation deductions to the lessor is computed by comparing the after-tax consequences of a lease with those of a loan for the equipment's cost at the same financing rate. In the example above, if the 120 rent payments of $1434.71 had instead been used to repay a $100,000 loan, the lender could have recovered the $100,000 principal tax free while the remaining $72,165 would have been taxable interest income. Similarly, the lessor can deduct $100,000 of depreciation from its aggregate rental income of $172,165. Hence over the ten-year term, the financing party's total taxable income from both loan and lease would be the same—the $72,165 remaining after nontaxable items of $100,000 are subtracted from total receipts of $172,165.

Because depreciation is accelerated, however, the lessor has a significant timing advantage: much of its rental income is taxed later than the lender's interest income. . . . [The] loan payments during the first years of the term are treated partly as taxable interest income and partly as a nontaxable amortization of the loan. The equivalent rental payments to the lessor are fully taxable, but depreciation deductions in each of the first . . . years greatly exceed the amount allocable by the lender to principal. The lessor defers tax to the extent that depreciation exceeds the lender's recovery of principal. As a result, the lessor realizes larger after-tax cash flows during the years it is taking depreciation. In the years following full depreciation of the equipment, the lessor's taxes exceed those of the lender, because rental payments remain fully taxable while only the interest component of the loan payments is taxable. Although total tax paid and total cash flows are equal by the end of the term, the lessor's initial deferral of tax weighs heavily in computing the discounted present value of the after-tax cash flow. . . . The higher present value of cash flow is the potential tax benefit to the lessor from leasing.

Users of equipment are, of course, loath to surrender the benefits of an accelerated write-off without receiving something in return. A user wishing to lease would seek bids from a number of potential lessors. If there were perfect competition among prospective lessors—a very large number of bidders with full knowledge of market conditions—the lessors would bid down the rent until the lessee recovered the exact equivalent of the tax benefits forgone. Even if competition is less than perfect, the lessee can recover part of the value of the tax benefits by negotiating a rent lower than the payments on an equivalent loan.

The investment tax credit is also an important bargaining point in the negotiation of equipment leases. Although only taxpayers that "acquire" qualified property receive investment credit, a lessor of new equipment can treat the lessee, for investment credit purposes, as the acquirer of the equipment. It is common for a leasing company to quote two rental rates—a lower charge if the lessor is to retain the investment credit and a higher charge if the lessee is to receive the credit. If it has sufficient tax liability to use the credit immediately, the lessee will want the credit. Otherwise, the lessee will permit the lessor to keep the credit in exchange for a reduction in the rent.

3. *Residuals.*—From a business standpoint, the parties to a long-term lease ordinarily have no incentive to make the residuals an important part of the lessor's return. Because the long-term finance lease is designed to substitute for purchasing on credit, the lessee, like a purchaser, typically seeks dominion over the property for virtually all of its useful life. The lessor, like a lender, prefers to recover its investment through cash payments rather than incur an "equipment risk," which makes its profit contingent upon the sale or second lease of the equipment.

Even so, under present law parties to a lease not within the safe harbor exception must provide that substantial residuals remain with the lessor to enable the lessor to take the depreciation deductions and investment credit. This requirement interposes a significant impediment to the use of leasing as a financing mechanism. In loan negotiations, the interest rate is the only factor (aside from length of term) affecting the sum the lender is to receive in each period. In lease transactions, however, the rental rate each party is willing to accept will also depend on an evaluation of the residuals. Bargaining over the residuals creates particularly vexatious problems when the lessee's estimate of the residual value is substantially greater than the estimate of the lessor. The lessee will want a large reduction in rent in compensation for surrendering the residuals, but the lessor will be unwilling to give a rent reduction worth more, in present value terms, than its own lower estimate. Thus, even when the parties settle on a financing rate, a dispute over the residual value may prevent them from coming to terms.

The Effect of Lease Financing on Tax Revenues

The revenue effect of transferring tax benefits from a user to a lessor depends upon the parties' respective tax brackets. If both parties are taxed at the same rate, leasing, rather than purchasing on credit, causes no loss or deferral of revenue. The government is indifferent about which of two taxpaying entities in the same bracket takes the depreciation deduction available for any given year. Similarly, lower rental payments result in less taxable income for the lessor but correspondingly lower deductions for the lessee. In short, if the lessor and lessee are in the same tax bracket, the allocation of tax benefits between them is a zero-sum game—what one gains, the other forgoes.

One or both of the parties profit at the expense of the Treasury, however, if the lessor is taxed at a higher rate than the lessee. The accelerated depreciation defers more tax liability for a high-bracket lessor than for a lower-bracket purchaser. If the rent is reduced based on transfer of depreciation allowances to the lessor, rental income will be lower and the lessor will pay less tax. Since the lessee is in a lower bracket, the lessee's reduced rent deductions will not increase its tax payments by an amount equal to the reduction in the lessor's taxes. Hence the Treasury loses revenue, because the rent reduction shifts income from a high-bracket taxpayer to one taxed at a lower rate, if at all. . . .

C. THE REVENUE CONSEQUENCES OF SHIFTING TAX PREFERENCES

Suppose that one party sells a second party the use of property. Does it matter whether the transfer is characterized as a sale or a lease? The net amount of taxable income reported by *both* transferor and transferee should be unaffected by sale or lease characterization. Therefore, provided that both transferor and transferee are taxed at the same rate, the answer is no.

To illustrate this proposition, consider the following example. One party sells to another the right to use a sprinkler system for five years. The system has a useful service life of five years; the purchase price is $4,000; the transferor's basis for the system is also $4,000; and the contract requires the transferee to pay $1,200 per year for five years. Assume that the "owner" of the asset will elect the double-declining balance method of depreciation and that the system is assigned a four-year POCR (one year shorter than its useful life). If the salvage value is estimated to be zero, then the depreciation schedule will be:

> year 1 — 2000
> year 2 — 1000
> year 3 — 500
> year 4 — 500

This schedule assumes that, after the third year, the owner will switch to the straight-line method.

1. Sale Form

The payments of $1,200 per year are viewed as installments paid to purchase the asset. Since the purchase price is $4,000 and the installments total $6,000, $2,000 of the latter figure represents a finance charge, that is, interest for deferring payment. Thus, of the $1,200 paid each year, $800 might be allocated to the purchase price and $400 to interest.

What are the tax consequences to the vendor and vendee under these assumptions? Because the purchase price is assumed to equal the asset's basis, the sale produces no gain to the vendor. But the vendor does have taxable income each year, attributable to $400 in interest income. Similarly, the vendee each year has $400 of deductible interest expense. *Notice that the vendor's interest income and the vendee's interest expense cancel each other out in the aggregate.* One has an income item, the other a deduction, of equal magnitude.

Ch. 40   Is the Tax Shelter an Abuse?   609

In addition, the vendee, as owner, will take accelerated depreciation over the asset's life. Table 40–1 lists the pattern of income and deductions:

TABLE 40-1.

Year	Vendor Interest Income	Vendee Interest Deduction	Depreciation
1	+400	−400	−2000
2	+400	−400	−1000
3	+400	−400	−500
4	+400	−400	−500
5	+400	−400	

2. Lease Form

The payments of $1,200 per year are viewed as rent. The lessee has $1,200 per year in deductible rental expense. The lessor has $1,200 per year in rental income. In addition, the lessor, retaining ownership, will claim accelerated depreciation. *Notice that the lessor's rental income and the lessee's rental expense cancel each other out in the aggregate.* Table 40–2 lists the pattern of income and deductions:

TABLE 40-2.

Year	Lessor Rent Income	Depreciation	Lessee Rent Deduction
1	+1200	−2000	−1200
2	+1200	−1000	−1200
3	+1200	−500	−1200
4	+1200	−500	−1200
5	+1200		−1200

3. Adjusting the Price for the Tax Preferences

In the real world, one would expect annual payments under the lease to be less than annual payments under a comparable installment sale. The reason is that a sale transfers everything the lease does—use of the asset—plus an additional valuable right—the right to take accelerated depreciation. A lessee who does not receive as much will insist on paying a lower price.

Suppose that while the installment sales price of the sprinkler system is $1,200 per year, the rental price is $1,175 per year. Will this change the proposition that overall tax revenue is unaffected by which party takes the accelerated depreciation, provided both parties are in the same tax bracket?

D. SAFE HARBOR LEASING

Staff of the Joint Committee on Taxation, 97th Cong., 2d Sess., General Explanation of the Revenue Provisions of the Tax Equity and Fiscal Responsibility Act of 1982 45–52 (Comm. Print 1982)

Overview

Prior to the enactment of the Economic Recovery Tax Act of 1981 (ERTA), the law contained rules (non-safe harbor lease rules) to determine who owns an item of property for tax purposes when the property is subject to an agreement which the parties characterize as a lease. Such rules are important because the owner of the property is the person entitled to claim cost recovery (depreciation) deductions and investment tax credits. The non-safe harbor lease rules attempted to distinguish between true leases, in which the lessor owned the property for tax purposes, and conditional sales or financing arrangements, in which the user of the property owned the property for tax purposes. These rules generally were not written in the Internal Revenue Code; instead they evolved over the years through a series of court cases and revenue rulings and revenue procedures issued by the Internal Revenue Service. Essentially, the law was that the economic substance of a transaction, not its form, determined who was the owner of property for tax purposes. Thus, if a transaction was, in substance, simply a financing arrangement, it would be treated that way for tax purposes regardless of how the parties chose to characterize it. Lease transactions could not be used solely for the purpose of transferring tax benefits. They had to have nontax economic substance. The specific prior law rules are discussed below.

ERTA provided a new set of rules which represented a major departure from the prior law. These provisions were intended to be a means of transferring tax benefits rather than a means of determining which person is in substance the owner of the property. Under these rules, certain transactions involving tangible personal property were treated as leases for Federal income tax purposes regardless of their nontax economic substance. If a transaction met these safe harbor requirements, the lessor in the agreement was treated as the property owner for Federal income tax purposes and was entitled to cost recovery deductions and investment credits. Under these rules, by entering into a nominal sale and safe-harbor leaseback, a person who acquired and used the property could have, in effect, sold some of the tax benefits associated with the property to a corporation, while retaining all other economic benefits and burdens of ownership. The non-safe harbor leasing rules continued to apply for transactions not qualifying for the safe harbor or when the safe harbor was not elected.

Non-safe harbor leasing rules

In general, the determination of lease treatment under the non-safe harbor leasing rules required a case-by-case analysis based on all facts and circumstances. Although the determination of whether a transaction was a lease was inherently factual, a series of general principles was embodied in court cases, revenue rulings, and revenue procedures. Those principles are still used in determining the character of transactions that are not eligible for the safe-harbor rules or for which the safe-harbor election is not made.

For a transaction to be a lease under non-safe harbor lease rules, the lessee could not hold title to or have an equity interest in the property. However, the fact that the lessor had title did not guarantee that the lessor was the owner for Federal income tax purposes. Both the courts and the IRS looked to additional criteria in determining whether a transaction was a lease. These criteria focused on the substance of the transaction rather than its form. The courts did not disregard the form of a transaction simply because tax considerations were a significant motive so long as the transaction also had a bona fide business purpose and the lessor retained sufficient burdens and benefits of ownership.

To be entitled to depreciation deductions as the owner of the property, the lessor had to show that the property was being used for a business or other income-producing purpose. To have had a business purpose, the person claiming ownership (i.e., the lessor) at least had to have a reasonable expectation that he would derive a profit from the transaction independent of tax benefits. This requirement precluded lease treatment for a transaction intended merely to reduce the user's costs by utilizing the lessor's tax base. For a sale-leaseback, other nontax business motives were considered in determining the substance of the transaction.

The fact that the lessor in a lease financing transaction could show a profit or business purpose, however, did not automatically result in lease treatment under prior law rules, since a profit or business motive could also exist in a financing arrangement. In addition, the lessor had to retain meaningful benefits and burdens of ownership. Thus, lease treatment was denied under prior law rules if the user had the option to obtain title to the property at the end of the lease for a price that either was nominal in relation to the value of the property at the time when the option could be exercised (as determined at the time the parties entered into the agreement) or which was relatively small when compared with the total payments required to be made.

Where the residual value of the property to the lessor was nominal, the lessor was viewed as having transferred full ownership of the property for the rental fee. Where the purchase option was more than nominal but relatively small in comparison with fair market value, the lessor was viewed as having transferred full ownership because of the likelihood that the lessee would exercise the bargain purchase option. Furthermore, if the lessor could force the lessee to purchase the property at the end of the lease (a "put"), the transaction might also be denied lease treatment under prior law because the put eliminated the risk borne by owners of property that there would be no market for the property at the end of the lease. . . .

Safe harbor leasing rules

The safe-harbor leasing provisions of ERTA were intended to permit owners of property who were unable to use depreciation deductions and investment credits to transfer those benefits to persons who were able to use them, without having to meet the prior law requirements for characterizing the transaction as a lease. The safe-harbor leasing provisions operated by guaranteeing that, for Federal income tax purposes, qualifying transactions were treated as leases, and that the nominal lessor was treated as the owner of the property, even though the lessee was in substance the owner of the property and the transaction otherwise would not have been considered a lease.

Eligibility requirements

To qualify for the safe harbor, a transaction had to meet the following requirements:

    1. All parties to the agreement had to elect to have the transaction treated as a lease for Federal income tax purposes;
    2. The nominal lessor had to be (a) a corporation (other than a subchapter S corporation or a personal holding company), (b) a partnership all of the partners of which were one of the corporations described in (a), or (c) a grantor trust with respect to which the grantor and all beneficiaries of the trust were corporations or a partnership comprised of corporations;
    3. The lessor had to have a minimum at-risk investment in the property at all times during the lease term of at least ten percent of the adjusted basis of the property;
    4. The lease term could not exceed the greater of 90 percent of the property's useful life or 150 percent of the ADR mid-point life of the property; and
    5. The property had to be "qualified leased property."

Qualified leased property

In general, qualified leased property meant new equipment eligible for both ACRS and the investment credit. The equipment could be leased within 3 months after the property was placed in service without violating the requirement that the equipment be new equipment (called the 3-month window).

Property used by a tax-exempt organization or a U.S. Federal, State, or local governmental unit generally was ineligible. However, under a special exception, qualified mass commuting vehicles financed in whole or in part by tax-exempt bonds were eligible even though the property was used by a tax-exempt organization or governmental unit. For mass commuting vehicles, the lessor was eligible for ACRS deductions but not the investment credit.

Factors disregarded

If a transaction met the safe-harbor requirements, the transaction was treated as a lease entered into by the parties to the agreement, and the nominal lessor was treated as the owner for Federal income tax purposes. Thus, the nominal lessor was entitled to the associated cost recovery allowances and investment credit. The following factors, therefore, were not taken into account in determining whether a transaction was a lease, as they had been under the non-safe harbor lease rules:

>   1. The fact the lessor or lessee had to take the tax benefits into account in order to realize a profit or positive cash flow from the transaction;
>   2. The fact the lessee had to be the owner of the property for State or local law purposes (e.g., had title to the property and retained the burdens, benefits, and incidents of ownership, such as payment of taxes and maintenance charges with respect to the property);
>   3. The fact that no person other than the lessee was able to use the property after the lease term;
>   4. The fact the property was, or had to have been, bought or sold at the end of the lease term at a fixed or determinable price or the fact that a rental adjustment was made upward or downward to reflect the difference between the expected residual value of the property and the actual sales price; and
>   5. The fact the lessee, or a related party, provided financing or guaranteed financing for the transaction (other than the lessor's minimum 10 percent investment). . . .

Tax benefit transfers

Treasury regulations contemplated that those who used the safe-harbor leasing rules for tax benefit transfers would structure their transactions as a particular kind of sale and leaseback. This type of transaction involved three steps. First, the seller/lessee (who may be either an individual or a corporation) acquired the property with its own funds or borrowed funds and then, within three months, transferred it in a nominal "sale" to the buyer/lessor. In exchange, the seller/lessee received cash for a part of the selling price and a level payment nonrecourse note for the balance. The seller/lessee continued to use the property and typically enjoyed all the economic benefits and burdens of ownership. In the standard transaction, the user of the property retained all incidents of State law ownership. For Federal income tax purposes, however, the buyer/lessor claimed the cost recovery deductions and investment credits allowable for the property. The second step was that the seller/lessee nominally leased the property back from the buyer/

lessor. The lease rental payments to the buyer/lessor were structured so as to equal the debt service payments to the seller/lessee arising from the nonrecourse note in stage one. Thus, no cash changed hands during this second stage. However, because the debt service payment consisted of both interest and principal, the excess of lease rent over interest for any taxable year (which equals the principal repaid in the year) was treated for Federal income tax purposes as income to the buyer/lessor and as a deduction for the seller/lessee. Third, at the end of the lease, the seller/lessee nominally repurchased the property for a token amount, such as $1.

The substantive effect of this sale-leaseback transaction was that the buyer/lessor had purchased a stream of tax benefits from the seller/lessee for an amount equal to the cash paid for the property during the first stage of the transaction. (This is the only cash which changed hands, apart from the nominal amount paid for repurchase of the property in stage three.) The stream of tax benefits purchased by the buyer/lessor equaled the ACRS cost recovery deductions, plus the investment tax credit (including the energy credit if applicable), minus the net rental income arising from the lease (the excess of lease rentals over interest on the nonrecourse note, which precisely equaled the principal payments on the note). . . .

E. NEW TAX LAW MAKES ONCE–UNUSABLE CREDITS A BOON FOR MANY FIRMS

The Wall Street Journal (August 27, 1981)

At the beginning of this year, Ford Motor Co. was sitting on $340 million in tax credits that it couldn't use. CSX Corp., which owns the Chessie railroad system, was holding $200 million of unusable credits, and Bethlehem Steel Corp. had nearly $150 million.

The companies couldn't use the tax breaks because they didn't owe enough taxes against which to apply the benefits. But starting with tax credits that the concerns accumulate this year, all that has changed.

Thanks to Congress and the Reagan administration, these companies and thousands like them can cash in on the generous corporate-tax reductions in the recently passed Economic Recovery Tax Act even if they don't owe any taxes. Essentially, they can sell their depreciation deductions and investment tax credits to well-heeled companies wanting to reduce their own taxes.

Such tax-break transfers could revolutionize corporate finance, experts say. The new tax rules greatly liberalize federal rules governing so-called leveraged tax leasing. Under such arrangements, a company with unusable tax breaks can lease equipment—usually through a leasing firm—and a profitable company can put up some of the cost of the equipment in return for the first company's tax credits.

The new rules can be used to transfer billions of dollars of tax credits from company to company through the loosest kinds of lease arrangements. Most of these arrangements will be leasing agreements on paper only. For example, a profitable energy company can "lease" assembly-line tooling to an ailing auto maker by swapping cash for tax benefits within the framework of a lease; the energy company doesn't physically lease equipment to the auto maker, but merely arranges for the lease through an agreement with the auto company or a third party acting as a broker.

The new law loosens, among other things, previous restrictions on what constitutes a lease, on the financing of the equipment or property, and on the profits to the firm arranging the lease. The law also makes it far cheaper for the company using the equipment to buy it when the lease expires. "It's no more a lease than you are my grandmother," quips one corporate tax expert. . . .

Helping Chrysler and other distressed companies was partly what Treasury Department officials had in mind when they developed the new leasing rules. The new rules were a compromise designed to placate corporate interests pushing for a "refundable" investment tax credit—that is, a credit that companies lacking tax liability could take in cash in lieu of tax reductions. That idea, pushed by former President Carter, didn't get very far.

Treasury officials also say the new rules were designed to nullify what some saw as a major problem stemming from President Reagan's corporate-tax reductions. Without the leasing provisions, they say, many companies holding unusable tax benefits generated by the bill would become targets of takeover bids by corporations seeking to latch on to the benefits and thus to reduce their taxes.

To forestall that, the administration offered to allow the easy transfer of tax benefits. In doing so, it gave business some financing tools that companies have wanted for years but that the old law barred.

The old tax-leasing rules, in effect, prohibited any kind of lease arrangement that seemed to be designed primarily to enable a company to trade its unusable tax breaks for cash. To set up a legitimate leasing agreement under the old law, for example, an airline could lease a new airplane through a leasing company for 15 years or so, with the leasing firm putting up at least 20% of the plane's cost and the other 80% coming from an unrelated third party.

Generally, the leasing firm had to hold title to the plane. It would reap the benefit of the 10% investment tax credit and of depreciation and, after the lease ended, would profit from the plane's market value. In addition, the law said that in figuring the profits from the lease, in order to establish its validity, the leasing firm couldn't look to the tax benefits alone; it had to make a profit apart from the tax benefits.

Also, to make sure that the lease was genuine, the old law prohibited the lease from extending throughout the useful life of the aircraft. After the lease expired, the airline could purchase the equipment at its fair market value, or the equipment could be sold to a third party. Finally, the law barred the airline from putting up any of the plane's original purchase price.

These rules, by favoring the leasing firms, "created an awful lot of profit" for them, Mr. Christian, the tax lawyer, says. The firms profited by retaining title to the equipment and selling it when the lease was up.

But the new law wipes away nearly all those requirements and, according to leasing-industry officials, restores the balance to transactions between leasing firms and companies that use the equipment. Other experts worry that the new law may go too far in favor of the companies using the equipment. They can hold title to the property. And not only doesn't the property have to have much usable life when the lease is up, but also the company using the asset may buy it for as little as one dollar, rather than at fair market value. In addition, the old requirement that the leasing firm put up at least 20% of the asset's cost is trimmed to 10%. And the leasing firm needn't make a profit apart from the tax benefits.

Here's an example of the form a lease could take. A money-losing auto maker purchases $10 million of assembly-plant tooling and thereby generates a $1 million investment tax credit that it can't use. A profitable company, seeking tax breaks, agrees to "lease" the tooling to the auto maker; it makes a minimum investment of $1 million, or 10%, and gives the auto maker a five-year note for the 90% balance of the cost of the tooling. In return, the profitable company can use immediately the $1 million in tax breaks and the depreciation on the tooling to cut its taxes.

Moreover, the lease is set up for a term of five years, and the payments, with interest, exactly match the note payments that the profitable company agreed to make for the 90% balance of the tooling. Hence, no funds need change hands between the money-making outfit and the ailing auto maker. The auto maker takes care of all the insurance, maintenance and taxes on the equipment and at the end of the lease can purchase the equipment for one dollar.

In short, the profitable company has swapped $1 million in cash for a $1 million investment tax credit, $460,000 in first-year depreciation allowances and the interest deductions on the note. Moreover, both the depreciation and the interest deductions extend through the life of the lease. The auto maker winds up with $10 million in tooling that actually cost it $9 million, thanks to the cash paid by the profitable company. . . .

The new law seems tailor-made for some companies. . . . One likely candidate for taking advantage of it is United Airlines, although its finance executives won't say whether the UAL Inc. unit will act under the new law during the three-month period in which already-purchased equipment can be refinanced. "We're looking hard at the new tax proposals," a spokesman says, but he declines to elaborate. At the beginning of this year, United leased about 22% of its aircraft.

United's predicament is shared by nearly all its domestic rivals. Despite losses, most airlines are jetting ahead with ambitious capital-spending programs to replace old and inefficient planes and equipment. United, for example, has scheduled more than $2 billion in spending over four years for new, fuel-thrifty Boeing 767s and for replacement engines for other planes.

But United hasn't made any profit since 1978, and without profits during those big-spending years the tax benefits can't be used. Under the new leasing laws, United can swap those benefits to a company with a big tax bill in return for a leased plane.

The new law holds plenty of advantages for profitable companies as well. For many of them, their profits and resultant tax bills aren't large enough to use all the tax benefits reaped from investments. "There is just so damn much investment required . . . we've never been able to use all the investment tax credits we've generated," says James T. Lyon, the vice-president for taxes of CSX.

CSX's Chessie hasn't done any significant leasing over the past decade or so for several reasons, including the old law's requirement that the leasing railroad had to pay market value to buy the asset when the lease expired—or part with it. "That was far too punitive," says Mr. Lyon, who joined a group of businessmen that included auto and steel executives to push for more lenient lease laws.

With the new laws, Chessie expects to lease about 80% of the more than $2 billion capital acquisitions that it plans over the next four years. Included may be rail cars, yard facilities, even bridges and signal equipment. "No holds are barred," Mr. Lyon says. "We can lease anything as far as the tax laws are concerned." When the tax law cleared Congress, CSX ordered an inventory of its purchases this year to see which ones could be leased.

For some projects, a decision whether to buy or lease a facility or equipment could make the difference between a profit or a loss, Mr. Lyon suggests. Leasing, he says, "is basically a financial mechanism. It increases our flexibility, liquidity and financial health."

Chrysler also is hopeful. It believes that the changes in the law, which it monitored intensively while legislation was being drafted, may go a long way toward narrowing the gap between its cost structure and that of its richest rival, General Motors Corp. "Our cost of equipment is being reduced. We think it restores fairness to our competitive position versus that of GM and others," says R. S. Miller, Jr., a Chrysler executive vice president and chief financial officer. "This is a major improvement in our ability to compete."

GM has usually been able to use the investment tax credits generated by its capital outlays to reduce its taxes and costs; but under the old law, Chrysler, because of its large losses, couldn't do that. Under the new law, Mr. Miller says, "we can realize, through leasing, the tax benefits that go with new investment." Chrysler also can get a quick infusion of badly needed cash from a leasing firm, which must put up at least 10% of the cost of the purchase to make the lease. . . .

F. FORD SELLS IBM $200 MILLION IN 1981 TAX BREAKS
The Washington Post (November 6, 1981)

In what appears to be the largest sale of corporate tax breaks to date under the 1981 tax law, Ford Motor Co. yesterday announced that it sold all 1981 investment credits and depreciation deductions to International Business Machines for somewhere between $100 million and $200 million. . . .

IBM, according to an official of the firm, also will make somewhere between $100 million and $200 million. This profit on the agreement would come from the difference between what IBM paid for the tax breaks and their value to the computer firm. IBM had net earnings after taxes of $2.2 billion through the third quarter of this year.

The tax sale, accomplished through controversial leasing provisions included in the tax cut enacted in July, will provide a major cash boost to Ford. Through the third quarter of this year, Ford reported total losses of $713 million.

"This transaction enables Ford to obtain the cash from these credits and deductions now," John Sagan, vice president and treasurer, said. "Otherwise, Ford would have to delay use of its investment tax credits and depreciation deductions on 1981 capital expenditures."

The leasing provisions in the 1981 tax bill were put in the legislation in an effort to spread some of the major corporate tax breaks to companies, like Ford, which have little or no profits.

Under terms of the legislation, a company like Ford buys needed equipment, then sells it to a profitable firm, such as IBM. This is accomplished through what amounts to a paper transaction involving only the tax breaks from the 10 percent investment tax credit and accelerated depreciation.

The profitable company then "leases" the equipment back to the actual user in an arrangement in which the rent exactly equals the cost of paying off the purchase. At the end of the term, the lease agreement would, in most circumstances, permit the low profit company to buy back the equipment at a nominal price. Ford would not disclose the precise terms of its agreement with IBM.

The leasing provisions were designed to benefit such industries as autos, steel, paper and railroad which are, in many cases, either running in the red or showing such low profits that the tax breaks in the 1981 tax bill are of no use. . . .

G. THE GREAT BUSINESS GIVEAWAY
The Washington Post (December 3, 1981)

Only now is the nation getting a fuller appreciation—and the final story hasn't been told—of just how bad a piece of legislation is the "Economic Recovery Act of 1981." In the guise of an investment-stimulus program, via super-generous business credits and write-offs, it constitutes the biggest tax giveaway in history. . . .

[A] company that doesn't have a tax liability against which to write off such expenditures can "lease" the tax break to somebody else through what former Internal Revenue Commissioner Sheldon S. Cohen has dubbed the "rent-a-deduction" provision.

This particular gimmick was dreamed up by Washington lobbyist Charls Walker—an unofficial adviser to the Reagan administration—when businessmen began to complain that the tax credits and depreciation allowances moving through Congress earlier this year were so generous they couldn't make full use of them. So, Walker reasoned, if Corporation A has tax benefits that it can't use, why not let it sell them for cash to Corporation B? . . .

The egregious and indefensible "rent-a-deduction" provision does more than enable red-ink corporations like Ford, Chrysler and International

Harvester to "sell" their tax losses to profitable companies that can use them to reduce their own tax burden.

Even worse (and the administration's tax experts never anticipated it), some companies, like Occidental Petroleum Co., have been able to use the loophole even though they themselves are profitable. Occidental, for example, has a surplus of foreign tax credits that wipe out its U.S. tax burden, and thus was able to sell off millions in investment and depreciation credits it couldn't otherwise have used.

The tremendous "market" in tax losses that has been generated is evidence. Sen. Nancy Kassebaum (R-Kan.) said the other day, that "we simply had no idea what we wrought with that" . . . .

To his credit, the influential Sen. Pete Domenici of New Mexico, Republican chairman of the Senate Budget Committee, has begun to speak out against this and other legalized frauds in the tax code. "We are going to have to look at such things as the loopholes, the legal tax breaks which are growing like crazy," Domenici said on "Face the Nation" over the weekend.

"If we're asking the average citizen to sacrifice, then we can't let the very rich and the very big corporations get extreme benefits through legal tax loopholes and tax breaks that don't have any social merit, and are not aimed at building the whole economy back up." . . .

What's wrong, of course, is that the tax-loss sale or lease is just one more form of government bail-out for companies that have flunked the test of the marketplace. Where is the vaunted dedication of the Reagan administration to a free-market philosophy? . . .

H. TESTIMONY OF JOHN CHAPOTON
Assistant Secretary of the Treasury for Tax Policy, before the Senate Finance Committee (December 10, 1981)

Mr. Chairman and Members of this Committee:

I am pleased to be here today to discuss the liberalized leasing rules of the Economic Recovery Tax Act of 1981 (ERTA). The leasing rules have generated a great deal of confusion and misunderstanding. I am happy for the opportunity to further explain these rules and to reemphasize their role in the President's program. . . .

"Safe harbor" leases allow all companies making new investments full access to the incentives in the recent tax bill. Without these rules, unequal competition for funds would have arisen, additional financial barriers would have been presented to new companies, and additional pressures for mergers and takeovers would have been created. The new leasing rules do not make otherwise bad investments into good investments, but they do make good investments equally profitable for companies in different tax situations.

The Investment Incentives of ERTA

To see the need for the new leasing rules, the operation of the investment incentives in the recent tax bill must first be clearly understood. The principal investment incentive in the new law is provided by the Accelerated Cost Recovery System (ACRS). ACRS allows firms to deduct the cost of their investment over a much shorter time period than before. This is a valuable incentive, for when firms must postpone deducting the cost of new assets, the value of those deductions is lowered. A dollar that a corporation can deduct today is usually worth $0.46, because the tax rate is 46 percent. If the company must delay taking the $1.00 deduction for five years, however, its present value is reduced to only $0.26 for a company earning 15 percent on investments. Conversely, accelerating the deductions for expenditures on new equipment increases the value of those deductions to the firm. Accelerating deductions effectively lowers the cost of buying the equipment and raises the after-tax rate of return on that investment.

The increase in after-tax return on equipment that comes from accelerating cost-recovery deductions is the major direct investment incentive in the President's tax program. But these early deductions may occur at a time when the new machine is producing little income. Thus, the deductions will serve their purpose only if they can offset other taxable income. If a company does not have other taxable income or cannot transfer its deductions to firms that can use them, then the accelerated deductions under ACRS will be postponed and much of the investment incentive will be permanently lost.

In any year, many active U.S. corporations are in the position of having no current U.S. tax liability. These include new and young corporations just starting up; companies with particularly large investment plans and, thus, large deductions for cost recovery; and firms with temporary domestic losses, but profitable investment opportunities. More rapid deductions for cost recovery will moderately increase the number of such currently nontaxable companies, and will also increase the number of companies that will reach the statutory limit on current use of the investment tax credit.

An Example

To see how one type of company may be excluded from the new investment incentives of ACRS, consider a new firm, Newco Manufacturing Company (Newco), making a $100,000 investment in equipment. In the first two years of that investment, Newco will be allowed under ACRS to take deductions of $37,000 and an investment credit of $10,000. To use all of these tax benefits Newco will need to have net income in those two years (before ACRS deductions) of approximately $59,000. Even highly profitable investments generally do not return income within two years equal to more than one-half of the cost of the investment. Without income from older assets, Newco would have to postpone using some or all of the ACRS benefit, and the new tax bill would have increased Newco's after-tax return on new investment by less than that of other companies. Newco's return from that investment would be lower than that of corporations that can use all the benefits currently.

The essence of the new leasing rules is that ACRS will provide incentives for firms, such as Newco, to invest in new equipment even though their investments have not yet produced large profits. Newco may allow some other firm, Taxable Corporation, which does have significant taxable income, to purchase Newco's $100,000 of new equipment for tax purposes and to lease that equipment back to Newco. This allows Newco to use the equipment in its business, but at the same time permits Taxable Corporation to take the resulting investment credit and accelerated deductions against its other income.

In this typical example, the user of the equipment (Newco, the lessee) provides financing for all but Taxable Corporation's downpayment. The terms of the agreement can be arranged so that rental payments owed by Newco to Taxable Corporation just match the reverse payments for debt service. In addition, the agreement may allow Newco to repurchase the asset at the end of the lease term for a token amount. In such a case, only the downpayment actually changes hands between the two companies. This payment is the agreed value of the tax benefits transferred by the lease. . . .

The Outcome of Leasing

There are three important aspects of such a lease . . . . First, no extra deductions or tax credits are ever created. The total deductions taken by both parties are just the same as would have been taken if Newco had taxable income from other investments or if Taxable Corporation made the investment directly. They are exactly equal to the legally prescribed ACRS deductions and investment tax credit. The Treasury loses no more revenues than those necessary to provide equal investment incentives to all firms. It might also be noted that an alternative, but much less desirable way to accomplish the same result, would be by actual merger of the two companies.

The second critical point is that virtually all of the tax benefits of ACRS will be passed through to the company actually making the new investment, i.e., Newco. This is because Taxable Corporation, and any other corporation interested in obtaining the investment credit and ACRS deductions, will bid for these by offering favorable lease terms. It is already apparent that the market for such deductions is becoming very competitive. . . .

This is a crucial result, for it means that the investment incentive inherent in ACRS has remained just where it should be—in the hands of the firm that will undertake the new investment and employ the new equipment. Although Taxable Corporation takes the credits and ACRS deductions on its tax returns, Taxable Corporation pays for those credits and accelerated deductions . . . . Newco ultimately receives all the benefits of ACRS except transaction fees.

The third essential point about the lease transaction is that it does not encourage Newco to undertake an investment unless that investment is expected to be economically profitable. Leasing does not encourage uneconomical or tax-motivated investment. . . . Leasing does not guarantee a profit for bad investments; it merely provides the same ACRS investment incentives to firms without current taxable income as provided to firms with taxable income. With those incentives equally available, firms can select investments on the basis of their economic profitability, not on the basis of tax circumstances.

Misconceptions About Leasing

I have dwelt at some length on the details of the lease transaction because misunderstanding of these transactions is apparently the basis of much recent criticism of the safe harbor provisions. It has been said, for example, that these leases are a "bonanza" for those profitable companies able to purchase deductions and credits as "tax shelters." The opposite is proving to be the case. We have already begun to see the new rules resulting in more of the benefits passing through to users of the new equipment.

Tax-oriented leasing has been a significant feature of the economy for many years. Prior law, however, restricted and unduly complicated lease arrangements. Consequently, lease transactions required complicated agreements and legal uncertainties resulting in high transaction costs, including large legal and brokerage fees. These high costs reduced the net tax benefit (investment incentive) available to companies making an investment. The new simpler and more precise rules are resulting in lower costs and thus substantially more of the tax benefit will remain with those making the investment and less will go to compensate brokers, lessors and lawyers for taking leasing risks or attempting to avoid them.

Others have said that the new leasing rules are just another way to "bail out" loss companies. However, the fact that tax leasing will aid companies with economic losses does not detract from the desirability of the new leasing rules. These companies cannot use leases unless they undertake new investment in machinery and equipment. They will not make new investments if they do not expect them to be profitable, with or without leasing. Further, with or without leasing, the marketplace will not provide these firms with the capital to make these investments unless the marketplace also believes the investments will be profitable. There is no sound reason to penalize these firms, once they have withstood the critical analysis of lenders and investors in the free market, by forcing them to incur a higher cost of capital than their competitors. Indeed, such a penalty is singularly counterproductive. For most loss firms to become profitable, they must be able to modernize their plant and equipment. Penalizing them when they do invest only serves to make it more difficult for them to become profitable.

If tax leasing were not allowed, inefficient investment decisions would result. Otherwise-identical firms would face different capital costs depending solely on whether they had income from older assets. For example, Newco . . . might not make a particular investment even though, with the same tax incentives as other firms, that investment would be profitable to Newco and valuable to society. Alternatively, Taxable Corporation, the firm with income from older assets, might undertake the same investment rather than Newco, because of greater tax incentives. This could occur even though Taxable Corporation might lack some of the expertise to pursue the investment as efficiently as Newco. Finally, Taxable Corporation might acquire Newco so as to take advantage of Newco's unused ACRS deductions. Such tax-motivated mergers would serve no economic purpose, but would lead to a greater concentration of economic power.

Some critics have agreed with the importance of investment incentives for distressed companies, but express dismay that profitable companies are also cashing in their unusable tax benefits through leasing. Leasing by profitable companies with no current tax liability is neither surprising nor undesirable. It isn't even new. Many companies with tax losses have routinely used tax leases to make use of depreciation allowances and the investment tax credit. However, such transactions were effectively limited to equipment with a ready resale market, such as airplanes, railroad cars, and oil rigs. The new rules will end this discrimination, making leasing available for all kinds of machinery and equipment, and in the process will provide a larger share of the benefits to the equipment-using company.

A company may be currently nontaxable and yet economically profitable for a number of reasons. Our hypothetical startup company, Newco, is one example. With ACRS, rapid investment growth can result in continuing tax losses for such companies as deductions outpace current incomes. In another case, a company might have worldwide profits subject to tax abroad, but also have losses from U.S. operations resulting in excess foreign tax credits. Leasing provides the incentives of ACRS to such companies for investment in the United States. Leasing may also be of benefit to companies with capital gains income, excess depletion allowances, and perhaps other conditions that limit the current use of deductions. In every case, the same two basic principles continue to hold: (1) every lease is associated with new investment expected to be profitable and (2) no more tax benefits are available to these companies than would be provided to their currently-taxable competitors.

In any year, a disproportionate number of companies with tax losses are small businesses. While such companies may not yet have made use of the leasing provisions because information reaches them more slowly and legal fees are initially large, there is every reason to believe that a ready market for small leases will become available through local financial institutions. Again, without leasing, the potential for job-creating investment by such businesses would be reduced and the market pressure for merger or takeover by mature taxable companies would be increased. . . .

I. TESTIMONY OF PROFESSOR PAUL MCDANIEL

Before the Senate Budget Committee (November 24, 1981)

The "Safe Harbor Leasing" Rules

. . . The safe harbor leasing rule (SHL) was enacted because the depreciation deductions awarded under ACRS were so excessive that many companies could find themselves in a tax loss position, unable to use currently their investment credits and perhaps even part of the ACRS deduction itself. That result was deemed undesirable by the administration and Congress, presumably because the permissible carryback and carryover of the excess tax benefits diluted the desired incentive effect of ACRS and the investment credit.

The solution to this issue would have been to have made the excess tax benefits refundable. As to ACRS, the Treasury could have been authorized to deliver a check to a business whose ACRS deductions exceeded income. The check would have represented an interest free loan repayable to the Treasury over a specified time period. Likewise, unused investment credits could have been refunded to a "tax loss" business. Since the investment credit is the functional equivalent of a direct Government grant, the business would simply have retained these Treasury funds. Refundable tax benefits are themselves, therefore, the functional equivalents of direct Federal transfer payment programs, such as food stamps, etc.

The SHL rules were viewed as an alternative to the refundability approach. Under SHL, the business receives its Federal transfer or welfare payment by selling its excess tax benefits to a profitable corporation. The program beneficiaries thus receive immediate cash and the profitable corporation reduces or eliminates its Federal corporate income tax by using its acquired tax deductions and credits.

But the SHL approach produces dramatically different results from refundability—differences which should be of critical concern to the Congressional Budget Committees.

First, the comparability of SHL to refundable tax benefits makes clear that SHL is simply a method of effecting Federal transfer payments to qualifying businesses. Instead of having the Treasury issue the business welfare checks directly to a tax loss company, profitable corporations were selected as the agents to deliver the Federal transfer payments. From a budgetary standpoint, the SHL approach thus introduced an alternative method for implementing Federal transfer payment programs. The important question is whether this alternative method is subject to the same budgetary scrutiny as are the direct transfer payment programs for individuals such as food stamps, Social Security, AFDC payments and the like. . . .

The Congressional Budget Committees thus urgently need to scrutinize the SHL provisions with particular attention to questions such as the following:

> — In times when Federal transfer payment programs must be reduced because of limited budget resources, why is the business transfer payment program exempted from any reductions so that the entire burden of program cuts must be borne by transfer programs that benefit low-income and elderly individuals?

> — In general, is it desirable virtually to exempt a Federal transfer program from the Budget process simply because a different method for delivering the program payments is adopted?

The SHL system also raises another question with which Congress generally and the Budget Committees in particular must be concerned. In an era of limited Federal resources, it is vital that Federal transfer payment programs operate as efficiently as possible. Thus, the SHL technique must be examined closely to see if it is cost-benefit effective. That is if the objective is to provide Federal payments to ailing businesses, is $1 of Federal revenue cost translated into $1 of benefit to the program beneficiary? . . .

Under the SHL system, profitable corporations are in effect designated as the agents to deliver the Federal transfer payments to loss corporations. The preliminary indications are that these delivery agents are siphoning off a substantial "commission" to compensate themselves for acting as delivery agents. This fact is readily apparent from an example that appeared in the recent explanation of the SHL provisions issued to the Staff of the Joint Committee on Taxation [JCT].

The JCT example assumed that X Corporation purchased equipment for $1 million. The present value of the ACRS depreciation deductions and the investment tax credit equalled $321,000. X Corporation sold those tax benefits to Y Corporation for $200,000. Thus, Y Corporation in effect received a $121,000 "commission" from the Treasury for delivering a $200,000 Treasury check to X Corporation. Or to put the matter another way, it cost the Treasury $1.60 to deliver each $1 dollar of transfer payment to X Corporation. Put still differently, if the objective is to deliver $200,000 to X Corporation, the Treasury could have saved $121,000 by just issuing the check itself (e.g., through a refundability mechanism). Or still differently, if the objective is to get $321,000 of tax benefits to X Corporation, almost 40% of that amount was wasted because of the delivery mechanism selected. . . .

J. NOTES AND QUESTIONS

1) The Context in Which SHL Emerged

The 1981 Economic Recovery Tax Act (ERTA) authorized vastly expanded tax incentives for capital investment in depreciable assets. The investment tax credit (ITC) rose to 10% and periods of cost recovery were radically shortened under the accelerated cost recovery system (ACRS) (Chapter 35).

One consequence of using the tax system, rather than direct expenditures, to promote investment is that companies with taxable income may receive a larger benefit than companies without such income. Consider two automobile manufacturers, General Motors and Ford, considering investing $200,000 in new equipment. Under ERTA, the ITC is 10% of $200,000, or $20,000, and can be used to reduce taxes due by that amount. Assume that the present value of tax savings from ACRS depreciation is $70,000. If General Motors purchases the equipment for $200,000 and has enough other taxable income, it realizes tax savings of $90,000 from ITC and ACRS, reducing the net, or after-tax, cost to $110,000. Suppose Ford, on the other hand, is experiencing losses and therefore must postpone using the tax incentives provided by ITC and ACRS. The present value of the tax benefits is *less* for Ford than for General Motors. If Ford purchases exactly the same equipment, its after-tax cost is considerably higher than General Motor's. Because the investment incentives are furnished through the tax system, Ford appears to be at a competitive disadvantage.

2) The Refundability Proposal

One way to eliminate this disadvantage is to make the tax incentives refundable. Refundability involves paying the taxpayer the amount that it would save in taxes if it had sufficient taxable income. For example, Ford would receive one dollar for every dollar of the ITC and 46 cents for every dollar of ACRS depreciation that it cannot use.

Why wasn't refundability adopted? At about the same time that the President and Congress enacted ERTA, they were cutting domestic programs, including food stamps, nutrition for pregnant women, and school lunches. (At one point, the Department of Agriculture proclaimed that catsup was a vegetable in order to prove that budget cuts had not affected the nutritional value of school lunches.) How would it have looked if refundability were enacted when the budget for such domestic programs was being reduced?

3) The SHL Solution

SHL was devised as a substitute for refundability. It was designed to enable loss companies to sell the tax benefits they could not use to another corporation. Ford, in the example above, purchases the equipment for $200,000, resells it to another party, and then leases the property back. The lease is on a net basis with Ford responsible for maintaining the property. The buyer puts down only a fraction of the purchase price. The balance, plus interest, is due in equal installments over the term of the lease, and each installment payment exactly equals rent due for the same period under the lease. Thus, rent under the lease exactly offsets installments due on the deferred purchase price, and the lease provides no net cash flow to the buyer. The only cash actually changing hands is the buyer's down payment. However, the buyer would be considered the owner of the property and entitled to the ITC and ACRS depreciation. In effect, the buyer purchases the tax benefits for the down payment.

As already noted, ERTA immunized SHL from conventional legal attacks. Even if the lessor neither retains a residual, nor has any prospect of a before-tax profit, the lessor is still considered the owner for tax purposes. The seller does not even have to transfer legal title. The transaction is designated a "tax sale," for tax purposes only.

4) Chapoton's Defense of SHL

How did Assistant Secretary Chapoton defend SHL from the conventional criticisms, described in the introductory note, of leasing tax shelters? How are the tax benefits passed through to the lessee, who is subject to the business risks associated with the property? Why is there no tax avoidance? (Remember under a safe-harbor lease only a corporation can act as purchaser-lessor.)

5) McDaniel's Critique

Professor McDaniel criticized SHL on two grounds. First, he argued that SHL received considerably less public scrutiny than refundability or other direct expenditure programs because it was in the form of an amendment to the tax code rather than legislation authorizing a direct outlay of government funds. Does this political process objection apply to SHL alone? Might it not be reason to object to tax incentives generally, including ITC and ACRS?

Professor McDaniel also argued that nearly 40% of revenues lost under SHL were wasted and never actually reached the intended recipient, the long-term lessee. The example, under 3), above, involving Ford's acquisition of capital equipment costing $200,000, assumes that the present value of the ITC plus ACRS is $90,000. Using McDaniel's estimates, only $54,000 actually reaches Ford in a SHL transaction and $36,000, or 40% of the value of the tax incentives, is wasted. (Later studies indicated waste of "only" 15%–25%.)

What might explain such waste? Is a small part attributable to the transaction costs of SHL? Is a larger part attributable to the lack of competitive bidding for safe harbor leases that may occur if there is an insufficient supply of companies with taxable income willing to engage in SHL transactions?

Suppose SHL had not been enacted and the lessee had to use an "ordinary" lease. The IRS' position was that the lease would be respected only if the lessor retained a significant residual and obtained some net cash flow (Chapter 39). But might not these requirements result in the lessor capturing even more of the benefits, with an even lower amount being passed on to the lessee than under SHL? Could SHL be defended as less wasteful than ordinary leasing?

Alternatively, does the possibility of 15%–40% waste under SHL—and perhaps even more under ordinary leasing—prove that investment incentives should be provided through direct grants or *refundable* tax benefits, rather than through the nonrefundable ITC and ACRS depreciation? Would direct grants or refundable tax incentives be likely to entail such enormous waste? If not, why was SHL chosen over them? In other words, what motivated Congress to choose the more wasteful program? Was it fear of appearing to provide "welfare" to corporations, while cutting domestic programs for individuals?

6) The Audit Argument for SHL Over Refundability

One argument for SHL over refundability was that it would lessen the audit burden on the IRS. The buyer-lessor could be counted on to ensure that capital equipment really was purchased in order to safeguard the tax breaks that it had acquired.

> A program of refundability ... might create significant audit problems. ... Would the Treasury simply issue checks to taxpayers on the tra-

ditional basis of self-assessment, given the possibility of fraudulent claims that recovery property had been purchased?

... Under safe harbor leasing, however, vesting federal tax ownership in lessors has necessarily made them Treasury surrogates for certain audit purposes.[1]

Do you find the audit argument persuasive? Is fraud any less likely when the purchaser has enough taxable income to use the tax benefits directly? Are fraudulent claims under refundability likely to exceed the amount wasted by SHL due to transaction costs and insufficient competitive bidding?

7) Is the Airplane Tax Shelter an Abuse?

Return to the question posed by the title of this chapter: Is the Airplane Tax Shelter an Abuse? Recall the conventional criticism that tax incentives go to the wrong party and wealthy investors avoid paying their fair share of taxes. What light does the debate about SHL shed on these criticisms? Despite their superficial appeal, the conventional criticisms may be overstated and, under certain assumptions, entirely misplaced. Consider their validity in the context of the airplane tax shelter.

a) Did tax incentives in the airplane tax shelter go to the wrong party? If Pan Am had bought the aircraft directly, it would have had to make a $3 million cash down payment but would also have received future tax benefits with a present value of about $3 million.[2] In effect, if Pan Am had bought the airplane, its down payment would have been funded by the tax benefits (assuming that Pan Am could use them). Under the tax shelter, Pan Am lost the tax benefits but saved the down payment. As a result, didn't Pan Am obtain roughly the same benefits through the tax shelter that it would have obtained if it had owned the airplane directly and had sufficient taxable income to use the accelerated depreciation and ITC? Under the leasing transaction, weren't the tax benefits passed on to Pan Am so that the user—the risk taker—in fact obtained them? If Pan Am had a history of losses, wasn't the tax shelter deal the only way to provide the same tax incentives to Pan Am as to profitable airlines? Is there a principled reason for affording such benefits to airlines with taxable income but denying them to airlines with losses?

b) Did wealthy investors in the airplane tax shelter avoid paying their fair share of taxes? While the investors obtained tax benefits, what about the $3 million they had to pay to get them? Couldn't that amount be viewed as offsetting their tax savings? As a kind of "implicit" tax? True, the inves-

---

1. Auerbach and Warren, Transferability of Tax Incentives and The Fiction of Safe Harbor Leasing, 95 Harv. Law Rev. 1752, 1777 (1982).

2. This $3 million figure is derived from Table 38-1 in Chapter 38, which calculated the present value of the benefits for a 50% bracket tax shelter investor. The tax rate on corporate income above $100,000 for the relevant period hovered at just above or below 50%.

tors saved "explicit" taxes—taxes otherwise due because they are explicitly assessed by the income tax system. But wasn't the saving in explicit taxes offset by the implicit tax imposed when the investors made a cash down payment of $3 million?

But what if the investors were in a significantly higher tax bracket than Pan Am (for example, 70% versus about 50%) so that their tax savings exceeded the tax shelter's cost? In that case, didn't the over 50% bracket investor avoid paying his or her fair share? And didn't that cause government revenues to be wasted? In the airplane tax shelter example, wasn't the implicit tax rate only about 50% so that investors in higher brackets realized a windfall?

Even if the investors' tax bracket was not significantly higher than the top corporate rate, not *all* the benefits might reach Pan Am, and the investors might avoid paying their fair share in taxes. In the absence of fully competitive bidding, the investors might pay less than the present value of the tax benefits. And the tax shelter promoters must take out some money for their transaction costs and might also demand a handsome profit. If, for example, there were an insufficient number of potential investors relative to the supply of tax shelters, they might agree to pay only $2.5 million instead of $3 million for the tax benefits. From that, the promoters might take another $300,000. This reduces the cash available for the down payment to $2.2 million, requiring a larger mortgage loan. Pan Am would then have to pay higher rent under the lease to cover the higher monthly mortgage payments that would be due.

To summarize, an equipment-leasing tax shelter might be viewed as "nonobjectionable"—and perhaps even desirable—if three conditions are met: if bidding for tax shelter benefits is competitive; if transaction costs are low; and if the lessor saves no more in explicit taxes than the lessee would save if it had taxable income. But to the extent that these conditions are not satisfied, tax incentives may not fully benefit the lessee and shelter investors may avoid their fair share of the tax burden.

8) The Relationship of the Economic Analysis of Tax Shelters to Sections 46(e)(3)(B) and 465

What light does this discussion cast on Code provisions that curb leasing tax shelters *only* for individual, and not for corporate, lessors? In 1981, the top individual tax rate on all income, earned or unearned, was lowered to 50%, only marginally above the corporate 46% rate.[3] Should provisions like Sections 46(e)(3)(B) and 465, which affected only individual lessors, therefore have been repealed? Wouldn't repeal have enabled individuals to bid for long-term leases, increasing competitive bidding and also possibly lowering transaction costs?

---

3. With the enactment of the 1986 Tax Reform Act, the top corporate rate fell to 34%, but the top individual rate fell even further, to 33%.

9) The Relationship of the Economic Analysis of Tax Shelters to Conventional Legal Doctrines

Is there any connection between the legal doctrine requiring the lessor to retain a residual and the factors (competitive bidding, low transaction costs, and no tax rate differential) indicating an unobjectionable tax shelter? Doesn't this doctrine make leasing a less efficient and more wasteful method of transferring tax benefits, because of uncertainty over the future value of the residual?

Similarly, is there any connection at all between the legal doctrine requiring the lessor to make a before-tax profit and the factors indicating an unobjectionable tax shelter? Doesn't a tax shelter provide benefits most efficiently to the true risk taker, the user of leased equipment, when the investors receive the future tax breaks but no other nontax economic value? Doesn't requiring a before-tax profit force the lessee to provide nontax benefits? Doesn't this also make leasing actually *less* efficient and *more* wasteful?

Is there a difference between requiring a before-tax profit in an equipment leasing tax shelter on the one hand and in a commodity straddle on the other? Might the requirement, although perhaps irrational in the first case, make sense in the second? Did Congress intend to provide tax incentives for investment in straddles? Did *Smith* (Chapter 16) interfere with the efficient sale of tax benefits by loss corporations engaged in capital formation? See Warren, The Requirement of Economic Profit in Tax Motivated Transactions, 59 Taxes 985 (1981).

K. GALPER AND LUBICK, THE DEFECTS OF SAFE HARBOR LEASING AND WHAT TO DO ABOUT THEM
14 Tax Notes 643, 643-646 (March 15, 1982)

The safe harbor leasing rules were enacted in the 1981 Tax Act (without hearings and with little discussion) as the mechanism to permit sale of cost recovery tax deductions and credits by one corporation to another. The widespread misgivings over these leasing rules, and serious concern expressed over the revenue loss from these transactions, usually overlook the true source of the problem: the substitution of cost recovery deductions under the Accelerated Cost Recovery System (ACRS) for a realistic set of depreciation deductions. Compared to prior law, ACRS has been estimated to cost $51.5 billion of corporate income tax receipts in 1986, of which less than 20 percent or $9.4 billion arises from the leasing rules.

The defects of leasing expose, and in large part derive from, the fact that ACRS combines into one allowance both the income measurement function of the depreciation deduction and the incentive function of a special cost recovery allowance over and above the existing investment credit (ITC). Safe harbor leasing permits the sale and transfer of more than the incentive; it allows the lessee to cash out a portion of an ordinary income measurement deduction. . . .

Objectives of Cost Recovery Allowances

To understand fully the problem addressed by the leasing rules and to evaluate their efficacy, we must review the two main objectives (other than administrative simplicity) of capital cost recovery allowances. They are as follows:

1. Income measurement. This is the traditional function of depreciation and is still the purpose of depreciation claimed for non-tax accounting purposes. The cost of equipment is appropriately charged as a series of deductions over its useful life against the income the equipment produces for the investor. It has also been argued that accurate income measurement requires an appropriate adjustment for inflation. This was in no small part a justification encouraging the enactment of fast write-offs under ACRS. With rapid inflation, the projected value of deferred deductions based on the original cost of the equipment when it was placed in service is seriously diminished. One aspect of ACRS is to allow earlier cost recovery deductions than would be appropriate in a noninflationary environment and thus to provide some rough compensation for the impact of inflation. Of course, such compensation may be either excessive or insufficient depending upon the rate of inflation.

2. Subsidy. To the extent that allowances exceed those obtained by proper measurement of income—in the case of ACRS the acceleration of tax benefits by greater deductions in the early years of an asset's use—a portion of the income generated by the asset is exempt from tax. The tax cost of the investment is thereby reduced and the investment becomes more profitable. Thus the excess of benefits over properly measured (economic) depreciation effectively removes a part of income from the tax base and is an implicit subsidy to the investor. The subsidy is reflected in an effective tax rate that is below the statutory tax rate. If the rate of subsidy is greater in one particular industry than in another, it will be more profitable to invest in the former industry. The flow of capital is thus encouraged toward those industries enjoying artificially high rates of return by reason of the tax subsidy. . . .

Scrambling of the Objectives

The defects in the operation of the safe harbor leasing rules are primarily caused by the amalgamation of income measurement and incentive subsidy into one cost recovery allowance under ACRS. ACRS is intended to give the allowance needed to measure income (including compensation for the erosion of depreciation allowances in periods of inflation) and at the same time to grant a subsidy in the form of reduced taxes as an incentive to invest in equipment. . . .

If the element of subsidy were separated from the element of income measurement, the objective of the leasing rules—delivery of the subsidy—

could be achieved easily. The straightforward solution would be to pay the subsidy to eligible recipients by an offset against taxes, or if there is no tax liability due, by direct Treasury check.

The investment credit delivers the subsidy in this way for profitable corporations. If corporation A invests $1,000,000 and the desired subsidy is 10 percent, it simply deducts $100,000 from the taxes it would otherwise pay the government. Corporation B, however, that has made the desired investment, but owes no taxes because it is struggling to become profitable (hence the investment in new equipment) cannot get its $100,000 by offset against its tax liability, which is zero. Of the two principal alternatives referred to above, the straightforward one of "refundability" would require corporation B to notify the Treasury that it made the investment, but owes no taxes. Then the IRS could send corporation B its $100,000. It is very simple and logical if the subsidy is in the form of a credit, since the credit represents subsidy and nothing else.

The other solution of "transferability" would permit corporation B to sell its unusable credit to corporation A. B gets its money and A gets the tax benefit as an offset to A's tax liability. By a round-about route, however, it is the IRS that pays whatever subsidy B receives. The safe harbor leasing rules adopt the latter solution of transferability for both ITC and ACRS but imperfectly and erroneously to the extent that transferability goes beyond the subsidy to include income measurement elements of the ACRS deduction. . . .

If under safe harbor leasing only the subsidy elements were transferred to A, the results would not be much different from refundability of a credit. Whether the Treasury gives B $100,000 by a refund check (refundability) or whether B gets its $100,000 by a sale of tax benefits to A (of course, this disregards the reality that A, its lawyers and its brokers, will each have to get a cut), and A gets the $100,000 from the Treasury by an offset to its tax liability (leasing) is of little import in theory.

In practice, safe harbor leasing leads to very different consequences from refundability.

The Shortcomings of Safe Harbor Leasing as a Subsidy Delivery Mechanism

Overgenerosity. The leasing rules permit corporation B to cash out much more than the subsidy. For this purpose we may define the subsidy to include the ITC (and the additional tax savings due to the ability of the taxpayer to depreciate the ITC, since there is no basis reduction on account of the ITC) and the tax savings from the excess of the present value of ACRS deductions over the present value of prior law . . . deductions. . . .

Since B can transfer to A the tax savings from the *whole* ACRS deduction, including the portion that represents prior law depreciation and hence measurement of income, A may be willing to make an up front cash payment that is *greater* than the subsidy element of the ITC and the ACRS deductions. . . .

B is thus able to cash out much more than the amount of the subsidy, even though B at the same time may have a properly measured economic loss from current operations. Suppose B had $10,000 of gross income before depreciation and expenses, $15,000 of ACRS deductions, of which $6,000 is subsidy and only $9,000 represents actual or economic depreciation under proper income measurement, and $8,000 of other expenses—wages, entertainment or any other business expense. The $9,000 of ACRS and $8,000 of other deductions equal $7,000 of excess deductions ($17,000 minus $10,000) and produce no immediate tax benefit to B, until it turns a profit in some other year. By the leasing rules, however, B can sell to A its entire $15,000 of ACRS deductions—both the $6,000 of subsidy and the $9,000 of income measurement deductions. B thus receives an immediate cash benefit from at least a portion of the tax value of the income measurement deductions, as well as the subsidy.

B can do this even though its other deductions also needed to properly measure income have no comparable immediate value. To the extent that B can sell deductions that represent more than the subsidy, i.e., that represent actual income measurement, B is able to accomplish through safe harbor leasing what other firms in similar economic circumstances, but with deductions resulting from wages, materials, rents and the like, cannot accomplish. This is patently unfair. It is one thing to make the subsidy available to all; it is something else again to cash out the actual economic costs that result only from the acquisition of depreciable assets without being able to cash out costs from any other source.

It is true that to equalize the cost of acquiring a physical asset between A with large taxable income and B with no taxable income (but with expected future profits and taxes), refundability (whether by leasing or directly) is required as to the whole tax benefit of the investment—the income measurement portion as well as the subsidy portion. That argument proves too much, however. Such equalization of opportunity from capital investment for profitable and loss corporations has never led to serious Congressional consideration of refundability for any other type of loss that is a function simply of proper income measurement.

To be consistent with the aspect of leasing that permits transferability of the value of an income measurement deduction, Congress would similarly have to provide that any business that has an economic loss, i.e., expenses greater than its income, even if that economic loss were the result of its own poor management, should receive a refund of 46 percent—a negative income tax for corporations. The rhetoric of the Administration on cutting back welfare payments could well and appropriately be directed to the feature of the leasing rules that permits such immediate refunds on account of business losses attributable to measurement of economic income. This amounts to a gigantic welfare program for corporations. Payments are even being granted to highly profitable corporations (as where a domestic loss would otherwise be wasted by offset against foreign source income). These bailouts represent more than a government-designed subsidy to invest. They represent, in effect, a refundable operating loss. . . .

L. AUERBACH AND WARREN, TRANSFERABILITY OF TAX INCENTIVES AND THE FICTION OF SAFE HARBOR LEASING
95 Harv. L. Rev. 1752, 1752–1762 (1982)

The Economic Recovery Tax Act of 1981 introduced a federal income tax "safe harbor" for leasing transactions in order to distribute the benefits of the investment tax credit (ITC) and the newly enacted Accelerated Cost Recovery System (ACRS) throughout the corporate sector. Although less than a year has passed since adoption of the 1981 Act, there is already considerable Congressional support for alteration or repeal of the leasing provisions.

This Article evaluates safe harbor leasing as a means of accomplishing the transfer of tax incentives. The focus here is not whether ACRS and the ITC are themselves desirable, but whether, given these provisions, the new rules for tax leasing are necessary and appropriate. . . .

I. THE INVESTMENT TAX CREDIT AND THE ACCELERATED COST RECOVERY SYSTEM

Adherence to the concept of income requires that the cost of an asset with a limited lifetime be deducted from the revenues produced by the asset over its useful life. In theory, these depreciation deductions, or capital costs, should match "economic depreciation"—the actual decline in value of the asset—as closely as possible. But to encourage investment, the Internal Revenue Code explicitly deviated from this principle in two significant ways before the 1981 Act was adopted. First, the Code granted an investment tax credit for purchases of qualified property, which could be described loosely as machinery and equipment. Second, the rate of depreciation was increased, and the depreciable life decreased, for certain assets; these changes resulted in faster recovery of capital costs for tax purposes than would have been consistent with economic depreciation.

The 1981 Act extended this deviation from economic depreciation by further disassociating the period over which an asset's cost is recovered from the asset's actual useful life. The Act divided all depreciable assets into four categories of "recovery property," with each category determining the period over which an asset's cost may be deducted. These periods are generally shorter than either actual economic lifetimes or the depreciation lives under prior law. The explicitly articulated rationale for these changes was to stimulate investment necessary for economic expansion, as well as to simplify the tax law.

The value of the new system to purchasers of eligible property is considerable. Perhaps the easiest way to demonstrate the significance of the change is to compare the present value (in the year in which the recovery property is purchased) of the tax savings that will result from future ACRS deductions and the ITC with the present value of the tax burden associated with income produced by the property involved. For example, at a discount rate of twelve percent and a corporate tax rate of forty-six percent, $100 of five-year property (which includes most industrial machinery and equipment) generates tax savings with a present value of $46.65.[4] For the marginal investment, the $100 cost is the present value of all future cash flows to be produced by the asset; hence the present value of the tax burden on those flows, at a tax rate of forty-six percent, is $46. A comparison of that burden with the $46.65 tax savings shows that there is no net income tax associated with income produced by the five-year property. Calculations such as this have led to statements, even by Treasury officials, that the 1981 Act reduced to zero the effective tax rate on income from certain capital investments.

In this example, the combined value of ACRS deductions and the ITC roughly equals the value of an immediate deduction for the entire cost of the equipment. As is well known, deducting (or, as it is sometimes called, "expensing") a capital cost has the effect of eliminating the tax burden on the taxpayer's investment because the tax savings from the deduction will fund all future taxes on income produced by the investment. . . .[5]

There is, however, nothing inherently limiting about a zero tax rate under ACRS and the ITC. Several studies have suggested that for some industries and some assets the effective rate of tax will actually be negative as a result of the 1981 Act. Indeed, the tax is somewhat negative in our example: the present value of tax benefits ($46.65) exceeds the present value of future tax liabilities ($46) by sixty-five cents.

Before turning to the problems that were created by these provisions and for which leasing was adopted as a solution, we should identify an ambiguity in the rationale for ACRS and the ITC, for it is an ambiguity that may affect evaluation of the safe harbor. In brief, the ITC and ACRS provisions can be seen either as structural components of the income tax that reduce the effective tax rate [on capital income to zero] or as government subsidies that are located in the Internal Revenue Code. . . .

If ACRS and the ITC were intended simply to eliminate [taxes on capital income, then] the lower limit of effective tax rates should be zero . . . .

---

4. Assuming that the property is purchased for $100 on the last day of year one and that the tax benefits for that year are immediately available, the present value of the 10% ITC . . . is $10. The rounded present value of the ACRS deductions, as computed below, is $79.68, which generates $36.65 in tax savings when the tax rate is 46% (.46 × $79.68 = $36.65). Thus, the present value of the combined tax benefits is $46.65 ($10 + $36.65).

TABLE I
Present Value of ACRS Deductions

Year	1 Discount Factor (@ 12%)	2 ACRS Deductions	3 Present Value [(1) × (2)]
1	1.000	15	15.00
2	.893	22	19.64
3	.797	21	16.74
4	.712	21	14.95
5	.636	21	13.35
Total		100	79.68

5. A 50% taxpayer with other income would, for example, be indifferent between (1) investing $100 in a perpetuity yielding an exempt return of 10% annually, and (2) investing $200 in a deductible perpetuity (with the tax savings from the deduction providing the additional $100) yielding a taxable return of 10% annually. Both investments would produce $10 annually after taxes.

Under the alternative explanation for ACRS and the ITC, the possibility of negative effective tax rates is not even relevant to tax policy, for ACRS and the ITC are not a part of the tax system at all. Rather, they constitute an expenditure program by which the government intends to reduce the price of recovery property in order to encourage its purchase, capital formation, and the economic benefits that are thought to ensue. The ITC involves a subsidy to the extent of the tax credit. . . . ACRS also creates a subsidy because the present value of the ACRS deductions exceeds the present value of economic depreciation. The ACRS subsidy can be viewed as an interest-free loan, under which the government makes available in earlier years the tax reductions investors would have obtained by deducting economic depreciation in later years. . . .

Unfortunately, the legislative history does not indicate which of these two views of ACRS and the ITC represents the intent of Congress. The relevant committee report speaks both of the effect of reductions in the real value of depreciation deductions on the profitability of investment and of "stimulating capital formation, increasing productivity and improving the nation's competitiveness in international trade"—language that is consistent with either perspective.

II. THE CASE FOR EXTENDING THE BENEFITS OF ACRS AND THE ITC TO COMPANIES WITHOUT TAXABLE INCOME

ACRS deductions and the ITC are valuable only if a taxpayer has taxable income against which the deductions can be taken and tax liability against which the ITC can be credited. There are, however, at least two types of taxpayers that do not meet these conditions.

A. *Start-Up Companies*

A company that purchases recovery property and has no other income or expenses (a "start-up company") generally has ACRS deductions and ITC in the initial years that exceed the income and tax liability produced by the property. . . . Thus, unless the recovery property produces large amounts of income in its early years, a start-up company does not receive the same present value of tax benefits as does a "profitable company" that can apply ACRS deductions against current income and the ITC against taxes on income from other assets. Even unlimited carryover of deductions and credits would not put a start-up company in the same position as a profitable company, because the profitable company would receive its benefits earlier than would the start-up company.

If ACRS and the ITC are to provide equivalent benefits to corporations investing equivalent amounts in the same categories of recovery property, some mechanism is needed to equate the tax benefits received by a start-up company with those received by a profitable company. Whether the combined effect of ACRS and the ITC is thought of as a form of tax reduction or as an investment subsidy, the desirability of equivalent benefits can be justified on two grounds. First, to avoid economic distortions, the government should be neutral among potential investors in similar projects.

Second, nonneutrality might stimulate tax-induced mergers of profitable and start-up companies. For example, a profitable retail company that owned little recovery property might merge with a start-up company so that the latter's ACRS deductions and ITC could be used to reduce the former's tax liability. We will refer generally to both grounds for extending the benefits of ACRS and the ITC as arguments to further "competitive neutrality."

B. *Loss Companies*

A second category of taxpayers that would not fully benefit from ACRS deductions and the ITC without some additional mechanism consists of corporations that have operating losses, net operating loss carryovers, or other tax attributes that immunize them from taxation in the foreseeable future. Such corporations will be called, rather loosely, "loss companies." Although loss companies were apparently the intended beneficiaries of safe harbor leasing as much as were start-up companies, the Treasury has generally used a hypothetical start-up company in post-enactment illustrations of how the safe harbor operates. To be sure, a loss company (like a start-up company) represents an extreme case, but the discussion that follows applies to other corporations to the extent they cannot use ACRS deductions and the ITC.

If the purpose of ACRS and the ITC is to reduce capital income taxation, loss companies should not be included among the beneficiaries of those provisions, because such companies are already effectively exempt. If, however, ACRS and the ITC are considered subsidies rather than a means of reducing capital income taxation, the principle of competitive neutrality supports extending these subsidies to loss companies for the same two reasons that it supports extension to start-up companies. First, payment of capital subsidies for investment in equipment by some companies but not by others may decrease economic welfare if the subsidized companies are not those best able to make the most socially desirable investments. This rationale is arguably subject to the objection that some loss companies may not be profitable because they are poorly managed, and therefore should not be subsidized. This objection assumes that competitive market pressures will fail to improve management and that government action is therefore necessary. If, however, the economy is basically competitive, it will provide incentives to minimize poor management and to eliminate the need for differential government subsidies.

The second argument for extending the subsidy to loss companies is that otherwise they may merge with profitable companies to obtain the subsidy. Although it is difficult to know precisely how much merger activity might occur, restricting the subsidies to companies with taxable income and tax liabilities would surely result in increased pressure for conglomeration. There is no reason to suppose that such mergers, which would not be attractive to the parties in the absence of tax incentives, would be beneficial to the economy. Nor will all tax-induced mergers be deterred by the prospect of consolidating with an unprofitable company. Loss companies include not only economically unprofitable corporations, but also successful corporations that have no *taxable* income or tax liability for whatever reason, including the use of tax incentives.

C. Summary

The combined effect of ACRS deductions and the ITC can be justified either as [eliminating] capital income taxation [that is, as reducing the effective tax rate on capital income to zero], or as an investment subsidy that has only a coincidental connection with the tax system. . . . Under either view, start-up companies should receive the benefits of ACRS deductions and the ITC to achieve either the same tax reduction or the same investment subsidy that profitable companies receive. Extension of these benefits to loss companies [through SHL] requires acceptance of the subsidy rationale.

Unfortunately, the assumptions regarding these provisions are not articulated well enough in the legislative history to support a clear conclusion about what was intended. Congress simply indicated that the benefits of ACRS deductions and the ITC should be available to loss and start-up companies, but not to exempt organizations or . . . to governmental units. . . .

M. NOTES AND QUESTIONS

1) Income Measurement versus Subsidy Losses

Galper and Lubick argue that leasing should enable a taxpayer to transfer only the excess of tax over economic depreciation, because it is only to that extent that depreciation is intended to provide a subsidy. However, SHL may enable a taxpayer to transfer more than that. Others have made the same point:

> [A] loss company should receive the excess of the present value of tax reductions resulting from ACRS deductions . . . over the present value of tax reductions that result from deductions for economic depreciation.
> The payments under leasing are too large because the down payment equals the excess of the present value of tax reductions . . . over the present value of taxes on income in the amount of principal repayments, rather than over the present value of tax reductions resulting from economic depreciation. The amortization of loan principal is slower than the best approximations of economic depreciation . . . Thus, the present value of principal repayments is smaller than the present value of economic depreciation, and the resulting down payments are larger than payments computed with regard to economic depreciation.[6]

How is the sale of such economic losses inconsistent with the principle of annual accounting, approved in Burnet v. Sanford & Brooks (see Chapter 24)? How does the sale enable companies to avoid the disadvantages of

---

6. Auerbach and Warren, Transferability of Tax Incentives and The Fiction of Safe Harbor Leasing, 95 Harv. L. Rev. 1752, 1769–1771 (1982).

Section 172, which permits the carryforward of net operating losses? Why is it, in the words of Lubick and Galper, "patently unfair"?

But don't conglomerates and other diversified corporations have a "patently unfair" advantage over the corporation that operates just one business? The diversified corporation can use current losses from one business to offset current profits from another business; however, the one-business corporation, by definition, cannot. Its losses may have to be carried forward, under Section 172, to later years, so that their present value is reduced. Doesn't the transfer of economic losses through leasing help reduce this unfair advantage? If transfer of the subsidy element through leasing is preferable to tax-motivated mergers, then why isn't transfer of economic losses through leasing also preferable to tax-motivated mergers?

Congress has enacted a number of provisions to prevent a profitable business from acquiring a company with large net operating losses simply in order to reduce taxes. Because these provisions are beyond the scope of this introductory casebook, they will be described only briefly. Section 269 disallows such losses altogether where the "principal purpose" of the acquisition is tax avoidance. In addition, Section 382 contains an objective test which reduces or denies the use of such losses when there is a substantial change in the ownership of a business.

Might the IRS requirements for a favorable ruling on a long-term leasing deal be understood as an attempt to curb the transfer of net operating losses through leasing? As a supplement to Sections 269 and 382?

2) The Zero Tax Rate versus Subsidy Objectives

Auerbach and Warren suggest that SHL should have been denied to "loss" companies if Congress' objective was to provide for a zero tax rate on new investment in, rather than a subsidy for, depreciable assets. Why? They also argue that whether Congress intended a zero tax rate or a subsidy is unclear from the legislative history. But isn't it made clear by the fact that Congress made SHL available to "loss" companies? Or could Congress have made a mistake in translating a zero tax rate objective into law?

If Congress wanted to eliminate the tax on new capital investment, why not expressly exempt that income from tax? What are the practical obstacles to implementing directly a zero tax rate on income from new investment, while at the same time, continuing to tax income from existing investment?

3) The Question of Appearances

Even if SHL were unobjectionable from the standpoint of economic analysis, what about the question of appearances? Won't taxpayer morale and voluntary compliance suffer if the public *believes* that unethical "trafficking in tax loopholes" allows wealthy corporations and individuals to avoid paying their fair share? (Consider the impact on public opinion of the newspaper articles included in this chapter's reading.) *SHL had only a brief existence and was repealed just one year after it was enacted.* The Senate Finance Committee explained:

Congress believed that the adverse public reaction to such practices and to the institutionalized commerce in tax deductions and credits was too likely to diminish respect for and compliance with the tax laws on the part of the general taxpayer.

Congress was also concerned that the revenue cost of the prior law safe-harbor rules was too large, in light of projected budget deficits [and] the uncertain public benefits . . . [7]

N. FORMAN, TAX CONSIDERATIONS IN RENTING A NAVY
26 Tax Notes 1192 (March 25, 1985)

On December 10, 1984, the IRS issued a 143 page private letter ruling declaring that a United States Navy ship financing deal put together by Salomon Brothers is a true lease for tax purposes. The ruling was released to the public last week. The financing deal involves one of the TAKX ships or T-5 tankers that the United States Navy leased rather than purchased. The ruling assures the Salomon Brothers investors that they are entitled to deduct interest and Accelerated Cost Recovery System (ACRS) depreciation based on a five year life for the ship. . . .

Rent-a-Navy

What happens when Congress passes a depreciation schedule that is so generous that it allows ships that are expected to last for over 30 years to be written off in just five years? That is exactly what the Economic Recovery Act of 1981 did when it replaced the old ADR depreciation system with ACRS. The result was that the tax advantages of leasing, rather than purchasing, became so great that even the Navy could not keep its hands off the back door of the Treasury. The Navy's arrangement to "charter" rather than purchase 13 TAKX ships and five T-5 tankers is reminiscent of Queen Elizabeth's chartering British pirates to defend England from the Spanish Armada.

Having failed to convince the U.S. Congress to let them buy the ships they wanted, the Department of the Navy, through the Naval Sea Systems Command, issued a Request for Proposals for TAKX Maritime Prepositioning Ships sufficient to provide lift capability for three Marine brigades. The Request for Proposals contemplated a chartering program, in which the contractor would arrange for the construction of a new vessel or the conversion of an existing vessel to meet the Navy's requirements, and upon completion, lease the vessel to the Navy for a total of 25 years. In his February 28, 1983 testimony before the House Ways and Means Subcommittee on Oversight, GAO Deputy Director Werner Grosshans dubbed this proposal as "Rent-a-Navy."

---

7. Staff of Joint Committee on Taxation, 97th Cong., 2d Sess., General Explanation of the Revenue Provisions of the Tax Equity and Fiscal Responsibility Act of 1982, 53 (Comm. Print 1982).

The Argent Group, Ltd. (Argent) of McLean, Virginia was engaged to assist the Navy "in structuring the transaction so as to obtain the most advantageous lease financing for the Navy." ... As part of its task, Argent compared the cost of chartering the TAKX vessels with the cost of purchasing the vessels. According to Argent's analysis, it was cheaper for the Navy to lease the ships than to buy them outright. Even taking into account the revenue loss to the Treasury as a result of the tax benefits to the lessors, Argent concluded that leasing the ships would be cheaper than buying them. Said Argent,

> Such an analysis, of course, assumes that the taxes payable by the potential investors in a TAKX charter would not otherwise be sheltered, which is a doubtful proposition. It can fairly be expected that the private sector lease financing sources would find alternative transactions producing tax benefits. Given that likelihood, the Treasury tax revenue effects cannot reasonably be considered as a cost of the TAKX program ...

GAO and Joint Tax Committee Analyses

At the request of several members of Congress, both the GAO and the Joint Tax Committee reviewed the Navy's ship-leasing program, and in 1983 both issued reports that were highly critical of the program. As a theoretical matter, the Joint Tax Committee's Report suggested that purchasing an asset should almost always be cheaper for the government than long-term leasing. When the government leases, the government's costs consist of rental payments and net tax benefits to the lessor sufficient to cover the lessor's capital costs. Because of the government's superior credit, however, the market rate of interest paid by the lessor and the rate of return expected by its shareholders are greater than the financing costs that the government would have borne if it had borrowed the funds and purchased the ship itself.

The Joint Tax Committee also did cost comparisons between purchasing a typical ship and chartering it. It found that while purchasing the ship would cost only $178.2 million, leasing the ship would cost the government even more. While the Navy's cost of leasing the ship would be $37 million less than purchasing it, the tax benefits associated with leasing the ship cost the Treasury $57.8 million for a net loss to the federal government of $20.8 million. Thus, leasing a ship cost about 12 percent more than buying the same ship outright.

Based on the Joint Tax Committee's estimate, leasing the 13 TAKX Navy ships and the five T-5 tankers will cost about 12 percent more than buying them. Since purchasing the ships would have cost about $2.7 billion according to the July 19, 1983 testimony of Everett Pyatt, Principal Deputy Assistant Secretary of the Navy, before the Senate Finance Committee, this means that the investors in those ships will receive additional tax benefits costing the United States almost $300 million.

The GAO report supported the Joint Tax Committee analysis and criticized the Navy for trying to set up a leasing program when its procurement efforts were blocked. The GAO also expressed concern about "the degree of control over the use of civilian and contractor personnel in time of mobilization or hostilities." GAO also recommended that Congress consider legislation that would require agencies to obtain congressional approval before entering into long-term leases.

Many tax analysts have suggested that the Navy ship lease deal and the similar sale-leaseback of Bennington College property were key in developing the political momentum for the restrictions on leasing by tax-exempt entities that were included in TRA 84. Also, the Department of Defense Authorization Act . . . imposed limits on military long-term leasing. Of note, however, these 18 ships were grandfathered free from the effects of these statutory changes. Said one former congressional aide, the transition rule for the Navy ships was largely the result of the "impassioned defense" of the transition rule by Rep. Sam Gibbons, D-Fla., "a distinguished member of the Ways and Means Committee in whose district [Tampa] many of the ships are being built."

Rub-a-dub-dub: Private Investors in the Navy's Tub

In its February 28, 1983 report entitled "Tax Aspects of Federal Leasing Arrangements," the Joint Tax Committee outlined the form of a typical Navy TAKX ship charter. The TAKX program was developed by the Navy in 1979 to provide sealift support for the rapid deployment of marine forces to crisis areas. The TAKX ships are designed for that purpose. Initially, the Navy had intended to buy the TAKX ships, but that proposal was replaced by the chartering approach.

In basic form, the charter arrangement involves an investor, a contractor, and the Navy. The investor arranges for the construction of a new ship or modification of an existing ship according to Navy specifications. The investor then leases the ship to the contractor. The contractor mans, equips and maintains the ship, transporting equipment, cargo, and personnel for the Navy. The Navy agreed to reimburse operating expenses and pay rent and capital charges sufficient to guarantee the investor an 11.745 percent guaranteed after-tax rate of return. The Navy also assumed economic risks of damage to or loss of the ship, risks that the ship will decline in value, and risks associated with interest rate and price fluctuations. And the Navy agreed to indemnify investors if some of the expected tax benefits of the transaction were lost. . . .

Conclusion

Leasing will frequently end up being cheaper for an agency than purchasing the same asset, whether it is a ship, a building, or a photocopier. However, when the tax costs associated with accelerated depreciation and the investment tax credit are also considered, leasing may be more expensive for the federal government. Congress needs to recognize this as it considers both the tax code and the budget process, lest another $300 million be lost to private investors.

O. NOTES AND QUESTIONS

1) The Issue of Backdoor Funding Through the Tax System

What is particularly objectionable about a leasing tax shelter when a federal department or agency is the lessee and the purpose of leasing is to circumvent Congressional spending limits? Do similar objections apply if the lessee is some other tax-exempt entity, such as a state or local government or charitable organization? How does the Navy's ship leasing program resemble the Federal Home Loan Bank Board's Memorandum R-49 Plan discussed in *Cottage Savings* (Chapter 17).

Chapter 41

THE SUPREME COURT STEPS IN

A. FRANK LYON CO. v. UNITED STATES
435 U.S. 561 (1978)

MR. JUSTICE BLACKMUN delivered the opinion of the Court.

This case concerns the federal income tax consequences of a sale-and-leaseback in which petitioner Frank Lyon Company (Lyon) took title to a building under construction by Worthen Bank & Trust Company (Worthen) of Little Rock, Ark., and simultaneously leased the building back to Worthen for long-term use as its headquarters and principal banking facility.

I....

A

Lyon is a closely held Arkansas corporation engaged in the distribution of home furnishings.... Worthen in 1965 was an Arkansas-chartered bank and a member of the Federal Reserve System. Frank Lyon was Lyon's majority shareholder and board chairman; he also served on Worthen's board. Worthen at that time began to plan the construction of a multistory bank and office building to replace its existing facility in Little Rock....

Worthen initially hoped to finance, to build, and to own the proposed facility at a total cost of $9 million.... Worthen's plan, however, had to be abandoned for two significant reasons:

1. As a bank chartered under Arkansas law, Worthen legally could not pay more interest on any debentures it might issue than that then specified by Arkansas law. But the proposed obligations would not be marketable at that rate.

2. Applicable statutes or regulations of the Arkansas State Bank Department and the Federal Reserve System required Worthen, as a state bank subject to their supervision, to obtain prior permission for the in-

vestment in banking premises of any amount (including that placed in a real estate subsidiary) in excess of the bank's capital stock or of 40% of its capital stock and surplus[1]. . . . Worthen, accordingly, was advised by staff employees of the Federal Reserve System that they would not recommend approval of the plan by the System's Board of Governors.

Worthen therefore was forced to seek an alternative solution that would provide it with the use of the building, satisfy the state and federal regulators, and attract the necessary capital. In September 1967 it proposed a sale-and-leaseback arrangement. The State Bank Department and the Federal Reserve System approved this approach, but the Department required that Worthen possess an option to purchase the leased property at the end of the 15th year of the lease at a set price, and the federal regulator required that the building be owned by an independent third party.

Detailed negotiations ensued with investors that had indicated interest, namely, Goldman, Sachs & Company; White, Weld & Co.; Eastman Dillon, Union Securities & Company; and Stephens, Inc. Certain of these firms made specific proposals.

Worthen then obtained a commitment from New York Life Insurance Company to provide $7,140,000 in permanent mortgage financing on the building, conditioned upon its approval of the titleholder. At this point Lyon entered the negotiations and it, too, made a proposal.

Worthen submitted a counterproposal that incorporated the best features, from its point of view, of the several offers. Lyon accepted the counterproposal. . . . Lyon in November 1967 was approved as an acceptable borrower by First National City Bank for the construction financing, and by New York Life, as the permanent lender. In April 1968 the approvals of the state and federal regulators were received.

In the meantime, on September 15, before Lyon was selected, Worthen itself began construction.

B

In May 1968 Worthen, Lyon, City Bank, and New York Life executed complementary and interlocking agreements under which the building was sold by Worthen to Lyon as it was constructed, and Worthen leased the completed building back from Lyon.

1. *Agreements between Worthen and Lyon.* Worthen and Lyon executed a ground lease, a sales agreement, and a building lease.

Under the ground lease dated May 1, 1968, . . . Worthen leased the site to Lyon for 76 years and 7 months through November 30, 2044. The first 19 months were the estimated construction period. The ground rents pay-

---

1. Worthen, as of June 30, 1967, had capital stock of $4 million and surplus of $5 million. During the period the building was under construction Worthen became a national bank subject to the supervision and control of the Comptroller of the Currency.

able by Lyon to Worthen were $50 for the first 26 years and 7 months and thereafter in quarterly payments:

    12/1/94 through 11/30/99 (5 years)   — $100,000 annually
    12/1/99 through 11/30/04 (5 years)   — $150,000 annually
    12/1/04 through 11/30/09 (5 years)   — $200,000 annually
    12/1/09 through 11/30/34 (25 years) — $250,000 annually
    12/1/34 through 11/30/44 (10 years) — $10,000 annually.

Under the sales agreement dated May 19, 1968 . . . Worthen agreed to sell the building to Lyon, and Lyon agreed to buy it, piece by piece as it was constructed, for a total price not to exceed $7,640,000, in reimbursements to Worthen for its expenditures for the construction of the building.[2]

Under the building lease dated May 1, 1968 . . . Lyon leased the building back to Worthen for a primary term of 25 years from December 1, 1969, with options in Worthen to extend the lease for eight additional 5-year terms, a total of 65 years. During the period between the expiration of the building lease (at the latest, November 30, 2034, if fully extended) and the end of the ground lease on November 30, 2044, full ownership, use, and control of the building were Lyon's, unless, of course, the building had been repurchased by Worthen. . . . The total rent for the building over the 25-year primary term of the lease thus was $14,989,767.24. That rent equaled the principal and interest payments that would amortize the $7,140,000 New York Life mortgage loan over the same period. When the mortgage was paid off at the end of the primary term, the annual building rent, if Worthen extended the lease, came down to the stated $300,000. Lyon's net rentals from the building would be further reduced by the increase in ground rent Worthen would receive from Lyon during the extension.[3]

The building lease was a "net lease," under which Worthen was responsible for all expenses usually associated with the maintenance of an office building, including repairs, taxes, utility charges, and insurance, and was to keep the premises in good condition, excluding, however, reasonable wear and tear.

Finally, under the lease, Worthen had the option to repurchase the building at the following times and prices:

---

2. This arrangement appeared advisable and was made because purchases of materials by Worthen (which then had become a national bank) were not subject to Arkansas sales tax. . . . Sales of the building elements to Lyon also were not subject to state sales tax, since they were sales of real estate. . . .

3. This, of course, is on the assumption that Worthen exercises its option to extend the building lease. If it does not, Lyon remains liable for the substantial rents prescribed by the ground lease. This possibility brings into sharp focus the fact that Lyon, in a very practical sense, is at least the ultimate owner of the building. If Worthen does not extend, the building lease expires and Lyon may do with the building as it chooses.

The Government would point out, however, that the net amounts payable by Worthen to Lyon during the building lease's extended terms, if all are claimed, would approximate the amount required to repay Lyon's $500,000 investment at 6% compound interest.

11/30/80 (after 11 years)—$6,325,169.85
11/30/84 (after 15 years)—$5,432,607.32
11/30/89 (after 20 years)—$4,187,328.04
11/30/94 (after 25 years)—$2,145,935.00

These repurchase option prices were the sum of the unpaid balance of the New York Life mortgage, Lyon's $500,000 investment, and 6% interest compounded on that investment.

2. *Construction financing agreement.* By agreement dated May 14, 1968, ... City Bank agreed to lend Lyon $7,000,000 for the construction of the building. This loan was secured by a mortgage on the building and the parking deck, executed by Worthen as well as by Lyon, and an assignment by Lyon of its interests in the building lease and in the ground lease.

3. *Permanent financing agreement.* By Note Purchase Agreement dated May 1, 1968 ... New York Life agreed to purchase Lyon's $7,140,000 6¾% 25-year secured note to be issued upon completion of the building. Under this agreement Lyon warranted that it would lease the building to Worthen for a noncancelable term of at least 25 years under a net lease at a rent at least equal to the mortgage payments on the note. Lyon agreed to make quarterly payments of principal and interest equal to the rentals payable by Worthen during the corresponding primary term of the lease. ... The security for the note was a first deed of trust and Lyon's assignment of its interests in the building lease and in the ground lease. ... Worthen joined in the deed of trust as the owner of the fee and the parking deck.

In December 1969 the building was completed and Worthen took possession. At that time Lyon received the permanent loan from New York Life, and it discharged the interim loan from City Bank. The actual cost of constructing the office building and parking complex (excluding the cost of the land) exceeded $10,000,000.

C

... On its 1969 return, Lyon ... asserted as deductions one month's interest to New York Life; one month's depreciation on the building; interest on the construction loan from City Bank; and sums for legal and other expenses incurred in connection with the transaction.

On audit of Lyon's 1969 return, the Commissioner of Internal Revenue determined that Lyon was "not the owner for tax purposes of any portion of the Worthen Building," and ruled that "the income and expenses related to this building are not allowable ... for Federal income tax purposes".... In other words, the Commissioner determined that the sale-and-leaseback arrangement was a financing transaction in which Lyon loaned Worthen $500,000 and acted as a conduit for the transmission of principal and interest from Worthen to New York Life.

All this resulted in a total increase of $497,219.18 over Lyon's reported income for 1969, and a deficiency in Lyon's federal income tax for that year in the amount of $236,596.36. The Commissioner assessed that amount, together with interest of $43,790.84, for a total of $280,387.20.

Lyon paid the assessment and filed a timely claim for its refund. The claim was denied, and this suit, to recover the amount so paid, was instituted in the United States District Court for the Eastern District of Arkansas within the time allowed by 26 U.S.C. § 6532(a)(1).

After trial without a jury, the District Court, in a memorandum letter-opinion setting forth findings and conclusions, ruled in Lyon's favor and held that its claimed deductions were allowable. . . . It concluded that the legal intent of the parties had been to create a bona fide sale-and-leaseback in accordance with the form and language of the documents evidencing the transactions. It rejected the argument that Worthen was acquiring an equity in the building through its rental payments. It found that the rents were unchallenged and were reasonable throughout the period of the lease, and that the option prices, negotiated at arm's length between the parties, represented fair estimates of market value on the applicable dates. It rejected any negative inference from the fact that the rentals, combined with the options, were sufficient to amortize the New York Life loan and to pay Lyon a 6% return on its equity investment. It found that Worthen would acquire an equity in the building only if it exercised one of its options to purchase, and that it was highly unlikely, as a practical matter, that any purchase option would ever be exercised. It rejected any inference to be drawn from the fact that the lease was a "net lease." It found that Lyon had mixed motivations for entering into the transaction, including the need to diversify as well as the desire to have the benefits of a "tax shelter." . . .

The United States Court of Appeals for the Eighth Circuit reversed. . . . It held that the Commissioner correctly determined that Lyon was not the true owner of the building and therefore was not entitled to the claimed deductions. It likened ownership for tax purposes to a "bundle of sticks" and undertook its own evaluation of the facts. It concluded, in agreement with the Government's contention, that Lyon "totes an empty bundle" of ownership sticks. It stressed the following: (a) The lease agreements circumscribed Lyon's right to profit from its investment in the building by giving Worthen the option to purchase for an amount equal to Lyon's $500,000 equity plus 6% compound interest and the assumption of the unpaid balance of the New York Life mortgage. (b) The option prices did not take into account possible appreciation of the value of the building or inflation.[4] (c) Any award realized as a result of destruction or condemnation of the building in excess of the mortgage balance and the $500,000 would be paid to Worthen and not Lyon. (d) The building rental payments during the primary term were exactly equal to the mortgage payments. (e) Worthen retained control over the ultimate disposition of the building through its various options to repurchase and to renew the lease plus its ownership of the site. (f) Worthen enjoyed all benefits and bore all burdens incident to the operation and ownership of the building so that, in the

---

4. Lyon challenges this observation by pointing out that the District Court found the option prices to be the negotiated estimate of the parties of the fair market value of the building on the option dates and to be reasonable.

Court of Appeals' view, the only economic advantages accruing to Lyon, in the event it were considered to be the true owner of the property, were income tax savings of approximately $1.5 million during the first 11 years of the arrangement.... The court concluded... that the transaction was "closely akin" to that in *Helvering* v. *Lazarus & Co.*.... "In sum, the benefits, risks, and burdens which [Lyon] has incurred with respect to the Worthen building are simply too insubstantial to establish a claim to the status of owner for tax purposes.... The vice of the present lease is that all of [its] features have been employed in the same transaction with the cumulative effect of depriving [Lyon] of any significant ownership interest."...

II

This Court, almost 50 years ago, observed that "taxation is not so much concerned with the refinements of title as it is with actual command over the property taxed—the actual benefit for which the tax is paid." *Corliss* v. *Bowers* [Chapter 45]. In a number of cases, the Court has refused to permit the transfer of formal legal title to shift the incidence of taxation attributable to ownership of property where the transferor continues to retain significant control over the property transferred.... In applying this doctrine of substance over form, the Court has looked to the objective economic realities of a transaction rather than to the particular form the parties employed. The Court has never regarded "the simple expedient of drawing up papers"... as controlling for tax purposes when the objective economic realities are to the contrary. "In the field of taxation, administrators of the laws, and the courts, are concerned with substance and realities, and formal written documents are not rigidly binding." *Helvering* v. *Lazarus & Co.*.... Nor is the parties' desire to achieve a particular tax result necessarily relevant. *Commissioner* v. *Duberstein* [Chapter 5].

In the light of these general and established principles, the Government takes the position that the Worthen-Lyon transaction in its entirety should be regarded as a sham. The agreement as a whole, it is said, was only an elaborate financing scheme designed to provide economic benefits to Worthen and a guaranteed return to Lyon. The latter was but a conduit used to forward the mortgage payments, made under the guise of rent paid by Worthen to Lyon, on to New York Life as mortgagee. This, the Government claims, is the true substance of the transaction as viewed under the microscope of the tax laws. Although the arrangement was cast in sale-and-leaseback form, in substance it was only a financing transaction, and the terms of the repurchase options and lease renewals so indicate. It is said that Worthen could reacquire the building simply by satisfying the mortgage debt and paying Lyon its $500,000 advance plus interest, regardless of the fair market value of the building at the time; similarly, when the mortgage was paid off, Worthen could extend the lease at drastically reduced bargain rentals that likewise bore no relation to fair rental value but were simply calculated to pay Lyon its $500,000 plus interest over the extended term. Lyon's return on the arrangement in no event could exceed 6% compound interest.... Furthermore, the favorable option and lease renewal terms made it highly unlikely that Worthen would abandon the building after it in effect had "paid off" the mortgage. The Government implies that the arrangement was one of convenience which, if accepted on its face, would enable Worthen to deduct its payments to Lyon as rent and would allow Lyon to claim a deduction for depreciation, based on the cost of construction ultimately borne by Worthen, which Lyon could offset against other income, and to deduct mortgage interest that roughly would offset the inclusion of Worthen's rental payments in Lyon's income. If, however, the Government argues, the arrangement was only a financing transaction under which Worthen was the owner of the building, Worthen's payments would be deductible only to the extent that they represented mortgage interest, and Worthen would be entitled to claim depreciation; Lyon would not be entitled to deductions for either mortgage interest or depreciation and it would not have to include Worthen's "rent" payments in its income because its function with respect to those payments was that of a conduit between Worthen and New York Life.

The Government places great reliance on *Helvering* v. *Lazarus & Co* . . . and claims it to be precedent that controls this case. The taxpayer there was a department store. The legal title of its three buildings was in a bank as trustee for land-trust certificate holders. When the transfer to the trustee was made, the trustee at the same time leased the buildings back to the taxpayer for 99 years, with option to renew and purchase. The Commissioner, in stark contrast to his posture in the present case, took the position that the statutory right to depreciation followed legal title. The Board of Tax Appeals, however, concluded that the transaction between the taxpayer and the bank in reality was a mortgage loan and allowed the taxpayer depreciation on the buildings. This Court, as had the Court of Appeals, agreed with that conclusion and affirmed. It regarded the "rent" stipulated in the leaseback as a promise to pay interest on the loan, and a "depreciation fund" required by the lease as an amortization fund designed to pay off the loan in the stated period. Thus, said the Court, the Board justifiably concluded that the transaction, although in written form a transfer of ownership with a leaseback, was actually a loan secured by the property involved.

The *Lazarus* case, we feel, is to be distinguished from the present one and is not controlling here. Its transaction was one involving only two (and not multiple) parties, the taxpayer-department store and the trustee-bank. The Court looked closely at the substance of the agreement between those two parties and rightly concluded that depreciation was deductible by the taxpayer despite the nomenclature of the instrument of conveyance and the leaseback. . . .

The present case, in contrast, involves three parties, Worthen, Lyon, and the finance agency. The usual simple two-party arrangement was legally unavailable to Worthen. Independent investors were interested in participating in the alternative available to Worthen, and Lyon itself (also independent from Worthen) won the privilege. Despite Frank Lyon's presence on Worthen's board of directors, the transaction, as it ultimately developed, was not a familial one arranged by Worthen, but one compelled by the realities of the restrictions imposed upon the bank. Had Lyon not appeared, another interested investor would have been selected. The ultimate solution would have been essentially the same. Thus, the presence of the third party, in our view, significantly distinguishes this case from *Lazarus* and removes the latter as controlling authority.

III

... There is no simple device available to peel away the form of this transaction and to reveal its substance. The effects of the transaction on all the parties were obviously different from those that would have resulted had Worthen been able simply to make a mortgage agreement with New York Life and to receive a $500,000 loan from Lyon. Then *Lazarus* would apply. Here, however, and most significantly, it was Lyon alone, and not Worthen, who was liable on the notes, first to City Bank, and then to New York Life. Despite the facts that Worthen had agreed to pay rent and that this rent equaled the amounts due from Lyon to New York Life, should anything go awry in the later years of the lease, Lyon was primarily liable. No matter how the transaction could have been devised otherwise, it remains a fact that as the agreements were placed in final form, the obligation on the notes fell squarely on Lyon. Lyon, an ongoing enterprise, exposed its very business well-being to this real and substantial risk.

The effect of this liability on Lyon is not just the abstract possibility that something will go wrong and that Worthen will not be able to make its payments. Lyon has disclosed this liability on its balance sheet for all the world to see. Its financial position was affected substantially by the presence of this long-term debt, despite the offsetting presence of the building as an asset. To the extent that Lyon has used its capital in this transaction, it is less able to obtain financing for other business needs.

In concluding that there is this distinct element of economic reality in Lyon's assumption of liability, we are mindful that the characterization of a transaction for financial accounting purposes, on the one hand, and for tax purposes, on the other, need not necessarily be the same.... Accounting methods or descriptions, without more, do not lend substance to that which has no substance. But in this case accepted accounting methods, as understood by the several parties to the respective agreements and as applied to the transaction by others, gave the transaction a meaningful character consonant with the form it was given.[5] Worthen was not allowed to enter into

---

5. We are aware that accounting standards have changed significantly since 1968 and that the propriety of Worthen's and Lyon's methods of disclosing the transaction in question may be a matter for debate under these new standards....

Then-existing pronouncements of the Internal Revenue Service gave Lyon very little against which to measure the transaction. The most complete statement on the general question of characterization of leases as sales, Rev. Rul. 55–540, 1955–2 Cum. Bull. 39, by its terms dealt only with equipment leases. In that ruling it was stated that the Service will look at the intent of the parties at the time the agreement was executed to determine the proper characterization of the transaction. Generally, an intent to enter into a conditional sales agreement will be found to be present if (a) portions of the rental payments are made specifically applicable to an equity acquired by the lessee, (b) the lessee will acquire a title automatically after certain payments have been made, (c) the rental payments are a disproportionately large

the type of transaction which the Government now urges to be the true substance of the arrangement. Lyon and Worthen cannot be said to have entered into the transaction intending that the interests involved were allocated in a way other than that associated with a sale-and-leaseback.

Other factors also reveal that the transaction cannot be viewed as anything more than a mortgage agreement between Worthen and New York Life and a loan from Lyon to Worthen. There is no legal obligation between Lyon and Worthen representing the $500,000 "loan" extended under the Government's theory. And the assumed 6% return on this putative loan—required by the audit to be recognized in the taxable year in question—will be realized only when and if Worthen exercises its options.

The Court of Appeals acknowledged that the rents alone, due after the primary term of the lease and after the mortgage has been paid, do not provide the simple 6% return which, the Government urges, Lyon is guaranteed. . . . Thus, if Worthen chooses not to exercise its options, Lyon is gambling that the rental value of the building during the last 10 years of the ground lease, during which the ground rent is minimal, will be sufficient to recoup its investment before it must negotiate again with Worthen regarding the ground lease. There are simply too many contingencies, including variations in the value of real estate, in the cost of money, and in the capital structure of Worthen, to permit the conclusion that the parties intended to enter into the transaction as structured in the audit and according to which the Government now urges they be taxed.

It is not inappropriate to note that the Government is likely to lose little revenue, if any, as a result of the shape given the transaction by the parties. No deduction was created that is not either matched by an item of income or that would not have been available to one of the parties if the transaction had been arranged differently. While it is true that Worthen paid Lyon less to induce it to enter into the transaction because Lyon anticipated the benefit of the depreciation deductions it would have as the owner of the building, those deductions would have been equally available to Worthen had it retained title to the building. The Government so concedes. . . . The fact that favorable tax consequences were taken into account by Lyon on entering into the transaction is no reason for disallowing those consequences. We cannot ignore the reality that the tax laws affect the shape of nearly every business transaction. . . .

---

amount in relation to the sum necessary to complete the sale, (d) the rental payments are above fair rental value, (e) title can be acquired at a nominal option price, or (f) some portion of the rental payments are identifiable as interest. . . .

The Service announced more specific guidelines, indicating under what circumstances it would answer requests for rulings on leverage[d] leasing transactions, in Rev. Proc. 75–21, 1975–1 Cum. Bull. 715. In general, "[u]nless other facts and circumstances indicate a contrary intent," the Service will not rule that a lessor in a leveraged lease transaction is to be treated as the owner of the property in question unless (a) the lessor has incurred and maintains a minimal investment equal to 20% of the cost of the property, (b) the lessee has no right to purchase except at fair market value, (c) no part of the cost of the property is furnished by the lessee, (d) the lessee has not lent to the lessor or guaranteed any indebtedness of the lessor, and (e) the lessor must demonstrate that it expects to receive a profit on the transaction other than the benefits received solely from the tax treatment. These guidelines are not intended to be definitive, and it is not clear that they provide much guidance in assessing real estate transactions. . . .

As is clear from the facts, none of the parties to this sale-and-leaseback was the owner of the building in any simple sense. But it is equally clear that the facts focus upon Lyon as the one whose capital was committed to the building and as the party, therefore, that was entitled to claim depreciation for the consumption of that capital. The Government has based its contention that Worthen should be treated as the owner on the assumption that throughout the term of the lease Worthen was acquiring an equity in the property. In order to establish the presence of that growing equity, however, the Government is forced to speculate that one of the options will be exercised and that, if it is not, this is only because the rentals for the extended term are a bargain. We cannot indulge in such speculation in view of the District Court's clear finding to the contrary. We therefore conclude that it is Lyon's capital that is invested in the building according to the agreement of the parties, and it is Lyon that is entitled to depreciation deductions.

IV

We recognize that the Government's position, and that taken by the Court of Appeals, is not without superficial appeal. One, indeed, may theorize that Frank Lyon's presence on the Worthen board of directors; Lyon's departure from its principal corporate activity into this unusual venture; the parallel between the payments under the building lease and the amounts due from Lyon on the New York Life mortgage; the provision relating to condemnation or destruction of the property; the nature and presence of the several options available to Worthen; and the tax benefits, such as the use of double declining balance depreciation, that accrue to Lyon during the initial years of the arrangement, form the basis of an argument that Worthen should be regarded as the owner of the building and as the recipient of nothing more from Lyon.

We, however, as did the District Court, find this theorizing incompatible with the substance and economic realities of the transaction: ... Worthen's undercapitalization; Worthen's consequent inability, as a matter of legal restraint, to carry its building plans into effect by a conventional mortgage and other borrowing; the additional barriers imposed by the state and federal regulators; the suggestion, forthcoming from the state regulator, that Worthen possess an option to purchase; the requirement, from the federal regulator, that the building be owned by an independent third party; the presence of several finance organizations seriously interested in participating in the transaction and in the resolution of Worthen's problem; the submission of formal proposals by several of those organizations; the bargaining process and period that ensued; the competitiveness of the bidding; ... the three-party aspect of the transaction; ... Lyon's being liable alone on the successive notes to City Bank and New York Life; the reasonableness, as the District Court found, of the rentals and of the option prices; the substantiality of the purchase prices; the presence of all building depreciation risks on Lyon; the risk, borne by Lyon, that Worthen might default or fail, as other banks have failed; the facts that Worthen could "walk away" from the relationship at the end of the 25-year primary term, and probably would do so if the option price were more than the then-current worth of the building to Worthen; the inescapable fact that if the building lease were not extended, Lyon would be the full owner of the building, free to do with it as it chose; Lyon's liability for the substantial ground rent if Worthen decides not to exercise any of its options to extend; the absence of any understanding between Lyon and Worthen that Worthen would exercise any of the purchase options; . . . and the absence of any differential in tax rates and of special tax circumstances for one of the parties—all convince us that Lyon has far the better of the case. . . .[6]

In short, we hold that where, as here, there is a genuine multiple-party transaction with economic substance which is compelled or encouraged by business or regulatory realities, is imbued with tax-independent considerations, and is not shaped solely by tax-avoidance features that have meaningless labels attached, the Government should honor the allocation of rights and duties effectuated by the parties. Expressed another way, so long as the lessor retains significant and genuine attributes of the traditional lessor status, the form of the transaction adopted by the parties governs for tax purposes. What those attributes are in any particular case will necessarily depend upon its facts. It suffices to say that, as here, a sale-and-leaseback, in and of itself, does not necessarily operate to deny a taxpayer's claim for deductions.

The judgment of the Court of Appeals, accordingly, is reversed.

MR. JUSTICE STEVENS, dissenting.

In my judgment the controlling issue in this case is the economic relationship between Worthen and petitioner, and matters such as the number of parties, their reasons for structuring the transaction in a particular way, and the tax benefits which may result, are largely irrelevant. The question whether a leasehold has been created should be answered by examining the character and value of the purported lessor's reversionary estate.

For a 25-year period Worthen has the power to acquire full ownership of the bank building by simply repaying the amounts, plus interest, advanced by the New York Life Insurance Company and petitioner. During that period, the economic relationship among the parties parallels exactly the normal relationship between an owner and two lenders, one secured by a first mortgage and the other by a second mortgage.[7] If Worthen repays both loans, it will have unencumbered ownership of the property. What

---

6. Thus, the facts of this case stand in contrast to many others in which the form of the transaction actually created tax advantages that, for one reason or another, could not have been enjoyed had the transaction taken another form. . . . Indeed, the arrangements in this case can hardly be labeled as tax-avoidance techniques in light of the other arrangements being promoted at the time. See, e.g., Zeitlin, Tax Planning in Equipment-Leasing Shelters, 1969 So. Cal. Tax Inst. 62. . . . (1974).

7. "[W]here a fixed price, as in *Frank Lyon Company*, is designed merely to provide the lessor with a predetermined fixed return, the substantive bargain is more akin to the relationship between a debtor and creditor than between a lessor and lessee." Rosenberg & Weinstein, Sale-leasebacks: An Analysis of these transactions after the *Lyon* decision, 45 J. Tax. 146, 149 (1976).

the character of this relationship suggests is confirmed by the economic value that the parties themselves have placed on the reversionary interest.

All rental payments made during the original 25-year term are credited against the option repurchase price, which is exactly equal to the unamortized cost of the financing. The value of the repurchase option is thus limited to the cost of the financing, and Worthen's power to exercise the option is cost free. Conversely, petitioner, the nominal owner of the reversionary estate, is not entitled to receive *any* value for the surrender of its supposed rights of ownership.[8] Nor does it have any power to control Worthen's exercise of the option. . . .[9]

"It is fundamental that 'depreciation is not predicated upon ownership of property *but rather upon an investment* in property.' No such investment exists when payments of the purchase price in accordance with the design of the parties yield no equity to the purchaser." *Estate of Franklin* v. *Commissioner* [Chapter 42].

Here, the petitioner has, in effect, been guaranteed that it will receive its original $500,000 plus accrued interest. But that is all. It incurs neither the risk of depreciation,[10] nor the benefit of possible appreciation. Under the terms of the sale-leaseback, it will stand in no better or worse position after the 11th year of the lease—when Worthen can first exercise its option to repurchase—whether the property has appreciated or depreciated.[11] And this remains true throughout the rest of the 25-year period.

Petitioner has assumed only two significant risks. First, like any other lender, it assumed the risk of Worthen's insolvency. Second, it assumed the risk that Worthen might *not* exercise its option to purchase at or before the end of the original 25-year term.[12] If Worthen should exercise that

---

8. It is worth noting that the proposals submitted by two other potential investors in the building, . . . did contemplate that Worthen would pay a price above the financing costs for acquisition of the leasehold interest. For instance, Goldman, Sachs & Company proposed that, at the end of the lease's primary term, Worthen would have the option to repurchase the property for either its fair market value or 20% of its original cost, whichever was the greater. . . . A repurchase option based on fair market value, since it acknowledges the lessor's equity interest in the property, is consistent with a lessor-lessee relationship. . . .

9. The situation in this case is thus analogous to that in *Corliss* v. *Bowers* [Chapter 45] where the Court held that the grantor of a trust who retains an unrestricted cost-free power of revocation remains the owner of the trust assets for tax purposes. Worthen's power to exercise its repurchase option is similar; the only restraints upon it are those normally associated with the repayment of a loan, such as limitations on the timing of repayment and the amount due at the stated intervals.

10. Petitioner argues that it bears the risk of depreciation during the primary term of the lease, because the option price decreases over time. . . . This is clearly incorrect. Petitioner will receive $500,000 plus interest, and no more or less, whether the option is exercised as soon as possible or only at the end of 25 years. Worthen, on the other hand, does bear the risk of depreciation, since its opportunity to make a profit from the exercise of its repurchase option hinges on the value of the building at the time.

11. After the 11th year of the lease, there are three ways that the lease might be terminated. The property might be condemned, the building might be destroyed by act of God, or Worthen might exercise its option to purchase. In any such event, if the property had increased in value, the entire benefit would be received by Worthen and petitioner would receive only its $500,000 plus interest. . . .

12. The possibility that Worthen might not exercise its option is a risk for petitioner because in that event petitioner's advance would be amortized during the ensuing renewal lease terms, totaling 40 years. Yet there is a possibility that Worthen would choose not to renew for the full 40 years or that the burdens of owning a building and paying a ground rental of $10,000 during the years 2034 through 2044 would exceed the benefits of ownership. . . .

right *not* to repay, perhaps it would *then* be appropriate to characterize petitioner as the owner and Worthen as the lessee. But speculation as to what might happen in 25 years cannot justify the *present* characterization of petitioner as the owner of the building. Until Worthen has made a commitment either to exercise or not to exercise its option,[13] I think the Government is correct in its view that petitioner is not the owner of the building for tax purposes. At present, since Worthen has the unrestricted right to control the residual value of the property for a price which does not exceed the cost of its unamortized financing, I would hold, as a matter of law, that it is the owner. I therefore respectfully dissent.

B. NOTES AND QUESTIONS

1) Applying the Residual Interest Analysis

Assume that Frank Lyon Co. seeks your tax advice before signing the sale and leaseback contract with Worthen. Would you advise your client that it will be able to deduct depreciation for the building, based on your reading of *Lazarus* and *Estate of Starr* (Chapter 39)?

a) Compare *Frank Lyon* with *Lazarus*. What is the relationship between the term of the lease and the useful life of the building in *Lazarus*? What is the relationship between those two variables in *Frank Lyon*? How is the relationship in *Frank Lyon* affected by whether the lease term is defined to include the renewal periods as well as the primary term? By whether the useful life of the building is more or less than 65 years? Is it harder or easier to say that the lessee is the real owner in *Frank Lyon* than it was in *Lazarus*?

b) Compare *Frank Lyon* with *Estate of Starr*. How does the formal residual, if any, retained by Frank Lyon Co. compare to the formal residual retained by the lessor in *Estate of Starr*? What has to happen in order for the residual to have real economic significance? How likely is that to happen? What is the option price at the end of the lease? (Use the table in Chapter 12 to compute the future value of $500,000 compounded at 6% interest for twenty-five years.) Is that option price likely to be greater or less than the market value of the building at that time? What did the building cost to construct? How much less will its value have to be in twenty-five years in order for the option price to exceed the value at the end of the lease's primary term? What forces will tend to cause the building's value to fall over twenty-five years? To rise? Is the lessor more or less likely to obtain the residual in *Frank Lyon* than in *Estate of Starr*?

---

13. In this case, the lessee is not "economically compelled" to exercise its option. . . . Indeed, it may be more advantageous for Worthen to let its option lapse since the present value of the renewal leases is somewhat less than the price of the option to repurchase. . . . But whether or not Worthen is likely to exercise the option, as long as it retains its unrestricted cost-free power to do so, it must be considered the owner of the building. . . .

In effect, Worthen has an option to "put" the building to petitioner if it drops in value below $500,000 plus interest. Even if the "put" appears likely because of bargain lease rates after the primary terms, that would not justify the present characterization of petitioner as the owner of the building.

c) *Frank Lyon* and IRS Ruling Practices—Would the IRS have been willing to rule in advance that Frank Lyon Co. was entitled to deduct depreciation for the building? See condition (7) in footnote 1 on page 596, in the list of conditions to be met before the IRS would grant favorable rulings on equipment leases during the 1960s. See also condition (b) in Rev. Proc. 75–15, cited in footnote 5 of the Supreme Court opinion in *Frank Lyon*.

d) *Frank Lyon* in the District Court—The taxpayer won. Given *Estate of Starr* and IRS ruling practices (which are suggestive although not binding on a court), how did the District Court justify treating Frank Lyon Co. as the real owner, especially under the terms of the lessee's option to repurchase? See footnote 4 of the Supreme Court's opinion. Does the District Court's finding make any sense? Is it, on its face, "clearly erroneous" under the Federal Rules of Civil Procedure? Might it reflect a District Court judge's sympathies for local business interests?

2) Applying the Risk Analysis

How does the doctrinal approach of *Estate of Starr* (which is to ask whether the lessor retains a significant residual interest) differ from the Supreme Court's approach in *Frank Lyon* (which is to ask whether the lessor incurs any significant risks)? Are the risks incurred by the lessor in *Frank Lyon* any greater than the risks usually incurred by an ordinary mortgagee? Than the risks incurred by the lessor in *Lazarus*? Than the risks incurred by the lessor in *Estate of Starr*? See Justice Stevens' dissent. Shouldn't Frank Lyon Co. be regarded as a second mortgagee who has also cosigned (or guaranteed) the first mortgage obligation?

Given *Lazarus* and *Estate of Starr*, how would you predict *Frank Lyon* would be decided on appeal to the Circuit Court? How could the taxpayer possibly convince the Supreme Court to reverse the Circuit Court of Appeals?

3) *Frank Lyon* as a "Good" Tax Shelter

After losing in the Circuit Court, the taxpayer hired a former Dean of Harvard Law School and Solicitor General of the United States, Erwin Griswold, to argue before the Supreme Court. Dean Griswold apparently argued that *Frank Lyon* involved a "good" tax shelter, because there were low transaction costs, competitive bidding, and no revenue loss (Chapter 40). Which of these three factors did the Court emphasize? Which did the Court refer to only in passing? Did the Court miss an opportunity to jettison the traditional legal doctrine, with its focus on "who is the real owner," and replace it with a focus on whether the leasing transaction achieves an efficient, nonwasteful transfer of tax benefits to the real user of property?

But are courts competent to judge leasing transactions by the latter standard? Can a court easily and adequately determine whether full value is paid for the transferred tax benefits, transaction costs are excessive, and revenue is lost?

Justice Blackmun's opinion notes that since both lessor and lessee were corporations, the leasing arrangement entailed no revenue loss to the Treasury. Did he cite any evidence that the bank had taxable income against which to offset depreciation deductions from the building? Even if there were such evidence, should a court take it into account? What about the possibility that, although the bank currently may have had taxable income, it might have little or none in the future? Is it advisable or practical to make the outcome in these cases turn on a *prediction* of whether there will be a revenue loss?

4) Two- versus Three-Party Transactions

Are you persuaded by the Court's attempt to distinguish *Lazarus* as involving a two-party, rather than a three-party, transaction? Does the number of parties bear any relation to the amount of risk incurred by the lessor?

5) The Regulatory Realities

How might the critical role played by state and federal banking authorities explain the outcome in *Frank Lyon*? Could the best reason for respecting the lease transaction be "cross-town" estoppel, that is, that a federal agency in one part of town is estopped from challenging a business transaction insisted on by a different federal agency in another part of town? Doesn't it violate "fundamental fairness" to allow Frank Lyon to be whipsawed between two agencies of the federal government?

Yet, perhaps it is fair to penalize Frank Lyon Co. for failing to notice the potential tax problems and to alert the bank and the regulatory authorities? Consider how the terms of the sale and leaseback might have been renegotiated to anticipate the IRS treating the bank as the owner for tax purposes. The purchase price might have been reduced or the rents might have been increased to reflect the fact that the seller-lessee would obtain the benefit of accelerated depreciation. Wouldn't such an arrangement satisfy both the banking authorities and the IRS? Shouldn't the bank be willing to be paid less for the building or to pay increased rent if it is treated as the "tax owner" and can fully use the depreciation? Would such a restructured deal be unacceptable to the bank only if (contrary to the Supreme Court's assertion) it does not expect to have enough taxable income to use the depreciation deductions generated by the building?

6) Nontax Aspects

What are the nontax reasons for leasing rather than owning property? When property is purchased with financing, the debt must be listed as a liability on the taxpayer's balance sheet. But when the same property is leased, the lease obligation may not have to appear on the balance sheet, or, if it must, it may be confined to a footnote at the bottom of the page. In reality, what is the difference between a twenty-five year mortgage obligation and a twenty-five year lease obligation? Why should one have to be listed as a liability and not the other? Why should balance sheet accounting rules treat the two obligations differently? See footnote 5 in *Frank Lyon*.

Why did the federal authorities want the bank to lease rather than own the building? A federal banking rule stated that a bank may not own and occupy premises with a value exceeding 40% of its net worth (capital stock and surplus). What is the purpose of such a rule? Is it any less violated by a leasehold interest (which presumably is not listed on the bank's books as an asset) than by fee simple title (which is)? Did the means adopted to avoid the federal banking rule do anything more than change appearances?

Why did the state authorities want the bank to lease rather than own the building? State usury laws limited the amount of interest that a bank could pay to 6%, but the lender required a higher rate of interest. Did characterizing the bank as a lessee paying rent change the underlying substance? Isn't there an implicit rate of interest built into the rent which might also exceed 6%?

C. SWIFT DODGE v. COMMISSIONER
692 F.2d 651 (9th Cir. 1982)

FARRIS, CIRCUIT JUDGE:

Swift Dodge, a California corporation, claimed an investment tax credit on its 1974 and 1975 federal income tax return for its investment in motor vehicles that were purchased for use under a "Lease Agreement". . . . After an audit of Swift Dodge, the Commissioner determined that the lease agreements were essentially conditional sales contracts. The Commissioner disallowed the claimed credit because he determined that the taxpayer was not the owner of the vehicles for which the credit was claimed.

The Internal Revenue Code permits a tax credit (7% during 1974–75) of a taxpayer's qualified investment in "Section 38" property. . . . Section 48(a) defines Section 38 property to include tangible personal property "with respect to which depreciation . . . is allowable and having a useful life . . . of 3 years or more." Property owned by a taxpayer and leased to others by him in his business is depreciable property and qualifies for the credit. Property purchased for resale is not depreciable under Section 167 and therefore is not Section 38 property eligible for the credit. Whether the investment tax credit was properly disallowed turns on whether, for purposes of federal tax law, the transactions between Swift Dodge and the vehicle users are leases or conditional sales contracts.

The taxpayer, Swift Dodge, operates an automobile dealership and sells automobiles, vans, and light trucks manufactured by the Chrysler Corporation. In addition to the usual sales business, the taxpayer offers vehicles of any manufacturer to its customers under a standard form lease provided by Chrysler. . . .

The typical lease lasted 36 months. Although the form permitted different terms, the typical agreement executed by Swift Dodge and its customers required the lessee to provide a specified amount of insurance for the benefit of Swift Dodge, to pay all taxes, and to perform all necessary maintenance and repairs for the vehicle. The agreement also contained provisions showing the amount of money which the lessee would have to pay Swift Dodge in the event of premature termination, loss due to theft or damage, or normal expiration of the agreement. The agreement shifted the risk of depreciable loss to the vehicle user. In contrast to a "close-ended" lease, under this "open-ended" type of lease . . . the lessee was required to pay, when the lease terminated, the amount, if any, by which the estimated "depreciated value" of the vehicle, as set forth in the agreement, exceeded its actual wholesale value. Similarly, if the actual wholesale value of the vehicle exceeded its estimated "depreciated value," the lessee would "receive any gain which result[ed] from final disposition of the vehicle." Although the lease did not contain an option to purchase, the tax court found that Swift Dodge's practice was to permit the lessee to retain the vehicle at the expiration of the agreement and to pay only the "depreciated value" to Swift Dodge—regardless of the actual value of the vehicle. Approximately one-half of the lessees paid the specified balance and retained the vehicle when the lease ended.

To purchase the vehicles, Swift Dodge borrowed money from the Bank of America[,] National Trust and Savings Association and the United California Bank. Swift Dodge usually borrowed an amount needed to cover the purchase price of the vehicles.

Swift Dodge contends that the questioned transactions are leases, and that it owned and leased the vehicles and therefore was entitled to the claimed investment tax credit. The Commissioner contends that the transactions are conditional sales contracts, and that Swift Dodge did not own the vehicles and was not entitled to the credit.

The tax court held that the agreements were leases. . . . The Commissioner appeals.

The parties do not dispute the specific factual findings of the tax court concerning the operation and terms of the agreements. The issue is whether the tax court erred by holding that these agreements were leases rather than conditional sales contracts. Whether the agreement is a "sale" or a "lease" for federal tax purposes is a question of law and is therefore fully reviewable on appeal. . . .

The characterization of a transaction for federal tax purposes is controlled by the substantive provisions of the agreement and the parties' conduct, rather than by the particular terminology used in the agreement. *Frank Lyon*. . . .

Before determining the nature of this transaction, we first note that this transaction was not a multiple-party sale and financing transaction in which Swift Dodge served merely as a conduit of funds from the vehicle users to the banks which loaned the money for the purchase of the vehicles. In *Frank Lyon* the Supreme Court determined that where the third-party participant in a multiple-party transaction assumed actual risks and therefore was not a mere conduit of funds, the sale and leaseback transaction was not a sham and the form of the transaction adopted by the parties governed for tax purposes.

In *Frank Lyon,* as in this case, the third-party (Swift Dodge) assumed risks that were both actual and significant. In both cases the taxpayer, and not the user of the asset, was liable on the loan instrument to the bank. . . .

Further, in both cases the user of the asset could walk away from the lease at its expiration. In this case the taxpayer, Swift Dodge, also had the responsibility of disposing of the asset when the lease ended. Swift Dodge was not merely a conduit in a financing transaction between the vehicle user and the bank.

The Commissioner, however, asserts that the transaction was a two-party sales transaction between Swift Dodge and the vehicle user. Swift Dodge counters that the transaction was a lease. In determining the economic realities of the transaction we look at the substantive provisions of the agreement and the parties' conduct with respect to it. We review the benefits, obligations, and rights of Swift Dodge and the user to determine whether they indicate the existence of a conditional sale or a lease. Under a conditional sale, the seller reserves title until the buyer pays for the goods. At that time, the condition is fulfilled and title passes to the buyer....

The user of the vehicle was required to insure for fire, theft, comprehensive, collision, public liability, and property damage, and was responsible for all operating and maintenance expenses except those covered by the manufacturer's warranty. The user was also responsible for all taxes, including licensing, sales, excise, and property taxes. Swift Dodge did not have similar burdens under the agreement. However, to minimize potential liability, it purchased excess insurance in case the vehicle user was not adequately insured. The *only* duty imposed on Swift Dodge was to find a purchaser for the vehicle when the agreement terminated.

The allocation of duties in the agreement is no different than they would be under a conditional sales contract....

The user had the right to use the vehicle as long as the terms of the agreement were satisfied and could keep the vehicle at the expiration of the agreement if the user paid an amount equal to the vehicle's depreciation value as specified in the agreement. A purchaser under a conditional sales contract with a balloon payment would have an identical right.

Next we analyze the parties' risks. The user assumed the risk of damage, theft, or destruction. More importantly, because this was an "open-ended" lease, the customer assumed the risk of depreciation.... If the vehicle did not depreciate as quickly as anticipated, the user had a gain when the vehicle was sold. But if the vehicle depreciated at a rate greater than anticipated, the user suffered a loss upon eventual sale. If the user decided to keep the vehicle, he made no gain or loss. These are the same risks a buyer assumes under a conditional sales contract....

The only risk Swift Dodge assumed was the risk of default by the purchaser. This is the same risk that would be assumed by the holder of a security interest in a conditional sale. In either case Swift Dodge incurred a loss only when the eventual sale of the vehicle did not produce sufficient funds to cover the amount owed.

Finally we examine the parties' intentions. The stated intention of both Swift Dodge and the users was to engage in lease agreements.

In spite of this, there are no essential differences between this transaction and a conditional installment sale with a lump sum final payment. Swift Dodge did not retain, in this two-party transaction, significant and genuine attributes of a lessor. We therefore are precluded from holding that the characterization given this transaction by the parties is controlling. *See generally, Frank Lyon* . . . (similar test in three-party transaction).

Reversed.

D. NOTES AND QUESTIONS

1) Applying the Law Before *Frank Lyon*

Given the law before *Frank Lyon,* how would you predict that *Swift Dodge* would turn out? Did the lessor retain a formal residual interest? Was it real? Was it any different from the residual retained by the lessor in *Estate of Starr*?

Did the lessor incur significant business risks? If the value of the residual was lower than its expected depreciated value, who suffered? If it was higher, who gained? What was the only risk assumed by the lessor? Is it any different from the risk incurred by the lessor in *Estate of Starr*?

2) Applying the Law After *Frank Lyon*

Given *Frank Lyon,* how might you expect *Swift Dodge* to turn out? Was the residual retained by the lessor in *Swift Dodge* any less significant than in *Frank Lyon*? Were the risks retained any less real? Could the most sensible way to distinguish *Frank Lyon* be "regulatory realities" that were absent in *Swift Dodge*?

3) The Rationale of *Swift Dodge*

How, in fact, did *Swift Dodge* distinguish *Frank Lyon*? Are you persuaded by the distinction? Does it comport with the facts?

4) Was *Swift Dodge* a "Bad" Tax Shelter?

Was there any revenue at stake in *Swift Dodge*? If the lessor was not the real owner, could the lessee claim the investment tax credit?

Chapter 42

ABUSIVE TAX SHELTERS: REAL ESTATE

A. ESTATE OF FRANKLIN v. COMMISSIONER
544 F.2d 1045 (9th Cir. 1976)

SNEED, CIRCUIT JUDGE:

This case involves another effort on the part of the Commissioner to curb the use of real estate tax shelters.[1] In this instance he seeks to disallow deductions for the taxpayers' distributive share of losses reported by a limited partnership with respect to its acquisition of a motel and related property. These "losses" have their origin in deductions for depreciation and interest claimed with respect to the motel and related property. These deductions were disallowed by the Commissioner on the ground either that the acquisition was a sham or that the entire acquisition transaction was in substance the purchase by the partnership of an option to acquire the motel and related property on January 15, 1979. The Tax Court held that the transaction constituted an option exercisable in 1979 and disallowed the taxpayers' deductions. . . . We affirm this disallowance although our approach differs somewhat from that of the Tax Court.

The interest and depreciation deductions were taken by Twenty-Fourth Property Associates (hereinafter referred to as Associates), a California limited partnership of which Charles T. Franklin and seven other doctors were the limited partners. The deductions flowed from the purported

---

1. An early skirmish in this particular effort appears in *Manuel D. Mayerson*, 47 T.C. 340 (1966), which the Commissioner lost. The Commissioner attacked the substance of a nonrecourse sale, but based his attack on the nonrecourse and long-term nature of the purchase money note, without focusing on whether the sale was made at an unrealistically high price. In his acquiescence to *Mayerson*, 1969–2 Cum. Bull. xxiv, the Commissioner recognized that the fundamental issue in these cases generally will be whether the property has been "acquired" at an artificially high price, having little relation to its fair market value. "The Service emphasizes that its acquiescence in *Mayerson* is based on the particular facts in the case and will not be relied upon in the disposition of other cases except where it is clear that the property has been acquired at its fair market value in an arm's length transaction creating a bona fide purchase and a bona fide debt obligation." Rev.Rul. 69–77, 1969–1 Cum.Bull. 59.

"purchase" by Associates of the Thunderbird Inn, an Arizona motel, from Wayne L. Romney and Joan E. Romney (hereinafter referred to as the Romneys) on November 15, 1968.

Under a document entitled "Sales Agreement," the Romneys agreed to "sell" the Thunderbird Inn to Associates for $1,224,000. The property would be paid for over a period of ten years, with interest on any unpaid balance of seven and one-half percent per annum. "Prepaid interest" in the amount of $75,000 was payable immediately; monthly principal and interest installments of $9,045.36 would be paid for approximately the first ten years, with Associates required to make a balloon payment at the end of the ten years of the difference between the remaining purchase price, forecast as $975,000, and any mortgages then outstanding against the property.

The purchase obligation of Associates to the Romneys was nonrecourse; the Romneys' only remedy in the event of default would be forfeiture of the partnership's interest. The sales agreement was recorded in the local county. A warranty deed was placed in an escrow account, along with a quitclaim deed from Associates to the Romneys, both documents to be delivered either to Associates upon full payment of the purchase price, or to the Romneys upon default.

The sale was combined with a leaseback of the property by Associates to the Romneys; Associates therefore never took physical possession. The lease payments were designed to approximate closely the principal and interest payments with the consequence that with the exception of the $75,000 prepaid interest payment no cash would cross between Associates and Romneys until the balloon payment. The lease was on a net basis; thus, the Romneys were responsible for all of the typical expenses of owning the motel property including all utility costs, taxes, assessments, rents, charges, and levies of "every name, nature and kind whatsoever." The Romneys also were to continue to be responsible for the first and second mortgages until the final purchase installment was made; the Romneys could, and indeed did, place additional mortgages on the property without the permission of Associates. Finally, the Romneys were allowed to propose new capital improvements which Associates would be required to either build themselves or allow the Romneys to construct with compensating modifications in rent or purchase price.

In holding that the transaction between Associates and the Romneys more nearly resembled an option than a sale, the Tax Court emphasized that Associates had the power at the end of ten years to walk away from the transaction and merely lose its $75,000 "prepaid interest payment." It also pointed out that a *deed* was never recorded and that the "benefits and burdens of ownership" appeared to remain with the Romneys. Thus, the sale was combined with a leaseback in which no cash would pass; the Romneys remained responsible under the mortgages, which they could increase; and the Romneys could make capital improvements. The Tax Court further justified its "option" characterization by reference to the nonrecourse nature of the purchase money debt and the nice balance between the rental and purchase money payments.

Our emphasis is different from that of the Tax Court. We believe the characteristics set out above can exist in a situation in which the sale imposes upon the purchaser a genuine indebtedness within the meaning of section 167(a), Internal Revenue Code of 1954, which will support both interest and depreciation deductions. They substantially so existed in *Hudspeth v. Commissioner* . . . in which parents entered into sale-leaseback transactions with their children. The children paid for the property by executing nonnegotiable notes and mortgages equal to the fair market value of the property; state law proscribed deficiency judgments in case of default, limiting the parents' remedy to foreclosure of the property. The children had no funds with which to make mortgage payments; instead, the payments were offset in part by the rental payments, with the difference met by gifts from the parents to their children. Despite these characteristics this court held that there was a bona fide indebtedness on which the children, to the extent of the rental payments, could base interest deductions. See also . . . *Manuel D. Mayerson* [discussed in footnote 1, above].

In none of these cases, however, did the taxpayer fail to demonstrate that the purchase price was at least approximately equivalent to the fair market value of the property. Just such a failure occurred here. The Tax Court explicitly found that on the basis of the facts before it the value of the property could not be estimated. . . .[2] In our view this defect in the taxpayers' proof is fatal.

Reason supports our perception. An acquisition such as that of Associates if at a price approximately equal to the fair market value of the property under ordinary circumstances would rather quickly yield an equity

---

2. The Tax Court found that appellants had "not shown that the purported sales price of $1,224,000 (or any other price) had any relationship to the actual market value of the motel property. . . ."

Petitioners spent a substantial amount of time at trial attempting to establish that, whatever the actual market value of the property, Associates acted in the good faith *belief* that the market value of the property approximated the selling price. However, this evidence only goes to the issue of sham and does not supply substance to this transaction. . . .

In oral argument, it was suggested by the appellants that neither the Tax Court nor they recognized the importance of fair market value during the presentation of evidence and that this hampered the full and open development of this issue. However, upon an examination of the record, we are satisfied that the taxpayers recognized the importance of presenting objective evidence of the fair market value and were awarded ample opportunity to present their proof; appellants merely failed to present clear and admissible evidence that fair market value did indeed approximate the purchase price. Such evidence of fair market value as was relied upon by the appellants, *viz.* two appraisals, one completed in 1968 and a second in 1971, even if fully admissible as evidence of the truth of the estimates of value appearing therein, does not require us to set aside the Tax Court's finding. As the Tax Court found, the 1968 appraisal was "error-filled, sketchy" and "obviously suspect." . . . The 1971 appraisal had little relevancy as to 1968 values. On the other side, there existed cogent evidence indicating that the fair market value was substantially less than the purchase price. This evidence included (i) the Romneys' purchase of the stock of two corporations, one of which wholly-owned the motel, for approximately $800,000 in the year preceding the "sale" to Associates ($660,000 of which was allocable to the sale property, according to Mr. Romney's estimate), and (ii) insurance policies on the property from 1967 through 1974 of only $583,200, $700,000, and $614,000. . . .

Given that it was the appellants' burden to present evidence showing that the purchase price did not exceed the fair market value and that he had a fair opportunity to do so, we see no reason to remand this case for further proceedings.

in the property which the purchaser could not prudently abandon. This is the stuff of substance. It meshes with the form of the transaction and constitutes a sale.

No such meshing occurs when the purchase price exceeds a demonstrably reasonable estimate of the fair market value. Payments on the principal of the purchase price yield no equity so long as the unpaid balance of the purchase price exceeds the then existing fair market value. Under these circumstances the purchaser by abandoning the transaction can lose no more than a mere chance to acquire an equity in the future should the value of the acquired property increase. While this chance undoubtedly influenced the Tax Court's determination that the transaction before us constitutes an option, we need only point out that its existence fails to supply the substance necessary to justify treating the transaction as a sale *ab initio*. It is not necessary to the disposition of this case to decide the tax consequences of a transaction such as that before us if in a subsequent year the fair market value of the property increases to an extent that permits the purchaser to acquire an equity. . . .

Authority also supports our perception. It is fundamental that "depreciation is not predicated upon ownership of property *but rather upon an investment in property.*" . . . No such investment exists when payments of the purchase price in accordance with the design of the parties yield no equity to the purchaser. . . . In the transaction before us and during the taxable years in question the purchase price payments by Associates have not been shown to constitute an *investment in the property*. Depreciation was properly disallowed. Only the Romneys had an investment in the property.

Authority also supports disallowance of the interest deductions. This is said even though it has long been recognized that the absence of personal liability for the purchase money debt secured by a mortgage on the acquired property does not deprive the debt of its character as a bona fide debt obligation able to support an interest deduction. . . . However, this is no longer true when it appears that the debt has economic significance only if the property substantially appreciates in value prior to the date at which a very large portion of the purchase price is to be discharged. . . . Prior to the date at which the balloon payment on the purchase price is required, and assuming no substantial increase in the fair market value of the property, the absence of personal liability on the debt reduces the transaction in economic terms to a mere chance that a genuine debt obligation may arise. This is not enough to justify an interest deduction. To justify the deduction the debt must exist; potential existence will not do. For debt to exist, the purchaser, in the absence of personal liability, must confront a situation in which it is presently reasonable from an economic point of view for him to make a capital investment in the amount of the unpaid purchase price. . . . Associates, during the taxable years in question, confronted no such situation. . . .

Our focus on the relationship of the fair market value of the property to the unpaid purchase price should not be read as premised upon the belief that a sale is not a sale if the purchaser pays too much. Bad bargains from the buyer's point of view—as well as sensible bargains from buyer's, but exceptionally good from the seller's point of view—do not thereby cease to be sales. . . . We intend our holding and explanation thereof to be understood as limited to transactions substantially similar to that now before us.

B. NOTES AND QUESTIONS

1) The Buyer's Perspective

The key to understanding the transaction is that the buyers expect to default on the balloon payment and to "lose" the motel when the lease ends. Assuming default, will the transaction make financial sense? What is the out-of-pocket cost to the buyers? How much of their own cash do they invest in the motel? If they are in a 50% bracket and expense the prepaid interest (that is, deduct it currently in full), what is their after-tax cost?

What benefits do they derive? Do they have any return before taxes? Is there any net cash flow during the lease? Do they anticipate any residual at the end of the lease? As "owners," do they anticipate anything other than tax benefits?

The tax benefits consist of the losses generated during the ten-year lease term. Ignoring nondepreciation expenses (if any), each year's loss equals rental income under Section 61(a), less deductions for interest on the installment payments under Section 163, and less deductions for depreciation under Section 167.

There is, in addition, an offsetting tax detriment when the buyers default on the balloon payment and the seller forecloses on its security, the motel. Why is foreclosure a realization event? What is the amount realized? Why is the adjusted basis of the motel certain to be much less than the amount realized? Will the gain realized on foreclosure be taxed as ordinary income or capital gain? Is the motel a capital or quasi-capital asset? How will the application of the recapture provisions on default affect the character of the gain? (Note that Section 1250 generally applies to all real estate placed in service before 1981, whether residential or nonresidential, to recapture only the excess of accelerated over straight-line method depreciation.)

To what extent is the combination of tax benefit and detriment provided by the motel investment equivalent to an interest-free loan? Equivalent to a loan that is partially forgiven?

2) A Financial Analysis

Assume that the purchase price of the motel is $1.2 million; the balloon payment due at the end of the lease is $1 million; the motel has a useful life (for tax purposes) of fifteen years; accelerated depreciation during the lease term equals $900,000; and the motel has a salvage value of $300,000.

Losses over the ten years then equal $700,000. How is this figure determined? Assume that losses equal rent minus interest minus depreciation. Depreciation is $900,000, and it can be demonstrated that rent minus interest equals $200,000. Rent due under the lease equals payments due on the note before maturity. Payments on the note consist of principal and interest. Thus, rent equals those payments of principal and interest. Subtracting interest from both sides of the equation, rent minus interest equals payments of principal. Payments of principal are $200,000, which is the difference between the $1.2 million purchase price and the $1 million balloon payment. Thus, rent minus interest equals $200,000.

On foreclosure after ten years, gain equals the amount realized minus the adjusted basis. Why does this exactly equal the $700,000 deducted as losses during the preceding ten years? Under the excess formula of Section 1250, how much of the gain will be recaptured as ordinary income, that is, what is the excess of actual over straight-line method depreciation?

In 1979, when the sale and leaseback transaction was signed, individuals were permitted to deduct 50% of capital gains. Assuming a 50% capital gains deduction, what is the net income reported from foreclosure? To what extent is the overall result equivalent to exclusion? To what extent is it equivalent to deferral?

Assume that the investors are in the 50% bracket. How much in taxes is saved? How much in taxes is deferred? Because the benefits accrue over a ten-year period, a rigorous financial analysis would require discounting the tax benefits to present value year by year. But a rough approximation can be calculated by taking the midpoint of the ten-year period and assuming that, on average, taxes saved are saved in five years and that, on average, taxes deferred are deferred for a five-year period. Using a discount rate of 6%, what is the present value of the taxes saved? What is the present value of the taxes deferred? Does the total present value of these benefits exceed the $37,500 after-tax cost of the prepaid interest?

3) The Seller's Perspective

Initially, the seller receives and must report the $75,000 of prepaid interest as ordinary income. If the seller's tax bracket is 50%, and if the gain is taxed immediately in full, the seller nets $37,500 after taxes.

Installment payments received are exactly offset by rent paid so that there is zero net cash flow to the seller. From the tax perspective, everything else is pretty much of a wash. The seller has income from each installment payment but also has an offsetting deduction from each payment of rent.[3] The installment method permits the seller to delay reporting gain from the motel's sale until payments of principal are actually received. Thus, assuming default on the balloon payment, most of the gain never has to be reported at all.

What is the effect of Section 453(i), enacted in 1981, on transactions of this type? What, if anything, is objectionable about a new purchaser beginning to depreciate an asset before the seller reports recapture gain?

---

3. In fact, deductions for rent may exceed income from the installment payments, which consist of interest and principal. First, part of the seller's basis in the motel property will reduce the income from payments of principal. (See the discussion of the installment method in Chapters 13 and 21.) Second, under the recapture formula of Section 1250, income attributable to payment of principal may be partly capital gain, 50% of which was deductible at the time.

4) The Incentive to Overvalue

In *Estate of Franklin*, ordinary laws of economics seem to be suspended. Ordinarily, when property is sold, the buyer wants to pay as little as possible. But here, *it is in the buyer's interest to pay as much as possible.* For example, if the purchase price doubles (assuming all other variables also double), how would the buyers benefit? How would the sellers benefit, provided they can rely on the installment method of reporting? What prevents buyers and sellers of the motel from agreeing to an even higher price? In this respect, how does *Estate of Franklin* resemble *Redwing Carriers* (Chapter 37)? Why is overvaluation of the motel an abuse?

5) Two-party versus Three-party Transactions

Suppose financing were provided by an independent third party instead of by the seller. Why might a third party indicate an absence of overvaluation? Consider the following criticism of the Supreme Court's distinction between two-party and three-party transactions in *Frank Lyon:*

> In distinguishing prior sale-leaseback cases, the Court accepted Lyon's notion that a three-party transaction is inherently different from a two-party transaction. Although the numbers are different absolutely, the significance of this difference is beyond grasp. If Lyon had had available cash of $7,640,000, not just $500,000, it could have invested the full building cost without the intervention of New York Life. Would that have made the case a *harder* one for Lyon? The Court seems to say so.
>
> Or suppose New York Life, desiring the depreciation deductions, had purchased the building and leased it back to Worthen. Would it fail to qualify as owner under the *Frank Lyon* rationale just because it had not brought another financing party into the transaction to make three? Again, the Court seems to say so. This aspect of the Court's opinion does nothing but signal tax lawyers that clients seeking tax shelter should never travel in pairs.[4]

But what about the possibility that a third party may indicate that property is not overvalued? Would a third party be willing to make a loan greater than the property's value without recourse if the lease is not a full payout lease? (On the other hand, a third party might not be deterred from lending more than the property's value without recourse, provided that the lease is a full payout lease and the lessee is creditworthy.)

In 1986, Congress distinguished between two-party and three-party transactions when it extended the "at risk" rules of Section 465 (Chapter 39) to real estate. Under Section 465(b)(6), the owner of real property is considered "at risk" with respect to nonrecourse financing only if provided by a third-party lender. Nonrecourse financing provided by the seller will not qualify. How do these changes in Section 465 affect the *Estate of Franklin* transaction?

---

4. Wolfman, The Supreme Court in The *Lyon*'s Den: A Failure of Judicial Process, 66 Cornell L. Rev. 1075, 1087–88 (1981).

6) The Rationale of *Estate of Franklin*

In *Estate of Franklin,* the rent covers the monthly installment payments owed during the term of the lease but does not fully pay off the loan. The purchasers must make an additional balloon payment of nearly $1 million after the lease terminates before they own the motel property "free and clear." The installment obligation is also without recourse. If the purchasers default on the balloon payment, they will not be personally liable for any deficiency that arises when the motel's value is less than the amount owed. Therefore, if the motel's value is less, they can be expected not to make the balloon payment. Why not? How does the nonrecourse obligation to make a balloon payment, not covered by lease rent, distinguish *Estate of Franklin* from the airplane tax shelter (Chapter 38) and from *Frank Lyon* (Chapter 41)?

While the large balloon payment in excess of the motel's current market value is obviously critical to the outcome in *Estate of Franklin,* there are at least *four* different explanations for why the buyers are not the real owners. The opinion mentions two. The Circuit Court itself emphasized that, since it was highly speculative whether the balloon payment would be made, the buyers had no equity in the property. The Circuit Court also referred to the Tax Court's theory that the buyers acquired no more than an option to buy the property. The Circuit Court did not mention a third possibility, that the buyers lacked a significant residual, like the lessor in *Estate of Starr.* Nor did it mention a fourth explanation, that the buyers incurred insignificant risks, like the lessor in *Swift Dodge.*

What are the relative strengths and weaknesses of these four different approaches? Which approach might apply to invalidate the transaction even if there were *no* overvaluation? Does the Circuit Court's emphasis (on the *un*likelihood that the purchaser will acquire an equity in the property by making the balloon payment) reflect a desire to invalidate only so-called "abusive" tax shelters, where overvaluation is present?

Suppose that real estate prices are expected to increase at an annual rate of 8%. At the end of ten years, how much will the motel be worth? (Consult the future value table in Chapter 12.) Under this assumption of fairly modest annual increases in real estate prices, will the buyers be likely to make the balloon payment? Does the Circuit Court's rationale still apply? What, therefore, is the possible weakness in the Circuit Court's approach?

7) Expensing Prepaid Interest

Was expensing the prepaid interest in *Estate of Franklin* consistent with *Idaho Power*? What is the effect of Section 461(g), enacted in 1976?

Chapter 43

ABUSIVE TEX SHELTERS: COPYRIGHTS

A. ABUSIVE TAX SHELTER RECIPE

How Julia Childs or the Galloping Gourmet might describe the transactions in this and the preceding chapter:

Ingredients

a) Sale of a depreciable asset at an artificially high price.
b) Payment of all or most of the price with a nonrecourse note, secured only by the asset.
c) Little or none of the principal due before maturity.
d) Leaseback of the asset to the seller on a net basis with the rent equaling payments of interest and principal (if any) due on the note before maturity.

Result

If you are the purchaser:
a) Each year, income equals rent, minus interest, minus depreciation. If rent equals interest, each year's loss equals depreciation deductions for that year. To the extent that rent exceeds interest (because principal is repaid), each year's loss is reduced.
b) When you default on the note at maturity, you "lose" the asset but are not personally liable. Income realized on foreclosure equals the unpaid principal of the note, minus the adjusted basis of the property. This equals losses that have been deducted over the years since the asset was "purchased."
c) The tax benefits are equivalent to an interest-free loan. You may deduct losses equal to accelerated depreciation (less principal repayments) during the term of the note but then you must report an equivalent amount on foreclosure at maturity. If there is less than complete recapture, some of the interest-free loan is, in effect, forgiven.

If you are the seller:

a) When the asset is sold, you receive and report an amount classified as either cash down payment or prepaid interest.
b) Otherwise, there are practically no tax consequences, provided the installment method of accounting applies to the sale. Over the life of the note, you report income from payment of interest and principal, but receive an offsetting deduction for rent. When you foreclose on the asset—after the mortgagor defaults on the note—there are no tax consequences for you as seller.[1]

FOR EXTRA LARGE PORTIONS:
Try doubling or even quadrupling the artificially high purchase price and all other "ingredients" to increase the size of the tax benefits.

B. DEAN v. COMMISSIONER
83 T.C. 56 (1984)

FEATHERSTON, JUDGE: This case was assigned to and heard by Special Trial Judge John J. Pajak, pursuant to the provisions of section 7456(c) of the Code and Rules 180 and 181. The Court agrees with and adopts the Special Trial Judge's opinion which is set forth below.

OPINION OF THE SPECIAL TRIAL JUDGE

PAJAK, SPECIAL TRIAL JUDGE: Respondent determined deficiencies in petitioners' Federal income taxes for 1976 and 1977 in the amounts of $9,042 and $4,051, respectively. Respondent disallowed the distributable share of losses from a limited partnership, The Season Co., claimed on petitioners' returns.

The issues for decision are: (1) Whether the partnership was engaged in for profit; (2) whether the partnership may deduct interest on certain nonrecourse indebtedness. . . .

This case is one of two groups of cases which were heard pursuant to test case procedures for purposes of judicial economy of benefit to petitioners, respondent, and the Court. For the same reason, since most of the witnesses had testimony relevant to each of the groups, the test cases of Fuchs, . . . and Genstein, . . . both decided this day in *Fuchs v. Commissioner* . . . were consolidated for trial at the same special session of the Court as was this case. The *Fuchs* case pertains to a limited partnership involving "The Chinese Ultimatum" original paperback book and rights thereto. This case pertains to a limited partnership involving "The Season" original paperback book and rights thereto.

---

1. Under certain circumstances, not relevant to this example, foreclosure can cause some recognition of gain to the seller under Section 1038.

FINDINGS OF FACT

Some of the facts have been stipulated. The stipulation of facts and the exhibits attached thereto are incorporated herein by this reference.

Petitioners John R. Dean and Florence Dean resided in Wexford, PA, when their petition was filed. On their 1976 and 1977 Federal income tax returns, petitioners deducted losses of $16,501 and $7,408, respectively, in connection with The Season Co. (Season Co.), a limited partnership formed under the laws of Pennsylvania. Respondent disallowed these loss deductions.

"The Season"; an Original Paperback Book

Patricia Hornung (Hornung) was the former spouse of Paul Hornung, the star halfback of the Vince Lombardi Green Bay Packers. Apparently in 1975, she contacted Robin Moore (Moore) to seek assistance in writing a book about professional football as seen through the eyes of the wives and girlfriends of the players. Moore is the author or coauthor of such best selling books as "The Green Berets," "The French Connection" (coauthor), and "The Happy Hooker" (coauthor), all three of which became highly successful motion pictures. Moore often used coauthors or ghostwriters to write books. Moore contacted Howard Liss (Liss) for his opinion and assistance. Liss is a professional writer who was the ghostwriter of several books for Moore.

Liss found Hornung's initial draft unpublishable. Liss and Hornung met in the summer of 1975 so that Liss could write an original paperback book, "The Season." Liss kept Hornung and Moore apprised of the progress being made on the draft, provided them with copies of work completed, and discussed with Moore future work on the paperback book. Moore did little, if any, of the actual writing. The cover of "The Season" lists as authors "Patricia Hornung & Robin Moore."

During early 1976, Liss accompanied Moore to the office of Jack Klein (Klein), Moore's accountant, where a discussion occurred involving tax shelters. In February 1976, Moore contacted Liss and requested that Liss complete the book as fast as he could do so. Liss finished the book in about 2 weeks and gave it to Moore toward the end of February 1976.

Moore had copyrighted 14 books in the 5 years 1971 through 1975. "The Season" was one of 24 books subject to copyright in Moore's name in 1976. Many more books were subject to copyright under Moore's name in subsequent years.

Babbitt Tax Shelter Department

Babbitt, Meyers & Co. (Babbitt) was a regional member firm of the New York Stock Exchange, with its headquarters in Pittsburgh, PA, and with branch offices located throughout western Pennsylvania. During 1976, Robert E. Rose (Rose) was the manager of Babbitt's tax shelter department. His function was to seek out, review, and coordinate the distribution of tax-advantaged investments to Babbitt's customers.

Babbitt's practice was to enter into an agreement on behalf of a partnership to be formed. If the offering was successful, the legal formalities of organizing a partnership were followed.

In late 1975 or early 1976, Babbitt began the development of tax shelter programs using books. Since neither Rose nor anyone else at Babbitt had any expertise in the publishing industry, Rose discussed the development of this program with George Mack (Mack) and others. Mack introduced Babbitt to the law firm of Regan, Goldfarb, Heller, Wetzler & Quinn (Regan Goldfarb), New York, NY. Marty Heller of Regan Goldfarb represented Moore. Heller introduced Rose to Moore in January or February 1976. Babbitt used Regan Goldfarb in developing book tax shelter programs. In 1976, Babbitt syndicated at least three limited partnerships which utilized paperback books bearing the name of Moore and different coauthors.

Season Co. Private Placement Memorandum

Babbitt offered $200,000 of limited partnership interests in the Season Co. by a private placement memorandum dated March 2, 1976. The Season Co. was established in the manner described in this memorandum. The memorandum stated in pertinent part that:

> THIS INVESTMENT IS AVAILABLE ONLY TO THOSE OFFEREES WHOSE NET WORTH EXCLUSIVE OF HOME AND PERSONAL EFFECTS IS AT LEAST $200,000 OR SOME PORTION OF WHOSE CURRENT ANNUAL GROSS INCOME WOULD BE SUBJECT TO FEDERAL INCOME TAX AT A RATE OF 50% OR HIGHER AND WHOSE NET WORTH IS $100,000 OR MORE. . . .
>
> *Offering:* $200,000 of Limited Partnership Interests to be offered by Babbitt, Meyers & Co. as exclusive agent for the Partnership; 25 Limited Partnership Interests of $8,000 each. Minimum purchase is one Limited Partnership Interest [which] requires (i) the payment of $2,000 in cash at the time of subscription, and (ii) the execution of a negotiable promissory note in the principal amount of $6,000 due in installments on September 1, 1976 and January 31, 1977. . . .
>
> *Partnership Business:* The acquisition, publication and other exploitation of the copyright to and the manuscript entitled THE SEASON written by ROBIN MOORE with PATRICIA (MRS. PAUL) HORNUNG ("THE WORK") . . .
>
> *Compensation to General Partner:* The General Partner will be paid a guaranteed initial management fee of $2,000 in 1977 which he will contribute to the capital of the Partnership. . . .
>
> • • •
>
> *Purchase Price and Leverage:* The Partnership will purchase the Work for $877,500, of which an aggregate of $135,000 is payable in cash and a short-term nonrecourse promissory note and the balance of $742,500 by delivery of the Partnership's 7-year, 8% nonrecourse purchase money note with required prepayments (i) to December 31, 1976 out of 100% of Partnership receipts attributable to the publication or other exploitation of the copyright and the Work associated therewith after the first $2,000 of such Partnership receipts to pay accrued interest to December 31, 1976 and out of 50% of

Partnership receipts in excess thereof to pay principal on the Partnership's 7-year nonrecourse note, (ii) from January 1, 1977 to March 31, 1977 (assuming a closing on April 1, 1977) out of 100% of such Partnership receipts to the extent of accrued interest on such 7-year nonrecourse note for such period and out of 50% of such Partnership receipts to pay principal on such note and (iii) thereafter out of 50% of such Partnership receipts to be applied first to the payment of interest on such 7-year nonrecourse note and then to the principal thereof. In addition, the Partnership may prepay interest in the amount of $5,050 . . .

• • •

Application of proceeds:

Gross proceeds	$200,000
Less selling commissions	30,000
Amount available for partnership	170,000
Cash payment for work	135,000
Guaranteed management fee	2,000
Legal fee	25,000
Accounting fee	2,000
Interest on 6% nonrecourse note	5,050
Working capital	950
Total application of proceeds	$200,000

• • •

The Partnership will secure its short-term nonrecourse promissory note in the amount of $110,000 due in installments on September 1, 1976 and January 31, 1977 to be delivered to the seller of the Work, by all of the investors' negotiable promissory notes. In addition, the Seller shall be granted a security interest in the Work as collateral for the due payment of the Partnership's short-term and long-term nonrecourse notes. Thus, if any one investor should fail to pay the Partnership the full amount of his Note so that the Partnership shall be unable to pay its short-term note to the seller of the Work, the copyright and the Work shall revert to the Seller. Such a reversion would constitute a disposition of the Work by the Partnership and would have a materially adverse effect on the Partnership including materially adverse tax consequences on the investors. . . .

• • •

Babbitt, Meyers & Co. . . . as exclusive agent for the Partnership, . . . will receive aggregate commissions of $30,000.

• • •

In any event, only a small percentage of all literary properties result in sales sufficient to return a profit . . . there is a substantial degree of risk that exploitation of the Work will not yield profits to the Partnership and the Limited Partners, and that investors may not recoup . . . their capital contributions . . .

• • •

The ultimate commercial success of the Work's publication will depend in large part on the quality of the Publisher of the Work and its ability to obtain sufficient retail shelf space . . .

• • •

the Publisher would be required to effect sales of approximately 1,700,000 copies of the Work for the royalties payable to the Partnership to be sufficient for the Limited Partners to recover their capital contributions and approximately 5,640,000 copies for the royalties payable to the Partnership to be sufficient to pay the principal and related interest on the Partnership's 8% nonrecourse purchase money note in the amount of $742,500. For the year ended December 31, 1975, approximately ten literary properties were published as paperback originals of which approximately four sold 1,000,000 copies and one sold 2,000,000 copies or more and none of which sold more than 5,000,000 copies.

• • •

The Partnership and its publisher will be in competition with numerous other literary property owners and publishers which have substantial financial resources, large distribution staffs and long established histories of publication of paperback originals, none of which may be possessed by the Partnership or its publisher.

• • •

William F. Aull, Jr., the General Partner, . . . has had no prior experience as an investor or otherwise in ventures created to exploit literary properties such as the Work.

The synopsis of the work to be purchased entailed 5½ lines in the private placement memorandum.

At least 32 of the 62 numbered pages of the private placement memorandum were devoted to the tax aspect of the transaction. In addition, Exhibit A contained 12 pages of tax projections and Exhibit C was a 47-page legal opinion about Federal income tax consequences.

The private placement memorandum contained a number of schedules entitled "PROJECTED NET AFTER TAX BENEFIT PER INVESTMENT UNIT." Those were based upon payments of $4,000 in 1976 and of another $4,000 in 1977 and were listed in a column captioned "Investment." These schedules included data as shown on page [677].

Petitioner's Subscription of Interest in Season Co.

Babbitt solicited petitioner John R. Dean (petitioner) and others to purchase interests in Season Co. After receipt of the private placement memorandum, petitioner signed a document captioned "SUBSCRIPTION AGREEMENT AND INVESTMENT LETTER." In that letter, he agreed to make a $2,000 downpayment to the Season Co.'s escrow account, to execute a promissory note in the amount of $6,000 due in installments on September 1, 1976, and January 31, 1977, and to deliver executed copies of the Certification Signature Page. On March 10, 1976, petitioner executed a document captioned "CERTIFICATION SIGNATURE PAGE." Apparently on the same day, petitioner executed the $6,000 promissory note and paid $2,000 to Babbitt by a check dated March 8, 1976.

Petitioner also executed a private placement questionnaire, which referred to his "participation in tax shelter offerings," and stated that his net

Projected copies sold 68,375 (minimal revenue)	Year	Investment	Taxable income or (loss)	Tax savings (detriment) at 50% bracket	Cash-flow	Net after-tax benefit (detriment) from investment Current	Cumulative
	1976	$4,000	($16,268)	$8,134	0	$4,134	$4,134
	1977	4,000	(15,461)	7,732	$33	3,765	7,899
	1978	0	(1,082)	541	7	548	8,447
	1979	0	(756)	378	8	386	8,833
	1980	0	(755)	377	8	385	9,218
	1981	0	(755)	378	8	386	9,604
	1982	0	(755)	377	8	385	9,989
	1983	0	29,177	(14,589)	8	(14,581)	(4,592)
Totals		8,000	(6,655)	3,328	80		
1,710,000 (number needed to cover cash payments made by partners)	1976	4,000	(9,401)	4,701	3,138	3,839	3,839
	1977	4,000	(8,816)	4,408	4,335	4,743	8,582
	1978	0	(911)	455	178	633	9,215
	1979	0	(565)	283	198	481	9,696
	1980	0	(565)	282	198	480	10,176
	1981	0	(565)	283	198	481	10,657
	1982	0	(565)	282	198	480	11,137
	1983	0	23,293	(11,647)	198	(11,449)	(312)
Totals		8,000	1,905	(953)	8,641		
5,640,000 (number needed to cover Season Co.'s $742,500 nonrecourse note)	1976	4,000	11,092	(5,546)	13,384	3,838	3,838
	1977	4,000	11,886	(5,943)	14,272	4,329	8,167
	1978	0	(98)	49	588	637	8,804
	1979	0	454	(227)	738	511	9,315
	1980	0	454	(227)	738	511	9,826
	1981	0	454	(227)	738	511	10,337
	1982	0	453	(227)	738	511	10,848
	1983	0	1,073	(536)	1,307	711	11,619
Totals		8,000	25,768	(12,884)	32,503		

worth was at least $200,000, his annual income was at least $50,000, and he was in a Federal income tax bracket of at least 50 percent.

Petitioner made two other payments, a $2,000 check dated August 23, 1976, and a $4,000 check dated January 8, 1977, to Babbitt to acquire a 3.96-percent interest in Season Co.

Season Co.

The Season Co. was formed by Babbitt in the manner described in the private placement memorandum.

One of the persons interested in "The Season" transaction was Moore. In December 1975, Klein, acting on behalf of Moore, asked Jack Letheren (Letheren) to serve as a consultant on a project. Moore and Letheren had at least one prior business dealing since Moore, Letheren, and another person were to share in sums due in connection with the publication of a book entitled "Valency Girl."

On March 18, 1976, a filing was made with the Pennsylvania Securities Commission pursuant to section 203(d) of the Pennsylvania Securities Act of 1972 regarding Season Co. in which it was stated that Monte E. Wetzler of Regan Goldfarb was the counsel of the issuer and the person to whom correspondence regarding the filing should be sent.

Moore hired Letheren to prepare a narrative report captioned "Current Practices and Conditions in the Paperback Industry" and to obtain three appraisals for "The Season." The narrative report, dated April 7, 1976, was sent to Rose at Babbitt. Rose had Letheren give a preliminary appraisal of "The Season" based on an outline of the book. Letheren's preliminary appraisal showed "The Season" as having a fair market value of 1.1 to 1.2 million dollars.

Babbitt used Regan Goldfarb to prepare a form "endorsement letter" which Letheren forwarded to three appraisers. The appraisers, Jill Hausrath, Herbert J. Moore, and Roger M. Darnio, filled in the blanks. By three separate letters, dated March 19, 1976, addressed to Season Co., each "appraiser" represented in prepared, identical language that "the present fair market value of the work is at least equal to the purchase price of $877,500 plus the contingent payment from release of the motion picture based on the work." Jill Hausrath, Herbert J. Moore, and Letheren were engaged in business together as Jack Letheren & Associates from about 1975 to 1979. Stanley B. Stetzer (petitioner's expert witness) began working with Letheren in 1976.

William F. Aull, Jr. (Aull), was the first general partner of Season Co. He had no experience in the publishing industry. He served as a general partner to facilitate the formation of the partnership for Babbitt's tax shelter department. Aull did not take part in any transactions relating to the acquisition of "The Season" nor with the publishing company. Aull merely reviewed and signed documents given to him by Rose of Babbitt. The duties and functions of the general partner were handled largely by personnel of Babbitt.

The 1976 Federal partnership return reported that Season Co. commenced business on March 31, 1976. As of that date, a certificate of limited partnership regarding Season Co. was signed by Aull as general partner and Sally Diehl as "nominee, limited partner." Diehl was a Babbitt employee.

Aull resigned as general partner on August 29, 1977, and until March 1979, Season Co. had no formal general partner. In March 1979, Robert C. Arthurs (Arthurs), a general partner of Babbitt, assumed the position of general partner of Season Co. Arthurs sometimes functioned in the guise of BMC Management Corp., a wholly owned subsidiary of Babbitt. During all relevant times, Arthurs managed 20 to 25 tax shelters.

Acquisition of Rights to "The Season" by Season Co.

Season Co. obtained all of the worldwide rights to "The Season" by two separately executed purchase agreements dated May 19, 1976, one signed by Moore and Hornung as the "Sellers" and the other by Aull as General Partner for Season Co., as the "Purchaser." These rights included motion picture, television, and commercial rights. All payments to sellers were to be made to Klein. Under the agreement, Season Co. was to enter into a contract whereby a publisher would publish "The Season" as a "paperback original" by July 1976, pay Season Co. 15 percent of the cover price of all such paperbacks sold, exclusive of returns, and pay royalties due with respect to sales through October 31, 1976, not later than December 31, 1976.

The agreement provided in part that:

> 12(a) In consideration of the rights and property sold to Purchaser hereunder, Purchaser agrees to pay to Sellers the sum of Eight Hundred Seventy-Seven Thousand, Five Hundred Dollars ($877,500.00) payable as follows:
>
> (i) The sum of Twenty-Five Thousand Dollars ($25,000.00) at the closing by bank or certified check.
>
> (ii) By delivery to the Sellers at the closing of a nonrecourse promissory note of the Purchaser in the amount of One Hundred Ten Thousand Dollars ($110,000.00) bearing interest at 6% per annum and payable in installments as follows: (a) Eighteen Thousand Dollars ($18,000.00) on September 1, 1976 and (b) Ninety-Two Thousand Dollars ($92,000.00) on January 31, 1977 with all interest due on this note to be paid on January 31, 1977 provided that the Purchaser shall have the right to prepay said interest at any time without penalty.
>
> (iii) The balance of the purchase price by delivery to Sellers at the closing of a non-recourse promissory note (the "Note") of the Purchaser in the amount of Seven Hundred Forty-Two Thousand Five Hundred Dollars ($742,500.00) in the form annexed hereto as Exhibit "A".
>
> (b) As security for the payment of the note referred to in (ii) of paragraph 12(a) above, the Purchaser hereby grants to Sellers a security interest in all of the recourse notes executed by the limited partners of the Purchaser in partial payment of their capital contributions to the limited partnership. . . .
>
> • • •
>
> (e) In the event a motion picture is produced based wholly or in part on the Property, then in addition to the above mentioned payments, Purchaser will pay to the Sellers a sum equal to five percent (5%) of Purchaser's

share of the gross receipts or net profits of the said motion picture, as the case may be, earned by the said motion picture within two (2) years of the general release of the picture in the United States of America.

• • •

[(f)(i)] When the [$742,500 nonrecourse] Note becomes due and payable upon maturity, if there remains any unpaid principal amount and accrued interest thereon Sellers shall be entitled to repossess the Property securing the Note and recover legal title thereto and Purchaser shall have no further interest in the Property or the receipts thereof. Sellers shall have no recourse whatsoever against the Purchaser, the Purchaser's other assets or the General or Limited Partners in the event of a default in the payment of the Note.

• • •

[13(b)] The share of the gross receipts received by Purchaser shall, after making the payments set forth in paragraph 12(e) above, be applied as follows:

(i) From the closing date to and including December 31, 1976 one hundred percent (100%) of such gross receipts in excess of the first Two Thousand Dollars ($2,000.00) will be paid to the Sellers to the extent of interest due on the Note for the period from the closing date to and including December 31, 1976. During the said period from the closing date to and including December 31, 1976 fifty percent (50%) of the balance of such gross receipts in excess of the said sum of Two Thousand Dollars ($2,000.00) and all of the foregoing interest paid to Sellers shall be paid to Sellers in reduction of the principal of the Note and fifty percent (50%) of such gross receipts shall be retained by the Purchaser.

(ii) From January 1, 1977 through and including a date occurring one year after the closing date, one hundred percent (100%) of the gross receipts shall be paid to the Sellers to the extent of interest due on the Note for such period and previously accrued but unpaid interest. After all such interest has been paid to the Sellers, fifty percent (50%) of gross receipts shall be paid to Sellers and fifty percent (50%) of such gross receipts shall be retained by the Purchaser, it being agreed that any such payments to Sellers shall be deemed first credited to interest and then to principal. Purchaser shall make such payments to Sellers of Sellers' share of the gross receipts (as set forth in subdivison (i) of this subparagraph (b)) on July 1 and December 1 of each year in respect of all receipts received during such periods commencing with the first publication of the Property. . . .[2]

• • •

20. . . . the sellers have agreed to pay to George Mack in consideration of Mr. Mack introducing the Sellers to the Purchaser a finder's fee in the amount of Thirty-Five Thousand Dollars ($35,000.00) . . . .

---

[2]. By its terms, the nonrecourse note was payable solely out of gross receipts as defined in par. 13 of the May 19, 1976, agreement. We note that the provisions of par. 13(b)(ii) of that agreement set forth above differ somewhat from those in the private placement memorandum set forth above under the heading *Purchase Price and Leverage*. The parties to the agreement apparently misunderstood the agreement and the memorandum as to the requirement for complete payment of accrued interest for the period beginning Jan. 1, 1977. On Dec. 29, 1980, Arthurs wrote to Frank Sturges, an agent of Moore, stating that: "Per the sales agreement and the offering memorandum we were to retain the first $2,000.00, pay the authors 100 percent of all revenues to April 30, 1977, and then 50 percent of any revenues beyond that point."

The $742,500 figure for the nonrecourse note was derived by multiplying 5.5 times the $135,000 cash payment. This formula was used by Babbitt with respect to a number of books bearing Moore's name involved in limited partnerships syndicated by Babbitt.

Two nonrecourse promissory notes payable to Moore and Hornung, dated May 19, 1976, were executed by Aull on behalf of the Season Co. as part of the closing. The first note was for $110,000 payable in installments of $18,000 and $92,000 on September 1, 1976, and January 31, 1977, respectively, together with interest at 6 percent per annum on the unpaid balance due on January 31, 1977. Under the agreement, this note was secured by the recourse notes of the limited partners. This note was paid to Moore and Hornung in accordance with its terms, including $3,886.68 as interest.

The second nonrecourse note for $742,500 was due on May 19, 1983, with interest at 8 percent on the balance outstanding. In 1977, Season Co. paid Moore and Hornung $37,311.10, of which $36,678.69 was applied to interest due on this note for the period May 19, 1976, through December 31, 1976, and $632.41 was applied against principal. In 1978, Season Co. paid Moore and Hornung $11,100.11 against interest due and in 1980 paid them $5,126.89 against interest due. Over almost the full 7-year period, Season Co. paid a total of $52,905.69 against the approximately $415,500 of interest accrued on the second note and $632.41 against the $742,500 principal.

The Publisher and Season Co.

Prior to Season Co.'s acquisition of "The Season," Moore had contacted Andrew Ettinger (Ettinger), vice president of Pinnacle Books Inc. (Pinnacle), with respect to several books, including "The Season" and "The Chinese Ultimatum."

During 1976, Pinnacle was in the bottom third of the 18 mass-market paperback publishers. Pinnacle then held about a 2-percent market share, generated 7 to 8 million dollars in sales, and published at least 144 titles of the approximately 3,000 paperbacks published annually.

Ettinger was willing to publish "The Season," even though two books bearing Moore's name and coauthored by Liss which previously were published by Pinnacle were not successful. These books were "The London Switch," which had final net sales of 37,000, and "The Italian Connection," which had only 20,000 in net sales. Eventually Mack, Rose, and others entered into the discussions with Ettinger about "The Season."

On March 10, 1976, a manuscript of "The Season" was delivered to Pinnacle. On March 17, 1976, an agreement naming Season Co. as the "Author" and Pinnacle as the publisher was signed by Aull on behalf of Season Co. Subsequently, that agreement was signed by Pinnacle. Ultimately, it was redated May 19, 1976, and two inconsequential changes were made.

The agreement provided for a $10,500 advance against all earnings from a 15-percent royalty on the retail price of all original paperback copies sold. Pinnacle paid the $10,500 advance to Season Co. The agreement also included a provision in which Season Co. agreed to share with Pinnacle 10 percent of the revenues derived from motion picture and television rights. It was not customary in the mass market industry to make royalty payments for the period August 1976 through October 31, 1976, by December 31, 1976. Pinnacle nevertheless agreed to make such payments to Season Co.

Pinnacle promoted "The Season" as an original paperback book to the best of its efforts. Hornung assisted Pinnacle in promoting the book by making publicity tours to 26 cities during August through October 1976.

Receipts from "The Season"

"The Season" was originally published by Pinnacle in August 1976 with an initial print of 390,000 copies. New cover art was used when 68,561 copies of "The Season" were republished by Pinnacle in September 1977. "The Season" was distributed throughout the United States and Canada by Independent News Co., a wholly owned subsidiary of Warner Communications, Inc. The book also had some export sales and sales to U.S. military posts which were also handled by Independent News. Sales of the German language rights were a minor source of revenue for Season Co.

The most current royalty figures provided by the Pinnacle to Season Co. for sales through June 30, 1982, indicated that 410,459 copies of "The Season" were distributed, with net sales of 196,252 units, a 47.8-percent sale.

The Season Co. also derived revenue from the sales of options to purchase motion picture/television rights to "The Season." During 1977–78, Zeitman Productions of Beverly Hills, CA, paid $7,500 for option rights. In 1980, Jack Haley Jr. Productions, Inc., paid $1,000 for a 3-month option. During 1980–81, Lorimar Productions paid a total of $4,100 for an option and extensions thereof. A total of $12,600 was generated from the sale of these options.

During the years 1976 through June 30, 1982, Season Co. received $58,065.10 in royalties from book sales. Through 1981, $12,600 was received from the sale of television/movie options. These figures total $70,665.10, of which $53,538.10 was paid to Moore and Hornung under the terms of the May 19, 1976, agreement.

Valuation of "The Season"

An April 8, 1983 valuation report by petitioner's witness, Stanley B. Stetzer (Stetzer), stated that in his opinion based on potential earnings foreseeable in the summer of 1976, the net proceeds from the sale of all rights to "The Season" could reasonably have been expected to be $927,484. An October 27, 1982, valuation report by respondent's witness, Robert Sachs (Sachs), estimated a fair market value for "The Season" as of May 19, 1976, at $16,700. A December 28, 1982, valuation report by respondent's witness, Stephen Conland (Conland), stated that his opinion was that the fair market value of "The Season" as of May 19, 1976, was $2,000. The reports of these three persons indicated the following in comparison to the actual figures:

	Stetzer	Conland	Sachs	Actual
"The Season" paperback				
Estimated print	1,675,000	100,000	none given	458,561.00
Net sales (copies)	1,500,800	50,000	160,000	196,252.00
return percentage (books not sold)	10.4%	50%	none given	57.2%
Value of book	none given	$ 2,000	$16,700	
Estimated receipts by Season Co. from rights to "The Season"				
Dollar value of royalties	$438,984	$14,625	$46,800	$57,343.52
Book club sales	55,000	0	0	0
Foreign language receipts	36,500	0	0	721.58
Serial excerpts receipts	22,000	0	0	0
Motion picture receipts	375,000	0	0	12,600.00
Total	927,484	14,625	46,800	70,665.10

On May 16, 1976, net sales of "The Season" would at best be expected to be in the 160,000 to 200,000 range. The value of other rights on that date was so speculative as to be unable to be estimated. On May 16, 1976, estimated receipts from all the rights to "The Season" did not exceed $58,500, and the value of all such rights was significantly less than $58,500. On that date, there was no possibility that Season Co. would generate enough revenues to return petitioners' cash payments and that the $742,500 nonrecourse note would be paid by its due date.

Season Co.'s Reported Losses

Season Co. . . . filed partnership returns for years ending December 31. For years 1976 through 1978, Season Co. elected the income forecast method of depreciation. Season Co. switched to the straight line method for 1979 and 1980. The partnership returns, Forms 1065, filed with the Internal Revenue Service by Season Co. for 1976 through 1980, reported the following:

	1976	1977	1978	1979	1980
Gross receipts	$39,944	$13,655	$10,098	0	$2,652
Interest income	0	895	917	$1,327	1,472
Other income	250	0	0	0	0
Total income	40,194	14,550	11,015	1,327	4,124
Interest expense	0	41,198	0	0	0
Depreciation	446,374	151,980	112,845	25,214	25,214
Amortization	0	6,000	0	0	0
Other deductions	10,500	2,457	500	4,640	1,658
Total deductions	456,874	201,635	113,345	29,854	26,872
Ordinary loss	(416,680)	(187,085)	(102,330)	(28,527)	(22,748)

Petitioners paid Babbitt $4,000 in 1976 and $4,000 in 1977 for their interest in "The Season." Petitioners deducted partnership losses from Season Co. in 1976 and 1977 in the amounts of $16,501 and $7,408, respectively. Respondent disallowed both deductions.

OPINION

Petitioners claim Season Co. was engaged in business for profit and that it was entitled to an interest deduction in 1977. Respondent contends, among other things, that Season Co. did not conduct its activities for profit and that it was not entitled to interest deductions on nonrecourse notes.

I. Section 183

At the outset, we accept the fact that Pinnacle, as the publisher, fully utilized its resources as a small mass-marketing publishing house to sell "The Season." Accordingly, we have not dwelt extensively upon that aspect of this case in our findings of fact. Our inquiry is not directed, as petitioners would have us believe, to the question of whether Pinnacle did its job. The first critical question before us is whether the partnership, Season Co., was an activity engaged in for profit within the meaning of section 183.

An "activity not engaged in for profit" is defined in section 183(c) as "any activity other than one with respect to which deductions are allowable for the taxable year under section 162 or under paragraph (1) or (2) of section 212." If the activity is not engaged in for profit, then section 183(b) separates the claimed deductions into two groups. Section 183(b)(1) allows only those deductions which are not dependent upon a profit objective, e.g., interest and taxes. Section 183(b)(2) allows the balance of the deductions which would otherwise be permitted if the activity was engaged in for profit, but only to the extent that the gross income derived from the activity exceeds the deductions allowed under paragraph (1).

It is well established that . . . the question of whether the partnership is "not engaged in for profit" under section 183 is determined at the partnership level. . . . Thus, petitioners' argument that they invested in the Season Co. with a bona fide objective to make a profit is of little significance to our analysis under the instant facts since a limited partner has no control over partnership activities or the business deductions of the partnership. . . .

. . . While a reasonable expectation of profit is not required, Season Co.'s actual and honest objective of making a profit must be bona fide. . . . Section 1.183–2(b), Income Tax Regs., lists some of the relevant factors to be considered in determining whether an activity is engaged in for profit.

The issue is one of fact to be resolved not on the basis of any one factor, but on the basis of all the facts and circumstances. . . . Greater weight is given to objective facts than to the parties' mere statement of their intent. . . .

In determining Season Co.'s intent, we focus on the intent of the general partner and the promotors of Season Co. since it is these individuals who actually controlled the partnership's activities. . . . In this case, it is clear that Babbitt organized and controlled Season Co. Aull was only a strawman for Babbitt which carried on the duties of the general partner. Eventually Arthurs, a Babbitt employee, formally assumed the mantle of the general partner.

Based on the record before us, we are convinced that Babbitt organized Season Co. as a limited partnership in order to create artificial losses which the limited partners could use to reduce their taxes. The essence of this transaction was to transfer all rights to "The Season" for 7 years to the partnership for a grossly inflated price in the form of an outright sale, to use the facade of the distribution of an original paperback book via Pinnacle, and to use a grossly exaggerated nonrecourse note to create large tax losses for the limited partners through unwarranted depreciation deductions.

Babbitt attempted to paper as a business activity the formation and operation of Season Co. Some of this paper was specious, as in the case of the three identical appraisals Letheren supplied to Babbitt. Babbitt made sure, contrary to normal publishing practices, that the initial royalties would be paid before December 31, 1976, so that a loss could be claimed in 1976 under the income forecast method of depreciation. . . . In addition, Babbitt puffed up the depreciation deductions by an excessive nonrecourse note which bore no relationship to reality other than that it equaled 5.5 times the cash payments made to Moore and Hornung, the same factor used by Babbitt with respect to a number of books bearing Moore's name.

Petitioners' expert witness so exaggerated his estimates of the value of the rights to "The Season" that his testimony was incredible, i.e., not credible. We found Sachs, one of respondent's expert witnesses, the most impressive in terms of his knowledge of the book business and valuation of the prospects of "The Season" as of May 1976. We are satisfied that on May 19, 1976, it was obvious that at best "The Season" would have modest net sales of 160,000 to 200,000 copies. Net sales of 200,000 copies with a royalty of 29.25 cents per copy would result in $58,500 in income. Most of the other rights were without value and the movie rights were so speculative as to be incapable of being valued. It is obvious that the value of all rights to "The Season" was significantly less than $58,500. We question whether, aside from tax motivations, Season Co., or anyone else in an arm's-length transaction, would agree on a price of $874,500 for a return of $58,500. We are convinced that the Season Co. transactions were not economically sound and lacked a commercial objective.

We can contrast what happened here with what would have happened in a straight economic transaction if Moore and Hornung had contracted directly with Pinnacle. Moore and Hornung would have received a total of about $71,000 over the 7-year period. Instead, via Season Co., Moore and Hornung received approximately $157,000, principally within the first year after publication. The interposition of Season Co. only served to fatten the purses of Moore, Hornung, Babbitt, Regan Goldfarb, and others by offering unwarranted paper losses to limited partners.

The factual sequence can be simplified. Hornung contacted Moore with respect to her rough draft of a concept for a book. Moore had Liss write a book for publication as a paperback original. Moore contacted Pinnacle to have it publish a mass-market paperback original. Pinnacle was willing to sign the requisite documents with a limited partnership.

Moore, Babbitt, Regan Goldfarb, and others engaged in a cooperative effort to set up the tax scheme known as Season Co. The private placement memorandum demonstrates that the sole purpose of Season Co. was to create substantial after-tax benefits in 1976 and 1977 no matter how many book sales actually occurred. Under the facts of this case, the only conclusion that could be drawn in 1976 was that these after-tax benefits would be substantial paper losses used to reduce other income of the limited partners.

Pinnacle published the original paperback after Moore and Hornung purportedly transferred *all* their rights in "The Season" to Season Co. Nevertheless, over 75 percent of the $70,655.10 of royalties and movie option income flowed to Moore and Hornung while these rights were held by Season Co. As anticipated, most of the revenues were derived in the first 2 years.

There was no prospect whatsoever that the $742,500 nonrecourse note would be paid off on or before May 19, 1983. The actual payments made by date of trial, which included nonsubstantial payments against interest due on that nonrecourse note and a de minimis payment against principal, were not such as to lend economic substance to that nonrecourse note.

In summary, based upon the facts in this record, petitioners have failed to sustain their burden of showing that Season Co. was engaged in the exploitation of the rights to "The Season" for profit. Accordingly, all deductions claimed by petitioners, other than intcrest expenses in 1977, are allowable only to the extent that gross income exceeds the deductions allowable under section 183(b)(1).

Since there were no section 183(b)(1) deductions in 1976, there was no distributable loss in 1976. Accordingly, respondent's determination is sustained as to 1976.

II. Section 163

For 1977, Season Co. claimed a total interest deduction of $41,197.78 which included $36,678.69 as interest on the $742,500 nonrecourse note. We agree with respondent that this $36,678.69 was not deductible interest under section 163.[3]

To qualify for a section 163 deduction, the taxpayer must pay for the use or forbearance of money upon a genuine indebtedness.... This Court explained in *Fox v. Commissioner* ... that "There are various approaches which may be taken in establishing whether a purchaser may treat a nonrecourse liability as a bona fide debt." The approach we follow is the one recently stated in *Flowers v. Commissioner* ... as follows:

> Where both the purchase price and the lesser principal amount of the nonrecourse note which makes up a portion of such purchase price unreasonably exceed the value of the property acquired, then no "genuine indebtedness" exists and no "investment in the property" occurs. *Estate of Franklin v. Commissioner*; ...

---

3. Also included in the total claimed deduction was $3,886.68 of interest paid on the $110,000 note. In light of our findings, we deem it unnecessary to consider whether the $3,886.68 is deductible under sec. 163 since it is less than the reported gross income of $14,550. The remaining $632.41 of the total claimed interest deduction is the principal payment made in 1977 on the $742,500 nonrecourse note. Obviously, that is not deductible interest.

Here, too, both the purchase price and the $742,500 nonrecourse note unreasonably exceeded the value of the property acquired.[4]

We have found that on May 16, 1976, the maximum estimated receipts from all rights to "The Season" totaled $58,500 and the value of such rights was substantially less than that amount. We contrast that with the purchase price of $877,500 and the nonrecourse note of $742,500. It is obvious that both the purchase price and the $742,500 nonrecourse obligation were both grossly inflated and far in excess of the value of the rights to "The Season." We have discussed above the tax factors motivating the structuring of the Season Co.'s activities and showing the artificial nature of the $742,500 nonrecourse note. Suffice it to say that that note is not a genuine indebtedness and does not support Season Co.'s claimed interest deduction.[5] Accordingly, there was no distributable loss for 1977 and respondent's determination for that year is sustained.

When we view this case as a whole we can only conclude that the recent statement by the Court of Appeals in *Barnard v. Commissioner* . . . is apposite:

> The long and short of it all is that the parties demeaned themselves in entering so dishonest a venture, unquestionably structured to garner for each of the taxpayers tax advantages to which they were not entitled and devoid of any realistic business purpose. In this case we confront only risk-takers who believed they proceeded on a no-loss path; if they got away with it, well and good from their misguided point of view, and, if they did not, they would be no worse off than had they never sought the unjustified benefits in the first place. We refrain from any expression of opinion as to whether the taxpayers have exposed themselves to the risk of criminal prosecution. However, even assuming that perhaps they have not, they, by their conduct, nevertheless reveal a malaise which a healthy United States of America cannot sanction. It is a frightening prospect when our wealthy citizens, those in the highest income tax brackets, seek to take indefensible

---

4. We note that in *Brannen v. Commissioner* . . . this Court stated that the test was whether the stated purchase price unreasonably exceeded the value of the property whereas in *Hager v. Commissioner* . . . this Court stated that the test was whether the principal amount of the nonrecourse indebtedness unreasonably exceeded the value of the property. We need not decide which test is appropriate on the facts before us . . . because we find that both the purchase price and the principal amount of the nonrecourse debt unreasonably exceeded the value of the rights to "The Season."

5. Our conclusion is not changed by the opinion of the Supreme Court in *Commissioner v. Tufts* [Chapter 24], which held that where a taxpayer disposes of property encumbered by nonrecourse indebtedness in an amount that exceeds the fair market value of the property, the Commissioner may require him to include the outstanding amount of the nonrecourse obligation in the amount realized by him. That case involved the symmetrical treatment to be accorded where nonrecourse liability has been properly included in basis initially and must thereafter also be included in the amount realized on disposition of the encumbered property. The Supreme Court, relying upon the Commissioner's treatment and over 35 years of judicial sanction, held that the nonrecourse loan should be treated as a true debt in that situation.

The instant case does not fit within the context of *Tufts* and *Crane v. Commissioner* [Chapter 24]. Our issue is whether or not the nonrecourse obligation is genuine indebtedness so that it can be properly included in basis at the front-end of the transaction. We have found that it was not genuine indebtedness and could not properly be included in the basis of the rights to "The Season." Our decision is based on the unreasonably and artificially inflated amount of the nonrecourse indebtedness at the outset. That was not the fact in either *Tufts* or *Crane*. . . .

advantage of the country and their fellow citizens, especially those who have far less from which to meet their tax responsibilities. . . .

C. BARNARD v. COMMISSIONER
731 F.2d 230 (4th Cir. 1984)

MURNAGHAN, CIRCUIT JUDGE:

Sixteen taxpayers (individuals or husband and wife) involved in the same transactions designed to provide them with income "tax shelters" found their cases consolidated before the United States Tax Court. In a comprehensive opinion filed May 18, 1983, Judge Arthur L. Nims, III upheld the assessments of income tax deficiencies for the years involved (1975, 1976 and 1977) in the case of each of the taxpayers. . . . Three . . . took appeals to this Court which were heard, and now are disposed of, on a consolidated basis.

While the facts are complicated, resolution is easy. Judge Nims convincingly demonstrated that a partnership created ostensibly to purchase and market a book manuscript was not engaged in an activity for profit. He further established that a nonrecourse note given by the partnership was not a genuine liability. . . .

Summarily, the tax-minimizing scheme, an evasion not a mere avoidance of tax liability, was structured so that, if not a single copy of the book were ever marketed, nevertheless, the "deductions" generated for income tax purposes would, for high bracket taxpayers which the Barnards . . . were, be so great that they would, if the fabricated "deductions" were allowed, reduce taxes by a substantially greater amount than the relatively small sums contributed in cash to the partnership by each taxpayer. The purchase of the book was made through issuance by the partnership of a non-recourse promissory note for $495,000.00 and a cash payment of $163,000.[6] The non-recourse characteristic of the note was for the benefit of the general partner and all of the limited partners.

Since the cash contributed was less than 25% of the total "purchase price," on a *pro rata* allocation of the deduction for the "indebtedness" represented by the non-taxpaying partnership's non-recourse note, each taxpayer picked up a "deduction" three times as great as his or their actual contribution in cash. The taxpayers made no other contributions. A fifty percent bracket taxpayer, consequently, deducted on his income tax returns an amount four times the actual contribution made in cash. Accordingly, the direct tax benefit, even if the book were a total bust, selling not so much as a single copy, was an amount two times greater than the only economic asset, the cash, actually put up. It was a paradigmatic case of how to win by losing. Putting up cash of $9,000, a taxpayer generated a "deduction"

---

6. It appears that originally the aggregate cash contribution was planned to be $165,000, since a) that sum, together with the principal amount of the non-recourse note would equal the agreed on purchase price for the book manuscript of $660,000, and b) the cash contribution would then amount to exactly 25% of the purchase price, i.e., would be one-third as large as the principal of the non-recourse note.

of approximately $36,000. The tax savings, accordingly, amounted to $18,000, bringing the taxpayer out way ahead, no matter what.

There was, however, a risk that something might go wrong: the book might actually sell. It would have taken the astronomical number of sales of between 800,000 and 1,300,000 copies, depending on the mix of hard cover and paperback sales as well as other factors, even to reach the point at which the non-recourse note could be paid off and retired. But, along the way, if something were not done, each sale of a copy of the book might reduce the "deductible loss" by the amount of the net proceeds of any sale. To preclude the situation's developing into one where the taxpayers, as partners, might lose through winning, the arrangement was so structured that ½ of the net proceeds of all book sales would be paid to the partners *pro rata*, the other ½ to the partnership for reduction of the outstanding amount due on the non-recourse note. On that basis, a partner would recapture a portion of his or their cash contribution just equal (after taxes) in amount to the economic worth of the diminution in "deduction" resulting from the sale. So sales, while they practically would not help, were treated so they would not hinder, insofar as the availability of the deduction, was concerned.

In short, the partnership's only purpose, as a practical matter, was the development of losses to be deducted for income tax purposes, not the marketing of the book. The partnership was not honestly engaged in an activity for profit. The non-recourse note was not a genuine liability.

It is instructive to reflect on the carefully fashioned, altogether merited observations of Judge Nims. He wrote in his opinion of May 18, 1983:

1. Was the "acquisition of book publishing rights ... a sham, serving no business purpose and lacking any economic substance ... ?" (The answer, he concluded, was in the affirmative.)

2. "The price was hardly arrived at through arm's length bargaining. The negotiators on behalf of J.W. Associates (the partnership) had little or no incentive to keep down the cost...."

3. "Romero, J.W. Associate's figurehead general partner, equally received, through Laurel, the benefit of any inflated price and so had no motive to reject on behalf of the partnership any excessive expenditure."

4. "[W]e find [one aspect of the negotiations] tainted with the pervasive disingenuousness characteristic of the entire series of transactions in this case. As long as the nonrecourse note was sufficiently large in comparison to the cash portion of the purchase price such as to achieve anticipated tax benefits, such benefits would make the limited partners essentially unconcerned about the nominal aggregate purchase price."

5. "The record is devoid of evidence showing that the purchase price for the book paid by J.W. Associates to Laurel was in any way determined with a 'true regard for the profitability of the activity.' "

6. "Whether the book's revenues could actually bear the burden of such a purchase price was of no apparent concern to the parties."

7. "The substance of these letters, totally acquiesced in by the petitioners for all that appears in the record before us, are tantamount to admissions by petitioners that unwarranted tax deductions solely motivated their participation in the J.W. Associates partnership."

8. "This arrangement makes no sense from a business point of view. . . ."

9. "[T]he publication of the book was not conducted with an actual and honest profit objective." . . .

D. NOTES AND QUESTIONS

1) Overvaluation: *Dean* versus *Estate of Franklin*

The property in *Estate of Franklin* was overvalued by a factor of two. The estimated fair market value of the motel was $600,000, whereas the purchase price was about $1.2 million. In comparison, by what factor was there overvaluation of the literary property in *Dean*?

Can you distinguish the following three acts: (a) intentionally not reporting salary income; (b) intentionally claiming depreciation deductions for an asset that has not, in fact, been purchased; and (c) intentionally paying an inflated price for a depreciable asset purchased with seller-provided nonrecourse financing. If (a) and (b) constitute criminal tax fraud, why doesn't (c)? Because overvaluation may reflect legitimate disagreements over appraisal, rather than intentional fraud? Is that distinction plausible when property is overvalued by a factor of *almost 18*, as in *Dean*?

2) The Intrastate Offering

The *Dean* transaction was structured as an intrastate offering in order to avoid federal regulation under the Securities and Exchange Act of 1933. Why? The Securities and Exchange Commission checks the accuracy of statements in the prospectus of offerings subject to federal regulation. What statements might the SEC have objected to as inaccurate?

3) Transaction Costs in *Dean*

Of the $200,000 cash invested by the partners, how much was spent to purchase the literary property and how much to pay the broker (Babbitt) and lawyer (Regan Goldfarb)? Of the amount ostensibly paid for the literary property, how much went to the real authors, Hornung and Liss, and how much was devoted to other packagers and promoters, such as George Mack and Robin Moore? (For purposes of your answer, assume that, after Mack is paid, the remaining amount is split evenly between Hornung, Liss, and Moore.)

Exactly what did Babbitt, Regan Goldfarb, Mack, and Moore each do? What was each paid for?

4) Financial Analysis of *Dean*

What does each partner acquire in return for his or her $8,000 cash investment? Assume that royalties are not expected to exceed interest on the note and that the partnership plans to default after seven years, when the note becomes unconditionally due.

Are there any before-tax benefits? The partnership is entitled to royalties from the publisher of the manuscript but must also pay interest on the seven-year note owed to Moore and Hornung. Note that during the 7-year period, interest is basically payable *only* to the extent of royalties. Will the partnership have any net cash flow to distribute to the partners? Does the partnership have a residual interest in the property?

What are the anticipated after-tax benefits? During years 1–7, each partner may deduct his or her share of partnership losses. Each year's loss equals royalties, minus interest paid on the seven-year note, minus other partnership deductions. Assuming that royalties never exceed interest, what is the measure of each year's loss? At the beginning of year 8, each partner must report his or her share of partnership gains arising from default on the seven-year note. What is the amount realized on default? What is the adjusted basis of the literary property? What is the character of the asset? How is the character of the gain transformed by Section 1245?

Table 43–1 uses figures from the *Dean* opinion to calculate the present value of the net after-tax benefits, assuming a tax bracket of 50% and an interest rate of 5%. Is the *Dean* tax shelter a sensible investment, judged solely from the financial perspective? Why not? How does this tax shelter differ in this respect from *Estate of Franklin*? Who really benefits from the abusive tax shelter in *Dean*?

TABLE 43-1. FINANCIAL ANALYSIS OF DEAN TAX SHELTER

50% Bracket Year	Tax Saving	5% Interest PV Multiplier	PV
1	8,134	.952	7,744
2	7,732	.907	7,013
3	541	.864	467
4	378	.823	311
5	377	.784	296
6	378	.746	282
7	377	.711	268
8	−14,589	.677	−9,877
TOTAL			6,504

5) Presentational Aspects

Each investor was required to provide $4,000 in 1976 and $4,000 in 1977. Why was the deal structured this way rather than simply requiring each investor to contribute about $8,000 in one payment? Given the way that the Dean transaction was structured, what was the ratio of cash paid to tax benefits in 1976? In 1977? How would requiring the entire $8,000 to be paid in 1976 have changed appearances?

> [O]ver its full course, the shelter will have pluses and minuses as any other investment transaction. But, at the beginning, all is roses. Who can

resist a deal where you get much or all your money back at the beginning? The topsy-turvy repayment-investment structure of tax shelters befogs the minds of ordinary mortals.[7]

6) Expensing of Deductions

The partnership expensed $65,000 in costs for brokers, lawyers, and miscellaneous expenses. Was expensing consistent with *Idaho Power*? See also Section 709(a) and (b)(1) requiring capitalization of amounts incurred to organize a partnership.

7) The Hazards of Success

What happens to the tax shelter if, contrary to expectations, the book is a "success," and royalties exceed interest on the seven-year partnership note? Recall that each year's losses equal royalty income, minus interest paid, minus depreciation and other business deductions. As long as royalties do not exceed interest, annual losses equal depreciation and other business deductions. For every dollar by which royalties exceed interest, the amount of loss is reduced by a dollar. For every dollar by which the loss is reduced, the tax shelter investors are unable to offset a dollar of income from other sources and, if they are in the 50% bracket, will owe 50 cents more in federal income taxes.

The agreement between the partnership and the sellers provides for funding any increased federal income tax liability of the partners caused by success. Under the terms of the note, 50% of royalties in excess of interest must be applied to repay the principal amount. The remaining 50% is available for distribution to the partners and will just equal the increased federal income tax liability imposed at the 50% rate.

In the event of success, what about the investors' increased liability for state income taxes? Does the agreement provide for funding this amount? Is this potential unfunded state tax liability a reason not to invest in the shelter, even if the out-of-pocket cost does not exceed the present value of the anticipated tax benefits, as described in Table 43–1? In this respect, does the *Dean* shelter recall the movie, "The Producers," directed by Mel Brooks?

8) Apportioning Blame

Dean, quoting *Barnard*, castigates the tax shelter investors. Do they really deserve the most blame? Who, in fact, received the lion's share of the benefits produced by the *Dean* tax shelter? Is their share directly affected by the case brought against Dean and the other investors? Weren't they in the best position to know that the copyright's price was being grossly inflated in order to provide tax benefits?

---

7. Cooper, The Taming of The Shrewd: Identifying and Controlling Income Tax Avoidance, 85 Colum. L. Rev. 657, 668 (1985).

If you had been an associate at Regan Goldfarb—the law firm hired by the promotors—should you have refused to work on this deal? See Treasurer Circular 230, 31 C.F.R. 203 (Sec. 10.33), promulgated in 1980, which sets out rules for attorneys who practice before the IRS. Under the rules, an attorney may use an appraisal to give a tax shelter opinion only if the appraisal "makes sense on its face."

9) Legal Rationales

How would the *Dean* tax shelter fare under the rationales of *Estate of Starr*, *Swift Dodge*, or *Estate of Franklin*? Do the investors have a significant residual? Bear significant risks? Have an equity in the literary property? What is the effect of the legal rationale of *Dean*? As a doctrine, do you find it satisfactory? As a matter of logic, can it be restricted to so-called "abusive" tax shelters, where overvaluation is present? Wouldn't the *Dean* rationale also apply to a "nonobjectionable" tax shelter with competitive bidding, low transaction costs, and no tax rate differential (Chapter 40)?

10) The Road Not Taken

A more satisfactory way to decide both *Estate of Franklin* and *Dean* may be to attack the overvaluation problem directly by reinterpreting the word "cost" in Section 1012. Usually, the buyer of property wants to pay as little as possible, and the seller wants to be paid as much as possible. Because the price is set by arm's length bargaining between parties with divergent interests, "cost" under Section 1012 can usually be interpreted to mean the price agreed to by the buyer and seller. But when financing is without recourse, it may be in both parties' interest to set as high a "price" as possible. In that event, might not "cost" under Section 1012 be given a meaning other than the price agreed to by buyer and seller? Could cost be interpreted to exclude nonrecourse financing (or stated purchase price) in excess of the asset's fair market value?

Won't such an interpretation of "cost" attack only abusive tax shelters, where overvaluation is present? And isn't this interpretation not subject to the weakness of the Circuit Court's rationale in *Estate of Franklin* (Chapter 42)?

But would this suggested approach be consistent with the holding in *Crane* (cited in *Tufts* in Chapter 24) that basis includes nonrecourse financing? With the decision in *Tufts* that the amount realized on the sale of property includes the principal amount of any nonrecourse financing encumbering the property, *even if* in excess of the property's fair market value?

How did the taxpayers in *Dean* apparently try to use the Supreme Court decision in *Tufts* to support their position? (See footnote 10 of the *Dean* opinion.) If, on foreclosure, the amount realized equals the full unpaid principal amount of the note, as *Tufts* requires, mustn't that amount also be included as part of the property's cost basis? Alternatively, if "cost" in Section 1012 were interpreted not to include nonrecourse financing (or stated purchase price) in excess of the property's fair market value—that is, if the longstanding *Crane* rule were modified—how should *Tufts* also be modified?

Is Section 465—limiting deductible losses from certain activities to the "amount at risk"—consistent with *Crane* and *Tufts*? Does it amount to a congressional decision to define the "cost" of property in certain instances as not including nonrecourse financing?

How did the taxpayers in *Dean* argue that they were not covered by Section 465? See Section 465(c)(1)(C). Would that argument be available after 1978? See Section 465(c)(3)(A), enacted in that year.

11) Statutory Reforms 1981–1984

During this period, Congress made piecemeal changes in the Code to try to limit "abusive" tax shelters using overvalued assets. Section 6659, enacted in 1981 and extended in 1984, imposes an extra penalty on taxpayers who overvalue assets. The size of the penalty varies with the amount of overvaluation. It is 10% of the underpayment of tax if the asset is overvalued by 50% to 100%; 20%, if overvalued by 100% to 150%; and 30%, if overvalued by more than 150%. The House Report explained:

> [T]here are about 500,000 tax disputes outstanding which involve property valuation questions of more than routine significance . . . .
> . . . [V]aluation issues frequently involve difficult questions of fact . . . . [T]axpayers have been encouraged to overvalue certain types of property and to delay the resolution of valuation issues. Because the tax interest rate has been below the prevailing cost of borrowing, this tendency probably has been accentuated somewhat.[8]

Section 6700, enacted in 1982, imposes a penalty on promoters who overvalue tax shelter property by more than 200%. See Section 6700(a)(2)(B) and (b)(1). The penalty equals the greater of $1,000 or 20% of the gross income derived from promoting the shelter. One critic complained about Section 6700's ineffectiveness, "[It] depends on a subjective definition that limits its application to situations that are virtually criminal."[9]

Section 6661, also enacted in 1982, imposes a penalty unless a taxpayer reasonably believed that claimed tax shelter benefits were "more likely than not . . . proper. . . ." The penalty equals 25% of the amount of underpayment of taxes. It applies only if the underpayment itself exceeds the greater of $5,000 or 10% of the tax due on the return.

The 1984 Deficit Reduction Act contained a number of measures designed to facilitate record-keeping and ease the administrative burden on the IRS. Section 6111 requires that the organizers of a tax shelter register the shelter with the IRS by the date it is offered to investors. Section 6112 requires the organizers to maintain lists of investors which must be available for IRS inspection. Section 6050J requires that a secured creditor report

---

8. H.R. Rep. No. 201, 97th Cong., 1st Sess. 243 (1981).
9. Cooper, The Taming of the Shrewd: Identifying and Controlling Income Tax Avoidance, 85 Colum. Law Rev. 657, 686 (1985).

any foreclosure of its security. The 1984 Act also increased the interest rate for underpaid taxes on certain tax-motivated transactions to 120% of the usual underpayment interest rate. Section 6621(c).

12) Why Piecemeal Reforms Fell Short

The statutory reforms enacted between 1969 and 1984, outlined here and in Chapter 39, did little to curb the growing tidal wave of tax shelter investments. To some extent, this failure was due to gaps in the legislation. The "at risk" rules of Section 465, for example, were not applied to real estate tax shelters until 1986. Congress may also have been at fault for expanding the tax incentives that feed shelters at the same time it purported to curb them.

> [W]hile all of this partially effective anti-shelter activity has been going on, Congress has been doing much that is counter-effective.... The 1981 Act ... introduced the ACRS system of capital recovery which augmented write-off allowances by a fifth or more, introduced large new tax credits for specialized investments in real estate and in research.... We have thus been throwing gasoline on the shelter fire while squirting extinguishers at it.... Although extreme abuses have been suppressed, the basic entitlements have been wonderfully enriched. Is it any wonder that the fire rages on?
>
> For example, I received, in November, 1984, a new prospectus for a post-1984 tax-sheltered investment in episodes of a major television series being licensed for broadcast.... Only nine percent of the purchase price is initially paid in cash. Another sixteen per cent is to be paid over the next three years. The balance of the price is financed with a long-term loan that will be fully serviced by large, virtually certain, revenue from existing network contracts. No economic return is projected for investors until final disposition of the assets in 1991. This transaction would be an economic disaster absent tax benefits. With a favorable final disposition ... a cash surplus can result ... but this small eventual return in 1991 contrasted with large outlays in early years ... makes the present value of the transaction highly negative ... The tax benefits, however, which are heavily weighted to early years, redress the balance....[10]

Another reason for the failure to eliminate abusive tax shelters was that the sheer volume overwhelmed the audit and litigation capabilities of the IRS, so that it was unable to use effectively the available arsenal of statutory weapons and legal arguments. This ineffectiveness encouraged even more investors to try their luck at the "audit lottery."

> [T]he tax shelter problem has continued to strain the resources of the IRS. A 1983 General Accounting Office report indicates that even with its new tools designed to stop the continued promotion of abusive tax shelters and the focus of the IRS on the problem, the IRS faced a backlog of 314,516 tax shelter returns as of March 1983. Even if no new cases were added to the inventory, it would take the IRS more than four years to process the backlog at its present pace of about 70,000 completed examinations annually.

10. Ibid. at 691–2 (1985).

... [I]t had become clear that traditional methods of enforcement were doing little to control abusive tax shelters, despite significant government victories in both criminal and civil tax shelter litigation. Civil tax shelter litigation focused upon investors and required waiting for the investors to file returns reporting tax shelter activity, causing years of delay and resulting in precedent not directly relevant to currently marketed tax shelters. Criminal proceedings against shelter promoters were also seen as a somewhat remote penalty that did not effectively deter current behavior. Criminal tax shelter investigations are generally lengthy and complex, and require more resources than other tax crimes . . . .[11]

As of March 31, 1983, tax shelter returns still in . . . inventory numbered 314,516, substantially all of which related to taxable years prior to 1980. Since there has been further proliferation of tax shelters since 1980, it is reasonable to expect that the true number of tax shelter returns already filed which will be audited . . . is perhaps twice as high.

The large number of tax shelter cases . . . has placed a heavy strain on the resources of the Service. . . . Commissioner of Internal Revenue . . . Roscoe Egger . . . likened the Service's position to Mickey Mouse in "The Sorcerer's Apprentice," e.g., each time the Service cut a broom in half even more came down the steps . . . .

At the end of 1983 over 20,000 tax shelter cases were docketed in the Tax Court, representing over one-third of its backlog. The Court's backlog now exceeds 55,000 cases. In fiscal 1982 the Tax Court closed 24,024 cases; thus, the backlog now exceeds two years. As a consequence, the Tax Court's resources have been heavily strained by such cases.[12]

E. PASSIVE ACTIVITY LOSSES

1) New Section 469

Congress adopted an entirely new approach to the problem of tax shelters in the 1986 Tax Reform Act. It enacted Section 469 to prevent tax shelter losses from offsetting nontax shelter income. Under this provision, losses from "passive activities" may be deducted *only* against income from "passive activities." Section 469(a)(1). Section 469 is one of the more complex provisions of the Code, and this introductory casebook will do no more than outline its general effect.

2) The Scope of "Passive Activity"

The linchpin of Section 469 lies in its definition of what does and does not constitute a "passive activity." Under Section 469(c), "passive activity" includes any rental activity and any trade or business in which the taxpayer "does not materially participate." "Material participation" is defined as involvement on a "regular, continuous, and substantial basis." Section 469(h)(1). The statute conclusively presumes that a limited partnership interest can

---

11. Feffer and Yingling, Prosecution and Defense of Abusive Tax Shelters, 36 Major Tax Planning 2-1, 2-3 to 2-4 (1984).
12. Martin, Tax Shelters: 1984 Style, 36 Major Tax Planning 6-1, 6-3 to 6-4 (1984).

never qualify as "material participation." Section 469(h)(2). In addition, Section 469(e) treats interest, dividends, and other gains and losses from securities as *not* arising from a "passive activity." The purpose of Section 469(e) is to prevent tax shelter losses from offsetting income from stocks, bonds, and other securities.

Can taxpayers avoid Section 469(e) by using the presumption of Section 469(h)(2)—that a limited partnership interest can never qualify as "material participation" and therefore must constitute a "passive activity"? Suppose that a taxpayer transfers all income-producing securities to a partnership consisting of the taxpayer and his or her spouse, in which the taxpayer is the limited, and the spouse, the general partner. Wouldn't the interest and dividend income—paid to the taxpayer as a limited partner—automatically be designated as "passive," so that it could be offset by "passive" tax shelter losses? Section 469(h)(2) empowers the Treasury to issue regulations to create exceptions to the limited partnership presumption to avoid such an outcome.

The limit on deducting "passive activity" losses applies to individuals, estates, trusts, and certain closely held corporations. Section 469(a)(2). Can large, public issue corporations still deduct tax shelter losses without limit? Was Congress oblivious to this form of abuse? Are such corporations unlikely to participate in "abusive" tax shelters?

3) The Effect of Section 469: Substantive and Administrative

What is the effect of Section 469 on losses generated by the *Dean* transaction? If it applies, can the losses be used to offset salary? To offset other dividend or interest income? How does Section 469 differ from the *Dean* "not for profit" test? Is the substantive outcome appreciably different? How does Section 469 simplify the audit and administrative burden on the IRS? Can the taxpayer in *Dean* argue that he "materially participates," so as to avoid the interest being considered a "passive activity"?

4) Qualifications and Exceptions

The complexity of Section 469 arises, in part, from its numerous qualifications and exceptions. First, oil and gas tax shelters emerged relatively unscathed. Under Section 469(c)(3)(A), "passive activity" does not include a working interest in oil or gas property *if* not held through a limited partnership interest.

Second, any disallowed passive activity loss may be carried forward *indefinitely* and applied against passive activity gains, if any, in future years.

Third, when the taxpayer disposes of his or her interest in a passive activity, a previously disallowed loss becomes immediately deductible.[13] Why permit an exception for such a disposition?

Fourth, a phase-in rule makes Section 469 fully effective only in 1991. The phase-in applies to any interest in a passive activity acquired on or

---

13. The disposition must be *fully* taxable. A partially taxable disposition, as in a Section 1031(b) exchange, is not enough.

before the enactment of Section 469 in 1986. Losses from passive activity investments made after the enactment date cannot benefit from the phase-in. If an activity qualifies, 35% of the loss is disallowed in 1987, 60% in 1988, 80% in 1989, and 90% in 1990.

Fifth, there is a special exception for the first $25,000 of losses generated by rental real estate. The exemption is not available to very high income taxpayers. It is reduced by 50% of the amount by which AGI exceeds $100,000 (or $200,000, in the case of certain low-income housing). In addition, to qualify for the rental real estate exemption, the taxpayer must "actively participate" in the activity. Active participation is envisioned as something less than "material participation." It is apparently satisfied by some involvement in management decisions even if not "regular, continuous, and substantial." However, even "active participation" is not required if the real estate is low-income housing. Does this exception from Section 469 explain why the 1986 Act extended the "at risk" rules of Section 465 to cover real estate?

5) Applying Section 469 to *Nickerson*

Would Section 469 apply to the loss in *Nickerson* (Chapter 31)? Does the farm constitute a "passive activity"? Is Nickerson's involvement on a "regular, continuous, and substantial basis," so as to constitute "material participation"? Or does the rental activity mean that the farm is conclusively presumed to be a "passive activity"? Even so, might Nickerson's involvement be regarded as "active participation," so that he qualifies for the limited exception for landlords?

6) Is There Life for Individual Tax Shelters After Section 469?

Is it still possible to construct a tax shelter so that an individual "materially participates" and therefore will not be prevented by Section 469 from deducting the losses in full? Consider the following.

F. INSTEAD OF A CONDO, A CABIN HOTEL SUITE
The New York Times (July 19, 1987)

A New York printing executive, whom we shall call Carl Michaels, spent months looking around the Northeast for a vacation home. What he settled on, however, was a vacation suite—a three-bedroom unit in the Ascutney Mountain Resort, a hotel in Brownsville, Vt.

Why did he choose a condominium hotel suite over a tree-shaded cabin? "This condo gives us a place of our own that we can use for the occasional vacation without all the responsibility of owning a house," Mr. Michaels said. "I don't want to worry about something happening to a house in an outlying area, when I'm not there." As for upkeep, "I can go back to New York on Sunday night and the maid will make up the room Monday morning." In addition, "we have a chance at cash flow, we'll get some tax deductions, and we may wind up with a good investment, too." . . .

Since passage of the Tax Reform Act last year, . . . "there has been a sudden burst of interest in condo hotels," said Martin Helpern, tax partner in the accounting firm of Laventhol & Horwath. One reason is that condo hotels were one of the few property investments not hurt by the new law; in addition, buyers have various options for tax purposes. Some, like Mr. Michaels, treat their unit as a second home, using it regularly and deducting the loan interest.

Other buyers use their condo less than 15 days during the year, treating the purchase mainly as an investment. A possible advantage of this, Mr. Helpern said, was established "as a result of a colloquy during tax reform." This "colloquy" was an on-the-record discussion between Bob Packwood, manager of the 1986 Tax Reform Act in the Senate, and fellow Oregon Senator Mark Hatfield. Their conversation, on the Senate floor, concluded that condo hotel buyers could be considered active rather than passive investors: This is an important benefit because active investors, who participate in management, can use losses on their investment to offset income from salaries, interest and dividends. Passive investors cannot.

Senator Hatfield spelled out 11 points that indicate "material participation" in management of a condo hotel, necessary for deducting losses. Condo owners must visit the site regularly, help with personnel policies, set room rates, and so on. "It's not easy to be a genuine material participant," said William Dowling, president of Dowmar Securities, which sponsors condo hotel investments. "Individuals will truly have to become involved. I estimate about half of our buyers will qualify." Some developers make an effort to facilitate this for their investors.

Several sponsors have been aggressive in promoting condo hotels as "the last real estate tax shelter," under the Tax Reform Act. But the word from Washington has been cautionary. "The Congressional Joint Committee on Taxation came out with its 'blue book' last spring, interpreting the Act," Mr. Helpern said. "It said that material participation is possible, in a condo hotel, but there is no 'safe harbor.' " That is, compliance with Senator Hatfield's 11 points will not automatically qualify a buyer for write-offs. . . .

Prospective buyers should also be aware that Condo hotels carry special risks: Participants do not have the "limited" liability protection that comes with a limited partnership investment. "Negative cash flow"—meaning that total expenses exceed current income—is likely with a start-up hotel. Some condo deals have guarantees or excess reserves to cover any shortfalls, but there is still a chance that condo owners will be called upon for more money. . . .

Chapter 44

THE ELUSIVE AND PUZZLING INTEREST DEDUCTION

A. INTRODUCTORY NOTE

The proper treatment of the cost of borrowing—usually referred to as interest expense—has bedeviled lawyers and economists since the inception of the income tax. From 1913 until 1969, interest was generally deductible whether incurred in connection with a "for profit" or a "for pleasure" activity, subject to only a few exceptions. During the past two decades, however, Congress has enacted a bewildering array of limits on the interest deduction.

The basic issue concerns a phenomenon known as *tax arbitrage*. Tax arbitrage occurs when deductible interest is combined with tax-exempt income. In other words, it involves the use of a loan, on which interest is deductible, to produce income that is *not* fully taxed. Some examples of tax arbitrage are: investing in a tax shelter with borrowed funds; mortgaging a personal residence; or borrowing to buy municipal bonds.

At a gut level, tax arbitrage *seems* objectionable for a simple reason. If the income from property is tax exempt, why allow a deduction for the costs of generating that income? For example, the income from personal consumption property is realized in imputed, tax-exempt form. Therefore, why allow deduction of the cost, whether depreciation (See Chapter 30) or interest expense?

Those who believe that tax arbitrage should be prevented usually favor limiting the interest deduction when a loan is used to produce tax-exempt income. But is tax arbitrage really a problem? While the subject has been hotly debated, particularly since the adoption of new limits in the 1986 Tax Reform Act, there is little or no consensus on whether there is actually a problem at all. Because the effect of the interest deduction is imperfectly understood, this chapter should be regarded as especially tentative and subject to modification.

Section 469—discussed at the end of the preceding chapter—is in some sense an antitax arbitrage provision. Under Section 469, interest on passive activity debt may be deducted only against passive activity income. Limits on the interest deduction in three other areas—investments in real estate and stock, personal consumption, and tax-exempt bonds—are discussed in this chapter. In addition, limits on deducting interest in connection with market discount bonds and insurance are discussed in Chapters 50 and 53, respectively.

B. INVESTMENTS IN REAL ESTATE AND STOCK

Section 163(d) allows noncorporate taxpayers to deduct investment interest only against investment income. When such interest expense exceeds such income, the deduction is deferred until investment income is produced in later years. Although Section 163(d) applies to all interest paid in connection with investments, the primary target is loans incurred in connection with land and stock held primarily for appreciation, rather than for current income.

To illustrate, a real estate investor might buy undeveloped farmland producing only nominal amounts of current rent in anticipation that the land could be sold at a profit for development some years later (see *Biedenharn Realty,* Chapter 27). Or a stock market investor might acquire shares of stock, paying only a small current dividend but with the prospect of significant growth and therefore appreciation in the stock's value. In both cases, assuming that the purchase is debt financed, annual interest expense would exceed rent on the land or dividends on the stock.

What is the effect of Section 163(d)?[1] Does it attempt to match expenses with income? How is it analogous to the capitalization requirement of Section 263?

C. PERSONAL CONSUMPTION

From 1913 until 1987, interest on loans to finance personal consumption (referred to as *personal interest,* for short) was deductible without exception or limit under Section 163(a). Since 1987, however, Section 163(h) has disallowed deductions for all personal interest, except "qualified residence interest." The disallowance is phased in over four years. Section 163(d)(6)(B).

The exception for qualified residence interest includes interest on mortgages used to acquire, construct, or improve the taxpayer's principal home and one other residence (for example, a vacation home). This exception is limited to interest on the portion of home mortgages *not* in excess of

---

1. Under Section 469(c)(2), passive activity is defined to include "any rental activity." However, Reg. § 1.469–1T(e)(iv)(B) states an exception where the principal purpose of holding land during the year is to realize gain from appreciation and gross rental income is the lesser of 2% of the unadjusted basis or the fair market value of the property. If these requirements are met, Section 163(d), rather than Section 469, will apply to the land.

$1 million. Section 163(h)(3)(A)(i) and (h)(3)(B).[2] Taxpayers are also permitted to deduct interest on an additional $100,000 in mortgage debt (so-called "home equity indebtedness") that may be incurred for any purpose. Section 163(h)(3)(A)(ii) and (h)(3)(C).

Section 163(h) has profound consequences for the large number of taxpayers who finance personal consumption by borrowing and therefore incur personal interest expense. Anyone who has a car loan, pays off a personal credit card bill in installments, or takes out a student loan to finance college or graduate school may find her interest deduction phased out and then eliminated by 1991. The interest on these obligations will continue to be fully deductible only if incurred in connection with a trade or business rather than personal consumption. For example, interest on a car loan will be deductible if the cost of the car is deductible in a trade or business (Chapter 5).

Was the allowance of a deduction for all personal interest before 1987 defensible? Why should personal interest *ever* be deductible when other personal consumption expenditures generally are not (Section 262)? One argument for permitting the deduction of personal interest is to prevent discrimination against income from labor as compared with income from property.

To illustrate, suppose A owns taxable bonds worth $500,000 and borrows $100,000 to finance personal consumption. Assume that A's taxable bonds earn 10% and that A can borrow at 10%. If interest is deductible, then A's income consists of $50,000 of bond income, less $10,000 of interest expense on the loan, or $40,000 net. If interest expense is not deductible, then A can sell bonds rather than borrow the money from another party. Selling $100,000 of bonds also reduces her income to $40,000, since she no longer receives the $10,000 in interest income from them. The result is the same as if she had borrowed $100,000 from someone else and deducted the interest expense.

Suppose B, who earns $50,000 a year in salary but owns no property, borrows $100,000 at 10% interest. If interest is deductible, then B's net income consists of his $50,000 salary, less $10,000 of interest expense on the loan, or $40,000. However, in this case, if the interest deduction is denied, B cannot duplicate its effect by selling property; he has no property to sell.

Denial of deductions for personal interest also discriminates against C, whose assets consist of a family business or unimproved land, both of which are illiquid and cannot easily be sold.

To sum up, disallowing the interest deduction would not hurt taxpayers who are able to use their own funds instead of borrowing (like A). But it would discriminate against taxpayers who cannot substitute their own funds for borrowing because they have not accumulated property (like B) or have accumulated illiquid assets (like C). Thus, one argument for allowing the deduction of personal interest is to prevent such discrimination.

---

2. Interest on a postacquisition, postconstruction, or postimprovement refinancing is deductible only to the extent that the new loan does not exceed the outstanding principal remaining on the original indebtedness.

A second argument for allowing the interest deduction in the specific case of home mortgage loans is to encourage owner-occupied housing. Owner-occupiers allegedly take better care of their homes and change residences less frequently than renters. This promotes better maintained and more stable communities.

Even if owner-occupied homes generally should be encouraged, why provide the subsidy through a tax deduction so that the amount of subsidy per dollar of mortgage interest varies with the homeowner's tax bracket? For example, the 15% bracket homeowner saves only 15 cents by deducting a dollar of mortgage interest, whereas the 33% bracket homeowner saves 33 cents. (See the discussion of tax expenditures in Chapter 11.)

In addition, why should the subsidy apply to *all* mortgage interest, no matter how expensive the house, or to *any* mortgage interest whatsoever on a second home? Providing a tax incentive for every family to acquire decent housing is one thing. Subsidizing the cost of $1 million homes and vacation residences is another. Is the $1 million limit on the amount of home mortgage loans qualifying for an interest deduction therefore too high? Should mortgage interest on a second home not qualify at all?

However, additional restrictions on deducting home mortgage interest would reintroduce the problem (described earlier) of discrimination in favor of income from property and against income from labor—although such discrimination may be more tolerable at higher income levels.

> The present policy of allowing the deduction of interest on home mortgages is objectionable on the ground, essentially, of its discriminatory effect. . . . [A]s between two taxpayers otherwise similarly situated, the one with the larger home investment receives the greater tax advantage. This discrimination is difficult to justify on the basis that home ownership should be favored over other forms of investment. . . . On the other hand, denial of the interest deduction, by whatever means, would merely alter the nature of the discrimination; the tax advantages of home ownership would continue to be available to those with funds available for investment. . . .
>
> The dilemma thus posed may be avoided only by eliminating the special tax advantage of this form of investment—that is, by the taxation of the imputed income from such investments [while continuing to permit the deduction of home mortgage interest].[3]

How would taxing imputed income from owner-occupied homes solve the dilemma? Suppose X, who earns $50,000 a year, borrows $100,000 at 10% interest (or $10,000 a year) to buy a $100,000 home. Assuming that housing also earns an imputed net return of 10%, X receives imputed income of $10,000 from her home but also deducts home mortgage interest of $10,000. Thus, her income remains at $50,000 a year.

Next, consider Y, who also earns $50,000 a year but borrows $200,000 to buy a $200,000 home. Y then receives imputed income of $20,000 from his home but also deducts mortgage interest of $20,000. Thus, his income also remains at $50,000 a year. Y, in other words, obtains no advantage over X by virtue of owning a larger home.

---

3. Klein, Borrowing To Finance Tax-Favored Investments, 1962 Wis. L. Rev. 608, 634.

Notice, however, what happens when imputed income is not taxed. As a result of buying a home, X's income falls from $50,000 to $40,000 ($50,000 in salary, less an interest deduction of $10,000). And Y's income falls from $50,000 to $30,000 ($50,000 in salary, less an interest deduction of $20,000). In effect, nontaxation of imputed income favors the individual with the more expensive house.

D. MUNICIPAL BONDS

The interest paid on municipal bonds is generally exempt from federal income tax (Section 103(a)).[4] However, interest expense on loans to "purchase or carry" municipal bonds has been nondeductible since 1917. Section 265(a)(2).

One argument for Section 265(a)(2) is that allowing a deduction for such interest would be inequitable. Owners of municipal bonds, the argument goes, already benefit from tax-exempt income. Why should they, in addition, get to deduct the cost of generating tax-preferred income?

This argument, however, ignores how market forces may respond to tax-preferred assets. Taxable bonds and tax-exempt bonds will tend to pay the same rate of interest *after taxes,* which means that taxable bonds will pay more than tax-exempt bonds *before taxes.*

> If a particular category of assets is [tax-preferred], taxpayers should respond by investing relatively more in the preferred assets and relatively less in other assets, until the after-tax return from an investment in preferred assets equals the after-tax return from other assets. The final market equilibrium will depend on a variety of factors . . . but the pre-tax return on preferred assets should be below the pre-tax return on otherwise comparable assets. . . . The best known example of this market effect is the lower rate of interest traditionally paid on tax-exempt bonds, relative to comparable bonds yielding taxable income. If the financial markets fully "capitalize," or take into account, the preferential treatment . . . , a new investor will not obtain any advantage from . . . the tax preference. . . .[5]

To illustrate, assume that a $1,000 taxable bond pays interest of $100; that a $1,000 municipal bond pays interest of $50; and that the highest tax bracket is 50%. An investor in the top bracket could then earn $50 after taxes by purchasing a taxable bond,[6] which is equivalent to purchasing a $1,000 municipal bond also yielding $50. In other words, for such an investor, municipal bonds would provide no advantage over taxable bonds.

---

4. There are, however, important limits on the amount of tax-free municipal bonds that can be issued for so-called "private purposes," such as financing capital investment by private industry. Section 103(b)(1). These restrictions, contained in Sections 141–148, are beyond the scope of this introductory casebook. In addition, even certain private purpose municipal bonds which qualify for exemption under the "regular" income tax, are nevertheless subject to the minimum tax (Chapter 35). Section 57(a)(5).

5. Warren, Accelerated Capital Recovery, Debt, and Tax Arbitrage, 38 Tax Lawyer 549, 564 (1985).

6. The $100 of interest before taxes, minus the tax due of $100 times 50% equals $50.

The advantage of the tax preference is said to be fully reflected in the lower municipal bond interest rate or *fully capitalized*.

The capitalization of the tax preference can also be described as imposing an *implicit* tax, equal to the difference between the return on taxable bonds and the return on municipal bonds. The tax is described as implicit because it is imposed by market forces, rather than by the government exacting an explicit payment from the investor. When there is full capitalization in the example above, the implicit tax is $50—the difference between the $100 interest on the $1,000 taxable bond and the $50 interest on the $1,000 tax-exempt bond. And the implicit tax rate—the percentage reduction in returns caused by market forces—is 50%. See Table 44–1.

TABLE 44-1. FULL CAPITALIZATION (MUNICIPAL BOND RATE IS 5%)

Investor Tax Bracket	Municipal Bond Interest	Implicit Tax	Implicit Tax Rate
50%	50	50	50%

Notice that although the explicit tax imposed on municipal bond interest is zero, the implicit tax—exacted in the form of the lower interest paid by municipal bonds—is a full 50%. Thus, the top bracket 50% investor in municipal bonds, although nominally tax exempt, in effect "pays" what would be his or her fair share according to the explicit tax rate schedule.

The conclusion that a fully capitalized tax preference offers investors no advantage has a corollary. If the preference is only *partially* capitalized, then higher bracket investors will obtain an advantage.

To illustrate, assume in the example above that a $1,000 municipal bond pays interest of $70. A 30% bracket investor could earn $70 after taxes from taxable bonds so that there is no advantage to tax-exempt bonds. But an investor in the 40% bracket, who could earn only $60 after taxes by purchasing a $1,000 taxable bond, gains an advantage. The 50% bracket investor could earn only $50 after taxes by purchasing the taxable bond and so gains even more. There is an advantage to higher bracket investors because the tax preference is only partially reflected in lower municipal bond interest or only partially capitalized.

The effects of partial capitalization can also be described in terms of implicit taxes. In the example above, there is an implicit tax of $30—the difference between the $100 interest on the $1,000 taxable bond and the $70 interest on the $1,000 municipal bond. And the implicit tax rate—the percentage reduction in returns caused by market forces—is 30%. See Table 44–2.

TABLE 44-2. PARTIAL CAPITALIZATION (MUNICIPAL BOND RATE IS 7%)

Investor Tax Bracket	Municipal Bond Interest	Implicit Tax	Implicit Tax Rate
30%	70	30	30%
40%	70	30	30%
50%	70	30	30%

Notice that the top 50% bracket investor, although nominally tax exempt, in fact "pays" a 30% tax. This implicit tax, however, is less than his or her fair share as determined under the explicit tax rate schedule, which would be the full 50%.

In the real world, for reasons that are not clearly understood, the tax preference for municipal bonds has been only partially capitalized. Historically, the tax-exempt bond interest rate has averaged about 70% of the taxable bond interest rate. When taxable bonds have paid 10% interest, tax-exempt bonds have earned about 7%. Thus, the implicit tax rate on municipal bonds has been about 30% during the period when the top individual rate has been at least 50% and as high as 70%.

But suppose interest expense incurred in connection with municipal bonds had been deductible. The demand for such bonds might have increased. If demand had increased, municipalities could have paid lower rates of interest. And a lower rate of interest would have meant a higher implicit tax rate on municipal bonds. Therefore, implicit taxes imposed on higher bracket investors in municipal bonds would have been closer to what should be their fair share according to the explicit tax rate schedule.

In the example above, the tax-exempt interest rate might have fallen from 7% to 6% so that a $1,000 municipal bond would have paid interest of $60 instead of $70. A 40% bracket investor, who could also earn $60 after taxes by purchasing a $1,000 taxable bond, would no longer gain any advantage. And the advantage to the 50% bracket investor from investing in a $1,000 municipal bond would be halved. Allowing the interest deduction, in other words, would tend to increase implicit taxes and to narrow the gap between the implicit tax rate imposed on municipal bonds and the explicit tax rate imposed on investors in the highest bracket. See Table 44–3. Thus, equity may argue *against*, not for, Section 265(a)(2).

TABLE 44-3. PARTIAL CAPITALIZATION (MUNICIPAL BOND RATE IS 6%)

Investor Tax Bracket	Municipal Bond Interest	Implicit Tax	Implicit Tax Rate
40%	60	40	40%
50%	60	40	40%

A second argument in favor of Section 265(a)(2) is that if interest expense in connection with municipal bonds were deductible, taxpayers would enter into transactions which would otherwise be uneconomic. To illustrate, assume that investors who borrow must pay a 10% interest rate and that tax-exempt bonds earn 7%. Would you ever borrow money at 10% to invest in tax-exempt bonds earning only 7%? If the interest is not deductible, the after-tax rate of interest remains at 10%, and it would clearly be a losing proposition to borrow at the 10% rate to earn a 7% return.

But suppose interest expense is deductible and your tax rate is 40%. In that event, the after-tax cost of borrowing is 6%,[7] which is less than the 7%

---

[7] When interest is deductible, the before-tax 10% rate has to be reduced by the benefit of the tax deduction to calculate the after-tax interest rate. If the investor's bracket is 40%, the benefit equals 40% of the 10% before-tax interest rate or 4%. The after-tax interest rate is therefore 10% minus 4%, which equals 6%.

that can be earned by investing the loan in municipal bonds. The losing proposition becomes a winner. Therefore, the argument goes, the interest deduction should be denied to prevent uneconomic transactions that would not otherwise occur.

This argument, however, also applies to the purchase of municipal bonds *without borrowed funds*. For example, but for the tax preference, why would you buy municipal bonds paying 7% if you could earn 10% on other investments? The very purpose of the tax preference is to encourage transactions that would not otherwise occur—in other words, to produce transactions that would be uneconomic, absent the preference. Criticizing such transactions as uneconomic implies that the preference itself is unwise. Indeed, some economists do argue that municipal borrowing should not be subsidized and that the tax exemption for municipal bond interest retards economic efficiency. But, if preference is the problem, why attack the interest deduction as the evil rather than the preference itself?[8]

One possible answer is political feasibility.

> [T]he present statute [Section 265(a)(2)] may be regarded as a necessary, though arbitrary, expedient. It might be argued that, as a matter of political reality, there is little hope of eliminating the tax advantage; that even though the effort to deny the interest deduction is an arbitrary and somewhat clumsy approach, it nevertheless serves to limit the availability of tax-free income; and therefore . . . such a device is justified even if it is by no means wholly satisfactory.[9]

In other words, attacking the preference directly might generate too much opposition from the beneficiaries and therefore fail. An indirect attack, via limits on the interest deduction, may be more likely to succeed and therefore may constitute a "second-best" alternative to a frontal assault. While not as effective as outright repeal of the exemption of municipal bonds interest, it would at least place some limits on the use of an unwise tax preference.

To summarize, there seem to be competing considerations at stake when one evaluates the disallowance of interest expense in connection with municipal bonds. Equity and efficiency considerations may be in conflict. If the exemption of municipal bond interest is an unwise tax preference not directly assailable, then disallowance of interest expense indirectly limits the amount of municipal bonds, improving economic efficiency. But disallowance also tends to decrease the degree of capitalization of the preference and to reduce the implicit tax on higher bracket investors, decreasing equity.

E. CATEGORIZING INTEREST

A major problem with implementing limits on interest deductions is determining how to categorize interest payments. To illustrate, suppose

---

8. On the other hand, if the preference is a desirable incentive for capital investment by state and local governments, then the charge that uneconomic transactions are encouraged is beside the point.
9. Klein, Borrowing To Finance Tax-Favored Investments, 1962 Wis. L. Rev. 608, 615.

that A and B each have $10,000 in cash savings and plan to buy $10,000 in corporate bonds and a $10,000 pleasure boat. A uses the cash to buy the bonds and borrows to buy the boat. B borrows to buy the bonds and uses the cash to buy the boat. In the end, each is in the same economic position, owning $10,000 of bonds and a $10,000 boat and owing $10,000.

One method categorizes interest by the use of the borrowed funds. A, having used his loan to acquire a boat, would have personal interest expense while B, having used her loan to acquire bonds, would have investment expense. This is known as a *tracing* rule, because interest is categorized by tracing the use of the borrowed funds.

Another possibility is to allocate the interest proportionately between the investment and personal consumption activities. Both A and B would be treated alike, with half the interest classified as personal and half as investment related. This is known as the *pro rata allocation* method. A third possibility is to allocate interest first to the bonds and last to the boat (or vice versa). Again, both A and B would be treated alike since all the interest would be investment related (or personal). This is called a *stacking* rule.

Temporary regulations, adopted under Section 163(h), provide for a tracing rule. Interest expenses are allocated among five basic categories, according to how the loan proceeds have been spent. The categories are listed below in ascending order of how restrictive the limits on interest deductions are:

1) Trade or business interest—generally deductible without limit;
2) Home mortgage interest—deductible within fairly liberal limits;
3) Investment interest—deductible only to the extent of investment income;
4) Tax shelter (or other passive activity) interest—deductible only against passive activity income; and
5) Interest on all other personal consumption loans—not deductible.

However, the tracing rule is superceded if a so-called "override" rule applies. For example, under Section 265(a)(2), a loan secured by municipal bonds is associated with the municipal bonds, even if the loan proceeds are spent on something else. The following materials explore the override rules that apply to interest expense in connection with municipal bonds.

F. THE WISCONSIN CHEESEMAN INC. v. UNITED STATES
388 F.2d 420 (7th Cir. 1968)

CUMMINGS, CIRCUIT JUDGE.

This lawsuit involves the proper construction of Section [265(a)(2)] of the Internal Revenue Code. The question for resolution is whether the taxpayer may deduct from its gross income the interest it paid on its mortgage and some of its short-term loans.

Taxpayer is located in Sun Prairie, Wisconsin, and is in the business of packaging fancy cheeses for sale as Christmas gifts. Its business is seasonal and is most active during the last three months of each calendar year. Its sales are solicited exclusively through a catalog mailed each October. It incurs high costs in the last three months of each calendar year. Funds are borrowed annually from September through early November to cover such costs.

During the three fiscal years ending July 31, 1960, 1961 and 1962, taxpayer obtained short-term bank loans to meet its recurring needs for working capital. These borrowings took place each fall and were repaid, from late November through January, out of the receipts of each year's sales. The balance of the receipts was used to purchase municipal bonds and treasury bills. The treasury bills were acquired with staggered maturity dates to meet the off-season needs of the business. They were reduced to cash by the middle of each July. The municipal bonds were used as collateral for the bank loans, enabling taxpayer to borrow almost 100% of their value. On August 1, 1959, taxpayer had municipal bond holdings of $138,168.29. By July 31, 1962, these holdings had increased to $218,542.70.

In the second of the fiscal years involved, in order to build a new plant, taxpayer borrowed $69,360 from a bank. This loan was secured by a mortgage upon its real estate. The proceeds of the loan were used to pay for construction and not directly to purchase municipal bonds.

For these taxable fiscal years, the Commissioner of Internal Revenue disallowed taxpayer's deductions of interest on the mortgage and on some of the short-term loans. The taxpayer paid the resulting assessments and later brought this refund suit against the United States.

The District Court held that taxpayer incurred the indebtedness to "carry obligations . . . the interest on which is wholly exempt" from Federal income tax within the meaning of Section [265(a)(2)] of the Internal Revenue Code. Therefore, judgment was entered for the United States. We agree as to the interest on the short-term loans but not as to the mortgage interest.

Interest on Short-Term Loans

During each fall in the years in question, taxpayer used its municipal bonds as collateral for short-term bank loans for essential working capital. Instead of resorting to bank loans, taxpayer could have sold its municipals to meet the high cost seasonal needs of its business. Because this alternative was available to taxpayer, the Government argues that the short-term indebtedness was automatically incurred in order to enable taxpayer to "carry [tax-exempt] obligations," so that the interest on this indebtedness would be non-deductible under Section [265(a)(2)] of the Internal Revenue Code. . . . The District Court construed Section [265(a)(2)] as forbidding the deduction of interest on indebtedness incurred or continued "in order to" or "for the purpose of" carrying tax-exempt obligations. We approve this construction but do not believe deduction is forbidden whenever taxpayer has an alternative of liquidating tax-exempts in lieu of borrowing.

The taxpayer contends that the short-term loans were incurred for the purpose of meeting its heavy fall seasonal financing needs, whereas the Government contends that the indebtedness was incurred for the purpose of making it possible for taxpayer to carry its municipal securities. In holding that the interest on the short-term loans could not be deducted, the District Court stated:

> To accomplish the purpose of obtaining cash to meet plaintiff's seasonal needs, it was not a condition precedent that indebtedness be incurred. To accomplish the purpose of carrying the municipal securities, it was a condition precedent that indebtedness be incurred.

In reaching its conclusion that no refund was due, the District Court construed the Congressional intent as not to grant a deduction for interest payments by a taxpayer who holds securities, the interest from which is not taxable. This is the double benefit prohibited by Section [265(a)(2)]. Stated another way, Congress sought to prevent a taxpayer from requiring the United States to finance its investments. . . .

In our view, the taxpayer is not *ipso facto* deprived of a deduction for interest on indebtedness while holding tax-exempt securities. The Government has not convinced us that interest deduction can be allowed only where the taxpayer shows that he wanted to sell the tax-exempt securities but could not. For example, Congress certainly did not intend to deny deductibility to a taxpayer who holds salable municipals and takes out a mortgage to buy a home instead of selling the municipals. As the Court of Claims stated in Illinois Terminal Railroad Company v. United States. . . :

> It is necessary [for the Commissioner] to establish a sufficiently direct relationship of the continuance of the debt for the purpose of carrying the tax-exempt bonds.

This construction flows from the use of "to" in Section [265(a)(2)]. In this case, this nexus or "sufficiently direct relationship" is established by the fact that the tax-exempt securities were used as collateral for the seasonal loans. Under Section [265(a)(2)], it is clear that a taxpayer may not deduct interest on indebtedness when the proceeds of the loan are used to buy tax-exempts. . . . Applying the rule that the substance of the transaction is controlling in determining the tax liability, the same result should follow when the tax-exempt securities are used as collateral for a loan. Surely one who borrows to buy tax-exempts and one who borrows against tax-exempts already owned are in virtually the same economic position. Section [265(a)(2)] makes no distinction between them.

In addition, our analysis of the statute and its legislative history convinces us that the deduction should not be allowed if a taxpayer could reasonably have foreseen at the time of purchasing the tax-exempts that a loan would probably be required to meet future economic needs of an ordinary, recurrent variety. This test would not permit this taxpayer to deduct the short-term loan interest, for its regular business pattern shows that it would have to go into debt each fall if it bought or kept municipals as a long-term investment.[10] This established course of conduct is con-

---

10. Under this test, the deduction would be disallowed here even if the municipals were not used as collateral for the short-term loans.

vincing proof that the underlying reason for these recurring loans was to carry the municipals....

As taxpayer contends, there should be no discrimination against seasonal businesses but neither should they be put in a preferred position. If a non-seasonal business borrowed to buy municipals, the interest on the loans would be non-deductible. There is no reason why a seasonal business should fare better....

Interest on Mortgage

The $69,360 construction loan was secured by a ten-year 6% mortgage on taxpayer's real estate. No municipal bonds were put up as collateral. The mortgage was for a new plant to meet a growing demand. The entire $69,360 mortgage proceeds were used to pay for this plant. According to the uncontroverted testimony, if taxpayer had sold municipal bonds to pay for the plant, it would have had fewer liquid assets to meet seasonal needs and would have had difficulty in borrowing to meet those needs. Plant construction is undeniably a major, non-recurrent expenditure and is usually financed over a long term. We cannot say that a reasonable person would sacrifice liquidity and security by selling municipals in lieu of incurring mortgage debt to finance a new plant. Business reasons dominated the mortgaging of the property. Therefore, we are unwilling to accept the Commissioner's view that taxpayer should have liquidated municipals instead of obtaining a real estate mortgage loan. There is an insufficient relationship between the mortgage indebtedness and the holding of the municipal bonds to justify denial of deduction of the mortgage interest. For non-deductibility, we have seen that the Commissioner must establish a sufficiently direct relationship between the debt and the carrying of the tax-exempt bonds. That has not been done as to the mortgage, so that the mortgage interest deductions must be allowed under Section 163(a) of the Internal Revenue Code....

G. REV. PROC. 72–18

1972–1 C.B. 740 Rev. Proc. 72–18

SEC. 1. PURPOSE.

The purpose of this Revenue Procedure is to set forth guidelines for taxpayers and field offices of the Internal Revenue Service for the application of section [265(a)(2)] of the Internal Revenue Code of 1954 to certain taxpayers holding state and local obligations the interest on which is wholly exempt from Federal income tax....

SEC. 2. BACKGROUND.

.01 Section [265(a)(2)] of the Code provides, with two exceptions not here relevant, that no deductions shall be allowed for interest on indebtedness "incurred or continued to purchase or carry obligations ... the interest on which is wholly exempt" from Federal income tax.

.02 . . . It is clear from the legislative history of those sections and of subsequent unsuccessful efforts to amend such sections (or their successors) that Congress intended to disallow interest under section [265(a)(2)] of the Code only upon a showing of a purpose by the taxpayer to use borrowed funds to purchase or carry tax-exempt securities. . . .

SEC. 3. GENERAL RULES.

.01 Section [265(a)(2)] of the Code is only applicable where the indebtedness is incurred or continued for the purpose of purchasing or carrying tax-exempt securities. Accordingly, the application of section [265(a)(2)] of the Code requires a determination, based on all the facts and circumstances, as to the taxpayer's purpose in incurring or continuing each item of indebtedness. Such purpose may, however, be established either by direct evidence or by circumstantial evidence.

.02 Direct evidence of a purpose to *purchase* tax-exempt obligations exists where the proceeds of indebtedness are used for, and are directly traceable to, the purchase of tax-exempt obligations. . . .

.03 Direct evidence of a purpose to *carry* tax-exempt obligations exists where tax-exempt obligations are used as collateral for indebtedness. "[O]ne who borrows to buy tax-exempts and one who borrows against tax-exempts already owned are in virtually the same economic position. Section [265(a)(2)] makes no distinction between them." *Wisconsin Cheeseman v. United States.* . . .

.04 In the absence of direct evidence linking indebtedness with the purchase or carrying of tax-exempt obligations as illustrated in paragraphs .02 and .03 above, section [265(a)(2)] of the Code will apply only if the totality of facts and circumstances supports a reasonable inference that the purpose to purchase or carry tax-exempt obligations exists. Stated alternatively, section [265(a)(2)] will apply only where the totality of facts and circumstances establishes a "sufficiently direct relationship" between the borrowing and the investment in tax-exempt obligations. See *Wisconsin Cheeseman.* . . .

.05 Generally, where a taxpayer's investment in tax-exempt obligations is insubstantial, the purpose to purchase or carry tax-exempt obligations will not ordinarily be inferred in the absence of direct evidence as set forth in sections 3.02 and 3.03. In the case of an individual, investment in tax-exempt obligations shall be presumed insubstantial only where during the taxable year the average amount of the tax-exempt obligations (valued at their adjusted basis) does not exceed 2 percent of the average adjusted basis of his portfolio investments (as defined in section 4.04) and any assets held in the active conduct of a trade or business. In the case of a corporation, an investment in tax-exempt obligations shall be presumed insubstantial only where during the taxable year the average amount of the tax-exempt obligations (valued at their adjusted basis) does not exceed 2 percent of the average total assets (valued at their adjusted basis) held in the active conduct of the trade or business. This paragraph shall not apply to a dealer in tax-exempt obligations.

SEC. 4. GUIDELINES FOR INDIVIDUALS.

.01 In the absence of direct evidence of the purpose to purchase or carry tax-exempt obligations (as set forth in sections 3.02 and 3.03), the rules set forth in this section shall apply.

.02 An individual taxpayer may incur a variety of indebtedness of a personal nature, ranging from short-term credit for purchases of goods and services for personal consumption to a mortgage incurred to purchase or improve a residence or other real property which is held for personal use. Generally, section [265(a)(2)] of the Code will not apply to indebtedness of this type, because the purpose to purchase or carry tax-exempt obligations cannot reasonably be inferred where a personal purpose unrelated to the tax-exempt obligations ordinarily dominates the transaction. For example, section [265(a)(2)] of the Code generally will not apply to an individual who holds salable municipal bonds and takes out a mortgage to buy a residence instead of selling his municipal bonds to finance the purchase price. Under such circumstances the purpose of incurring the indebtedness is so directly related to the personal purpose of acquiring a residence that no sufficiently direct relationship between the borrowing and the investment in tax-exempt obligations may reasonably be inferred.

.03 The purpose to purchase or carry tax-exempt obligations generally does not exist with respect to indebtedness incurred or continued by an individual in connection with the active conduct of trade or business (other than a dealer in tax-exempt obligations) unless it is determined that the borrowing was in excess of business needs. However, there is a rebuttable presumption that the purpose to *carry* tax-exempt obligations exists where the taxpayer reasonably could have foreseen at the time of purchasing the tax-exempt obligations that indebtedness probably would have to be incurred to meet future economic needs of the business of an ordinary, recurrent variety. See *Wisconsin Cheeseman v. United States*.... The presumption may be rebutted, however, if the taxpayer demonstrates that business reasons, unrelated to the purchase or carrying of tax-exempt obligations, dominated the transaction.

.04 Generally, a purpose to *carry* tax-exempt obligations will be inferred, unless rebutted by other evidence, wherever the taxpayer has outstanding indebtedness which is not directly connected with personal expenditures (see section 4.02) and is not incurred or continued in connection with the active conduct of a trade or business (see section 4.03) and the taxpayer owns tax-exempt obligations. This inference will be made even though the indebtedness is ostensibly incurred or continued to purchase or carry other portfolio investments.

Portfolio investment for the purposes of this Revenue Procedure includes transactions entered into for profit (including investment in real estate) which are not connected with the active conduct of a trade or business....

A sufficiently direct relationship between the incurring or continuing of indebtedness and the purchasing or carrying of tax-exempt obligations will generally exist where indebtedness is incurred to finance portfolio investment because the choice of whether to finance a new portfolio investment through borrowing or through the liquidation of an existing investment in tax-exempt obligations typically involves a purpose either to maximize profit or to maintain a diversified portfolio. This purpose necessarily involves a decision, whether articulated by the taxpayer or not, to incur (or continue) the indebtedness, at least in part, to purchase or carry the existing investment in tax-exempt obligations.

A taxpayer may rebut the presumption that section [265(a)(2)] of the Code applies in the above circumstances by establishing that he could not have liquidated his holdings of tax-exempt obligations in order to avoid incurring indebtedness. The presumption may be overcome where, for example, liquidation is not possible because the tax-exempt obligations cannot be sold. The presumption would not be rebutted, however, by a showing that the tax-exempt obligations could only have been liquidated with difficulty or at a loss; or that the taxpayer owned other investment assets such as common stock that could have been liquidated; or that an investment advisor recommended that a prudent man should maintain a particular percentage of assets in tax-exempt obligations. Similarly, the presumption would not be rebutted by a showing that liquidating the holdings of tax-exempt obligations would not have produced sufficient cash to equal the amount borrowed.

The provisions of this paragraph may be illustrated by the following example:

> Taxpayer *A*, an individual, owns common stock listed on a national securities exchange, having an adjusted basis of $200,000; he owns rental property having an adjusted basis of $200,000; he has cash of $10,000; and he owns readily marketable municipal bonds having an adjusted basis of $41,000. *A* borrows $100,000 to invest in a limited partnership interest in a real estate syndicate and pays $8,000 interest on the loan which he claims as an interest deduction for the taxable year. Under these facts and circumstances, there is a presumption that the $100,000 indebtedness which is incurred to finance *A*'s portfolio investment is also incurred to carry *A*'s existing investment in tax-exempt bonds since there are no additional facts or circumstances to rebut the presumption. Accordingly, a portion of the $8,000 interest payment will be disallowed....

See section 7 concerning the amount to be disallowed....

SEC. 6. GUIDELINES FOR CORPORATIONS THAT ARE NOT DEALERS IN TAX-EXEMPT OBLIGATIONS.

.01 Where there is no direct evidence of the purpose to purchase or carry tax-exempt obligations (as set forth in sections 3.02 and 3.03), the rules set forth in this section shall apply to a corporation which is not a dealer in tax-exempt obligations.

The purpose to purchase or carry tax-exempt obligations will generally not be inferred with respect to indebtedness incurred or continued to provide funds for carrying on an active trade or business, not involving the holding of tax-exempt obligations, unless it is determined that the borrowing was in excess of business needs. Thus the purpose may be present where the borrowings exceed the reasonable needs of business or provide funds for portfolio investments. For example, where indebtedness is incurred and the proceeds are used, directly or indirectly, to purchase tax-exempt obligations which are retained for a substantial period of time as an investment, the purpose to purchase or carry tax-exempt obligations may be inferred. Similarly, where the taxpayer invests a disproportionately large portion of its liquid assets in tax-exempt obligations and there are no facts indicating that such investment is related to the reasonable needs of the taxpayer's business operations or is required on the basis of the financial conditions prevailing with respect thereto, the required purpose may also be inferred with respect to indebtedness of the taxpayer. On the other hand, temporary, short-term, investment of working capital in tax-exempt obligations, particularly where such obligations are of a nature suited for such investment (such as 90 day tax anticipation notes), and where such investments are liquidated frequently to provide funds for use in the taxpayer's business, normally provides no basis for inferring that the purpose to purchase or carry tax-exempt obligations exists with respect to indebtedness of the taxpayer. An inference may arise, however, with respect to indebtedness which is itself short-term and is incurred other than in the normal course of the taxpayer's trade or business.

.02 Generally, the purpose to *carry* tax-exempt obligations will be inferred unless rebutted by other evidence where the taxpayer could reasonably have foreseen at the time of purchasing the tax-exempt obligations that indebtedness probably would have to be incurred to meet future economic needs of the corporation of an ordinary, recurrent variety. For example, a purpose to carry tax-exempt obligations can be inferred in a case (such as *Wisconsin Cheeseman,* supra) where the regular business pattern of a corporation shows that it would be required to borrow funds to meet its recurring needs for working capital if it bought or retained tax-exempt obligations as a long-term investment. The presumption will not apply, however, if the taxpayer demonstrates that business reasons unrelated to the purchase or carrying of tax-exempt obligations dominated the transaction. For example, the purpose to carry tax-exempt obligations generally cannot be inferred where a mortgage debt is incurred to finance a new plant which is a nonrecurrent major expenditure. In such cases, a dominant business purpose, other than the purchase or carrying of tax-exempt obligations will normally exist and, accordingly, any inference will be rebutted. On the other hand, the purpose to *carry* tax-exempt obligations can be inferred where a corporation *continues* indebtedness which it could discharge, in whole or in part, by liquidating its holdings of tax-exempt obligations without withdrawing any capital which is committed to, or held in reserve for, the corporation's regular business activities. . . .

SEC. 7. PROCEDURES.

.01 When there is direct evidence under sections 3.02 and 3.03 establishing a purpose to purchase or carry tax-exempt obligations (either because tax-exempt obligations were used as collateral for indebtedness or the proceeds of indebtedness were directly traceable to the holding of particular tax-exempt obligations) no part of the interest paid or incurred on such indebtedness may be deducted. However, if only a fractional part of the indebtedness is directly traceable to the holding of particular tax-exempt obligations, the same fractional part of the interest paid or incurred on such indebtedness will be disallowed. For example, if A borrows $100,000 from a bank and invests $75,000 of the proceeds in tax-exempt obligations, 75 percent of the interest paid on the bank borrowing would be disallowed as a deduction.

.02 In any other case where interest is to be disallowed in accordance with this Revenue Procedure, an allocable portion of the interest on such indebtedness will be disallowed. The amount of interest on such indebtedness to be disallowed shall be determined by multiplying the total interest on such indebtedness by a fraction, the numerator of which is the average amount during the taxable year of the taxpayer's tax-exempt obligations (valued at their adjusted basis) and the denominator of which is the average amount during the taxable year of the taxpayer's total assets (valued at their adjusted basis) minus the amount of any indebtedness the interest on which is not subject to disallowance to any extent under this Revenue Procedure. . . .

H. NOTES AND QUESTIONS

1) The Results in *Wisconsin Cheeseman* and *Rev. Proc. 72–18*

Try to describe the different methods for categorizing interest in these decisions. When is a tracing method used? When is a pro rata allocation method used? Does there seem to be a reason why one method rather than another may be used in a particular circumstance?

2) Economic Substance in *Wisconsin Cheeseman*

The court states that "one who borrows to buy tax-exempts and one who borrows against tax-exempt bonds are in virtually the same economic position." What about (a) one who borrows to buy tax-exempt bonds and buys other assets with cash and (b) one who buys tax-exempt bonds with cash and borrows to buy other assets? Aren't both also in virtually the same economic position? Is the fact that one person used the loan to buy tax-exempt bonds and the other used his own money to do the same a meaningful distinction? Do your answers suggest that pro rata allocation is the conceptually correct method for categorizing interest?

What are the practical obstacles to implementing a pro rata allocation rule? Would it require annual appraisals of all a taxpayer's assets? If annual appraisal is too difficult, would the adjusted basis of assets be a satisfactory surrogate for market value?

Are there circumstances in which pro rata allocation is not even conceptually correct? For example, suppose you buy an office building with nonrecourse financing. Should the nonrecourse loan be prorated among all your assets?

*

PART FIVE

Assignment of Income

Part Five deals with attempts to assign or shift income from higher bracket to lower bracket taxpayers. The terms *assignment* and *shifting* are used interchangeably to mean the taxation of income to one person in place of another. The advantage of assigning income has decreased very substantially with the cutback in the top individual rate from 70% to 50% in 1981 and then to 33% in 1986. The advantage also is limited by the relatively modest size of the 15% brackets and by the fact that the marginal tax rate on all income above a certain level is only 28% (Chapter 1).

To illustrate, suppose a wealthy taxpayer in the 28% bracket assigns income to her fourteen-year-old grandchild, whose other income equals the standard deduction plus personal exemption. Only the first $17,850 of the income shifted to the grandchild is taxable at the 15% rate rather than the 28% rate. See Section 1(c). Thus, the tax savings available from shifting the grandparent's income to the grandchild are limited to 13% (28% − 15%) of $17,850, or $2,320.50.

Some significant incentives for shifting do remain. First, even in a system under which individuals face marginal rates of only 0%,[1] 15%, 28%, and 33%, taxpayers stand to gain up to 33 cents for each dollar of income successfully assigned from a higher to a lower bracket individual taxpayer.

Second, a taxpayer with net gains may still try to assign income to a taxpayer with net losses.

Third, the Code allows some entities to be exempt from paying federal income taxes and thus creates an incentive for the shifting of income from taxable persons to tax-exempt organizations.

---

1. An amount of each individual's income, equal to the standard deduction plus personal exemptions, is tax-exempt and therefore effectively taxed at a zero rate. For 1988, the tax-exempt amount equals $4,950 for a single person with no dependents. See Chapter 1.

Fourth, even though the top corporate rate of 34% is slightly higher than the top individual rate of 33%, the first $50,000 of corporate income is taxed at only 15% and the next $25,000 at only 25%. Section 11. Thus, an individual taxpayer might still gain by assigning up to $75,000 of income to a corporation.[2]

---

2. This benefit, however, was substantially limited by the Revenue Act of 1987. Lower corporate rates no longer apply to personal service corporations, for example, an architect, lawyer, or physician who incorporates. See Chapter 46.

SUBPART A

Intrafamily Transactions

Subpart A deals with attempts to shift income within the family. This subject has already been discussed in several earlier chapters. Chapter 10 analyzed deductible compensation paid to one's children as shifting income from parent to child. Chapters 22 and 23 examined the basis provisions of Section 1015(a), which permit unrealized appreciation in property to be shifted by gift but prohibit the shifting of unrealized losses.

Chapter 45

THE COMMON LAW

A. INTRODUCTORY NOTE

This chapter focuses on the evolution of judicial principles limiting the assignment of income between family members. When the assignment succeeds, it is said to produce a *valid* assignment of income; when it fails, an *invalid* assignment. Note that the question of whether an assignment is valid for federal tax purposes is generally different from, and should not be confused with, the question of whether the assignment is valid under state property law.

The seven Supreme Court decisions in this chapter set out the basic law on assignment of income. The reasons offered by the Court to justify the results in these cases are mostly incoherent. The reader might therefore be advised "to stress the *results* [rather] than to linger over the reasoning."[1]

B. LUCAS v. EARL
281 U.S. 111 (1930)

MR. JUSTICE HOLMES delivered the opinion of the Court.

This case presents the question whether the respondent, Earl, could be taxed for the whole of the salary and attorney's fees earned by him in the years 1920 and 1921, or should be taxed for only a half of them in view of a contract with his wife which we shall mention. The Commissioner of Internal Revenue and the Board of Tax Appeals imposed a tax upon the whole, but their decision was reversed by the Circuit Court of Appeals. . . . A writ of certiorari was granted by this Court.

By the contract, made in 1901, Earl and his wife agreed "that any property either of us now has or may hereafter acquire . . . in any way, either by earnings (including salaries, fees, etc.), or any rights by contract

---

1. M. Chirelstein, Federal Income Taxation 180 (3d ed. 1982)

or otherwise, during the existence of our marriage, or which we or either of us may receive by gift, bequest, devise, or inheritance, and all the proceeds, issues, and profits of any and all such property shall be treated and considered and hereby is declared to be received, held, taken, and owned by us as joint tenants, and not otherwise, with the right of survivorship." The validity of the contract is not questioned, and we assume it to be unquestionable under the law of the State of California, in which the parties lived. Nevertheless we are of opinion that the Commissioner and Board of Tax Appeals were right.

... A very forcible argument is presented to the effect that the statute seeks to tax only income beneficially received, and that taking the question more technically the salary and fees became the joint property of Earl and his wife on the very first instant on which they were received. We well might hesitate upon the latter proposition, because however the matter might stand between husband and wife he was the only party to the contracts by which the salary and fees were earned, and it is somewhat hard to say that the last step in the performance of those contracts could be taken by anyone but himself alone. But this case is not to be decided by attenuated subtleties. It turns on the import and reasonable construction of the taxing act. There is no doubt that the statute could tax salaries to those who earned them and provide that the tax could not be escaped by anticipatory arrangements and contracts however skilfully devised to prevent the salary when paid from vesting even for a second in the man who earned it. That seems to us the import of the statute before us and we think that no distinction can be taken according to the motives leading to the arrangement by which the fruits are attributed to a different tree from that on which they grew.

C. CORLISS v. BOWERS
281 U.S. 376 (1930)

MR. JUSTICE HOLMES delivered the opinion of the Court. . . .

The question raised by the petitioner is whether . . . the Revenue Act can be applied constitutionally to him upon the following facts. In 1922 he transferred the fund from which arose the income in respect of which the petitioner was taxed, to trustees, in trust to pay the income to his wife for life with remainder over to their children. By the instrument creating the trust the petitioner reserved power "to modify or alter in any manner, or revoke in whole or in part, this indenture and the trusts then existing, and the estates and interests in property hereby created" &c. It is not necessary to quote more words because there can be no doubt that the petitioner fully reserved the power at any moment to abolish or change the trust at his will. The statute referred to provides that "when the grantor of a trust has, at any time during the taxable year, . . . the power to revest in himself title to any part of the corpus of the trust, then the income of such part of the trust for such taxable year shall be included in computing the net income of the grantor." . . . There can be no doubt either that the statute purports to tax the plaintiff in this case. But the net income for 1924 was paid over to the petitioner's wife and the petitioner's argument is that however it might have been in different circumstances the income never was his and he cannot be taxed for it. The legal estate was in the trustee and the equitable interest in the wife.

But taxation is not so much concerned with the refinements of title as it is with actual command over the property taxed—the actual benefit for which the tax is paid. If a man directed his bank to pay over income as received to a servant or friend, until further orders, no one would doubt that he could be taxed upon the amounts so paid. It is answered that in that case he would have a title, whereas here he did not. But from the point of view of taxation there would be no difference. The title would merely mean a right to stop the payment before it took place. The same right existed here although it is not called a title but is called a power. The acquisition by the wife of the income became complete only when the plaintiff failed to exercise the power that he reserved. . . . Still speaking with reference to taxation, if a man disposes of a fund in such a way that another is allowed to enjoy the income which it is in the power of the first to appropriate it does not matter whether the permission is given by assent or by failure to express dissent. The income that is subject to a man's unfettered command and that he is free to enjoy at his own option may be taxed to him as his income, whether he sees fit to enjoy it or not. . . .

D. POE v. SEABORN
282 U.S. 101 (1930)

MR. JUSTICE ROBERTS delivered the opinion of the Court.

Seaborn and his wife, citizens and residents of the State of Washington, made for the year 1927 separate income tax returns. . . .

During and prior to 1927 they accumulated property comprising real estate, stocks, bonds and other personal property. While the real estate stood in his name alone, it is undisputed that all of the property real and personal constituted community property and that neither owned any separate property or had any separate income.

The income comprised Seaborn's salary, interest on bank deposits and on bonds, dividends, and profits on sales of real and personal property. He and his wife each returned one-half the total community income as gross income and each deducted one-half of the community expenses to arrive at the net income returned.

The Commissioner of Internal Revenue determined that all of the income should have been reported in the husband's return, and made an additional assessment against him. Seaborn paid under protest, claimed a refund, and on its rejection, brought this suit.

The District Court rendered judgment for the plaintiff . . . ; the Collector appealed, and the Circuit Court of Appeals certified to us the question whether the husband was bound to report for income tax the entire income, or whether the spouses were entitled each to return one-half thereof. This Court ordered the whole record to be sent up.

The case requires us to construe . . . the Revenue Act of 1926, and apply [it], as construed, to the interests of husband and wife in community property under the law of Washington. These sections lay a tax upon the net income of every individual. The Act goes no farther, and furnishes no other standard or definition of what constitutes an individual's income. The use of the word "of" denotes ownership. It would be a strained construction, which, in the absence of further definition by Congress, should impute a broader significance to the phrase.

The Commissioner concedes that the answer to the question involved in the cause must be found in the provisions of the law of the State, as to a wife's ownership of or interest in community property. What, then, is the law of Washington as to the ownership of community property and of community income, including the earnings of the husband's and wife's labor?

The answer is found in the statutes of the State, and the decisions interpreting them.

These statutes provide that, save for property acquired by gift, bequest, devise or inheritance, all property however acquired after marriage, by either husband or wife, or by both, is community property. On the death of either spouse his or her interest is subject to testamentary disposition, and failing that, it passes to the issue of the decedent and not to the surviving spouse. While the husband has the management and control of community personal property and like power of disposition thereof as of his separate personal property, this power is subject to restrictions which are inconsistent with denial of the wife's interest as co-owner. The wife may borrow for community purposes and bind the community property. . . . Since the husband may not discharge his separate obligation out of community property, she may, suing alone, enjoin collection of his separate debt out of community property. . . . She may prevent his making substantial gifts out of community property without her consent. . . . The community property is not liable for the husband's torts not committed in carrying on the business of the community. . . .

The books are full of expressions such as "the personal property is just as much hers as his" . . . ; "her property right in it [an automobile] is as great as his" . . . ; "the title of one spouse . . . was a legal title as well as that of the other". . . .

Without further extending this opinion it must suffice to say that it is clear the wife has, in Washington, a vested property right in the community property, equal with that of her husband; and in the income of the community, including salaries or wages of either husband or wife, or both. . . .

The taxpayer contends that if the test of taxability . . . is ownership, it is clear that income of community property is owned by the community and that husband and wife have each a present vested one-half interest therein.

The Commissioner contends, however, that we are here concerned not with mere names, nor even with mere technical legal titles; that calling the wife's interest vested is nothing to the purpose, because the husband has such broad powers of control and alienation, that while the community lasts, he is essentially the owner of the whole community property, and ought so to be considered. . . . He points out that as to personal property the husband may convey it, may make contracts affecting it, may do anything with it short of committing a fraud on his wife's rights. And though the wife must join in any sale of real estate, he asserts that the same is true, by virtue of statutes, in most States which do not have the community system. He asserts that control without accountability is indistinguishable from ownership, and that since the husband has this, *quoad* community property and income, the income is that "of" the husband under . . . the income tax law.

We think, in view of the law of Washington above stated, this contention is unsound. The community must act through an agent. This Court has said with respect to the community property system . . . that "property acquired during marriage with community funds became an acquêt of the community and not the sole property of the one in whose name the property was bought, although by the law existing at the time the husband was given the management, control and power of sale of such property. This right being vested in him, not because he was the exclusive owner, but because by law he was created the agent of the community."

In that case, it was held that such agency of the husband was neither a contract nor a property right vested in him, and that it was competent to the legislature which created the relation to alter it, to confer the agency on the wife alone, or to confer a joint agency on both spouses, if it saw fit,—all without infringing any property right of the husband. . . .

The reasons for conferring such sweeping powers of management on the husband are not far to seek. Public policy demands that in all ordinary circumstances, litigation between wife and husband during the life of the community should be discouraged. Law-suits between them would tend to subvert the marital relation. The same policy dictates that third parties who deal with the husband respecting community property shall be assured that the wife shall not be permitted to nullify his transactions. The powers of partners, or of trustees of a spendthrift trust, furnish apt analogies.

The obligations of the husband as agent of the community are no less real because the policy of the State limits the wife's right to call him to account in a court. Power is not synonymous with right. Nor is obligation coterminous with legal remedy. The law's investiture of the husband with broad powers, by no means negatives the wife's present interest as a co-owner.

We are of opinion that under the law of Washington the entire property and income of the community can no more be said to be that of the husband, than it could rightly be termed that of the wife.

We should be content to rest our decision on these considerations. Both parties have, however, relied on executive construction and the history of the income tax legislation as supporting their respective views. We shall, therefore, deal with these matters.

The taxpayer points out that, following certain opinions of the Attorney General, the Decisions and Regulations of the Treasury have uniformly made the distinction that while under California law the wife's interest in community property amounts to a mere expectancy contingent on her husband's death and does not rise to the level of a present interest, her interest under the laws of Washington, Arizona, Texas and some other states is a present vested one. They have accordingly denied husband and wife the privilege of making separate returns of one-half the community income in California, but accorded that privilege to residents of such other states. . . .

The *Corliss* case raised no issue as to the intent of Congress, but as to its power. We held that where a donor retains the power at any time to revest himself with the principal of the gift, Congress may declare that he still owns the income. While he has technically parted with title, yet he in fact retains ownership, and all its incidents. But here the husband never has ownership. That is in the community at the moment of acquisition.

In the *Earl* case a husband and wife contracted that any property they had or might thereafter acquire in any way, either by earnings (including salaries, fees, etc.), or any rights by contract or otherwise, "shall be treated and considered and hereby is declared to be received held taken and owned by us as joint tenants . . . " We held that, assuming the validity of the contract under local law, it still remained true that the husband's professional fees, earned in years subsequent to the date of the contract, were his individual income, "derived from salaries, wages, or compensation for personal services" under . . . the Revenue Act of 1918. The very assignment in that case was bottomed on the fact that the earnings would be the husband's property, else there would have been nothing on which it could operate. That case presents quite a different question from this, because here, by law, the earnings are never the property of the husband, but that of the community.

Finally the argument is pressed upon us that the Commissioner's ruling will work uniformity of incidence and operation of the tax in the various states, while the view urged by the taxpayer will make the tax fall unevenly upon married people. This argument cuts both ways. When it is remembered that a wife's earnings are a part of the community property equally with her husband's, it may well seem to those who live in states where a wife's earnings are her own, that it would not tend to promote uniformity to tax the husband on her earnings as part of his income. The answer to such argument, however, is, that the constitutional requirement of uniformity is not intrinsic, but geographic. . . . And differences of state law, which may bring a person within or without the category designated by Congress as taxable, may not be read into the Revenue Act to spell out a lack of uniformity. . . .

The District Court was right in holding that the husband and wife were entitled to file separate returns, each treating one-half of the community income as his or her respective income, and its judgement is

Affirmed. . . .

E. BLAIR v. COMMISSIONER
300 U.S. 5 (1937)

Mr. Chief Justice Hughes delivered the opinion of the Court.

This case presents the question of the liability of a beneficiary of a testamentary trust for a tax upon the income which he had assigned to his children prior to the tax years and which the trustees had paid to them accordingly.

The trust was created by the will of William Blair, a resident of Illinois who died in 1899, and was of property located in that State. One-half of the net income was to be paid to the donor's widow during her life. His son, the petitioner Edward Tyler Blair, was to receive the other one-half and, after the death of the widow, the whole of the net income during his life. In 1923, after the widow's death, petitioner assigned to his daughter, Lucy Blair Linn, an interest amounting to $6000 for the remainder of that calendar year, and to $9000 in each calendar year thereafter, in the net income which the petitioner was then or might thereafter be entitled to receive during his life. At about the same time, he made like assignments of interests, amounting to $9000 in each calendar year, in the net income of the trust to his daughter Edith Blair and to his son, Edward Seymour Blair, respectively. In later years, by similar instruments, he assigned to these children additional interests, and to his son William McCormick Blair other specified interests, in the net income. The trustees accepted the assignments and distributed the income directly to the assignees.

The question first arose with respect to the tax year 1923 and the Commissioner of Internal Revenue ruled that the income was taxable to the petitioner. The Board of Tax Appeals held the contrary.... The Circuit Court of Appeals reversed the Board, holding that under the law of Illinois the trust was a spendthrift trust and the assignments were invalid.... We denied certiorari....

Thereupon the trustees brought suit in the Superior Court of Cook County, Illinois, to obtain a construction of the will with respect to the power of the beneficiary of the trust to assign a part of his equitable interest and to determine the validity of the assignments he had made. The petitioner and the assignees were made defendants. The Appellate Court of Illinois, First District, after a review of the Illinois decisions, decided that the trust was not a spendthrift trust and upheld the assignments.... Under the mandate of the appellate court, the Superior Court of Cook County entered its decree which found the assignments to be "voluntary assignments of a part of the interest of said Edward Tyler Blair in said trust estate" and as such adjudged them to be valid.

At that time there were pending before the Board of Tax Appeals proceedings involving the income of the trust for the years 1924, 1925, 1926 and 1929. The Board received in evidence the record in the suit in the state court and, applying the decision of that court, the Board overruled the Commissioner's determination as to the petitioner's liability.... The Circuit Court of Appeals again reversed the Board. That court recognized the binding effect of the decision of the state court as to the validity of the assignments but decided that the income was still taxable to the petitioner upon the ground that his interest was not attached to the corpus of the estate and that the income was not subject to his disposition until he received it. . . .

First. The Government contends that the judgment relating to the income for 1923 is conclusive in this proceeding as *res judicata.* . . . Petitioner insists that this question was not raised before the Board of Tax Appeals and hence was not available before the Circuit Court of Appeals. . . .

Here, after the decision in the first proceeding, the opinion and decree of the state court created a new situation. The determination of petitioner's liability for the year 1923 had been rested entirely upon the local law. . . . The supervening decision of the state court interpreting that law in direct relation to this trust cannot justly be ignored in the present proceeding so far as it is found that the local law is determinative of any material point in controversy. . . .

Second. The question of the validity of the assignments is a question of local law. The donor was a resident of Illinois and his disposition of the property in that State was subject to its law. By that law the character of the trust, the nature and extent of the interest of the beneficiary, and the power of the beneficiary to assign that interest in whole or in part, are to be determined. The decision of the state court upon these questions is final. . . . It matters not that the decision was by an intermediate appellate court. . . . In this instance, it is not necessary to go beyond the obvious point that the decision was in a suit between the trustees and the beneficiary and his assignees, and the decree which was entered in pursuance of the decision determined as between these parties the validity of the particular assignments. Nor is there any basis for a charge that the suit was collusive and the decree inoperative. . . . The trustees were entitled to seek the instructions of the court having supervision of the trust. That court entertained the suit and the appellate court, with the first decision of the Circuit Court of Appeals before it, reviewed the decisions of the Supreme Court of the State and reached a deliberate conclusion. To derogate from the authority of that conclusion and of the decree it commanded, so far as the question is one of state law, would be wholly unwarranted in the exercise of federal jurisdiction.

In the face of this ruling of the state court it is not open to the Government to argue that the trust "was, under the Illinois law, a spendthrift trust." The point of the argument is that, the trust being of that character, the state law barred the voluntary alienation by the beneficiary of his interest. The state court held precisely the contrary. The ruling also determines the validity of the assignment by the beneficiary of parts of his interest. That question was necessarily presented and expressly decided.

Third. The question remains whether, treating the assignments as valid, the assignor was still taxable upon the income under the federal income tax act. That is a federal question.

Our decisions in *Lucas* v. *Earl* . . . and *Burnet* v. *Leininger* . . . are cited. In the *Lucas* case the question was whether an attorney was taxable for the whole of his salary and fees earned by him in the tax years or only upon one-half by reason of an agreement with his wife by which his earnings were to be received and owned by them jointly. We were of the opinion that the case turned upon the construction of the taxing act. We said that "the statute could tax salaries to those who earned them and provide that the tax could not be escaped by anticipatory arrangements and contracts however skilfully devised to prevent the same when paid from vesting even for a second in the man who earned it." That was deemed to be the meaning of the statute as to compensation for personal service, and the one who earned the income was held to be subject to the tax. In *Burnet v. Leininger* ... a husband, a member of a firm, assigned future partnership income to his wife. We found that the revenue act dealt explicitly with the liability of partners as such. The wife did not become a member of the firm; the act specifically taxed the distributive share of each partner in the net income of the firm; and the husband by the fair import of the act remained taxable upon his distributive share. These cases are not in point. The tax here is not upon earnings which are taxed to the one who earns them. . . .

In the instant case, the tax is upon income as to which, in the general application of the revenue acts, the tax liability attaches to ownership. . . .

The Government points to the provisions of the revenue acts imposing upon the beneficiary of a trust the liability for the tax upon the income distributable to the beneficiary. But the term is merely descriptive of the one entitled to the beneficial interest. These provisions cannot be taken to preclude valid assignments of the beneficial interest, or to affect the duty of the trustee to distribute income to the owner of the beneficial interest, whether he was such initially or becomes such by valid assignment. The one who is to receive the income as the owner of the beneficial interest is to pay the tax. If under the law governing the trust the beneficial interest is assignable, and if it has been assigned without reservation, the assignee thus becomes the beneficiary and is entitled to rights and remedies accordingly. We find nothing in the revenue acts which denies him that status.

The decision of the Circuit Court of Appeals turned upon the effect to be ascribed to the assignments. The court held that the petitioner had no interest in the corpus of the estate and could not dispose of the income until he received it. Hence it was said that "the income was *his*" and his assignment was merely a direction to pay over to others what was due to himself. The question was considered to involve "the date when the income became transferable". . . . The Government refers to the terms of the assignment,—that it was of the interest in the income "which the said party of the first part now is, or may hereafter be, entitled to receive during his life from the trustees." From this it is urged that the assignments "dealt only with a right to receive the income" and that "no attempt was made to assign any equitable right, title or interest in the trust itself." This construction seems to us to be a strained one. We think it apparent that the conveyancer was not seeking to limit the assignment so as to make it anything less than a complete transfer of the specified interest of the petitioner as the life beneficiary of the trust, but that with ample caution he was using words to effect such a transfer. That the state court so construed the assignments appears from the final decree which described them as voluntary assignments of interests of the petitioner "in said trust estate," and it was in that aspect that petitioner's right to make the assignments was sustained.

The will creating the trust entitled the petitioner during his life to the net income of the property held in trust. He thus became the owner of an equitable interest in the corpus of the property.... By virtue of that interest he was entitled to enforce the trust, to have a breach of trust enjoined and to obtain redress in case of breach. The interest was present property alienable like any other, in the absence of a valid restraint upon alienation.... The beneficiary may thus transfer a part of his interest as well as the whole....

We conclude that the assignments were valid, that the assignees thereby became the owners of the specified beneficial interests in the income, and that as to these interests they and not the petitioner were taxable for the tax years in question....

F. HELVERING v. CLIFFORD
309 U.S. 331 (1940)

MR. JUSTICE DOUGLAS delivered the opinion of the Court.

In 1934 respondent declared himself trustee of certain securities which he owned. All net income from the trust was to be held for the "exclusive benefit" of respondent's wife. The trust was for a term of five years, except that it would terminate earlier on the death of either respondent or his wife. On termination of the trust the entire corpus was to go to respondent, while all "accrued or undistributed net income" and "any proceeds from the investment of such net income" was to be treated as property owned absolutely by the wife. During the continuance of the trust respondent was to pay over to his wife the whole or such part of the net income as he in his "absolute discretion" might determine. And during that period he had full power (a) to exercise all voting powers incident to the trusteed shares of stock; (b) to "sell, exchange, mortgage, or pledge" any of the securities under the declaration of trust "whether as part of the corpus or principal thereof or as investments or proceeds and any income therefrom, upon such terms and for such consideration" as respondent in his "absolute discretion may deem fitting"; (c) to invest "any cash or money in the trust estate or any income therefrom" by loans secured or unsecured, by deposits in banks, or by purchase of securities or other personal property "without restriction" because of their "speculative character" or "rate of return" or any "laws pertaining to the investment of trust funds"; (d) to collect all income; (e) to compromise, etc., any claims held by him as trustee; (f) to hold any property in the trust estate in the names of "other persons or in my own name as an individual" except as otherwise provided. Extraordinary cash dividends, stock dividends, proceeds from the sale of unexercised subscription rights, or any enhancement, realized or not, in the value of the securities were to be treated as principal, not income. An exculpatory clause purported to protect him from all losses except those occasioned by his "own wilful and deliberate" breach of duties as trustee. And finally it was provided that neither the principal nor any future or accrued income should be liable for the debts of the wife; and that the wife could not transfer, encumber, or anticipate any interest in the trust or any income therefrom prior to actual payment thereof to her.

It was stipulated that while the "tax effects" of this trust were considered by respondent they were not the "sole consideration" involved in his decision to set it up, as by this and other gifts he intended to give "security and economic independence" to his wife and children. It was also stipulated that respondent's wife had substantial income of her own from other sources; that there was no restriction on her use of the trust income, all of which income was placed in her personal checking account, intermingled with her other funds, and expended by her on herself, her children and relatives; that the trust was not designed to relieve respondent from liability for family or household expenses and that after execution of the trust he paid large sums from his personal funds for such purposes.

Respondent paid a federal gift tax on this transfer. During the year 1934 all income from the trust was distributed to the wife who included it in her individual return for that year. The Commissioner, however, determined a deficiency in respondent's return for that year on the theory that income from the trust was taxable to him. The Board of Tax Appeals sustained that redetermination.... The Circuit Court of Appeals reversed.... We granted certiorari because of the importance to the revenue of the use of such short term trusts in the reduction of surtaxes.

Sec. 22(a) of the Revenue Act of 1934 . . . includes among "gross income" all "gains, profits, and income derived . . . from professions, vocations, trades, businesses, commerce, or sales, or dealings in property, whether real or personal, growing out of the ownership or use of or interest in such property; also from interest, rent, dividends, securities, or the transaction of any business carried on for gain or profit, or gains or profits and income derived from any source whatever." The broad sweep of this language indicates the purpose of Congress to use the full measure of its taxing power within those definable categories. . . . Hence our construction of the statute should be consonant with that purpose. Technical considerations, niceties of the law of trusts or conveyances, or the legal paraphernalia which inventive genius may construct as a refuge from surtaxes should not obscure the basic issue. That issue is whether the grantor after the trust has been established may still be treated, under this statutory scheme, as the owner of the corpus. See *Blair v. Commissioner.* . . . In absence of more precise standards or guides supplied by statute or appropriate regulations, the answer to that question must depend on an analysis of the terms of the trust and all the circumstances attendant on its creation and operation. And where the grantor is the trustee and the beneficiaries are members of his family group, special scrutiny of the arrangement is necessary lest what is in reality but one economic unit be multiplied into two or more by devices which, though valid under state law, are not conclusive so far as § 22(a) is concerned.

In this case we cannot conclude as a matter of law that respondent ceased to be the owner of the corpus after the trust was created. Rather, the short duration of the trust, the fact that the wife was the beneficiary, and the retention of control over the corpus by respondent all lead irresistibly to the conclusion that respondent continued to be the owner for purposes of § 22(a).

So far as his dominion and control were concerned it seems clear that the trust did not effect any substantial change. In substance his control over the corpus was in all essential respects the same after the trust was created, as before. The wide powers which he retained included for all practical purposes most of the control which he as an individual would have. There were, we may assume, exceptions, such as his disability to make a gift of the corpus to others during the term of the trust and to make loans to himself. But this dilution in his control would seem to be insignificant and immaterial, since control over investment remained. If it be said that such control is the type of dominion exercised by any trustee, the answer is simple. We have at best a temporary reallocation of income within an intimate family group. Since the income remains in the family and since the husband retains control over the investment, he has rather complete assurance that the trust will not effect any substantial change in his economic position. It is hard to imagine that respondent felt himself the poorer after this trust had been executed or, if he did, that it had any rational foundation in fact. For as a result of the terms of the trust and the intimacy of the familial relationship respondent retained the substance of full enjoyment of all the rights which previously he had in the property. That might not be true if only strictly legal rights were considered. But when the benefits flowing to him indirectly through the wife are added to the legal rights he retained, the aggregate may be said to be a fair equivalent of what he previously had. To exclude from the aggregate those indirect benefits would be to deprive § 22(a) of considerable vitality and to treat as immaterial what may be highly relevant considerations in the creation of such family trusts. For where the head of the household has income in excess of normal needs, it may well make but little difference to him (except income-tax-wise) where portions of that income are routed—so long as it stays in the family group. In those circumstances the all-important factor might be retention by him of control over the principal. With that control in his hands he would keep direct command over all that he needed to remain in substantially the same financial situation as before. Our point here is that no one fact is normally decisive but that all considerations and circumstances of the kind we have mentioned are relevant to the question of ownership and are appropriate foundations for findings on that issue. Thus, where, as in this case, the benefits directly or indirectly retained blend so imperceptibly with the normal concepts of full ownership, we cannot say that the triers of fact committed reversible error when they found that the husband was the owner of the corpus for the purposes of § 22(a). To hold otherwise would be to treat the wife as a complete stranger; to let mere formalism obscure the normal consequences of family solidarity; and to force concepts of ownership to be fashioned out of legal niceties which may have little or no significance in such household arrangements....

We should add that liability under § 22(a) is not foreclosed by reason of the fact that Congress made specific provision in § 166 for revocable trusts, but failed to adopt the Treasury recommendation in 1934 . . . that similar specific treatment should be accorded income from short term trusts. Such choice, while relevant to the scope of § 166 . . . cannot be said to have subtracted from § 22(a) what was already there. Rather, on this evidence it must be assumed that the choice was between a generalized treatment under § 22(a) or specific treatment under a separate provision (such as was accorded revocable trusts under § 166); not between taxing or not taxing grantors of short term trusts. In view of the broad and sweeping language of § 22(a), a specific provision covering short term trusts might well do no more than to carve out of § 22(a) a defined group of cases to which a rule of thumb would be applied. The failure of Congress to adopt any such rule of thumb for that type of trust must be taken to do no more than to leave to the triers of fact the initial determination of whether or not on the facts of each case the grantor remains the owner for purposes of § 22(a).

In view of this result we need not examine the contention that the trust device falls within the rule of *Lucas* v. *Earl* . . . and *Burnet* v. *Leininger* . . . relating to the assignment of future income; or that respondent is liable under § 166, taxing grantors on the income of revocable trusts.

MR. JUSTICE ROBERTS, dissenting:

I think the judgment should be affirmed.

The decision of the court disregards the fundamental principle that legislation is not the function of the judiciary but of Congress.

In every revenue act from that of 1916 to the one now in force a distinction has been made between income of individuals and income from property held in trust. It has been the practice to define income of individuals, and, in separate sections, under the heading "Estates and Trusts," to provide that the tax imposed upon individuals shall apply to the income of estates or of any kind of property held in trust. A trust is a separate taxable entity. The trust here in question is a true trust.

While the earlier acts were in force creators of trusts reserved power to repossess the trust corpus. It became common also to establish trusts under which, at the grantor's discretion, all or part of the income might be paid to him, and to set up trusts to pay life insurance premiums upon policies on the grantor's life. The situation was analogous to that now presented. The Treasury, instead of asking this court, under the guise of construction, to amend the act, went to Congress for new legislation. Congress provided . . . that if the grantor set up such a life insurance trust, or one under which he could direct the payment of the trust income to himself, or had the power to revest the principal in himself *during any taxable year,* the income of the trust, for the taxable year, was to be treated as his.

After the adoption of these amendments taxpayers resorted to the creation of revocable trusts with a provision that more than a year's notice of revocation should be necessary to termination. Such a trust was held not to be within the terms . . . of the Revenue Act of 1924, because not revocable within the taxable year.

Again, without seeking amendment in the guise of construction from this court, the Treasury applied to Congress, which met the situation by adopting § 166 of the Revenue Act of 1934, which provided that, in the case of a trust under which the grantor reserved the power *at any time* to revest the corpus in himself, the income of the trust should be considered that of the grantor.

The Treasury had asked that there should also be included in that act a provision taxing to the grantor income from short term trusts. After the House Ways and Means Committee had rendered a report on the proposed bill, the Treasury, upon examination of the report, submitted a statement to the Committee containing recommendations for additional provisions; amongst others, the following: "(6) The income from short-term trusts and trusts which are revocable by the creator at the expiration of a short period after notice by him should be made taxable to the creator of the trust." Congress adopted an amendment to cover the one situation but did not accept the Treasury's recommendation as to the other. The statute, as before, clearly provided that the income from a short term irrevocable trust was taxable to the trust, or the beneficiary, and not to the grantor.

The regulations under § 166 of the Act of 1932 contained no suggestion that term trusts were taxable to the creator. . . . Thus though the Treasury realized that irrevocable short term trusts did not fall within the scope of § 166, instead of going to Congress for amendment of the law it comes here with a plea for interpretation which is in effect such amendment.

Its claim, in support of this effort, that a reversionary interest in the grantor is a "power to revest" the corpus within the meaning of § 166 so as to render the income taxable to the grantor is plainly untenable. That theory was first advanced in a regulation issued under the 1934 act, but was abandoned March 7, 1936, when the regulation was revised to read substantially in its present form. . . .

I think it clear that the administrative interpretation has not been consistent and that reënactment of § 166 is, therefore, not a ratification by Congress of the present construction.

The revised regulations indicating that in some circumstances the separate taxability of the trust may be ignored are said to rest on § 166, and also on § 22(a) which defines income. The regulation is not only without support in the statute but contrary to the entire statutory scheme and, as it now stands, is vague and meaningless, as respects the taxability to the grantor of income from an irrevocable term trust.

To construe either § 166 or § 22(a) of the statute as justifying taxation of the income to respondent in this case is, in my judgment, to write into the statute what is not there and what Congress has omitted to place there.

If judges were members of the legislature they might well vote to amend the act so as to tax such income in order to frustrate avoidance of tax but, as judges, they exercise a very different function. They ought to read the act to cover nothing more than Congress has specified. Courts ought not to stop loopholes in an act at the behest of the Government, nor relieve from what they deem a harsh provision plainly stated, at the behest of the taxpayer. Relief in either case should be sought in another quarter.

No such dictum as that Congress has in the income tax law attempted to exercise its power to the fullest extent will justify the extension of a plain provision to an object of taxation not embraced within it. If the contrary were true, the courts might supply whatever they considered a deficiency in the sweep of a taxing act. I cannot construe the court's opinion as attempting less. . . .

. . . As far back as 1922, Parliament amended the British Income Tax Act, so that there would be no dispute as to what short term trust income should be taxable to the grantor, by making taxable to him any income which, by virtue of any disposition, is payable to, or applicable for the benefit of, any other person for a period which cannot exceed six years.

If some short term trusts are to be treated as nonexistent for income tax purposes, it is for Congress to specify them. . . .

G. HELVERING v. HORST
311 U.S. 112 (1940)

MR. JUSTICE STONE delivered the opinion of the Court.

The sole question for decision is whether the gift, during the donor's taxable year, of interest coupons detached from the bonds, delivered to the donee and later in the year paid at maturity, is the realization of income taxable to the donor.

In 1934 and 1935 respondent, the owner of negotiable bonds, detached from them negotiable interest coupons shortly before their due date and delivered them as a gift to his son who in the same year collected them at maturity. The Commissioner ruled that . . . the interest payments were taxable, in the years when paid, to the respondent donor. . . . The Circuit Court of Appeals reversed the order of the Board of Tax Appeals sustaining the tax. . . .

The Court below thought that as the consideration for the coupons had passed to the obligor, the donor had, by the gift, parted with all control over them and their payment, and for that reason the case was distinguishable from *Lucas v. Earl* . . . where the assignment of compensation for services had preceded the rendition of the services, and where the income was held taxable to the donor.

The holder of a coupon bond is the owner of two independent and separable kinds of right. One is the right to demand and receive at maturity the principal amount of the bond representing capital investment. The other is the right to demand and receive interim payments of interest on the investment in the amounts and on the dates specified by the coupons. Together they are an obligation to pay principal and interest given in exchange for money or property which was presumably the consideration for the obligation of the bond. Here respondent, as owner of the bonds, had acquired the legal right to demand payment at maturity of the interest specified by the coupons and the power to command its payment to others, which constituted an economic gain to him.

Admittedly not all economic gain of the taxpayer is taxable income. From the beginning the revenue laws have been interpreted as defining "realization" of income as the taxable event, rather than the acquisition of the right to receive it. . . . Where the taxpayer does not receive payment of income in money or property realization may occur when the last step is taken by which he obtains the fruition of the economic gain which has already accrued to him....

... [T]he rule that income is not taxable until realized has never been taken to mean that the taxpayer ... who has fully enjoyed the benefit of the economic gain represented by his right to receive income, can escape taxation because he has not himself received payment of it.... The rule, founded on administrative convenience, is only one of postponement of the tax to the final event of enjoyment of the income, usually the receipt of it by the taxpayer, and not one of exemption from taxation where the enjoyment is consummated by some event other than the taxpayer's personal receipt of money or property.... This may occur when he has made such use or disposition of his power to receive or control the income as to procure in its place other satisfactions which are of economic worth. The question here is, whether because one who in fact receives payment for services or interest payments is taxable only on his receipt of the payments, he can escape all tax by giving away his right to income in advance of payment. If the taxpayer procures payment directly to his creditors of the items of interest or earnings due him ... he does not escape taxation because he did not actually receive the money....

Underlying [this] reasoning is the thought that income is "realized" by the assignor because he, who owns or controls the source of the income, also controls the disposition of that which he could have received himself and diverts the payment from himself to others as the means of procuring the satisfaction of his wants. The taxpayer has equally enjoyed the fruits of his labor or investment and obtained the satisfaction of his desires whether he collects and uses the income to procure those satisfactions, or whether he disposes of his right to collect it as the means of procuring them....

Although the donor here, by the transfer of the coupons, has precluded any possibility of his collecting them himself, he has nevertheless, by his act, procured payment of the interest as a valuable gift to a member of his family. Such a use of his economic gain, the right to receive income, to procure a satisfaction which can be obtained only by the expenditure of money or property, would seem to be the enjoyment of the income whether the satisfaction is the purchase of goods at the corner grocery, the payment of his debt there, or such nonmaterial satisfactions as may result from the payment of a campaign or community chest contribution, or a gift to his favorite son. Even though he never receives the money, he derives money's worth from the disposition of the coupons which he has used as money or money's worth in the procuring of a satisfaction which is procurable only by the expenditure of money or money's worth. The enjoyment of the economic benefit accruing to him by virtue of his acquisition of the coupons is realized as completely as it would have been if he had collected the interest in dollars and expended them for any of the purposes named....

In a real sense he has enjoyed compensation for money loaned or services rendered, and not any the less so because it is his only reward for them. To say that one who has made a gift thus derived from interest or earnings paid to his donee has never enjoyed or realized the fruits of his investment or labor, because he has assigned them instead of collecting them himself and then paying them over to the donee, is to affront common understanding and to deny the facts of common experience. Common understanding and experience are the touchstones for the interpretation of the revenue laws.

The power to dispose of income is the equivalent of ownership of it. The exercise of that power to procure the payment of income to another is the enjoyment, and hence the realization, of the income by him who exercises it. We have had no difficulty in applying that proposition where the assignment preceded the rendition of the services, *Lucas v. Earl,* supra; *Burnet v. Leininger,* supra, for it was recognized in the *Leininger* case that in such a case the rendition of the service by the assignor was the means by which the income was controlled by the donor and of making his assignment effective. But it is the assignment by which the disposition of income is controlled when the service precedes the assignment, and in both cases it is the exercise of the power of disposition of the interest or compensation, with the resulting payment to the donee, which is the enjoyment by the donor of income derived from them.

This was emphasized in *Blair v. Commissioner* . . . on which respondent relies, where the distinction was taken between a gift of income derived from an obligation to pay compensation and a gift of income-producing property. In the circumstances of that case, the right to income from the trust property was thought to be so identified with the equitable ownership of the property, from which alone the beneficiary derived his right to receive the income and his power to command disposition of it, that a gift of the income by the beneficiary became effective only as a gift of his ownership of the property producing it. Since the gift was deemed to be a gift of the property, the income from it was held to be the income of the owner of the property, who was the donee, not the donor—a refinement which was unnecessary if respondent's contention here is right, but one clearly inapplicable to gifts of interest or wages. Unlike income thus derived from an obligation to pay interest or compensation, the income of the trust was regarded as no more the income of the donor than would be the rent from a lease or a crop raised on a farm after the leasehold or the farm had been given away. *Blair v. Commissioner.* . . . We have held without deviation that where the donor retains control of the trust property the income is taxable to him although paid to the donee. *Corliss v. Bowers,* supra. Cf. *Helvering v. Clifford,* supra.

The dominant purpose of the revenue laws is the taxation of income to those who earn or otherwise create the right to receive it and enjoy the benefit of it when paid. See, *Corliss v. Bowers.* . . . The tax laid by the 1934 Revenue Act upon income "derived from . . . wages, or compensation for personal service, of whatever kind and in whatever form paid, . . .; also from interest . . . " therefore cannot fairly be interpreted as not applying to income derived from interest or compensation when he who is entitled to receive it makes use of his power to dispose of it in procuring satisfactions which he would otherwise procure only by the use of the money when received.

It is the statute which taxes the income to the donor although paid to his donee. *Lucas v. Earl,* supra; *Burnet v. Leininger,* supra. True, in those cases the service which created the right to income followed the assignment, and it was arguable that in point of legal theory the right to the compensation vested instantaneously in the assignor when paid, although he never received it; while here the right of the assignor to receive the income antedated the assignment which transferred the right and thus precluded such an instantaneous vesting. But the statute affords no basis for such "attenuated subtleties." The distinction was explicitly rejected as the basis of decision in *Lucas v. Earl*. It should be rejected here; for no more than in the *Earl* case can the purpose of the statute to tax the income to him who earns, or creates and enjoys it be escaped by "anticipatory arrangements however skilfully devised" to prevent the income from vesting even for a second in the donor.

Nor is it perceived that there is any adequate basis for distinguishing between the gift of interest coupons here and a gift of salary or commissions. The owner of a negotiable bond and of the investment which it represents, if not the lender, stands in the place of the lender. When by the gift of the coupons, he has separated his right to interest payments from his investment and procured the payment of the interest to his donee, he has enjoyed the economic benefits of the income in the same manner and to the same extent as though the transfer were of earnings, and in both cases the import of the statute is that the fruit is not to be attributed to a different tree from that on which it grew. See *Lucas v. Earl*, supra. . . .

Reversed.

The separate opinion of Mr. Justice McReynolds.

The facts were stipulated. In the opinion of the court below the issues are thus adequately stated—

> The [taxpayer] owned a number of coupon bonds. The coupons represented the interest on bonds and were payable to bearer. In 1934 he detached unmatured coupons of face value of $25,182.50 and transferred them by manual delivery to his son as a gift. The coupons matured later on in the same year, and the son collected the face amount, $25,182.50, as his own property. There was a similar transaction in 1935. . . . [The taxpayer] did not include any part of the moneys collected on the coupons in his income tax returns for these two years. The son included them in his returns. The Commissioner added the moneys collected on the coupons to the petitioner's taxable income and determined a tax deficiency for each year. The Board of Tax Appeals, three members dissenting, sustained the Commissioner, holding that the amounts collected on the coupons were taxable as income to the petitioner.

The decision of the Board of Tax Appeals was reversed and properly so, I think.

The unmatured coupons given to the son were independent negotiable instruments, complete in themselves. Through the gift they became at once the absolute property of the donee, free from the donor's control and in no way dependent upon ownership of the bonds. No question of actual fraud or purpose to defraud the revenue is presented.

Neither *Lucas v. Earl* . . . nor *Burnet v. Leininger* . . . support [the Commissioner's] view. *Blair v. Commissioner* . . . shows that neither involved an unrestricted completed transfer of property.

Helvering v. Clifford . . . decided after the opinion below, is much relied upon by [the Commissioner] but involved facts very different from those now before us. There no separate thing was absolutely transferred and put beyond possible control by the transferror. The Court affirmed that Clifford, both conveyor and trustee, "retained the substance of full enjoyment of all the rights which previously he had in the property." "In substance his control over the corpus was in all essential respects the same after the trust was created, as before." "With that control in his hands he would keep direct command over all that he needed to remain in substantially the same financial situation as before."

The general principles approved in *Blair v. Commissioner* . . . are applicable and controlling. The challenged judgment should be affirmed. . . .

H. HARRISON v. SCHAFFNER
312 U.S. 579 (1941)

MR. JUSTICE STONE delivered the opinion of the Court.

In December, 1929, respondent, the life beneficiary of a testamentary trust, "assigned" to certain of her children specified amounts in dollars from the income of the trust for the year following the assignment. She made a like assignment to her children and a son-in-law in November, 1930. The question for decision is whether, under the applicable 1928 Revenue Act . . . the assigned income, which was paid by the trustees to the several assignees, is taxable as such to the assignor or to the assignees.

The Commissioner ruled that the income was that of the life beneficiary and assessed a deficiency against her for the calendar years 1930 and 1931, which she paid. In the present suit to recover the tax paid as illegally exacted the district court below gave judgment for the taxpayer, which the Court of Appeals affirmed. . . . We granted certiorari . . . to resolve an alleged conflict in principle of the decision below with those in *Lucas v. Earl* . . . , *Burnet v. Leininger* . . . and *Helvering v. Clifford*. . . .

Since granting certiorari we have held, following the reasoning of *Lucas v. Earl*, supra, that one who is entitled to receive, at a future date, interest or compensation for services and who makes a gift of it by an anticipatory assignment, realizes taxable income quite as much as if he had collected the income and paid it over to the object of his bounty. . . . Decision in these cases was rested on the principle that the power to dispose of income is the equivalent of ownership of it and that the exercise of the power to procure its payment to another, whether to pay a debt or to make a gift, is within the reach of the statute taxing income "derived from any source whatever." In the light of our opinions in these cases the narrow question presented by this record is whether it makes any difference in the application of the taxing statute that the gift is accomplished by the anticipatory assignment of trust income rather than of interest, dividends, rents and the like which are payable to the donor.

Respondent, recognizing that the practical consequences of a gift by assignment, in advance, of a year's income from the trust, are, so far as the use and enjoyment of the income are concerned, no different from those of the gift by assignment of interest or wages, rests his case on technical distinctions affecting the conveyancing of equitable interests. It is said that since by the assignment of trust income the assignee acquires an equitable right to an accounting by the trustee which, for many purposes, is treated by courts of equity as a present equitable estate in the trust property, it follows that each assignee in the present case is a donee of an interest in the trust property for the term of a year and is thus the recipient of income from his own property which is taxable to him rather than to the donor. See *Blair* v. *Commissioner*. . . .

Section 22 (a) of the 1928 Revenue Act provides, " 'Gross income' includes gains, profits, and income derived from . . . interest, rent, dividends, securities or the transactions of any business carried on for gain or profit, or gains or profits, and income derived from any source whatever." By §§ 161(a) and 162(b) the tax is laid upon the income "of any kind of property held in trust," and income of a trust for the taxable year which is to be distributed to the beneficiaries is to be taxed to them "whether distributed to them or not." In construing these and like provisions in other revenue acts we have uniformly held that they are not so much concerned with the refinements of title as with the actual command over the income which is taxed and the actual benefit for which the tax is paid. See *Corliss* v. *Bowers* . . . *Lucas* v. *Earl,* supra; *Helvering* v. *Horst,* supra; . . . *Helvering* v. *Clifford,* supra. It was for that reason that in each of those cases it was held that one vested with the right to receive income did not escape the tax by any kind of anticipatory arrangement, however skillfully devised, by which he procures payment of it to another, since, by the exercise of his power to command the income, he enjoys the benefit of the income on which the tax is laid.

Those decisions are controlling here. Taxation is a practical matter and those practical considerations which support the treatment of the disposition of one's income by way of gift as a realization of the income to the donor are the same whether the income be from a trust or from shares of stock or bonds which he owns. It is true, as respondent argues, that where the beneficiary of a trust had assigned a share of the income to another for life without retaining any form of control over the interest assigned, this Court construed the assignment as a transfer *in praesenti* to the donee, of a life interest in the corpus of the trust property, and held in consequence that the income thereafter paid to the donee was taxable to him and not the donor. *Blair* v. *Commissioner,* supra. But we think it quite another matter to say that the beneficiary of a trust who makes a single gift of a sum of money payable out of the income of the trust does not realize income when the gift is effectuated by payment, or that he escapes the tax by attempting to clothe the transaction in the guise of a transfer of trust property rather than the transfer of income, where that is its obvious purpose and effect.

We think that the gift by a beneficiary of a trust of some part of the income derived from the trust property for the period of a day, a month or a year involves no such substantial disposition of the trust property as to camouflage the reality that he is enjoying the benefit of the income from the trust of which he continues to be the beneficiary, quite as much as he enjoys the benefits of interest or wages which he gives away as in . . . *Horst*. . . . Even though the gift of income be in form accomplished by the temporary disposition of the donor's property which produces the income, the donor retaining every other substantial interest in it, we have not allowed the form to obscure the reality. Income which the donor gives away through the medium of a short term trust created for the benefit of the donee is nevertheless income taxable to the donor. *Helvering v. Clifford*. . . . We perceive no difference, so far as the construction and application of the Revenue Act is concerned, between a gift of income in a specified amount by the creation of a trust for a year . . . and the assignment by the beneficiary of a trust already created of a like amount from its income for a year.

Nor are we troubled by the logical difficulties of drawing the line between a gift of an equitable interest in property for life effected by a gift for life of a share of the income of the trust and the gift of the income or a part of it for the period of a year as in this case. "Drawing the line" is a recurrent difficulty in those fields of the law where differences in degree produce ultimate differences in kind. . . . It is enough that we find in the present case that the taxpayer, in point of substance, has parted with no substantial interest in property other than the specified payments of income which, like other gifts of income, are taxable to the donor. Unless in the meantime the difficulty be resolved by statute or treasury regulation, we leave it to future judicial decisions to determine precisely where the line shall be drawn between gifts of income-producing property and gifts of income from property of which the donor remains the owner, for all substantial and practical purposes. Cf. *Helvering v. Clifford*, supra.

I. NOTES AND QUESTIONS

1) The Basic Principles of Assignment of Income Law

What are the basic legal principles fashioned by the preceding seven Supreme Court decisions? May income from labor (that is, compensation for personal services) be shifted for tax purposes? See Lucas v. Earl. Ordinarily, who is taxable on income from property? See Corliss v. Bowers. How do community property laws modify these principles? See Poe v. Seaborn.

What distinguishes the gift of property in *Blair* from the gifts of property in Corliss v. Bowers and *Clifford*? Why does *Blair* involve a valid assignment of income from property, while Corliss v. Bowers and *Clifford* do not? What distinguishes the gift of property in *Blair* from the gifts of property in *Horst* and Harrison v. Schaffner? Why does *Blair* involve a valid assignment of income from property, while *Horst* and Harrison v. Schaffner do not?

2) Lucas v. Earl

Did the taxpayer have a tax avoidance purpose? When was the contractual assignment of future income effected? When was the income tax statute enacted? What do you suppose motivated the contractual arrangement?

3) Corliss v. Bowers

Technically, this is not a common law case at all but rather a case involving the constitutionality of a statute. Nevertheless, common law principles appear to be articulated in the opinion. What are those principles?

Why was this opinion cited in later cases involving sale and leaseback transactions? What is the analytic connection between, for example, the issue in Corliss v. Bowers and the issue in *Frank Lyon* (Chapter 41)? See footnote 9 in Justice Stevens' dissent in *Frank Lyon*.

4) Poe v. Seaborn

Is the reasoning of this opinion consistent with the reasoning in the two preceding opinions? In Lucas v. Earl, the Court said that cases were "not to be decided by attenuated subtleties." In Corliss v. Bowers, it stated, "taxation is not so much concerned with the refinements of title as it is with command over the property taxed." Does Poe v. Seaborn square with these admonitions? What are the distinctions made between the community property laws of California, on the one hand, and Arizona, on the other, if not "attenuated subtleties"? In disregarding the husband's virtually unfettered power over community property in Washington, is the Supreme Court concentrating on "actual command," rather than on "refinements of title"? Is Poe v. Seaborn best explained by an unstated concern with principles of federalism and respect for state community property laws, which does not extend to private contractual arrangements (even though the latter are also given effect by state law)?

5) *Blair*

What is the relationship in this case between state property law and federal taxation? What is a "spendthrift trust"? See Black's Law Dictionary. Why is the assignment invalid for federal tax purposes if the trust is a spendthrift trust?

Why were the Board of Tax Appeals and the Federal Circuit Court initially called on to interpret Illinois law? How did the taxpayer circumvent their unfavorable interpretation?

6) *Clifford*

What facts result in the grantor in *Clifford* being considered the owner of the property? Do any facts appear more significant than others? If taken seriously, where do the references in Justice Douglas' opinion to the family group lead? In a direction consistent with the outcome in *Blair?*

7) *Horst*

What is the relationship between the realization principle and the question of who is taxable in *Horst?* Is *Horst* consistent with the principle that a transfer by gift is not ordinarily a realization event (Chapter 22)? How does interest income, already earned on a bond, differ from appreciation in the value of stock? Will the latter ordinarily be realized by the donor when a gift is made? If not, what is different about the unrealized appreciation in *Horst?* What are the implications of *Horst* for gifts of property subject to Section 1245 or Section 1250? But see Sections 1245(b)(1) and 1250(d)(1).

8) Harrison v. Schaffner

Why is the reasoning in this opinion especially incoherent? Does the Court convincingly distinguish *Blair?* Would it make more sense to distinguish *Blair* by holding that a donor is considered to "own" any property with respect to which he or she retains a future or reversionary interest? Can such a rule be deduced from the principles articulated in Corliss v. Bowers and *Clifford?*

Chapter 46

CIRCUMVENTING THE COMMON LAW: FAMILY PARTNERSHIPS, SELF-CREATED PROPERTY, AND PROFESSIONAL SERVICE CORPORATIONS

A. COMMISSIONER v. CULBERTSON
337 U.S. 733 (1949)

Mr. Chief Justice Vinson delivered the opinion of the Court.

This case requires our further consideration of the family partnership problem. The Commissioner of Internal Revenue ruled that the entire income from a partnership allegedly entered into by respondent and his four sons must be taxed to respondent, and the Tax Court sustained that determination. The Court of Appeals for the Fifth Circuit reversed. . . .

Respondent taxpayer is a rancher. From 1915 until October 1939, he had operated a cattle business in partnership with R. S. Coon. Coon, who had numerous business interests in the Southwest and had largely financed the partnership, was 79 years old in 1939 and desired to dissolve the partnership because of ill health. To that end, the bulk of the partnership herd was sold until, in October of that year, only about 1,500 head remained. These cattle were all registered Herefords, the brood or foundation herd. Culbertson wished to keep these cattle and approached Coon with an offer of $65 a head. Coon agreed to sell at that price, but only upon condition that Culbertson would sell an undivided one-half interest in the herd to his four sons at the same price. His reasons for imposing this condition were his intense interest in maintaining the Hereford strain which he and Culbertson had developed, his conviction that Culbertson was too old to carry on the work alone, and his personal interest in the Culbertson boys. Culbertson's sons were enthusiastic about the proposition, so respondent thereupon bought the remaining cattle from the Coon and Culbertson partnership for $99,440. Two days later Culbertson sold an undivided one-half interest to the four boys, and the following day they gave their father a note for $49,720 at 4 per cent interest due one year from date. Several months later a new note for $57,674 was executed by the boys to replace the earlier note. The increase in amount covered the purchase by Culbertson and his sons of other properties formerly owned by Coon and Culbertson. This note was paid by the boys in the following manner:

Credit for overcharge	$5,930
Gifts from respondent	21,744
One-half of a loan procured by Culbertson & Sons partnership	30,000

The loan was repaid from the proceeds from operation of the ranch.

The partnership agreement between taxpayer and his sons was oral. The local paper announced the dissolution of the Coon and Culbertson partnership and the continuation of the business by respondent and his boys under the name of Culbertson & Sons. A bank account was opened in this name, upon which taxpayer, his four sons and a bookkeeper could check. At the time of formation of the new partnership, Culbertson's oldest son was 24 years old, married, and living on the ranch, of which he had for two years been foreman under the Coon and Culbertson partnership. He was a college graduate and received $100 a month plus board and lodging for himself and his wife both before and after formation of Culbertson & Sons and until entering the Army. The second son was 22 years old, was married and finished college in 1940, the first year during which the new partnership operated. He went directly into the Army following graduation and rendered no services to the partnership. The two younger sons, who were 18 and 16 years old respectively in 1940, went to school during the winter and worked on the ranch during the summer.[1]

The tax years here involved are 1940 and 1941. A partnership return was filed for both years indicating a division of income approximating the capital attributed to each partner. It is the disallowance of this division of the income from the ranch that brings this case into the courts.

First. The Tax Court read our decisions in *Commissioner* v. *Tower* . . . and *Lusthaus* v. *Commissioner* . . . as setting out two essential tests of partnership for income-tax purposes: that each partner contribute to the partnership either vital services or capital originating with him. Its decision was based upon a finding that none of respondent's sons had satisfied those requirements during the tax years in question. . . .

The Court of Appeals, on the other hand, was of the opinion that a family partnership entered into without thought of tax avoidance should be given recognition tax-wise whether or not it was intended that some of the partners contribute either capital or services during the tax year and whether or not they actually made such contributions, since it was formed "with the full expectation and purpose that the boys would, in the future, contribute their time and services to the partnership."[2] We must consider,

---

1. A daughter was also made a member of the partnership some time after its formation upon the gift by respondent of one-quarter of his one-half interest in the partnership. Respondent did not contend before the Tax Court that she was a partner for tax purposes.

2. . . . The court further said: "Neither statute, common sense, nor impelling precedent requires the holding that a partner must contribute capital or render services to the partnership prior to the time that he is taken into it. These tests are equally effective whether the capital and the services are presently contributed and rendered or are later to be contributed or to be rendered." . . .

therefore, whether an intention to contribute capital or services sometime in the future is sufficient. . . .

In the *Tower* case we held that, despite the claimed partnership, the evidence fully justified the Tax Court's holding that the husband, through his ownership of the capital and his management of the business, actually created the right to receive and enjoy the benefit of the income and was thus taxable upon that entire income. . . . In such case, other members of the partnership cannot be considered "Individuals carrying on business in partnership" and thus "liable for income tax . . . in their individual capacity" within the meaning of § [701]. If it is conceded that some of the partners contributed neither capital nor services to the partnership during the tax years in question, as the Court of Appeals was apparently willing to do in the present case, it can hardly be contended that they are in any way responsible for the production of income during those years.[3] The partnership sections of the Code are, of course, geared to the sections relating to taxation of individual income, since no tax is imposed upon partnership income as such. To hold that "Individuals carrying on business in partnership" includes persons who contribute nothing during the tax period would violate the first principle of income taxation: that income must be taxed to him who earns it. *Lucas* v. *Earl* . . . *Helvering* v. *Clifford*. . . .

Furthermore, our decision in *Commissioner* v. *Tower* . . . clearly indicates the importance of participation in the business by the partners during the tax year. We there said that a partnership is created "when persons join together their money, goods, labor, or skill for the purpose of carrying on a trade, profession, or business and when there is community of interest in the profits and losses." . . . This is, after all, but the application of an often iterated definition of income—the gain derived from capital, from labor, or from both combined—to a particular form of business organization. A partnership is, in other words, an organization for the production of income to which each partner contributes one or both of the ingredients of income—capital or services. . . . The intent to provide money, goods, labor, or skill sometime in the future cannot meet the demands . . . of the Code that he who presently earns the income through his own labor and skill and the utilization of his own capital be taxed therefor. The vagaries of human experience preclude reliance upon even good faith intent as to future conduct as a basis for the present taxation of income.[4]

Second. We turn next to a consideration of the Tax Court's approach to the family partnership problem. It treated as essential to membership in a family partnership for tax purposes the contribution of either "vital services" or "original capital." Use of these "tests" of partnership indicates, at best, an error in emphasis. It ignores what we said is the ultimate question for decision, namely, "whether the partnership is real within the meaning

---

3. Of course one who has been a bona fide partner does not lose that status when he is called into military or government service, and the Commissioner has not so contended. On the other hand, one hardly becomes a partner in the conventional sense merely because he might have done so had he not been called.

4. The *reductio ad absurdum* of the theory that children may be partners with their parents before they are capable of being entrusted with the disposition of partnership funds or of contributing substantial services occurred in *Tinkoff* v. *Commissioner*. . . . where a taxpayer made his son a partner in his accounting firm the day the son was born.

of the federal revenue laws" and makes decisive what we described as "circumstances [to be taken] into consideration" in making that determination.

The *Tower* case thus provides no support for such an approach.... The question is not whether the services or capital contributed by a partner are of sufficient importance to meet some objective standard supposedly established by the *Tower* case, but whether, considering all the facts—the agreement, the conduct of the parties in execution of its provisions, their statements, the testimony of disinterested persons, the relationship of the parties, their respective abilities and capital contributions, the actual control of income and the purposes for which it is used, and any other facts throwing light on their true intent—the parties in good faith and acting with a business purpose intended to join together in the present conduct of the enterprise. There is nothing new or particularly difficult about such a test. Triers of fact are constantly called upon to determine the intent with which a person acted....[5] Whether the parties really intended to carry on business as partners is not, we think, any more difficult of determination or the manifestations of such intent any less perceptible than is ordinarily true of inquiries into the subjective.

But the Tax Court did not view the question as one concerning the bona fide intent of the parties to join together as partners. Not once in its opinion is there even an oblique reference to any lack of intent on the part of respondent and his sons to combine their capital and services "for the purpose of carrying on the business." Instead, the court, focusing entirely upon concepts of "vital services" and "original capital," simply decided that the alleged partners had not satisfied those tests when the facts were compared with those in the *Tower* case. The court's opinion is replete with such statements as "we discern nothing constituting what we think is a requisite contribution to a real partnership," "we find no son adding 'vital additional service' which would take the place of capital contributed because of formation of a partnership," and "the sons made no capital contribution, within the sense of the *Tower* case."...

Unquestionably a court's determination that the services contributed by a partner are not "vital" and that he has not participated in "management and control of the business" or contributed "original capital" has the effect of placing a heavy burden on the taxpayer to show the bona fide intent of the parties to join together as partners. But such a determination is not conclusive, and that is the vice in the "tests" adopted by the Tax Court. It assumes that there is no room for an honest difference of opinion as to whether the services or capital furnished by the alleged partner are of sufficient importance to justify his inclusion in the partnership. If, upon a consideration of all the facts, it is found that the partners joined together in good faith to conduct a business, having agreed that the services or capital to be contributed presently by each is of such value to the partnership that the contributor should participate in the distribution of profits, that is sufficient. The *Tower* case did not purport to authorize the Tax Court to

---

5. Nearly three-quarters of a century ago, Bowen, L. J., made the classic statement that "the state of a man's mind is as much a fact as the state of his digestion."....

substitute its judgment for that of the parties; it simply furnished some guides to the determination of their true intent. Even though it was admitted in the *Tower* case that the wife contributed no original capital, management of the business, or other vital services, this court did not say as a matter of law that there was no vital partnership. We said, instead, that "There was, thus, more than ample evidence to support the Tax Court's finding that no genuine union for partnership business purposes *was ever intended* and that the husband earned the income." . . .

Third. The Tax Court's isolation of "original capital" as an essential of membership in a family partnership also indicates an erroneous reading of the *Tower* opinion. We did not say that the donee of an intra-family gift could never become a partner through investment of the capital in the family partnership, any more than we said that all family trusts are invalid for tax purposes in *Helvering* v. *Clifford,* supra. The facts may indicate, on the contrary, that the amount thus contributed and the income therefrom should be considered the property of the donee for tax, as well as general law, purposes. In the *Tower* and *Lusthaus* cases this Court, applying the principles of *Lucas* v. *Earl,* supra; *Helvering* v. *Clifford,* supra; and *Helvering* v. *Horst* . . . found that the purported gift, whether or not technically complete, had made no substantial change in the economic relation of members of the family to the income. In each case the husband continued to manage and control the business as before, and income from the property given to the wife and invested by her in the partnership continued to be used in the business or expended for family purposes. We characterized the results of the transactions entered into between husband and wife as "a mere paper reallocation of income among the family members," noting that "The actualities of their relation to the income did not change." . . . This, we thought, provided ample grounds for the finding that no true partnership was intended; that the husband was still the true earner of the income.

But application of the *Clifford-Horst* principle does not follow automatically upon a gift to a member of one's family, followed by its investment in the family partnership. If it did, it would be necessary to define "family" and to set precise limits of membership therein. We have not done so for the obvious reason that existence of the family relationship does not create a status which itself determines tax questions, but is simply a warning that things may not be what they seem. It is frequently stated that transactions between members of a family will be carefully scrutinized. But, more particularly, the family relationship often makes it possible for one to shift tax incidence by surface changes of ownership without disturbing in the least his dominion and control over the subject of the gift or the purposes for which the income from the property is used. He is able, in other words, to retain "the substance of full enjoyment of all the rights which previously he had in the property." *Helvering* v. *Clifford.* . . .

The fact that transfers to members of the family group may be mere camouflage does not, however, mean that they invariably are. The *Tower* case recognized that one's participation in control and management of the business is a circumstance indicating an intent to be a bona fide partner despite the fact that the capital contributed originated elsewhere in the family. If the donee of property who then invests it in the family partnership exercises dominion and control over that property—and through that control influences the conduct of the partnership and the disposition of its income—he may well be a true partner. Whether he is free to, and does, enjoy the fruits of the partnership is strongly indicative of the reality of his participation in the enterprise. In the *Tower* and *Lusthaus* cases we distinguished between active participation in the affairs of the business by a donee of a share in the partnership on the one hand, and his passive acquiescence to the will of the donor on the other.[6] This distinction is of obvious importance to a determination of the true intent of the parties. It is meaningless if "original capital" is an essential test of membership in a family partnership.

The cause must therefore be remanded to the Tax Court for a decision as to which, if any, of respondent's sons were partners with him in the operation of the ranch during 1940 and 1941. As to which of them, in other words, was there a bona fide intent that they be partners in the conduct of the cattle business, either because of services to be performed during those years, or because of contributions of capital of which they were the true owners, as we have defined that term in the *Clifford, Horst,* and *Tower* cases? No question as to the allocation of income between capital and services is presented in this case, and we intimate no opinion on that subject. . . .

MR. JUSTICE BURTON, concurring, states that, upon remand of the cause to the Tax Court, there is nothing in the facts which have been presented here which, as a matter of law, will preclude that court from finding that the 1940 and 1941 income was properly taxable on a partnership basis. The physical absence of some of the Culbertson boys from the ranch does not necessarily preclude them or others from the obligations or the benefits of the partnership for tax purposes. Their contributions of capital, their participation in the income and their commitments to return to the ranch or otherwise to render service to the partnership are among the material factors to be considered. A present commitment to render future services to a partnership is in itself a material consideration to be weighed with all other material considerations for the purposes of taxation as well as for other partnership purposes. . . .

MR. JUSTICE FRANKFURTER, concurring.

The Court finds that the Tax Court applied wrong legal standards in determining that the arrangement in controversy did not constitute a partnership. It remands the case to the Tax Court because it is for that court, and not for the Court of Appeals, to ascertain, on the basis of appropriate legal criteria, the existence of a partnership. . . . With these conclusions I agree. I think, however, that it is due to the Tax Court, the Courts of

---

6. There is testimony in the record as to the participation by respondent's sons in the management of the ranch. Since such evidence did not fall within either of the "tests" adopted by the Tax Court, it failed to consider this testimony. Without intimating any opinion as to its probative value, we think that it is clearly relevant evidence of the intent to carry on business as partners.

Appeals, the Treasury and the bar to make more explicit what the appropriate legal criteria are.

The Tax Court's decision rested on a misconception of our decision in *Commissioner v. Tower*. . . . It is, however, fair to say that it was led into that misconception by phrases which it culled from the *Tower* opinion with inadequate attention to the opinion in its entirety—both what it said and what it significantly did not say. The *Tower* opinion did not say what the Government now urges upon this Court; the Court's opinion did not take the position of the concurring opinion. In short, the opinion did not say that family partnerships are not to be regarded as partnerships for income-tax purposes even though they be genuine commercial partnerships; the opinion did not even announce hobbling presumptions under the income-tax law against such partnerships.

On the contrary, in defining the relevant considerations for determining the existence of a partnership, the Court in the *Tower* case relied on familiar decisions formulating the concept of partnership for purposes of various commercial situations in which the nature of that concept was decisive. . . . [T]he Court did not purport to announce a special concept of "partnership" for tax purposes differing from the concept that rules in ordinary commercial-law cases. . . .

. . . Men may put on the habiliments of a partnership whenever it advantages them to be treated as partners underneath, although in fact it may be a case of "The King has no clothes on" to the sharp eyes of the law. Since there are special temptations to appear as a partnership in order to avoid the hardships of heavy taxation, the tribunal which presumably is gifted with superior discernment in differentiating between the real thing and the imitation—the Tax Court—will naturally be on the alert against being taken in. Therefore, a finding by the Tax Court that that which has the outward appearance of an arrangement to engage in a common enterprise is not in fact such an associated business venture ought to be respected when challenged in another court, unless such a determination is wholly without warrant in fact or, as in this case, the wrong standards for judgment have been applied. . . .

. . . While recognizing the importance of the question "who actually owned a share of the capital attributed to the wife on the partnership books," the *Tower* opinion states the ultimate issue to be "whether this husband and wife really intended to carry on business as a partnership." . . . . To that determination it was of course relevant that no new capital was brought into the business as a result of the formation of the partnership, that the wife drew on income of the partnership only to pay for the type of things she had previously bought for the family, and that the consequence was a mere paper reallocation of income. But these circumstances were not cited as giving the term "partnership" a content peculiar to the Internal Revenue Code. They were characterized, rather, simply as "more than ample evidence to support the Tax Court's finding that no genuine union for partnership business purposes was ever intended" and, as a corollary, "that the husband earned the income." . . .

Recognition of the importance . . . of the appraisal of facts makes manifest why . . . a determination by a State court should not . . . foreclose a contrary determination by a federal tribunal charged with administration of the tax laws. Such an inconsistency would not mean that the legal standards applied by each were inconsistent; it would be a result simply of the commonplace that no finder of fact can see through the eyes of any other finder of fact. . . . Nor would inconsistency be created by a State court's concern for the protection of creditors which lead it to seize upon adoption of the outward form as the vital fact. So, indeed, might the taxing authorities refuse to be precluded from holding the taxpayer to his election to adopt the form of a partnership. . . . The need for guarding against misuse of the outward form of a partnership as a device for obtaining tax advantages is properly satisfied by reliance on the vigilance of the Tax Court, not by distorting the concept of partnership. It is not for this Court, by redefinition or the erection of presumptions, to amend the Internal Revenue Code so as virtually to ban partnerships composed of the members of an intimate family group.

The present case, nevertheless, is not the first manifestation of an impression that the *Tower* opinion had precisely such an effect. It seems to me important, therefore, to make crystal clear that there is no special concept of "partnership" for tax purposes, while at the same time recognizing that in view of the temptations to assume a virtue that they have not for the sake of tax savings, men and women may appear in a guise which the gimlet eye of the Tax Court is entitled to pierce. We should leave no doubt in the minds of the Tax Court, of the Courts of Appeals, of the Treasury and of the bar that the essential holding of the *Tower* case is that there is "no reason" why the "general rule" by which the existence of a partnership is determined "should not apply in tax cases where the Government challenges the existence of a partnership for tax purposes."

In plain English, if an arrangement among men is not an arrangement which puts them all in the same business boat, then they cannot get into the same boat merely to seek the benefits of §§ [701 and 702]. But if they are in the same business boat, although they may have varying rewards and varied responsibilities, they do not cease to be in it when the tax collector appears.

B. NOTES AND QUESTIONS

1) Using Family Partnerships to Circumvent the Common Law

Each of the following examples raises an assignment of income issue in the context of a partnership. For each example, consider whether the allocation of partnership profits circumvents the assignment of income principles established by the Supreme Court decisions in the preceding chapter. Pay attention to whether the principal input to the partnership is services, property, or both, and how that affects your answers.

a) A, B, and C—all unrelated parties—form a partnership to operate a construction business. A, an architect, and B, a builder, will contribute services. C, a wealthy investor, will finance the venture. After discussing the relative contributions of each, they sign a partnership agreement which provides that A and B each will receive 40% of the profits and that C will receive 20%. See Section 704(a).

b) Parent owns and operates a construction business. Other than a few items of office furniture and a pickup truck, Parent rents all machinery used in the business. The day after Parent's Child is born, Parent and Child "agree" to own and operate the construction business as partners. The partnership agreement provides that Parent and Child each will receive 50% of partnership profits. (See footnote 4 in *Culbertson*.) Hint: How does the agreement contravene the principle of Lucas v. Earl?

c) Parent is a highly successful attorney in sole practice. The day after Child graduates from law school, Parent hires Child as an associate. Child receives a full salary during the three months that Child is studying for the bar exam and not working. One year after becoming an associate, Child is made a full partner, entitled to one-half of the partnership's profits. Hint: Why is it more difficult to argue in this example, than it was in the preceding one, that the allocation of partnership income contravenes the principle of Lucas v. Earl?

d) A, B, C, D, and E are law partners, each entitled to 20% of the partnership's profits. If any partner becomes disabled for a period not to exceed one year, the partner shall continue to be entitled to a 20% share. Hint: *Should* it matter whether the partners are unrelated or related?

e) Parent owns a shopping center, which is managed by a full-time employee. Parent devotes, on the average, two hours per week to the shopping center business. The day after Parent's Child is born, Parent gives a one-half interest in the property to Child, and Parent and Child "agree" to own the property as partners. The partnership agreement provides that Parent and Child are each to receive 50% of partnership profits. Hint: Does this arrangement more closely resemble that in *Blair* or that in *Clifford*?

f) Parent owns and operates a construction business. The business owns all machinery used in construction, the total value of which is over $1 million. When Child enters college, Parent gives Child a one-half interest in the business, and Parent and Child agree to operate the business as partners. The partnership agreement provides that each partner will receive 50% of partnership profits. Child expects to work for the business during summers until graduation and full time after graduation. Hint: Would two unrelated partners be likely to agree to share partnership profits equally, when each contributes one-half of the capital, but one partner plans to work full time and the other only part time? When would unrelated partners who contribute equal amounts of capital most likely agree to an equal division of profits?

Why do the facts of example f) resemble *Culbertson*? Did the IRS argue that *Culbertson* involved an attempt to shift personal services income? Should it have? See the last sentence of the Court's opinion.

2) The Tax Court in *Culbertson*

What legal principle did the Tax Court apply to determine whether the allocation of income under the Culbertson family partnership should be respected? Was this principle consistent with *Blair* (Chapter 45)? If not, can the principle be defended as necessary to prevent special abuses more likely to arise in family partnerships than in other arrangements?

3) The Circuit Court

How did the legal principle applied by the Circuit Court differ from the Tax Court's? Was it consistent with the principle of Lucas v. Earl? If an unrelated party might be made a partner in return for a promise to provide future services, why not a related party?

4) The Supreme Court

Is the Supreme Court's basic rule for testing the allocation of family partnership income too vague? Do you agree with the sentiments expressed in footnote 5 of the Court's opinion? Justice Frankfurter's separate opinion bemoans the lack of more explicit legal criteria in the Court's opinion. But does his concurrence provide explicit criteria for determining whether the allocation of family partnership income is valid? (Note that Justice Frankfurter made an identical complaint about the "detached and disinterested generosity" test of *Duberstein* in Chapter 5.)

Does the Court distinguish meaningfully between "active participation" and "passive acquiescence" by the donee of a partnership share? How actively do limited partners participate in ordinary nonfamily partnerships? In general, don't they passively acquiesce in the management decisions of the general partner? Is the active versus passive distinction consistent with *Blair*? Is this distinction suggested by some of the language of *Clifford*? Is it consistent with the limits on deducting passive activity losses (Chapter 43)?

5) Congress Acts: Section 704(e)

Congress attempted to provide more explicit criteria by enacting Section 704(e) in 1951. Is Section 704(e)(1) consistent with *Blair*? How does Section 704(e)(2) attempt to prevent a family partnership from circumventing Lucas v. Earl? According to the Senate Finance Committee Report,

> [Section 704(e)] is intended to harmonize the rules governing interests in the so-called family partnership with those generally applicable to other forms of property or business. Two principles governing attribution of income have long been accepted as basic: (1) income from property is attributable to the owner of the property; (2) income from personal services is attributable to the person rendering the services. There is no reason for applying different principles to partnership income. If an individual makes a bona fide gift of real estate, or of a share of corporate stock, the rent or dividend income is taxable to the donee. Your committee's amendment makes it clear that, however the owner of a partnership interest may have acquired such interest, the income is taxable to the owner, if he is the real owner....
>
> Although there is no basis under existing statutes for any different treatment of partnership interests, some decisions in this field have ignored the principle that income from property is to be taxed to the owner of the

property. Many court decisions since the decision of the Supreme Court in Commissioner v. Culbertson . . . have held invalid for tax purposes family partnerships which arose by virtue of a gift of a partnership interest from one member of a family to another, where the donee performed no vital services for the partnership. . . .

The amendment leaves the Commissioner and the courts free to inquire in any case whether the donee or purchaser actually owns the interest in the partnership which the transferor purports to have given or sold him . . . . [C]ases will arise where the transferor retains so many of the incidents of ownership that he will continue to be recognized as a substantial owner of the interest which he purports to have given away, as was held by the Supreme Court in an analogous trust situation involved in the case of Helvering v. Clifford. . . . The same standards apply in determining the bona fides of other transactions between family members. . . .

Not every restriction upon the complete and unfettered control by the donee of the property donated will be indicative of sham in the transaction. . . . Substantial powers may be retained by the transferor as a managing partner . . . which, when considered in the light of all the circumstances, will not indicate any lack of true ownership in the transferee.

Since . . . a gift of a family partnership interest is to be respected for tax purposes . . . , it is considered appropriate at the same time to provide specific safeguards . . . against the use of the partnership device to accomplish the deflection of income from the real owner.

Therefore . . . when the [partnership] shares are allocated without proper allowance of reasonable compensation for services rendered . . . by the donor [of a partnership interest], and . . . [when] the allocation to the donated capital is proportionately greater than that attributable to the donor's capital . . . a reasonable allowance will be made for the services rendered . . . and the balance of the income will be allocated according to the amount of capital . . . invested. However, the distributive share of a partner in the earnings . . . will not be diminished because of absence due to military service. . . .

[A]ll interests purchased by one member of the family from another will be treated as though the transfer were made by gift.[7]

Is it possible to distinguish the "substantial powers" that may be retained by a managing partner from powers "indicative of sham"? For a heroic attempt, see Reg. § 1.704-1(e)(2). Why does the Report mention a special exemption for absence due to military service? Why are purchased partnership interests treated as "gifts" under Section 704(e)(3) when buyer and seller are related parties?

C. HEIM v. FITZPATRICK
262 F.2d 887 (2d Cir. 1959)

SWAN, CIRCUIT JUDGE. . . .

Plaintiff was the inventor of a new type of rod end and spherical bearing. In September 1942 he applied for a patent thereon. On November 5, 1942

---

7. S. Rep. No. 781, 82d Cong., 1st Sess. 38-40 (1951).

he applied for a further patent on improvements of his original invention. Thereafter on November 17, 1942 he executed a formal written assignment of his invention and of the patents which might be issued for it and for improvements thereof to The Heim Company. This was duly recorded in the Patent Office and in January 1945 and May 1946 plaintiff's patent applications were acted on favorably and patents thereon were issued to the Company. The assignment to the Company was made pursuant to an oral agreement, subsequently reduced to a writing dated July 29, 1943, by which it was agreed (1) that the Company need pay no royalties on bearings manufactured by it prior to July 1, 1943; (2) that after that date the Company would pay specified royalties on 12 types of bearings; (3) that on new types of bearings it would pay royalties to be agreed upon prior to their manufacture; (4) that if the royalties for any two consecutive months or for any one year should fall below stated amounts, plaintiff at his option might cancel the agreement and thereupon all rights granted by him under the agreement and under any and all assigned patents should revert to him, his heirs and assigns; and (5) that this agreement is not transferable by the Company.

In August 1943 plaintiff assigned to his wife "an undivided interest of 25 per cent in said agreement with The Heim Company dated July 29, 1943, and in all his inventions and patent rights, past and future, referred to therein and in all rights and benefits of the First Party [plaintiff] thereunder...." A similar assignment was given to his son and another to his daughter. Plaintiff paid gift taxes on the assignments. The Company was notified of them and thereafter it made all royalty payments accordingly. As additional types of bearings were put into production from time to time the royalties on them were fixed by agreement between the Company and the plaintiff and his three assignees.

The Commissioner of Internal Revenue decided that all of the royalties paid by the Company to plaintiff's wife and children during the taxable years in suit were taxable to him....

The appellant contends that the assignments to his wife and children transferred to them income-producing property and consequently the royalty payments were taxable to his donees, as held in Blair v. Commissioner.... Judge Anderson, however, was of opinion that...:

> The income-producing property, i.e. the patents, had been assigned by the taxpayer to the corporation. What he had left was a right to a portion of the income which the patents produced. He had the power to dispose of and divert the stream of this income as he saw fit.

Consequently he ruled that the principles applied by the Supreme Court in Helvering v. Horst ... required all the royalty payments to be treated as income of plaintiff.

The question is not free from doubt, but the court believes that the transfers in this case were gifts of income-producing property and that [Horst does not require] the contrary view. In the Horst case the taxpayer detached interest coupons from negotiable bonds, which he retained, and made a gift of the coupons, shortly before their due date, to his son who collected them in the same year at maturity. Lucas v. Earl . . . which held that an assignment of unearned future income for personal services is taxable to the assignor, was extended to cover the assignment in Horst, the court saying . . . :

> Nor is it perceived that there is any adequate basis for distinguishing between the gift of interest coupons here and a gift of salary or commissions.

In the Eubank case the taxpayer assigned a contract which entitled him to receive previously earned insurance renewal commissions. In holding the income taxable to the assignor the court found that the issues were not distinguishable from those in Horst. No reference was made to the assignment of the underlying contract.

In the present case more than a bare right to receive future royalties was assigned by plaintiff to his donees. Under the terms of his contract with The Heim Company he retained the power to bargain for the fixing of royalties on new types of bearings, i.e. bearings other than the 12 products on which royalties were specified. This power was assigned and the assignees exercised it as to new products. Plaintiff also retained a reversionary interest in his invention and patents by reason of his option to cancel the agreement if certain conditions were not fulfilled. This interest was also assigned. The fact that the option was not exercised in 1945, when it could have been, is irrelevant so far as concerns the existence of the reversionary interest. We think that the rights retained by plaintiff and assigned to his wife and children were sufficiently substantial to justify the view that they were given income-producing property.

In addition to Judge Anderson's ground of decision appellee advances a further argument . . . in support of the judgment, namely, that the plaintiff retained sufficient control over the invention and the royalties to make it reasonable to treat him as owner of that income for tax purposes. Commissioner of Internal Revenue v. Sunnen . . . is relied upon. There a patent was licensed under a royalty contract with a corporation in which the taxpayer-inventor held 89% of the stock. An assignment of the royalty contract to the taxpayer's wife was held ineffective to shift the tax, since the taxpayer retained control over the royalty payments to his wife by virtue of his control of the corporation, which could cancel the contract at any time. The argument is that, although plaintiff himself owned only 1% of The Heim Company stock, his wife and daughter together owned 68% and it is reasonable to infer from depositions introduced by the Commissioner that they would follow the plaintiff's advice. Judge Anderson did not find it necessary to pass on this contention. But we are satisfied that the record would not support a finding that plaintiff controlled the corporation whose active heads were the son and son-in-law. No inference can reasonably be drawn that the daughter would be likely to follow her father's advice rather than her husband's or brother's with respect to action by the corporation. . . .

D. NOTES AND QUESTIONS

1) Making an Exception to the Common Law Principles

The court analogizes the assignment of income in this case to that in *Blair*. Is the analogy valid? How does the assignment in Heim v. Fitzpatrick contravene the principle of Lucas v. Earl? What kind of exception to that principle is condoned? To what other kinds of self-created property would the exception apply? How can the exception be justified as a matter of policy? Is congressional acceptance of the exception implicit in Section 1221(3)(C)?

2) Did the Donor Retain Too Many Strings?

The court notes that the donor retained no reversionary interest in the property given away. Why? Does that fact indicate that the assignment does not run afoul of the principle of Harrison v. Schaffner?

The court also notes that the donor did not control the corporate licensee. Even if the donor did, should that change the outcome? In that event, is the donor in the same position as someone who has sold property and then leased it back for its entire useful life?

E. FOGLESONG v. COMMISSIONER
621 F.2d 865 (7th Cir. 1980)

CUDAHY, CIRCUIT JUDGE.

This is an appeal from a decision of the United States Tax Court, . . . determining that the bulk of the commission income of a personal service corporation, Frederick H. Foglesong Co., Inc. (the "Corporation"), set up by a steel tubing sales representative, Frederick H. Foglesong (the "taxpayer"), was taxable to the taxpayer and not to the Corporation. The Tax Court for various reasons, which will appear, chose essentially to disregard the corporate form and, under Section 61 of the Internal Revenue Code and the assignment of income doctrine of *Lucas v. Earl* . . . to treat the bulk of the commission income as having been earned by, and as taxable to, the taxpayer. . . . We reverse and remand.

I

The facts here are not in substantial dispute. Frederick H. Foglesong, the taxpayer, was a sales representative for the Plymouth Tube division of the Van Pelt Corporation ("Plymouth Tube") and for the Pittsburgh Tube Company ("Pittsburgh Tube"), two manufacturers of cold drawn steel tubing. Taxpayer entered into an agreement to become the Eastern sales representative of Plymouth Tube in 1962. He sold Plymouth Tube's products within a defined territory for a commission. In 1963, taxpayer entered into a similar agreement with Pittsburgh Tube.

As a sales representative, taxpayer sought out prospective customers for steel tubing and tried to persuade them to use the products of Plymouth Tube or Pittsburgh Tube in their manufacturing processes. Taxpayer answered technical questions about the products he was selling, and after his customers had placed orders, he was available to respond to questions and to service any complaints. There was evidence that taxpayer had an impressive reputation as a salesman, and this was one of the principal reasons he was retained as a sales representative by Plymouth Tube and Pittsburgh Tube.

On August 30, 1966, taxpayer incorporated his business as Frederick H. Foglesong Company, Inc. He, his wife and his accountant were listed as the incorporators on the certificate of incorporation. Of the one hundred shares of common stock issued by the Corporation (for a total subscription price of $1,000), taxpayer held 98 shares and his wife and accountant held 1 share each. The Corporation paid no dividends on its common stock during the taxable years in question, 1966 through 1969.

The Corporation also issued preferred stock to the taxpayer's four minor children (for which the total subscription price was $400). The four children received dividends totaling $32,000 over the period beginning September 1, 1966 and ending December 31, 1969.

At or about the time the Corporation was organized, the taxpayer notified Plymouth Tube and Pittsburgh Tube that the Corporation was being formed and asked that any commissions due under his agreements with them be paid to the Corporation. Both suppliers agreed to this request. As a result, certain commissions earned for services rendered before the date of incorporation were paid to the Corporation. In addition, the Corporation adopted a fiscal year ending August 31, and the taxpayer received no salary from the Corporation during the months of September through December 1966 although he continued to work as a salesman servicing Plymouth Tube and Pittsburgh Tube during that period.

On his personal income tax return for the calendar year 1966, taxpayer reported a net profit from his business as a sales representative in the amount of $86,665.88, all of which was derived from commissions paid to him personally during the months of January through August, 1966, by his principals. The Corporation made its first salary payment to taxpayer on January 9, 1967, and he received a regular monthly salary after that date during the years which are relevant here. Taxpayer's salary income from the Corporation during calendar year 1967 was $56,500. In that year and in the succeeding relevant calendar years, he reported no personal income from any business as a sole proprietor. The respective net receipts of the Corporation from sales commissions and its deductions for compensation paid to taxpayer for the four taxable years in question are as follows:

Taxable Year Ending	Net Receipts from Commissions Before Payment of Compensation to Taxpayer	Compensation to Taxpayer Deducted
August 31, 1967	$148,486.70	$41,500.00
August 31, 1968	100,482.23	55,000.00
August 31, 1969	99,429.35	65,000.00
August 31, 1970	121,018.24	73,700.00

After the formation of the Corporation, all commissions from Plymouth Tube and Pittsburgh Tube were paid to the Corporation. But a written agreement with Pittsburgh Tube was not executed until May 19, 1969, or with Plymouth Tube until January 1, 1971.

Taxpayer testified that he wished to incorporate his business in order to obtain the limited liability protection afforded by a corporate structure and also to provide a better vehicle for his planned expansion into several new business ventures. Subsequent to the formation of the Corporation, taxpayer interviewed a prospective salesman to help him in the New England area, but these negotiations were unsuccessful. The Corporation did, however, employ a secretary during its taxable years ending August 31, 1969 and 1970, paid her a salary and took corresponding deductions. Taxpayer asserted that he had unsuccessfully attempted to expand his sales business into other areas such as steel warehousing, transportation of steel tubing and the exporting of steel tubes to Europe but produced no documentation of these efforts.

The Corporation paid taxpayer a regular salary as a salesman, paid all of taxpayer's expenses incurred in connection with his sales activities, maintained a bank account, carried its own insurance coverage, maintained a company automobile and complied with all the formalities required of corporations in the state of New Jersey. The Corporation adopted bylaws, held an initial meeting of incorporators, at which the board of directors was elected, and conducted periodic board of directors' and stockholders' meetings as required by its bylaws. Taxpayer served as chairman of the board of directors as well as president and treasurer of the Corporation.

During the years in question here taxpayer did not enter into any written employment contracts with the Corporation nor did he enter into a covenant not to complete [sic] with the Corporation.

During these years taxpayer's only gainful activity was as an employee of the Corporation. He had no legal rights under the representation contracts with Plymouth Tube and Pittsburgh Tube subsequent to the formation of the Corporation. Taxpayer testified that during the period at issue he did not engage in any business activity other than as an employee of the Corporation.

The Tax Court, *inter alia*, concluded on balance that . . . tax avoidance considerations "far outweighed any genuine business concerns taxpayer may have had in setting up [the Corporation]." Nonetheless, the Commissioner conceded, and the Tax Court found, that the Corporation was a viable, taxable entity and not a mere sham during the years in issue.

But, in spite of its finding of viability (and strongly influenced by the apparent flagrancy of the tax avoidance), the Tax Court, in effect, substantially disregarded the Corporation for tax purposes. It found that during the years in question control over 98% of the commission income remained with taxpayer so as to cause such income to be taxable to him (as the person who earned it through his personal sales efforts) and not to the Corporation. The Tax Court based this result on Section 61 of the Internal Revenue Code and the assignment of income doctrine of *Lucas v. Earl*, supra. With respect to those commissions which were received by taxpayer solely because of the exclusive territorial rights assigned to the

Corporation under its agreement with Plymouth Tube and Pittsburgh Tube (amounting to approximately 2% of the total), the Tax Court held that the Corporation, not the taxpayer, was the party earning this income, and, hence, such commissions should be taxed to it. . . .

II

Personal service corporation tax cases reveal a tension between "the principle of a graduated income tax . . . and the policy of recognizing the corporation as a taxable entity distinct from its shareholders in all but extreme cases." . . . The impact of the graduated income tax is eroded when income is split artificially among several entities or over several tax years. The assignment of income doctrine under Section 61 of the Internal Revenue Code (as formulated in *Lucas v. Earl*) seeks to recognize "economic reality" by cumulating income diffused among several recipients through "artificial" legal arrangements. The attribution of income to its "true earner" is simply a species of recognizing "substance" over "form." . . .

But, if the issue is one of attributing the income of a corporation to its sole stockholder-employee who "really" earned it, we encounter the important policy of the law favoring recognition of the corporation as a legal person and economic actor. As Mr. Justice Holmes said . . . :

> But it leads nowhere to call a corporation a fiction. If it is a fiction it is a fiction created by law with intent that it should be acted on as if true. The corporation is a person and its ownership is a nonconductor that makes it impossible to attribute an interest in its property to its members.

In the instant case, the following circumstances, among others, are present: (1) the Corporation and not the taxpayer is the party to the contracts under which services are performed, (2) the Corporation is recognized to be a viable, taxable entity and not a mere sham, (3) non-tax business purposes are present even though tax avoidance is apparently a major concern, (4) the Corporation has not been formed for the purpose of taking advantage of losses incurred by a separate trade or business, (5) the corporate form (and the status of the Corporation as an actual operating enterprise) has been consistently honored by the taxpayer and other parties to the transactions giving rise to the income, (6) the taxpayer does not render services as an employee to any entity other than the Corporation, (7) the Corporation is not disqualified from performing the Services required of it by contract because the law requires these services to be performed by an individual, (8) the entities paying or providing the income are not controlled or dominated by the taxpayer, and (9) as will appear, other and more appropriate legal bases exist for attacking apparent tax avoidance than broad-scale disregard of the corporate form through application of assignment of income theory. We note especially that the Tax Court did not find the Corporation to be a pure tax avoidance vehicle.

Under the circumstances of the instant case, we think it inappropriate to attempt to weigh "business purposes" against "tax avoidance motives" in a determination whether the assignment of income doctrine of *Lucas v. Earl* should apply, in effect, to substantially disregard the corporate form . . . . [T]o apply *Lucas v. Earl* in this fashion under the circumstances present here is effectively (and more realistically) to nullify the determination that the Corporation is a viable, taxable entity and not a sham. . . .

In *Moline Properties v. Commissioner* . . . the Supreme Court confronted the question whether the gain on sale of certain real estate held by a corporation as security was to be taxed to the corporation or to its sole shareholder. The Court perceived the problem as determining whether the corporate form might be disregarded for tax purposes as a sham or unreal. The Court said that the corporation was a viable taxable entity *so long as the purpose of its creation is the equivalent of business activity or its creation is followed by the carrying on of business by the corporation*. . . . We think it inappropriate, in light of *Moline Properties* . . . except on more extreme facts than appear here, to achieve, through recourse to the assignment of income doctrine, essentially the same result as would follow from treating the Corporation as a "sham" for tax purposes. . . .

Although we do not regard the point as decisive, the Tax Court here found that, with respect to the contracts to perform sales services for Plymouth Tube and Pittsburgh Tube, there had been not only an assignment but a novation, with the corporation's becoming the sole party obligated to perform sales services and entitled to be compensated for such performance. Hence, this case is in essential concept quite distinguishable from *Lucas v. Earl*, where only income was assigned. . . . Here not only the fruit but the tree itself was transferred to the Corporation.

In *Rubin v. Commissioner*, . . . the Tax Court held that income was taxable to an individual who owned a 70% interest in a personal service corporation, which performed management services for another company. The same individual also controlled the company for which services were to be performed. The Tax Court attempted to analyze the problem both as one in which form differed from substance (the individual being held to work "directly" for the company) and in which the earning of the income was controlled by the individual rather than his corporation and was, therefore, taxable to the individual under the doctrine of *Lucas v. Earl*. In *Rubin*, the Tax Court suggested that the difference between the form over substance analysis and the assignment of income approach was only semantic. Thus it attempted to determine whether the form of the transaction, involving the personal service corporation, served any economic purpose and also whether the individual, in fact, controlled the earning of the income. The Tax Court found, first, that the income was properly taxable to the individual [because] the taxpayer was not contractually bound to (and in fact did not) render services exclusively to the personal service corporation. . . . Second, in *Rubin*, the taxpayer controlled not only the personal service corporation, but also the corporation to which services were rendered. . . .

We think that the Tax Court determination in *Rubin* might be easily distinguished here on the grounds that the taxpayer in the instant case worked exclusively for his personal service corporation (although he was not under contract to do so). Further, he did not own or control Pittsburgh Tube or Plymouth Tube, the entities to which services were rendered. . . .

Roubik v. Commissioner . . . on which the Tax Court . . . relies, involved a professional corporation consisting of four radiologists, where the question raised was whether the business of the four principals was carried on by the corporation or outside it. In *Roubik,* the individual radiologists, not the corporation, maintained contractual relationships with the institutions for which services were rendered. The corporation did not own equipment nor did it incur the great bulk of operating expenses. It did not assign its shareholders to institutions or to tasks. In short, the corporate form was repeatedly flouted. Indeed, it would be fair to say that the corporation was not an operating enterprise and, in fact, to conclude (although the Tax Court did not do so in *haec verba*) that the corporation was a sham. The instant case is clearly distinguishable in that the Corporation here assumed the contractual obligations to provide sales services for Pittsburgh Tube and Plymouth Tube, paid any expenses that were associated with the rendition of such services and otherwise honored the corporate form with respect to all matters of operating concern. Unlike *Roubik,* the Tax Court has specifically found here that the Corporation is not a sham and is a viable taxable entity.

Another type of case clearly distinguishable from the case at bar is illustrated by *Jones v. Commissioner,* . . . where an individual set up a professional service corporation, with himself as the sole shareholder and only employee, to carry on work as an official court reporter of a federal district court. In that case, the individual and not the corporation was held to be the "true earner" of the income, primarily because federal law required that court reporting services be performed by an individual, not a corporation. Thus, in *Jones,* the corporation was legally disabled from performing the work and earning the income; no such infirmity affected the corporation here. . . .

We believe that, where the issue is application of the assignment of income doctrine to effectively set aside the corporation, under the particular circumstances of this case (which we have carefully delineated), an attempt to strike a balance between tax avoidance motives and "legitimate" business purposes is an unproductive and inappropriate exercise. Such an approach places too low a value on the policy of the law to recognize corporations as economic actors except in exceptional circumstances. This is true whether the analysis used to dismantle the corporation pursues the rubric of assignment of income or substance over form. Here there are other more precise devices for coping with the unacceptable tax avoidance which is unquestionably present in this case. But there is no need to crack walnuts with a sledgehammer. . . .

. . . [S]tatutory provisions and "common law" doctrines, structured for more limited application, may . . . be available to remedy potential tax abuse. Thus, the dividends paid to taxpayer's children, . . . the assignment of commissions already earned before formation of the Corporation on September 1, 1966, and nonpayment of taxpayer's salary for the balance of 1966 after September 1 may each be subject to attack via . . . the assignment of income doctrine . . . . We think that the very aggressive tax avoidance measures which taxpayer employed here are vulnerable, but we express no opinion as to what statutory provisions or "common law" principles may properly address them.

We believe that, where all of the criteria set forth here are met, it is inappropriate to weigh "legitimate" business purposes against tax avoidance motivations in determining the application of the *Lucas v. Earl* assignment of income doctrine essentially to set aside a corporation for tax purposes. In the instant case, the Tax Court did not find that the Corporation was organized as a pure tax avoidance vehicle. Nor has the Tax Court perceived any flouting of the corporate form in the way business has been conducted. Pittsburgh Tube and Plymouth Tube entered into contracts requiring the Corporation to provide them services, for which they paid the Corporation. Taxpayer then worked exclusively for the Corporation in enabling it to carry out its responsibilities as a sales representative. The corporate tree seems sturdy enough to become fruit-bearing, subject, of course, to whatever pruning (radical or otherwise) by the tax collector appears appropriate.

We think that our approach in this case of recognizing some vitality in personal service corporations accords with congressional intent. ". . . [T]he absence of any special exclusion of such corporations from corporate taxation . . . indicate[s] that to some extent Congress has sanctioned the incorporation of service businesses for tax purposes. . . ."

HARLINGTON WOOD, JR., CIRCUIT JUDGE, dissenting.

As both sides of the issue are fully and fairly set forth in the majority opinion, little need be added in registering my dissent. Although I view it as a close case, I prefer in general the view of the United States Tax Court. . . .

This corporation is nothing more than a few incorporating papers lying in a desk drawer of no significance except when a tax return is due. Mr. Foglesong continued to conduct his original one-man sales representative business as he always did, except he has become insulated by those incorporating papers from the taxes he should have been paying. For a subscription price of $400 for all the preferred stock, this "should-be" taxpayer accomplished, among other things, the diversion to his children of at least $8,000 of his own income for each of the four taxable years. His make-believe corporation is too transparent for me to accept for tax purposes under Section 61 of the Code. I respectfully dissent.

F. NOTES AND QUESTIONS

1) The Incentive to Incorporate

What precise advantage does Foglesong gain by incorporating? How would his earnings have been taxed if he had *not* incorporated? If all corporate earnings are paid to Foglesong as salary, what difference does incorporation make? In that event, are corporate receipts subject to a separate corporate level tax?

When corporate receipts exceed the amount paid Foglesong as salary, what difference does incorporation make? Is the excess subject to a corporate level tax? If Foglesong's individual tax rate is *lower* than or equal to the corporate tax rate, will there be any tax advantage in paying him a salary less than corporate receipts?

If after-tax corporate income is distributed as dividends on preferred stock held by Foglesong's children, what additional shareholder level tax is imposed? What must be true of the combined effect of the corporate tax and shareholder level tax in order for incorporation to provide a net tax advantage?

If after-tax corporate income is accumulated and reinvested, what additional shareholder level tax is imposed? When will it be imposed? Is that additional shareholder level tax significant?

2) Changes in the Rate Structure Since *Foglesong*

During the tax years involved in *Foglesong*, the flat rate on corporate income above $100,000 hovered around 50%, while the top individual tax rate was 70%. In 1969, the top individual rate on earned income fell to 50%. How did that change affect the incentive to form a personal services corporation, paying the owner-employee a salary less than corporate receipts?

Today, the flat corporate rate on income above $75,000 is 34%, and the top individual rate is 33%. How does that affect the incentive to incorporate and to have the corporation pay the owner-employee a salary less than corporate receipts (after other expenses)?

Also, see Section 11(b)(2), enacted in 1987. Why was it enacted? To prevent individuals from taking advantage of the graduated rates on the first $75,000 of corporate income? Would it have applied to Foglesong? Would his corporation have been considered a "personal service corporation"?

3) Should the Lucas v. Earl Principle Have Been Applied in *Foglesong*?

What would have been the effect of applying the Lucas v. Earl principle to *Foglesong*, as the Tax Court wished to do? What was the effect of the Circuit Court's refusal to apply the principle? Why might this refusal be acceptable in the context of personal service corporations but not partnerships? Corporate income is subject to tax both at corporate and shareholder levels. Perhaps the two-level tax (even at a lower combined rate) is viewed as an adequate substitute for a one-level individual ordinary income tax.

4) More Limited Doctrines

The Circuit Court suggested that the "real" abuse in *Foglesong* could be prevented by more limited principles than Lucas v. Earl. Consider the following possibilities:

a) How would the *Horst* principle affect income earned by Foglesong before incorporation, paid to the corporation after it was formed?

b) The children invested $400 in preferred stock, which received annual dividends of $8,000. What is the rate of return, or interest rate, on the preferred? Would third parties, dealing at arm's length, be able to purchase preferred with a comparably high return? How might preferred dividends in excess of a market rate of return be recast? As a dividend on common stock, followed by a gift of the dividend? Or as additional salary to Foglesong, followed by a gift of the salary? Would this recasting be available if the corporation had issued the children 100% of the common instead of preferred?

5) The Business Purpose Doctrine in *Foglesong*

Is the business purpose doctrine a reasonable way to decide whether to respect the corporate form? Is it practical to administer? Does it lend itself to abuse? Consider the following statements:

> [B]usiness purposes are often manufactured in the offices of attorneys.[8]

> [S]uch tests actually stack the cards [against the IRS]; . . . the evidence as to motive is almost entirely in the possession of the taxpayer, unless psychology devises a better mental X-ray than has so far been discovered.[9]

6) The Taxable Year: Calendar or Fiscal?

Although taxes are assessed annually, business taxpayers may choose to calculate taxes on the basis of a fiscal year, that is, a year which does not correspond to the calendar year, beginning on January 1 and ending on December 31. See Section 441(a)–(e). A fiscal year may be chosen because it ends during a slow business period, when it is easier to complete accounting operations, such as the taking of inventory, needed to calculate taxable income.

A fiscal year may also be chosen in order to defer reporting taxes. In *Foglesong*, the corporation's first fiscal year did not end until August 31, 1967. If there had been no incorporation, when would Foglesong have had to pay taxes on his personal service income for the last four months of 1966? Why did Foglesong arrange to have the corporation not pay him any salary during the last four months of 1966? If it had, when would he have had to pay taxes on that income? What did he gain by having the corporation defer paying him such income until 1967?

Also, see Section 441(i)(1), enacted in 1986, which prohibits personal service corporations from using a fiscal year, "unless the corporation establishes, to the satisfaction of the Secretary [of the Treasury], a business purpose for having a different period for its taxable year."

---

8. Michaelson, "Business Purpose" and Tax-Free Reorganization, 61 Yale L.J. 14, 25 (1952).

9. R. Paul, Selected Studies in Federal Taxation 301 (2d Ser. 1938).

Chapter 47

STATUTORY MODIFICATION OF COMMON LAW PRINCIPLES

A. JOINT RETURNS

Section 1 of the Code provides different tax rate schedules for:
a) married individuals filing jointly;
b) heads of households;[1]
c) single individuals; and
d) married individuals filing separately.

When spouses file jointly, the tax is based on the combined income of husband and wife. The actual distribution of income between them is irrelevant. Married couples with the same combined income pay the same tax.

The Code does permit married couples to file separate returns, but it rarely pays to do so because separate filing almost always either increases the tax or produces no tax saving compared to joint filing.[2] Because most married couples file joint returns, incentives for shifting income to one's spouse[3] and for residing in a common law rather than in a community property state have been virtually eliminated.[4]

It is impossible for the tax system to be marriage neutral, that is, to have no impact whatsoever on a couple's decision to marry, if we wish to have both joint returns *and* progressive tax rates.[5] Currently, our tax system

---

1. Defined as a single individual who supports and has living with him or her a dependent.
2. Only in unusual circumstances will a couple save taxes by filing separately. One example is where one spouse has large unreimbursed medical expenses which will nevertheless be nondeductible under joint filing, because the expenses will not exceed 7.5% of the couple's combined AGI. See Section 213(a). Depending on the relative magnitude of each spouse's income, separate filing might make a substantial portion of such expenses deductible.
3. See Lucas v. Earl, Corliss v. Bowers, and *Clifford* (Chapter 45).
4. See Poe v. Seaborn (Chapter 45).
5. Suppose that A and B each earn $30,000 a year, that C earns $60,000 a year, and that D earns zero. If tax rates are progressive, the tax owed by C should be more than twice the tax owed by either A or B. But if A marries B and C marries D, each couple's total income

results in varying degrees of marriage "bonuses" and "penalties" depending on a couple's total income and on the distribution of that income between spouses. Generally speaking, couples in which one member has all the income receive the greatest bonus, and couples in which spouses have equal incomes are penalized the most.

To illustrate, suppose that X and Y have a combined 1988 gross income (GI) of $40,000 and take no deductions other than the standard deduction and their own personal exemptions (Chapter 1). Table 47–1 indicates taxes owed by X and Y together, depending on how much of the combined income is earned by each and depending on their filing status as well.

TABLE 47-1.

	Married, Separate Filing	Married, Joint Filing	Unmarried, Individual Filing
X earns $10,000, Y earns $30,000	$6,052.75[6]	$4,840.50[7]	$5,451.00[8]
X earns $20,000, Y earns $20,000	$4,840.50[9]	$4,840.50[10]	$4,515.00[11]

Notice that when X and Y file joint returns, the distribution of income between them is irrelevant. The total tax bill remains at $4,840.50 (the

---

is the same, and, with joint returns, each couple should pay the same amount in taxes. This is possible only if:

a) after the marriage, C's taxes (paid jointly with D) fall, in which case the system provides a "marriage bonus;" or

b) after marriage, the tax imposed on A and B rises, in which case the system imposes a "marriage penalty."

6. X's $10,000 GI, minus the $2,500 standard deduction and one $1,950 personal exemption, equals Taxable Income (TI) of $5,550. Section 1(d) imposes a tax of 15% of this figure or $832.50 due from X.

Y's $30,000 GI, minus the $2,500 standard deduction and one $1,950 personal exemption, equals TI of $25,550. When an individual's TI exceeds $14,875, Section 1(d) imposes a tax of $2,231.25 plus 28% of the excess. Y has excess TI of $10,675 ($25,550 minus $14,875); 28% of the excess equals $2,989. This figure plus $2,231.25 equals the tax due from Y of $5,220.25.

Thus, the total due from both X and Y together equals $832.50 plus $5,220.25 or $6,052.75.

7. Their $40,000 GI, minus the $5,000 standard deduction and two $1,950 personal exemptions, equals taxable income (TI) of $31,100. When TI exceeds $29,750, Section 1(a) imposes a tax of $4,462.50 plus 28% of the excess. X and Y have excess TI of $1,350 ($31,100 minus $29,750); 28% of the excess equals $378. This figure plus $4,462.50 equals the tax due of $4,840.50.

8. X's GI of $10,000, minus the $3,000 standard deduction and one $1,950 personal exemption, equals TI of $5,050. Section 1(c) imposes a tax of 15% of this amount so that X owes $757.50

Y's GI of $30,000, minus the $3,000 standard deduction and one $1,950 personal exemption, equals TI of $25,050. Section 1(c) imposes a tax of $2,677.50 plus 28% of the excess over $17,850; 28% of the $7,200 excess equals $2,016. This figure plus $2,677.50 equals the tax due from Y of $4,693.50.

Together, X and Y owe $757.50 plus $4,693.50 or a total of $5,451.

9. X and Y each have GI of $20,000. GI minus the $2,500 standard deduction and one personal exemption of $1,950, equals TI of $15,550. When TI exceeds $14,875, Section 1(d) imposes a tax of $2,231.25, plus 28% of the excess. Each has excess income of $675 ($15,550 minus $14,875). 28% of the excess equals $189. This figure plus $2,231.25 equals the tax due from each of $2,420.25. Together, X and Y owe double this amount or $4,840.50.

10. See footnote 7.

11. X and Y each have GI of $20,000, minus the $3,000 standard deduction and one $1,950 personal exemption, for TI of $15,050. The tax due under Section 1(c) from each is 15% of this amount or $2,257.50. Together, they owe twice this much or $4,515.

center column). If X and Y are married, filing separately is disadvantageous when they have unequal incomes and of no advantage when they have equal incomes (the left-hand column). When X and Y have unequal incomes, joint filing provides a marriage bonus. In this example, over $600 is saved compared to the total that they would have paid had they not married. But if X and Y have equal incomes, the Code imposes a marriage penalty. In this example, X and Y pay about $325 less in taxes if they "live together" than if they marry, leading some critics to accuse the Code of providing a "sin" bonus.

The marriage penalty (or sin bonus) has been described as unintended:

> It would be altogether absurd to suppose that Congress . . . had any invidious intent to discourage or penalize marriage—an estate enjoyed by the vast majority of its members. [It] is simply impossible to design a progressive tax regime in which all married couples of equal aggregate income are taxed equally and in which an individual's tax liability is unaffected by changes in marital status.[12]

Do you agree with the characterization of the marriage penalty as "unintended"? An income tax system with both progressive rates and joint returns could either favor marriage, penalize marriage, or do some of both. However, while marriage neutrality is impossible, a marriage penalty is not inevitable. From 1948 to 1969, for example, rate schedules were structured to provide for a marriage bonus only and no marriage penalty.[13]

How does the amount of progression in the rate structure affect the magnitude of the marriage penalty or bonus? What was the impact of the deduction for two-earner couples (Chapter 9), which is no longer in effect? How did the flattening of rates in the 1986 Tax Reform Act (Chapter 1) affect both marriage bonuses and penalties? Suppose imputed income from household services (Chapter 8) were taxed. What would be the impact on marriage bonuses and penalties?

B. THE TAXABLE UNIT

1) Choosing the Taxable Unit

The taxable unit means the person, group, or entity on which taxes are imposed according to the unit's income. Originally, the income tax treated

---

12. Druker v. Commissioner, 697 F.2d 46, 50 (2d Cir. 1982).
13. From the beginning of the income tax in 1913 until 1948, there was only one individual rate schedule. Each individual was taxed on his or her own income regardless of marital status. In 1948, Congress enacted a second rate schedule for married couples filing jointly in order to eliminate the advantage afforded by Poe v. Seaborn (Chapter 45) to couples living in community property states. Under the 1948 provision, married couples were taxed as if they were two *single* individuals, each of whom received one-half of the couple's income.

The other side of the marriage bonus was that it placed taxpayers who remained single at a serious disadvantage. In 1969, Congress responded to the complaints of singles by increasing the number of tax schedules from two to four, as listed above. The schedules were set so that a single person's tax liability would never be more than 120% of that of a married couple filing jointly with the same income. But the other side of relief for singles was to impose a marriage penalty on relatively equal-income couples.

the individual as the basic taxable unit and imposed taxes at rates determined by the individual's income. The choice of the individual as the taxable unit has been modified by the provision for joint returns, which, in effect, treats the married couple as a taxable unit. An alternative would be to treat the nuclear family as the taxable unit and to impose taxes at rates determined by the total income of all family members, children as well as parents.

If the family was defined as the taxable unit, would the distribution of income among family members matter? What are the conceptual and administrative obstacles to treating the family as the taxable unit? Until what point should a child be regarded as belonging to the same unit as his or her parents? When the child reaches the age of majority? Occupies a separate residence? Finishes college? Would an aging parent who moves in with his or her children also be regarded as belonging to their taxable unit?

2) New Section 1(i): Unearned Income of Certain Minor Children

In 1986, Congress enacted Section 1(i) to provide that *un*earned income of children under 14 years of age be taxed at the parents' rate. Section 1(i) applies only to "net unearned income." Net unearned income is defined as unearned income in excess of $500 plus the greater of $500 or deductions for the cost of producing the unearned income.

How do you feel about Section 1(i)? Do you agree with excluding a child's *earned* income from being taxed at the parents' rate? Is 14 years the right age to start to tax a child's unearned income at the child's rate? Should the age be higher or lower? What opportunities for shifting or assigning income among family members still exist? To what extent does the Code now tax the nuclear family as a single unit?

C. GRANTOR TRUSTS

1) The Grantor Trust Sections

Corliss v. Bowers, *Clifford, Blair,* and Harrison v. Schaffner (Chapter 45) set out common law principles for determining when the transfer of property to a trust effects a valid assignment of the income from the property. To implement this common law, Congress has enacted Sections 671–677, which specify in detail when the grantor will be treated as the "real" owner of the trust property and therefore taxable on the trust income. These sections deserve careful study as an example of an attempt by Congress to provide a comprehensive legislative solution to a perceived abuse.

2) Section 671: The Jurisdiction of the Grantor Trust Sections

Read the last sentence of Section 671. What is its purpose? How does it affect the statutory basis of the decision in *Clifford*? Without this language in Section 671, how might Section 61(a) be used to tax the grantor on trust income even though the grantor might not be treated as the owner of the trust property under Sections 672–677?

3) Section 673: Reversionary Interests

Section 673(a) may treat the grantor as owner of any portion of a trust in which the grantor has a reversionary interest. Prior to 1987, Section 673(a) applied only if the reversion could be expected to vest within ten years of its inception. Grantors could be certain that a more than ten-year reversionary interest would not render the assignment invalid. Thus, under the prior version of Section 673(a), it was commonplace for trusts to be created for a period just over ten years, with reversion to the grantor.

The new version, enacted in 1986, is much stricter. It applies if the value of the reversion (at its inception) "exceeds 5% of the [present] value of that portion." The present value of a reversion will depend on the interest rate as well as on how soon after inception it is expected to vest. At an interest rate of 12%, a grantor reversion is less than 5% of value and avoids Section 673(a) only if it is not expected to vest for twenty-six years. At an interest rate of 10%, the period before vesting must be thirty-one years, and at 8%, the period must be forty years.

4) Section 674: Power to Control Beneficial Enjoyment

Section 674(a) appears to treat the grantor as owner if either she or a nonadverse party can affect the beneficial enjoyment of trust property or income. Section 674, like Sections 675, 676, and 677, imputes to the grantor any power held by a nonadverse party. What is a nonadverse party? See the definitions in Sections 672(a) and (b). What is the unstated assumption made in these sections about such parties? Why does Section 674(a) not apply if an adverse party must consent to the exercise of a power over trust property or income?

Section 674(a)'s broad reach—treating the grantor as owner if either the grantor or a nonadverse party has any power to affect beneficial enjoyment of income or corpus—is subject to numerous qualifications and exceptions, contained in Section 674(b) and (c).

Suppose that Parent transfers property in trust. The income is payable to Children for the rest of Parent's life. When Parent dies, the trust property is to be distributed to beneficiaries named in Parent's will. Does Section 674(a) apply to treat the grantor as owner? See Section 674(b)(3).

Suppose that Parent may also distribute trust property to the other Parent for the other Parent's "reasonable comfort and support"? See Section 674(b)(5)(A) and Reg. § 1.674(b)–1(b)(5)(i).

Suppose that Parent may withhold income from any Child and add it to the corpus? See Section 674(b)(6).

Suppose that Parent's lawyer and housekeeper are trustees and that the trustees have unfettered discretion to distribute either income or corpus to the named beneficiaries. See Section 674(c). What is the definition of an "independent trustee"? See Section 672(c).

Are these exceptions to Section 674(a) consistent with the spirit of Justice Douglas' opinion in *Clifford* (Chapter 45)? In Corliss v. Bowers and *Clifford*, the donors could have shifted income to the donees simply by making an absolute (or outright) gift of the property. Why did the donors choose not to adopt this method? In some circumstances, a potential conflict may exist between the goal of minimizing taxes and the goal of controlling family members. A donor who does not trust his or her spouse, for example, or who wants leverage to control the behavior of his or her children, may choose not to make an outright gift. A donor who is confident of controlling the donees through other means (guilt, for example) may not hesitate to shift taxation of income from property by making a "no strings" gift. Are the exceptions contained in Section 674(b) and (c) defensible as putting parents who are not adept at emotional manipulation on more or less the same footing as parents who are?

5) Section 675: Administrative Powers

Section 675 treats the grantor as owner if the grantor or a nonadverse party possesses any of the listed administrative powers. For example, Section 675(1) applies to a power to buy or to sell trust property for less than adequate consideration. And Section 675(2) applies to a power to make a loan to the grantor without adequate interest or security.

6) Section 676: Power to Revest

Section 676 treats the grantor as owner if the grantor or a nonadverse party has the power to revest trust property in the grantor. If the power to revest is limited to a portion of a trust, Section 676(a) applies only to that portion.

7) Section 677: Income for Benefit of Grantor

Section 677(a) treats the grantor as owner if the grantor or a nonadverse party may distribute income or accumulate income for future distribution to the grantor or the grantor's spouse. However, trust income that may be used to support the grantor's children is taxable to the grantor only to the extent that it *is* so used. See the first sentence of Section 677(b). What is the definition of support? Does it extend to luxuries as well as to necessities? Suppose that trust income pays for trips to Europe or private school tuition for the grantor's children. Is the grantor taxable on the income?

8) Nongrantor Trusts

If Sections 672–677 do not apply—and the grantor is not treated as the owner—to whom is trust income taxed? The taxation of so-called nongrantor trusts is a complex, detailed subject and therefore this introductory casebook will set out only the broad outlines. Ordinarily, distributed trust income is taxed directly to the beneficiaries. Accumulated income is taxable to the trust at rates determined under Section 1(e). When ultimately distributed, income that had been accumulated and taxed to the trust is taxed again to the beneficiaries. However, the beneficiary is given credit for the tax already paid by the trust.

Taxing accumulated income twice—first to the trust and then a second time to the beneficiary—approximates a one-level tax at the beneficiary level. The key word is "approximates" since the time period between accumulation and distribution may provide deferral value. If the beneficiary's tax bracket is higher than the trust's, the additional tax owed by the beneficiary is deferred for that period—although again the potential benefit has been greatly diminished by the substantially flatter rate schedules in the 1986 Tax Reform Act.

9) Section 1(i) and the Grantor Trust Sections

The reader should note the relationship between Section 1(i) and the grantor trust sections. Even if the grantor is not taxable under Sections 671–677, the trust arrangement may be affected by the new "Unearned Income of Minor Children" provisions. When the beneficiary is under fourteen years of age, the beneficiary's income will be taxed under Section 1(i) at the parents' rate.

D. BELOW–MARKET INTEREST GIFT LOANS

1) Using Loans to Avoid Section 673(a)

If Parent tries to assign income from property to Child for a short period by creating a short-term trust, Parent will be taxable on the income under Section 673(a). For example, suppose Parent transfers cash or property in trust for five years, with the investment income payable to Child and remainder to Parent. Under either the old or the new version of Section 673(a), the retention of a reversionary interest to vest in five years after the trust's inception means that Parent will be taxable on the trust income.

For many years, however, interest-free and below-market interest loans were successfully used to make short-term assignments of income without running afoul of Section 673(a). For example, suppose Parent lends Child $100,000, payable in five years, at zero interest and that the market rate of interest is 10%. In effect, why has Parent assigned $10,000 of income a year for five years to Child? Or suppose the loan carries an interest rate of 5%. In effect, why has Parent assigned $5,000 of income a year for five years to Child?

How might the IRS have tried to prevent the assignment of income through related party loans? By arguing that the loan is economically equivalent to a trust and therefore subject to the grantor trust provisions? What is the weakness of such an argument? By arguing that interest be imputed to both lender and borrower as if paid? Could the IRS argue that the lender be treated as if he or she made a gift each year to the borrower, which the borrower then used to pay interest on the loan? How would such imputation of interest prevent the assignment of income? For reasons discussed in Chapters 51–53, the courts refused to accept such imputation arguments.

2) The Statutory Solution: Section 7872

Section 7872, enacted in 1984, imputes interest flows to lender and borrower on below-market interest loans. Section 7872(a) applies where the purpose of the below-market interest loan is to make a gift.[14] According to a congressional report:

> A below-market loan is the economic equivalent of a loan bearing a market rate of interest, and a payment by the lender to the borrower to fund the payment of interest by the borrower. The Congress believed that, in many instances, the failure of the tax laws to treat these transactions in accordance with their economic substance provided taxpayers with opportunities to circumvent well-established tax rules.
>
> Under prior law, loans between family members (and other similar loans) were being used to avoid the assignment of income rules and the grantor trust rules. A below-market loan to a family member, for example, generally involves a gratuitous transfer of the right to use the proceeds of the borrowing until repayment is demanded (in the case of a demand loan) or until the end of the term of the loan (in the case of a term loan). If the lender had assigned the income from the proceeds to the borrower instead of lending the proceeds to the borrower, the assignment of income doctrine would have taxed the lender (and not the borrower) on the income. If the lender had transferred the principal amount to a trust established for the benefit of the borrower that was revocable at will (similar to a demand loan), or that would terminate at the end of a period of not more than 10 years (similar to a term loan with a term of not more than 10 years), the income earned on trust assets would have been taxed to the lender under the grantor trust provisions set forth in Code secs. 671–679.[15]

Congress, however, did not close the loophole completely. Section 7872(d)(1)(A) contains an exception for gift loans of less than $100,000. The exception is unavailable if *one* principal purpose of the loan is tax avoidance. Section 7872(d)(1)(B). Can you imagine circumstances in which this is not the case?

---

14. Interest is also imputed when the lender provides a below-market rate of interest in consideration for an economic benefit received from the borrower. See Chapter 53.

15. Staff of Joint Committee on Taxation, 98th Cong., 2d Sess., General Explanation of the Revenue Provisions of the Deficit Reduction Act of 1984 527 (Comm. Print 1984).

Chapter 48

GIFT AND LEASEBACK

A. ROSENFELD v. COMMISSIONER
706 F.2d 1277 (2d Cir. 1983)

IRVING R. KAUFMAN, CIRCUIT JUDGE:

For as long as governments have taxed their citizens, individuals have sought to minimize their tax burdens. On occasion, members of the public have employed elaborate devices to defer taxes or shift income to their associates and relatives in lower tax brackets. When such schemes completely lack legitimate purposes and affect no real economic or beneficial interests, courts have not hesitated to pierce the formal arrangements and examine the substance of the underlying transaction. At the same time, judges have recognized that taxpayers are generally free to order their investment and business decisions to reduce their tax liability. As Judge Learned Hand eloquently noted, "one may so arrange his affairs that his taxes shall be as low as possible; he is not bound to choose that pattern which will best pay the Treasury; there is not even a patriotic duty to increase one's taxes." . . .

This case calls upon us to draw, once again, the fine line between valid business transactions and illegitimate tax avoidance ploys. We are required to determine, as a matter of first impression within this Circuit, whether a taxpayer who gives property to his children in trust may lease back that property for use as a professional office, and deduct the rent payments from his income pursuant to I.R.C. § 162(a)(3). Because we believe these transactions involved real transfers of economic interests, and for other reasons set forth below, we affirm the Tax Court's order allowing the rent deductions.

I

Since the underlying facts are important to the resolution of this dispute, we set them forth in some detail.

775

In 1963 George B. Rosenfeld, a doctor practicing in Cheektowaga, New York, purchased a parcel of land in that town. Shortly thereafter, Rosenfeld arranged for a building to be constructed on the property, intended for use as a medical office. Since the completion of the building in 1964, Rosenfeld has been its sole occupant.

In 1969 Rosenfeld decided to establish a trust for the benefit of his three daughters, and to transfer the land and medical office to the trust. Prior to executing this transaction, he arranged for an independent firm, Grant Appraisal & Research Corporation, to value the property. After the appraiser concluded that the fair rental of the property was $14,000 per year, Rosenfeld created an irrevocable trust, and arranged for Samuel Goldman, his accountant, and Ira Powsner, his attorney, to act as trustees. Pursuant to the terms of the agreement, the trustees were responsible for collecting income produced by the property and investing it, until the termination of the trust, at which time the accumulated proceeds would be distributed to the beneficiaries.

The trust was to have a term of 10½ years, and Rosenfeld retained a reversionary interest in the corpus. During the period of the trust, he remained liable for the mortgage payments and general upkeep of the property. The trustees were responsible for the payment of real estate taxes. Rosenfeld had no right to alter the terms of the trust, and was legally obligated to fulfill its requirements.

The trust agreement was executed on July 1, 1969, and on that same date, Rosenfeld entered into a lease with the trustees. Rosenfeld agreed to rent the medical property for the entire term of the trust for annual payments of $14,000, the amount fixed by the appraisers as fair and reasonable. The lease also required Rosenfeld to pay utility and other incidental expenses, and granted him the right to construct additions to the building at his expense.

In 1973, Rosenfeld decided to transfer his reversionary interest in the trust property to his wife. Two years later, appellee and the trustees agreed upon further changes and amended the trust to extend its termination date for 5 years, from 1980 to 1985. Also in 1975 the lease agreement was modified to increase the annual rent to $15,000, and alter the rental term to one year, renewable for an additional year at Rosenfeld's option.

We now approach the core of this dispute. In his tax returns for 1974 and 1975, Rosenfeld claimed a deduction for his rent payments to the trust pursuant to I.R.C. § 162(a)(3), which allows a taxpayer to deduct from his income "ordinary and necessary" rent expenses incurred as a condition of the taxpayer's trade or business. The trust ... reported the amounts paid by appellee as income. The trust also claimed deductions for real estate taxes and depreciation on the property. After auditing Rosenfeld's returns, the Commissioner disallowed the deductions for the rent expenses in 1974 and 1975. In October 1977, appellee received a statutory notice of deficiency, and, as one would anticipate under these circumstances, he challenged the Commissioner's assessment. . . .

II

While, as we have noted, this appeal raises a question of first impression in this Circuit, we are not writing on a *tabula rasa*. The issue on this appeal has not suffered from lack of consideration by various tribunals. The Tax Court has been confronted with this problem on numerous occasions, and several other Circuits have also expressed their views. These authorities, however, have been divided on the proper tax treatment of a claimed deduction in a gift-leaseback situation. Generally the Tax Court's recent decisions have allowed deductions in similar situations. But we find the Courts of Appeals have split on this issue. The Third, Seventh, Eighth and Ninth Circuits have held in favor of the taxpayer, while the Fourth and Fifth Circuits have adopted the Commissioner's view. It is against this background of divergent views that we are called upon to exercise our Solomonic powers and resolve the instant dispute, by determining which of the conclusions reached among the Circuits accords with the law, and, indeed, is the fairer course to follow. . . .

In considering the validity of a claimed deduction in a gift-leaseback situation, we have been given some guidance by the Tax Court which has devised a four-prong test. To receive the deduction, "1) [t]he grantor must not retain substantially the same control over the property that he had before he made the gift, 2) [t]he leaseback should normally be in writing and must require the payment of a reasonable rent, 3) [t]he leaseback (as distinguished from the gift) must have a bona fide business purpose, [and] 4) [t]he grantor must not possess a disqualifying 'equity' in the property. . . .

. . . Pursuant to the terms of the trust agreement, the trustees were authorized to mortgage or sell the property, grant easements, and exercise other powers traditionally associated with ownership. Moreover, Rosenfeld was obligated to pay rent, and although the initial lease granted a right of occupancy for the entire term of the trust, the amended lease was only for a single year, renewable for one additional year. Rosenfeld was also prohibited from subletting the property or assigning his rights under the lease. . . .

The Commissioner . . . claims, as we have indicated, that the entire transaction, and not merely the leaseback, must be imbued with a valid business purpose. But we are of the view that such a requirement is too harsh for it would lead inevitably to a denial of the rent deduction, despite its clear business purpose, because the gift of the land was not *ipso facto* a business transaction. The Commissioner's argument calls for a test which is overly stringent, particularly in the circumstances here. Many financial decisions are motivated by the prospect of legitimate tax savings, rather than business concerns, and we have already expressed our agreement with Judge Learned Hand's view that a transaction which is otherwise legitimate, is not unlawful merely because an individual seeks to minimize the tax consequences of his activities. . . .

. . . Congress has explicitly considered the gift aspect of this transaction which the Commissioner finds objectionable. The so-called Clifford trust provisions of the Internal Revenue Code, 26 U.S.C. §§ 671–678, specifically address the creation of short-term trusts, and impose minimum requirements which must be satisfied before the trust income can be taxed to the beneficial owner. While these provisions are not dispositive of the issue whether payments to the trust may be deducted . . . we cannot blind ourselves to the interplay between these provisons and § 162(a)(3). . . .

The Commissioner's position that both the trust and the leaseback must have a legitimate business purpose, ignores the Congressional policy inherent in the Clifford sections. It is difficult to imagine a case in which the establishment of such a trust could be viewed as furthering a taxpayer's business objectives. Quite simply, Clifford trusts are income-shifting devices designed to shelter income, and we cannot lightly overlook the legislative determination that trusts which comply with §§ 671–678 are legitimate. Accepting the Commissioner's view . . . "would produce a benefit only in cases where investment property—not used in the grantor's trade or business—is placed in trust. Persons whose assets consist largely of business property would be excluded from a tax benefit clearly provided by Congress."

Accordingly, we decline appellant's invitation to adopt a business purpose standard of review. Rather, we believe our inquiry should focus on whether there has been a change in the economic interests of the relevant parties. If their legal rights and beneficial interests have changed, there is no basis for labeling a transaction a "sham" and ignoring it for tax purposes. . . .

It is readily apparent here that there has been a real change in the legal rights and interests of the parties. As we noted, the trustees were granted broad powers over the corpus of the trust, which necessarily reduced Rosenfeld's authority. Moreover, during the years in issue, Rosenfeld had no present or future interest in the property. When he deeded his reversion in 1973, he retained no legal or equitable right to the trust property. . . . The trustees were required to collect a fixed rent which the Commissioner concedes is fair, and also to discharge their fiduciary duties to the trust beneficiaries. Although the lease was initially coterminous with the trust, the lease amendments required renegotiation on an annual basis if Rosenfeld was to continue to occupy the building, and there is nothing presented to us to cause us to believe that this bargaining would not be carried out at arm's length.

In addition to these substantial changes in the economic positions of the parties, there were legitimate non-tax motives for the creation of the trust and the leaseback. Rosenfeld understandably wanted to guarantee his children's financial well-being, and the trust helped assure realization of this objective. . . .

While recognizing these factors, the Commissioner asserts, nonetheless, that nothing changed because Rosenfeld was occupying the same premises as a lessee which he previously used as the owner. This argument is disingenuous. Rosenfeld could have given the property to his children in trust and leased property from a third party for an amount equally fair and reasonable for his medical office. It is clear, and indeed, counsel conceded at oral argument, that a rent deduction would have been entirely proper in such a case. *See Frank Lyon Co. v. United States,* supra. In real terms, there is little difference between this hypothetical case and the events the Commissioner challenges. In both cases Rosenfeld would have voluntarily relinquished his right to occupy his offices rent-free, and created the need to lease other premises. It can hardly be a matter of concern for the Commissioner whether Rosenfeld rents from the trust rather than from some third party. In either situation he would be required to pay rent, and the trust could receive rental income from the property it owned.

III

In sum, we believe the gift-leaseback transaction substantially altered Rosenfeld's economic and beneficial rights, and accordingly, the arrangement, which was otherwise proper under both the Clifford sections of the Internal Revenue Code and § 162(a)(3), was not rendered objectionable merely because Rosenfeld's rent payments were made to a trust which he established for the benefit of his children. The Tax Court properly concluded that Rosenfeld had a right to deduct his rent expenses pursuant to I.R.C. § 162(a)(3). . . .

MacMahon, District Judge, dissenting:

I respectfully dissent. It is fundamental that in determining liability for income taxes courts consider the economic reality, not the form, of financial transactions. In the words of Judge Learned Hand:

> The Income Tax Act imposes liabilities upon taxpayers based upon their financial transactions, and it is of course true that the payment of the tax is itself a financial transaction. *If, however, the taxpayer enters into a transaction that does not appreciably affect his beneficial interest except to reduce his tax, the law will disregard it;* for we cannot suppose that it was part of the purpose of the act to provide an escape from the liabilities that it sought to impose.

. . . Since I find that the transaction here does not appreciably affect the beneficial interest of the taxpayer, except to reduce his tax, I cannot agree with the majority. Nor can I find either a business purpose in the transaction or a significant transfer of control over the property.

I. *Business Purpose* . . .

The total payments made by Dr. Rosenfeld were far in excess of the reasonable rental value of the office. This court previously has recognized, in a gift-leaseback, the significance of the fact that the transaction is disadvantageous to the business. . . . In the instant case, Dr. Rosenfeld initially paid $14,000 per year, which was the gross rental, as determined by an independent appraiser, necessary to carry the building's fair market value. However, the appraiser determined that the highest and best use of the building was as a professional office, with the unfinished one-third of the building "finished and occupied." But Dr. Rosenfeld paid the full appraised rent while using the one-third unfinished space not for an office but for storage. In addition, Dr. Rosenfeld remained liable on the mortgage and continued to make the monthly payments. The standard in this court for determining whether a business expense is "ordinary and necessary," 26

U.S.C. § 162(a), and therefore deductible, is whether a hard-headed businessman, under the circumstances, would have incurred the expense.... These terms, I submit, are not the terms on which a hard-headed businessman would sign a lease for an office he already owned and occupied. Dr. Rosenfeld remained liable on the mortgage so that the gift of the building to the trust would be of greater value to his daughters and, presumably, because the interest deductions were of more value to him than to the trust. He was willing to pay a high rent because the greater the rent, the greater the gift to his daughters and the lower the family's taxes....

Dr. Rosenfeld's scheme amounts in substance to an assignment of $14,000 of his yearly income to the trust. Such an assignment would not be recognized by the tax law.... In the instant case, Dr. Rosenfeld in effect diverted $14,000 of his income to the trust by taking a business deduction for rent. The only conclusion that can be drawn from these facts is that the trust, deed and lease were conceived and executed at the same time and for the same purpose and that the purpose was to make gifts to Dr. Rosenfeld's children.... The majority offers the validity of the trust as the sole "other factor" to be considered. In addition, the majority concludes that the test to be applied to the gift is whether the gift was a "sham." In other words, if the gift is valid, the deduction is allowed; if the gift is a sham, the deduction is denied.... However, the majority's reliance on the validity of the trust does not withstand analysis.

First, the legislative history plainly states that the Clifford trust sections are irrelevant in determining the deductibility of Dr. Rosenfeld's rental payments. The Senate Finance Committee Report states:

> The effect of this provision is to insure that taxability of Clifford type trusts shall be governed solely by this subpart [rather than by 26 U.S.C. § 61]. However, this provision does not affect the principles governing the taxability of income to a grantor or assignor other than by reason of his dominion and control over the trust.... *This subpart also has no application in determining the right of a grantor to deductions for payments to a trust under a transfer and leaseback arrangement.*

... This language could hardly be clearer.

Second, the majority relies on the argument ... that to deny a deduction here "would produce a benefit only in cases where investment property—not used in the grantor's trade or business—is placed in trust. Persons whose assets consist largely of business property would be excluded from a tax benefit clearly provided by Congress."... The infirmities of this argument are many.... [It] ignores the fact that this "benefit clearly provided" is not "provided" to the majority of taxpayers who do not have assets lying around that they can give away for ten years at a time.... [There] would be no such "unfairness" if the taxpayer had assets other than business property which could form the corpus of a Clifford trust. The record does not indicate ... whether the respective taxpayers had other assets substantial enough to form the corpus of a Clifford trust....

The majority also argues, later in its opinion, that there is no difference "in real terms" between this case and the hypothetical case where Dr. Rosenfeld leases office space somewhere else and the trust property is leased to a third party. But there is a difference, as shown in Part II of this dissent. Dr. Rosenfeld exerted substantial control over the property by remaining in a building he previously owned and that he, and later his wife, would own in the future, and by dealing with trustee-lessors who were his personal advisors, and later his daughter. Although his legal interest in the property was a leasehold, he acted as both tenant and landlord and claimed the tax deductions available to both a tenant (rent) and an owner (interest on the mortgage). In short, Dr. Rosenfeld wants to have his cake, or more accurately the Treasury's, and eat it too.

In sum, Dr. Rosenfeld began paying rent on July 1, 1969, not in order to have an office in which to practice medicine, because he already had such an office. He began paying rent so that the trust would have income and his purpose of making a lifetime gift to his children would be fulfilled. There was simply no business purpose in this transaction. . . .

II. *Retention of Control*

The government argues that . . . Dr. Rosenfeld should not be granted a deduction for his rental payments. The government bases this argument on the principles that transactions lacking in economic substance cannot form the basis for tax deductions, . . . and that transactions entered into among family members for the purpose of splitting income must be examined with strict scrutiny. . . . *Helvering v. Clifford* . . . . The majority ignores these principles, applying instead the first prong of the Tax Court's special four-part test. This prong requires that the grantor, in order to receive a deduction, must not retain "substantially the same control over the property that he had before he made the gift." Because I believe that even this requirement has not been met, I must dissent on this ground also.

The original trustees, Mr. Powsner and Mr. Goldman, were Dr. Rosenfeld's advisors. They were the individuals who concocted the gift-leaseback scheme, and it is to be expected that they would want Dr. Rosenfeld to be satisfied with the arrangement. Nor surprisingly, the trustees never spoke with another potential tenant in 1969, and there is no evidence that they did so in 1975 when the new lease was signed. The trustees' purpose obviously was to satisfy both their fiduciary duties and Dr. Rosenfeld, and, indeed, Mr. Goldman testified that he saw no reason for contacting other potential tenants and "disturbing the doctor's practice." Moreover, it is fair to say that the original trustees, if not bosom buddies, certainly were located less than an arm's length from Dr. Rosenfeld. . . .

The lease also granted Dr. Rosenfeld the right to build onto the building, an indicia of ownership one would not expect to find in a tenant's hands. Moreover, as explained in Part I, supra, the total payments made by Dr. Rosenfeld were excessive. Dr. Rosenfeld was willing to pay a premium because he was more than a tenant.

In 1973 Dr. Rosenfeld deeded his reversion in the trust corpus to his wife. The possibility, urged by Dr. Rosenfeld's counsel, that the Rosenfelds might obtain a divorce in the future is mere speculation, while the question before us is one of fact. The reversion in Dr. Rosenfeld's wife is of little relevance because the question is one of control, not one of equity.... In short, that Dr. Rosenfeld became wise enough in 1973 to deed the reversion to his wife does nothing to weaken the substantial control he retained.

In 1975 Dr. Rosenfeld amended the trust, extending its term five and one-half years. He was able to extend the trust even though, having already deeded his reversion to his wife, he had no beneficial interest in the corpus. By extending the trust, Dr. Rosenfeld shifted from his wife to his daughters the income of the property for the period covered by the extension. And there is little chance that Dr. Rosenfeld would be opposed in another attempt to extend the trust: his daughters would not object, and his wife is not likely to object because her income from the property would be taxed to him.... Dr. Rosenfeld, for all practical purposes, has the power to determine who receives the income from the property.

Moreover, when Dr. Rosenfeld amended the trust, he appointed his daughter Barbara and Robert Swados, an attorney, as trustees.[1] The amendment provided that the trustees could act by majority vote, but only if Barbara Rosenfeld was among the majority. In other words, the trustees could take no action opposed by Barbara Rosenfeld, who was, of course, the grantor's daughter, a beneficiary of the trust and a recipient of her father's largesse.

In sum, the question before us is not what amount of control Dr. Rosenfeld gave to the trustees, but whether the control he retained was "substantially the same [as] he had before he made the gift." Dr. Rosenfeld determined whether to improve the unfinished space in the building, and he had the right to build onto the building. He paid all expenses of the land and building except real estate taxes and structural repairs, the deduction which he shifted to his family. He faced no competitors either time he signed a lease with the trustees. The trustees were his advisors and, later, his daughter Barbara, one of the recipients of his largesse. Dr. Rosenfeld extended the trust once, installing his daughter as a trustee with an essential vote, and might do so again. This, I think, is enough control over the building to be "substantially the same ... [as] he had before he made the gift," and to make Dr. Rosenfeld ... the "actual enjoyer and owner of the property." ... As this court recently stated, " '*for tax purposes,* there was not a sufficient severance of the [taxpayer's] ownership over the assets for the transaction to create the tax consequence' intended for her." ...

B. NOTES AND QUESTIONS

1) Applying the Grantor Trust Sections

Are the trustees in *Rosenfeld* adverse or nonadverse parties under Section 672(a) and (b)? Why isn't the grantor treated as the owner of the trust property under Sections 673(a), 674(a), 675, 676(a), or 677(a)? How does

---

[1] Mr. Powsner had died before this.

modifying the trust five years after its creation affect application of the grantor trust sections?

2) Applying the Judicial Doctrines of *Estate of Starr* and *Frank Lyon*

Suppose that (a) Rosenfeld had simply given the real estate to his daughters; (b) the daughters had then leased the property back to Rosenfeld for ten and one-half years, under a net lease; and (c) the daughters had also granted Rosenfeld an option to repurchase the property at the lease's end for a nominal amount. Does this hypothetical gift and leaseback arrangement differ significantly from the trust and leaseback in *Rosenfeld*?

In such a gift and leaseback, would the daughters be treated as the owners under *Estate of Starr* or *Frank Lyon*? Would they possess a significant residual? Would they bear significant risks? Should it make any difference if their mother, rather than their father, held the repurchase option? Hint: The mother holding the repurchase option in the hypothetical gift and leaseback is analogous to the mother holding the reversionary interest in the modified trust and leaseback.

3) The Relationship Between the Grantor Trust Sections and the Judicial Doctrines

Why do the grantor trust sections, on the one hand, and judicial doctrines for determining who is the real owner of leased property, on the other, appear to conflict? How do the two approaches differ in determining who really owns property? How does the 1986 amendment of Section 673(a) tend to eliminate this difference? In order to avoid Section 673(a) as amended, how much time must Rosenfeld allow to pass before his reversionary interest vests? (See Chapter 47.)

If the trust must exist for at least thirty years, will the typical grantor even bother to retain a reversion? Can a grantor avoid Section 673(a) by setting up a shorter term trust and naming his or her spouse as remainderperson, as Rosenfeld did when he extended the trust term for five years? See Section 672(e), enacted in 1986.

4) Equitable Considerations

The majority argues that it would be inequitable to treat Rosenfeld as owner. As compared to whom? Why? How does the dissent answer the majority's fairness argument? What different comparison does it make? How do the grantor trust sections (as well as the principles of assignment of income law in general) favor income from property over income from labor?

5) Owning (and Depreciating) versus Renting

When Rosenfeld transferred the property in trust, he relinquished the right to depreciate the building. Why did it become advantageous to shift ownership to his children at this particular time? Why was depreciation likely to exceed rent under a lease during the early years when he owned the building? At about what point would rent begin to exceed depreciation?

6) Tax Consequences on the Transfer of Mortgaged Property

What tax detriment should have arisen if, when Rosenfeld transferred the building, it was subject to a nonrecourse mortgage? Or to an ordinary mortgage for which the trust assumed responsibility? In that event, would the transfer be considered partly a sale? See *Diedrich* (Chapter 22).

If the transfer relieved Rosenfeld of a mortgage liability so that gain was realized, would the gain be ordinary income or capital gain? (Note that Section 1250 applies only to real property placed in service after 1964, apparently too late for the building in *Rosenfeld*.) To the extent that the gain is capital, is there another advantage to the transaction in addition to the shifting of income? Why might it also allow ordinary income to be transformed into capital gain? Compare with *Redwing Carriers* (Chapter 37).

Chapter 49

PRIVATE ANNUITIES AND ALIMONY

A. LAFARGUE v. COMMISSIONER
689 F.2d 845 (9th Cir. 1982)

CANBY, CIRCUIT JUDGE:

Taxpayer appeals from a decision of the Tax Court . . . [and] contends that the court improperly characterized the transfer of her property to a trust. . . .

. . . In 1971 Taxpayer established a trust with $100. The trust agreement provided for independent trustees and taxpayer's daughter was the named beneficiary. Taxpayer was neither a trustee nor a beneficiary under the terms of the trust. A few days after establishing the trust, taxpayer executed an Annuity Agreement with the trustees. Pursuant to that agreement she transferred property worth $335,000 to the trustees in exchange for annual lifetime payments of $16,502. The property she transferred included non-income producing land, proceeds from the liquidation of a business, and assorted stocks and municipal bonds. The actuarial value of the $16,502 annuity was significantly less than the value of the property transferred, since the annuity amount was calculated without giving effect to any time discount factor. Both the initial creation of the trust and the subsequent transfer of the property were integral parts of a prearranged plan, the details of which were designed to minimize Taxpayer's tax liability.

The Tax Court characterized the $16,502 annual payments as distributions of trust income, taxable to the grantor under I.R.C. §§ 677(a) and 671. In the terms of § 677(a), Taxpayer was treated as the grantor of "a trust . . . whose income . . . is, or . . . may be—(1) distributed to the grantor . . . [or] (2) held or accumulated for future distribution to the grantor. . . ." The alternative was to treat the original transfer of the property to the trust as a sale, perhaps with a gift component, and to view taxpayer as receiving the fixed annual payments in the capacity of an annuitant and creditor of the trust, subject to the income tax provisions of I.R.C. § 72.

The Tax Court's analysis is heavily dependent upon factual determinations. We cannot disturb these, absent clear error. We do not believe, however, that the facts are sufficient to justify the Tax Court's recharacterization of the transfer of the property. We are convinced that the annuity characterization comports with the formal structure of the transaction and accurately reflects its substance. The formal agreement concerning the transfer of Taxpayer's property to the trustees . . . establishes her status as a creditor of the trust. She must transfer the property; in exchange, the trustees must pay her $16,502 annually. The $16,502 payments have been made each year and the payments have not fluctuated with the income of the trust. Thus the fundamental annuity obligation has not been ignored or modified. Under these circumstances, absent some indication that the annuity payment agreed upon is a mere disguise for transferring the income of the trust to the grantor, rather than a payment for the property transferred, we cannot justify disregarding the formal structure of the transaction as a sale in exchange for an annuity. Accordingly, we reverse.

In reaching this conclusion, we have reviewed the factors considered by the Tax Court. We accept the Tax Court's conclusion that Taxpayer sold the property for less than she might have had the beneficiary of the trust been a stranger. But this factor does not alter the fundamental structure of the transaction as a sale in exchange for an annuity. At most it suggests that the transfer was partially a gift . . . posing certain questions concerning the income tax ramifications of the transaction.

The Tax Court also concluded that Taxpayer viewed herself as the beneficial owner of the property rather than as a creditor of the trust, on the basis of certain "informalities" in the administration of the trust and the transfer of the property to it. Particularly in the context of non-arm's length sales and trust arrangements, it is important to scrutinize whether the parties actually did what they purported to do in the formal documents. . . . In the present case, such scrutiny is appropriate because the Trustees were friends of Taxpayer and Taxpayer's daughter was the beneficiary of the trust. But the "informality" the Tax Court found did not justify disregarding taxpayer's formal characterization of the entire transaction as a sale in exchange for an annuity. The Tax Court observed that the issuers of most of the transferred stock were not notified of the transfer until November 1973, and that as a result Taxpayer received approximately $2,200 in dividends each year during 1971, 1972, and 1973. The stock, however, represented only a fraction of the total property transferred and the Tax Court's decision did not confine itself to taxing Taxpayer on these dividends. We do not believe that a temporary defect in the transfer of this stock should serve as a basis for recasting the entire transaction from a sale or gift, taxable as such, to a transfer in trust. The Tax Court also observed that taxpayer did not assert her contractual right to a penalty when the annuity payments were a few months late. However, waiver of a late charge, without more, does not show that the trustees intended to ignore the fundamental contractual obligation to pay $16,502 annually, or that Taxpayer did not intend to enforce it. Finally, the Tax Court observed that Taxpayer expected to be kept informed on trust matters. Had she taken an active role in trust investment decisions or held some power to manage the trust or control the trustees, we might [reach a different result]. But the record demonstrates that Taxpayer was not well-informed concerning trust investments, did not take an active role in trust management, and held no power to manage the trust or in any way control the trustees. Thus the "informalities" considered by the Tax Court do not justify disregarding Taxpayer's characterization of the transaction as a sale in exchange for an annuity. Taken as a whole, the facts clearly show that the fundamental transfer and annuity obligations of the contract were being met, and that Taxpayer relinquished control over the property transferred.

The Tax Court concentrated its analysis on the factual similarities between the present case and *Lazarus v. Commissioner*. . . . In *Lazarus,* as here, the taxpayers met with their advisor to devise a method for disposing of their assets for the benefit of their children, while minimizing tax consequences. Pursuant to a prearranged plan, they entered into a trust agreement establishing an irrevocable trust with independent trustees, and with their children as beneficiaries. The trust was funded with $1,000. Seven months later, as planned, they transferred their shopping center stock to the trust, under a formal "Annuity Agreement." The agreement entitled them to a joint and survivor "annuity" of $75,000 and the present value of the annuity was considerably less than the value of the property transferred. But this was not the end of the *Lazarus* plan. Almost immediately after transferring the stock, the trust sold it in exchange for a note. The note was then the *only* asset in the trust and just happened to yield $75,000 in interest income annually, exactly enough to pay the "annuity" payments to the taxpayers. The trust contained no other income producing property and none of the income from the note could accumulate to provide for other trust investments. Since the note was non-negotiable and could not be assigned, there was no fund from which to collect the $75,000 "annuity" except for the annual interest on the note. The payment would consume the trust's income—no more, no less. It could never be paid out of the trust corpus.

Affirming the Tax Court, this circuit determined that to recharacterize the transaction was reasonable . . . and agreed that the grantor had transferred the property to the trust retaining a life estate in the trust's income, rather than selling it to the trust in exchange for an annuity. . . . Although the payment amount was fixed, as an annuity arising out of a sale would be, it was obviously a "mere conduit" for transmitting the income of the trust to the grantor . . . and not a payment for the property transferred. Congress specifically provided for taxing such income reservations under I.R.C. § 677.

The fundamental rationale of *Lazarus* simply cannot apply to Taxpayer's annuity arrangement since the fixed annuity payments were not a conduit for the income of the trust. In the case before us there was no evidence indicating that the payments are anything other than payments for the property transferred. There was no "tie-in" between the income of the trust and the amount of the annuity. . . . Certainly, in both the present case and *Lazarus,* there was a discrepancy between the fair market value of the property transferred and the actuarial value of the annuity the taxpayers received. But in the present case, this discrepancy was due to Taxpayer's failure to account for a time discount factor, not an attempt to provide her with the income of the trust.

We also recognize that in both the present case and *Lazarus* the property the Taxpayers transferred constituted the bulk of the trust assets, and that the *Lazarus* opinion accorded significance to this factor. We believe, however, that in *Lazarus*, its principal effect was to bolster the court's determination that the annuity represented a reservation of trust income. The trust's only asset was a single note which was non-assignable and non-negotiable, so the interest income on the note was the only practical source for the "annuity" payment. . . . In contrast to *Lazarus*, here the trust corpus was assessable for payment of the annuity, and, in fact, some corpus was used. In years when trust income exceeded the annuity amount the excess was available to the trustees for further investment or distribution to beneficiaries. The payment simply did not represent a camouflaged transfer of trust income, and the fact that the bulk of the trust's assets were obtained under the agreement has not been shown to have any practical or legal bearing on the trustee's obligation or ability to comply with the terms of the annuity contract. Under these circumstances, an otherwise valid sale and annuity agreement should not be disregarded for tax purposes.

The Tax Court also relied on *Samuel v. Commissioner* . . . but we do not believe that it controls here. In *Samuel*, Archbishop Athanasius Samuel transferred the "Dead Sea Scrolls" to a trust for which he was a co-trustee. The original trust provided that all of the trust's income and 90% of the principal should be disposed of at Samuel's direction. Samuel also retained full power to amend and revoke the trust. The trust was subsequently amended to provide for payments to Samuel of $15,000 to reimburse him for the scrolls, $15,000 for his future expenses in connection with the scrolls, and an additional $10,000 per year. Samuel remained the co-trustee with the right to reduce the annual payments although the trust was no longer otherwise amendable or revocable. All documents were formally cast as a trust agreement and the trust made no distributions to Samuel in years when there was no income. The court applied I.R.C. § 677(a) to the trust income, rejecting Samuel's argument that the payments to him should be regarded as "annuity" payments on his "sale" of the scrolls to the trust.

Several important factors distinguish the *Samuel* case from the instant one. First, in *Samuel* none of the documents supported Samuel's contention that a sale had occurred or that an annuity was intended or contemplated. . . . The court stated that in the context of a non-commercial annuity "conspicuously garbed in all of the external manifestations of a trust arrangement," " 'the instruments evidencing the agreement ought to spell out in detail the intent of the parties that there is contemplated an annuity venture.' " . . . Second, Samuel was also the trustee. As such, he was asserting a debtor-creditor relationship against himself. . . . Third, in his capacity as trustee he controlled the property, unlike the typical annuitant. . . . Fourth, the trust did not make the payments in years in which there was no income, which is uncharacteristic of a debtor-creditor relationship. . . . Clearly Samuel was a beneficial owner rather than an annuitant-creditor. His contention that the formal trust characterization should be ignored for tax purposes was unsupportable. But none of these factors are present in the instant case.

The present case involves a sales transaction of clearer substance than the one in *Lazarus* or *Samuel*. Not only did the formal documents reflect a sale in exchange for an annuity, but the annuity was not calculated to approximate or bear any mathematical relationship to the property's annual income, and the taxpayer, like a seller, did not actually continue to control the property sold. Taxpayer had traded certain property, with the management problems it presented, for a fixed life annuity. As in any sale, she would no longer share in the earnings of the property, its appreciation, or its actual management. Her only right was to a fixed annual payment; subsequent gains in the property's value would inure to the trust, not Taxpayer. As with any annuity taken in exchange for property, the risk of Taxpayer's early death lay with the taxpayer, whereas the risk of Taxpayer's late demise lay with the trust and its trustees. In these circumstances, Taxpayer's formal characterization of the transaction as a sale in exchange for an annuity should not be disregarded for tax purposes. . . .

B. NOTES AND QUESTIONS

1) A Hypothetical Based on *LaFargue*

Assume that a taxpayer, with a life expectancy of five years, transfers property, worth $1 million and with a $500,000 basis, to a trust. In return, the trust promises to pay the taxpayer $100,000 a year for life. If the appropriate discount rate is 10%, then the present value of the promise is about $380,000. (See the present value table in Chapter 12.)

Lafargue states that there are two possible ways to characterize the transaction: as if property has been transferred to pay for an annuity or as if there has been a gift of property in trust, with the donor retaining the right to the income for life. To understand the stakes, the reader needs to consider two separate aspects of the transaction: first, the transfer of property, and second, the annual payments to the taxpayer for life.

2) The Transfer of Property

Under the view that the property was transferred in exchange for an annuity, how much gain or loss is realized on the exchange? Hint: Consider the part sale, part gift rule of *Diedrich* (Chapter 22). Suppose that the property's basis is zero rather than $500,000. How much gain is realized? When is it recognized? When the transfer of property occurs? Or might the taxpayer claim that, under the installment method, she is taxable only when payments are actually received under the annuity contract? Assuming that gain is taxed only as annuity payments are received, how much should the taxpayer report each year? See Chapter 13.

Under the alternative view that there has been a gift of property in trust, how much gain would arise from the transfer?

3) Payments to the Taxpayer

Under the view that the annual payments constitute an annuity, the taxpayer's income would be determined under Section 72. Annuity payments in excess of the annuity's cost, spread ratably over the taxpayer's life expectancy, are taxed as ordinary income. See Section 72(b)(1) and (2) (Chapter 35). Why does the cost of the private annuity in this hypothetical equal its present value of $380,000? How much of each year's payment should be reported as ordinary income by the taxpayer? Under the annuity characterization, how much of the $100,000 paid annually to the taxpayer should be deductible to the trust? Taxable to the trust?

Under the alternative view that there has been a gift of property in trust, how much income would the taxpayer report each year from the annual payments? Note that if the transaction is treated as a grantor trust, the trust itself would not be taxable on any of the $100,000 paid annually to the taxpayer. See Chapter 47.

4) The Overall Stakes in *Lafargue*

From your answers to the questions under 2) and 3), above, try to describe what was at stake in Lafargue. Why might the private annuity characterization be described as shifting income from the transferor of property to the beneficiaries of the trust?

C. BERNATSCHKE v. UNITED STATES
364 F.2d 400 (Ct. Cl. 1966)

... The sole issue is whether Section 72 or Section 71(a)(1) of the Internal Revenue Code of 1954 governs the taxability of the sum of $25,000 received each year by plaintiff under certain annuity contracts for which the consideration was paid by her former husband, Cornelius Crane, pursuant to an Agreement of February 20, 1940 incident to a divorce.

In general, annuity payments are taxable under the rules of Section 72 of the Code. . . . These rules, however, are not applicable to payments under an annuity contract which are includible in the income of the wife under Section 71; such payments are wholly includible in the wife's gross income. . . .

The substance of Section 71 was first enacted in 1942 to allow the husband to deduct "payments in the nature of or in lieu of alimony or an allowance for support" and to tax such payments to the wife who receives them. . . . Section 7.71–1(b)(4) of the Regulations states that "Section 71(a) applies only to payments made because of the family or marital relationship in recognition of the general obligation to support which is made specific by the decree, instrument, or agreement. . . . "

Against this background, plaintiff contends that all or part of the cost of the annuity contracts was paid by Cornelius Crane for reasons other than his obligation to support plaintiff and hence that the annual payments of $25,000 received pursuant to the contracts were taxable in whole or in part under the rules set forth in Section 72 of the Code. Defendant argues, on the other hand, that the annual payments of $25,000 received by plaintiff constituted periodic payments in discharge of a legal obligation incurred by her former husband because of the marital or family relationship, and not in settlement of any property rights, and thus were wholly includible in her gross income under Section 71(a)(1) of the Code.

The nub of the problem is thus to determine whether or not plaintiff's former husband, Cornelius Crane, paid the consideration for the annuities by virtue of an obligation to support plaintiff which was imposed on him by their marital relationship. This is a question that depends upon the substance of the transaction and the true intent of the parties, rather than on the labels or formal provisions of the written contract or divorce decree....

Plaintiff, who was born in 1906, is a housewife and has never been gainfully employed. Her father was a naval medical officer who came from a family of well-to-do professional people; her mother also had considerable means in her own right due largely to her skill as an investor. In 1922 plaintiff was married to a naval flyer but the marriage ended in divorce some seven years later. They had one child, a daughter.

In 1929 plaintiff married Cornelius Crane (hereafter referred to as "Cornelius"), the grandson of the founder of the Crane Company (a manufacturer of plumbing equipment and valves) and the only son of R. T. Crane, Jr., the president and controlling stockholder of that company. The Crane family was possessed of great wealth and its members—including Cornelius and plaintiff—lived on a lavish scale in family mansions in Chicago (their primary residence), Massachusetts and Georgia, and a family apartment at the Ritz in New York. Cornelius, who himself possessed substantial wealth through gifts and inheritance, and also received income from trusts established by his father, was not interested in the family business and at no time in his life held a position for which he received a salary. As a young man he decided he did not want to go to college, but would like to go around the world on a yacht and explore parts of the world which others had not reached. Accordingly, his father bought him a sailing ship which was about 140 feet in length and carried a crew of 26. From this trip he developed an interest in archeology and anthropology, and financed and conducted several expeditions in his vessel to the South Seas. His other interests consisted of hunting, fishing, walking through the woods and reading.

Cornelius' personal budget (as well as that of the entire Crane family) was managed by J. K. Prentice, who had been his father's private secretary, who served as a confidant to the entire family and who stood in place of a father to Cornelius after R. T. Crane, Jr. died. Cornelius had a different attitude toward money than most people. For example, very early in his marriage to plaintiff he became "sick" of Bermuda and suddenly sold for the extraordinarily low price of $25,000 a 26-acre island he owned at the entrance to the harbor in Bermuda, together with a restored house thereon and four boats. He purchased property in Tahiti without ever having seen it. Withal, Cornelius and plaintiff were more alike than different in various respects. Neither had ever been gainfully employed. While Cornelius occupied himself with his interests in archeology and anthropology, plaintiff occupied herself with giving singing concerts (which were artistic successes rather than profitable ventures) and with charitable endeavors. Both were unconcerned with, and uninterested in, finances and property. Thus, until her marriage to Cornelius, plaintiff relied on her mother completely to manage stocks and bonds which her mother and grandmother had given her; after the marriage she turned her investments over to the Crane family to manage. During her marriage to Cornelius, her stock and bond holdings were augmented by gifts from Cornelius and his father, and as of February 1940 had a market value of about $347,000, which produced a yield of about $13,000 in that year.

Throughout his marriage to plaintiff, Cornelius continued his sailing expeditions and was away for extended periods of time; plaintiff did not accompany him on these trips. After February 1936, Cornelius and plaintiff did not live together as man and wife, although he continued to support her and her daughter by her first marriage. By 1939, plaintiff was considering getting a divorce and retained an attorney, but did not pursue the matter further at that time. In the latter part of that year, Cornelius adopted plaintiff's daughter, the adoption being prompted at least in part by his desire to effect a reconciliation with plaintiff. (Plaintiff and Cornelius had no children of their own.) Thereafter, upon the happening of some incident, plaintiff finally reached a firm decision to go ahead with the divorce and filed a divorce action in the Circuit Court of Cook County, Illinois, on February 19, 1940. The divorce was granted on the ground of desertion on February 23, 1940. Up to the final day of the divorce, Cornelius tried to dissuade plaintiff from going through with it. Plaintiff and Cornelius remained friendly at all times during, before and after the divorce proceedings.

At the time that she finally decided to proceed with the divorce, plaintiff's attorney indicated to her that she had a dower right and that such right was a third of an estate. Plaintiff told her attorney that she wanted a lump-sum settlement and asked him to find out from Cornelius what would be fair. She felt that having been a good wife something was due her and she wanted any settlement in a lump sum so that she would never again have to go back to Cornelius and ask for anything—for household money and things like that in the future; she wanted all ties cut.

Meanwhile, Cornelius discussed the matter with his advisers and stated that he would be willing to make a reasonable property settlement, based on his assets, to take care of plaintiff and that he wanted to be, if anything, liberal in the amount of such settlement. He requested one of his advisers to ascertain the amount of income-producing assets he had under his control and it was determined that they were worth about $2,000,000. Cornelius thereupon indicated to his attorney that if he died without a will, plaintiff would get one-third of that amount. The attorney said that that would probably be right by virtue of her dower rights. Cornelius then stated to his advisers that he and plaintiff had been married for ten years; that he thought he should make a property settlement which substantially represented her dower rights in his assets; and that he would give her $650,000, approximately one-third of his assets of $2,000,000. After having so decided (and also determining what he would give to plaintiff's daughter whom he had adopted), he told his advisers to work out the details.

J. K. Prentice (who, as previously indicated, managed Cornelius' personal budget) approved of Cornelius' decision to make a liberal settlement for plaintiff, but opposed turning over liquid assets to her since he was afraid she might give them away or that someone might take them from her. Consequently, he felt strongly that the sum to be paid should be so invested that she could not dissipate her principal, and he urged that annuities be used for that purpose. He mentioned the subject to plaintiff; she respected and trusted Prentice and when he recommended annuities to her, she accepted this recommendation and asked Cornelius to take care of buying the annuities for her, insisting, however, that Cornelius be given a contingent right to receive refunds under the annuity contracts in the event of her death. The actual arrangements for the purchase of annuities were handled by Cornelius' advisers who made inquiries of insurance companies to ascertain how much of an annuity for a person of plaintiff's age and description could be bought for $650,000 and were informed by such insurance companies that approximately $647,000 would buy an exact or round amount of $25,000 per year. The amount of the income to be paid was the result of the determination of the approximate amount of the principal to be paid, not the cause of such amount.

In the discussions Cornelius had with his advisers there was no mention of alimony; Cornelius simply determined that he would give plaintiff part of his assets. Nor did anyone at any time mention alimony in the discussions in which plaintiff participated with her attorney, Cornelius or any of his advisers. During the course of the negotiations, Cornelius told her she would receive a lump sum and plaintiff understood that she would get a "one-time payment."

At the time of the divorce, plaintiff did not transfer any of her property to Cornelius, except for such items as primitive artifacts that had no great intrinsic value. Nor, with the exception of some household items, did Cornelius transfer any property to plaintiff at the time of the divorce other than the amount provided in the Agreement of February 20, 1940.

Following the divorce, plaintiff in March 1940 married her present husband, a portrait painter, who has been successful artistically though not financially.

Subsequently, in accordance with the Agreement of February 20, 1940, plaintiff (and her present husband) granted to Cornelius quitclaim deeds and released to him all rights in property Cornelius owned in Massachusetts and Tahiti. Cornelius fulfilled his obligations under the Agreement by liquidating a substantial portion of his income-producing assets and having one of his advisers in the months following the divorce purchase 13 annuity policies from various insurance companies to provide total annual payments of $25,000 to plaintiff.

Plaintiff's standard of living changed markedly after her divorce from Cornelius since she could no longer live in the kind of lavish luxury produced by the Crane family's great wealth. In the tax years here involved, plaintiff has received dividend and interest income from her stocks and bonds (which are now worth about $1,000,000) of from $23,000 to $30,000 a year, which income is over and above the $25,000 each year received under the annuity contracts. The $25,000 annuity is commingled with her dividend income and is used for normal living expenses, taxes, investments, savings, etc.

In summary, the record shows that at no time during the negotiation of the Agreement of February 20, 1940 was there any mention of alimony. Plaintiff did not request it and Cornelius did not mention it. Nor was there any attempt to determine the extent or the dollar value of Cornelius' obligation to support plaintiff or to pay alimony. The record shows, rather, that the amount which plaintiff received pursuant to the Agreement was derived solely on the basis of the income-producing property then owned outright by Cornelius and what the parties understood to be plaintiff's intestate share in his estate or "dower" rights; and that such amount was determined without reference to any obligation to support or pay alimony. Thus, it seems evident that the amounts paid by Cornelius for the annuity contracts were not based on the marital obligation to support and were not intended to be payments in discharge of such an obligation but rather were intended to be in the nature of a property settlement under which plaintiff's inchoate interests in Cornelius' property under Illinois law were extinguished.

In addition to these considerations, other factors present here provide further indication that the annuity payments to plaintiff do not have the usual characteristics of alimony or support. . . . First, the fact that the payments were to continue for the lifetime of the plaintiff, without regard to her remarriage or the death of her ex-husband, tends to show that they were not intended as alimony or in discharge of a marital obligation to support. . . . It is relevant, also, that plaintiff received and exercised the right to determine the beneficiary of refunds that might be payable after her death. It would appear that if the annuity payments had been intended as support payments for plaintiff, Cornelius, rather than plaintiff, would have retained and exercised the power to determine the recipient of any part of the sum not needed for that purpose.

In addition, it is customary for support payments to be related to the husband's income and, frequently, to vary if there is a substantial change in such income. . . . The wife is ordinarily entitled to be supported in the same style of living to which she was accustomed during the marriage. . . . The amount of the wife's own income is, obviously, also a factor in determining her need for support. Here the payments were not related in any way to Cornelius' substantial income. The parties agreed on a lump sum based entirely on assets which he owned outright, without reference to the trust income he received, and then fixed the amount of the annual payments on the basis of what annuities the lump sum would buy. There could be no variation, of course, because of changes in Cornelius' income (or because of any property which he might later inherit). Nor was plaintiff's income considered in any way as a factor in determining the amount to be paid. Furthermore, the amount of the annuity payments, even when combined with plaintiff's income from her stocks and bonds, could not possibly allow her to live in a style which would in any way approach that to which she had been accustomed as Cornelius' wife, and the record in fact shows that her standard of living changed markedly after the divorce.

Another factor of significance is whether or not there is a fixed sum the husband is required to pay; the absence of such a fixed sum is considered to indicate that support was intended.... Here the contract itself specifically provides the amount which the husband was required to pay and the record shows that the settlement was determined on the basis of his paying such amount.

In conclusion, the record establishes that Cornelius Crane did not pay the consideration for the annuity contracts because of any marital obligation to support plaintiff and, accordingly, the annuity payments are not taxable under Section 71. Plaintiffs are entitled to a refund of income tax for the years involved based on the application of the rules of Section 72 to the annuity payments received in each year.

D. NOTES AND QUESTIONS

1) The Tax Treatment of Alimony

Under Sections 71(a) and 215(a), alimony is generally deductible by the payor and taxable to the payee. However, since 1984, the parties have been able to elect to treat alimony as nondeductible (and therefore taxable) to the payor and excludable by the payee. See Section 71(b)(1)(B). In other words, the parties may choose who will bear the tax. (Child support, on the other hand, is always treated as nondeductible to the payor and excludable by the payee.)

The basic issue surrounding alimony, therefore, has been formulated as *who* should be taxable, the payor or the payee? Do you agree with this formulation? Can an argument be made that alimony should be both nondeductible by the payor *and* taxable to the payee? Even if such an argument appears unreasonable, why allow divorced or separated spouses the option to choose whether the payor or the payee will be taxed?

2) Alimony versus Property Settlement

Bernatschke distinguishes alimony, which is deductible by the payor and includable by the payee, from a property settlement, which is not. The difference between the two is clear enough in simple examples, but becomes less clear when the arrangements are more complicated. If one spouse transfers a fixed amount of property to the other spouse when divorce occurs and there is no provision for any future payments, then the transfer obviously qualifies as a property settlement. At the other extreme, where one spouse agrees to pay the other a stated amount each year until the payee spouse dies, then the future payments obviously constitute alimony.

Suppose, however, that one spouse agrees to pay the other $50,000 a year for five years. Is the payment a property settlement or alimony? Should the agreement be regarded as a property settlement that is paid off in installments over five years? Or as alimony that lasts for only five years, perhaps on the assumption that, by the end of the five-year period, the payee spouse should have sufficient time and opportunity to become self-supporting?

Section 71(f) draws the line by defining alimony as occurring when payments over the three years following divorce or separation are relatively equal in amount. Section 71(f) contains a complex set of rules under which the payor is taxed on excess amounts where payments are subject to substantial fluctuation during the three-year period.

3) Alimony versus Annuity

Suppose that, in a divorce, one spouse agrees to pay the other $25,000 a year for life. Why isn't this arrangement characterized and taxed as a private annuity? If it were, would there be any need to distinguish alimony from property settlements? Isn't the annuity characterization the most accurate? Or should it depend on whether alimony is being paid out of income from property or income from services?

When periodic payments qualify as alimony and a Section 71(b)(1)(B) election has not been made, the effect of not adopting the annuity characterization is to shift income from payor to payee. Why? Where periodic payments do *not* qualify as alimony (or when they do and a Section 71(b)(1)(B) election has been made), the effect is to shift income from payee to payor. Why? Does any of this matter?

SUBPART B

Time Value of Money Transactions

This subpart deals with transactions that misstate the amount of interest actually being charged on a loan. The primary consequence of misstating interest is to shift income from borrower to lender or vice versa. When interest is *under*stated, the lender reports less income but the borrower has lower deductions and consequently more income. The net result is to shift income from lender to borrower. When interest is *over*stated, the lender reports more income but the borrower has larger deductions and consequently less income. The net result is to shift income from borrower to lender.[1]

If both borrower and lender face the same tax rates, the misstatement of interest will not affect revenues. However, most of the transactions discussed below involve attempts to misstate interest in order to take advantage of differences between the borrower's and the lender's tax rate. They are referred to as *Time Value of Money Transactions* because interest is the charge for the use of funds over time.

Most of these transactions depend on the manipulation of accounting methods to achieve the desired tax savings. The two basic methods of tax accounting are the *cash receipts and disbursements method* (or *cash method*) and the *accrual method*. The difference between these two methods is one of timing. Under the cash method, income is reported only when payment is actually received. Under the accrual method, income is reported when it is earned—that is, when the right to be paid accrues—even if actual payment occurs at a later date.

There is a similar difference between the two methods when a taxpayer seeks to deduct a business expense. Under the cash method, the deduction is available only when the taxpayer actually pays for the expense. Under the accrual method, the deduction may be taken when the obligation to pay arises—that is, when it accrues—even if actual payment occurs at a later date.

---

1. Shifting will occur whenever the interest in question may be deducted by the borrower. When the interest is not deductible, the effect of understating interest is to understate income and the effect of overstating interest is to overstate income.

Chapter 50

BOND DISCOUNT

A. INTRODUCTORY NOTES AND QUESTIONS

1) What Is a Bond?[1]

A bond is a legal document that records the borrowing of funds by a debtor from a creditor. How is a bond different from other loan transactions? The bond is an instrument that permits the debtor, usually a corporation or a government, to borrow funds *in one transaction* from a large number of separate lenders, rather than from a single lender. For example, suppose that AT&T wishes to borrow $100 million. One possibility is to obtain a loan from a single lender, such as a bank, insurance company, or pension fund. Another is to borrow a relatively small amount from each of tens of thousands of investors, typically individuals rather than institutions, by selling $100 million worth of AT&T bonds.

Bonds are usually issued in denominations (referred to as *principal amounts*) of $1,000. The bond itself consists of promises by the debtor to make payments to the creditor. There are two kinds of promises: first, a promise to pay *interest,* which is *stated* as a percentage of the principal amount (and thus referred to as *stated interest*); and second, a promise to pay back the principal amount, due at a specified future time or maturity date. For example, suppose that in 1989, AT&T issues a bond promising to pay 10% annual interest and principal amount of $1,000 at maturity, five years from the issue date. Each year until maturity, AT&T must pay the stated annual interest of 10% of the principal amount, or $100 a year. In addition, AT&T is obligated to pay the bondholder the $1,000 principal amount in 1994.

---

1. Some readers may notice that the first two paragraphs of this chapter appear earlier in the section on premium bonds in Chapter 34. To spare readers the inconvenience of having to flip back and forth through the casebook, they are reprinted here.

2) Identifying the Bondholder's Income

The proper identification and treatment of the bondholder's income from making a loan has persisted as a difficult problem. As a matter of definition, the income from any loan equals the difference between the amount loaned and the amount paid back. For example, if you lend $1,000 and are paid back $1,200, then your income is $200.

In the specific case of a bond, the amount loaned is the price for which the bond initially sells, referred to as the *issue price*. The amount paid back consists of stated interest plus the principal amount. Thus, the bondholder's income equals the stated interest, plus the principal amount, minus the issue price of the bond.

Perhaps most difficult to grasp is that income from a bond may sometimes *exceed* the stated interest. *This will occur whenever the principal amount due at maturity exceeds the issue price.* Suppose the AT&T bond, described under question 1), above, is issued for $950, then the bondholder's profit equals stated interest of $500 ($100 a year for five years), plus principal amount of $1,000, minus the sales price of $950—or $550—rather than simply the stated interest of $500.

3) Calculating the Issue Price

The *issue price* is what the bond sells for when it is issued and, in effect, represents the amount loaned. What determines the issue price? A bond consists of the right to receive stated interest plus principal amount in the future. The issue price equals the sum of each of these future amounts, discounted to present value at the market rate of interest.

To illustrate, suppose that AT&T issues a bond with a principal amount of $1,000 and maturity in five years and that the market rate of interest is 10%. What is the issue price of the bond if it pays stated interest of 10%? If stated interest is only 8%? If stated interest is zero? To calculate the issue price, discount the future payments of stated interest and principal, using the present value table in Chapter 12. Your answers should correspond to Table 50–1 on page 800.

4) The Relationship Between the Issue Price and the Principal Amount

Note in Table 50–1 that when the market rate of interest and the stated interest on the bond are both 10%, the issue price equals the $1,000 principal amount. But when stated interest falls to 8%, the issue price also falls to $925. And when stated interest falls even further, to zero, the issue price drops to $621. Table 50–1 thus illustrates two basic propositions about the relationship between a bond's issue price and its principal amount. First, when the stated interest on the bond *equals* the market rate of interest, the issue price *equals* the principal amount. Second, when the stated interest is *less* than the market rate of interest, the issue price is *less* than the principal amount.

TABLE 50-1. CALCULATING THE ISSUE PRICE OF A FIVE-YEAR $1,000 BOND, WITH VARYING AMOUNTS OF STATED INTEREST, GIVEN A MARKET INTEREST RATE OF 10%

Year	10% Stated Interest	PV @ 10%	8% Stated Interest	PV @ 10%	Zero Stated Interest	PV @ 10%
1	100	91	80	73	0	
2	100	83	80	66	0	
3	100	75	80	60	0	
4	100	68	80	55	0	
5	100	62	80	50	0	
5	1000	621	1000	621	1000	621
Total (Issue Price)		1000		925		621

5) The Definition of Original Issue Discount (OID)

Original issue discount, or OID, is defined as the excess of the principal amount due at maturity over the issue price. If the principal amount equals the issue price, then there is no OID. If the principal amount exceeds the issue price, then OID is measured by the difference. For example, suppose that an AT&T bond with a principal amount of $1,000 is issued at a price of $928. Then the amount of OID is $1,000 minus $928, or $72. What is the amount of OID for each of the three bonds described in Table 50–1, above?

6) What Does OID Represent?

OID represents additional interest, required by bondholders, when the stated interest on a bond is too low (that is, low relative to the market interest rate). Thus, there will be no OID if the stated interest rate on a bond equals the market rate of interest when the bond is issued. In that event, the issue price of a bond will equal its face amount.

But OID will arise whenever the stated interest is less than what the market demands. In that event, the price of a bond will be less than its principal amount. The reduction in the issue price from the principal amount—or OID—supplies the extra interest required by the market. At maturity, therefore, only part of the principal amount represents a repayment of "true" principal. To the extent of OID, the principal amount represents the additional interest that must be paid in order to induce bondholders to make the loan.

OID, in other words, is simply interest in another form. It is sometimes referred to as *un*stated interest to distinguish it from the stated interest explicitly provided for in the bond contract.

7) The Economics of OID

Continue with the example of the AT&T bond with a principal amount of $1,000, five year maturity, and zero stated interest, which will be issued at a price of $621 when the market rate of interest is 10% (see the fifth and sixth columns in Table 50–1, above). How much is the bond expected to be worth one year after it is issued? Two years, three years, four years, and five years after it is issued? Hint: Use a 10% discount rate to calculate the anticipated present value of the bond when maturity is four, three, two, one, and zero years away. Your answers should correspond to the figures in Table 50–2.

TABLE 50-2. VALUE OF $1,000 PRINCIPAL AMOUNT, ZERO STATED INTEREST, FIVE YEAR BOND, GIVEN A MARKET INTEREST RATE OF 10%

Years To Maturity	Value	Increase in Value During Preceding Year
5	621	
4	683	62
3	751	68
2	826	75
1	909	83
0	1000	91
TOTAL		379

In Table 50–2, why does the value of the bond rise over time as the maturity date approaches? What does the annual increase in the bond's value represent? Why do the total annual increases equal the amount of OID? Why is the annual increase smaller in early years and larger in later years, rather than evenly spread over the life of the bond? Why can purchasing the bond (when it is issued) be analogized to depositing $621 in a savings account, which pays 10% interest, for five years? (You might work through the numbers, calculating how much the $621 so deposited will grow each year.) If interest represented by OID is taxed *as it is earned,* how much would the bondholder be required to report each year?

8) Economic Accrual Taxation of OID

A method that takes account of OID interest as it is actually earned, or as it *accrues,* is known as *economic accrual.* Since 1982, the Code has applied this method to bonds.[2] OID interest is taxable to bondholders and deductible for the issuer, as it actually accrues. Sections 1272(a)(1) and 163(e)(1). The amount of OID is determined under Section 1273(a)(1). There is an exception when the amount of OID is *de minimis.* Section 1273(a)(3).

9) Problems with Economic Accrual Taxation

The economic accrual solution to the problem of OID on bonds raises two different problems. First, it represents a departure from the cash method

---

2. The economic accrual method applies only to bonds issued after July 1, 1982. OID on bonds issued on or before that date but after May 27, 1969 is accounted for under the ratable accrual method which is discussed below. Section 1272(b)(1). OID on bonds issued on or before May 27, 1969 is accounted for under the taxpayer's usual accounting method.

of accounting. Individual bondholders—who are virtually always on the cash method—are taxed on OID interest as it accrues, even though they are actually not paid—and therefore receive nothing of the OID—until maturity.

Second, economic accrual is complicated. Interest represented by OID accrues in uneven amounts, smaller in early years and larger in later years. Although the total amount of OID is known when the bond is issued, allocating the OID as it accrues over the bond's life requires computations that take account of the phenomenon of the compounding of interest. See Sections 1272(a)(3)–(5).

It would be much simpler either to tax OID only when it is paid or to allocate OID interest in even amounts over the life of the bond. This latter method, known as *ratable accrual,* involves simply dividing the total amount of OID by the term of the bond in order to determine how much OID interest is taxable to the bondholder and deductible for the issuer each year.[3] In the case of the $1,000, five year, zero stated interest AT&T bond, the $379 total OID interest, spread over five years, would be accounted for at the rate of $75.80 a year. (This might be rounded off to $76 a year in years 1–4 and $75 in year 5.)

Why did Congress adopt the system of economic accrual, despite these drawbacks? The taxation of OID on bonds has a long and convoluted history. The materials that follow explore that history and the reasons why we have ended up where we have.

B. COMMISSIONER v. CAULKINS
144 F.2d 482 (6th Cir. 1944)

ALLEN, CIRCUIT JUDGE.

This case arises upon petition to review a decision of the Tax Court of the United States . . . which sustained the taxpayer in reporting an increment received within the taxable year 1939 as a capital gain. The primary question is whether the excess amount received by the taxpayer over the aggregate payment made by him under a contract with Investors Syndicate constitutes ordinary income or capital gain.

The taxpayer in 1928 purchased an "Accumulative Installment Certificate" under the terms of which Investors Syndicate agreed to pay him $20,000 at the expiration of ten years, if the payments provided for therein were made. The taxpayer paid $15,043.33 on the certificate prior to November 7, 1938. On April 11, 1939, the taxpayer surrendered the certificate and received $20,000 from the company. In its information return for the year 1939, the company reported the difference between the total amount paid by the taxpayer and the $20,000 paid to the taxpayer, namely, $4,956.67, as interest paid by the company. In his income tax return for the year 1939 the taxpayer reported $4,956.67 as a long-term capital gain. . . . The Com-

---

3. OID on bonds issued after May 27, 1969 but before July 2, 1982 is accounted for under this method, as described below.

missioner determined a deficiency as to this item, upon the ground that the increment received by the taxpayer constituted ordinary income.... [T]he Tax Court found that the certificate was in registered form and that it was an evidence of indebtedness covered by § [1271(a)(1)] which provides:

[Amounts received by the holder on retirement of any debt instrument shall be considered as amounts received in exchange therefore.]

The Tax Court concluded that the taxpayer had correctly reported his profit....

The Commissioner contends that the difference between the total amount paid by the taxpayer and the amount received by him on the maturity of the certificate is taxable in its entirety as ordinary income....

The certificate provides that in consideration of the payment by the taxpayer of $1,512 annually in advance for the period of ten years, the company, at the expiration of the period and on surrender of the certificate, will pay the sum of $20,000. At the bottom of the first page of the certificate and on the cover page are printed the figures 5½%....

The decisive question is whether the amount received by the taxpayer falls within § [1271(a)(1)] which provides that amounts received by the holder upon retirement of the securities named shall be considered as amounts received in exchange therefor. If it does, the decision of the Tax Court is correct.... [P]rior to the enactment of § [1271(a)(1)] in 1934, the redemption before maturity of corporate bonds [was] not a sale and exchange of capital assets within the commonly accepted meaning of the words. The gain realized prior to 1934, the court held, was not a capital gain.... The Revenue Act of 1934 made a radical change in the prior law when it provided ... that amounts received on retirement of the securities listed should be calculated as capital gain or capital loss.

The inherent difficulty in construing § [1271(a)(1)] is presented in cases like this, where the amount received upon retirement of the security is calculated under the capital gains statute, although the transaction presents no true aspect of capital gain....

While granting that the security held by the taxpayer is an evidence of indebtedness of the character described in § [1271(a)(1)], the Commissioner contends that that section was not intended to cover the gain from interest, but only capital gain. It is pointed out that the increment here is identical with interest compounded at 5½% during the agreed period; that the issuing company in its information return considered it as interest, and that the certificate bears the symbols 5½% in two places. The Commissioner hence urges that the increment in value of the certificate constitutes compensation for the use of the taxpayer's money ... and that as such it must be taxed in its entirety as ordinary income....

Congress might well have made the differentiation urged by the Commissioner, since it is difficult to perceive any practical reason for taxing [an] increment of the type involved here differently from ordinary income. The fact that the contract does not provide for equal amounts of interest to be set aside each year, available to the holder, does not affect the question. The increment is consideration paid for the use of the amounts paid in. Unfortunately for the Commissioner's contention, Congress has not made the differentiation.

Where statutory standards are lacking, statutory language is to be read in its natural and common meaning.... In the present case, the promise was to pay $20,000 at the expiration of the ten-year period. Clearly $20,000 was the amount received on the retirement of the certificate, and under the plain wording of § [1271(a)(1)], it was taxable as a capital gain. A provision that the increment in such cases should be taxable [as ordinary income] might or might not have been wise and fair; but Congress has not enacted it, and the courts cannot supply it by judicial legislation. Because of the application of the capital gains tax to securities which on their retirement may not result in capital gain, inconsistencies and inequalities may well result from the application of § [1271(a)(1)]. If this is so, the correction of this defect in the operation of the statute is for Congress and not for the courts....

C. UNITED STATES v. MIDLAND-ROSS CORP.
381 U.S. 54 (1965)

MR. JUSTICE BRENNAN delivered the opinion of the Court.

The question for decision is whether, under the Internal Revenue Code of 1939, certain gains realized by the taxpayer are taxable as capital gains or as ordinary income. The taxpayer bought noninterest-bearing promissory notes from the issuers at prices discounted below the face amounts.... [Each] of the notes ... was sold for less than its face amount but more than its issue price. It is conceded that the gain in each case was the economic equivalent of interest for the use of the money to the date of sale but the taxpayer reported the gains as capital gains. The Commissioner of Internal Revenue determined that the gains attributable to original issue discount were but interest in another form and therefore were taxable as ordinary income....

The more favorable capital gains treatment applied only to gain on "the sale or exchange of a capital asset." §[1222]. Although original issue discount becomes property when the obligation falls due or is liquidated prior to maturity and § [1221] defined a capital asset as "property held by the taxpayer," we have held that

> not everything which can be called property in the ordinary sense and which is outside the statutory exclusions qualifies as a capital asset. This Court has long held that the term 'capital asset' is to be construed narrowly in accordance with the purpose of Congress to afford capital-gains treatment only in situations typically involving the realization of appreciation in value accrued over a substantial period of time, and thus to ameliorate the hardship of taxation of the entire gain in one year.

... In applying this principle, this Court has consistently construed "capital asset" to exclude property representing income items or accretions to the value of a capital asset themselves properly attributable to income. ... [E]arned original issue discount cannot be regarded as "typically involving the realization of appreciation in value accrued over a substantial period of time . . . [given capital gains treatment] to ameliorate the hardship of taxation of the entire gain in one year."

Earned original issue discount serves the same function as stated interest, concededly ordinary income and not a capital asset; it is simply "compensation for the use or forbearance of money." . . . Unlike the typical case of capital appreciation, the earning of discount to maturity is predictable and measurable, and is "essentially a substitute for . . . payments which § [61(a)] expressly characterizes as gross income [;thus] it must be regarded as ordinary income, and it is immaterial that for some purposes the contract creating the right to such payments may be treated as 'property' or 'capital.' ". . . The $6 earned on a one-year note for $106 issued for $100 is precisely like the $6 earned on a one-year loan of $100 at 6% stated interest. The application of general principles would indicate, therefore, that earned original issue discount, like stated interest, should be taxed . . . as ordinary income.

The taxpayer argues, however, that administrative practice and congressional treatment of original issue discount under the 1939 Code establish that such discount is to be accounted for as capital gain when realized. . . . [T]he Internal Revenue Code of 1954 provides that "upon sale or exchange of . . . evidences of indebtedness issued after December 31, 1954, held by the taxpayer more than 6 months, any gain realized . . . [up to the prorated amount of original issue discount] shall be considered as gain from the sale or exchange of property which is not a capital asset," that is, it is to be taxed at ordinary income rates. From this the taxpayer would infer that Congress understood prior administrative and legislative history as extending capital gains treatment to realized original issue discount. If administrative practice and legislative history before 1954 did in fact ignore economic reality and treat stated interest and original issue discount differently for tax purposes, the taxpayer should prevail. . . .

The taxpayer refers us to various statutory provisions treating original issue discount as ordinary income in specific situations, arguing that these establish a congressional understanding that in situations not covered by such provisions, original issue discount is entitled to capital gains treatment. Even if these provisions were merely limited applications of the principle . . . , they may demonstrate, not that the general rule was to the contrary, but that the general rule was unclear . . . and that Congress wished to avoid any doubt as to its treatment of particular situations. . . .

. . . [T]he taxpayer has not demonstrated that, in specifying ordinary income treatment for original issue discount in particular situations, Congress evinced its understanding that such discount would otherwise be entitled to capital gains treatment. Therefore we turn to the question whether Treasury practice and decisional law preclude ordinary income treatment.

The taxpayer premises this part of his argument primarily upon the case of *Caulkins v. Commissioner.* . . . The Tax Court upheld the taxpayer . . . but its discussion of the capital gains question is at best opaque. The Court of Appeals acknowledged that "the transaction presents no true aspect of capital gain" and that "Congress might well have made the differentiation urged by the Commissioner, since it is difficult to perceive any practical reason for taxing increment of the type involved here differently from ordinary income ... [as] consideration paid for the use of the amounts paid in".... Nevertheless it construed the words "amounts received by the holder upon ... retirement " in § [1271(a)(1)] as unsusceptible of partition, and therefore as including the increment attributable to interest, which, with the principal amount, was thus taxable only as capital gain.

Caulkins did not unambiguously establish that original issue discount was itself a "capital asset" entitled to capital gains treatment. It held only that under § [1271(a)(1)] Congress had not provided that the "amount" received on retirement might be broken down into its component parts. ... The Tax Court has consistently regarded *Caulkins* as having erroneously read § [1271(a)(1)] to preclude differentiation of the sources of proceeds on redemption.... The Commissioner, in addition to withdrawing his acquiescence in *Caulkins*, has also rejected the interpretation of "amount" under § [1271(a)(1)] as not subject to apportionment under general principles. ...

The concept of discount or premium as altering the effective rate of interest is not to be rejected as an "esoteric concept derived from subtle and theoretic analysis." ... For, despite some expressions indicating a contrary view, this Court has often recognized the economic function of discount as interest. [For] example, the Court [has] regarded it as "no longer open to question that amortized bond discount may be deducted in the separate return of a single taxpayer.". . .

For these reasons we hold that earned original issue discount is not entitled to capital gains treatment under the 1939 Code.

D. NOTES AND QUESTIONS

1) Early Taxation of Bond OID

Under *Caulkins*, how and when was OID taxed to the bondholder? Under *Midland-Ross*? Did the two opinions disagree about the proper characterization of OID as a matter of economics? If not, what was the basis of the disagreement? Which opinion adopted the more plausible interpretation of Section 1271(a)'s predecessor?

2) The Mismatching of Interest Income and Interest Deductions Under the 1954 Code

In 1954, Congress amended the Code to provide explicitly for taxing as ordinary income the gain attributable to OID when a bond is sold or redeemed. Section 1271(c)(2)(A)(i). Even though OID was correctly identified as interest income taxable at ordinary rates, was tax avoidance still possible? The answer is yes, due to mismatching the *inclusion* of interest by the bondholder with the *deduction* of interest by the issuer. The mismatching occurred because of the different accounting methods used by bondholders on the one hand and issuers on the other. Many bondholders were individuals, on the cash method of accounting, and therefore not taxable on OID until the bond was either paid at maturity or sold to another investor.

Most issuers were corporations, on the accrual method, and deducted OID interest as it arose over the life of the bond—according to economic or even ratable accrual—rather than at maturity when it was actually paid. Table 50–3 illustrates mismatching with the five year, zero stated interest bond from Table 50–2.

TABLE 50-3. MISMATCHING OF INTEREST INCOME AND DEDUCTIONS UNDER THE 1954 CODE FOR A $1,000 PRINCIPAL AMOUNT, FIVE YEAR, ZERO STATED INTEREST BOND, GIVEN A MARKET INTEREST RATE OF 10%

Year	OID Income—Cash Method	OID Deductions—Economic Accrual	OID Deductions Ratable Accrual
1	0	−62	−76
2	0	−68	−76
3	0	−75	−76
4	0	−83	−76
5	+379	−91	−75
Total	+379	−379	−379

3) The Adoption of Ratable Accrual

Section 1271(b)(1) and (2), enacted in 1969, mandated the ratable accrual of original issue discount for both issuer and bondholder. The Senate Finance Committee explained both mismatching and outright nonreporting as requiring the change:

> The present treatment of original issue discount results in a nonparallel treatment of the corporation issuing the bond and the person acquiring the bond. The corporation is allowed a deduction each year with respect to the discount. On the other hand, the holder is not required to report any income with respect to the original issue discount until he disposes of the bond. While it is quite likely that the discount always will be deducted by the corporation, it is probable that much of the ordinary income is not being reported by the owner of the bonds. Not only is the fact that this discount is taxable at the time of disposition likely to be forgotten, but also the fact that it is ordinary income rather than capital gain is likely to be overlooked.[4]

Under ratable accrual, the bondholder reports and the borrower deducts the same amount of OID each year that the bond is outstanding. This annual amount equals the total amount of OID divided by the term of the bond. Under ratable accrual, how much OID interest does the bondholder report and the lender deduct each year for a five-year bond, with zero stated interest, where the market interest rate is 10% (see Table 50–2). How does this correspond to the amount of interest income actually accruing (that is, to economic accrual) during each of these years? The answers are indicated in Table 50–4, below.

---

4. S. Rep. No. 552, 91st Cong., 1st Sess. 146–147 (1969).

TABLE 50-4. RATABLE VERSUS ECONOMIC ACCRUAL, FIVE YEAR BOND, WITH $379 OID

Year	Ratable Accrual	Economic Accrual	Difference
1	76	62	+14
2	76	68	+8
3	76	75	+1
4	76	83	−7
5	75	91	−16
Total	379	379	0

4) Ratable Accrual and Economic Accrual Compared

How do ratable and economic accrual differ? Over the life of the bond, the entire amount of OID is unchanged. But timing—when OID interest is taken into account—is affected. During the early years (1–3), ratable accrual overstates the amount of interest. During the later years (4–5), ratable accrual understates the amount of interest.

Why does ratable accrual overstate the issuer's interest deductions—and therefore understate the issuer's income? Why does ratable accrual overstate the bondholder's interest income? Why is the understatement of income to the issuer exactly matched by the overstatement of income to the bondholder? Why is the result of ratable accrual (as compared with economic accrual) to shift income from issuer to bondholder?

5) Does the Shifting of Income Under Ratable Accrual Matter?

Does the shifting of income produced by ratable accrual matter if both bondholder and issuer are in the same tax bracket? In that event, wouldn't the relative overtaxation of the bondholder be exactly offset by the relative undertaxation of the issuer? Under what circumstances might ratable accrual lead to tax avoidance? What if the bondholder's tax rate is significantly less than the issuer's? What if, for example, the bondholder is a tax-exempt entity? Consider the following transaction, as described in a 1982 congressional report on the decision to replace ratable accrual of bond OID with the economic accrual method.

E. AMORTIZATION OF ORIGINAL ISSUE DISCOUNT ON BONDS

Staff of Joint Committee on Taxation, 97th Cong., 2d Sess., General Explanation of the Revenue Provisions of the Tax Equity and Fiscal Responsibility Act Of 1982, 158–161 (Comm. Print 1982)

Prior Law

Tax treatment of corporate original issue discount bonds

Normally, a bond is issued at a price approximately equal to the amount for which the bond will be redeemed at maturity, and the return to the holder of the bond is entirely in the form of periodic interest payments. However, in the case of original issue discount (OID) bonds, the issue price is below the redemption price, and the holder receives some or all of his return in the form of price appreciation. The spread between the issue price and redemption price is the original issue discount. The extreme case of an OID bond is a zero-coupon bond, on which there are no periodic interest payments, and the holder's entire return comes from price appreciation.

Under prior law, for bonds issued by a corporation and for which the period between the issue date and the stated maturity date exceeded one year, the original issue discount was treated as accruing in equal monthly installments over the life of the bond. Thus, an issuer of an OID bond deducted, as interest, both any periodic interest payments and a ratable portion of the original issue discount each year, and the holder of the bond included this same amount in income. For example, if a corporation issued a $1,000, 25-year bond paying a $70 annual coupon for an issue price of $500, it would deduct $90 for each full year over the life of the bond ($70 annual coupon plus 1/25th of the $500 original issue discount). The original holder of the bond would also report $90 of income for each full year he held the bond. The basis of the bond in the hands of the holder was adjusted for the discount required to be included in income. . . .

Example comparing corporate OID and ordinary bonds

Assume a 15-percent interest rate. Suppose a business wants to borrow $1 and then borrow at the end of the year to pay all interest charges for the year, and repeat this sequence each year for 30 years. Its interest payments would be 15 cents in the first year, 17.3 cents the second year (15 percent interest on the outstanding balance of $1.15), and so on, and would grow exponentially, eventually equaling $8.64 in the 30th year. At the end of 30 years, the overall debt would mount up to $66.21. A total of $65.21 in interest would be paid, and deducted, over the period, but the deductions would start small and grow.

The taxpayer could achieve the same substantive result by issuing a zero-coupon bond at a price of $1 redeemable for $66.21 in 30 years. However, by using the OID bond, the taxpayer could obtain a deduction of $2.17 each year ($65.21 divided by 30). Thus, the OID bond allowed larger interest deductions in early years than borrowing the same amount with ordinary loans. In this example, the taxpayer deducted in the first year more than twice the amount borrowed and more than 14 times the real interest. Conversely; the purchaser of the OID bond included more interest in his income in early years than the purchaser of an ordinary bond. [But if the bondholder was tax exempt—as was often the case—it would not care about the overstatement of its interest income.]

[The table below] shows the different patterns of deductions for the issuer and income inclusion for the holder between a zero-coupon bond and borrowing with ordinary loans under prior law.

COMPARISON OF INTEREST DEDUCTIONS AND INCOME INCLUSION BETWEEN BORROWING $1 WITH ZERO-COUPON BONDS AND WITH ORDINARY LOANS UNDER PRIOR LAW

Year	Ordinary loans	Zero-coupon bond	Difference
1982	0.150	2.174	2.024
1983	.173	2.174	2.001
1984	.198	2.174	1.976
1985	.228	2.174	1.946
1986	.262	2.174	1.912
1987	.302	2.174	1.872
1988	.347	2.174	1.827
1989	.399	2.174	1.775
1990	.459	2.174	1.715
1991	.528	2.174	1.646
1992	.607	2.174	1.567
1993	.698	2.174	1.476
1994	.803	2.174	1.371
1995	.923	2.174	1.251
1996	1.061	2.174	1.113
1997	1.221	2.174	.953
1998	1.404	2.174	.770
1999	1.614	2.174	.560
2000	1.856	2.174	.318
2001	2.135	2.174	.039
2002	2.455	2.174	−.281
2003	2.823	2.174	−.649
2004	3.247	2.174	−1.073
2005	3.734	2.174	−1.560
2006	4.294	2.174	−2.120
2007	4.938	2.174	−2.764
2008	5.679	2.174	−3.505
2009	6.530	2.174	−4.356
2010	7.510	2.174	−5.336
2011	8.636	2.174	−6.462
Total	65.212	65.212	0
Present value (computed at 8.1 percent after-tax rate)	11.738	24.245	12.505

Assumptions ...

  Ordinary bond: Taxpayer borrows $1 in 1981 and borrows every year to pay the interest on the outstanding indebtedness. Interest rates remain at 15 percent. All debt repaid in 2011.

  Zero-coupon bond: Taxpayer issues bond for price of $1 with no coupon, maturing in 30 years at a price of $66.21 (15-percent yield to maturity).

Reasons for Change

The larger deductions allowed to issuers of OID bonds in the early years of a bond's term relative to deductions allowed issuers of interest-bearing bonds not issued at a discount were a substantial tax advantage to the former, an advantage that increased with the term of the bonds. The ratable OID amortization formula was adopted at a time when interest rates were considerably lower than at present and when the formula involved a much smaller distortion. The formula was significantly different from the formula which issuers use to compute interest deductions on financial statements and did not represent a proper measurement of interest costs to the issuer. . . .

F. NOTES AND QUESTIONS

1) The Zero Stated Interest Bond as Tax Shelter

The table in the reading above indicates the present value of ratable accrual of interest deductions, as compared with economic accrual, when $1 is borrowed for thirty years. How does ratable accrual of deductions for OID resemble accelerated depreciation of capital expenditures? What is the present value of the extra tax savings produced by ratable accrual for a 50% bracket issuer? How does this amount compare with the amount borrowed?

Suppose that the issuer of the zero stated interest bond can invest the proceeds in thirty-year tax exempt bonds earning 10%. How much does it have to put aside when the zero stated interest bond is issued to fund the obligation to pay the face amount of about $65 on maturity? (Use the present value table in Chapter 12.) How does the amount put aside compare with the present value of the tax savings generated by ratable accrual? How much does the issuer "net" from the transaction?

What limits the number of such bonds that a corporation will be willing to issue? How do the long-term, zero stated interest bonds issued by taxable corporations to tax-exempt entities resemble the "abusive" tax shelters of *Estate of Franklin* and *Dean* (Chapters 42 and 43)?

What happens to the tax advantage of ratable accrual if the bondholder is also in a 50% bracket, instead of tax exempt? How does the 1986 reduction in tax rates affect the calculations in the table in the Joint Committee Report?

2) The Realization Principle and Accrual Taxation of OID

Can either ratable or economic accrual of OID be reconciled with the realization principle? If Congress can tax the annual appreciation in a bond's value attributable to OID, then why not tax the annual increase in the value of unimproved land attributable to market forces?

3) An Alternative Solution

Instead of requiring economic accrual of OID on bonds, suppose that Congress had required issuers to defer deducting OID interest until actually paid. Notice that this alternative solution is tantamount to treating the issuer as if it used the cash method of accounting and could only deduct interest expense when paid. Would this prevent mismatching of the reporting of OID interest income by bondholders and the deduction of OID interest expense by issuers?

How does this alternative solution compare with economic accrual? Why does it understate the bondholder's income and overstate the issuer's income by exactly offsetting amounts? Why is the net effect to shift interest income from bondholder to issuer? If both parties are in the same tax bracket, will the shifting of income matter? How likely is it that a corporate issuer will be in a lower tax bracket than the bondholder, given the structure of rates today?

Might adoption of this alternative solution encourage tax-exempt institutions to issue zero stated interest bonds? Why might such institutions then be able to issue OID bonds to wealthy investors at lower than market rates of interest? Could a tax-exempt entity take the proceeds from issuing such a bond, invest just enough in fully taxable corporate bonds to fund the principal amount due on the maturity of its own obligation, and pocket the difference? Is there any limit to the number of such bonds that a tax-exempt organization could issue, provided that bondholders were assured (through an escrow arrangement, for example) that enough of the proceeds would be immediately invested in corporate bonds to fund repayment at maturity?

4) Nonoriginal Issue Discount

Suppose that AT&T issues a $1,000 principal amount bond paying 10% stated interest and that 10% is also the market rate of interest when the bond is issued, so that the issue price equals the face amount. Assume that the bond will mature in ten years and that, five years after issue, the market rate of interest for the bond rises to 20%. Why might this rise occur? How will it affect the value of the AT&T bond? (Use the present value tables in Chapter 12.) Will you be able to buy the bond in the market at a discount from the $1,000 principal amount? What does this nonoriginal issue discount, or so-called *market discount*, represent? (And why is market discount a misnomer?)

The tax law has treated market discount on bonds differently from OID. Before 1984, market discount was taxed only when a bond was sold or exchanged and then only as capital gain. Section 1276(a)(1), enacted in 1984, provides that market discount is taxable as ordinary income but still only when a bond is sold or exchanged. It does not require *accrual* of market discount. In addition, Section 1276 applies only to bonds issued after July 18, 1984.

Is the difference between the treatment of market discount and the treatment of OID defensible? Is the difference consistent with the treatment of bond premiums (Chapter 34)?

Readers should also note Section 1277, which limits the deduction of interest expense on loans incurred in connection with market discount bonds. Under Section 1277, such interest expense may not be deducted to the extent of market discount allocable to the taxable year in question. Any disallowed deductions may be taken when the bond is sold or retired.

Chapter 51

UNSTATED INTEREST ON SALES FOR DEFERRED PAYMENT

A. INTRODUCTORY NOTES AND QUESTIONS

1) Allocating Deferred Payments Between Purchase Price and Interest

Suppose that property with a fair market value of $100,000 is sold for deferred payments of $30,000 a year for five years, that is, for a total of $150,000. As a matter of economics, $50,000—the difference between the market value of the property and total deferred payments—represents interest. It is the extra amount paid for the privilege of deferring payment. In effect, the sale for deferred payment can be recast as two transactions. First, property is sold for its fair market value of $100,000. Second, the seller loans the buyer the $100,000 purchase price in return for the buyer's promise to repay $150,000 over the next five years.

If the basis of the property is $80,000, then the seller's overall gain equals $70,000 (total deferred payments of $150,000 minus the basis). This $70,000 gain consists of two separate components. One part, $20,000, represents appreciation in the value of the property that has been sold. The other part, $50,000, represents the difference between the amount loaned and the amount repaid, or interest, and arguably should be taxable to the seller as ordinary income.

Before 1964, if the sales contract did not explicitly label any part of the deferred payment as interest—that is, if the stated interest was zero—then the entire $150,000 was generally treated as an amount paid for the property and none of it as interest. Provided that the property was a capital or quasi-capital asset and provided that the "extra" property gain was not recaptured as ordinary income (Chapter 36), the seller was allowed to convert ordinary income into capital gain.

The buyer on the other hand appeared to suffer an offsetting disadvantage—the loss of a deduction against ordinary income for interest expense. However, this disadvantage could often be disregarded. If the buyer was tax exempt, the loss of a deduction was irrelevant. If the property was depreciable, an ordinary income deduction for interest expense was lost, but the property acquired a higher basis and therefore higher depreciation deductions against ordinary income. This could even produce a net advantage for the buyer if depreciation was deducted more rapidly than interest, because of an artificially short useful life assigned to the property (Chapter 35). Thus, by providing for zero interest, a deferred payment sale could produce considerable tax savings for either one or both parties.

2) Sales for Deferred Payment Compared to OID Bonds

The seller of property for deferred payment in the example under 1), above, is in a position analogous to that of a bondholder with OID in *Caulkins* and *Midland-Ross* (Chapter 50). The $150,000 stated purchase price is like the principal amount of the bond. The $100,000 fair market value of the property is like the bond's issue price. The $50,000 difference between the stated purchase price and the property's value represents unstated interest and is like bond OID.

In *Midland-Ross,* the Supreme Court recognized that OID on bonds should be characterized as interest income. But the courts still generally accepted the taxpayers' characterization of unstated interest in sales of property for deferred payment as part of the price of the property. Unstated interest on such sales began to be taxed as interest only after Congress amended the Code to provide explicitly for such a result.

Can this difference in results be explained by problems of measurement? Why is it easy to measure the amount of OID on bonds? Why is it often more difficult to measure unstated interest in a sale of property for deferred payment? Why in the latter case does it require specifying either (a) the fair market value of the property when the sale occurs or (b) the real interest rate being charged by the seller? Why might this require a subjective estimate? Why is the amount of OID objectively determinable in the case of bonds? (Chapter 34 made a similar comparison between premium leases and premium bonds.)

3) Imputing Interest: Section 483

In 1964, Congress enacted Section 483, providing for interest to be *imputed* whenever the stated interest in a sale for deferred payment was below a certain minimum rate, prescribed in regulations. The effect of *imputation* is to recharacterize a portion of the property's purchase price as interest. However, the minimum stated interest required in order to avoid imputation was still considerably below commercial interest rates. Provided only that stated interest equaled the minimum, it could still be substantially less than the real interest being charged and therefore provide opportunities for tax avoidance.[1] In addition, even when interest was imputed, Section 483 had no impact whatsoever on the mismatching of interest

---

1. This was aggravated by the fact that, until 1984, Section 483 required interest to be computed only on a simple basis, without compounding.

income and interest deductions. A cash method purchaser could still report the imputed interest only when paid, whereas an accrual method buyer would deduct the imputed interest as it accrued.

4) Applying the OID Analysis to Deferred Payment Sales: Section 1274

Section 1274, enacted in 1984, has radically changed the treatment of unstated interest in sales of property for a deferred payment. First, unstated interest is accounted for according to an economic accrual schedule. The seller reports unstated interest income and the buyer takes unstated interest deductions as the interest is earned—in the same manner as bond OID. Second, interest is imputed at a much more realistic rate. Unless the stated interest equals the so-called "federal rate," interest will be imputed at that rate. See Sections 1274(a), 1274(b)(1) and (2), 1274(c)(1) and (2), and 1274(d)(1).

Section 1274 describes how to determine the "issue price" of "any debt instrument given in consideration for the sale or exchange of property." The issue price is computed by discounting the deferred payments to present value, using the federal interest rate. Section 1274(b)(1) and (2). Any difference between the stated purchase price and the issue price, so computed, is defined as OID. Section 1273(a)(1). The seller is required to report OID as it accrues by Section 1272, the same provision that requires bondholders to report OID on bonds. Section 1272(a)(1) (the reference to "any debt instrument"). The buyer deducts interest according to an economic accrual schedule. Section 163(e)(1).

Section 1274 is described in the following congressional report.

B. IMPUTING INTEREST ON SALES FOR DEFERRED PAYMENT [SECTION 1274]

> Staff of the Joint Committee on Taxation, 98th Cong., 2d Sess., General Explanation of the Revenue Provisions of the Deficit Reduction Act of 1984, 108–112 (Comm. Print 1984).

If, in a lending transaction, the borrower receives less than the amount to be repaid at the loan's maturity, the difference represents "discount." Discount performs the same function as stated interest; that is, it compensates the lender for the use of its money. . . . [P]rior law . . . required the holder of a discount debt obligation to include in income annually a portion of the original issue discount on the obligation, and allowed the issuer to deduct a corresponding amount, irrespective of whether the cash method or the accrual method of accounting was used.

Original issue discount was defined as the excess of an obligation's stated redemption price at maturity over its issue price. This amount was allocated over the life of the obligation . . . .

The OID rules did not apply to obligations issued by individuals . . . or obligations issued in exchange for property where neither the obligation nor the property received for it was traded on an established securities exchange . . . .

A deferred-payment sale of property exempt from the OID rules was generally subject to the unstated interest rules of Section 483. If the parties to the transaction failed to state a minimum "safe-harbor" rate of interest . . . , section 483 recharacterized a portion of the principal amount as unstated interest. This "imputation" of interest was performed by assuming that interest accrued at a rate higher than the safe-harbor rate . . . .

Enacted in 1969, the OID rules were designed to eliminate the distortions caused by the mismatching of income and deductions by lenders and borrowers. . . . Prior to that time, an accrual method borrower could deduct deferred interest payable to a cash method lender prior to the period in which the lender included the interest in income. Although the OID rules prevented mismatching in many situations, the potential for distortion continued to exist where the obligation was excepted from the OID rules. Some taxpayers attempted to exploit these exceptions, particularly the exception relating to nontraded obligations issued for nontraded property . . . .

For example, in a typical transaction, real estate, machinery, or other depreciable property was purchased for a promissory note providing that interest accrued annually but was not payable until the note matured. The issuer, who used the accrual method of accounting, would claim annual interest deductions for accrued but unpaid interest. The holder, a cash method taxpayer, would defer interest income until it was actually received.

Such a mismatching of income and deductions had serious revenue consequences, since the present value of the income included by the lender in the later period was less than the present value of the deductions claimed by the borrower. . . .

. . . Congress believed it appropriate to extend the [OID rules] to nontraded debt instruments issued for nontraded property. The same policy objectives that led to the application of these rules to . . . traded debt instruments—namely, better compliance by holders and clearer reflection of income—were believed to apply equally in the case of nontraded instruments issued for nontraded property. . . .

The principal obstacle to applying the OID rules to a transaction in which neither side is traded is the difficulty of determining the issue price of the debt instrument directly. Both the issue price and the redemption price of an instrument must be known to compute the amount of OID. In a transaction involving the issuance of a note for cash, the issue price is simply the amount of cash received. Where the issuer receives nontraded property, however, the fair market value of the property determines the obligation's issue price. Using a . . . case-by-case analysis to determine fair market value in these situations was considered impracticable. Congress believed that the valuation problem could best be resolved by incorporating into the OID rules a mechanism for testing the adequacy of [stated] interest in a sale of property . . . . An approximation of the maximum fair market value of property (and hence the issue price of the obligation issued in exchange for it) could be arrived at by assuming a minimum rate of interest which parties . . . could be expected to agree upon . . . .

Congress recognized that, under prior law, it was possible for taxpayers in a sale of nontraded property for nontraded debt to achieve unwarranted tax benefits not only by mismatching interest income and deductions, but by manipulating the principal amount of the debt. This could be accomplished by artificially fixing interest at a below-market rate. Although economically the parties were in the same position as if interest had been accurately stated, significant tax advantages often resulted from characterizing the transaction as involving a lower rate of interest and a larger principal amount. If recognized for tax purposes, this mischaracterization of interest as principal resulted in an overstatement of the sales price and tax basis of the property. In cases where the property was a capital asset in the hands of the seller, the seller was able to convert interest income ... into capital gain ....

... Section 483 of prior law failed to control this overstatement of purchase price and tax basis ... because both the test rate and the imputation rate were frequently less than prevailing market rates. The section 483 rates were inadequate for three reasons. First, although the rates were changed periodically, they failed to keep pace with market interest rates. Second, the simple interest computation used in testing the adequacy of stated interest ignored the compounding of interest on unpaid interest ... Finally, the use of a single rate for all obligations regardless of maturity failed to reflect the fact that lenders typically demand different returns on investment depending on the term of the loan.

Congress believed that the solution was to provide a mechanism for bringing the test and imputation rates closer to market rates ....

C. NOTES AND QUESTIONS

1) Exceptions to Section 1274

Although Section 1274 generally applies to all sales of property where at least one payment is "due more than 6 months after the sale" (Section 1274(c)(1)(B)), it contains numerous exceptions. Section 1274(c)(3). Certain sales of farms for no more than $1 million, sales of a taxpayer's principal residence, sales involving total payments of less than $250,000, certain sales of patents, and certain sales of land between related parties all escape Section 1274's and therefore Section 1272's reach. Section 1274(c)(3)(A), (B), (C), (E), and (F).[2]

Many of these excepted transactions, however, remain subject to the imputed interest rules of Section 483, which were considerably strengthened. Section 483(b) adopts the imputation formula of Section 1274. Unless the stated interest equals the federal rate, interest will be imputed at the federal rate.

What, then, is the advantage of having interest imputed under Section 483 rather than Section 1274 when both sections impute interest at the federal rate? The answer is that only Section 1274 requires accrual reporting of interest income as it is earned. Unstated interest on items ex-

---

2. The exception for publicly traded debt (Section 1274(c)(3)(D)) provides only illusory relief. The amount of unstated interest on such instruments is determined under Section 1273 and subject to accrual taxation under Section 1272.

cepted from Section 1274, therefore, need not be reported by a seller who uses the cash method until paid. Is there any principled way to explain why these particular exceptions to Section 1274 were made?

2) Exceptions to Section 483

Certain sales of patents are exempted from Section 483, as are sales for less than $3,000. Sections 483(d)(2) and (4). In addition, interest on certain sales of land between related parties may not be imputed at a rate above 6%. Section 483(e)(1).

3) And Even More Exceptions!—Section 1274A

If all this were not complicated enough, Congress has provided further exceptions to the rules of Sections 1274 and 483. See Section 1274A, enacted in 1985. First, if the stated principal amount does not exceed $2,800,000, then the rate at which interest is imputed may not exceed 9%. Second, if the principal amount does not exceed $2,000,000 and if the seller uses the cash method of accounting (and also is not a dealer in the property), then both seller and buyer may escape the accrual of interest mandated by Section 1274. Both parties may elect to have interest accounted for only when paid so that the seller reports interest income and the buyer deducts interest expense according to the cash method of accounting.

Section 1274A is supposed to represent an attempt to balance the hardships caused by accrual taxation of interest against the need to prevent tax avoidance. Does it go too far?

4) The *Clay Brown* Decision

In *Clay Brown* (which follows), the taxpayer sold a lumber business to a charity for a deferred payment, under a contract that provided for no interest. Because the transaction occurred before 1964, unstated interest was not imputed by the Code.

D. COMMISSIONER v. [CLAY] BROWN
380 U.S. 563 (1965)

MR. JUSTICE WHITE delivered the opinion of the Court.

In 1950, when Congress addressed itself to the problem of the direct or indirect acquisition and operation of going businesses by charities or other tax-exempt entities, it was recognized that in many of the typical sale and leaseback transactions, the exempt organization was trading on and perhaps selling part of its exemption. . . . For this and other reasons the Internal Revenue Code was accordingly amended in several respects, of principal importance for our purposes by taxing as "unrelated business income" the profits earned by a charity in the operation of a business, as well as the income from long-term leases of the business. The short-term lease, however, of five years or less, was not affected and this fact has moulded many of the transactions in this field since that time, including the one involved in this case.

The Commissioner, however, in 1954, announced that when an exempt organization purchased a business and leased it for five years to another corporation, not investing its own funds but paying off the purchase price with rental income, the purchasing organization was in danger of losing its exemption; that in any event the rental income would be taxable income; ... and finally, and most important for this case, that the payments received by the seller would not be entitled to capital gains treatment. . . .

This case is one of the many in the course of which the Commissioner has questioned the sale of a business concern to an exempt organization. The basic facts are undisputed. Clay Brown, members of his family and three other persons owned substantially all of the stock in Clay Brown & Company, with sawmills and lumber interests near Fortuna, California. Clay Brown, the president of the company and spokesman for the group, was approached by a representative of California Institute for Cancer Research in 1952, and after considerable negotiation the stockholders agreed to sell their stock to the Institute for $1,300,000, payable $5,000 down from the assets of the company and the balance within 10 years from the earnings of the company's assets. It was provided that simultaneously with the transfer of the stock, the Institute would liquidate the company and lease its assets for five years to a new corporation, Fortuna Sawmills, Inc., formed and wholly owned by the attorneys for the sellers. Fortuna would pay to the Institute 80% of its operating profit without allowance for depreciation or taxes, and 90% of such payments would be paid over by the Institute to the selling stockholders to apply on the $1,300,000 note. This note was noninterest bearing, the Institute had no obligation to pay it except from the rental income and it was secured by mortgages and assignments of the assets transferred or leased to Fortuna. If the payments on the note failed to total $250,000 over any two consecutive years, the sellers could declare the entire balance of the note due and payable. The sellers were neither stockholders nor directors of Fortuna but it was provided that Clay Brown was to have a management contract with Fortuna at an annual salary and the right to name any successor manager if he himself resigned.[3]

The transaction was closed on February 4, 1953. Fortuna immediately took over operations of the business under its lease, on the same premises and with practically the same personnel which had been employed by Clay Brown & Company. Effective October 31, 1954, Clay Brown resigned as general manager of Fortuna and waived his right to name his successor. In 1957, because of a rapidly declining lumber market, Fortuna suffered severe reverses and its operations were terminated. Respondent sellers did not repossess the properties under their mortgages but agreed they should be sold by the Institute with the latter retaining 10% of the proceeds. Accordingly, the property was sold by the Institute for $300,000. The

---

3. Clay Brown's personal liability for some of the indebtedness of Clay Brown & Company, assumed by Fortuna, was continued. He also personally guaranteed some additional indebtedness incurred by Fortuna.

payments on the note from rentals and from the sale of the properties totaled $936,131.85. Respondents returned the payments received from rentals as the gain from the sale of capital assets. The Commissioner, however, asserted the payments were taxable as ordinary income and were not capital gain. . . .

In the Tax Court, the Commissioner asserted that the transaction was a sham and that in any event respondents retained such an economic interest in and control over the property sold that the transaction could not be treated as a sale resulting in a long-term capital gain. A divided Tax Court . . . found that there had been considerable good-faith bargaining at arm's length between the Brown family and the Institute, that the price agreed upon was within a reasonable range in the light of the earnings history of the corporation and the adjusted net worth of its assets, that the primary motivation for the Institute was the prospect of ending up with the assets of the business free and clear after the purchase price had been fully paid, which would then permit the Institute to convert the property and the money for use in cancer research, and that there had been a real change of economic benefit in the transaction.[4] Its conclusion was that the transfer of respondents' stock in Clay Brown & Company to the Institute was a bona fide sale arrived at in an arm's-length transaction and that the amounts received by respondents were proceeds from the sale of stock and entitled to long-term capital gains treatment under the Internal Revenue Code. The Court of Appeals affirmed . . . and we granted certiorari. . . .

Having abandoned in the Court of Appeals the argument that this transaction was a sham, the Commissioner now admits that there was real substance in what occurred between the Institute and the Brown family. The transaction was a sale under local law. The Institute acquired title to the stock of Clay Brown & Company and, by liquidation, to all of the assets of that company, in return for its promise to pay over money from the operating profits of the company. If the stipulated price was paid, the Brown family would forever lose all rights to the income and properties of the company. Prior to the transfer, these respondents had access to all of the income of the company; after the transfer, 28% of the income remained with Fortuna and the Institute. Respondents had no interest in the Institute nor were they stockholders or directors of the operating company. Any rights to control the management were limited to the management contract between Clay Brown and Fortuna, which was relinquished in 1954.

Whatever substance the transaction might have had, however, the Commissioner claims that it did not have the substance of a sale within the meaning of § 1222(3). His argument is that since the Institute invested nothing, assumed no independent liability for the purchase price and promised only to pay over a percentage of the earnings of the company, the entire risk of the transaction remained on the sellers. Apparently, to qualify as a sale, a transfer of property for money or the promise of money must be to a financially responsible buyer who undertakes to pay the purchase

---

4. The Tax Court found nothing to indicate that the arrangement between the stockholders and the Institute contemplated the Brown family's being free at any time to take back and operate the business.

price other than from the earnings or the assets themselves or there must be a substantial down payment which shifts at least part of the risk to the buyer and furnishes some cushion against loss to the seller.

To say that there is no sale because there is no risk-shifting and that there is no risk-shifting because the price to be paid is payable only from the income produced by the business sold, is very little different from saying that because business earnings are usually taxable as ordinary income, they are subject to the same tax when paid over as the purchase price of property. This argument has rationality but it places an unwarranted construction on the term "sale," is contrary to the policy of the capital gains provisions of the Internal Revenue Code, and has no support in the cases. We reject it.

"Capital gain" and "capital asset" are creatures of the tax law and the Court has been inclined to give these terms a narrow, rather than a broad, construction. *Corn Products Co. v. Commissioner* [Chapter 26]. A "sale," however, is a common event in the non-tax world; and since it is used in the Code without limiting definition and without legislative history indicating a contrary result, its common and ordinary meaning should at least be persuasive of its meaning as used in the Internal Revenue Code. "Generally speaking, the language in the Revenue Act, just as in any statute, is to be given its ordinary meaning, and the words 'sale' and 'exchange' are not to be read any differently."...

"A sale, in the ordinary sense of the word, is a transfer of property for a fixed price in money or its equivalent,".... The transaction which occurred in this case was obviously a transfer of property for a fixed price payable in money.

Unquestionably the courts, in interpreting a statute, have some "scope for adopting a restricted rather than a literal or usual meaning of its words where acceptance of that meaning would lead to absurd results ... or would thwart the obvious purpose of the statute.".... But it is otherwise "where no such consequences would follow and where ... it appears to be consonant with the purposes of the Act ...." We find nothing in this case indicating that the Tax Court or the Court of Appeals construed the term "sale" too broadly or in a manner contrary to the purpose or policy of capital gains provisions of the Code.

Congress intended to afford capital gains treatment only in situations "typically involving the realization of appreciation in value accrued over a substantial period of time, and thus to ameliorate the hardship of taxation of the entire gain in one year.".... It was to "relieve the taxpayer from ... excessive tax burdens on gains resulting from a conversion of capital investments" that capital gains were taxed differently by Congress....

As of January 31, 1953, the adjusted net worth of Clay Brown & Company as revealed by its books was $619,457.63. This figure included accumulated earnings of $448,471.63, paid in surplus, capital stock and notes payable to the Brown family. The appraised value as of that date, however, relied upon by the Institute and the sellers, was $1,064,877, without figuring interest on deferred balances. Under a deferred payment plan with a 6% interest figure, the sale value was placed at $1,301,989. The Tax Court found the sale price agreed upon was arrived at in an arm's-length transaction, was the result of real negotiating and was "within a reasonable range in light of the earnings history of the corporation and the adjusted net worth of the corporate assets.". . .

Obviously, on these facts, there had been an appreciation in value accruing over a period of years . . . and an "increase in the value of the income-producing property.". . . This increase taxpayers were entitled to realize at capital gains rates on a cash sale of their stock; and likewise if they sold on a deferred payment plan taking an installment note and a mortgage as security. Further . . . the gain itself could be reported on the installment basis.

In the actual transaction, the stock was transferred for a price payable on the installment basis but payable from the earnings of the company. Eventually $936,131.85 was realized by respondents. This transaction, we think, is a sale, and so treating it is wholly consistent with the purposes of the Code to allow capital gains treatment for realization upon the enhanced value of a capital asset.

The Commissioner, however, embellishes his risk-shifting argument. Purporting to probe the economic realities of the transaction, he reasons that if the seller continues to bear all the risk and the buyer none, the seller must be collecting a price for his risk-bearing in the form of an interest in future earnings over and above what would be a fair market value of the property. Since the seller bears the risk, the so-called purchase price *must* be excessive and *must* be simply a device to collect future earnings at capital gains rates.

We would hesitate to discount unduly the power of pure reason and the argument is not without force. But it does present difficulties. In the first place, it denies what the tax court expressly found—that the price paid was within reasonable limits based on the earnings and net worth of the company; and there is evidence in the record to support this finding. We do not have, therefore, a case where the price has been found excessive.

Secondly, if an excessive price is such an inevitable result of the lack of risk-shifting, it would seem that it would not be an impossible task for the Commissioner to demonstrate the fact. However, in this case he offered no evidence whatsoever to this effect; and in a good many other cases involving similar transactions, in some of which the reasonableness of the price paid by a charity was actually contested, the Tax Court has found the sale price to be within reasonable limits, as it did in this case.

Thirdly, the Commissioner ignores as well the fact that if the rents payable by Fortuna were deductible by it and not taxable to the Institute, the Institute could pay off the purchase price at a considerably faster rate than the ordinary corporate buyer subject to income taxes, a matter of considerable importance to a seller who wants the balance of his purchase price paid as rapidly as he can get it. The fact is that by April 30, 1955, a little over two years after closing this transaction, $412,595.77 had been paid on the note and within another year the sellers had collected another $238,498.80, for a total of $651,094.57.

Furthermore, risk-shifting of the kind insisted on by the Commissioner has not heretofore been considered an essential ingredient of a sale for tax purposes . . . . To require a sale for tax purposes to be to a financially responsible buyer who undertakes to pay the purchase price from sources other than the earnings of the assets sold or to make a substantial down payment seems to us at odds with commercial practice and common understanding of what constitutes a sale. The term "sale" is used a great many times in the Internal Revenue Code and a wide variety of tax results hinge on the occurrence of a "sale." To accept the Commissioner's definition of sale would have wide ramifications which we are not prepared to visit upon taxpayers, absent congressional guidance in this direction. . . .

There is another reason for us not to disturb the ruling of the Tax Court and the Court of Appeals. In 1963, the Treasury Department, in the course of hearings before the Congress, noted the availability of capital gains treatment on the sale of capital assets even though the seller retained an interest in the income produced by the assets. The Department proposed a change in the law which would have taxed as ordinary income the payments on the sale of a capital asset which were deferred over more than five years and were contingent on future income. Payments, though contingent on income, required to be made within five years would not have lost capital gains status nor would payments not contingent on income even though accompanied by payments which were . . . .

Congress did not adopt the suggested change but it is significant for our purposes that the proposed amendment did not deny the fact or occurrence of a sale but would have taxed as ordinary income those income-contingent payments deferred for more than five years. If a purchaser could pay the purchase price out of earnings within five years, the seller would have capital gain rather than ordinary income. The approach was consistent with allowing appreciated values to be treated as capital gain but with appropriate safeguards against reserving additional rights to future income. In comparison, the Commissioner's position here is a clear case of "overkill" if aimed at preventing the involvement of tax-exempt entities in the purchase and operation of business enterprises. There are more precise approaches to this problem as well as to the question of the possibly excessive price paid by the charity or foundation. And if the Commissioner's approach is intended as a limitation upon the tax treatment of sales generally, it represents a considerable invasion of current capital gains policy, a matter which we think is the business of Congress, not ours.

The problems involved in the purchase of a going business by a tax-exempt organization have been considered and dealt with by the Congress. Likewise, it has given its attention to various kinds of transactions involving the payment of the agreed purchase price for property from the future earnings of the property itself. In both situations it has responded, if at all, with precise provisions of narrow application. We consequently deem it wise to "leave to the Congress the fashioning of a rule which, in any event, must have wide ramifications.". . .

Mr. Justice Harlan, concurring.

Were it not for the tax laws, the respondents' transaction with the Institute would make no sense, except as one arising from a charitable impulse. However the tax laws exist as an economic reality in the businessman's world, much like the existence of a competitor. Businessmen plan their affairs around both, and a tax dollar is just as real as one derived from any other source. The Code gives the Institute a tax exemption which makes it capable of taking a greater after-tax return from a business than could a nontax-exempt individual or corporation. Respondents traded a residual interest in their business for a faster payout apparently made possible by the Institute's exemption. The respondents gave something up; they received something substantially different in return. If words are to have meaning, there was a "sale or exchange."

Obviously the Institute traded on its tax exemption. The Government would deny that there was an exchange, essentially on the theory that the Institute did not put anything at risk; since its exemption is unlimited, like the magic purse that always contains another penny, the Institute gave up nothing by trading on it.

One may observe preliminarily that the Government's remedy for the so-called "bootstrap" sale—defining sale or exchange so as to require the shifting of some business risks—would accomplish little by way of closing off such sales in the future. It would be neither difficult nor burdensome for future users of the bootstrap technique to arrange for some shift of risks. If such sales are considered a serious abuse, ineffective judicial correctives will only postpone the day when Congress is moved to deal with the problem comprehensively. Furthermore, one may ask why, if the Government does not like the tax consequences of such sales, the proper course is not to attack the exemption rather than to deny the existence of a "real" sale or exchange.

The force underlying the Government's position is that the respondents did clearly retain some risk-bearing interest in the business. Instead of leaping from this premise to the conclusion that there was no sale or exchange, the Government might more profitably have broken the transaction into components and attempted to distinguish between the interest which respondents retained and the interest which they exchanged. The worth of a business depends upon its ability to produce income over time. What respondents gave up was not the entire business, but only their interest in the business' ability to produce income in excess of that which was necessary to pay them off under the terms of the transaction. The value of such a residual interest is a function of the risk element of the business and the amount of income it is capable of producing per year, and will necessarily be substantially less than the value of the total business. Had the Government argued that it was that interest which respondents exchanged, and only to that extent should they have received capital gains treatment, we would perhaps have had a different case.

I mean neither to accept nor reject this approach, or any other which falls short of the all-or-nothing theory specifically argued by the petitioner, specifically opposed by the respondents, and accepted by the Court as the premise for its decision. On a highly complex issue with as wide ramifications as the one before us, it is vitally important to have had the illumination provided by briefing and argument directly on point before any particular path is irrevocably taken. Where the definition of "sale or exchange" is concerned, the Court can afford to proceed slowly and by stages. The illumination which has been provided in the present case convinces

Mr. Justice Goldberg, . . . dissenting.

The essential facts of this case which are undisputed illuminate the basic nature of the transaction at issue. Respondents conveyed their stock in Clay Brown & Co., a corporation owned almost entirely by Clay Brown and the members of his immediate family, to the California Institute for Cancer Research, a tax-exempt foundation. The Institute liquidated the corporation and transferred its assets under a five-year lease to a new corporation, Fortuna, which was managed by respondent Clay Brown, and the shares of which were in the name of Clay Brown's attorneys, who also served as Fortuna's directors. The business thus continued under a new name with no essential change in control of its operations. Fortuna agreed to pay 80% of its pretax profits to the Institute as rent under the lease, and the Institute agreed to pay 90% of this amount to respondents in payment for their shares until the respondents received $1,300,000, at which time their interest would terminate and the Institute would own the complete beneficial interest as well as all legal interest in the business. If remittances to respondents were less than $250,000 in any two consecutive years or any other provision in the agreements was violated, they could recover the property. The Institute had no personal liability. In essence respondents conveyed their interest in the business to the Institute in return for 72% of the profits of the business and the right to recover the business assets if payments fell behind schedule.

At first glance it might appear odd that the sellers would enter into this transaction, for prior to the sale they had a right to 100% of the corporation's income, but after the sale they had a right to only 72% of that income and would lose the business after 10 years to boot. This transaction, however, afforded the sellers several advantages. The principal advantage sought by the sellers was capital gain, rather than ordinary income, treatment for that share of the business profits which they received. Further, because of the Tax Code's charitable exemption and the lease arrangement with Fortuna,[5] the Institute believed that neither it nor Fortuna would have to pay income tax on the earnings of the business. Thus the sellers would receive free of corporate taxation, and subject only to personal taxation at capital gains rates, 72% of the business earnings until they were paid $1,300,000. Without the sale they would receive only 48% of the business earnings, the rest going to the Government in corporate taxes, and this 48% would be subject to personal taxation at ordinary rates. In effect the Institute sold the respondents the use of its tax exemption, enabling the

---

5. This lease arrangement was designed to permit the Institute to take advantage of its charitable exemption to avoid taxes on payment of Fortuna's profits to it, with Fortuna receiving a deduction for the rental payments as an ordinary and necessary business expense, thus avoiding taxes to both. Though unrelated business income is usually taxable when received by charities, an exception is made for income received from the lease of real and personal property of less than five years. See I.R.C. § 514. . . .

respondents to collect $1,300,000 from the business more quickly than they otherwise could and to pay taxes on this amount at capital gains rates. In return, the Institute received a nominal amount of the profits while the $1,300,000 was being paid, and it was to receive the whole business after this debt had been paid off. In any realistic sense the Government's grant of a tax exemption was used by the Institute as part of an arrangement that allowed it to buy a business that in fact cost it nothing. I cannot believe that Congress intended such a result.

The Court today legitimates this bootstrap transaction and permits respondents the tax advantage which the parties sought. The fact that respondent Brown, as a result of the Court's holding, escapes payment of about $60,000 in taxes may not seem intrinsically important—although every failure to pay the proper amount of taxes under a progressive income tax system impairs the integrity of that system. But this case in fact has very broad implications. We are told by the parties and by interested *amici* that this is a test case. The outcome of this case will determine whether this bootstrap scheme for the conversion of ordinary income into capital gain, which has already been employed on a number of occasions, will become even more widespread. It is quite clear that the Court's decision approving this tax device will give additional momentum to its speedy proliferation. In my view Congress did not sanction the use of this scheme under the present revenue laws to obtain the tax advantages which the Court authorizes. Moreover, I believe that the Court's holding not only deviates from the intent of Congress but also departs from this Court's prior decisions.

The purpose of the capital gains provisions . . . is to prevent gains which accrue over a long period of time from being taxed in the year of their realization through a sale at high rates resulting from their inclusion in the higher tax brackets. . . . These provisions are not designed, however, to allow capital gains treatment for the recurrent receipt of commercial or business income. In light of these purposes this Court has held that a "sale" for capital gains purposes is not produced by the mere transfer of legal title. . . . Rather, at the very least, there must be a meaningful economic transfer in addition to a change in legal title. . . . Thus the question posed here is not whether this transaction constitutes a sale within the terms of the Uniform Commercial Code or the Uniform Sales Act—we may assume it does—but, rather, the question is whether, at the time legal title was transferred, there was also an economic transfer sufficient to convert ordinary income into capital gain by treating this transaction as a "sale" within the terms of I.R.C. § 1222(3).

In dealing with what constitutes a sale for capital gains purposes, this Court has been careful to look through formal legal arrangements to the underlying economic realities. . . .

. . . The sellers were to be paid only out of the proceeds of the business. If the business made money they would be paid; if it did not, they would not be paid. In the latter event, of course, they could recover the business, but a secured interest in a business which was losing money would be of dubious value. There was no other security. The Institute was not bound to pay any sum whatsoever. The Institute, in fact, promised only to channel to the sellers a portion of the income it received from Fortuna.

Moreover, in numerous cases this Court has refused to transfer the incidents of taxation along with a transfer of legal title when the transferor retains considerable control over the income-producing asset transferred. . . . *Helvering v. Clifford* [Chapter 45], *Corliss v. Bowers* [Chapter 45]. Control of the business did not, in fact, shift in the transaction here considered. Clay Brown, by the terms of the purchase agreement and the lease, was to manage Fortuna. Clay Brown was given power to hire and arrange for the terms of employment of all other employees of the corporation. The lease provided that "if for any reason Clay Brown is unable or unwilling to so act, the person or persons holding a majority interest in the principal note described in the Purchase Agreement shall have the right to approve his successor to act as general manager of Lessee company." Thus the shareholders of Clay Brown & Co. assured themselves of effective control over the management of Fortuna. Furthermore, Brown's attorneys were the named shareholders of Fortuna and its Board of Directors. The Institute had no control over the business.

I would conclude that on these facts there was not a sufficient shift of economic risk or control of the business to warrant treating this transaction as a "sale" for tax purposes. Brown retained full control over the operations of the business; the risk of loss and the opportunity to profit from gain during the normal operation of the business shifted but slightly. If the operation lost money, Brown stood to lose; if it gained money Brown stood to gain, for he would be paid off faster. Moreover, the entire purchase price was to be paid out of the ordinary income of the corporation, which was to be received by Brown on a recurrent basis as he had received it during the period he owned the corporation. I do not believe that Congress intended this recurrent receipt of ordinary business income to be taxed at capital gains rates merely because the business was to be transferred to a tax-exempt entity at some future date. For this reason I would apply here the established rule that, despite formal legal arrangements, a sale does not take place until there has been a significant economic change such as a shift in risk or in control of the business.[6]

To hold as the Court does that this transaction constitutes a "sale" within the terms of I.R.C. § 1222(3), thereby giving rise to capital gain for the income received, legitimates considerable tax evasion. Even if the Court restricts its holding, allowing only those transactions to be § 1222(3) sales in which the price is not excessive, its decision allows considerable latitude for the unwarranted conversion of ordinary income into capital gain. Valuation of a closed corporation is notoriously difficult. The Tax Court in the present case did not determine that the price for which the corporation was sold represented its true value; it simply stated that the price "was the result of

---

6. The fact that respondents were to lose complete control of the business after the payments were complete was taken into account by the Commissioner, for he treated the business in respondents' hands as a wasting asset, see I.R.C. 1954, § 167, and allowed them to offset their basis in the stock against the payments received.

real negotiating" and "within a reasonable range in light of the earnings history of the corporation and the adjusted net worth of the corporate assets.". . . The Tax Court, however, also said that "[i]t may be . . . that petitioner [Clay Brown] would have been unable to sell the stock at as favorable a price to anyone other than a tax-exempt organization.". . . Indeed, this latter supposition is highly likely, for the Institute was selling its tax exemption, and this is not the sort of asset which is limited in quantity. Though the Institute might have negotiated in order to receive beneficial ownership of the corporation as soon as possible, the Institute, at no cost to itself, could increase the price to produce an offer too attractive for the seller to decline. Thus it is natural to anticipate sales such as this taking place at prices on the upper boundary of what courts will hold to be a reasonable price—at prices which will often be considerably greater than what the owners of a closed corporation could have received in a sale to buyers who were not selling their tax exemptions. Unless Congress repairs the damage done by the Court's holding, I should think that charities will soon own a considerable number of closed corporations, the owners of which will see no good reason to continue paying taxes at ordinary income rates. It should not be necessary, however, for Congress to address itself to this loophole, for I believe that under the present laws it is clear that Congress did not intend to accord capital gains treatment to the proceeds of the type of sale present here.

Although the Court implies that it will hold to be "sales" only those transactions in which the price is reasonable, I do not believe that the logic of the Court's opinion will justify so restricting its holding. If this transaction is a sale under the Internal Revenue Code, entitling its proceeds to capital gains treatment because it was arrived at after hard negotiating, title in a conveyancing sense passed, and the beneficial ownership was expected to pass at a later date, then the question recurs, which the Court does not answer, why a similar transaction would cease to be a sale if hard negotiating produced a purchase price much greater than actual value. . . .

Further, a bootstrap tax avoidance scheme can easily be structured under which the holder of any income-earning asset "sells" his asset to a tax-exempt buyer for a promise to pay him the income produced for a period of years. The buyer in such a transaction would do nothing whatsoever; the seller would be delighted to lose his asset at the end of, say, 30 years in return for capital gains treatment of all income earned during that period. It is difficult to see, on the Court's rationale, why such a scheme is not a sale. And, if I am wrong in my reading of the Court's opinion, and if the Court would strike down such a scheme on the ground that there is no economic shifting of risk or control, it is difficult to see why the Court upholds the sale presently before it in which control does not change and any shifting of risk is nominal.

I believe that the Court's overly conceptual approach has led to a holding which will produce serious erosion of our progressive taxing system, resulting in greater tax burdens upon all taxpayers. The tax avoidance routes opened by the Court's opinion will surely be used to advantage by the owners of closed corporations and other income-producing assets in order to evade ordinary income taxes and pay at capital gains rates, with a resultant large-scale ownership of private businesses by tax-exempt organizations. While the Court justifies its result in the name of conceptual purity,[7] it simultaneously violates long-standing congressional tax policies that capital gains treatment is to be given to significant economic transfers of investment-type assets but not to ordinary commercial or business income and that transactions are to be judged on their entire substance rather than their naked form. Though turning tax consequences on form alone might produce greater certainty of the tax results of any transaction, this stability exacts as its price the certainty that tax evasion will be produced. In *Commissioner v. P. G. Lake, Inc.*, [Chapter 52] this Court recognized that the purpose of the capital gains provisions of the Internal Revenue Code is " 'to relieve the taxpayer from. . .excessive tax burdens on gains resulting from a conversion of capital investments, and to remove the deterrent effect of those burdens on such conversions.' . . . And this exception has always been narrowly construed so as to protect the revenue against artful devices." I would hold in keeping with this purpose and in order to prevent serious erosion of the ordinary income tax provisions of the Code, that the bootstrap transaction revealed by the facts here considered is not a "sale" within the meaning of the capital gains provisions of the Code, but that it obviously is an "artful device," which this Court ought not to legitimate. The Court justifies the untoward result of this case as permitted tax avoidance; I believe it to be a plain and simple case of unwarranted tax evasion.

E. NOTES AND QUESTIONS

1) *Clay Brown* Compared With *Miller* and *Ferrer*

In *Miller* (Chapter 28), the taxpayer sold Universal Pictures the right to make a movie about her deceased husband in return for a share of the movie profits. In *Ferrer* (Chapter 29), the taxpayer sold an interest in a literary property in return for a share of movie profits. Both claimed capital gain treatment of the sale proceeds. How would they have been affected by the IRS argument in *Clay Brown* that no real sale occurs if the seller is still "at risk" with respect to the property purportedly sold?

2) The Significance of an Excessive Purchase Price

The IRS argued that the sale occurred in form only. Why? The IRS emphasized the fact that the price was effectively 100% seller-financed with a nonrecourse loan. What is the analytic relationship between that fact and the argument that there was no sale in substance? Given the Supreme Court decision in *Crane* (cited in *Tufts* Chapter 24), why was that fact alone unlikely to convince the Court that no real sale had occurred? Why did the IRS

---

[7]. It should be noted, however, that the Court's holding produces some rather unusual conceptual results. For example, after the payout is complete the Institute presumably would have a basis of $1,300,000 in a business that in reality cost it nothing. If anyone deserves such a basis, it is the Government, whose grant of tax exemption is being used by the Institute to acquire the business.

argue, in addition, that the purchase price was excessive? What is the analytic relationship between the question of whether a "real" sale has occurred and the existence of an excessive purchase price when most of the purchase price is financed without recourse?

In finding that there was a "real" sale, Justice White emphasized that, after the purchase price was paid, the buyer would possess the business and be "at risk." What is the analytic connection between the likelihood that such risks have been shifted and the existence of an excessive purchase price when most of the purchase price is financed without recourse?

Why did the Supreme Court refuse to find that no sale occurred in *Clay Brown*? Why, given the Tax Court findings of fact, was the IRS argument a "loser"? Didn't the Supreme Court acknowledge that an excessive price, coupled with a nonrecourse obligation and little or no down payment, might indicate the absence of a true sale? How did this acknowledgment anticipate the decision in *Estate of Franklin* (Chapter 42)?

3) Recasting *Clay Brown* as the Sale of a Future Interest

Justice Harlan suggests that the transaction might be recast as the sale of a residual or future interest in the lumber business. How does this approach avoid the Tax Court finding that the purchase price was not excessive? Is it consistent with *Lazarus* and *Estate of Starr* (Chapter 39)?

How does this recasting prevent tax avoidance? Will the business income be taxable to the sellers until the future interest vests? When will vesting occur?

Gain on the sale of stock ordinarily equals the amount realized minus the adjusted basis. May the sellers, under this suggested recasting, allocate the stock basis between the future interest and the retained interest? Is the retained interest a wasting asset? May the sellers deduct basis allocated to the retained term interest over its remaining life? Does that deduction, if allowed, mean that some ordinary income generated by the business will escape taxation?

4) Denying Tax-exempt Status to the Purchaser

Justice Harlan also suggests that the IRS might have attacked the buyer for misusing its tax-exempt status. The Court majority refers to 1950 legislation, taxing charities on "unrelated business income." Section 511(a)(1). However, "unrelated business income" was defined *not* to include income from leasing property if the lease term was five years or less. Is it defensible to penalize the charity for taking advantage of an exception specifically allowed by Congress? Might the IRS have argued that the real (rather than the formal) lease term was probably longer than five years? If the total purchase price had not been paid by the end of five years, wasn't the lease likely to be renewed? And shouldn't the probable renewal be counted in determining the real term of the lease?

5) Unstated Interest in *Clay Brown*

Is there unstated interest in the transaction? How, as an economic matter, should the amount of unstated interest be determined? How would the amount be determined under Section 1274? Would recharacterizing part of the principal as interest offer an alternative solution to the *Clay Brown* problem? Is the existence of unstated interest dependent on the existence of an excessive purchase price?

After *Clay Brown* was decided, Congress expanded the definition of a charity's "unrelated business income" subject to tax. Under Section 514(a), it includes income from property to the extent that the property is debt-financed. What is the effect of Section 514(a) on the *Clay Brown* transaction? Suppose that stated interest is "adequate," that is, it equals the market rate. In that event, to the extent that property is debt-financed, income will have to be reported, but there should be a roughly offsetting interest deduction, so that the net effect on the charity is zero.

On the other hand, suppose that stated interest is too low. To that extent, the charity's unrelated business income will not be offset by an interest deduction, and the charity will report taxable income. In other words, the effect of Section 514(a) is to tax the charity as a substitute or surrogate, whenever insufficient interest is taxed to the seller. By understating interest, the parties have attempted to shift income from seller to buyer. Where the seller is taxable and the buyer is tax exempt, the shifting of income would produce tax avoidance, save for Section 514(a).

Does Section 514(a) eliminate all tax avoidance potential? Charities are taxed on unrelated business income at corporate rates. Under the 1986 Tax Reform Act, is the charity's tax rate likely to be less than the seller's? In what circumstances? See the Notes and Questions following *Foglesong* (Chapter 46). Suppose that the tax rate applicable to the charity is *less* than the tax rate applied to the seller. Won't understating interest, in that event, continue to produce tax avoidance, notwithstanding Section 514(a)? Or has that possibility been rendered moot by Section 1274? Suppose, however, that the "applicable federal rate," imputed by Section 1274(d) is less than the actual interest rate being charged? How likely is it, after all, that a charity's credit (or that of any other buyer, for that matter) will be as good as the federal government's?

6) Illustrating *Clay Brown*: A Numerical Example

Suppose Clay Brown pays $1,000 for a bond with a $1,000 face amount, 16% stated interest, and a twenty-year term. Assume that Brown is in the 50% tax bracket and that capital gains are taxable at 20%. Brown sells the bond to a charity in return for a note promising to pay $154 a year for ten years. The note carries zero interest and is secured by the bond but is otherwise without recourse.

What is the present value of the note? After taxes, Brown will net about $143 a year for ten years. (Assume that Brown gets to deduct the bond's basis of $1,000 at the rate of $100 a year against the ten equal installments of $154, producing a capital gain of $54. Taxes due are 20% of $54, or about $11, leaving $143 after taxes.) Assume that Brown can borrow at 16% before taxes, or 8% after taxes if his interest payments are deductible. The present value of $143 a year for ten years, discounted at the 8% after-tax interest rate, is about $1,000.

If the deal is structured in this way, how does the charity gain? Why is Brown no worse off? Why might Brown be able to convince the charity to pay more, say, $150 a year for twenty years? Under that arrangement, how much would Brown net each year after taxes? The present value of the after-tax income stream for twenty years is about $1,500. How is Brown made better off by this restructured deal? Why does the charity still gain?

How does the *Clay Brown* transaction with an excessive purchase price differ from the *Clay Brown* transaction without one? In how the benefits of tax avoidance are allocated between the seller and the charity? Even if the purchase price is not excessive, why is there still an abuse?

If Section 514 applied, how would it affect the transaction? Would the charity still be able to pay Clay Brown out of the annual interest earned by the bond?

Suppose that the excess of total payments over the value of the bond were taxed to the seller as interest income. How would that affect the viability of the deal? Would Clay Brown still be willing to sell the bond for $154 a year for ten years? How much of the interest and principal would the charity have to agree to pay over to Brown in order for the present after-tax value of the installment note to remain at $1,000?

Chapter 52

OID ON FUTURE INTERESTS: IGNORING THE TEMPORAL DIVISION

A. INTRODUCTORY NOTES AND QUESTIONS

1) What Is a Future Interest?

A future interest can be defined as the right to property at some time in the future. For example: The right to possess an acre of land in five years is a future interest in land; the right to possess IBM stock in ten years is a future interest in stock; and the right to $1,000 in cash in three years is a future interest in cash. A present interest, in contrast, would consist of immediate possession of land, stock, or cash without having to wait for an interval of time to pass.

2) Dividing Property Temporally to Create a Future Interest

Assume that you own an acre of land worth $1,000. You can divide the land physically, that is, across physical dimensions. For example, the one acre can be divided into two one-half acre plots. You can also divide the land temporally, that is, across the dimension of time.[1] For example, the acre can be divided into the right to the land for the next five years and the right to the land after five years. The first right is referred to as a term interest in the land, the second right as a future (or remainder) interest.

Why is property sometimes temporally divided? Occasionally, the owner of property may wish to sell only a future interest, while retaining a term interest (or vice versa). For example, the owner of the Booth property in Starker v. Commissioner (Chapter 18) sold a future interest in his home, retaining the right to own and occupy the property for his life. However,

---

1. The word temporal is derived from the possessive case of the Latin word for time, *temporis*.

such sales—although common in Great Britain—occur only infrequently in the United States.

A more common reason for a temporal division of property is to make gifts of the term interest and future interest to different donees. In that case, the donee who receives the term interest in the property is called the *income beneficiary,* and the donee who possesses the future (or remainder) interest is the *remainderperson.*

3) The Impact of Having to Wait to Take Possession on the Value of a Future Interest in Property

Suppose you own a future interest consisting of the right to an acre of land in five years. If the land is expected to be worth $1,000 in five years, and if the appropriate interest rate is 10%, then the value of the future interest is the same as the present value of the right to $1,000 in five years or $621. (See the present value table in Chapter 12.)

What happens to the value of this future interest in land over time? After one year has passed, and only four years remain until possession, what is the value of the future interest? After two years have passed, and only three years remain until possession? After three years have passed? After four years have passed? After five years have passed? How much does the future interest increase in value with each passing year? Your answers should correspond to Table 52-1 below.

TABLE 52-1. VALUE OF RIGHT TO LAND IN FIVE YEARS, WHICH IS EXPECTED TO BE WORTH $1,000 IN FIVE YEARS, DISCOUNTED AT 10%

Years To Vesting	Value	Increase in Value During Preceding Year
5	621	
4	683	62
3	751	68
2	826	75
1	909	83
0	1,000	91
TOTAL		379

4) The Economics of Income Arising From a Future Interest

In Table 52-1, what does the annual 10% increase in value represent? Can the acquisition of the future interest be analogized to depositing $621 in a savings account, which pays 10% interest, for five years? Why is the increase in the value of the future interest over time analogous to interest being earned on the savings account?

Why can the future interest also be analogized to a zero stated interest bond with a $1,000 face amount that matures in five years and is discounted by the market at 10%? How can the increase in the value of the future interest over time be analogized to the increase in value of the bond over time? Why does the future interest, like the bond, generate income in the form of original issue discount (OID)?

5) The Taxation of Income Arising From a Future Interest: The Problem of Measuring OID

Should the increase in the value of a future interest over time be taxed like bond OID? Can the OID on a future interest be measured as easily as bond OID, which equals the difference between the bond's issue price and the principal amount and can be objectively determined (Chapter 50)?

With a future interest in land, the "issue price" is the value of the future interest when it is created, and the "principal amount" is the expected value of the land when the future interest vests. If the future interest is created by gift, can either amount be determined except by subjective estimates?

Even if a future interest is created by sale—so that the "issue price" is set by an objective market transaction—how can the "principal amount" be determined, except by estimating either the appropriate interest rate or the future value of the property? A similar problem arises when property is sold for deferred payment (Chapter 51). Section 1274 measures OID on such sales by assuming that the deferred payments should be discounted to present value by the "applicable federal rate." Is this solution also applicable to future interests in land or other property?

6) The *Jones* Case

The IRS has had one success arguing that OID on a future interest in real estate should be taxed as ordinary income. In Jones v. Commissioner, 330 F.2d 302 (3d Cir. 1964), the taxpayer purchased and later sold future interests in real estate. The issue was whether gain, when the property interests were sold, should be ordinary income or capital gain. The Third Circuit sustained the IRS position that the gain on sale attributable to "discount" should be taxed as ordinary income. *Jones* is therefore similar to *Caulkins* and *Midland-Ross* (see Chapter 50), where the issue was whether gain on the redemption of a bond should be ordinary income to the extent that it represented OID.[2]

7) An Alternative Approach: Ignoring the Temporal Division

In *Caulkins, Jones,* and *Midland-Ross*, the IRS argued that bond OID or its equivalent should be taxed as ordinary interest income. In other cases involving future interests, however, the IRS has taken an alternative ap-

---

2. The reader should note, however, that the IRS never argued in these cases that OID should be taxable as it accrued. Moreover, given the Code's recognition of the cash method of accounting, the chance of such an argument succeeding was low. It took congressional action in Sections 1272-1274 to authorize accrual taxation of cash method taxpayers on OID from bonds and other debt (Chapters 50 and 51). And although Congress could conceivably subject *all* future interests in property to the OID rules of Section 1272, it has *not* chosen to do so outside of the special case of debt.

proach. Instead of confronting the problem of taxing future interests directly, the IRS has treated the transaction in question as if no temporal division of property had occurred—and, therefore, as if no future interest had been created. How this fiction prevents tax avoidance—and how variations of this fiction have been applied in different situations—is explored in the materials that follow.

B. ALSTORES REALTY CORP. v. COMMISSIONER
46 T.C. 363 (1966)

HOYT, JUDGE: [The issues] are: (1) Whether petitioner realized $253,090.75 of rent income as a result of a transaction in which it purchased a warehouse property for $750,000 cash plus a simultaneous agreement to permit the seller to retain occupancy of a portion of the building rent free for 2½ years, and (2) if petitioner did realize rent income as determined by respondent, is it entitled to increase its cost basis in the property by the amount so realized, and accordingly increase its annual depreciation of the building?

FINDINGS OF FACT . . .

STEINWAY & SONS, a NEW YORK corporation (hereinafter sometimes referred to as Steinway), was, prior to February 1, 1957, owner of certain real property. . . .

Steinway's original asking price for the subject premises was $1,250,000; this was later lowered to $1 million. However, because Steinway at the time of these negotiations was not yet prepared to remove its manufacturing operations from the subject building, it would not at that time have agreed to a sale unless an arrangement could be made permitting it to retain possession of a portion of the building until its new plant would be ready for occupancy. Eventually, in 1956, the parties agreed to a transaction under which petitioner (Alstores) would pay $750,000 cash for title to the building and Steinway would retain occupancy of a portion of the building for 2½ years from the date of conveyance, without further payment of rent. . . .

. . . Prior to delivery of the deed to petitioner, Steinway's attorney affixed to the deed revenue stamps in the amount of $1,103.85, reflecting a consideration for the transaction of $1,003,090.75. The difference between $1,003,090.75 and the $750,000 total cash consideration, or $253,090.75, was the fair rental value of the space in the subject premises which Steinway was to occupy "without further payment. . . ."

[Steinway] made an entry in its general ledger showing prepaid rent as of February 1, 1957, in the amount of $253,090.75. . . . No cash rental payments were ever made by Steinway to petitioner.

Respondent determined in the deficiency notice that petitioner realized $253,090.75 additional taxable income from rents from Steinway & Sons in its 1958 fiscal year which was not reported in its income tax return for that year. Petitioner assigns error to that determination and in its petition alleges alternatively that if this determination should be sustained, petitioner's cost basis for the property (purchase price) should be increased by this amount to $1,003,090.75 and additional depreciation allowed. . . .

. . . Petitioner [originally] regarded the cost of the entire parcel (both land and building) acquired from Steinway to be $750,000 (the total cash paid). This total was allocated between land and building according to the ratio of valuations assessed for real estate tax purposes by the City of New York, $95,000 for the land and $355,000 for the buildings. Petitioner assigned to the building a 30-year useful life with no salvage value. The respondent has not challenged petitioner's computation of depreciation as claimed in its return, however, he has made no adjustment in the notice of deficiency increasing cost basis and allowable depreciation as a result of his determination that petitioner realized rental income.

The parties have stipulated certain facts, some of which are detailed above. The stipulated facts are adopted as our findings and incorporated herein by this reference.

ULTIMATE FINDINGS OF FACT

The fair market value as of February 1, 1957, of Steinway's rights of occupancy under the space-occupancy agreement was $253,090.75. The fair market value of the subject premises on February 1, 1957, was $1,003,090.75, and petitioner's cost basis in the property was $1,003,090.75, the total purchase price paid when the cash consideration of $750,000 is added to the fair market value of the leaseback to Steinway. Petitioner received rental income of $253,090.75 on February 1, 1957, when the transaction was closed and the subject property was deeded to it by Steinway & Sons.

OPINION

It is respondent's contention that petitioner realized taxable rent income as a result of the transaction described in our findings. Petitioner contends simply that Steinway's occupancy was expressly made rent free and that petitioner never received any rent payments from Steinway for occupancy of the subject premises in the taxable year in question or any other year.

Steinway & Sons reported the transaction as a sale on which the "amount realized" within the meaning of section 1001(b) was not only the $750,000 cash received, but also included the fair market value of the rent-free space-occupancy agreement; said fair market value was determined to be $253,090.75. This amount was "capitalized" on the books of Steinway and amortized . . . over the 2½-year term of the space-occupancy agreement.

The Commissioner has also challenged this treatment of the subject transaction on the part of Steinway by disallowing Steinway's claimed rent expense deductions resulting from its writeoff of the capitalized fair value of the 2½-year space-occupancy agreement. Steinway is contesting this determination . . . in this Court. . . . The Commissioner has taken a protective position between the two parties, arguing that the petitioner herein, Alstores, received $253,090.75 rent income from its transaction with Steinway, and arguing in the Steinway cases (which were not consolidated with the instant case) that Steinway incurred no deductible rent expense as a result of the transaction.

There are two approaches to analyzing the transaction here involved. One approach is to say that there was a purchase by petitioner of the entire fee interest in the subject premises and at the same time a lease of a portion of the premises back to the seller for a 2½-year term. This is the approach taken by the respondent herein.

Petitioner contends that even if the space-occupancy agreement should be regarded as a lease, there was, nonetheless, no income produced to the "lessor" since the "lease" was rent free. While it may be true that no rent was due or to be paid after Steinway's occupancy was to begin as petitioner's tenant, the agreement of the parties recognizes that it was because prepayment had been made by Steinway. . . . The answer to petitioner's contention here is that although there were no cash payments to petitioner designated as rent after the property was deeded to it, Steinway's right of occupancy thereafter was a valuable one for which petitioner must have received consideration in some form, and that consideration was in the form of Steinway's conveyance to petitioner of fee title to the entire building—to the extent that the purchase price of the building exceeded the $750,000 cash paid therefor, or $253,090.75, as determined by respondent. . . .

The alternative analysis of the situation looks to the substance of the transaction. Petitioner here argues that, although in form there may have been a sale and leaseback, in substance there was a conveyance of a *future interest* with Steinway reserving to itself, or carving out, a term of 2½ years in a portion of the property. Hence, Steinway in substance retained its right to occupancy not as a lessee of petitioner, but as a legal owner of a reserved term for years. . . .

Although at first blush petitioner's argument is an appealing one, we conclude that it must be rejected and we must hold for respondent. Steinway did not in form or substance reserve an estate for years. . . .

. . . Petitioner, the buyer, assumed control of the premises and the benefits of ownership. Petitioner, the buyer, specifically agreed to pay for and supply to Steinway, the seller, heat, electricity, and water. The space-occupancy agreement stated that in the event the property was damaged or destroyed and Steinway's occupancy was thereby destroyed or impaired the burden of loss would be upon *petitioner* (with petitioner agreeing to pay Steinway 6¼ cents per square foot per month for space so affected). It is clear in the instant case that the buyer bore the risks and burdens of ownership during the term of the space-occupancy agreement. . . .

Furthermore, the rights of Steinway, the seller, as occupant were not those of a holder of a legal estate for years but were specifically limited to those of a lessee. The standard terms and conditions of a New York Real Estate Board form lease were imposed. For example, Steinway could not alter or improve the building nor sublet or assign its interest without the consent of petitioner.

Of key significance in this case is the fact that petitioner was required to pay to Steinway 6¼ cents per square foot per month for space which Steinway was entitled to occupy but which it may have been unable to occupy by reason of an act of God or the fault of petitioner, or which it may have elected to vacate during the last one-half year of the space occupancy agreement. This arrangement is entirely inconsistent with the theory that Steinway had a reserved estate for years; why would petitioner, the alleged remainderman, be required to make payments to Steinway, the alleged owner of an estate for years, as a result of nonoccupancy by the latter? What we really have here is a provision for reimbursement of prepaid rent in the event the tenant is denied (or, during the last one-half year of the term, elects abandonment of) its right of unfettered occupancy, the prepaid rent being in the form of the value of the property received by petitioner in excess of the $750,000 cash paid therefor.

Petitioner emphasizes the fact that it received no cash rental payments at any time; it merely purchased real estate for cash. This is partly true, but one need not receive cash to have received income. . . . In the instant case petitioner received, in exchange for the lease interest granted to Steinway, rent income in the amount of the excess of the value of the property that petitioner received over the cash which it paid.

Rather than to rely on its argument that it received no cash payments labeled as rent, petitioner might have attempted to show that it did not receive on the purchase any value in excess of the cash consideration paid so that it received nothing which could be considered rent, even constructively. However, such a showing has not been made and we have found as an ultimate fact that the property had a fair market value of $1,003,090.75 at the time of transfer.

The president of Steinway testified for respondent that his original asking price for the property was $1,250,000, and later $1 million, and that he agreed to accept $750,000 cash only with the concomitant rent-free space-occupancy agreement, which the evidence indicates had a fair market value of $253,090.75. The parties were both intimately familiar with the property and were dealing at arm's length, and in the absence of evidence to the contrary, it must be concluded that the value of the property conveyed to petitioner was equal to the value of what was received by Steinway as consideration, $1,003,090.75. Petitioner, on whom rests the burden of proof, made no attempt at trial to establish the fair market value of the property.

Possibly the result in the instant case would be different if the parties had in fact *intended* to carve out a reserved term for years in Steinway and had structured their transaction in that form. . . . We do not agree with petitioner, however, that to hold that there was a sale of the fee and a simultaneous leaseback here is to exalt form over substance. The so-called space-occupancy agreement placed the two parties' rights, obligations, and risks as they would be allocated in a typical lease arrangement. Hence, the arrangement was a lease in substance as well as in form.

. . . Since we have held that a lease did exist in substance and in form, we sustain respondent's determination that petitioner received taxable rent income in the taxable year in question in the amount of $253,090.75.

Petitioner has raised the alternative argument that if it is deemed to have received rent income upon purchase of the subject premises its cost basis of said premises should be increased by the amount of such income and, consequently, its annual depreciation deduction increased. Petitioner originally treated the entire premises as having a basis of $750,000, the amount of cash paid, and it had taken depreciation on the portion of that amount allocable to the depreciable building. Respondent objects to any increase in petitioner's basis as a result of a determination that petitioner realized rent income, however, he presents no argument on this point.

Respondent's position is entirely inconsistent with the theory upon which his principal argument is grounded. We have held above, sustaining respondent, that petitioner acquired a parcel of improved real estate for which it paid not only $750,000 cash, but the grant of a 2½-year lease on a portion of the premises. The fair market value of this lease was $253,090.75, which amount is as much a cost of acquiring the property as the cash consideration. . . .

We hold that petitioner's cost basis in the subject premises includes the $253,090.75 fair market value of the space-occupancy agreement. This sum must be allocated between the land and the building in the same proportions as the $750,000 cash consideration was allocated. . . .

C. NOTES AND QUESTIONS

1) Ignoring the Temporal Division

In *Alstores*, the taxpayer argued that it had purchased a future interest in real estate. In other words, the taxpayer argued that the real estate should be treated as temporally divided, with the seller retaining a term interest. The court instead characterized the transaction as a sale and leaseback, with the taxpayer purchasing the real estate outright and then leasing it back to the seller for two and one-half years. *Why does the court's characterization amount to treating the real estate as not being temporally divided?*

2) The Stakes in *Alstores*

To illustrate the stakes in *Alstores* using a simplified example, assume that Steinway owns land worth $1 million. Alstores pays $750,000 for the land, with Steinway retaining the right to occupy the land for the next two years. What is the effect of sale and leaseback characterization on the buyer? How is the $250,000 difference between the stated $750,000 price and the property's $1 million value characterized? How and *when* is this $250,000 amount taxable to the buyer?

Suppose that Alstores were treated as purchasing a future interest. Assuming *Jones* (discussed above) would not apply, would the $250,000 be ordinary income or capital gain? Even if *Jones* applied, *when* would it be taxed? Only if and when Alstores decided to sell the real estate?

What is at stake in this simplified example? Both deferral and the conversion of ordinary income into capital gain?

In the actual case, Alstores purchased not just land but land and a building. How does sale and leaseback or purchase of a future interest characterization affect the basis allocable to the building and therefore depreciation deductions to which Alstores is entitled? How does that change the overall stakes in *Alstores*?

3) *Alstores* Today: Would Section 1274 Apply?

Today, how might a taxpayer restructure the *Alstores* transaction so it would not be recast as a sale and leaseback under the test articulated by the Tax Court (and would therefore be treated as creating a future interest)? In that event, could the IRS apply Section 1274 to tax the increase in the value of the future interest over time? For example, by arguing that the taxpayer had sold property, namely $750,000 in cash, in return for a deferred payment consisting of the right to the real estate in two and one-half years? If Section 1274 applies, how and when would the difference between the $750,000 in cash and the market value of the real estate be taxed to the buyer?

4) When Should Investment Gain Be Treated as OID? Some Questions and Observations

Suppose you purchase undeveloped land for $621, which can be leased for only a nominal amount. It is expected that, in five years, the land will appreciate in value to $1,000. If you sell the land for the expected $1,000 in five years, in theory shouldn't the gain be taxed as ordinary income? Isn't the gain analogous to bond OID?

Or suppose the property purchased were not land but shares of stock. Should the answers be any different? Whenever property is purchased with the expectation that it will appreciate in value, should the *expected* appreciation be taxed as OID rather than capital gain? What effect would such a rule have on the capital gains preference?

5) The Treatment of the Seller

Suppose that Steinway's adjusted basis for the real estate sold in *Alstores* was $1 million. With the transaction recast as a sale and leaseback, how much gain should Steinway report from the sale? Hint: What is Steinway's amount realized?

Suppose that the transaction were viewed as the sale of a future interest by Steinway. Should Steinway be forced to allocate the property's basis between the future interest sold and the term interest retained?

If the basis is so allocated, *should* Steinway be entitled to amortize the basis assigned to the term interest? Or would denying Steinway an amortization deduction for the term interest compensate for failing to tax Alstores on OID? Note: This is a truly hard question. Hint: Denying the amortization deduction would overstate Steinway's income. But failing to tax OID on the future interest understates Alstores' income. Under what assumptions might the overstatement of Steinway's income compensate for the understatement of Alstore's income?

D. COMMISSIONER v. P.G. LAKE, INC.
356 U.S. 260 (1958)

MR. JUSTICE DOUGLAS delivered the opinion of the Court....

... Lake is a corporation engaged in the business of producing oil and gas. It has a seven-eighths working interest in two commercial oil and gas leases. In 1950 it was indebted to its president in the sum of $600,000 and in consideration of his cancellation of the debt assigned him an oil payment right in the amount of $600,000, plus an amount equal to interest at 3 percent a year on the unpaid balance remaining from month to month, payable out of 25 percent of the oil attributable to the taxpayer's working interest in the two leases. At the time of the assignment it could have been estimated with reasonable accuracy that the assigned oil payment right would pay out in three or more years. It did in fact pay out in a little over three years.

In its 1950 tax return Lake reported the oil payment assignment as a sale of property producing a profit of $600,000 and taxable as a long-term capital gain.... The Commissioner determined a deficiency, ruling that the purchase price (less deductions not material here) was taxable as ordinary income....

The purpose of § [1221] was "to relieve the taxpayer from ... excessive tax burdens on gains resulting from a conversion of capital investments, and to remove the deterrent effect of those burdens on such conversions." ... And this exception has always been narrowly construed so as to protect the revenue against artful devices. See *Corn Products Refining Co. v. Commissioner* [Chapter 26].

We do not see here any conversion of a capital investment. The lump sum consideration seems essentially a substitute for what would otherwise be received at a future time as ordinary income. The pay-out of these particular assigned oil payment rights could be ascertained with considerable accuracy.... [C]ash was received which was equal to the amount of the income to accrue during the term of the assignment, the assignee being compensated by interest on his advance. The substance of what was assigned was the right to receive future income. The substance of what was received was the present value of income which the recipient would otherwise obtain in the future. In short, consideration was paid for the right to receive future income, not for an increase in the value of the income-producing property.

These arrangements seem to us transparent devices. Their forms do not control. Their essence is determined not by subtleties of draftsmanship but by their total effect. See *Helvering v. Clifford* [Chapter 45]; *Harrison v. Schaffner* [Chapter 45]. We have held that if one, entitled to receive at a future date interest on a bond or compensation for services, makes a grant of it by anticipatory assignment, he realizes taxable income as if he had collected the interest or received the salary and then paid it over. That is the teaching of *Helvering v. Horst* [Chapter 45], and *Harrison v. Schaffner* [Chapter 45]; and it is applicable here. As we stated in *Helvering v. Horst* ... "The taxpayer has equally enjoyed the fruits of his labor or investment and obtained the satisfaction of his desires whether he collects and uses the income to procure those satisfactions, or whether he disposes of his right to collect it as the means of procuring them." There the taxpayer detached interest coupons from negotiable bonds and presented them as a gift to his son. The interest when paid was held taxable to the father. Here, even more clearly than there, the taxpayer is converting future income into present income. . . .

E. NOTES AND QUESTIONS

1) The Inadequacy of the Rationale

The formal legal issue in *P.G. Lake* is whether Section 1221 "property" has been sold, thereby entitling the gain to preferential treatment. The rationale offered by the opinion for denying preferential capital gains treatment is that Section 1221 "property" does not include something that is a "substitute for future income."

As a matter of logic, this rationale makes no sense. A basic principle of economics holds that the market price of an asset equals its future earnings discounted to present value. Therefore, any and every capital gain *is* future income valued from the perspective of the present. In other words, any and every capital gain is a "substitute for future ordinary income." If taken literally, therefore, the rationale would eliminate the entire Section 1221 capital gains preference.

Because the formal legal issue is whether Section 1221 "property" has been sold, *P.G. Lake* has traditionally been taught along with other materials on capital gains and losses. This casebook departs from tradition because the formal capital gains issue masks the real problem: how to treat OID on a future interest in property.

2) The Hidden Meaning of *P.G. Lake*: The Carving-out Rule

Tax lawyers understand that a better explanation for *P.G. Lake* is the so-called "carving-out rule." The rule is not articulated as such in opinions but is inferred from the results. The carving-out rule applies when there is a temporal division of property and a term interest is "carved-out" and sold, with the original owner retaining a future interest, as in *P.G. Lake*.

Under the carving-out rule:

a) The seller is not permitted to allocate any of the basis of the property to the part sold; instead, the entire basis remains with the unsold future interest; and

b) the proceeds are taxed as ordinary income, even if all other requirements for preferential capital gain treatment are satisfied.

3) Why Is the Carving-out Rule Needed?

The increase in the value of the retained future interest over time represents OID which, in principle, should be taxed as ordinary income. The carving-out rule, in effect, taxes this increase indirectly.

To illustrate, assume that you pay $1,000 for land producing annual net rent of $100; that in five years the land is expected still to be worth $1,000; and that the appropriate discount rate is 10%. Suppose that you sell the right to the net rent of $100 for the next five years for $379 (the present value discounted at 10%).

a) If there were no carving-out rule, how much income would you report from the sale of the term interest? (Don't forget to allocate an appropriate portion of the basis of the whole to the part sold.) How much income would the purchaser of the term interest report over five years, after allowing deductions for the cost of the term interest?

During the same five-year period, what is the increase in the value of the future interest retained by the seller? Why is this increase analogous to interest on a savings account or to bond OID? Will it be taxed as ordinary income as it accrues?

Why is too little ordinary income being taxed? Note that, in the absence of a temporal division, the land would have generated $500 in taxable income over the five-year period. How does this $500 figure compare with the amount of ordinary income reported by both the purchaser and seller in the absence of a carving-out rule?

b) Now assume that the carving-out rule applies. How does it eliminate the avoidance problem? By overtaxing the seller? Why does the carving-out rule assume, in effect, that the property has not been temporally divided?

c) Is there a better solution to the "carving-out" problem? Suppose that we recast the sale of the term interest as a loan, with the seller as the borrower and the buyer as the lender. The $380 received by the borrower is then the principal amount loaned; the $500 paid to the lender over five years is repayment of principal with interest. See *Lazarus* (Chapter 39), where a sale was also recast as a loan. *With this recasting, the sale of the term interest—and therefore any temporal division—is imagined out of existence.*

What are the tax consequences? Having sold nothing, the owner remains taxable on the $500 net rental income earned over the five-year period. As a borrower, however, the owner may deduct $121 in interest, equal to the difference between the principal amount loaned and the total amount repaid. The lender, on the other hand, must report interest income in the same amount.

With the sale of the term interest recast as a loan, what is the net income reported by both parties over the five-year period? How does this recasting prevent tax avoidance without overtaxing the seller of the term interest?

d) Does Section 636(a) adopt the solution proposed in c), above? Would it change the result in *P.G. Lake*?

4) Hort v. Commissioner

In 1927, a bank signed a fifteen-year lease for office space at a fixed annual rent of $15,000. Six years later, in 1933, the bank paid the landlord $140,000 to cancel the lease. In Hort v. Commissioner, 313 U.S. 28 (1941), the Supreme Court held that the entire amount paid to the landlord was taxable as ordinary income under the "substitute for ordinary income" rationale.

Does *Hort* present a carving-out problem? Perhaps superficially. The lump sum payment compensates the landlord for rent lost under the lease. Therefore, the landlord may appear to have sold a term interest, namely the right to occupy the property for a stated term consisting of the remaining nine years of the lease, and retained a future interest, namely the underlying fee.

It is, however, a mistake to view *Hort* as involving temporally divided property. To understand why, consider the following questions. Would the landlord have been able to charge a new tenant in 1933 as high a rent as under the 1927 lease with Irving Trust? How might you describe the asset consisting of the right to receive an above-market rent from Irving Trust? When the taxpayer received the lump-sum payment from Irving Trust, didn't it sell that entire asset, without any carving-out?

F. IRWIN v. GAVIT
268 U.S. 161 (1925)

MR. JUSTICE HOLMES delivered the opinion of the Court. . . .

The question is whether the sums received by the plaintiff under the will of Anthony N. Brady in 1913, 1914 and 1915, were income and taxed. The will, admitted to probate August 12, 1913, left the residue of the estate in trust to be divided into six equal parts, the income of one part to be applied so far as deemed proper by the trustees to the education and support of the testator's granddaughter, Marcia Ann Gavit, the balance to be divided into two equal parts and one of them to be paid to the testator's son-in-law, the plaintiff, in equal quarter-yearly payments during his life. But on the granddaughter's reaching the age of twenty-one or dying the fund went over, so that, the granddaughter then being six years old, it is said, the plaintiff's interest could not exceed fifteen years. The Courts below held that the payments received were property acquired by bequest, were not income and were not subject to tax.

. . . If these payments properly may be called income by the common understanding of that word and the statute has failed to hit them it has missed so much of the general purpose that it expresses at the start. Congress intended to use its power to the full extent. . . . [Taxable] income is to include 'gains or profits and income derived from any source whatever, including the income from but not the value of property acquired by gift, bequest, devise or descent.' . . . [I]f a fund were given to trustees for A for life with remainder over, the income received by the trustees and paid over to A would be income of A under the statute. It seems to us hardly less clear that even if there were a specific provision that A should have no interest in the corpus, the payments would be income none the less, within the meaning of the statute and the Constitution, and by popular speech.

In the first case it is true that the bequest might be said to be of the corpus for life, in the second it might be said to be of the income. But we think that the provision of the act that exempts bequests assumes the gift of a corpus and contrasts it with the income arising from it, but was not intended to exempt income properly so-called simply because of a severance between it and the principal fund. . . .

The Courts below went on the ground that the gift to the plaintiff was a bequest and carried no interest in the corpus of the fund. We do not regard those considerations as conclusive, as we have said, but if it were material a gift of the income of a fund ordinarily is treated by equity as creating an interest in the fund. Apart from technicalities we can perceive no distinction relevant to the question before us between a gift of the fund for life and a gift of the income from it. The fund is appropriated to the production of the same result whichever form the gift takes. Neither are we troubled by the question where to draw the line. That is the question in pretty much everything worth arguing in the law. . . . Day and night, youth and age are only types. But the distinction between the cases put of a gift from the corpus of the estate payable in instalments and the present seems to us not hard to draw, assuming that the gift supposed would not be income. This is a gift from the income of a very large fund, as income. It seems to us immaterial that the same amounts might receive a different color from their source. We are of opinion that quarterly payments, which it was hoped would last for fifteen years, from the income of an estate intended for the plaintiff's child, must be regarded as income within the meaning of the Constitution and the law. . . .

MR. JUSTICE SUTHERLAND, dissenting.

By the plain terms of the Revenue Act of 1913, the value of property acquired by gift, bequest, devise, or descent is not to be included in net income. Only the income derived from such property is subject to the tax. The question, as it seems to me, is really a very simple one. Money, of course, is property. The money here sought to be taxed as income was paid to respondent under the express provisions of a will. It was a gift by will,—a bequest. . . . It, therefore, fell within the precise letter of the statute; and, under well settled principles, judicial inquiry may go no further. The taxpayer is entitled to the rigor of the law. There is no latitude in a taxing statute,—you must adhere to the very words. . . .

The property which respondent acquired being a bequest, there is no occasion to ask whether, before being handed over to him, it had been carved from the original corpus of, or from subsequent additions to, the estate. The corpus of the estate was not the legacy which respondent received, but merely the source which gave rise to it. The money here sought to be taxed was not the fruits of a legacy; it was the legacy itself. . . .

With the utmost respect for the judgment of my brethren to the contrary, the opinion just rendered, I think without warrant, searches the field of argument and inference for a meaning which should be found only in the strict letter of the statute.

G. NOTES AND QUESTIONS

1) Taxing the Income Produced by Gifts of Temporally Divided Property

Assume that land worth $1,000 is expected to produce $100 of rental income annually. A temporally divided gift is made of the land to an income beneficiary for five years and to a remainderperson after five years. During the first five years, to whom would the annual income be taxed under the decision in Irwin v. Gavit? After the remainder vests? See also Sections 102(a) and (b)(1).

2) An Alternative to Irwin v. Gavit and the Section 102 System of Taxing Temporally Divided Gifts: Economic Accrual

Why should the income beneficiary ordinarily be taxable on *all* the current income from a temporally divided gift? Is there an argument for splitting the income between the income beneficiary and the remainderperson? Consider the implications of the following questions using the numerical example in question 1), above.

Assuming a discount rate of 10%, what are the values of the income and remainder interests when the gifts are made? Hint: The income beneficiary has the right to $100 a year for five years; the remainderperson has the right to land worth $1,000 in five years. Use the present value table in Chapter 12.

How much gain accrues on the income beneficiary's interest over the five-year term? Hint: At the beginning, what is the value of the term interest? Over the five years, how much does the income beneficiary receive? What is the difference or gain?

How much gain accrues on the remainder interest during the interval between the time the interest is created and the time it vests? Hint: At the beginning, what is the value of the remainder interest? At the end of five years, what is the value expected to be?

Under a system of economic accrual, how much gain should be allocated over the five years to the income beneficiary and to the remainderperson, respectively?

3) The Fiction of Section 102

By taxing the income beneficiary on all of the trust's income, Section 102 treats that party as if he or she owned the property outright. *In other words, the fact that the property has been temporally divided is ignored.*

What problem is avoided when this fiction is adopted? What are the practical obstacles to adopting economic accrual taxation as described in 2), above? Why might a remainderperson object to being taxed under the economic accrual system?

4) The Effect of Section 102

Why might the effect of Section 102 be described as shifting income from remainderperson to income beneficiary? Does this shifting of income ordinarily provide the potential for tax avoidance? What if property is placed in trust, with income to a charity for fifteen years and remainder to the grantor's grandchildren?

5) Section 102 versus Section 673

Under Section 102, the income beneficiary is generally taxable on all, and the remainderperson on none, of a trust's income. But if the remainderperson is also the donor and if the remainder interest vests within a specified period, the opposite occurs. Section 673(a) will override Section 102 so that the remainderperson is taxable on all of the current income and the income beneficiary on none. Why should it matter whether the remainderperson is a second donee or the original donor?

Chapter 53

INSURANCE, INTEREST-FREE LOANS, AND PREPAYMENTS

A. ANNUITIES AND LIFE INSURANCE

1) The Savings Component of Insurance Contracts

Most readers should be familiar with the insurance aspect of annuity and life insurance contracts. An annuity protects the annuitant who lives beyond his or her life expectancy by providing retirement income no matter how long the annuitant lives. Life insurance protects the family of the beneficiary who fails to live out his or her life expectancy by providing a payment on the insured's death. See Chapter 2.

In addition to providing insurance, annuity and life insurance contracts also include a savings component. The savings earn unstated interest income, which is analogous to OID on bonds (Chapter 50) or to OID on sales of property for deferred payment (Chapter 51). However, unlike OID on bonds and deferred payment sales, the unstated interest on insurance contracts is not taxed on an economic accrual schedule. In some instances, taxation is deferred; in others, the unstated interest is never taxed at all.

This unstated interest can be difficult to separate out from the gain or loss that arises from the insurance component of such investments. It is therefore helpful to illustrate the analogy to OID with examples in which the insured just lives out his or her life expectancy and therefore neither wins, nor loses, the "bet" with the insurance company. (The footnotes modify the examples in the text for instances in which the insured either dies earlier or later than expected.) It also simplifies matters to assume a single premium policy, which means that the purchaser pays for the insurance contract with one lump sum (see *Drescher* in Chapter 2).

2) Unstated Interest on Annuities

Suppose that Y purchases a single premium annuity policy on January 1, 1995, which promises to pay Y $100 on January 1 of each year until Y dies, beginning in the year 2001. The price of the policy will depend on (a) how much longer Y is expected to live; (b) the rate of interest that the company expects to earn; and (c) the amount that the company charges for providing its services.

Assume that Y is expected to live until the end of 2005, that the insurance company can earn a 10% return, and that the service charge can be ignored. Given Y's life expectancy, the insurance company can expect to pay out $100 a year for five years or a total of $500. The price of the policy should equal the present value of $100 a year for five years, beginning in six years, discounted at 10%, which equals $235. (See the present value table in Chapter 12.)

The annuity which costs $235 in 1996 will be worth $417 at the close of the year 2000, just before payments begin. The $182 difference represents unstated interest and is the economic equivalent of bond OID. It is as if Y deposited $235 in a savings account for six years at 10%. But taxation of this interest income is deferred until the years 2001 through 2005 as the annuitant is paid. See Section 72(a). The longer the interval between acquisition of the annuity and the date when payments begin, the longer the period of deferral and the greater the benefit.

In addition, once payments do start, the annuitant is allowed to deduct the annuity's cost under an "accelerated" straight-line method, whereas a slower sinking fund method would probably be more accurate (Chapter 35). See Section 72(b). This faster-than-economic depreciation further defers the taxation of interest income.[1]

Not surprisingly, insurance companies have tried to provide taxpayers with the opportunity to disguise conventional investments in money market accounts and mutual funds as tax-preferred annuities. After initially condoning such arrangements, the IRS ruled that where the insurance company permits the annuitant to designate how premiums should be invested, the investment income will not qualify for deferral and will be taxed directly to the annuitant.[2] The IRS has also ruled that investment income will be taxed directly to the annuitant when the annuity simply duplicates an investment product generally available in nonannuity form.[3] What is the purpose of these rulings? How do they affect the willingness of taxpayers to substitute tax-preferred annuities for other conventional investments?

---

1. The tax system currently does take account of the gain or loss that results from the annuitant winning or losing the "bet" with the insurance company as to whether the annuitant will die earlier or later than expected. If Y dies earlier, that is before 2005, then Y loses the "bet" and receives less than the expected $500 in payments. The adjusted basis of the annuity, which reflects this loss, may be deducted in his or her final tax return. Conversely, if Y dies later, that is after 2005, then Y wins the "bet" and receives more than the expected $500 in payments. The annuity's basis will have fallen to zero so that additional payments, reflecting the gain, are taxed in their entirety.

Before 1986, mortality losses and gains were ignored. A short-lived annuitant was not allowed to deduct the remaining adjusted basis in his or her final return. A long-lived annuitant was permitted to continue taking annual deductions—equal to the annuity's cost divided by the annuitant's life expectancy—even after the cost had already been fully deducted.

2. Rev. Rul. 77–85, 1977–1 C.B. 12.

3. Rev. Rul. 80–274, 1980–2 C.B. 27 and Rev. Rul. 81–225, 1981–2 C.B. 13.

3) Unstated Interest on Life Insurance

With modifications, the same basic analysis can be applied to illustrate the existence of unstated interest, which is analogous to OID, in the case of life insurance. Suppose that X purchases a single-premium life insurance policy which promises to pay $1,000 when X dies. Again, the price of the policy will depend on (a) how much longer X is expected to live; (b) the rate of interest that the company expects to earn; and (c) the amount that the company charges for providing its services. Assume that X's life expectancy is twenty years, that the insurance company can earn a 10% return, and that the service charge can be ignored. Then, the price of the policy should equal the present value of $1,000 in twenty years, discounted at 10%, or $148. (See the present value table in Chapter 12.)

If X lives for exactly twenty years after purchasing the policy—that is, exactly for his life expectancy—the difference between the $148 price and the $1,000 face amount paid to the beneficiary represents unstated interest and is the economic equivalent of bond OID. It is as if X made a loan to the insurance company and the $1,000 of insurance on X's death represents repayment of the principal plus accrued interest. This interest income is not only exempt from accrual taxation under the OID rules. If paid by reason of the insured's death, it is never taxed at all by virtue of Section 101(a), which excludes life insurance proceeds from the beneficiary's gross income.[4]

In the 1970s, new kinds of life insurance contracts began to be marketed, which combined a minor amount of actual insurance with conventional investment products. In 1984, Congress enacted a definition of life insurance in Section 7702 to exclude such contracts from receiving preferential treatment. If a contract fails to meet the definition, the investment interest is taxed to the policyholder as it accrues.

4) Early Withdrawals From Annuity and Life Insurance Policies

Many annuity and life insurance contracts permit the investor to withdraw funds by cashing in the policy before the scheduled payment date. The amount which may be withdrawn is referred to as the *cash* or *loan value*. Under Section 72(e), the excess of the cash value of the contract over its cost in premiums is taxable.[5]

In the case of annuities, early withdrawals are also subject to an additional 10% penalty tax. Section 72(q). What is the purpose of the penalty? Why might an "average" investor—anticipating the possible need to make

---

[4]. What happens if we modify the example so that X dies either earlier or later than expected? If X dies earlier—before the 20 years are up—then X has won the "bet" with the insurance company (albeit in a macabre sense) and X's beneficiary will receive the $1,000 early. Conversely, if X dies later—after the expected 20 years—then has lost the "bet" (probably happily) and X's beneficiary will receive the $1,000 late. In the aggregate, the gains of taxpayers who die earlier than expected should equal the losses of taxpayers who die later than expected. In either case, these gains and losses on the insurance component, like the unstated interest on the savings component, are ignored.

[5]. See Section 72(e)(2)(B) and (e)(3).

an early withdrawal in case of an emergency—be deterred from substituting a tax-preferred annuity for other conventional investments? Why might wealthier investors—with access to other liquid assets in case of an emergency—not be similarly deterred?

In addition, early withdrawals from annuity contracts are taxable even if the policyholder borrows against the policy rather than cashing it in. Section 72(e)(4)(A). Is this provision consistent with the rule of *Woodsam* (Chapter 13) that mortgaging appreciated property is generally not a taxable event? Or is *Woodsam* different because it involved investment property with potential capital gains income whereas the early withdrawals from an insurance contract reflect unstated interest, usually taxable as ordinary income?

Early withdrawals from life insurance policies are treated more favorably. Except for a limited class of policies, there is no penalty imposed, and loans are not treated as producing realization. Section 72(e)(5)(A) and (C).

5) Policy Considerations

A 1984 Treasury Report proposed that the unstated interest on annuity and life insurance policies be taxed as it accrues:

> The benefit of deferring or avoiding tax on the inside interest build-up on life insurance policies goes only to individuals with excess disposable income that enables them to save, and particularly to individuals in high tax brackets. . . .
>
> Investment income earned on deferred annuities is similar to investment income earned on other savings instruments with other financial institutions. Interest on savings accounts and certificates of deposits is taxed currently, however, while investment income earned on annuities is not taxed until withdrawal. . . .
>
> The deferral of tax on investment income credited to deferred annuities is available only to persons with disposable income available for savings and is of greatest benefit to persons in the highest tax brackets. The tax deferral thus favors wealthier individuals. . . .[6]

Is the failure to tax the unstated interest on insurance policies defensible? Consider the following justification (made with reference to life insurance, but which applies to annuities as well):

> The savings element in life insurance grows without being currently taxed to the policyholder, but that is also true of alternative investments if the growth consists of unrealized appreciation rather than taxable interest or dividends. . . .
>
> It is often asserted that the interest element in life insurance . . . receives preferential tax treatment. If viewed as unrealized appreciation, however, its exclusion from the policy owner's taxable income illustrates the effect of the realization concept. . . .[7]

---

6. U.S. Treasury Department, 2 Tax Reform for Fairness, Simplicity, and Economic Growth, 259, 266 (1984).

7. B. Bittker, 1 Federal Taxation of Income, Estates and Gifts, p. 12–5 (1981).

How persuasive do you find this defense? Is the savings component of life insurance really comparable to unrealized appreciation in stock and real estate? Or is it more analogous to unstated interest on bonds and sales for deferred payment which is now taxed on an economic accrual basis (Chapters 50 and 51)? In evaluating whether the comparison with unrealized appreciation on stock is appropriate, consider the significance of the fact that corporate earnings are generally taxed twice—first to the corporation and second to the shareholders—whereas insurance companies are generally not taxable on income set aside for the benefit of policyholders.

Can the realization concept *still* be invoked to defend the failure to tax unstated interest on insurance policies as it accrues? How did enactment of Sections 1272–1274 (taxing OID on bonds and sales for deferred payment), in effect, modify concepts of realization?

6) Interest Expense in Connection With Life Insurance and Annuities

Section 264(a)(2) prohibits the deduction of interest incurred to "purchase or carry" a single-premium life insurance or annuity contract.[8] The purpose is to prevent taxpayers from combining fully deductible interest with the tax-preferred return on such investments (see Chapter 44).

B. DEAN v. COMMISSIONER
35 T.C. 1083 (1961)

RAUM, JUDGE: . . .

Income From Interest-Free Loans

The Commissioner's amended answer charged petitioners with income equal to interest at the alleged legal rate in Delaware (6 percent) with respect to loans which they had obtained upon non-interest-bearing notes from their controlled corporation, Nemours Corporation, and which were outstanding during 1955 and 1956. The theory of the amended answer was that the petitioners realized income to the extent of the economic benefit derived from the free use of borrowed funds from Nemours, and that such economic benefit was equal to interest at the legal rate in Delaware, alleged to be 6 percent per annum. However, the Commissioner's brief has reduced the amount of his additional claim so that the income thus attributed to petitioners is measured, not by the legal rate of interest, but by the prime rate, since it is stipulated that petitioners could have borrowed the funds at the prime rate. . . .

The theory of the Commissioner's amended answer, as modified in his brief, undoubtedly had its origin in a statement by this Court in a Memorandum Opinion involving certain gift taxes of these taxpayers . . . , where it was said:

---

8. Note that under Section 264(b), the disallowance applies to more than literally single payment policies.

> Viewed realistically, the lending of over two million dollars to petitioners without interest might be looked upon as a means of passing on earnings (certainly potential earnings) of Nemours in lieu of dividends, to the extent of a reasonable interest on such loans. . . .

The amended answer herein was filed within several months after the foregoing Memorandum Opinion had been promulgated. The statement quoted above was mere dictum and we have not been directed to any case holding or even suggesting that an interest-free loan may result in the realization of taxable income by the debtor, or to any administrative ruling or regulation taking that position. Although the question may not be completely free from doubt we think that no taxable income is realized in such circumstances.

In support of its present position, the Government relies primarily upon a series of cases holding that rent-free use of corporate property by a stockholder or officer may result in the realization of income. . . . These cases bear a superficial resemblance to the present case, but reflection convinces us that they are not in point. In each of them a benefit was conferred upon the stockholder or officer in circumstances such that had the stockholder or officer undertaken to procure the same benefit by an expenditure of money such expenditure would not have been deductible by him. Here, on the other hand, had petitioners borrowed the funds in question on interest-bearing notes, their payment of interest would have been fully deductible by them under section 163, I.R.C. 1954. Not only would they not be charged with the additional income in controversy herein, but they would have a deduction equal to that very amount. We think this circumstance differentiates the various cases relied upon by the Commissioner, and perhaps explains why he has apparently never taken this position in any prior case.

We have heretofore given full force to interest-free loans for tax purposes, holding that they result in no interest deduction for the borrower, . . . nor interest income to the lender. . . . We think it to be equally true that an interest-free loan results in no taxable gain to the borrower, and we hold that the Commissioner is not entitled to any increased deficiency based upon this issue.

BRUCE, J., dissenting: I respectfully dissent from the opinion of the majority. . . . In my opinion the present case is not distinguishable in principle from . . . cases cited by the majority, wherein it was held that the rent-free use of corporate property by a stockholder or officer resulted in the realization of income. "Interest" in the sense that it represents compensation paid for the use, forbearance, or detention of money, may be likened to "rent" which is paid for the use of property.

. . . I do not wish to infer [sic] that the interest-free loan of money should be construed as resulting in taxable income to the borrower in every instance. However, it is difficult to believe that the interest-free loan of in excess of $2 million ($2,563,098.07 throughout 1956) by a personal holding company to its majority stockholders (its only stockholders prior to December 17, 1954) did not result in any economic benefit to the borrower.

In my opinion, the statement that "had petitioners borrowed the funds in question on interest-bearing notes, their payment of interest would have been fully deductible by them under section 163, I.R.C. 1954," is likewise too broad a generalization to make here.

Section 163(a) states the "General Rule" to be that "There shall be allowed as a deduction all interest paid or accrued within the taxable year on indebtedness." Section [265(a)(2)] provides, however, that—

No deduction shall be allowed for—

• • •

(2) INTEREST.—Interest on indebtedness incurred or continued to purchase or carry obligations . . . the interest on which is wholly exempt from the taxes imposed by this subtitle.

Section [265(a)(2)] is specifically included in the cross references contained in subsection (c) of section 163 and is therefore clearly intended as an exception to, or limitation upon, section 163(a). . . .

. . . It was incumbent upon the petitioners, if such were the facts, to plead and establish that had they been required to pay interest on the loans in question they would have been entitled to deduct such interest from their gross income. They have done neither. It is well established that deductions are matters of legislative grace and must be clearly established.

On the record presented herein, I do not agree that "had petitioners borrowed the funds in question on interest-bearing notes, their payment of interest would have been fully deductible by them under section 163," and that the inclusion in the gross income of the petitioners of an amount representing a reasonable rate of interest on the loans in question would therefore result in no deficiency.

C. NOTES AND QUESTIONS

1) Recasting (or Imputing Interest on) Interest-free Loans

Does a so-called "interest-free" loan truly involve the payment of zero interest by the borrower? The loan could be recast as involving two separate transactions: (a) a loan is extended on which the borrower pays the lender interest at the market rate and (b) the lender pays the borrower an amount equal to the market rate interest due on the loan. This recasting of an interest-free loan is often referred to as *imputing interest* on the loan.

To illustrate, the interest-free loan from a corporation to its shareholders in *Dean* could be recast as (a) a market interest rate loan, with (b) the corporation paying the shareholders an amount equal to the market rate interest due on the loan. Given the corporate-shareholder relationship between lender and borrower, the payment in (b) should probably be characterized as a dividend.

Similarly, an interest-free loan from an employer to an employee could be recast as (a) a market interest rate loan, with (b) the employer paying the employee an amount equal to the market rate interest due on the loan. In this example, given the employer-employee relationship between lender and borrower, the payment in (b) should probably be characterized as compensation.

2) The Stakes

Why might recasting (that is, imputing interest on) an interest-free loan from a corporation to a shareholder have no consequences for the shareholder but permit tax avoidance by the corporation? Why might the shareholder's deduction and income items offset each other? Why don't the corporation's?

Did the IRS litigate against the wrong party in *Dean*? If it wanted to succeed in imputing interest, why might it have been better advised to litigate against the corporation?

3) Limits on Deducting Interest

Why did the majority decide not to impute interest on the loan from the corporation to its shareholders in *Dean*? Why did the dissent disagree? Which opinion made the better argument?

How do the various limits on deducting interest, contained in Section 265 and elsewhere (Chapter 44), affect the argument that imputing interest to the borrower is not necessary because income and deduction items are offsetting?

D. INTEREST-FREE AND BELOW-MARKET INTEREST LOANS

Staff of Joint Committee on Taxation, 98th Cong., 2d Sess., General Explanation of the Revenue Provisions of the Deficit Reduction Act of 1984, 528 (Comm. Print 1984).

[L]oans from corporations to shareholders [are] being used to avoid rules requiring the taxation of corporate income at the corporate level. A below-market loan from a corporation to a shareholder is the economic equivalent of a loan by the corporation to the shareholder requiring the payment of interest at a market rate, and a [dividend from] the corporation to the shareholder . . . equal to the amount of interest required to be paid under . . . the loan. If a transaction were structured as a [dividend] and a loan, the borrower would have dividend income and an offsetting interest deduction. The lender would have interest income. . . . [I]f the transaction was structured as a below-market loan, the lender avoided including in income the interest that would have been paid by the borrower. As a result, the lender was in the same economic position as . . . if it had deducted . . . dividends. . . .

[In addition], loans to persons providing services [are] being used to avoid . . . rules restricting the deductibility of interest in certain situations by the person providing the services. A below-market loan to a person providing services is the economic equivalent of a loan requiring the payment of interest at a market rate, and a payment . . . of compensation equal to the amount of interest required to be paid under . . . the loan. [A] transaction structured as a loan and a payment . . . of compensation often did not result in [tax avoidance] for either the lender or borrower because each would have offsetting income and deductions. However, there were a number of situations in which the payment of compensation and a loan requiring the payment of interest . . . did not offset. For example, if a taxpayer used the proceeds of an arms'-length loan to invest in tax-exempt obligations, the deduction for interest paid on the loan would be disallowed under Section 265.

E. NOTES AND QUESTIONS

1) Section 7872

Enacted in 1984, Section 7872 imputes interest on below-market interest loans, including loans between a corporation and its shareholders and between an employer and employee.[9] Section 7872 distinguishes between two kinds of loans: demand loans, where the principal is repayable at the lender's demand, and term loans, where the principal is repayable only after a fixed term.

2) Demand Loans

Section 7872 applies to demand loans when the stated interest is below the "applicable federal rate." In that event, on the last day of each calendar year, two payments are simultaneously imputed by Section 7872(a). First, the borrower is treated as paying the lender the excess of "applicable federal rate" interest over the stated interest on the loan. Second, the lender is treated as simultaneously paying the borrower exactly the same amount.

The payment from borrower to lender is characterized as interest. The characterization of the payment from lender to borrower depends on the relationship between the parties. If they are corporation and shareholder, the payment will be characterized as a dividend. If they are employer and employee, the payment will be characterized as salary. What is the effect of Section 7872 on a demand loan of $100,000 from a corporation to its sole shareholder, where the loan carries a 4% interest rate and the applicable federal rate is 12%? Suppose that instead the parties are employer and employee. What is the effect of Section 7872?

3) Term Loans

Term loans are treated in a somewhat more complex fashion. The present value of the future payments of stated interest and principal is calculated using the "applicable federal rate." This present value is designated the actual amount of the loan.

The excess of the stated principal over this actual loan amount is defined as original issue discount (OID) and, as such, is subject to economic accrual

---

9. Section 7872 also applies to below-market interest gift loans (as discussed in Chapter 47) and to other designated tax avoidance transactions.

taxation for both lender and borrower under Sections 1272(a)(1) and 163(e)(1). In addition, the excess is treated as a nonloan payment, from lender to borrower, *that is made at exactly the same time as the loan is extended.* Again, the characterization of this payment depends on the relationship between the parties. If they are corporation and shareholder, it is a dividend; if they are employer and employee, it is salary.

To illustrate, suppose that an employer loans an employee $1,000 for five years at zero stated interest and that the applicable federal rate is 10%. The present value of the stated interest and principal is $621, which is treated as the actual amount of the loan. (See the present value table in Chapter 12.) The excess of stated principal over this actual loan amount is $1,000 minus $621, or $379. Given the fact that it is an employer who makes a loan to an employee, this excess will probably be characterized as compensation. In addition, the employer reports $379 in interest income over the five-year period and the employee deducts $379 as interest expense, according to an economic accrual schedule (see Chapter 50).

Why are term loans treated differently from demand loans? Suppose the interest-free loan in *Dean* was a term, *rather than a demand,* loan. If interest were imputed under Section 7872, would the shareholder's income and deduction items offset each other? Was the *Dean* majority wrong to imply that they would be offsetting, regardless of the type of loan?

A congressional report on Section 7872 explained that it is impossible for the imputed payments on a term loan to create offsetting income and deduction items in the same year:

> [I]f a term loan extended beyond the taxable year in which it was made, income and deductions did not offset because the . . . income was includible in the year the loan was made. In such circumstances, substantial tax [avoidance] could be derived by structuring the transaction as a [no interest or] below-market [interest rate] loan.[10]

F. RCA CORP. v. UNITED STATES

664 F.2d 881 (2d Cir. 1981), cert. denied, 457 U.S. 1133 (1982)

KEARSE, CIRCUIT JUDGE:

I

This appeal requires us to determine whether the Commissioner of Internal Revenue ("Commissioner") properly exercised his discretion when he rejected as "not clearly reflect[ing] income" within the meaning of § 446(b) of the Internal Revenue Code of 1954 ("I.R.C."), 26 U.S.C. § 446(b) (1976), the accrual method of accounting used in 1958 and 1959 by plaintiff RCA Corporation ("RCA") to account for revenues received from the prepay-

---

10. Staff of Joint Committee on Taxation, 98th Cong., 2d Sess., General Explanation of the Revenue Provisions of the Deficit Reduction Act of 1984, 528 (Comm. Print 1984).

ment of fees associated with certain service contracts entered into with purchasers of its products. . . .

. . . In the typical service arrangement, the purchaser of an RCA product would contract, at the time of purchase, to receive service and repair of the product for a stated period in exchange for prepayment of a single lump sum. Under these agreements, service was available to the purchaser on demand at any time during the contract term, which might range from three to twenty-four months.

. . . RCA, employed an accrual method of accounting for service contract revenues on their books. For each group of service contracts of a given duration entered into in a given month, the seller credited to current income a sum that represented the actual cost of selling and processing the contracts, plus a profit. The balance of the revenues derived from each group of contracts, i.e., the portion to be earned through future performance under them, was credited to a deferred income account. Each month thereafter, [RCA] journaled from the deferred income account to current income that proportion of the revenues from each group of contracts that the seller estimated had been earned in the month through actual performance. For the most part, [RCA's] estimates of its rate of performance for a particular class of contracts were based on its past experience in the business, and took into account such factors as seasonal repair patterns, variations in average daily workloads, and the number of working days in each month. Although these forecasts were not perfect and may have rested to some extent on untested assumptions, they matched service contract revenues and related expenses with reasonable accuracy.

After an audit of RCA's tax returns for 1958 and 1959, the Internal Revenue Service ("IRS") required RCA to report its service contract revenues upon receipt, rather than deferring recognition of any portion of them. . . .

At trial, RCA contended, first, that its accrual method of tax accounting for prepaid service contract revenues "clearly reflect[ed] income" within the meaning of I.R.C. § 446(b), and that the Commissioner had therefore abused his discretion in rejecting that method. . . .

For its part, the government argued that under a trio of Supreme Court cases, *Automobile Club of Michigan v. Commissioner* . . . ; *American Automobile Association v. United States* . . . and *Schlude v. Commissioner* . . . methods of accrual accounting based on projections of customers' demands for services do not "clearly reflect income," and that in view of these decisions the Commissioner did not abuse his discretion in rejecting RCA's method. . . .

After reviewing the stipulated facts and hearing the testimony of the one live witness, an accounting expert, the district court ruled for RCA. The court read *Michigan, AAA,* and *Schlude,* supra, to proscribe, as "not clearly reflect[ing] income," only those methods of deferring recognition of income that are not based on demonstrably accurate projections of future expenses required to earn the income. . . . Finding that RCA's accrual method matched service contract revenues and related expenses "with reasonable precision" and therefore "clearly reflect[ed] income," the court held that the Commissioner had abused his discretion under I.R.C. § 466(b) in rejecting RCA's method and imposing on RCA a cash method of accounting. . . .

... We conclude that the district court erred in holding ... that the Commissioner abused his discretion in rejecting RCA's accrual method of accounting for prepaid service contract revenues. ...

II

This case well illustrates the fundamental tension between the purposes of financial accounting and those of tax accounting. As the Supreme Court has recognized, these two systems of accounting have "vastly different objectives":

> The primary goal of financial accounting is to provide useful information to management, shareholders, creditors, and others properly interested; the major responsibility of the accountant is to protect these parties from being misled. The primary goal of the income tax system, in contrast, is the equitable collection of revenue; the major responsibility of the Internal Revenue Service is to protect the public fisc. Consistently with its goals and responsibilities, financial accounting has as its foundation the principle of conservatism, with its corollary that "possible errors in measurement [should] be in the direction of understatement rather than overstatement of net income and net assets." In view of the Treasury's markedly different goals and responsibilities, understatement of income is not destined to be its guiding light.

Thor Power Tool Co. v. Commissioner [Chapter 15]. The case also highlights the fundamentally different perspective that courts must adopt when reviewing the propriety of an exercise of administrative discretion rather than deciding a naked question of substantive law. We conclude that the district court gave too little weight to the objectives of tax accounting and to the Commissioner's wide discretion in implementing those objectives.

Section 446 of the Internal Revenue Code of 1954 provides that "[t]axable income shall be computed under the method of accounting on the basis of which the taxpayer regularly computes his income in keeping his books," unless "the method used does not clearly reflect income"; in the latter event "the computation of taxable income shall be made under such method as, in the opinion of the Secretary [of the Treasury], does clearly reflect income." I.R.C. § 446(a), (b). It is well established that the Commissioner enjoys "broad discretion" to determine whether, " 'in [his] opinion,' " a taxpayer's accounting methods clearly reflect income, *Thor Power Tool* ... and the Commissioner's exercise of his discretion must be upheld unless it is clearly unlawful. ... The task of a reviewing court, therefore, is not to determine whether in its own opinion RCA's method of accounting for prepaid service contract income "clearly reflect[ed] income," but to determine whether there is an adequate basis in law for the Commissioner's conclusion that it did not. Our review of the relevant decisions persuades us that the law adequately supports the Commissioner's action.

In *Michigan*, supra, the first Supreme Court ruling on tax accounting for income received in respect of services to be performed in the future upon demand, the taxpayer received income in the form of prepaid membership dues and promised, in exchange, to perform various services for its members upon demand at any time during the twelve-month term of the membership agreement. In order to match prepaid dues revenues with related expenses, the taxpayer assumed that members would demand services at a constant rate during the contract term and credited prepaid membership dues to current income on a monthly pro rata basis to match the hypothetical rate of demand for services. The Supreme Court upheld the Commissioner's rejection of this method, reasoning that it was "purely artificial and [bore] no relation to the services which [the taxpayer] may in fact be called upon to render." . . .

Not long after *Michigan* was decided, however, this Court, in *Bressner Radio, Inc. v. Commissioner,* supra, upheld a method of deferral accounting for prepaid service contract income that resembled the method rejected in *Michigan.* The taxpayer in *Bressner Radio* contracted to service television sets on demand for a period of one year in exchange for prepayment of a stated fee; the taxpayer recognized 25% of the prepayment as income upon receipt and the remainder over the twelve-month contract term. Although the *Bressner* taxpayer's method of accounting for service contract income was thus nearly identical to that employed by the taxpayer in *Michigan,* this Court distinguished *Michigan,* and ruled for the taxpayer, on the ground that the taxpayer had shown that it experienced "a reasonably uniform demand for services," so that its recognition of income on a pro rata basis predicted its costs of performance with reasonable accuracy and was not "purely artificial" within the meaning of *Michigan.* . . .

Subsequently, in *AAA,* supra, a Supreme Court case that involved a method of deterring recognition of prepaid membership dues income "substantially identical" . . . to that employed by the taxpayer in *Michigan,* the taxpayer argued that the Commissioner had abused his discretion in rejecting its deferral method of accounting because it had shown at trial that its method accorded with generally accepted accounting principles and was justified by its past experience in providing services. Despite this showing, the Court upheld the Commissioner's rejection of the method. The Court stated as follows:

> When [the] receipt [of prepaid dues] as earned income is recognized ratably over two calendar years, without regard to correspondingly fixed individual expense or performance justification, but consistently with overall experience, their accounting doubtless presents a rather accurate image of the total financial structure, but fails to respect the criteria of annual tax accounting and may be rejected by the Commissioner.
>
> • • •
>
> [F]indings merely reflecting statistical computations of average monthly cost per member on a group or pool basis are without determinate significance to our decision that the federal revenue cannot, without legislative consent and over objection of the Commissioner, be made to depend upon average experience in rendering performance and turning a profit. . . .

Finally, in *Schlude,* supra, the third Supreme Court case on the subject, the taxpayers, operators of a dance studio, contracted with some of their students to provide a specified number of dancing lessons in exchange for a prepaid fee; the lessons were to be given from time to time, as the student specified, during the contract term. For both tax and book accounting purposes, the taxpayers credited contract prepayments to a deferred income account, and then at the end of each fiscal period credited to current income for that period the fraction of the contract price that represented the fraction of the total number of hours of instruction available under the contract that the student had actually used during the period. In addition, if for more than a year a student failed to request any lessons, the taxpayer treated the contract as cancelled and recognized gain to the extent of the amount of the student's prepayment. Despite the fact that the taxpayer's method of accounting was based largely on its actual performance of services during the taxable year, the court upheld the Commissioner's rejection of the method, viewing the case as "squarely controlled" by *AAA*, . . . because the taxpayer was required to perform services under its contracts only at the student's demand. . . .

The policy considerations that underlie *Michigan*, *AAA*, and *Schlude* are quite clear. When a taxpayer receives income in the form of prepayments in respect of services to be performed in the future upon demand, it is impossible for the taxpayer to know, at the outset of the contract term, the amount of service that his customer will ultimately require, and, consequently, it is impossible for the taxpayer to predict *with certainty* the amount of net income, i.e., the amount of the excess of revenues over expenses of performance, that he will ultimately earn from the contract. For purposes of financial accounting, this uncertainty is tolerable; the financial accountant merely estimates future demands for performance and defers recognition of income accordingly. Tax accounting, however, "can give no quarter to uncertainty." *Thor Power Tool*. . . . The entire process of government depends on the expeditious collection of tax revenues. Tax accounting therefore tends to compute taxable income on the basis of the taxpayer's present ability to pay the tax, as manifested by his current cash flow, without regard to deductions that may later accrue. . . . By the same token, tax accounting is necessarily hostile to accounting practices that defer recognition of income, and thus payment of the tax on it, on the basis of estimates and projections that may ultimately prove unsound.

In view of the relevant Supreme Court decisions and the policies they reflect, we cannot say that the Commissioner abused his discretion in rejecting RCA's method of accounting for service contract income. Like the service agreements at issue in *Michigan*, *AAA*, and *Schlude*, RCA's service contracts obligated it to perform services only upon the customer's demand. Thus, at the beginning of the contract term, RCA could not know the extent of the performance that the customer might ultimately require, and it could not be certain of the amount of income that it would ultimately earn from the contract. The Commissioner was not required to subject the federal revenues to the vicissitudes of RCA customers' future demands for services. Accordingly, he acted within his discretion in requiring RCA to report its prepaid service contract income upon receipt.

RCA's arguments against the Commissioner's exercise of his discretion are unpersuasive. RCA contends principally that its accounting method must be upheld on the basis of our decision in *Bressner Radio*, supra, which, as noted above, upheld an accounting system that was based on reasonably accurate predictions of the demand for services. We think, however, that the Supreme Court's post-*Bressner* decisions in *AAA* and *Schlude* have deprived *Bressner* of controlling force. First, the *AAA* Court seems to have believed that it was overruling *Bressner,* for the Court stated that it had granted certiorari to review the lower court's decision in *AAA* because it perceived "a conflict between" that decision, which the Court affirmed, and our contrary ruling in *Bressner.* . . . Second, the holdings of *AAA* and *Schlude* are sufficiently contrary to that of *Bressner* that we must regard *Bressner* as invalid even if *AAA* did not expressly overrule it. As *AAA* and *Schlude* make plain, it is not simply the "artificiality" of a taxpayer's method of deferring recognition of income from services performable on demand that offends the clear reflection principle of § 446(b), but rather the uncertainty inherent in any method that relies on prognostications and assumptions about the future demand for services. The method upheld by us in *Bressner* relied on such prognostications as much as did the methods rejected in *AAA* and *Schlude.* Because the latter cases underscore the Commissioner's discretion to disallow accounting methods that subject the federal revenues to such uncertainty, we cannot invoke *Bressner* to invalidate the Commissioner's exercise of his discretion here.

Equally unpersuasive are RCA's efforts to distinguish *AAA* and *Schlude.* RCA contends that the accounting practices at issue in those cases, which were based on the past demand for services, differ significantly from its own, which was based on relatively scientific projections of the future demand for services, and that its accounting method was valid under *AAA* and *Schlude* even if *Bressner* is disregarded. We think, however, that the differences between RCA's method and the others are immaterial in the present context. As noted above, the vice of the systems treated in *AAA* and *Schlude* was their tendency to subject government revenues to the uncertainties inherent in prognostications about the rate at which customers would demand services in the future. RCA's system shared this vice. Although RCA's predictions may have been more accurate than those of the taxpayers in *AAA* and *Schlude,* they were predictions nonetheless, and the Commissioner was not required to accept them as determinants of the federal revenue. . . .

G. NOTES AND QUESTIONS

1) The Rationale of *RCA*

Does the rationale of *RCA* (and the Supreme Court precedents cited in the opinion) make any sense? Isn't there sufficient statistical data to allocate the prepaid income over future periods without too much uncertainty? Doesn't the decision treat RCA as if it were on the cash method of accounting?

2) The Scope of *RCA*

The scope of the *RCA* decision has been somewhat limited. Payments received in one taxable year for services to be supplied in the next taxable year may be reported by accrual method taxpayers when earned, rather than when received. Rev. Proc. 71–21, 1971–2 C.B. 549. Warranties, however, are explicitly excluded from this special rule. In addition, advance payments for goods may be reported by accrual method taxpayers when the goods are shipped. Reg. § 1.451–5.

3) Analogizing Prepayment to a Loan

How does the analysis of interest-free and below-market loans suggest that the *RCA* transaction might be recast? Consider the following:

> In every transaction involving the delivery of goods or services, there is a time of "actual economic performance," when the buyer obtains the benefit of the goods or services that are being purchased. . . . [I]f payment is made before the time of actual economic performance, the buyer has made an implicit loan to the seller, and the seller will reduce the price charged to reflect the interest implicitly due the buyer. As in the case of interest-free loans, the transaction can be disaggregated into two separate components—a payment for goods or services and a disguised loan.[11]

Suppose that RCA is paid for agreeing to provide $1,000 worth of services in two years. The prepayment can be recast as involving two separate transactions, a loan and a service contract. First, RCA borrows an amount equal to the prepayment, promising to repay principal plus accrued interest in two years. Second, RCA agrees to sell the lender services in two years for an amount equal to the principal plus accrued interest due on the loan at that time.

What are the consequences of failing to impute interest on the implicit loan? The lender reports no interest income, while the borrower, RCA, loses interest deductions. Why is the effect to shift interest income from the lender to RCA? Will this matter if both parties face the same tax rate? But suppose RCA is in a lower tax bracket than the payor? According to Professor Halperin:

> [I]n the absence of full imputation [of interest through an implicit loan analysis], accelerated payments offer opportunities for shifting income similar to those offered by original issue discount obligations and interest-free loans. Yet the Code has not taken a full imputation approach in the case of prepayments.[12]

In light of this comment, consider the following prepayment transaction.

---

11. Halperin, Interest in Disguise: Taxing the "Time Value of Money," 95 Yale L. J. 506, 515–516 (1986).

12. Ibid. at 518. According to Prof. Halperin, "Whether this ultimately leads to [tax avoidance] depends on (1) whether the payment is deductible by the buyer; (2) when we take account of the buyer's business deductions and the seller's business income; and (3) whether both parties face the same tax rates." Ibid. at 516. Courageous readers, interested in pursuing this subject further, might consult Prof. Halperin's article at 515-519.

5) Tuition Prepayment Plans

To help parents beat the high cost of college tuition, a growing number of educational institutions are offering tuition prepayment plans, under which parents can prepay college tuition at a significantly reduced rate. Under one such plan:

> Michigan parents with newborn babies [would] invest roughly $3,000 in future tuition with a new state authority. In return, the children would be guaranteed a full four years at any of the 15 colleges in the state system. . . . For the state, meanwhile, the money would have ballooned in a way that private investments rarely can. "We have tax-exempt status that we can share with our people," explains Michigan Governor James Blanchard. "E.F. Hutton can't do that."[13]

What is the tax effect of the prepayment of tuition? To shift interest income from the student's parents (who are taxable) to the school (which is tax exempt)? Why does this ordinarily lead to tax avoidance? How does the prepaid tuition arrangement resemble the *Clay Brown* transaction (Chapter 51)?

To illustrate, suppose that Georgetown University estimates tuition will be $10,000 a year in five years and that the University can invest excess cash at 10%. Georgetown—a tax-exempt institution—might offer parents of prospective students the opportunity to prepay tuition five years in advance for $10,000, discounted at 10% for five years, or $6,210. Suppose a parent who is in the 40% bracket and can also invest funds at 10% before taxes, earns only 6% after taxes. In order to accumulate $10,000 after five years, the parent would have to invest $7,470. Georgetown's prepayment plan saves the parent $1,260.

Should Congress require that interest be imputed on prepaid tuition? What would be the effect on the payor and payee? Does Section 1274 arguably apply? Can the payor be viewed as transferring property, in the form of cash, in return for a deferred payment, consisting of educational services? Or might Section 7872 apply? Does it depend on whether the prepayment is characterized as a "loan"?

The IRS has issued a ruling that would destroy the viability of tuition prepayment plans in which prepayments are placed in a specially designated trust fund *and* a cash refund is provided should the prospective student not attend a state school. Under the ruling, the trust would be taxed currently on the income earned from investing the prepayments. Moreover, if the student does attend a state school, she would be taxed on the difference between (a) the value of education services received under a tuition prepayment plan and (b) the amount of the prepayment. Private Letter Ruling 8825027 (March 29, 1988). The IRS has not, however, ruled on a plan when the prepayments are not placed in trust and there is no right to a refund.

---

13. "How to Ease the Tuition Load," Time, August 4, 1986, p. 62.

6) Education Savings Bonds

Cash method taxpayers have been permitted to *defer* reporting the interest earned on U.S. Series EE Savings Bonds until the bond is sold or redeemed. Section 1272(a)(2)(B). In the 1988 Technical and Miscellaneous Corrections Act, Congress provided for *exemption* of such interest income if the proceeds from redemption are spent on tuition for post-secondary education for the taxpayer or the taxpayer's spouse or dependents. Section 135(a). Why do education savings bonds achieve the same result as that intended by Michigan's tuition prepayment plan, described above?

The exemption is phased-out for higher income levels and applies only to bonds issued after 1989. Section 135(b)(2) and (c)(1)(A). In addition, the taxpayer must have purchased the bonds after reaching 24 years of age. Section 135(c)(1)(B). In most cases, this means that the parents of a student, rather than the student herself, will have to purchase and own the bonds in order to qualify for the exemption. The age requirement prevents high-income parents from avoiding the phase-out by arranging for their low-income child to own the bond.

Chapter 54

PREMATURE ACCRUALS, THE ALL EVENTS TEST, AND ECONOMIC PERFORMANCE

A. MOONEY AIRCRAFT, INC. v. UNITED STATES
420 F.2d 400 (5th Cir. 1969)

CASSIBRY, DISTRICT JUDGE. . . .

This is yet another case in the continuing conflict between commercial accounting practice and the federal income tax. The facts, as accepted by the parties for the purpose of the motion for summary judgment, may be summarized as follows:

During the years 1961 through 1965 taxpayer was in the business of manufacturing and selling single-engine, executive aircraft. The taxpayer's practice was to sell exclusively to regional distributors throughout the United States and Canada. These distributors sold to more localized dealers who in turn sold to the ultimate consumers.

During the fiscal years ending October 31, 1961, 1963, 1964 and 1965 taxpayer issued, with each aircraft which it manufactured and sold, a document captioned "Mooney Bond" setting out an unconditional promise that taxpayer would pay to the bearer the sum of $1,000 when the corresponding aircraft should be permanently retired from service. By far the great majority of the "Mooney Bonds" issued by the taxpayer were retained by the distributors to whom they were originally issued, or by persons related to such distributors as the result of reorganizations, liquidations, etc. By October 31, 1965 many distributors had accumulated quite large holdings in the certificates; one distributor, for example, held no fewer than 122.

Taxpayer seeks to exclude or deduct from gross income the face value of either all Mooney Bonds, or those Mooney Bonds which it is estimated will ultimately be redeemed, in the year the instruments were issued. It is the Government's position that the Mooney Bonds may be deducted only in the year the aircraft to which they relate are in fact permanently retired from service. The Government has alleged, and the taxpayer has not denied, that perhaps 20 or more years may elapse between issuance of the Bonds and retirement of the aircraft. The district court sustained the Government's position and, for the reasons to be discussed, we affirm the judgment of the district court.

The issue in this case is whether the taxpayer's "accrual" system of accounting is acceptable for tax purposes. In order to better understand this issue it may be helpful to first discuss the purpose and techniques of accrual accounting as they relate to the federal income tax.

"Income" has been defined as "a net or resultant determined by matching revenues with related expenses." Since the Internal Revenue Code allows the deduction of substantially all business expenses it seems reasonably clear that Congress intended to tax only net business income. This objective, however, is complicated by the fact that the tax is exacted on an annual basis whereas business transactions are often spread over two or more years. A business may receive payment for goods or services in one tax year but incur the related expenses in subsequent tax years. The result is that the expenses cannot be used to offset the receipts, and the full amount of the receipts is taxed as though it were all net "profit."

The purpose of "accrual" accounting in the taxation context is to try to alleviate this problem by matching, in the same taxable year, revenues with the expenses incurred in producing those revenues. Accurate matching of expenses against revenues in the same taxable year may occur either by "deferring" receipts until such time as the related expenses are incurred or by "accruing" estimated future expenses so as to offset revenue. Under the deferral concept present receipts are not recognized as "income" until they are "earned" by performing the related services or delivering goods. It is thus not the actual receipt but the *right* to receive which is controlling; and, from an accounting (if not from a tax) point of view, that "right" does not arise until the money is "earned." A corresponding principle states that expenses are to be reported in the year the related income is "earned" whether or not actually paid in that year.

Another accounting technique for matching expenses and revenues is the "accrual" of estimated future expenses which has been described as follows:

> The professional accountant recognizes estimated future expenses when the current performance of a contract to deliver goods or render services creates an *incidental* obligation in the seller which may require him to incur additional expenses at some future time. Instead of deferring the recognition of a portion of the revenue from the sale transaction until such time as the future expenses are incurred, accepted accounting procedures require inclusion of the total revenue in the current determination of income when the contract has been substantially performed, and the simultaneous deduction of all the related expenses, including a reasonable estimate for future expenses.

The early Revenue Acts of 1909 and 1913 did not recognize accounting techniques designed to match receipts and expenses in the same taxable year, but required the reporting of income on the basis of actual receipts and disbursements. It was soon realized that such a requirement could seriously distort income—especially in a business of any complexity in which payment is frequently received in a different accounting period than that in which expenses attributable to such payment are incurred. In order to alleviate the situation the Commissioner of Internal Revenue permitted some departures from the strict receipts and disbursements basis. . . . Finally, in the Revenue Act of 1916, Congress provided that a corporation keeping its books upon any basis other than actual receipts and disbursements could report its income on the same basis, "unless such other basis does not clearly reflect its income. . . . " The substance of this provision was carried forward into the Internal Revenue Code of 1939 and the present Internal Revenue Code of 1954. The 1954 Code specifically permitted the reporting of income under the "accrual" method, unless the Commissioner determines that such method "does not clearly reflect income."

These provisions seemed designed to reconcile the tax laws with commercial accounting practice, but unfortunately they have failed to do so. The Commissioner has consistently opposed deferral of prepaid income, or accrual of estimated future expenses, on the ground that for tax purposes such methods do not clearly reflect income. In the "deferral" cases he has argued that when the taxpayer receives payment under "claim of right,"—i.e., without restriction as to disposition—deferring such payments to a future year violates the annual accounting concept, and they must therefore be reported in the year received. Similarly, in the "accrual" cases, the Commissioner has maintained that it is equally violative of the annual accounting concept to allow present deduction of a future expense unless "all the events" fixing the fact and the amount of the liability occur in the taxable year. Both of these positions are legal crystalizations of the Commissioner's discretionary power under § 461(b) of the Code to reject an accounting method when it does not clearly reflect income. The principal question in the present case is whether, in the light of the statutory policies these doctrines are intended to implement, the Commissioner was justified in disallowing a present deduction of the Mooney Bonds as "not clearly reflecting income."

Although the Government admits that the retirement of the aircraft in this case is inevitable, it contends, nevertheless, that taxpayer cannot deduct the bonds in the year of issuance because the obligation they represent is contingent upon the happening of a future event—retirement of the related aircraft. Therefore, "all the events" creating the liability have not occurred in the taxable year. We cannot agree. In all the cases cited by the Government there was uncertainty as to whether the future event would actually happen; here there is none. There is no contingency in this case as to the *fact* of liability itself; the only contingency relates to *when* the liability will arise. To be sure, technically, the liability is "created" by the event of the retirement of a particular plane; if a plane lasted forever there would be no liability. But taxation has been called a "practical field," and we do not see how the technical position the Government takes is designed to further the purpose of the statute. One commentator has argued, and we think justly, that the all events test is designed to protect tax revenues by "[insuring] that the taxpayer will not take deductions for expenditures that might never occur. . . . " If there is any doubt whether the liability will occur courts have been loath to interfere with the Commissioner's discretion in disallowing a deduction.... But here there is no doubt at all that the liability will occur since airplanes, like human beings, regrettably must cease to function....

The "all events test," however, is not the only basis upon which the Commissioner can disallow a deduction. Under § 446(b) he has discretion to disallow any accounting method which does not clearly reflect income....

... Was there reasonable basis for the Commissioner's action in this case? It appears to us there was ample basis.

The most salient feature in this case is the fact that many or possibly most of the expenses which taxpayer wishes to presently deduct will not actually be paid for 15, 20 or even 30 years (the taxpayer has not attempted to deny this). In no other case coming to our attention have we found anything even comparable to the time span involved in this case. In virtually all these other cases, even though a taxpayer may have received money under "claim or right" and had unrestricted use of the funds, there was still some relationship between those funds and related expenses which, more or less proximately, had to be borne. If there were no actual strings there were at least invisible strings attached to the money. Taxpayers could not use the money without at least an eye to the upcoming expenses or services to be performed. In this case, however, the related expenditure is so distant from the time the money is received as to completely attenuate any relationship between the two. For all practical purposes the revenue taxpayer received from the sale of the planes is his to use as he pleases. Rather than being set up as a reserve to pay an impending expense it is far more probable that the money will be used as capital to expand the business. In what sense, then, is it an accurate reflection of income to regard it as an expense of doing business in the current year? To so regard it is to let an accounting fiction obscure the business and fiscal realities that are the heart of this case. In exercising his discretion the Commissioner need not close his eyes to these realities. We feel that from both a business and tax standpoint the accounting systems rejected by the Supreme Court in *Schlude* and *AAA* were much more reasonable than the one involved here, and that to allow a present deduction in this case would distort rather than reflect income. We therefore find no difficulty in concluding that the Commissioner had a reasonable basis for disallowing the deduction as not clearly reflecting income.

There is yet another reason why the time span is too long. The longer the time the less probable it becomes that the liability, though incurred, will ever in fact be *paid*.... [The] very purpose of the "all events test" is to make sure that the taxpayer will not deduct expenses that might never occur.... [The] longer the time interval between receipt of money and payment of the related expense the greater the chance that the money will be dissipated and never paid. If it is never paid, it is not an expense and should have been taxed. In the present case the taxpayer could in good faith use the monies it has received as capital to expand its business; if one day it became insolvent the expense might never be paid, yet the money would have been used as tax-free income. We repeat that because of the inordinate length of time involved in this case the Commissioner was clearly within his discretion in disallowing deduction of the "Mooney Bonds" as a *current* expense. . . .

Likewise, the taxpayer's contention that the Mooney Bonds qualify as excludable premium coupons within the applicable regulations also lacks merit. See Treas.Reg. § 1:451–4(a). Unlike a trading stamp or a premium coupon, which is immediately redeemable upon issuance, the Mooney Bond cannot be redeemed until some distant date in the future when the related plane is retired. To treat the instruments as premium coupons would violate the intent of the regulations, which envision premium coupons which are in fact redeemed shortly after the related sales. . . . This is, we think, conclusively proved by the fact that the regulations allow a present deduction for only that portion of the stamps issued in a given year which will eventually be redeemed, and that this percentage is to be determined on the basis of the taxpayer's redemption experience during the preceding *five years*. Treas.Reg. § 1:451–4(a). This shows that the regulations contemplate that all the stamps of a given year will be redeemed within the following five year period (except of course, those that will never be redeemed). Mooney, on the other hand, would have to show redemption experience over a twenty year period (at least). . . .

B. NOTES AND QUESTIONS

1) Accrual Accounting of Deductions

Under the accrual method of accounting, a taxpayer ordinarily can deduct a noncapital cost when the obligation arises rather than when it is paid. For example, suppose that in November, 1984, a law firm performs $1,000 of services for Mooney Aircraft, but Mooney doesn't pay the bill until January, 1985. When can Mooney deduct the expense if it uses the accrual method of accounting? If it uses the cash method?

2) The Rationale of *Mooney Aircraft*

Whenever Mooney sells a plane, it incurs an obligation to pay $1,000 on the plane's retirement from service. Thus, the obligation can be said to arise when the plane is sold. But the court delays Mooney's deduction until the plane is retired, because "of the inordinate length of time" between when the obligation arises and when payment is made. Why should the length of time between the attempt to accrue the deduction and actual payment make a difference?

3) The Economics of *Mooney Aircraft*

Suppose that Mooney is allowed an immediate deduction for the future payment. If the company is in a 50% bracket, what are the current tax savings from the $1,000 deduction? If Mooney Aircraft can earn 5% after taxes, how much does it need to invest in order to have $1,000 available in twenty years (the expected life of its planes)? Consult the present value table in Chapter 12.

What is the difference between: (a) the tax savings from an immediate $1,000 deduction and (b) the amount that the company needs to invest at 5% in order to have $1,000 in twenty years? Why does this difference represent a net benefit to Mooney Aircraft?

What happens to the net benefit if Mooney decides to double the amount it pays on the retirement of its planes? How are normal laws of economics disrupted? Also, how does *Mooney Aircraft* resemble the abusive tax shelters in *Estate of Franklin* (Chapter 42) and *Dean* (Chapter 43)?

4) Codification of *Mooney Aircraft*: The Requirement of "Economic Performance" Under Section 461(h)

The result in *Mooney Aircraft* has been codified in Section 461(h), enacted in 1984. Under Section 461(h)(2)(B), Mooney would not be allowed a deduction until the cash rebate was paid. A congressional report explained:

> The courts generally have held that the length of time between accrual and performance does not affect whether an amount is properly accruable. However, in *Mooney Aircraft* . . . the court held that a taxpayer who gave to purchasers of its airplanes a bond redeemable when the plane was permanently retired from service, was not allowed a deduction because the possible interval between accrual and payment was "too long"; the court concluded that the likelihood of payment decreases as the time interval between accrual and payment increases. . . .
>
> Congress believed that the rules relating to the time for accrual of a deduction . . . should be changed to take into account the time value of money . . . . Recent court decisions in some cases permitted accrual method taxpayers to deduct currently expenses that were not yet economically incurred (i.e., that were attributable to activities to be performed or amounts to be paid in the future). Allowing a taxpayer to take deductions currently for an amount to be paid in the future overstates the true cost of the expense to the extent that the time value of money is not taken into account; the deduction is overstated by the amount by which the face value exceeds the present value of the expense. The longer the period of time involved, the greater is the overstatement.
>
> Congress was concerned about the potential revenue loss from such overstated deductions. In many everyday business transactions, taxpayers incur liabilities to pay expenses in the future. Congress believed that because of the large number of transactions in which deductions may be overstated and because of the high interest rates in recent years, the magnitude of the revenue loss could be significant . . . .[1]

Try to explain the reference to "high interest rates in recent years" in the last paragraph of the quoted excerpt. As interest rates go up, why does the magnitude of the revenue loss increase? Hint: Suppose that interest rates rise and that Mooney can earn 10% after taxes. How does that rise

---

1. Staff of Joint Committee on Taxation, 98th Cong., 2d Sess., General Explanation of the Revenue Provisions of the Deficit Reduction Act of 1984, 259–260 (Comm. print 1984).

affect the gap between (a) an immediate deduction of $1,000 and (b) the present value of deducting $1,000 in twenty years?

5) Deferring the Deduction versus Deducting the Present Value

It can be demonstrated that (a) permitting an immediate deduction for the present value of the future payment is equivalent to (b) deferring the deduction until economic performance under Section 461(h). To illustrate, suppose that Mooney is in a 50% bracket and can invest funds at 5% after taxes. The present value of a $1,000 rebate in twenty years, discounted at 5%, equals $377. An immediate deduction of $377—the present value of the future payment—saves Mooney about $189 in taxes. If invested at 5% after taxes, the $189 will grow in twenty years to $500. This $500 amount equals the tax savings available in twenty years if the $1,000 deduction is deferred until that time under Section 461(h).

In other words, instead of deferring the full deduction until economic performance under Section 461(h), Congress might have permitted an immediate deduction of the present value of the future payment, discounted at the after-tax rate of interest. Why wasn't this option adopted? A congressional report explained:

> [I]n the case of noncapital items, a taxpayer, theoretically, should be allowed a deduction for either the full amount of a liability when the liability is satisfied or a discounted amount at an earlier time. However, ... determining the discounted values for all kinds of future expenses would be extraordinarily complex and would be extremely difficult to administer. For instance, [such] a system ... would have to ... recalculat[e] overstated and understated deductions when the future liabilities ... are actually satisfied at a time or in an amount, different from that originally projected. Furthermore ... an appropriate discounting system [might] be equally complex. Therefore ... Congress believed that expenses should be accrued only when economic performance occurs.[2]

The congressional report makes two separate objections to allowing a deduction for the present discounted value of a future expense. First, it notes that an immediate deduction may turn out to have been overstated (or understated) because future obligations are "actually satisfied at a time or amount, different from that originally projected." But, in that event, why not recapture and tax the overstated amount, just as excess depreciation is recaptured under Section 1245 and 1250 (or allow a deduction for the understated amount)? Second, the report states that discounting future payment obligations would be "overly complex." But why would it be any more complex than discounting to determine unstated interest on sales for a deferred payment under Section 1274 (Chapter 51)? Why not use the same "applicable federal rate" as Section 1274, after reducing the federal rate to an after-tax rate by applying the taxpayer's marginal bracket?

---

2. Ibid. at 261.

Congress has permitted certain taxpayers in special situations to deduct the present discounted value of future payment obligations. For example, a nuclear power plant operator is obligated to pay for the cost of cleaning up (or "decommissioning") when the plant's useful life is over. Under Section 468A, nuclear power plant operators may deduct the present discounted value of future decommissioning expenses when the plant begins operating.

6) Mismatching of Income and Deduction Items

The purchaser of a plane from Mooney would probably report the rebate only when the plane is retired. This follows as a matter of course for a cash method purchaser. But one suspects that even an accrual method purchaser would not treat the right to the rebate as accruing until the plane's retirement. Thus, permitting Mooney Aircraft an immediate deduction while allowing the purchaser to defer reporting until payment creates a mismatching of deduction and income items. How is this similar to the mismatching of interest deductions and income from bond OID before 1969? (See Chapter 50.)

Perhaps the *Mooney Aircraft* decision (and Section 461(h)) can be understood as imposing a matching requirement. Mooney may not deduct the rebate until the plane is retired because it is assumed that the purchaser will not report the rebate until that time.

Notice, however, that matching is not needed to prevent tax avoidance in *Mooney Aircraft*. Another option would be to permit Mooney an immediate deduction of the present value equivalent of the future payment, as explained above.

7) An Alternative Matching Requirement: Should the Purchaser Report the Rebate When the Plane Is Acquired?

Suppose that Mooney is permitted to deduct the full amount of the $1,000 future payment obligation when the plane is purchased, *provided* that the purchaser—whether on the cash or accrual method—agrees to report the full $1,000 rebate at the same time? Would this alternative matching requirement prevent tax avoidance?

If the purchaser is in a 50% bracket, what is the tax due on the future rebate? Suppose the purchaser can earn 5% after taxes. What is the present value of receiving the $1,000 rebate in twenty years, discounted at 5%?

What is the difference between: (a) the immediate tax due on the future $1,000 rebate and (b) the present value of the rebate? Why, under these circumstances, would a 50% bracket purchaser refuse to accept the right to a future rebate? If the purchaser refuses to accept the right to a rebate, no future payment obligation would exist for Mooney to deduct.

But would such a matching requirement prevent tax avoidance if the purchaser is tax exempt? How does the failure of matching in this circumstance resemble the failure of matching under ratable accrual of bond OID where the bondholder is tax exempt? (See Chapter 50.)

8) Damage Settlements

Suppose that a tortfeasor agrees to pay an accident victim $100,000 a year for twenty years (or $2 million total) in satisfaction of a personal injury claim. If the tortfeasor is in the 50% bracket and accrues a deduction for the obligation to pay $2 million when the agreement is made, how much will be saved in taxes? How much does the tortfeasor have to invest in tax-exempt bonds earning 8% in order to fund the obligation? Hint: The present value of $100,000 a year for twenty years, discounted at 8%, is $982,000. What is the net benefit to the tortfeasor? How, in fact, does Section 461(h)(2)(C)(i) and (ii) treat the tortfeasor?

C. UNITED STATES v. HUGHES PROPERTY, INC.
476 U.S. 593 (1986)

JUSTICE BLACKMUN delivered the opinion of the Court.

This case concerns the deductibility for federal income tax purposes, by a casino operator utilizing the accrual method of accounting, of amounts guaranteed for payment on "progressive" slot machines but not yet won by playing patrons.

I

A

... Respondent Hughes Properties, Inc., is a Nevada corporation. It owns Harolds Club, a gambling casino, in Reno, Nev. It keeps its books and files its federal income tax returns under the accrual method of accounting. During the tax years in question (the fiscal years that ended June 30 in 1973 to 1977, inclusive), respondent owned and operated slot machines at its casino. Among these were a number of what are called "progressive" machines. A progressive machine, like a regular one, pays fixed amounts when certain symbol combinations appear on its reels. But a progressive machine has an additional "progressive" jackpot, which is won only when a different specified combination appears. The casino sets this jackpot initially at a minimal amount. The figure increases, according to a ratio determined by the casino, as money is gambled on the machine. The amount of the jackpot at any given time is registered on a "payoff indicator" on the face of the machine. That amount continues to increase as patrons play the machine until the jackpot is won or until a maximum, also determined by the casino, is reached.

The odds of winning a progressive jackpot obviously are a function of the number of reels on the machine, the number of positions on each reel, and the number of winning symbols. The odds are determined by the casino, provided only that there exists a possibility that the winning combination of symbols can appear.[3]

The Nevada Gaming Commission closely regulates the casino industry in the State, including the operation of progressive slot machines. In September 1972, the Commission promulgated § 5.110 of the Nevada Gaming Regulations. . . . This section requires a gaming establishment to record at least once a day the jackpot amount registered on each progressive machine. § 5.110.5. Furthermore,

> [n]o payoff indicator shall be turned back to a lesser amount, unless the amount by which the indicator has been turned back is actually paid to a winning player, or unless the change in the indicator reading is necessitated through a machine malfunction, in which case an explanation must be entered on the daily report. . . .

The regulation is strictly enforced. Nevada, by statute, authorizes the Commission to impose severe administrative sanctions, including license revocation, upon any casino that wrongfully refuses to pay a winning customer a guaranteed jackpot. . . .

It is respondent's practice to remove the money deposited by customers in its progressive machines at least twice every week and also on the last day of each month. The Commission does not regulate respondent's use of the funds thus collected, but, since 1977, it has required that a casino maintain a cash reserve sufficient to provide payment of the guaranteed amounts on all its progressive machines available to the public. . . .

B

At the conclusion of each fiscal year, that is, at midnight on June 30, respondent entered the total of the progressive jackpot amounts shown on the payoff indicators as an accrued liability on its books. From that total, it subtracted the corresponding figure for the preceding year to produce the current tax year's increase in accrued liability. On its federal income tax return for each of its fiscal years 1973, 1974, 1975, and 1977, respondent asserted this net figure as a deduction under § 162(a) of the Internal Revenue Code . . . as an ordinary and necessary expense "paid or incurred during the taxable year in carrying on any trade or business."[4] There is no dispute as to the amounts so determined or that a progressive jackpot qualifies for deduction as a proper expense of running a gambling business. . . .

---

3. A 1976 study of the 24 4-reel progressive machines then in operation at respondent's casino revealed that the average period between payoffs was approximately 4½ months, although one machine had been in operation for 13 months and another for 35 months without a payoff as of September 1, 1976. The payoff frequency of the other 22 machines ranged from a high of 14.3 months to a low of 1.9 months.

4. No deduction was asserted for fiscal 1976 because the aggregate accrued liability at the end of fiscal 1976 was less than that at the end of fiscal 1975.

On audit, the Commissioner of Internal Revenue disallowed the deduction. He did so on the ground that, under Treas. Reg. § 1.461–1(a)(2), ... an expense may not be deducted until "all the events have occurred which determine the fact of the liability and the amount thereof can be determined with reasonable accuracy." In his view, respondent's obligation to pay a particular progressive jackpot matures only upon a winning patron's pull of the handle in the future. According to the Commissioner, until that event occurs, respondent's liability to pay the jackpot is contingent and therefore gives rise to no deductible expense. Indeed, until then, there is no one who can make a claim for payment. ... Accordingly, the Commissioner determined deficiencies in respondent's income taxes for the years in question in the total amount of $433,441.88, attributable solely to the denial of these progressive jackpot deductions. Respondent paid the asserted deficiencies and filed timely claims for refund. When the claims were denied, respondent brought this suit for refunds in the Claims Court.

C

Each side moved for summary judgment. ... Respondent contended that the year-end amounts shown on the payoff indicators of the progressive slot machines were deductible, claiming that there was a reasonable expectation that payment would be made at some future date, that the casino's liability was fixed and irrevocable under Nevada law, that the accrual of those amounts conformed with generally accepted accounting principles, and that deductibility effected a timely and realistic matching of revenue and expenses.

The Claims Court denied the Government's motion for summary judgment but granted respondent's motion. ... It concluded that, under the Nevada Commission's rule, respondent's liability to pay the amounts on the progressive jackpot indicators became "unconditionally fixed," ... at "midnight of the last day of the fiscal year" .... The final event was "the last play (successful or not) of the machine before the close of the fiscal year, that is, the last change in the jackpot amount before the amount is recorded for accounting purposes." ... A contrary result would mismatch respondent's income and expenses. The court acknowledged that, if respondent were to go out of business, it would not owe the jackpot amount to any particular person. ... Nevertheless, the jackpot indicator amount "would still continue to be an *incurred* liability fixed by state law, for which [respondent] would continue to be responsible" (emphasis in original). ...

The Claims Court further acknowledged that its ruling was in conflict with the decision of the Court of Appeals for the Ninth Circuit in *Nightingale v. United States* ... having to do with another Nevada casino, but it declined to follow that precedent and specifically disavowed its reasoning. ...

The Court of Appeals for the Federal Circuit affirmed the judgment "on the basis of the United States Claims Court opinion." ... It ruled that, under the accrual method of accounting, an expense is deductible in the tax year in which all the events have occurred that determine the fact of liability and the amount thereof can be determined with reasonable accuracy, and that liability exists "if there is an obligation to perform an act and the cost of performance can be measured in money." . . . The liability here was not contingent upon the time of payment or the identity of the jackpot winner. Rather, it was fixed by the Commission's regulation. The "contrary conclusion" of the Ninth Circuit in *Nightingale* was noted. . . .

Because of the clear conflict between the two Circuits, we granted certiorari. . . .

II

Section 162(a) of the Internal Revenue Code allows a deduction for "all the ordinary and necessary expenses paid or incurred during the taxable year in carrying on any trade or business." Section 446(a) provides that taxable income "shall be computed under the method of accounting on the basis of which the taxpayer regularly computes his income in keeping his books." Under the "cash receipts and disbursements method," specifically recognized by § 446(c)(1), a taxpayer is entitled to deduct business expenses only in the year in which they are paid. . . . The Code also permits a taxpayer to compute taxable income by the employment of "an accrual method." § 446(c)(2). An accrual-method taxpayer is entitled to deduct an expense in the year in which it is "incurred," § 162(a), regardless of when it is actually paid.

For a number of years, the standard for determining when an expense is to be regarded as "incurred" for federal income tax purposes has been the "all events" test prescribed by the Regulations. . . . This test appears to have had its origin in a single phrase that appears in this Court's opinion in *United States v. Anderson,* . . . ("[I]t is also true that in advance of the assessment of a tax, all the events may occur which fix the amount of the tax and determine the liability of the taxpayer to pay it.") Since then, the Court has described the "all events" test "established" in *Anderson* as "the 'touchstone' for determining the year in which an item of deduction accrues," and as "a fundamental principle of tax accounting." . . .

Under the Regulations, the "all events" test has two elements, each of which must be satisfied before accrual of an expense is proper. First, all the events must have occurred which establish the fact of the liability. Second, the amount must be capable of being determined "with reasonable accuracy." Treas. Reg. § 1.446–1(c)(1)(ii). This case concerns only the first element, since the parties agree that the second is fully satisfied.

III

The Court's cases have emphasized that "a liability does not accrue as long as it remains contingent." . . . Thus, to satisfy the all-events test, a liability must be "final and definite in amount," . . . must be "fixed and absolute," . . . and must be "unconditional," . . . . And one may say that "the tax law requires that a deduction be deferred until 'all the events' have occurred that will make it fixed and certain." *Thor Power Tool Co. v. Commissioner*, [Chapter 15].

A

The Government argues that respondent's liability for the progressive jackpots was not "fixed and certain," and was not "unconditional" or "absolute," by the end of the fiscal year, for there existed no person who could assert any claim to those funds. It takes the position, quoting *Nightingale v. United States*, . . . that the indispensable event "is the winning of the progressive jackpot by some fortunate gambler." It says that, because respondent's progressive jackpots had not been won at the close of the fiscal year, respondent had not yet incurred liability. Nevada law places no restriction on the odds set by the casino, as long as a possibility exists that the winning combination can appear. Thus, according to the Government, by setting very high odds respondent can defer indefinitely into the future the time when it actually will have to pay off the jackpot. The Government argues that if a casino were to close its doors and go out of business, it would not owe the jackpots to anyone. Similarly, if it were to sell its business, or cease its gaming operations, or go into bankruptcy, or if patrons were to stop playing its slot machines, it would have no obligation.

B

We agree with the Claims Court and with the Federal Circuit and disagree with the Government for the following reasons:

1. The effect of the Nevada Gaming Commission's regulations was to fix respondent's liability. Section 5.110.2 forbade reducing the indicated payoff without paying the jackpot, except to correct a malfunction or to prevent exceeding the limit imposed. . . . Respondent's liability, that is, its obligation to pay the indicated amount, was not contingent. That an extremely remote and speculative possibility existed that the jackpot might never be won,[5] did not change the fact that, as a matter of state law, respondent had a fixed liability for the jackpot which it could not escape. The effect of Nevada's law was equivalent to the situation where state law requires the amounts of the jackpot indicators to be set aside in escrow pending the ascertainment of the identity of the winners. The Government concedes that, in the latter case, the liability has accrued, . . . even though the same possibility would still exist that the winning pull would never occur.

2. The Government misstates the need for identification of the winning player. That is, or should be, a matter of no relevance for the casino op-

---

5. An affidavit of the president of respondent's Harolds Club Division, submitted in the Claims Court in support of respondent's motion for summary judgment, states that all the progressive machine jackpots unpaid as of June 30, 1977, "were subsequently won and paid to customers." . . .

erator. The obligation is there, and whether it turns out that the winner is one patron or another makes no conceivable difference as to basic liability.

3. The Government's heavy reliance on *Brown v. Helvering*, . . . in our view, is misplaced. That case concerned an agent's commissions on sales of insurance policies, and the agent's obligation to return a proportionate part of the commission in case a policy was canceled. The agent sought to deduct from gross income an amount added during the year to his reserve for repayment of commissions. This Court agreed with the Commissioner's disallowance of the claimed deduction because the actual event that would create the liability—the cancellation of a particular policy in a later year— "[did] not occur during the taxable year," . . . but rather occurred only in the later year in which the policy was in fact canceled. Here, however, the event creating liability, as the Claims Court recognized, was the last play of the machine before the end of the fiscal year, since that play fixed the jackpot amount irrevocably. . . . That event occurred during the taxable year.

4. The Government's argument that the fact that respondent treats unpaid jackpots as liabilities for financial accounting purposes does not justify treating them as liabilities for tax purposes is unpersuasive. Proper financial accounting and acceptable tax accounting, to be sure, are not the same. Justice Brandeis announced this fact well over 50 years ago: "The prudent business man often sets up reserves to cover contingent liabilities. But they are not allowable as deductions." . . . The Court has long recognized "the vastly different objectives that financial and tax accounting have." *Thor Power Tool Co. v. Commissioner* . . . . The goal of financial accounting is to provide useful and pertinent information to management, shareholders, and creditors. On the other hand, the major responsibility of the Internal Revenue Service is to protect the public fisc. Ibid. Therefore, although § 446(c)(2) permits a taxpayer to use an accrual method for tax purposes if he uses that method to keep his books, § 446(b) specifically provides that if the taxpayer's method of accounting "does not clearly reflect income," the Commissioner may impose a method that "does clearly reflect income." Thus, the "Commissioner has broad powers in determining whether accounting methods used by a taxpayer clearly reflect income." . . . The Regulations carry this down specifically to "the accounting treatment of any item." Treas. Reg. § 1.446–1(a)(1).

Granting all this—that the Commissioner has broad discretion, that financial accounting does not control for tax purposes, and that the mere desirability of matching expenses with income will not necessarily sustain a taxpayer's deduction, . . . —the Commissioner's disallowance of respondent's deductions was not justified in this case. As stated above, these jackpot liabilities were definitely fixed. A part of the machine's intake was to be paid out, that amount was known, and only the exact time of payment and the identity of the winner remained for the future. But the accrual method itself makes irrelevant the timing factor that controls when a taxpayer uses the cash receipts and disbursements method.

5. The Government suggests that respondent's ability to control the timing of payouts shows both the contingent nature of the claimed de-

ductions and a potential for tax avoidance. It speaks of the time value of money, of respondent's ability to earn additional income upon the jackpot amounts it retains until a winner comes along, of respondent's "virtually unrestricted discretion in setting odds," . . . and of its ability to transfer amounts from one machine to another with the accompanying capacity to defer indefinitely into the future the time at which it must make payment to its customers. All this, the Government says, unquestionably contains the "potential for tax avoidance." See *Thor Power Tool Co. v. Commissioner* . . . . And the Government suggests that a casino operator could put extra machines on the floor on the last day of the tax year with whatever initial jackpots it specifies and with whatever odds it likes, and then, on the taxpayer's theory, could take a current deduction for the full amount even though payment of the jackpots might not occur for many years, citing *Nightingale* . . . .

None of the components that make up this parade of horribles, of course, took place here. Nothing in this record even intimates that respondent used its progressive machines for tax-avoidance purposes. Its income from these machines was less than 1% of its gross revenue during the tax years in question. . . . Respondent's revenue from progressive slot machines depends on inducing gamblers to play the machines, and, if it sets unreasonably high odds, customers will refuse to play and will gamble elsewhere. Thus, respondent's economic self-interest will keep it from setting odds likely to defer payoffs too far into the future.[6] Nor, with Nevada's strictly imposed controls, was any abuse of the kind hypothesized by the Government likely to happen. In any event, the Commissioner's ability, under § 446(b) of the Code, . . . to correct any such abuse is the complete practical answer to the Government's concern. If a casino manipulates its use of progressive slot machines to avoid taxes, the Commissioner has the power to find that its accounting does not accurately reflect its income and to require it to use a more appropriate accounting method. Finally, since the casino of course must pay taxes on the income it earns from the use of as-yet-unwon jackpots, the Government vastly overestimates the time value of respondent's deductions.

6. There is always a possibility, of course, that a casino may go out of business, or surrender or lose its license, or go into bankruptcy, with the result that the amounts shown on the jackpot indicators would never be won by playing patrons. But this potential nonpayment of an incurred liability exists for every business that uses an accrual method, and it does not prevent accrual. . . . "The existence of an absolute liability is necessary; absolute certainty that it will be discharged by payment is not." . . . And if any of the events hypothesized by the Government should occur, the deducted amounts would qualify as recaptured income subject to tax. Treas. Reg. § 1.461–1(a)(2).

---

6. Respondent also is unlikely to set extremely high initial jackpots on its machines, since that practice would increase the casino's risk. The initial progressive jackpot amount is the casino's money. If a patron gets the winning combination soon after the machine goes into service, the casino will not have time to recoup the initial jackpot from money gambled by the public. Thus, casinos will tend to set rather low initial jackpots, relying on a percentage of the funds gambled by previous players to contribute the bulk of the progressive jackpot.

7. Finally, the result in *United States v. Anderson*, . . . a case to which the Government makes repeated reference, is itself instructive. The issue there was the propriety of the accrual of a federal munitions tax prior to its actual assessment. The assessment was required before the tax became due. The Government's position, in contrast to its position in the present case, was that the tax liability accrued before assessment. The Court held that the absence of the assessment did not prevent accrual of the tax. It recognized that the taxpayer's "true income for the year . . . could not have been determined without deducting . . . the . . . expenses attributable to the production of that income during the year." . . . One of the expenses that necessarily attended the production of munitions income was the commitment of a particular portion of the revenue generated to a "reserve for munitions taxes." . . . Similarly, one of the expenses that necessarily attends the production of income from a progressive slot machine is the commitment of a particular portion of the revenue generated to an irrevocable jackpot. Respondent's true income from its progressive slot machines is only that portion of the money gambled which it is entitled to keep.

JUSTICE STEVENS . . . dissenting.

Unlike the Court, . . . I believe that the distinction between the nonpayment of an existing obligation and the nonexistence of an obligation is of controlling importance in this case.

It is common ground that the taxpayer can accrue as a deduction the jackpots in its progressive slot machines only if "all the events have . . . occurred which fix the liability." Treas. Reg. § 1.461–1(a)(2), . . . The question is whether an "obligation" created by the rules of a state gaming commission and defeasible at the election of the taxpayer is "fixed" within the meaning of the Treasury Regulation. To me, the answer is clearly "no."

"Under Nevada law," if the taxpayer in this case "were to surrender its gaming license, it would no longer be subject to the gaming laws and regulations and could thus avoid the payment of the liability." . . . Thus, "the bankruptcy of the [taxpayer], or the surrender of its gaming license could relieve it of its obligation." . . .

On these facts, the taxpayer has no present liability to accrue. Rather, the taxpayer's obligation to pay the jackpots in this case resembles the taxpayer's obligation to pay the cost of overhauling its aircraft engines and airframes in *World Airways, Inc. v. Commissioner*. . . . In that case, the Tax Court held that the taxpayer, an airline, did not satisfy the "all events" test and hence could not accrue and deduct any portion of these costs, . . . despite the existence of contracts obligating the taxpayer to pay, upon the completion of an overhaul, an amount for each hour of flight time since the previous overhaul, . . . and a statutory obligation to overhaul its engines and airframes after a specified number of flight hours. . . . Of critical importance to the decision before us today, the court distinguished between the *nonpayment* of a legal obligation and the *nonexistence* of an obligation by considering the taxpayer's liability in the event of a bankruptcy:

> The bankruptcy of petitioner [the taxpayer] or the crash or permanent grounding of an aircraft might conceivably relieve petitioner of the payment of overhaul costs. The occurrences of any of these contingencies, however, would not relieve petitioner of an *existing* obligation to pay any overhaul costs. Rather, the occurrence would mean that no obligation to pay would ever come into existence. Petitioner has not shown that its liability for the accrued overhaul costs was absolutely fixed in the year of accrual. The contingencies referred to would act to prevent a potential liability from coming into existence. . . .

The court recognized that the risk of bankruptcy or disaster was remote. But it added that "there exists another contingency whose occurrence is not unlikely": "Petitioner has sold five piston aircraft and one jet aircraft since 1965. The five piston aircraft owned by petitioner during 1965, and 1966, were sold prior to the time when major airframe overhaul was required." . . .

Here, too, the taxpayer has no obligation that could be discharged in a bankruptcy court—a fact that confirms that it has no present liability to pay the jackpots on its progressive slot machines. And there likewise exists a contingency under which it is not at all unlikely that a slot machine owner would elect to escape its liability. If the gross amount of the accruals on these machines should ever exceed the net value of the business—perhaps as a result of shrewd management—it could liquidate at a profit without having any liability to anyone for what the Court mistakenly describes as a "fixed liability." By simply tendering its gaming license the taxpayer would avoid its liability on the jackpots. This option is exercisable in the sole discretion of the taxpayer at any point in time. My research has revealed no other instance in which the Commissioner has been forced to allow accrual of a deduction when the expense deducted may be avoided entirely at the election of the taxpayer. This feature of the deduction before us unquestionably contains the "potential for tax avoidance," *Thor Power Tool Co. v. Commissioner,* . . . and I think it lies well within the Commissioner's authority to interpret the Regulation to forbid it . . . .

D. UNITED STATES v. GENERAL DYNAMICS
481 U.S. 239 (1987)

JUSTICE MARSHALL delivered the opinion of the Court.

The issue in this case is whether an accrual basis taxpayer providing medical benefits to its employees may deduct at the close of the taxable year an estimate of its obligation to pay for medical care obtained by employees or their qualified dependents during the final quarter of the year, claims for which have not been reported to the employer.

I

Taxpayers, respondents herein, are the General Dynamics Corporation and several of its wholly-owned subsidiaries (General Dynamics). General

Dynamics uses the accrual method of accounting for federal tax purposes; its fiscal year is the same as the calendar year. From 1962 until October 1, 1972, General Dynamics purchased group medical insurance for its employees and their qualified dependents from two private insurance carriers. Beginning in October, 1972, General Dynamics became a self-insurer with regard to its medical care plans. Instead of continuing to purchase insurance from outside carriers, it undertook to pay medical claims out of its own funds, while continuing to employ private carriers to administer the medical care plans.

To receive reimbursement of expenses for covered medical services, respondent's employees submit claims forms to employee benefits personnel, who verify that the treated persons were eligible under the applicable plan as of the time of treatment. Eligible claims are then forwarded to the plan's administrators. Claims processors review the claims and approve for payment those expenses that are covered under the plan.

Because the processing of claims takes time, and because employees do not always file their claims immediately, there is a delay between the provision of medical services and payment by General Dynamics. To account for this time lag, General Dynamics established reserve accounts to reflect its liability for medical care received, but still not paid for, as of December 31, 1972. It estimated the amount of those reserves with the assistance of its former insurance carriers.

Originally, General Dynamics did not deduct any portion of this reserve in computing its tax for 1972. In 1977, however, after the IRS began an audit of its 1972 tax return, General Dynamics filed an amended return, claiming it was entitled to deduct its reserve as an accrued expense, and seeking a refund. The IRS disallowed the deduction, and General Dynamics sought relief in the Claims Court.

The Claims Court sustained the deduction, holding that it satisfied the "all events" test . . . since "all events" which determined the fact of liability had taken place when the employees received covered services, and the amount of liability could be determined with reasonable accuracy. . . . The Court of Appeals for the Federal Circuit affirmed, largely on the basis of the Claims Court opinion. . . .

The United States sought review of the question whether all the events necessary to fix liability had occurred. . . . We reverse.

II

. . . [W]hether a business expense has been "incurred" so as to entitle an accrual method taxpayer to deduct it under § 162(a) . . . is governed by the "all events" test. . .[7]

---

7. . . . Section 461(h) does not apply in this case. It became effective as of July 18, 1984, the date of the enactment of the Deficit Reduction Act. . . . We do not address how this case would be decided under § 461(h), but note that the legislative history of the Act indicates that, "[i]n the case of . . . employee benefit liabilities, which require a payment by the taxpayer to another person, economic performance occurs as the payments to such person are made." . . .

... It is fundamental to the "all events" test that, although expenses may be deductible before they have become due and payable, liability must first be firmly established. This is consistent with our prior holdings that a taxpayer may not deduct a liability that is contingent, ... or contested .... Nor may a taxpayer deduct an estimate of an anticipated expense, no matter how statistically certain, if it is based on events that have not occurred by the close of the taxable year. ...

We think that this case ... involves a mere estimate of liability based on events that had not occurred before the close of the taxable year, and therefore the proposed deduction does not pass the "all events" test. We disagree with the legal conclusion of the courts below that the last event necessary to fix the taxpayer's liability was the receipt of medical care by covered individuals. A person covered by a plan could only obtain payment for medical services by filling out and submitting a health expense benefits claim form. ... Employees were informed that submission of satisfactory proof of the charges claimed would be necessary to obtain payment under the plans. ... General Dynamics was thus liable to pay for covered medical services *only* if properly documented claims forms were filed. Some covered individuals, through oversight, procrastination, confusion over the coverage provided, or fear of disclosure to the employer of the extent or nature of the services received, might not file claims for reimbursement to which they are plainly entitled. Such filing is not a mere technicality. It is crucial to the establishment of liability on the part of the taxpayer. Nor does the failure to file a claim represent the type of "extremely remote and speculative possibility" that we held in *Hughes*, ... did not render an otherwise fixed liability contingent. ... Mere receipt of services for which, in some instances, claims will not be submitted does not, in our judgment, constitute the last link in the chain of events creating liability for purposes of the "all events" test.

The parties stipulated in this case that as of December 31, 1972, the taxpayer had not received all claims for medical treatment services rendered in 1972, and that some claims had been filed for services rendered in 1972 that had not been processed. ... The record does not reflect which portion of the claims against General Dynamics for medical care had been filed but not yet processed and which portion had not even been filed at the close of the 1972 tax year. The taxpayer has the burden of proving its entitlement to a deduction. ... Here, respondent made no showing that, as of December 31, 1972, it knew of specific claims which had been filed but which it had not yet processed. Because the taxpayer failed to demonstrate that any of the deducted reserve represented claims for which its liability was firmly established as of the close of 1972, all the events necessary to establish liability were not shown to have occurred, and therefore no deduction was permissible.

This is not to say that the taxpayer was unable to forecast how many claims would be filed for medical care received during this period, and estimate the liability that would arise from those claims. Based on actuarial data, General Dynamics may have been able to make a reasonable estimate of how many claims would be filed for the last quarter of 1972. But that alone does not justify a deduction. In *Brown*, . . . the taxpayer, a general agent for insurance companies, sought to take a deduction for a reserve representing estimated liability for premiums to be returned on the percentage of insurance policies it anticipated would be cancelled in future years. The agent may well have been capable of estimating with a reasonable degree of accuracy the ratio of cancellation refunds to premiums already paid and establishing its reserve accordingly. Despite the "strong probability that many of the policies written during the taxable year" would be cancelled, . . . the Court held that "no liability accrues during the taxable year on account of cancellations which it is expected may occur in future years, since the events necessary to create the liability do not occur during the taxable year." . . . A reserve based on the proposition that a particular set of events is likely to occur in the future may be an appropriate conservative accounting measure, but does not warrant a tax deduction. . . .

General Dynamics did not show that its liability as to any medical care claims was firmly established as of the close of the 1972 tax year, and is therefore entitled to no deduction. . . .

JUSTICE O'CONNOR . . . dissenting.

Section 446(a) of the Internal Revenue Code of 1954 provides that taxable income "shall be computed under the method of accounting on the basis of which the taxpayer regularly computes his income in keeping his books." The Code specifically recognizes the use of "an accrual method," . . . under which a taxpayer is permitted to deduct an expense in the year in which it is "incurred," regardless of when it is actually paid. § 162(a). Under the "all events" test, long applied by this Court and the Internal Revenue Service, an expense may be accrued and deducted when all the events that determine the fact of liability have occurred, and the amount of the liability can be determined with reasonable accuracy. . . . Because the Court today applies a rigid version of the all events test that retreats from our most recent application of that test, and unnecessarily drives a greater wedge between tax and financial accounting methods, I respectfully dissent.

This case calls for the Court to revisit the issue addressed only last Term in *United States v. Hughes Properties, Inc.*, ...

In my view, the circumstances of this case differ little from those in *Hughes Properties*. The taxpayer here is seeking to deduct the amounts reserved to pay for medical services that are determined to have been provided to employees in the taxable year, whether or not the employees' claims for benefits have been received. The taxpayer's various medical benefits plans provided schedules for the medical and hospital benefits, and created a contractual obligation by the taxpayer to pay for the covered services upon presentation of a claim. The courts below found that the obligation to pay became fixed once the covered medical services were received by the employee. . . . Once the medical services were rendered to an employee while the relevant benefit plan was in effect,

General Dynamics could not avoid liability by terminating the plan prior to the filing of a claim. . . . Neither could General Dynamics extinguish its liability by firing an employee before the employee filed a claim for benefits. . . .

It is true, of course, that it was theoretically possible that some employees might not file claim forms. In my view, however, this speculative possibility of nonpayment differs not at all from the speculation in *Hughes Properties* that a jackpot might never be paid by a casino. As we observed in *Hughes Properties,* the potential of nonpayment of a liability always exists, and it alone does not prevent accrual. The beneficiary of a liability always has the option of waiving payment, but a taxpayer is still unquestionably entitled to deduct the liability. An injured employee entitled absolutely to reimbursement for medical services under a worker's compensation statute, for example, may fail to utilize the medical services. The employer, however, has been held to be entitled to deduct the expected medical expenses because the worker's compensation law creates liability. . . . Similarly, any business liability could ultimately be discharged in bankruptcy, or a check might never be cashed by its recipient. There can be no doubt, however, that these remote possibilities alone cannot defeat an accrual basis taxpayer's right to deduct the liability when incurred.

The Claims Court found that the processing of the employees' claims was "routine" and "ministerial in nature," . . . and the majority does not question that finding. . . . Instead, the majority holds that "as a matter of law, the filing of a claim was necessary to create liability." . . . Even if, in a technical sense, the Court is correct that the filing of a claim is a necessary precondition to liability as a matter of law, the failure to file a claim is at most a "merely formal contingenc[y], or [one] highly improbable under the known facts," that this Court has viewed as insufficient to preclude accrual and deductibility. . . .

The holding of the Court today unnecessarily burdens taxpayers by further expanding the difference between tax and business accounting methods without a compelling reason to do so. Obviously, tax accounting principles must often differ from those of business accounting. The goal of business accounting "is to provide useful and pertinent information to management, shareholders, and creditors," while the responsibility of the Internal Revenue Service is to protect the public fisc. *United States v. Hughes Properties, Inc.* . . . Therefore, while prudent businesses will accrue expenses that are merely reasonably foreseeable, for tax purposes the liability must be fixed. But Congress has expressly permitted taxpayers to use the accrual method of accounting, and from its inception . . . the all-events test has been a practical adjustment of the competing interests in permitting accrual accounting and protecting the public fisc. Unfortunately, the Court today ignores the pragmatic roots of the all events test and instead applies it in an essentially mechanistic and wholly unrealistic manner. Because the liability in this case was fixed with no less certainty than the range of expenses both routinely accrued by accrual method taxpayers and approved as deductible for tax purposes by this Court and other courts in a variety of circumstances, I respectfully dissent.

888　　　　　　　　　Assignment of Income　　　　　　　　Part 5

E. NOTES AND QUESTIONS

1) The All Events Test

Did the Supreme Court apply the all events test consistently in *Hughes Property* and *General Dynamics*? Is the obligation in *General Dynamics* any less fixed and definite than the obligation in *Hughes Property*? Is there greater uncertainty about the amount of the obligations in *General Dynamics*? Or is any uncertainty adequately accounted for by the use of actuarial data? Is there greater uncertainty about the period of delay between accrual and payment in *General Dynamics* than in *Hughes Property*? Or is there arguably less?

Do the other opinions cited in *Hughes Property—Anderson, Brown*, and *World Airways*—appear to have applied the all events test in a consistent fashion?

2) Economic Performance

Both *General Dynamics* and *Hughes Property* were decided under the all events test because they involved tax years *before* the effective date of Section 461(h) (July 18, 1984). Will Section 461(h) change the results of these cases for tax years *after* its effective date?

a) *General Dynamics*—Could "economic performance" under Section 461(h) occur when the medical services are provided? Or only when the employees are reimbursed? See footnote 7 to the Court's opinion.

b) *Hughes Property*—Could "economic performance" under Section 461(h) arguably occur before the progressive jackpot is won? See the definition of "economic performance" in Section 461(h)(2).

c) Even if "economic performance" is lacking in both cases, might the taxpayer qualify under the exception of Section 461(h)(3) for "certain recurring items"? A committee report explained this exception:

> Congress recognized that in many ordinary business transactions, economic performance may not occur until the year following the year in which the deduction may be taken under the all events test. Therefore, to avoid disrupting normal business and accounting practices and imposing undue burdens on taxpayers, Congress believed that an exception . . . should be provided for certain recurring items.[8]

Is there another possible justification for this exception for recurring items? Would the "steady state" analysis of expensing capital costs, discussed by Judge Posner in *Encyclopaedia Brittanica* (Chapter 33), also apply to an immediate deduction for future costs?

3) Other Aspects of the Court's Reasoning in *Hughes Property*

In permitting an immediate deduction in full of the future payoff, the Court noted that "a contrary result would mismatch the [taxpayer's] income

---

8. See note 2, supra.

and expenses." What did the Court mean by "mismatch" in this context? Why was it necessarily a problem? Assuming it was, couldn't the problem be solved by permitting the taxpayer to accrue the present value of the future payoff, discounted at the after-tax rate of interest, rather than the full future amount?

The Court also notes that if Hughes Property had deposited in escrow an amount required to fund the jackpot, it would have been entitled to an immediate deduction. But, in that event, would Hughes Property have placed the *full* amount in escrow? Or only the present discounted value?

4) Mismatching of the Casino's Deduction and the Winner's Income in *Hughes Property*

Hughes Property appears to permit tax avoidance by allowing the casino to deduct the full amount of the future cost without discounting to present value. Could a matching requirement solve the problem? Why couldn't the winner be required to report the full amount of the jackpot as income when the casino takes its deduction under *Hughes Property*? Is the problem that the identity of the winner will be known only when the jackpot is won?

But suppose that, when the casino accrues its deduction, it is also required to pay taxes, at the top individual rate, on behalf of the eventual winner. Whoever wins would then be paid the jackpot amount, less the taxes paid on his or her behalf. If the winner's tax rate is lower than the top individual rate, the winner would also receive a tax refund. Would this kind of matching requirement prevent tax avoidance?

Chapter 55

PREMATURE ACCRUALS AS IMPLICIT LOANS

A. THE IMPLICIT LOAN ANALYSIS

1) Should the Obligation to Make a Future Payment Be Recast as an Immediate Payment, Plus a Zero Stated Interest Loan?

The creation of an obligation to make a future payment in *Mooney Aircraft*, *Hughes Property*, and *General Dynamics* (Chapter 54) could be recast as two separate transactions. First, the obligor makes an immediate payment, equal to the present discounted value of the future obligation. Second, the obligor issues a zero stated interest note for which the obligor is loaned an amount equal to the immediate payment.

In effect, this recasting views the obligor as taking out a loan, with the future payment obligation representing the obligation to repay principal plus accrued interest at maturity. For this reason, it will be referred to as the *implicit loan analysis*.

The implicit loan analysis provides a different solution to the problem of premature accruals from that adopted by the all events test and by Section 461(h). An example based on *Mooney Aircraft* will be used to illustrate those differences.

Assume that Mooney promises to rebate $1,000 five years after an airplane is sold and that the *before-tax* interest rate—at which money is loaned—equals 10%. The present value of the promise to pay $1,000 in five years, discounted at 10%, equals $621. (See the present value table in Chapter 12.) The promise can be recast as two transactions. First, Mooney pays the purchaser an immediate rebate of $621. Second, Mooney issues a zero stated interest note, promising to pay $1,000 in five years, for which Mooney is loaned the present value, discounted at 10%, or $621.

Under the implicit loan analysis, what amount should Mooney be allowed to deduct as the expense of making the immediate rebate when the plane is sold? What amount should the buyer report from receiving the rebate? What interest expense would Mooney be entitled to deduct, and what interest income should the buyer report over the term of the loan?

(Assume that the OID rules of Sections 1272 and 163(e), which provide for economic accrual accounting of interest income and deductions, would apply.)

Table 55–1 compares how Mooney and the buyer would fare under the implicit loan analysis with how they actually are taxed under Section 461(h). Table 55–1 makes the critical assumption that, under the implicit loan analysis, an immediate rebate increases the buyer's income by the amount of the rebate. The tax results of the implicit loan analysis and Section 461(h) will be compared, first given this assumption and, second, after changing it.

TABLE 55-1. COMPARING THE IMPLICIT LOAN ANALYSIS WITH SECTION 461(h)

	Implicit Loan		Section 461(h)	
Year	Mooney	Buyer	Mooney	Buyer
1	−621	+621		
2	−62	+62		
3	−68	+68		
4	−75	+75		
5	−83	+83		
6	−91	+91	−1000	+1000
Total	−1000	+1000	−1000	+1000

2) The Implicit Loan Analysis versus Section 461(h)

Using Table 55–1, try to answer the following questions. What is the effect of Section 461(h) compared to the implicit loan analysis? Why does Section 461(h) overstate Mooney's income? Why does it understate the buyer's income? Why is the overstatement of Mooney's income exactly offset by the understatement of the buyer's income? Why is the result of Section 461(h)—as compared with the implicit loan analysis—to shift income from the buyer to Mooney?

Does the shifting of income matter if both parties are in the same tax bracket? Does the shifting of income by Section 461(h) appear to provide opportunities for tax avoidance? Are those opportunities comparable to those that had been afforded by ratable accrual of OID on bonds (Chapter 50) and by sales of property for deferred payment (Chapter 51) before enactment of Sections 1272(a) and 1274?

3) Changing the Critical Assumption

Table 55–1 treats an immediate rebate as increasing the buyer's income by an amount equal to the $621 rebate. Is that necessarily correct? The effect of the immediate rebate is to reduce the price of the aircraft and therefore the buyer's basis. If the holder of the Mooney Bond is an airplane distributor (and the opinion indicates that such was usually the case), then the rebate lowers the cost of inventory and increases the distributor's income by a corresponding amount.

What if, on the other hand, the holder of the Mooney bond is the ultimate user of the airplane? Assume that the user is entitled to depreciation deductions and an investment tax credit. If the present value of both depreciation and the credit approximates expensing, as was the case from 1981 through 1986 (Chapter 35), then a $621 reduction in the buyer's basis is the equivalent of losing a current $621 deduction or increasing income in the same amount, exactly the effect indicated in Table 55–1.

However, under current law, there is no generally available investment tax credit, and the present value of depreciation is less than expensing. Thus, the effect of a $621 reduction in the buyer's basis is the equivalent of losing *less* than a current deduction of $621. Suppose that the present value of $621 of depreciation deductions is $500. Then a $621 reduction in the buyer's basis is the equivalent of losing a current deduction of $500 or increasing income by the same amount. Table 55–2 compares the results of the implicit loan analysis and Section 461(h) in these circumstances.

TABLE 55-2. COMPARING THE IMPLICIT LOAN ANALYSIS WITH SECTION 461(h) WHERE THE PRESENT VALUE OF DEPRECIATION AND THE ITC IS LESS THAN EXPENSING

Year	Implicit Loan Mooney	Buyer	Section 461(h) Mooney	Buyer
1	−621	+500		
2	−62	+62		
3	−68	+68		
4	−75	+75		
5	−83	+83		
6	−91	+91	−1000	+1000
Total	−1000	+879	−1000	+1000

What is the effect of Section 461(h) relative to the implicit loan analysis? The effect is still to shift income to Mooney from the buyer. But there is an additional complication. The overstatement of Mooney's income now exceeds the understatement of the buyer's. In these circumstances, the effect of Section 461(h) is not only to shift income but also to increase the total amount reported by both parties together and therefore probably to increase the total taxes owed. Even if both parties face the same tax rate, Section 461(h) will fail to produce the correct overall result.

Does this overtaxation really matter? Can taxpayers design around it by providing explicitly for an immediate cash rebate, followed by a loan?

4) The Implicit Loan Analysis and Damage Settlements

Recall the damage settlement discussed in the notes and questions following *Mooney Aircraft* (Chapter 54) in which a tortfeasor agrees to pay an accident victim $100,000 a year for twenty years. How might this agreement be recast as involving an immediate payment of lump sum damages, followed by a loan from the victim to the tortfeasor (with the loan to be repaid over twenty years)? If the implicit loan analysis is correct, how should the parties be treated under the economic accrual rules of Sections 1272 and 163(e)? How does Section 461(h) overattribute income to the tortfeasor and underattribute income to the victim? Why is the overall effect to shift income from victim to tortfeasor? Does it matter if both parties are in the same tax bracket? Does it appear to create opportunities for tax avoidance?

5) The Implicit Loan Analysis and *Hughes Property*

Should the implicit loan analysis be applied to *Hughes Property* (Chapter 54)? The casino's obligation to pay a future jackpot could be recast as two transactions. First, the casino makes an immediate payment to the eventual winner of an amount equal to the present value of the future jackpot. Second, the casino borrows that amount back in exchange for a zero stated interest note.

Both the due date and the principal amount of the note are uncertain. The note becomes due when the slot machine turns up a winning combination. The stated principal amount is determined by the number of times that the slot machine is played before there is a winner. Each time a gambler plays the machine, he or she, in effect, "lends" a small amount, which the casino is obligated to repay only if the gambler's play turns up a winning combination.

Is it plausible to recast *Hughes Property* as involving an implicit loan? How can the eventual winner be regarded as earning anything before his or her identity is known? But does it matter which approach is adopted— the implicit loan analysis or Section 461(h)—if both parties face the same marginal tax rate?

6) The Implicit Loan Analysis and *General Dynamics*

Should *General Dynamics* be recast as a current payment by the company to its employees, followed by a loan from the employees to the company? By unilaterally delaying the filing of a claim to which they are currently entitled, are the employees making a loan on which they earn interest income? Does that mean that any time a payee delays collecting an obligation that is due, an implicit loan is extended? Or does an implicit loan exist only when the payee bargains for and obtains some consideration— namely interest income—in return for agreeing to delay collection?

Again, does it matter which approach is adopted—the implicit loan analysis or Section 461(h)—if both parties are in the same tax bracket?

B. DEFERRED COMPENSATION

The following material explores the tax treatment of deferred compensation arrangements under which an employer defers paying an employee for services rendered in one year until some later year. The same issues arise as in the comparison of Section 461(h) and the implicit loan analysis as different approaches to taxing the deferred rebate in *Mooney Aircraft*.

1) Matching the Tax Treatment of Employer and Employee

Suppose that E. Iacocca works for Chrysler Corporation. If Chrysler paid Iacocca in 1980 for services rendered during 1980, Chrysler would have a salary deduction and Iacocca would have salary income during that year.

Suppose, however, that Chrysler contracts to pay Iacocca for these services two years later, in 1982. Chrysler, which is presumably using the accrual method of accounting, might try to deduct the salary expense in 1980, when the obligation accrues. On the other hand, Iacocca, who is presumably a cash method taxpayer, will delay reporting the salary until 1982 when he is paid.

Should mismatching of deduction and reporting of the same item be allowed? Or should Chrysler be required to delay deducting the salary until Iacocca reports it as income? Section 404(a)(5) provides for matching by delaying Chrysler's deduction. Section 404(a)(5) was enacted in 1942, over forty years before Section 461(h). Why can it be understood as having the same basic purpose as Section 461(h), namely preventing premature accrual of a deduction by forcing accrual method taxpayers to deduct the expense only when payment occurs?

Does Section 404(a)(5) produce a correct result if the deferred payment arrangement *should* be viewed as involving an implicit loan? If not, is the result of Section 404(a)(5) (like Section 461(h)) to shift income from Iacocca to Chrysler? In answering these questions, consider the following examples.

2) The Tax Advantage of Deferred Compensation

Assume that Iacocca renders $2,000 worth of services to Chrysler in December of 1980, that both Chrysler and Iacocca are in a 50% bracket, and that both Chrysler and Iacocca can invest money at a before-tax rate of interest of 10%. What are the tax consequences of the following arrangements:

Example #1—*No deferral*—Under a no-deferral arrangement, Chrysler pays Iacocca $2,000 at the end of 1980. After taxes, Iacocca has $1,000, which he invests for two years at an after-tax rate of 5%. At the end of two years, the $1,000 will have grown to $1,102.50. (Consult the future value table in Chapter 12.)

Example #2—*Deferred compensation*—Suppose that Chrysler agrees to defer paying Iacocca for two years and to set aside and invest the deferred amount. How much will Chrysler set aside? Since it loses the immediate deduction under Section 404(a)(5), Chrysler will presumably set aside only $1,000. Note that, had Iacocca been paid in 1980, the after-tax cost of $2,000 to Chrysler would have been only $1,000—the $2,000 salary less the $1,000 in taxes saved by deducting the salary payment. Thus, the example assumes that Chrysler will be willing to defer payment, provided that its after-tax cost does not increase.

Over a two-year period, the $1,000 set aside will grow to $1,102.50, after taxes. When it is paid out at the end of 1982, Chrysler should be willing to double this amount to $2,205. Why? Because when the amount is paid to the employee, Chrysler becomes entitled to a deduction under Section 404(a)(5). Thus, the $2,205 paid out will be funded by the $1,102.50 set aside, plus the $1,102.50 saved in taxes by deducting $2,205. After Iacocca is paid the $2,205, he will have left $1,102.50 after taxes—precisely the same amount that he would have had under example #2, when there is no deferral.

Example #3—*Deferred compensation invested in dividend paying stock*—Suppose that Chrysler invests the deferred amounts in common stock of a public utility paying annual dividends at a rate of 10%. At the time, under Section 243, 85% of Chrysler's dividend income was excluded from tax.[1] In effect, the dividends would be taxed to Chrysler at a rate of only 7.5% (15% of the dividend income taxed at a 50% rate). Over a two year period, the $1,000 invested at 10% before taxes, or 9¼% after taxes, will grow to about $1,194. When paid out at the end of 1982, Chrysler should be willing to double the amount to $2,388. Why? When Iacocca is paid the $2,388, he will have $1,194 left after taxes. Why is he better off than if he had made the investment himself?

Example #4—*No deferral, with special tax rate applied to Iacocca's investment income*—Suppose that Iacocca is paid $2,000 at the end of 1980 and that he invests the after-tax proceeds of $1,000 in public utility common stock, paying annual dividends at a rate of 10%. Over two years, this might be expected to grow, at an after-tax rate of 5%, to $1,102.50. Suppose, however, that in recognition of Iacocca's contribution to his country, Congress passes an amendment to the Code, allowing him to be taxed on investment income at a special low rate of only 7.5%. Over the two-year period, the $1,000 will grow, at an annual after-tax rate of 9¼%, to $1,194—precisely the same amount he would have had under example #3.

3) Applying the Implicit Loan Analysis

What causes the tax avoidance in example #3, above? Is it Section 404(a)(5), which, like Section 461(h), shifts income from the payee to the payor (in this case from Iacocca to his employer)? Is the shifting of income irrelevant in example #2, above, where both parties face the same tax rate but relevant in #3, where the employer is almost effectively tax exempt?

Shouldn't the deferred compensation arrangement be broken down into immediate payment of salary followed by a loan from Iacocca to his employer? Won't this recharacterization prevent tax avoidance?

---

1. Today, the dividend exclusion is 70%. See Section 243.

4) The Purpose of Section 243(a)(1)

What do you suppose is the purpose of Section 243(a)(1)? To prevent the triple taxation of corporate-shareholder income? What is the effect of Section 243(a)(1) in example #3, above? Is it applied in arguably unintended circumstances? If it did not apply to amounts set aside under deferred compensation arrangements, what would happen to the tax advantage obtained in example #3 by Iacocca?

5) Focusing on the Precise Difference Between Section 404(a)(5) and the Implicit Loan Analysis: Who Is Taxed on Investment or Interest Income?

This chapter has attempted to make three basic analytic points. First, the problem of premature accruals can be dealt with either by: (a) delaying the deduction under Section 461(h) or 404(a)(5); or (b) treating the deferred payment as involving an implicit loan. Second, the effect of Sections 461(h) and 404(a)(5), when implicit loan treatment is appropriate, is to shift income from payee to payor. Third, the shifting of income produces tax avoidance whenever the payor's tax rate is less than the payee's.

The precise nature of this shifting of income will now be examined more closely. It has been left for last, because it is counterintuitive and difficult to grasp. The basic idea, however, is easily stated. The critical difference between the two analyses is simply *who* is taxable on the interest income earned on the amounts deferred or set aside. Under the implicit loan analysis, investment or interest income is taxable to the payee. Under Section 461(h) or Section 404(a)(5), this income is taxable to the payor.

Perhaps the easiest way to illustrate this idea is to return to the Iacocca examples from above and to suppose that Iacocca's employer is not Chrysler but a tax-exempt institution. (Note that if Chrysler has more deductions than it can possibly use—perhaps as a result of net operating loss carryovers under Section 172—then its effective tax rate is zero, and it is effectively tax exempt.) Recall that these examples assume that Iacocca earns $2,000 in 1980 and is in a 50% tax bracket.

Example #5—*Deferred compensation with a tax-exempt employer*—Suppose that a tax-exempt employer agrees to defer paying Iacocca for two years and to set aside and invest the deferred amounts. How much will the tax-exempt employer be willing to set aside? The entire $2,000? Why is the employer in this case not affected by the loss of a current deduction under Section 404(a)(5)?

Over a two-year period, the $2,000 set aside will grow at a 10% interest rate, both before and after taxes, assuming that no tax is currently imposed on the investment income because the employer is tax exempt. Thus, over two years, the $2,000 initially set aside will grow to $2,420. After Iacocca is paid the $2,420, he will have $1,210 left after taxes—and is considerably better off, as compared with examples #1 and #2, above.

Example #6—*No deferral, with 100% exemption of investment income*—Under a no-deferral arrangement, Iacocca is paid $2,000 at the end of 1980.

After taxes, Iacocca has $1,000, which he invests for two years at a before-tax interest rate of 10%. Suppose that, in recognition of Iacocca's contributions to his country, Congress passes an amendment to the Code, granting him a special tax exemption for his investment income. Over the two-year period, the $1,000 will grow to $1,210. This is exactly the same result as in example #5, above.

Example #7—*Deferred compensation with a tax-exempt employer taxed on investment income at the employee's rate*—Suppose that in example #5, the tax-exempt employer were to be taxed on the interest earned on the amounts set aside at the employee's rate. Then, the advantage of shifting investment income to the employer would be eliminated! To illustrate, if such a tax were applied, the tax-exempt employer would earn an after-tax return of only 5% so that $2,000 set aside in 1980 would grow over two years to $2,205. When paid out to Iacocca, he will retain $1,102.50 after taxes.

In sum, the preceding examples illustrate several important ideas. The effect of Section 404(a)(5) (and Section 461(h))—deferring the payor deduction until economic performance—is tantamount to taxing interest income to the payor, rather than the payee. Where a deferred payment should *not* be recast as involving an implicit loan, deferring the payor's deduction under Sections 404(a)(5) and 461(h) appears correct. But where the implicit loan analysis should be applied, Section 461(h) shifts interest income from payee to payor and may produce opportunities for tax avoidance whenever the payor's tax rate is lower. Tax avoidance, however, can be prevented by taxing interest income earned by the payor at the payee's tax rate.

Although it seems highly technical, this analysis has profound implications for public policy in a number of areas where an accrual method taxpayer seeks a current deduction for a future payment. The next (and final) chapter examines those implications for national policies concerning retirement income.

Chapter 56

ACCOUNTING METHODS, DEFERRED COMPENSATION, AND QUALIFIED PENSION PLANS

A. AMEND v. COMMISSIONER
13 T.C. 178 (1949), acq. 1950–1 C.B. 1

FINDINGS OF FACT.

... Petitioners employed the cash basis method of accounting and filed their returns on that basis.

From 1942 to 1946, inclusive, petitioner, a wheat farmer, annually contracted to sell a portion of his wheat in one year for delivery and payment in January of the subsequent year. ...

At the time the contract was made in each of the five transactions, the purchaser either had the grains in storage or received them prior to January 1, pursuant to a contemporaneous agreement as to shipping date. Under the terms of the contract made in each of the five transactions, petitioner was to receive his money for the wheat in January of the year following the contract of sale. The contracts of sale in each year were oral. These contracts were bona fide arm's-length transactions between the seller and the buyer.

Petitioner did not attempt to obtain payment, nor was it represented to him or his attorney in fact that he could obtain payment, prior to January of the following year under the contract made in each of the five transactions. ...

... In the grain business the actual contract is generally oral.

OPINION.

BLACK, JUDGE: ...

In each of the taxable years there is one common issue and that is whether the doctrine of constructive receipt should be applied to certain payments which petitioner received from the sale of his wheat. There is no controversy as to the amounts which petitioner received or as to the time when he actually received them. Petitioners, being on the cash basis, returned these amounts as part of their gross income in the years when petitioner actually received them. As heretofore explained, the Commissioner has refused to accept petitioner's treatment of the payments and has applied the doctrine of constructive receipt and determined that such amounts were income of the prior years. . . .

In *Loose v. United States* . . . the rule providing for the taxation of income constructively received is stated as follows:

> . . . the strongest reason for holding constructive receipt of income to be within the statute is that for taxation purposes income is received or realized when it is made subject to the will and control of the taxpayer and can be, except for his own action or inaction, reduced to actual possession. So viewed, it makes no difference why the taxpayer did not reduce to actual possession. The matter is in no wise dependent upon what he does or upon what he fails to do. It depends solely upon the existence of a situation where the income is fully available to him. . . .

Respondent, in his brief, relies upon the *Loose* case, from which the above quotation is taken, and several other cases which deal with the doctrine of constructive receipt. Needless to say, each of those cases depends upon its own facts. In the *Loose* case, for example, interest coupons had matured prior to the decedent's death. The decedent had not presented them for payment because of his physical condition. It was held that, even though the decedent had not cashed them, the interest coupons represented income to him in the year when they matured, under the doctrine of constructive receipt.

It seems clear to us that the facts in the instant case do not bring it within the doctrine of *Loose v. United States,* supra, and the other cases cited by respondent dealing with constructive receipt.

In discussing the situation which we have in the instant case, we turn our attention first to the contract of sale which petitioner made of his 1944 wheat crop to Burrus. The testimony was that 1944 was a bumper wheat crop year and that petitioner produced and harvested about 30,000 bushels, some of which was lying out on the ground and some of which was stored on the farm. Petitioner . . . sold this wheat to Burrus for January 1945 delivery at $1.57 per bushel. It was the understanding that petitioner would ship his wheat to Burrus at once and that Burrus would pay him for it in January of the following year. The contract was carried out. Some time during the month of August 1944, after August 2, petitioner shipped the 30,000 bushels to Burrus. Burrus received it, put it in its elevator, and paid petitioner for it by check dated January 17, 1945.

Respondent's contention seems to be based primarily on the fact that petitioner could have sold Burrus the wheat at the same price for immediate cash payment in August 1944 and that although he did not do so, he should be treated in the same manner as if he had and the doctrine of constructive receipt should be applied to the payments received. We do not think the doctrine of constructive receipt goes that far. Porter Holmes, who was the manager of the Burrus Panhandle Elevator in Amarillo at the time of the 1944 transaction, testified at the hearing. He testified that it was the usual custom of Burrus to pay cash for wheat soon after it was delivered and that the transaction between Burrus and petitioner for January 1945 delivery and settlement was unusual and that he telephoned the manager at Dallas, Texas, for authority to make the deal that way and secured such authority and the deal was made. He testified that when Burrus' check for $40,164.08 was mailed to petitioner January 17, 1945, it was done in pursuance of the contract. So far as we can see from the evidence, petitioner had no legal right to demand and receive his money from the sale of his 1944 wheat until in January 1945. Both petitioner and Burrus understood that to be the contract. Such is the substance of the testimony of both petitioner, who was the seller of the wheat, and Holmes, who acted for the buyer. Such also is the testimony of Paul Higgs, who represented the seller in the negotiations for the sale. During 1944 all that petitioner had in the way of a promise to pay was Burrus' oral promise to pay him for the wheat in January 1945. Burrus was a well known and responsible grain dealer and petitioner testified that he had not the slightest doubt that he would receive his money in January 1945, as had been agreed upon in the contract. Such a situation, however, does not bring into play the doctrine of constructive receipt. See *Bedell* v. *Commissioner* . . . wherein the court said:

> While, therefore, we do not think that the case is like a promise to pay in the future for a title which passes at the time of contract, we would not be understood as holding by implication that even in that case the profit is to be reckoned as of the time of sale. If a company sells out its plant for a negotiable bond issue payable in the future, the profit may be determined by the present market value of the bonds. But if land or a chattel is sold, and title passes merely upon a promise to pay money at some future date, to speak of the promise as property exchanged for the title appears to us a strained use of language, when calculating profits under the income tax. . . . it is absurd to speak of a promise to pay in the future as having a "market value," fair or unfair. . . .

The doctrine that a cash basis taxpayer can not be deemed to have realized income at the time a promise to pay in the future is made was reiterated by the Circuit Court of Appeals for the Eighth Circuit in the more recent case of *Perry* v. *Commissioner.* . . . In that case it was stated:

> These cases seem to be predicated upon the fact that in a contract of sale of property containing a promise to pay in the future, but not accompanied by notes or other unqualified obligations to pay a definite sum on a day certain, the obligation to pay and the obligation to pass title both being in the future, there is an element of uncertainty in the transaction and the promise has no "market value", fair or unfair. This theory is supported by the decision of the Supreme Court in *Lucas* v. *North Texas Co.* . . .

The Commissioner in the instant case is not contending that Burrus' contract to pay petitioner for his wheat in January 1945 had a fair market value equal to the agreed purchase price of the wheat when the contract was made in August 1944. What he is contending is that petitioner had the unqualified right to receive his money for the wheat in 1944; that all he had to do to receive his money was to ask for it; and that, therefore, the doctrine of constructive receipt applies. . . .

. . . If petitioner had begun this method of selling his wheat in 1944, when he had a bumper crop, there might be reason to doubt the *bona fides* of the contract, but what we have said about the 1944 transaction between Burrus and petitioner is based upon the finding that the contract between Burrus and petitioner was bona fide in all respects, though it was initiated by petitioner, and each party was equally bound by its terms. Petitioner did not begin this method of selling his wheat in 1944—he began it in 1942 and continued it through 1946. No doubt his taxes were more in some years and less in others than they would have been if petitioner had sold and delivered his wheat for cash in the year when it was produced. . . .

Petitioner was asked at the hearing why he adopted the manner of selling his wheat which has been detailed in our findings of fact. His answer was as follows:

> Well, that had been my practice, to handle that wheat that way since 1942 and I have handled my wheat that way, '42, '43, '44, '45, '46, '47 and into 1948. It is still my practice to do that and there have been some years in that interval that I would certainly have paid less income had I handled it the other way, but that is a semi-arid country and we are uncertain about our wheat crops and our expenses are always pretty well set and we know they are going to be high and we need for our own protection to carry part of this wheat forward.
>
> • • •
>
> As I have already explained, it's been a matter of making my income more uniform and even; about five of those years had it all been set back and sold in the year that it was supposed to have been sold in, my income tax would have been less and in the other two it would have been more. I merely emphasize that to show the consistency of my policy and not as a matter of paying any tax.

Whether the reasons advanced by petitioner in his testimony quoted above are good or bad as a business policy, we do not undertake to decide. The question we think we have to decide is whether the contracts detailed in our findings of fact were bona fide arm's-length transactions and whether under them the petitioner had the unqualified right to receive the money for his wheat in the year when the contracts were made and whether petitioner's failure to receive his money was of his own volition. Our conclusion, as already stated, is that the contracts were bona fide arm's-length transactions and petitioner did not have the right to demand the money for his wheat until in January of the year following its sale. This being true, we do not think the doctrine of constructive receipt applies. . . .

B. REV. RUL. 60–31
1960–1 C.B. 174

Advice has been requested regarding the taxable year of inclusion in gross income of a taxpayer, using the cash receipts and disbursements method of accounting, of compensation for services received under the circumstances described below.

(1) On January 1, 1958, the taxpayer and corporation X executed an employment contract under which the taxpayer is to be employed by the corporation in an executive capacity for a period of five years. Under the contract, the taxpayer is entitled to a stated annual salary and to additional compensation of $10x$ dollars for each year. The additional compensation will be credited to a bookkeeping reserve account and will be deferred, accumulated, and paid in annual installments equal to one-fifth of the amount in the reserve as of the close of the year immediately preceding the year of first payment. The payments are to begin only upon (a) termination of the taxpayer's employment by the corporation; (b) the taxpayer's becoming a part-time employee of the corporation; or (c) the taxpayer's becoming partially or totally incapacitated. Under the terms of the agreement, corporation X is under a merely contractual obligation to make the payments when due, and the parties did not intend that the amounts in the reserve be held by the corporation in trust for the taxpayer.

The contract further provides that if the taxpayer should fail or refuse to perform his duties, the corporation will be relieved of any obligation to make further credits to the reserve (but not of the obligation to distribute amounts previously contributed); but, if the taxpayer should become incapacitated from performing his duties, then credits to the reserve will continue for one year from the date of the incapacity, but not beyond the expiration of the five-year term of the contract. There is no specific provision in the contract for forfeiture by the taxpayer of his right to distribution from the reserve; and, in the event he should die prior to his receipt in full of the balance in the account, the remaining balance is distributable to his personal representative at the rate of one-fifth per year for five years, beginning three months after his death.

(2) The taxpayer is an officer and director of corporation A, which has a plan for making future payments of additional compensation for current services to certain officers and key employees designated by its board of directors. This plan provides that a percentage of the annual net earnings (before Federal income taxes) in excess of $4,000x$ dollars is to be designated for division among the participants in proportion to their respective salaries. This amount is not currently paid to the participants; but, the corporation has set up on its books a separate account for each participant and each year it credits thereto the dollar amount of his participation for the year, reduced by a proportionate part of the corporation's income taxes attributable to the additional compensation. Each account is also credited with the net amount, if any, realized from investing any portion of the amount in the account.

Distributions are to be made from these accounts annually beginning when the employee (1) reaches age 60, (2) is no longer employed by the company, including cessation of employment due to death, or (3) becomes totally disabled to perform his duties, whichever occurs first. The annual distribution will equal a stated percentage of the balance in the employee's account at the close of the year immediately preceding the year of first payment, and distributions will continue until the account is exhausted. However, the corporation's liability to make these distributions is contingent upon the employee's (1) refraining from engaging in any business competitive to that of the corporation, (2) making himself available to the corporation for consultation and advice after retirement or termination of his services, unless disabled, and (3) retaining unencumbered any interest or benefit under the plan. In the event of his death, either before or after the beginning of payments, amounts in an employee's account are distributable in installments computed in the same way to his designated beneficiaries or heirs-at-law. Under the terms of the compensation plan, corporation A is under a merely contractual obligation to make the payments when due, and the parties did not intend that the amounts in each account be held by the corporation in trust for the participants.

(3) On October 1, 1957, the taxpayer, an author, and corporation Y, a publisher, executed an agreement under which the taxpayer granted to the publisher the exclusive right to print, publish and sell a book he had written. This agreement provides that the publisher will (1) pay the author specified royalties based on the actual cash received from the sale of the published work, (2) render semiannual statements of the sales, and (3) at the time of rendering each statement make settlement for the amount due. On the same day, another agreement was signed by the same parties, mutually agreeing that, in consideration of, and notwithstanding any contrary provisions contained in the first contract, the publisher shall not pay the taxpayer more than $100x$ dollars in any one calendar year. Under this supplemental contract, sums in excess of $100x$ dollars accruing in any one calendar year are to be carried over by the publisher into succeeding accounting periods; and the publisher shall not be required either to pay interest to the taxpayer on any such excess sums or to segregate any such sums in any manner.

(4) In June 1957, the taxpayer, a football player, entered into a two-year standard player's contract with a football club in which he agreed to play football and engage in activities related to football during the two-year term only for the club. In addition to a specified salary for the two-year term, it was mutually agreed that as an inducement for signing the contract the taxpayer would be paid a bonus of $150x$ dollars. The taxpayer could have demanded and received payment of this bonus at the time of signing the contract, but at his suggestion there was added to the standard contract form a paragraph providing substantially as follows:

> The player shall receive the sum of $150x$ dollars upon signing of this contract, contingent upon the payment of this $150x$ dollars to an escrow agent designated by him. The escrow agreement shall be subject to approval by the legal representatives of the player, the Club, and the escrow agent.

Pursuant to this added provision, an escrow agreement was executed on June 25, 1957, in which the club agreed to pay $150x$ dollars on that date to the Y bank, as escrow agent; and the escrow agent agreed to pay this amount, plus interest, to the taxpayer in installments over a period of five years. The escrow agreement also provides that the account established by the escrow agent is to bear the taxpayer's name; that payments from such account may be made only in accordance with the terms of the agreement; that the agreement is binding upon the parties thereto and their successors or assigns; and that in the event of the taxpayer's death during the escrow period the balance due will become part of his estate. . . .

Section 1.451–1(a) of the Income Tax Regulations provides in part as follows:

> Gains, profits, and income are to be included in gross income for the taxable year in which they are actually or constructively received by the taxpayer unless includible for a different year in accordance with the taxpayer's method of accounting. . . .

And, with respect to the cash receipts and disbursements method of accounting, section 1.446–1(c)(1)(i) provides in part—

> Generally, under the cash receipts and disbursements method in the computation of taxable income, all items which constitute gross income (whether in the form of cash, property, or services) are to be included for the taxable year in which actually or constructively received. . . .

As previously stated, the individual concerned in each of the situations described above, employs the cash receipts and disbursements method of accounting. Under that method, as indicated by the above-quoted provisions of the regulations, he is required to include the compensation concerned in gross income only for the taxable year in which it is actually or constructively received. Consequently, the question for resolution is whether in each of the situations described the income in question was constructively received in a taxable year prior to the taxable year of actual receipt.

A mere promise to pay, not represented by notes or secured in any way, is not regarded as a receipt of income within the intendment of the cash receipts and disbursements method. . . . "Taxpayers on a receipts and disbursements basis are required to report only income actually received no matter how binding any contracts they may have to receive more."

This should not be construed to mean that under the cash receipts and disbursements method income may be taxed only when realized in cash. For, under that method a taxpayer is required to include in income that which is received in cash or cash equivalent. . . . And, as stated in the above-quoted provisions of the regulations, the "receipt" contemplated by the cash method may be actual or constructive.

With respect to the constructive receipt of income, section 1.451–2(a) of the Income Tax Regulations . . . provides, in part, as follows:

> Income although not actually reduced to a taxpayer's possession is constructively received by him in the taxable year during which it is credited to his account or set apart for him so that he may draw upon it at any time. However, income is not constructively received if the taxpayer's control of its receipt is subject to substantial limitations or restrictions. Thus, if a cor-

poration credits its employees with bonus stock, but the stock is not available to such employees until some future date, the mere crediting on the books of the corporation does not constitute receipt.

Thus, under the doctrine of constructive receipt, a taxpayer may not deliberately turn his back upon income and thereby select the year for which he will report it. . . . Nor may a taxpayer, by a private agreement, postpone receipt of income from one taxable year to another. . . .

However, the statute cannot be administered by speculating whether the payor would have been willing to agree to an earlier payment. See, for example, *J. D. Amend, et ux., v. Commissioner.* . . .

Consequently, it seems clear that in each case involving a deferral of compensation a determination of whether the doctrine of constructive receipt is applicable must be made upon the basis of the specific factual situation involved.

Applying the foregoing criteria to the situations described above, the following conclusions have been reached:

(1) The additional compensation to be received by the taxpayer under the employment contract concerned will be includible in his gross income only in the taxable years in which the taxpayer actually receives installment payments in cash or other property previously credited to his account. To hold otherwise would be contrary to the provisions of the regulations and the court decisions mentioned above.

(2) For the reasons in (1) above, it is held that the taxpayer here involved also will be required to include the deferred compensation concerned in his gross income only in the taxable years in which the taxpayer actually receives installment payments in cash or other property previously credited to his account. . . .

(3) Here the principal agreement provided that the royalties were payable substantially as earned, and this agreement was supplemented by a further concurrent agreement which made the royalties payable over a period of years. This supplemental agreement, however, was made before the royalties were earned; in fact, it was made on the same day as the principal agreement and the two agreements were a part of the same transaction. Thus, for all practical purposes, the arrangement from the beginning is similar to that in (1) above. Therefore, it is also held that the author concerned will be required to include the royalties in his gross income only in the taxable years in which they are actually received in cash or other property.

(4) In arriving at a determination as to the includibility of the $150x$ dollars concerned in the gross income of the football player, under the circumstances described, in addition to the authorities cited above, consideration also has been given to . . . the decision in *E. T. Sproull v. Commissioner,* 16T.C.244. . . .

In *E. T. Sproull v. Commissioner* . . . the petitioner's employer in 1945 transferred in trust for the petitioner the amount of $10,500. The trustee was directed to pay out of principal to the petitioner the sum of $5,250 in 1946 and the balance, including income, in 1947. In the event of the petitioner's prior death, the amounts were to be paid to his administrator, executor, or heirs. The petitioner contended that the Commissioner erred in including the sum of $10,500 in his taxable income for 1945. In this connection, the court stated:

> ... it is undoubtedly true that the amount which the Commissioner has included in petitioner's income for 1945 was used in that year for his benefit ... in setting up the trust of which petitioner, or, in the event of his death then his estate, was the sole beneficiary....
>
> The question then becomes ... was "any economic or financial benefit conferred on the employee as compensation" in the taxable year. If so, it was taxable to him in that year. This question we must answer in the affirmative. The employer's part of the transaction terminated in 1945. It was then that the amount of the compensation was fixed at $10,500 and irrevocably paid out for petitioner's sole benefit...."

Applying the principles stated in the *Sproull* decision to the facts here, it is concluded that the 150x-dollar bonus is includible in the gross income of the football player concerned in 1957, the year in which the club unconditionally paid such amount to the escrow agent. ...

In the application of [the Code] to unfunded plans, no deduction is allowable for any compensation paid or accrued by an employer on account of any employee under such a plan except in the year when paid and then only to the extent allowable under section 404(a). Thus, under an unfunded plan, if compensation is paid by an employer directly to a former employee, such amounts are deductible under section 404(a)(5) when *actually* paid *in cash or other property to the employee,* provided that such amounts meet the requirements of section 162 or section 212.

C. NOTES AND QUESTIONS

1) Cash Method: A Misnomer?

Suppose that during 1990 a professional tennis player has earnings from the following sources:

a) She is paid $200,000 cash for playing in various tournaments.

b) She is under a one-year contract (effective January 1, 1990 to December 31, 1990) to make commercial endorsements of Canon cameras. In return, Canon is to pay her $30,000 a year for twenty years, beginning in 1991.

c) She is under a one-year contract (effective January 1, 1990 to December 31, 1990) to make commercial endorsements of Canon cameras. In return, Canon is to pay her $50,000 a year for twenty years, beginning in 2010.

d) She receives a new sports car, worth $12,000, for winning a tournament sponsored by Volvo.

e) She receives ten shares of IBM stock for winning a tournament sponsored by IBM.

Assuming that she uses the cash method of accounting, which items must be reported on her 1990 tax return? If not in 1990, then when? Do your answers suggest that the "cash receipts" method of accounting is misnamed? Does it apply only to the receipt of cash? What would be a more accurate description?

If she uses the accrual method, when should the items be reported? Even if she uses the cash method, could the IRS require that any of the items be reported when earned under Section 446(b), particularly c), above?

2) The Stakes in *Amend*

Why did the taxpayer in *Amend* defer payment for the wheat? What is the significance of the fact that in 1944 Amend had a "bumper crop"? Assume that Amend expects to harvest and sell $30,000 of wheat in 1944 and $10,000 of wheat in 1945. Suppose that the first $20,000 of his receipts are taxable at a rate of 20% and the second $20,000 at a rate of 40%. If Amend makes no attempt to postpone payment, his tax bill will be:

1944	$20,000	x	20%	=	$ 4,000
	10,000	x	40%	=	4,000
			Subtotal		$ 8,000
1945	$10,000	x	20%	=	$ 2,000
			Total		$10,000

On the other hand, if Amend arranges to be paid in 1945 for $10,000 of wheat, delivered in 1944 (and if his use of the cash method is respected), then he will owe:

1944	$20,000	x	20%	=	$4,000
1945	$20,000	x	20%	=	$4,000
			Total		$8,000

If rates were proportional, rather than progressive, would Amend arrange for deferred payment? Does the cash method ease the rigor of accounting for Amend's income on an annual basis by spreading income more evenly over the years? Would the installment method achieve the same result? Despite Sections 453(b)(2)(A) and 453(*l*)(1)—enacted in 1987 to deny the installment method to businesses that sell to customers for deferred payment—there is an exception for farm products in Section 453(*l*)(2)(A).

3) Constructive Receipt

The doctrine of constructive receipt requires taxpayers to report amounts that they have the right to receive even if they have failed to collect them. For example, a cash method taxpayer must report interest that accumulates on a savings account (whether or not the interest is withdrawn) and amounts for which the taxpayer has received a check (even if not cashed or deposited). In *Amend,* the IRS tried to extend the doctrine of constructive receipt. What did the IRS find objectionable about Amend's claim that the cash method allowed deferral in his case? By implication, in what circumstances would the IRS—had it won in *Amend*—have continued to allow deferral under the cash method? Would the IRS' position, if accepted, have affected items b) and c) in question 1), above? Is the distinction that the IRS tried to make in *Amend* enforceable? How?

4) Rev. Rul. 60–31

Are the limits imposed on the cash method in Rev. Rul. 60–31 easier to administer than the limits proposed by the IRS in *Amend*? Are they fair or unfair? Who would feel discriminated against?

5) Special Rules for Qualified Pension Plans

When compensation is deferred under a *qualified pension plan*, the rules set out in Rev. Rul. 60–31 and Section 404(a) are suspended. Even though the deferred amounts are put into trust, the employee is not taxed on them until he or she is actually paid (contrary to the principal of Rev. Rul. 60–31 that employees are immediately taxable on deferred compensation that is secured or placed in escrow). And even though the employee is not taxable until some future date, the employer is granted an immediate deduction for amounts contributed to the plan (contrary to the principle of Section 404(a) that the employer deduction is deferred until the employee is taxed).

Besides being exempt from Rev. Rul. 60–31 and Section 404(a), qualified pension plans enjoy additional tax advantages. By far the most important is that the investment income of such plans—the income earned on the investment of the deferred amounts—is exempt from tax.[1]

What is a "qualified pension plan"? A "pension" can be defined as a regular payment made to a worker after he or she retires. A "pension plan" is an arrangement under which a portion of a worker's earnings are set aside in order to provide for a retirement pension.

A pension plan is "qualified" if it meets certain requirements. For purposes of this discussion, three requirements are most important. First, the plan must be broadly based so that it covers certain categories of workers. The plan may not simply benefit a select group of employees. Second, the plan must allocate pension benefits in a nondiscriminatory fashion. It cannot, for example, favor selected employees, in particular the more highly paid. Third, the plan must be funded, that is, the amounts set aside must be placed in a separate escrow or trust account so that they are not subject to the business risks of the employer. The exact requirements are specified in Sections 401–419A of the Code, which are among the most difficult, detailed, and technical provisions of the Code.

---

1. These investment earnings, however, are taxable to plan beneficiaries when distributed. See the discussion in Section E, below.

7) The Social Policy Behind Qualified Pension Plans

What is the purpose of this complex and carefully constructed system? Why are the requirements (broad coverage, nondiscrimination, and funding) imposed as a condition for special tax treatment? Why not let each individual employee decide how much to save for retirement up to a certain limit and provide tax benefits on that basis? For example, why not let every worker deduct up to $30,000 for earnings placed in a retirement fund and exempt the investment earnings of the fund from tax?

Instead, why are tax benefits conditioned on mandatory participation in a plan by all employees in certain categories? What is the implicit assumption about individual decision making? About how everyday pressures of supporting a family affect saving for retirement, even when promoted with tax incentives? Does the system assume that top executives will seek to provide for their own retirement, while middle and lower income employees may not?

D. STATEMENT OF DANIEL HALPERIN
Deputy Assistant Secretary of the Treasury for Tax Policy, Before the Senate Finance Committee Subcommittee on Private Pension Plans and Employee Fringe Benefits (March 15, 1978).

Proposed Deferred Compensation Regulations

I would like to turn now to the second issue for discussion today, the regulations on nonqualified deferred compensation arrangements proposed by the Internal Revenue Service on February 3, 1978.

The proposed regulations are concerned with situations in which the recipient of compensation is given the choice of receiving compensation currently or in a later year under a nonqualified deferred compensation arrangement. Qualified retirement plans are not affected. The proposed regulations apply to cases where the compensation is fixed, such as by statute or contract, and *then* the employer says to the employee, in effect, "Tell me when you want it paid." The proposed regulations provide that even if the employee elects deferral, the compensation will nevertheless be treated as received when the employee would have received it in the absence of an election to postpone payment. . . .

. . . In the context of deferred compensation arrangements, the Service stated in Revenue Ruling 60–31 that it could not administer the law "by speculating whether the payor would have been willing to agree to an earlier payment". However, with arrangements of the type affected by the proposed regulation, no such speculation is required. If an employee is in complete control of the disposition of part of his or her compensation and the employer is willing to pay or withhold that amount at the direction of the employee, the fact that the employee elects deferral should not, in the absence of statutory authorization, result in exclusion of the amount from gross income. In similar instances, no exclusion would result if the employee directed the employer to withhold an amount from compensation and pay the amount into a savings account or as a premium on an annuity contract owned by the employee. . . .

E. DEFERRED COMPENSATION PLANS [SECTION 457]

H.R. Report No. 1445, 95th Cong., 2d Sess. 50–58 (1978)

... In 1960, the Internal Revenue Service published Revenue Ruling 60–31 which set forth a broad policy statement regarding the application of the constructive receipt and cash equivalent doctrines to nonqualified deferred compensation arrangements. Revenue Ruling 60–31 set forth a number of general principles regarding the constructive receipt and cash equivalent doctrines and then provided ... examples of their application to deferred compensation arrangements.

The ... examples set forth in the ruling made it clear that the constructive receipt and cash equivalent doctrines would not be applied to certain deferred compensation arrangements between an employee and an employer even though the employee might have obtained an agreement from the employer to make an immediate cash payment following the performance of services. Subsequent published rulings continued to confirm that the constructive receipt and cash equivalent doctrines would not be applied merely because an employee was permitted to elect, before the compensation was earned, to defer the compensation to a later time or receive it currently. In addition, some of these subsequent rulings indicated that a cash method employee would not be considered to have current income even though the employer set aside assets to fund its obligation to pay deferred compensation, as long as the employee did not acquire a present interest in either the amounts deferred or the assets used as the employer's funding medium.

In 1972, the Internal Revenue Service issued the first favorable private letter ruling with respect to an unfunded deferred compensation arrangement where a State or local government unit was the employer. Subsequently, many States and local governments have obtained private rulings with respect to their deferred compensation plans which provide that participating employees who use the cash method will include in income benefits payable under the deferred compensation plan only in the taxable year in which such benefits are received or otherwise made available.

Because these plans are not designed to be qualified for special treatment under the tax law, they need not comply with Internal Revenue Code rules prohibiting benefits or contributions which discriminate in favor of employees who are officers, shareholders, or highly compensated. Also, nonqualified plans are not subject to the limitations on contributions or benefits which apply to qualified plans. ...

In April 1977, the Internal Revenue Service stopped issuing private rulings dealing with the income tax treatment of individuals under certain nonqualified deferred compensation plans, the type of unfunded deferred compensation plans typically established by State and local governments, and began advising applicants for rulings that their applications would be delayed pending study. The plans involved permitted individuals to elect to defer a portion of salary that would otherwise be payable. Later, the Service publicly announced the suspension pending a review of the area.

After completion of its review of this area, the Internal Revenue Service issued proposed regulations which provide generally that, if under a plan or arrangement (other than a qualified retirement plan), payment of an amount of a taxpayer's fixed basic or regular compensation is deferred at the taxpayer's individual election to a taxable year later than that in which the amount would have been payable but for the election, the deferred amount would be treated as received in the earlier taxable year. These proposed regulations would apply to plans maintained by States and local governments and tax-exempt organizations as well as plans maintained by taxable employers.

Reasons for change

The committee believes that the regulations concerning nonqualified deferred compensation plans involving an individual election to defer compensation proposed by the Internal Revenue Service on February 3, 1978, if adopted in final form, would seriously impact upon the employees of many States and localities. If adopted, the regulations would prohibit employees of States and local governments and employees of tax-exempt rural electric cooperatives and their tax-exempt affiliates from participating in salary-reduction deferred compensation plans as a means of providing retirement income.

The committee believes that limitations should be imposed on the amounts of compensation that can be deferred under these arrangements and allowed to accumulate on a tax-deferred basis. The committee realizes that the denial of a compensation deduction to a non-taxable entity until an amount is includible in the income of the person providing services does not act as a restraint on the amounts that non-taxable entities are willing to let employees defer as it does when a taxable entity is involved. Accordingly, the committee believes that a percentage-of-compensation limit on amounts that can be deferred, as well as an absolute dollar limitation to prevent excessive deferrals by highly-compensated employees, is necessary.

Explanation of provisions

The committee's bill adds a new provision to the Code (sec. 457) to provide certainty with respect to unfunded deferred compensation plans maintained by States and local governments. . . . Thus, under this provision, employees and independent contractors who provide services for one of these entities that maintains an eligible deferred compensation plan will be able to defer compensation as long as such deferral does not exceed the prescribed annual limitations.

In general

Amounts of compensation deferred by a participant in an eligible State deferred compensation plan, plus any income attributable to the investment of such deferred amounts, will be includible in the income of the participant or his beneficiary only when it is paid or otherwise made available. . . .

Plan requirements

To qualify as an eligible State deferred compensation plan, the plan must be maintained by . . . a State, a political subdivision of a State, an agency or instrumentality of a State or one of its political subdivisions. . . . In addition, the plan by its terms must not allow the deferral of more than

$7,500, or 33⅓ percent of the participant's includible compensation for the taxable year, whichever is less. . . .

F. NOTES AND QUESTIONS

1) Qualified Pension Plans and Tax-exempt Employers

How may tax incentives fail to encourage qualified pension plans with broad and nondiscriminatory coverage when the employer is tax exempt? How did the Treasury propose to respond to the problem of nonqualified unfunded plans established by tax-exempt employers? What losing argument did the Treasury try to resurrect?

2) Section 457

How did Congress attack nonqualified pension plans of tax-exempt employers? See Sections 457(a), (b), (f)(1)(A), and (f)(3)(B). As originally enacted in 1978, Section 457 covered only state and local government employers. In 1986, it was extended to nongovernmental tax-exempt employers as well.

G. NONQUALIFIED DEFERRED COMPENSATION

Halperin, Interest in Disguise: Taxing the "Time Value of Money", 95 Yale L.J. 506, 539–545 (1987).

. . . [Deferred] compensation that does not qualify for preferential treatment under the Internal Revenue Code [is] referred to as "nonqualified" deferred compensation. . . . This [article] makes the case for a special tax on investment income earned on nonqualified deferred compensation, and describes how such a tax might operate.

The Case for a Special Tax on Investment Income

Under the current taxing scheme, investment income earned on deferred compensation in a nonqualified plan often goes untaxed. This unwarranted subsidy undermines the incentives created by Congress to establish qualified retirement plans. Furthermore, because nonqualified plans usually benefit highly paid individuals, the subsidy violates the rationale for giving a tax preference to retirement savings, namely to benefit low and middle income wage earners. To eliminate this subsidy, a special tax must be imposed on the investment income generated by nonqualified plans.

1. *Treatment of Qualified and Nonqualified Plans*

Specific types of employer-established retirement programs, generally referred to as "qualified plans," are not taxed on investment income. To promote adequate retirement income for low and moderate wage earners, Congress required that qualified plans be available to a broad group of employees. Thus, retirement plans which are only offered to highly paid employees are not eligible for the statutory tax exemption on investment income afforded to qualified plans.

The benefit of exemption, however, is often achieved in practice by such nonqualified plan sponsors. Tax-exempt employers can realize the exemption by investing retirement assets on behalf of the employees. Because the employer is tax-exempt, the investment income earned on the retirement assets is similarly not taxed. Congress has responded to this tax avoidance technique by imposing a $7,500 annual limit on the amount of deferred compensation that can be allocated to an employee of a governmental unit under a nonqualified plan. Congress, however, ignored [until 1986] the larger problem of tax-exempt employers other than government.

Taxable employers may effectively exempt investment income from tax to the extent that they have excess loss carryovers. Alternatively, these employers can invest deferred compensation in securities that pay dividends, which are 85% [today 70%] exempt from tax. . . .

Since comparable benefits can be achieved under nonqualified plans that do not meet the statutory coverage requirements, employers may choose to provide benefits only for their highly paid employees, thus circumventing the congressional mandate to protect low and moderate wage earners. Even if such nonqualified plans do not impact significantly on the establishment of qualified plans, they provide an unwarranted and unintended subsidy to high-income individuals.

2. *Inadequacy of Alternative Approaches*

To maintain the incentives for qualified plans and to avoid subsidizing highly compensated employees, nonqualified plans must be taxed on their investment income. This Section demonstrates the inadequacy of the principal alternatives to a special tax on investment income—full accrual taxation of compensation and expansion of the doctrine of constructive receipt.

a. *Accrual Taxation of All Compensation*

The tax benefits of nonqualified deferred compensation could be eliminated if compensation were taxed to the employee upon performance of services. Since most employees rely on W-2 forms furnished by the employer, calculating the amount of accrued income would not unduly burden employees. Measurement of accrued income could, of course, require assumptions as to interest rates and mortality risks, but the IRS could provide tables for this purpose. Resources to pay the tax could be provided by requiring employer withholding on accrued compensation. The employer could derive funds for withholding either out of the tax savings resulting from the allowance of an immediate salary deduction or from the funds which would otherwise be set aside for the employee.

In some circumstances, however, such as when benefits are forfeited if death occurs before normal retirement age, full accrual would tax employees on benefits they might never receive. For example, if $10,000 deferred compensation were set aside for an employee who survives to age 65 and there were an 80% chance that the employee would reach that age, the employee would be charged with current income of $8,000. Although this is analogous to receiving cash compensation of $8,000 followed by the purchase of an annuity contract that might never pay benefits, employees might find it difficult to understand why they should be taxed on money that they may never receive.

Another problem with full accrual taxation is the potential bunching of income which could cause higher than normal rates to apply. For example, a state university may adopt a special retirement program for a football coach who has been successful over many years. If the value of all of the past years' benefits were allocated to the year the plan is implemented, the amount would likely far exceed the $7,500 limit applicable to government plans and accrual would inflate the marginal rate of tax. In other circumstances, by properly allocating income to the year in which it is earned, full accrual taxation would eliminate the tax saving that results from the reduction in the employee's marginal tax bracket after retirement. To the extent that the averaging possibilities of current law are thought to be desirable, such a result would be a disadvantage.

In sum, there are serious obstacles to immediate accrual taxation of all compensation. These include the real or imagined inability to pay the tax, problems of measurement, and significant bunching of income. A lack of employee understanding of the accrual method, however, may be the most serious obstacle to implementing such a system.

b. *Constructive Receipt*

The constructive receipt doctrine provides another possible avenue for eliminating the tax benefits of nonqualified deferred compensation. Current income tax regulations view income as constructively received if an individual has an opportunity to claim it. If the employee could have received cash had she wished to do so, many of the problems generated by a scheme of accrual taxation would disappear. The amount of current income could readily be measured, and cash would, at least presumably, be available to pay the tax. It might also be easier to justify current taxation to employees.

Nevertheless, the IRS has not been aggressive in asserting the constructive receipt doctrine in the context of deferred compensation. At present, as long as an employee agrees to deferral before services are performed, constructive receipt is not applied. A later election to defer may also be permissible, particularly if the amount of compensation remains uncertain at the time of performance or if the day of payment is not immediate.

In 1978, the Treasury responded to perceived abuses in plans adopted by state and local governments and other tax-exempt employers by urging a broader application of the constructive receipt doctrine. The Treasury suggested that when it is clear that the compensation has been withheld at the direction of the employee or when there has been a specific set-aside, the employee should not be permitted to exclude that amount from current gross income. Constructive receipt might also be established by focusing on whether the employee has significant control over investment or distribution.

Nevertheless, it seems unlikely that expansion of the constructive receipt doctrine would be very successful. This approach would undoubtedly foster administrative difficulty and uncertainty as tax advisors develop ways to disguise the election or the set-aside. Moreover, if the employee were not permitted to demonstrate that, despite the set-aside, the employer was unwilling or unable to pay currently, the result would be tantamount to accrual accounting.

Because compensation may be deferred for reasons other than tax avoidance, it is impractical to overcome these difficulties by a harsh bright-line standard which makes deferred compensation impossible. Legitimate nontax reasons for deferring payment of compensation by an employer include a shortage of current funds and the stimulation of savings for retirement above the amounts permitted by qualified plans, either to promote an employer's image as socially responsible or to encourage retirement while making room for younger employees. Ideally, deferred compensation should be neither favored nor disfavored relative to the tax treatment of current compensation.

Thus, neither full accrual taxation of deferred compensation nor the expansion of the doctrine of constructive receipt seems likely to eliminate the potential for tax savings under current law with respect to nonqualified deferred compensation plans. Instead, a special tax on the investment income generated by such plans is needed.

A Special Tax on Investment Income

A special tax on investment income designed to capture the tax that would have been paid by the employee can accomplish the goal of accrual taxation while avoiding most of the difficulties described above. Despite deferral, an employee *will* pay the proper amount of tax with respect to the deferred *compensation;* she will not, however, pay tax on the *interest* earned on that compensation during the period of deferral. Denial of the employer's deduction for compensation until paid increases the employer's taxable income by the amount of such interest. This "matching" approach, however, does not prevent the parties from taking advantage of the employer's lower rate of tax. It seems preferable, therefore, to allow the employer a deduction for interest credited to the employee while at the same time imposing a tax on an equal amount of investment income. Such a tax would be paid by the employer, but at a special rate.

The feasibility of a special tax on investment income earned on deferred compensation in nonqualified plans depends upon being able to determine the appropriate tax rate . . .

The rate of tax applied to investment income should ideally be the rate applicable to the beneficiaries of the deferred compensation arrangement. By using the beneficiaries' tax rate, the deferral of compensation is neither encouraged nor penalized. When the amount of investment income allocable to each employee can be determined, the proper tax could be assessed by applying the rate from the employee's filed tax return. When contingencies such as mortality rates or future service make individual allocation difficult, the weighted average marginal rate of all participants could be used.

In practice, however, the rate of tax applied to the investment income would probably have to be the top marginal rate for individuals. While undoubtedly erring on the high side in some cases, this rate preserves the maximum incentive for deferral through qualified plans. Furthermore, employees may always avoid the special tax by opting out of the plan.

H. NOTES AND QUESTIONS

1) Section 1274 and Deferred Compensation

Suppose that Section 1274 were amended to apply to the sale of services for deferred payment (as well as to the sale of property). Would the problem described by Professor Halperin in the preceding article still exist? Why is imposing a special tax on the employer's investment income, as Prof. Halperin proposes, equivalent to imputing interest income on deferred compensation to the employee and taxing such interest under the accrual method? See the discussion of deferred compensation in Chapter 55.

I. A LAST WORD

Readers may notice a similarity between the subject of this final chapter, unfunded deferred compensation plans, and *Drescher*, the very first case in this book. In *Drescher*, the issue was whether an annuity was taxable to the executive when it was earned. In Rev. Rul. 60–31, the issue was similar—whether deferred salary should be taxable when earned.

Analysis of time value of money transactions has taught some counterintuitive lessons about the relative importance of this issue. Even if the employee is not taxed immediately, there is *no* unfair advantage if the interest on the deferred payment is taxed at the appropriate rate. Conversely, even if the employee is taxed immediately, there is an unfair advantage if the interest income is preferentially taxed. See the E. Iacocca examples in Chapter 55.

These lessons apply whether current earnings are deferred through an unfunded plan or a funded arrangement such as an annuity. Thus, we can return to *Drescher* with an unsettling question. Did the issue in the case—whether the annuity should be immediately taxed to the employee—distract us from asking a different and possibly more critical question: How is income earned by the annuity investment taxed?

Once we focus on this second question, we might note the tax-preferred status granted annuity income by Congress under Section 72 (Chapter 53). And we might also note that annuities, like unfunded deferred compensation plans, may be purchased by highly compensated employees in order to avoid the broad coverage and nondiscrimination requirements imposed on qualified pension plans. In other words, both unfunded deferred compensation and annuities may diminish incentives for providing retirement income for middle-income and low-income taxpayers.

We end with the same problem with which we began, but with a different, and hopefully deeper, understanding of the interplay of technical tax provisions, financial analysis, and important social issues.

TABLE OF CASES

Principal cases are in italic type. Non-principal cases are in roman type. References are to Pages.

Adam v. Commissioner, 417
Alderson v. Commissioner, 295, 299, 592
Alice Phelan Sullivan Corp. v. United Statees, 556, 564
Alstores Realty Corporation v. Commissioner, 836, 840, 841
Amend v. Commissioner, 898, 907, 908
Anderson, United States v., 888
Arkansas Best Corp. v. Commissioner, 394, 398, 399, 401
Armantrout v. Commissioner, 71, 76

Barnard v. Commissioner, 688, 692
Benaglia v. Commissioner, 33, 36, 37, 38, 39, 42, 43, 68
Bernatschke v. United States, 790, 795
Biedenharn Realty Co., Inc. v. United States, 402, 411, 412, 413, 416, 417, 439, 567, 701
Biggs v. Commissioner, 294
Bingler v. Johnson, 62, 68, 69
Blair v. Commissioner, 728, 742, 744, 753, 754, 758, 770
Bob Jones University v. United States, 159
Boswell v. Commissioner, 270
Bowers v. Kerbaugh–Empire Co., 322, 324, 325, 329
Bradford v. Commissioner, 325, 329, 343
Briarcliff Candy Corp. v. Commissioner, 511
Brown v. Helvering, 888
Brown, Commissioner v., 818, 829, 830, 831, 832, 865
Bruun, Helvering v., 311, 313, 314, 325, 518
Burnet v. Commonwealth Improvement Co., 294, 592
Burnet v. Logan, 334, 336, 337, 425, 441
Burnet v. Sanford & Brooks Co., 324

Carpenter v. Commissioner, 456, 459
Caulkins, Commissioner v., 802, 806, 814, 835
Central Texas Sav. & Loan Ass'n v. United States, 506, 510, 511
Century Electric v. Commissioner, 292
Clifford, Helvering v., 731, 742, 743, 744, 753, 754, 767, 770, 771
Coit v. Green, 158

Commissioner v. ———(see opposing party)
Committee for Public Ed. and Religious Liberty v. Nyquist, 157
Corliss v. Bowers, 723, 742, 743, 744, 767, 770, 771
Corn Products Refining Co. v. Commissioner, 388, 391, 393, 394, 398, 399, 401, 411, 431
Correll, United States v., 52
Cottage Savings Assoc. v. Commissioner, 274, 284, 285, 286, 293, 643
Coughlin v. Commissioner, 172
Crane v. Commissioner, 365, 366, 603, 693, 694, 829
Culbertson, Commissioner v., 745, 753

Davis, United States v., 197
Dean v. Commissioner, 35 T.C. 1083, pp. 853, 855, 856, 858, 872
Dean v. Commissioner, 83 T.C. 56, pp. 672, 690, 691, 692, 693, 694, 697, 811
Diedrich v. Commissioner, 340, 343, 344, 345, 346, 349, 365, 424, 589, 784, 789
Drescher, United States v., 16, 20, 21, 22, 38, 76, 103, 116, 174, 313, 537, 849, 916
Druker v. Commissioner, 769
Duberstein, Commissioner v., 164, 173, 174, 175, 176, 178, 328, 754

Eisner v. Macomber, 314, 378, 385, 386
Eller v. Commissioner, 161, 163, 164
Encyclopaedia Britannica, Inc. v. Commissioner, 491, 495, 496, 511, 529, 888
Estate of (see name of party)
Excelsior Printing Co. v. Commissioner, 563

Faura v. Commissioner, 495, 496
Ferrer, Commissioner v., 432, 438, 439, 440, 441, 467, 512, 519, 829
First Federal Sav. & Loan Ass'n of Temple v. United States, 286, 287
Flowers, Commissioner v., 44, 50, 52
Foglesong v. Commissioner, 758, 765, 766, 831
Foster, Estate of v. Commissioner, 602
Franklin's Estate v. Commissioner, 663, 669, 670, 690, 691, 693, 811, 830, 872

919

920   Table of Cases

Frank Lyon Co. v. United States, 644, 656, 657, 658, 662, 669, 670, 743, 783

General Artists Corp. v. Commissioner, 431
General Dynamics Corp., United States v., 883, 888, 890, 893, 897
Generes, United States v., 399
Gevirtz v. Commissioner, 452, 454, 459
Golonsky, Commissioner v., 431
Green v. Connally, 158
Greenberg v. Commissioner, 57, 69, 467
Gregory v. Helvering, 598
Griffiths v. Helvering, 211

Hanrahan v. Commissioner, 22
Hantzis v. Commissioner, 53
Harrison v. Schaffner, 740, 742, 758, 770
Haverly v. United States, 564, 566
Heim v. Fitzpatrick, 755, 758
Hellermann v. Commissioner, 371
Helvering v. ——— (see opposing party)
Hewitt Realty Co. v. Commissioner, 314
Higgins v. Smith, 215, 220, 221, 222, 223, 269, 274, 291, 292, 293, 294, 314, 572, 592
Hillsboro Nat. Bank v. Commissioner, 558, 564
Hilton v. Commissioner, 601
Horne v. Commissioner, 223, 269, 274, 286, 288
Horst, Helvering v., 736, 742, 744, 765
Hort v. Commissioner, 844, 845
Hughes Properties, Inc., United States v., 875, 888, 889, 890, 893, 897

Idaho Power Co., Commissioner v., 480, 485, 486, 487, 490, 511, 525, 549, 670, 692
Inaja Land Company, Ltd. v. Commissioner, 331, 334, 336, 344, 345, 346, 349
International Shoe Mach. Corp. v. United States, 413, 416, 425, 567
Irwin v. Gavit, 845, 847

J. H. Baird Publishing Company v. Commissioner, 309
Jones v. Commissioner, 835, 840
Jordan Marsh Company v. Commissioner, 288, 291, 292, 293, 294, 299, 308, 573, 592

Keeton, United States v., 42
Kirby Lumber Co., United States v., 323, 324, 325
Kowalski, Commissioner v., 42

Lafargue v. Commissioner, 785, 789, 790
Lazarus & Co., Helvering v., 590, 591, 592, 594, 595, 600, *656,* 657, 658, 830, 844
Laird v. United States, 513
Liant Record, Inc. v. Commissioner, 315
Lo Bue, Commissioner v., 24, 28, 29, 30, 31, 38, 103, 186
Lochner v. People of State of New York, 386
Lucas v. Earl, 722, 742, 743, 753, 754, 758, 765, 767

Malat v. Riddell, 400, 401, 412
Mattes v. Commissioner, 141, 144

McCue Bros & Drummond, Inc., Commissioner v., 431, 519
McFall v. Commissioner, 418, 420, 431
McWilliams v. Commissioner, 224, 225, 226, 274, 288
Midland Empire Packing Company v. Commissioner, 475, 479, 480
Midland-Ross Corp., United States v., 804, 806, 814, 835
Miller v. Commissioner, 420, 423, 424, 431, 441
Miller v. Gearin, 314, 829
Minzer, Commissioner v., 101, 102, 103, 117
Mooney Aircraft, Inc. v. United States, 867, 871, 872, 874, 890, 892, 894
Moore, Commissioner v., 514, 518, 519, 520, 522, 524
Moss v. Commissioner, 97, 100
Murphy v. Commissioner, 157

NCNB Corp. v. United States, 498, 510, 511
Nickerson v. Commissioner, 461, 467, 468, 470, 698
Nowland v. Commissioner, 5
Nye v. United States, 206, 210, 211, 212, 220, 221

Oppewal v. Commissioner, 153, 157
Owens, Helvering v., 460

Parker v. Delaney, 366
Pittston Company, Commissioner v., 426, 431, 438, 440
P. G. Lake, Inc., Commissioner v., 842, 843, 844
Poe v. Seaborn, 724, 742, 743, 767, 769

RCA Corp. v. United States, 858, 863, 864
Redwing Carriers, Inc. v. Tomlinson, 293, 308, 567, 572, 669, 784
Roemer v. Commissioner, 316
Rosenfeld v. Commissioner, 775, 782, 783, 784
Rosenpan v. United States, 40, 42, 43, 49, 50, 468
Rudolph v. United States, 77, 83, 96, 467

Schulz v. Commissioner, 85, 90
Smith v. Commissioner, 40 B.T.A. 1038, 128, 129, 130
Smith v. Commissioner, 78 T.C. 350, 255, 269, 270, 286, 601, 630
Stanton v. United States, 173, 174, 175, 176, 177
Starker v. Commissioner, 833
Starker v. United States, 602 F.2d 1341, 293, *302,* 308, 309, 316, 441, 572
Starker v. United States, 432 F.Supp. 864, *300*
Starr Bros, Commissioner v., 431
Starr's Estate v. Commissioner, 592, 594, 595, 600, 656, 657, 662, 670, 693, 783, 830
Swift Dodge v. Commissioner, 659, 662, 670, 693

Tax Analysts and Advocates v. Internal Revenue Service, 2
Thor Power Tool Co. v. Commissioner, 234, 242, 243, 285, 467, 486, 487, 511, 549

Table of Cases

Town and Country Food Co. Inc. v. Commissioner, 212
Tufts, Commissioner v., *358*, 365, 366, 367, 589, 603, 693, 694, 829

United States v. ——— (see opposing party)
United Surgical Steel Co., Inc. v. Commissioner, 212

Walz v. Tax Commission of City of New York, 157
Weiss v. Stearn, 386

Welch v. Helvering, *471*, 473, 474, 479, 518
Western Contracting Corporation v. Commissioner v., 595
Wilson v. United States, 42
Wisconsin Cheeseman, Inc. v. United States, 708, 716
Woodsam Associates v. Commissioner, 213, 221, 269, 367, 368, 852
World Airways Inc. v. Commissioner, 888

Young v. Commissioner, 520

TABLE OF INTERNAL REVENUE CODE SECTIONS

Sec.	Page	Sec.	Page
1	767	61(a)(12)	319
1(a)	9	61a	5
1(a)–(d)	7		6
1(a)–(e)	7		22
	8		31
1(c)	8		32
	768		42
1(d)	768		52
1(e)	772		69
1(f)	7		103
1(g)	8		447
	9		582
1(g)(2)	8		667
1(g)(3)	8		770
1(i)	770	62	6
	773		444
11	7	62(a)	6
	9		444
	97	62(a)(1)	43
	176	62(a)(2)(A)	6
	720		43
11(b)(2)	765	62(a)(2)(B)	43
21	133	62(a)(4)	444
	134	62(b)	43
	136	63	6
21(a)(2)	133		145
21(b)(2)	133	63(b)	444
21(c)	133	63(c)	6
	134	63(c)(4)	130
32	135	63(d)(1)	43
46(e)(3)(B)	602		444
	603	67	43
	604		62
	629		96
55(a)	548		468
55(b)	548		469
56–58	548	67(a)	43
	549		444
56(a)(1)(ii)	548	67(b)	43
56(f)(1)	549	71(a)	795
56(g)(1)	549	71(b)(1)(B)	795
56(g)(4)(A)(i)	549		796
57(a)(2)	604	71(f)	796
57(a)(3) (former)	602	72	790
57(a)(5)	704		916
61(a)(1)	15	72(a)	850
	103	72(b)	850
61(a)(3)	193	72(b)(1)	537
	196		790
61(a)(7)	174	72(b)(2)	790

923

Table of Internal Revenue Code Sections

Sec.	Page	Sec.	Page
72(e)	851	111	564
72(e)(2)(B)	851	117	62
72(e)(3)	851		68
72(e)(4)(A)	852		69
72(e)(5)(A)	852		70
72(e)(5)(C)	852		75
72(q)	851		76
74	178		321
74(c)	177	117(a)	68
	178	117(b)(2)	62
	179		69
79	126	117(c)	62
83	22		76
83(a)	22	117(d)	118
	23	119	39
	28		41
	30		42
	31		43
	32		96
	76	119(a)	5
	116	119(a)(1)	39
	174	119(a)(2)	39
	432	120	126
83(d)(2)	22	121	316
83(h)	187		452
85	69	124	51
86	69		126
89	126	124(c)	51
102	847	125	127
	848	127	70
102(a)	164		126
	174	127(c)(1)(B)	70
	178	129	126
	179		134
	326		145
	328	129(a)(2)	134
	847	129(b)	134
102(b)(1)	847	129(d)	134
102(c)	178	132	70
	179		104
103(a)	205		115
	704		117
103(b)(1)	704		118
104	144		126
	315	132(a)(1)	117
	321		118
104(a)(2)	315	132(a)(2)	116
105	144	132(a)(3)	5
106	126		38
	146		115
	147	132(b)	117
106(a)	145		118
108	320	132(b)(2)	117
	321	132(c)	116
	460	132(d)	5
108(a)	320		38
	321	132(e)	178
108(e)(5)	321		179
108(f)	321	132(e)(2)	117
108(f)(1)	321	132(f)(3)	118
108(f)(2)	321	132(h)(4)	51
108(g)	320	132(h)(5)	117
109	314	135(b)(2)	866
	321	135(c)(1)(A)	866

Table of Internal Revenue Code Sections

Sec.	Page	Sec.	Page
135(c)(1)(B)	866	165(b)	460
141–148	704	165(c)	447
151	8		475
151(a)	6		476
151(b)	6	165(c)(1)	447
151(c)(1)(B)	130		448
151(d)(1)(B)	6		454
151(d)(1)(C)	6	165(c)(2)	447
151(d)(3)	6		448
	130		453
152(a)	130		454
162	38	165(c)(3)	455
	48		459
	50		460
162(a)	50		479
	51		480
	57	165(d)	470
	116		470
	129	165(h)	459
	444	165(h)(1)	459
	473	165(h)(2)	459
	474	165(h)(4)	459
	475	165(h)(4)(E)	459
	476	166	399
	566	166(a)	399
	593		563
162(a)(1)	88	166(d)	399
	89	167	583
	90		667
	163	167(a)	444
162(a)(2)	42		447
	44		485
	46	167(g)	518
	47	168	553
	48		554
	51	168(b)	548
	52		553
	96		555
162(c)	443	168(c)	548
162(e)	443		553
162(e)(2)	443		555
162(f)	443	168(d)(1)	551
162(g)	443	168(d)(2)	551
163	583	168(d)(4)	551
	667	168(g)	548
	856		549
163(a)	701	170	159
163(d)	701	170(a)	10
163(d)(6)(B)	701		157
163(e)	891		346
	893	170(c)(1)	157
163(e)(1)	801	170(c)(2)(D)	157
	815	170(c)(3)	157
	858	170(c)(4)	157
163(h)	701	170(c)(5)	157
	702	170(e)(1)	566
163(h)(3)(A)(i)	702		589
163(h)(3)(A)(ii)	702	170(e)(1)(A)	246
163(h)(3)(B)	702		370
163(h)(3)(C)	702	171(a)(1)	522
164	10		522
	159	171(b)(3)(A)	537
165(a)	220	172	470
	223		564

Table of Internal Revenue Code Sections

Sec.	Page	Sec.	Page
	582		708
	639		709
	896		710
172(a)	324		711
172(b)(1)(A)	324		712
172(b)(1)(B)	324		713
174(a)(1)	475		714
179	566		855
179(b)(2)	566	267	223
182	468		224
183	468		225
	469		270
183(a)	468		274
	469		291
183(b)	468		348
	469		350
183(c)	468	267(a)	350
	469	267(a)(1)	223
183(d)	468	267(b)	226
195	511	267(b)(1)–(b)(10)	223
212(1)	444	267(b)(2)	223
213	144	267(d)	350
	145	269	639
213(a)	6	274	178
	144	274(a)	90
	145	274(a)(1)(A)	90
	767		91
214	132		96
	133	274(b)	176
	134		177
	136		487
215(a)	795	274(b)(1)	176
221	131	274(c)	84
243	895	274(d)	90
243(a)(1)	896	274(e)	90
262	46	274(e)(1)	91
	51		96
	69	274(h)(1)	84
	89	274(h)(2)	85
	128	274(j)	178
	329	274(j)(1)	177
	447	274(j)(2)(A)	177
	448	274(j)(2)(B)	177
	459		178
	460	274(j)(3)(A)(ii)	177
	702	274(j)(3)(B)(i)	177
263	474	274(j)(3)(B)(ii)	177
	701	274(m)(1)	85
263(a)(1)	480	274(n)	96
	486		97
263(c)	475		177
263A	468		469
	488	280A	469
	498	280A(c)	469
263A(a)	496	280A(c)(5)	469
263A(a)(1)(A)	490	280B	520
263A(a)(2)(A)	490	318(a)	211
263A(b)(1)	496	368	212
263A(d)(1)(A)	468	368(a)	310
264(a)(2)	853	382	639
264(b)	853	401–419A	908
265(a)(2)	704	402(a)(1)	5
	706	404(a)	908
	707	404(a)(5)	894

Table of Internal Revenue Code Sections

Sec.	Page	Sec.	Page
	895	461(h)(2)(C)(i)	875
	896	461(h)(2)(C)(ii)	875
	897	461(h)(3)	888
404(b)	896	465	367
415(c)(1)	5		603
421(a)(2)	187		604
422A	31		629
	187		669
422A(a)	186		694
422A(b)	186		695
435(j)(2)	337		698
441(a)–(e)	766	465(a)(1)	603
441(i)(1)	766	465(b)(1)	603
446(b)	467	465(b)(2)	603
	537	465(b)(6)	669
	907	465(c)(1)(C)	603
453	206		694
	210	465(c)(3)	603
	211	465(c)(3)(A)	694
	336	468A	874
453(b)(2)(A)	210	469	696
453(c)	211		697
	336		698
453(e)(1)	211		700
	818		701
453(e)(2)(A)	211	469(a)(1)	696
453(f)(1)	211	469(a)(2)	697
453(i)	370	469(c)	696
	573	469(c)(2)	701
	668	469(c)(3)(A)	697
453(j)	211	469(e)	697
	336	469(h)(1)	696
	337	469(h)(2)	697
453(j)(2)	211	472(c)	232
453(k)	211		243
453(*l*)(1)	210	483	814
	907		817
453(*l*)(2)(A)	907		818
453A(a)(1)	210	483(b)	817
453A(b)(1)	213	483(d)(2)	818
453A(c)(1)	210	483(d)(4)	818
453A(d)(1)	213	501(c)(3)	157
453B(a)	212		157
	214		158
457	910	511(a)(1)	830
	912	514	832
457(a)	912	514(a)	831
457(b)	912	551	386
457(f)(1)(A)	912	636(a)	844
457(f)(3)(B)	912	671	770
461(g)	670	671–677	770
461(h)	872		772
	873		773
	874	672(a)	771
	888		782
	891	672(b)	771
	892		782
	893	672(c)	771
	894	672(e)	783
	895	673	771
	896		848
	897	673(a)	771
461(h)(2)	888		773
461(h)(2)(B)	872		782

Table of Internal Revenue Code Sections

Sec.	Page	Sec.	Page
	783		522
	848	1016(a)(5)	522
674	771	1017	460
674(a)	771	1023	357
	782	1031	285
674(b)	771		289
	772		290
674(b)(3)	771		292
674(b)(5)(A)	771		293
674(b)(6)	771		294
674(c)	771		295
	772		299
675	771		308
	772		309
	782		310
675(1)	772		314
675(2)	772		316
676	771		348
	772		349
676(a)	772		368
	782		376
677	771		572
	772	1031(a)	349
677(a)	772	1031(a)(1)	289
	782	1031(a)(2)(A)–(a)(2)(C)	310
677(b)	772	1031(a)(2)(B)	285
704(a)	753	1031(a)(2)(C)	285
704(e)	754	1031(a)(3)	309
704(e)(1)	754	1031(b)	290
704(e)(2)	754		349
704(e)(3)	755		697
709(a)	692	1031(c)	289
709(b)(1)	692		292
951	386	1031(d)	348
1001(a)	330		349
1001(b)	330	1031(e)	310
1011	447	1033	315
1011(a)	330		316
1011(b)	345		321
	346	1033(a)	314
	589		315
1012	330	1033(a)(1)	314
	424	1033(a)(1)(B)	316
	447	1033(a)(2)(A)	314
	693	1033(g)	315
1014(a)	348	1034	316
	357		317
	385		318
	424		321
	518		452
	589	1034(a)	316
1014(a)(1)	351	1034(h)(1)	318
	522	1034(h)(2)(A)	318
	523	1038	672
	524	1041	350
1015(a)	348		424
	350	1041(a)	411
	424	1041(a)(1)	212
	518	1041(a)(2)	197
	721	1056(d)	513
1016(a)(2)	553	1091	223
1016(a)(2)(A)	447		225
	480		269
	519		270

Table of Internal Revenue Code Sections

Sec.	Page	Sec.	Page
	274		567
	348		572
	350		573
1091(a)	223		589
	224		691
	349		744
1091(d)	350		873
1092	270	1245(a)(1)	554
1092(b)	269	1245(a)(3)(A)	554
1211	227	1245(b)(1)	744
	230	1250	554
	233		555
	244		563
	270		567
	470		667
1211(b)	227		668
1212	564		744
1221	227		784
	230		873
	388	1250(a)(1)(A)	555
	389	1250(b)(1)	555
	390	1250(c)	555
	391	1250(d)(1)	744
	393	1256	270
	425	1271(a)	806
	431	1271(a)(1)	806
	438	1271(b)(1)	807
	441	1271(b)(2)	807
	842	1271(c)(2)(A)(i)	806
	843	1272	815
1221(1)	230		817
	388		835
	411		891
	412		893
	416	1272–1274	835
	424		853
	425	1272(a)	891
	438	1272(a)(1)	801
1221(2)	416		815
	554		858
1221(3)	424	1272(a)(2)(B)	866
	435	1272(a)(3)–(a)(5)	802
1221(3)(A)	424	1273	817
	438	1273(a)(1)	801
1221(3)(C)	424		815
	425	1273(a)(3)	801
	438	1274	815
	758		817
1222	227		818
	388		831
	420		835
1231	416		841
1231(a)(1)	416		865
1231(a)(2)	416		873
1231(b)	416		891
	554		916
1235	424	1274(a)	815
1236	399	1274(b)(1)	815
1237	413	1274(b)(2)	815
	420	1274(c)(1)	815
1241	431	1274(c)(1)(B)	817
1245	554	1274(c)(2)	815
	555	1274(c)(3)	817
	563	1274(c)(3)(A)	817

Table of Internal Revenue Code Sections

Sec.	Page
1274(c)(3)(B)	817
1274(c)(3)(C)	817
1274(c)(3)(D)	817
1274(c)(3)(E)	817
1274(c)(3)(F)	817
1274(d)	831
1274(d)(1)	815
1274(d)(1)(C)(i)	175
1274A	818
1276	812
1276(a)(1)	812
1277	812
1348	602
1361(b)(1)	604
1363(a)	604
1366(a)(1)	604
6050	694
6111	694
6112	694
6601(a)	175

Sec.	Page
6621(a)(2)	175
6621(c)	695
6659	694
6661	694
6700	694
6700(a)(2)(B)	694
6700(b)(1)	694
7441	36
7701(g)	367
7702	851
7704	603
7872	774
	857
	858
	865
7872(a)	774
	857
7872(d)(1)(A)	774
7872(d)(1)(B)	774

TABLE OF TREASURY REGULATIONS

Reg.	Page	Reg.	Page
1.61–2(d)(2)	103	1.162–5(b)(3), Ex. 4	62
1.61–6	286	1.162–5(e)	69
	333	1.162–12	467
	334	1.165–7(a)(5)	454
	336	1.165–7(b)(1)	460
	344		480
	345	1.165–7(b)(1)(ii)	480
	349	1.167(a)–3	474
1.61–6(a)	5		475
	193		490
	196		511
1.61–6(a), Ex.(2)	334		518
1.83–7(a)	29	1.183–2(b)	467
1.83–7(b)(1)	29	1.183–2(c)	467
	31	1.274–2(c)(4)	90
1.119–1(a)(2)(ii)(a)	39	1.274–4(g), Ex. 7	84
1.119–1(a)(2)(ii)(b)	39	1.274–5T(f)(2)	6
1.119–1(a)(2)(ii)(c)	39	1.446–1(a)(4)(ii)	474
1.119–1(b)	39	1.451–5	864
1.119–1(e)	41	1.469–1T(e)(iv)(B)	701
1.119–1(f), Exs. 5–7	39	1.471–1	394
1.161–1	480	1.471–2(b)	232
1.162–2(b)(2)	83	1.471–4	232
1.162–2(e)	50	1.674(b)–1(b)(5)(i)	771
1.162–5	56	1.704–1(e)(2)	755
	57	1.1001–1(a)	287
	61	1.1031	289
	68	1.1031(a)–1(b)	292
	69		310
	70	1.1031(b)–1(c)	367
1.162–5(a)	56		368
1.162–5(b)(1)	57	1.1031(d)–2, Ex. 1	367
1.162–5(b)(2)	56	1.1031(d)–2, Ex. 2	368
1.162–5(b)(3)	56	1.1031–1(a)–(c)	310
	61	15A.453–1(c)	337
1.162–5(b)(3), Ex. 1	62		

REVENUE RULINGS AND PROCEDURES

Rev. Rul.	Page	Rev. Proc.	Page
55–422	177	77–85	850
56–181	474	77–185	253
60–31	*902*		269
	908	77–263	70
	916		71
63–144	91	80–274	850
63–232	*458*	81–225	850
67–167	214	83–82	52
70–217	69	71–21	864
76–62	62	*72–18*	*711*
76–63	69		716
76–144	69	75–15	657

933

INDEX

Editor's Note: The page references in the index are to material written by the author in the Notes and Questions and other Note material. The reader will usually find excerpted material on the same subject—from judicial opinions, articles, or congressional reports—immediately preceding the Note material referred to by page numbers in the index.

ABILITY-TO-PAY PRINCIPLE, 12

ACCOUNTING
Accrual method, 797–798, 906–908
All events test, 888
Annual principle, 324–325, 564
Cash method, 797–798, 863, 906–908
Nontax, 243, 285, 487, 511
Premature accruals, 871–875, 880–888 890–894
Tax year, 766

ACQUIESCENCE, 223

ADJUSTED GROSS INCOME, 6

ADVERTISING, 474–475

ALIMONY, 795–796

ALL EVENTS TEST, 888

AMORTIZATION, 518–519, 521–522

ANNUITIES,
As compensation, 20–23, 916–917
Cost recovery, 537
Private, 789–790, 796
Unstated interest, 849–853

APPRAISAL,
Depreciation, 536
Generally, 29–30, 196
Stock options, 29–30

ASSIGNMENT OF INCOME,
Corporations, 764–766
Generally, 719–720
Intrafamily, 721–722, 742–744
Partnerships, 753–755
Patents, 758

AT RISK RULES, 603, 694, 698

AWARDS, EMPLOYEE ACHIEVEMENT, 177–178

BAD DEBTS, 399, 563

BASIS,
Allocation, 333–334, 439–441, 512–513
Effect of mortgage, 365–367, 693–694
Gifts, 350–351
Installment sales, 336–337
Like-kind exchanges, 348–349
Part gift, part sale, 344–346
Personal consumption property, 447–448, 451–452, 454
Related party sales, 350
Wash sales, 349–350

BELOW-MARKET INTEREST LOANS, 773–774, 855–857, 865

BENEFIT PRINCIPLE, 11–12

BOARD OF TAX APPEALS, 36–37

BONDS
Discount, 798–902, 806–809, 811–812
Premium, 520–522, 537

BUSINESS EXPENSES, 44, 443–444

CAFETERIA PLANS, 127

CAPITAL EXPENDITURES,
Education, 56–57
Generally, 471, 473–475, 485–488
Interest expense, 701
Salaries, 490–491, 495–496, 510–511

Index

CAPITAL GAINS,
Dual character assets, 401, 411–413, 416–417
Generally, 369–371
Hedging transactions, 391–394
Inventory versus investment, 388, 391–394, 398–399
Justifications, 375–378, 386
Property definition, 420, 423–424, 431, 438
Quasi-capital assets, 416–417
Versus compensation, 420, 423–425

CAPITAL LOSSES, 227–230

CARVING OUT RULE, 843–845

CASUALTY LOSSES, 458–460

CHARITABLE CONTRIBUTIONS, 156–159, 345–346, 589

CHILD CARE EXPENSES, 129–135

CHURCH AND SYNAGOGUE DUES, 157

COMMODITY STRADDLES, 263–265

COMMUTING, 50–54

CONSTRUCTIVE RECEIPT, 907–908

CONSUMPTION TAX BASE, 12

CORPORATE-SHAREHOLDER TAXATION, 386–387, 764–766

COURT OF CLAIMS, 175

CREDITS, 133–134, 135

DAMAGES, 315–316, 875, 892–893

DEFERRED COMPENSATION, 893–897, 912, 916–918

DEPLETION, 337–338

DEPRECIABLE INTEREST, 524–525

DEPRECIATION,
Economic, 529–530, 535–537
Generally, 526–529, 548, 551–552

EARNED INCOME CREDIT, 135

ECONOMIC PERFORMANCE, 872–873, 888

EDUCATION EXPENSES, 55–57, 61–62, 865–866

EDUCATION SAVINGS BONDS, 866

EMPLOYEE DISCOUNTS, 116–117

ENTERTAINMENT EXPENSES, 90–91, 96–97

EXPENSING, 444, 471, 474–475, 490–491, 495, 692

FAMILY CORPORATIONS, 764–766

FAMILY PARTNERSHIPS, 752–755

FORM AND SUBSTANCE, 221–222

"FOR PROFIT" ACTIVITIES, 443–444

FORGIVENESS OF DEBT, 318–321, 328–329, 460

FRINGE BENEFITS,
Generally, 115–118, 126–127
Nonstatutory, 103–104, 115–116

FUTURE INTERESTS, 833–836, 840–841, 843–845, 847–848

GAMBLING LOSSES, 470

GIFTS,
Basis, 350–351
Generally, 164, 174, 176–179
Installment contracts, 214
Leaseback, 782–784
Temporally divided, 847–848

GRANTOR TRUSTS, 770–773

GROSS INCOME, 6

HEAD TAX, 11

HOBBY LOSSES, 467–470

HOME OFFICES, 469–470

IMPUTED INCOME,
Property, 447–448, 703–704
Services, 102–103, 130–131

INCOME EFFECT, 131–132

INCOME IN KIND,
Generally, 21–22
Limited choice, 21–22, 116
Restricted property, 22–23

INSTALLMENT SALES,
Basis, 336–337
Definition, 206
Policy, 209–211
Unstated interest, 813–815, 817–818, 829–832

INTANGIBLE DRILLING COSTS, 475

Index

INTEREST EXPENSE, 700–708, 716–717, 853

INVENTORY, 230–234

INVOLUNTARY CONVERSION, 314–315

ITEMIZED DEDUCTIONS, 6–7

JOINT RETURNS, 767–769

LIFE INSURANCE, 849–853

LIKE-KIND EXCHANGES, 285, 287–288, 292–293, 294–295, 299–300, 308–310, 314, 348–349, 367–368

LOSSES,
Capital, 227–230
Casualty, 458–460
Hobby, 467–470
Personal consumption, 447–448, 451–452, 454, 467–470
Related party sales, 220–224
Wash sales, 223–226, 269, 314

MARITAL PROPERTY SETTLEMENTS, 197, 795

MARRIAGE BONUSES AND PENALTIES, 767–769

MEALS AND LODGING, 38–39, 41–43, 100–101

MEDICAL EXPENSES, 144–147

MEDICAL INSURANCE, 145–147

MINIMUM TAX, 548–550, 602

MORTGAGES, 365–368

MUNICIPAL BONDS, 704–707

NO ADDITIONAL COST SERVICE, 117

NONWASTING ASSETS, 444, 471, 474, 490, 510–511, 512–514

OVERVALUATION, 573, 669, 690, 811, 871–872

PARTNERSHIPS, 603–604, 752–755

PASSIVE ACTIVITY LOSSES, 696–699, 700–701, 708

PATENTS, 424, 758

PREMATURE ACCRUALS, 871–875, 880–888, 890–894

PREMIUM LEASE, 513–514, 518–519, 537

PREPAYMENTS, 863–865

PRESENT VALUE, 197–199, 201–205

QUALIFIED PENSION PLANS, 908–909, 912, 916–918

QUALIFIED TUITION REDUCTION, 118

QUASI-CAPITAL ASSETS, 416–417, 567

RATES,
After-tax, 10
Before-tax, 10
History, 7
Progressive, proportional, and regressive, 12–14
Surcharge, 8–9

REALIZATION,
Casualty, 459–460
Definition, 193
Generally, 286–287
Gifts, 196–197, 339–343
Marital property settlements, 197
Mortgaging of property, 212–214, 784
Stock dividends, 385–386
Tenant forfeiture of lease, 314

RECAPTURE, 553–555, 567, 572–573

RECOGNITION,
Forgiveness of debt, 328–329
Involuntary conversion, 314–315
Like-kind exchanges, 285, 287–288, 292–293, 294–295, 299–300, 308–310, 314
Personal residence sale, 316–318
Related party sales, 220–224
Wash sales, 223–226, 269, 314

RELATED PARTY SALES, 220–224, 350

REPAIRS, 479–480

RESEARCH AND DEVELOPMENT, 475

SALE AND LEASEBACK, 292, 525, 591–592, 594–595, 643, 656–659, 840–841

SAVINGS AND LOANS, 284–288

SCHOLARSHIPS, 68–71, 75–76

SEGREGATED PRIVATE SCHOOLS, 157–159

STANDARD DEDUCTION, 6–7

STATE AND LOCAL TAXES, 159–160, 692

STOCK APPRECIATION RIGHTS, 188–189

STOCK DIVIDENDS, 384–386

STOCK OPTIONS,
As compensation, 27–32, 186–189
Incentive or qualified, 31, 186–189
Valuation, 29–30

SUBSTITUTION EFFECT, 131–132

TAX AVOIDANCE PURPOSE, 222–223, 226, 270, 693

TAX BENEFIT RULE, 563–564, 566

TAX COURT, 174–175

TAX EXEMPT ORGANIZATIONS, 157–159, 811–812, 830–832, 874, 896–897, 912

TAX EXPENDITURES, 135–137, 288

TAX SHELTERS,
Abusive, 667–670, 690–696
Basic structure, 581–585, 588–589
Economic analysis, 608–610, 625–630, 638–639

TAX SHELTERS —Cont'd
Equipment-leasing, 581–585, 588–589, 662
Generally, 575
Legality, 599–604, 694–698
Real estate, 656–659

TAXABLE INCOME, 6

TAXABLE UNIT, 769–770

TRAVEL EXPENSES, 83–85

TUITION PREPAYMENT PLANS, 865

UNEARNED INCOME OF MINOR CHILDREN, 740

VACATION HOMES, 469–470

WASH SALES, 223–226, 269, 314, 349–350

WORKING CONDITIONS, 37–38